Editorial Staff

Editors
Douglas J. Murray Paul R. Viotti

Associate for Research
Harold M. Maynard

Research and Editorial Assistants
Thomas Drohan Dean Habrun
Mark Graper Mark Hefferly
Douglas Gregory Henry Johnson
James Kinzer

THE DEFENSE POLICIES OF NATIONS

A Comparative Study

Edited by

Douglas J. Murray and Paul R. Viotti

THE JOHNS HOPKINS UNIVERSITY PRESS
Baltimore and London

Printed in the United States of America

The Johns Hopkins University Press, Baltimore, Maryland
21218
The Johns Hopkins Press Ltd., London

The views and conclusions expressed by military and other government personnel in material contained in this volume are those of the authors and not necessarily those of the U.S. Air Force Academy, the Department of Defense, any particular service thereof, or any other government agency.

Library of Congress Cataloging in Publication Data
Main entry under title:

The Defense policies of nations.

Bibliography
Includes index.
1. Military policy—Case studies. 2. Armed Forces—Case studies. I. Murray, Douglas J. II. Viotti, Paul R.
UA11.D387 355'.0335 81-3790
ISBN 0-8018-2636-5 AACR2
ISBN 0-8018-2637-3 (pbk.)

To Richard F. Rosser and the late Fred Sondermann, whose contributions to international relations and security studies have given impetus to the development of the comparative study of defense policy

Contents

Foreword

The study of defense policy from a comparative perspective is a natural corollary to the more common focus on defense policies of single nation-states. However, while the study of American defense policy in particular has achieved substantial progress during the past twenty years, comparative perspective remains embryonic. For a variety of reasons, scholars and, indeed, policy makers have tended to view such issues as strategy, doctrine, force posture, defense decision making, and civil-military relations only as they pertain to single actors in the international arena. The task of relating these issues across national borders has fallen largely to the student.

In 1973 several members of the political science department at the United States Air Force Academy coedited a volume entitled *Comparative Defense Policy,* which directed its attention to six themes: military profession, military doctrine, force posture, weapons acquisition, structure/process, and the use of force. The editors chose not to attempt a parallel examination of countries in relation to the six themes but, rather, to examine each theme relative to a variety of nation-states. The volume remains a successful publication used in college classrooms as well as by defense officials.

To determine more about the future direction of comparative policy studies, in late 1977 Maj. Harold Maynard conducted an extensive survey of academicians and policy makers. That survey indicated the need for a new book, one that would be oriented to a larger audience (i.e., both undergraduate and graduate students, as well as policy makers), would be organized according to countries rather than topics, and would include distinct chapters on the United States and the Soviet Union.

This book, then, is substantively and methodologically different from the earlier one. Indeed, it is founded upon a comparative country study approach that employs a common outline or framework for analysis, focusing on four dimensions of a state's defense policy: first, the international environment in which the state exists and, in particular, the threats it perceives as coming from that environment; second, the state's national objectives as specified in its national strategy and military doctrine; third, the process of defense decision making; and finally, the recurrent issues or defense policy outputs of that process. The countries examined include the United States, the Soviet Union, the United Kingdom, France, West Germany, Sweden, Romania, Israel, the People's Republic of China, and Japan. These countries were selected because of their dominant or unique positions within the international milieu. Moreover, all of the countries identified in our survey as essential to comparative defense studies have been included. Throughout, our efforts have been to make this volume useful to both the student and the policy maker. In addition, we have included readings designed to supplement the country study chapters, and short bibliographical essays to facilitate further in-depth research or analysis. Finally, because this volume contains a section on American defense policy, designed to be both a basis for comparison and a primer on the subject, it complements *American Defense Policy,* also edited by members of the Department of Political Science at the Air Force Academy and currently going into its fifth edition.

Lt. Col. Douglas Murray and Lt. Col. Paul Viotti, editors of this volume, have brought superb backgrounds of experience to their task. Both have been deeply involved in various research efforts and have taught a variety of American, international, and comparative politics courses, as well as a highly successful course in comparative defense policy. Both editors also have practical experience in comparative defense policy as a result of earlier assignments in the Washington area. Finally, I should like to point with pride to the fact that the distinguished contributors of chapters for this volume include Col. John E. Endicott, Mr. William R. Heaton, Lt. Col. Bard E. O'Neill, and Lt. Col. Edward L. Warner, all former members of the Department of Political Science.

Ervin J. Rokke, Colonel, U.S.A.F.
Professor and Head
Department of Political Science
United States Air Force Academy

Acknowledgments

As would be expected in an enterprise of this magnitude, our debts are many. Not only do we thank all of our contributors for their efforts, but we also wish to acknowledge the collaboration of Harold Maynard during the early and very important conceptualization phase of this project. His good fortune in securing an assignment to Indonesia necessarily ended his direct participation in this project, although he remains a strong advocate for the comparative defense policy field. In particular, we would like to acknowledge his efforts in surveying many of our colleagues for their inputs on research and countries to be selected for examination. Moreover, he also participated in the very lengthy discussions that resulted in the framework for analysis ultimately used by our country study authors.

In soliciting manuscripts for this volume, we have quite consciously sought both a mix of civilian and military authors and a similar blend of American and foreign contributors. Not only was such a balance our own preference, but it was also the consensus that emerged from the already mentioned survey of over 400 academicians and policy makers.

Also active in the earliest stage of this project were two of our research assistants, Dean Habrun and Mark Hefferly, who spent seemingly endless hours reviewing the existing literature and providing copies of books and journal articles for our use and for use by our contributors. Picking up this task and helping us organize the conference of our contributors were two more research assistants, Henry Johnson and Thomas Drohan. Finally, Mark Graper, Douglas Gregory, and James Kinzer joined us to work on the glossary.

Later in the project we have relied on still others for help. William Berry and Kenneth Stoehrmann oversaw the final proofreading of galleys. Other colleagues who so willingly gave of their time to read and critique manuscripts and engage in the laborious tasks of proofreading galleys are too numerous to mention here. Suffice it to say that without the support of our colleagues in the Department of Political Science at the Air Force Academy, this volume would not have been possible.

Secretarial support was invaluable. In particular, we would like to acknowledge the efforts of Aline Rankin, Nellie Dykes, Linda Belcher, and Pat Mitchell. Illustrations prepared by Richard Mohr and other members of the academy's academic support staff were an invaluable contribution.

Finally, but certainly one of the most important considerations that has made this effort possible, was financial backing for copyright permissions and clerical support from the Johns Hopkins University Press and the Air Force Academy's Academic Support Fund. In addition, a contribution by the National Security Education Program at New York University, directed by Professor Frank Trager, enabled us to convene a meeting of our authors in October 1979. As noted above, we have relied heavily on their comments in writing our concluding essay.

Contributors

The Editors

Douglas J. Murray, formerly associate professor of political science and director of comparative and area studies at the Air Force Academy, is currently assigned to the Pentagon as deputy chief of the secretary of the air force's staff group. He is the author of articles and studies on U.S.-Canadian relations and other defense issues. Murray has a Ph.D. from the University of Texas at Austin.

Paul R. Viotti, currently on sabbatical in a political advisory position with the U.S. European Command, is an associate professor of political science at the Air Force Academy, where he has served as director of international and defense studies. A contributor to the 1974 volume *Comparative Defense Policy,* he is the author of articles and studies on national security and international economic questions. Viotti has a Ph.D. from the University of California, Berkeley.

Foreword

Ervin J. Rokke is professor and head, Department of Political Science, U.S. Air Force Academy. Currently serving as the U.S. air attaché to the United Kingdom, Colonel Rokke was the coeditor of the third edition of *American Defense Policy*. He holds a doctorate from Harvard University.

Country Studies

David P. Burke holds a doctorate from Harvard University and has served on the faculty of the Naval Postgraduate School at Monterey, California. Formerly a member of the Air Force Academy's political science department, he has also served in staff positions with the Strategic Air Command and the Joint Chiefs of Staff. Professor Burke has published numerous articles on national security topics and is coeditor of *Eurocommunism: Between East and West*.

John E. Endicott, formerly deputy head of the Air Force Academy's Department of Political Science, is currently associate dean, National War College, Washington. The author of *Japan's Nuclear Option,* coauthor of *The Politics of East Asia,* and coeditor of the fourth edition of *American Defense Policy,* he received his Ph.D. from the Fletcher School of Law and Diplomacy, Tufts University.

David Greenwood is the director of the Centre for Defence Studies at the University of Aberdeen, Scotland. He is an economist with degrees from the University of Liverpool. A former member of the Royal Air Force, he has served as economic adviser to the Ministry of Defence, as visiting fellow at the International Institute for Strategic Studies, and in numerous governmental advisory posts concerned with national security and arms control. The author of numerous publications in these fields, Greenwood is particularly noted for his work on defense budgeting.

William R. Heaton, Jr., holds a doctorate in political science from the University of California, Berkeley. Formerly a faculty member at the Air Force Academy and a research fellow at the National Defense University, Heaton is currently an analyst with the Foreign Broadcast Information Service in Washington. Having traveled extensively in China and lived for several years in Hong Kong, he is the author of numerous articles and books, including *The Politics of East Asia* (coauthor) and *Insurgency in the Modern World* (coeditor and contributor).

CATHERINE MCARDLE KELLEHER is a foremost student of European politics in general and NATO and West German security relations in particular. She has served on the faculties of the University of Michigan, the University of Denver, and the National Defense University. Among her scholarly publications are *Germany and the Politics of Nuclear Weapons, American Arms and Changing Europe* (coauthor), and *Political-Military Systems: Comparative Perspectives* (editor). Professor Kelleher received her Ph.D. from the Massachusetts Institute of Technology.

LAWRENCE J. KORB, formerly a faculty member at the Naval War College and director of Defense Policy Studies at the American Enterprise Institute for Public Policy Research, in Washington, D.C., is assistant secretary of defense for manpower, reserve affairs and logistics. Prior to assuming this position, he also served as coeditor of the *AEI Foreign Policy and Defense Review*. Among his many contributions to the national security field are *The Joint Chiefs of Staff, The Price of Preparedness, The System for Educating Military Officers,* and *The Fall and Rise of the Pentagon: American Defense Policies in the 1970s*. Korb holds a Ph.D. from the State University of New York at Albany.

BARD E. O'NEILL is a permanent member of the National War College faculty and a fellow of the Research Directorate of the National Defense University. He is the author of several books and numerous articles, including the recently published *Armed Struggle in Palestine* and *Insurgency in the Modern World* (coeditor and contributor). Professor O'Neill has a Ph.D. from the Graduate School of International Studies, University of Denver.

ALAN NED SABROSKY is an associate professor of politics at Catholic University, in Washington, D.C., and general editor of the quarterly *International Security Review*. Among his many contributions are *The Conventional-Revisionist Controversy and the U.S. Role in World Affairs, Blue-Collar Soldiers? Unionization and the U.S. Military, and Defense Manpower Policy: A Critical Reappraisal*. Professor Sabrosky received his Ph.D. in political science from the University of Michigan.

WILLIAM J. TAYLOR, JR., is professor of social sciences at the U.S. Military Academy at West Point, where he teaches courses in American national security and foreign policy. Among his scholarly contributions is *U.S. National Security: Policy and Process* (coauthor). A frequent contributor to journals and conferences, Taylor is particularly well known for his work on the defense policies of Scandinavian countries. He holds a Ph.D. from the American University.

EDWARD L. WARNER III holds a Ph.D. from Princeton University. Formerly a faculty member in political science at the Air Force Academy and later assistant air attaché in Moscow, he is currently head of the staff group that assists the Air Force chief of staff in Washington. Among his numerous scholarly publications is *The Military in Contemporary Soviet Politics: An Institutional Analysis*.

Readings

ARTHUR J. ALEXANDER is an economist with the RAND Corporation. He holds an M.S. degree from the London School of Economics and a Ph.D. from The Johns Hopkins University. He has been a junior staff member of the President's Council of Economic Advisors and has published extensively on the Soviet Union.

GRAEME P. AUTON, a scholar in the foreign and defense policy fields, has served on the faculties of Whitman College, the University of California at Santa Barbara, and Occidental College. Among his contributions is *The Foreign Policies of West Germany, France, and Britain*.

FRITZ W. ERMARTH was a member of the National Security Council staff during the Carter administration. He has also served as an analyst with both the RAND Corporation and the Central Intelligence Agency, focusing his attention on strategy and arms control questions.

PIERRE M. GALLOIS is a retired French air force general who is well known internationally for his work on strategic questions. He has also served as professor of international relations at the Sorbonne.

STANLEY HOFFMANN is professor of government at Harvard University. He is well known for his numerous articles and books in the international relations and foreign policy fields, including *Contemporary Theory and International Relations, The State of War, Gulliver's Troubles: The Setting of American Foreign Policy,* and *Primacy or World Order*. Professor Hoffmann received a doctorate in law from the University of Paris.

MICHAEL E. HOWARD is Regius Professor of Modern History at All Souls College, Oxford, where he also held the Chichelle professorship of the history of war. He is the author of many historical as well as policy-oriented studies, including *The Franco-Prussian War* and *Studies in War and Peace*.

CHRIS L. JEFFERIES, currently assigned as a defense policy analyst and planner with the U.S. Mission to NATO, was previously an assistant professor of political science at the Air Force Academy. He has also served as a research consultant to the Office of the Joint Chiefs of Staff and has participated in research and policy analysis with the U.S. Air Force. Graduate work was done at the University of Pittsburgh. A frequent contributor of articles on public administration, Jefferies has a particular interest in the politics of the defense budgetary process.

HENRY A. KISSINGER, now associated with the Georgetown University Center for Strategic Studies, was secretary of state and national security adviser to Presidents Nixon and Ford. Before assuming these positions he was professor of government at Harvard University, where he received his Ph.D. His publications include *Nuclear Weapons and Foreign Policy, The Necessity for Choice, The Troubled Partnership,* and *American Foreign Policy.*

BENJAMIN S. LAMBETH is a senior staff member of the RAND Corporation. He received his graduate education at Harvard University and served previously in the Office of National Estimates and the Office of Political Research, Central Intelligence Agency. Lambeth has published extensively on Soviet military matters and is coauthor of *The Soviet Union and Arms Control: A Superpower Dilemma.*

The late HANS J. MORGENTHAU was a key figure in the post–World War II "realist" school of international politics. He is best known for his now classic *Politics among Nations.* Born and educated in Germany, Morgenthau taught in several European universities before emigrating to the United States in 1937.

HISAHIKO OKAZAKI, a member of the Japanese Defense Ministry, is director general for foreign relations. He is the author of *A Japanese View of Détente.*

RICHARD PIPES, professor of history and director of the Russian Research Center at Harvard University, is now serving as a member of the National Security Council staff. During the Ford administration he served as chairman of "Team B," a group of private citizens appointed by the Foreign Intelligence Advisory Board to prepare an alternative to the CIA estimate of Soviet strategic objectives.

KENNETH N. WALTZ is Ford Professor of Political Science at the University of California, Berkeley. He is the author of numerous articles and books, including *Theory of International Politics, Foreign Policy and Democratic Politics,* and *Man, the State, and War.* Professor Waltz received his Ph.D. from Columbia University.

Bibliographies and Bibliographical Essays

JAMES H. BUCK, a Far East specialist, has served as professor of international affairs at the Air War College in Alabama.

MARK G. EWIG did his graduate work in Middle East studies at the University of Utah. He is currently an assistant professor of political science at the Air Force Academy.

SCHUYLER FOERSTER, an assistant professor of political science at the Air Force Academy, is completing doctoral work at Oxford University. He specializes in Soviet and national security affairs.

TERRY L. HEYNS is a graduate of St. Louis University and the University of Kansas. He has written several articles on NATO and other security matters. Formerly assistant professor of political science at the Air Force Academy, he is now at the National Defense University.

CHRIS L. JEFFERIES. See listing above under "Readings."

RICHARD J. LATHAM is currently a Ph.D. candidate at the University of Washington. He has served as assistant air attaché to Hong Kong and on the political science faculty at the Air Force Academy, where he will return upon completion of doctoral studies.

JEROME V. MARTIN is an instructor in the military studies department at the Air Force Academy and has a particular interest in Soviet defense policy. He has served as an intelligence analyst in the Federal Republic of Germany and in Thailand.

LESTER G. PITTMAN, a faculty member at the Air Force Academy, did his graduate work at the University of Southern California. A student of comparative European defense policy, he is currently working on a history of French military thought.

BARBARA U. RILEY did graduate work in German at Michigan State University. An intelligence officer, she has also taught German at the Air Force Academy.

A Note on Format

This book has been designed to be used both as an introductory text in comparative defense policy and as a book of readings. All material written especially for this book and serving as an introduction to the subject—i.e., all chapters on the various defense policies and bibliographical essays—is set in serif type. All material reprinted from other sources—the readings—is set in sans serif type.

Part one

DEFENSE POLICY:
The international environment

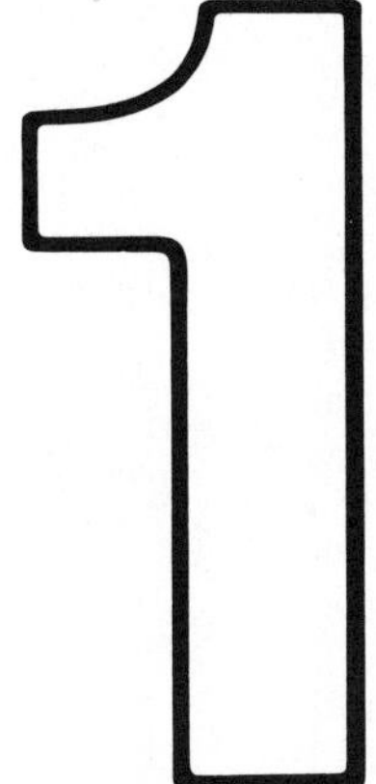

DEFENSE POLICY IN COMPARATIVE PERSPECTIVE: AN INTRODUCTION

Douglas J. Murray and Paul R. Viotti

The field of *comparative* defense or national security policy[1] is a relatively new one. To our knowledge, the first study that introduced this field in America was a volume based on contributions to a 1973 conference and edited by our colleagues Barry Horton, Edward L. Warner, and Anthony Rogerson.[2] Subsequently, there has been substantial evidence of growing interest in this field.

In 1975, for example, John Baylis and several of his colleagues published a volume of comparative essays which examined the defense policies of the United States, the Soviet Union, China, the United Kingdom, and France.[3] In 1978, another effort to advance this growing field was made by a well-attended conference of the International Studies Association's section on military studies, the entire proceedings of which were devoted to comparative defense policy.[4] A related enterprise has been the study of comparative military-political sociology, led by Morris Janowitz, Charles Moskos, Sam Sarkesian, Catherine Kelleher, and others. A useful product from that endeavor was a 1974 volume edited by Kelleher on "political-military" systems.[5] The semiannual *Journal of Political and Military Sociology* and the Inter-University Seminar's quarterly, *Armed Forces and Society,* have been primary vehicles for promoting further research in this area. Another, more recent addition to this literature is an anthology edited by Sheldon Simon.[6] Finally, credit must be given to works produced primarily in the 1950s and 1960s which examine military elites, particularly in the Third World, where they are often seen as agents of modernization and political development.[7]

This work is built upon the foundation laid by these earlier studies. At the same time, it attempts to expand this emerging field by taking the first few steps toward developing a conceptualization or paradigm to organize the knowledge of this field and develop the methodology to study it. What follows is not theory, but, we hope, the prelude to it.

Approaches to the comparative study of defense policy

In the period since 1973, several approaches to comparative defense studies have appeared. One such approach is to select such recurring issues as military doctrine, force posture, the decision-making process, and weapons acquisition and then to compare and contrast how different countries deal with these issues. This, in essence, was the organizational device used in the 1973 edition of *Comparative Defense Policy*.

An alternative approach, used by Aaron Wildavsky and others, is to focus upon the budget.[8] Two of the contributors to this volume—Lawrence Korb and David Greenwood—have a demonstrated preference for such a methodology. Greenwood has even asserted that expenditure *is* policy. To the extent that policy involves the allocation of scarce resources expressed in monetary terms, the budget is a handy device for comparative description. Understanding how the budget comes to be, furthermore, engages one in the politics of the budgetary process—a relevant focus for the theoretical task of developing defense policy explanation.

Comparing the budget to policy statements is a tactic investigated in a short article by our colleague, Chris Jefferies. Of course, a substantial limitation associated with any budget-oriented methodology is data availability. Intentionally or unintentionally, some countries conceal defense expenditures in other budget categories; others do not publish such data at all. Indeed, much of what we say we know of Soviet budget allocations is inferred from observed force posture, weapons acquisition, and research and development programs. Needless to say, numerous assumptions are made in estimating the Soviet budget. As a result, conclusions are almost always subject to considerable dispute.

The approach that we have adopted in this volume is a "country study," one using a common framework for analysis. This framework is founded upon our perception of defense policy as a dynamic process that can best be understood by studying it from several different dimensions. Samuel Huntington writes that defense policy is Janus-like—existing in the worlds of both international and domestic politics.[9] At the same time, it involves a threat frequently generated in the international politico-economic environment and responded to in the domestic or national one. Glenn Snyder adds a further dimension by arguing that national security policy involves two concepts—deterrence and defense. He writes:

> Essentially, deterrence means discouraging the enemy from taking military action by posing for him a prospect of cost and risk which outweighs his prospective gain. Defense means reducing our own prospective costs and risks in the event that deterrence fails. Deterrence works on the enemy's intentions; the deterrent value of military forces is their effect in reducing the likelihood of enemy military moves.
>
> Defense reduces the enemy's capability to damage or deprive us; the defense value of military forces is their effect in mitigating the adverse consequences for us of possible enemy moves, whether such consequences are counted as losses of territory or war damage. . . .
>
> Perhaps the crucial difference between deterrence and defense is that deterrence is primarily a peacetime objective while defense is a wartime value. Deterrence value and defense value are directly employed in different time periods.[10]

Given these views of national security policy concerns, we constructed a four-part framework that we asked our contributors to use to describe the defense policy of an individual state. The four parts are: (1) the international environment as it is perceived by the state; (2) the particular national objectives, strategy, and military force employment doctrine of that state; (3) the state's defense policy-making process; and (4) various recurring issues—force posture, the use of force, weapons acquisition, arms control, and civil-military relations. The framework is discussed in greater detail in the next section.

As editors, we are quite pleased that the contributors were willing to follow this framework as closely as they have. We make no claim to have developed a comprehensive theory of comparative defense or national security policy any more than this has been achieved in other fields of inquiry in political science; nevertheless, we do hope to have identified at least some of the important variables or factors that would likely be part of such a theory.

A framework for analysis

The security dilemma in which all states find themselves (and with which all governments must cope) arises from the absence of any authority over states—no guarantor of order among states. The defense policy of any state, then, is closely tied to its position within what we refer to as an international system of interacting states. This international environment can be understood as both the source of "opportunities" the state may wish to pursue and the source of "threats" to its security. Certainly, it is our view that the study of a country's defense policy should begin with an assessment of the country's position within the international system.

The second part of our organizational outline or framework conforms fairly closely to a rational actor model of national security policy decision making. Given national objectives, possessing certain capabilities, and facing various constraints, decision makers acting for the state establish national strategy and military force employment doctrine. We do not claim that national strategy, force posture, military doctrine, or other elements of national security policy necessarily conform to this logical pattern. We asked our contributors to examine objectives, strategies, and doctrines in the various countries they chose to study with an eye toward identification of both consistencies and contradictions. It may be, for example, that national strategy, force employment doctrine, and the range of feasible national objectives they serve are determined by capabilities provided by the existing force posture. In short, do strategy and doctrine give rise to a given force posture, or does the latter determine the former? Or, under what circumstances do these different relationships obtain? Whatever may be the case, we asked our contributors to provide an exposition of these factors as they saw them in the separate empirical realms they chose to examine.

In the third part of the framework, we address many of the questions raised by the first and second parts. How does the defense policy process actually work? How important are organizational processes or bureaucratic politics among agencies (or bureaucrats representing these agencies)? What is the relative importance of domestic and international factors in determining defense policy outcomes?

Finally, we address what we call the recurring defense policy issues (civil-military relations, weapons acquisition, force posture, arms control, and the use of force), treating them in the context of the conceptual discussion in the first three parts of the framework for analysis. These recurring issues are the substance of defense policy outputs—the decisions and actions made by government officials. Rather than discuss them at the end, some of our contributors exercised the option of incorporating these recurring issues in the main body of the chapter. Often these issues are used as empirical illustrations of conceptual arguments related to the first three parts of the framework. To facilitate any comparative analysis in which our readers might wish to engage, we are including the framework or outline used by our contributors as an appendix to this chapter.

The organization in this book reflects a view strongly held by the editors that any defense or national security study must begin with some consideration of factors external to the state. Thus, we begin our effort with the part entitled "Defense Policy: The International Environment." In the readings that follow this introductory chapter, we present some different perspectives on the nature of the international political system. These are followed by a reading that addresses the various dimensions of strategy.

Part two is an examination of the American and Soviet superpowers. Following that are country studies collected under regional labels: Europe (part three), the Middle East (part four), and East Asia (part five). We conclude with a comparative essay that represents our effort to summarize some of the findings in this collective effort. In this regard, we have been assisted by the written work of our contributors, as well as by their comments during our conference.

One of our aims in this book is to provide readers with bibliographic sources, a choice of methodological tools, and empirical data on various countries in order to facilitate any comparative analysis in which they may wish to engage. Our own modest attempt is contained in the concluding chapter. In addition to this aim of providing a stimulus to further work in the field of comparative defense policy, we hope that this book will be of use to both policy makers and academics concerned with such matters. The policy maker who wishes a broad overview of a given country's defense policy will find that what he or she wants is in this volume. Those engaged in national security and defense studies should also find this book to be a useful source even if their efforts are concentrated solely on American national security issues, since a cursory knowledge of the defense policies and processes of other states is important in understanding those of the United States.

The student of foreign policy or comparative and international politics should also find use for this volume. Security, though by no means the only important issue, is clearly a core concern in any country's foreign policy. Those interested in political institutions and processes will find considerable resource material in this book for European, East Asian, and other Northern Hemisphere studies.

Finally, we should point out that this volume and the earlier *Comparative Defense Policy* book are complementary. The earlier work remains useful as a collection of essays which can be integrated with the country study chapters of this volume.

Appendix: organizational outline

I. International Environment
  - A. Relative Position in the International System
    1. Power and status
    2. Relative capabilities
  - B. Threats
    1. Internal and external threats
    2. Nature of the threat (military, political, cultural, economic, etc.)

3. Source of the threat
4. Perceptions of the threat by decision makers
5. Vulnerabilities of the state

C. Self-perceived Role and Opportunities for the State within the International System (World View)
1. Role in the past
2. Changes in the role since World War II
3. Changes in the role in the next five to ten years

D. Linkages and Interdependencies
1. Alliances
2. Dependencies and interdependencies

II. National Objectives, National Strategy, and Military Doctrine

A. National Security Objectives
1. Changes in objectives over time
2. Degree of consensus or dissensus
   a. Voicing of dissent
   b. Effectiveness of dissent
3. Direction of objectives
   a. Internal (domestic affairs)
   b. External (state's actions in international system)
   c. Relative importance of internal versus external objectives

B. Determining National Objectives
1. Relative importance of ideology, culture, and capabilities
2. The effect of national experiences and "lessons" learned

C. Capabilities for Accomplishing National Security Objectives
1. Military capabilities
2. Economic capabilities
3. Technological capabilities
4. Political capabilities
5. Psychosocial capabilities

D. National Strategy for Achieving National Security Objectives
1. Formally (and publicly) stated versus implicit (must be inferred from observation of actual practice)
2. Degree of consensus or dissensus among individuals, factions, and bureaucratic agencies

E. Domestic Determinants of National Strategy
1. Political system type
2. Economic system type
3. Geography
4. Public opinion
5. National "will"
6. Level of political and economic development
7. Technology
8. Population size and educational level
9. Other factors

F. Military Doctrine (Force Employment Doctrine)
1. Conventional forces
2. Nuclear forces
3. Relation between doctrine and national strategy
4. Relation between doctrine and national security objectives
5. Formally (and publicly) stated versus implicit military doctrine (must be inferred from observation of actual practice)
6. Degree of consensus or dissensus on military doctrine among individuals, factions, and bureaucratic agencies

III. The Defense Decision-Making Process

A. The Nature of the Process

B. Degree of Concentration or Fragmentation of Power Domestically
1. Effect of concentration or fragmentation on comprehensiveness and responsiveness of policy outputs
2. The important actors in the process

C. Relative Importance of Bureaucratic Politics in the Process
1. Domestic and external influences on policy choices
2. Relative importance of different bureaucratic actors
3. Resolution of disputes among bureaucratic actors

D. Relative Importance of Personality in the Process; Other Idiosyncratic Factors

E. Constraints on Defense Decision Makers
1. Opposition from other states
2. Economic and budgetary limitations
3. Technological insufficiencies
4. Manpower
   a. Number, age, sex
   b. Conscripted or "volunteer" forces
   c. Reserves
   d. Capability for mobilization of reserves
5. Military hardware
   a. Weapons systems
   b. Spare parts
   c. Fuel
   d. Logistical capabilities
   e. Defense industry capability
   f. Foreign dependencies
6. Implementation difficulties (bureaucratic opposition and delaying tactics)
7. Public opinion, interest groups, and political parties as sources of opposition
8. Ideological and cultural orientations
9. Past lessons "learned"
10. Law and ethical norms

IV. Recurring Issues: Defense Policy Outputs

A. Civil-Military Relations
1. Domestic role of the military
2. Alienation or integration of the military and society
3. Recruitment and social groups
4. Social status of the military

B. Weapons Acquisition
1. Domestic industry production
2. Technology level (degree of domestic autonomy or foreign dependency)
3. Foreign supply
   a. Dependency on foreign supply
   b. Reliability of foreign supply
4. Cooperative production projects
5. Percentage of GNP spent on weapons acquisition

C. Force Posture
1. Weapons systems and military units maintained
2. Deployment

3. Effectiveness of the recruitment program
4. Effectiveness of force employment
5. Responsiveness of force posture to national objectives, strategy, and military doctrine (doctrine determines posture, or vice versa)

D. Arms Control
1. Feasibility
   a. Quantitative restrictions
   b. Qualitative restrictions
2. Threat perceptions
3. Existing agreements
4. Future prospects

E. The Use of Force
1. Type and extent of employment
   a. Passive role (deterrent)
   b. Active role (fighting)
2. Objectives sought through use of the military instrument
3. Constraints on the use of force posed by other countries
4. Technological developments and the use of force
5. Domestic constraints on the use of force

F. Other Issues

Notes

1. In this volume we use the terms *national security policy* and *defense policy* interchangeably. Some would disagree, arguing that *national security policy* is the broader term, covering a wide range of political, social, economic, and military issues, whereas the term *defense policy* refers primarily to military-political concerns. Although a case can be made for such differentiation, we prefer to regard the terms as synonyms. Indeed, preference for this usage was also the consensus at a conference of our country study contributors.

2. See Frank B. Horton III, Anthony C. Rogerson, and Edward L. Warner III, eds., *Comparative Defense Policy* (Baltimore: Johns Hopkins University Press, 1974).

3. See John Baylis et al., *Contemporary Strategy: Theories and Policies* (New York: Holmes & Meier, 1975).

4. Many of the papers presented at that conference have been published in a volume edited by James Roherty. His efforts focus primarily, although not exclusively, on Southern Hemisphere countries. As such, given the emphasis in this volume on the superpowers and other major states of the Northern Hemisphere, the two efforts would appear to be complementary. See James Roherty, ed., *Defense Policy Formation: Towards Comparative Analysis* (Durham, N.C.: Carolina Academic Press, 1979).

5. See Catherine Kelleher, ed., *Political Military Systems: Comparative Perspectives* (Beverly Hills, Calif.: Sage Publications, 1974).

6. See Sheldon Simon, ed., *The Military and Security in the Third World: Domestic and International Impacts* (Boulder, Colo.: Westview Press, 1978).

7. For example, see Lucian Pye, "Armies in the Process of Political Modernization," *Archives Europeans de Sociologie* 2 (1961); John J. Johnson, ed., *The Role of the Military in Underdeveloped Countries* (Princeton: Princeton University Press, 1962); idem, *The Military and Society in Latin America* (Stanford: Stanford University Press, 1964); Samuel E. Finer, *The Man on Horseback: The Role of the Military in Politics* (New York: Penguin, 1962); Morris Janowitz, *The Military in the Political Development of New Nations* (Chicago: University of Chicago Press, 1964); Robert J. Alexander, "The Army in Politics," in *Government and Politics in Latin America,* ed. Harold Eugene Davis (New York: Ronald, 1958); Edwin Lieuwen, *Arms and Politics in Latin America* (New York: Praeger, 1964); J. C. Hurewitz, *Middle East Politics: The Military Dimension* (New York: Praeger, 1969); and Amos Perlmutter, "The Praetorian State and the Praetorian Army," *Comparative Politics* 1 (April 1969): 382–404. For a critique of the military elite as modernizer, see Eric A. Nordlinger, "Soldiers in Mufti: The Impact of Military Rule upon Economic and Social Change in the Non-Western States," *American Political Science Review* 64 (December 1970): 1131–48. Certainly, if one is to explain defense policy outcomes or the defense policy process in various countries, one cannot ignore the military as an institutional actor and the entire range of civil-military issues; however, our focus on comparative defense policy in this volume is broader in scope than the concerns of comparative military-political sociology, although these concerns do form a vital part of our effort.

8. See Aaron Wildavsky, *Budgeting: A Comparative Theory of Budgetary Process* (Boston: Little, Brown, 1975), and his earlier *Politics of the Budgetary Process* (1964; reprinted, Boston: Little, Brown, 1979).

9. See Samuel Huntington, *The Common Defense* (New York: Columbia University Press, 1961).

10. See Glenn H. Snyder, "Deterrence and Defense: A Theoretical Introduction," in *American Defense Policy,* ed. John E. Endicott and Roy W. Stafford, Jr., 4th ed. (Baltimore: Johns Hopkins University Press, 1977), pp. 39–40.

The international system: Structural causes and military effects

Kenneth N. Waltz

How should we count poles, and how can we measure power? These questions must be answered in order to identify variations of structure. Almost everyone agrees that at some time since World War II, the world was bipolar. Few seem to believe that it remains so. For years Walter Lippmann wrote of the bipolar world as being perpetually in the process of rapidly passing away.[1] Many others now carry on the tradition he so firmly established. To reach the conclusion that bipolarity is passing, or past, requires some odd counting. The inclination to count in funny ways is rooted in the desire to arrive at a particular answer. Scholars feel a strong affection for the balance-of-power world of Metternich and Bismarck, on which many of their theoretical notions rest. That was a world in which five or so Great Powers manipulated their neighbors and maneuvered for advantage. Great Powers were once defined according to their capabilities. Students of international politics now seem to look at other conditions. The ability or inability of states to solve problems is said to raise or lower their rankings. The relations of states may be examined instead of their capabilities, and, since the former are always multilateral, the world is said to be multipolar. Thus, the dissolution of blocs was said to signal the end of bipolarity even though to infer bipolarity from the existence of blocs in itself confuses the relations with the capabilities of states. The world was never bipolar because two blocs opposed each other, but because of the preeminence of bloc leaders.

In addition to confusion about what to count, one often finds that those who try to identify Great Powers by gauging their capabilities make their measurements strangely. Of all the ways of playing the numbers game the favorite is probably this: to separate the economic, military, and political capabilities of nations in gauging their ability to act. For example, Henry Kissinger, while secretary of state, observed that although militarily "there are two superpowers," economically "there are at least five major groupings." Power is no longer "homogeneous." Throughout history, he added, "military, economic, and political potential were closely related. To be powerful a nation had to be strong in all categories." This is no longer so. "Military muscle does not guarantee political influence. Economic giants can be militarily weak, and military strength may not be able to obscure economic weakness. Countries can exert political influence even when they have neither military nor economic strength."[2]

If the different capabilities of a nation no longer reinforce each other, one can focus on a nation's strengths and overlook its weaknesses. Nations are then said to be superpowers even though they have only some of the previously required characteristics. China has more than 800 million people; Japan has a strong economy; Western Europe has the population and the resources and lacks only political existence. As commonly, the wanted number of Great Powers is reached by projecting the future into the present. When Europe unites . . . ; if Japan's economy continues to grow . . . ; once China's industrious people have developed their resources. . . . Then, although the imagined future lies some decades ahead, we hear that the world is no longer bipolar. A further variant is to infer another country's status from our policy toward it. Thus Nixon, when he was president, slipped easily from talking of China's becoming a superpower to conferring superpower status on it. In one of the statements that smoothed the route to Peking, he accomplished this in two paragraphs.[3] The headlines of various news stories before, during, and after his visit confirmed China's new rank. This was the greatest act of creation since Adam and Eve, and a true illustration of the superpower status of the United States. A country becomes a superpower if we treat it like one. We create other states in our image.

Many of those who have recently hailed the world's return to multipolarity have not unexpectedly done so because they confuse structure and process. How are capabilities distributed? What are the likely results of a given distribution? These are distinct questions. The difficulty of counting poles is rooted in the failure to observe the distinction. A systems theory requires one to define structures partly by the distribution of capabilities across units. Because states are in a self-help system, they have to use their combined capabilities to serve their interests. The economic, military, and other capabilities of nations cannot be sectored and separately weighed. States are not placed in the top rank because they excel in one way or another. Their rank depends on how they score on *all* of the following items: size of population and territory, re-

Some parts of this chapter were written as a study of interdependence for the Department of State, whose views may differ from my own.

source endowment, economic capability, military strength, political stability, and competence. States spend a lot of time estimating one another's capabilities, especially their abilities to do harm. States have different combinations of capabilities which are difficult to measure and compare, the more so since the weight to be assigned to different items changes with time. We should not be surprised if wrong answers are sometimes arrived at. Prussia startled most foreigners, and most Prussians, by the speed and extent of its victories over Austria in 1866 and over France in 1870. Ranking states does not, however, require predicting their success in war or in other endeavors. We need only rank them roughly by capability. Any ranking at times involves difficulties of comparison and uncertainties about where to draw lines. Historically, despite the difficulties, one finds general agreement about who the great powers of a period are, with occasional doubt about marginal cases. The recent inordinate difficulty of counting Great Powers arose not from problems of measurement, but from confusion about how polarities should be defined.

Counting the Great Powers of an era is about as difficult, or as easy, as saying how many major firms populate an oligopolistic sector of an economy. The question is an empirical one, and common sense can answer it. Economists agree that, even when the total number of firms in a sector is large, their interactions can be understood, though not fully predicted, through theories about oligopoly if the number of consequential firms reduces to a small number by virtue of the preeminence of a few of them. International politics can be viewed in the same way. The 150-odd states in the world appear to form a system of fairly large numbers. Given the inequality of nations, however, the number of consequential states is small. From the Treaty of Westphalia to the present, eight major states at most have sought to coexist peacefully or have contended for mastery. Viewed as the politics of the powerful, international politics can be studied in terms of the logic of small-number systems.

STABILITY, BIPOLARITY, AND MULTIPOLARITY

The stability of pairs—of corporations, of political parties, of marriage partners—has often been appreciated. Although most students of international politics probably believe that systems of many Great Powers would be unstable, they resist the widespread notion that two is the best of small numbers. Are they right to do so? For the sake of stability, peace, or whatever, should we prefer a world of two Great Powers or a world of at least several? Problems of national security in multipolar and bipolar worlds do clearly show the advantages of having two Great Powers, and only two, in the system.

To establish the virtues of two-party systems requires comparing systems of different number. By what criteria do we determine that an international-political system changes, and conversely, by what criteria do we say that a system is stable? Political scientists often lump different effects under the heading of stability. I did this in essays of 1964 and 1967,[4] using stability to include also peacefulness and the effective management of international affairs. It is important, I now believe, to keep different effects separate so that we can accurately locate their causes.

Anarchic systems* are transformed only by changes in organizing principle and by consequential changes in the number of their principal parties. To say that an international-political system is stable means two things: first, that it remains anarchic; second, that no consequential variation takes place in the number of principal parties that constitute the system. "Consequential" variations in number are changes of number that lead to different expectations about the effect of structure on units. The stability of the system, then, as long as it remains anarchic, is closely linked with the fate of its principal members. The close link is established by the relation of changes in number of Great Powers to transformation of the system. The link does not bind absolutely, however, because the number of Great Powers may remain the same or fail to vary consequentially even while some powers fall from the ranks of the great ones only to be replaced by others. International-political systems are remarkably stable, as table 1 graphically shows. The multipolar system lasted three centuries because as some states fell from the top rank others rose to it through the relative increase of their capabilities. The system endured even as the identity of its members changed. The bipolar system has lasted three decades because no third state has been able to develop capabilities comparable to those of the United States and the Soviet Union. The system appears robust, although unlikely to last as long as its predecessor.

The link between the survival of particular Great Powers and the stability of systems is also weakened by the fact that not all changes of number are changes of system. That bipolar and multipolar systems are distinct is widely accepted. Systems of two have qualities distinct from systems of three or more. What is the defining difference? The answer is found in the behavior required of parties in self-help systems: namely, balancing. Balancing is done differently in multipolar and bipolar systems. Though many students of international politics believe that the balance-of-power game requires at least three or four players, two will do. Where two powers contend, imbalances can be righted only by their internal efforts. With more than two, shifts in alignment provide an additional means of adjustment, adding flexibility to the system. This is a crucial difference between multipolar and bipolar systems. Beyond two, what variations of number are consequential? Three and four are threshold numbers. They mark the transition from one system to another because the opportunities offered for balancing through combining with others vary in ways that change expected out-

*By *anarchy,* the author is referring to the absence of any superordinate authority over states within the international system. As a consequence, it is a "self-help" system in which the state must act in its own behalf, to assure its own security or for other purposes. By contrast to this "flat" or horizontal structure of the international system, domestic political systems tend to be hierarchic or vertical in structure (there is a real hierarchy of authority over the citizens of a state).—Ed.

Table 1
Great Powers, 1700 to the present

Country	1700	1800	1875	1910	1935	1945
Turkey	X					
Sweden	X					
Netherlands	X					
Spain	X					
Austria (Austria-Hungary)	X	X	X	X		
France	X	X	X	X	X	
England (Great Britain)	X	X	X	X	X	
Prussia (Germany)		X	X	X	X	
Russia (Soviet Union)		X	X	X	X	X
Italy			X	X	X	
Japan				X	X	
United States				X	X	X

Source: Adapted from Quincy Wright, *A Study of War* (Chicago: University of Chicago Press, 1965), appendix 20, table 43.

comes. Systems of three have distinctive and unfortunate characteristics. Two of the powers can easily gang up on the third, divide the spoils, and drive the system back to bipolarity. In multipolar systems, four is then the lowest acceptable number, for it permits external alignment and promises considerable stability. Five is thought of as another threshold number, being the lowest number that promises stability while providing a role for a balancer; and I shall examine that claim. Beyond five, no threshold appears. We know that complications accelerate as numbers grow because of the difficulty everyone has in coping with the uncertain behavior of many others and because of the ever larger number and variety of coalitions that can be made, but we have no grounds for saying that complications pass a threshold as we move from, say, seven to eight. Luckily, as a practical matter, no increase in the number of Great Powers is in prospect.

Until 1945 the nation state system was multipolar, and always with five or more powers. In all of modern history, the structure of international politics has changed but once. We have only two systems to observe. By inference and analogy, however, some conclusions can be drawn about international systems with smaller or larger numbers of Great Powers. The next part of this article shows that five parties do not constitute a distinct system and considers the different implications of systems of two and of four or more.

THE BALANCE OF POWER

With only two Great Powers, a balance-of-power system is unstable; four powers are required for its proper functioning. For ease and nicety of adjustment, a fifth power, serving as balancer, adds a further refinement. This is the conventional wisdom. Should we accept it? Is five a nice compromise between the simplest possible system of two and numbers so large as to make anarchic systems hopelessly complex?

The notion of a balancer is more a historical generalization than a theoretical concept. The generalization is drawn from the position and behavior of Britain in the eighteenth and nineteenth centuries. British experience shows what conditions have to prevail if the role of balancer is to be effectively played. The first of these was that the margin of power on the side of the aggressor not be so large that British strength added to the weaker side would be insufficient to redress the balance. When the states of the Continent were nearly in balance, Britain could act with effect. The second condition was that Britain's ends on the Continent remain negative, for positive ends help to determine alignments. A state that wishes to secure a piece of territory ordinarily has to ally with states that do not already have it. The goals of the state then lessen the scope of its diplomatic maneuver. Finally, to be effective in the role of balancer, Britain required a status in power at least equal to that of the mightiest. British weakness vis-à-vis European countries has to the present day meant entanglement with them. Only when Continental powers were nearly in balance or when Britain was impressively strong was it able to remain aloof until the moment arrived when its commitment could be diplomatically decisive. These are highly special conditions, made more so by the fact that political preferences must not lead the balancer to identify with any actual or potential grouping of states. Balance-of-power theory cannot incorporate the role of balancer, because the playing of the role depends on such narrowly defined and historically unlikely conditions. The number five has no special charm, for there is no reason to believe that the odd party will be able and willing to serve as balancer.

Such considerations lead to more general doubts about the vaunted advantages of flexible alliances. To be helpful, flexibility has to mean that, where one or more states threaten others, some state will join one side or defect from the other in order to tilt the balance against the would-be aggressors. The old balance-of-power system here looks suspiciously like the new collective-security system of the League and the United Nations. Either system depends for its maintenance and functioning on neutrality of alignment at the moment of serious threat. To preserve the system, at least one powerful state must overcome the pressure of ideological preference, the pull of previous ties, and the conflict of present interests in order to add its weight to the side of the peaceful. It must do what the moment requires.

Since one of the interests of each state is to avoid domination by other states, why should it be difficult for one or a few states to swing to the side of the threatened? The answer has two parts. First, the members of a group sharing a common interest may well not act to further it. *A* and *B*, both threatened by *C*, may unite to oppose the latter. After all, they experience a common danger. But *A* may instead say to *B:* "Since the threat is to you as well as to me, I'll stand aside and let you deal with the matter." If *B* acts effectively, *A* gains free benefits. If *B*, having become resentful, does not, *A* and *B* both lose. Contemplation of a common fate may not lead to a fair division of labor—or to any labor at all. Whether or not it does depends on the size of the group and the inequalities within it, as well as on the character of its members.[5]

One sees the difficulties in any multipolar system where some states threaten others while alignments are uncertain. French Foreign Minister Flandin told British Prime Minister Baldwin that Hitler's military occupation of the Rhineland in 1936 provided the occasion for Britain to take the lead in opposing Germany. As the German threat grew, some British and French leaders could hope that, if their countries remained aloof, Russia and Germany would balance each other off or fight each other to the finish.[6] Uncertainties about who threatens whom, about who will oppose whom, and about who will gain or lose from the actions of other states accelerate as the number of states increases. Even if one assumes that the goals of most states are worthy, the timing and content of the actions required to reach them become more and more difficult to calculate. Rather than making the matter simpler, prescribing general rules for states to follow simply illustrates the impossibility of believing that states can reconcile two conflicting imperatives—to act for their own sakes, as required by their situations, and to act for the system's stability or survival, as some scholars advise them to do. Political scientists who favor flexibility of national alignment have to accept that flexibility comes only as numbers increase and thus also as complexities and uncertainties multiply.

With more than two states, the politics of power turn on the diplomacy by which alliances are made, maintained, and disrupted. Flexibility of alignment means both that the country one is wooing may prefer another suitor and that one's present alliance partner may defect. Flexibility of alignment narrows one's choice of policies. A state's strategy must please a potential or satisfy a present partner. A comparable situation is found where political parties compete for votes by forming and re-forming electoral coalitions of different economic, ethnic, religious, and regional groups. The strategy, or policy, of a party is made for the sake of attracting and holding voters. If a party is to be an electoral success, its policy cannot simply be the one that its leaders believe to be best for the country. Policy must be made at least partly for the sake of winning elections. Similarly, with a number of approximately equal states, strategy is made at least partly for the sake of attracting and holding allies. If alliances may form, states will want to look like attractive partners. Suitors alter their appearance and adapt their behavior to increase their eligibility. Those who remain unattractive, finding that they compete poorly, are likely to try all the harder to change their appearance and behavior. One has to become attractive enough in personality and policy to be considered a possible choice. The alliance diplomacy of Europe in the years before World War I is rich in examples of this. Ever since the Napoleonic Wars, many had believed that the "Republican" and the "Cossack" could never become engaged, let alone contract a marriage. The wooing of France and Russia, with each adapting somewhat to the other, was nevertheless consummated in the alliance of 1894 and duly produced the Triple Entente as its progeny when first France and England, and then Russia and England, overcame their long-standing animosities in 1904 and 1907, respectively.

If pressures are strong enough, a state will deal with almost anyone. Litvinov remarked in the 1930s that, to promote its security in a hostile world, the Soviet Union would work with any state, even with Hitler's Germany.[7] It is important to notice that states will ally with the devil to avoid the hell of military defeat. It is still more important to remember that the question of who will ally with which devil may be the decisive one. In the end, Hitler's acts determined that all of the Great Powers, besides Italy and Japan, would unite against him.[8]

In the quest for security, alliances may have to be made. Once made, they have to be managed. European alliances beginning in the 1890s hardened as two blocs formed. The rigidity of blocs contributed strongly, it is thought, to the outbreak of World War I. The view is a superficial one. Alliances are made by states that have some but not all of their interests in common. The common interest is ordinarily a negative one: fear of other states. Divergence comes when positive interests are at issue. Consider two examples. Russia would have preferred to plan and prepare for the occasion of war against Austria-Hungary. Russia could hope to defeat Austria-Hungary, but not Germany, and Austria-Hungary stood in the way of Russia's gaining control of the straits linking the Mediterranean and the Black Seas. France, however, could regain Alsace-Lorraine only by defeating Germany. Perception of a common threat brought Russia and France together. Alliance diplomacy, and a large flow of funds from France to Russia, helped to hold them together and to shape an alliance strategy more to the taste of France than of Russia. Alliance strategies are always the product of compromise, since the interests of allies and allies' notions of how to secure them are never identical. In a multipolar system, moreover, despite the formation of blocs, one's allies may edge toward the opposing camp. If a member of one alliance tries to settle differences, or to cooperate in some ways, with a member of another alliance, its own allies become uneasy. Thus, British-German cooperation in 1912 and 1913 to dampen Balkan crises, and the settling of some colonial questions between them, may have been harmful. The reactions of their allies dissuaded Britain and Germany from playing similar roles in Southeastern Europe in 1914, yet gave each of them some hope that the other's alliance would not hold firm.[9] Greater cohesion of blocs would have permitted greater flexibility of policy. But then the cohesion of blocs, like the discipline of parties, is achieved through expert and careful management; and the management of blocs is exceedingly difficult among near-equals, since it must be cooperatively contrived.

If competing blocs are seen to be closely balanced, and if competition turns on important matters, then to let one's side down risks one's own destruction. In a moment of crisis, the weaker or the more adventurous party is likely to determine its side's policy. Its partners can afford neither to let the weaker member go to the wall nor to advertise their disunity by failing to back a venture even while deploring its risks. The prelude to World War I provides striking examples. The approximate equality of alliance partners made them closely interdependent. The interdependence of allies, plus the keenness of competition between the two camps, meant that while any country could commit its associates, no one country on either side could exercise control. If Austria-Hungary marched, Germany had to follow; the dissolution of the Austro-Hungarian Empire would have left Germany alone in the middle of Europe. If France marched, Russia had to follow; a German victory over France would be a defeat for Russia. And so it was all around the vicious circle. Because the defeat or the defection of a major ally would have shaken the balance, each state was constrained to adjust its strategy and the use of its forces to the aims and fears of its partners. In one sense, the unstable politics of the Balkans carried the world into war. But that statement rather misses the point. Destabilizing events and conditions abound internationally. The important questions to ask are whether they are likely to be managed better, and whether their efforts are absorbed more readily, in one system than in another.

The game of power politics, if really played hard, presses the players into two rival camps, though so complicated is the business of making and maintaining alliances that the game may be played hard enough to produce that result only under the pressure of war. Thus, the six or seven Great Powers of the interwar period did not move into a two-bloc formation until more than two years after World War II began. The forming of two blocs, moreover, did not make the multipolar system into a bipolar one any more than the forming of opposing coalitions for the purpose of fighting an election turns a multiparty system into a two-party system. Even with the greatest of external pressure, the unity of alliances is far from complete. States or parties in wartime or in electoral alliance, even as they adjust to one another, continue to jockey for advantage and to worry about the constellation of forces that will form once the contest is over.

In multipolar systems there are too many powers to permit any of them to draw clear and fixed lines between allies and adversaries and too few to keep the effects of defection low. With three or more powers, flexibility of alliances keeps relations of friendship and enmity fluid and makes everyone's estimate of the present and future relation of forces uncertain. As long as the system is one of fairly small numbers, the actions of any of the powers may threaten the security of others. There are too many to enable anyone to see for sure what is happening, and too few to make what is happening a matter of indifference. Students of international politics have traditionally thought that the uncertainty that results from flexibility of alignment generates a healthy caution in everyone's foreign policy.[10] Conversely, they have also believed that bipolar worlds are doubly unstable—that they easily erode or explode. This conclusion is based on false reasoning and scant evidence. Military interdependence varies with the extent to which, and the equality with which, Great Powers rely on others for their security. In a bipolar world, military interdependence declines even more sharply than economic interdependence. Russia and America depend militarily mainly on themselves. They balance each other by "internal" instead of "external" means, relying on their own capabilities rather than on the capabilities of allies. Internal balancing is more reliable and precise than external balancing. States are less likely to misjudge their relative strengths than they are to misjudge the strength and reliability of opposing coalitions. Rather than making states properly cautious and forwarding the chances of peace, uncertainty and miscalculation cause wars.[11] In a bipolar world, there is less uncertainty and calculations are easier to make.

Much of the skepticism about the virtues of bipolarity arises from thinking of a system as being bipolar if two blocs form within a multipolar world. A bloc unskillfully managed may indeed fall apart. In a multipolar world, the leaders of both blocs must be concerned at once with alliance management—since the defection of an ally may be fatal to its partners—and with the aims and capabilities of the opposing bloc. The prehistory of two world wars dramatically displays the dangers. The fair amount of effort that now goes into alliance management may obscure the profound difference between old-style and new-style alliances. In alliances among equals, the defection of one party threatens the security of the others. In alliances among unequals, the contributions of the lesser members are at once wanted and of relatively small importance. Where the contributions of a number of parties are highly important to all of them, each has strong incentive both to persuade others to its views about strategy and tactics and to make concessions when persuasion fails. The unity of major partners is likely to endure because they all understand how much they depend on it. Before World War I, Germany's acceptance of Italy's probable defection from the Triple Alliance signaled its relative unimportance. In alliances among unequals, alliance leaders need worry little about the faithfulness of their followers, who usually have little choice anyway. Contrast the situation in 1914 with that of the United States and Britain and France in 1956. The United States could dissociate itself from the Suez adventure of its two principal allies and subject them to heavy financial pressure. Like Austria-Hungary in 1914, these allies tried to commit or at least immobilize their alliance partner by presenting a *fait accompli*. Enjoying a position of predominance, the United States could continue to focus its attention on the major adversary while disciplining its allies. The ability of the United States, and the inability of Germany, to pay a price measured in intraalliance terms is striking. It is important, then, to distinguish sharply between the formation of two blocs in a multipolar world and the structural bipolarity of the present system.

In bipolar as in multipolar worlds, alliance leaders may try to elicit maximum contributions from their associates. The contributions are useful even in a bipolar world, but they are not indispensable. Because they are not, the policies and strategies of alliance leaders are ultimately made according to the leaders' own calculations and interests. Disregarding the views of an ally makes sense only if military cooperation is fairly unimportant. This is the case both in the Warsaw Treaty Organization (WTO) and in the North Atlantic Treaty Organization (NATO). In 1976, for example, the Soviet Union's military expenditures were well over 90 percent of the WTO total, and those of the United States were about 75 percent of the NATO total. In fact if not in form, NATO consists of guarantees given by the United States to its European allies and to Canada. The United States, with a preponderance of nuclear weapons and as many troops as the West European states combined, may be able to protect them; they cannot protect it. Because of the vast differences in the capabilities of member states, the roughly equal sharing of burdens found in earlier alliance systems is no longer possible.

Militarily, interdependence is low in a bipolar world and high in a multipolar one. Great Powers in a multipolar world depend on one another for political and military support in crises and war. To assure oneself of steadfast support is vital. This cannot be the case in a bipolar world, for third parties are not able to tilt the balance of power by withdrawing from one alliance or by joining the other. Thus, two "losses" of China in the postwar world—first by the United States and then by the Soviet Union—were accommodated without disastrously distorting, or even much affecting, the balance between America and Russia. Nor did France, in withdrawing its forces from NATO, noticeably change the bipolar balance. That American policy need not be made for the sake of France helps to explain France's partial defection. The gross inequality between the two superpowers and the members of their respective alliances makes any realignment of the latter fairly insignificant. The leader's strategy can therefore be flexible. In old-style balance-of-power politics, flexibility of alignment made for rigidity of strategy or limitation of freedom of decision. In new-style balance-of-power politics, the obverse is true: rigidity of alignment in a two-power world makes for flexibility of strategy and enlargement of freedom of decision. Although concessions to allies are sometimes made, neither the United States nor the Soviet Union alters its strategy or changes its military dispositions simply to accommodate associated states. Both superpowers can make long-range plans and carry out their policies as best they see fit, for they need not accede to the demands of third parties.

In a multipolar world, states often pool their resources in order to serve their interests. Roughly equal parties engaged in cooperative endeavors must look for a common denominator of their policies. They risk finding the lowest one and easily end up in the worst of all possible worlds. In a bipolar world, alliance leaders make their strategies mainly according to their own calculations of interests. Strategies can be designed more to cope with the main adversary and less to satisfy one's allies. Alliance leaders are free to follow their own line, which may of course reflect their bad as well as their good judgment, their imaginary as well as their realistic fears, their ignoble as well as their worthy ends. Alliance leaders are not free of constraints. The major constraints arise, however, from the main adversary and not from one's own associates.

STRATEGIC RELATIONS OF THE UNITED STATES AND THE SOVIET UNION

Neither the United States nor the Soviet Union has to make itself acceptable to other states, but they do have to cope with each other. In the Great-Power politics of multipolar worlds, who is a danger to whom, and who can be expected to deal with threats and problems, are matters of uncertainty. In the Great-Power politics of bipolar worlds, who is a danger to whom is never in doubt. This is the first big difference between the politics of power in the two systems. The United States is the obsessing danger for the Soviet Union, and the Soviet Union for the United States, since each can damage the other to an extent no other state can match. Any event in the world that involves the fortunes of either automatically elicits the interest of the other. President Truman, at the time of the Korean invasion, could not very well echo Neville Chamberlain's words in the Czechoslovakian crisis by claiming that the Koreans were a people far away in the East of Asia of whom Americans knew nothing. We had to know about them or quickly find out. In the 1930s France lay between England and Germany. The British could believe, and the United States could too, that their frontier and ours lay on the Rhine. After World War II, no third Great Power could lie between the United States and the Soviet Union, for none existed. The statement that peace is indivisible was controversial, indeed untrue, when it was made by Litvinov in the 1930s. Political slogans express wishes better than realities. In a bipolar world, the wish becomes reality. A war or threat of war anywhere is a concern to both of the superpowers if it may lead to significant gains or losses for either of them. In a two-power competition, a loss for one power appears as a gain for the other. Because this is so, the powers in a bipolar world promptly respond to unsettling events. In a multipolar world, dangers are diffused, responsibilities unclear, and definitions of vital interests easily obscured. Where a number of states are in balance, the skillful foreign policy of a forward power is designed to gain an advantage over one state without antagonizing others and frightening them into united action. At times, in modern Europe, possible gains seemed greater than likely losses. Statesmen could hope to push an issue to the limit without causing all of the potential opponents to unite. When possible enemies are several in number, unity of action among them is difficult to arrange. National leaders could therefore think—or desperately hope, as did Bethmann Hollweg and Adolf Hitler before two world wars—that no united opposition would form. Interdependence of parties, diffusion of dangers, confusion of responses—these are the characteristics of Great-Power politics in multipolar worlds.

If interests and ambitions conflict, the absence of crises is more worrisome than the recurrence of crises. Crises are produced by the determination of a state to resist a change that another state tries to make. The situation of the United States and of the Soviet Union disposes them to do the resisting, for in important matters they cannot hope that others will do it for them. Political action in the postwar world has reflected this condition. Communist guerrillas operating in Greece prompted the Truman Doctrine. The tightening of the Soviet Union's controls over the states of Eastern Europe led to the Marshall Plan and the Atlantic Defense Treaty, and these in turn gave rise to the Cominform and the Warsaw Pact. The plan to form a West German government produced the Berlin Blockade. And so on through the 1950s, 1960s, and 1970s. Our responses are geared to the Soviet Union's actions, and theirs to ours, which has produced an increasingly solid bipolar balance.

In a bipolar world there are no peripheries. With only two powers capable of acting on a world scale, anything that happens anywhere is potentially of concern to both of them. Bipolarity extends the geographic scope of both powers' concern. It also broadens the range of factors included in the competition between them. Because allies add relatively little to the superpowers' capabilities, they concentrate their attention on their own dispositions. In a multipolar world, who is a danger to whom is often unclear; the incentive to regard all disequilibrating changes with concern and to respond to them with whatever effort may be required is consequently weakened. In a bipolar world, changes may affect each of the two powers differently, and this means all the more that few changes in the world at large or within each other's national realm are likely to be thought irrelevant. Competition becomes more comprehensive as well as more widely extended. Not just military preparation but also economic growth and technological development become matters of intense and constant concern. Self-dependence of parties, clarity of dangers, certainly about who has to face them—these are the characteristics of Great Power politics in a bipolar world.

Miscalculation by some or all of the Great Powers is the source of danger in a multipolar world; overreaction by either or both of the great powers is the source of danger in a bipolar world. Bipolarity encourages the United States and the Soviet Union to turn unwanted events into crises, while rendering most of them relatively inconsequential. Each can lose heavily only in war with the other; in power and in wealth, both gain more by the peaceful development of internal resources than by wooing and winning—or by fighting and subduing—other states in the world. A 5 percent growth rate sustained for three years increases the American gross national product by an amount exceeding one-half of West Germany's GNP, and all of Great Britain's (base year 1976). For the Soviet Union, with one-half of the U.S. GNP, imaginable gains double in weight. They would still be of minor importance. Only Japan, Western Europe, and the Middle East are prizes that if won by the Soviet Union would alter the balance of GNPs and the distribution of resources enough to be a danger.

Yet, since World War II the United States has responded expensively in distant places to wayward events that could hardly affect anyone's fate outside of the region. Which is worse: miscalculation or overreaction? Miscalculation is more likely to permit the unfolding of a series of events that finally threatens a change in the balance and brings the powers to war. Overreaction is the lesser evil because it costs only money and the fighting of limited wars.

The dynamics of a bipolar system, moreover, provide a measure of correction. In a hot war or a cold war—as in any close competition—the external situation dominates. In the mid-1950s, John Foster Dulles inveighed against the immoral neutralists. Russian leaders, in like spirit, described neutralists as either fools themselves or dupes of capitalist countries. But ideology did not long prevail over interest. Both Russia and America quickly came to accept neutralist states and even to lend them encouragement. The Soviet Union aided Egypt and Iraq, countries that kept their Communists in jail. In the late 1950s and throughout the 1960s, the United States, having already given economic and military assistance to Communist Yugoslavia, made neutralist India the most favored recipient of economic aid.[12] According to the rhetoric of the Cold War, the root cleavage in the world was between capitalist democracy and godless communism. But by the size of the stakes and the force of the struggle, ideology was subordinated to interest in the policies of America and Russia, who behaved more like traditional Great Powers than like leaders of messianic movements. In a world in which two states united in their mutual antagonism far overshadow any other, the incentives to a calculated response stand out most clearly, and the sanctions against irresponsible behavior achieve their greatest force. Thus, two states, isolationist by tradition, untutored in the ways of international politics, and famed for impulsive behavior, soon showed themselves—not always and everywhere, but always in crucial cases—to be wary, alert, cautious, flexible, and forbearing.

Some have believed that a new world began with the explosion of an atomic bomb over Hiroshima. In shaping the behavior of nations, the perennial forces of politics are more important than the new military technology. States remain the primary vehicles of ideology. The international brotherhood of autocrats after 1815, the cosmopolitan liberalism of the middle nineteenth century, international socialism before World War I, international communism in the decades following the Bolshevik revolution—in all of these cases, international movements were captured by individual nations, adherents of the creed were harnessed to the nation's interest, international programs were manipulated by national governments, and ideology became a prop to national policy. So the Soviet Union in crisis became Russian, and American policy, liberal rhetoric aside, came to be realistically and cautiously constructed. By the force of events, they and we were impelled to behave in ways belied both by their words and by ours. Political scientists, drawing their inferences from the characteristics of states, were slow to appreciate the process. Inferences drawn from the characteristics of small-number systems are better borne out politically. Economists have long known that the passage of time makes peaceful coexistence among major competitors easier. They become accustomed to one another; they learn how to interpret one another's moves and how to accommodate or counter them. "Unambiguously," as Oliver Williamson puts it, "experience leads to a higher level of adherence" to agreements made and to commonly accepted practices.[13] Life becomes more predictable.

Theories of perfect competition tell us about the market and not about the competitors. Theories of oligopolistic competition tell us quite a bit about both. In important ways, competitors become like one another as their competition continues. This applies to states as well as to firms. Thus, William Zimmerman found not only that the Soviet Union in the 1960s had abandoned its Bolshevik views of international relations but also that its views had become much like ours.[14] The increasing similarity of competitors' attitudes, as well as their experience with one another, eases the adjustment of their relations.

These advantages are found in all small-number systems. What additional advantages do pairs enjoy in dealing with each other? As a group shrinks, its members face fewer choices when considering whom to deal with. Partly because they eliminate the difficult business of choosing, the smallest of groups manages its affairs most easily. With more than two parties, the solidarity of a group is always at risk because the parties can try to improve their lots by combining. Interdependence breeds hostility and fear. With more than two parties, hostility and fear may lead *A* and *B* to seek the support of *C*. If they both court *C*, their hostility and fear increase. When a group narrows to just two members, choice disappears. On matters of ultimate importance, each can deal only with the other. No appeal can be made to third parties. A system of two has unique properties. Tension in the system is high because each can do so much for and to the other. But because no appeal can be made to third parties, pressure to moderate behavior is heavy.[15] Bargaining among more than two parties is difficult. Bargainers worry about the points at issue. With more than two parties, each also worries about how the strength of his position will be affected by combinations he and others may make. If two of several parties strike an agreement, moreover, they must wonder if the agreement will be disrupted or negated by the actions of others.

Consider the problem of disarmament. To find even limited solutions, at least one of the following two conditions must be met. First, if the would-be winner of an arms race is willing to curtail its program, agreement is made possible. In the 1920s the United States—the country that could have won a naval arms race—took the lead in negotiating limitations. The self-interest of the would-be losers carried them along. Such was the necessary, though not the only, condition making the Washington Naval Arms Limitation Treaty possible. Second, if two powers can consider their mutual interests and fears without giving much thought to how the military capabilities of others affect them, agreement is made possible. The 1972 treaty limiting the deployment of antiballistic missiles is a dramatic example of this. Ballistic missile defenses, because they promise to be effective against missiles fired in small numbers, are useful against the nuclear forces of third parties. Because of their vast superiority, the United States and the Soviet Union were nevertheless able to limit their defensive weaponry. To the extent that the United States and the Soviet Union have to worry about the military strength of others, their ability to reach bilateral agreements lessens. So far those worries have been small.[16]

The simplicity of relations in a bipolar world and the strong pressures that are generated make the two Great Powers conservative. Structure does not, however, by any means explain everything. I say this again because the charge of structural determinism is easy to make. To explain outcomes, one must look at the capabilities, the actions, and the interactions of states, as well as at the structure of their systems. States armed with nuclear weapons may have stronger incentives to avoid war than states armed conventionally. The United States and the Soviet Union may have found it harder to learn to live with each other in the 1940s and 1950s than more experienced and less ideological nations would have. Causes at both the national and the international level make the world more or less peaceful and stable. I concentrate attention at the international level because the effects of structure are usually overlooked or misunderstood and because I am writing a theory of international politics, not of foreign policy.

In saying that the United States and the Soviet Union, like duopolists in other fields, are gradually learning how to cope with each other, I do not imply that they will interact without crises or find cooperation easy. The quality of their relations did, however, perceptibly change in the 1960s and 1970s. Worries in the 1940s and 1950s that tensions would rise to intolerable levels were balanced in the 1960s and 1970s by fears that America and the Soviet Union would make agreements for their mutual benefit at others' expense. West Europeans—especially in Germany and France—have fretted. Chinese leaders have sometimes accused the Soviet Union of seeking world domination through collaboration with the United States. Worries and fears on any such grounds are exaggerated. The Soviet Union and the United States influence each other more than any of the states living in their penumbra can hope to do. In the world of the present, as in that of the recent past, a condition of mutual opposition may require rather than preclude the adjustment of differences, yet first steps toward agreement do not lead to second and third steps. Instead, they mingle with other acts and events that keep the level of tension quite high. This is the pattern set by the first major success enjoyed by the Soviet Union and the United States in jointly regulating their military affairs—the Test Ban Treaty of 1963. The test ban was described in the United States as possibly a first big step toward wider agreements that would increase the chances of maintaining peace. In the same breath, it was said that we cannot lower our guard, for the Soviet Union's aims have not changed.[17] Because they must rely for their security on their own devices, both countries are wary of joint ventures. Since they cannot know that benefits will be equal, and since they cannot be certain that arrangements made will reliably bind both of them, each shies away from running a future risk for the sake of a present benefit. Between parties in a self-help system, rules of reciprocity and caution prevail. Their concern for peace and stability draws them together; their fears drive them apart. They are rightly called *frère ennemi* and adversary partners.

May not the enmity obliterate the brotherhood and the sense of opposition obscure mutual interests? A small-number system can always be disrupted by the actions of a Hitler and the reactions of a Chamberlain. Since this is true, it may seem that we are in the uncomfortable position of relying on the moderation, courage, and good sense of those holding positions of power. Given human vagaries and the unpredictability of the individual's reaction to events, one may feel that the only recourse is to lapse into prayer. We can nonetheless take comfort from the thought that, like others, those who direct the activities of great states are by no means free agents. Beyond the residuum of necessary hope that leaders will respond sensibly lies the possibility of estimating the pressures that encourage them to do so. In a world in which two states united in their mutual antagonism far overshadow any other, the incentives to a calculated response stand out most clearly, and the sanctions against irresponsible behavior achieve their greatest force. The identity as well as the behavior of leaders is affected by the presence of pressures and the clarity of challenges. One may lament Churchill's failure to gain control of the British government in the 1930s, for he knew what actions were required to maintain a balance of power. Churchill was brought to power not by the diffused threat of war in the 1930s, but only by the stark danger of defeat after war began. If people representing one pole of the world now tolerate inept rulers, they run clearly discernible risks. Leaders of the United States and the Soviet Union are presumably chosen with an eye to the tasks they will have to perform. Other countries can enjoy, if they wish to, the luxury of selecting leaders who will most please their peoples by the way in which internal affairs are managed. The United States and the Soviet Union cannot.

It is not that one entertains the utopian hope that all future American and Russian rulers will combine in their persons a complicated set of nearly perfect virtues, but rather that the pressures of a bipolar world strongly encourage them to act internationally in ways better than their characters may lead one to expect. I made this proposition in 1964; Nixon as president confirmed it. It is not that one is serenely confident about the peacefulness, or even about the survival, of the world, but rather that cautious optimism is justified so long as the dangers to which each must respond are so clearly present. Either country may go berserk or succumb to inanition and debility. That necessities are clear increases the chances that they will be met, but gives no guarantees. Dangers from abroad may unify a state and spur its people to heroic action; however, as with France facing Hitler's Germany, external pressures may divide the leaders, confuse the public, and increase their willingness to give way. It may also happen that the difficulties of adjustment and the necessity for calculated action simply become too great. The clarity with which the necessities of action can now be seen may be blotted out by the blinding flash of nuclear explosions. The fear that this may happen strengthens the forces and processes I have described.

A MOST EXCLUSIVE CLUB: THE DURABILITY OF BIPOLARITY

A system of two has many virtues. Before explaining any more of them, the question of the durability of today's bipolar world should be examined. The system is dynamically stable, as I have shown. I have not, however, examined the many assertions that America and Russia are losing, or have lost, their effective edge over other states, as has happened to previous Great Powers and surely may happen again. Let us first ask whether the margin of American and Soviet superiority is seriously eroding, and then examine the relation between military power and political control.

Surveying the rise and fall of nations over the centuries, one can only conclude that national rankings change slowly. War aside, the economic and other bases of power change little more rapidly in one major nation than they do in another. Differences in economic growth rates are neither large enough nor steady enough to alter standings except in the long run. France and its major opponents in the Napoleonic Wars were also the major initial participants in World War I, with Prussia having become Germany and with the later addition of the United States. Even such thorough defeats as those suffered by Napoleonic France and Wilhelmine Germany did not remove those countries from the ranks of the great powers. World War II did change the cast of Great-Power characters; no longer could others compete with the United States and the Soviet Union, for only they combine great scale in geography and population with economic and technological development. Entering the club was easier when Great Powers were larger in number and smaller in size. With fewer and bigger powers, barriers to entry have risen. Over time, however, even they can be surmounted. How long a running start is needed before some third or fourth state will be able to jump over the barriers? Just how high are they?

Although not as high as they once were, they are higher than many would have us believe. One of the themes of recent American discourse is that we are a "declining industrial power." C. L. Sulzberger, for example, announced in November of 1972 that "the U.S. finds itself no longer the global giant of twenty years ago." Our share of global production, he claimed, "has slipped from 50 to 30 percent." Such a misuse of numbers would be startling had we not become accustomed to hearing about America's steady decline. In the summer of 1971, President Nixon remarked that twenty-five years ago "we were number one in the world militarily" and "number one economically" as well. The United States, he added, "was producing more than 50 percent of all the world's goods." But no longer. By 1971, "instead of just America being number one in the world from an economic standpoint, the preeminent world power, and instead of there being just two superpowers, when we think in economic terms and economic potentialities, there are five great power centers in the world today."[18]

The trick that Sulzberger and Nixon played on us,

and no doubt on themselves, should be apparent. In 1946, Nixon's year of comparison, most of the industrial world outside of the United States lay in ruins. By 1952, Sulzberger's year of comparison, Britain, France, and Russia had regained their prewar levels of production, but the German and Japanese economic miracles had not been performed. In the years just after the war, the United States naturally produced an unusually large percentage of the world's goods. Now again, as before the war,[19] we produce about one quarter of the world's goods, which is two and three times as much as the two next-largest economies—namely, the Soviet Union's and Japan's. And that somehow means that rather than being number one, we have become merely one of five?

A recovery growth rate is faster than a growth rate from a normal base. The recovery rates of other economies reduced the huge gap between America and other industrial countries to one still huge, but less so. No evidence suggests further significant erosion of America's present position. Much evidence suggests that we became sufficiently accustomed to our abnormal postwar dominance to lead us now to an unbecoming sensitivity to others' advances, whether or not they equal our own. In the economic/technological game, the United States holds the high cards. Economic growth and competitiveness depend heavily on technological excellence. The United States has the lead, which it maintains by spending more than other countries on research and development. Here again, recent statements mislead. The *International Economic Report of the President,* submitted in March of 1976, warned the Congress that "the United States has not been keeping pace with the growth and relative importance of R&D efforts of some of its major foreign competitors, especially Germany and Japan."[20] This should be translated to read as follows: Germany's and Japan's increases in R&D expenditures brought them roughly to the American level of spending by 1973. Much of America's decline in expenditure over the decade reflects reduced spending on space and defense-related research and development, which have little to do with economic standing anyway. Since expenditure is measured as a percentage of GNP, moreover, America's national expenditure is still disproportionately large. The expenditure is reflected in results, as several examples suggest. In the twenty-nine years following the 1943 resumption of Nobel Prize awards in science, Americans won 86 of the 178 given.[21]

In 1976 we became the first country ever to sweep the Nobel Prizes. (This led, of course, to articles in the press warning of an approaching decline in America's scientific and cultural eminence, partly because other countries are catching up in research expenditures in ways that I have just summarized. One suspects that the warning is merited; we can scarcely do better.) Between 1953 and 1973, the United States produced 65 percent of 492 major technological innovations. Britain was second, with 17 percent. In 1971, of every 10,000 employees in the American labor force, 61.9 were scientists and engineers. The comparable figures for the next ranking noncommunist countries were 38.4 for Japan, 32.0 for West Germany, and 26.2 for France. Finally, our advantage in the export of manufactured goods has depended heavily on the export of high-technology products. In the three years from 1973 through 1975, those exports grew at an annual average rate of 28.3 percent.

However one measures, the United States is the leading country. One may wonder whether the position of leader is not a costly one to maintain. Developing countries, Russia and Japan, for example, have gained by adopting technology expensively created in countries with more advanced economies. For four reasons, this is no longer easily possible. First, the complexity of today's technology means that competence in some matters can seldom be separated from competence in others. How can a country be in the forefront of any complicated technology without full access to the most sophisticated computers? Countries as advanced as the Soviet Union and France have felt the difficulties that the question suggests. Second, the pace of technological change means that lags lengthen and multiply. "The countries only a little behind," as Victor Basiuk has said, "frequently find themselves manufacturing products already on the threshold of obsolescence."[22] Third, even though the United States does not have an internal market big enough to permit the full and efficient exploitation of some possible technologies, it nevertheless approaches the required scale more closely than anyone else does. The advantage is great, since most projects will continue to be national rather than international ones. Fourth, economic and technological leads are likely to become more important in international politics. This is partly because of the military stalemate. It is also because in today's world, and more so in tomorrow's, adequate supplies of basic materials are not easily and cheaply available. To mine the seabeds, to develop substitutes for scarce resources, to replace them with synthetics made from readily available materials—these are the abilities that will become increasingly important in determining the prosperity, if not the viability, of national economies.

I have mentioned a number of items that have to be entered on the credit side of the American ledger. Have I not overlooked items that should appear as debit entries? Have I not drawn a lopsided picture? Yes, I have, but then, it's a lopsided world. It is hard to think of disadvantages we suffer that are not more severe disadvantages for other major countries. The Soviet Union enjoys many of the advantages that the United States has and some that we lack, especially in natural resource endowments. With half of our GNP, the Soviet Union nevertheless has to run hard to stay in the race. One may think that the question to ask is not whether a third or fourth country will enter the circle of Great Powers in the foreseeable future, but whether the Soviet Union can keep up.

The Soviet Union, since the war, has been able to challenge the United States in some parts of the world by spending a disproportionately large share of its smaller income on military means. Already disadvantaged by having to sustain a larger population than America's on one half the product, the Soviet Union also spends from that product proportionately more than the United States does on defense—perhaps 11 to 13 percent, as compared to roughly 6 percent of GNP that the United States spent in the years 1973 through 1975.[23] The burden of such high military spending is heavy. Only Iran and the confrontation states of the Middle East have spent proportionately more. Some have worried that the People's Republic of China may follow such a path, that it may mobilize the nation in order to increase production rapidly while simultaneously acquiring a large and modern military capability. It is doubtful that it can do either, and surely not both, and surely not the second without the first. As a future superpower, the People's Republic of China is dimly discernible on a horizon too distant to make speculation worthwhile.

Western Europe is the only candidate for the short run—say, by the end of the millennium. Its prospects may not be bright, but at least the potential is present and needs only to be politically unfolded. The nine states of Western Europe have a total population slightly larger than the Soviet Union's and a GNP that exceeds the USSR's by 25 percent. Unity will not come tomorrow, and, if it did, Europe would not instantly achieve stardom. A united Europe that developed political competence and military power over the years would one day emerge as the third superpower, ranking probably between the United States and the Soviet Union.

Unless Europe unites, the United States and the Soviet Union will remain economically well ahead of other states, but does that in itself set them apart? In international affairs, force remains the final arbiter. Thus, some have thought that by acquiring nuclear weapons third countries reduce their distance from the Great Powers. "For, like gunpowder in another age," so one argument goes, "nuclear weapons must have the ultimate result of making the small the equal of the great."[24] Gunpowder did not blur the distinction between the Great Powers and the others, however, nor have nuclear weapons done so. Nuclear weapons are not the great equalizers they were sometimes thought to be. The world was bipolar in the late 1940s, when the United States had few atomic bombs and the Soviet Union had none. Nuclear weapons did not cause the condition of bipolarity; other states cannot change the condition by acquiring them. Nuclear weapons do not equalize the power of nations because they do not change the economic bases of a nation's power. Nuclear capabilities reinforce a condition that would exist in their absence: even without nuclear technology, the United States and the Soviet Union would have developed weapons of immense destructive power. These countries are set apart from the others not by particular weapons systems, but by their ability to exploit military technology on a large scale and at the scientific frontiers. Had the atom never been split, each would far surpass others in military strength, and each would remain the greatest threat and source of potential damage to the other.

Because it is so research intensive, modern weaponry has raised the barriers that states must jump over if they are to become members of the superpower club. Unable to spend on anywhere near the American or Russian level for research, development, and production, middle powers who try to compete find themselves constantly falling behind.[25] They are in the second-ranking powers' customary position of imitating the more advanced weaponry of their wealthier competitors, but their problems are now much bigger. The pace of the competition has quickened. If weaponry changes little and slowly, smaller countries can hope over time to accumulate weapons that will not become obsolete. In building a nuclear force, Britain became more dependent on the United States. Contemplating the example, de Gaulle nevertheless decided to go ahead with France's nuclear program. He may have done so believing that missile-firing submarines were the world's first permanently invulnerable force, that for them military obsolescence had ended. The French are fond of invulnerability. Given the small number of submarines France has planned, however, only one or two will be at sea at any given time. Continuous trailing makes their detection and destruction increasingly easy. France's eighteen land-based missiles can be blanketed by Russia's intermediate-range ballistic missiles, which it has in abundant supply. French officials continue to proclaim the invulnerability of their forces, as I would do if I were they. But I would not find my words credible. With the United States and the Soviet Union, each worries that the other may achieve a first-strike capability, and each works to prevent that. The worries of lesser nuclear powers are incomparably greater, and they cannot do much to allay them.

In the old days, weaker powers could improve their positions through alliance, by adding the strength of foreign armies to their own. Cannot some of the middle states do together what they are unable to do alone? For two decisive reasons, the answer is no. Nuclear forces do not add up. The technology of warheads, of delivery vehicles, of detection and surveillance devices, of command and control systems, count more than the size of forces. Combining separate national forces is not much help. To reach top technological levels would require complete collaboration by, say, several European states. To achieve this has proved politically impossible. As de Gaulle often said, nuclear weapons make alliances obsolete. At the strategic level he was right. That is another reason for calling NATO a treaty of guarantee rather than an old-fashioned alliance. To concert their power in order to raise their capabilities to the level of the superpowers, states would have to achieve the oligopolists' unachievable "collusive handling of all relevant variables." We know that this they cannot do. States fear dividing their strategic labors fully—from research and development through production, planning, and deployment. This is less because one of them might in the future be at war with another, and more because anyone's decision to use the weapons against third parties might be fatal to all of them. Decisions to use nuclear weapons may be decisions to commit suicide. Only a national authority can be entrusted with the decision, again as de Gaulle always claimed. The reasons Europeans fear American unwillingness to retaliate on their behalf are the reasons middle states cannot enhance their power to act at the global and strategic levels through alliances compounded among themselves.[26] I leave aside the many other impediments to nuclear cooperation. These are impediments enough. Only by merging and losing their political identities can middle states become superpowers. The nonadditivity of nuclear forces shows again that in our bipolar world, efforts of lesser states cannot tilt the strategic balance.

Saying that the spread of nuclear weapons leaves bipolarity intact does not imply indifference to proliferation. It will not make the world multipolar; it may have other good or bad effects. The bad ones are easier to imagine. Bipolarity has been proof against war between the Great Powers, but enough wars of lesser scale have been fought. The prospect of a number of states having nuclear weapons that may be ill-controlled and vulnerable is a scary one, not because proliferation would change the system but because of what lesser powers might do to one another. In an influential 1958 article, Albert Wohlstetter warned of the dangers of a "delicate balance of terror." Those dangers may plague countries having small nuclear forces, with one country tempted to fire its weapons preemptively against an adversary thought to be momentarily vulnerable. One must add that these dangers have not appeared. Reconsideration of nuclear proliferation is called for, but not here, since I want only to make the point that an increase in the number of nuclear states does not threaten the world's bipolar structure.

Limitations of technology and scale work decisively against middle states competing with the Great Powers at the nuclear level. The same limitations put them even further behind in conventional weaponry. Conventional weaponry has become increasingly unconventional. Weapons systems of high technology may come to dominate the battlefield. One American officer describes an escort plane, under development for tactical strike missions, that "will throw an electronic blanket over their air defenses that will allow our aircraft to attack without danger from anything more than lucky shots." Another describes electronic-warfare capability as "an absolute requirement for survival in any future conflicts."[27]

Though the requirement may be an absolute one, it is a requirement that only the United States and, belatedly, the Soviet Union will be able to meet. From rifles to tanks, from aircraft to missiles, weapons have multiplied in cost. To buy them in numbers and variety sufficient for military effectiveness exceeds the economic capability of most states. From about 1900 onward, only Great Powers, enjoying economies of scale, could deploy modern fleets. Other states limited their ships to older and cheaper models, while their armies continued to be miniatures of the armies of Great Powers. Now armies, air forces, and navies alike can be mounted at advanced levels of technology only by Great Powers. Countries the size of prewar Germany or Great Britain enjoy economies of scale in manufacturing steel and refrigerators, in providing schools, health services, and transportation systems. They no longer do so militarily. Short of the electronic extreme, the cost and complication of conventional warfare exclude middle states from developing the full range of weapons for land, air, and sea warfare.[28]

Great Powers are strong not simply because they have nuclear weapons but also because their immense resources enable them to generate and maintain power of all types, military and other, at strategic and tactical levels. The barriers to entering the superpower club have never been higher and more numerous. The club will long remain the world's most exclusive one.

POWER AND THE USE OF FORCE

No one doubts that capabilities are now more narrowly concentrated than ever before in modern history. Many argue, however, that the concentration of capabilities does not generate effective power. Military power no longer brings political control. Despite its vast capability, is the United States "a tied Gulliver, not a master with free hands"?[29] Does the Soviet Union also fit the description? The two superpowers, each stalemated by the other's nuclear force, are for important political purposes effectively reduced to the power of lesser states. That is a common belief. The effective equality of states emerges from the very condition of their gross inequality. We read, for example, that the

> "change in the nature of the mobilizable potential has made its actual use in emergencies by its unhappy owners quite difficult and self-defeating. As a result, nations endowed with infinitely less can behave in a whole range of issues as if the difference in power did not matter." The conclusion is driven home by adding that the United States thinks in "cataclysmic terms," lives in dread of all-out war, and bases its military calculations on the forces needed for the ultimate but unlikely crisis rather than on what might be needed in the less spectacular cases that are more likely to occur.[30]

In the widely echoed words of John Herz, absolute power equals absolute impotence, at least at the highest levels of force represented by the American and Russian nuclear armories.[31] At lesser levels of violence, many states can compete as though they were substantially equal. The best weapons of the United States and the Soviet Union are useless, and the distinct advantage of those two states is thus negated. But what about American or Russian nuclear weapons used against minor nuclear states or against states having no nuclear weapons? Here again the "best" weapon of the most powerful states turns out to be the least usable. The nation that is equipped to "retaliate massively" is not likely to find the occasion to use its capability. If amputation of an arm were the only remedy available for an infected finger, one would be tempted to hope for the best and leave the ailment untreated. The state that can move effectively only by commiting the full power of its military arsenal is likely to forget the threats it has made and acquiesce in a situation formerly described as intolerable. Instruments that cannot be used to deal with small cases—those that are moderately dangerous and damaging—remain idle until the big case arises. But then the use of major force to defend a vital interest would run the grave risk of retaliation. Under such circumstances, the powerful are frustrated by their strength; and although the weak do not thereby become strong, they are, it is said, able to behave as though they were.

Such arguments are repeatedly made and have to be taken seriously. In an obvious sense, part of the contention is valid. When Great Powers are in a stalemate, lesser states acquire an increased freedom of movement. That this phenomenon is now noticeable tells us nothing new about the strength of the weak or the weakness of the strong. Weak states have often found opportunities for maneuver in the interstices of a balance of power. In a bipolar world, leaders are free to set policy without acceding to the wishes of lesser alliance members. By the same logic, the latter are free not to follow the policy that has been set. As the United States once did, lesser alliance members enjoy the freedom of the irresponsible, since their security is mainly provided by the efforts that others make. To maintain both the balance and its by-product requires the continuing efforts of America and Russia. Their instincts for self-preservation call forth such efforts. The objective of both states must be to perpetuate an international stalemate as a minimum basis for the security of each of them—even if this should mean that the two big states do the work while the small ones have the fun.

Strategic nuclear weapons deter strategic nuclear weapons (though they may also do more than that). Where each state must tend to its own security as best it can, the means adopted by one state must be geared to the efforts of others. The cost of the American nuclear establishment, maintained in peaceful readiness, is functionally comparable to the cost incurred by a government in order to maintain domestic order and provide internal security. Such expenditure is not productive in the sense that spending to build roads is, but it is not unproductive either. Its utility is obvious, and should anyone successfully argue otherwise, the consequences of accepting the argument would quickly demonstrate its falsity. Force is least visible where power is most fully and most adequately present.[32] Power maintains an order; the use of force signals a possible breakdown. The better ordered a society and the more competent and respected its government, the less force its police are required to employ. Less shooting occurs in present-day Sandusky than did on the western frontier. Similarly, in international politics, states supreme in their power have to use force less often. "Nonrecourse to force"—as both Eisenhower and Kruschchev seem to have realized—is the doctrine of powerful states. Powerful states need to use force less often than their weaker neighbors because the strong can more often protect their interests or work their wills in other ways—by persuasion and cajolery, by economic bargaining and bribery, by the extension of aid, and, finally, by posing deterrent threats. Since states with large nuclear armories do not actually "use" them, force is said to be discounted. Such reasoning is fallacious. Possession of power should not be identified with the use of force, and the usefulness of force should not be confused with its usability. To introduce such confusions into the analysis of power is comparable to saying that the police force that seldom if ever employs violence is weak or that a police force is strong only when its members are shooting their guns. To vary the image, it is comparable to saying that a man with large assets is not rich if he spends little money or that a man is rich only if he spends a lot of it.

The argument, which we should not lose sight of, is that just as the miser's money may depreciate grossly in value over the years, so the Great Powers' military strength has lost much of its usability. If military force is like currency that cannot be spent or money that has lost much of its worth, then is not forbearance in its use merely a way of disguising its depreciated value? Conrad von Hötzendorf, Austrian chief of staff prior to World War I, looked at military power as though it were a capital sum, useless unless invested. In his view, to invest military force is to commit it to battle.[33] In the reasoning of Conrad, military force is most useful at the moment of its employment in war. Depending on a country's situation, it may make much better sense to say that military force is most useful when it dissuades other states from attacking—that is, when it need not be used in battle at all. When the state with the strongest military force is also a status-quo power, nonuse of force is a sign of its strength. Force is most useful, or best serves the interests of such a state, when it need not be used in the actual conduct of warfare. Throughout a century that ended in 1914, the British navy was powerful enough to scare off all comers, while Britain carried out occasional imperial ventures in odd parts of the world. Only as Britain's power weakened were its military forces used to fight a full-scale war. In being used, its military power surely became less useful.

Force is cheap, especially for a status-quo power, if its very existence works against its use. What does it mean, then, to say that the cost of using force has increased while its utility has lessened? It is highly important, indeed useful, to think in "cataclysmic terms," to live in dread of all-out war, and to base military calculations on the forces needed for the ultimate but unlikely crisis. That the United States does so, and that the Soviet Union apparently does too, makes the cataclysm less likely to occur. The web of social and political life is spun out of inclinations and incentives, deterrent threats and punishments. Eliminate the latter two, and the ordering of society depends entirely on the former—a utopian thought impractical this side of Eden. Depend entirely on threat and punishment, and the ordering of society is based on pure coercion. International politics tends toward the latter condition. The daily presence of force and recurrent reliance on it mark the affairs of nations. Since Thucydides in Greece and Kautilya in India, the use of force and the possibility of controlling it have been the preoccupations of international-political studies.[34]

John Herz coined the term *security dilemma* to describe the condition in which states, unsure of one another's intentions, arm for the sake of security and, in doing so, set a vicious circle in motion. Having armed for the sake of security, states feel less secure and buy more arms because the means to anyone's security is a threat to someone else, who in turn responds by arming.[35] Whatever the weaponry, and however many states in the system, states have to live with their security dilemma, which is produced not by their wills, but by their situations. A dilemma cannot be solved; it can more or less readily be dealt with. Force cannot be eliminated. How is peace possible when force takes its awesome nuclear form? I have discussed in this article that two powers can deal with the dilemma better than three or more. Second-strike nuclear forces are the principal means used. Those means look almost entirely unusable. Is that a matter of regret? Why is "usable" force preferred—so that the United States and the Soviet Union would be able to fight a war such as Great Powers used to do on occasion? The whole line of reasoning implied in assertions that the United States and the Soviet Union are hobbled by the unusability of their forces omits the central point. Great Powers are best off when the weapons they use to cope with the security dilemma are ones that make the waging of war among them unlikely. Nuclear forces are useful, and their usefulness is reinforced by the extent to which their use is forestalled. The military forces of Great Powers are most useful and least costly if they are priced only in money and not also in blood.

Odd notions about the usability and usefulness of force result from confused theory and a failure of historical recall. Great Powers are never "masters with free hands." They are always "Gullivers," more or less tightly tied. They usually lead troubled lives. After all, they have to contend with one another, and, because Great Powers have great power, that is difficult to do. In some ways their lot may be enviable; in many ways it is not. To give a sufficient example, they fight more wars than lesser states do.[36] Their involvement in wars arises from their position in the international system, not from their national characters. When they are at or near the top, they fight; as they decline, they become peaceful—think of Spain, Holland, Sweden, and Austria. Those who have declined more recently enjoy a comparable benefit. Some people seem to associate great powers with great good fortune, and when fortune does not smile, they conclude that power has evaporated. One wonders why.

As before, Great Powers find ways to use force, although now not against each other. Where power is seen to be balanced, whether or not the balance is nuclear, it may seem that the resultant of opposing forces is zero; however, this is misleading. The vectors of national force do not meet at a point, if only because the power of a state does not resolve into a single vector. Military force is divisible, especially for states that can afford a lot of it. In a nuclear world, contrary to some assertions, the dialectic of inequality does not produce the effective equality of strong and weak states. Nuclear weapons deter nuclear weapons; they also serve to limit escalation. The temptation of one country to employ increasingly larger amounts of force is lessened if its opponent has the ability to raise the ante. Force can be used with less hesitation by those states able to parry, to thrust, and to threaten at varied levels of military endeavor. For more than three decades, power has been narrowly concentrated, and force has been used, not orgiastically, as in the world wars of this century, but in a controlled way and for conscious political purposes, albeit not always the right ones. Power may be present when force is not used, but force is also used openly. A catalogue of examples would be both complex and lengthy. On the American side of the ledger, it would contain such items as the garrisoning of Berlin, its supply by airlift during the blockade, the stationing of troops in Europe, the establishment of bases in Japan and elsewhere, the waging of war in Korea and Vietnam, and the "quarantine" of Cuba. Seldom if ever has force been more variously, more persistently, and more widely applied; and seldom has it been more consciously used as an instrument of national policy. Since World War II, we have seen the political organization and pervasion of power, not the cancellation of force by nuclear stalemate.

Plenty of power has been used, although at times with unhappy results. Just as the state that refrains from applying force is said to betray its weakness, so the state that has trouble in exercising control is said to display the defectiveness of its power. In such a conclusion, the elementary error of identifying power with control is evident. If power is identical with control, then those who are free are strong, and their freedom has to be taken as an indication of the weakness of those who have great material strength. The weak and disorganized are, however, often less amenable to control than those who are wealthy and well disciplined. Here again old truths need to be brought into focus. One old truth, formulated by Georg Simmel, is this: when one "opposes a diffused crowd of enemies, one may oftener gain isolated victories, but it is very hard to arrive at decisive results which definitely fix the relationships of the contestants."[37]

A still older truth, formulated by David Hume, is that "force is always on the side of the governed." "The soldan of Egypt or the emperor of Rome," he went on to say, "might drive his harmless subjects like brute beasts against their sentiments and inclination. But he must, at least, have led his *mamalukes* or *praetorian bands,* like men, by their opinion."[38] The governors, being few in number, depend for the exercise of their rule on the more or less willing assent of their subjects. If sullen disregard is the response to every command, no government can rule. If a country, because of internal disorder and lack of coherence, is unable to rule itself, no body of foreigners, whatever the military force at its command, can reasonably hope to do so. If insurrection is the problem, then it can hardly be hoped that an alien army will be able to pacify a country that is unable to govern itself. Foreign troops, though not irrelevant to such problems, can be of only indirect help. Military force, used internationally, is a means of establishing control over a territory, not of exercising control within it. The threat of a nation to use military force, whether nuclear or conventional, is preeminently a means of affecting another state's external behavior, of dissuading a state from launching a career of aggression and of meeting the aggression if dissuasion should fail.

Dissuasion, whether by defense or by deterrence, is easier to accomplish than *compellence,* to use an apt term invented by Thomas C. Schelling.[39] Compellence is more difficult to achieve, and its contrivance is a more intricate affair. In Vietnam, the United States faced the task not merely of compelling a particular action, but of promoting an effective political order. Those who argue from such a case that force has depreciated in value fail in their analyses to apply their own historical and political knowledge. The master builders of imperial rule, such men as Bugeaud, Galliéni, and Lyautey, played both political and military roles. In like fashion, successful counterrevolutionary efforts have been directed by such men as Templer and Magsaysay, who combined military resources with political instruments.[40] Military forces, whether domestic or foreign, are insufficient for the task of pacification, the more so if a country is rent by faction and if its people are politically engaged and active. Some events represent change; others are mere repetition. The difficulty experienced by the United States in trying to pacify Vietnam and establish a preferred regime is mere repetition. France fought in Algeria between 1830 and 1847 in a similar cause. Britain found Boers terribly troublesome in the war waged against them from 1898 to 1903. France, when it did the fighting, was thought to have the world's best army, and Britain, an all-powerful navy.[41] To say that militarily strong states are feeble because they cannot easily bring order to minor states is like saying that a pneumatic hammer is weak because it is not suitable for drilling decayed teeth. It is to confuse the purpose of instruments and to confound the means of external power with the agencies of internal governance. Inability to exercise *political* control over others does not indicate *military* weakness. Strong states cannot do everything with their military forces, as Napoleon acutely realized, but they are able to do things that militarily weak states cannot do. The People's Republic of China can no more solve the problems of governance in some Latin American country than the United States can in Southeast Asia. But the United States can intervene with great military force in far quarters of the world while wielding an effective deterrent against escalation. Such action exceeds the capabilities of all but the strongest of states.

Differences in strength do matter, although not for every conceivable purpose. To deduce the weakness of the powerful from this qualifying clause is a misleading use of words. One sees in such a case as Vietnam not the *weakness* of great military power in a nuclear world, but instead a clear illustration of the *limits* of military force in the world of the present as always.

Within the repeated events, an unmentioned difference lurks. Success or failure in peripheral places now means less in material terms than it did to previous Great Powers. That difference derives from the change in the system. Students of international politics tend to think that wars formerly brought economic and other benefits to the victors and that in contrast the United States cannot now use its military might for positive accomplishment.[42] Such views are wrong on several counts. First, American successes are overlooked. Buttressing the security of Western Europe is a positive accomplishment; so was defending South Korea, and one can easily lengthen the list. Second, the profits of past military ventures are overestimated. Before 1789, war may have been "good business"; it has seldom paid thereafter.[43]

Third, why the United States should be interested in extending military control over others when we have so many means of nonforceful leverage is left unspecified. America's internal efforts, moreover, add more to its wealth than any imaginable gains scored abroad. The United States, and the Soviet Union as well, have more reason to be satisfied with the status quo than most earlier Great Powers had. Why should we think of using force for positive accomplishment when we are in the happy position of needing to worry about using force only for the negative purposes of defense and deterrence? To fight is hard, as ever; to refrain from fighting is easier because so little is at stake. Léon Gambetta, French premier after France's defeat by Prussia, remarked that because the old continent is stifling, such outlets as Tunis are needed. This looks like an anticipation of Hobson. The statement was merely expediential, for as Gambetta also said, Alsace-Lorraine must always be in Frenchmen's hearts, although for a long time it could not be on their lips. Gains that France might score abroad were valued less for their own sake and more because they might strengthen France for another round in the Franco-German contest. Jules Ferry, a latter premier, argued that France needed colonies lest it slip to the third or fourth rank in Europe.[44] Such a descent would end all hope of retaking Alsace-Lorraine. Ferry, known as *Le Tonkinoise,* fell from power in 1885, when his southeast Asian ventures seemed to be weakening France rather than adding to the strength it could show in Europe. For the United States in the same part of the world, the big stake, as official statements described it, was internally generated—our honor and credibility, although the definition of those terms was puzzling. As some saw early in that struggle, and as most saw later on, little was at stake in Vietnam in terms of global politics.[45] The international-political insignificance of Vietnam can be understood only in terms of the world's structure. America's failure in Vietnam was tolerable because neither success nor failure mattered much internationally. Victory would not make the world one of American hegemony. Defeat would not make the world one of Russian hegemony. No matter what the outcome, the American-Soviet duopoly would endure.

Military power does not bring political control, but then it never did. Conquering and governing are different processes, yet public officials and students alike conclude from the age-old difficulty of using force effectively that force is now obsolescent and that international structures can no longer be defined by the distribution of capabilities across states.

How can one account for the confusion? In two ways. The first, variously argued earlier, is that the usefulness of force is mistakenly identified with its use. Because of their favored positions, the United States and the Soviet Union need to use force less than most earlier Great Powers did. Force is more useful than ever for upholding the status quo, though not for changing it, and maintaining the status quo is the minimum goal of any Great Power. Moreover, because the United States has much economic and political leverage over many other states, and because both the United States and the Soviet Union are more nearly self-sufficient than most earlier Great Powers were, they need hardly use force to secure ends other than their own security. Nearly all unfavorable economic and political outcomes have too little impact to call for their using force to prevent them, and strongly preferred economic and political outcomes can be sufficiently secured without recourse to force. For achieving economic gains, force has seldom been an efficient means anyway. Because the United States and the Soviet Union are secure in the world, except in terms of each other, they find few international-political reasons for resorting to force. Those who believe that force is less useful reach their conclusion without asking whether there is much reason for today's Great Powers to use force to coerce other states.

The second source of confusion about power is found in its odd definition. We are misled by the pragmatically formed and technologically influenced American definition of power—a definition that equates power with control. Power is then measured by the ability to get people to do what one wants them to do when otherwise they would not do it.[46] That definition may serve for some purposes, but it ill fits the requirements of politics. To define "power" as "cause" confuses process with outcome. To identify power with control is to assert that only power is needed in order to get one's way. That is obviously false, for else what would there be for political and military strategists to do? To use power is to apply one's capabilities in an attempt to change someone else's behavior in certain ways. Whether *A*, in applying its capabilities, gains the wanted compliance of *B* depends on *A*'s capabilities and strategy, on *B*'s capabilities and counterstrategy, and on all of these factors as they are affected by the situation at hand. Power is one cause among others, from which it cannot be isolated. The common relational definition of power omits consideration of how acts and relations are affected by the structure of action. To measure power by compliance rules unintended effects out of consideration, and that takes much of the politics out of politics.

According to the common American definition of power, a failure to get one's way is proof of weakness. In politics, however, powerful agents fail to impress their wills on others in just the ways they intend to. The intention of an act and its result will seldom be identical because the result will be affected by the person or object acted on and conditioned by the environment within which it occurs. What, then, can be substituted for the practically and logically untenable definition? I offer the old and simple notion that an agent is powerful to the extent that he affects others more than they affect him. The weak understand this; the strong may not. Prime Minister Trudeau once said that, for Canada, being America's neighbor "is in some ways like sleeping with an elephant. No matter how friendly or even tempered is the beast . . . one is affected by every twitch and grunt."[47] As the leader of a weak state, Trudeau understands the meaning of our power in ways that we overlook. Because of the weight of our capabilities, American actions have tremendous impact whether or not we fashion effective policies and consciously put our capabilities behind them in order to achieve certain ends.

How is power distributed? What are the effects of a given distribution of power? These two questions are distinct, and the answer to each of them is extremely important politically. In the definition of power just rejected, the two questions merge and become hopelessly confused. Identifying power with control leads one to see weakness wherever one's will is thwarted. Power is a means, and the outcome of its use is necessarily uncertain. To be politically pertinent, power has to be defined in terms of the distribution of capabilities; the extent of one's power cannot be inferred from the results one may or may not get. The paradox that some have found in the so-called impotence of American power disappears if power is given a politically sensible definition. Defining power sensibly, and comparing the plight of present and of previous Great Powers, shows that the usefulness of power has increased.

CONCLUSION

International politics is necessarily a small-number system. The advantages of having a few more Great Powers is at best slight. The advantages of subtracting a few and arriving at two are decisive. The three-body problem has yet to be solved by physicists. Can political scientists or policy makers hope to do better in charting the courses of three or more interacting states? Cases that lie between the simple interaction of two entities and the statistically predictable interactions of very many are the most difficult to unravel. We have seen the complications in the military affairs of multipolar worlds. The fates of Great Powers are closely linked. The Great Powers of a multipolar world, in taking steps to make their likely fates happier, at times need help from others. Friedrich Meinecke described the condition of Europe at the time of Frederick the Great this way: "A set of isolated power-States, alone yet linked together by their mutually grasping ambitions—that was the state of affairs to which the development of the European State-organism had brought things since the close of the Middle Ages."[48] Militarily and economically, interdependence developed as the self-sufficient localities of feudal Europe were drawn together by modern states. The Great Powers of a bipolar world are more self-sufficient, and interdependence loosens between them. This condition distinguishes the present system from the previous one. Economically, America and Russia are markedly less interdependent and noticeably less dependent on others than earlier Great Powers were. Militarily, the decrease of interdependence is more striking still, for neither Great Power can be linked to any other Great Power, given "their mutually grasping ambitions."

Two Great Powers can deal with each other better than more can.

NOTES

1. For example, see Walter Lippmann, "Break-up of the Two Power World," *Atlantic Monthly,* April 1950; idem, "NATO Crisis—and Solution: Don't Blame De Gaulle," *Boston Globe,* 5 December 1963.

2. See "At Pacem in Terris Conference," News Release, U.S. Department of State, Bureau of Public Affairs, 10 October 1973, p. 7.

3. See "Transcript of the President's News Conference on Foreign and Domestic Matters," *New York Times,* 5 August 1971, p. 16.

4. See Kenneth N. Waltz, "The Stability of a Bipolar World," *Daedalus* 93 (Summer 1964); idem, "International Structure, National Force, and the Balance of World Power," *Journal of International Affairs* 21 (1967); idem, "The Relation of States to Their World" (Paper delivered at the 63rd Annual Meeting of

the American Political Science Association, Chicago, September 1967); and idem, "The Politics of Peace," *International Studies Quarterly* 11 (September 1967).

5. Cf. Mancur Olson, Jr., *The Logic of Collective Action* (Cambridge, Mass.: Harvard University Press, 1965), pp. 36, 45.

6. See Nigel Nicolson, ed., *Harold Nicolson: Diaries and Letters, 1930-1939* (London: Collins, 1966), pp. 247-49, and Kenneth C. Young, *Stanley Baldwin* (London: Weidenfeld & Nicolson, 1976), pp. 128-30.

7. Barrington Moore, Jr., *Soviet Politics: The Dilemma of Power* (Cambridge, Mass.: Harvard University Press, 1950), pp. 350-55.

8. As Winston Churchill said to his private secretary the night before Germany's invasion of Russia, "If Hitler invaded Hell I would make at least a favorable reference to the Devil in the House of Commons." See Winston S. Churchill, *The Grand Alliance* (Boston: Houghton Mifflin, 1950), p. 370.

9. See Robert Jervis, *Perception and Misperception in International Politics* (Princeton: Princeton University Press, 1976), p. 110.

10. Cf. Morton A. Kaplan, *System and Process in International Politics* (1957; New York: Wiley, 1964), pp. 22-36, and Hans J. Morgenthau, *Politics among Nations,* 3rd ed. (New York: Knopf, 1960), part 4.

11. Cf. Geoffrey Blaney, *The Causes of War* (London: Macmillan, 1970), pp. 108-19.

12. From 1960 to 1967, America's economic aid to India exceeded its combined economic and military aid to any other country (U.S. Agency for International Development, various years).

13. Oliver E. Williamson, "A Dynamic Theory of Inter-Firm Behavior," in *Economic Theories of International Politics,* ed. Bruce M. Russett (Chicago: Markham, 1968), p. 227.

14. William Zimmerman, *Soviet Perspectives on International Relations, 1956-1967* (Princeton: Princeton University Press, 1969), pp. 135, 282.

15. Georg Simmel, "The Number of Members As Determining the Social Form of the Group," *Journal of Sociology* 8 (July 1902); and Robert F. Bales and Edgar F. Borgatta, "Size of Group As a Factor in the Interaction Profile" (1953), in *Small Groups: Studies in Social Interaction,* ed. A. Paul Hare, Borgatta, and Bales (New York: Knopf, 1965).

16. Richard Burt has carefully considered some of the ways in which the worries are growing. See *New Weapons Technologies: Debate and Directions,* Adelphi Papers, no. 26 (London: International Institute for Strategic Studies, 1976).

17. See "Text of Rusk's Statement to Senators about Test Ban Treaty," *New York Times,* 13 August 1963.

18. See C. L. Sulzberger, "New Balance of Peace," *New York Times,* 15 November 1972, p. 47; also see "President's Remarks to News Media Executives, July 6, 1971," *Weekly Compilation of Presidential Documents,* 12 July 1971.

19. Nixon and Sulzberger do, however, overestimate American postwar economic dominance. W. S. and E. S. Woytinsky credit the United States with 40.7 percent of world income in 1948, compared to 26 percent in 1938. Theirs seems to be the better estimate. See W. S. and E. S. Woytinsky, *World Population and Production* (New York: Twentieth Century Fund, 1953), pp. 389, 393-95.

20. See *International Economic Report of the President* (Washington, D.C.: Government Printing Office, 1976), pp. 119-20.

21. See Bruce L. R. Smith and Joseph J. Karlesky, *The State of Academic Science,* vol. 1 (New Rochelle, N.Y.: Change Magazine Press, 1977), p. 4.

22. Victor Basiuk, "Technology, Western Europe's Alternative Futures, and American Policy" (New York: Columbia University Institute of War and Peace Studies, n.d.), p. 489.

23. Some estimates of the Soviet Union's spending are higher. Cf. Donald G. Brennan, "The Soviet Military Build-up and Its Implications for the Negotations on Strategic Arms Limitations," *Orbis* 21 (Spring 1977).

24. Edmund O. Stillman and William Pfaff, *The New Politics: America and the End of the Postwar World* (New York: McCann, 1961), p. 135.

25. Between 1955 and 1965, Britain, France, and West Germany spent 10 percent of the American total on military R&D; between 1970 and 1974, 27 percent. As Richard Burt concludes, unless European countries collaborate on producing and procuring military systems and the United States buys European, exploitation of new technology will widen the gap in the capabilities of allies. See Burt, *New Weapons Technologies,* pp. 20-21.

26. For the same reasons, a lagging superpower cannot combine with lesser states to compensate for strategic weakness.

27. Drew Middleton, "Growing Use of Electronic Warfare Is Becoming a Source of Major Concern for World's Military Powers," *New York Times,* 13 September 1976, p. 7.

28. Vital has made these points nicely for small states. They apply to middle states as well. See David Vital, *The Inequality of States* (Oxford: Oxford University Press, 1967), pp. 63-77.

29. See Stanley Hoffmann, "Going toward a New World Order," *New York Times,* 11 January 1976, sec. 4, p. 1.

30. See Stanley Hoffmann, "Europe's Identity Crisis: Between the Past and America," *Daedalus* 93 (Fall 1964): 1279, 1287-88. Cf. Klaus Knorr, *On the Uses of Military Power in the Nuclear Age* (Princeton: Princeton University Press, 1966).

31. John H. Herz, *International Politics in the Atomic Age* (New York: Columbia University Press, 1959), pp. 22, 169.

32. Edward Hallet Carr, *The Twenty Years' Crisis: 1919-1939,* 2nd ed. (1946; New York: Harper & Row, 1964), pp. 103, 129-32.

33. "The sums spent for the war power is money wasted," he maintained, "if the war power remains unused for obtaining political advantages. In some cases the mere threat will suffice and the war power thus becomes useful, but others can be obtained only through the warlike use of the war power itself, that is, by war undertaken in time; if this moment is missed, the capital is lost. In this sense, war becomes a great financial enterprise of the State." See Alfred Vagts, *Defense and Diplomacy: The Soldier and the Conduct of Foreign Relations* (New York: King's Crown Press, 1956), p. 361.

34. See Robert J. Art and Kenneth N. Waltz, "Technology, Strategy, and the Uses of Force," in *The Use of Force,* ed. Art and Waltz (Boston: Little, Brown, 1971), p. 4.

35. See John H. Herz, "Idealist Internationalism and the Security Dilemma," *World Politics* 2 (January 1950).

36. Wright, *A Study of War,* pp. 221-23 and table 22; see also Frederick Adams Woods and Alexander Baltzly, *Is War Diminishing?* (Boston: Houghton Mifflin, 1915), table 46.

37. Georg Simmel, "The Sociology of Conflict, II," *American Journal of Sociology* 9 (March 1904).

38. David Hume, "Of the First Principles of Government" (1741), in *Hume's Moral and Political Philosophy,* ed. Henry D. Aiken (New York: Hafner, 1948), p. 307.

39. Thomas Schelling, *Arms and Influence* (New Haven: Yale University Press, 1966), pp. 70-71.

40. Cf. Samuel P. Huntington, "Patterns of Violence in World Politics," in *Changing Patterns of Military Politics,* ed. Huntington (New York: Free Press, 1962), p. 28.

41. Blainey, *The Causes of War,* p. 205.

42. For example, see Hans J. Morgenthau, *Politics among Nations,* 5th ed. (New York: Knopf, 1973), p. 325, and A.F.K. Organski, *World Politics,* 2nd ed. (New York: Knopf, 1968), pp. 328-29.

43. Joseph A. Schumpeter, "The Sociology of Imperalism" (1919), in *Imperialism and Social Classes,* ed. Schumpeter, trans. Heinz Norden (New York: Meridian Books, 1955), p. 18.

See also Albert Sorel, "Europe under the Old Regime," in *L'Europe et la Rèvolution Française* (1885), trans. Francis H. Herrick (New York: Harper & Row, 1964), pp. 1-70; and Robert E. Osgood and Robert W. Tucker, *Force, Order, and Justice* (Baltimore: Johns Hopkins Press, 1967), p. 40.

44. Thomas F. Power, *Jules Ferry and the Renaissance of French Imperialism* (New York: Octagon Books, 1944), p. 192.

45. Stoessinger shows that this was Kissinger's view. See John G. Stoessinger, *Henry Kissinger: The Anguish of Power* (New York: W. W. Norton, 1976), chap. 8.

46. Cf. Robert A. Dahl, "The Concept of Power," *Behavioral Science* 2 (July 1957).

47. Quoted in Louis Turner, *Invisible Empires* (New York: Harcourt, Brace, Jovanovich, 1971), p. 166.

48. Friedrich Meinecke, *Machiavellism,* trans. Douglas Scott (1924; London: Routledge & Kegan Paul, 1957), p. 321.

A world of complexity

Stanley Hoffmann

Communism and antiimperialism are still on the ideological offensive against the liberal industrial powers. But one of the most bitter rifts of all opposes the two leading communist states—the former Mecca of communism, Moscow, and the Rome of the capitalist world, Washington, negotiate on military matters—and the antiimperalist nations show a remarkable ability at double bookkeeping. They denounce the unfair order imposed by the rich nations of the West, yet they deal profitably with several if not all of these, and they pursue their own rivalries and grievances in ways that turn the common front of the developing nations into a mass of bitter conflicts. A given country can, depending on the issue, be a member of a host of coalitions. Brazil is both a military ally of the United States and, occasionally, a champion of the Third World; the same is true of the Philippines. Military alignments seem reasonably stable: United States forces have not left Europe, Japan has not denounced its alliance with the United States, there is still no West European defense system, the Arab-Israeli stalemate persists. But there has been frenzy over economic matters. Not only has their politicization put them on top of the statesmen's agenda, but it has been accompanied by monetary crises, energy warfare, collective confrontations, cycles of inflation and recession, anguish over limits of growth or resource shortages, and the like. Can one make sense of all of this?[1]

CHANGES

One way of trying to understand the present is to try to fit it into, and to compare it with, the analytic models of international politics that we find in classical political theory.[2] Classical philosophers may have reflected more often on the good state than on the right international order, but they did have views on it and on how it might come about, and they had implicit or explicit interpretations of the dynamics of world affairs.

CLASSICAL MODELS

There are two radically different interpretations. The first is the model of the imperfect community, which prevails in Christian political thought from Augustine to Grotius at the end of the sixteenth century. It treats mankind as a community ruled by princes who are themselves submitted to the rule of law, and not arbitrary and willful masters. There is God's law and there is natural law, the product of human participation in divine reason. Behind this model lies a double postulate: the princes' community of spirit and sense of obligation, the decisive role of the church in interpreting and enforcing the norms of natural law. Being human, this community is imperfect. Hence the ever-present risk of a violation, by princes or by their subordinates, of the dictates of natural law, that is, the possibility of war. Since mankind is deemed a community—a group welded, not by mere ties of mutual interest, but by common beliefs, values, and goals, and ruled not by wills but by higher law—the use of force is not a morally neutral act. In modern parlance, it is either a delict or a sanction, a delict when it violates the conditions of a just war laid down by theologians, a sanction when it meets these criteria, which deal with the prince's intention, the cause (or goals), and the means. In this conception, in which the princes are not the shapers of separate sovereign entities, but the shepherds of the various flocks that form mankind, the obligations of natural law and of the just war theory apply not merely to states but to all individuals.

A second model prevails in modern political thought, from Grotius (whose work shows traces of, and contradictions between, the earlier and the new conceptions) and Hobbes to the present. But its real founding father was a historian, not a philosopher or legal theorist: Thucydides, whose study of the Peloponnesian War aimed not only at making future readers understand a singular event, but also and above all at laying out the necessary logic of a certain kind of human behavior. For while his impeccable staging of the principles describes the singular through such universal concepts as honor, interest, fear, or power, he was most eager for, and proudly conscious of, reaching the universal through the singular. His ambition was to show how the combination of human nature, a certain structure of power, and the specific properties of rival states creates an inescapable logic characteristic of a vital and permanent realm of human affairs: world politics. It is the model and the dynamics of fragmentation. There is no world community; there is the domestic order and the international order, and a double contrast exists between them. The citizen's allegiance is to the state; the state's highest allegiance is to its own survival, security, and power. The state has at its disposal a domestic monopoly of force, but there is no force superior to the state's. Hence, the ever-present possibility of war was conceived, not as a punishable revenge of human wickedness over natural law, or as the marshaling of human violence for a rightful cause, but as an inevitable outcome of human nature uncorseted by the norms and force of the state.

Hence also the very special problems of order in international affairs.[3] First, in the realm of politics. Within the state, power, whether it is exercised by political leaders or by social groups, is often at the service of common ideals; this restricts the scope of "power politics," and indeed the essence of the polity is—ideally—the prevalence of cooperation over conflict. The opposite is true in world affairs. There is no aspect of interstate relations that cannot be claimed or reclaimed by politics, even if it appears "depoliticized" (i.e., as not requiring for its management or solution the intervention of the wielders of political power, due to the intrinsic importance of the issue for their policies, or to the concern expressed by domestic political forces). Moreover, politics here means generally "power politics," the politics of confrontation, for in this realm even cooperation exists only because of conflict (allies coalesce against an enemy), or evolves primarily through conflict (as, indeed, in most alliances). The fundamental cause is psychological: domestic affairs are the realm of mutual understanding and predictability (even among adversaries); world affairs is the realm of mutual suspicions, misconceptions, and projections.[4] Second, in the realm of law. The domestic order is a domain of vast regulation; its members are the subjects of commands and of sanctions imposed directly on them by the state with the help of justice and the police. On the international scene, rights and duties apply only to the states, and they result from contracts, not from superior rule; there are vast gaps and ambiguities in the regulations, the authority of the world judge is limited, and enforcement is a polite word for self-help. In institutions, in authority, in substance, international law is weak. Third, in the realm of ethics, international politics suffers particularly from the lack of integration. The range of moral conflict, that is, of conflicts between moral conceptions, is a frequent threat to whatever solidarities survive across borders. The state's range of moral opportunities is narrow, since its first priorities are survival and security, not the good life—without survival, there can be no quest for it—yet the requirements of survival often clash with the requirements of ethics.[5] Hence a tragic separation of order and justice. The existence of order in the state gives license to the quest for justice, and the order reflects—or imposes—a dominant conception of justice. But in world affairs, order has to be achieved first; it is often established at the cost of justice—international law is a frequent consecration of state might, the balance of power is the rule of the Great Powers, the balance of terror is the threat of the unthinkable—and attempts at establishing justice often breed utter chaos.

A second distinction has to be made, for there are two different models of fragmentation. One might be called the model of troubled peace. It sees in the contrasts between the domestic and the international realms differences in degree rather than essence. The international milieu is not pure anarchy. There are forces capable of ensuring a minimum of order. They result from common sociability (Locke's notion) or mutual interests (Hume's), and they can result in common norms. Therefore, there remains a distinction between the international "state of nature" and the state of war. The former finds its cause in the absence of central power and is responsible for the weakness of the common norms: each state interprets them itself and resorts to self-help. But a state of war is a state of general malevolence and will to dominate, with no common norms. The state of nature is inferior to a well-ordered civil society, but preferable to a common despotism.

The other model is precisely that which sees international politics as a state of war. Not the absence of a common superior, but the existence of war is the essence, for everything in world affairs is the struggle, or its preparation, or its sequels. Thus, whatever common norms appear to exist are but fragile and temporary products of a momentary configuration of power or convergence of interests backed by power. The many authors of this model never agreed on the cause of the state of war. Is it human nature itself (Hobbes, Kant)? Is it civil society that has corrupted human nature (Rousseau)? Is it a certain kind of civil society: capitalism (Marx)? Is it fragmentation itself, that is, the structure of power, or all these factors acting together (Thucydides, Raymond Aron)?[6] And there is a final disagreement. Some deem this state of war ultimately bearable, like Hobbes, who saw in the existence of the state—long before nuclear weaponry or mass terrorism—a cushion for the individuals, hence in the international state of war less of a calamity for them than a "war of all against all" among equally weak and puny individuals. Others, such as Rousseau and Kant—and Marx—thought the state of war would be unbearable.

Where does the present international system fit? The systems of the past centuries—what has been called the post-Westphalian order of nation states, although the treaties of Westphalia (1648) merely crystallized trends that had existed for a long time—have all corresponded to the model of fragmentation. Sometimes they have vindicated its more optimistic version. In periods of international "legitimacy," when states agreed on the rules of the game, practices developed that moderated state ambitions, and international law flourished. Sometimes, in the revolutionary periods, fragmentation meant the state of war. This distinction fits Clausewitz's notion of two types of war, depending on how the "remarkable trinity" of "primordial violence, free play of the creative spirit, and pure reason," that is, the mix of instinct, skill, and political control, turns out: there are limited wars and wars of annihilation.[7] The greatest contemporary Clausewitzian, Raymond Aron, in his magnum opus on the Prussian theorist of war, argues that the old model of fragmentation still applies. The decisive actors are still the states; the game is still a contest of separate units endowed with the means of violence and saddled with survival as the necessary overriding goal. International relations is still an arena of conflict. There remains something distinctive about war (i.e., collective, organized, armed violence), which characterizes the world scene, and it should not be drowned in an undifferentiated notion of social violence, lumped together with either social coercion or social control.[8] Thus, the problem of world order remains, as before, that of creating troubled peace rather than a "state of war."

This may be true, but at so skeletal a level that it tells us nothing about the new flesh and blood of world affairs. In order to appreciate the degree of novelty (and without deciding yet whether novelty means merely greater complexity, which would affect the *varieties* of behavior on the stage, or a radical transformation of the *logic* of behavior itself), I will begin with the ideal type of interstate relations that one finds in most of the texts of the fifties and sixties, particularly in Aron's own *Peace and War.*

1. The game is played by a small number of actors: independent states, in control of their instruments of action (dependent states who had, in effect, transferred some of these instruments to their masters were pawns, not players). This does not mean that there was no interconnection between states, or no interpenetration between societies; but the connections were voluntary and removable, and the penetration (by trade or travel) did not affect the sphere of political decisions, that is, the realm and tools of power available to the state for action abroad (military might, economic aid, regulation of trade or investments, subversion, and so forth) or at home (fiscal, credit, welfare, educational, industrial, and agricultural policies, thought control, and so on).
2. The actors define their national interest, not on the basis of domestic political concerns, but by giving primacy to their foreign policy needs and greeds: in terms of the geopolitical situation of the country, its external rivalries, ambitions, and drives, and its diplomatic traditions. The main objectives are possession goals, that is, the effective control of territories, populations, resources, and markets capable of increasing the overall power, of improving the geopolitical position, and of raising the rank of the player.
3. They play in a single international system, dominated by the possibility of armed conflict. Their game is the strategic-diplomatic contest, whose main structure is the military alliance, a concert or coalition of forces aimed at deterring and eventually defeating an enemy. The key distinction is that between adversaries and allies, even if they change over time.
4. Consequently, the decisive means is military might or strategic power (often identified with power altogether). Power as a set of resources is defined above all in terms of military supplies (troops, material, and bases) and of the capacity to mobilize the society for war production and combat. Power as a relation of control is seen as the ability to wrest from others the possessions one wants, or to protect one's own possessions from their grasp.
5. The hierarchy of the system is geomilitary. The Great Powers are those that have the greatest military capabilities (such as France and Russia in the eighteenth and nineteenth centuries, Austria in the eighteenth, Prussia and later Germany in the nineteenth), or (as Britain did) an inexpugnable home base, the power to conquer and protect key positions across the world, and the financial and economic power to support allies in a military coalition.

In other words, it is a tournament of distinctive knights. Their alliances do not jeopardize their independence; they are supposed to preserve it. They may need to acquire their resources abroad, but either these are brought in from areas under the player's control or else they are bought on the free market, in a depoliticized trade protected by classical international law (even interstate war was not allowed to interrupt it). To be sure, reality was always more complex. Yet this ideal type did schematize rather than distort reality's main features. Today, however, the distance between this ideal type and world politics is enormous. The drama lies in the following points. One, since the states remain the main actors, there is still a prevalence of conflict and a poverty of common norms. Two, technology and the universal quest for economic growth have created, if not a world society, at least an unprecedented interdependent milieu. Three, the combination of an interdependent world economy and an international system without central direction means an entirely original tension between the "objective" need for global solutions to problems that threaten the future of mankind and the uneven splintering of the centers of decision. In other words, what operates at present is not a mere juxtaposition, but an interplay of the old and the new. This can best be understood as a series of changes, contradictions, and races.

THE OLD AND THE NEW: AN OVERVIEW

There are five major changes. They concern the actors, their goals, their power, the international hierarchy, and the international system itself.

Actors and objectives. One, there is a change in the number and nature of actors. This is one of the reasons why a purely "structural" analysis of the international system that focuses only on the number of Great Powers and "the distribution of capabilities among units" tells us little.[9] On the one hand, there are more than 150 states. This means, of course, that the "group" that comprises the main players, or the main subjects of rights and duties, is still small by comparison with a domestic society. But it represents a considerable increase by comparison with international systems of the past (which were usually limited to parts of the globe). Some of these actors have limited resources, but other factors of the system, such as the role of "collectives"—international organizations and groupings—and the relative decline of force (to be discussed later), compensate, to some degree, for such weakness, and make even more formal sovereignty an asset: intangible assets are a form of power.

On the other hand, nonstate actors, even though they may not be "sovereign," which means essentially that they are not constituted according to the principle of territorial organization characteristic of the state system, can nevertheless be players. As such, they can be considered part of the system's "structure" and not merely of the "processes that go on within it."[10] They are not merely members of a transnational society separate from the interstate system, whose behavior may affect a given state insofar as what happens in its society affects the state's policy. They are endowed with power over resources essential to the state; they can bargain directly with the legitimate wielders of political power (or try to undermine them); and even when they are the mere emanation of a state, or a creation of states, they have a de facto autonomy within certain ranges. It is true that they are not "a new phenomenon in world politics, and no present-day corporation has yet an impact comparable with that of the English East India Company, which employed its own armed forces and controlled territory."[11] But the question is not whether they are new. It is whether their importance in world affairs has increased sufficiently to require their inclusion even into an ideal type of present world politics, whereas they did not need to be so included in the past.

If we use a traditional definition of actors (or of power also), we shall not understand what is happening. Yesterday, it was roughly true that only states were actors; hence, we defined the actors as those endowed with a legitimate monopoly of force over a territory and population. If we define actors as those whose autonomous decisions affect resources and values, and who interact with other similar players *across* state lines,[12] we shall be able to take changes into account. The definition creates two difficulties, however. It introduces heterogeneity into the category of actors (some have a territory and population, others do not), and it raises a problem of ambiguity: are the nonstate actors as autonomous as the states, even within their range of jurisdiction? One can answer, first, that the heterogeneity is an essential fact of life today. Second, although it is, of course, true that nonstate actors can operate "only in conditions in which a modicum of peace and security has been provided by the action of states,"[13] the problem of ultimate autonomy (which could always be raised even in the relation among states, given their uneven power) is one for empirical research. What matters for an analysis of world politics is that the actors behave as if they had such autonomy, even if, in a crunch, some will discover that they do not. A third problem—that a nonstate actor can be both largely autonomous and used as an instrument by (or bring advantages to) a state—is, again, in the nature of present world affairs.

These nonstate actors are, first, such transnational agents as multinational enterprises, and also Internationales of religion, ideas, interests, or scientific organizations, or private groups operating across borders (whether they are airline companies, terrorists, or foundations).[14] Second, there are international and regional organizations endowed with powers and secretariats capable of initiative or management. One consequence of this increase and diversification in the nature of the actors is the intensity of contacts, both among governments and among societies, in world affairs today. Needless to say, one would need a map describing the unevenness of these contacts, for the world of transnational agents is not the whole world, and a society's degree of penetration or openness is still controllable by regimes determined to preserve their impermeability.

The nature of the states' objectives has also changed. The old ones still exist, of course. But foreign policy has ceased being the preserve of the diplomat and the soldier. It is no longer a specialized activity, and what used to be its essence—the integration of force and policy, the use of coercion on behalf of external goals—is now only one of its aspects. Foreign policy has never been divorced from domestic politics. (Bismarck's diplomacy was aimed, in part, at preserving the power of conservative forces in Germany, and he knew how to manipulate the internal affairs of others.) Insofar as the old ideal type assumed such a divorce, it was merely normative—it was a prescription, not a description, an ideology, not an analysis. But what used to be a connection has become a fusion. Foreign policy has become the external dimension of the universally dominant concern for economic development and social welfare. All economic and social issues have an external dimension, since, with few exceptions, none of the state actors is self-sufficient and all the other actors still depend on the states for their operations. The old definition of the national interest is far too narrow; international politics becomes a collision of economic and social policies, in addition to being what it has always been. This means an end to specialization, and a second cause of the huge increase in scope. Every ministry, every agency, has its foreign policy, and the constituencies of foreign policy have broadened along with the sphere of decision makers; they include not only the foreign policy establishments or the "military industrial complex," but all the groups whose interests are affected by what happens abroad. Therefore, it is not surprising if coalitions of interests, ideas, or even bureaucratic fragments appear across borders. The old "primacy of foreign policy" loses much of its meaning under these conditions, for that imperative assumed specialization and separation.

While possession goals have not disappeared in a world in which the "struggle for the world product"[15] is intense, one notices a double shift. Possession goals become, so to speak, repatriated—states want *domestic* control over their resources, or aim at increasing self-sufficiency, or define their national ambition as the development of their economy. Abroad, states, as well as nonstate actors whose means of power are usually less complete, less blunt, or more fragile, seek milieu goals: an atmosphere in which multinationals can operate safely, or a set of rules allowing for the stable promotion of exports or for the security of supplies. Moreover, who gets what possession depends on the rules of the milieu. These goals require a modicum of cooperation, for the coveted possessions can best be enjoyed if there is common consent. In other words, *influence* rather than *control* is at the heart of the process. There are too many actors for any one of them to exert a decisive importance on all fronts or for very long, especially as the use of force is limited.

There are immediate, or intermediate, stakes. Procedural goals must be reached if the ultimate objectives are to be attained. First, there is the determination, or the transformation, of the rules of play, that is, the balance of burdens and rights, advantages and costs that will accrue to the various players and their powers of control. Second, the framework in which a given issue will be discussed must be set. It can be more or less favorable to a given actor or group of actors, depending on this framework's degree of specificity or generality, on its degree of openness, and on its degree of democracy or oligarchic control. Lastly, once the framework of discussion or decision has been settled, the agenda itself must be set, which often slants or even shapes the outcome. These immediate stakes are means to the end—the modeling of the milieu—and are substitutes of the traditional means, the use or threat of war, toward possession ends.

The transformation of power. Power remains the capacity of affecting the behavior of others, or the outcome of an issue, whether or not its use was deliberately aimed at doing so.[16] But there has been a radical change in the nature of power. One is in its *diffusion,* which has resulted from the increase in the number of actors and from the immense increase in foreign policy issues. A second change is the *diversification* of power. The kinds of supplies needed to exert influence are so varied that the old quasidentification with military might has become absurd.

A third change is a fundamental *heterogeneity* between two ways of using these supplies. One is the use of power according to the logic of separateness and the rules of interaction; the other is the use of power according to the logic of integration and the rules of interdependence. In the former, the central assumption of the contest is that, ultimately, "my gain is your loss," even if it is so only ultimately, that is, if we pursue mixed interests for a while. What is distinctive is that the moment may always come when the gain I am after will be perceived by you as an unacceptable loss, and the only "compensation" you would get if you accepted my gain is the absence of war. The even greater losses that you might incur if you fought my gain you may well deem worth risking, if you think my gain too dangerous or believe that war could bring a gain for you. The perspective is that of the *ultimate* test of strength, of the zero-sum game, which requires a constant calculation of force. My interest consists either in preventing or eliminating your gain, or, should the costs prove too high, in extracting a concession in return for my acceptance of your gain. I have to take your power into account because of what you might otherwise do to me, not because I could not live without you—indeed, I wish you did not exist. Two powers cannot be number one simultaneously. Since I am in control of my instruments of power, how I react to your moves is my sovereign business; your moves may constrain my choices, the way a city's maze of streets constrains my walk to a destination. Some choices may thus be costlier than others, but they are still mine. This is the traditional logic of interstate politics.

The "modern" logic does not deny conflict and competition. It starts from the awareness of increased contacts and mutual vulnerability. Even if my first concern is my absolute gain (for instance, the industrialization of my country), I may want to gain at your expense, or I may seek my gain in a way that inflicts a loss on you (cf. Iran's oil strategy versus the industrialized world). There are elements of a zero-sum game here; there is assuredly no permanent premium on "constructive" cooperation, and nothing necessarily benign about the interdependence of sovereigns. But the *ultimate* perspective is one of solidarity; the dynamics of the world economy, of world science and technology, is, for better (growth and welfare) or worse (population explosion, pollution, depletion, inflation, and recession) a dynamics of integration. If I push too far, your loss risks becoming mine. We may all lose, if we all become victims of inflation, recession, shortages, or an epidemic of protectionist moves. The only difference may be degrees of loss. (This explains why a world economy dominated by a hegemonic state, such as Britain in the nineteenth century, may be more advantageous, say, to a middle or small power than a world in which the hegemony breaks up; a hegemonic state, if it is enlightened, may take the interests of others into account in setting the rules, but as its power declines and insecurity grows, all the participants in the world economy may suffer from the breakdown of the rules, the deficiencies of the international financial and monetary system, speculative capital movements, or the loss of national control over credit or monetary policies.) Inversely, even when there is a test of wills, there is a joint incentive, not merely to split the difference, but somewhat to "upgrade the common interest."[17] The best way for me to maximize my gain, even if I inflict a loss on you, is to see to it that you gain something, too—either because this will give you an incentive to help me increase my gain or because you will otherwise be tempted to erase it. So, what is distinctive here is not so much the quest for absolute gains,[18] but the interest in a joint gain: your loss (or my gain) will be at least partly compensated by some gain for you.

To be sure, this need not be the case in situations of extreme dependence, where one side's domination results in actual and total exploitation. Nor does the "compensatory" gain need to be equal to the loss. It merely has to be sufficient to prevent the actor that suffers the loss from seeking revenge. In the kinds of relations that theorists of imperialist dependency usually describe, the imperialist actor obtains his gains less often by inflicting a loss on his colony or client than by preventing the development of his dependent, or by slanting it in a way profitable mainly to himself. But the situation lasts only as long as at least one important group in the colony or client state makes a gain—the "comprador" group, the social elite tied to the ruler of the imperialist actor. Thus, the notion of a joint gain says nothing about the evenness of distribution, the fairness of the game, or the possibility of better alternatives for one or even both partners. But it points to a game *different* from the traditional one.

Interdependence results not merely from the interpenetration of societies, but from the way in which this interpenetration concerns and constrains the actors. It is "policy interdependence"[19] that matters, and it results from both the very scope of "societal interdependence," which cannot fail to affect the actors, and the increasing control governments try to exert over society, given the predominance of economic and social issues in the domestic political agenda. The consequence is clear: the loss by state actors of some instruments of control, such as monetary, credit and taxation policies.[20] Choices are not merely constrained, they are sometimes eliminated (a state like Japan cannot "choose" economic self-sufficiency) by either external or domestic imperatives. Thus, the "interdependent" use of power both is less free (or full) and follows a different strategy than the traditional one. In the conventional logic, if my enemy became my friend, I would no longer have to worry (see the relation between the United States and Canada). In an interdependent world, the more intensely you are my friend, the more I may have to worry (think of the propagation of recessions, or United States-Saudi or United States-Iranian relations). There was some truth to a statement made, around 1973, by Helmut Sonnenfeldt: we had more difficulties in relations between Washington and its partners than in those with the USSR and China, to which the logic of interdependence does not fully apply.

Obviously, the ideal type of the first use of power is the diplomatic-strategic game; the ideal type of the second, the modern world economy. But reality is more complex. The uses of power form a continuum, and they can be subtly mixed. Moreover, because today's military power has a large economic component—arms industries—some of the second type of logic appears in relations between military allies, or arms buyers and sellers; because the open world economy is not as extensive as the planet, there are states that, to protect their separateness even in the economic realm, refrain from following the logic of solidarity, prefer autarky, or may even prefer to use the logic of interaction in the old mercantilist tradition. Conversely, even a state that observes the logic of interdependence in the world economy has two series of choices.

First, it can choose a more or a less cooperative strategy, by trying to maximize its relative gain, or to preserve a sizable joint gain even if its relative advantage is smaller, because it hopes that future benefits will be greater thereby. Second, it can try to improve its position in the sphere of interdependence by bringing to bear on it the assets it enjoys in the realm of interaction, such as military might others may want to draw on for their security. The mode of operation depends on the components of power at one's disposal. (Indeed, one may have no choice if one is ideologically committed to separateness and surrounded by foes, or, at the other extreme, if one is in a condition not merely of interdependence but of one-sided dependence on another nation). In most instances, the choice is largely determined by one's objectives.

To sum up: in the traditional usage of power, states were like boiled eggs. War, the minute of truth, would reveal which ones were hard or soft. Interdependence breaks eggs into a vast omelet. It does not mean the end of conflict: I may want *my* egg to contribute a larger part of the omelet's size and flavor than *your* egg—or I may want you to break yours into it first, etc. But we all end in the same omelet.

A fourth change of power lies in the existence of new *restraints* that affect the old logic of interaction and are built into that of interdependence. They make power less calculable than ever, for there is an increasing difference between supply and usability and a growing distance between uses and achievements. I shall return to this later.

New hierarchies and multiple systems. These transformations of power have also affected the nature of the international hierarchy. There is no longer one hierarchy based on military or geomilitary power. There are separate functional hierarchies, and in each one the meaning of being "top dog" is far from simple. Here again, the restraints on power operate, and their effects range from an attenuation of hierarchy to an outright subversion. In other words, it is a trying world for the top dogs, because of the general difficulty (the interference of other actors and one's own domestic accidents) of using one's might to achieve desired results, because of the difficulty of making might in one area affect outcomes in another (linkage), and because of the handicaps proper to each area.

The international system itself has been transformed. For the first time, there is a single international system, symbolized by the United Nations, in which all state actors have to take, or pretend to take, stands on huge quantities of issues. This singleness is also illustrated by the way in which action on one issue—such as oil—affects the military and financial capabilities of states, their stands and claims on the world monetary system, on other raw materials, on aid and technology transfers, and so on; however, the very intensity of contacts, number of issues, and transformations of power allow one to establish two distinctions. One, there is still a distinctive strategic-diplomatic system, dominated by the possibility of violent conflict and characterized by the threat or the use of force. The same actors participate, however, in other systems, or games, where the threat or use of force is remote—a *distant* possibility, not a merely *latent* one (as it often is in the strategic-diplomatic arena), an improbable event even when the game's framework reflects the hierarchy of force. This improbability results from the costs of a resort to force, which would exceed by far any likely gain, or, even more, from irrelevance (force simply not being the means to the desired end), or from both. America's abstention from force against the Organization of Petroleum-Exporting Countries (OPEC) resulted from the political and economic losses such an expedition would have entailed, from the doubt that even a "successful" conquest would force a lasting reduction in the price of oil, and from the obvious fact that there are more appropriate ways of securing supplies of oil than through military conquest. (It also resulted, in part, from ethical restraints, although their reach is not universal.)[21] Finally, the United States, the greatest possessor of military power, could afford to restrain this might because it depends much less on imported oil for its industrial production than countries insufficiently endowed with military supplies. The two superpowers, despite their different choices with respect to interdependence, are not in desperate need of external resources.

Second, there are many different functional systems in the nonstrategic realms, and it is not easy to produce an inventory. There are nonstrategic games of economic interaction (but not interdependence) between East and West, for instance. Mainly, there are specialized games of "complex interdependence," to use the expression of Joseph Nye and Robert Keohane.[22] Some crystallize around an issue—territorial, such as the oceans, or functional, such as international trade. Others crystallize around an issue and an international organization such as the world monetary system (International Monetary Fund [IMF]) or food (Food and Agricultural Organization [FAO]). Other games seem to have as a primary object the creation of the framework in which they will take place. For instance, should energy problems be dealt with separately or along with other raw materials? Should each commodity have its own arena? Thus, there is both some fluidity and room for additions, because some issues are not yet the objects of real collective games, even if they are put on the international agenda either for symbolic reasons, or, like the matter of human rights, as weapons in the diplomatic-strategic contest. Thus, the unity of the international system contains a bewildering differentiation.

THE DIPLOMATIC-STRATEGIC CHESSBOARD

A survey of the changes cannot stop here. One must take a closer look at the "traditional" diplomatic-strategic chessboard and at the "modern" systems. In the traditional one, power remains above all a stock of national capabilities and forces that each state uses as it sees fit, to preserve or acquire the maximum possible freedom of action. The states are practically the only actors, along with groups (such as terrorists) struggling to form or to control states. The game of power remains what it has always been: my aim is to increase my ability to harm you and to decrease your ability to harm me; and this game is played with alacrity by many states, quite noticeably the new ones.[23] The structure of the game is still the military alliance. A partial *and perhaps temporary* transformation has, however, been brought about by the nuclear revolution. It has introduced into the competition of those states that now possess nuclear weapons an element of solidarity that tempers the very logic of separateness that gave rise to the nuclear race in the first place: it is solidarity for survival. The rules that apply are no longer the old rules of interaction, but it would be excessive to say that we are now in the same realm as that of economic interdependence, which entails not merely the vulnerability of one actor to the other's moves, but also a certain volume of transactions. "Policy interdependence" results from "societal interdependence." Nuclear solidarity does not come from the interpenetration of societies, but the effect is somewhat similar, and we can therefore talk about nuclear interconnection. It means that, for each of the present nuclear powers, the supreme form of military might is not usable in the daily course of world politics; given the risks of escalation, this also dampens their resort to conventional force among themselves. Hence the prevalence of oblique, indirect, or latent uses of force; the concern for arms control and the phobia of nuclear proliferation; and the desire, even when the struggle for influence unfolds in the traditional mode, to prevent third-party disputes from triggering a state of war between themselves. In other words, this fear of force not only makes the "minute of truth" more hypothetical, but also privileges other kinds of power.

This has, in turn, led to three changes. The first is a change in the rules of the "game of power," now a strange blend of arms race and restraints. On the one hand, at the nuclear level, the old Clausewitzian formula, "War is the continuation of state policy by other means," has become invalid. The peril of escalation is such that, first, the search for limited nuclear war strategies that might bring the formula back as a guideline is still most likely to fail or merely to reinforce deterrence;[24] and that, second, even at the conventional level, only limited, not "knock-out," wars make sense. For the nuclear level, the blend has produced the paradoxes of deterrence: I stop you from wanting to attack me by threatening suicide. We must both be concerned about injecting some stability into the race, and thus formally or informally coordinate our separate contributions to it, to allow ourselves to pursue our ordinary competitive pursuits without risk of annihilation. We must also respect some Alice in Wonderland precepts to protect deterrence's foundations. I must make sure that your retaliatory force can survive any attack by me, and I shall leave my population exposed to your retaliatory blows. Thus, we have not only an exclusion of the old logic of the zero-sum game from the nuclear and even the large conventional war levels, but also the introduction of mixed strategies at the nuclear level.

On the other hand, the nonnuclear actors experience two kinds of restraints. One is traditional: insofar as they are members of a Great Power's network of alliances, or as their enemies are protected by another network, they are inhibited in their resort to force by the need not to antagonize their guardian or the guardian of their foe. The other restraint is more original. Because the agenda of world politics is now crowded by issues that do not involve the use or threat of force, and because there are many games with varied alignments, the total hostility that usually brings reality closest to the model of the zero-sum game, and antagonists closest to the minute of truth, may be less frequent (although we still find it in the Middle East). Even states that are on opposite sides on some issues may be on the same side on others, or be sufficiently interdependent economically for violence to be suspended (see the relations between several black African nations and Praetoria).

The second change affects the hierarchy of states. The strategic-diplomatic game is the only truly bipolar one. But there are now different levels of strategic action. At the nuclear level, since atomic weapons are so far only weapons of deterrence, there has been fortunately general abstention. Large numbers of wars have been waged at the level of conventional conflict, however; interstate limited wars, wars of national liberation which remain limited on the defender's side, and all-out civil wars. Finally, there is the new level of terrorism. It all amounts to a decline in the actual ability of those who have the biggest supplies to use their military power, and the very inhibitions that weigh on them give greater opportunity to smaller states and nonterritorial groups to resort to violence. Moreover, the well-endowed states compete to sell arms to or to license arms production by lesser ones. Thus, in various ways, the hierarchy is being subverted.

The third change concerns the structure of the game. On the one hand, the classical structure—the military alliance—has shown far greater resiliency than, say, General Gallois's prediction of the dissolution of the alliance by the purely national character of nuclear weaponry would have led one to believe. This is because alliances have usually been not fusions but additions. Yet the formidable issue of the credibility of deterrence for the protection of an ally, the steps taken by nuclear powers themselves to replace deterrence-by-the-threat-of-doing-the-irrational with deterrence-by-the-threat-that-leaves-something-to-chance, to use Thomas Schelling's terms, and to replace even the latter with elaborate strategies of war fighting—all this has created serious strains among allies. Unless one nuclear power places its forces at the service of another (as Britain alone has done, or rather has had to do, given the technological dependence of its "independent" deterrent), alliances between nuclear states are difficult. The weaker state's asset lies precisely in its independence, that is, in its forces' eventual use *not* being aligned and merged with the planned use of the superior one's. One such alliance has exploded: that between the USSR and China. For alignment or merger makes the smaller deterrent unnecessary and creates no special problem for the potential enemy. But nonalignment, separateness, creates one for both the enemy and the senior ally. Alliances between a nuclear power and nonnuclear states become means by which the former controls the behavior of the latter. On the other hand, as Kissinger has recognized, the stability of the central nuclear balance has led to a splintering of the world into partial military balances along regional lines or around specific conflicts. There are, in effect, two kinds of fragments in the strategic-diplomatic puzzle: those that remain subdued, because an explosion there might lead to general war, given the sizable and direct involvement of superpower's forces (the prime example is Europe); and those that, so to speak, can afford turbulence.

THE GAMES OF INTERDEPENDENCE

Modern games—those in which the use of force is unlikely—are extraordinarily complex. This is partly because of the great variety of economic capabilities and of the ways they can be used. There are many natural resources and all the means to exploit them (technology, skilled labor, fleets . . .). There is real capital and financial capital. There is what has sometimes been called the *force de frappe* of a nation's exports and also that of investments abroad—portfolio investments or enterprises. One can use economic power as a stock to be kept under one's control or to gain control over others without giving up anything of one's own freedom (see Soviet sales of natural gas), or one can weave with one's economic power a seamless web made of inextricably intertwined national threads—indeed, not merely national threads, since these are games played by nonstate actors as well. This latter possibility becomes a necessity for a state whenever the level of transactions and the actor's sensitivity to them create that web, and for nonstate actors, which cannot usually resort to the logic of strategic and diplomatic interaction.

This use of power, which is not universal, interests us most here, because of both its originality and its importance. With the end of empires—the subjugation of needed resources or markets—with the sweeping internationalization of economies because of the communications revolution, the worldwide spread of technology and entrepreneurship, and the projection of the effects of consumption and production outside the nation's borders; with the resulting disappearance of the radical separation between interstate affairs and international economic transactions which was characteristic both of liberal theory and of much nineteenth-century practice, and given the role played by the state in economic development and welfare, the states themselves are interdependent. This explains why the debate among experts about whether the ratio of foreign trade to GNP or the level of foreign investments has much increased since 1914,[25] misses the point. Even if the figures are not higher, the political significance of such interdependence is entirely different.

The rules of the game. This interdependence, the possibility or obligation to weave one's power into the web, is both an opportunity for and a restraint on the actor. It is an opportunity to exert influence almost literally on a global scale. It is a restraint, not only on domestic autonomy but also on the hostile use of economic power, not just because of the actor's interest in promoting joint gains, but for three other reasons. One has to do with objectives. Let us take the case of a state actor whose aim is to maximize economic development, however defined (whether in terms of aggregate growth, or with priority given to those components of national power that can best be used for gains on the world scene, or in such a way as to overcome a rival, etc.). The level and nature of interdependence may well be such that this state could not reach its goal unless others (its rival included) reach their own development and welfare goals. Thus, a joint gain is not only in the actor's interest; it is a necessity. This is the case, at present, among the nations of Western Europe, the United States, and Japan. Even the USSR, which in the traditional strategic-diplomatic game tries to reduce America's power and does not play the games of complex interdependence, is sufficiently in need of American wheat, technology, and credits to have been highly ambivalent about the recent "crisis of capitalism." Some East European countries, far more eager to play these games in order to escape from Russia's clasp, were not ambivalent at all about wishing capitalism well.

The second reason has to do with the impact of foreign policy on domestic affairs in a realm where the old, partial separation has vanished. An actor's hostile or aggressively competitive use of his economic power may well backfire at home. De Gaulle's accumulation of gold reserves in his fight against the privileges of the dollar, and his determination to keep wages from rising too fast so as to improve the competitiveness of French industry in the Common Market, created social frustrations that led to the explosion of 1968.

This points to the third restraint, which results from the game itself: a state's uninhibited use of economic power could hurt it, for it might backfire internationally. In monetary matters, de Gaulle himself, far from waging an all-out war on the dollar, "was (contrary to much popular mythology . . .) pulling punches."[26] He wanted to dethrone the dollar; he did not want to destroy the principles of Bretton Woods—fixed rates, convertibility—which he approved and which he accused Washington of undermining. Similarly, he pulled his punches in his effort to limit the entry of American multinationals, for if they had been kept away from France, they would have invested their capital in the economy of France's European Economic Community (EEC) partners, and their products would have been imported into France.[27] Thus, the motto, quite different from that of traditional interaction, becomes, "You can harm me, and I you, but neither one of us can retaliate fully without harming himself." The recognition of the capacity to harm acknowledges, so to speak, the conflictual part of the process. After all, even among interdependent "partners" whose might is not drastically imbalanced, interdependence, being divisible, is seldom homogeneously even, and being constraining, it is often resented. The formula also acknowledges the ultimate non-zero-sum game aspects. Even when I try unilaterally to increase my share of the pie, I should not endanger its existence; even when I resort to conflict to exploit my advantage, ultimately I need, if not your cooperation, at least your consent.

Hence, here also, a triple change. First, in the rules of the game of power. Its name becomes the manipulation of interdependence: I pull on your thread, you pull on mine; I need you, but you need me—even when you are, either generally or even in the area that concerns us specially, much stronger than I am. The stakes of the games are multiple: specific gains (for instance, a certain level of oil prices, or an agreement to protect exporters of raw materials against losses resulting from price fluctuations, or the wiping out of the debts of certain nations), but also the determination of the rules of a game (Who has the power to license the exploration of the seabeds? Who controls the IMF?), and the possibility of linking separate games to redress one's weakness in one through one's strength in another. Clearly, the calculation of power, always a difficult exercise, becomes almost impossible.

One can weigh capabilities of power, but whether, and on how broad a front, they will be usable, and with what results, is largely a function of one's own skill, that of one's opponents, one's internal cohesion, the circumstances, and so on. The pace of technology, the ups and downs of the world economy, and monetary fluctuations make even the evaluation of capabilities difficult. Power tends to be disaggregated abroad, into the various functional systems of interdependence. Each system tends to involve only a certain element of power (money, a given raw material, source of energy, and the like). At home, it is fragmented into a variety of bureaucratic services. Moreover, to make calculations even more complex, the formal power of governments or public institutions to deal with issues is divorced from the substantive power of private actors to empty that formal power of much of its content. For example, the oil multinationals thwarted the Arab embargo of most of its effect, with Japan receiving far more oil than before.[28] The irrelevance of using force to reap benefits or erase disadvantages also introduces vast uncertainties about the outcomes of contests, by removing one traditional trenchant way of ending them. Finally, the very nature of the web makes an accounting of power difficult: you and I may be so entangled that we do not clearly know where your power ends and mine begins. Or else, whether my power (defined as my capacity to reach my goal) exceeds yours depends on third party reactions. For instance, in the contest between Saudi Arabia and Iran (the two chief antagonists in the split over oil prices among OPEC members in December 1976), whether one camp prevailed over the other depended, in large part, on how many of the consumers' orders switched to the cheaper oil. All of this in turn becomes an incentive to further testing one's power and that of one's rivals—or partners.

A twisted hierarchy of players. Second, there is a change in the hierarchy of players. As many hierarchies exist as games, and none of them is bipolar, since, on the whole, the USSR remains absent or hesitant. On top of each, one finds not necessarily the state that has the greatest amount of overall power, but those states that, in this particular realm, individually or collectively enjoy a monopoly or oligopoly. Thus, the United States was able to change the rules of the monetary system in August 1971, because of the international role of the dollar. In a monopoly or oligopoly of a sufficiently vital resource, those states that depend on it [that is, an external supply of the resource -Ed.] may be forced to accept the linkage even of a game in which they are stronger, to that [that is, the "game" or issue area -Ed.] in which this monopoly or oligopoly operates. For years, the United States has obtained economic concessions from the EEC and the Federal Republic, or has prevented them from making "unfriendly" decisions about the American multinationals or the Eurodollar market, by linking its military protection to the economic issues. OPEC not only changed the rules of the world oil game, but forced—in alliance with other developing nations—the United States to accept, in 1975, the linkage of energy needs to all the other economic demands raised by the Third World. Saudi Arabia, more subtly, is coaxing a linkage between the realm of oil and the Arab-Israeli conflict.

This has the following effects on the international hierarchy. The games of interdependence obviously favor the United States; its economic capabilities are huge, its threads are all over the tapestry. Moreover, the loss of its external sources of supply, of its outlets, of its means of action abroad, while dealing a serious blow to its influence, would not be fatal—in contrast to the situation of Japan, West Germany, or the OPEC countries. And yet, serious inhibitions on the use of America's power limit its capacity to obtain outcomes proportional to its capabilities (and provoke dismay in a public that is not used to vulnerabilities, dependencies, and forced restraints). These inhibitions also weigh on the power of other "monopolists." Here are some instances:

"I could theoretically use my advantages at your expense on a given issue, but must refrain from doing so because I need your support on another." This could be called "self-deterring linkage," as opposed to "enforced" linkage. For instance, both in the International Energy Agency and in the huge recycling facility Kissinger proposed in 1975, the United States could try to impose its technology on partners eager for substitutes for oil and its preferences for economic policies to be followed by them, in exchange for its help. But the United States, in turn, needs their support in dealing with the oil-producing countries, and it therefore has to behave more like a senior partner than a hegemonic master, if a common front of consumer countries is to be achieved. Similarly, the Third World countries cannot stabilize their export earnings if the United States refuses to, but the United States, or at least its multinationals, needs, sooner or later, an agreement on the rules of the game: the Great Power's interest in predictability and order operates as a restraint. The oligopolists of OPEC, in turn, need the support of the oil-importing states of the Third World, both in order to resist the pressure of the rich oil-importing countries eager for guarantees of supply and concessions on price and in order to wrest a larger share of the management of world economic institutions. This puts some brakes on the pricing policies of OPEC, and obliges the cartel to provide at least some aid to the poorer victims of its price increases.

"I cannot push my advantage too far, because my power is partly your hostage." Multinationals have an incentive to respect the laws and customs of their host countries; otherwise they risk expropriation. The OPEC countries cannot increase the price of oil beyond reason, not just because this might provoke a military response, but because of their own interest in investing their huge revenues in the economies of their clients and in receiving goods and services from them. Their ambition for power and economic growth will force them to help their clients remain prosperous, and it will certainly refrain them from inciting their victims to confiscate OPEC investments or wiping out their debts to OPEC. In this respect, an oil embargo is a perfectly sensible strategy *before* mutual entanglement has gone too far, that is, as long as your short-term need for oil exceeds my short-term need to earn revenue. Once I have begun to put my earnings into your domain, however, a new embargo could hurt me as much as you. If some oil-producing countries propose new price increases that could further depress the world economy (and perpetuate the vicious cycle, since the proposed increases are partly aimed at compensating for the failure to earn as many petrodollars as had been expected, due to the consumers' slump), then the common front risks splitting, as it did in December 1976.

"If I push my advantage too far, you can copy me, and thereby wipe it out." This might be called deterrent linkage. It is, for instance, the problem of competitive devaluations, or export subsidies, or import restrictions. (To be sure, there is not always perfect reciprocity. The United States has been able to change the rules, to devalue twice, and to force others into a system of floating rates, this meant, in exchange, the end of the U.S. privilege of obliging its partners to absorb unlimited amounts of inconvertible dollars.)

"I cannot go too far, because I fear unwelcome domestic consequences on both your turf and mine." There are, unevenly distributed over the world, striking inhibitions on the use of force over economic matters. In the United States there is growing opposition to the use of food as an instrument of foreign policy, or even to the use of economic aid to shore up politically shaky and dubious allies. In other words, there is a restraint that comes from a somewhat inchoate, not always fair, but undeniable sense of legitimacy. In a very different vein, having to do not with moral scruples but with political prudence, Washington could not encourage an unlimited expansion of its "cosmocorps," without fomenting a revolt of labor unions and domestic industries within the United States. It almost happened with the Burke-Hartke Bill. It would also foster a reaction from the "penetrated" foreign societies. Here we come to the impact on foreign turf: if you are a friend, I must make sure that I do not behave as a rogue elephant, for instance, that my antiinflation policy does not induce a recession that could cripple you and aggravate my own condition. Even if you are an opponent, I must be careful not to bring about the advent of an even more intractable regime. Thus, arguments in favor of a United States military intervention in Arab countries to force a reduction in the price of oil left conveniently aside the issue of the regime that might take over, were the Saudi king overthrown or humiliated. Saudi Arabia has pleaded for restraint in oil pricing, lest radical regimes rise over the depressed economies of Italy and France.

The capacity of the strong to exploit fully the favorable asymmetries of interdependence is thus limited. The United States may be at the top of almost every hierarchy of economic power, but here, as in the strategic realm, it is a Gulliver tied, not a master with free hands. Insult can be added to injury: I refer to what might be called the *revenge* of the weaker. All those aspects of the new game can be seen, if not as factors of egalitarianism, at least as correctives to overall asymmetries.

The most obvious example is that lesser actors, devoid of military might or vast industrial resources, yet endowed with an asset (such as oil, bauxite, copper, or uranium) indispensable to the most advanced nations, can extract, through cartels and coalitions, a price that will help them narrow the gap in the race for development. The same relationship exists among unevenly powerful advanced countries: de Gaulle's great skill lay in exploiting such French assets as geography, or France's veto power in the EEC, to wrest advantages from the North Atlantic Treaty Organization (NATO) without losing the American guarantee or to obtain a common agricultural policy (CAP) maximizing French advantages.

Other assets of a weaker power eager to block policies of a larger one reside in what Joseph S. Nye calls "the asymmetry of attention" and the "greater cohesion and concentration"[29] of the weaker government compared to the more powerful state. The latter has to disperse its attention over a huge number of chessboards and players and cannot always keep its own internal bureaucratic coalitions together. The examples Nye gives come from American-Canadian relations.

In the cases of Canada and France, *in*dependence allowed a weaker state, by exploiting its assets, to decrease an "asymmetrical interdependency." Such a state can, however, narrow the asymmetry another way. It consists of accentuating the *inter*dependency, even if it entails an apparent loss of autonomy or "separateness." For in certain relationships, the stronger state is obliged to transfer wealth or other resources to the weaker. Thus, the United States and its allies were transferring technological know-how to Iran; the United States is selling to Arab countries weapons that will provide them with a military panoply capable of reinforcing their economic *force de frappe*—and of making United States military intervention more difficult. In a world of interdependence, your desire to influence me may force you to help me get stronger. There is yet another way to accentuate interdependence in favor of the weaker partner. Keohane and Nye have found that Canada has done better than Australia in its relations with the United States because of the greater role played, in Canadian-American affairs, by transnational actors (for example, auto and oil companies) whose interests "did not always coincide with the United States government's."[30]

There is a corollary: the new games provide new opportunities for a very old exercise, the blackmail of weakness, or "since you need me, and since my collapse would hurt you, you have to save me." For your possession of assets that are in demand (for instance: America's and West Germany's currencies; American weapons, grain, or technology; Bonn's current surpluses) turns out to be double edged. It gives you some power, but you cannot either refuse to give (or sell) what your partner desperately needs or impose such conditions that your partner in trouble would try to get help from your opponents. Thus, Bonn's interest—political and economic—in preserving the Common Market has led the Federal Republic to keep financing the CAP, to keep Italy afloat, to establish a regional fund, and so on. Washington, despite its hostility to gold, has had to allow its European allies to revalue their stocks to meet their new financial obligations to OPEC. Similarly, one can expect the OPEC countries to increase their aid to the Fourth World, whose support they need in their own contest of wills with the industrial nations.

The players who are in the most uncomfortable position are the industrialized middle powers. They have no monopoly or oligopoly, and, separately or jointly, they cannot force either linkages or changes in rules of the game (hence the anemia of the EEC). Nor do they have the weapons of the weak: they are stopped from fully exploiting the assets they *do* have—technology, capital goods, or financial resources—by their need to get the potential "victim's" support in another game, or by the fact that their might is another's hostage, that is, they suffer the same inhibitions as the strong. Their economies are too entangled in the web of interdependence to allow them to choose the Soviet or the Chinese way.

Indeed, the refusal to play power-as-entanglement, still characteristic of the two main Communist states, is, for them, a source of embarrassment as well as a strength. If a nation plays the game of entanglement and bargaining with all the other players, it creates both great chances for self-enhancement and great risks in a contest of constant uncertainty where no gain is ever final, no setback fatal. A loss may be a gain at the same time (as when the United States "lost" power to OPEC yet "regained" power toward Western Europe and Japan). Conversely, an undeniable gain (such as the obtainment, for instance, by Iran, of all the traditional trappings of power, weapons, factories, investments abroad, and the like) can also become a trap, since the preservation of power now means permanent and universal worry about the other actors' welfare and resources. Most nations, not being self-sufficient, have no choice: they must play, if only to try to increase their margin of self-sufficiency or their measure of control over the uncertainties of insufficiency. On the other hand, if a nation tries to be self-sufficient to preserve itself from the risks of the game, the compromises of the bargains, and the contagion of the other players' diseases, then it may well be able to increase its power by its own means, but its influence abroad is likely to be limited. Even Moscow's military cornucopia, and its skillful political exploitation of quarries of radicalism, are no substitutes for the influence derived from interdependence. The power of example may be its own reward, but it is not a tangible one, especially since it is not an example many countries can follow. Thus, playing the game of power on the world scene means an endless chase after elusive achievements, but trying to build power away from that scene means a temporary abdication from, or limitation of, an impact of events.

To be sure, there is ample room for halfway houses. China can try, so to speak, for discrete effects—without entanglement—for instance, through oil exports to well-selected targets of influence (such as Japan). The USSR, while trading with the rest of the world, tries to reduce the risks of interdependence by buying goods and technology only if the transaction creates no lasting dependence on a supplier, or no foreign right of overseeing Moscow's domestic policies. But such halfway houses are not stable. The Soviets, in order better to control their satellites, do practice entanglement in Eastern Europe, where its inconvenience is discounted by the presence of Soviet military force. Yet it is not abolished thereby: force can be used or brandished only at exceptional moments, and entanglement involves some constraints for the USSR (for instance, in the matter of East European oil supplies). Raw materials delivered to Eastern Europe are not available for export to Western countries. Just as the West often has to subsidize its exports to Russia, Moscow has to grant credits to its East European partners, or else import from them industrial goods it does not badly need.

And a new structure. Third, a change, or rather a double innovation, has transformed the structure of the game. On the one hand, many more actors and a new type of game also bring with them a new grouping. As ever, indeed even more than before, the contests—those of interdependence as well as those of interaction—are fluid bets and plots among shifting partners. However, there is now a generally recognized need for structures of bargaining, such as institutions, agencies, and organized coalitions. The actors need them to maximize *their* disaggregated or dispersed power and to minimize mutual interference, or at least make it predictable and maybe even beneficial; the issues require them because of the mixed interests of the players. (This, in turn, creates another restraint on an actor's itch to use his economic power aggressively. Some of the partners he needs are likely to cool him down or to thwart him: witness Kissinger's gradual shift to conciliation in North-South affairs, due to West European and Japanese misgivings about the earlier hard line, or Iran's difficulties with Saudi Arabia in OPEC.) To be sure, part of the contest is *about* such structures. In areas where I alone am strong, it is in my interest to dodge the harness; in areas where I alone am weak, it is in my interest not only to join those whose alliance with me will add up to collective strength but also to slip a harness on you. This in itself is a new element, and—again—it contributes to uncertainty. Will the structure last? If it rests on a mere convergence of different calculations, how solid will it be? Moreover, it consecrates a kind of power that, to be sure, requires a "stock" or ingredient of some kind to be more than a *trompe-l'oeil,* yet, like most modern economies based on paper currencies, it depends more on trust, reputation, or faith than on any fixed ratio of gold to bank notes: the power to organize coalitions, define acceptable rules of the game, change these and force linkages. States are unevenly skillful at cementing a beneficial coalition, or dissolving a hostile one. The choice of an actor for one alignment over another often depends not only on its interests in the case at issue, but also on its regime at a given moment. The very disaggregation of power may lead the same player to belong to diverse coalitions, depending on which game is being played—Harold Wilson once joked (was it a joke?) about the future British membership in OPEC, but when it comes to raw materials, Britain is surely not a member of the Group of 77. Thus, these groupings contribute to a certain defusing of world politics—states group to bargain, not to shoot—and to its complexity. They can be no more than interstate pressure groups, but they can also, like OPEC, become cartels controlling prices and quantities, or they can become even a mix of cartel and alliance, like the Arab members of OPEC. They can be highly specialized and deal with just one product, or be very general (like the Group of 77) and aimed, a bit like a political party, at putting some fire under a collection of demands. They can be ideological groups, like the Islamic Conference, or institutionalized groups, like the EEC. This brings us to the second structural innovation.

In world affairs, as in domestic societies in the earlier part of this century, the magnitude of the issues as well as the concern for some stability or moderation now brings about a shift from a system in which the management of interdependence was sought through the observance by states of a set of rules (such as those of the General Agreement on Tariffs and Trade [GATT] or Bretton Woods), to a system in which joint management will be required through international institutions, the pooling of sovereignties, and the coordination of policies and goals. Rules prescribing states what to do and not to do are no longer enough; yet governments remain unwilling to let, for instance, indicators determine automatically when to eliminate their payments surpluses or deficits. Whether one considers the regime of the oceans, the problem of food, or the future international monetary system, one sees no way of avoiding the establishment of international organizations with considerable powers either of administration or even of policy making.

Coalitions and international agencies mean an enormous expansion of the scope of multilateral diplomacy; this, in turn, contributes to the transformation of the international hierarchy. Multilateral diplomacy boosts the influence of small states, both because of their numbers and because of the ability of even very weak states to obtain vicarious power through coalition. This is a fact that the smaller members of the European Community discovered long ago, and which the Soviets know, fear, and resist. On the traditional chessboard, small powers can exploit, at Washington's expense, either the security link or the ties created by the existence of an ethnic pressure group within the United States (as in the case of Israel). In the arenas of interdependence, it is multilateral diplomacy that dilutes the full use of American power because Washington faces not discrete weak players, but groups of actors tied together by convergent interests. Saudi Arabia has known how to exploit both the security link and multilateral games.

THE POSITION OF THE NATION STATE

All these transformations affect the position of the state in international affairs. They can be understood by looking at three terms of the traditional diplomatic vocabulary: sovereignty, the national interest, and independence. Sovereignty, the state's privilege of carrying no obligations other than those it has accepted (whether this acceptance is truly voluntary or the result of a *Diktat*), the state's mastery of its own territory, population, and resources, is at the same time bolstered and undermined. It is bolstered by the rise in the number of states and by attempts of these states to control all their resources; it is undermined by the mutual and constant interference of the players. Everyone, from the lowliest to the most eminent, tries to find, develop, and exploit some asset either to maximize his influence or to ensure his security, but when all do this simultaneously, the outcome is, inevitably, frustration for many and a threat of chaos for all. With hierarchies constantly reshuffled, and with an unprecedented proliferation of pieces moving all at once on the board, the exercise of safe external or even internal control is difficult, evanescent, and shaky. Although each state tries to make itself less, and others more vulnerable, or to turn the relation of interdependence into one in which it will be less, and others more dependent, these "neomercantilist" strategies collide with the current world economy, which has invalidated two key premises of old mercantilism: that the economic contest among states is a zero-sum game and that the right policy for each is autarky. Moreover, they collide with a highly nonmercantilist phenomenon: the loss of national control over essential ingredients of power or over vital tools of policy. This loss is experienced not merely (as in the relations between oil-importing countries and OPEC) by some states to the advantage of others, but by all (witness Iran's economic troubles). It is due partly to the role of actors that are not states and partly to phenomena: short-term capital movements, speculations against weak currencies, the spread of inflations and recessions, which the international economy conveys and which states either do not know how to check or else fear trying to control by unilateral measures that might cut them off from the international economy on which they depend. National measures to curb inflation and payments deficits easily boomerang: the West German and American moves to cut demand created a deep recession because they were simultaneous. One's own policy-making autonomy can be ravaged by the moves of others: Japan's post-OPEC limitation on imports restored its balance at the expense of other nations' exports, that is, of their payments balance. As a result, sovereignty becomes both a frantic quest for extending control wherever it is still possible (see the oceans and the new wave of creeping protectionism) and a last defense against the thrusts of all those forces that have turned the old armor into a sieve.

The concept of the national interest was inseparable from a relatively hard, calculable, and stable idea of power and the international system. There was always something oversimplified and wrongheadedly dogmatic about it. But the old uncertainties about physical survival and military safety look simple next to the new ones. The modern games offer so many alternatives, mysteries, and complexities that an "objective" definition of the national interest makes even less sense than before. In the first place, although many nations—especially ones newly rich—obviously act on the belief that their *interest* lies in behaving in a traditional way, that is, to imitate the patterns of the past by maximizing their military might and by becoming industrial powers; this may not be the wisest path. Military might may turn out to be hard to use—given the restraints watchfully observed or imposed by the Great Powers—as well as dangerous to the domestic stability. While industrialization, investments abroad, and a large trading role allow one to splash in the sea of interdependence, one's lifejacket is tied to those of the other swimmers, there remains a permanent peril of sinking, and the longer one stays in the water the less one can break out of the chain and reach the shore where one could be tranquil, if alone. In the second place, the old concept of the *national* interest is clearly being dissolved, so to speak, from below, from the side, and from above. From below, it is dissolved through the transgovernmental bureaucratic alliances along functional lines that recent studies have begun to describe; from the side, through the subversion of sovereignty either by transnational alliances of barons and bureaus or by transnational agents, especially corporations that often create in the host country a dilemma between regulation on behalf of the "national" development of priorities, and openness or even incentives to penetration on behalf of rapid growth; from above, through interstate or transnational bargaining solidarities (it would be a mistake to describe these as mere clusters of material interests, for ideological and psychological factors often determine the alignments), or through international or regional organizations that the state must either enlist or enfeeble.

The concept of the national interest was supposed to provide the state with a compass for an independent course. There seemed to be a clear choice between independence and dependence, but today the fluidity of games without any necessary single minute of truth or clearcut boundaries, games played by so many players over so many issues, gives each player a choice among several strategies. Each one has its risks. Each one corresponds to a different priority (for instance, independence as the maximum of impenetrability compatible with welfare, or independence as the maximum of influence abroad) or to the preference for a particular kind of solidarity. Material solidarity alone does not explain, for instance, why in the winter of 1973-74 eight out of the nine members of EEC preferred Henry Kissinger's strategy to Michel Jobert's, or why, in most of the North-South meetings, the oil-rich and the poor nations of the Third World have tended to vote together. Or else the choice depends on the internal balance of political and social forces, which can shift. Precisely because very few nations are able or eager to be self-sufficient in every realm, even a country eager to maximize its independence, to eliminate one-sided dependence on a single "big brother" on all the playing fields, and to fragment its dependencies would have a variety of alternatives. (Is it more important to spend resources on military autonomy, or on the creation of a heavy modern civilian industry? to give top priority to reducing imports of energy or to reducing dependence on foreign computers? Who should be one's partner in the effort? And so on.) Each state is thus adrift on a sea of guesses.

Sovereignty as Sisyphean abstraction, a battle against loss of control, yet waged over a broader front than in the days when control was safer, but politicization less prevalent; the national interest splintered into many alternatives, yet with no assurance that any one course would lead the state to the Erewhon of independence: does this mean the decline of the nation state? Let us, once more, be prudent and observe that the present scene is the triumph of ambiguity. There are nonstate actors, but not, on the whole, in the traditional arena. In the modern arenas, the very perils of loss of control, the determination of new states to assert themselves, the fear of most states to have interdependence turn into costly dependence on a master or on an extortionist—all this and the politicization of economic issues give the state enormous resilience, the will to curb the nonstate actors, and the desire to curtail one's vulnerability even by reducing the openness of the society. International interdependence may frustrate a state's ambition, but it is not irreversible. It provides opportunities for manipulation and rebellion, and the nature of the issues often gives to the state's action abroad, however handicapped, the dynamism that comes from domestic needs. Thus, the state has been neither superseded nor tamed. Many states are threatened by secessions, but these would create more states. Individuals or groups may not agree on the limits of the national community, but it is still to the state that they turn for protection, welfare, and justice.

PROBLEMS

Any international system has three dimensions: horizontal (the relations between major players), vertical (the hierarchical aspects), and functional (the subject matter of international political transactions). As in a surrealistic dream, the three dimensions move at once and into each other. To what extent are the current restraints among the big powers tied to a long period of growth and prosperity? Would these powers survive the centrifugal domestic pressures toward autarky or aggressive nationalism which worldwide economic dislocations might provoke? What would be the effects of a frequent reshuffling of the hierarchy or, rather, hierarchies of power, since different pyramids of players correspond to different kinds of assets? Can there be a reasonably stable system with inconsistent hierarchies, that is, wildly disparate "top dogs," depending on the component of power? Are the same principles of management and rules of bargaining valid on all the chessboards? Is there, as Alastair Buchan had suggested in the 1973 Reith lectures,[31] a domain for balancing power and a distinct one for collective management? Is the traditional strategic-diplomatic chessboard still the decisive one? How extensive are linkages between games likely to be? One's inability to answer these questions suggests that the outcome of the struggle between the separate drives of the players and their groping toward joint management is far from clear. Let me now draw some conclusions from the preceding analysis. The present international system is a theater of three contradictions and three races.

CONTRADICTIONS

A first contradiction exists, quasi-universally, between ideologies and interests. It is not total, since interests tend to wrap themselves in ideological rationalizations. A good example is antiimperialist ideology, especially the so-called theory of *dependencia,* with its view of a world periphery bled white by the centers of industrial and financial power. It reflects and elevates the interest in emancipation of those "peripheral" areas most subjected to foreign investment, most devoid of local entrepreneurs, and least endowed with modern technology and industry. Also, ideologies, when they provide the basis of a regime's legitimacy, create interests—as in the case of Soviet political dominance in Eastern Europe. Similarly, as George Kennan has pointed out, Soviet ideology requires "the protection of the image of the Soviet Union as the central bastion of revolutionary socialism throughout the world,"[32] and therefore dictates support for "progressive forces" in the Third World. Still, ideology and interests are often in conflict. As development proceeds, especially when it does so according to a capitalist model and through reliance on the world economy, antiimperialist ideology conflicts with the need for cooperation, bargains, and imports of advanced technology. Opposition to a traditional law of the seas which served the interests of the most advanced nations no longer overcomes the clear difference in interest between coastal developing nations and landlocked ones. Soviet ideology suggests alignment with the Third World against the liberal industrial nations, but nuclear interconnection puts the Soviets and the Americans on the same side of the proliferation issue. The competitive yet convergent interests of the world's two largest fleets lead to joint Soviet and American stands for an unimpeded right-of-transit passage in the territorial sea or in straits, and for freedom of scientific research within the new two-hundred-mile economic zone. The interests of the USSR as an industrial society, joined with its internal economic difficulties that would in any case curtail the contributions Moscow could make to the development of the Third World, have incited the Soviets to remarkable abstinence in general North-South discussions.

Many of the world's regional organizations are founded on some ideological solidarity and have foundered on clashes of interest among their members, the Organization of African Unity (OAU) being the most recent example. OPEC itself is torn between states with huge oil resources and small populations, whose first concern is the profitability of their huge capital abroad, and states with smaller oil reserves and large populations, whose first concern is to maximize resources for their internal development. A world of highly conflicting interests is not orderly per se. A world of self-righteous and uncompromising ideologies would, however, be hopeless, even if physical annihilation were avoided. Some nations (Algeria, for instance) are very good at pragmatic dealing behind unfurled ideological banners. But nothing, except obtuse faith, guarantees that pragmatic leaders will everywhere prevail over romantics or revolutionaries. Nothing tells us that pragmatic deals, aimed at making economic interdependence hasten national development, will not put more potent fuel into the motor of ideological strife. If the world's multiple tyrannies have to show some material progress to their peoples, they also often need to cover pure and simple meanness with an ideological fig leaf. For every Nasser or Sukarno who disappears, there seems to be a Khadafi who comes, or a Kim il Sung or a Park who stays.

A second contradiction exists between the various kinds of fragmentation and the unity of the international system. I have mentioned regional fragmentation, produced by the very multiplicity of players, and the central balance of military power, functional splintering that corresponds to the different games played, and the different functional hierarchies. These partitions can easily be seen as providential safeguards against worldwide disasters, a tentative haphazard equivalent of the federalist system, which sees (by contrast, say, with French centralization) that every local trouble, far from leaping to the top of the world agenda, clogging channels, or spreading into chaos, remains well circumscribed. Unfortunately, two forces work the other way. One is miscalculation. A local war or act of terrorism can spread beyond regional bounds through the dialectic of the commitments made by extraneous powers, along the lines described by Thucydides, or through the reprisals of the terrorists' target state. The failure of states to agree on the rules of the game in one functional area—the monetary system, say, or the oceans—can lead to a snowballing of conflict into other economic realms (trade) or even to armed conflicts (e.g., Greco-Turkish tension over the respective rights of the two nations in the Aegean Sea).

The other force of reescalation is quite deliberate state will. Not only interdependence but also the willed manipulation of it make "decoupling" the global system from its fragments difficult. Remember that what could be called the oil spill from the Arab-Israeli war of October 1973 was provoked first by the Arab countries, then by OPEC. Similarly, the attractiveness of military might—including its supreme form, nuclear weapons—for states that are weak in the strategic-diplomatic game, but on or near the top of the hierarchy in other games, may lead to a kind of rapprochement between these hierarchies on the plateau of greatest peril. Less dangerous, but still of an escalatory nature, is the desire of poorer states or states with limited assets to compensate for their weakness in some of the functional areas by exploiting international egalitarianism.

Whether it takes the form of miscalculation or of a deliberate decision, this risk of contagion shows that the beneficial effects of fragmentation—its potential as a way of ordering a complex world and in cushioning its members against the excesses of interdependence—are neither assured nor unlimited. On the traditional chessboard, each Great Power is torn between its desire for stability and domestic progress, which induces caution abroad, and the worldwide involvement dictated by its ideology as well as its interests. Whenever the latter prevails, fragmentation fades. In the modern arenas, the very logic of the world economy makes fragmentation—if it should lead to protectionist goals and beggar-thy-neighbor policies—a peril, not a buffer. Remember the 1930s.

These dangers point to a key flaw of the world system. Unity exists, not at the top in the guise of a superior, but only at the level of the actors—one might say at the level of (potential) mischief-making. It is the actors who decide how to distribute their efforts and whether to try to create links.

A third contradiction follows from another kind of heterogeneity. On the one hand, the players participate in a simultaneous set of games. On the other, they belong to different ages of world politics. I am not referring again to ideological splits. I am trying to describe something that results from a mix of differences in economic levels, degrees of nationhood and statehood, dates of formal independence, and content of ideological dogmas. I am also referring to basic attitudes, tested more by crisis situations than by daily behavior, in which routine or practicality often prevails.

Some actors seem to live, more or less schizophrenically, in the world I have tried to describe: a potpourri of conflict and cooperation, anxious interaction and confusing interdependence, national selfishness and vague concern for a wider order. Others, even when caught in the economic web, or remote from the Great Powers' strategic maneuvers, seem to live in an age that seems past to the "sages" in the first category but is very much present to their leaders. These actors have just emerged from subjugation, they are still struggling to reduce dependencies, or they believe in philosophies of revolution. To them, the nation state is not a familiar structure whose recent inadequacies are revealed in ever-growing cracks, but a new shelter and a new springboard.[33] One group sees national control waning, the other grabs it at last, whatever its imperfections. This is true even for states—like those in Latin America—that are not new, yet are trying for the first time to act on the world stage and to develop their economies. Our nineteenth century is very much their twentieth, and, consequently, their view of order is unlikely to be the same as ours. It is often less concerned with long-term problems (population growth, pollution, depletion of resources, preservation of "commons") than with the achievement of power and autonomy. This achievement is seen as, at worst, the triumph through battle of the righteous over the miscreants, at best, the final flowering of Wilsonianism, a world order of harmony through self-determination and rather little collective management, unless the righteous can control it and use it against the big and rich. Another consequence is that the problems of borders, the difficulties of social integration (with the risk of an external diversion of internal troubles), and the festering of traditional rivalries, in other words, proneness to violence, have to be given different weights depending on the area.

I am not suggesting that there shall be no peace or order until those whose present is our past have been lifted to our lofty level. After all, we too carry the past into our present, for the simple reason that the past lives on both in the logic of much world politics and in our own minds. (Hurrah for the Mayaguez! And the beatitudes of Wilsonianism are not unknown in Washington.) I am merely suggesting that different ranges of experience raise one more obstacle. Even though there is a growing economic differentiation in the "new" group—between rich and poor, almost industrialized and backward—and a bewildering variety of regimes, there is no comparable mental diversity insofar as the approach to world politics is concerned. Here, it is difficult to skip stages (and let us remember the fragility, or even reversibility, of our own mental stage).

RACES

The future of world order may well depend on how these contradictions will be smoothed out. It may also depend on the outcome of three races, besides the race, described throughout the last section, between the logic of conflict, whose range has been widened by the increase in the scope of international relations and by the intensity of interstate contacts, and the new restraints of nuclear interconnection and economic interdependence. Even though the latter do not constrain actors to cooperation, and even though de facto solidarity is not a solidarity of commitments, there are imperatives of prudence that dampen at least interstate conflicts; and all of world politics tends to become the testing of the uncertain and shifting limits of these restraints.

Domestic politics, technology, and world order. There is a race between the domestic priorities that govern the political life of states and the external imperatives of order. Everywhere, domestic pressure groups, parties, such public services as the military, or the guardians of official orthodoxy do their best to influence or control the definition of the nation's policy, to capture, so to speak, the national interest. Leaders, whether tyrannical or democratic, have to take care, if not of the needs of their people—a concept as vague as that of the national interest—at least of the demands of those from whom their power comes or on whom its survival rests. When this happens to fit the interests of world order, it is a happy coincidence. At any rate, the criterion of national policy remains, at best, the interest of the nation or of a fragment of mankind with which it identifies; more usually, it is that of a group within the society, whether this interest is primarily material ("the American farmer") or ideological. Either the global interest is not taken into account at all (for it remains an abstraction: what is peace, or peaceful change, next to the drive for black self-determination in Southern Africa or the defense of shrinking white supremacy?), or it is not yet a felt reality (say, in matters of population control), or it is more or less candidly equated with the national interest (see the American ideology of the free market for world development), or it clearly clashes with a state's or a group of states' conviction about its own interest (as when OPEC pushed an admittedly low price of oil so high that not only was a serious blow administered both to the industrial nations and, even more, to the poorer developing countries, but the earnings of the oil producers outran their capacities of absorption or induced excessive development plans that dragged them into debt). Thus the breakdown of the great divide between foreign policy and domestic politics turns out to be, like so many other changes, a mix of good and evil. It is good insofar as it results from a change in the political agenda that has brought to the fore issues that ordinarily cannot be resolved by violence; bad, insofar as the late, unlamented, and partly mythical primacy of foreign policy, for all its brutal consequences, had the uncelebrated virtue of sometimes protecting diplomacy from the parochialisms and the contradictory passions of domestic politics—whereas interdependence today provides the leaders and interest groups of one state with countless opportunities to manipulate domestic forces elsewhere.

There is a second race, this one between technology and the capacity of the fragmented international milieu to master it. In the realm of nuclear energy, both among the nuclear powers and among those states that are on the threshold of, or are tempted by, the status of nuclear statehood, the progress of technology, military and peaceful, has already outstripped diplomacy. I have mentioned it apropos of the Strategic Arms Limitation Talks (SALT). The current arguments about slowing down the spread of the capacity to produce nuclear bombs through the development of peaceful nuclear energy often have a tone of desperation. The progress of peaceful nuclear power and the bomb can, no doubt, be slowed down; mastery, in the sense of curtailing the harmful potential, seems increasingly difficult. Technological progress also risks putting increasingly more accurate missiles at the disposal of the superpowers, with dangerous consequences for the taboo on direct military contests between them; it risks putting sophisticated conventional technology at the disposal of many states; it risks blurring the essential distinction between conventional and nuclear weapons (as it does in the case of cruise missiles), a distinction that has been crucial for the self-restraint of the nuclear powers. Inversely, in many other areas—the exploration of the seabeds, techniques for improving food production, or for reducing population growth—the beneficial potential of technology is being held back both by the nature of international politics and by domestic political or social obstacles.

Dimensions of insecurity. A third race exists between the universal desire for security—nourished by the abundance of means of mass destruction and by a fear of a scarcity of resources (or of restriction to their access)—and what might be called the proliferation of insecurity. I shall not mention at length the obvious insecurity of terrorist groups; international agencies submitted to the financial whimsy and political pressures of states; and multinational enterprises coping with monetary fluctuations, demands from their parent state, and restrictions imposed by their host states. I shall concentrate on the state's three dimensions of insecurity. There is, as before, physical unsafety, the product of the risk of war, the need to protect oneself from it, or the urge to wage it. Despite the worldwide interest in survival, and the inhibitions observed by the present nuclear powers on the use of certain kinds of force in direct confrontations, this fear has been heightened by all the new ways in which violence can either penetrate the "inviolable" state or subvert it from within. It is intensified by the spread of nuclear weapons (and the risk of theft of nuclear fuels); the surge of terrorism; the universality of intelligence work, espionage, and covert operations; and the ideological, financial, and often overtly symbiotic links between domestic forces and foreign foes.

Second, economic unpredictability,[34] the newest and most insidious of these dimensions, may appear less deadly than military unsafety, but may well be even more unsettling insofar as it is less manageable and calculable. The ingredients one needs to develop one's economic power may depend on someone else's good will: the industrial world, and part of the developing world, have discovered the cost of dependence on imported oil, or they may depend on someone else's wisdom: the Third World (rich and poor) has discovered the cost of having to import manufactured products from the industrial world at a time of inflation.

Some of the new, interdependent power is passing almost by essence, because whoever exerts it at the moment has little control over how long he will be able to exploit it. This is particularly true of the ability to bargain and forge coalitions. Thus, for several years, French policy consisted of trying to build, in the EEC, a structure whose base would be a de facto alliance between France, aiming for common policies, and the EEC's, eager to extend the scope of its activities. That alliance collapsed, however, in the mid-1960s because de Gaulle was forced to choose between, on the one hand, accepting Britain's entry or else reinforcing the supranational aspects of the Community—two very different developments, yet both leading to a loss of French control over the common policies—and, on the other hand, the pursuit by France alone of some of the objectives it had tried to get its partners to share. He chose the latter course, which led to a blind alley both for France and for the EEC. The alliance of France and the commission was forged again under Pompidou, thanks to his decision in favor of Britain's entry. This time, the energy crisis broke it up, when France's eight partners chose, in effect, a United States-led structure, the International Energy Agency (IEA), rather than the EEC as the framework for that overarching issue.[35] Bargaining power and the art of shaping coalitions also depend heavily on individual leadership skills that may not be transmissible.

The lack of control over one's momentary power is not limited to bargaining situations. One's investments abroad can be confiscated. One's surpluses or reserves may be wiped out, by a sudden external action that one can not affect (cf., the effect of United States devaluations, in 1971 and 1973, on Washington's allies; or the impact on Britain, France, Italy, and Japan of the quadrupling of the price of oil); by a sudden domestic drama, such as May 1968, in France; by internal mismanagement, as in Italy; by the domestic policies of a major client (cf. the impact of United States inflation and recession on America's trading partners, or the effect on French economic growth of the failure by Bonn and Washington to stimulate their economies sufficiently in 1976); by the perfectly "rational" calculations of huge private companies moving their capital from one place to another; or even by the boomeranging outcome of one's own external policy (cf. the ultimate impact on America's inflation of America's monetary practices of the 1960s and early 1970s, leading to the deterioration of the international monetary system). Technologically based assets—such as a nation's aeronautic or electronic industry—are susceptible to obsolescence and to the superior competition of latecomers. Inversely, the exploitation in America of domestic oil reserves and of alternatives to oil that were unprofitable before the OPEC decisions has become a potential source of increased power for the United States, for reasons entirely independent of American will. Finally, there is insecurity even when one's bargaining power rests on a tangible asset, if it is nonrenewable. Algeria's resources of natural gas and Iran's and Algeria's oil reserves are limited, and the difference between them and Saudi Arabia in this respect puts a question mark on the future of OPEC.

When I no longer know where your power ends and mine begins; when yours is partly my hostage; when the more I try to force you to depend on me, the more I depend on you; when world politics becomes a test of vulnerability, and degrees of vulnerability are not identical with power supplies, who can feel secure? There is, as before, yet in far more complex ways, psychological uncertainty. It is partly due to the depth of ideological cleavages, to the abysses of miscomprehension between opposed camps, and to the resulting tendency to see in the other side a devil rather than a member of mankind. It is partly due to the elusiveness, fragmentation, and frequent ineffectiveness of power, to the complexity of the games nations play, to the dilemmas of choice among possible strategies. Not only do we live in a world full of enemies, but we cannot rely entirely on our friends, because those who are "on our side" in one arena may play against us in another game. It is partly due to the existence of a single international system, which obliges each state to cope with issues far beyond its reach and, indeed, beyond its psychological resources. It is partly due to the rapidity and uncontrollability of social change. It is partly due to the importance of milieu goals, which, almost by definition, can never be reached in their entirety or for long by anyone. It is partly due to the rules of nuclear deterrence, which require states to search for "credibility," to test their will even in unlikely places, and to replace iron with image. Very often, therefore, a statesman who tries to chart his nation's course for the various games of world politics does not know what cards he has, what his cards are worth, or for how long. Cards on which he may count heavily could turn out to be liabilities (think of Britain's Blue Streak and Sky Bolt missiles, the Concorde's misadventures, the troubles of the European space programs, or the European monetary "snake," once a key French objective). Cards that may have been treated with indifference turn out to be assets (think of German or Polish coal). New cards may appear out of the deep blue sea (think of the North Sea oil). Conversely, foreign statesmen trying to predict a friend's or a rival's behavior are often left with question marks. Precisely because many alternative strategies are open, one can be sure that the next government will follow the same approach, or that even a few changes in the top bureaucracy will not lead to a different way of using whatever power may be available? Yet the statesman must act, and neither he nor the average citizen has the time to look constantly at all the implications of these acts.

Let me return to my original question: which of the models of international politics does the present system resemble? One thing is clear. The model of community is as irrelevant as it has been for more than four centuries. There is no equivalent of the universal church: "nonterritorial central guidance"[36] remains fragmentary and controlled by modern princes of highly divergent faiths. There may be some universal norms, such as self-determination, but they are so vague and so distorted by self-interpretation as to be pathetic. There are some imperatives of prudence—no nuclear war, no economic disaster, some aid to development—but they correspond to calculations and convergences of interests rather than beliefs. As Robert W. Tucker has pointed out, wealthy citizens of a nation may feel some sense of obligation to the poorer ones, but rich nations feel no such duty toward the poorer countries, partly because of the vast difference between individual equality and the equality of states, which may never benefit their members.[37] There may, in some parts of the world, have been a decline in the acceptability of force, a result of liberal values, but it remains limited in scope and depth. The highest allegiance of each actor remains either to himself or to a fragment of humankind—a bloc he belongs to out of necessity or conviction.

We are still among the models of fragmentation,

then. But which model? State of war or troubled peace? The originality of the postwar bipolar system was that it blended the two. The bipolar contest seemed straight out of Thucydides, but nuclear weapons, the legitimacy of the nation state, the obstacles posed by the heterogeneity of the world to the annexation of all other issues by the Cold War served as moderating factors in the strategic-diplomatic arena, while the restraints of economic interdependence developed in the other ones. Where are we now, and where are we going? The present is still a blend of the two ideal types. Precisely because of the fragility of common norms, the prodigious progress of weaponry, the multiple ideological, ethnic, tribal, and national hostilities, and the uneven distribution of power, there are still many features of the state of war. The modern games themselves are, to a large extent, conflictual. They are struggles around the two key issues of all politics, who benefits and who commands—struggles in which, as we all know today (and as the truly dependent or exploited have always known), blows are inflicted and losses imposed. Nevertheless, because of the restraints on the use of force and those that result from mutual economic interests, because of the need to blend hostility and cooperation, or to move from hostility to cooperation, which nuclear interconnection and economic interdependence induce, it would be excessive to speak of universal malevolence or a complete absence of common rules, even if those that exist are "rules of the game," not moral commands. But can such a blend be stable?

I have listed changes, contradictions, races, ambiguities—all facts of an increasingly complex world. One must not only analyze, but also evaluate. What do the dynamics of this intricate system portend for world order?

NOTES

1. Few people still believe that the United States can disentangle itself from the world. The author of a distinguished plea for a new isolationism, written a few years ago, has since moved on to schemes for the American invasion of the Persian Gulf and, as a way of reducing Israeli dependence on the United States, for a nuclear Middle East, which is easier to see as a recipe for disaster involving the Great Powers than as a panacea for their disengagement. See Robert W. Tucker, *A New Isolationism* (New York: Universe Books, 1972); "Oil: The Issue of American Intervention," *Commentary,* January 1975; "Israel and the United States: From Dependence to Nuclear Weapons," *Commentary,* November 1975.

2. For a comparable but more thorough exercise, published after this one had been drafted, see Edward L. Morse, *Modernization and the Transformation of International Relations* (New York: Free Press, 1976), esp. chaps. 2 to 4.

3. See, for further elaboration, my *State of War* (New York: Praeger, 1965), esp. chap. 2.

4. See Robert Jervis, *Perception and Misperception in International Politics* (Princeton: Princeton University Press, 1976).

5. See Arnold Wolfers, *Discord and Collaboration* (Baltimore: Johns Hopkins Press, 1962).

6. See Kenneth N. Waltz, *Man, the State, and War* (New York: Columbia University Press, 1954); and my *State of War,* chap. 3.

7. Clausewitz, *On War* (Baltimore: Pelican Books, 1968), vol. 1, chaps. 1 and 2. See Raymond Aron's monumental two-volume work, *Penser la guerre, Clausewitz* (Paris: Gallimard, 1976), esp. vol. 1, chap. 3.

8. Aron, *Penser la guerre,* vol. 2, chap. 6.

9. Cf. Robert Keohane and Joseph S. Nye, Jr., *Power and Interdependence* (Boston: Little, Brown, 1977), chap. 3. This is at the heart of my disagreements with Kenneth N. Waltz. In his incisive essay, "Theory in International Relations," in *International Politics,* ed. Fred I. Greenstein and Nelson W. Polsby, vol. 8 of *Handbook of Political Science* (Reading, Mass.: Addison-Wesley, 1976), he indicts my conception of the international system for being "so rigged" as not to explain anything. This may be true, but on the one hand, I find his "purely positional" definition of structure (pp. 46-47) too narrow. To understand a structure requires that one know not only "the principle by which a system is ordered" (coordinate units versus super and subordinate ones) and "the arrangement of parts," but also whether those parts are, so to speak, all apples, or a mix of apples, oranges, and stones. Power as capabilities cannot be assessed otherwise; hence the importance of knowing whether the actors are all states, and, even if they are, whether they are of the same type. On the other hand, to limit one's concern to showing how the level of the structure (A), narrowly defined, and the level of the interacting units (B) "operate and interact" (p. 45), "how A and B affect each other," is also much too narrow. I agree with Waltz that "to define a structure requires ignoring how units relate with each other" (even if "concentrating on how they stand in relation to each other"—his definition of structure—demands, in my opinion, more than a "purely positional picture," since I need to know *who* is "positioned"). But "how units relate with each other" results not only from the structure (defined in his way, or even in my broader one), but also from other elements, such as the domestic regimes and the transnational forces, and in turn affects not only the structure but also these elements. Moreover, changes in those regimes and forces affect the structure, insofar as they also change the "distribution of capability among units" (think of the passage from Weimar to Hitler). I have other, minor quarrels with Waltz's critique of my writings. For instance, when I say that the existence of a system is certain, I do not mean that the system is a reality. I mean exactly what he does when (pp. 8-9) he talks about theories as being instruments to apprehend some part of the real world. In his critique of my notion of structure, he confuses homogeneity or heterogeneity of the structure (i.e., is it composed only of nation states, or of a mix of empires, nation states, and city states?) with homogeneity or heterogeneity of a given state. Whether "outcomes" are "unit determined" or "system influenced," is, for me, a matter of empirical research. Obviously, a superpower usually can affect the system more easily than a tiny actor, but the superpower can also be mightily "system influenced" (see below). (Incidentally, to say, as he does in his critique of Morton Kaplan, that what Kaplan calls a "subsystem dominant system," i.e., one in which the units determine the outcome, is "no system at all," is as absurd as saying that a domestic system shaped by a "subsystem" such as a dominant party or institution is no system.) And while Waltz now (by contrast with his analysis in *Man, the State, and War*) interprets Rousseau correctly, he thoroughly misreads my interpretation of Jean-Jacques—to which he has come around.

10. Waltz, *Man, the State, and War,* p. 74.

11. Hedley Bull, *The Anarchical Society* (New York: Columbia University Press, 1977), p. 271.

12. Cf. the definition by Robert Keohane and Joseph S. Nye in *Transnational Relations and World Politics* (Cambridge, Mass.: Harvard University Press, 1972), introduction and chap. 4.

13. Bull, *Anarchical Society,* p. 272.

14. These forces are not to be deemed "actors" unless they meet the definition given above. If they do not have autonomy (i.e., they are merely the tool of a totalitarian state), and if they have no power to make decisions affecting resources and val-

ues across borders, but merely that of making suggestions that can influence governments because of the interaction between each society and its state, then we are still in transnational society, not in world politics.

15. See Helmut Schmidt, "The Struggle for the World Product," *Foreign Affairs* 52, no. 3 (April 1974).

16. Cf. Susan Strange, "What Is Economic Power, and Who Has It?" *International Journal* 30, no. 2 (Spring 1975); and Jeffrey Hart, "Three Approaches to the Measurement of Power in International Relations," *International Organization* 3, no. 2 (Spring 1976).

17. Cf. Ernst B. Haas, "International Integration: The European and the Universal Process," *International Organization* 15 (1961); and *The Uniting of Europe* (Stanford, Calif.: Stanford University Press, 1958).

18. Here I differ slightly with Keohane and Nye (see their "World Politics and the International Economic System," in *The Future of the International Economic Order: An Agenda for Research,* ed. C. Fred Bergsten (Lexington, Mass.: Lexington Books, 1973), p. 127.

19. Ibid., p. 122ff.

20. Cf. Morse, *International Relations,* p. 104ff.

21. Cf. my "The Acceptability of Military Force," in *Force in Modern Societies,* Adelphi Papers, no. 102 (London: International Institute of Strategic Studies, 1974); and the discussion in Klaus Knorr, *The Power of Nations* (New York: Basic Books, 1975), chap. 5.

22. It is characterized by multiple channels connecting societies, an absence of hierarchy among issues, and abstention from the use of force.

23. Cf. Klaus Knorr, "Is International Coercion Waning or Rising?," *International Security* 1, no. 4 (Spring 1977): 92-110.

24. Whether this will be the case forever is not sure.

25. Cf. Kenneth N. Waltz, "The Myth of Interdependence," in *The International Corporation,* ed. Charles Kindleberger (Cambridge, Mass.: Harvard University Press, 1970); Peter Katzenstein, "International Interdependence: Some Long-term Trends and Recent Changes," *International Organization* 29, no. 4 (Autumn 1975); and R. Rosecrance and A. Stein, "Interdependence: Myth or Reality?," *World Politics* 26 (October 1973).

26. Susan Strange, "Economic Power," p. 213.

27. On the respective effects of domestic policies and international interdependence on foreign economic policy, see Peter Katzenstein's brilliant essay, "International Relations and Domestic Structures: Foreign Economic Policies of Advanced Industrial States," *International Organization* 30, no. 1 (Winter 1976).

28. Cf. the issues of *Daedalus* on the oil crisis (Fall 1975).

29. "Transnational Relations and Interstate Conflicts; An Empirical Analysis," *International Organization* 28 (Autumn 1974): 992. See also Keohane and Nye, *Power and Interdependence,* chap. 7.

30. Ibid., p. 207.

31. Cf. Alastair Buchan, *Change without War* (New York: St. Martin's Press, 1975).

32. *The Cloud of Danger* (Boston: Atlantic-Little, Brown, 1977), p. 187.

33. Cf. Morse, *International Relations,* p. 111ff.

34. See Wolfgang Hager, *Europe's Economic Security,* Atlantic Papers (Paris: Atlantic Institute, 1975).

35. See Robert J. Lieber, "Oil and the Middle East War: Europe in the Energy Crisis," *Harvard Studies in International Affairs,* no. 35 (1976).

36. Cf. Richard A. Falk, "The Sherrill Hypothesis" (manuscript, Princeton University).

37. See his "Egalitarianism and International Politics," *Commentary,* September 1975, and *The Inequality of Nations* (New York: Basic Books, 1977).

The forgotten dimensions of strategy

Michael E. Howard

The term *strategy* needs continual definition. For most people, Clausewitz's formulation "the use of engagements for the object of the war," or, as Liddell Hart paraphrased it, "the art of distributing and applying military means to fulfill the ends of policy," is clear enough. Strategy concerns the deployment and use of armed forces to attain a given political objective. Histories of strategy, including Hart's own *Strategy of Indirect Approach,* usually consist of case studies, from Alexander the Great to Douglas MacArthur, of the way in which this was done. Nevertheless, the experience of the past century has shown this approach to be inadequate to the point of triviality. In the West the concept of "grand strategy" was introduced to cover those industrial, financial, demographic, and societal aspects of war that have become so salient in the twentieth century; in Communist states all strategic thought has to be validated by the holistic doctrines of Marxism-Leninism. Without discarding such established concepts, I shall offer here a somewhat different and perhaps slightly simpler framework for analysis, based on a study of the way in which both strategic doctrine and warfare itself have developed over the past 200 years. I shall also say something about the implications of this mode of analysis for the present strategic posture of the West.

Clausewitz's definition of strategy was deliberately and defiantly simplistic. It swept away virtually everything that had been written about war (which was a very great deal) over the previous 300 years. Earlier writers had concerned themselves almost exclusively with the enormous problems of raising, arming, equipping, moving, and maintaining armed forces in the field—an approach that Clausewitz dismissed as being as relevant to fighting as the skills of the swordmaker were to the art of fencing. None of this, he insisted, was significant for the actual conduct of war, and the inability of all previous writers to formulate an adequate theory had been due to their failure to distinguish between the *maintenance* of armed forces and their *use.*

By making this distinction between what I shall term the *logistical* and the *operational* dimensions in warfare, Clausewitz performed a major service to strategic thinking; but the conclusions he drew from that distinction were questionable and the consequences of those conclusions have been unfortunate. In the first place, even in his own day, the commanders he so much admired—Napoleon, Frederick the Great—could never have achieved their operational triumphs if they had not had a profound understanding of the whole range of military activities that Clausewitz excluded from consideration. In the second place, no campaign can be understood, and no valid conclusions drawn from it, unless its logistical problems are studied as thoroughly as the course of operations; and, as Dr. Martin van Creveld has recently pointed out in his book *Supplying War,* logistical factors have been ignored by ninety-nine military historians out of a hundred—an omission that has warped their judgments and made their conclusions in many cases wildly misleading.

Clausewitz's dogmatic assertion of priorities—his subordination of the logistical element in war to the operational—may have owed something to a prejudice common to all fighting soldiers in all eras. It certainly owed much to his reaction against the supercautious "scientific" generals whose operational ineptitude had led Prussia to defeat in 1806. But it cannot be denied that in the Napoleonic era it *was* operational skill rather than sound logistical planning that proved decisive in campaign after campaign. And since Napoleon's campaigns provided the basis for all strategic writings and thinking throughout the nineteenth century, "strategy" became generally equated in the public mind with *operational* strategy.

But the inadequacy of this concept was made very clear, to those who studied it, by the course of the American Civil War. There the masters of operational strategy were to be found, not in the victorious armies of the North, but among the leaders of the South. Lee and Jackson handled their forces with a flexibility and an imaginativeness worthy of a Napoleon or a Frederick; nevertheless they lost. Their defeat was attributed by Liddell Hart, whose analyses seldom extended beyond the operational plane, primarily to operational factors, in particular, to the "indirect approach" adopted by Sherman. But, fundamentally, the victory of the North was due not to the operational capabilities of its generals but to its capacity to mobilize its superior industrial strength and manpower into armies, which such leaders as Grant were able, thanks largely to road and river transport, to deploy in such strength that the operational skills of their adversaries were rendered almost irrelevant. Ultimately the latter were ground down in a conflict of attrition in which the *logistical* dimension of strategy proved more significant than the operational. What proved to be of the greatest importance was the capacity to bring the largest and best-equipped forces into the operational theater and to maintain them there. It was an experience that has shaped the strategic doctrine of the U.S. armed forces from that day to this.

But this capacity depended upon a third dimension of strategy, one to which Clausewitz was the first major thinker to draw attention: the *social,* the attitude of the people upon whose commitment and readiness for self-denial this logistical power ultimately depended. Clausewitz had described war as "a remarkable trinity," composed of its political objective, of its operational instruments, and of the popular passions, the social forces it expressed. It was the latter, he pointed out, that made the wars of the French Revolution so different in kind from those of Frederick the Great, and that would probably so distinguish any wars in the future. In this he was right.

With the end of the age of absolutism, limited wars of pure policy fought by dispassionate professionals became increasingly rare. Growing popular participation in government meant popular involvement in war, and so did the increasing size of the armed forces, which nineteenth-century technology was making possible and therefore necessary. Management of, or compliance with, public opinion became an essential element in the conduct of war. Had the population of the North been as indifferent to the outcome of the Civil War as the leaders of the Confederacy had initially hoped, the operational victories of the South in the early years might have decisively tipped the scales. The logistical potential of the North would have been of negligible value without the determination to use it. But given equal resolution on both sides, the capacity of the North to mobilize superior forces ultimately became the decisive factor in the struggle. Again Clausewitz was proved right: *all other factors being equal,* numbers ultimately proved decisive.

In one respect, in particular, other factors were equal. The Civil War was fought with comparable if not identical weapons on both sides, as had been the revolutionary wars in Europe. The possibility of decisive *technological* superiority on one side or the other was so inconceivable that Clausewitz and his contemporaries had discounted it. But within a year of the conclusion of the American Civil War, just such a superiority made itself apparent in the realm of small arms, when the Prussian armies equipped with breech-loading rifles defeated Austrian armies, which were not so equipped. Four years later, in 1870, the Prussians revealed an even more crushing superiority over their French adversaries, thanks to their steel breech-loading artillery. This superiority was far from decisive: the Franco-Prussian War in particular was won, like the American Civil War, by superior logistical capability based upon a firm popular commitment. But technology, as an independent and significant dimension, could no longer be left out of account.

In naval warfare, the crucial importance of technological parity had been apparent since the dawn of the age of steam, and in colonial warfare the technological element was to prove quite decisive. During the latter part of the nineteenth century, the superiority of European weapons turned what had previously been a marginal technological advantage over indigenous forces, often counterbalanced by numerical inferiority, into a crushing military ascendancy, which made it possible for European forces to establish a new imperial dominance throughout the world over cultures incapable of responding in kind. As Hilaire Belloc's Captain Blood succinctly put it: "Whatever happens, we have got/The Maxim gun, and they have not." Military planners have been terrified of being caught without the contemporary equivalent of the Maxim gun from that day to this.

So by the beginning of this century, war was conducted in these four dimensions: the *operational,* the *logistical,* the *social,* and the *technological.* No successful strategy could be formulated that did not take account of them all, but under different circumstances one or another of these dimensions might dominate. When, in 1914-15, the operational strategy of the Schlieffen Plan, for the one side, and of the Gallipoli campaign, for the other, failed to achieve the decisive results expected of them, then the logistical aspects of the war, and with them the social basis on which they depended, assumed even greater importance as the opposing armies tried to bleed each other to death. As in the American Civil War, victory was to go, not to the side with the most skillful generals and the most courageous troops, but to that which could mobilize the greatest mass of troops and firepower and sustain it with the strongest popular support.

The inadequacy of mere numbers without social cohesion behind them was demonstrated by the collapse of the Russian Empire in 1917. But the vulnerability even of logistical and social power if the adversary could secure a decisive technological advantage was equally demonstrated by the success of the German submarine campaign in the spring of 1917, when the Allies came within measurable distance of defeat. Those in the German Empire decided to gamble on a technological advantage to counter the logistical superiority that American participation gave to their enemies. But they lost.

From the experiences of the First World War, different strategic thinkers derived different strategic lessons. In Western Europe, the most adventurous theorists considered that the technological dimension of war would predominate in the future. The protagonists of armored warfare in particular believed that it might restore an operational decisiveness unknown since the days of Napoleon himself—the first two years of the Second World War were to prove them right. Skillfully led and well-trained armed forces operating against opponents who were both militarily and morally incapable of resisting them achieved spectacular results.

But another school of thinkers who placed their faith in technology fared less well; this school included those who believed that the development of air power would enable them to eliminate the operational dimension altogether and to strike directly at the roots of the enemy's *social* strength, at the will and capacity of the opposing society to carry on the war. Instead of wearing down the morale of the enemy civilians through the attrition of surface operations, air power, its protagonists believed, would be able to attack and pulverize it directly.

The events of the war were to disprove this theory. Technology was not yet sufficiently advanced to be able to eliminate the traditional requirements of operational and logistical strategy in this manner. Neither the morale of the British nor that of the German people was to be destroyed by air attack; indeed, such attack was found to demand an operational strategy of a new and complex kind in order to defeat the opposing air forces and to destroy their logistical support. But operational success in air warfare, aided by new technological developments, did eventually enable the Allied air forces to destroy the entire logistical framework that supported the German and Japanese war effort, and rendered the operational skills, in which the Germans excelled until the very end, as ineffective as those of Jackson and Lee.

Technology had not in fact transformed the nature of strategy. It, of course, remained of vital importance to keep abreast of one's adversary in all major aspects of military technology, but, given that this was possible, the lessons of the Second World War seemed little different from those of the first. The social base had to be strong enough to resist the psychological impact of operational setbacks and to support the largest possible logistical build-up by land, sea, and air. The forces thus raised had then to be used progressively to eliminate the operational options open to the enemy and ultimately to destroy his capacity to carry on the war.

The same conclusions, set out in somewhat more turgid prose, were reached by the strategic analysts of the Soviet Union—not least those who in the late 1940s and early 1950s were writing under the pen name of J. V. Stalin. But Marxist military thinkers, without differing in essentials from their contemporaries in the West, naturally devoted greater attention to the social dimension of strategy—the structure and cohesiveness of the belligerent societies. For Soviet writers this involved, and still involves, little more than the imposition of a rigid stereotype on the societies they study. Their picture of a world in which oppressed peoples are kept in a state of backward subjection by a small group of exploitative imperialist powers, themselves domestically vulnerable to the revolutionary aspirations of a desperate proletariat, bears little resemblance to the complex reality, whatever its incontestable value as a propagandistic myth. As a result their analysis is often hilariously inaccurate, and their strategic prescriptions either erroneous or banal.

But the West is in no position to criticize. The stereotypes that we have imposed, consciously or unconsciously, on the political structures that surround us have in the past been no less misleading. The Cold War image of a world that would evolve peacefully, if gradually, toward an Anglo-Saxon style of democracy under western tutelage if only the global Soviet-directed Marxist conspiracy could be eradicated was at least as naïve and ill-informed as that of the Russian dogmatists. It was the inadequacy of the sociopolitical analysis of the societies with which we were dealing that lay at the root of the failure of the Western powers to cope more effectively with the revolutionary and insurgency movements that characterized the postwar era, from China in the 1940s to Vietnam in the 1960s. For in these, more perhaps than in any previous conflicts, war really was the continuation of political activity with an admixture of other means; and that political activity was itself the result of a huge social upheaval throughout the former colonial world which had been given an irresistible impetus by the events of the Second World War. Of the four dimensions of strategy, the social was here incomparably the most significant, and it was the perception of this that gave the work of Mao Zedong and his followers its abiding historical importance.

Military thinkers in the West, extrapolating from their experience of warfare between industrial states, naturally tended to seek a solution to what was essentially a conflict on the social plane either by developing operational techniques of "counterinsurgency" or in the technological advantages provided by such developments as helicopters, sensors, or "smart" bombs. When these techniques failed to produce victory, military leaders, both French and American, complained, as had the German military leaders in 1918, that the war had been "won" militarily but "lost" politically—as if these dimensions were not totally interdependent.

In fact, these operational techniques and technological tools were now as ancillary to the main sociopolitical conflict as the tools of psychological warfare had been to the central operational and logistical struggle in the two world wars. In those conflicts, fought between remarkably cohesive societies, the issue was decided by logistic attrition. Propaganda and subversion had played a marginal role, and such successes as they achieved were strictly geared to those of the armed forces themselves. Conversely, in the conflicts of decolonization which culminated in Vietnam, operational and technological factors were subordinate to the sociopolitical struggle. If that was not conducted with skill and based on a realistic analysis of the societal situation, no amount of operational expertise, logistical backup, or technical know-how could possibly help.

If the social dimension of strategy has become dominant in one form of conflict since 1945, in another it has, if one is to believe the strategic analysts, vanished completely. Works about nuclear war and deterrence normally treat their topic as an activity taking place almost entirely in the technological dimension. From their writings not only the sociopolitical but the operational elements have quite disappeared. The technological capabilities of nuclear arsenals are treated as being decisive in themselves, involving a calculation of risk and outcome so complete and discrete that neither the political motivation for the conflict nor the social factors involved in its conduct—nor indeed the military activity of fighting—are taken into account at all. In their models, governments are treated as being absolute in their capacity to make and implement decisions, and the reaction of their societies are taken as little into account as were those of the subjects of the princes who conducted warfare in Europe in the eighteenth century. Anatole Rapoport, in a rather idiosyncratic introduction to a truncated edition of Clausewitz's *On War,* called these thinkers "neo-Clausewitzians."It is not easy to see why. Every one of the three elements that Clausewitz defined as being intrinsic to war—political motivation, operational activity, and social participation—is completely absent from their calculations. Drained of political, social, and operational content, such works resemble rather the studies of the eighteenth-century theorists whom Clausewitz was writing to confute, and whose influence he considered, with good reason, to have been so disastrous for his own times.

But the question insistently obtrudes itself: in the terrible eventuality of deterrence failing and hostilities breaking out between states armed with nuclear weapons, how will the peoples concerned react, and how will their reactions affect the will and the capacity of their governments to make decisions? And what form will military operations take? What, in short, will be the social and the operational dimensions of a nuclear war?

It is not, I think, simply an obsession with traditional problems that makes a European thinker seek an answer to these questions. If nuclear war breaks out at all, it is quite likely to break out here. In Europe such a conflict would involve not simply an exchange of nuclear missiles at intercontinental range but a struggle between armed forces for the control of territory, and rather thickly populated territory. The interest displayed by Soviet writers in the conduct of such a war, which some writers in the West find so sinister, seems to me no more than common sense. If such a war does occur, the operational and logistical problems it will pose will need to have been thoroughly thought through. It is not good enough to say that the strategy of the West is one of deterrence, or even of crisis management. It is the business of the strategist to think what to do if deterrence fails, and if Soviet strategists are doing their job and those in the West are not, it is not for us to complain about them.

Not only must the operational and logistical dimensions be taken into account; so also must the societal. Here the attention devoted by Soviet writers to the importance of the stability of the social structure of any state engaged in nuclear war also appears to me to be entirely justifiable, even if their conclusions about contemporary societies, both their own and ours, are ignorant caricatures.

About the operational dimension in nuclear war, Western analysts have until recently been both confused and defeatist. In spite of the activities of Defense Secretary Robert McNamara and his colleagues nearly twenty years ago, and in spite of the lip service paid to the concept of "flexible response," the military forces in Western Europe are still not regarded as a body of professionals, backed up where necessary by citizen soldiers whose task it will be to repel any attack upon their own territories and those of their allies. Rather, they are considered as an expendable element in a complex mechanism for enhancing the credibility of nuclear response. Indeed, attempts to increase the operational effectiveness of these forces are still sometimes opposed on the grounds that to do so would be to reduce the credibility of nuclear retaliation.

But such credibility depends not simply on a perceived balance, or imbalance, of weapons systems, but on perceptions of the nature of the society whose leaders are threatening such retaliation. Peoples who are not prepared to make the effort necessary for operational defense are even less likely to support a decision to initiate a nuclear exchange from which they will themselves suffer almost inconceivable destruction, even if that decision is made at the lowest possible level of nuclear escalation. And if such a decision were made over their heads, they would be unlikely to remain sufficiently resolute and united to continue to function as a cohesive political and military entity in the aftermath. The maintenance of adequate armed forces in peacetime, and the will to deploy and support them operationally in war, is in fact a symbol of that social unity and political resolve that is as essential an element in nuclear deterrence as any invulnerable second-strike capability.

So although the technological dimension of strategy has certainly become of predominant importance in armed conflict between advanced societies in the second half of the twentieth century—as predominant as the logistical dimension was during the first half—the growing political self-awareness of those societies and, in the West at least, their insistence on political participation have made the social dimension too significant to be ignored. There can be little doubt that societies that have developed powerful mechanisms of social control, such as those of the Soviet Union and the People's Republic of China, enjoy an apparent initial advantage over those of the West, which operate by a consensus reached by tolerating internal disagreements and conflicts—though how great that advantage would actually prove under pressure remains to be seen.

Whatever one's assessment of their strength, these are factors that cannot be left out of account in any strategic calculations. If we do take account of the social dimension of strategy in the nuclear age, we are likely to conclude that Western leaders might find it much more difficult to initiate nuclear war than would their Soviet counterparts—and, more important, would be perceived by their adversaries as finding it more difficult. If this is the case, and if on their side the conventional strength of the Soviet armed forces makes it unnecessary for their leaders to take such an initiative, the operational effectiveness of the armed forces of the West once more becomes a matter of major strategic importance, both in deterrence and in defense.

Most strategic scenarios today are based on the least probable of political circumstances—a totally unprovoked military assault by the Soviet Union, with no shadow of political justification, on Western Europe. But Providence is unlikely to provide us with anything so straightforward. Such an attack, if it occurred at all, would be likely to arise out of a political crisis in Central Europe over the rights and wrongs of which Western public opinion would be deeply and perhaps justifiably divided. Soviet military objectives would probably extend no farther than the Rhine, if indeed that far. Under such conditions, the political will of the West to initiate nuclear war might have to be discounted entirely, and the defense of West Germany would depend not on our nuclear arsenals but on the operational capabilities of our armed forces, fighting as best they could and for as long as they could without recourse to nuclear weapons of any kind. And it need hardly be said that hostilities breaking out elsewhere in the world are likely, as they did in Vietnam, to arise out of political situations involving an even greater degree of political ambiguity, in which our readiness to initiate nuclear war would appear even less credible.

The belief that technology has somehow eliminated the need for operational effectiveness is, in short, no more likely to be valid in the nuclear age than it was in the Second World War. Rather, as in that war, technology is likely to make its greatest contribution to strategy by improving operational weapons systems and the logistical framework that makes their deployment possible. The transformation in weapons technology which is occurring under our eyes with the development of precision-guided munitions suggests that this is exactly what is now happening. The new weapons systems hold out the possibility that operational skills will once more be enabled, as they were in 1940–41, to achieve decisive results, either positive in the attack or negative in the defense. But whether these initial operational decisions are then accepted as definitive by the societies concerned will depend, as it did in 1940–41 and in all previous wars, on the two other elements in Clausewitz's trinity: the importance of the political objective, and the readiness of the belligerent communities to endure the sacrifices involved in prolonging the war.

These sacrifices might or might not include the experience, on whatever scale, of nuclear war, but they would certainly involve living with the day-to-day, even hour-to-hour, possibility that the war might "go nuclear" at any moment. It is not easy to visualize a greater test of social cohesion than having to endure such a strain for a period of months, if not years, especially if no serious measures had been taken for the protection of the civil population.

Such measures were projected in the United States two decades ago, and they were abandoned for a mixture of motives. There was, on the one hand, the appreciation that not even the most far-reaching of preparations could prevent damage being inflicted on a scale unacceptable to the peoples of the West. On the other hand was the reluctance of those peoples to accept, in peacetime, the kind of social disruption and the diversion of resources which such measures would involve. The abandonment of these programs was then rationalized by the doctrine of mutually assured destruction. And any attempt by strategic thinkers to consider what protective measures might have to be taken if the war that everyone hoped to avoid actually came about was frowned on as a weakening of deterrence. But here again, there seem to have been no such inhibitions in the Soviet Union; their civil defense program, which some Western thinkers find so threatening, like that of the Chinese, seems to me no more than common sense. It is hard not to envy governments that have the capacity to carry through such measures, however marginally they might enhance the survivability of their societies in the event of nuclear war.

The Western position, on the other hand, appears both paradoxical and, quite literally, indefensible, as long as our operational strategy quite explicitly envisages the initiation of a nuclear exchange. The use of theater nuclear weapons within Western Europe, on any scale, would involve agonizing self-inflicted wounds for which our societies are ill-prepared, while their extension to Eastern European territory would invite retaliation against such legitimate military targets as the ports of Hamburg, Antwerp, or Portsmouth, for which we have made no preparations at all. The planned emplacement of nuclear weapons in Western Europe capable of matching in range, throw-weight, and accuracy those that the Russians have targeted onto that area may be necessary to deter the Soviet Union from initiating such an exchange. But it will not solve the problem as long as the Russians are in a position to secure an operational victory without recourse to nuclear weapons at all. Deterrence works both ways.

It cannot be denied that the strategic calculus I have outlined in the above pages has disquieting implications for the defense of the West. We appear to be depending on the technological dimension of strategy to the detriment of its operational requirements, while we ignore its societal implications altogether—something that our potential adversaries, very wisely, show no indication of doing. But the prospect of nuclear war is so appalling that we no less than our adversaries are likely, if war comes, to rely on "conventional" operational skills and the logistical capacity to support them for as long as possible, no less than we have in the past.

Hostilities in Europe would almost certainly begin with the engagement of armed forces seeking to obtain or to frustrate an operational decision. But as in the past—as in 1862, or in 1914, or in 1940–41—social factors will determine whether the outcome of these initial operations is accepted as decisive, or whether the resolution of the belligerent societies must be further tested by logistical attrition, or whether governments will feel sufficiently confident in the stability and cohesion of their own peoples, and the instability of their adversaries, to initiate a nuclear exchange. All of this gives us overwhelming reasons for praying that the great nuclear powers can continue successfully to avoid war. It gives us none for deluding ourselves as to the strategic problems such a war would present to those who would have to conduct it.

Part two

THE SUPERPOWERS

THE DEFENSE POLICY OF THE UNITED STATES

Lawrence J. Korb

Since the end of World War II, the process and substance of American defense policy have been topics of intense interest to students, scholars, policy makers, and statesmen, both in the United States and around the world. The reason for this intense concern is easy to understand. Because of the American position within the international political system, the defense policies of the United States have (and will continue to have) a profound impact upon international relations. American perceptions, national security objectives, military strategy, alliances, force employment doctrine, and force structure cannot but influence the course of human events.

International environment

THE RELATIVE POWER POSITION

There is little doubt that the United States emerged from World War II as the world's preeminent power; no other nation on earth could rival the United States economically or militarily. At the close of World War II, the United States had a GNP of $217 billion and accounted for almost half of the world's exports. It was essentially self-sufficient in strategic raw materials and was a net exporter of energy. The country's armed forces numbered about 12 million people. The Army Air Corps possessed 218 operational strategic and tactical combat groups and the world's only strategic nuclear weapons. The American navy consisted of approximately 1,200 major combatant ships. In addition, the Navy Department had more than 40,000 aircraft and almost 500,000 marines, giving it the world's most effective power projection force. Finally, the U.S. Army had approximately 6 million troops organized into over 100 combat-ready divisions.

The pre–World War II centers of world power had been virtually destroyed by the war. The defeated Axis powers literally lay in ruins. The victorious British and Russians were not in much better shape. The six long years of war had bankrupted the British Empire, and the Soviet Union had suffered almost twenty million casualties and severe damage to its industrial base.

The United States remained the world's preeminent economic and military power throughout the next two decades. Although its chief adversary, the Soviet Union, made great strides economically and militarily during the 1950s, the early 1960s still found it far behind the United States in economic and military power. As late as 1965 the Soviet GNP was less than half that of the United States, that is, $329 billion compared to $688 billion. Moreover, while the Soviets had very capable ground forces, they lagged far behind the United States in strategic nuclear forces and naval capabilities. In 1965, the United States possessed over 2,000 strategic delivery vehicles with some 6,000 nuclear warheads, while the Soviets possessed only 400 delivery vehicles equipped with approximately 450 warheads. In 1965, the United States had more major surface ships and submarines than the Russian navy, displaced 72 million more tons, and maintained an overseas operating tempo fifteen times greater than that of the Soviets. Many have argued that it was this overwhelming American strategic and naval dominance that forced the Soviet Union to acquiesce to American demands during the Cuban Missile Crisis in 1962. In the mid-1960s, the United States was still such a preeminent power in the international system that most analysts were referring to the period as one of American hegemony.[1]

Today, at the start of the 1980s, the situation has changed dramatically. The United States is still an economic and military superpower, but it is no longer the world's preeminent power. It still has the world's largest GNP, but no longer dominates the world trade scene. Indeed, despite the fact that it exports over $150 billion in manufactured and agricultural goods annually, the United States has run a negative trade balance almost every year since 1971. Moreover, as shown in table 1, the United States is now heavily dependent upon other nations for critical raw materials, and now imports about half of its petroleum needs;[2] its annual bill for foreign oil rose from $3 billion in 1970 to almost $70 billion in 1979. Finally, inflation in the United States, which had averaged less than 3 percent a year through 1972, climbed as high as 7 percent or more per year during the remainder of the decade, reaching double digits in some years, while its real growth rate dropped from 5 percent to below 2 percent.

Table 1
U.S. dependence upon foreign sources for critical raw materials

Raw Material	1950	1970	1985	2000
Aluminum	64%	85%	96%	98%
Chromium	NA	100	100	100
Copper	31	0	34	56
Iron	8	30	55	67
Lead	39	31	62	67
Manganese	88	95	100	100
Phosphorus	8	0	0	2
Potassium	14	42	47	61
Sulfur	2	0	28	52
Tin	77	NA	100	100
Tungsten	NA	50	87	97
Zinc	38	59	72	84

Source: Lester Brown, *The Global Politics of Resource Scarcity,* Overseas Development Council, Development Paper 17 (April 1974), pp. 20-21.

The United States still possesses a formidable amount of military power. Its armed forces have some 2,100 delivery vehicles equipped with about 10,000 strategic nuclear weapons, 13,000 tactical nuclear weapons, 450 ships, 38 tactical air wings, and 19 active and 9 reserve ground divisions. Nonetheless, the country's military might is equaled, if not surpassed, by that of the Soviet Union. At the beginning of the 1980s the Soviets surpassed the United States in most quantitative indicators of military power. The best that can be said about U.S. forces today is that they are in a state of rough equivalence with those of the USSR. Given military spending trends in the 1970s, some observers questioned whether the United States could cling to military parity with the Soviets much longer. During the 1970s, the Russians were increasing defense spending by about 5 percent a year in real terms.[3] By contrast, the U.S. defense budget remained level until the end of the decade, when the Carter administration committed itself to achieving 3 percent real growth in annual expenditures for defense. (See figure 1.)

THREATS FACING THE UNITED STATES

The external threats facing the United States may be categorized as military or economic. The primary military threat to the United States is posed by the Soviet Union. Beginning in the early 1960s, the Soviets undertook a rapid expansion of their military capabilities. As indicated in figure 1, if one excludes the incremental costs of the war in Southeast Asia, by 1968 the Soviets had forged ahead of the United States in the amount of money allocated annually to defense. Moreover, because the Pentagon was forced to expend a large percentage of its budget first for prosecuting the war in Southeast Asia and then for paying the additional personnel costs caused by the changeover to the all-volunteer force (AVF), the Kremlin began to outstrip the United States in outlays for a wide spectrum of military capabilities.[4] As a recent study has shown, during the 1970s, the Soviets spent $104 billion more than the United States on new weapons systems and produced six times as many tanks, twice as many combat aircraft, and three times as many ships, while developing twice as many new strategic systems.[5] This huge investment in military hardware has enabled the Soviets to make American land-based ICBMs vulnerable to a preemp-

Figure 1. Comparison of U.S. defense outlays and estimated dollar cost of Soviet defense programs

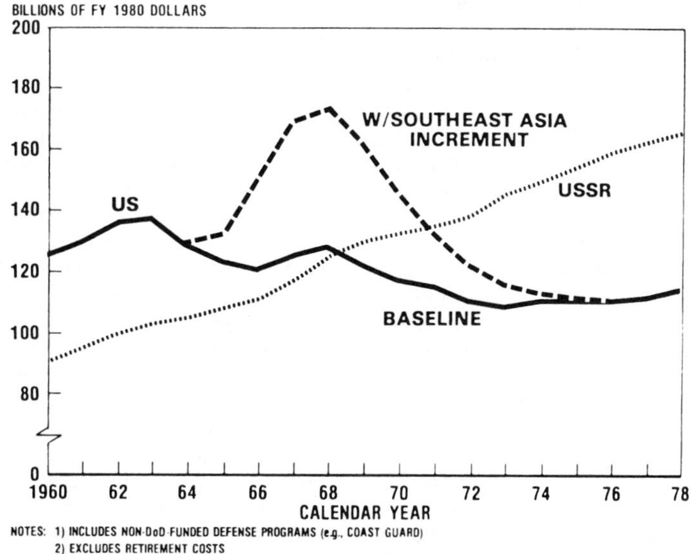

Source: Harold Brown, *Annual Defense Department Report, FY 1980,* p. 33. For a further explanation of these estimates, see notes 3 and 4.

tive first strike, to place in jeopardy the ability of the U.S. Navy to perform its sea control mission, and to undermine U.S. and NATO ability to withstand a sudden attack by the Soviet Union and its Warsaw Pact allies on Western Europe.

At the close of the 1970s, the gravity of the military threat posed by the growing Soviet armada had finally begun to impress the American people and their leaders. Opinion polls consistently showed that, for the first time since the Vietnamese Tet offensive of 1968, the majority of American people perceived that American military power was declining relative to that of the Soviet Union and that the U.S. defense budget would have to increase.[6] To deal with this situation, the Carter administration, which had planned to cut defense spending by $5 billion to $7 billion, actually raised the FY 1979 and 1980 defense budgets by 3 percent in real terms, and pledged to maintain continued real increases of that magnitude for the foreseeable future. Congress, which had been hostile to absolute or relative increases in defense spending throughout 1969–78, ultimately appropriated the 3 percent increase requested by the administration and urged the president to devote even more resources to areas like strategic nuclear forces and naval combatants.

It was not so much that the American people and their leaders feared that the Soviet Union might use its superior military forces to launch a direct attack on the United States or its allies; rather, they were concerned that the Soviets might attempt to exploit their military advantages to achieve political gains—as W. Averell Harriman, former U.S. Ambassador to the Soviet Union, has said, "in a bullying process."[7] This state of affairs would place the United States in the difficult position of having either to back down or to risk hostilities with the Soviet Union.

The economic threat facing the United States as it entered the 1980s was the increasing dependence of the nation and its major allies on foreign sources for materials critical to the functioning of their economies. This dependence is most acute in the case of oil. The United States now imports half of its petroleum needs, and its allies Japan and Western Europe (with the notable exception of the United Kingdom), are dependent on foreign sources for nearly all of their oil. Moreover, 68 percent of the petroleum needs of the United States and its allies come from the Persian Gulf alone.[8] Any sudden disruption of the oil flow could bring western economies crashing down. As the secretary of defense has noted: "Protecting the oil flow from the Middle East is clearly part of our vital interest, which warrants any action that's appropriate including the use of force."[9] Even threats of such cutoffs hinder U.S. ability to pursue freely its national security interests in such places as the Middle East and Africa. In 1979, for example, pressure from Saudi Arabia complicated U.S. efforts to arrange a settlement between the Egyptians and the Israelis, while threats from Nigeria became a factor in U.S. policy toward Rhodesia and South Africa.

SELF-PERCEPTION

To understand the self-perception of the appropriate role that the United States feels it should play in the international system in the 1980s, it is necessary to sketch briefly the role it has played up to now.[10] The United States is still a comparatively young nation. For most of its 200 years, it has tended to play a minor or passive role within the international system, under the assumption that such a course of action could most effectively promote its national security. During the first 100 years of its existence, the United States tried to remain free of entangling alliances and disengaged from the balance of power politics practiced by the major European states. Since it was in the interest of Great Britain that the United States remain unallied, the British fleet was used to enforce the American wish. Many U.S. leaders who were unaware of the role that British naval power played in allowing them to pursue this course of action felt themselves morally superior to those European states forced to indulge in power politics.

When the United States did become a major actor within the international system, it always felt the need to do so under the guise of moral self-righteousness. Although, in many cases, the United States was acting primarily to enhance its economic interests, some form of moral justification was always explicitly or implicitly invoked. Thus, when the United States wrested control of Cuba and the Philippines from Spain, it referred to its Christian responsibilities toward the pagans. Similarly, the United States entered World War I to make the world safe for democracy and attempted to make the post-World War I period free from secret diplomacy. Finally, during the period between the world wars, when the American people discovered that the so-called merchants of death had profited from the war, the United States again vowed to avoid involvement in the international system to the maximum extent possible. Not even Hitler's blitzkrieg attack on Poland could galvanize the United States into becoming active in the world arena. It took the Japanese attack on Pearl Harbor to shake the American populace from its isolationist lethargy.

With one exception, the experience of World War II completely changed the American perception of its appropriate role in foreign affairs. In the immediate postwar period, the United States saw itself as the world's policeman, charged with containing monolithic communism whenever and wherever it appeared outside the Soviet orbit. To accomplish this task, the United States was willing to apply its economic, political, military, and paramilitary resources all around the globe. The nation, which had remained disengaged from world politics, now ringed the communist world with alliances, poured hundreds of billions of dollars into military and economic assistance to noncommunist regimes, intervened covertly in countries from Guatemala to Iran, attempted to influence the outcome of elections in such widely diverse nations as Italy and the Philippines, employed military force without war (for political purposes) on more than 200 occasions,[11] and fought two long, bitterly divisive, and costly wars on the Asian mainland.

The one element that remained constant in U.S. post-World War II defense policy was the strong moral component. The conflict with the Soviet Union and its allies was depicted as a fight against the godless atheists in the Kremlin. Military and nonmilitary intervention was justified in terms of defending freedom, championing democracy, and liberating captive peoples.

With their overwhelming economic and military strength and a sense of moral self-righteousness, the American people and many of their leaders felt that there were no limits to their capabilities to influence events around the globe. This "arrogance of power" eventually led "the best and the brightest"* into overextending the nation in Vietnam, bringing about a dramatic change in American self-perception.

By the close of the 1960s, the United States realized that there were limits to its power and consequently to its ability to influence events around the globe. While the United States could certainly provide for its own security needs, it could not single-handedly preserve the freedom and independence of noncommunist governments throughout the world. Nor was such a state of affairs vital to American national security. This new perception was given its clearest expression by President Richard M. Nixon on Guam on November 3, 1969. In what later became known as the Guam or Nixon doctrine, the Republican president proclaimed that although the United States would honor all the commitments it had made in the quarter of a century since the end of World War II, its allies, outside of Western Europe and Japan, would henceforth bear the primary responsibility for their own security. The United States would provide some assistance to these nations, but in the final analysis, they, not the United States, would determine their own fates.[12]

At about the same time, the United States began to perceive that it was not engaged in a zero-sum struggle with a monolithic Communist enemy. As the 1960s drew to a close, it became clear to U.S. policy makers that the split between the Soviet Union and the People's Republic of China (PRC) was real and that the many other Marxist governments and parties around the world often acted independently of both Communist giants. Moreover, the United States shared certain common interests with both the USSR and the PRC and considered nationalism, not ideol-

*This is a reference to David Halberstam's critique of the American elite, *The Best and the Brightest* (New York: Random House/Fawcett Crest, 1969, 1972). *Arrogance of power* is a term popularized by former Senator J. W. Fulbright, Chairman of the Senate Foreign Relations Committee in the 1960s.—Ed.

ogy, to be the dominant motive in the behavior of those nations.

Accordingly, President Nixon and his national security adviser, Henry Kissinger, began to move the United States in the direction of a limited form of détente with the Soviet Union, recognition of the Communist government in Peking as the legitimate rulers of China, and improving trade and cultural relations with other communist governments. These policies were quite successful. Détente with the Soviet Union led to the SALT I Treaty in 1972, the Vladivostok Accords of 1974, the Helsinki Agreement of 1975, and SALT II in 1979. Recognition of Communist China and full diplomatic relations with the Peking government took effect on January 1, 1979.

Trade with the Communist nations also grew rapidly. The Soviet Union became one of the biggest customers for American wheat, while China imported American technology. By the end of the 1970s, U.S. exports to communist nations amounted to more than five billion dollars.[13] Nonetheless, the Nixon-Ford-Kissinger policy was not without its critics.

Throughout the early part of the 1970s, while the United States was moving away from its role of world policeman, there were many who wished to see it return almost to its pre–World War II isolationist posture, or "fortress America" strategy, and to reemphasize the moral component of its national security policy. In 1972 these neoisolationists succeeded in helping Senator George McGovern capture the Democratic presidential nomination. McGovern's campaign theme was "Come Home, America," and to make sure that Americans stayed home, the South Dakota senator proposed a 40 percent reduction in the size of the defense budget, which was already 10 percent below its pre-Vietnam level.[14] Similarly, other neoisolationists in Congress repeatedly attempted to circumscribe the ability of the executive branch to employ military force overseas. The War Powers Act of 1972 limited to sixty days the president's power to use the armed services outside the United States. The legislature also used the power of the purse to prevent the commander in chief from intervening militarily in such areas as Angola and Indochina.

The neoisolationists were defeated in the 1972 presidential campaign. Throughout the 1976 Carter campaign the candidate railed against a foreign policy that was contrary to what he believed were America's longstanding beliefs and principles. As candidate Carter noted on October 6, 1976: "We've lost in our foreign policy the character of the American people."[15] Once in office, he set out to define a new policy with a strong emphasis on human rights.[16]

The 1970s were years in which the United States adjusted its self-perceptions and tried to rebuild the foreign policy consensus that had been shattered during the American involvement in Vietnam. There was no doubt that America was no longer able or willing to play the role of the world's policeman. Yet no consensus developed on whether it could play the subtle, and at times amoral, game of balance-of-power politics or whether it should embrace some type of neoisolationism buttressed by some form of moral superiority.

During the 1980s, the United States will probably move toward the former position. Neoisolationism is simply unrealistic, as is a national security policy based *solely* on a moral principle like human rights. The United States will continue to be a world power with concrete, definable interests in the international arena that cannot be supported without an activist foreign policy backed by a strong military force. Like it or not, the American political leadership and people must recognize that American military power does defend open societies in Europe. It enables Israel to maintain the status quo and Japan not to rearm. It gives Communist China a reason for not making a settlement with the USSR on Moscow's terms. Similarly, in order to protect American national security, the United States must deal with nations whose moral values differ substantially. As one observer has noted, raising such issues as human rights can actually foster conflict rather than cooperation among nations.[17]

Ironically, the most accurate view of the likely new self-perception is expressed in Presidential Decision (PD) 18 of August 1977. In it President Carter, who had campaigned on a platform of cutting the defense budget and making the quest for human rights the foundation of his foreign policy, pledged to increase defense spending by 3 percent a year in real terms and not to pursue human rights at the cost of injuring American relations with the Soviet Union.[18]

INTERDEPENDENCIES

As discussed above, the U.S. perception of the appropriate role it ought to play in the international system underwent a complete reversal after World War II. Nowhere was this change more evident than in the American attitude toward alliances. Between the Revolutionary War and World War II, the United States had almost scrupulously heeded Washington's advice to remain free of entangling alliances. It even fought its wars alone. The War of 1812, the Mexican War, and the Spanish-American War were all conducted without the assistance of other nations. The United States even entered World War I and World War II for its own reasons, rather than because of formal alliance commitments. After World War I, the Senate refused to ratify the Treaty of Versailles and thus effectively kept the nation out of the collective security arrangements of the League of Nations.

In the post-1945 period, however, the United States actively sought to become involved throughout the world. Before the war came to a close, it took the initiative in founding the United Nations and was primarily responsible for those provisions in the U.N. charter that provided for collective security through the use of multinational military force, if necessary. Then, in response to what it perceived as Soviet expansionism, the United States initiated and joined a number of regional alliances.[19] In the Rio Treaty of 1947, the United States joined with twenty Central and South American nations to form a multilateral pact that prohibited intervention by foreign states in Latin American affairs and provided for consultations among the nations with regard to the external threat. While the Rio Pact could be considered a normal outgrowth of the Monroe Doctrine and an expression of traditional U.S. concern about its own hemisphere, the North Atlantic Treaty Organization (NATO) Pact of 1949 marked a sharp change from previous practices. The NATO Pact was an open-ended, multilateral, peacetime alliance between the United States, Canada, and thirteen Western European nations that committed the United States to consider an attack on any of these nations as an attack on itself. In addition, the NATO Pact provided for the establishment of a permanent multinational military force and the basing of American forces in and around the European continent.

NATO was primarily a response to Soviet actions in Czechoslovakia, Berlin, and Greece. However, the Communist takeover of mainland China in 1949, the Sino-Soviet Pact of 1950, and the North Korean attack that same year caused the United States to focus on the Communist threat to Asia as well. In 1951 the United States signed bilateral mutual defense treaties with Japan and the Philippines and a trilateral pact with Australia and New Zealand (the ANZUS Treaty). In 1953 and 1954 the United States entered into bilateral arrangements with South Korea and the Republic of China (Taiwan), respectively. In 1954 the United States, along with France, Britain, and seven Asian nations, signed the Manila Pact, which created the South East Asia Treaty Organization (SEATO). Although not as demanding as the NATO Treaty, this pact pledged the signatories to assist one another when their peace and safety were threatened. In 1959 the United States completed its "ring around the communist world" by concluding bilateral agreements with Iran, Pakistan, and Turkey. In addition, it became a silent partner in the Central Treaty Organization (CENTO), which formally consisted of Iran, Iraq, Turkey, Pakistan, and the United Kingdom.

The alliances that the United States put together so carefully in the 1940s and 1950s eroded throughout the 1960s in both form and substance. The first to show signs of coming apart was SEATO. Although it was not officially disbanded until 1977, SEATO began to disintegrate much sooner. In 1962 Laos was removed from SEATO's area of concern when the country was declared neutral by international agreement. Cambodia dropped out of the alliance in 1964 after breaking diplomatic relations with the United States. Moreover, in 1965, when the United States began to intervene massively in South Vietnam, it did so with no visible support from its SEATO allies. Finally, the other major powers, France and Britain, dropped out of SEATO in 1966 and 1967, respectively, and Pakistan formally withdrew in 1972.

CENTO officially lasted until the overthrow of the shah of Iran in 1979. However, its fate was sealed in 1967 when Great Britain formally abandoned all interests east of Suez. The bilateral treaty between the United States and Taiwan was officially abrogated by the Carter administration in late 1978, but actually began to unravel when Nixon visited Peking in May 1972.

NATO still endures, but it too has suffered some severe strains over the past three decades. In 1966 France withdrew militarily because of its concern over the U.S. domination of the alliance, particularly U.S. control over the use of nuclear weapons by NATO. A decade later Greece took the same step because of its difficulties with Turkey over Turkish occupation of Cyprus. During the late 1960s many of the country's NATO allies became disenchanted when the United States redeployed troops from Europe to the Southeast Asia theater. The alliance members also became concerned when the United States concluded strategic arms agreements with the Soviet Union in 1972, consulting only minimally with its NATO allies, and when the Americans sent military supplies from the NATO stockpile to Israel during the 1973 Middle East War. There was some fear among the NATO allies that agreements with the USSR could undermine the American resolve to use its strategic nuclear weapons to defend Europe, while U.S. aid to Israel might have resulted in a cutoff of oil supplies to Western Europe by some Arab states.

However, as the 1970s came to a close, NATO appeared to be experiencing a revitalization. Faced with growing Soviet military strength, the members of the alliance pledged to increase defense spending by 3 percent a year in real terms for the foreseeable future. Moreover, they pledged to move toward greater standardization, interoperability, and cost sharing in their force structure. In addition, the United States once again placed the primary emphasis in the allocation of the resources within its defense budget and in the development of its force structure upon defending Europe, while having substantially cut back its military forces in the Pacific after the end of the Vietnam War. Finally, in the SALT II talks with the USSR, the United States began to focus on topics that were of prime concern to members of NATO, such as theater nuclear weapons.

Because of its overwhelming military and economic power, the United States dominates all its mutilateral and bilateral associations. For example, it accounts for about 60 percent of NATO's military expenditures. At this writing, the United States has only six bonafide alliances remaining: NATO, the Rio Pact, the ANZUS Pact, and bilateral agreements with Japan, Korea, and the Philippines. (In addition, the United States has overseas base rights agreements with Portugal, Spain, and Turkey.) These arrangements signal to potential adversaries and to the American people what are vital interests of the United States. In themselves these alliances do not restrict or alter the American world view or strategy. Rather, they are a reflection of it. Just as the pactomania of the late 1940s and 1950s was a reflection of the containment policy, so the smaller number of alliances gives evidence of the more limited security objectives of the United States as it enters the 1980s.

National objectives, national strategy, and military doctrine

NATIONAL SECURITY OBJECTIVES AND THREAT PERCEPTIONS

The United States has four principal national security objectives. The first is to deter both nuclear and conventional attacks on the country and its allies, particularly attacks on Western Europe and Japan by the Soviet Union and its Warsaw Pact allies. Second is the objective to keep open the sea and air lines of communication between the United States and its allies and trading partners. The third objective is to provide an international environment in which democratic development is encouraged, human rights are promoted, and free access to overseas markets for American business is maintained. Fourth, the United States desires to conclude any hostilities that may occur with a minimum amount of U.S. losses and on terms favorable to the United States and its allies.[20]

These objectives have narrowed substantially in the wake of the post-Vietnam reassessment of America's role in the world. As discussed above, prior to the debacle in Southeast Asia, the primary objective of American national security policy was to contain or prevent the spread of communism in any area of the globe. American policy makers did not make very much of a distinction between those areas that were vital to the protection of national security and those that were merely desirable; nor did policy makers make much of a distinction between those Communist movements controlled by the Soviet Union and those independent of it.

Generally speaking, the leaders of the United States consider that there are three distinct threats to the security and economic well-being of the United States and its allies. The first is the challenge posed by the arms build-up of the Soviet Union and its Warsaw Pact allies. Second are the various forms of instability that exist in the Third World that could be exploited by such outside powers as the Soviet Union. And third are the potential disruptions of the global economy that could seriously jeopardize the economic health and well-being of the United States and its allies. The most pressing issue in this third area is energy.[21]

The current objectives of American national security policy are likely to remain essentially the same for the foreseeable future. But the appropriate means of achieving those objectives are likely to be subject to continuous debate and thus are more susceptible to change. Indeed, the whole history of post-World War II American defense policy has consisted of a struggle over how to achieve national security objectives most efficiently.

During the Eisenhower administration it was felt that a policy of "massive retaliation" based upon an overwhelming American superiority in strategic nuclear forces would most efficiently and effectively deter communist aggression and provide the desired international environment. In the Kennedy-Johnson years, the policy was changed to flexible response. This policy (which dictated that the United States have sufficient nuclear weapons to fight theater wars* or engage in a strategic exchange, adequate conventional forces to fight two major wars and one smaller, or "brush fire," war simultaneously—two and one-half wars—and forward deployment of a substantial theater nuclear and conventional warfighting capability) was considered a more credible deterrent than the less expensive massive retaliation strategy.

In the last decade, the Nixon-Ford and Carter administrations have refined, but not changed, the essentials of the Kennedy-Johnson strategy of flexible response. Nuclear *sufficiency* has been interpreted to mean *essential equivalence;* that is, U.S. nuclear forces are in fact, and are perceived to be, equivalent to those of the Soviet Union because any Soviet advantage in a particular area is offset by corresponding U.S. advantages in some other area. The two-and-one-half-war strategy has been narrowed to one and one-half wars, and overseas deployments, especially in the Pacific, have been reduced substantially from Korea and Vietnam wartime levels.

During this same period, there has been considerable debate over what constitutes essential equivalence, what mix of forces is needed to handle one major and one minor contingency simultaneously, and how much forward deployment is actually needed. There are two extreme positions on these questions. On the one hand, there are those who belong to what might be called the school of "minimum

*The term *theater* refers to a specific region of the world where conflict takes place, such as the European "theater."—Ed.

deterrence." Members of this group argue that nuclear deterrence requires no more than perhaps 100 land-based ICBMs and 31 fleet ballistic submarines equipped with 496 SLBMs, that conventional forces could achieve their objectives with perhaps 11⅓ ground divisions, 200 ships, 30 tactical air wings, 1.3 million people, and forward deployments cut in half.[22] On the other hand, there are those who would like to see a force of larger proportions than the present level (perhaps 1,200 land-based missiles, 824 SLBMs, 500 bombers, 20 ground divisions, 40 tactical air wings, and 600 ships).[23]

Battles over these differing views of how best to achieve national security objectives are fought in the executive and legislative phases of the annual defense budget process, as well as among the research corporations ("think tanks") specializing in defense matters. Normally, the Joint Chiefs of Staff and the military departments support increased capabilities, while the Office of Management and Budget (OMB) and the Arms Control and Disarmament Agency (ACDA) contend that lesser levels would be quite acceptable. The Office of the Secretary of Defense (OSD) and the Department of State normally take a middle-ground position, with OSD leaning more toward the maximum end of the spectrum and the State Department favoring the minimum pole.* Within Congress, the Armed Services Committees normally support the JCS positions, while the Appropriations and Budget Committees favor the middle ground. Minimum deterrence often draws strong support from some members of the Foreign Relations and International Affairs Committees.

Outside the government there is an increasing number of "think tanks" or research groups that focus a substantial amount of effort on security matters. These groups represent nearly every shade of opinion on defense issues, ranging from unilateral disarmament to maximum deterrence. Those favoring less defense include the Institute for Policy Research, the Center for Defense Information, the Federation of American Scientists, and the Arms Control Association. Those favoring increased preparedness include the National Strategy Information Center, the Committee on Present Danger, and the American Security Council. In between these two extremes stand the Brookings Institution and the American Enterprise Institute for Public Policy Research (AEI). The former favors making incremental changes in the present posture that would have the effect of producing a smaller force, while the latter supports small changes in the opposite direction.

These nongovernmental organizations express their dissent primarily through the publication of periodicals. For example, the Center for Defense Information publishes monthly the *Defense Monitor;* Brookings, a series called *Studies in Defense Policy;* and AEI, the monthly *Foreign Policy and Defense Review*. In addition, most of these groups issue an annual analysis of the current defense budget and often supply expert witnesses for sympathetic Congressional committees.

The ideas of these groups often enter directly into the defense debate and occasionally form the basis on which the issues are examined within the Congress. For example, during the B-1 debate, various Congressmen referred to studies made by Brookings and AEI.[24] However, their overall impact upon policy is diluted because their positions are often contradictory. For example, a congressman who quotes a Brookings study supporting the elimination of a particular program will likely find a colleague citing an AEI study that draws the opposite conclusion.

In addition to these nongovernmental research groups, others, such as the RAND Corporation, the Institute for Defense Analyses (IDA), and the Hudson Institute, engage in research projects commissioned by various bureaucratic elements within the Defense Department itself. Finally, government agencies such as the General Accounting Office (GAO) and the Library of Congress also publish reports that have an impact on the political process.

IDEOLOGY, CULTURE, AND CAPABILITIES

The approach that nations take toward the international system generally is a mixture of their ideology, culture, and capabilities. However, for each nation the relative importance of each of these three factors is markedly different. For the United States, ideology and culture have had a relatively large impact in determining the objectives it pursues in the international arena.[25]

In the minds of Americans, the United States is more than just the world's first new nation, it is the world's first democracy and the first nation in the history of mankind that has devoted itself to improving the lot of the common man. As such, many Americans consider the country morally superior to other nations. Moreover, in the American view, peace is seen as the natural state of affairs, and wars are caused primarily through the abuse of power. Just as power has to be restricted at home, so it must be restricted in international affairs. Similarly, just as the United States prospered at home through a laissez-faire economic policy, so the international system would flourish through free trade. To put it bluntly, in American ideology, economics is good and politics is bad. Therefore, using power and force within the domestic or international system can be justified only by appealing to some higher moral principle. Thus, the United States claimed that it entered World War I not for the quite legitimate pur-

*Although these are the usual bureaucratic positions, deviations can sometimes be explained by the preferences of politically appointed agency heads.—Ed.

pose of protecting its own security from a European continent dominated by Germany, but because the Germans had engaged in unrestricted and morally reprehensible submarine warfare and, therefore, deserved to be punished. Even in the post-World War II period, American support for *realpolitik* (policy guided by national interest and power considerations—Ed.) could be gained only by disguising it as *idealpolitik* (policy guided by moral principle—Ed.). Anticommunism served as a useful justification for full-scale American involvement in power politics and its use of force in such places as Korea, Vietnam, the Dominican Republic, and the Middle East.

Finally, because of the impact of ideology and culture, when the United States finds it necessary to use its military power, it is usually plagued with a sense of guilt afterward. Thus, after every major war, the reasons for the nation's involvement have been reinterpreted. These revisionist histories have certain common themes: the conflicts in which the United States became involved did not, in fact, threaten its security interests; the United States became involved primarily because the politicians saw a threat where none really existed, and this illusion was promoted by propagandists who aroused and manipulated public opinion, by civilian and military bureaucrats concerned with promoting the interests of their own organizations, and by bankers and industrialists whose economic interests benefited from the struggle.

Americans traditionally attempt to assuage this feeling of guilt in two ways. First, they withdraw from the international system and focus on problems at home. As noted above, this was the theme promoted by Senator George McGovern toward the end of the war in Vietnam. Second, to ensure that the policy makers will not become too involved internationally again, restrictions are placed upon their ability to involve the United States overseas. The Ludlow Amendment after World War I, the Bricker Amendment after Korea, and the Congressional War Powers Act after Vietnam were similar attempts to restrain policy makers from overextension in international politics.

In the post-Vietnam period, ideology and culture still remain a significant factor in justifying continuing involvement by the United States in the international system. As Secretary of Defense Donald Rumsfeld noted in his report to Congress in January 1977, the United States has "a duty both to advocate democratic principles and to encourage those societies where freedom grows or continues to flourish."[26] However, this moral justification has been placed in its proper context, that is, the United States no longer pretends that moral principle is the primary driving force behind the country's security policy. Rather, it is economics and politics that require the maintenance of a large military establishment. As recent secretaries of defense have bluntly told the Congress, the American standard of living is now tied to the country's ability to control events within the international system, that is, to engage in power politics.[27]

Total imports and exports by the United States equal $300 billion annually, while international investments by American companies approach $200 billion. In addition, the United States imports more than 50 percent of its needs of twelve vital strategic materials. Because of this, it is often necessary for the United States to associate with regimes that do not share American values and to use military force for economic reasons. Contemporary international politics no longer permit the United States the luxury of ideological purity or of guilt feelings about using military force in support of vital interests.

NATIONAL STRATEGY

The United States possesses a number of capabilities that can be directed toward accomplishing its national security objectives. As it enters the last two decades of this century the country has some 13,000 theater nuclear weapons, 29 land-based tactical air wings, 12 sea-based or carrier air wings, 19⅓ ground divisions, and 450 ships. The GNP of the United States is more than twice that of any other nation in the world, and the United States is technologically the most advanced nation on earth. Finally, political and social arrangements within the American system provide the best model to those interested in preserving human dignity and freedom within a stable society.

Although not specifically stated in any one document, the American national strategy is to employ creative diplomacy to direct all of these assets toward the accomplishment of national security objectives.[28] U.S. military capabilities provide the essential backdrop or psychological milieu in which American diplomats attempt to negotiate arms control accords and trade agreements. In addition, since World War II the United States has actually employed its armed forces over 200 times to influence the behavior of other nations. Similarly, it has given out over $200 billion in economic and military aid and employed technological exports and access to its vast markets as weapons in an attempt to control events in the international arena. Finally, the United States has used its military and economic leverage, as well as its own example, to promote in other nations the values for which it stands.

Within the American political system there is basic agreement upon this strategy. There is disagreement, however, about the extent to which each of these capabilities should be employed in particular circumstances. Some favor almost total reliance on the moral or economic instruments, while others support using the military instrument more aggressively. This disagreement is largely a function of the domestic factors that influence U.S. national strategy.

DOMESTIC DETERMINANTS

Over a century ago, the French political philosopher Alexis de Tocqueville observed that the institutions and processes of American democracy make it difficult to achieve excellence in foreign policy. Tocqueville noted that "foreign politics demand scarcely any of those qualities which are peculiar to a democracy; they require, on the contrary, the perfect use of almost all those in which it is deficient." Nonetheless, democracies, like the United States, can and do pursue policies designed to protect their national security. Unlike those of other forms of government, the policies and strategies employed by a democracy are strongly affected by domestic factors. In the case of the United States, the principal factors are its political system, economic system, geography, public opinion, and national strategy.

The political system. The primary domestic determinant of U.S. national strategy is the nature of the American political system. Even in the area of national security policy, powers are shared by the executive and legislative branches of the federal government. Through its power of the purse, its confirmation powers, and the prerogatives to declare war and raise an army and navy, Congress can restrict the type of strategy that the president can develop. It can affect policy directly, for example, by prohibiting aid to certain countries like Turkey or by banning military operations in areas like Cambodia. In addition, it often has an indirect, but important, impact in that the president and his advisers must take into account the effect that a particular action will have on the Congress and how they will respond to Congressional questions about particular situations.

The courts can have an impact on national strategy. For example, the Supreme Court refused to allow President Truman to seize the steel mills in Youngstown, Ohio, during the Korean War. During the war in Southeast Asia, the courts heard several challenges from reservists who argued that they were called up illegally, that is, without a national emergency having been declared. It is to be expected that, in the near future, issues involving the drafting of women or using women in combat may reach the courts.

A second characteristic of the political system that has an impact upon national strategy is the fact and timing of elections. Foreign policy decisions, such as SALT I and the normalization of relations with China, are often timed for maximum impact upon upcoming elections. Concerns about challenges in the primary or general elections can have a great impact upon policy makers' decisions on issues such as the size of the defense budget or aid to nations that have large ethnic constituencies in the United States. For example, in 1976 President Ford reduced the defense budget by $7 billion from prior projections in order to keep his election year budget below $400 billion. That same year the "Greek lobby" in Congress prevented the executive from giving military aid to Turkey.[29]

The openness of the American political system is a third factor affecting national strategy. Not even the most serious and delicate national issues can be kept secret. Negotiating positions, force planning doctrines, and crisis action plans are normally revealed and thus debated openly in the Congress and the media. For example, on July 23, 1971, the *New York Times* carried an article outlining the U.S. negotiating position one day before it was scheduled to be presented to the Soviet Union, and on August 3, 1977, the *Washington Post* summarized the minutes of a National Security Council meeting that concluded that the Carter administration would concede one-third of West Germany to a Soviet invasion rather than seek increased defense spending.[30]

The U.S. system of checks and balances is the final factor within the political system impinging upon strategy. It normally prevents any radical changes in strategy, even if such changes are necessary to meet new or different international requirements. The advantage within the American political system is always with those seeking to preserve the status quo. New policies can be killed by bureaucratic inertia, denied funding within the Congress, amended, filibustered, and even challenged in court.

The economic system. As discussed above, one of the objectives of American national security policy is to maintain an environment in which U.S. companies have access to overseas markets for trade and investment. This objective arises from two sources: the American beliefs that, first, unrestricted free trade will do for the international system what laissez-faire economics did for this nation, and, second, the U.S. standard of living depends upon the ability to secure certain raw materials, invest overseas, and have access to foreign markets.

There is no doubt that the American economic system and its underlying philosophy play a role in determining national strategy. The United States would not stand idly by while a raw material cartel undermined the country's economy. However, it is not true, as some have argued, that the strategic behavior of the United States is primarily determined by the interests of the American economy.[31] In fact, the United States has often acted contrary to its own best economic interests. For example, the United States poured over $200 billion and 2 million troops into Southeast Asia from 1964 to 1972, but did not intervene in Indonesia during its 1965 revolution, despite the fact that the latter area had many more raw materials than the nations of South Vietnam, Cambodia, and Laos combined. In the Middle East, the United

States has consistently supported Israel despite the fact that the United States has become increasingly dependent on Arab oil. In fact, during the 1973 war, the United States continued to send massive amounts of aid to Israel after the Arab nations had embargoed American oil. For nearly three decades after World War II the U.S. government severely restricted trade with the Soviet Union, mainland China, and Eastern Europe despite great pressures from the business community that clamored for access to these large markets.[32] Even today such trade accounts for less than 2 percent of American trade.

Geography. The United States is essentially an "island" nation. Over 60 percent of its borders is shoreline. Although it has neighbors directly on its northern and southern borders, these nations have never posed a threat to U.S. national security. Moreover, the orientation of America has always been more east-west than north-south. Its potential opponents lie overseas and the majority of its trade has always been overseas, not overland.

Thus, for the greater part of this century, the United States has regarded a maritime strategy as the best hope of providing for its national defense. For example, during the 1930s, the U.S. Navy was among the three strongest in the world, while the American army ranked seventeenth. The maritime strategy, which owed its intellectual rigor to Alfred Thayer Mahan, dictated that the United States control the seas in order to ensure prosperity in peacetime and victory in war. Controlling the seas required a large navy and suitable overseas bases.[33] This maritime strategy meant that even when it demobilized its navy between the Spanish-American War and World War I and between world wars I and II, the United States maintained a comparatively large force.

Many have argued, quite convincingly, that, in the age of intercontinental ballistic missiles and huge air transports, maritime strategy is no longer important and that geography should no longer be a determinant of U.S. strategy. Yet such traditions die hard. When confronted with a crisis, policy makers almost instinctively turn toward naval forces. In over 80 percent of the cases in which military forces were employed for political purposes in the post–World War II period, naval units were the chosen instrument.[34] The top priority of the Nixon-Ford administration in the area of conventional forces was to rebuild American naval capability so that the United States could maintain maritime superiority. One of President Ford's last acts in office was to present to the Congress a five-year shipbuilding program that would have built 157 ships at a cost of $50 billion.[35] When President Carter cut this program in half, he was heavily criticized.[36] Moreover, to prevent the building of a $2.5 billion nuclear-powered aircraft carrier in FY 1979, President Carter took the unprecedented step of vetoing the entire FY 1979 defense authorization bill. Nevertheless, the Carter administration spent the largest portion of its defense budget on the Navy Department. In FY 1980, for example, the Navy received $44 billion, while the Air Force received $39 billion and the Army $34 billion.

Public opinion and national will. One of the greatest paradoxes of the American political system is the fact that the public is not informed about national security issues, yet public support is necessary to carry out national strategy, particularly one that carries risks. For example, in January 1979, 77 percent of the American people could not identify the participants in the SALT talks, yet many senators up for reelection in 1980 were concerned that their position on the SALT II Treaty might send the wrong message to their constituents.[37]

Generally speaking, public opinion sets limits or boundaries on national strategy. The American public is not particularly concerned over whether the United States pursues a maritime or continental strategy for its conventional forces, or a counterforce or countervalue strategy* for its strategic nuclear component. However, the people do set limits on how much of their resources ought to go to defense or on how much the United States should allow the military balance vis-à-vis the USSR to deteriorate.

On specific issues, such as aid to Israel or Turkey, special or single interest groups can have a great impact on policy. The existence of certain groups within the American public has affected American strategy in areas like the Middle East and the eastern Mediterranean. For example, as former President Ford notes in his memoirs: "The Israeli lobby . . . is strong, vocal, and healthy."[38]

National will becomes a factor when Americans are asked to make sacrifices of blood and treasure to support specific policies. A change in the national mood in the late 1960s was the dominant factor in forcing the United States to attempt to negotiate its way out of the Vietnam War, end the draft, and cut defense spending. As the "Vietnam hangover" recedes, however, the willingness of people to sacrifice again for national security is increasing. By the end of the 1970s, support for defense spending reached an eighteen-year high, and a majority of Americans stated that they would support military involvement by U.S. troops in Western Europe.[39]

Other factors. The United States is a large, technologically advanced, comparatively wealthy, and politically stable nation with a highly educated populace. All of these characteristics have had some impact upon U.S. national strategy. Because of its size and wealth, the United States has little choice but

*Counterforce targeting is against largely military or military-related targets, whereas countervalue targeting is generally directed against industrial or population centers.—Ed.

to help maintain the balance of power. Its advanced technology has enabled it to maintain rough military parity with the Soviet Union even though its force size and weapons inventory are considerably smaller, and even though it devotes a smaller portion of its resources to the task. Its political stability has enabled the country to focus on external threats to national security and all but ignore internal threats, while its great wealth has allowed it to spend over one trillion dollars on national security since the end of World War II without seriously neglecting the social needs of its people.

FORCE EMPLOYMENT DOCTRINE

The force employment doctrine of the United States is spelled out annually in the report of the secretary of defense to the Congress. This document, which is known throughout the government as the Posture Statement, is presented to the Congress in January of each year as a justification for the current Department of Defense (DoD) budget. From time to time throughout the year, the doctrines set forth in the Posture Statement are expanded upon or clarified by speeches and other public statements of the president and members of the national security apparatus. Nonetheless, the annual posture statements remain the basic source for U.S. force employment doctrine.

In theory, national security objectives, policy, force structure, and employment doctrine should be interdependent. The force structure ought to be configured and the employment doctrine ought to be designed to support the prescribed policy. On the other hand, the policy is not created in a vacuum. At any given time it is constrained by the forces already in existence or the forces the nation is willing to develop and procure. In practice, the fit among policy, structure, and doctrine is rarely perfect; however, these elements are usually connected, albeit loosely. With this caveat in mind, I shall review, as an example, the policy assumptions under which the national security policy of the Carter administration was developed and assess the fit among the policy, force structure, and employment doctrine.

In their first months in office, administrations normally develop a statement of national security policy objectives that are to be used as a basic guide in formulating force posture throughout the duration of the administration. The national security policy objectives and assumptions of the Carter administration are contained in a document known as Presidential Document 18 (PD-18), which was promulgated in August 1977. Within the Department of Defense, the objectives and assumptions of PD-18 were operationalized in a comprehensive program document known as the Consolidated Guidance (CG). This document, which is prepared annually by the Assistant Secretary of Defense for Program Analysis and Evaluation (PA&E), is circulated in draft form throughout the Pentagon in January and February of each year and is presented to the President each April. Although both PDs and CGs are classified documents, there are usually enough references to them in the posture statements and public utterances of administration officials to reveal their contents.[40]

According to PD-18 and the Consolidated Guidance, the military forces supported by the Carter defense program budget were to be configured for both deterrence and war fighting. These forces were to be designed to deter four specific contingencies: nuclear attacks on the United States and its allies, principally by the Soviet Union; conventional attacks by the Warsaw Pact nations on Western Europe; smaller contingencies in areas where the United States has vital interests and in which conflict could precede, and even set off, a crisis or conflagration in Western Europe; and disruption of the main sea and air lines of communication to American allies in Europe and Northeast Asia.

Deterrence of nuclear war is the fundamental objective of U.S. national security policy. It requires that the United States have the capability to carry out a true, countervailing strategy.[41] This strategy requires that, whatever the nature of the attacks that might be made against the United States, the country should possess the capability to respond in such a way that the enemy can have no expectation of achieving any rational objective—no illusion of making any gain without offsetting losses. Achievement of such a strategy requires the attainment of four general conditions.

1. The United States must have forces in sufficient numbers and quality that they can:
   a. survive a well-executed surprise attack (first strike);
   b. react with the timing needed to assure the necessary deliberation and control;
   c. penetrate any enemy defenses; and
   d. destroy their designated targets.
2. The United States must have the redundancy and diversity built into its forces to insure against the failure of any one component, to permit the cross-targeting of key enemy facilities, and to complicate the enemy's defenses as well as his attack.
3. American forces must have targeting flexibility, that is, they must be capable of covering, or being withheld from, a substantial list of both hard targets (missile silos, command bunkers, and nuclear weapons storage items) and soft targets (cities and industrial sites).
4. The United States must also possess a survivable command, control, and communications network; weapons with high accuracy and low yield; and some measure of civil defense evacuation capability. (In the view of the administration, the Defense Department had sufficient forces to execute this "countervailing" strategy and thus insure deterrence for the foreseeable future.)

The general purpose, or conventional, forces of the United States are configured primarily to handle the strong and growing military power of the Communist bloc in Europe. These forces must be capable of handling two types of operations. First, the primary mission of American nonnuclear forces is to be able to conduct, along with the forces of its NATO allies, a large-scale, intense, conventional war in Central Europe of relatively short duration against the Soviet Union and its Warsaw Pact allies. In short, the mission is to resist a blitzkrieg attack by the Communist forces in Europe for up to thirty days. Second, the nonnuclear forces must be capable of responding effectively and simultaneously to a minor war or contingency in an area like the Persian Gulf, because conflict in that area could undermine the situation in Europe.

In the view of the Carter administration, American general purpose forces were not equipped to handle the European scenario. Both PD-18 and the Consolidated Guidance therefore advised the components of DoD to plan on a 3 percent real growth in the level of defense spending and to give priority to those forces that could be used on the central front in NATO. The Carter administration argued that by 1983 the NATO forces would be able to conduct an intensive war in Europe for up to thirty days.

The strategic nuclear and general purpose policies of the Carter administration reflected both continuity with and change from the policies of previous years. The expression *countervailing strategy,* as applied to strategic policy, was new. However, the concept was not entirely new. Since the early 1960s the keystone of U.S. strategic nuclear policy has been an assured second-strike capability, that is, the ability to inflict unacceptable damage upon an enemy who might attack the United States first. Until the early 1970s, U.S. policy had been one of assured destruction through maintaining the capability to direct massive attacks primarily against population and industry (a countervalue strategy). However, during the Nixon administration the Defense Department developed the capability to engage in a controlled or limited nuclear exchange and to attack hard targets (a counterforce strategy) as well as soft targets. For its part, the Carter administration formally acknowledged limited nuclear war-fighting options in PD-59, a document approved in the summer of 1980.

What was new about the countervailing strategy was that it dropped the criteria of balance or sufficiency or essential equivalence as force-sizing criteria. Previously, the United States configured its strategic forces not only so that they could carry out their missions, but also so that they would be perceived to be equal to those of the country's principal adversary, the Soviet Union. For example, in 1978, Secretary of Defense Brown told Congress that he could not see how we could do otherwise than to insist on and maintain essential equivalence with the Soviet Union in strategic offensive capabilities.[42] By "essential equivalence," he meant the achievement of four general conditions: that the Soviets do not see their strategic nuclear forces as usable instruments for political leverage, diplomatic coercion, or military superiority; that nuclear stability, especially in crisis, is maintained; that any advantages in force characteristics or configuration enjoyed by the Soviets are offset by other U.S. advantages; and that the U.S. posture is not in fact (and is not perceived to be) inferior in performance to Soviet forces.

The policy of equipping U.S. general purpose forces primarily to wage a short, intensive, conventional war on the central front in Europe reflected a change in emphasis from the post-Vietnam policies of previous administrations. This change can be demonstrated in two ways. First, while both the Nixon and Ford administrations were concerned about resisting a Communist attack in Europe, they did not give the same overwhelming priority to the short, intensive war scenario on the central front in Europe. Presidents Nixon and Ford were equally concerned with maintaining the capability for conducting a longer war and for conducting operations on the northern and southern flanks of NATO and opening up a second front in the Pacific. Second, the "half-war," or minor contingency—the Persian Gulf scenario—was not necessarily NATO related. The general purpose forces of the Nixon and Ford administrations planned to deal simultaneously with a European war and a half-war in Northeast Asia, which might or might not be related to the conflict in Europe.

As were those of previous administrations, the force employment doctrines of the Carter administration for both nuclear and nonnuclear forces were attacked as being both too demanding and not demanding enough. Some critics of the strategic doctrine argue that deterrence could be achieved through the maintenance of a much smaller force—for example, 100 land-based and 400 sea-based missiles. Those holding this view note that one Poseidon submarine contains enough firepower to destroy the fifty largest cities in the USSR.[43] Proponents of minimum deterrence usually feel that it is sheer folly to talk about conducting limited nuclear wars. In their view, once the nuclear threshold is breached, the dreaded holocaust will occur.[44]

Those who maintained that the Carter doctrine for strategic nuclear forces was not demanding enough argued that superiority, not equivalence, is the only sure way to deter the Soviets or to win a nuclear war with them. Proponents of nuclear superiority are uncomfortable with the current Soviet lead in the number of missiles, and the total throw-weight and destructive power of the forces.[45] They feel that the Russians are likely to try to exploit their advantages diplomatically and militarily. These individuals note that Soviet military writers constantly talk about conducting and winning nuclear wars and that the Soviets have invested substantial resources in civil defense.

The force employment doctrine of the Carter administration for conventional forces was also criticized on two counts. On the one hand, the administration was criticized for not doing enough to maintain the balance in Central Europe. Proponents of this view pointed to the advantages of the Warsaw Pact in tactical nuclear weapons, personnel, tanks, tactical aircraft, and armored vehicles.[46]

On the other hand, the NATO first strategy was criticized for "putting too many eggs into one basket." Proponents of this view argue that since the American people have never in peacetime been willing to pay the full cost of providing the forces necessary to support the nation's military strategy, the United States ought to compensate, as it has in the past, by developing flexible forces—forces capable of being used in more than one place and for many purposes. In their view, the force employment doctrine of the Carter administration would have brought about the worst of all possible worlds. The NATO emphasis was not sufficient to offset the Warsaw Pact build-up, while the lack of flexibility prevented the United States from employing its military forces effectively to achieve its objectives in non-NATO areas like the Arabian (or Persian) Gulf. In response to this criticism, the Carter Doctrine announced early in 1980 led to the creation of a "quick reaction" or "rapid deployment" force that could be sent to trouble spots. Indeed, in his January 1980 State of the Union Address, President Carter asserted: "An attempt by any outside force to gain control of the Persian Gulf region will be regarded as an assault on the vital interests of the United States of America and such an assault will be repelled by any means necessary, including military force."

For its part, the new Reagan administration that assumed office in January 1981 committed itself to a strong national defense. Although at this writing the precise lines of the Reagan defense policy have not been definitely elaborated, the administration does appear committed to higher defense outlays for both strategic and conventional force modernization, improved readiness, and increased compensation for military personnel. On the other hand, substantially higher defense outlays may conflict with other commitments such as reducing the overall size of the federal budget and cutting taxes.

The defense decision-making process

EXECUTIVE BRANCH

Within the executive branch of the federal government, decisions affecting national security objectives, strategy, policy, and force employment are made in two principal forums: the National Security Council (NSC) system and the defense budget process. The goal of these two processes is to develop a force structure that supports the policy of a given administration. The best way to accomplish this task is to ensure that the military experts make meaningful inputs, but that they do not dominate the process (where civilian leaders maintain control of the process). When such a situation prevails, it is normally referred to as a civil-military balance.

The NSC system.[47] Although the organization varies from administration to administration, the National Security Council structure employed by the Carter administration is included here as an example. As indicated in figure 2, the system was divided into three main parts: the council itself; the two council committees—the Policy Review Committee (PRC) and the Special Coordination Committee (SCC); and the interdepartmental and ad hoc groups. In addition, at least two interagency committees were appended to the system on an informal but more or less permanent basis: one to monitor U.S.-Soviet activities and the other to keep track of the SALT negotiations. If they were displayed in figure 2, these two interagency committees would fall somewhere below the PRC and SCC but above the interdepartmental and ad hoc groups.

Issues or problems for NSC consideration can be proposed by a civilian or military member of the national security bureaucracy, with presidential approval sometimes being required before the issue is placed into the NSC process. In the Carter administration, the process began with the promulgation of a Presidential Review Memorandum (PRM), which defined the problem, set a deadline, and assigned it to either the PRC or the SCC. In addition, if the issue were assigned to the PRC, the PRM designated the chairman. (As indicated in figure 2, the SCC was always chaired by the assistant to the president for national security affairs, while the chairmanship of the PRC rotated according to the issue area.) Normally policy issues without short-term deadlines were analyzed by the PRC, while "short-fuse," or crisis, issues and arms control questions have been handled by the SCC. In 1977 and 1978 President Carter approved the promulgation of 44 PRMs, two-thirds of which were handled by the PRC. A list of these presidentially directed studies for 1977–78 is contained in table 2; even though issues change over time, this table is included as an example of the kinds of questions considered by the National Security Council.

The PRM was first analyzed by an interdepartmental or ad hoc group headed by someone at the assistant secretary or deputy assistant secretary level. For example, the interdepartmental group that worked on PRM-10, the comprehensive review of U.S. military force posture, was headed by the deputy assistant secretary of defense for national security affairs,

Figure 2. The NSC system

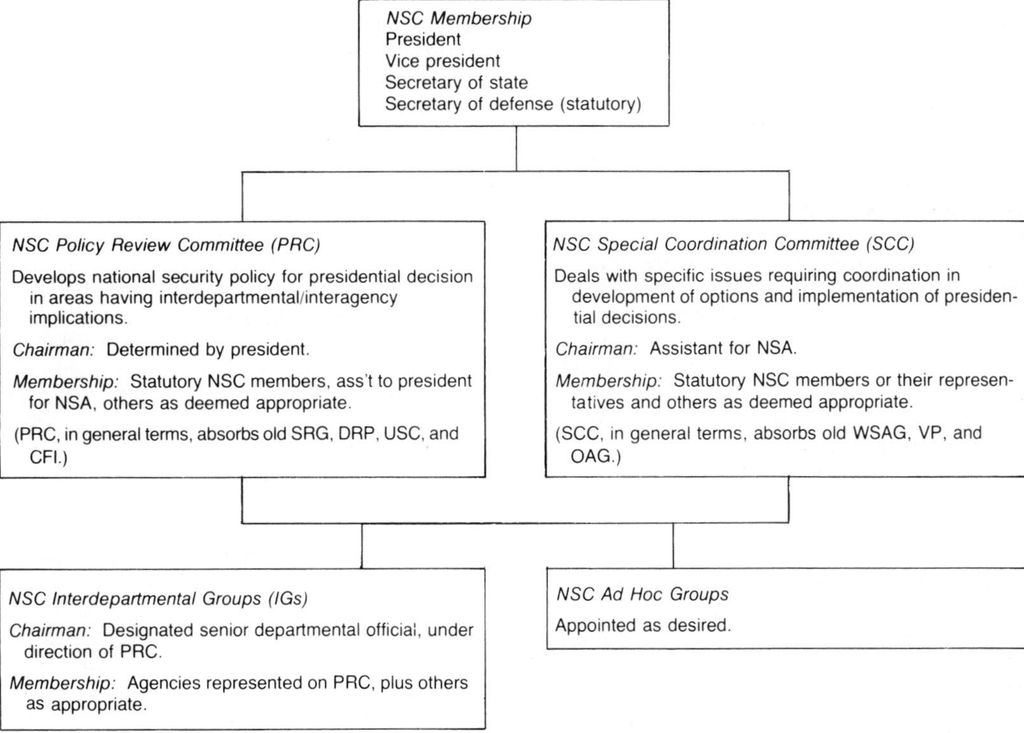

Source: PD/NSC-2, 20 January 1977

Table 2
NSC studies, 1977–78

PRM	Subject	PRM	Subject
1	Panama	26	ABM treaty review
2	SALT	27	Chemical warfare
3	Middle East	28	Human rights
4	South Africa and Rhodesia	29	Review of classification
5	Cyprus/Aegean	30	Terrorism
6	MBFR	31	Export control of U.S. technology
7	International summit	32	Civil defense
8	North/South strategy	33	Science and technology in developing countries
9	Review European issues	34	U.S. policy in North Africa
10	Net assessment force posture	35	International communications policy
11	Intelligence structure/mission	36	Soviet/Cuban presence in Africa
12	Arms transfer policy review	37	Chemical weapons
13	Korea	38	Long-range theater nuclear capabilities and arms control (C)
14	Philippine base negotiations	39	Economic implications of a Middle East peace settlement
15	Nuclear proliferation	40	Military survey teams
16	Nuclear testing	41	Review of U.S. policies toward Mexico
17	U.S. policy: Latin America	42	(Sensitive subject)
18	Law of the sea	43	(Sensitive subject)
19	Micronesian status	44	Export of oil and gas production technology to the USSR
20	Cooperation with France		
21	Horn of Africa		
22	National integrated telecom protection policy		
23	Coherent U.S. space policy		
24	People's Republic of China		
25	Arms control in Indian Ocean		

while the ad hoc group working on PRM-2 was headed by David Aaron, the deputy assistant for national security affairs. When the interdepartmental or ad hoc group completed its work, it forwarded its recommendations to the PRC or SCC for review. After holding a formal PRC or SCC meeting on the subject, a committee recommendation was made to the President. On some occasions President Carter accepted the recommendations as presented, on others he consulted with individuals on the NSC staff before making a decision, and on still other occasions he convened a meeting of the full NSC. Most of the decisions were made by means of the first two methods. In his first two years in office the president held only ten meetings of the full NSC.[48] When the president decided on a course of action, a Presidential Decision (PD) is promulgated. A list of these directives for 1977 is included in table 3 as an example of the kinds of national security decisions made by the president in a given year.

Formally, the NSC system provides for an almost ideal civil-military balance. The chairman of the Joint Chiefs of Staff (JCS) is an adviser to the NSC itself and in the Carter administration participated in all the meetings of the PRC and SCC. In addition, representatives of the JCS and the individual military services had an input to the analyses of the interdepartmental and ad hoc groups. However, the council itself, the PRC, the SCC, the interagency committees, and the interdepartmental groups were all chaired by civilian leaders. None of the groups within the NSC was under the control of a military officer.

The reality, however, is somewhat different. In various ways the impact of the military participation in the NSC process was reduced. Indeed, many important issues were handled outside the formal NSC apparatus. Thirty PRMs were issued during President Carter's first six months in office, seventeen of these in his first week as president. Subsequently, the president relied less and less on formal mechanisms to reach his national security decisions. The main coordinating mechanism for national security affairs turned out to be a Friday morning breakfast in the cabinet room with the president, Vice President Walter Mondale, Secretary of State Cyrus Vance, Secretary of Defense Harold Brown, and presidential assistants Zbigniew Brzezinski and Hamilton Jordan. No member of the JCS was in attendance. As a result, on some occasions, decisions were made without seeking or permitting JCS input. One such case involved the issue of the length of a comprehensive test ban treaty with the USSR. In mid-1978 the president made a decision to accept a Soviet proposal for a five-year ban, apparently without consulting the chairman of the JCS or any other uniformed military officer.[49] (Eventually, on the advice of then Secretary of Energy Schlesinger, who also had not been consulted, the president changed his position.)

Another case involved the PRM-12 analysis of arms transfers. In making the decision to reduce the volume of American arms transfers, the president and his advisers were influenced by CIA data that appeared to demonstrate that U.S. arms sales were twice as high as those of the Soviet Union. They did not ask for (nor did they receive) a Defense Intelligence Agency study that showed that the two figures were not comparable because the U.S. figures included the cost of advisory and support teams, logistic and infrastructure facilities, support equipment, construction, and spares, while the CIA cost data on the Soviet arms transfers included only the cost of the major combat equipment itself.[50]

The defense budget process. Figure 3 outlines the defense budget process as it existed under the Ford administration; the system was modified somewhat during the Carter administration, as is shown in figure 4. Comparison of these two charts makes it appear that only minor changes occurred, that is, some documents were renamed and others eliminated. The charts indicate that the policy and planning and the planning and programming guidance memoranda drawn up by the Office of the Secretary of Defense (OSD) were replaced by the Consolidated Guidance (CG), while the Joint Strategic Objectives

Table 3
Presidential directives, 1977

PD/NSC	
1	Establishment of presidential review and directive series/NSC
2	The National Security Council system
3	Disposition of national security decision memoranda
4	The law of the sea policy review
5	Southern Africa
6	Cuba (not circulated; limited access)
7	No information available
8	Nuclear nonproliferation
9	Army special operations field office in Berlin
10	Instructions for the tenth session of the Standing Consultative Commission
11	Micronesian status negotiations
12	U.S. policy in Korea
13	Conventional arms transfer policy
14	Disposition of national security action memoranda and national security decision memoranda
15	Chemical warfare
16	Law of the sea
17	Reorganization of the intelligence community
18	PRM-10
19	Intelligence structure and mission
20	SALT
21	Policy toward Eastern Europe
22	ABM treaty review
23	Standing Consultative Commission
24	Telecommunications protection policy
25	Scientific or technological experiments with possible large-scale adverse environmental effects and launch of nuclear system into space

Figure 3. Ford DoD management system

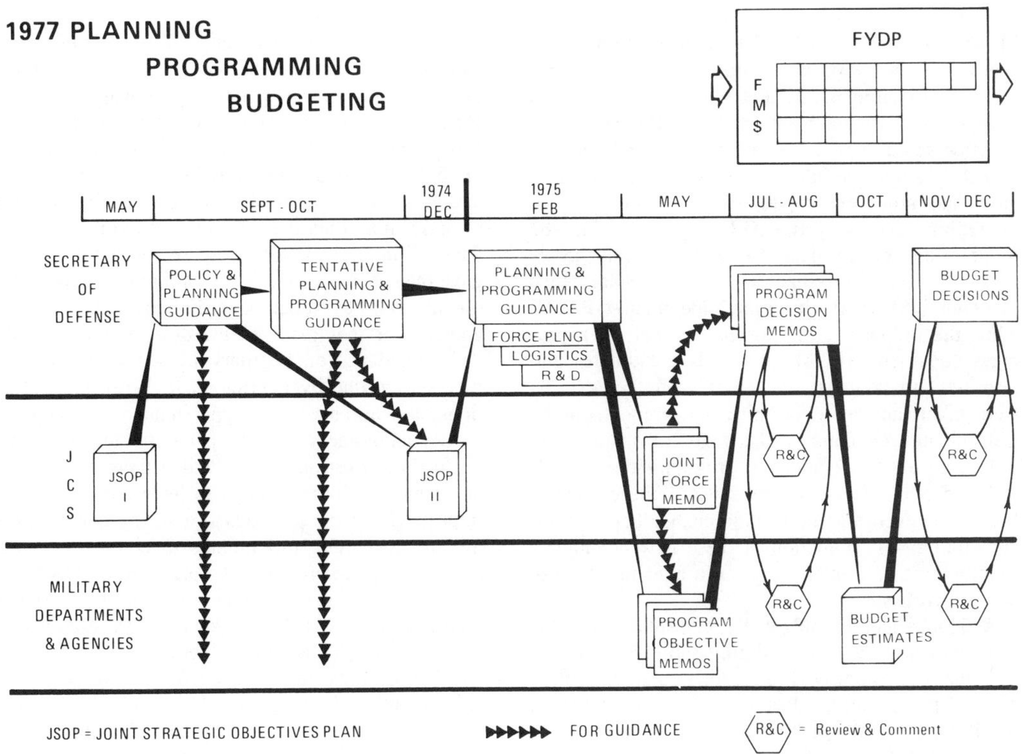

Figure 4. Carter DoD management system

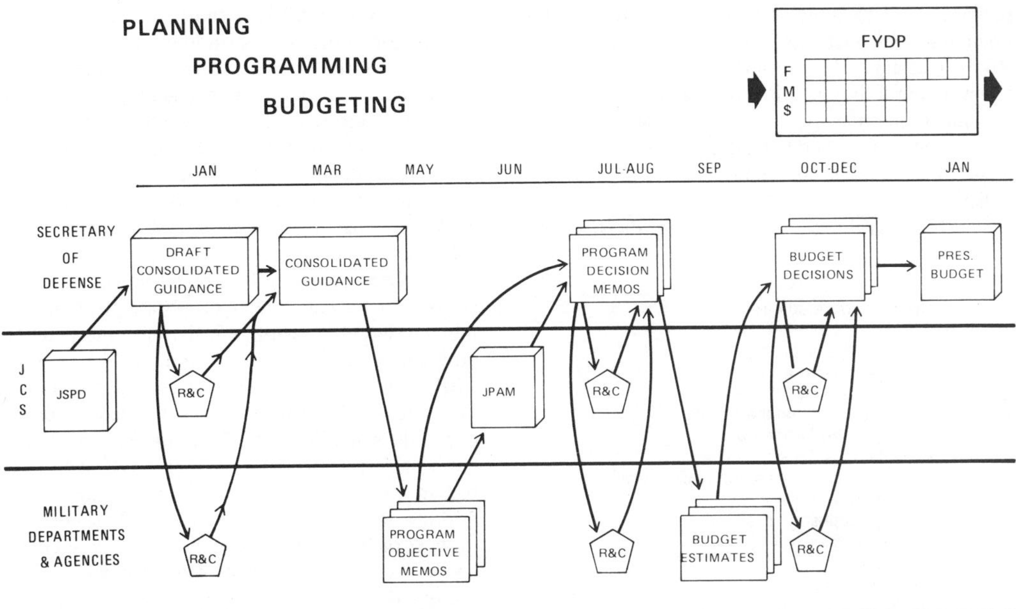

Plan (JSOP), volumes I and II, and the Joint Force Memorandum (JFM) were supplanted by the Joint Strategic Planning Document (JSPD) and the Joint Program Assessment Memorandum (JPAM).

As depicted in figure 4, in the Carter administration the various military elements would appear to have had numerous inputs to the planning, programming, and budgeting (PPB) process, but the program and budget decisions were made at the secretary of defense (civilian) level. The JCS drew up a planning (JSPD) and program document (JPAM), while the military services prepared their own program documents (POM) and budget estimates and priorities. In addition, the chiefs and the services were given ample opportunity to comment on the Consolidated Guidance and ask for reconsideration (reclama) of the secretary's programmatic (PDM) and budgetary decisions. In spite of these appearances, however, a great deal did change between administrations. Introduction of these new documents and some other subtle changes did alter the defense budget process.[51]

As is indicated in table 4, the Consolidated Guidance, which in the Carter administration was drafted in January and approved in April, was an extremely detailed programming document. It covered fifteen specific areas of the defense budget and put down in the minutest detail what the military services were to procure in each of these fifteen areas over the next five fiscal years. In fact, some have argued that the Consolidated Guidance did not provide an explicit policy or a clear strategic underpinning for its programming guidance other than reference back to PD-18 (see table 3) and other policy guidance. By contrast, the Policy and Planning and Programming documents that the Consolidated Guidance replaced were much more general in nature, but did attempt to relate force structure to overall national security and policy.

The JCS and the individual services did have the opportunity to comment on a draft version of the Consolidated Guidance before it was finalized; however, for two reasons, their impact was negligible. First, since there was no separate policy section in the Consolidated Guidance, it was difficult to challenge on policy grounds. Second, because of time constraints, it was difficult for the services and the JCS to make more than marginal changes to the Consolidated Guidance. Indeed, the secretary of defense gave them only two weeks to send in their comments on this 500-page document. For example, the JCS and the services received the draft of the Consolidated Guidance on February 12, 1979. Their comments were due by February 28. As in most situations, the initiative and upper hand were with the individual or agency that prepared the document, but when time constraints were added there was almost no chance for other groups to have any significant impact. Under the previous system, by contrast, the military had three full months to comment on the policy and planning guidance prepared by OSD.

Table 4
Draft consolidated guidance, FY 1981-85

A	Overview and summary
B	Strategic nuclear forces
C	Forces for NATO
D	Forces for Asia and the Pacific
E	Forces for the Middle East
F	Forces for the Persian Gulf
G	Theater nuclear forces, the nuclear stockpile, and chemical warfare
H	General purpose forces
I	Mobility programs
J	Land forces
K	Tactical air forces
L	Naval forces
M	Logistics planning and programming guidance
N	Manpower
O	Communications, command, control, and intelligence
P	Research, development, and acquisition

The professional military input to the defense budget process was also weakened by the elimination of the JSOP. Written in the absence of concern for fiscal constraints, the JSOP contained detailed threat assessments and outlined the forces that the JCS felt were necessary to deal adequately with that threat. While the JCS objective force was about twice the size that could be afforded, it did provide a useful benchmark for the remainder of the process. By contrast, under the Carter administration, the JSOP was replaced by the JSPD, a short executive summary that described the JCS position on a planning or reduced risk force—that is, a force no more than ten billion dollars above certain budgetary limits. The difference between the two documents can be illustrated by comparing the JSOP objective force level for navy carriers with the carrier level in the JSPD: the former called for a total of twenty large-deck carriers, while the latter requested only fifteen (the actual level was thirteen).[52]

The charts depicting the budget processes also do not take into account completely the impact of grafting zero-based budgeting (ZBB) onto the planning, programming, and budgeting system (PPBS). While ZBB did not live up to the president's expectations in the Defense Department or other federal agencies, one of the side effects of ZBB in the Pentagon was to diminish further the role of the military leaders in the budget process. The ultimate rank ordering, or prioritizing, of defense programs was done not by the services or JCS, but rather at the secretary of defense level. Thus, the secretary of defense can kill a high-priority JCS program not by arguing against the program on its merits, but simply by giving it a lower ranking than funds for other projects.[53]

The attempt to prevent the JCS from establishing a benchmark for evaluating the administration's defense budget carried over into the congressional phase as well. In the Nixon-Ford years, the annual Military Posture Statement, made by the chairman of the JCS to Congress, would contain eight measures of the strategic balance and six of the general purpose forces balance. These balances clearly demonstrated that the military posture of the United States vis-à-vis the Soviet Union was deteriorating. In December 1978, Secretary of Defense Brown eliminated these fourteen balances from the JCS Military Posture Statement. Indeed, the statement that reached the Congress in January 1979 was a bland overview without much substance or real meaning.

THE CONGRESS

Congress becomes involved in the defense decision-making process in two principal ways. First, it votes on funds for the defense program. Second, it places some restrictions on how the military power of the United States can be used. It can do this through the appropriations process or through separate substantive legislation.

In the post-Vietnam period, the Congress has attempted to play a more active role in the defense decision-making process. During the Nixon-Ford administration, the legislative branch of the federal government tried to apply a brake to the activist national security policies of the administration. The legislators attempted to accomplish this goal by pruning over fifty billion dollars from the defense budget requests of the executive, by restricting the areas of the world to which military force could be applied, and by limiting the time that the president could employ U.S. military forces overseas.

After President Carter took office, some elements within the legislature tried to prod the executive branch into doing more in the area of national security. Congress used its power of the purse to push the executive branch into accelerating such programs as aircraft carriers, the XM-1 main battle tank, and the MX mobile ICBM, while cutting back on other programs.[54]

Although it is difficult to measure the exact influence of the legislature on policy, it seems fair to conclude that even in the post-Vietnam period Congress has had only a marginal impact on policy and force structure. It did not affect to any significant degree the Nixon doctrine, the one-and-one-half-war strategy, or the strategic sufficiency concept of presidents Nixon and Ford. Although the votes were often close, particularly in the Senate, the Nixon administration received funding for such controversial and expensive systems as Trident and the B-1. Similarly, Congress had relatively little impact upon the countervailing strategy or the NATO emphasis of the Carter administration. Moreover, Congress could not force President Carter to build the B-1 manned bomber.

BUREAUCRATIC POLITICS

Prior to Graham Allison's pioneering work on the Cuban Missile Crisis,* decisions affecting national security or defense policy were thought by many to involve very little bureaucratic politics. As Allison himself noted, it is the U.S. public's image that it is un-American to play bureaucratic politics with national security. Americans need to believe that defense decisions are made by the president unilaterally and rationally.[55]

In the decade since the first publication of Allison's analysis, however, many people have come to view bureaucratic politics as the primary determinant of national security policy outcomes within the American political system. What Allison referred to as the rational and organizational models, or what John Steinbruner referred to as the cybernetic model,[56] are thought by others to have almost no bearing on the outcome of the policy process.

The truth, as in most cases, lies somewhere in between. Bureaucratic politics do affect all decisions, even those involving vital national security interests. However, rational, organizational, and cybernetic factors are also involved. The mix of these factors depends upon such things as the type of the decision and the background and experiences of the players. For example, political considerations are normally more important in choosing contractors for individual weapons systems, while rational factors become more important in deciding on force employment doctrines.

Choices made by individuals within the policy processes of the executive branch are affected by both domestic and international considerations. Chief among the domestic considerations is the impact of certain key members of Congress. Basic decisions are made and weapons contractors are chosen with an eye to their potential reception on Capitol Hill. In addition, defense decisions are often influenced by their impact upon domestic economic policy. For example, because the defense budget is controllable,[57]† it can be used relatively easily to affect such things as the money supply, the size of the deficit, and the rates of employment and inflation. Policy makers, thus, often vary the defense total regardless of international events.

A second domestic influence upon defense decision makers is the mass communications media. Adverse comments by writers and columnists appearing

*See Allison's *Essence of Decision* (Boston: Little Brown and Company, 1971) and his "Conceptual Models and the Cuban Missile Crisis," *American Political Science Review* 63, no. 3 (September 1969). Cf. Allison and Morton Halperin, "Bureaucratic Politics: A Paradigm and Some Policy Implications," *World Politics* 24 (Spring 1972).—Ed.

†A greater proportion of the Defense Department budget involves programs that can be increased or decreased in expenditure compared to other agencies that administer programs such as welfare that are fixed by law.—Ed.

in such widely read newspapers as the *Washington Post* and the *New York Times* influence the decision-making process. In addition, leaks to the media before a decision often have an impact on the final product. It is no accident that the secretary of defense begins each work day with a review of *Current News,* a compilation of news items of interest to the Defense Department.

External influences such as alliances also affect the choices made by U.S. policy makers. The pledge by President Carter to increase the size of the U.S. defense budget by 3 percent a year in real terms was brought about by pressure from members of the NATO alliance.[58] Decisions on forward deployment of U.S. forces in Europe and the Pacific are strongly affected by such factors as American membership in NATO, the country's defense treaty with Japan, and the U.S. understanding with Israel.

Disputes among bureaucratic agencies on national security issues are normally resolved the same way as domestic disputes, that is, through negotiation, bargaining, and compromise among the concerned agencies. Some contentious issues do reach the president for a final decision, but this is the exception rather than the rule. Disputes among the services are normally resolved within the JCS system through compromise. Conflicts among the military and civilian elements of the Defense Department are normally resolved through the intervention of the secretary of defense or his deputy, while disputes among the Defense Department and other agencies are resolved through the NSC system, primarily at the PRC or SCC level.

Which actors prevail in policy disputes is a result not only of the individual's power base and access to the key decision makers but also of his or her skill in exploiting these resources and his or her expertise in the area. In the 1950s, the views of Secretary of State John Foster Dulles usually prevailed in serious disputes among the agencies. During the Kennedy-Johnson years Secretary of Defense Robert McNamara was the dominant figure. Henry Kissinger, the executive assistant for national security affairs and later the secretary of state, was clearly the key actor in the Nixon-Ford era. Secretary of Defense Harold Brown appears to have been the first among equals in the defense policy processes of the Carter administration.

IDIOSYNCRATIC FACTORS

Throughout the post–World War II period, the personalities and backgrounds of the key decision makers have had a profound impact upon the defense decision-making process. Indeed, as discussed above, the personality of the individuals, rather than the office per se, has determined the key actors in the different administrations.

The president is usually the key actor in the policy process. Even if he himself does not make a decision, he sets the broad guidelines or the tone or the atmosphere in which the decisions are made. His presence is felt throughout the process. The impact of the personality and ideological background of the chief executive have again been vividly demonstrated in the case of President Carter.

With less background and fewer preformed ideas about national security matters than any of his immediate predecessors, President Carter nonetheless put his stamp on the policy process and policy outputs. He wanted an "open administration" and, even in the area of national security policy, he attempted to maintain this commitment. Similarly, throughout his administration, President Carter has held weekly breakfast meetings with his national security advisers and met more frequently with the Joint Chiefs of Staff than any recent president.[59]

Mr. Carter took office feeling that he had a moral obligation to keep his campaign promises and to do something about what he perceived to be a dangerous arms race. The impact of these two factors can be seen in the outputs of his defense decision-making process. Early in the administration, as part of an attempt to fulfill campaign promises, the B-1 was canceled, a Korean troop withdrawal was commenced, a slowdown in the rate of growth in defense spending was undertaken, a human rights policy was proclaimed, and an attempt was made to reduce the volume of arms sales to Third World countries. The president's moral imperative to slow the arms race was reflected in his comprehensive proposal to the Soviets in March 1977 for a 20 percent cutback in existing levels of strategic offensive weapons and a complete freeze on modernization and testing.[60]

Likewise, the personality and background of Presidents Nixon, Johnson, Kennedy, and Eisenhower influenced the way in which each structured his National Security Council decision-making process, ranging from the loose, free-wheeling, informal Kennedy-Johnson arrangements to the very structured approaches of Nixon and Eisenhower. These same personality factors contributed to the desire of Presidents Nixon and Johnson to "see it through" in Vietnam and, by contrast, to the apparent willingness of Presidents Eisenhower and Kennedy to allow Vietnam to fall, if necessary.[61]

Nonetheless, personality and position, while important, are often constrained by systemic and other realities. The Soviet build-up forced President Carter to back away from his campaign promise to cut five to seven billion dollars from the defense budget, while rapidly rising inflation and large Congressional cuts made it difficult for him to fulfill completely his promise to the country's NATO allies to raise defense spending by 3 percent a year in real terms. Both Mr. Carter and his immediate predecessors have been limited in the size of the armed forces that they can develop due to the end of conscription and the consequent need to compete for volunteers in a competitive market with a declining labor pool. All presidents must contend with opposition from bureaucratic elements within the government. In part to obtain the support of the Joint Chiefs of Staff for the SALT II agreement, for example, President Carter authorized construction of a multibillion dollar MX mobile missile system. Another constraint is that in the aftermath of the Vietnam War, it has been difficult for American presidents to consider direct military intervention in the Third World as a viable option. Finally, moral and ethical concerns of certain segments within the American polity limit the president's ability to use covert means to accomplish policy goals, while laws, like the War Powers Act, make it difficult to use even shows of military force.

Recurring issues: defense policy outputs

CIVIL-MILITARY RELATIONS

Up until the era of World War II, the United States did not have a large standing military force. It maintained a small professional cadre and augmented it during wartime with reservists and conscripts—that is, citizen soldiers. However, in the three decades since the end of World War II, the United States has maintained a large military, first through conscription and now on a volunteer basis.

Not surprisingly, during this same period, there has been an intense concern about civil-military relations. This concern has focused not simply on the problem of maintaining effective civilian control, but on the impact of military concerns upon the policy process, for example, the power of the so-called military-industrial complex.[62]

Some analysts, like Samuel Huntington, have argued that the best way to preserve civilian control with a large standing military is through objective means, such as by establishing an autonomous and politically neutral military profession that would be at once self-policing and isolated from society.[63] However, the consensus among Americans is that subjective control is the preferred option—achieving control by civilianizing the military so that it in effect mirrors civilian society. This is accomplished through a rapid turnover in the membership of armed forces and extensive education programs for careerists, especially those in the officer corps.[64]

The concerns of the American military establishment (except for the National Guard) are primarily external. The professional military compete within the internal decision-making processes to gain personnel and materiel to deal with the external threat. Traditionally, the uniformed military has not reacted favorably to suggestions that it perform even humanitarian domestic roles on a regularized basis because of a fear that these functions would degrade combat readiness.

Even in the era of the all-volunteer force (AVF), the American military prefers to maintain the citizen-soldier concept and seeks to retain its identity with civilian society. Moreover, even without the draft, the aggregate force remains broadly representative of U.S. society. A report on the AVF published at the end of 1978 noted that in fiscal year 1977: (*a*) blacks comprised about 18 percent of active-duty personnel, (*b*) the twenty most populated states (which had 71 percent of the seventeen- to twenty-one-year-old population) provided 74 percent of the accession, while the top ten states (which had 52 percent of the population) provided 53 percent of the enlistees, and (*c*) both the upper and lower income levels were underrepresented, in about the same proportion as during conscription.[65]

However, beneath the surface there were some disturbing trends in the AVF. Blacks still comprised only 4 percent of the officer corps but 40 percent of the first-line combat forces. Moreover, new recruits increasingly viewed the military not as a calling or profession but as an occupation.[66]

Nonetheless, the American public still has a predominantly positive image of military service and a generally sympathetic view of the military. Public opinion polls consistently show the military as one of the most admired institutions in American society,[67] and career military officers are continually appointed to high government posts. For example, the Carter administration appointed retired military officers to the head of the Central Intelligence Agency, the Arms Control and Disarmament Agency, and the General Services Administration.

WEAPONS ACQUISITION

The United States spends $50 billion or more each year for the development and production of complex weapons systems, and has, in various stages of development, over $500 billion worth of new systems. This represents a significant amount of the nation's resources and will involve a significant commitment of federal expenditures in future years.

Because of the large amount of funds and large number of people involved, there has been a great concern over the process by which the DoD buys its weapons. Many people have argued that unnecessary weapons are procured and that poor management practices have driven up costs unnecessarily.[68] Reforms of the process have been suggested by everyone from the General Accounting Office (GAO) to Harvard Business School, but the criticisms still persist.

Policies currently governing the weapons systems acquisition processes are contained in directives from the Office of Management and Budget (OMB) and the Department of Defense. An OMB directive (circular no. A-109) establishes the policies to be followed by governmental agencies in the acquisition of major systems. This directive, which grew out of the recommendations proposed in 1972 by the Commission on Government Procurement, applies to: management of the acquisition system; analysis of missions; determination of mission needs; setting of program objectives; determination of requirements; planning and budgeting; funding; research; engineering, test, and development; test and evaluation; contracting; and production and management control.

OMB circular A-109 specifies that each agency acquiring systems should: ensure that the system fulfills mission needs, operates effectively, and otherwise demonstrates its justification for acquisition; ensure that competition exists between the new system and other similar systems; investigate trade-offs; provide strong checks and balances through test and evaluation, independent of developers; ensure agency planning, built on mission analysis results; develop an acquisition strategy for each program to ensure that competition is encouraged and guidelines are developed for evaluation and acceptance or rejection of proposals; maintain a capability to predict, review, and assess costs for development, test, and evaluation over the predicted life of the system; and appoint a program manager for each major acquisition program who is to be given budget guidance and a written charter of his or her authority, responsibility, and accountability.

According to the OMB circular, the key to an effective acquisition process is the agency's ability to determine and develop those needs required to perform its specific tasks based on its mission, reconciled with its overall capabilities, priorities, and resources. To achieve the most effective military posture, each service is required to identify mission area needs and to develop systems to meet those needs *at the right time*. Plans must also identify those systems for which future development or procurement can be canceled. As Secretary of Defense Brown noted: "DoD is looking for ways to respond more quickly to the threat while still being assured that the system program doesn't entail unwarranted technological, cost, or schedule risks."[69]

DoD has developed an elaborate process to ensure that it buys only needed weapons at the cheapest possible price. This process has two main steps.[70] The first step is the development of the Mission Element Need Statement (MENS). The MENS for each major new system describes succinctly the mission and justification for a new system, and must include: the mission area and needs in terms of tasks to be performed; an assessment of the projected threat through the time frame for which the capability is required; an identification of existing DoD capabilities to accomplish the mission; an assessment of the needs in terms of deficiencies, capabilities, and costs; statements of known constraints and alternative solutions; assessments of the impact of not acquiring the system; and a plan exploring competitive alternatives.

The second phase involves program reviews by the Defense Systems Acquisition Review Council (DSARC) at four milestones. These milestones are as follows:

Milestone 0—program initiation
- a. Service submits MENS to secretary of defense.
- b. Secretary states conditions under which the program may begin, if at all.

Milestone 1—demonstration and validation
- a. Competitive identification and exploration of alternative design concepts.
- b. Design concept plan prepared recommending preferred alternatives.
- c. DSARC reviews completed plan and makes recommendations to secretary.

Milestone 2—full-scale engineering
- a. Selection of alternative for full-scale engineering development.
- b. DSARC review.

Milestone 3—production and deployment

Figure 5 outlines the weapons system acquisition process just described. Obviously this is an idealized version. In reality no program ever flows that smoothly. Requirements often change as development continues, and information acquired during one stage of development does and should feed back to earlier phases. Specifications change, new components appear, performance does not conform to expectations, retesting is necessary, and other departures from plans are frequent.

Except for the need to import strategic materials and a limited number of parts, weapons system production for DoD is almost exclusively an American enterprise. At the present time there are more than 20,000 prime contractors and some 100,000 subcontractors engaged in defense work in the United States. Moreover, nearly 2 million people are employed in defense-related industry.

While every state in the union has some defense-related industry, the vast majority of weapons systems are produced by firms with headquarters or manufacturing plants in five major metropolitan areas: southern California, San Francisco, New York, Boston, and Washington, D.C. Moreover, some of America's largest corporations subsist largely on defense contracts. For example, 98 percent of the Lockheed Corporation's business is defense related, while General Dynamics does over four billion dollars a year in defense business.

Research and development of weapons systems for DoD is done almost exclusively within the United States, both in government and in private corporations. In FY 1980, for example, planned expenditures on R&D amounted to about 10 percent of the

Figure 5. The weapons systems acquisitions process

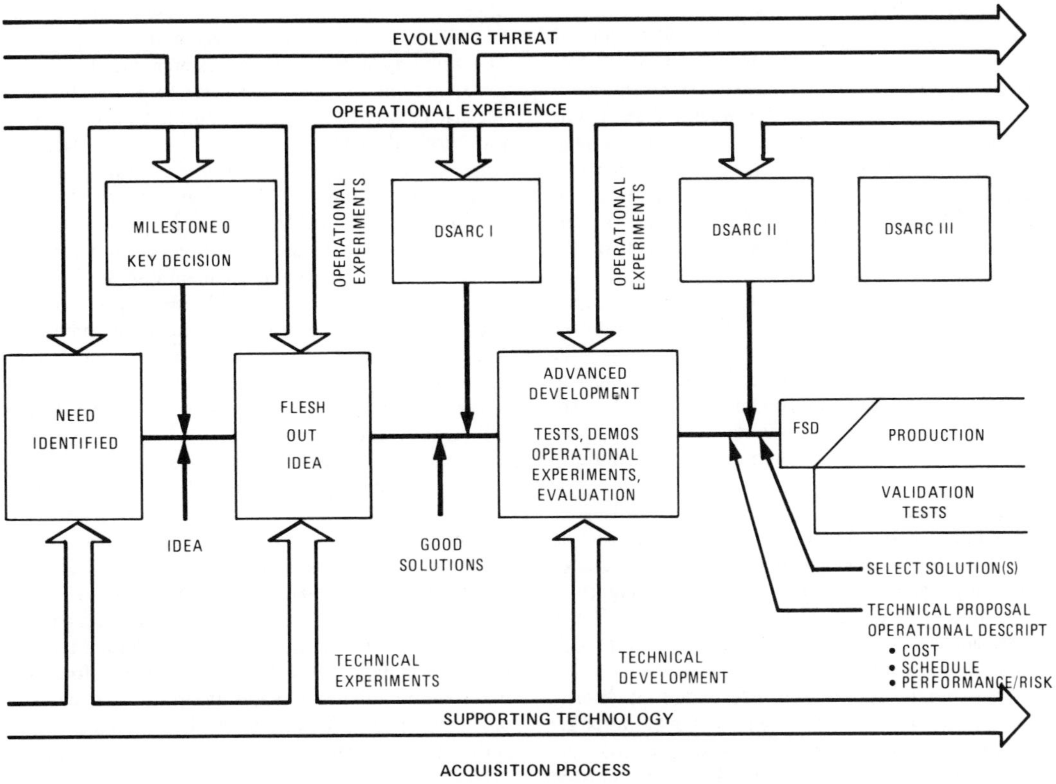

Source: OMB Circular A-109 and DoD Instruction 5000.1

entire defense budget. During the 1970s, the Defense Department spent over $100 billion in this area, a figure that amounts to about 40 percent of the total of all U.S. expenditures for R&D for this period. Total spending for weapons acquisition in FY 1980, on the order of $49 billion, equates to about 35 percent of the defense budget and 1.8 percent of the entire gross national product. Moreover, 40 percent of the nation's engineers and scientists direct their full-time attention to military research and development.

The tremendous impact of the development of a single large weapons system on the U.S. economy can be seen through an analysis of the potential benefits of the MX mobile missile program. If this $30 to $40 billion project is completed, it is estimated that approximately 130,000 new aerospace and supporting service jobs will be created nation-wide. In California alone the MX could create 46,000 new jobs and infuse $8.5 billion into the state's economy; in Washington it could mean 6,600 jobs and $350 million in revenues; in Colorado, 2,400 jobs and $119 million; and in Utah, 2,100 jobs and $90 million. New York, New Jersey, and Connecticut could realize up to $1 billion in revenues and 21,000 new jobs.

As indicated in table 1, the United States is becoming increasingly dependent upon foreign sources to supply the thirteen basic raw materials required for defense production. Thirty years ago this nation imported more than half of its required supply of four materials; ten years ago, the number increased to six. By 1985 the United States is expected to depend primarily on imports for its supply of nine of the basic raw materials, including such critical ones as iron, tin, and bauxite. By the end of this century, estimates are that the United States will be dependent upon foreign sources for the majority of its needs for twelve of these thirteen critical materials; the country will be self-sufficient only in phosphorus.

The main sources of supply for these essential materials are Third World countries. In time of war or national emergency, many of these sources of supply would probably prove to be unreliable if the interest of those nations did not coincide with those of the United States. As the Arab countries demonstrated in the 1973 mideast war, withholding of needed materials can be a powerful weapon. The United States can lessen its dependence somewhat through such methods as stockpiling, developing synthetics, and substitution, but these actions will not change the essential fact that the United States can now be held hostage by some smaller nations.

The United States engages in a limited amount of cooperative production with its NATO allies. Between 1956 and 1977, more than sixty-five coproduction agreements were signed between NATO countries and U.S. firms. Most of these agreements have increased the licensing of U.S.-developed weapons for production in allied countries, for example, the F-16, F-5A, and F-104 aircraft, ME-113 armored personnel carrier, and M-109A1 self-propelled 155 MM howitzer. However, on a few occasions, U.S. firms have been licensed to build European-developed systems, such as the Roland surface-to-air point defense missile and the AV-8B Harrier. The impetus behind these coproduction agreements has been the desire for standardization and interoperability of NATO weapons systems and for reduction of unit costs through production of larger quantities.

FORCE POSTURE

The military forces of the United States consist of two million active and about one million ready reservists. They are broken down into three categories: conventional, strategic, and theater nuclear. These forces are stationed on U.S. soil and forward deployed in many different parts of the globe.[71]

Conventional forces. Since the end of World War II, the United States has stationed a large number of military forces abroad, primarily in Europe and the Far East. In Central Europe, mostly in the Federal Republic of Germany, the United States currently maintains approximately 230,000 soldiers and air forces staffing combat and support elements capable of waging full-scale conventional and tactical nuclear war. These forces include five and two-thirds army division equivalents and eight air force fighter/attack wings. In the Mediterranean the dominant allied naval force is the U.S. Sixth Fleet, which, like its land and air counterparts, is a force in being and capable, on immediate notice, of conducting full-scale offensive and defensive operations, including amphibious operations. Throughout the western and northern Mediterranean littoral, the United States maintains in excess of 100 military facilities engaged in diverse missions ranging from logistics to intelligence-collecting activities.

The stationing of U.S. troops is not as extensive in the Far East in terms of the numbers of personnel assigned, but the geographic area covered is quite large. The air force currently maintains major bases in the Philippines, Okinawa, South Korea, Guam, and the Japanese main islands. Of these, three operate tactical fighter/attack wings (one in the Philippines and two in South Korea); the remainder are major command headquarters and support bases for the Strategic Air Command. Although Guam is not a foreign base in the strictest sense, it is the only strategic bomber base outside the continental United States. The primary U.S. Army presence in the Far East is the Second Infantry Division in South Korea. The withdrawal of this force was announced in early 1977, but the decision was later reversed, in part because of revised estimates of the size of the opposing North Korean force. As a result, the bulk of American forces are expected to remain in place for the immediate future.[72] The marines have one Marine Amphibious Force (MAF) in the Far East, which includes a division, a tactical air wing, and combat support units. This comprises about one-third of the active combat element of the Marine Corps. Rounding out the U.S. force structure in the Western Pacific is the U.S. Seventh Fleet. Like its opposite number in the Mediterranean, this fleet is the cutting edge of American naval forces and is on call to perform the full range of naval operations.

The Seventh and Sixth fleets are quite similar in structure. Both are built around two carrier task groups, but because of the larger area covered by the Seventh Fleet, it has a slightly larger number of surface combatants (nineteen as compared to fourteen) and 50 percent more attack submarines (six as compared to four). In addition, the amphibious capability is greater in the Pacific because the Third MAF is stationed in Japan. The Seventh Fleet therefore deploys two amphibious ready groups, while there is only one in the Mediterranean. This balance might shift, however, because a U.S. Fifth Fleet or a permanent naval presence may be established in the Indian Ocean around the Persian Gulf area. Seen as a force to protect vital U.S. interests in the Middle East, an Indian Ocean fleet would greatly tax the navy's logistic train and would likely reduce the effectiveness of the Seventh Fleet, at least initially, as Pacific units would be the first to be assigned.

Balancing these forward-deployed forces, the majority of conventional U.S. military strength is routinely based in the United States. Approximately half of the active army and two-thirds of the active Marine Corps are based at home. In addition, the army has eight National Guard divisions and twenty-four National Guard and army reserve separate brigades (a total of forty-eight brigades); the Marine Corps has one division and one air wing in reserve. The air force has fifteen active fighter/attack wings and approximately ten and one-half reserve tactical fighter wings based in the continental United States. The naval forces of the Second Fleet (western Atlantic) and the Third Fleet (eastern Pacific) comprise approximately 65 percent of the total fleet strength. At any given time about 30 percent of the total fleet strength (just under one-half of the fleet located in the United States) is in a reduced operational status for maintenance and overhaul.

Strategic forces. Since the early 1960s the U.S. strategic offensive capability has been built around three complementary systems for the delivery of nuclear weapons. Referred to collectively as the Triad, these systems are land-based ICBMs, sea-based SLBMs, and manned bombers.

Two of the legs of the Triad, the ICBMs and the manned bombers, comprise the combat elements of the Strategic Air Command. They are under a single commander in chief who reports to the secretary of defense through the Joint Chiefs of Staff. The ICBM force consists of 450 Minuteman IIs, 550 Minuteman IIIs, and 54 Titan IIs, all based within the continental United States. A mobile ICBM (the MX), designed as a replacement for increasingly vulnerable, fixed-position ICBMs, is currently being developed.

The bomber force includes two wings of FB-111s and seventeen wings of B-52s in the continental United States, and one B-52 wing in Guam. About half of the B-52 force is expected to be armed with cruise missiles beginning in the early to middle 1980s.

The Navy's fleet ballistic missile submarines are the third leg of the Triad. These Polaris/Poseidon ships will be gradually replaced by the Trident submarines, the first of which was launched in 1979. The older Poseidon ships are being modified to join the Trident ships in carrying the 7,400-kilometer-range Trident I missile. If the Trident II missile is developed, the Trident ships will be back-fitted with the improved Trident II in the late 1980s.

Finally, the United States possesses a small strategic defense force. At the present time it consists of just 141 active and 190 reserve fighter-interceptor aircraft based in the continental United States and one deactivated Safeguard antiballistic missile complex at Grand Forks, North Dakota.

Theater nuclear forces. The United States currently possesses about 13,000 theater or tactical nuclear weapons. These consist of battlefield systems for use by the artillery, bombs carried by aircraft, and fleet defensive systems. Approximately 7,000 of these weapons are dedicated to the European theater. The majority of them are in the hands of U.S. forces, while the remainder are deployed with the forces of the NATO allies, but subject to American control. Another 3,000 are afloat or deployed in the Pacific, while the remaining weapons are based in the United States.

In order to maintain its active duty force size, the armed services need to recruit some 400,000 individuals annually. Between the end of conscription in 1973 and mid-1978, the services met their recruiting goals for the active forces, but fell considerably short of fulfilling their reserve requirements, particularly in the individual ready reserve, where the Defense Department is short by over 100,000 personnel.

Beginning in the second half of 1978, however, all of the services began to have difficulty meeting the recruiting goals for the active forces as well. Moreover, since the number of males between the ages of seventeen and twenty-one has begun a period of rapid decline (it is expected to decline from 2.14 million in 1978 to about 1.6 million in 1990), the situation will probably continue to deteriorate. The Joint Chiefs of Staff and many Congressional leaders have become so concerned at this prospect that they are urging reinstatement of the draft or, as a minimum, registration for selective service.

Quality of forces. In order for the United States to employ its forces effectively, these forces must possess three characteristics: sufficiency, flexibility, and readiness. At the present time there is some doubt about all three of these characteristics.

Forward-deployed U.S. forces in Central Europe, even augmented by the forces of the NATO allies, are no match for their Warsaw Pact adversaries in a purely conventional (nonnuclear) engagement. To be sufficient to deal with the threat, the United States must be able to reinforce and resupply Europe by air and by sea. In addition, the United States must have sufficient prepositioned materials and war reserves in place on the European continent. One view is that the United States will not have the capacity to reinforce Europe adequately by air until 1983 at the earliest, nor will it have sufficient prepositioned stocks of war supplies until the mid-1980s.[73] For example, at the present time the United States can only lift two divisions and twenty air squadrons to Europe within thirty days. Some have argued that the country needs to have the capability to bring in five divisions and sixty air squadrons.

Doubt has been expressed as to whether the navy has a sufficient number of ships to move the supplies necessary to fight a prolonged war in Europe, or whether it has enough naval forces to counter the massive Soviet submarine threat in the Atlantic. Finally, should the United States attain an expanded airlift and sealift capability to reinforce and resupply Europe, shortages in the selected reserve and individual ready reserve army forces could bring these efforts to naught. Indeed, some army estimates are that in a European conflict it would likely run out of trained infantry, tank crews, and artillery personnel before conscripts could be ready for battle.

The armed services have not only a quantitative shortfall in their active and reserve establishment but a qualitative one as well. Because of the increasing complexity of modern weapons systems, all of the armed services, even the army and the Marine Corps, need high-quality personnel. Yet the majority of volunteers tested mentally in the lower half of the U.S. population and are unable to read at a high school level.[74] In addition to these personnel problems, the armed services have also experienced difficulties due to budgetary constraints on expenditures for maintenance of and logistics support for the equipment of the operating forces.

In an ideal world, force posture would be completely responsive to the demands of objectives, strategy, and doctrine. However, in the real world the relationship is more complex and the opposite is often true—that is, the prior existence of a given force posture largely determines the doctrine. For example, the bedrock of American strategic doctrine is the Triad (three different strategic offensive systems, each of which has unique capabilities that complement the other two, and each of which presents unique problems for any potential attacker). Yet this doctrine was developed after—not before—each of the three legs was built independently, primarily for reasons of organizational enhancement rather than doctrine. Similarly, the doctrine of forward deployment was developed to justify the fact that as a result of the position of U.S. conventional forces at the end of World War II, the Defense Department already had forces permanently deployed outside the United States.

On the other hand, force structure does sometimes change to support changes in strategy. For example, the strategy of preparing for a short intensive war on the central front in Europe has led to a new emphasis on "heavy," or mechanized, divisions in the army and a doubling of the equipment prepositioned in Europe.

ARMS CONTROL

In the post–World War II period, the United States has occasionally engaged in negotiations on the control of conventional arms such as the Mutual Balanced Force Reductions (MBFR) talks in Europe and discussions on the limitation of naval forces in the Indian Ocean. However, its main focus in arms limitation has been in the area of strategic nuclear weapons. The United States has concentrated on the strategic arms for three reasons. First, these weapons represent the only real threat to the physical security of the United States. Second, given the level of technological advancement in the Soviet Union, there is the expectation that the United States can be matched and offset by the Soviet Union. Thus, the United States could find itself in the position of spending vast sums of money without purchasing any additional security. Third, since the first two factors can also be applied to the Soviet Union, both sides see strategic nuclear weapons as an issue with considerable arms control potential. Therefore, in the past fifteen years, the United States and the Soviet Union have concluded various arms control agreements, including the Nuclear Test Ban Treaty of 1963, SALT I in 1972, and SALT II in 1979.[75]

Although the overall policy of the United States for the past two decades has been to seek strategic arms control agreements with the USSR, there is considerable disagreement within the American political system over the specifics of that policy. Both Democratic and Republican administrations have been committed to maintaining a strategic posture of essential equivalence with the Soviets. Essential equivalence is defined to be the continuing maintenance of the following conditions: (1) that Soviet strategic nuclear forces do not become usable instruments of political leverage, diplomatic coercion, or military advantage; (2) that nuclear stability, especially in crisis, is maintained; (3) that any advantages in force characteristics enjoyed by the Soviets are offset by U.S. advantages in other characteristics; and (4) that the U.S. posture is not in fact, and is not seen as, inferior in performance to the nuclear forces of the Soviet Union.[76] In the abstract, this policy enjoys nearly unanimous support within the nation as a whole. However, there are substantial differences over such questions as what constitutes an inferior posture or what constitutes an advantage in force characteristics.

On one extreme, there are those who feel that the Soviet Union is still bent on world domination and hence will exploit SALT to attain military superiority over the United States. On the other extreme is a group that feels that true détente between the superpowers is possible regardless of differences, and hence, the United States should rely on Soviet good will in its negotiations.[77] Obviously, there are also many who hold positions between these two extremes.

No single actor has been able to dominate the arms control policy process. Any treaty must conform to the world view of the chief executive, while simultaneously proving acceptable to the Joint Chiefs of Staff, the Arms Control and Disarmament Agency, the State Department, informed public opinion, and at least sixty-seven senators,* each of whom has his or her own perception of the motivations of the Soviet Union and the meaning of essential equivalence.

Strategic arms control between the two superpowers is feasible to the extent that it will benefit both sides. However, quantitative restrictions are much easier to achieve than qualitative ones, in part because the former are more easily measured and verified. Thus, the two superpowers could agree relatively easily to halting testing in the atmosphere and limiting the number of ABM sites, missile launchers, and ballistic missile submarines. But qualitative restrictions such as range, lifting capacity, accuracy, and mission are more difficult to measure and are much more difficult to detect. For example, there is no visible or electronic way to detect with certainty the maximum range of a cruise missile or whether it has a nuclear warhead. SALT II moved into the qualitative area of arms control and thus took twice as

*That is, the minimum number of votes required to ratify treaties in the U.S. Senate.—Ed.

long to negotiate as SALT I, even though the basic negotiation principles had been settled beforehand. Moreover, SALT II was subject to a much more rigorous examination by the U.S. Senate. Indeed, the SALT II Treaty signed by President Carter was never ratified. Nevertheless, SALT II did show that qualitative restrictions are at least possible.

Certain aspects of the force posture maintained by the United States appear threatening to other nations, primarily those that are suspicious of American intentions. Some Soviet strategists perceive that recent improvements in the accuracy and yield of the American land- and sea-based missile force, and development of the cruise missile for the country's manned bombers, could lead to a preemptive first strike by the United States. Similarly, the Soviet Union and its Warsaw Pact allies may wonder if the forward deployment of large numbers of U.S. land and air forces in Europe and naval forces in the Mediterranean signifies some aggressive designs on the territory of Soviet bloc nations. However, some of the NATO allies of the United States and "neutrals," like the Chinese, are concerned about the relative decrease in U.S. strategic and conventional capabilities vis-à-vis the Soviet Union. Consequently, they wish to see the United States develop a more formidable posture and increase its forward deployments.[78]

To a certain extent, the force posture currently maintained by the United States is a reaction to the threat perceived from the Soviet force posture. The qualitative improvements in American strategic forces over the past decade have been primarily a response to the quantitative and qualitative build-up of the strategic nuclear forces of the USSR, while American conventional and theater nuclear forces are sized primarily to deal with a sudden blitzkrieg attack by the Warsaw Pact nations in Central Europe. Indeed, during the post-Vietnam period, the United States drew down its force structure dramatically. Were it not for the rapid Soviet build-up, it is doubtful that a consensus would have emerged in the late 1970s on increasing U.S. force structure.

USE OF FORCE

In the post–World War II period, the United States has fought two large and prolonged wars in Asia. From 1950 to 1953, the nation poured a total of over 1 million people and $50 billion into the fight against the forces of North Korea and the People's Republic of China. (Actual troop strength at any one time peaked at 325,000 in 1953.) In the period from 1964 through 1973, the United States sent a total of over 2 million citizens and spent some $200 billion in a futile effort to thwart the attempt of the North Vietnamese to expand their control over the rest of Indochina. (Actual troop strength in Vietnam peaked at 579,000 in 1968.)

In addition, since World War II the United States has employed its forces over 200 times as a political instrument, that is, in a deliberate attempt to influence the specific behavior of other states without engaging in a prolonged contest of violence such as Korea and Vietnam.[79] These employments have ranged from the low-key, but highly publicized, cancellation of a carrier visit to Chile during the Marxist presidency of Salvador Allende in the early 1970s to the massive naval blockade of Cuba that brought the United States to the brink of war with the Soviet Union in October 1962.

In fighting its wars in Korea and Vietnam, as well as in using forces as political instruments, the United States has usually sought limited and rather specific objectives. The primary purpose of sending troops to Korea and Vietnam was to prevent the Communist governments in those areas from imposing their will on their southern neighbors by force. Even in the Cuban Missile Crisis, the United States sought merely to compel the Soviet Union to remove its missiles from Cuba and pledge not to use Cuba as a base for strategic weapons systems.

Similarly, the United States has limited the military means it has used so that they would be commensurate with the objectives sought. In Korea and Vietnam, the United States refrained from using strategic and tactical nuclear weapons, spared the hydroelectric facilities in North Korea and the dams in North Vietnam, and avoided actions that would provoke China and the Soviet Union, even though those countries were actively supplying the forces of North Korea and North Vietnam.

The vast majority of the cases in which forces were employed for political purposes involved very limited use of force. About 32 percent of the time the forces simply provided a presence; another 40 percent involved participation in port visits or exercises; only 17 percent of the cases involved the actual use of firepower or the landing of ground forces. Moreover, in only 9 percent of the cases did the United States threaten to use or maneuver its nuclear forces, for example, by putting them on a higher alert posture.

In Korea and Vietnam, the level of U.S. involvement was no doubt influenced and limited by the threatened actions of the Chinese and Russians. The United States allowed China to remain a sanctuary in both wars and refused to interdict Soviet supply bases in either Korea or Vietnam because it did not wish to expand the war beyond those areas. Similarly, it was primarily ethical and legal concerns that prevented the United States from destroying things like dikes and population centers in North Korea and North Vietnam.

On the other hand, the level of U.S. effort, when employing forces as a political instrument, has increased as Soviet and Chinese involvement or threats of involvement have increased. The Soviets and

Chinese were involved in only 40 percent of the total number of incidents, but these incidents accounted for the majority of cases in which the United States employed major nuclear and nonnuclear force elements.

In using its forces for political purposes, the United States has generally tried to follow the precepts of international law, even if only after the fact. Thus, it sought OAS approval for its actions in Cuba in 1962 and in the Dominican Republic in 1965.

Domestic political pressures and public opinion have had an impact on the use of force by American political leaders. For example, President Truman's decision to intervene in Korea, as well as those of Presidents Kennedy and Johnson to become involved in Vietnam, were influenced by their fear of the reaction of conservatives in Congress and the public if they failed to take decisive action. Paradoxically, it was the opinion of the public, tired of absorbing high casualties in seemingly futile struggles, that forced Presidents Truman and Johnson to seek a negotiated settlement on terms less than their original objectives may have been in those Asian wars.

Because of its limited duration, the impact of domestic politics and public opinion on the political use of armed forces is more difficult to assess. However, there does exist a significant relationship between the popularity of a president and the nation's sense of confidence and the frequency of incidents. Generally speaking, the more popular the president and the higher the people's sense of confidence in him, the greater is his flexibility or freedom of choice in responding to threats and, as a result, the more frequent is the employment of military forces for political purposes.

In Korea and Vietnam and in the 220 political uses of U.S. armed forces, the fact that the United States has had a large, technologically advanced military force has made it easier to rely on these forces for policy goals. It is no accident that since the Soviet Union has achieved military parity, the United States has grown increasingly reluctant to employ military force for political purposes.

Conclusion

As the United States enters the last two decades of this century, its national security policy is clearly in a state of flux. Its relative position within the international system as well as its perception of the role that it ought to play in that system are changing. Its national security objectives, strategy, force structure, arms control policy, and employment doctrine are subjects of intense debate among a somewhat weakened executive, a resurgent Congress, and an informed but divided public. The American people, still suffering from the trauma of the Vietnam debacle, are unsure of the kind of defense policies that they want their leaders to pursue.

The future direction of the defense policies of the United States is difficult to determine with certainty at this time. The only thing that can be said with any degree of assurance is that, whatever they are, the policies will have a profound effect upon the relations among nations. The choices that were open to the United States before 1941 are no longer relevant. Whether it wishes to or not, the United States will remain a major actor in the world arena. But it will need strong and informed leadership to ensure that there is congruence among its perceptions, strategy, policy, force structure, arms control policy, and force employment doctrine.

Notes

1. See, for example, Raymond Aron, *The Imperial Republic* (Cambridge, Mass: Winthrop, 1974), p. 92; and George Liska, *Imperial America* (Baltimore: Johns Hopkins Press, 1967), p. 10.

2. Lester Brown, *The Global Politics of Resource Scarcity,* Overseas Development Council, Development Paper 17 (April 1974), pp. 20–21.

3. Central Intelligence Agency, *Estimated Soviet Defense Spending: Trends and Prospects,* June 1978, p. 1. There has, of course, been some dispute with the CIA's estimate; however, most concede that it is correct in depicting the trend toward increasing defense outlays. Most debate has centered on the actual percentage estimate of expenditure growth and on the data base and methodology used in preparing this estimate.

4. Between 1965 and 1973, the Department of Defense spent $135 billion prosecuting the war in Southeast Asia. Personnel costs rose from 42 percent of the defense budget in 1968 to 55 percent in 1976, even though manpower in the post-Vietnam period was cut from 3.5 to 2.1 million persons. Perhaps even more important than AVF costs, however, are inflated purchase costs of material.

5. Arthur Alexander, "The Significance of Divergent U.S.-USSR Military Expenditures," *A Rand Note* (N-1000-AF), February 1979, p. viii.

6. Polling data on these subjects is summarized in "Americans and the World," *Public Opinion,* March/May 1979, pp. 21–27.

7. Harriman's remarks were made before the Senate Foreign Relations Committee on 19 July 1979. They are quoted in Charles Cordry, "Baker Appears in Film Attacking SALT Treaty," *Baltimore Sun,* 20 July 1979, p. 2.

8. R. L. Janisch, "U.S. Military Options to Protect Persian Gulf Oil Are Limited," *Armed Forces Journal,* July 1979, p. 24.

9. Ibid. Harold Brown's opinion is shared by Secretary of State Cyrus Vance and Senator Frank Church (D-Idaho), Chairman of the Senate Foreign Relations Committee. John Gosmok, "Vance and Church Indicate That the U.S. Would Act to Protect Saudi Oil Supply," *Washington Post,* 10 March 1979, p. A1.

10. There are many excellent sources on U.S. self-perceptions. Chapter 1 in John Spanier, *American Foreign*

Policy Since World War II (New York: Praeger, 1973), is particularly good.

11. Barry Blechman and Stephen Kaplan, *Force without War: U.S. Armed Forces As a Political Instrument* (Washington, D.C.: Brookings Institution, 1978), p. 16.

12. Richard Nixon, *U.S. Foreign Policy for the 1970s*, 18 February 1970, p. 27.

13. Gerald Ford, *International Economic Report of the President*, January 1977, p. 154.

14. The two best sources on McGovern's perception of the appropriate role of the United States in world affairs are his remarks in the *Congressional Record*, 24 January 1977, pp. 1-5; and his statement before the Subcommittee on Priorities and Economy in Government, Joint Economic Committee, 16 June 1972.

15. Quoted in Gerald Ford, *A Time to Heal* (New York: Harper & Row, 1970), p. 421.

16. An excellent source on Carter's view of the role of human rights in American foreign policy is his "Remarks at a Fundraising Dinner for Abraham Beame," New York, 5 December 1978.

17. Stanley Hoffmann, "The Hell of Good Intentions," *Foreign Policy*, Winter 1977-78, pp. 7-8.

18. The best source on PD-18 is a speech by Secretary of Defense Harold Brown to the Thirty-fourth Annual Dinner of the National Security Industrial Association, Washington, D.C., 15 September 1977.

19. For an excellent analysis of the U.S. alliance policy, see Robert Osgood, *Alliances and American Foreign Policy* (Baltimore: Johns Hopkins Press, 1968), and Congressional Quarterly, *Global Defense: U.S. Military Commitments Abroad* (September 1969).

20. These objectives are drawn from the following sources: *Annual Defense Department Reports* (FY 1978, 1979, and 1980) and speeches by President Carter at Wake Forest on 17 March 1978, and at Georgia Tech on 20 February 1979.

21. Anthony Lake, "The International Security Environment" (Paper presented at Senior Conference 17, West Point, N.Y., 15 June 1979), summarizes these threats quite succinctly.

22. See, for example, Philip Morrison and Paul Walker, "A New Strategy for Military Spending," *Scientific American*, October 1978, pp. 48-63. Examples of individuals clustering around this position include Vice President Walter Mondale, Senator Mark Hatfield, Congressman Les Aspin, and former Director of the Arms Control and Disarmament Agency Paul Warnke.

23. Benjamin Schemmer, "Secretary of Defense Annual Report at Odds with His Budget Guidance for Next Year," *Armed Forces Journal*, March 1978, pp. 37-39. This "maximum deterrence" position is supported by the Joint Chiefs of Staff and such individuals as Senator Sam Nunn, Congressman Jack Kemp, and former Deputy Secretary of Defense Paul Nitze.

24. Alton Quanbeck and Archie Wood, *Modernizing the Strategic Bomber Force* (Washington, D.C.: Brookings Institution, 1975), and David Ott et al., *Federal Budget Options for the Last Half of the Seventies* (Washington, D.C.: American Enterprise Institute, 1973).

25. This account is drawn primarily from Spanier, *Foreign Policy*, pp. 7-21.

26. Donald Rumsfeld, *Annual Defense Department Report, FY 1978*, 17 January 1977, p. 27.

27. The first secretary to put the issue squarely before the American people was James Schlesinger, in his *Annual Defense Department Report, FY 1976 and 1977*, 5 February 1975, pp. I-2 through I-4.

28. See Michael Howard, "The Forgotten Dimensions of Strategy," *Foreign Affairs*, Summer 1979, for an excellent analysis of strategy and warfare.

29. Ford, *A Time to Heal*, pp. 302-4.

30. William Beecher, "U.S. Asks Soviets to Join in Missile Moratorium," *New York Times*, 23 July 1971, p. 1; and Rowland Evans and Robert Novak, "Conceding Defeat in Europe," *Washington Post*, 3 August 1977, p. A-19.

31. For example, see Harry Magdoff, *The Age of Imperialism: The Economics of United States Foreign Policy* (New York: Monthly Review Press, 1969); and Gabriel Kolko, *The Roots of American Foreign Policy* (Boston: Beacon Press, 1969).

32. For an excellent critique of the economic imperative argument, see Aron, *Imperial Republic*, pp. 159-87.

33. Alfred Thayer Mahan, *The Influence of Seapower upon History, 1660-1783* (Annapolis: Naval Institute, 1890).

34. Blechman and Kaplan, *Force without War*, p. 38.

35. Rumsfeld, *Defense Department Report, FY 1978*, p. 190. Since Congress's approved ship construction averaged 14 percent for over a decade, it may have been a bit optimistic to assume that the legislature would approve on the order of thirty new ships per year.

36. For example, Senator Robert Taft (R-Ohio) and Senator Gary Hart (D-Colorado), *A Modern Military Strategy for the United States, White Paper on Defense*, March 1978; and Gary Hart, "The U.S. Senate and the Future of the Navy," *International Security*, Spring 1978, pp. 175-84.

37. CBS News/*New York Times* Poll, 23-26 January 1979.

38. Ford, *A Time to Heal*, p. 247.

39. *Public Opinion*, March/May 1979, p. 26.

40. For example, see Harold Brown, *Annual Defense Department Report, FY 1980*, 25 January 1979, pp. 1-9; Bernard Weinraub, "Brown Seeks to Cut Involvement of the Navy in Nonnuclear War," *New York Times*, 26 January 1978, p. 1; George Wilson, "New U.S. Military Plan: European, Persian Focus," *Washington Post*, 27 January 1978, p. A-1.

41. Brown, *FY 1980*, p. 77.

42. Harold Brown, *Annual Defense Department Report, FY 1979*, January 1978, p. 56.

43. President Jimmy Carter, State of the Union Address, 16 January 1979.

44. Daniel Seligman, "Our ICBMs Are in Danger," *Fortune*, 2 July 1979, p. 50, discusses the position of the advocates of minimum deterrence.

45. In 1979 the Soviet missile force was 38 percent larger than that of the United States, and possessed 163 percent more throw-weight and 72 percent more equivalent megatonnage (*FY 1980 Posture Statement*, pp. 65-74).

46. U.S., Congress, House of Representatives, Committee on Armed Services, *NATO Standardization Interoperability and Readiness*, 95th Cong., 2d sess., pp. 2-3.

47. The best published sources on the structure and process of the Carter NSC system are Dom Bonafede, "Brzezinski: Stepping Out of His Backstage Role," *National Journal*, 15 October 1977, pp. 1596-1601; and Don Ober-

dorfer, "Carter as Foreign Policy Manager: He Does Good Things Badly," *Washington Post*, 18 February 1979, p. C-1. See also my "National Security Organization and Process in the Carter Administration," in *Carter's Defense Policies*, ed. Sam Sarkesian (Boulder, Colo.: Westview Press, 1979), pp. 111-37.

48. Oberdorfer, "Carter as Foreign Policy Manager," p. C-1.

49. George Wilson, "Carter to Seek Five-Year Ban on Atomic Tests," *Washington Post*, 22 May 1978, p. A-1; and Rowland Evans and Robert Novak, "Test Ban Bypassing the Chiefs," *Washington Post*, 26 May 1978, p. A-21.

50. Bridget Gail, "The Fine Old Game of Killing: Comparing U.S. and Soviet Arms Sales," *Armed Forces Journal*, September 1978, pp. 16-24; and Drew Middleton, "Heavy Arms Sales Show Soviets Ahead," *New York Times*, 7 January 1979, p. 2.

51. For an analysis of civil-military relations in the Defense Budgetary Process in the Nixon-Ford period, see my *Joint Chiefs of Staff: The First Twenty-five Years* (Bloomington: Indiana University Press, 1976), pp. 121-28; and "The Budget Process in the Department of Defense, 1947-1977," *Public Administration Review*, July/August 1977, pp. 334-46.

52. Interview with official in OSD, May 1978.

53. See the "Memorandum for the Secretary of Defense," 10 December 1977, from R. James Woolsey, Undersecretary of the Navy, *Armed Forces Journal*, March 1978, p. 42.

54. For example, language in the FY 1979 Supplemental Defense Authorization Bill directs the DoD to begin immediate development of the MX.

55. Graham Allison, *Essence of Decision* (Boston: Little, Brown, 1971), p. 146.

56. John Steinbruner, *Cybernetic Theory of Decision: New Dimensions of Political Analysis* (Princeton: Princeton University Press, 1974).

57. Changes in the defense budget can be made without changing the law. In FY 1980, defense accounted for 58 percent of the discretionary funds in the entire federal budget.

58. For an analysis of this decision, see Herschel Kanter, "That '3 Percent' for Defense," *Washington Post*, 27 December 1978, and my *FY 1980-1984 Defense Program: Issues and Trends* (Washington, D.C.: American Enterprise Institute, 1979), pp. 27-30.

59. Oberdorfer, "Carter as Foreign Policy Manager," p. C-1.

60. The comprehensive plan is spelled out in Herbert Scoville, Jr., "A Starting Point for a New SALT Agreement," *Arms Control Today*, April 1977, pp. 4-5.

61. For the classic study of the impact of personality characteristics on individual presidents, see James Barber, *The Presidential Character* (Englewood Cliffs, N.J.: Prentice-Hall, 1972).

62. There is a rich literature on this subject. For a good sampling, see the following: Richard Kaufman, "We Must Guard against the Unwarranted Influence by the Military Industrial Complex," *New York Times Magazine*, 22 June 1969, pp. 10, 68-72; Seymour Melman, *Pentagon Capitalism* (New York: McGraw-Hill, 1970); Jack Raymond, "The Military Industrial Complex," *Harvard Business Review*, May-June 1968, pp. 53-64; Charles Wolf, "Military-Industrial Complexities," *Bulletin of the Atomic Scientists*, February 1971, pp. 19-22; and Adam Yarmolinsky, *The Military Establishment* (New York: Harper & Row, 1974).

63. Samuel Huntington, *The Soldier and the State* (Cambridge, Mass.: Harvard University Press, 1957).

64. See, for example, Morris Janowitz, *The Professional Soldier* (New York: Free Press, 1960).

65. U.S. Department of Defense, *America's Volunteers: A Report on the All-Volunteer Forces*, 31 December 1978, pp. 35-37.

66. Charles Moskos, "The Emergent Military: Calling, Profession, or Occupation," in *The Changing World of the American Military*, ed. Franklin Margiotta (Boulder, Colo.: Westview Press, 1978), pp. 199-206.

67. David Segal and John Blair, "Public Confidence in the U.S. Military," *Armed Forces and Society*, November 1976, p. 3.

68. The most detailed analysis of the weapons system acquisition process is J. Ronald Fox, *Arming America* (Cambridge, Mass.: Harvard University Press, 1974).

69. Brown, *Defense Department Report, FY 1979*, p. 100.

70. These steps are outlined in Department of Defense Instruction 5000.1, 18 January 1977.

71. Current U.S. force posture is spelled out in Brown, *Defense Department Report, FY 1980*, pp. 114, 125, 136, 140, 159, 178, 181, and 195. See also *The Military Balance, 1978-1979* (London: International Institute for Strategic Studies, 1978), pp. 5-8.

72. "Carter Said Ready to Drop Korea Troop Withdrawals," *Washington Post*, 20 July 1979, p. 4.

73. U.S., Congress, House of Representatives, Committee on Armed Services, *NATO Standardization*, pp. 2-3. See also "The Fireman and the Flanks," *Sea Power Magazine*, June 1979, p. 6.

74. Harold Brown, *Annual Defense Department Report, FY 1980*, p. 281; Morris Janowitz and Charles Moskos, "Five Years of the All-Volunteer Force," *Armed Forces and Society*, Winter 1979, pp. 171-219; and Robin Beard, "The All-Volunteer Military," *Strategic Review*, Summer 1979, p. 43.

75. The essence of these agreements is contained in U.S., Department of State, "The Strategic Arms Limitation Talks," Special Report 46, May 1979.

76. *Annual Defense Department Report, FY 1979*, pp. 5-6.

77. These positions are spelled out in J. William Fulbright, "The Significance of SALT II," *AEI Defense Review* 2, no. 4, pp. 2-4.

78. See, for example, Flora Lewis, "Seminar in Europe Views U.S. As Weak," *New York Times*, 3 June 1979, p. 8.

79. The data in this section are drawn from Blechman and Kaplan, *Force without War*.

THE DEFENSE POLICY OF THE SOVIET UNION

Edward L. Warner III

International environment

The Soviet Union enters the 1980s as one of the world's two superpowers. After over sixty years of Communist rule, the aging leaders in the Kremlin are bound to view the nation's domestic and international accomplishments with considerable satisfaction. Within their lifetime the country has weathered the self-inflicted human losses of Stalin's forced collectivization campaign and bloody purges of the 1930s as well as the catastrophic devastation of the Second World War. They have seen the Soviet Union come back from the very brink of defeat at the hands of Hitler's armies in 1941–42 to become the most powerful nation in Europe and Asia.

The current leaders have also witnessed the realization of many of the most cherished foreign policy goals of their czarist predecessors. These include: (1) the expansion of the country's frontiers during the course of World War II and its immediate aftermath with the forcible annexation of the Baltic states, portions of Poland, Czechoslovakia, and Romania in the West, and the southern half of Sakhalin Island and the Kurile Islands in the Far East; (2) the establishment of subservient client regimes throughout most of Eastern Europe in the immediate postwar period; and (3) greatly increased Russian presence and influence in many other areas, including the Middle East, South and Southeast Asia, and Africa, as the result of sustained efforts since the mid-1950s. Finally, over the past twenty years, they have presided over a seemingly inexorable expansion of Soviet military power which has succeeded in establishing the Soviet Union as a coequal with the United States in this critical dimension of power potential and has helped them promote their foreign policy interests aggressively throughout the world.

RELATIVE POWER POSITION

It has become commonplace to attribute the superpower status of the Soviet Union almost exclusively to its massive military might. Indisputably, defense efforts enjoy unrivaled primacy within the Soviet economy. Moreover, military power has played a critical role in the growth of Soviet influence in the world. Yet, Soviet claims to superpower status are not based solely on the country's obvious military prowess.

The Soviet Union is one of the world's leading industrial nations. With a gross national product of approximately $1.2 trillion in 1978,[1] the USSR ranks second in the world, behind the United States. Moreover, the Soviet Union leads the world in several economic categories, including annual production of iron ore, steel, cement, petroleum, lumber, and machinery, and trails only the United States in coal and natural gas production and electrical power generation.[2] Soviet economic achievements, however, are considerably less impressive when computed on a per capita basis. Viewed from this perspective, the Soviet Union, much as czarist Russia did on the eve of the Revolution in 1917,[3] ranks behind not only the United States but also most of the industrial nations of Western Europe and Asia.[4]

Soviet superpower status has a substantial political and ideological component. Undoubtedly, the international appeal of the Soviet political system has dimmed somewhat in recent years as the shortcomings of the system in individual freedoms and the standard of living of the general populace have become widely known. Nevertheless, the USSR still enjoys considerable influence, particularly in the Third World, as the leader of the world Communist movement and the self-proclaimed champion of the fight against Western imperialism.

THREATS FACING THE SOVIET UNION

The Soviets have a deep-seated and historically well-founded concern about foreign military invasion. As former U.S. Ambassador to the Soviet Union Malcolm C. Toon has noted, "Centuries of invasions from both East and West have left their mark on the outlook of the Russian people and its rulers."[5]

Soviet concern about foreign invasion is not based simply on bitter Russian historic experience at the hands of such aggressors as the Mongol hordes of Ghengis Khan and Napoleon's *grande armée*. This wariness also reflects direct experience during the Soviet period. The Soviets assiduously keep alive the memory of several foreign incursions: the invasion by imperial Germany just weeks after the Bolsheviks seized power in November 1917; the military interventions of Britain, France, the United States, and Japan on behalf of the rival "White" forces who battled the Bolsheviks during the Russian Civil War, 1918–20; the border clashes with imperial Japan in 1938 and 1939; and, most significantly, the devastating effects of the Nazi invasion and brutal occupation in 1941–44.[6] This Soviet "siege mentality"[7] is further intensified by the strong emphasis in Marxist-Leninist ideology on the inevitable hostility of the capitalist powers toward the socialist states and the Soviets' own repeated warnings about the dangers posed by "capitalist encirclement."

Soviet statements since the end of World War II have left no doubt that the United States has become the USSR's principal enemy. Soviet propaganda has consistently identified the United States as the leading force of "imperialist reaction," dedicated to the defeat of socialism and eagerly poised to attack the Soviet Union at the first opportunity. The only other Western nation that has merited such Soviet concern is the Federal Republic of Germany. The regular Soviet attacks on the "revanchist" goals of the West Germans reflect the deep scars left by two devastating German invasions in this century.

Since the mid-1960s, the Soviets have increasingly come to describe the People's Republic of China as a dangerous external threat. Soviet concern about China has several roots. These include historical distrust that can be traced back to the Mongol dominance of medieval Russia, racial antipathy, intense rivalry for leadership of the international Communist movement, and strongly conflicting foreign policy aspirations, particularly in Asia. This distrust also reflects justifiable Soviet anxiety about the long-term threat posed by a mammoth neighbor with whom they share a 4,500-mile frontier and that has a population of over a billion, a growing nuclear capability, and a decidedly hostile attitude toward the USSR.

Having noted the Soviet obsession with defense and the threat of foreign invasion, one must not overlook the degree to which the Soviets and their czarist predecessors have successfully employed offensive military power to promote their foreign policy interests and to expand their frontiers. Neighboring countries such as Finland, Poland, Bulgaria, and Turkey, to say nothing of the formerly independent Baltic states of Lithuania, Latvia, and Estonia and, most recently, Afghanistan have periodically been the victims of Russian coercion and invasion. Buoyed by the apparent political utility of their growing military power, the Soviet leaders today almost certainly view the international scene more as an arena of substantial opportunity for the advancement of their interests than as a source of threats to the security of the USSR.

The national security concerns of the leaders in the Kremlin are not limited to external considerations. They also take very seriously the threat of internal political opposition. Their anxieties in this regard include concerns about oppositional political movements and the nationalistic aspirations of several of the minorities within the Soviet multinational state. Soviet spokesmen have traditionally attributed such opposition to the "diversionary activities" of foreign adversaries. Harsh internal security measures to deal with the subversive activities of so-called rotten capitalist elements were especially prominent in the early years of the Bolshevik regime. Fears of "class enemies" were manipulated by Stalin in particular to justify the ruthless suppression of political opposition groups in a series of bloody purges in the 1930s.

These fears of subversion and the attendant internal security measures to deal with this threat are still present today, although in much attenuated form compared with the days of Stalin's paranoia and terror. Nevertheless, the Soviet leadership remains vigilant and determined to deal ruthlessly with serious internal opposition, as evidenced in the wave of repression in the 1970s against dissidents of various persuasions undertaken by the secret police, the KGB. Despite its determined pursuit of détente with the West since the late 1960s, the Soviet regime has made it absolutely clear that there will be no relaxation of ideological or political controls on the domestic scene. Rather, it is precisely in such an atmosphere, with its attendant increased contacts with foreigners and their culture, that the Soviet leaders have insisted that tight social controls are most necessary and thus must be intensified.

SELF-PERCEPTION OF THE SOVIET LEADERSHIP

The Soviet perspective on world affairs contains an amalgam of traditional Russian and Marxist-Leninist ideological elements. Much has been written about the relative weight of these two factors in Soviet foreign policy. These discussions are of limited value since, to a considerable extent, the two traditions reinforce Soviet inclinations toward expansionism on the world scene.

Both the Russian imperial heritage and the Marxist-Leninist tradition provide support for a highly centralized, authoritarian government and a heavily regulated economy. Both traditions also call for defense of the ruling regime as the most fundamental objective of the Soviet state. Both are also marked by strong messianic strains. The Russian tradition included a centuries-old belief that the Russian Empire was the "third Rome," the successor to Byzantium, and the defender of the true orthodox Christian faith. Moreover, Russia was viewed as having a special right to exercise hegemony throughout the Slavic areas of southeastern Europe. The imperial tradition was also marked by a paradoxical mix of attitudes about Russia and the West. It combined an almost mystical veneration of things Russian with a nagging sense of inferiority regarding the economic and technological achievements of the industrially advanced West.

Marxist-Leninist ideology provides the Soviets, as the leading Communist power, with a similar sense of being historically chosen. It also provides an element of long-term optimism by positing that communism will inevitably triumph over capitalism. This ideological self-confidence was well captured in Nikita Khrushchev's famous boast that Soviet communism would eventually "bury" the capitalist West.

Both the Russian imperialist tradition and Marxism-Leninism reinforce Soviet tendencies toward an expansionist foreign policy. The czarist pattern of territorial aggrandizement was largely characterized by the forcible incorporation of contiguous areas along Russia's lengthy European and Asian frontiers. The imperial Russian regimes were not, however, without longer range ambitions, as evidenced by various diplomatic initiatives and involvements in Western Europe, the Far East, the Middle East, and even Africa.[8] Moreover, it is perfectly reasonable to expect that any twentieth-century Russian government, having industrialized and thus begun to realize the country's immense geopolitical potential,[9] would have broadened its horizons and sought to extend its influence on a global scale.

Some observers, nevertheless, attribute Soviet expansionist international behavior almost solely to a Marxist-Leninist drive for world domination. This school of thought asserts that the fundamental teachings of Marx and Lenin about the inevitable defeat of capitalism and the global triumph of socialism remain the key operative foreign policy goals of the Soviet leadership. From this perspective, the Communist leaders of the USSR are viewed as thoroughly committed to a protracted life and death struggle for power and as determined to expand their influence at every possible opportunity.

Regardless of whether one is inclined toward the traditional Russian great power or ideological interpretations of Soviet motivations in the world, there is little doubt that the Soviet leadership today perceives the USSR as a major international actor with a right to be heard, if it chooses, on virtually any issue. Moreover, proud of its status as one of the world's two nuclear superpowers and the recognized leader of the world Communist movement, the Soviet leadership is virtually certain to believe that the Soviet Union should play an even greater role in world politics in the 1980s and beyond.

INTERDEPENDENCIES

The Soviet Union has an extensive series of treaty commitments, as befits a superpower. The most prominent of these is the multilateral Treaty of Friendship, Mutual Assistance, and Cooperation signed in Warsaw, Poland, on 14 May 1955. This alliance, commonly known as the Warsaw Pact, commits the Soviet Union and the Communist regimes of Poland, Hungary, East Germany, Czechoslovakia, Bulgaria, and Romania to the joint defense of their European territories.* Originally conceived

*The USSR also has close ties with these countries and Cuba through the Council for Economic Mutual Assistance (usually abbreviated as CEMA or COMECON).—Ed.

as a response to the rearmament of the Federal Republic of Germany and its admission into NATO, this treaty has become, over the years, a major policy instrument for the Soviets' domination of their Communist client states in Eastern Europe.

The common defense commitments of the Warsaw Pact are reinforced by bilateral treaties of friendship and mutual assistance between the Soviet Union and each of the other member states. The Soviets have also signed bilateral status of forces agreements with East Germany, Poland, Hungary, and Czechoslovakia that provide for the stationing of Soviet troops in these countries. Soviet military forces permanently deployed in Eastern Europe include two tank divisions and a tactical air army within the Northern Group of Forces in Poland, five divisions (three motorized rifle and two tank) and a tactical air army within the Central Group of Forces in Czechoslovakia, four divisions (two motorized rifle and two tank) and a tactical air army in Hungary, and twenty divisions (ten motorized rifle and ten tank) and a tactical air army in the Group of Soviet Forces Germany (GSFG).[10]

There are a series of high-level military and political consultative bodies associated with the Warsaw Pact. All are thoroughly dominated by the Soviet Union. The most important are the Political Consultative Committee (whose membership includes the Communist party first secretaries, heads of governments, and defense and foreign ministers from each member state) and the Council of Defense Ministers. Both of these bodies convene on an average of twice a year. The military command structure of the Warsaw Pact is led by the Joint High Command, headquartered in Moscow. This command is headed by a senior Soviet officer, who serves as commander in chief of the Warsaw Pact. This post is currently occupied by Marshal V. G. Kulikov, who is also a Soviet first deputy minister of defense. The military command also includes a chief of staff (currently General of the Army A. I. Gribkov), who traditionally serves simultaneously as a deputy chief of the Soviet General Staff. In addition, general officers from each of the member states represent their nations at the Warsaw Pact headquarters in Moscow.

The Soviets have bilateral "friendship" treaties with several other states. The oldest is with the Mongolian Peoples' Republic, which has been allied with the Soviet Union since the creation of this vassal state under direct Soviet sponsorship in 1921. Soviet military cooperation with the regime in Ulan Bator is currently governed by a treaty of friendship, cooperation, and mutual aid signed on January 16, 1966. This pact provides for the permanent stationing of several Soviet divisions in Mongolia.[11] Over the past decade, the Soviets have signed ten other treaties of friendship and cooperation. These treaties have allied the Soviets with several Third World countries, including Egypt (May 1971), India (August 1971), Iraq (April 1972), Somalia (July 1974), Angola (October 1976), Mozambique (March 1977), Vietnam (November 1978), Ethiopia (November 1978), Afghanistan (December 1978), and South Yemen (October 1979). The treaties with Egypt and Somalia are no longer in effect, having been terminated by those countries in March 1976 and November 1977, respectively, after their relations with the Soviet Union had deteriorated severely.

Most of these treaties contain provisions calling for military cooperation between the parties, the only exceptions being the pacts with India and Vietnam. All ten were accompanied by varying degrees of Soviet military assistance, Soviet utilization of basing facilities, and, in some cases, the substantial presence of Soviet military personnel. Most recently, the treaty with Afghanistan was invoked by the Soviets in December 1979 to justify their invasion that toppled the Amin regime. It is likely that the treaty will also be utilized as the legal basis for the prolonged stationing of several Soviet divisions within Afghanistan. The eight treaties of friendship and cooperation remaining in effect provide dramatic evidence of expanding Soviet involvement in Africa, the Middle East, and Asia.

National objectives, national strategy, and military doctrine

NATIONAL SECURITY OBJECTIVES

The most fundamental security objectives of the Soviet leaders are the defense of the Communist regime and the territorial integrity of the USSR. The bitter experience of the Nazi invasion during World War II and the deep-seated patriotism of the Russian people provide a solid basis for a shared commitment between the Communist party leadership and the Soviet people regarding the primacy of defense considerations.

The Soviet near-obsession with defense has provided a powerful impetus for the accumulation of military power and for the steady expansion of Soviet political and military control beyond the nation's political frontiers. Motivated by what some observers have called a quest for "absolute security," the Soviets have, for over forty years, accorded the highest investment priority to defense. In addition, they have sought to establish and enlarge a territorial buffer, particularly in Europe, between themselves and their prospective enemies. This drive to erect a *cordon sanitaire* lay behind the Soviet establishment of its first Communist satellite regime in Outer Mongolia in 1921 and the Soviet absorption of the Baltic states and eastern portions of Poland, Finland,

Czechoslovakia, and Romania in 1939–45. It also lay behind the subsequent westward extension of this buffer zone via the forcible establishment of "baggage train" Communist regimes, which were imposed throughout most of Eastern Europe in the wake of the advance of the Red Army at the end of World War II.

Retention of subservient Communist governments throughout Eastern Europe has remained a high-priority Soviet security objective throughout the postwar period. This unrelenting Soviet determination has been visibly demonstrated in the Soviet army's brutal suppression of would-be defector regimes in Hungary in 1956 and Czechoslovakia in 1968. The Soviets demonstrated a similar willingness to employ armed force to maintain a "friendly" Communist regime in power in neighboring states in Asia, as evidenced by their 1979 invasion of Afghanistan. This apparent application of the so-called Brezhnev Doctrine, which justifies Soviet armed intervention to defend allied "socialist" regimes endangered by "counterrevolution,"[12] beyond the previous bounds of Eastern Europe does not augur well for other Third World states that have allied themselves with the Soviet Union.

Soviet national security objectives are not confined to these broadly construed "defensive" concerns. As noted earlier, Russian great power and Marxist-Leninist drives combine to underwrite a strong impulse to expand Soviet influence in areas adjacent to the USSR and throughout the world. Soviet leaders, like their Russian predecessors, have evidenced consistent interest in gaining increased influence in Western Europe, the Middle East, and the energy-rich Persian Gulf. Moreover, during the past two decades, Soviet political and military spokesmen have increasingly come to speak about and utilize military power as a primary instrument for the promotion of their state interests.[13]

The Soviets are intensely concerned about their relative position in the international area. They regularly assess their overall position in the world in terms of what they call the "correlation of forces" (*sootnosheniye sil*). In Soviet usage, this correlation refers to the overall balance of economic, military, scientific, and sociopolitical capabilities between two competing states or coalitions of states. Soviet analysts frequently calculate the correlation of forces between both themselves and their leading rival, the United States, and between the socialist and capitalist camps.

The Soviets are invariably optimistic about the long-term trends in the correlation of forces. This optimism reflects the basic tenet of Marxism-Leninism that socialism/communism will inevitably triumph over the capitalist order. Since the close of World War II, the Soviets have consistently claimed that the correlation of forces is shifting inexorably in the favor of the socialist states led by the Soviet Union. Given their relentless accumulation of military power over the past fifteen years, the Soviets have considerable basis to support this contention.

Undoubtedly, the Soviet leaders aspire to be the world's dominant political, military, and economic power. Soviet military experts frequently analyze the narrower military balance, which they describe as the "correlation of military forces and means," between themselves and their prospective enemies.[14] Discussions in this regard range from simple quantitative comparisons of the East-West balance of strategic nuclear or general purpose forces to sophisticated dynamic analyses of relative military capabilities in various scenarios, often using complex mathematical force effectiveness calculations.[15]

Soviet declarations regarding the state of the military balance and Soviet objectives in the military competition with the West have varied considerably. For several decades, dating as far back as declarations accompanying their early five-year economic and defense plans of the 1930s, the Soviets openly declared their intention to acquire military superiority over their prospective enemies. Moreover, in the late 1950s and early 1960s, Soviet political and military figures asserted that Soviet military capabilities were superior to those of the West. The most prominent example of such claims was the series of outspoken assertions by Party First Secretary Nikita Khrushchev in the late 1950s that the Soviet Union was superior to the United States in strategic missile strength. These boasts, made against the backdrop of dramatic Soviet sputnik launches, helped spur the United States into determined efforts to overcome what was later revealed to have been an illusory "missile gap."[16] The fact that the resultant surge of U.S. strategic missile deployments placed the Soviets at a distinctly inferior position throughout the 1960s may help explain the Soviet avoidance of such bold claims of military advantage since that time.

The Soviets have exhibited increased circumspection in public declarations regarding their goals in the East-West arms competition over the past decade. Military figures wrote openly in the 1960s and on into the mid-1970s of the need to attain military-technological superiority over their adversaries.[17] Nevertheless, Soviet claims of the possession of such superiority tapered off significantly in the early 1970s and virtually disappeared from Soviet public discourse in the latter half of the 1970s. This occurred at the very time when the unrelenting momentum of Soviet arms programs was leading many Western observers to argue that the Soviet Union was, in fact, embarked upon a drive to attain clear-cut military superiority. The Soviet declaratory stance since 1977 has become, instead, one of strongly rebutting these

Western charges and of asserting that the Soviet Union seeks nothing more than military parity with the West.[18] Whatever their public position, the combination of military doctrinal incentive, residual siege mentality, and their apparent conviction regarding the political utility of vast military power are such that the Soviet leaders are almost certain to continue to seek and to attain substantial military advantage over their capitalist foes.

The Soviet armed forces make important contributions to the fulfillment of the regime's internal objectives as well. The military forces of the Ministry of Defense have infrequently been involved in the maintenance of domestic order. Over the past two decades their activity in this regard has been limited to occasional use in extraordinary circumstances, such as their reported involvement in the forcible suppression of striking workers in Novocherkassk in 1962[19] and the quelling of rioters protesting food shortages in Rostov in 1963.[20]

The regular troops of the Ministry of Defense are unlikely to see this type of action often because such incidents occur extremely infrequently in the Soviet Union. Moreover, responsibility for the maintenance of public order rests primarily with the Ministry of Internal Affairs (MVD), and the Committee of State Security (KGB), both of which have sizable forces organized in regular military formations available for such contingencies. These internal security troops are, interestingly, included by the Soviets as an element of the Soviet armed forces.

By far the most important domestic political role played by the Soviet military establishment occurs in the area of political socialization. Some two million young men are inducted into the Soviet armed forces annually for terms of service of one and a half to three years.[21] During their stints in the military, these young men are exposed to an intensive indoctrination effort supervised by the political officers of the Main Political Administration, whose organization and activities will be discussed below in greater detail. A combination of compulsory attendence at five hours of weekly political instruction conducted by the political officers and mandatory participation in the activities of the Young Communist League, the Komsomol, are utilized in a determined effort to inculcate the desired domestic and foreign policy perspectives. These experiences within the armed forces represent the final phase of a sustained, Party-controlled political indoctrination campaign, begun in the nursery schools and elementary schools, that is designed to meet the regime's long-term objective of developing properly oriented "new Soviet men."

The Soviet armed forces also contribute in various ways to the functioning of the Soviet economy. Soviet army personnel stationed in agricultural regions within the USSR are regularly called upon to aid in the harvest. In addition, contingents of the 400,000-person Construction Troops, although predominantly involved in the construction of defense-related facilities, are also employed to build a variety of civilian projects, such as Moscow State University, Sheremetovo Airport, and multistory apartment buildings in Moscow.[22] Both the Construction Troops and the Ministry of Defense's Railroad Troops are working on the Soviet showcase construction project of the late 70s and early 80s, the new rail line, called the Baikal-Amur Magistral (BAM), which will run parallel to the legendary Transiberian Railroad through Siberia and the Far East to the Pacific.

NATIONAL SECURITY STRATEGY

Despite the Soviet penchant for authoritative programmatic statements and the voluminous output of their sizable communities of political commentators and professional military theoreticians, there is no single, publicly available document or group of documents that sets forth the Soviet strategy for pursuing its national security objectives. It is quite likely that, even within the inner councils of the Kremlin, no such document exists. Nevertheless, on the basis of the statements of Soviet political and military spokesmen and the many defense-related activities of the Soviet government, it is possible to piece together what appears to be the broad guidelines of the Soviet national security strategy.

The central element of the Soviet national security strategy is quite straightforward: the Soviets relentlessly expand and improve their large and diverse military arsenal and then utilize these capabilities to protect and advance their interests on the world scene. First and foremost, the Soviet leaders rely upon their steadily growing military power to deter attack on the Soviet Union itself and on their allies and friends. They accomplish this by maintaining a full spectrum of strategic and general purpose forces.

The Soviets assign the highest priority to the deterrence of nuclear war. Over the past three decades, Soviet spokesmen have repeatedly made deterrent threats, directed primarily at the United States and its NATO allies. Their approach to deterrence has a decidedly traditional military tone. Soviet military and political figures have consistently warned that any state that dares to attack the Soviet Union or its allies will receive a "crushing rebuff" and suffer certain military defeat.

Soviet military doctrine fully supports this war-winning approach to deterrence. It commits the Soviet armed forces, in the event of a war, to a combination of offensive and defensive operations designed to allow the Soviet Union to survive and prevail in any conflict, including a world-wide nuclear war. Moreover, Soviet force deployments—from the fielding of large numbers of accurate ICBM weapons, which are increasingly capable of successful "counterforce" strikes against U.S. silo-based ICBMs, to the steady upgrading of their vast active and passive defenses, which are designed to limit damage to the Soviet homeland—are consistent with this war-fighting orientation.

This victory-oriented Soviet approach differs markedly from the American perspective on strategic deterrence, which has consistently emphasized a threat to punish any aggressor by devastating his urban-industrial base with retaliatory strikes.[23] This is not to say that the Soviet war-fighting perspective lacks a substantial punishment dimension. Soviet military writings on general nuclear war clearly assign the highest priority to attacks on the enemy's military forces, in particular, his nuclear delivery systems. Yet at the same time, Soviet doctrinal writings also call for extensive strikes against key industrial and political facilities throughout an enemy's homeland with the stated objective of disrupting and devastating his economy and political-administrative apparatus and breaking the morale of his people.

The Soviets have evidenced little interest in restraining their strategic programs in the interest of maintaining a stable nuclear deterrent stand-off based on mutual societal vulnerability. From time to time, Soviet diplomats, civilian academics, and even military writers have acknowledged the existence of such a state of mutual vulnerability.[24] Nevertheless, Soviets' doctrinal pronouncements, their unwillingness to constrain significantly their growing hard-target counterforce capabilities in SALT, and, most importantly, their unrelenting drive to acquire survivable forces with comprehensive war-fighting capabilities all point toward an abiding concern for the security of Soviet deterrent capabilities. Nevertheless, the Soviets show little interest in exercising restraint that would assist the United States in maintaining its assured retaliatory capability.

This is not to say that the Soviets have succeeded or are close to succeeding in denying the United States its very substantial nuclear retaliatory capabilities. But it is to recognize that, their periodic disclaimers notwithstanding, the Soviets show strong inclinations to do so. The Soviet view of strategic nuclear stability appears to be, quite simply, that the more powerful the USSR is, the more stable the international situation.

The threat to defeat any aggressor in a general nuclear war is the cornerstone of Soviet deterrent policy. It is complemented by a clear determination to acquire the capabilities to fight and win lesser conflicts in major theaters of war along the periphery of the Soviet Union. Soviet preparations to fight successfully in such theater conflicts include a readiness to engage in conventional, chemical, or nuclear warfare supported by the combination of a well-developed combined-arms force employment doctrine and a panoply of impressive military capabilities.

Throughout their history, the Soviets have confronted a serious "two-front" security challenge due to the presence of hostile, militarily significant adversaries on their extended European and Far Eastern borders. Consequently, the Soviets have long adhered to a "two-war" policy in the sense that they have sought to maintain sufficient forces in both theaters with the capability, at a minimum, to defend these areas independently. This "two-war" policy, or "two-major-contingency approach" in the language of contemporary American defense policy planning, has become increasingly evident since the severe deterioration of Sino-Soviet relations in the early 1960s. Over the past fifteen years, Soviet forces facing China in the Far East and Central Asia have more than doubled in strength. Yet this was accomplished at the same time that Soviet forces stationed in Eastern Europe and the western portions of the Soviet Union were being significantly expanded and upgraded.

In the 1970s, the Soviets dramatically improved their capabilities to project forces by air and sea far beyond the traditional peripheral reach of the Red Army. In this same period, Soviet military writers increasingly touted the role of the Soviet armed forces in advancing Soviet foreign policy interests throughout the world. These enhanced Soviet force projection capabilities, combined with the Soviet occupation of Afghanistan and its resultant strengthening of Soviet forces in Southwest Asia, suggest the emergence of a new "half-war" or lesser contingency objective in Soviet national security strategy. This new strategy and attendant capability appear to be directed primarily toward possible operations in the Middle East and Persian Gulf, with further potential for supporting longer range projection of Soviet military power into Africa or Southeast Asia as well.

Soviet national security strategy is not confined to the accumulation of military power to support its deterrence and theater warfare objectives. It also includes the utilization of arms control negotiations and military assistance programs of various types to support the achievement of Soviet foreign policy goals.

The Soviets have participated in virtually all of the important international arms control negotiations since the close of World War II. A major objective of this participation has been the Soviet determination to gain widespread recognition as one of the world's two leading powers. The Soviets have also used these negotiations to support their claims of peace-loving intent on the international scene.

The Soviet pursuit of what they call "military détente" became a central element in their broader policy of promoting political détente with the West during the 1970s. In addition to the motivations cited above, Soviet arms control efforts have been designed to foster mutual East-West commitments to avoid nuclear conflict. Despite the clearly stated war-winning objectives of their doctrine and the periodic claims by military figures that victory is possible in a nuclear conflict, Soviet military and political commentators have repeatedly acknowledged the catastrophic consequences of general nuclear war and are certain to support its avoidance. The Soviets also seek to use arms control negotiations and agreements to constrain the military activities of their adversaries while maintaining maximum flexibility for themselves. Arms control efforts in pursuit of these objectives are likely to remain a fundamental element of the Soviet national security strategy.

For over fifty years, the Soviets have employed military assistance programs to aid factions struggling to gain power and to support friendly regimes in power against internal opposition or international foes. These programs have frequently proven useful as a means to gain political influence in the recipient nation and, in many cases, to maneuver the recipient into a position of dependence on the Soviet Union for economic support or for maintenance and logistic support of the military equipment provided.

Since the mid-1950s, the Soviets have had considerable experience in this area. Major infusions of military assistance have by no means guaranteed success for the Soviets in their dealing with Third World countries. Despite extensive Soviet military aid programs over several years, the Soviets suffered major setbacks in their dealings with Indonesia in the mid-1960s and Egypt in the mid-1970s. Nevertheless, the Soviets clearly intend to continue to use this instrument to strengthen their ties and create further dependencies with old clients and to seek to move other countries into the Soviet sphere of influence.

Soviet military assistance programs complement their growing capabilities for long-range power projection activities discussed earlier. Arms aid has frequently facilitated initial Soviet acquisition of basing, staging, and transit rights that are critical to operations in distant areas. Military assistance efforts often result in the establishment of substantial stockpiles of modern Soviet weapons in distant areas that can readily be utilized in short order by Soviet-sponsored surrogates like the Cubans or East Germans, or directly by Soviet military personnel. Regional and internal tensions that appear inevitable in the Third World in the years ahead suggest that military assistance diplomacy will remain a vital element of Soviet foreign and defense policy.

DOMESTIC DETERMINANTS

The Soviet national security strategy is the product of many diverse influences. These include not only the aspirations and concerns derived from Imperial Russian and Soviet historical experience and Marxist-Leninist ideology noted above, but also the geographical character of the USSR and various aspects of the Soviet political and economic systems.

CHARACTER OF THE POLITICAL SYSTEM

Defense matters are clearly one of the highest priority policy issues within the Soviet system. As such, they are carefully overseen by the top Soviet leadership. Consequently, all key defense decisions are apparently made (or at least reviewed) by the twenty-three-member Party Politburo, which sits atop the combined Communist party and Soviet government hierarchies. The priority of defense matters is also evident in the fact that each time a single dominant Soviet political leader has emerged, he has personally taken charge of defense matters. Iosif Stalin, Nikita Khrushchev, and Leonid Brezhnev all chose to confirm their personal responsibility for defense by assuming the post of supreme commander in chief of the Soviet armed forces.[25]

This centralization of authority at the top regarding defense matters has several important consequences. First, it means that there are no significant checks built into the system once the decision is taken within the Politburo. Second, given the lengthy tenure of the senior Soviet political leaders—Stalin dominated the Soviet political scene from the mid-1920s until 1953, Khrushchev from 1957 to 1964, and Brezhnev from 1964 until this article was written (early 1980)—this centralization has provided a pronounced element of continuity in Soviet military policy. Third, the reverse side of this highly personalized pattern is that when a period of leadership transition occurs, it clearly carries with it considerable potential for significant change in defense policy. Consequently, during these struggles for power, which are inevitable due to the absence of a regularized procedure for Soviet leadership succession, the leading contenders are virtually certain to be particularly attentive to defense issues. Conflict over defense matters was evident in the struggle between Khrushchev and Malenkov during the post-Stalin succession in 1953–54, and it appears to have surfaced briefly in 1965 following Khrushchev's political demise.[26] Fully aware of this, the constituencies with substantial stakes in defense matters, the professional military and their allies in the defense production ministries, are certain to defend and promote their interests actively during such succession periods.

The closed nature of Soviet political processes is another aspect of the Soviet political system that influences both the formulation of Soviet defense policy and our understanding of it in the West. Soviet policy making in all issue areas is conducted in considerable secrecy. This pattern is most pronounced with regard to national security matters. U.S. suspicions about the strict compartmentalization of defense-related information within the Soviet system were dramatically confirmed in an often-recounted incident that occurred during the early phases of the Strategic Arms Limitation Talks. At that time, the leading Soviet military representative, then Colonel General N. V. Ogarkov (he is now a marshal of the Soviet Union and chief of the General Staff), asked the U.S. negotiators not to discuss the details of Soviet strategic weapons deployments with Soviet civilian representatives, who, he said, were not authorized access to such information.[27] This denial of information to those outside the professional military establishment and a small circle of senior Soviet leaders is similarly evident in the limited knowledge of Soviet defense information found among the civilian national security policy analysts of the world affairs institutes of the Academy of Sciences.[28]

The consequences of this closed policy-making pattern and compartmentalization of defense information are twofold. First, in such an environment, those with access to the controlled information, in this case for the most part officers of the Ministry of Defense, are in an excellent position to influence decisively the formulation and implementation of defense policy. This new monopoly of relevant information and expertise is a crucial factor that strengthens the hand of the armed forces on the Soviet political scene. Secondly, this secrecy effectively limits the data available to both internal Soviet and foreign observers about defense policy making. It compels Western analysts to rely upon a variety of partial sources, including a smattering of memoir accounts, observable activities such as major weapons deployments, and Kremlinological analyses of various Soviet official publications, in order to piece together plausible explanations of Soviet defense policy.

THE ECONOMIC SYSTEM

The Soviet defense effort has long been the primary beneficiary of the Soviet command economy. The extent of this priority has been such that some have been prompted to argue that the accumulation of military power has been the primary social product of the Soviet economic system, while the production of other goods and services is nothing more than necessary social overhead.[29] Although this may be somewhat overstated, there is no doubt that military weaponry has consistently been accorded the highest priority in a host of inputs, including direct budgetary support, the infusion of the highest quality equipment such as advanced computers and machine tools, and the recruitment of talented scientific and technical personnel.

Throughout the Soviet period, the economy has been largely autarkic. Consequently, questions of access to imports or markets for exports have had little influence on Soviet foreign or defense policy. In recent years, however, various difficulties in the functioning of the Soviet economy have begun to surface that may alter this situation. These problems include: a steady decline in the overall rate of economic growth, the prospect that Soviet oil production will peak in the early 1980s and then decline for the next several years at the same time that domestic energy demand is projected to rise steadily,[30] continuing poor performance in agriculture (the economy's endemically weak area), and declining worker productivity.[31]

Many of these problems have been evident for several years. They were almost certainly major factors behind the decision of Mr. Brezhnev and his colleagues to pursue a "policy of selective economic interdependence" as a key element of Soviet détente with the West throughout the 1970s.[32] While by no means abandoning their pronounced tendency toward economic self-reliance, the Soviets have significantly expanded their involvement in the world economy over the past decade. However, substantial technology imports, joint ventures in the expansion of motor transport, and major grain imports have failed to reverse the adverse trends in the performance of the Soviet economy. Thus, it appears that if the Soviets are to address these deficiencies effectively, they must reexamine both their external trade relations and the structure and working of their highly centralized command economy.

Continuing economic difficulties could, of course, have significant impact on Soviet defense policy. Some have suggested that these difficulties will prompt the leaders in the Kremlin to reduce their investments in defense. Soviet defense expenditures are estimated by the Central Intelligence Agency to have run at approximately 13–14 percent of the Soviet GNP for the past several years and to have increased steadily at an average of 4–5 percent per year.[33] Barring a very dramatic downturn in the performance of the overall economy, however, cuts in defense spending do not appear likely, at least over the next several years. Ever since the fall of Khrushchev in 1964, the Brezhnev-led leadership has proved itself prepared to accept declining overall economic growth and to continue to suppress the consumer demands of the Russian people in order to sustain the relentless expansion of Soviet military strength. And they are very likely to continue to do so.

GEOGRAPHY

The Soviet Union occupies a central geographic position, straddling the continents of Europe and Asia. Spanning approximately 170 degrees of longitude, the USSR directly borders on twelve neighboring states and looks out across enclosed seas at an additional seven. Thus, Soviet interests and concerns range from the Scandinavian neighbors of Norway and Finland in the northwest, through the Communist client regimes of Eastern Europe, on to Turkey, Iran, and Afghanistan in the Near East, to Pakistan and India in South Asia, and China, North Korea, and Japan in the Far East. The majority of these frontiers are marked by no significant geographical barriers, thus contributing to the historical perceptions and reality of Russian vulnerability to overland invasion. From the critical "heartland" location, the leaders in the Kremlin, like their czarist predecessors, confront a multitude of challenges and opportunities along this lengthy frontier.

The Soviet Union is richly endowed with natural resources. Its deposits of precious metals, petroleum, natural gas, coal, iron, and several other minerals are among the largest in the world. However, many of these deposits are located in relatively inaccessible regions of Siberia, thus significantly complicating successful exploitation. Another important geographic characteristic is the northerly latitude of the Soviet Union. Most of the country lies above 40°N. Consequently, the amount of arable land available for sustained cultivation is quite small for a country of such vast size and has proven consistently inadequate to meet the needs of the nation's more than 260 million people.

PUBLIC OPINION

The authoritarian character of the Soviet political system is such that public opinion plays no direct role in the shaping of the nation's foreign or domestic policies. Nevertheless, the prevailing views of the Soviet citizens on defense matters are not without importance.

By all evidence, the Russians are an intensely patriotic people with a genuine commitment to the defense of the *rodina,* the motherland. Whatever their views about the domestic policies of the Soviet regime, the vast majority of Soviet people are intensely proud of their nation's political, economic, and military accomplishments and are prepared to support the Kremlin unquestioningly in the name of the defense of Mother Russia. This is not to say that many Soviet citizens would not prefer a reduction in defense spending—Soviet dissident literature has periodically included calls for this. But such matters are not the business of the Soviet people, who are expected to (and largely do) accept their nation's massive defense exertions silently.

NATIONALITY ISSUES

The Soviet leaders, like the czars before them, face a significant "nationalities problem." The USSR is a multinational state composed of over 130 national groups. This polyglot population can be usefully divided into two major ethnic groupings: the European nationalities, including the Great Russians, Ukrainians, Byelorussians, Moldavians, Latvians, Lithuanians, and Estonians; and the non-Europeans, such as the Uzbeks, Tartars, Kazakhs, Azeri, Turkmen, Kirgiz, Tadzhiks, Armenians, and Georgians.

The multinational character of the Soviet state is reflected in the federal structure of the Union of Soviet Socialist Republics, with its fifteen union-republics that are organized along national lines and a host of smaller nationality-based autonomous republics and autonomous regions. Yet despite the formal lip service paid to the rights and traditions of the constituent nationalities, the Soviet leadership has always demanded full subordination of these groups to the will of the Communist party center in Moscow. This Party core has been and remains thoroughly dominated by the Great Russians, with substantial assistance from the other Slavs, the Ukrainians and Byelorussians.

Nevertheless, the national identities have persisted and remain a substantial concern to the regime. The primary problem posed by the nationalities to the Kremlin authorities today is not one of incipient political separatism, but rather a demand from many of the nationality groups for a larger voice within the national system and for somewhat greater autonomy in the handling of local issues. These matters have no clear-cut impact upon defense matters.[34]

However, in recent years the Soviet nationalities issue has taken on a new dimension due to the pronounced disparities in the population growth rates of the European and non-European groups. The non-European nationalities of Central Asia have produced far higher birth rates over the past few decades, and this disparity is virtually certain to remain in the years ahead. This trend is bound to have significant impact on Soviet economic choices in the years ahead. It has already raised what one author calls the specter of the demographic "yellowing" of the Soviet population as the Asiatic peoples become a larger and larger share of the populace. The leaders in Moscow must either succeed in encouraging a migration of the more numerous Asiatics into the labor-short manufacturing centers of the Urals and European Russia or take the necessary steps to expand greatly the industrial facilities of Central Asia.[35]

The increased numbers of Asians within the annual cohorts that are inducted into the Soviet armed forces will be likely to necessitate major adjustments in assignment policies within the armed forces. Up to this time, Central Asians, whose mastery of the Russian language is often rudimentary, have generally been excluded from most prestigious, high-technology military career fields. They are commonly found, instead, to make up the majority of pick-and-shovel soldiers of the Construction Troops as one encounters these units in Moscow and other major cities.

In sum, despite the various problems raised by the nationalities issue, it currently does not appear to pose a significant threat to the political integrity of military preparedness of the USSR.

FORCE EMPLOYMENT DOCTRINE

Over the years, the Soviets have developed a distinctive style of warfare that reflects a variety of influences. These include: imperial Russian military tradition (transmitted to the Red Army by a sizable core of former czarist officers who were particularly active in the development of Soviet military doctrine in the 1920s and 1930s), the geographic setting of the USSR, the numbers and types of weapons made available by the pampered defense sector of the Soviet economy, and a unique Soviet approach to theater war that emerged from the military scientific specialists working in the General Staff and the prestigious senior military academics in Moscow beginning in the early 1930s.[36]

The Soviets devote enormous attention to the study and elaboration of military doctrine. This activity falls fully within the purview of the professional military establishment. Successive generations of officers attached to the Military Science Directorate of the General Staff and the military science and history faculties of such academies as the Voroshilov Academy of the General Staff and the Frunze Academy have developed an elaborate and highly formalized body of military doctrinal concepts. These concepts are presented in a host of journals and books that steadily pours out of the Ministry of Defense's military publishing house (*Voenizdat*), and in classified publications such as the General Staff's *Military Thought* (*Voennaia mysl'*).

The contemporary Soviet approach to theater war, and, to a considerable extent, intercontinental conflict as well, clearly reflects key elements that were already evident in the Soviet doctrine for massed, armored warfare called the theory of operations in depth, developed almost fifty years ago.[37] These guiding principles include a commitment to seize the initiative at the outset of hostilities and to conduct bold offensive operations with massed, armor-heavy forces at high tempo in order to annihilate completely the enemy's military forces. At the same time, Soviet doctrine calls for all possible offensive and defensive efforts to limit the damage that the Soviet Union itself would suffer in a war. Soviet military theory categorically rejects the dominance of a single weapon or branch of the service in the conduct of these operations. It calls instead for the reinforcing efforts of all ground, sea, and air forces to achieve victory via the so-called combined-arms concept.[38]

Contemporary Soviet military writings deal primarily with various facets of a complex scenario for general nuclear war. This literature describes several aspects of this global clash between the opposing socialist and capitalist social systems, including: (1) a major theater land and air battle; (2) war at sea; (3) both regional and intercontinental missile and bomber exchanges; and (4) extensive efforts to defend the Soviet homeland. While a comprehensive review of these variegated operations is beyond the scope of this study, some of the highlights of the distinctive Soviet force employment doctrine are given below.

Theater war. Soviet doctrine exhibits a readiness to conduct massive ground-air offensive operations against NATO and, presumably, the People's Republic of China, using only conventional weapons for an opening period of indeterminant length. The Soviets say they are prepared to initiate, at the same time, extensive nuclear operations either at the very outset of the conflict or at any time during its conduct. For the latter case, the Soviets maintain a high state of nuclear readiness and clearly intend to preempt any enemy resort to the use of nuclear weapons with massed missile and aircraft strikes of their own throughout the depth of the theater.

In either a conventional or a nuclear environment, the Soviets plan to mass their armor-heavy forces along selected main axes of attack and to make a series of simultaneous breakthroughs of the enemy's defenses. These breakthroughs are to be exploited immediately by the continuous introduction of additional echelons that are to advance rapidly in order to encircle and destroy the enemy's main formations and occupy his territory in a matter of days.[39]

This land offensive is to be supported by extensive "air operations" that combine units from tactical ("frontal") and strategic ("long-range") aviation to destroy enemy forces, especially nuclear delivery systems, throughout the theater.[40] In a nuclear conflict, these air forces will be supplemented by operational-tactical and regional strategic missile forces in the conduct of massive strikes both on the battlefield and throughout the enemy's rear area.

War at sea. Primary emphasis will be devoted to efforts to destroy enemy naval combatants, in particular aircraft carriers and ballistic missile submarines, that are capable of striking Soviet forward-deployed forces or targets on Soviet territory. These efforts will involve coordinated attacks by cruise-missile–equipped surface ships, submarines, and land-based bomber aviation.

Over the past decade the Soviets have also developed a concept calling for the employment of combined antisubmarine warfare assets—attack submarines, surface ships, and aircraft—in a "bastion defense" or "strategic support mission" to help protect their own strategic ballistic missile submarines, deployed in nearby waters, from U.S. attack submarines.[41]

The forces of the Soviet navy are expected to conduct amphibious operations using naval infantry and ground force units along the maritime flanks in support of theater land offensives. They must also be prepared to execute coastal defense operations to deny the enemy the ability to mount successful amphibious assaults against the Soviet Union.

Soviet naval air and submarine forces are also tasked to interdict enemy sea lines of communications, although this appears to be a secondary mission.

Intercontinental nuclear warfare. In the event that a strategic nuclear exchange occurs, Soviet doctrine includes a strong predisposition to launch a preemptive strike against U.S. strategic forces if U.S. preparations to commence nuclear operations can be detected.[42] If preemption is not achieved, there are hints that the Soviets might employ a "launch under attack" tactic[43] or, failing this, simply retaliate after absorbing the U.S. strike.

In any case, Soviet ICBMs, SLBMs, and strategic bombers would be employed to strike simultaneously such targets as U.S. strategic forces (ICBMs, SSBNs in port, and bombers), key military command and control facilities, major groupings of general purpose forces, and a variety of economic and political objectives, including electrical power systems, stocks of strategic raw materials, and large industrial and transport centers.[44]

These strikes, executed in the so-called initial period of a general nuclear war, are said to be capable of having a decisive influence upon the outcome of a war, although "final victory" is said to be achievable only with the combined efforts of all arms and services.

Soviet doctrinal writings have displayed no interest in the possibility of limited nuclear warfare at either the central strategic or theater level. The Soviets have expressly rejected U.S. concepts of limited nuclear war as artificial "rules of the game" and continue to embrace instead a concept of massive nuclear strikes for maximum military and political effectiveness. Nevertheless, growing Soviet capabilities could support a wide spectrum of controlled nuclear operations, which they could choose to employ in a crisis.[45]

The Soviets also speak of their intentions to conduct active antiair, antimissile, and antispace (antisatellite) measures in combination with extensive civil defense activities to reduce the damage inflicted on the USSR by those enemy forces that survive the vigorous Soviet counterforce attacks.

The defense decision-making process

THE ORGANIZATIONAL SETTING

As described earlier, political power in the Soviet Union is concentrated within the hands of the few who control the Soviet Communist party. The small group who determine the nation's destiny from atop the twin organizational networks of the Communist party and the Soviet government clearly exercise control over national security policy as one of their highest priority activities.

In analyzing the pattern of defense policy making and implementation in the USSR, it is useful to think in terms of a "decisional trajectory" model, which has been developed by two students of Soviet foreign policy.[46] This approach analyzes policy making as a sequence of events beginning with problem identification, then proceeding with information collection and interpretation, the development and analysis of alternative courses of action, decision making (i.e., selection of a course of action), policy elaboration, and, finally, policy implementation. The trajectory aspect of the metaphor is used to indicate that during the course of this sequence, these stages generally take place at successively higher levels of authority on the path upward toward decision and then drop down once again to lower levels during the process of policy elaboration and implementation. When combined with examination of the roles, resources, and tactics of the various organizations and individuals involved, the decisional trajectory model can significantly assist us in understanding the dynamics of Soviet defense policy.

There is a constellation of organizations in which Soviet defense policy is made. It includes specialized defense-related organizations and generalist bodies, whose involvements in national security issues constitute only a portion of their overall activities. Some of these organs are active across the full range of national security matters, while the activities of others are limited to involvement in a single defense issue area, such as weapons acquisition. The various organizations within the vast Party and government bureaucracies that are engaged in defense policy development, decision making, and execution often serve as arenas for political competition among key individuals and groups interested in shaping Soviet defense policy.

On the Party side, the bodies of note are the topmost elements of the Party bureaucracy, including the Politburo, the Secretariat, and certain departments of the Party apparatus that are formally attached to the Central Committee. The most important of these is the twenty-three-member Politburo. This small body, with fourteen full voting members and nine nonvoting "candidates," is a generalist organ that exercises ultimate decisional authority on all issues of consequence in the Soviet Union. It can be presumed to have the prerogative of formally approving all key defense decisions. This places the Politburo at the apogee of the decisional trajectory for such diverse defense matters as the formulation of Soviet military strategy, the development and acquisition of weaponry, and, of course, the threat to use or the actual employment of Soviet military power.

Although it has ultimate decisional authority, the full Politburo is almost certainly unable to maintain close supervision of defense matters on a regular basis. The highest level body with this responsibility is the Defense Council (*Soviet Oborony*). This organization, although officially linked to the Presidium of the Supreme Soviet within the governmental structure by Article 121 of the 1977 Soviet Constitution, appears to function as a defense subcommittee for the Politburo.

The Defense Council is the latest in a long line of high-level councils, or "soviets," with combined civilian and military membership that have supervised Soviet defense matters. Soviet publications have only recently acknowledged the existence of the Defense Council and have never disclosed its membership beyond announcing that the regime's most powerful figure, Leonid Brezhnev, is its chairman. Western observers speculate that Brezhnev is very likely to be joined by other key Politburo members: almost certainly (prior to his death in 1980) by Alexei Kosygin (chairman of the Presidium of the Council of Ministers),* Andrei Kirilenko (party secretary), Dmitri Ustinov (minister of defense), and perhaps Yuri Andropov (head of the KGB), Andrei Gromyko (foreign minister), and Mikhail Suslov (Party secretary) as well.

Staff support for the Defense Council may be provided by those elements of the central Party apparatus that support the Politburo, perhaps with the assistance of the General Staff of the Soviet armed forces. Such General Staff involvement would provide the basis for the regular participation of Marshal N. V. Ogarkov, the chief of the General Staff and the ranking professional military officer within the Ministry of Defense. Whatever its permanent membership, other senior Party, government, and military figures are likely to be invited to attend the deliberations of the Defense Council when issues within their special competence are under consideration.

There is no information available on the activities of the Defense Council. However, memoir accounts of the activities of its predecessors, known variously as the Council of Workers' and Peasants' Defense, the Council of Labor and Defense, and the Supreme Military Council, indicate that it probably serves as the forum within which such matters as significant weapons development and procurement programs, defense budgets, and major force deployments are discussed. These deliberations, carefully orchestrated in accordance with Brezhnev's consensus-oriented style, are likely to culminate in preliminary decisions that are, in turn, considered and almost certainly approved by the full Politburo. During wartime, the Defense Council would almost certainly provide the nucleus for the formation of a new State Defense Committee, similar to the body of that name created during World War II, which would oversee the total Soviet defense effort.

While these two top-level bodies play critical roles in all major defense decisions, they are not involved in the myriad of activities that surrounds the critical tasks of gathering and interpreting information, developing and analyzing defense policy alternatives, and implementing the courses of action selected by the senior Party leadership. These activities are largely the responsibility of the various components of the Ministry of Defense, and, to a lesser degree, the industrial ministries engaged in the design and production of armaments, and a few other specialized Party and government organizations.

The Ministry of Defense has by far the largest role in policy formulation and execution. It is a central actor in virtually all aspects of Soviet defense activity. The most important elements within the ministry are the Main Military Council, the General Staff, the five "services" of the Soviet armed forces—the Strategic Rocket Forces, National Air Defense (*PVO Strany*), navy, ground forces, and air forces—and a series of central directorates, including Rear Services, Civil Defense, Armaments, Construction and Billeting, and the Main Inspectorate.

This key ministry is run by the minister of defense, Marshal D. F. Ustinov, who is assisted by three first deputy ministers and ten deputy ministers. The former group consists of Marshal N. V. Ogarkov, chief of the General Staff; Marshal V. G. Kulikov, commander in chief of the Warsaw Pact; and Marshal S. L. Sokolov, who apparently supervises the day-to-day administration of the ministry. The latter group includes all the service commanders in chief and the heads of the important central directorates.

Marshal Ustinov and his collection of deputies, joined by the chief of the ministry's Main Personnel Directorate, General of the Army I. N. Shkadov, the chief of the Main Political Administration, General of the Army A. A. Yepishev, and perhaps even the chairman of the Defense Council, Leonid Brezhnev, make up the membership of Defense Ministry's Main Military Council. This collective organ is the most senior of an extensive network of military councils ("soviets") that are found throughout the services and the major regional commands—the military and air defense districts, groups of forces and fleets that are discussed below. The Main Military Council is a high-level advisory body that apparently serves as a forum for the discussion of key policy issues. It

*The position is now held by N. A. Tikhonov.—Ed.

would almost certainly become the *Stavka,* or general headquarters, in time of war.

Defense Minister Dmitri Ustinov, although he carries the rank of marshal of the Soviet Union, is not a career military professional. Rather, he has, for over forty years, been a major figure in Soviet armaments development and production. He served as commissar of armaments under Stalin during World War II and then occupied other key defense production posts in the Party and government before being named to succeed a veteran professional soldier, Marshal A. A. Grechko, as defense minister upon Grechko's sudden death in April 1976. Ustinov's tenure as minister of defense is rather short in comparison with the majority of his deputies, whose terms average more than ten years. The most senior of these is Admiral S. G. Gorshkov, who has commanded the Soviet navy since 1956. Despite Ustinov's likely sympathy for Soviet military viewpoints on such matters as the priority of defense spending, the professional military would almost certainly prefer a career officer in this key post.

Another important figure in the senior leadership cadre of the Ministry of Defense is General of the Army A. A. Yepishev, who heads the Main Political Administration (MPA) of the Soviet army and navy. Although General Yepishev is neither a first deputy nor a deputy minister of defense, he is accorded the fourth-ranked protocol position within the ministry, standing between first deputies Marshals Kulikov and Sokolov. This reflects the importance accorded the MPA, whose political officers, serving throughout the armed forces, are the descendants of the Bolshevik political commissars that were employed during the Civil War to monitor the reliability of the Red Army's military commanders. The MPA has operated since 1925 in the unique position of having "the rights of a department of the Central Committee." It is responsible, as discussed in greater detail below, for the political indoctrination of the Soviet officer corps and enlisted personnel.

Within the Soviet military establishment, the General Staff is unquestionably the most important single element. As the central, directing force of the Soviet armed forces, its role is well described by the title of a lengthy study by one of its most important founding figures, Marshal Boris Shaposhnikov, who described the role of the General Staff as that of "the brain of the army."[47]

The Soviet General Staff directs and controls virtually all the military activities of the Soviet armed forces. Its many components, including the Main Operations, Main Intelligence, Main Organization and Mobilization, Main Foreign Military Assistance, and Military Science Directorates, play the dominant role in such diverse undertakings as the formulation of doctrinal concepts, the refinement of Soviet military organization, the development of mobilization and military contingency plans, as well as the peacetime training and, if need be, the wartime operational direction of the Soviet armed forces.

The General Staff is manned by both a cadre of career staff officers, many of whom spend decades in its directorates, and some of the most promising command figures drawn from all of the services, who usually attend the prestigious Voroshilov Academy of the General Staff in Moscow prior to their posting in the General Staff. During the Second World War, representatives of the General Staff were sent out to monitor the activities of the staffs of the fronts and armies in the field.[48] It is quite possible that the General Staff continues to reinforce its control today by placing its representatives on the staffs of the military district, the groups of forces in Eastern Europe, and the main staffs of the five services during peacetime.

Those services are responsible for the peacetime training and equipping of their various subelements. Their activities are overseen by the service commanders in chief (CInCs), who are deputy ministers of defense. These prestigious figures are assisted by military councils, whose members include their several deputy commanders, chiefs of staff, and deputies for political affairs, as well as the main staffs of the services.

The operational responsibilities of the services are not clear. In peacetime the headquarters of the navy, Strategic Rocket Forces, and National Air Defense may exercise operational control over their respective forces in the field. This does not appear to be the case for the air forces or the ground forces, however. In time of war the service CInCs would be actively involved in the direction of combat operations as members of the foremost collective military command organ, the *Stavka.* The service main staffs would likely be involved in directing continuing service training and equipping functions, in providing specialized staff support to the CInCs, and, as an alternative channel of operational command and control, in supplementing the primary command channels run by the General Staff.

Each of the central directorates of the Defense Ministry is responsible for a particular defense function. The Armaments Directorate, headed by Marshal of Signal Troops N. N. Alekseyev, for example, plays an important role in the management of weapons research, development, and production, while the Civil Defense Directorate, led by General of the Army A. T. Altunin, directs the extensive national civil defense program. Soviet civil defense efforts involve not only a substantial cadre of regular troops assigned to civil defense duties but also a vast regional network that combines the efforts of local Party and government organizations, economic enterprises, and educational institutions.

In both peace and war, most Soviet forces are deployed and directed by a series of geographically organized commands. The intercontinental- and regional-range ballistic missiles of the Strategic Rocket Forces, for example, are deployed in several missile armies scattered throughout the USSR. Similarly, the strategic bombers of Long-Range Aviation are assigned to regional bomber commands. The surface-to-air missile troops, radar-technical troops, and interceptor aviation of National Air Defense (*PVO Strany*) are controlled by a network of air defense districts, while the some 170 tank, motorized rifle, and airborne divisions of the ground forces and their supporting tactical air armies of Air Force Frontal Aviation are controlled by the commanders of the sixteen military districts within the Soviet Union[49] and the four groups of Soviet forces in Eastern Europe.[50] The majority of these military districts and groups would become "fronts" in wartime. They would fall either directly under the control of the *Stavka* and its working organ, the General Staff, in Moscow or, alternatively, under the control of a senior figure commanding a theater of war. Finally, the increasingly active Soviet navy is divided into four widely separated fleets, the Northern, Baltic, Black Sea, and Pacific fleets, with headquarters in Severomorsk, Kaliningrad, Sevastopol, and Vladivostok, respectively.

Although the Ministry of Defense dominates the policy preparation and implementation stages in most defense-related matters, several civilian organizations outside the Ministry of Defense play active roles in these phases of Soviet weapons development and production. While the dynamics of this process are discussed in greater detail in another portion of this volume,[51] it is worth noting some of the key organizations involved in the weapons acquisition process. The largest organizations in this regard are the various industrial ministries engaged in defense research, development, and production. This group includes nine defense production ministries whose primary products are military equipment and several others that provide important support to the armaments effort.[52] Basic research in defense-related technologies is conducted within the research establishments of the Ministry of Defense and the defense production ministries as well as many institutes of the Academy of Sciences.

The relations between these defense research and production organizations and their steady customer, the Ministry of Defense, have been traditionally supervised by the Military-Industrial Commission (the "VPK," according to its Russian acronym), on the government side, and by a secretary specializing in defense production within the central Party apparatus. The occupant of the latter position, which apparently has been left unfilled since Y. P. Ryabov moved on to a top post in Gosplan in 1979, had long played, with the help of the Defense Industries Department of the Central Committee, a critical role in personally directing Soviet defense production.

Its previous occupants prior to Ryabov's brief tenure included Leonid Brezhnev in the late 1950s, and the long-time czar of the Soviet armaments industry, D. F. Ustinov, who held the job from 1965 until 1976. With this post apparently unfilled in early 1980, it is interesting to speculate on who may be performing this function—perhaps Ustinov, while simultaneously serving as Minister of Defense, or A. P. Kirilenko, the rumored patron of Ryabov, who has often been identified by Western observers as the most likely successor to Brezhnev as general secretary of the Party.

Within the organizational setting just discussed, the professional military officers of the Ministry of Defense have enormous influence. Although top civilian organizations such as the Politburo and the Defense Council clearly have the right of final decision in all defense matters, the processes of policy formulation, analysis, and implementation in the national security policy area are thoroughly dominated by the Ministry of Defense. The military's influence is reinforced by the fact that the top-level civilian decision makers have no significant alternative sources of relevant defense information or expertise outside the Ministry of Defense.[53] Consequently, even should the Party leaders be inclined to pursue a defense policy at variance with that recommended by the Soviet military, they would have considerable difficulty gathering the sensitive information or critical expertise required to develop plausible alternatives. This does not rule out the possibility of dynamic defense policy initiatives sponsored by leading political figures—witness the vigorous attempts of Khrushchev to reshape Soviet military policy radically between 1958 and 1964. It underscores, nevertheless, the serious obstacles that any would-be innovator in this area, acting without the support of the Ministry of Defense, would confront.

THE DEFENSE BUDGET PROCESS

The Soviet defense establishment, like all of the Soviet system, operates within the confines of both a five-year and an annual economic plan. These plans are formulated by the Ministry of Defense and by the key defense production ministries with the assistance of the Military-Industrial Commission, the State Planning Commission (Gosplan), and the Party Secretariat. In the Ministry of Defense, defense budget plans are apparently prepared by the ubiquitous General Staff, which must reconcile the budgetary demands of the services and the other elements of the Soviet armed forces. Given the generous support that defense spending has received since the fall of Khrushchev, this is unlikely to have been a particularly difficult task in recent years. Just a few years earlier, however, when Khrushchev was determinedly seeking to reduce defense expenditures, this process was almost certainly accompanied by significant interservice conflict in a "scarcity" environment.

After preparation and coordination by the responsible Party and government agencies, the annual and periodic five-year defense plans must ultimately be considered and approved by the Defense Council and the Politburo. As noted earlier, over this past sixteen years these bodies have consistently been willing to expend steadily increasing amounts on defense. This pattern has persisted despite significant Soviet economic difficulties, including a substantial decline in the rate of overall economic growth, low worker productivity, and endemic shortcomings in agriculture.

In marked contrast to the situation in the Western democracies, there is no significant legislative review of the Soviet defense budget or, for that matter, any other aspect of Soviet political life. Although the bicameral Supreme Soviet is, in theory, the dominant element in the Soviet parliamentary system, it is convened infrequently and has no impact whatsoever on defense or other issues. Thus, the shape of the Soviet defense budget is purely the product of bureaucratic politics within the government and Party hierarchies.

THE IMPACT OF PERSONALITY

Due to the extreme centralization of political power in the Soviet system, a few key individuals have enormous impact on the political process. Consequently, the personal preferences and idiosyncracies of these men can be exceptionally important—witness the impacts of Stalin's suspicious nature, Khrushchev's rambunctious "hare-brained scheming," and Brezhnev's conservative, consensus-oriented style on Soviet politics during their respective tenures.

With regard to defense, the styles and perspectives of key Soviet leaders have had their effect. Iosif Stalin extended his personal domination of Soviet politics into defense matters, where he personally controlled the weapons acquisition process and, during World War II, forcefully supervised from Moscow in considerable detail Soviet military operations against Nazi Germany and imperial Japan. Khrushchev's personal preferences and style were similarly important once he had firmly established his political preeminence. His rise to power between 1953 and 1957 was aided critically by his outspoken support of heavy industry and defense spending (in contrast to Malenkov's incipient consumerism) and his personal links with several senior military commanders with whom he had worked closely while serving as a senior political commissar during World War II. Nevertheless, from the late 1950s until his removal from power in October 1964, Khrushchev engaged in a determined effort to reshape Soviet military strategy and force posture in conformance with his personal views on the dominant role of nuclear-armed missiles, the decreased requirements for large theater ground and air forces, the uselessness of large naval combatants, and, in general, the need to reduce inherently "wasteful and unproductive" defense expenditures.[54] However, due to the determined opposition of the professional military and their like-minded "metal eaters" (as Khrushchev called them), he never achieved his major objectives. Yet the defense policy conflicts he initiated have had lasting impact on Soviet force posture and military doctrine.

Brezhnev's personal influence on defense policy has been less evident. He is obviously proud of his accomplishments as a political commissar during World War II, when he rose to the rank of major general and saw extensive combat along the southern front. Over the past few years, Brezhnev has increasingly sought public recognition of his military prowess by having himself awarded the rank of marshal of the Soviet Union and being publicly identified as the supreme commander in chief of the armed forces and chairman of the Defense Council. Yet with regard to the substance of Soviet defense policy, Brezhnev does not appear to have had strong personal impact beyond his unstinting support for the steady expansion of Soviet military power.

While the marshals have by no means "taken over" in Moscow during the Brezhnev period, they appear to be enjoying great influence in an environment that has been exceptionally supportive of their interests. The Soviet military is virtually certain to be highly pleased with Brezhnev and this pattern. The senior military leadership is likely to be strongly inclined to fight bureaucratically to retain its privileged position during the inevitable post-Brezhnev succession maneuvering.

Recurring issues: defense policy outputs

CIVIL-MILITARY RELATIONS

The Soviet military is a significant element not only in the bureaucratic struggles of Soviet politics but also in the broader aspects of Soviet life. As just discussed, thanks to its near monopoly of relevant information and expertise, the military wields substantial influence on the development and implementation of Soviet defense policy. Moreover, the sheer size of the Soviet defense effort, in terms of the personnel involved, its far-flung activities, and its vast expenditures, is such that the Soviet military establishment has multiple direct and indirect effects beyond the sphere of defense-related activities.

The Party leadership has found it advantageous to encourage the military to play a major role in the socialization of Soviet youth. These activities go beyond the compulsory political indoctrination to which each of the some 1.8 million new recruits conscripted annually into the armed forces are subjected. They also include an extensive "military-patriotic education" campaign directed at Soviet young people, the many paramilitary activities of the Voluntary Society for the Support of the Army, Navy, and Air Force ("DOSAAF," according to its Russian acronym), and the compulsory civil defense and preinduction training programs conducted within the school system.[55] All of these efforts, although they involve a wide range of Party and government organizations, are directed and actively supported by the Ministry of Defense.

While most of these types of programs have been in existence since the 1920s, their scope was expanded significantly in the late 1960s. At that time, it appears that the Party and the military struck a bargain that brought an expansion of the military-patriotic education effort and the initiation of compulsory preinduction training programs in exchange for military acquiescence to a one-year reduction in the compulsory service obligation of Soviet conscripts.

These extensive programs reflect the genuine community of interest between the senior Party and military leadership. Both groups are determined to do all they can to foster intense patriotic commitment to the nation, a proper Marxist-Leninist viewpoint, a sense of discipline, and basic military skills among Soviet youth. Their general desires in this regard are probably intensified by their common perceptions of the need to combat vigorously the amilitary and apolitical attitudes that have emerged among Soviet urban youth in the past several years.

While the military has considerable impact on the Soviet domestic scene due to the budgetary priority accorded its substantial armament programs and its broader defense preparedness activities, the military leadership does not appear to play a direct role in shaping Soviet domestic policies beyond the defense sphere. Senior defense figures, including Defense Minister Ustinov, infrequently comment publicly on nondefense matters. The presence of Ustinov on the Politburo provides an opportunity for the minister of defense to be heard in critical deliberations on the full range of domestic issues. Nevertheless, there is little reason to believe that the military participates actively in the formulation, analysis, decision, or implementation of policies with regard to such matters as economic reform, agricultural policy, or cultural policy. Their quiescence in this regard reflects a well-established tradition that allows the Soviet military significant participation and influence in those defense matters directly affecting their corporate interests while discouraging them from involvement in broader issues.

This pattern is reinforced by the fact that the Soviet regime provides significant benefits to the Soviet officer corps in the form of generous pay and material benefits, personal security, high status, substantial career mobility opportunities, and unstinting support of the nation's defense efforts. One student of Soviet politics has argued that the military's lack of involvement in broader societal issues is further reinforced by the fact that, despite its presence in garrisons, bases, and headquarters throughout the country, the military is largely a self-sufficient organization that has only minimal ties with the local community or with regional government and Party organizations.[56]

The military profession enjoys a good reputation within Soviet society. In the wake of the Second World War, the standing of the Soviet officer corps in the eyes of the general public was especially high in recognition of its role in repelling the Nazi invaders. By the mid-1960s, two opinion surveys of Soviet secondary school students and teachers indicated that the military officer career ranked at approximately the 25 percent point in terms of attractiveness among a wide range of occupations evaluated.[57] Over the years, the standing of the Soviet military appears to have declined somewhat, almost certainly as a result of the spread of amilitary attitudes among the urbanized segments of Soviet youth. It is precisely this undesirable trend that has prompted the Soviet military leadership to devote substantial efforts to try to propagate a positive view of the role of the armed forces within the Soviet system.[58]

Any review of Soviet civil-military relations must include a discussion of the activities of the Main Political Administration. In the first years of Soviet rule, the political commissars, the predecessors of today's political officers, were assigned two important tasks: monitoring the political reliability of the officer corps, many of whom had served in the Russian imperial army, and indoctrinating both enlisted men and officers with the proper Communist outlook. Within the first decade, a third task was added: the political officers came to share the responsibilities of the military commanders for the combat readiness and military discipline of their units.[59]

Over the years, the watchdog function of the political officers has declined considerably. This task has largely fallen upon the so-called special sections of the KGB, which guard against espionage and anti-Soviet activity within the military through a network of KGB officers and their recruited informers found throughout the armed forces. Rather than serving as an alien checking agency within the military, the political officers of the MPA have become an integral part of the Soviet military establishment. Political officers today are, in their own right, career military professionals who have chosen to pursue the indoctrinational and organizational specialities of the MPA. Their professional military orientation is reflected in the patterns of political officer recruitment. For several decades, the majority of young political officers has been drawn from the ranks of junior officers in the combat services. Since 1971, new political officers have also been supplied each year by the graduating classes of the MPA's seven higher military commissioning schools first opened in 1967.

Although the political officers are career military professionals, they may occasionally find themselves in conflict with their line officer compatriots. The commanders and their political deputies, the *zampolits,* share mutual interests in having units that are well trained, disciplined, and properly politically indoctrinated. Nevertheless, there is bound to be periodic conflict between the commanders and the political officers over a scarce commodity, the time of the personnel that both seek to train.

The political officers must attend to a host of duties: the conduct of political education for all personnel, the maintenance of morale and discipline, care for individual welfare, the encouragement of technical competence, and the supervision of the operation of the Party and the Young Communist League (*Komsomol*) organizations that are found throughout the armed forces.[60] Although many of these activities are likely to be supported by the commanders, the time required to do all of them may well impinge on the time the commanders would like to devote to improving the military skills and combat readiness of their forces. Consequently, there is likely to be friction between commanders and present-day commissars, but it is relatively unimportant and far different from the model of intense Party-military conflict between two strongly opposed entities that has sometimes been depicted.[61]

Finally, Soviet civil-military relations have often included the important element of personal ties between important civilian figures and the senior military leadership. During wartime, in particular, Party politicians have found themselves in close contact with key military commanders, and political alliances have sometimes emerged. Such was the case for both Stalin and Khrushchev, who developed lasting patronage ties with military officers during the defense of the same city, called first Tsaritsyn, then Stalingrad, during the Civil War and World War II, respectively.[62] Thirty-five years after the end of World War II, these wartime clusterings have largely lost their significance. One might anticipate a somewhat weaker set of alliance patterns of the same general character to emerge in peacetime between regional Party secretaries and the commanders of the military districts. Regional Party secretaries, are, in fact, members of the military councils of these military districts; yet if Colton is right about the largely autarchic tendencies of the military units, the Party-military contacts in the field are likely to be largely inconsequential.

Personal contacts between senior civilians and key military officers are likely to occur more often, to be more substantive and thus more important at the center. Several memoir accounts testify to the existence of close Party-military working relationships in Moscow, where the senior military leaders promote their corporate and individual views on defense matters in routine contacts with key Party and government officials.[63] Western speculations regarding Marshal Ogarkov's somewhat surprising selection as chief of the General Staff in January 1977 often centered, for example, on rumors of the respect he was reported to have earned from Defense Minister Ustinov in the course of their joint involvement in Soviet policy making regarding the Strategic Arms Limitation Talks during the previous several years. Whatever the truth concerning the "Ustinov-Ogarkov connection," there is no doubt that such personal relationships are likely to play an important role in the selection of senior officers to fill the key posts within the Ministry of Defense.

WEAPONS ACQUISITION

Over the years, the Soviets have built up a large complex of organizations engaged in the research, development, and production of armaments. The many elements involved, some of which were noted earlier in this section, include research institutes, weapons design bureaus, and series production facilities as well as a group of military, government, and Party bodies that help manage various phases of the weapons acquisition process.

Western scholarship regarding the dynamics of Soviet weapons acquisition has increased substantially in recent years.[64] Since major sections of a recent definitive study on this subject by Arthur Alexander are reprinted in this volume, this chapter will not dwell upon the details of the organizational arrangements or processes involved in this endeavor. Instead, the following general observations are offered.

(*a*) The Soviet Union clearly possesses a powerful, well-entrenched "military-industrial complex" that has been continuously involved in the design and production of the full spectrum of military weapons for over five decades.

(*b*) The dynamics of Soviet weapons acquisition includes a mixture of "demand-pull" developments in which the design and production organs of the defense industrial ministries develop and produce weapons in response to specifications laid down by the Soviet armed forces and cases of "design push" in which armaments are produced as a result of the entrepreneurial initiatives of the major designers who "sell" their latest weapons ideas to their military customers and key political leaders.

(*c*) The nine ministries predominantly engaged in weapons production represent the most privileged sector of the Soviet economy. They are supplied with the most advanced equipment, the most talented scientific and technical personnel, priority access to scarce resources, and high status, high pay, and other material benefits for their employees.

(*d*) There are several links between the design and production facilities of the defense production ministries and their military customers, one of the most important of which is the strict quality control of defense-related products enforced by the military representatives from the weapons directorates of the services, who are attached to each major production plant and design bureau.[65]

(*e*) Over the years, the Soviets have developed well-established patterns of weapons development. These include: widespread use of competitions among two or more design bureaus that extend through the competitive testing of full-scale prototypes; simplicity in the use of austere, uncomplicated, and frequently crudely finished subsystems; and significant conservatism in the development of new weapons reflected in the high degree of design inheritance from one generation of weapons to another manifested in the frequent use of proven components and incrementalism.[66]

(*f*) Most of the key participants in Soviet weapons development and production, including the leading designers, industrial ministers, and Party and government overseers, have spent decades in their senior posts, thus adding important elements of close personal ties, extensive experience, and continuity to the acquisition process.[67]

FORCE POSTURE

The systems that emerge from the weapons acquisition process represent a major input into the aggregate of military capabilities fielded by the Soviet Union. Consequently, the size and quality of this force posture reflect both the predominant design practices that characterize Soviet weapons development and acquisition and the considerable political clout of the Soviet military-industrial complex. Other factors that influence the character of Soviet force posture include the views of the political and military leadership regarding the threats and opportunities facing the Soviet Union, their judgments regarding the most effective military force deployments to respond to this environment, and the tenets of Soviet Military doctrine that help guide the Ministry of Defense, particularly the General Staff, in establishing requirements for both the production and the possible employment of specific military capabilities.

STRATEGIC NUCLEAR FORCES

Since entering the nuclear age in 1949, the Soviets have consistently striven to develop and deploy offensive and defensive forces that could add nuclear muscle to their military power and reduce the damage any adversary might inflict upon them in the event of war. In the course of three decades, they have deployed a full spectrum of nuclear weapons with virtually all of their forces, ranging from various tactical weapons deployed with the navy, ground, and air forces to the multimegaton warheads associated with their very large, intercontinental ballistic missiles (ICBMs). In the process, they have created two new military services, National Air Defense (*PVO Strany*) in 1948 and the Strategic Rocket Forces (SRF) in 1959, whose primary wartime missions would be to defend against and mount attacks with strategic nuclear weapons.

As they enter the 1980s, Soviet strategic offensive nuclear strike capabilities include both regional and intercontinental range components. In both cases, these capabilities include a mix of land-based ballistic missiles under the control of the SRF, submarine-borne missiles of the navy, and strategic bombers of the air forces' Long-Range Aviation (LRA). There are differing balances among those elements of the Soviet "triad," or perhaps more appropriately, *troika*. The ICBM component, including the third-generation SS-9s, SS-11s, and SS-13s as well as the fourth-generation SS-17s, SS-18s and SS-19s, provides approximately 70 percent of the Soviet Union's intercontinental range weapons, thus making it the predominant element among the so-called central strategic forces. The submarine-launched ballistic missiles (SLBMs) of the Yankee and Delta class nuclear-powered submarines armed with the SS-N-6, SS-N-8, and SS-N-18 missiles account for some 25 percent of the intercontinental strike forces, while LRA's Bear and Bison bombers provide the remaining 5 percent of these forces among the central strategic forces. The Badgers, Blinders, and Backfires of LRA and Soviet Naval Aviation account for 63 percent of the regional strategic strike forces, while the SFR's intermediate- and medium-range ballistic missiles, the older SS-4s and 5s and newer, mobile SS-20s, provide 34 percent and the Golf and Hotel class subs carrying the SS-N-4 and SS-N-5 provide the remaining 3 percent.[68]

Over the years, the Soviets have steadily sought to improve both the survivability and the attack effectiveness of their strategic nuclear forces. The quest for survivability has led them to deploy their land-based missiles in successive generations of increasingly harder, reinforced concrete silos and, in the case of their intermediate-range SS-20, in a road-mobile configuration. In the same vein, they have sought to provide a highly survivable command and control apparatus to direct these forces by deploying a host of hardened command bunkers, mobile command posts, and redundant communications facilities.

The Soviet quest for improved military effectiveness in the strategic missile force has been concentrated on efforts to increase the numbers of warheads carried by these missiles and to improve the accuracy of these weapons. The centerpiece of this effort has been their deployment of increasingly accurate, multiple independently targetable reentry vehicles, or "MIRVs," which began in the mid-1970s.

The Soviet MIRV program has been assisted significantly by the tradition of developing and deploying large, heavy-payload strategic missiles, which dates back to the earliest days of Soviet rocket development. In the 1950s, the Soviets were forced to develop large rocket boosters for their military and space programs in order to compensate for their relative backwardness in both nuclear weapons design and electronics miniaturization. They continued this pattern in the 1960s, developing ICBMs as large as the "heavy" SS-9, which carries either a single large multimegaton warhead or a "triplet" consisting of three reentry vehicles (RVs) that dispense in a cluster pattern without an independent targeting capability for the individual RVs. With the dawn of the Soviet MIRV era in the 1970s, the Soviets were able to take advantage of the high payload capacity, or "throw-weight," of their fourth-generation ICBMs, in particular the SS-19 and the massive SS-18, which carry up to six and ten MIRVs, respectively.

At the same time that they were rapidly expanding their ICBM-borne weapons inventory, the Soviets made major improvements in the accuracy of these weapons. By the late 1970s, they had acquired the capability to place at risk a substantial share of hardened U.S. military facilities, the most numerous of which are the fixed silos housing the Minuteman and Titan II ICBMs. Thus, by 1980, the Soviets were rapidly achieving one of their highest priority doctrinal objectives, the ability to attack effectively the ICBM component of the U.S. strategic nuclear arsenal.[69]

As they entered the 1980s, the Soviet ICBM force consisted of 1,398 missiles: 100 SS-9s, 638 SS-11s, and 60 SS-13s (all carrying single RV equivalents); and 100 SS-17s (four RVs), 200 SS-18s (up to ten RVs), and 300 SS-19s (up to six RVs) within the MIRVed portion of their force.[70] There have been reports for several years that the Soviet missile design bureaus were working on several modifications to the fourth-generation systems as well as some completely new, fifth-generation ICBMs. The SALT II Treaty would have imposed significant constraints on these developments. It would have permitted the flight testing and deployment of only one new "light" ICBM, no larger than SS-19 class, and have limited this missile to no more than ten MIRVs. It would also have confined modifications of the current fourth-generation missile within specific parameters, including allowing the modifications to carry no more RVs than those already tested on these missiles as of May 1, 1979.[71] In the absence of these SALT II constraints, the Soviets are clearly free to pursue whatever modernization measures they might desire, including the possibility of deploying considerably greater numbers of warheads—perhaps twenty or more—on the very large SS-18 ICBM or a follow-on system of that general character.

Over the years the Soviets have produced several combinations of ballistic missiles and missile-carrying submarines. These include: the 350-mile-range SS-N-4 on the diesel-powered Z-V class submarines in 1957; the SS-N-4 and SS-N-5 on the diesel-powered Golf and Hotel class subs; the development in the late 1960s and early 1970s of the numerous Yankee class nuclear subs (SSBNs) carrying the 1750- to 2000-mile-range SS-N-6; the Delta 1 and Delta 2 classes with the 4800-mile-range SS-N-8 in the middle to late 1970s; and finally the Delta 3 SSBNs with the over-5000-mile-range SS-N-18 that carries three or seven MIRVs.[72]

For a variety of geographical, technological, and logistical reasons, the Soviets have consistently deployed a small portion of their SSBN force on peacetime patrols within striking distance of the United States. They have only recently achieved an at sea, day-to-day alert rate of between 11 and 18 percent of their SSBN force.[73] The Soviets apparently continue to count upon the occurrence of a period of heightened tensions preceding any major conflict that will allow them to deploy rapidly from their Northern and Pacific Fleet home ports the considerable number of SSBNs that are not inoperable due to major refit or overhaul. The long range of the SS-N-8 and SS-N-18, which allows them to cover targets in the United States immediately after leaving port, gives added credibility to this strategy. However, barring such a force generation in crisis, the majority of Soviet strategic missile submarines are routinely tied up in port and thus highly vulnerable.

Once at sea, all of the Soviet strategic missile submarines are much noisier than U.S. SSBNs or attack submarines (SSNs). This makes them vulnerable to possible acoustic detection and attack by U.S. antisubmarine warfare (ASW) systems, an area in which the United States is reported to have a considerable technological edge.[74] Recognizing this, the Soviets have developed the "bastion" or "enclave" defense approach noted earlier, in which submarine, surface ship, and airborne ASW assets are employed in combination to protect the Delta SSBNs, which can hold U.S. targets at risk from the nearby waters of the Barents and Norwegian seas or the Sea of Okhotsk in the Far East.

The Soviet long-range strategic submarine force at the opening of the 1980s consisted of nine Delta 3 subs, each with sixteen SS-N-18 (three or seven

MIRVs); five Delta 2s, each with sixteen SS-N-8 (single RV); fifteen Delta 1s, each with twelve SS-N-8; and thirty-three Yankees, each carrying sixteen SS-N-6 (single RV).[75] In the years ahead, the number of weapons carried by this element of the Soviet strategic *troika* will increase substantially with the continuing deployment of the MIRVed SS-N-18 on the Delta 3 sub and the anticipated deployment of the new MIRVed SLBM that began flight testing in February 1980, which will be deployed on the new large "Typhoon" submarine.

The least powerful element of the Soviet long-range strategic arsenal is the small intercontinental bomber force, which has remained largely unchanged since the mid-1950s. It consists of 113 Tu-95 Bear and 43 Mya-4 Bison bombers, both of which carry gravity bombs or first-generation cruise missiles.[76] These bombers are supported by a modest aerial refueling tanker force of 44 converted Mya-4 Bison and 9 converted Tu-16 Badger bombers.[77] Looking toward the future, there have been various reports that during the course of the SALT II negotiations, Soviet representatives indicated that they have under development three new long-range bomber or cruise missile carrier designs that could enter production in the 1980s.[78]

The Soviets have also been significantly upgrading their regional strategic forces. The land-based element is being appreciably strengthened with the addition of the road-mobile, three-MIRV SS-20 intermediate-range ballistic missile, which is being deployed in garrisons in the western, central, and eastern USSR. Similarly, the bomber component is being improved with the addition of the Tu-22M Backfire bomber to both Long-Range Aviation and Soviet naval aviation. The Backfire has, of course, been the subject of considerable controversy in the West because, although its range is sufficient to permit it to strike targets in the United States without refueling on one-way "range" missions or on two-way missions with in-flight refueling, it is not included in the aggregate ceilings of the SALT II Treaty.[79] These new systems are being added to the some 450 older SS-4 MRBMs and 90 SS-5 IRBMs of the SRF, to the LRA's 463 Tu-16 Badgers and Tu-22 Blinders, and to the Soviet naval aviation's 325 Tu-16 Badgers and Tu-95 Bears.

STRATEGIC DEFENSE

The Soviets have long maintained a large and expensive strategic air and missile defense capability. In 1980, the troops of *PVO Strany* fielded a combined force of some 10,000 surface-to-air missiles, 2,600 fighter-interceptors, a comprehensive radar warning and control network to engage enemy aircraft, 64 antiballistic missile launchers in the "Galosh" ABM-1 system deployed around Moscow since the late 1960s, and an antisatellite capability that has been repeatedly tested against low-altitude target satellites.[80]

Despite their extensive antiaircraft defenses, the Soviets have not been able to mount an effective defense against enemy bombers penetrating at low levels. They continue to seek to remedy this critical deficiency and are reportedly developing: (1) a modern airborne warning and control system (AWACS) based on the Il-76 Candid; (2) a "look down, shoot down" radar capability, improved air-to-air missiles for the modified Mig-25 Foxbat, Mig-23 Flogger, and a new air superiority fighter; and (3) a new low-level surface-to-air missile, the SA-X-10.[81] With the deployment of these systems in substantial numbers, Soviet strategic air defenses are likely to become considerably more effective against low-altitude penetrating aircraft in the latter part of the 1980s.[82]

The prospects for improvements in Soviet ABM capabilities are less clear. The ABM Treaty, signed at the conclusion of SALT I in May 1972, and the 1974 Protocol to that agreement ban the construction of more than 100 ABM launchers defending either the national capital or an ICBM deployment complex. Consequently, barring abrogation of the treaty, the Soviets will not be able to deploy a substantial ABM system in the years ahead. Nevertheless, the Soviets have apparently pursued several ballistic missile defense development efforts, including a rapidly deployable conventional interceptor system, ground-based and space-based lasers, and possibly a charged particle-beam weapon as well.[83] With regard to antisatellite warfare, the Soviets appear determined to continue to test their low-orbit interceptor and are unlikely to surrender this capability despite their extended involvement in bilateral negotiations with the United States on an antisatellite (ASAT) agreement.

Other strategic defensive programs include Soviet antisubmarine warfare efforts and the damage limitation measures associated with their extensive civil defense program. Soviet acoustic ASW capabilities are, by all reports, grossly inadequate for the task of locating U.S. SSBNs. This shortcoming almost certainly lies behind the Soviet decision to reorient the use of these ASW forces to help defend the Soviet SSBNs using the bastion defense concept. Despite this failure, or perhaps spurred on by it, the Soviets are reported to be investigating a variety of nonacoustic submarine detection means.[84] Given the magnitude of the U. S. effort in SLBMs and the high priority the Soviets assign to damage limitation, there is little doubt that they will continue to devote substantial efforts in an attempt to make a breakthrough in strategic ASW.

Soviet civil defense efforts, as noted earlier, although supervised by a directorate in the Ministry of

Defense, involve the participation of many other organizations, including elements of the Party and government bureaucracies as well as most urban-based economic enterprises and educational institutions. The Soviets have developed a policy that provides fallout shelters in or near major urban areas for the political and military leadership and a share of the essential work force. They apparently intend to rely upon large-scale dispersal and evacuation followed by the construction of temporary shelters for the protection of the majority of the populace. The books and pamphlets published by the full-time Soviet civil defense bureaucracy are generally optimistic about the ability of the Soviet Union to survive and function effectively in a post–nuclear war environment. Western analyses are less optimistic, although it is generally agreed that if circumstances permitted the Soviets a week or so to implement their full range of protective measures, they could appreciably limit fatalities, perhaps to a few tens of millions. These efforts could not, however, prevent them from suffering massive industrial damage.[85]

THEATER FORCES

The backbone of Russian military power has traditionally been its large armies, staffed by masses of hardy peasants and frequently supported by large concentrations of field artillery. The Soviet army today continues to reflect its Russian heritage: it is large, its soldiers are tough, and it has impressive firepower, both conventional and nuclear. But it is much more than that, having been fully motorized and equipped with a wide variety of highly effective tanks and armored fighting vehicles as well as some of the world's most modern tactical missiles and mobile air defense missiles and guns. Moreover, it is supported by a large and increasingly capable air arm, whose major elements are the interceptors, fighter-bombers, and armed helicopters of Frontal Aviation. The net result is the world's largest and most powerful standing army, led by a well-trained, dedicated officer corps and prepared to wage armor-heavy, blitzkrieg warfare in various theaters around the Soviet periphery.

As the USSR entered the 1980s, the Soviet army fielded a total of 173 divisions, of which 47 were tank divisions, 118 motorized rifle, and 8 airborne. These divisions are deployed throughout the USSR, in Eastern Europe, Mongolia, and, since December 1979, in the army of occupation within Afghanistan. Within the Soviet Union, the heaviest concentrations are in the European USSR (the Baltic, Byelorussian, Carpathian, Kiev, Leningrad, and Moscow military districts), where 66 divisions are posted. Facing China (the Central Asian, Siberian, Transbaikal, and Far Eastern military districts plus Mongolia) there are 46 divisions.[86]

The Soviet divisions have differing compositions. A fully equipped motorized rifle division contains approximately 12,500 troops and up to 265 medium tanks, while a fully equipped tank division is staffed by 9,800 personnel and equipped with up to 320 tanks.[87] The eight airborne divisions are much smaller, with approximately 7,000 troops, equipped with their own specially designed, light-armored fighting vehicles and artillery, and supported by the transport aircraft of Military Transport Aviation (VTA).

Not all of the 173 divisions of the Soviet armed forces are fully staffed. The Soviets maintain three degrees of readiness: category 1 divisions are at least 75 percent staffed and fully equipped; category 2 divisions are between 50 percent and 75 percent staffed and fully stocked; and category 3 divisions are only 25 percent staffed and, if fully equipped, much of the equipment is obsolete.[88] The category 3 divisions can be brought up to full strength in a matter of weeks by the mobilization of the extensive reserve system, as was done in the late fall of 1979 to provide the bulk of the troops for the forces that invaded Afghanistan.[89]

The distribution of Soviet divisions is such that all thirty-one divisions in Eastern Europe and half of those in the European USSR and the Far East are category 1. In contrast, most of the divisions in the Central USSR (the Volga and Ural Military Districts) and the Southern USSR (North Caucasus, Transcaucasus, and Turkestan military districts), at least prior to the invasion of Afghanistan, were category 3.[90]

In peacetime these divisions, along with their supporting Frontal Aviation elements, are controlled by the group of forces or military district commanders, both of which operate under the direction of the General Staff. In time of war, all of the groups of forces and most of the military districts would be converted to "fronts," composed of three or four combined-arms armies and a tank army, that is, approximately twenty to twenty-five motorized rifle and tank divisions, along with a tactical air army and a host of combat and support elements.[91] The airborne divisions, although an element of the ground forces, appear to fall under the direct control of the minister of defense. In wartime they may be attached to a field command—a front or a theater of military operations (TVD)—or remain under the direct control of the Supreme Headquarters in Moscow.

The level of Soviet investment in defense is amply reflected in the steady improvement of the armaments of the armed forces. Not only have the Soviets purchased the large numbers of weapons systems needed to equip this two-million-man army but they have steadily improved the quality of these armaments. As a result, the latest Soviet tanks, the T-64 and T-72, the BMP fighting vehicle, the self-propelled 122-mm and 152-mm howitzers, the mobile air defense systems—the SA-4, SA-6, SA-8, and SA-11 missile systems and ZSU23/4 self-propelled antiaircraft gun—and their SS-21 tactical missiles are all among the most modern and capable in the world.[92] In addition, the Soviets have taken very seriously the prospects of warfare with weapons of mass destruction, that is chemical, biological, and nuclear weapons, and their forces are extensively trained and equipped to fight in these environments.[93]

In sum, the continuing accumulation of new equipment has significantly increased both the firepower and the mobility of the Soviet combined-arms assault formations to the point where they are considerably more capable of massing the large numbers of armored vehicles and conventional fire support on the main axes of attack in order to meet the armament norms, that is, the 3:1 to 5:1 margins of local superiority, called for by their conservative military doctrine.[94] Consequently, the Soviets are prepared to undertake their multiple breakthrough offensive strategy either relying solely upon conventional firepower or with the support of nuclear weapons.

Soviet tactical or "frontal" aviation is similarly impressive. This force, largely designed to support the land battle, also reflects the Russian penchant for large numbers: it is made up of some 4,350 combat aircraft.[95] In recent years, the quality of Frontal Aviation, like that of all the other elements of Soviet military power, has improved dramatically. With the addition of the third-generation aircraft—the multipurpose Mig-23 Flogger B; the late-model Mig-21 Fishbed J, K, L, and N; the Su-17 Fitter C; the Mig-27 Flogger D; and the Su-19 Fencer—the range and payload capabilities of Frontal Aviation have been increased enormously.[96] In addition, during the 1970s the Soviets, clearly emulating U.S. developments of the 1960s, began to deploy the highly capable MI-24 Hind A and Hind D and a version of the MI-8 Hip as armed helicopter gunships, equipped for antitank and other fire support missions.[97]

Frontal Aviation is organized into sixteen air armies, one each deployed with the groups of forces in East Germany, Poland, Czechoslovakia, and Hungary and the remaining twelve spread among the sixteen military districts in the USSR.[98] The largest of these, the Sixteenth Air Army attached to the Group of Soviet Forces in East Germany, is reported to have over 1,200 aircraft.[99] The commanders of these air armies serve as the deputy commanders for air with the military district, group, or, in time of war, frontal command. The aircraft of these air armies may be employed in combination with the medium bombers of Long-Range Aviation in the large-scale "air operations," as discussed earlier,[100] or independently, in efforts to maintain air superiority over the main axes of attack or to provide close air support near or at the forward edge of the battle area.

NAVAL FORCES

While all of the elements of the Soviet armed forces have steadily increased their capabilities over the past two decades, none has done so more dramatically than the Soviet navy. Not only has the navy's nuclear striking power expanded enormously with the deployment of the Yankee and Delta class submarines discussed above, but the general purpose naval capabilities have been significantly improved as well. In particular, the Soviets have attained a genuine blue water capability based upon a force of 270 surface warships of the light frigate class or larger. These include: two Kiev class light aircraft carriers equipped with vertical take-off landing (VTOL) Yak-36 Forger aircraft; two Moskva class ASW cruisers; a host of guided missile-equipped Kara, Kresta I, and Kresta II cruisers; several classes of destroyer, including the Krivak II; improved logistics support and amphibious ships, including the Berezina class fleet oiler and the Ivan Rogov class amphibious assault transport; and a variety of cruise missile and torpedo-equipped attack submarines the most impressive of which is the high-speed, titanium-hulled Alpha class.[101] At the same time, land-based Soviet naval aviation has been improved with the addition of the Backfire bomber.

These ships have allowed the Soviet Union to increase significantly its visible peacetime presence throughout the world's oceans. More important, they provide the Soviet navy with greatly enhanced capabilities to fulfill its various wartime missions—mounting nuclear strikes against the United States, neutralizing U.S. carrier task forces, combating American strategic and attack submarines, interdicting the enemy's sea lines of communications, repelling any amphibious assault attempted against the USSR, and conducting amphibious operations along the flanks of its advancing land armies.

Looking to the future, the Soviets face a problem of bloc obsolescence with regard to their destroyer forces. Nevertheless, additional improvements are apparently in the offing in the form of possibly a new, large aircraft carrier, a third Kiev class carrier, a new 27,000–30,000-ton class nuclear-powered battle cruiser, and three other new classes of cruiser.[102]

Improved naval vessels and aircraft are by no means the full expression of the changing character of the Soviet navy. Its operational concepts and deployment patterns have also been altered dramatically. These shifts are well captured in the analysis by Michael MccGwire, a leading Western expert on Soviet naval policy, who describes a steady expansion of the "Soviet maritime defense perimeter" over the past two decades. According to this construct, U.S. carrier and long-range SLBM deployments have compelled the Soviets to expand their operations beyond their traditional "inner defense zone," that is, the waters close to the USSR where local superiority readily permits them command of these seas. They have been forced, instead, to extend greatly their normal operating areas, thus creating an "outer defense zone" that reaches into the North Atlantic, the Mediterranean, the Indian Ocean, and the Western Pacific in order to counter these U.S. strike systems.[103] This process has resulted in a truly ocean-going Soviet naval capability, with obvious potential wartime applications and peacetime uses that have been clearly recognized and increasingly utilized by the Soviet leadership.

FORCE PROJECTION

The Soviets have also made significant improvements in their ability to project military power. Their capability for contiguous force projection, that is, the ability to move military power into areas along the periphery of the Soviet Union, is inherent in the extensive theater warfare capabilities discussed earlier. The Soviets' moves into Czechoslovakia in 1968 and Afghanistan in 1979, for example, simply involved the application of those land and air forces that were trained and equipped to wage theater warfare on the Soviet periphery. Thus, Soviet contiguous force projection capabilities have grown apace as part and parcel of the steady improvement of the theater forces.

The more dramatic improvements in Soviet force projection have occurred with regard to their ability to move military forces over long distances. This improvement has involved the acquisition of new, long-range air and sea transport, as well as the development of an embryonic basing infrastructure and the accumulation of greatly increased experience in undertaking such operations. On the capabilities side, the major developments have been the addition of the An-22 Cock heavy turboprop transport aircraft and the Il-76 Candid jet medium transport within the Military Transport Aviation (VTA) and, on the naval side, the addition of improved transports, including "roll on, roll off" ships within the Soviet merchant marine (MORFLOT) and several new vessels within the Soviet navy that can be used to project power ashore, including the Kiev class carriers and the Ivan Rogov class amphibious ships.[104] These improved airlift and sealift capabilities are well suited for use by the eight Soviet airborne divisions or by the naval infantry, the 12,000-troop component of the Soviet navy that is specifically trained and equipped for amphibious assault operations.[105]

Soviet long-distance power projection has been enhanced by the USSR's increased political and military involvement in several Third World countries. These involvements have resulted in significant experience in long-distance movements of troops and equipment, for example, Soviet assistance in air transporting Cuban troops to Angola in 1975–76 and in Soviet movements of military advisers and equipment by air and sea to such arms assistance clients as Ethiopia, Libya, Vietnam, Iraq, and South Yemen.[106] The latter activities have often been accompanied by the build-up of significant overseas stockpiles of modern Soviet weaponry. These stockpiles represent *de facto* prepositioned stocks of armaments that might be available to Soviet forces rapidly inserted into these areas in the event of a regional crisis or conflict. This combination of improved long-range transport, increased experience in mounting distant operations, and the development of an overseas facilities infrastructure to assist in such activities provides the Kremlin with greatly increased flexibility in the possible use of Soviet military power to advance Soviet interests in the Third World.

ARMS CONTROL

The Soviet Union has been a vocal champion of arms control and disarmament for many years. Since the late 1950s, the Soviets have been involved, virtually continuously, in a series of international arms control negotiations. Within these negotiations and outside them, the Soviets have consistently asserted that they favor dramatic progress toward substantial disarmament. Yet they have proved, in practice, willing to agree to only moderately restrictive limitations, largely confined to those areas where they do not appear to have promising prospects for their own military forces. At the same time, they have strongly resisted large-scale force reductions or tight constraints upon their own major weapons programs.

The development of arms control policy appears to be an area in Soviet defense policy making that is open to a wider circle of organizations beyond the familiar line-up of the Ministry of Defense, the defense-industrial organs, and the senior Party leadership described earlier. Since contemporary arms control involves extended international negotiations, a major role has been played by the Ministry of Foreign Affairs. There has also been a substantial involvement of various scientists and scholars connected within the Academy of Sciences.[107] Senior representatives from the Foreign Ministry have been in charge of all Soviet negotiating delegations and, in most cases, have provided the majority of the delegates. This latter pattern was most notably breached during the two lengthy rounds of the Strategic Arms Limitations Talks, SALT I and SALT II, when the military provided two of the six chief Soviet delegates and the defense-industrial sector an additional two.[108] Nevertheless, even in SALT, the delegation chief was a career diplomat.[109]

Despite its prominence in the negotiations process,

it is clear that the Ministry of Foreign Affairs is by no means the dominant institution in the formulation of Soviet arms control policy in Moscow. Its role appears to be largely one of faithfully implementing rather than developing Soviet negotiating strategies. The formulation of Soviet arms control objectives and bargaining positions is done in a manner much closer to that followed in handling other defense issues, with the key roles played by the Ministry of Defense, in particular, the General Staff, the defense-industrial organs, the Defense Council, and, ultimately, the Politburo.[110]

During the 1970s, the major efforts of Soviet arms control policy were focused on the bilateral SALT negotiations with the United States and the multilateral East-West talks on Mutual and Balanced Force Reductions in Central Europe.[111] In these negotiations, the Soviets sought to attain both broad political goals and narrower security-related objectives. On the political side, they sought to confirm visibly the position of the Soviet Union as one of the world's two superpowers, being treated as fully equal by the United States. In addition, the Soviet leadership clearly recognized, and thus supported, the key arms control negotiations as the centerpiece of their efforts to cultivate East-West détente, which was intended to yield a variety of additional political and economic benefits. Finally, with regard to SALT in particular, despite their doctrinal preparations and ideological assertions about the "winnability" of a general nuclear war, the Soviets are undoubtedly interested in avoiding such a conflict and are likely to view the major arms limitation talks as a useful means to promote this objective.

On the military side, despite their repeated calls for agreements based on the principle of equal security, the Soviets have persistently sought to gain the most advantageous terms possible within the negotiations. They have consistently tried to eliminate or reduce current or projected Western military capabilities—such as the air-launched cruise missile, U.S. forward-based fighter bombers, or NATO's proposed deployments of ground-launched cruise missiles and Pershing IIs—while seeking to avoid any constraints on their own extensive force modernization efforts. Nevertheless, when confronted by steadfast resistance to these demands, the Soviets have proved grudgingly willing to agree to compromises that involved reciprocal limits on both sides. Such was the pattern that emerged in the development of the SALT I and SALT II agreements, although there is considerable dispute in the West regarding the overall equity of the agreements that were eventually signed.[112]

Looking to the future, the Soviets appear determined to continue to pursue arms control as a major dimension of their foreign and defense policy. Despite the serious chill in U.S.-Soviet relations triggered by the Soviet invasion of Afghanistan, continuing Soviet interests in détente, in the avoidance of war, and in the possibility of placing advantageous constraints on Western military capabilities are likely to keep them at the negotiating table in any international atmosphere short of full-scale resumption of the Cold War.

USE OF FORCE

Since the superpower status of the USSR rests, to a considerable degree, on its massive military power, it is not surprising that the Soviets have frequently used this power to protect and advance their interests on the world scene. As noted earlier, the Soviet leaders, like their czarist predecessors, have employed their armed forces as an effective instrument of foreign policy. They have, for example, used the force of arms to expand the frontiers of the Soviet Union—to absorb the Baltic states and portions of Finland, Poland, Czechoslovakia, Romania, and Japan—and to impose and maintain subservient Communist regimes beyond these borders in Mongolia, Eastern Europe, and, most recently, Afghanistan.

The Soviets have also used their military capabilities in manners other than such straightforward armed expansionism. During the Russian Civil War, during the border skirmishes with Japan in the late 1930s,[113] and, of course, following the German invasion in 1941, they were forced to rely upon the Red Army to defend their control of Soviet territory. Moreover, their steadily expanding military capabilities have provided a useful backdrop of Soviet diplomacy and have also been used effectively in the form of peacetime demonstrations, shows of force during crises, and various types of military assistance both to woo incumbent governments and to aid insurgent movements fighting to gain power.

The frequency with which the Soviets have employed their military capabilities for foreign policy ends in situations short of armed conflict was investigated in a study published by the Brookings Institution. This lengthy analysis found that between June 1944 and June 1979, Soviet military units were used as a policy instrument to influence other international actors on 187 occasions. Among these incidents, 155 involved the deliberate manipulation of Soviet forces as a means to coerce other states, while the remaining 32 cases involved cooperative moves in support of other actors.[114]

The various types of Soviet external military involvements are well reflected in their relations with the Communist movements in China and Vietnam over the past several decades. In both cases the Soviets provided arms and advisers to these parties when they were struggling to control their nations and again after they had gained power and were at war with major powers—the Chinese with the United States in Korea, 1950–53; the Vietnamese with the

United States, 1964–73; and the Vietnamese with the Chinese, 1979. In the Chinese case, the Sino-Soviet relationship went on to shift from extensive and close cooperation to bitter conflict, culminating in the armed border clashes along the Ussuri River in the spring of 1969. This relationship has remained one of substantial rivalry and tension since that time.[115]

While Soviet military assistance activities have their antecedents in the early years of Bolshevik rule, they have increased dramatically in the past twenty-five years. In the post-Stalin era, the Soviets have come to use arms aid more and more as a means to gain entry to Third World nations. This development is reflected organizationally in the growth of the Tenth Directorate of the General Staff from an organization established to oversee Soviet defense cooperation with its Eastern European Communist allies to a body supervising Soviet military assistance to a host of Asian, African, and Latin American nations.[116]

Soviet military assistance has taken various forms, ranging from small-scale weapons sales to massive arms transfers accompanied by large numbers of Soviet advisory personnel. In some cases, it has led to the direct involvement of Soviet military personnel in regional conflicts, as was the case, for example, with Soviet pilots in China flying with the nationalists against the Japanese in the 1930s and in Egypt in dogfights with the Israelis over the Suez Canal in July 1970.[117]

More recently, the Soviets have diversified their military assistance repertoire by combining their own efforts with those of their Cuban allies in joint ventures undertaken in Angola and in Ethiopia. In these cases the Soviets apparently provided the arms, air transport, and financial backing to allow large-scale Cuban troop involvements that were vital to the success of their local clients, Neto's MPLA faction in Angola and the Mengistu government in Ethiopia, against internal and regional foes.[118] In Ethiopia, moreover, the successful campaign to drive the Somalis from the Ogaden in 1978 was reportedly planned and directed on the scene by a high-level Soviet military delegation led by the deputy CInC of the ground forces, General V. I. Petrov.[119]

As discussed in the preceeding section, Soviet military assistance activities over the past decade have been accompanied by and have themselves facilitated significant improvements in Soviet long-range power projection. The Soviet desire to play an active and often interventionary role in trouble spots in Africa and Asia has been clearly evident for many years. Now, however, the Soviet potential for such involvement has increased substantially. Soviet military and political writings amply reflect their growing interest in the peacetime political utility of the armed forces.[120] Thus, in 1974, the minister of defense, Marshal A. A. Grechko, wrote, with typical hyperbole:

> At the present stage, the historical function of the Soviet Armed Forces is not restricted merely to their function in defending our Motherland and other socialist countries. In its foreign policy activity, the Soviet state actively and purposefully opposes the export of counterrevolution and the policy of oppression, supports the national liberation struggle and resolutely resists imperial aggression in whatever distant region of our planet it may occur.[121]

The commander in chief of the navy, Admiral S. G. Gorshkov, has been particularly outspoken regarding this matter. On numerous occasions, Gorshkov has touted the particular virtues of the navy as a means to promote the "state interests" of the Soviet Union on the international scene.[122] Gorshkov's claims have not been simply idle boasts—witness the increased manipulation of naval forces in support of Soviet foreign policy in a wide variety of cases including the establishment of the so-called Guinea Patrol, composed of two destroyers and an oiler, to support the beleaguered Sekou Touré government in December 1970, the convoy movement of Moroccan troops to Syria in 1973, and the reactive deployments of Soviet naval task forces to the Bay of Bengal during the Indo-Pakistani War in 1971, off Angola in 1975, in the Mediterranean during the Middle East crises in 1967, 1970, and 1973, and, most recently, in response to the build-up of U.S. naval forces in the Indian Ocean in 1979–80 following the seizure of the U.S. embassy personnel in Tehran.[123]

It appears likely that the Soviet's military assistance activities as well as their various peacetime manipulations of military power will continue to serve as a major dimension of Soviet foreign policy in the years ahead. While not without their setbacks—for example, in Egypt and Indonesia[124]—these efforts have assisted the Soviets significantly in expanding their international influence and prestige. Moreover, given the declining international appeal of the Marxist-Leninist ideology and the economic and political systems of the Soviet Union, these military instrumentalities are likely to be called upon to play a larger and larger role in the promotion of Soviet interests abroad.

Conclusion

The Soviet Union enters the 1980s as one of the world's most powerful nations. For nearly two decades, its leaders have been embarked upon a sustained, expensive, across-the-board build-up of Soviet military capabilites. In this same period, they have derived considerable benefits from their growing arsenal in terms of increased international prestige and a repertoire of military activities that has been used effectively to advance Soviet interests on the international scene.

This growth in military power has had significant impact on the Soviet domestic scene. It appears to have strengthened the political leverage of those groups most directly involved in the development, production, and day-to-day management of the Soviet military machine. This is not to say that the marshals or the munitions designers and producers are in control of the Soviet system; ultimate power continues to reside with the senior Party leadership. However, there appears to be such a congruence of views among the senior Party oligarchs and the leading figures of the Soviet military-industrial complex that policy conflict among these groups has been minimal over the past several years. However, such conflict has emerged in the past—witness Khrushchev's extended clashes with the military in the late fifties and early sixties. And it could emerge once again, particularly if the already troubled Soviet economy were to decline drastically. Even in this circumstance, the well-connected Soviet defense "lobby," both civilian and military, could be expected to resist vigorously any attempt to shift investment priorities substantially away from the defense area.

It appears highly likely that the Soviets will continue to seek to translate their impressive military capabilities into foreign political advantage. There is little doubt that the leaders in the Kremlin would be willing, if required, to use overwhelming military force to retain the Soviet hold on client regimes in Eastern Europe. One is less certain about the manner in which the Soviets are likely to use their military power in dealing with other neighboring states or in more distant areas. Their invasion and subsequent pacification activities in Afghanistan are an ominous sign that the 1980s may witness an increased Soviet willingness to resort to the direct use of armed forces when circumstances indicate that this can be done without serious risk of effective military resistance or response. Given the marked growth in Soviet power projection potential discussed above and the virtual certainty that the international political scene will continue to be characterized by a myriad of unstable situations, the prospect of a more adventuristic Soviet Union, emboldened by its expanding military power, is both very real and very disturbing. Nevertheless, it is precisely such a prospect that the world faces in the years ahead.

Notes

1. *Handbook of Economic Statistics, 1979* (Washington, D.C.: Central Intelligence Agency, 1979), p. 10.
2. Ibid., pp. 11, 128, 130, 150.
3. This point has been documented in the modernization research of Professor Cyril Black of Princeton University.
4. *Handbook of Economic Statistics*, pp. 10, 11. Today the Soviets and the industralized nations of the West have been surpassed in GNP per capita by a few of the oil-rich states of the Middle East.
5. Statement of Ambassador Malcolm C. Toon, in U.S., Senate, *The SALT II Treaty*, Hearings before the Committee on Foreign Relations, 96th Cong., 1st sess. (Washington, D.C.: Government Printing Office, 1978), part 3, p. 6.
6. The efforts of the Soviet regime to perpetuate popular awareness of the massive suffering of the "Great Fatherland War," as the Soviets call their involvement in World War II, is well captured in the title of Hedrick Smith's chapter on this subject, "Patriotism: World War II Was Only Yesterday," in *The Russians* (New York: Quadrangle, 1976), pp. 303-25.
7. Helmut Sonnenfeldt and William G. Hyland, *Soviet Perspectives on Security*, Adelphi Papers, no. 150 (London: International Institute of Strategic Studies, 1979), p. 9.
8. See Ivo J. Lederer, ed., *Russian Foreign Policy* (New Haven: Yale University Press, 1962).
9. An especially prescient observation about Russia's power potential was made almost 150 years ago by Alexis de Tocqueville, who predicted that Russia and the United States were destined to be the world's dominant powers, with the Russian position resting primarily on its military capabilities.
10. International Institute of Strategic Studies, *The Military Balance, 1979-1980* (London: International Institute of Strategic Studies, 1979), p. 13.
11. The Soviets maintained two divisions in Mongolia until 1975, then increased this number to three divisions, where it has remained until the present. See *The Military Balance, 1974-1975* (London: International Institute of Strategic Studies, 1974) and *The Military Balance, 1979-1980* (London: International Institute of Strategic Studies, 1979).
12. The so-called Brezhnev Doctrine justifying Soviet intervention in the "defense" of socialism, first appeared in a *Pravda* editorial on 26 September 1968, a month after the Soviet invasion of Czechoslovakia in August 1968. It was repeated by General Secretary Brezhnev at the Polish Party Congress in Warsaw on 12 November 1968.
13. The most outspoken military figure in this regard has been the commander in chief of the navy, Fleet Admiral of the Soviet Union S. G. Gorshkov. Over the past fifteen years he has regularly touted the navy's ability to serve Soviet foreign policy—for example, he asserted that "the Navy is, to the greatest degree, capable of operationally supporting the state's interest beyond its borders" (S. G. Gorshkov, *Morskaia moshch' gosudarstva* [Sea power of the state] [Moscow: Voenizdat, 1976], p. v).
14. M. Ellen Jones, "The Correlation of Forces in Soviet Decision-Making" (Paper delivered to the 1978 Biennial Conference, Section on Military Studies, International Studies Association, November 1978).
15. For example, Maj. Gen. I. Anureyev, "Determining the Correlation of Forces in Terms of Nuclear Weapons," *Voennaia Mysl'* [Military thought], no. 6 (1967), pp. 35-45.
16. See Arnold L. Horelick and Myron Rush, *Strategic*

Power and Soviet Foreign Policy (Chicago: University of Chicago Press, 1966).

17. Cf. Lt. Col. V. M. Bondarenko, "Military Technological Superiority: The Most Important Factor in the Reliable Defense of the Country," *Kommunist Vooruzhennykh Sil* [Communist of the armed forces], no. 17 (September 1966), pp. 7–14; and *Sovetskaia voennaia entsiklopediia* [Soviet military encyclopedia], vol. 2 (Moscow: Voenizdat, 1976): 253.

18. Brezhnev himself keynoted this campaign to refute Western assertions that the Soviet Union seeks military superiority over the United States and its NATO allies in his major address to Tula in January 1977 (*Pravda*, 19 January 1977). Marshal N. V. Ogarkov, first deputy minister of defense and chief of the General Staff, has lent the authority of the professional military to this claim in various public statements and his authoritative article, "Military Strategy," in *Sovetskaia voennaia entsiklopediia* [Soviet military encyclopedia], vol. 7 (Moscow: Voenizdat, 1979): 563.

19. Timothy Colton, *Commissars, Commanders, and Civilian Authority: The Structure of Soviet Military Politics* (Cambridge, Mass.: Harvard University Press, 1979), p. 251.

20. Harriet Fast Scott and William F. Scott, *The Armed Forces of the USSR* (Boulder, Colo.: Westview Press, 1979), p. 176.

21. For most Soviet draftees, the period of compulsory military service is two years. However, this term is three years for certain naval components, while most deferred students who have received institute or university degrees serve for a year and a half (Scott and Scott, *Armed Forces of the USSR*, p. 305).

22. A. I. Romashko, *Voennye stroiteli na stroikakh Moskvy* [The military builders in the building of Moscow] (Moscow: Voenizdat, 1972).

23. For an excellent comparison of many aspects of U.S. and Soviet military doctrines, see Fritz Ermath's "Contrasts in American and Soviet Strategic Thought," *International Security*, Fall 1978, pp. 142–53.

24. Cf. Raymond L. Garthoff, "Mutual Deterrence and Strategic Arms Limitation in Soviet Policy," *International Security*, Summer 1978, pp. 112–47.

25. Stalin assumed this position after the German invasion in 1941. Khrushchev apparently did so in the late 1950s or early 1960s as he sought to impose his will on the military regarding doctrinal and budgetary issues. Brezhnev's accession to the post, date unknown, was acknowledged in the course of a routine article in the military press in the fall of 1977.

26. There were signs of disagreement on defense investment priorities within the Brezhnev-led collective leadership that succeeded Khrushchev in early 1965. See T. W. Wolfe, *The Soviet Military Scene: Institutional and Defense Policy Considerations*, Rm-4913 (Santa Monica, Calif.: Rand Corporation, 1966), pp. 64–67.

27. John Newhouse, *Cold Dawn: The Story of SALT* (New York: Holt, Rinehart & Winston, 1973), p. 192.

28. Personal observations in contacts with Soviet staff members of the Institute for the Study of the USA and Canada and the Institute of World Economics and International Relations, Moscow, 1976–78.

29. This point has been made by William E. Odom and Robert G. Kaiser in *Russia: The People and the Power* (New York: Pocket Books, 1976), p. 380.

30. J. Richard Lee and James R. Lecky, "Soviet Oil Developments," in Joint Economic Committee, *The Soviet Economy in a Time of Change: A Compendium of Papers*, 96th Congr. (Washington, D.C.: Government Printing Office, 10 October 1979), pp. 581–99.

31. Paul K. Cook, "The Political Setting," in Joint Economic Committee, *Soviet Economy in a Time of Change*, pp. 38–50.

32. John P. Hardt, "Soviet Economic Capabilities and Defense Resources," in *The Soviet Threat: Myths and Realities*, ed. G. Kirk and N. H. Wessell (New York: Academy of Political Science, 1978), p. 124.

33. *Estimated Soviet Defense Spending: Trends and Prospects*, SR-78-10121 (Washington, D.C.: Central Intelligence Agency, 1978).

34. Jeremy Azrael, *Emergent Nationality Problems in the USSR*, R-2172-AF (Santa Monica, Calif.: Rand Corporation, 1977), p. v.

35. S. Enders Wimbush and Dmitry Ponomareff, *Alternatives for Mobilizing Soviet Central Asian Labor: Outmigration and Regional Development*, R-2476-AF (Santa Monica, Calif.: Rand Corporation, 1979).

36. For an excellent review of these and other factors, see Benjamin S. Lambeth, "The Sources of Soviet Military Doctrine," in *Comparative Defense Policy*, ed. F. B. Horton, A. C. Rogerson, and E. L. Warner III (Baltimore: Johns Hopkins University Press, 1974), pp. 200–215.

37. See Marshal M. V. Zakharov, ed., *Voprosy strategii i operativnogo iskusstva v sovetskikh voennykh trudakh, 1917–1940* [Problems of strategy and operational art in Soviet military works, 1917–1940] (Moscow: Voenizdat, 1965), pp. 17–24; John Erickson, *The Soviet High Command: A Military-Political History, 1918–1941* (New York: St. Martin's Press, 1962), pp. 349–54, 404–11; Marshal N. V. Ogarkov, "Deep Operations (Battle)," in *Sovetskaia voennaia entsiklopediia* [Soviet military encyclopedia], vol. 2 (Moscow: Voenizdat, 1976): 574–78.

38. Cf. Marshal N. V. Ogarkov, "Military Strategy," in *Sovetskaia voennaia entsiklopediia* [Soviet military encyclopedia], vol. 7 (Moscow: Voenizdat, 1979): 559–63; Marhsal A. A. Grechko, *Vooruzhennye sili Sovetskogo gosudarstva* [The armed forces of the soviet state] (Moscow: Voenizdat, 1976); Marshal V. D. Sokolovskiy, ed., *Voennaia strategiia* [Military strategy], 3rd ed., rev. (Moscow: Voenizdat, 1968); and commentaries such as Benjamin S. Lambeth, *How to Think about Soviet Military Doctrine*, P-5939 (Santa Monica, Calif.: Rand Corporation, 1978).

39. Cf. A. A. Sidorenko, *Nastuplenie* [The offensive] (Moscow: Voenizdat, 1970); John Erickson, "The Soviet Concept of Land Battle," in *The Soviet Union in Europe and the Near East*, ed. John Erickson (London: Royal United Services Institution, 1970), pp. 26–32.

40. Y. G. Veraka and M. N. Kozhevnikov, "Air Operations," *Sovetskaia voennaia entsiklopediia* [Soviet military encyclopedia], vol. 2 (Moscow: Voenizdat, 1976): 281–82; Robert P. Berman, *Soviet Air Power in Transition* (Washington, D.C.: Brookings Institution, 1978), pp. 11, 66–73; Chief Marshal of Aviation P. Kutakhov, "The Conduct of Air Operations," *Voenno-istoricheskii zhurnal* [Military history journal], no. 6 (June 1972), pp. 20–28.

41. Michael MccGwire, "Naval Power and Soviet Global Strategy," *International Security*, Spring 1979, pp. 170–73; Robert P. Berman and John C. Baker, *Soviet Strategic Forces: Requirements and Responses*

(Washington, D.C.: Brookings Institution, forthcoming), pp. IV-80 to IV-86.

42. Soviet doctrinal writings spoke openly of such preemption in the 1950s. Since that time, however, they have not expressly stated the intention to strike preemptively but have often used suggestive euphemisms such as claiming a readiness to "nip in the bud" any Western nuclear missile attack. See Edward L. Warner III, *The Military in Contemporary Soviet Politics: An Institutional Analysis* (New York: Praeger Publishers, 1977), p. 151.

43. Cf. Marshal N. I. Krylov, "The Nuclear Shield of the Soviet State," *Voennaia mysl'* [Military thought], no. 11 (November 1967), p. 20; Gen. S. Ivanov, "Soviet Military Doctrine and Strategy," *Voennaia mysl'*, no. 5 (May 1969), p. 48; Maj. Gen. N. Vasendin and Col. N. Kuznetsov, "Modern Warfare and Surprise Attack," *Voennaia mysl'*, no. 6 (June 1968), pp. 46–47.

44. Maj. Gen. V. Zemskov, "Characteristic Features of Modern Wars and Possible Methods of Conducting Them," *Voennaia mysl'* [Military thought], no. 7 (July 1969), p. 20; Joseph D. Douglas and Amoretta M. Hoeber, *Soviet Strategy for Nuclear War* (Palo Alto: Hoover Institution Press, 1979), pp. 14–33.

45. Benjamin S. Lambeth, *Selective Nuclear Options in American and Soviet Policy*, R-2034-SSEW (Santa Monica, Calif.: Rand Corporation, 1976).

46. David D. Finley and Jan F. Triska, *Soviet Foreign Policy* (New York: Macmillan Co., 1968), pp. 72–74.

47. Shaposhnikov's three-volume classic, *Mozg armii* [The brain of the army], published in 1927–29, is a historical treatise on the role of the Austro-Hungarian General Staff prior to and during World War I, which makes the case for a powerful general staff as a key element of a nation's military power. Earlier, M. V. Frunze, a leading Red Army commander during the Civil War and subsequently the people's commissar of defense, had described the staff of the Workers' and Peasants' Red Army in 1925 as "the brain of the army."

48. These men were members of a Corps of Officers, representatives of the General Staff, a group operating under the control of the Operations Directorate that was in existence only during World War II.

49. These, in alphabetical order, are the Baltic, Byelorussian, Carpathian, Central Asian, Far Eastern, Kiev, Leningrad, Moscow, North Caucasus, Odessa, Siberian, Transbaikal, Transcaucasus, Turkestan, Ural, and Volga military districts.

50. These groups are the Group of Soviet Forces Germany (GSFG) in East Germany, the Northern Group in Poland, the Central Group in Czechoslovakia, and the Southern Group in Hungary.

51. See Arthur J. Alexander, "Decision-Making in Soviet Weapons Procurement," pp. 153–94, excerpted from his Adelphi Papers, 147 and 148 (London: International Institute of Strategic Studies, 1978/79), of the same title.

52. The nine defense production ministries and their primary products are: the Ministry of Defense Industries, conventional weapons; the Ministry of Aviation Industry, aircraft and cruise missiles; the Ministry of Shipbuilding Industry, ships and submarines; the Ministry of Electronics Industry, electronic components; the Ministry of Radio Industry, electronic products; the Ministry of Medium Machine Building, ballistic missiles; the Ministry of Machine Building, ammunition; and the Ministry of the Means of Communication, telecommunication equipment.

53. In recent years there have been speculations, including my own, that an alternative source of nonmilitary expertise on defense issues might be provided by the two leading foreign affairs institutes of the Academy of Sciences, G. A. Arbatov's Institute for the Study of the USA and Canada, and N. N. Inozemtsev's Institute of World Economics and International Affairs. Both institutes have departments specializing in political-military and arms control matters whose most prominent staff are retired military officers. While these bodies may provide analytical support to top Party leaders on arms control matters and the latest developments in Western defense policies, they do not appear to have a meaningful role in the development of Soviet defense policy. For further discussion of this issue, see my *Military in Contemporary Soviet Politics*, pp. 130–33, and William F. Scott and Harriet Fast Scott, "The Social Sciences Institutes of the Soviet Academy of Sciences," *Air Force Magazine*, March 1980, pp. 60–65.

54. For discussions of Khrushchev's style and beliefs regarding defense issues, see Warner, *Military in Contemporary Soviet Politics*, pp. 137–46, and Khrushchev's memoirs, *Khrushchev Remembers: The Last Testament* (Boston: Little, Brown, 1974), pp. 18–22, 25–26, 40–42, 46, 50, 540.

55. For descriptions of these programs, see Herbert Goldhammer, *The Soviet Soldier: Soviet Military Management at the Troop Level* (New York: Crane & Russak, 1975), pp. 39–88.

56. Colton, *Commissars, Commanders, and Civilian Authority*, pp. 254–55, 284.

57. Ibid., pp. 264, 267.

58. Warner, *Military in Contemporary Soviet Politics*, pp. 100–102.

59. Colton, *Commissars, Commanders, and Civilian Authority*, pp. 35–44, and E. H. Carr, *Socialism in One Country, 1924–1926*, vol. 2 (Baltimore: Penguin Books, 1970): 432–33.

60. Colton, *Commissars, Commanders, and Civilian Authority*.

61. The most prominent advocate of this view has been Roman Kolkowicz, whose most detailed presentation is found in *The Soviet Military and the Communist Party* (Princeton: Princeton University Press, 1967).

62. Stalin's "Tsaritsyn group" included K. E. Voroshilov, S. K. Timoshenko, and S. M. Budenny of the famous First Cavalry Army, all of whom became marshals of the Soviet Union under Stalin's sponsorship. Khrushchev's comrades in arms at the Stalingrad include such figures as Marshals V. I. Chuikov, S. S. Biriuzov, and R. Y. Malinovskiy, all of whom rose to key posts in the Ministry of Defense while Khrushchev dominated Soviet politics in the late 1950s and early 1960s.

63. Cf. *Khrushchev Remembers;* Marshal G. K. Zhukov, *The Memoirs of Marshal Zhukov* (New York: Delacorte Press, 1971); Gen. S. M. Shtemenko, *General 'ny shtab v gody voiny* [*The General Staff during the war years*], vols. 1 and 2 (Moscow: Voenizdat, 1968 and 1973); and S. Bialer, ed., *Stalin and His Generals: Soviet Military Memoirs of World War II* (New York: Pegasus, 1969).

64. Major works in this regard are Arthur J. Alexander's "Weapons Acquisition in the Soviet Union, United States and France," in *Comparative Defense Policy*, ed. Horton, Rogerson, and Warner, pp. 426–44; and Alexander's *Decision-Making in Soviet Weapons Procurement;* David Holloway, "Technology and Political Decision in Soviet

Armaments Policy,'' *Journal of Peace Research*, no. 4 (1976); John McConnell, ''The Soviet Defense Industry As a Pressure Group,'' in *Soviet Naval Policy*, ed. M. MccGwire, K. Booth, and J. McConnell (New York: Praeger, 1975), pp. 91–101; and Berman and Baker, *Soviet Strategic Forces*.

65. Odom, personal conversation with author; Robert Kaiser emphasizes the critical *quality control* function performed by these military representatives in his *Russia*, pp. 378–83.

66. Alexander, ''Weapons Acquisition,'' pp. 430–31; and idem, *Decision-Making in Soviet Weapons Procurement*, pp. 33, 34, 41.

67. Karl F. Spielmann, ''Defense Industrialists in the USSR,'' *Problems of Communism*, September–October 1976, pp. 52–69.

68. All of these percentages are based on data from the International Institute of Strategic Studies's *Military Balance, 1979–1980*, p. 9.

69. The Soviets probably sought to achieve this objective, at least partially, with their third-generation ICBMs by targeting the powerful warheads of the relatively inaccurate SS-9 against the 100 Minuteman launch control centers. The United States countered this possible tactic in the late 1960s by deploying launch control aircraft that can be kept on continuous airborne alert (Berman and Baker, *Soviet Strategic Forces*, pp. IV-30 to IV-34).

70. International Institute of Strategic Studies, *Military Balance, 1979–1980*, p. 9.

71. These constraints are found in articles IV-9, IV-10, and IV-11 of the *SALT II Agreement: Selected Documents no. 12A* (Washington, D.C.: Department of State, 1979), pp. 34–36.

72. International Institute of Strategic Studies, *Military Balance, 1979–1980*, p. 9.

73. Berman and Baker, *Soviet Strategic Forces*, appendix B, p. 6.

74. Ibid., pp. IV-64 to IV-67; ''ASW: Is the US Lead Slipping,'' *Armed Forces Journal International*, April 1980, pp. 46–47.

75. International Institute of Strategic Studies, *Military Balance, 1979–1980*, p. 9.

76. Ibid.

77. Ibid.

78. ''Gallery of Soviet Aerospace Weapons,'' *Air Force Magazine*, March 1980, p. 119.

79. Constraints on the Backfire are provided by a statement made by General Secretary Brezhnev to President Carter at the June 1979 summit in Vienna when the SALT II agreements were signed. This exchange limits the Soviet annual Backfire production rate to not more than thirty per year and commits the Soviets not to increase the range of the Backfire to enable it to strike the United States (*SALT II Agreement*, p. 50).

80. International Institute of Strategic Studies, *Military Balance, 1979–1980*, p. 9.

81. Ibid.; Berman and Baker, *Soviet Strategic Forces*, pp. IV-68, 86–88.

82. Edgar Ulsamer, ''Moscow's Goal in Military Superiority,'' *Air Force Magazine*, March 1980, and William T. Lee, ''The Soviet Defense Establishment in the 1980s,'' *Air Force Magazine*, March 1980, pp. 50, 104–5, 122, 126; Harold Brown, *Department of Defense Annual Report, FY 1980* (Washington, D.C.: Government Printing Office, 1979), p. 73.

83. ''Gallery of Soviet Aerospace Weapons,'' p. 134; Richard Burt, ''US Says Russians Develop Satellite Killing Laser,'' *New York Times*, 22 May 1980; Alexander, *Decision-Making in Soviet Weapons Procurement*, pp. 37–39; Harold Brown, *Department of Defense Annual Report, FY 1981* (Washington, D.C.: Government Printing Office, 1980), p. 82.

84. ''ASW: Is the US Lead Slipping,'' pp. 46–47.

85. Results of an interagency U.S. government study released by the director of central intelligence in July 1978 and published in *Soviet Civil Defense*, Special Report no. 47 (Washington, D.C.: Department of State, 1978).

86. International Institute of Strategic Studies, *Military Balance, 1979–1980*, pp. 9–10.

87. Ibid., p. 10; Brown, *Department of Defense Annual Report, FY 1981*, p. 101.

88. International Institute of Strategic Studies, *Military Balance, 1979–1980*, p. 10.

89. ''The Red Army's New Look,'' *Newsweek*, 11 February 1980, p. 46.

90. International Institute of Strategic Studies, *Military Balance, 1979–1980*, p. 10.

91. *Handbook on the Soviet Armed Forces* (Washington, D.C.: Defense Intelligence Agency, 1978), p. 8–5.

92. Ibid., pp. 8–22 to 8–27; J. V. Braddock and N. F. Wikner, *An Assessment of Soviet Forces Facing NATO: The Central Region and Suggested NATO Initiatives* (McLean, Va.: Braddock, Dunn, McDonald, 1978); Ray Bonds, ed., *The Soviet War Machine* (London: C. Hartwell Books, 1976), pp. 168–85; General David G. Jones, *United States Military Posture, FY 1980* (Washington, D.C.: Government Printing Office, 1980), p. 54.

93. John Erickson, ''The Soviet Union's Growing Arsenal of Chemical Warfare,'' *Strategic Review*, Fall 1979, pp. 63–71.

94. John Erickson, ''Doctrine, Technology and Style,'' in *Soviet Military Power and Performance*, ed. John Erickson and E. J. Fuechtwanger (London: Macmillan Press, 1979), pp. 20–22; and ''Soviet Breakthrough Operations: Resources and Restraints,'' *Royal United Services Institution Journal*, September 1976, p. 74.

95. International Institute of Strategic Studies, *Military Balance, 1979–1980*, p. 11.

96. Berman, *Soviet Air Power in Transition*, p. 32; William Schneider, Jr., ''Trends in Soviet Frontal Aviation,'' *Air Force Magazine*, March 1979, pp. 76–81.

97. Lynn M. Hansen, ''Soviet Combat Helicopter Operations,'' *International Defense Review*, August 1978, pp. 1242–46.

98. International Institute of Strategic Studies, *Military Balance, 1979–1980*, p. 11.

99. Schneider, ''Soviet Frontal Aviation,'' p. 80.

100. See the discussion above in the force employment doctrine section.

101. Brown, *Department of Defense Annual Report, FY 1981*, pp. 103–4; Jones, *United States Military Posture, FY 1980*, pp. 23, 55.

102. Brown, *Department of Defense Annual Report, FY 1981*, p. 103; Michael MccGwire, ''Soviet Naval Developments'' (Personal paper, April 1980), pp. 7–8.

103. Michael MccGwire, ''Naval Power and Soviet Global Strategy,'' in *Soviet Military Thinking*, ed. D. Leebaerd (London: Allen & Unwin, forthcoming).

104. Ibid., p. 106; International Institute of Strategic Studies, *Military Balance, 1979–1980*, pp. 5, 11; Peter Bogart, ''The Soviet Transport Air Force: Aircraft and

Capabilities," *International Defense Review*, June 1979, pp. 945–50.

105. International Institute of Strategic Studies, *Military Balance, 1979–1980*, p. 11.

106. David Halevy, "Soviet Airlift in Ethiopia, Aden Reported," *Washington Star*, 23 September 1979, p. 3; Stephen S. Kaplan, "The Historical Record," and Colin Legum, "Angola and the Horn of Africa," in *Diplomacy of Power: Soviet Armed Forces As a Political Instrument*, Stephen S. Kaplan, ed. (Washington, D.C.: Brookings Institution, 1981), pp. 3-66 to 3-70, 5-70 to 5-80, and 13-1 to 13-94.

107. The latter group, led by the Commission for Scientific Problems of Disarmament, includes several prominent Soviet scientists, scholars, and members of the academy's social science institutes. Apparently these people are consulted on arms control matters and frequently participate in international conferences such as those sponsored annually by the Pugwash US-USSR Study Group on Arms Control and Disarmament. See Warner, *Military in Contemporary Soviet Politics*, pp. 222–24.

108. The military delegates have included such important military figures as Marshal N. V. Ogarkov and Col. Gen. N. N. Alekseyev, both of whom were active in SALT I. The defense industry figures included academician A. N. Shchukin, a leading weapons development scientist, and Petr Pleshakov, then a deputy minister and subsequently the minister of radio industry.

109. The post was held by Deputy Minister of Foreign Affairs V. S. Semyonov from 1969 until 1978 and subsequently by Ambassador V. P. Karpov, who served through the completion of the SALT II negotiations in June 1979.

110. For discussions of Soviet organizations involved in SALT, see Warner, *Military in Contemporary Soviet Politics*, pp. 237–44; Newhouse, *Cold Dawn;* Raymond L. Garthoff, "SALT and the Soviet Military," *Problems of Communism*, January–February 1975, pp. 21–37; and Thomas W. Wolfe, *The SALT Experience* (Cambridge, Mass.: Ballinger Publishing Co., 1979).

111. Others included negotiations with the United States and the United Kingdom on a comprehensive nuclear test ban, with the United States on an antisatellite warfare regime, limitations on conventional arms transfers, and chemical warfare limits, and participation in the United Nations' continuing Conference on Disarmament in Geneva.

112. For descriptions of Soviet proposals and U.S.-Soviet bargaining, see Newhouse, *Cold Dawn;* and Strobe Talbott, *End Game: The Inside Story of SALT II* (New York: Harper & Row, 1979).

113. These were the battles of Lake Khasan in the Far East in 1938 and of Khalgin-gol in Mongolia in 1939, in which the Red Army more than held its own against armed probes by the Japanese Kwantung Army, thus apparently helping convince the Japanese that a full-fledged war with the Soviet Union would not be an inviting prospect. See Erickson, *Soviet High Command*, pp. 494–99, 517–22, 532–37.

114. Kaplan, ed., *Diplomacy of Power*, pp. 2-1 to 2-5. The study represents a follow-on effort to similar Brookings examination of U.S. peacetime uses of force in the post–World War II period. See also Barry M. Blechman and Stephen S. Kaplan, *Force without War: U.S. Armed Forces As a Political Instrument* (Washington, D.C.: Brookings Institution, 1977).

115. For accounts of the Sino-Soviet and Soviet-Vietnamese military relationships, see Raymond L. Garthoff, ed., *Sino-Soviet Military Relations* (New York: Praeger, 1966); Kaplan, "Historical Record"; William Zimmerman, "The Korean and Vietnam Wars," and Thomas W. Robinson, "The Sino-Soviet Border Conflict," in *Diplomacy of Power*, ed. Kaplan, pp. 3-42 to 3-57, 3-69 to 3-73, 8-1 to 8-67, and 7-1 to 7-66.

116. Oleg Penkovskiy, *The Penkovskiy Papers*, trans. Peter Deriabin (New York: Avon Books, 1966), p. 88; *Directory of USSR Ministry of Defense and Armed Forces Officials* (Washington, D.C.: Central Intelligence Agency, 1978), p. 4.

117. Kaplan, "Historical Record," p. 5-31; and Ken Booth, *The Military Instrument in Soviet Foreign Policy* (London: Royal United Services Institute, 1973), p. 35.

118. Legum, "Angola and the Horn of Africa," pp. 13-1 to 13-44.

119. Kaplan, "Historical Record," in *Diplomacy of Power*, ed. Kaplan, pp. 5-7, 5-9.

120. For a review of these, see William F. Scott and Harriet Fast Scott, *A Review and Assessment of Soviet Policy and Concepts on the Projection of Military Presence and Power* (McLean, Va.: General Research Corporation, 1979).

121. Marshal A. A. Grechko, "The Leading Role of the CPSU in Building the Army of a Developed Socialist Society," *Voprosy istorii Kpss* [Problems of history of the CPSU] (May 1974), p. 38.

122. These parochial proclamations include: "The Navy is, to the greatest degree, capable of operationally supporting the state interests of the country beyond its borders" (Gorshkov, *Morskaia moshch' gosudarstva*, p. v).

123. David K. Hall, "Naval Diplomacy in West African Waters," in *Diplomacy of Power*, ed. Kaplan, pp. 12-1 to 12-74; MccGwire, "Naval Power and Soviet Global Strategy," pp. 52-53. For a comprehensive survey of Soviet naval force projection, see James M. McConnell and Bradford N. Dismukes, eds., *Soviet Naval Diplomacy: From the June War to Angola* (New York: Pergamon Press, 1981).

124. Indonesia, despite receiving some three billion dollars in arms assistance from the Soviet Union in the late 1950s and early 1960s, turned abruptly away from Moscow following an abortive communist coup attempt in 1965. In the Egyptian case, despite some fifteen years of Soviet military assistance valued at over five billion dollars, in 1971 President Sadat chose to terminate his arms aid relationship and dramatically alter Cairo's relations with the Soviet Union. For further comments on these incidents and other shortcomings of Soviet military assistance efforts, see "Soviet Weapons Exports: Russian Roulette in the Third World," *Defense Monitor*, Center for Defense Information (January 1979).

SOVIET DEFENSE POLICY: A BIBLIOGRAPHICAL ESSAY

Schuyler Foerster

Soviet defense policy is rarely viewed by scholars in its totality. More often than not, the literature includes, in recurring publications, articles dealing with more specific aspects of Soviet security affairs. In viewing this literature, the reader must realize that such articles may reflect institutional interests, editorial bias, or policy advocacy on the part of the journal or individual author. The reader can only hope to rectify this inevitable slant in the literature by reading broadly and critically. Although this is true for most policy-related writings, it is especially true for the literature on Soviet defense policy because of the high degree of uncertainty that characterizes our knowledge of the Soviets and because of the policy stakes that may exist on any particular issue.

United States sources

Within the United States, virtually any journal that deals in any way with international security issues will contain articles on Soviet defense policy. Four academic journals do so on a regular basis: *Orbis,* published quarterly by the Foreign Policy Research Institute in association with the International Relations Graduate Group of the University of Pennsylvania; *International Security,* published quarterly by the Program for Science and International Affairs at Harvard University; *Armed Forces and Society,* published quarterly by the Inter-University Seminar on Armed Forces and Society; and *Comparative Strategy,* a journal published quarterly for the Strategic Studies Center by Crane, Russak, & Co. Two additional U.S. journals have consistently opposing perspectives on Soviet defense policy, particularly insofar as these views relate to U.S. defense policy issues: *Strategic Review,* published quarterly by the United States Strategic Institute, and the *Defense Monitor,* published monthly by the Center for Defense Information. Both of these organizations conduct research and advocate policy positions within Washington, D.C.; the former tends to take a more pessimistic view of Soviet military power, while the latter tends to take a somewhat more optimistic perspective.

Another set of journals addresses Soviet defense policy more indirectly, dealing with broader issues of international politics. Yet, they are worth consulting on a regular basis because the specifics of Soviet defense policy are often better understood in this broader context. These include *Foreign Affairs,* now published five times a year by the Council on Foreign Relations; *Foreign Policy,* published quarterly by the Carnegie Endowment for International Peace; *International Studies Quarterly,* published by SAGE Publications; and *World Politics,* published quarterly by Princeton University Press.

U.S. government agencies also publish relevant materials on a recurring basis, particularly *Problems of Communism,* published six times annually by the International Communications Agency and distributed by the Government Printing Office. In addition, each of the service schools of the army, navy, and air force publishes a journal on defense policy issues: *Military Review* (monthly), *Naval War College Review* (quarterly), and *Air University Review* (bimonthly).

Soviet sources

Soviet writers on defense policy issues have always been prolific in elaborating their particular world view, interpreting international security issues, and codifying the complex body of knowledge that they refer to as "military science." Yet the analysis of these primary sources has long been the province of a few select scholars who, by virtue of linguistic ability and experience, were capable of detecting nuances and sharing their insights with other scholars in the field. This body of literature has lately become more accessible and comprehensible to students of defense policy.

Although the reader faces disadvantages in studying the defense policy of a closed society, there is one notable advantage: Soviet press reporting reflects Soviet policy, and a reader can gain insight into Soviet behavior by charting responses to specific events. One avenue of gaining access to this literature is through indices and digests that routinely screen, translate, and publish the Soviet press. Within the U.S. government there are two vehicles for doing this. The most familiar is the *Foreign Broadcast Information Service* (FBIS) daily report, which includes not only press but also radio and television coverage. On a more inclusive (if not unwieldy) scale, the *Joint Publications Research Service* (JPRS) translates books, articles, and monographs on a variety of subjects. While not normally available in libraries, JPRS reports are accessible through the National Technical Information Service of the Department of Commerce. The most useful guide to the Soviet press is the *Current Digest of the Soviet Press,* published weekly by the American Association for the Advancement of Slavic Studies. It is available in most libraries, and there is a very usable quarterly index.

Soviet sources themselves tend to be intimidating in style, ponderous to read, and pregnant with propaganda. The three most important newspaper sources, in as much as they reflect officialdom, are *Pravda* ("truth"), published by the Communist party of the Soviet Union; *Izvestia* ("news"), the organ of the Soviet Council of Ministers; and *Krasnaya Zvezda* ("red star"), a product of the Soviet armed forces. The most important periodic journal on defense policy issues is *Kommunist Vooruzhennykh Sil* ("Communist of the armed forces"), published twice monthly by the Main Political Administration of the Soviet armed forces. While this is an official journal for internal professional consumption, the *Soviet Military Review* (published monthly in English, French, and Arabic—but not Russian) is intended for foreign consumption. To help readers identify these and other Soviet sources, William F. Scott, former U.S. air attaché to Moscow, has written a compendium entitled *Soviet Sources of Military Doctrine and Strategy,* a National Strategy Information Center product (New York: Crane, Russak & Co., 1975). The book's utility derives from its comprehensive coverage of basic Soviet sources, books, and publishers since 1960; a review of available English translations of Soviet military writings; and a thoughtful commentary on the nature and validity of Soviet military writing. As an annotated bibliography, it also serves as a superb documentary on the milestones of post-Stalinist doctrinal developments.

While Scott's book on Soviet sources is now a few years old, one continuing source for major Soviet military writings is the *Soviet Military Thought* series, available from the U.S. Government Printing Office. Translated and published under the auspices of the U.S. Air Force, this series presently comprises sixteen volumes, including Sidorenko's classic 1970 treatise on *The Offensive* (vol. 1), a useful *Dictionary of Basic Military Terms* (vol. 9), a handbook on *Civil Defense* (vol. 10), the late Minister of Defense Marshal Grechko's *Armed Forces of the Soviet State* (vol. 12), and *The Officer's Handbook* (vol. 13). Although perhaps alien to the novice reader, these provide—with commentary—a worthwhile means to view defense issues through a Soviet lens.

Of course, one should not overlook the now classic collective study under the editorship of V. D. Sokolovskiy entitled *Military Strategy.* It was originally published in 1962, and subsequent revised editions appeared in 1963 and 1968. In particular, the reader may wish to consult the English version edited by Harriet F. Scott (New York: Crane, Russak & Co. 1975), which compares the 1968 edition with the earlier versions.

European sources

While European publications pertinent to Soviet defense policy undoubtedly suffer from the same criticisms that American sources do, there appears to be less concern for policy advocacy and, hence, more objectivity and depth of analysis in some of them. Indeed, perhaps the most consistently objective and insightful publications on Soviet defense policy and related international security issues are those that emanate from the International Institute of Strategic Studies (IISS) in London. There are four useful publications from IISS: a bimonthly journal, *Survival,* which includes articles and important primary source documents; occasional Adelphi Papers on a variety of security issues by single authors; the annual *Strategic Survey,* reviewing events of the previous year; and the annual *Military Balance,* which remains the best unclassified source of national and alliance force postures.

While each European country has its own litany of publications that pertain to Soviet defense policy, it is beyond the scope of this essay to name them all. Four European journals do deserve mention, however: the relatively new *Journal of Strategic Studies,* published quarterly by Frank Cass & Co., London; *NATO Review,* published bimonthly by the NATO Information Service in Brussels; the *RUSI Journal,* published quarterly by the Royal United Services Institute for Defense Studies in London; and *International Defense Review,* published nine times annually by Interavia in Geneva. While the first three generally include articles on Soviet doctrine and military organization, *International Defense Review* is primarily devoted to a review of force posture and weapons system issues.

It should be clear to the reader that the literature on Soviet defense policy is vast and continues to build. The following section seeks to direct the reader to a small but representative portion of that literature.

A selective review of Soviet defense policy literature

Since the Soviets view military force as an extension of both internal and external policy, any review of Soviet defense policy should begin with an understanding of the broader policy contexts in which the military operates. To begin that understanding, a particularly useful text on Soviet politics is *The Soviet*

Polity: Government and Politics in the U.S.S.R. (2nd ed.), by John S. Reshetar, Jr. (New York: Harper & Row, 1978). The book includes two features pertinent to this essay: first, an excellent annotated bibliography, and, second, an analysis of six alternative models of Soviet behavior. Its emphasis on understanding the unique Russian political culture serves as a helpful introduction to the more specific study of Soviet defense policy.

While much has been written on Soviet foreign policy—that broad category of which defense policy is but a violent subset—two works stand out. First, for an in-depth history of Soviet foreign policy, is the incomparable *Expansion and Coexistence: Soviet Foreign Policy, 1917-1973* (2nd ed.), by Adam B. Ulam (New York: Praeger Publishers, 1974). Complementing Ulam's massive work, Robin Edmonds's *Soviet Foreign Policy, 1962-1973: The Paradox of Super Power* (New York: Oxford University Press, 1975) is a brief, highly readable, insightful, and occasionally witty review of the Brezhnev foreign policy, prefaced by a superb analysis of the Khrushchev period. While both appear dated, they in fact are not, for Soviet styles, objectives, and use of policy instruments have remained remarkably consistent, a reflection of the conservatism of the current Soviet leaders, if not all of them.

Similarly incompatible with any narrower categorization of Soviet defense policy elements, there are a handful of works that treat Soviet defense policy as a generic instrument of policy and projection of power. While some are by individual authors, others are edited books with several contributors; this in itself is a useful introduction to the field and the authors who publish in it. In this latter category, Laurence L. Whetten has edited *The Future of Soviet Military Power* (New York: Crane, Russak & Co., 1976), which includes separate chapters on various dimensions of Soviet military power. Particularly recommended are William R. VanCleave's chapter on the evolving American perception of Soviet strategic doctrine and John Erickson's chapter on Soviet theater war capability. More recently, the Academy of Political Science has published its *Proceedings* (vol. 33, no. 1), edited by Grayson Kirk and Nils H. Wessell, entitled *The Soviet Threat: Myths and Realities* (Montpelier, Vt.: Capital City Press, 1978). Like Whetten's work, it brings together a number of authors who discuss, in a single volume, the multifaceted nature of Soviet defense policy.

A unique contribution to the literature, *Contemporary Strategy: Theories and Policies,* by John Baylis, Ken Booth, John Garrett, and Phil Williams (New York: Holmes & Meier Publishers, 1975), discusses Soviet defense policy, not only by itself but in a comparative and theoretical context. Ken Booth's chapter on Soviet defense policy is lucid and concise, and it contains a useful bibliography on both Soviet and Western sources. In addition, three smaller pieces reflect on the nature of Soviet power and provide insights into the Soviet security "mind-set." Thomas W. Wolfe's *Military Power and Soviet Policy* (Rand Paper P-5388 [March 1975]) discusses the relationship between evolving Soviet military power and broader policy. On a more conceptual level, Helmut Sonnenfeldt and William G. Hyland have produced their *Soviet Perspectives on Security* (Adelphi Papers, no. 150 [Spring 1979]), a thoughtful review of how Soviet views on the need for military force have evolved since the early revolutionary years. Finally, Robert Legvold's article, "The Nature of Soviet Power," in *Foreign Affairs* (vol. 56, no. 1 [October 1977]: 49-71), reminds us that military power is only one dimension of a country's overall power. While force may be the most usable dimension for the Soviets in terms of strength, it may also be the least usable by virtue of its inherent risks.

DOCTRINE AND FORCE POSTURE

While I suggested earlier that doctrine is best considered an input and force posture an output of defense decision making, most authors tend to combine the two as reflections of each other. Thus, most of the works cited in this part of the essay discuss both of these elements together. Interestingly enough, there appears to be a decided difference in style between those authors who view Soviet military power either pessimistically or optimistically. Those in the former category tend more readily to cite primary Soviet military sources in the open literature that call for an open-ended accumulation of military force; moreover, they conclude that the Marxist-Leninist world view—specifically the inherent antagonisms of global class struggle and the continued relevance of Clausewitz's formulation that war is merely "the extension of politics by violent means"—creates an incentive for persistent emphasis on superiority and war fighting with no moderating desire for long-term strategic stability or mutual deterrence. The result, then, is a focus on military capabilities, with a presumption of intent to use those capabilities.

On the other hand, those authors who write with greater optimism (or at least less pessimism) tend less to cite primary Soviet military sources, assuming these sources to be a relatively unreliable guide to intent and as much rhetoric for internal bureaucratic bargaining and external propaganda purposes as realistic calls for action. In the past few years, this group of authors has largely come to accept that Soviet doctrine is different from American doctrine, particularly strategic nuclear doctrine. Yet the Soviet emphasis on Clausewitz is interpreted more as a conservative device to preclude the use of force unless external and internal political considerations both demand and allow it. In short, the more optimistic writers tend to accept Soviet military capabilities as a natural outgrowth of a distinctive doctrinal and organizational context. While these capabilities are hardly discounted, the focus of analysis remains centered on intent, either by viewing the Soviet use of force in a historical perspective or by assessing the political dynamics of the entire system.

Because the United States holds Soviet strategic nuclear forces as the primary concern, this aspect of Soviet doctrine and force posture has received the most attention in the literature. Indicative of the more pessimistic perspective is a series of books published by the University of Miami's Center for Advanced International Studies. Two representative and pertinent works are *The Role of Nuclear Forces in Current Soviet Strategy,* by Leon Goure, Foy D. Kohler, and Mose L. Harvey (Washington, D.C.: Center for Advanced International Studies, 1975), and *War Survival in Soviet Strategy: USSR Civil Defense,* by Leon Goure (Washington, D.C.: Center for Advanced International Studies, 1976). Both books relate complementary aspects of Soviet strategic doctrine. While the former details the development of Soviet offensive weaponry in the wake of the first Strategic Arms Limitation Accord and the Vladivostok guidelines, the latter relates a fundamentally war-fighting aspect of Soviet doctrine that seeks to make nuclear war "winnable" and therefore "thinkable." A concise and articulate summary of this thesis is Richard Pipes's controversial article, "Why the Soviet Union Thinks It Could Fight and Win a Nuclear War," *Commentary* (July 1977), reprinted in *Air Force Magazine* (vol. 60, no. 9 [September 1977]: 54-66).* An example of an opposing view, Fred Kaplan's article, "Soviet Civil Defense: Some Myths in the Western Debate," in *Survival* (vol. 20, no. 3 [May/June 1978]: 113-20), discounts Soviet civil defense programs as an impractical solution to the essentially insoluble problem of damage limitation.

Until recently, the debate over Soviet strategic doctrine centered on whether the Soviets accepted the Western concept of deterrence or preferred the more ominous alternative of a war-fighting posture. While Soviet doctrine appears distinct from U.S. doctrine, the nature of that distinction is held by some as one of differing concepts of deterrence, rather than a rejection of deterrence altogether. Three articles in this vein appeared in 1978. The first, "SALT and Soviet Nuclear Doctrine," by Stanley Sienkiewicz, in *International Security* (vol. 2, no. 4 [Spring 1978]: 84-100), argues that difficulties in negotiating with the Soviets on limiting strategic arms stem from the fact that, while the Soviets emphasize deterrence as a criterion for formulating their strategic nuclear posture, their deterrence concept does not include a desire for long-term mutual stability. Dennis Ross, in "Rethinking Soviet Strategic Policy: Inputs and Implications," the lead article in the *Journal of Strategic Studies* (vol. 1, no. 1 [May 1978]: 3-30), refines the differing concepts of deterrence, distinguishing between Soviet "deterrence by denial" and American "deterrence by punishment." While the former concept is more oriented toward a war-fighting posture, Ross views this as a product of a policy process in which the Soviet military has a monopoly on technical expertise; the American concept, he argues, partly derives from the heavy civilian participation in doctrinal formulation in the United States. Completing this trilogy, Fritz W. Ermarth provides a concise review of these doctrinal differences in "Contrasts in American and Soviet Strategic Thought," in *International Security* (vol. 3, no. 2 [Fall 1978]: 138-55).* Ermarth cites differing views, not only on the nature of deterrence but also on the consequences of a strategic nuclear war, the desirability of strategic stability, the linkage between intercontinental and regional security concerns, and the dynamics of conflict limitation.

Bridging the gap between strategic nuclear and general purpose forces, one particularly good study has focused on the integration of nuclear weapons into Soviet doctrine for a war in Europe: Joseph D. Douglass, Jr., *The Soviet Theater Nuclear Offensive,* vol. 1 in the *Studies in Communist Affairs* series published under the auspices of the U.S. Air Force (Washington, D.C.: Government Printing Office, 1976). Douglass draws a great deal from Soviet doctrinal writings, particularly Sidorenko's *Offensive* (cited earlier). While Sidorenko viewed the preemptive use of nuclear weapons as a crucial determinant of victory, Soviet doctrine has, more recently, considered it possible that a theater war in Europe could stay at the conventional level. Not surprisingly, most of the Western literature on Soviet capabilities in Europe has focused on the growth and modernization of Soviet conventional forces. Richard Pipes has edited *Soviet Strategy in Europe* (New York: Crane, Russak & Co., 1976), which includes two particularly pertinent chapters by Thomas W. Wolfe and John Erickson. In the same vein, William Schneider, Jr., concisely reviews both doctrine and forces in "Soviet General Purpose Forces," in *Orbis* (vol. 21, no. 1 [Spring 1977]: 95-105). Wolfe's *Soviet Power in Europe, 1945-1970* (Baltimore: Johns Hopkins University Press, 1970) remains a classic source for the background and evolution of the Soviet military presence in Eastern Europe.

Before the 1970s, the Soviet navy received very

*See below, pp. 134-46.

*See below, pp. 126-33.

little attention, largely because, from a strategic point of view, it did not deserve very much. Soviet naval development represents, perhaps, a classic case in which a major change in Soviet doctrine has led to the deployment of forces hitherto considered largely irrelevant for anything but coastal defense. Reviewing a series of articles by Soviet Naval Commander-in-Chief Admiral Gorshkov in 1972–73, "The Gorshkov Papers: Soviet Naval Doctrine for the Nuclear Age," by E. T. Wooldrige, Jr. (*Orbis* 28, no. 4 [Winter 1975]: 1153–75), outlines the evolution of Soviet doctrine for a "blue water" navy. Perhaps the most detailed review of the modern Soviet navy is Paul J. Murphy's *Naval Power in Soviet Policy,* vol. 2 in the *Studies in Communist Affairs* series (Washington, D.C.: Government Printing Office, 1978). For the most part a compendium of naval and naval air capabilities, it is comprehensive, providing the reader with a useful handbook of naval forces designed to fill a variety of missions.

The growth of the Soviet navy, its potential for sea denial, and its expanded capability to project military power for political purposes have all provided new impetus to concerns about Soviet presence around the globe. Soviet activity in Africa, the Middle East, the Indian Ocean littoral, Afghanistan, and Southeast Asia remain subjects of controversy. One school of thought views these efforts as part of a plan to integrate regional politicomilitary ties into a single collective security system. This thesis is the subject of *The Evolution of Soviet Security Strategy,* by Avigdor Haselkorn (New York: Crane, Russak & Co., 1976), and is summarized in his article "The Soviet Collective Security System," published in *Orbis* (vol. 19, no. 1 [Spring 1975]: 231–54). While most authors do not openly subscribe to the notion of such a deliberate and integrated strategy, Haselkorn's work is worth reviewing, if for no other reason than that it contains a tremendous body of empirical data and case studies.

To conclude this review of Soviet doctrinal literature, mention must be made of one particular work that cuts across the framework used so far in this essay. The *Soviet Aerospace Handbook* (Washington, D.C.: Government Printing Office, 1978, published as Air Force Pamphlet 200–21) is a comprehensive unclassified review of the Soviet air force, Strategic Missile Forces, National Air Defense Forces, Naval Aviation, and space programs: their place within the overall organization of the Soviet Ministry of Defense, their command interrelationships, their doctrine and force postures, and their research and development programs. The book also includes a section on "Life in the Soviet Air Force," a useful bibliography, and biographies of key military leaders. While not an analytical work, it stands as a worthwhile source for background information and data on force capabilities.

DEFENSE DECISION MAKING

Until the last decade, Soviet defense policy was generally analyzed as the product of a unitary decision maker. This reliance on a single level of analysis began to change, however, as Western analysts began to view policy outcomes as the product of multiple actors in the decision-making process. This new emphasis on bureaucratic bargaining, organizational routine, and selective perception on the part of decision makers was particularly applicable when viewing a pluralistic system like the United States. The Soviet Union, however, was another matter. While the Soviet Union remains a heavily bureaucratized state, strongly authoritarian party control might preclude the formation and expression of organizational interests. Thus, the application of bureaucratic politics models to the Soviet Union might be no more than mirror imaging of questionable validity.

Roman Kolkowicz's classic book, *The Soviet Military and the Communist Party* (Princeton: Princeton University Press, 1967), was the first substantial attempt at using interest group competition as a framework for analyzing Soviet Party-military relations. Viewing this relationship largely in the pre-Brezhnev eras, Kolkowicz concluded that there was an inherent antagonism between the Party and the military, each pursuing antithetical values (elitism versus egalitarianism, autonomy versus subordination to the Party, nationalism versus proletarian internationalism, detachment from society versus social involvement, and heroic symbolism versus anonymity). A good summary of Kolkowicz's thesis is his article, "Interest Groups in Soviet Politics: The Case of the Military," in *Comparative Politics* (vol. 2, no. 3 [April 1970]: 445–72).

The essence of Kolkowicz's thesis is an interest group model in which the Party and the military are each viewed as unitary interests competing for influence on a horizontal plane. More recently, however, the Party and the military have each been viewed as bureaucratic actors in which the respective leaders seek to maintain vertical control over bureaucratic subelements. Representative of this view, William E. Odom has concluded that Party and military leaders, particularly in the Brezhnev era, actually exist in a mutually interdependent, symbiotic relationship, each cooperating in the control of their respective bureaucracies. Odom's first article on this thesis, "The Party Connection," published in *Problems of Communism* (vol. 22, no. 5 [September/October 1973]: 12–26), critiques Kolkowicz's theory of antithetical traits, arguing that the Party and military leaders actually agree on their respective goals and values. Odom's "Who Controls Whom in Moscow," in *Foreign Policy* (no. 19 [Summer 1975], pp. 109–22), expands this Party-military symbiosis to include the defense industry managers.

The literature currently tends to view Party-military-industrial relations as essentially cooperative, evidenced by more recent works on defense decision making. Thomas W. Wolfe's *The SALT Experience: Its Impact on U.S. and Soviet Strategic Policy and Decision-Making* (Washington, D.C.: U.S. Air Force Project Rand Report R-1686-PR, September 1975) includes a comprehensive review of these organizational actors. Like Igor S. Glagolev's "The Soviet Decision-Making Process in Arms Control," in *Orbis* (vol. 21, no. 4 [Winter 1978]: 767–776), Wolfe's article cites a significant participation by Soviet military officers in the decision process. Yet, for all this attention, little is known about the interaction of these actors in strategic policy decisions. As a surrogate measure of this interaction, the Soviet weapons acquisition process serves as a useful and tangible area of inquiry. Undoubtedly the most complete treatment of this particular aspect of defense decision making is Arthur J. Alexander's *Decision-Making in Soviet Weapons Procurement,* published by IISS as a double Adelphi Paper, no. 147/148 (Winter 1978/79).* As a supplement to Alexander's definitive work, Karl F. Spielmann has focused more narrowly on the defense industry manager in "Defense Industrialists in the USSR" (*Problems of Communism* 25 [September/October 1976]: 52–69).

To round out this review of the study of the Soviet defense establishment, one needs to realize that most of the literature focuses on organizational interaction, which entails looking at how the leaders of these organizations interact. A fuller understanding of the bureaucratic model of Soviet decision making requires study of how the leaders control pressures for autonomy within their respective bureaucracies. At this level, Kolkowicz's earlier works remain useful. A more recent work along this line is Michael J. Deane's "The Main Political Administration As a Factor in Communist Party Control over the Military in the Soviet Union," published in *Armed Forces and Society* (vol. 3, no. 2 [February 1977]: 295–323). Much remains to be learned in this area, however.

USE OF FORCE

Presumably, one can gauge a country's defense policy by how that country employs military force. This is difficult in the Soviet case, however, because the Soviet use of force has, for the most part, been indirect and characterized by caution. Despite Soviet ideological support for "wars of national liberation," the USSR has used force directly only on the periphery of its territory. The Soviets have tended toward a less direct use of force when away from their own borders. The consistency of this behavior is the subject of Christopher D. Jones's "Just Wars and Limited Wars: Restraints on the Use of the Soviet Armed Forces," in *World Politics* (vol. 28, no. 1 [October 1975]: 44–68). This superbly articulate article explains the inherent conservatism of Soviet views on the use of force, pointing out that the security of the Soviet homeland is the primary criterion for a "just war." Indeed, Jones unearths quite candid Soviet comments on the possibility that initial defeat in war might well create conditions for domestic turmoil, an admission that public opinion (the "moral-political factor") does weigh heavily, at least in issues of war and peace.

Case studies on the use of force by the Soviet Union have borne out this conclusion and given rise to a small body of literature on Soviet crisis management behavior. Hannes Adomeit, in *Soviet Risk-Taking and Crisis Behaviour: From Confrontation to Coexistence* (Adelphi Papers, no. 101 [Autumn 1973]), argues that Soviet crisis behavior is distinctive because risk assessment is based on an antagonistic world view that sees crises as zero-sum gain situations. More recently, the Cybernetics Technology Office of the Defense Advanced Research Projects Agency (DARPA) has conducted a major study program on Soviet crisis management behavior. The *Analysis of the Soviet Crisis Management Experience: Technical Report,* published by DARPA (30 September 1978), is notable, not only because it confirms the intuitive conclusion of Soviet conservatism but because it brings together a vast empirical data base and a very useful annotated bibliography on both Soviet and American sources.

Except in the case of Afghanistan, the direct use of force by the Soviets in the postwar period has been confined to East Germany, Hungary, Czechoslovakia, and the border disputes with China. However, even in Eastern Europe Soviet behavior remains conservative and sensitive to the demands of a doctrinaire ideology. Nish Jamgotch, Jr., in "Alliance Management in Eastern Europe: The New Type of International Relations," in *World Politics* (vol. 27, no. 3 [April 1975]: 405–29), explains how détente has affected Soviet behavior in Eastern Europe, causing the Soviets to rely on ideological justification and persuasion and normally to avoid brute application of force.

Three case studies on the Soviet use of force are notable because they each differ in scenario and the way force was used. "The Sparrow in the Cage," by Richard Lowenthal, in *Problems of Communism* (vol. 17, no. 6 [November/December 1968]: 2–28), remains the best concise source on the Soviet invasion of Czechoslovakia in 1968. Lowenthal paints a picture of tremendous orchestration by the Soviet leaders so that force could be applied effectively, in a limited setting, under control with assurance of success, and with a minimum of adverse political and diplomatic effects. William B. Quandt's study,

*See below, pp. 153–94.

Soviet Policy in the October 1973 War (Rand Report R-1864-ISA [May 1976], prepared for the Office of the Assistant Secretary of Defense for International Security Affairs) shows similar cautious orchestration on the Soviets' part, but in this case avoiding the direct use of force and threatening its limited use only temporarily. Such calculated caution, however, is not as evident in a third case study, which looks not at past events but at a possible future scenario. *The Third World War: August 1985* (New York: Macmillan Publishing Co., 1979), by General Sir John Hackett et al., is an example of what might happen were Soviet conservatism and measured control over the use of force to be lost. All three "case studies," for both their similarities and their differences, make compelling reading.

ROLE OF THE MILITARY IN SOVIET SOCIETY

The final section of this bibliographical essay highlights an indirect aspect of Soviet defense policy—the link of the military to the broader society. One of the best sources for the life, training, and background of the Soviet soldier is Herbert Goldhammer's *The Soviet Soldier: Soviet Military Management at the Troop Level* (Rand Report R-1513/1-PR [New York: Crane, Russak & Co., 1975]). The Soviet military not only affects the individual Soviet soldier, but is profoundly intertwined with the fabric of Soviet society. Reflecting on his thesis that the military supports the Party by performing a heroic role and being involved with society, William E. Odom has called this "The Militarization of Soviet Society," in *Problems of Communism* (vol. 25 [September/October 1976]: 34–51). In fact, Odom traces two themes: the first is the increasing professionalism of the officer corps, and the second is the expansion of paramilitary training into the secondary school system. In like fashion, Leon Goure's *Military Indoctrination of Soviet Youth* (National Strategy Information Center Agenda Paper [New York: Crane, Russak & Co., 1976]) portrays what the Soviets call "military-patriotic" education as a means of enhancing the legitimacy of the Soviet regime through the vehicle of the military to those who are too young to have been affected by the "Great Patriotic War" of 1941–45. By the same token, the proliferation of paramilitary organizations throughout Soviet life helps insure that the society remains cognizant of a threat, rationalizes the continued heavy investment on defense, maintains the framework for social mobilization when necessary, and provides a vehicle for control now.

This emphasis on the military in Soviet society is not to suggest that the military is the dominant political influence. The Party retains that position, despite the fact that it needs institutions like the military to sustain its dominance. Thus, the logical extension of Odom and Goure's position is to suggest that, while the leadership hopes to militarize the society, it also hopes to politicize the military. I have found such a generalization useful in understanding the nature of Party primacy in this complex system. Two final books that may help the reader understand the delicate balance of power and influence that the Party maintains are Hedrick Smith's *Russians* (New York: Ballantine Books, 1976) and Robert G. Kaiser's *Russia: The Power and the People* (New York: Pocket Books, 1976).

Conclusion

It is perhaps fitting that this review of the literature on Soviet defense policy end with two nominally "nonacademic" books. Much of the Soviet Union and its policy dynamics is closed to us. The case studies of today become the histories of tomorrow. But there remains a consistency in Soviet behavior that seems derived from the Soviet "mind-set," "world view," or other political or cultural values. It is my impression that the kind of human insight that journalists give us are as valuable as the most probing scholarly treatises. Indeed, if this essay has shown nothing else, it has shown that an author's views about Soviet defense policy are often critically dependent upon the assumptions that the author makes to begin with. Thus, a proper review of Soviet defense policy literature might well begin by an examination of assumptions and continue with wide and critical reading.

Consistent with this view, I have not sought to catalog all important works on Soviet defense policy. Rather, I have tried to provide a framework for viewing the literature, to review the most common pertinent publications, and to highlight the more insightful and representative works in the field. Clearly, virtually every aspect of Soviet defense policy is fraught with controversy, and opposing views often differ in initial assumptions and interpretations of the same facts. The field is ripe for fresh analysis and insight, and I hope this essay is an aid to that process.

SELECTED BIBLIOGRAPHY ON THE SOVIET MILITARY ESTABLISHMENT

Jerome V. Martin

General

Alexander, Arthur J. *Decision-making in Soviet Weapons Procurement*. Adelphi Papers, no. 147 and 148. Winter 1978.

Baylis, John. *Contemporary Strategy*. New York: Holmes & Meier, 1975.

Bonds, Ray, ed. *Soviet War Machine*. New York: Hamlyn Publishing Group, 1977.

Collins, John M. *American and Soviet Military Trends since the Cuban Missile Crisis*. Washington, D.C.: Center for Strategic and International Studies, 1978.

Cordier, Sherwood W. *Calculus of Power: The Current Soviet-American Conventional Military Balance in Central Europe,* 3d ed. Washington, D.C.: University Press of America, 1980.

Davis, Jaquelyn K. *Soviet Theatre Strategy*. Washington, D.C.: U.S. Strategic Institute, 1978.

Deane, Michael J. *Political Control of the Soviet Armed Forces*. New York: Crane, Russak & Co., 1977.

Douglass, Joseph D., Jr. *The Soviet Theater Nuclear Offensive*. Washington, D.C.: Government Printing Office, 1976.

Douglass, Joseph D., Jr., and Hoebel, Amoretta M. *Soviet Strategy for Nuclear War*. Stanford, Calif.: Hoover Institute Press, 1979.

Erickson, John. *The Soviet High Command: A Military-Political History*. New York: St. Martin's Press, 1962.

———. *Soviet Military Power*. Washington, D.C.: United States Strategic Institute, 1973.

Erickson, John, and Feuchtwanger, E. J. *Soviet Military Power and Performance*. Hamden, Conn.: Shoe String Press, 1979.

Garthoff, Raymond L. *Soviet Military Policy: A Historical Analysis*. New York: Praeger, 1966.

Goure, Leon. *Soviet Civil Defense in the Seventies*. Coral Gables, Fla.: Center for Advanced International Studies, 1975.

———. *War Survival in Soviet Strategy: USSR Civil Defense*. Washington, D.C.: Center for Advanced International Studies, 1976.

Goure, Leon, et al. *The Role of Nuclear Forces in Current Soviet Strategy*. Coral Gables, Fla.: Center for Advanced International Studies, 1974.

Jacobs, Walter. *Frunze: The Soviet Clausewitz, 1885–1925*. The Hague: Martinus Nijhoff, 1969.

Jukes, Geoffrey. *The Development of Soviet Strategic Thinking since 1945*. Canberra: Australian University Press, 1972.

Kolkowicz, Roman. *The Soviet Military and the Communist Party*. Princeton, N.J.: Princeton University Press, 1967.

Longworth, Philip. *The Art of Victory: The Life and Achievements of Field Marshall Suvorov, 1729–1800*. New York: Holt, Rinehart & Winston, 1965.

The Mechanics of War Series. London: Almark Publishing Co. (Distributed in the United States by Squadron/Signal Publications, Warren, Mich.) Includes *Tank Tactics, 1939–1945; Ground Attack* (World War II Air Support); *Artillery Tactics, 1939–1945; Infantry Tactics, 1939–1945; Russian Armor, 1941–1943*.

Penkovskiy, Oleg. *The Penkovskiy Papers*. Garden City, N.Y.: Doubleday & Co., 1965.

Pipes, Richard, ed. *Soviet Strategy in Europe*. New York: Crane, Russak & Co., 1976.

Prospects of Soviet Power in the 1980s, Adelphi Papers, no. 151 and 152. Summer 1979.

Scott, Harriet Fast. *Soviet Military Doctrine*. Menlo Park, Calif.: Stanford Research Institute, 1971.

———. *Soviet Military Doctrine: Its Continuity, 1960–1970*. Menlo Park, Calif.: Stanford Research Institute, 1971.

———. *Soviet Military Doctrine: Its Formulation and Dissemination*. Menlo Park, Calif.: Stanford Research Institute, 1971.

Scott, Harriet Fast, and Scott, William F. *The Armed Forces of the USSR*. Boulder, Colo.: Westview Press, 1979.

Scott, William F. *Soviet Sources of Military Doctrine and Strategy*. New York: Crane, Russak & Co., 1975.

Sokolovskiy, V. D. *Soviet Military Strategy*. Edited by Harriet Fast Scott. 3d ed. New York: Crane, Russak & Co., 1975.

Sonnenfeldt, Helmut, and Hyland, William G. *Soviet Perspectives on Security*. Adelphi Papers, no. 150. Spring 1979.

Warner, Edward L. *The Military in Contemporary*

Soviet Politics: An Institutional Analysis. New York: Praeger, 1977.

Weiner, Freidrich. *The Armies of the Warsaw Pact Nations*. Translated by William J. Lewis. 2d ed. Vienna: Carl Ueberreuter Publishers, 1978.

Whetten, Lawrence L., ed. *The Future of Soviet Military Power*. New York: Crane, Russak & Co., 1976.

Wolfe, Thomas W. *Soviet Power in Europe, 1945–1970*. Baltimore: Johns Hopkins University Press, 1970.

Ground forces

Gardner, Michael. *History of the Soviet Army*. New York: Praeger, 1966.

Goldhammer, Herbert. *The Soviet Soldier*. New York: Crane, Russak & Co., 1975.

Handbook on Soviet Ground Forces. U.S. Army Field Manual 30-40. Washington, D.C.: Government Printing Office, 1976.

Liddell Hart, Basil Henry. *The Red Army*. New York: Harcourt Brace, 1956.

Lototskiy, V. K. *The Soviet Army*. Moscow: Progress Publishers, 1971.

MacKintosh, Malcolm. *Juggernaut: A History of the Soviet Armed Forces*. New York: Macmillan Co., 1967.

O'Ballance, Edgar. *The Red Army: A Short History*. New York: Praeger, 1964.

Record, Jeffrey. *Sizing up the Soviet Army*. Washington, D.C.: Brookings Institution, 1975.

Air forces

Barron, John. *Mig Pilot: The Escape of Lieutenant Belenko*. New York: Reader's Digest Press, 1980.

Berman, Robert P. *Soviet Air Power in Transition*. Washington, D.C.: Brookings Institution, 1975.

Boyd, Alexander. *The Soviet Air Force since 1918*. New York: Stein & Day, 1977.

Gunston, Bill, and Sweetman, Bill. *Soviet Air Power*. New York: Crescent Publications, 1978.

Highham, Robin, and Kipp, Jacob W. *Soviet Aviation and Air Power*. Boulder, Colo.: Westview Press, 1977.

Jackson, Robert. *Red Falcons: The Soviet Air Force in Action, 1919–1969*. New York: International Publications Service, 1970.

Kilmarx, Robert A. *A History of Soviet Air Power*. New York: Praeger, 1962.

Lee, Asher, ed. *The Soviet Air and Rocket Forces*. New York: Praeger, 1959.

Peterson, Phillip A. *Soviet Air Power and the Pursuit of New Military Options*. Washington, D.C.: Government Printing Office, 1979.

Soviet Aerospace Handbook. Air Force Pamphlet 200-21. Washington, D.C.: Government Printing Office, 1978.

The Soviet Air Forces in World War II: The Official History Originally Published by the Minister of Defense of the USSR. Translated by Leland Fetzer and edited by Ray Wagner. Garden City, N.Y.: Doubleday & Co., 1973.

Naval forces

Breyer, Siegfield. *Guide to the Soviet Navy*. Translated by M. W. Henley. Annapolis, Md.: Naval Institute Press, 1970.

Gorshkov, Sergei G. *Red Star Rising at Sea*. Annapolis, Md.: Naval Institute Press, 1979.

———. *The Sea Power of the State*. Annapolis, Md.: Naval Institute Press, 1979.

Herrick, Robert Waring. *Soviet Naval Strategy*. Annapolis, Md.: Naval Institute Press, 1968.

McGruther, Kenneth R. *The Evolving Soviet Navy*. Newport, R.I.: Naval War College Press, 1978.

Murphy, Paul J., ed. *Naval Power in Soviet Policy: USAF Studies in Communist Affairs*. Vol. 2. Washington, D.C.: Government Printing Office, 1978.

Polmar, Norman. *Soviet Naval Developments*. Annapolis, Md.: Nautical and Aviation Publishing Company of America, 1979. (Update of naval pamphlet below.)

Understanding Soviet Naval Developments. 3d ed. U.S. Navy Pamphlet. Washington, D.C.: Government Printing Office, 1978.

The *Soviet Military Thought* series, translated and published under the auspices of the United States Air Force by the Government Printing Office, Washington, D.C., 1973–79:

1. *The Offensive*
2. *Marxism-Leninism on War and Army*
3. *Scientific-Technical Progress and the Revolution in Military Affairs*
4. *The Basic Principles of Operational Art and Tactics*
5. *The Philosophical Heritage of V. I. Lenin and Problems of Contemporary War*
6. *Concept, Algorithm Decision*
7. *Military Pedagogy*
8. *Military Psychology*
9. *Dictionary of Basic Military Terms*
10. *Civil Defense*
11. *Selected Soviet Military Writings, 1970–1975*
12. *The Armed Forces of the Soviet State*
13. *The Officer's Handbook*
14. *The People, the Army, the Commander*
15. *Long-Range Missile-Equipped*
16. *Forecasting in Military Affairs*

The future of NATO

Henry A. Kissinger

At the beginning of the conference, the most useful thing I can do is to outline the concerns that I have about the future of NATO, the problems that in my estimation require solution if we are to retain our vitality and if we are to remain relevant to the challenge before us. Since the early 1960s, every new American administration that has come into office has promised a new look at Europe, a reappraisal and a reassessment. Each of these efforts has found us more or less confirming what already existed and what had been created in the late 1940s and early 1950s, with just enough alliance adaptation to please the endlessly restless Americans who can never restrain themselves from new attempts at architecture.

Without going into which of these proposals were right, or if any of these specific proposals was necessary, I think the fact that in the late 1970s we are operating an alliance machinery and a force structure under a concept more or less unchanged from the 1950s should indicate that we have been depleting capital. Living off capital may be a pleasant prospect for a substantial period of time, but inevitably a point will be reached where reality dominates. My proposition to this group is that NATO is reaching a point where the strategic assumption on which it has been operating, the force structure that it has been generating, and the joint policies it has been developing will be inadequate for the 1980s.

I have said in the United States, in my SALT testimony, that if present trends continue, the 1980s will be a period of massive crisis for all of us. We have reached this point not through the mistakes of any single administration. Just as the commitment to NATO is a bipartisan American effort, the dilemmas that I would like to put before this group—admittedly in a perhaps exaggerated form—have been growing up over an extended period, partly as the result of American perceptions, partly as a result of European perceptions.

This is not to deny that NATO, by all of the standards of traditional alliances, has been an enormous success. To maintain an alliance in peacetime without conflict for a generation is extremely rare in history. And it is inherent in a process in which an alliance has been successful, in which deterrence has worked, that no one will be able to prove why it has worked. Was it because we conducted the correct policy? Was it because the Soviet Union never had any intention to attack us in the first place? Was it because of the policies of strength of some countries, or the policies of accommodation of other countries? So, what I say should not be taken as a criticism either of any particular American administration (even granting that there was one period of eight years in the past in which no mistakes were made) or of any specific policies of European nations, but rather as an assessment of where we are today.

THE GLOBAL ENVIRONMENT

Let me first turn to the strategic situation. The dominant fact of the current military balance is that the NATO countries are falling behind in every significant military category, with the possible exception of naval forces, where the gap in our favor is closing. Never in history has it happened that a nation achieved superiority in all significant weapons categories without seeking to translate it at some point into some foreign policy benefit. It is, therefore, almost irrelevant to debate whether there is some tragic date at which Soviet armies will head in some direction or another. I am willing to grant that there is no particular master plan nor is there any specific deadline; I do not even consider that the present Soviet leaders are superadventurous. That is fundamentally irrelevant.

In a world of upheaval and rapid changes, enough opportunities will arise in which the relative capacity and the relative willingness of the two sides to understand their interests and to defend their interests will be the key element. I do not believe that the Soviet Union planned Angola, or created the conditions for intervention in Ethiopia, or necessarily had a deadline for the revolution in Afghanistan. But all of these events happened to the detriment of general stability. I would consider it a rash Western policy that did not take into account that in the decade ahead we will face simultaneously an unfavorable balance of power, a world in turmoil, a potential economic crisis, and a massive energy problem. To conduct business as usual is to entrust one's destiny to the will of others and to the self-restraint of those whose ideology highlights the crucial role of the objective balance of forces.

This is my fundamental theme. I would now like to discuss it in relation to specific issues.

THE SHIFTING STRATEGIC BALANCE

First, at the risk of repeating myself, let me state once again what I take to be the fundamental change in

These remarks were made to a NATO conference held in September 1979. Kissinger's speech is reprinted here with permission from the *Washington Quarterly* 2, no. 4 (Autumn 1979).

the strategic situation as far as the United States is concerned, and then examine the implications for NATO.

When the North Atlantic Treaty Organization was created, the United States possessed an overwhelming strategic nuclear superiority. That is to say, for a long period of time we were likely to prevail in a nuclear war: certainly if we struck first and for a decade perhaps even if we struck second, we were in a position to wipe out the Soviet strategic forces and to reduce any possible counterblow against us to an acceptable level. That situation must have looked even more ominous to the Soviet Union than it looked favorable to us.

Thinking back to the Cuban Missile Crisis of 1962, which all the policy makers of the time were viewing with a consciousness of an approaching Armageddon, one is almost seized with nostalgia for the ease with which the decisions were made. At that time the Soviet Union had about seventy long-range missiles that took ten hours to fuel, which was a longer period of time than it would take our airplanes to get to the Soviet Union from forward bases. Even at the time of the Middle East crisis of 1973 (the alert), we had a superiority of about eight to one in missile warheads. Comparing this with the current and foreseeable situation, we are approaching a point where it is difficult to assign a clear military objective to American strategic forces in a strategic nuclear exchange.

In the 1950s and for much of the 1960s, NATO was protected by a preponderance in American strategic striking power that was capable of disarming the Soviet Union, and by a vast American superiority in theater nuclear forces, although, as I will discuss, we never had a comprehensive theory for using theater nuclear forces. Since all intelligence services congenitally overestimate the rationality of the decision-making process that they are analyzing, it is probable that the Soviet Union made more sense out of our nuclear deployment in Europe than we were able to make ourselves. In any event, it was numerically superior. It was in that strategic framework that the allied ground forces on the Continent were deployed.

No one disputes any longer that in the 1980s the United States will no longer be in a strategic position to reduce a Soviet counterblow against the United States to tolerable levels. Indeed, one can argue that the United States will not be in a position in which attacking the Soviet strategic forces makes any military sense, because it may represent a marginal expenditure of our own strategic striking force that does not help greatly to ensure the safety of our forces.

Since the mid-1960s the Soviet strategic force has grown immensely. It grew from 220 intercontinental ballistic missiles in 1965 to 1,600 around 1972-73. Soviet submarine-launched missiles grew from negligible numbers to over 900 in the 1970s. And the amazing phenomenon that historians will ponder is that all of this has happened without the United States making a significant effort to rectify that state of affairs. One reason was that it was not easy to rectify. But another reason was the growth of a school of thought to which I myself, and many around this conference table, contributed, which considered that strategic stability was a military asset, and in which the historically amazing theory developed that vulnerability contributed to peace and invulnerability contributed to risks of war.

Such a theory could develop and be widely accepted only in a country that had never addressed the problem of the balance of power as a historical phenomenon—and, if I may say so, only on a continent that was looking for any excuse to avoid analysis of the perils it was facing and that was looking for an easy way out. When the administration with which I was connected sought to implement an antiballistic missile (ABM) program inherited from our predecessors, it became the subject of the most violent attacks from those who held the theory that it was destabilizing, provocative, and an obstacle to arms control; initially the ABM could be sold only as a protection against the Chinese and not against the Soviet threat. In any case, the ABM was systematically reduced by the Congress in every succeeding session to the point where we wound up with a curious coalition of the Pentagon and the arms controllers, both finally opposed to it: the Pentagon because it no longer made any military sense to put resources into a program that was being systematically deprived of military utility, and the arms control community because it saw in the strategic vulnerability of the United States a positive asset. It cannot have occurred often in history that it was considered an advantageous military doctrine to make your own country deliberately vulnerable.

Now we have reached that situation so devoutly worked for by the arms control community: we are indeed vulnerable. Moreover, our weapons had been deliberately designed, starting in the 1960s, so as to not threaten the weapons of the other side. Under the doctrine of "assured destruction," nuclear war became not a military problem but one of engineering; it depended on theoretical calculations of the amount of economic and industrial damage that one needed to inflict on the other side, and was therefore essentially independent of the forces the other side was creating.

This general theory suffered two drawbacks. One is that the Soviet did not believe it. The other is that we have not yet bred a race of supermen that can implement it. While we were building "assured destruction" capabilities, the Soviet Union was building forces for traditional military missions capable of destroying the military forces of the United States. So in the 1980s we will be in a position where (1) many of our own strategic forces, including all of our land-based ICBMs, will be vulnerable, and (2) such an insignificant percentage of Soviet strategic forces will be vulnerable as not to represent a meaningful strategic attack option for the United States. Whether that means that the Soviet Union intends to attack the United States or not is certainly not my point. The point I am making is that the change in the strategic situation that is produced by our limited vulnerability is more fundamental for the United States than even total vulnerability would be for the Soviet Union because our strategic doctrine has relied extraordinarily, perhaps exclusively, on our superior strategic power. The Soviet Union has never relied on its superior strategic power. It has always depended more on its local and regional superiority. Therefore, even an equivalence in destructive power, even "assured destruction" for both sides, is a revolution in the strategic balance as we have known it. It is a fact that must be faced.

I have recently urged that the United States build a counterforce capability of its own. The answer of our NATO friends to the situation that I have described has invariably been to demand additional reassurances of an undiminished American military commitment. And I have sat around the NATO Council table in Brussels and elsewhere and have uttered the magic words that had a profoundly reassuring effect and that permitted the ministers to return home with a rationale for not increasing defense expenditures. My successors have uttered the same reassurances. Yet if my analysis is correct, these words cannot be true indefinitely; if my analysis is correct, we must face the fact that it is absurd in the 1980s to base the strategy of the West on the credibility of the threat of mutual suicide.

One cannot ask a nation to design forces that have no military significance, whose primary purpose is the extermination of civilians, and expect that these factors will not affect a nation's resoluteness in crisis. We live in the paradoxical world in which it is precisely the liberal, human. progressive community that is advocating the most bloodthirsty strategies and insisting that there is nothing to worry about as long as the capacity exists to kill a hundred million people. It is this approach that argues that we should not be concerned about the vulnerability of our missile forces, when, after all, we can always launch them on warning of an attack. Any military person at this conference will tell you that launching strategic forces on warning can be accomplished only by delegating the authority to the proverbially "insane colonel" about whom so many movies have been made. Nobody who knows anything about how our government operates would believe that it is possible for our president to get the secretary of state, secretary of defense, chairman of the joint chiefs of staff, and director of the CIA to a conference called in the fifteen minutes that may be available to make a decision, much less issue an order, which then travels down the line of command in the fifteen minutes. So the only way you can implement that strategy is by delegating the authority to some field commander, who must be given discretion so that when he thinks a nuclear war has started, he can retaliate. Is that the world we want to live in? Is that where "assured destruction" will finally take us?

Therefore, I would say—what I might not say in office—that our European allies should not keep asking us to multiply strategic assurances that we cannot possibly mean, or, if we do mean, we should not want to execute because if we execute them, we risk the destruction of civilization. Our strategic dilemma is not solved by verbal reassurances; it requires redesigning our forces and doctrine. There is no point in complaining about declining American will, or criticizing this or that American administration, for we are facing an objective crisis and it must be remedied.

THEATER NUCLEAR FORCES

The second part of this problem is the imbalance that has grown up in theater nuclear forces. In the 1950s and 1960s we put several thousand nuclear weapons into Europe. To be sure, we had no very precise idea of what to do with them, but I am sure that Soviet intelligence figured out some purpose for these forces; in any event it was a matter for this disquiet. Now one reason we did not have a rational analysis for the use of these factors was the very reason that led to the strategic theory of "assured destruction." Let us face it: the intellectually predominant position in the United States was that we had to retain full control of the conduct of nuclear war and we therefore had a vested interest in avoiding any "firebreak" between tactical nuclear weapons and strategic nuclear weapons. The very reasoning that operated against setting a rational purpose for strategic forces also operated against giving a military role to tactical nuclear forces. This was compounded by the fact that—to be tactless—the secret dream of every European was, of course, to avoid a nuclear war, but if there had to be a nuclear war, to have it conducted overhead by the strategic forces of the United States and the Soviet Union. Be that as it may, the fact is that the strategic imbalance that I have predicted for the 1980s will also be accompanied by a theater imbalance. How is it possible to survive with these imbalances in the face of the already demonstrated inferiority in conventional forces?

If there is no theater nuclear establishment on the continent of Europe, we are writing the script for selective blackmail in which our allies will be threatened and in which we will be forced into a decision whereby we can respond only with a strategy that has no military purpose but only the aim of destruction of populations.

I ask any of you around this conference table, if you were secretary of state or security adviser, what would you recommend to the president of the United States to do in such circumstances? How would he improve his relative military position? Of course, he could threaten a full-scale strategic response, but is it a realistic course? It is senseless to say that dilemma shows that Americans are weak and irresolute. This is not the problem of any particular administration, but it is a problem of the doctrines that has developed.

Therefore, I believe that it is urgently necessary either that the Soviets be deprived of their counterforce capability in strategic forces or that a U.S. counterforce capability in strategic forces be rapidly built. It is also necessary either that the Soviet nuclear threat in theater nuclear forces against Europe be eliminated (which I do not see as possible) or that an immediate effort be made to build up our theater nuclear forces. Just as I believe it is necessary that we develop a military purpose for our strategic forces and move away from the senseless and demoralizing strategy of massive civilian extermination, so it is imperative that we finally try to develop some credible military purposes for the tactical and theater nuclear forces that we are building.

THE ROLE OF GROUND FORCES

Third, it is time that we decide exactly what role we want for our ground forces on the Continent. These forces were deployed in the 1950s when American strategic superiority was so great that we could defend Europe by the threat of general nuclear war. They were deployed in Europe, as I have often said, as a means of ensuring the automaticity of our response. Our forces were in Europe as hostages. Everybody had a vested interest in not making the forces too large. We wound up with the paradox that they were much too large for what was needed for a tripwire yet not large enough for a sustained conventional defense. I tried for the years that I was in office to get some assessment of just what was meant by the ninety-day stockpile that we were supposed to have, and what the minimum critical categories were. I know that my friend General Alexander Haig, whom I admire greatly, has done enormous work in improving the situation; nevertheless, I would be amazed if even he believed that we can now say that our ground forces by themselves can offer a sustained defense without massive, rapid improvements.

THE POLITICAL CONTEXT

If the chairman will permit, I will move to a few political considerations. Everything that I have said about the military situation would be difficult enough to remedy, but the situation is compounded by theories to which, again, I myself have no doubt contributed. In 1968, at Reykjavik, NATO developed the theory—which I believe is totally wrong—that the alliance is as much an instrument of détente as it is of defense. I think that this is simply not correct. NATO is not equipped to be an instrument of détente; for example, every time we attempted to designate the secretary general of NATO as a negotiating partner with the Warsaw Pact, it was rejected. But this is a minor problem, and détente is important. It is important because, as the United States learned during Vietnam, in a democracy you cannot sustain the risk of war unless your public is convinced that you are committed to peace. Détente is important because we cannot hold the alliance together unless our allies are convinced that we are not seeking confrontation for its own sake. Détente is important because I cannot accept the proposition that it is the democracies that must concede the peace issue to their opponents. And détente is important so that if a confrontation proves unavoidable, we will have elaborated the reasons in a manner that permits us to sustain a confrontation.

So I have always been restless with those who define the issue as "détente" or "no détente." All Western governments must demonstrate and must conduct a serious effort to relax tensions and to negotiate outstanding differences. But something deeper is involved in the West. There is in the West a tendency to treat détente quite theatrically, that is to say, not as a balancing of national interests and negotiations on the basis of strategic realities but rather as an exercise in strenuous good will, in which one removes by understanding the suspiciousness of a nation that is assumed to have no other motive to attack. This tendency to treat détente as an exercise in psychotherapy, or as an attempt at good personal relations, or as an effort in which individual leaders try to gain domestic support by proving that they have a special way in Moscow—this is disastrous for the West. It is the corollary to the "assured destruction" theory, in the sense that it always provides an alibi for not doing what must be done.

Against all evidence, we were told that the ABM would ruin the chances of arms control. The fact was that Premier Kosygin in 1967 told President Johnson at Glassboro, New Jersey, that the idea of not engaging in defense was one of the most ridiculous propositions that he had ever heard. By 1970, when we had an ABM program, however inadequate, it was the only subject the Soviet Union was willing to discuss with us in SALT. When we gave up the B-1 bomber, we asked the Soviets to make a reciprocal gesture. We have yet to see it. When we gave up the neutron weapon, we were told that this was in correlation with the deployment of the SS-20. (If so, the result was in inverse correlation with the SS-20.) Now we are told that of course we are all for theater nuclear forces, but first let us have another effort at negotiation. I saw a report about a distinguished American senator returning from Moscow the other day who said: "It is virtually certain that cruise missiles will be deployed and that NATO will undertake a build-up of its own unless negotiations to a new treaty are begun soon." If this is our position, all the Soviets have to do is to begin a negotiation to keep us from doing what they are already doing, negotiation or no negotiation.

Such a version of détente leads to unilateral disarmament for the West. I favor negotiation on theater nuclear forces, but the talks will accelerate the more rapidly as we build such theater nuclear forces. Then we can consider some numerical balance or some deployment pattern, but we cannot defer the strategic decisions we must make for the sake of initiating a negotiation. We must have détente, but the détente must be on a broad front in the sense that all of the NATO nations must pursue comparable policies. The illusion that some countries can achieve a preferential position with the USSR is theoretically correct, but it is the best means of dividing the alliance. The illusion that some subjects can be separated for individual treatment of détente, while conflict goes on in all other areas, turns détente into a safety valve for aggression.

My fundamental point is that we need a credible strategy; we need an agreed strategy and we urgently need to build the required forces. We cannot wait two or three more years. We cannot conduct a foreign policy, even though each of our political systems encourages such a policy, in which we ease the domestic positions of the individual countries by pretending that single forays to Moscow can solve our problems.

Unfortunately, the time frame of the evolution of programs that I have described is longer than the electoral period of most of our leaders. Therefore, our leaders in all of our countries have an enormous temptation to celebrate the very successes that lead to a differential détente either as to subject or as to region. How is it possible that the states that have 70 percent of the world's gross national product will not conduct a common energy policy? This is not just because it has become a shibboleth that "we must not have confrontation"; when have nations been confronted by a massive decline of their economies without being willing to confront those who are contributing significantly to the decline? And, after all, it takes two to make a confrontation.

How is it possible that in the Middle East, two totally conflicting theories on how to proceed are being carried out simultaneously? How can it be that both Egypt and the PLO must simultaneously be encouraged, sometimes, I confess, by our own government? But fundamentally the Europeans are playing one card and we are playing another, so that both the radical and the moderate elements are being strengthened simultaneously. One of us has got to be wrong, and it is just an evasion to pretend that we work one side of the street and the Europeans work another side of the street, because what is really involved in Europe is an attempt to gain special advantages. Yet it is a situation in which the market conditions do not permit special advantages, but where, on the contrary, once it is accepted that oil is a political weapon, even the moderates have no excuse for *not* using it as a political weapon.

I am not trying to suggest what the correct answer is, but I am saying that the nations represented around this table ought to ask themselves whether the two years of special advantages that any of them might gain are worth the ten years' disaster that could easily befall them.

I know we have many alibis. We have the alibi that none of the things I have said is inevitable because there is China. And we have the alibi that, after all, the Soviets have never stayed anywhere and they're in deep trouble themselves. And we have the alibi that we can make such great progress in the Third World that all of this is irrelevant.

In my view the Chinese have survived for three thousand years by being the most unsentimental practitioners of the balance of power, the most sophisticated, and the most free of illusion. China will be an alibi for us only if we do what is necessary. China, as the victim of the forces that we have unleashed, will not defend the barricades that we refuse to defend. So it is certain that we can have cooperation with China only if we create a balance of power.

Now the theory that the Soviets can never stay where they have been is amazingly widely held and supported by exactly one example: Egypt. (I do not count Somalia-Ethiopia because I consider the Soviet departure from Somalia as a voluntary switch from one client to a larger client.) In Egypt the fact of the matter is that the balance of power was in favor of those that we supported and those who learned in three wars (in two of which we approached a U.S.-Soviet confrontation) that they could not achieve their aims by Soviet arms. Only after that demonsration was there an Egyptian switch. So we are right back to our original problem.

The final nostalgia is that of the "noble savage," the Third World: that we're going to sweep them over to our side. (I have to confess that I cannot give this an operational definition.) As for the Third World nations now meeting in Cuba, when I was in office I never read their resolutions, I regret to tell you, which is just as well, because I might have said something rather nasty. But I would think it is statistically impossible that over the years that these Third World nations have been meeting, the United States has never done anything right. Even by accident we're bound to do something right. I defy anybody to read through these documents to find one reference on even the most minor thing to something that the United States has ever done right. What are the prospects of progress in a world in which the Cubans can host the nonaligned conference?

It seems to me a nostalgia, not a policy, to appeal to radical elements in the Third World to change their operational politics. They cannot, because the radical element is required for their bargaining position, a position between us and the Soviets, and because its ideology is hostile to us. Therefore, paradoxically, the more we approach them the more they are likely to pull away from us.

I am not saying that we should not deal with the radical elements of the Third World or that we should not do the best we can in the Third World. All I am saying is that the Third World is not our alibi, it is not our escape route; we may not lose there, but we are not likely to win there by repeating their slogans.

CONCLUSION

This is not intended to be a depressing account of difficulties. It is not to say that we have no favorable prospects. It is simply to point out that problems neglected are crises invited.

In the thirtieth year of NATO we have come far and have achieved our principal purpose. If we do not address ourselves immediately to at least some of the problems I have mentioned, we will face the potentiality of debacles. And the weird aspect of it is that there is absolutely no necessity for it: the nations assembled in this room have three times the gross national product of the Soviet Union and four times the population. The Soviet Union has leadership problems, social problems, minority problems; all they have in their favor is the ability to accumulate military power and perhaps that only for a transitory period.

So looking ahead for ten years, if we do what is necessary, all the odds are in our favor. The challenges I have put before this group do not indicate that we are bound to be in difficulties, but only that we can defeat ourselves. By contrast, we have an extraordinary opportunity to rally our people, to define new positive programs even for negotiations with the East if we do what is necessary.

To put it another way, our adversaries are really not in control of their own future. Their system and their conditions in many ways make them victims of their past. We around this table are in the extraordinary position that we can decide a positive future for ourselves if we are willing to make the effort. We are in the position to say that the kind of world in which we want to live is largely up to us.

Contrasts in American and Soviet strategic thought

Fritz W. Ermarth

We are having trouble with Soviet strategic doctrine. Soviet thinking about strategy and nuclear war differs in significant ways from our own. To the extent one should care about this—and that extent is a matter of debate—we do not like the way the Soviets seem to think. Before 1972, appreciation of differences between Soviet and American strategic thinking was limited to a small number of specialists. Those who held it a matter of high concern for policy were fewer still. Since that time, concern about the nature, origins, and consequences of these differences is considerably more widespread, in large measure as a result of worry about the Soviet strategic arms build-up and the continued frustrations of achieving a real breakthrough in SALT.

Heightened attention to the way the other side thinks about strategic nuclear power is timely and proper. The nature of the Soviet build-up and some of our own previous choices have locked us out of pure "hardware solutions" to our emerging strategic security problems that are independent of the other side's values and perceptions. Whatever one thinks about the wisdom or folly of the manner in which we have pursued SALT so far, it is desirable that management of the U.S.-Soviet strategic relationship have a place for an explicit dialogue. That dialogue should include more attention to strategic concepts than we have seen in past SALT negotiations. Moreover, whatever the role of SALT in the future, the existence of "rough parity" or worse almost by definition means that we cannot limit strategic policy to contending merely with the opponent's forces. In the cause of deterrence, crisis management, and, if need be, war, we must thwart his strategy. That requires understanding that opponent better.

THE NEED TO UNDERSTAND STRATEGIC DOCTRINE

Let us define "strategic doctrine" as a set of operative beliefs, values, and assertions that in a significant way guide official behavior with respect to strategic research and development (R&D), weapons choice, forces, operational plans, arms control, etc. The essence of U.S. "doctrine" is to deter central nuclear war at relatively low levels of arms effort ("arms race stability") and strategic anxiety ("crisis stability") through the credible threat of catastrophic damage to the enemy should deterrence fail. In that event, this doctrine says it should be the aim and ability of U.S. power to inflict maximum misery on the enemy in his homeland. Making the world following the outbreak of nuclear war more tolerable for the United States is, at best, a lesser concern. Soviet strategic doctrine stipulates that Soviet strategic forces and plans should strive in all available ways to enhance the prospect that the Soviet Union could survive as a nation and, in some politically and militarily meaningful way, defeat the main enemy should deterrence fail—and by this striving help deter or prevent nuclear war, along with the attainment of other strategic and foreign policy goals.

These characterizations of U.S. and Soviet strategic doctrine and the differences between them are valid and important. Had U.S. strategic policy been more sensitive over the last ten years to the asymmetry they express, we might not find ourselves in so awkward a present situation. We would have been less sanguine than we were about prospects that the Soviets would settle for an easily defined, nonthreatening form of strategic parity. We would not have believed as uncritically as we did that the SALT process was progressing toward a common explication of already tacitly accepted norms of strategic stability.

It is, if anything, even more important that these asymmetries be fully appreciated today. They are a crucial starting point for strategic diagnosis and therapy. But they are only a starting point. The constellations of thought, value, and action that we call U.S. and Soviet strategic doctrine or policy are much more complicated, qualified, and contradictory than the above characterizations admit by themselves. To be aware of these other ramifications without fully understanding them could lead to dangerous discounting, on one hand, or distorting, on the other, of the real differences between U.S. and Soviet strategic thinking.

COMPARATIVE STRATEGIC DOCTRINE

The following discussion is intended only to suggest some of the contrasts that exist between U.S. and Soviet strategic thinking. The issues raised are not treated exhaustively, and the list itself is not exhaustive. Our appreciation of these matters is not adequate

This article was first published in *International Security,* Fall 1978, pp. 138–55.

to the critical times in the U.S.-Soviet strategic relationship we are facing. It would be highly desirable to develop the intellectual discipline of comparative military doctrine, especially in the strategic sphere. Systematic comparative studies of strategic doctrine could serve to clarify what we think and how we ourselves differ on these matters, as well as to organize what we know about Soviet strategic thinking.

Although many studies have done so and express views on how both the United States and the Soviet Union deal with strategic problems, there is in fact little systematic comparison of the conceptual and behavioral foundations of our respective strategic activity. In this area, more than in other comparative inquiries into Communist and non-Communist politics, there are the obstacles of secrecy in the path of research. Perhaps as vital, neither government nor academic institutions appear to have cultivated many people with the necessary interdisciplinary skills and experience.

The most influential factor that has inhibited lucid comparisons of U.S. and Soviet strategic thinking has been the uncritically held assumption that they had to be very similar, or at least converging with time. Many of us have been quite insensitive to the possibility that two very different political systems could deal very differently with what is, in some respects, a common problem. We understood the problem of keeping the strategic peace on equitable and economical terms—or so we thought. As reasonable people the Soviets, too, would come to understand it our way.

Explaining this particular expression of our cultural self-centeredness is itself a fascinating field for speculation. I think it goes beyond the American habit of value projection. It may result from the fact that postwar developments in U.S. strategy were an institutional and intellectual offspring of the natural sciences that spawned modern weapons. Scientific truth is transnational, not culturally determined. But, unfortunately, strategy is more like *politics* than like science.

The next five to ten years of the U.S.-Soviet strategic relationship could well be characterized by mounting U.S. anxieties about the adequacy of our deterrent forces and our strategic doctrine. There seems to be little real prospect that the SALT process, as we have been conducting it, will substantially alleviate these anxieties. Even if a more promising state of affairs emerges, however, it is hard to see us managing it with calm and confidence unless we develop a more thorough appreciation of the differences between U.S. and Soviet strategic thinking. Things have progressed beyond the point where it is useful to have the three familiar schools of thought on Soviet doctrine arguing past each other: one saying, "Whatever they say, they think as we do;" the second insisting, "Whatever they say, it does not matter;" and the third contending, "They think what they say, and are therefore out for superiority over us."

Comparative strategic doctrine studies should address systematically a series of questions:

—What are the central decisions about strategy, force posture, and force employment or operations that doctrine is supposed to resolve for the sides examined?

—What are the prevailing categories, concepts, beliefs, and assertions that appear to constitute the body of strategic thought and doctrine in question?

—What are the hedges and qualifications introduced to modify the main theses of official thinking?

—What are the "nonstrategic," e.g., propagandistic, purposes that might motivate doctrinal pronouncements? Does the doctrinal system recognize a distinction between what ideally ought to be and what practically is (a serious problem in the Soviet case)?

—In what actions, e.g., force posture, does apparent doctrine have practical effect? Where does it lie dormant?

—To what extent are doctrinal pronouncements the subject of or the guise for policy dispute?

—What perceptions does one side entertain as to the doctrinal system of the other side? With what effect?

Answering these questions for both the United States and the Soviet Union is admittedly no easy matter, especially in a highly politicized environment in which many participants have already made up their minds how they want the answers to come out with respect to assumed impact on U.S. strategic policy. But we have the data to do a good deal better than we have done to date.

U.S. AND SOVIET DOCTRINE CONTRASTED

What is U.S. strategic doctrine and policy? What is Soviet strategic doctrine and policy? The Soviets provide definitions of doctrine (*doktrina*) and policy (*politika*) that state they are official principles, guidance, and instructions from the highest governing authorities to provide for the building of the armed forces and for their employment in war.

The most useful thing about these definitions is that they remind us—or should—that we do not have direct and literal access to Soviet strategic doctrine and policy through the most commonly available sources, i.e., Soviet military literature and various pronouncements of authoritative political and military figures. Our insight into Soviet strategic policy is derived by inference from such sources, along with inferences from observed R&D and force procurement behavior, what we manage to learn about peacetime force operations and exercises, and occasional direct statements in more privileged settings, such as SALT, by varyingly persuasive spokesmen.

The value of all these sources is constrained by the limitations of our perceptive apparatus, technical and intellectual, and the fact that Soviet communications on strategic subjects serve many purposes other than conveying official policy, such as foreign and domestic propaganda. For all that, we have gained over the years a substantial degree of understanding of the content of Soviet strategic thinking, of the values, standards, objectives, and calculations that underlie Soviet decisions. It is this total body of thinking and its bearing on action that are of concern here.

Where lack of access complicates understanding of Soviet strategic doctrine, an overabundance of data confuses understanding of the American side, a point that Soviets make with some justice when berated with the evils of Soviet secrecy. If, in the case of the United

States, one is concerned about the body of thinking that underlies strategic action, it is clearly insufficient to rely on official statements or documents at any level of classification or authority. Such sources, for one reason or another, may not tell the whole story or may paper over serious differences of purpose behind some action.

One of the difficulties in determining the concepts or beliefs that underlie U.S. strategic action is that strategic policy is a composite of behavior taking place in at least three distinguishable but overlapping arenas. The smallest, most secretive, and least significant over the long term, assuming deterrence does not fail, is the arena of operational or war planning. The second arena is that of system and force acquisition; it is much larger and more complex than the first. The most disorganized and largest, but most important for the longer-term course of U.S. strategic behavior is the arena of largely public debate over basic strategic principles and objectives. Its participants range from the most highly placed executive authorities to influential private elites, and occasionally the public at large. Strategy making is a relatively democratic process in the United States.

To be sure, many areas of public policy making can be assessed in terms of these overlapping circles of players and constituents. But the realm of U.S. strategic policy may be unusual in the degree to which different rules, data, concerns, and participants dominate the different arenas. These differences make it difficult to state with authority what U.S. strategic policy is on an issue that cuts across the arenas. For example, public U.S. policy may state a clear desire to avoid countersilo capabilities on stability grounds. The weapons acquisition community may, for a variety of reasons, simultaneously be seeking a weapons characteristic vital to countersilo capability, improved ballistic missile accuracy. As best they can with weapons available, meanwhile, force operators may be required by the logic of their task to target enemy missile silos as a high priority.

Despite these complexities, however, it is possible to generalize a body of policy concepts and values that governs U.S. strategic behavior. There are strong tendencies that dominate U.S. strategic behavior in the areas of declaratory policy, force acquisition, and arms control policy. Again, the case of U.S. countersilo capabilities may be cited. Today, the United States lacks high confidence capabilities against Soviet missile silos; it may continue to lack them for some time or indefinitely. This is in part the result of technological choice, the early selection of small ICBMs and the deployment of low-yield MIRV weapons. It is also the result of Soviet efforts to improve silo hardness. But the main reason for this lack is that we have abided by a conscious judgment that a serious countersilo capability, because it threatens strategic stability, is a bad thing for the United States to possess.

The situation seems more straightforward, if secretive, on the Soviet side. Soviet strategic policy making takes place in a far more vertical and closed system. Expertise is monopolized by the military and a subset of the top political leadership. Although elites external to this group can bid for its scarce resources to some extent, they cannot seriously challenge its values and judgments. Matters of doctrine, force acquisition, and war planning are much more intimately connected within this decision group than in the United States. Policy arguments are indeed possible. Public evidence suggests a series of major Soviet debates on nuclear strategy from the mid-1950s to the late 1960s, although identification of issues, alternatives, and parameters in these debates must be somewhat speculative.

These considerations make difficult, but not impossible, the comparative treatment of U.S. and Soviet strategic belief systems and concepts. One may describe with some confidence how the two very different decision systems deal with certain concerns central to the strategic nuclear predicament of both sides. Much about U.S. and Soviet strategic belief systems can be captured by exploring how they treat five central issues: (1) the consequences of an all-out strategic nuclear war, (2) the phenomenon of deterrence, (3) stability, (4) distinctions and relationships between intercontinental and regional strategic security concerns, and (5) strategic conflict limitation.

CONSEQUENCES OF NUCLEAR WAR

For a generation, the relevant elites of both the United States and the Soviet Union have agreed that an unlimited strategic nuclear war would be a sociopolicital disaster of immense proportions. Knowing the experiences of the peoples of the Soviet Union with warfare in this century and with nuclear inferiority since 1945, one sometimes suspects that the human dimensions of such a catastrophe are more real to Russians, high and low, than to Americans, for whom the prospect is vague and unreal, if certainly forbidding.

For many years the prevailing U.S. concept of nuclear war's consequences has been such as to preclude belief in any military or politically meaningful form of victory. Serious effort on the part of the state to enhance the prospect for national survival seemed quixotic, even dangerous—hence stems our relative disinterest in air defenses and civil defenses over the last fifteen years, and our genuine fear that ballistic missile defenses would be severely destabilizing. Growth of Soviet nuclear power has certainly clinched this view of nuclear conflict among critical elements of the U.S. elite. But even when the United States enjoyed massive superiority, when the Soviet Union could inflict much less societal damage on the United States, and then only in a first strike (through the early 1960s), the awesome destructiveness of nuclear weapons had deprived actual war with these weapons of much of its strategic meaning for the United States.

The Soviet system has, however, in the worst of times, clung tenaciously to the belief that nuclear war cannot—indeed, must not—be deprived of strategic meaning, i.e., some rational relationship to the interests of the state. It has insisted that, however awful, nuclear war must be survivable and some kind of meaningful victory attainable. As most are aware, this issue was debated in various ways at the beginning and end of the Khrushchev era, with Krushchev on both sides of the issue. But the system decided it *had* to believe in survival and victory of some form. Not to believe so would mean that the most basic processes of history, on which Soviet ideology and political legitimacy are founded, could be derailed by the technological works of man and the caprice of a historically doomed opponent. Moreover, as the defenders of doctrinal rectitude continued to point out, failure to believe in the "manageability" of nuclear disaster would lead to pacificism, defeatism, and lassitude in the Soviet military effort. This should not be read as the triumph of ideological will over objective science and practical reason. From the Soviet point of view, nuclear war with a powerful and hostile America was a real danger. Could the state merely give up on its traditional responsibilities to defend itself and survive in that event? Their negative answer hardly strikes one as unreasonable. Their puzzlement, alternating between contemptuous and suspicious, over U.S. insistence on a positive answer is not surprising.

In recent years the changing strategic balance has had the effect of strengthening rather than weakening the asymmetry of the two sides' convictions on this matter. Dubious when the United States enjoyed relative advantage, strategic victory and survival in nuclear conflict have become the more incredible to the United States as the strategic power of the Russians has grown. For the Soviets, however, the progress of arms and war-survival programs has transformed what was in large measure an ideological imperative into a more plausible strategic potential. For reasons to be examined below, Soviet leaders possibly believe that, under favorable operational conditions, the Soviet Union could win a central strategic war today. Notwithstanding strategic parity or essential equivalence of force, they may also believe that they could lose such a conflict under some conditions.

DETERRENCE

The concept of deterrence early became a central element of both U.S. and Soviet strategic belief systems. For both sides the concept had extended or regional dimensions, and a good deal of political content. There has, in short, been some functional symmetry between the deterrence thinking of the two sides: restraint of hostile action across a spectrum of violence by the threat of punishing consequences in war. Over time and with shifts in the overall military balance, latent asymmetries of thinking have become more pronounced. For the United States, strategic deterrence has tended to become the only meaningful objective of strategic policy, and it has become progressively decoupled from regional security. For the Soviets, deterrence—or war prevention—was the first, but not the only and not the last objective of strategy. Deterrence also meant the protection of a foreign policy that had both offensive and defensive goals. And it was never counterposed against the ultimate objective of being able to manage a nuclear war successfully should deterrence fail. The Soviet concept of deterrence has evolved as the strategic balance has improved for the Soviet Union from primary emphasis on defensive themes of war prevention and protection of prior political gains to more emphasis on themes that include the protection of dynamic processes favoring Soviet international interests. Repetition of the refrain that détente is a product of Soviet strategic power, among other things, displays this evolution.

STABILITY

Strategic stability is a concept that is very difficult to treat in a comparative manner because it is so vital to U.S. strategic thinking but hardly identifiable in Soviet strategic writings. In U.S. thinking, strategic stability has meant a condition in which incentives inherent in the arms balance to initiate the use of strategic nuclear forces and, closely related, to acquire new or additional forces, are weak or absent. In an environment dominated by powerful offensive capabilities and comparatively vulnerable ultimate values, i.e., societies, stability was thought to be achievable on the basis of a contract of mutually vulnerable societies and survivable offensive forces. Emphasis on force survivability followed, as did relative uninterest in counterforce, active, and passive defenses.

Soviet failure to embrace these notions is sufficiently evident not to require much elaboration. One may argue about Soviet ability to overturn stability in U.S. terms, but not about Soviet disinclination to accept the idea as a governing principle of strategic behavior. Soviet acceptance of the ABM agreement in 1972 is still frequently cited as testimony to some acceptance of this principle. It is much more probable, however, that the agreement was attractive to Moscow because superior U.S. ABM technology plus superior U.S. ABM penetrating technology would have given the United States a major advantage during the middle to late 1970s. In a unilateral sense, the Soviets saw the ABM agreement as stabilizing a process of strategic catch-up against a serious risk of reversal. But it did not mean acceptance of the U.S. stability principle.

The United States has always been relatively sensitive to the potential of technology to jeopardize specific formulas for achieving stability, although it has been relatively slow to perceive the pace and extent to which comparative advantage has shifted from passive survivability to counterforce technologies. The Soviets have also been sensitive to destabilizing technologies. But they have tended to accept the destabilizing dynamism of technology as an intrinsic aspect of the strategic dialectic, the underlying engine of which is a political competition not susceptible to stabilization. For the Soviets, arms control negotiations are part of this competitive process. Such negotiation can help keep risks within bounds and also, by working on the U.S. political process, restrain U.S. competitiveness.

Soviet failure to embrace U.S. strategic stability notions as strategic norms does not mean, as a practical matter, that the Soviets fail to see certain constellations of weapons technology and forces as having an intrinsic stability, in that they make the acquisition of major advantages very difficult. What they reject is the notion that, in the political and technical world as they see it, those constellations can be frozen and the strategic competition dimension thereby factored out of the East-West struggle permanently or for long periods.

INTERCONTINENTAL AND REGIONAL POWER

Defining the boundary line between strategic and nonstrategic forces has been a troubling feature of

SALT from the beginning. It is one of diplomacy's minor ironies that the United States is hard pressed to exclude from negotiations the forward capabilities that it considers as general purpose forces. But peripheral strike forces that the Soviets have systematically defined and managed as strategic seem very difficult to bring into the picture.

Geography imparted an intercontinental meaning to the term *strategic* for the United States. The same geography dictated that. for the Soviet Union, strategic concern began at the doorstep. Soviet concern about the military capabilities in the hands of and on the territory of its neighbors is genuine, although Soviet arguments for getting the United States to legitimatize and pay for those concerns at SALT in terms of its own central force allowances have been a bit contrived. They are tantamount to penalizing the United States for having friends, while rewarding the Soviet Union for conducting itself in a manner that has left it mostly vassals and opponents on its borders.

Underlying these definitional problems are more fundamental differences between U.S. and Soviet doctrines on what is generally called "coupling." It has long been U.S. policy to assure that U.S. strategic nuclear forces are seen by the Soviets and our NATO allies as tightly coupled to European security. Along with conventional and theater nuclear forces, U.S. strategic nuclear forces constitute an element of the NATO "triad." The good health of the alliance politically and the viability of deterrence in Europe have been seen to require a very credible threat to engage U.S. strategic nuclear forces once nuclear weapons come into play above the level of quite limited use. For more than twenty years NATO's official policy has had to struggle against doubts that this coupling could be credible in the absence of clear U.S. strategic superiority. Yet the vocabularly we commonly employ itself tends to strain this linkage in that theater nuclear forces are distinguished from strategic. Ironically, the struggle to keep so-called Forward Based Systems out of SALT, because we could not find a good way to bring in comparable Soviet systems, tended to underline the distinction. In our thinking about the actual prosecution of a strategic conflict, once conflict at that level begins we tend to forget about what might be the local outcome of the regional conflict that probably precipitated the strategic exchange.

The Soviets, on the other hand, appear to take a more comprehensive view of strategy and the strategic balance. Both in peacetime political competition and in the ultimate test of a central conflict, they tend to see all force elements as contributing to a unified strategic purpose, national survival and the elimination or containment of enemies on their periphery. The USSR tends to see intercontinental forces, and strategic forces more generally, as a means to help it win an all-out conflict in its most crucial theater, Europe. Both institutionally and operationally, Soviet intercontinental strike forces are an outgrowth and extension of forces initially developed to cover peripheral targets. Land combat forces, including conventional forces, are carefully trained and equipped to fight in nuclear conditions. In the last decade, the emergence of a hostile and potentially powerful China has more firmly riveted the "rimland" of Eurasia into the Soviet strategic perspective.

Whatever the consequence of a central U.S.-Soviet nuclear conflict for their respective homelands, it could well have the effect of eliminating U.S. power and influence on the Eurasian landmass for a long time. If, by virtue of its active and passive damage-limitation measures, the Soviet Union suffered measurably less damage than did the United States, and it managed to intimidate China or destroy Chinese military power, the resultant Soviet domination of Eurasia could represent a crucial element of "strategic victory" in Soviet eyes. In any case, regional conflict outcomes seem not to lose their significance in Soviet strategy once strategic nuclear conflict begins.

CONFLICT LIMITATION

Nuclear conflict limitation is a theme on which influential American opinion is divided. After much thought and argument, the Ford administration adopted a more explicit endorsement of limited strategic nuclear options as a hedge against the failings of a strategy solely reliant on all-out war plans for deterrence or response in the event of deterrent failure. The Carter administration appeared more doubtful about the value of limited nuclear options because it appeared generally to doubt the viability of nuclear conflict limitations. It may also have shared the fear of some critics that limited options could seem to make nuclear use more tolerable and therefore detract from deterrence.

Theories of nuclear conflict limitation entertained in the United States tend to rest on concepts of risk management and bargaining with the opponent. We are interested in limited options because they are more credible than unlimited ones in response to limited provocation. Whether or not they can be controlled is uncertain; hence, their credible presence enhances the risk faced by the initiator of conflict. Should conflict come about, then limited options might be used to change the risk, cost, and benefit calculus of the opponent in the direction of some more or less tolerable war termination. This would not be a sure thing, but better to have the limited options than not.

How the Soviets view the matter of nuclear conflict limitations is obscure. The least one can say is that they do not see it in the manner described above. From the early 1960s, after McNamara's famed Ann Arbor speech, Soviet propagandists have denounced limited nuclear war concepts as U.S. contrivances to make nuclear weapons use more "acceptable" and to rationalize the quest for counterforce advantages. They have replayed the criticism that such concepts weaken deterrence and cannot prevent nuclear war from becoming unlimited.

To some degree, Soviet propaganda on this theme is suspect for being aimed at undermining U.S. strategy innovations that detract from the political benefits of Soviet strategic force improvement. Given differences of view in the United States on this subject, moreover, the Soviets could hardly resist the temptation to fuel the U.S. argument. There are several reasons why Soviet public pronouncements should not be taken as entirely reflecting the content of operative Soviet strategic thinking and planning regarding limited nuclear use.

For one thing, qualified acceptance in doctrine and posture of a nonnuclear scenario, or at least a nonnuclear phase, in theater conflict displays some Soviet willingness to embrace conflict limitation notions previously rejected. Soviet strategic nuclear force growth and modernization, in addition, have given Soviet operational planners a broader array of employment options than they had in the 1960s and may have imparted some confidence in Soviet ability to *enforce* conflict limitations. It would not be surprising, therefore, to find some Soviet contingency planning for various kinds of limited nuclear options at the theater and, perhaps, at the strategic level.

One may seriously doubt, however, whether Soviet planners would approach the problem of contingency planning for limited nuclear options with the conceptual baggage the U.S. system carries. It would seem contrary to the style of Soviet doctrinal thinking to emphasize bargaining and risk management. Rather, the presence of limited options planning in the Soviet system would seem likely to rest on more traditional military concepts of economizing on force use, controlling actions and their consequences, reserving options, and leaving time to learn what is possible in the course of a campaign. The Soviet limited options planner would seem likely to approach his task with a more strictly unilateral set of concerns than his American counterpart.

METHODS OF ASSESSING THE STRATEGIC BALANCE

Comparative study of U.S. and Soviet strategic doctrine should give attention to a closely related matter: how we perceive and measure force balances. Allusion has already been made to asymmetries between U.S. and Soviet definitions of strategic forces, what should be counted in SALT, etc. This is by no means the heart of the matter. U.S. and Soviet methodologies for measuring military strength appear to differ significantly.

Many rather amateurish and misleading beliefs about the way the Soviets measure and value military strength prevail: for example, that the Soviets have some atavistic devotion to mass and size. Mass they do believe in, because both experience and analysis show that mass counts. They can be quite choosey about size, however, as a look at their tank and fighter designs reveals. Within the limits of their technological potential, they have been quite sensitive and in no way primitive in their thinking about quality/quantity tradeoffs.

Another widespread notion is that the Soviets have an unusual propensity for worst-case planning or military overinsurance. This is hard to demonstrate convincingly in Soviet behavior. The Soviet theory of war in Central Europe, for example, is daring, not conservative. Despite much rhetoric on the danger of surprise and the need for high combat readiness, Soviet strategic planning has not accorded nearly the importance to "bolt from the blue" surprise attack that the United States has. This does not look like overinsurance.

The problem of measuring strength goes more deeply, to differing appreciations of the processes of conflict and how they bear on force measurement. U.S. measures of the overall strategic balance tend to be of two general types. First come the so-called static measures of delivery vehicles, weapons, megatonage and equivalent megatonage, throw-weight, and, perhaps, some measure of hard-target kill potential (such as weapon numbers times a scaled yield factor divided by the square of circular error probability). Comparisons of this type can display some interesting things about differing forces. But they say very little about how those forces, much less the nations that employ them, will fare in war. By themselves, static measures can be dangerously misleading.

We then move on to the second, or quasi-dynamic, class of measures. Here the analyst is out to capture the essential features of a "real war" in terms general enough to allow parametric application, frequent reiteration of the analysis with varying assumptions, and easy swamping of operational and technical details that he may not be able to quantify or of which he may be ignorant. Typically, certain gross attributes of the war "scenario" will be determined, e.g., levels of alert, who goes first, and very general targeting priorities. Then specified "planning factor" performance characteristics are attributed to weapons. Because it is relatively easy (and fun), a more or less elaborate version of the ICBM duel is frequently conducted. The much more subtle and complicated, but crucial, engagement of air- and sea-based forces is usually handled by gross assumption, e.g., *n* percent of bomber weapons get to target, all SSBNs at sea survive. Regional conflicts and forces are typically ignored. Of course, all command/control/communications systems are assumed to work as planned—otherwise the forces and, even worse, the analyst would be out of business. Finally, "residuals" of surviving forces, fatality levels, and industrial damage are totaled up. A popular variant is to run a countermilitary war in these terms and then see whether residual forces are sufficient to inflict "unacceptable damage" on cities. If so, then deterrence is intact, according to some. Others point to grossly asymmetric levels of surviving forces to document an emerging strategic imbalance.

Most specialists agree and explicitly admit that this kind of analysis does not capture the known (much less the unknown) complexities, uncertainties, and fortuities of a real strategic nuclear conflict of any dimension. Such liturgical admissions are usually offered to gain absolution from their obvious consequences, namely, that the analysis in question could be not illuminating, but quite wrong. However, more heroic analytic attempts at capturing the real complexity and operational detail of a major nuclear exchange usually are not made because they are: (*a*) usually beyond the expertise of single analysts or small groups, (*b*) not readily susceptible to varied and parametric application, and (*c*) *still* laden by manifold uncertainties and unknowns that are very hard to quantify. Hence, they are very hard to apply to the tasks of assessing strategic force balances or the value of this or that force improvement. The more simplistic analysis is more convenient. The analyst can conduct it many times, and talk over his results with other analysts who do the same thing. The whole methodology thereby acquires a reality and persuasiveness of its own.

The influence of this kind of analysis in our strategic decision system has many explanations. It has sociological origins in the dominance of economists and engineers over soldiers in the conduct of our strategic affairs. It conforms with the needs of a flat and argumentative policy process in which there are many and varied participants, from generals to graduate students. They need a common idiom that does not soak up too much computer time and can be unclassified. And finally, in part because of the first explanation cited, when it comes to nuclear strategy, we do not believe much in "real" nuclear war anyway. We are after a standard of sufficiency that is adequate and persuasive in a peacetime setting.

Two things about this style of strategic analysis merit stating in the context of this article. First, on the face of it, the value of simplistic, operationally insensitive methodologies is assuredly less in the present strategic environment than it was when the United States enjoyed massive superiority. Not only are weapons, force mixes, and scenarios more complicated than these methodologies can properly illuminate, but the relative equality of the two sides going into the conflict makes the subtleties, complexities, and uncertainties all the more important for how they come out. Second, the Soviets do not appear to do their balance measuring in this manner.

One can gain a fair insight into the manner of Soviet force balance analysis from public sources, particularly Soviet military literature. Additional inferences can be drawn from the organization and professional composition of the Soviet defense decision system, and from some of the results of Soviet decisions. On the whole it appears that Soviet planners and force balance assessors are much more sensitive than we are to the subtleties and uncertainties—what we sometimes call "scenario dependencies"—of strategic conflict seen from a very operational perspective. The timing and scale of attack initiation, tactical deception and surprise, uncertainties about weapons effects, the actual character of operational plans and targeting, timely adjustment of plans to new information, and, most important, the continued viability of command and control—these factors appear to loom large in Soviet calculations of conflict outcomes.

The important point, however, is a conceptual one: unlike the typical U.S. planner, the Soviet planner does not appear to see the *force* balance prior to conflict as a kind of physical reification of the war outcome and therefore as a measure of strategic strength by itself. Rather, he seems to see the force balance, the "correlation of military forces," as one input to a complex combat process in which other factors of great significance will play, and the chief aim of which is a new, more favorable balance of forces. The sum of these factors is strategy, and strategy is a significant variable to the Soviet planner.

As a generalization, then, the Soviet planner is very sensitive to operational details and uncertainties. Because these factors can swing widely, even wildly, in different directions, a second generalization about Soviet force analysis emerges: a given force balance in peacetime can yield widely varying outcomes to war depending on the details and uncertainties of combat. Some of those outcomes could be relatively good for the Soviet Union, others relatively bad. The planner's task is to improve the going-in force balance, to be sure. But it is also to develop and pursue ways of waging war that tend to push the outcome in favorable directions.

This kind of thinking occasions two very unpleasant features in Soviet military doctrine: a strong tendency to preempt and a determination to suppress the enemy's command and control system at all costs. The Soviets tend to see any decision to go to nuclear war as being imposed on them by a course of events that tells them "war is coming," a situation they bungled memorably in June 1941. It makes no difference whose misbehavior started events on that course. Should they find themselves on it, their operational perspective on the factors that drive war outcomes places a high premium on seizing the initiative and imposing the maximum disruptive effects on the enemy's forces *and* war plans. By going first, and especially disrupting command and control, the highest likelihood of limiting damage and coming out of the war with intact forces and a surviving nation is achieved, virtually independent of the force balance.

This leads to a final generalization. We tend rather casually to assume that, when we talk about parity and "essential equivalence" and the Soviets about "equal security," we are talking about the same thing: functional strategic stability. We are not. The Soviets are talking about a going-in force balance in which they have an equal or better chance of winning a central war, if they can orchestrate the right scenario and take advantage of lucky breaks. It is the job of the high command to see that they can. If it fails to do so, the Soviet Union could possibly lose the war. This is not stability in our terms.

Again, this is not to argue that the Soviets do not foresee appalling destruction as the result of any strategic exchange under the best of conditions. In a crisis, Soviet leaders would probably take any tolerable and even some not very tolerable exits from the risk of such a war. But their image of strategic crisis is one in which these exits are closing up, and the "war is coming." They see the ultimate task of strategy to be the provision of forces and options for preempting that situation. This then leads them to choose strategies that, from a U.S. point of view, seem not particularly helpful in keeping the exits open, and even likely to close them off.

It is frequently argued—more frequently as we become more anxious about the emerging force balance—that the Soviets could not have confidence in launching a strategic attack and achieving the specific objectives that theoretical analysis might suggest to be possible, such as destruction of Minuteman. Particularly because they are highly sensitive to operational uncertainties they would not, in one of the more noteworthy phrases of the latest Defense Department posture statement, gamble national survival on a "single cosmic throw of the dice." This construction of the problem obscures the high likelihood that decisions to go to strategic war will be made under great pressure and in the face of severe perceived penalty if the decision is not made and the war comes anyway. They are not likely to come about in a situation in which the choice is an uncertain war or a comfortable peace. It also obscures the fact that the heavy weight of uncertainty will also rest on the shoulders of U.S. decision makers in a crisis.

DANGERS OF MISUNDERSTANDING

In sum, there are fundamental differences between U.S. and Soviet strategic thinking, both at the level of value and at the level of method. The existence of these differences and, even more, our failure to recognize them have had dangerous consequences for the U.S.-Soviet strategic relationship.

One such might be called the "hawk's lament." Failing to appreciate the character of Soviet strategic thinking in relation to our own views, we have underestimated the competitiveness of Soviet strategic policy and the need for competitive responsiveness on our part. This is evident in both our SALT and our strategic force modernization behavior.

A second negative effect might be termed the "dove's lament." By projecting our views onto the Soviets, and failing to appreciate their real motives and perceptions, we have underestimated the difficulties of achieving genuine strategic stability through SALT and oversold the value of what we have achieved. This has, in turn, set us up for profound, perhaps even hysterical, disillusionment in the years ahead, in which the very idea of negotiated arms control could be politically discredited. If present strategic trends continue, it is not hard to imagine a future political environment in which it would be difficult to argue for arms control negotiations even of a very hard-nosed sort.

The third and most dangerous consequence of our misunderstanding of Soviet strategy involves excessive confidence in strategic stability. U.S. strategic behavior, in its broadest sense, has helped to ease the Soviet Union onto a course of more assertive international action. This has, in turn, increased the probability of a major East-West confrontation, arising not necessarily by Soviet design, in which the United States must forcefully resist a Soviet advance or face collapse of its global position, while the Soviet Union cannot easily retreat or compromise because it has newly acquired global power status to defend and the matter at issue could be vital. In such conditions, it is all too easy to imagine a "war is coming" situation in which the abstract technical factors on which we rest our confidence in stability, such as expected force survival levels and "unacceptable damage," could crumble away. The strategic case for "waiting to see what happens," for conceding the operational initiative to the other side—which is what crisis stability is all about—could look very weak. Each side could see the great operational virtues of preemption, be convinced that the other side sees them too, and be hourly more determined that the other side not have them. This, in any case, could be the Soviet way of perceiving things. Given the relative translucence of U.S. versus Soviet strategic decision processes, however, our actual ability to preempt is likely to be less than the Soviets', quite apart from the character of the force balance. Add to that the problem of a vulnerable Minuteman ICBM force and you have a potentially very nasty situation.

What we know about the nature of our own strategic thinking and that of the Soviet Union is not at all comforting at this juncture. The Soviets approach the problem of managing strategic nuclear power with highly competitive and combative instincts. Some have argued that these instincts are largely fearful and defensive, others that they are avaricious and confident. My own reading of Russian and Soviet history is that they are both, and, for that, the more difficult to handle.

The United States and the Soviet Union share two awesome problems in common, the creation of viable industrial societies and the management of nuclear weapons. Despite much that is superficially common to our heritages, however, these two societies have fundamentally different political cultures that determine how they handle these problems. The stamp of a legal, commercial, and democratic society is clearly seen in the way the United States has approached the task of managing nuclear security. Soviet styles of managing this problem bear the stamp of an imperial, bureaucratic, and autocratic political tradition. While the United States is willing to see safety in a compact of "live and let live" under admittedly unpleasant conditions, the Soviet Union operates from a political tradition that suspects the viability of such deals and expects them, at best, to mark the progress of historically ordained forces to ascendancy.

It is not going to be easy to stabilize the strategic competition on this foundation of political traditions. But if we understand the situation clearly, there should be no grounds for fatalism. Along with a very uncomfortable degree of competitiveness, Soviet strategic policy contains a strong element of professionalism and military rationalism with which we can do business in the interest of a common safety if we enhance those qualities in ourselves. The Soviets respect military power and they take warfare very seriously. When the propaganda and polemics are pared away, they sometimes wonder if we do. We can make a healthy contribution to our own future, and theirs, by rectifying this uncertainty.

Why the Soviet Union thinks it could fight and win a nuclear war

Richard Pipes

In an interview with the *New Republic,* Paul Warnke, then head of the Arms Control and Disarmament Agency, was asked how the United States ought to react to indications that the Soviet leadership thinks it possible to fight and win a nuclear war. "In my view," he replied, "this kind of thinking is on a level of abstraction which is unrealistic. It seems to me that instead of talking in those terms, which would indulge what I regard as the primitive aspects of Soviet nuclear doctrine, we ought to be trying to educate them into the real world of strategic nuclear weapons, which is that nobody could possibly win."[1]

Even after allowance has been made for Mr. Warnke's notoriously careless syntax, puzzling questions remain. On what grounds does he, a Washington lawyer, presume to "educate" the Soviet General Staff composed of professional soldiers who thirty years ago defeated the Wehrmacht about, of all things, the "real world of strategic nuclear weapons" of which they happen to possess a considerably larger arsenal than we? Why does he consider them children who ought not to be "indulged"? And why does he chastise for what he regards as a "primitive" and unrealistic strategic doctrine not those who hold it, namely, the Soviet military, but Americans who worry about their holding it?

Be all that as it may, even if Mr. Warnke refuses to take Soviet strategic doctrine seriously, it behooves us to take his views of Soviet doctrine seriously. He not only will head our SALT II team; his thinking as articulated in the above statement and on other occasions reflects all the conventional wisdom of the school of strategic theory dominant in the United States, one of whose leading characteristics is scorn for Soviet views on nuclear warfare.

American and Soviet nuclear doctrines, it needs stating at the outset, are starkly at odds. The prevalent U.S. doctrine holds that an all-out war between countries in possession of sizable nuclear arsenals would be so destructive as to leave no winner; thus, resort to arms has ceased to represent a rational policy option for the leaders of such countries vis-à-vis one another. The classic dictum of Clausewitz, that war is politics pursued by other means, is widely believed in the United States to have lost its validity after Hiroshima and Nagasaki. Soviet doctrine, by contrast, emphatically asserts that while an all-out nuclear war would indeed prove extremely destructive to both parties, its outcome would not be mutual suicide: the country better prepared for it and in possession of a superior strategy could win and emerge a viable society. "There is profound erroneousness and harm in the disorienting claims of bourgeois ideologies that there will be no victor in a thermonuclear world war," thunders an authoritative Soviet publication.[2] The theme is mandatory in the current Soviet military literature. Clausewitz, buried in the United States, seems to be alive and prospering in the Soviet Union.

The predisposition of the American strategic community is to shrug off this fundamental doctrinal discrepancy. American doctrine has been and continues to be formulated and implemented by and large without reference to its Soviet counterpart. It is assumed here that there exists one and only one "rational" strategy appropriate to the age of thermonuclear weapons, and that this strategy rests on the principle of "mutual deterrence" developed in the United States some two decades ago. Evidence that the Russians do not share this doctrine, which, as its name indicates, postulates reciprocal attitudes, is usually dismissed with the explanation that they are clearly lagging behind us: given time and patient "education," they will surely come around.

It is my contention that this attitude rests on a combination of arrogance and ignorance; that it is dangerous; and that it is high time to start paying heed to Soviet strategic doctrine, lest we end up deterring no one but ourselves. There is ample evidence that the Soviet military say what they mean, and usually mean what they say. When the recently deceased Soviet minister of defense, Marshal Grechko, assured us: "We have never concealed, and do not conceal, the fundamental, principal tenets of our military doctrine,"[3] he deserved a hearing. This is especially true in view of the fact that Soviet military deployments over the past twenty years make far better sense in the light of Soviet doctrine, "primitive" and "unrealistic" as the latter may appear, than when reflected in the mirror of our own doctrinal assumptions.

Mistrust of the military professional, combined with a pervasive conviction, typical of commercial societies, that human conflicts are at bottom caused by misunderstanding and ought to be resolved by negotiations rather than force, has worked against serious attention to military strategy by the United States. We have no General Staff; we grant no higher degrees in "military science"; and, except for Admiral Mahan, we have produced no strategist of international repute. America has tended to rely on its insularity to protect it from aggressors, and on its unique industrial capacity to help crush its enemies once war was under way. The United States is accustomed to waging wars of its own choosing and on its own terms. It lacks an ingrained strategic tradition. In the words of one historian, Americans tend to view both military strategy and the armed forces as something to be "employed intermittently to destroy occasional and intermittent threats posed by hostile powers."[4]

This approach to warfare has had a number of consequences. The United States wants to win its wars quickly and with the smallest losses in American lives. It is disinclined, therefore, to act on protracted and indirect strategies, or to engage in limited wars and wars of attrition. Once it resorts to arms, it prefers to mobilize the great might of its industrial plant to produce vast quantities of the means of destruction with which in the shortest possible time to undermine the enemy's will and ability to continue the struggle. Extreme reliance on technological superiority, characteristic of U.S. warfare, is the obverse side of America's extreme sensitivity to its own casualities; so is indifference to the casualties inflicted on the enemy. The strategic bombing campaigns waged by the U.S. Air Corps and the RAF against Germany and Japan in World War II excellently implemented this general attitude. Paradoxically, America's dread of war and casualties pushes it to adopt some of the most brutal forms of warfare, involving the indiscriminate destruction of the enemy's homeland with massive civilian deaths.

These facts must be borne in mind to understand the way the United States reacted to the advent of the nuclear bomb. The traditional military services—the army and the navy—whose future seemed threatened by the invention of a weapon widely believed to have revolutionized warfare and rendered conventional forces obsolete, resisted extreme claims made on behalf of the bomb. But they were unable to hold out for very long. An alliance of politicians and scientists, backed by the air force, soon overwhelmed them. "Victory through Air Power," a slogan eminently suited to the American way of war, carried all before it once bombs could be devised whose explosive power was measured in kilotons and megatons.

The U.S. Army tried to argue after Hiroshima and Nagasaki that the new weapons represented no fundamental breakthrough. No revolution in warfare had occurred, its spokesman claimed: atomic bombs were merely a more efficient species of the aerial bombs used in World War II, and in themselves no more able to ensure victory than the earlier bombs had been. As evidence, they could point to the comprehensive U.S. Strategic Bombing Surveys carried out after the war to assess the effects of the bombing campaigns. These had demonstrated that saturation raids against German and Japanese cities had neither broken the enemy's morale nor paralyzed his armaments industry; indeed, German productivity kept on rising in the face of intensified Allied bombing, attaining its peak in the fall of 1944, on the eve of capitulation.

And when it came to horror, atomic bombs had nothing over conventional ones: as against the 72,000 casualties caused by the atomic bomb in Hiroshima, conventional raids carried out against Tokyo and Dresden in 1945 had caused 84,000 and 135,000 fatalities, respectively. Furthermore, those who sought to minimize the impact of the new weapon argued, atomic weapons in no sense obviated the need for sizable land and sea forces. For example, General Ridgway, as chief of staff in the early 1950s, maintained that war waged with tactical nuclear weapons would demand larger rather than smaller field armies, since these weapons were more complicated, since they would produce greater casualities, and since the dispersal of troops required by nuclear tactics called for increasing the depth of the combat zone.[5]

As I shall note below, similar arguments disputing the revolutionary character of the nuclear weapon surfaced in the Soviet Union, and there promptly came to dominate strategic theory. In the United States, they were just as promptly silenced by a coalition of groups each of which it suited, for its own reasons, to depict the atomic bomb as the "absolute weapon" that had, in large measure, rendered traditional military establishments redundant and traditional strategic thinking obsolete.

Once World War II was over, the United States was most eager to demobilize its armed forces. Between June 1945 and June 1946, the U.S. Army reduced its strength from 8.3 to 1.9 million troops; comparable manpower cuts were achieved in the navy and air force. Little more than a year after Germany's surrender, the military forces of the United States, which at their peak had stood at 12.3 million troops, were cut down to 3 million; two years later they declined below 2 million. The demobilization proceeded at a pace (if not in a manner) reminiscent of the dissolution of the Russian army in the revolutionary year of 1917. Nothing could have stopped this mass of humanity streaming homeward. To most Americans, peacetime conditions meant reversion to a skeletal armed force.

Yet, at the same time, growing strains in the wartime alliance with the Soviet Union, and mounting evidence that Stalin was determined to exploit the chaotic conditions brought about by the collapse of the Axis powers to expand his domain, called for an effective military force able to deter the Soviets. The United States could not fulfill its role as leader of the Western coalition without an ability to project its military power globally.

In this situation, the nuclear weapon seemed to offer an ideal solution: the atomic bomb could hardly have come at a better time from the point of view of U.S. international commitments. Here was a device so frighteningly destructive, it was believed, that the mere threat of its employment would serve to dissuade would-be aggressors from carrying out their designs. Once the air force received the B-36, the world's first intercontinental bomber, the United States acquired the ability to threaten the Soviet Union with devastating punishment without, at the same time, being compelled to maintain a large and costly standing army.

Reliance on the nuclear deterrent became more imperative than ever after the conclusion of the Korean war, in the course of which U.S. defense expenditures had been driven sharply up. President Eisenhower had committed himself to a policy of fiscal restraint. He wanted to cut the defense budget appreciably, and yet he had to do so without jeopardizing either America's territorial security or its worldwide commitments. In an effort to reconcile these contradictory desires, the president and his Secretary of State, John Foster Dulles, enunciated in the winter of 1953/54 a strategic doctrine that to an unprecedented degree based the country's security on a single weapon, the nuclear deterrent. In an address to the United Nations in December 1953, Eisenhower argued that since there was no defense against nuclear weapons (i.e., thermonuclear or hydrogen bombs, which both countries were then beginning to produce), war between the two "atomic colossi" would leave no victors and probably cause the demise of civilization. A month later, Dulles enunciated what came to be known as the doctrine of "massive retaliation." The United States, he declared, had decided "to depend primarily upon a great capacity to retaliate, instantly, by means and at places of our choosing." Throughout his address, Dulles emphasized the fiscal benefits of such a strategy, "more basic security at less cost."

The Eisenhower-Dulles formula represented a neat compromise between America's desires to reduce the defense budget and simultaneously to retain the capacity to respond to Soviet threats. The driving force was not, however, military but budgetary: behind "massive retaliation" (as well as its offspring, "mutual deterrence") lay *fiscal* imperatives. In the nuclear deterrent, the United States found a perfect resolution of the conflicting demands of domestic and foreign responsibilities. For this reason alone its adoption was a foregone conclusion: the alternatives were either a vast standing army or forfeiture of status as a leading world power. The air force enthusiastically backed the doctrine of massive retaliation. As custodian of the atomic bomb, it had a vested interest in a defense posture of which that weapon was the linchpin. And since in the first postwar decade the intercontinental bomber was the only available vehicle for delivering the bomb against an enemy like the Soviet Union, the air force could claim a goodly share of the defense budget built around the retaliation idea.

Although the Soviet Union exploded a fission bomb in 1949 and announced the acquisition of a fusion (or hydrogen) bomb four years later, the United States still continued for a while longer to enjoy an effective monopoly on nuclear retaliation, since the Soviet Union lacked the means of delivering quantities of such bombs against U.S. territory. That situation changed dramatically in 1957 when the Soviets launched the Sputnik. This event, which their propaganda hailed as a great contribution to the advancement of science (and ours as proof of the failures of the American educational system!), represented in fact a significant military demonstration, namely, the ability of the Russians to deliver nuclear warheads against the United States homeland, until then immune from direct enemy threats. At this point massive retaliation ceased to make much sense and before long yielded to the doctrine of "mutual deterrence." The new doctrine postulated that inasmuch as both the Soviet Union and the United States possessed (or would soon possess) the means of destroying each other, neither country could rationally contemplate resort to war. The nuclear stockpiles of each were an effective deterrent that ensured that they would not be tempted to launch an attack.

This doctrine was worked out in great and sophisticated detail by a bevy of civilian experts employed by various government and private organizations. These physicists, chemists, mathematicians, economists, and political scientists came to the support of the government's fiscally driven imperatives with scientific demonstrations in favor of the nuclear deterrent. Current U.S. strategic theory was thus born of a marriage between the scientist and the accountant. The professional soldier was jilted.

A large part of the U.S. scientific community had been convinced as soon as the first atomic bomb was exploded that the nuclear weapon, which that community had conceived and helped to develop, had accomplished a complete revolution in warfare. This conclusion was reached without much reference to the analysis of the effects of atomic weapons carried out by the military, and indeed without consideration of the traditional principles of warfare. It represented, rather, an act of faith on the part of an intellectual community that held strong pacifist convictions and felt deep guilt at having participated in the creation of a weapon of such destructive power. As early as 1946, in an influential book sponsored by the Yale Institute of International Affairs, under the title *The Absolute Weapon,* a group of civilian strategic theorists enunciated the principles of the mutual-deterrence theory, which subsequently became the official U.S. strategic doctrine. The principal points made in this work may be summarized as follows:

1. Nuclear weapons are "absolute weapons" in the sense that they can cause unacceptable destruction, but also and above all because there exists against them no possible defense. When the aggressor is certain to suffer the same punishment as his victim, aggression ceases to make sense. Hence, war is no longer a rational policy option, as it had been throughout human history. In the words of Bernard Brodie, the book's editor: "Thus far the chief purpose of our military establishment had been to win wars. From now on its chief purpose must be to avert them. It can have almost no other useful purpose" (p. 76).

2. Given the fact that the adjective *absolute* means, by definition, incapable of being exceeded or surpassed, in the nuclear age military superiority has become meaningless. As another contributor to the book, William T. R. Fox, expressed it: "When dealing with the absolute weapon, arguments based on relative advantage lose their point" (p. 181). From this it follows that the objective of modern defense policy should be not superiority in weapons, traditionally sought by the military, but "sufficiency": just enough nuclear weapons to be able to threaten a potential aggressor with unacceptable retaliation—in other words, an "adequate" deterrent, no more, no less.

3. Nuclear deterrence can become effective only if it restrains mutually—i.e., if the United States and the

Soviet Union each can deter the other from aggression. An American monopoly on nuclear weapons would be inherently destabilizing, both because it could encourage the United States to launch a nuclear attack, and, at the same time, by making the Russians feel insecure, cause them to act aggressively. "Neither we nor the Russians can expect to feel even reasonably safe unless an atomic attack by one were certain to unleash a devastating atomic counterattack by the other," Arnold Wolfers maintained (p. 135). In other words, to feel secure the United States actually required the Soviet Union to have the capacity to destroy it.

Barely one year after Hiroshima and three years before the Soviets were to acquire a nuclear bomb, *The Absolute Weapon* articulated the philosophical premises underlying the mutual-deterrence doctrine that today dominates U.S. strategic thinking. Modern strategy, in the opinion of its contributors, involved preventing wars rather than winning them, securing sufficiency in decisive weapons rather than superiority, and even ensuring the potential enemy's ability to strike back. Needless to elaborate, these principles ran contrary to all the tenets of traditional military theory, which had always called for superiority in forces and viewed the objective of war to be victory. But then, if one had decided that the new weapons marked a qualitative break with all the weapons ever used in combat, one could reasonably argue that past military experience, and the theory based on it, had lost relevance. Implicit in these assumptions was the belief that Clausewitz and his celebrated formula proclaiming war an extension of politics were dead. Henry Kissinger, who can always be counted upon to utter commonplaces in the tone of prophetic revelation, announced Clausewitz's obituary nearly twenty years after *The Absolute Weapon* had made the point, in these words: "The traditional mode of military analysis which saw in war a continuation of politics but with its own appropriate means is no longer applicable."[6]

American civilian strategists holding such views gained the dominant voice in the formulation of U.S. strategic doctrine with the arrival in Washington in 1961 of Robert S. McNamara as President Kennedy's secretary of defense. A prominent business executive specializing in finance and accounting, McNamara applied to the perennial problem of American strategy—how to maintain a credible global military posture without a large and costly military establishment—the methods of cost analysis. These had first been applied by the British during World War II under the name *operations research* and subsequently came to be adopted here as *systems analysis*. Weapons procurement was to be tested and decided by the same methods used to evaluate returns on investment in ordinary business enterprises. Mutual deterrence was taken for granted: the question of strategic posture reduced itself to the issue of which weapons systems would provide the United States with effective deterrence at the least expense. Under McNamara the procurement of weapons, decided on the basis of cost effectiveness, came in effect to direct strategy, rather than the other way around, as had been the case through most of military history. It is at this point that applied science in partnership with budgetary accountancy—a partnership that had developed U.S. strategic theory—also took charge of U.S. defense policy.

As worked out in the 1960s, and still in effect today, American nuclear theory rests on these propositions: all-out nuclear war is not a rational policy option, since no winner could possibly emerge from such a war. Should the Soviet Union nevertheless launch a surprise attack on the United States, the latter would emerge with enough of a deterrent to devastate the Soviet Union in a second strike. Since such a retaliatory attack would cost the Soviet Union millions of casualties and the destruction of all its major cities, a Soviet first strike is most unlikely. Meaningful defenses against a nuclear attack are technically impossible and psychologically counterproductive; nuclear superiority is meaningless.

In accord with these assumptions, the United States in the mid-1960s unilaterally froze its force of ICBMs at 1,054 and dismantled nearly all its defenses against enemy bombers. Civil defense was all but abandoned, as was in time the attempt to create an ABM system that held out the possibility of protecting American missile sites against a surprise enemy attack. The Russians were watched benignly as they moved toward parity with the United States in the number of intercontinental launchers, and then proceeded to attain numerical superiority. The expectation was that as soon as the Russians felt themselves equal to the United States in terms of effective deterrence, they would stop further deployments. The frenetic pace of the Soviet nuclear build-up was explained first on the ground that the Russians had a lot of catching up to do, then that they had to consider the Chinese threat, and finally on the grounds that they are inherently a very insecure people and should be allowed an edge in deterrent capability.

Whether mutual deterrence deserves the name of a strategy at all is a real question. As one student of the subject puts it:

> Although commonly called a "strategy," "assured destruction" was by itself an antithesis of strategy. Unlike any strategy that ever preceded it throughout the history of armed conflict, it ceased to be useful precisely where military strategy is supposed to come into effect: at the edge of war. It posited that the principal mission of the U.S. military under conditions of ongoing nuclear operations against [the continental United States] was to shut its eyes, grit its teeth, and reflexively unleash an indiscriminate and simultaneous reprisal against all Soviet aim points on a preestablished target list. Rather than deal in a considered way with the particular attack on hand so as to minimize further damage to the United States and maximize the possibility of an early settlement on reasonably acceptable terms, it had the simple goal of inflicting punishment for the Soviet transgression. Not only did this reflect an implicit repudiation of political responsibility, it also risked provoking just the sort of counterreprisal against the United States that a rational wartime strategy should attempt to prevent.[7]

I cite this passage merely to indicate that the basic postulates of U.S. nuclear strategy are not as self-evident and irrefutable as its proponents seem to believe and that, therefore, their rejection by the Soviet military is not, in and of itself, proof that Soviet thinking is "primitive" and devoid of a sense of realism.

The principal differences between American and Soviet strategies are traceable to different conceptions of the role of conflict and its inevitable concomitant, violence, in human relations and, secondly, to different functions that the military establishment performs in the two societies.

In the United States, the consensus of the educated and affluent holds all recourse to force to be the result of an inability or an unwilingness to apply rational analysis and patient negotiation to disagreements: the use of force is *prima facie* evidence of failure. Some segments of this class not only refuse to acknowledge the existence of violence as a fact of life, they have even come to regard fear—the organism's biological reaction to the threat of violence—as inadmissible. "The notion of being threatened has acquired an almost class connotation," Daniel P. Moynihan notes in connection with the refusal of America's "sophisticated" elite to accept the reality of a Soviet threat. "If you're not very educated, you're easily frightened. And not being ever frightened can be a formula for self-destruction."[8]

Now this entire middle-class, commercial, essentially Protestant ethos is absent from Soviet culture, whose roots feed on another kind of soil, and which has had for centuries to weather rougher political climes. The Communist revolution of 1917, by removing from positions of influence what there was of a Russian bourgeoisie (a class Lenin was prone to define as much by cultural as by socioeconomic criteria), in effect installed in power the *muzhik,* the Russian peasant. And the *muzhik* had been taught by long historical experience that cunning and coercion alone ensured survival: one employed cunning when weak, and cunning coupled with coercion when strong. Not to use force when one had it indicated some inner weakness. Marxism, with its stress on class war as a natural condition of mankind so long as the means of production were privately owned, has merely served to reinforce these ingrained convictions. The result is an extreme Social Darwinist outlook on life which today permeates the Russian elite as well as the Russian masses, and which only the democratic intelligentsia and the religious dissenters oppose to any significant extent.

The Soviet ruling elite regards conflict and violence as natural regulators of all human affairs: wars between nations, in its view, represent only a variant of wars between classes, recourse to the one or the other being dependent on circumstances. A conflictless world will come into being only when the socialist (i.e., Communist) mode of production spreads across the face of the earth.

The Soviet view of armed conflict can be illustrated with another citation from the writings of the late Marshal Grechko, one of the most influential Soviet military figures of the post-World War II era. In his principal treatise, Grechko refers to the classification of wars formulated in 1972 by his U.S. counterpart, Melvin Laird. Laird divided wars according to engineering criteria—in terms of weapons employed and the scope of the theater of operations—to come up with four principal types of war: strategic-nuclear, theater-nuclear, theater-conventional, and local-conventional. Dismissing this classification as inadequate, Grechko applies quite different standards to come up with his own typology:

> Proceeding from the fundamental contradictions of the contemporary era, one can distinguish, according to *sociopolitical criteria,* the following types of wars: (1) wars between states (coalitions) of two contrary social systems—capitalist and socialist; (2) civil wars between the proletariat and the bourgeoisie, or between the popular masses and the forces of the extreme reaction supported by the imperialists of other countries; (3) wars between imperialist states and the peoples of colonial and dependent states fighting for their freedom and independence; and (4) wars among capitalist states.[9]

This passage contains many interesting implications. For instance, it makes no allowance for war between two Communist countries, like the Soviet Union and China, though such a war seems greatly to preoccupy the Soviet leadership. Nor does it provide for war pitting a coalition of capitalist and Communist states against another capitalist state, such as actually occurred during World War II when the United States and the Soviet Union joined forces against Germany. But for our purposes, the most noteworthy aspect of Grechko's system of classification is the notion that social and national conflicts *within* the capitalist camp (that is, in all countries not under Communist control) are nothing more than a particular mode of class conflict of which all-out nuclear war between the superpowers is a conceivable variant. In terms of this typology, an industrial strike in the United States, the explosion of a terrorist bomb in Belfast or Jerusalem, the massacre by Rhodesian guerrillas of a black village or a white farmstead, differ from nuclear war between the Soviet Union and the United States only in degree, not in kind. All such conflicts are calibrations on the extensive scale by which to measure the historic conflict that pits communism against capitalism and imperialism. Such conflicts are inherent in the stage of human development which precedes the final abolition of classes.

Middle-class American intellectuals simply cannot assimilate this mentality, so alien is it to their experience and view of human nature. Confronted with the evidence that the most influential elements in the Soviet Union do indeed hold such views, they prefer to dismiss the evidence as empty rhetoric, and to regard with deep suspicion the motives of anyone who insists on taking it seriously. Like some ancient Oriental despots, they vent their wrath on the bearers of bad news. How ironic that the very people who have failed so dismally to persuade American television networks to eliminate violence from their programs nevertheless feel confident that they can talk the Soviet leadership into eliminating violence from its political arsenal!

Solzhenitsyn grasped the issue more profoundly as well as more realistically when he defined the antithesis of war not as the absence of armed conflict between nations—i.e., "peace" in the conventional meaning of the term—but as the absence of all violence, internal as well as external. His comprehensive definition, drawn from his Soviet experience, obversely matches the comprehensive Soviet definition of warfare.

We know surprisingly little about the individuals and institutions whose responsibility it is to formulate Soviet military doctrine. The matter is handled with the utmost secrecy, which conceals from the eyes of outsiders the controversies that undoubtedly surround it. Two assertions, however, can be made with confidence.

Because of Soviet adherence to the Clausewitzian principle that warfare is always an extension of politics—i.e., subordinate to overall political objectives (about which more below)—Soviet military planning is carried out under the close supervision of the country's highest political body, the Politburo. Thus, military policy is regarded as an intrinsic element of "grand strategy," whose arsenal also includes a variety of nonmilitary instrumentalities.

Secondly, the Russians regard warfare as a science (*nauka,* in the German sense of *Wissenschaft*). Instruction in the subject is offered at a number of university-level institutions, and several hundred specialists, most of them officers on active duty, have been accorded the Soviet equivalent of the Ph.D. in military science. This means that Soviet military doctrine is formulated by full-time specialists: it is as much the exclusive province of the certified military professional as medicine is that of the licensed physician. The civilian strategic theorist who since World War II has played a decisive role in the formulation of U.S. strategic doctrine is not in evidence in the Soviet Union, and probably performs at best a secondary, consultative function.

Its penchant for secrecy notwithstanding, the Soviet military establishment does release a large quantity of unclassified literature in the form of books, specialist journals, and newspapers. Of the books, the single most authoritative work at present is unquestionably the collective study, *Military Strategy,* edited by the late Marshal V. D. Sokolovskii, which summarizes Soviet warfare doctrine of the nuclear age.[10] Although published fifteen years ago, Sokolovskii's volume remains the only Soviet strategic manual publicly available—a solitary monument confronting a mountain of Western works on strategy. A series called "The Officer's Library" brings out important specialized studies.[11] The newspaper *Krasnaia zvezda* [Red star] carries important theoretical articles that, however, vie for the reader's attention with heroic pictures of Soviet troops storming unidentified beaches and firing rockets at unnamed foes. The flood of military works has as its purpose indoctrination, an objective to which the Soviet high command attaches the utmost importance: indoctrination both in the psychological sense, designed to persuade the Soviet armed forces that they are invincible, as well as of a technical kind, to impress upon the officers and ranks the principles of Soviet tactics and the art of operations.

To a Western reader, most of this printed matter is unadulterated rubbish. It not only lacks the sophistication and intellectual elegance that he takes for granted in works on problems of nuclear strategy; it is also filled with a mixture of pseudo-Marxist jargon and the crudest kind of Russian jingoism, which is one of the reasons why it is hardly ever read in the West, even by people whose business it is to devise a national strategy against a possible Soviet threat. By and large the material is ignored. Two examples must suffice. *Strategy in the Missile Age,* an influential work by Bernard Brodie, one of the pioneers of U.S. nuclear doctrine, which originally came out in 1959 and was republished in 1965, makes only a few offhand allusions to Soviet nuclear strategy, and then either to note with approval that it is "developing along lines familiar in the United States" (p. 171), or else, when the Russians prefer to follow their own track, to dismiss it as a "ridiculous and reckless fantasy" (p. 215). Secretary of Defense McNamara perused Sokolovskii and "remained unimpressed," for nowhere in the book did he find "a sophisticated analysis of nuclear war."[12]

The point to bear in mind, however, is that Soviet military literature, like all Soviet literature on politics broadly defined, is written in an elaborate code language. Its purpose is not to dazzle with originality and sophistication but to convey to the initiates messages of grave importance. Soviet policy makers may speak to one another plainly in private, but when they take pen in hand they invariably resort to an "Aesopian" language, a habit acquired when the forerunner of today's Communist party had to function in the Czarist underground. Buried in the flood of seemingly meaningless verbiage, nuggets of precious information on Soviet perceptions and intentions can more often than not be unearthed by a trained reader. In 1958-59 two American specialists employed by the RAND Corporation, Raymond L. Garthoff and Herbert S. Dinerstein, by skillfully deciphering Soviet literature on strategic problems and then interpreting this information against the background of the Soviet military tradition, produced a remarkably prescient forecast of actual Soviet military policies of the 1960s and 1970s.[13] Unfortunately, their findings were largely ignored by U.S. strategists from the scientific community who had convinced themselves that there was only one strategic doctrine appropriate to the age of nuclear weapons, and that therefore evidence indicating that the Soviets were adopting a different strategy could be safely disregarded.

This predisposition helps explain why U.S. strategists persistently ignored signs indicating that those who had control of Soviet Russia's nuclear arsenal were not thinking in terms of mutual deterrence. The calculated nonchalance with which Stalin at Potsdam reacted to President Truman's confidences about the American atomic bomb was a foretaste of things to come. Initial Soviet reactions to Hiroshima and Nagasaki were similar in tone: the atomic weapon had not in any significant manner altered the science of warfare or rendered obsolete the principles that had guided the Red Army in its victorious campaigns against the Wehrmacht. These basic laws, known as the five "constant principles" that win wars, had been formulated by Stalin in 1942. They were, in declining order of importance: "stability of the home front," followed by morale of the armed forces, quantity and quality of the divisions, *military equipment,* and, finally, ability of the commanders.[14] There was no such thing as an "absolute weapon"—weapons altogether occupied a subordinate place in warfare; defense against atomic bombs was entirely possible.[15] This was disconcerting, to be sure, but it could be explained away as a case of sour grapes. After all, the Soviet Union had no atomic bomb, and it was not in its interest to seem overly impressed by a weapon on which its rival enjoyed a monopoly.[16]

In September 1949 the Soviet Union exploded a nuclear device. Disconcertingly, its attitude to nuclear weapons did not change, at any rate not in public. For the remaining four years, until Stalin's death, the Soviet high command continued to deny that nuclear weapons required fundamental revisions of accepted military doctrine. With a bit of good will, this obduracy could still have been rationalized: for although the Soviet Union now had the weapon, it still lacked adequate means of delivering it across continents insofar as it had few intercontinental bombers (intercontinental rockets were regarded in the West as decades away). The United States, by contrast, possessed not only a fleet of strategic bombers but also numerous air bases in countries adjoining Soviet Russia. So once again one could find a persuasive explanation of why the Russians refused to see the light. It seemed reasonable to expect that as soon as they had acquired both a stockpile of atomic bombs and a fleet of strategic bombers, they would adjust their doctrine to conform with the American.

Events that ensued immediately after Stalin's death seemed to lend credence to these expectations. Between 1953 and 1957 a debate took place in the pages of Soviet publications which, for all its textural obscurity, indicated that a new school of Soviet strategic thinkers had arisen to challenge the conventional wisdom. The most articulate speaker for this new school, General N. Talenskii, argued that the advent of nuclear weapons, especially the hydrogen bomb that had just appeared on the scene, did fundamentally alter the nature of warfare. The sheer destructiveness of these weapons was such that one could no longer talk of a socialist strategy automatically overcoming the strategy of capitalist countries: the same rules of warfare now applied to both social systems. For the first time doubt was cast on the immutability of Stalin's "five constant principles." In the oblique manner in which Soviet debates on matters of such import are invariably conducted, Talenskii was saying that perhaps, after all, war had ceased to represent a viable policy option. More important yet, speeches delivered by leading Soviet politicians in the winter of 1953/54 seemed to support the thesis advanced by President Eisenhower in his United Nations address of December 1953 that nuclear war could spell the demise of civilization. In an address delivered on March 12, 1954, and reported the following day in *Pravda,* Stalin's immediate successor, Georgii Malenkov, echoed Eisenhower's sentiments: a new world war would unleash a holocaust that "with the present means of warfare, means the destruction of world civilization."[17]

This assault on its traditional thinking—and, obliquely, on its traditional role—engendered a furious reaction from the Soviet military establishment. The Red Army was not about to let itself be relegated to the status of a militia whose principle task was averting war rather than winning it. Malenkov's unorthodox views on war almost certainly contributed to his downfall; at any rate, his dismissal in February 1955 as party leader was accompanied by a barrage of press denunciations of the notion that war had become unfeasible. There are strong indications that Malenkov's chief rival, Khrushchev, capitalized on the discontent of the military to form with it an alliance with whose help he eventually rode to power. The successful military counterattack seems to have been led by the World War II hero Marshal Georgii Zhukov, whom Khrushchev made his minister of defense and brought into the Presidium. The guidelines of Soviet nuclear strategy, still in force today, were formulated during the first two years of Khrushchev's tenure (1955-57), under the leadership of Zhukov himself. They resulted in the unequivocal rejection of the notion of the "absolute weapon" and all the theories that U.S. strategists had deduced from it. Stalin's view of the military "constants" was implicitly reaffirmed. Thus, the re-Stalinization of Soviet life, so noticeable in recent years, manifested itself first in military doctrine.

To understand this unexpected turn of events—so unexpected that most U.S. military theorists thus far have not been able to come to terms with it—one must take into account the function performed by the military in the Soviet system.

Unlike the United States, the Soviet government needs and wants a large military force. It has many uses for it, at home and abroad. As a regime that rests neither on tradition nor on a popular mandate, it sees in its military the most effective manifestation of government omnipotence, the very presence of which discourages any serious opposition from raising its head in the country as well as in its dependencies. It is, after all, the Red Army that keeps Eastern Europe within the Soviet camp. Furthermore, since the regime is driven by ideology, internal politics, and economic exigencies steadily to expand, it requires an up-to-date military force capable of seizing opportunities that may present themselves along the Soviet Union's immensely long frontier or even beyond. The armed forces of the Soviet Union thus have much more to do than merely protect the country from potential aggressors: they are the mainstay of the regime's authority and a principal instrumentality of its internal and external policies. Given the shaky status of the Communist regime internally, the declining appeal of its ideology, and the noncompetitiveness of its goods on world markets, a persuasive case can even be made that, ruble for ruble, expenditures on the military represent for the Soviet leadership an excellent and entirely "rational" capital investment.

For this reason alone (and there were other compelling reasons too, as we shall see), the Soviet leadership could not accept the theory of mutual deterrence.[18] After all, this theory, pushed to its logical conclusion, means that a country can rely for its security on a finite number of nuclear warheads and on an appropriate quantity of delivery vehicles, so that, apart perhaps from some small mobile forces needed for local actions, the large and costly traditional military establishments can be disbanded. Whatever the intrinsic military merits of this doctrine may be, its broader implications are entirely unacceptable to a regime like the Soviet one for whom military power serves not only (or even primarily) to deter external aggressors, but also and above all to ensure internal stability and permit external expansion. Thus, ultimately, it is *political* rather than strictly strategic or fiscal considerations that may be said to have determined Soviet reactions to nuclear weapons and shaped the content of Soviet nuclear strategy. As a result, Soviet advocates of mutual deterrence like Talenskii were gradually silenced. By the mid-1960s the country adopted what in military jargon is referred to as a "war-fighting" and "war-winning" doctrine.

Given this fundamental consideration, the rest followed with a certain inexorable logic. The formulation of Soviet strategy in the nuclear age was turned over to the military, who are in complete control of the Ministery of Defense. (Two American observers describe this institution as a "uniformed empire.")[19] The Soviet General Staff had only recently emerged from winning one of the greatest wars in history. Immensely confident of their own abilities, scornful of what they perceived as the minor contribution of the United States to the Nazi defeat, inured to casualties running into tens of millions, the Soviet generals tackled the task with relish. Like their counterparts in the U.S. Army, they were professionally inclined to denigrate the exorbitant claims made on behalf of the new weapon by strategists drawn from the scientific community; unlike the Americans, however, they did not have to pay much heed to the civilians. In its essentials, Soviet nuclear doctrine as it finally emerged is not all that different from what American doctrine might have been had military and geopolitical rather than fiscal considerations played the decisive role here as they did there.

Soviet military theorists reject the notion that technology (i.e., weapons) decides strategy. They perceive the relationship to be the reverse: strategic objectives determine the procurement and application of weapons. They agree that the introduction of nuclear weapons has profoundly affected warfare, but deny that nuclear weapons have altered its essential quality. The novelty of nuclear weapons consists not in their destructiveness—that is, after all, a matter of degree, and a country like the Soviet Union, which, as Soviet generals proudly boast, suffered in World War II the loss of over 20 million casualties as well as the destruction of 1,710 towns, over 70,000 villages, and some 32,000 industrial establishments to win the war and emerge as a global power, is not to be intimidated by the prospect of destruction.[20] Rather, the innovation consists of the fact that nuclear weapons, coupled with intercontinental missiles, can by themselves carry out strategic missions that previously were accomplished only by means of prolonged tactical operations:

> Nuclear missiles have altered the relationship of tactical, operational, and strategic acts of the armed conflict. If in the past the strategic end-result was secured by a succession of sequential, most often long-term, efforts [and] comprised the sum of tactical and operational successes, strategy being able to realize its intentions only with the assistance of the art of operations and tactics, then today, by means of powerful nuclear strikes, strategy can attain its objectives directly.[21]

In other words, military strategy, rather than a casualty of technology, has, thanks to technology become more central than ever. By adopting this view, Soviet theorists believe themselves to have adapted modern technological innovations in weaponry to the traditions of military science.

Implicit in all this is the idea that nuclear war is feasible and that the basic function of warfare, as defined by Clausewitz, remains permanently valid, whatever breakthroughs may occur in technology. "It is well known that the essential nature of *war as a continuation of politics does not change with changing technology and armament.*"[22] This code phrase from Sokolovskii's authoritative manual was certainly hammered out with all the care that in the United States is lavished on an amendment to the Constitution. It spells the rejection of the whole basis on which U.S. strategy has come to rest: thermonuclear war is not suicidal, it can be fought and won, and thus resort to war must not be ruled out.

In addition (though we have no solid evidence to this effect) it seems likely that Soviet strategists reject the mutual-deterrence theory on several technical grounds of a kind that have been advanced by American critics of this theory like Albert Wohlstetter, Herman Kahn, and Paul Nitze:

1. Mutual deterrence postulates a certain finality about weapons technology: it does not allow for further scientific breakthroughs that could result in the deterrent's becoming neutralized. On the offensive side, for example, there is the possibility of significant improvements in the accuracy of ICBMs or striking innovations in antisubmarine warfare; on the defensive, satellites that are essential for early warning of an impending attack could be blinded and lasers could be put to use to destroy incoming missiles.
2. Mutual deterrence constitutes "passive defense," which usually leads to defeat. It threatens punishment to the aggressor after he has struck, which may or may not deter him from striking; it cannot prevent him from carrying out his designs. The latter objective requires the application of "active defense"—i.e., nuclear preemption.
3. The threat of a second strike, which underpins the mutual-deterrence doctrine, may prove ineffectual. The side that has suffered the destruction of the bulk of its nuclear forces in a surprise first strike may find that it has so little of a deterrent left, and the enemy so much, that the cost of striking back in retaliation would be exposing its own cities to total destruction by the enemy's third strike. The result could be a paralysis of will, and capitulation instead of a second strike.

Soviet strategists make no secret of the fact that they regard the U.S. doctrine (with which, judging by the references in their literature, they are thoroughly familiar) as second rate. In their view, U.S. strategic doctrine is obsessed with a single weapon that it "absolutizes" at the expense of everything else that military experience teaches soldiers to take into account. Its philosophical foundations are "idealism" and "metaphysics"—i.e., currents that engage in speculative discussions of objects (in this case, weapons) and of their "intrinsic" qualities, rather than relying on pragmatic considerations drawn from experience.[23]

Since the mid-1960s, the proposition that thermonuclear war would be suicidal for both parties has been used by the Russians largely as a commodity for export. Its chief proponents include staff members of the Moscow Institute of the USA and Canada, and Soviet participants at Pugwash, Dartmouth, and similar international conferences, who are assigned the task of strengthening the hand of antimilitary intellectual circles in the West. Inside the Soviet Union, such talk is generally denounced as "bourgeois pacifism."[24]

In the Soviet view, a nuclear war would be total and go beyond formal defeat of one side by the other: "War must not simply [be] the defeat of the enemy, it must be his destruction. This condition has become the basis of Soviet military strategy," according to the *Military-Historical Journal.*[25] Limited nuclear war, flexible response, escalation, damage limiting, and all the other numerous refinements of U.S. strategic doctrine find no place in its Soviet counterpart (although, of course, they are taken into consideration in Soviet operational planning).

For Soviet generals the decisive influence in the formulation of nuclear doctrine was the lessons of World War II, with which, for understandable reasons, they are virtually obsessed. This experience they seem to have supplemented with knowledge gained from professional scrutiny of the record of Nazi and Japanese offensive operations, as well as the balance sheet of British and American strategic bombing campaigns. More recently, the lessons of the Israeli-Arab wars of 1967 and 1973, in which they indirectly participated, seem also to have impressed Soviet strategists, reinforcing previously held convictions. They also follow the Western literature, tending to side with the critics of mutual deterrence. The result of all these diverse influences is a nuclear doctrine that assimilates into the main body of the Soviet military tradition the technical implications of nuclear warfare without surrendering any of the fundamentals of this tradition.

The strategic doctrine adopted by the USSR over the past two decades calls for a policy diametrically opposite to that adopted in the United States by the predominant community of civilian strategists: not deterrence but victory, not sufficiency in weapons but superiority, not retaliation but offensive action. The doctrine has five related elements. (1) preemption (first strike), (2) quantitative superiority in arms, (3) counterforce targeting, (4) combined-arms operations, and (5) defense. I shall take up each of these elements in turn.

PREEMPTION

The costliest lesson that the Soviet military learned in World War II was the importance of surprise. Because Stalin thought he had an understanding with Hitler, and because he was afraid to provoke his Nazi ally, he forbade the Red Army to mobilize for the German attack of which he had had ample warning. As a result of this strategy of "passive defense," Soviet forces suffered frightful losses and were nearly defeated. This experience etched itself very deeply on the minds of the Soviet commanders: in their theoretical writings no point is emphasized more consistently than the need never again to allow themselves to be caught in a surprise attack. Nuclear weapons make this requirement especially urgent because, according to Soviet theorists, the decision in a nuclear conflict in all probability will be arrived at in the initial hours. In a nuclear war the Soviet Union, therefore, would not again have at its disposal the time that it enjoyed in 1941-42 to mobilize reserves for a victorious counteroffensive after absorbing devastating setbacks.

Given the rapidity of modern warfare (an ICBM can traverse the distance between the USSR and the United States in thirty minutes), not to be surprised by the enemy means, in effect, to inflict surprise on him. Once the latter's ICBMs have left their silos, once his bombers have taken to the air and his submarines to sea, a counterattack is greatly reduced in effectiveness. These considerations call for a preemptive strike. Soviet theorists draw an insistent, though to an outside observer very fuzzy, distinction between "preventive" and "preemptive" attacks. They claim that the Soviet Union will never start a war—i.e., it will never launch a preventive attack—but once it had concluded that an attack upon it was imminent, it would not hesitate to preempt. They argue that historical experience indicates that outbreaks of hostilities are generally preceded by prolonged diplomatic crises and military preparations that signal to an alert command an imminent threat and the need to act. Though the analogy is not openly drawn, the action that Soviet strategists seem to have in mind is that taken by the Israelis in 1967, a notably successful example of "active defense" involving a well-timed preemptive strike. (In 1973, by contrast, the Israelis pursued the strategy of "passive defense," with unhappy consequences.) The Soviet doctrine of nuclear preemption was formulated in the late 1950s and described at the time by Garthoff and Dinerstein in the volumes cited above.

A corollary of the preemption strategy holds that a country's armed forces must always be in a state of high combat readiness so as to be able to go over to active operations with the least delay. Nuclear warfare grants no time for mobilization. Stress on the maintenance of a large ready force is one of the constant themes of Soviet military literature. It helps explain the immense land forces that the USSR maintains at all times and equips with the latest weapons as they roll off the assembly lines.

QUANTITATIVE SUPERIORITY

There is no indication that the Soviet military shares the view prevalent in the U.S. that in the nuclear age numbers of weapons do not matter once a certain quantity has been attained. They do like to pile up all sorts of weapons, new on top of old, throwing away nothing that might come in handy. This propensity to accumulate hardware is usually dismissed by Western observers with contemptuous references to a Russian habit dating back to Czarist days. It is not, however, as mindless as it may appear. For although Soviet strategists believe that the ultimate outcome in a nuclear war will be decided in the initial hours of the conflict, they also believe that a nuclear war will be of long duration: to consummate victory—that is, to destroy the enemy—may take months or even longer. Under these conditions, the possession of a large arsenal of nuclear delivery systems, as well as of other types of weapons, may well prove to be of critical importance. Although prohibited by self-imposed limitations agreed upon in 1972 at SALT I from exceeding a set number of ICBM launchers, the Soviet Union is constructing large numbers of so-called intermediate range ballistic missile launchers (i.e., launchers of less than intercontinental range), not covered by SALT. Some of these could be rapidly converted into regular intercontinental launchers should the need arise.[26]

Reliance on quantity has another cause, namely, the peculiarly destructive capability of modern missiles equipped with multiple independently targetable reentry vehicles, or MIRVs. The nose cones of MIRVed missiles, which both superpowers possess, when in midcourse, split like a peapod to launch several warheads, each aimed at a separate target. A single missile equipped with three MIRVs of sufficient accuracy, yield, and reliability can destroy up to three of the enemy's missiles—provided, of course, it catches them in their silos, before they have been fired (which adds another inducement to preemption). Theoretically, assuming high accuracy and reliability, should the entire American force of 1,054 ICBMs be MIRVed (so far only half of them have been MIRVed), it would take only 540 American ICBMs, each with three MIRVs, to attack the entire Soviet force of 1,618 ICBMs. The result would leave the United States with 514 ICBMs and the USSR with few survivors. Unlikely as the possibility of an American preemptive strike may be, Soviet planners apparently prefer to take no chances; they want to be in a position rapidly to replace ICBMs lost to a sudden enemy first strike. Conversely, given its doctrine of preemption, the Soviet Union wants to be in a position to destroy the largest number of American missiles with the smallest number of its own, so as to be able to face down the threat of a U.S. second strike. Its most powerful ICBM, the SS-18, is said to have been tested with up to ten MIRVs (compared to three of the Minuteman 3, America's only MIRVed ICBM). It has been estimated that 300 of these giant Soviet missiles, authorized under SALT I, could seriously threaten the American arsenal of ICBMs.

COUNTERFORCE

Two terms commonly used in the jargon of modern strategy are *counterforce* and *countervalue.* Both terms refer to the nature of the target of a strategic nuclear weapon. Counterforce means that the principal objectives of one's nuclear missiles are the enemy's forces—i.e., his launchers as well as the related command and communication facilities. Countervalue means that one's principal targets are objects of national "value," namely, the enemy's population and industrial centers.

Given the predominantly defensive (retaliatory) character of current U.S. strategy, it is naturally predisposed to a counter*value* targeting policy. The central idea of the U.S. strategy of deterrence holds that should the Soviet Union dare to launch a surprise first strike at the United States, the latter would use its surviving missiles to lay waste Soviet cities. It is taken virtually for granted in this country that no nation would consciously expose itself to the risk of having its urban centers destroyed—an assumption that derives from British military theory of the 1920s and 1930s, and that influenced the RAF to concentrate on strategic bombing raids on German cities in World War II.

The Soviet high command has never been much impressed with the whole philosophy of countervalue strategic bombing, and during World War II resisted the temptation to attack German cities. This negative attitude to bombing of civilians is conditioned not by humanitarian considerations but by cold, professional assessments of the effects of that kind of strategic bombing as revealed by the Allied Strategic Bombing Surveys. The findings of these surveys were largely ignored in the United States, but they seem to have made a strong impression in the USSR. Not being privy to the internal discussions of the Soviet military, we can do no better than consult the writings of an eminent British scientist noted for his pro-Soviet sympathies, P. M. S. Blackett, whose remarkable book *Fear, War, and the Bomb,* published in 1948-49, indicated with great prescience the lines that Soviet strategic thinking were subsequently to take.

Blackett, who won the Nobel Prize for Physics in 1948, had worked during the war in British Operations Research. He concluded that strategic bombing was ineffective and wrote his book as an impassioned critique of the idea of using atomic weapons as a strategic deterrent. Translating the devastation wrought upon Germany into nuclear terms, he calculated that it represented the equivalent of the destruction that would have been caused by 400 "improved" Hiroshima-type atomic bombs. Yet despite such punishment, Nazi Germany did not collapse. Given the much greater territory of the Soviet Union and a much lower population density, he argued, it would require "thousands" of atomic bombs to produce decisive results in a war between American and Russia.[27] Blackett minimized the military effects of the atomic bombing on Japan. He recalled that in Hiroshima trains were operating forty-eight hours after the blast; that industries were left almost undamaged and could have been back in full production within a month; and that if the most elementary civil defense precautions had been observed, civilian casualties would have been substantially reduced.

Blackett's book ran so contrary to prevailing opinion and was furthermore so intemperately anti-American in tone that its conclusions were rejected out of hand in the West—too hastily, it appears in retrospect. For while it is true that the advent of hydrogen bombs a few years later largely invalidated the estimates on which he had relied, Blackett correctly anticipated Soviet reactions. Analyzing the results of Allied saturation bombing of Germany, Soviet generals concluded that it was largely a wasted effort. Sokolovskii cites in his manual the well-known figures showing that German military productivity rose throughout the war until the fall of 1944, and concludes: "It was not so much the economic struggle and economic exhaustion [i.e., countervalue bombing] that were the causes for the defeat of Hitler's Germany, but rather the armed conflict and the defeat of its armed forces [i.e., the counterforce strategy pursued by the Red Army]."[28]

Soviet nuclear strategy is counter*force* oriented. It targets for destruction—at any rate, in the initial strike—not the enemy's cities but his military forces and their command and communication facilities. Its primary aim is to destroy not civilians but soldiers and their leaders, and to undermine not so much the will to resist as the capability to do so. In the words of Grechko:

> The Strategic Rocket Forces, which constitute the basis of the military might of our armed forces, are designed to annihilate the means of the enemy's nuclear attack, large groupings of his armies, and his military bases; to destroy his military industries; [and] to disorganize the political and military administration of the aggressor as well as his rear and transport.[29]

Any evidence that the United States may contemplate switching to a counterforce strategy, such as occasionally crops up, throws Soviet generals into a tizzy of excitement. It clearly frightens them far more than the threat to Soviet cities posed by the countervalue strategic doctrine.

COMBINED-ARMS OPERATIONS

Soviet theorists regard strategic nuclear forces (organized since 1960 into a separate arm, the Strategic Rocket Forces) to be the decisive branch of the armed services, in the sense that the ultimate outcome of modern war would be settled by nuclear exchanges. But since nuclear war, in their view, must lead not only to the enemy's defeat but also to his destruction (i.e., his incapacity to offer further resistance), they consider it necessary to make preparations for the follow-up phase, which may entail a prolonged war of attrition. At this stage of the conflict, armies will be needed to occupy the enemy's territory, and navies to interdict his lanes of communications. "In the course of operations [battles], armies will basically complete the final destruction of the enemy brought about by strikes of nuclear rocket weapons."[30] Soviet theoretical writings unequivocally reject reliance on any one strategy (such as the *Blitzkrieg*) or on any one weapon, to win wars. They believe that a nuclear war will require the employment of all arms to attain final victory.

The large troop concentrations of Warsaw Pact forces in Eastern Europe—well in excess of reasonable defense requirements—make sense if viewed in the light of Soviet combined-arms doctrine. They are there not only to have the capacity to launch a surprise land attack against NATO but also to attack and seize Western Europe with a minimum of damage to its cities and industries *after* the initial strategic nuclear exchanges have taken place, partly to keep Europe hostage, partly to exploit European productivity as a replacement for that of which the Soviet Union would have been deprived by an American second strike.

As for the ocean-going navy that the Soviet Union has now acquired, it consists primarily of submarines and ground-based naval air forces, and apparently would have the task of cleaning the seas of U.S. ships of all types and cutting the sea lanes connecting the United States with allied powers and sources of raw materials.

The notion of an extended nuclear war is deeply embedded in Soviet thinking, despite its being dismissed by Western strategists who think of war as a one-two exchange. As Blackett noted sarcastically already in 1948-49: "Some armchair strategists (including some atomic scientists) tend to ignore the inevitable counter-moves of the enemy. More chess playing and less nuclear physics might have instilled a greater sense of the realities."[31] He predicted that a World War III waged with the atomic bombs then available would last longer than either of its predecessors and require combined-arms operations—which seems to be the current Soviet view of the matter.

DEFENSE

As noted, the U.S. theory of mutual deterrence postulates that no effective defense can be devised against an all-out nuclear attack: it is this postulate that makes such a war appear totally irrational. In order to make this premise valid, American civilian strategists have argued against a civil defense program, against the ABM, and against air defenses.

Nothing illustrates better the fundamental differences between the two strategic doctrines than their attitudes to defense against a nuclear attack. The Russians agreed to certain imprecisely defined limitations on ABM after they had initiated a program in this direction, apparently because they were unable to solve the technical problems involved and feared the United States would forge ahead in this field. However, they then proceeded to build a tight ring of antiaircraft defenses around the country while also developing a serious program of civil defense.

Before dismissing Soviet civil defense efforts as wishful thinking, as is customary in Western circles, two facts must be emphasized.

One is that the Soviet Union does not regard civil defense to be exclusively for the protection of ordinary civilians. Its chief function seems to be to protect what in Russia are known as the "cadres," that is, the political and military leaders as well as industrial managers and skilled workers—those who could reestablish the political and economic system once the war was over. Judging by Soviet definitions, civil defense has as much to do with the proper functioning of the country during and immediately after the war as with holding down casualties. Its organizations, presently under Deputy Minister of Defense Colonel General A. Altunin, seems to be a kind of shadow government charged with responsibility for administering the country under the extreme stresses of nuclear war and its immediate aftermath.[32]

Second, the Soviet Union is inherently less vulnerable than the United States to a countervalue attack. According to the most recent Soviet census (1970), the USSR had only nine cities with a population of 1 million or more; the aggregate population of these cities was 20.5 million, or 8.5 percent of the country's total. The United States 1970 census showed thirty-five metropolitan centers with over 1 million inhabitants, totaling 84.5 million people, or 41.5 percent of the country's aggregate. It takes no professional strategist to visualize what these figures mean. In World War II, the Soviet Union lost 20 million inhabitants out of a population of 170 million (i.e., 12 percent), yet the country not only survived but emerged stronger politically and militarily than it had ever been. Allowing for the population growth that has occurred since then, this experience suggests that as of today the USSR could absorb the loss of 30 million of its people and be no worse off, in terms of human casualties, than it had been at the conclusion of World War II. In other words, all of the USSR's multimillion cities could be destroyed without trace or survivors, and, provided that its essential cadres had been saved, it would emerge less hurt in terms of casualties than it was in 1945.

Such figures are beyond the comprehension of most Americans. But clearly a country that since 1914 has lost, as a result of two world wars, a civil war, famine, and various "purges," perhaps up to 60 million citizens must define "unacceptable damage" differently from the United States, which has known no famines or purges and whose deaths from all the wars waged since 1775 are estimated at 650,000—fewer casualties than Russia suffered in the 900-day siege of Leningrad in World War II alone. Such a country tends also to assess the rewards of defense in much more realistic terms.

How significant are these recondite doctrinal differences? It has been my invariable experience when lecturing on these matters that during the question period someone in the audience will get up and ask: "But is it not true that we and the Russians already possess enough nuclear weapons to destroy each other ten times over" (or fifty, or a hundred—the figures vary)? My temptation is to reply: "Certainly. But we also have enough bullets to shoot every man, woman, and child, and enough matches to set the whole world on fire. The point lies not in our ability to wreak total destruction: it lies in intent." And insofar as military doctrine is indicative of intent, what the Russians think to do with their nuclear arsenal is a matter of utmost importance that calls for close scrutiny.

Enough has already been said to indicate the disparities between American and Soviet strategic doctrines of the nuclear age. These differences may be most pithily summarized by stating that whereas we view nuclear weapons as a deterrent, the Russians see them as a "compellant"—with all the consequences that follow. Now it must be granted that the actual, operative differences between the two doctrines may not be quite as sharp as they appear in the public literature: it is true that our deterrence doctrine leaves room for some limited offensive action, just as the Russians include elements of deterrence in their "war-fighting" and "war-winning" doctrine. Admittedly, too, a country's military doctrine never fully reveals how it would behave under actual combat conditions. And yet the differences here are sharp and fundamental enough, and the relationship of Soviet doctrine to Soviet deployments sufficiently close, to suggest that ignoring or not taking seriously Soviet military doctrine may have very detrimental effects on U.S. security. There is something innately destabilizing in the very fact that we consider nuclear war unfeasible and suicidal for both, and our chief adversary views it as feasible and winnable for himself.

SALT misses the point at issue as long as it addresses itself mainly to the question of numbers of strategic weapons: equally important are qualitative improvements within the existing quotas, and the size of regular land and sea forces. Above all, however, looms the question of intent: as long as the Soviets persist in adhering to the Clausewitzian maxim on the function of war, mutual deterrence does not really exist. And unilateral deterrence is feasible only if we understand the Soviet war-winning strategy and make it impossible for them to succeed.

NOTES

1. "The Real Paul Warnke," *New Republic,* 26 March 1977, p. 23.

2. N. V. Karabanov in N. V. Karabanov et al., *Filosofskoe nasledie V. I. Lenina i problemy sovremennoi voiny* [The philosophical heritage of V. I. Lenin and the problems of contemporary war] (Moscow, 1972), pp. 18-19, cited in Leon Goure, Foy D. Kohler, and Mose L. Harvey, eds., *The Role of Nuclear Forces in Current Soviet Strategy* (Coral Gables, Fla.: University of Miami Center for Advanced International Studies, 1974), p. 60.

3. A. A. Grechko, *Vooruzhonnye sily sovetskogo gosudarstva* [The armed forces of the Soviet state] (Moscow, 1975), p. 345.

4. Russell F. Weigley, *The American Way of War* (New York: Macmillan, 1973), p. 368.

5. Matthew B. Ridgway, *Soldier* (1956), pp. 296-97.

6. In Michael Howard, ed., *The Theory and Practice of War* (London: Cassell, 1965), p. 291.

7. Benjamin S. Lambeth, *Selective Nuclear Options in American and Soviet Strategic Policy,* Paper R-2034-DDRE (Santa Monica, Calif.: Rand Corporation, 1976), p. 14. This study analyzes and approves of the refinement introduced into the U.S. doctrine by James R. Schlesinger as secretary of defense in the form of "limited-response options."

8. Interview with *Playboy,* March 1977, p. 72.

9. Grechko, *Vooruzhunnye sily,* pp. 347-48, emphasis added.

10. *Voennaia strategiia* (Moscow, 1962). Since 1962 there have been two revised editions (1963 and 1968). The 1962 edition was immediately translated into Englsh, but currently the best version is that edited by Harriet Fast Scott (New York: Crane, Russak, 1975), which renders the third edition but collates its text with the preceding two.

11. To date, twelve volumes in this series have been translated into English and made publicly available through the U.S. Government Printing Office.

12. William W. Kaufmann, *The McNamara Strategy* (New York: Harper & Row, 1964), p. 97.

13. Garthoff's principal works are *Soviet Military Doctrine* (Glencoe, Ill.: Free Press, 1953), *Soviet Strategy in the Nuclear Age* (New York: Praeger, 1962), and *The Soviet Image of Future War* (Washington, D.C.: Public Affairs Press, 1959). Herbert S. Dinerstein wrote *War and the Soviet Union* (New York: Praeger, 1959).

14. Cited in J. M. Mackintosh, *The Strategy and Tactics of Soviet Foreign Policy* (London: Oxford University Press, 1962), pp. 90-91, emphasis added.

15. Articles in the *New Times* for 1945-46 cited in P. M. S. Blackett, *Fear, War and the Bomb* (New York: Whittlesey House, 1949), pp. 163-65.

16. We now know that orders to proceed with the development of a Soviet atomic bomb were issued by Stalin in June 1942, probably as a result of information relayed by Klaus Fuchs concerning the Manhattan Project, on which he was working at Los Alamos (*Bulletin of the Atomic Scientists* 23, no. 10 [December 1967]: 15).

17. Dinerstein, *War and the Soviet Union,* p. 71.

18. I would like to stress the word *theory,* for the Russians

certainly accept the *fact* of deterrence. The difference is that whereas American theorists of mutual deterrence regard this condition as mutually desirable and permanent, Soviet strategists regard it as undesirable and transient: they are entirely disinclined to allow us the capability of deterring them.

19. Matthew P. Gallagher and Karl F. Spielmann, Jr., *Soviet Decision-Making for Defense* (New York: Praeger, 1972), p. 39.

20. The figures are from Grechko, *Vooruzhonnye sily*, p. 97.

21. *Methodologicheskie problemy voennoi teorii i praktiki* [Methodological problems of military theory and practice] (Moscow: Ministry of Defense of the USSR, 1969), p. 288.

22. V. D. Sokolovskii, *Soviet Military Strategy* (Santa Monica, Calif.: Rand Corporation, 1963), p. 99, emphasis added.

23. See, e.g., *Methodologicheskie problemy*, pp. 289-90.

24. Goure et al., *The Role of Nuclear Forces*, p. 9.

25. Cited in ibid., p. 106.

26. I have in mind the SS-20, a recently developed Soviet rocket. This is a two-stage version of the intercontinental SS-16 that can be turned into an SS-16 with the addition of a third booster and fired from the same launcher. Its production is not restricted by SALT I and not covered by the Vladivostok Accord.

27. Blackett, *Fear*, p. 88. As a matter of fact, recent unofficial Soviet calculations stress that the United States dropped on Vietnam the TNT equivalent of 650 Hiroshima-type bombs—also without winning the war: *Kommunist Vorruzhonnykh Sil* [The Communist of the armed forces], no. 24 (December 1973), p. 27, cited in Goure et al., *The Role of Nuclear Forces*, p. 104.

28. Sokolovskii, *Soviet Military Strategy*, 3d ed., p. 21.

29. A. A. Grechko, *Na strazhe mira i stroitel'stva Kommunizma* [Guarding peace and the construction of communism] (Moscow, 1971), p. 41.

30. *Methodologicheskie problemy*, p. 288.

31. Blackett, *Fear*, p. 79.

32. On the subject of civil defense, see Leon Goure, *War Survival in Soviet Strategy* (Coral Gables, Fla.: University of Miami Center for Advanced International Studies, 1976).

How to think about Soviet military doctrine

Benjamin S. Lambeth

INTRODUCTION

Throughout most of the past two decades, Western analysis of Soviet military doctrine was largely the esoteric preserve of a relatively small body of specialists in Soviet strategic affairs. Since the emergence of SALT and the ambitious Soviet military build-up that first became apparent during the late 1960s, however, Soviet doctrine has increasingly become a topic of widespread discussion throughout the Western defense research community as a whole. Moreover, with the mounting popular disenchantment over détente and the rising concern over what many regard as a disturbing trend in Soviet weapons modernization, Soviet military philosophy—with its avowed emphasis on war fighting—has additionally surfaced as a touchstone of growing attention and controversy among journalistic commentators and the public at large.

This resurgent concern over what the Soviets are up to and what the United States should do about it is a healthy trend. For years, the U.S. defense community remained substantially oblivious to the content of Soviet military thought, relying primarily on Western strategic logic and what were widely held to be "objective" principles of nuclear strategy as the guiding criteria for U.S. strategic planning and force design. As long as the United States enjoyed a commanding lead in military technology and a position of clear numerical preeminence in the strategic balance, that was an approach that we could afford to employ with little operational consequence. Today, with the Soviet force posture roughly equivalent to our own in size and capability, it has become far more difficult to ignore the enunciated principles of Soviet doctrine with equanimity.

Now that the past asymmetries between U.S. and Soviet forces have largely been eradicated and strategic equivalence has become a declared goal of both superpowers' defense policies, the respective force employment concepts of the two sides have risen markedly in importance as factors affecting each country's overall strategic prowess. It is almost axiomatic that in any confrontation between matched opponents, the side that commands the more astute array of strategic concepts is the side more likely to dominate in crises and war. The Soviets are keenly attentive to developments in U.S. strategic policy and are fond of intimating that, in their view, the USSR possesses a superior military strategy. Whether or not that is the case, there is little denying that doctrinal adroitness and the operational effectiveness of war plans can make a great deal of difference in the outcome of confrontations between otherwise equal opponents. Soviet military doctrine, in marked contrast to prevailing U.S. strategic orthodoxy, is highly systematic, unambiguously martial, and explicitly geared to a belief that should deterrence fail, some recognizable form of victory is theoretically attainable through the skillful exploitation of initiative, surprise, and shock. Coupled with the dramatic Soviet force expansion and modernization effort that has been steadily under way since the mid-1960s, this robust image of nuclear war and the seemingly confident belief in the military utility of strategic weaponry that informs it warrant legitimate concern about Soviet intentions and serious attention to what the Soviets have to say about deterrence and war.

At the extremes, one finds two opposing views on the significance of Soviet doctrine prevalent in contemporary American strategic discourse. The first view holds that the essentials of official Soviet thought on deterrence and war are abundantly evident in a large body of translated Soviet military writings readily available to any observer willing to take the time to read them. Those of this persuasion argue that the Soviets mean what they say, that their declared views on the importance of being able to fight and win a nuclear war are inseparably linked to their ongoing strategic force improvements, and that simple prudence requires us to heed Soviet doctrine not only as a valid indicator of underlying Soviet strategic beliefs but also as an important baseline from which U.S. strategic force planning should be conducted.

At the opposite end of the spectrum, there is the school of thought that maintains that whatever Soviet doctrine may superficially say should not be taken at face value because it emanates solely from professional military men and, as such, cannot reflect the real beliefs of those authoritative civilians on the Politburo who are ultimately responsible for Soviet strategic programs and behavior. Those espousing this viewpoint maintain that the Soviet weapons acquisition process is driven primarily not by a priori doctrinal imperatives, but by such institutional factors as program momentum, bureaucratic politics, technological determinism, and reactions to perceived external threats—factors that, by and large, shape the defense policies of all modern industrial powers, the United States not excluded. Moreover, they assert, the principles of doctrine represent, at best, merely a reflection of desiderata that Soviet military leaders regard as optimum in warfare rather than any codification of actual Soviet military expectations or rigid rules the Soviet leadership would feel compelled to follow in a real military showdown. As exemplified by both the ABM Treaty and the traditional pattern of Soviet circumspection in past crises, this school argues, Soviet political leaders, at bottom, accept mutual deterrence as the only solution to the East-West nuclear dilemma, notwithstanding the militancy and bombast of Soviet doctrinal writings.

It is not the purpose here to adjudicate these countervailing arguments or to take sides in the debate, although, as it will become clear presently, the following discussion will tend to treat the former view somewhat more sympathetically than the latter. Nor is it to reconstruct in detail the specific axioms and principles of Soviet military doctrine, which have already been dealt with at great length in the academic literature and are by now generally familiar to most attentive students of strategic affairs. Rather, its objective is to highlight the key themes and propositions of Soviet doctrine and offer some perspectives on how—and with what reservations—they should be used as a basis for understanding broader Soviet strategic programs and behavior.

Protagonists on both sides of the debate may well bridle at the dichotomy of views etched out above and maintain that it unfairly reduces their highly nuanced arguments into easily demolishable straw men. While there is doubtless ample room for such criticism, the device nonetheless has its uses in defining the boundaries of contention on the issue. In fact, it is the thesis of this essay that both points of view contain important elements of truth and that reality consists of a complex amalgam of the two. It is a further argument of this essay that there is much we do not know—and cannot know—about Soviet motivations, either from formal doctrine or from other observables such as Soviet forces and deployment rates, and that all analyses of Soviet intentions based on these incomplete and frequently ephemeral indicators should be advanced with a seemly measure of diffidence and caution. The essential argument here is that while Soviet military doctrine tells us far less than we need to know about the motive forces behind Soviet behavior (and can be dangerously misleading if read out of context as a "master plan" of Soviet strategic goals), it nonetheless reveals a great deal about the general mind-set of the Soviet leadership regarding the preconditions of deterrence, the technical requirements for maintaining it, and the military responsibilities that would be energized in the event of its catastrophic failure.

KEY THEMES IN SOVIET DOCTRINE

In the formal taxonomy of Soviet military thought, military doctrine is typically defined as "the sum total of scientifically based views accepted by the country and its armed forces on the nature of contemporary wars that might be unleashed by the imperialists against the Soviet Union, on the goals and missions of the armed forces in such a war, on the methods of waging it, and also on the demands, which flow from such views, for the preparation of the country and the armed forces for war." This conception of doctrine constitutes the central component of a complex system of military thought that is stimulated by the inputs of military science (the lessons derived from reflection on past wars and the opportunities provided by modern weapons technology) and, in turn, provides inspiration and guidance for the development of military art (the actual strategy and tactics of wartime force application). Were one to delve deeply into the scholastic disquisitions of Soviet writers on the specific content of these interconnected categories and attempt to uncover the precise interaction and feedback relationships between them, one would quickly become ensnared in a philosophical byzantium and lose sight of the more practical question of what it is that constitutes the mainstream of Soviet thinking on war and peace. For the purpose of this discussion, it is enough to note that official Soviet views on deterrence and war are highly formulaic, aimed at providing broad criteria for peacetime weapons acquisition and wartime force employment. These views are continuously refined by theoreticians in the senior service academies, the Main Political Administration of the armed forces, and the Main Operations Directorate of the General Staff, and are integrated into finished doctrine at the Ministry of Defense level for review and formal approval by the Party leadership.

Reduced to its essentials, Soviet doctrine accords closely with the Clausewitzian dictum that war is simply a violent extension of politics and must be constantly conducted with sensitivity to the political objectives at stake. Soviet military writers fully appreciate that modern weapons technology, with its vast destructive potential, has dramatically altered the traditional *character* of war and elevated deterrence to a level of unprecedented importance in the Soviet hierarchy of national objectives. They steadfastly deny, however, that nuclear weapons have altered the *essence* of war as a political event or the long-standing responsibility of the national leadership to take every measure for assuring the survival of the Soviet state should it occur. From the vast body of published Soviet writings on military doctrine, we can extract the following propositions as constituting the most fundamental tenets of declared Soviet strategic thought.

THE BEST DETERRENT IS AN EFFECTIVE WAR-FIGHTING CAPABILITY

During the past fifteen years, American defense policy has increasingly come to rest on the belief that nuclear war is both irrational and unwinnable in any meaningful sense. We have adopted as our principal goal the maintenance of a survivable "assured destruction" capability so as to guarantee that any Soviet nuclear attack against the United States would cost a prompt retaliation that would visit unacceptable damage on Soviet society. In effect, this policy has placed abiding faith in the durability of deterrence and the assumption that the Soviet leadership would always remain circumspect under duress. In doing so, it has fixated almost exclusively on the preservation of deterrence at the expense of those concepts and capabilities that might be required to cope successfully in the event of war. It has also led to the adoption of a fairly explicit set of "sufficiency" criteria stipulating that an arsenal that projects an image of "equivalence" with Soviet forces and guarantees the capacity to inflict a specified level of retaliatory damage following the worst imaginable Soviet attack is adequate for underwriting U.S. national security.

There is nothing in known Soviet military thought that even approximates this American pattern of logic. Soviet strategic pronouncements typically maintain that the only acceptable deterrent is one that rests on the intrinsic capabilities of Soviet forces rather than on the rationality and good will of the enemy. In practical terms, this reduces to a doctrinal requirement for an inventory of forces and battle management infrastructure that could rapidly escalate to a level of high readiness in a crisis, carry out the necessary actions dictated by the circumstances, and retain control of the situation throughout, blunting the enemy's military initiatives and exerting every effort to assure the Soviet Union's emergence in a position of net advantage.

The principal difference between this strategic orientation and that of the United States is that American deterrence theory places primary stress on the required measures for preventing nuclear war in the first place, whereas Soviet thinking concentrates largely on the requirements for responding effectively and surviving in the event deterrence fails. This orientation can be seen across a wide range of observable features in the current Soviet strategic posture. It is also apparent in the absence of any discernible criteria of strategic "sufficiency" in Soviet force development. Soviet military planning adheres to no known yardsticks of strategic adequacy in any way comparable to the American "assured destruction" concept. Instead, it allows for an open-ended process of arms accumulation constrained only by domestic economic and technological resources, U.S. forbearance, and the formal protocols of negotiated arms limitation agreements. It would not be overly facetious to suggest that for Soviet military planners, the favored standard of sufficiency is the notion that "too much is not enough." This is not to say that the Soviet leaders have inexorably committed themselves to strategic superiority over the United States whatever the cost. They well understand the obstacles that would confront any such policy and doubtless appreciate that by precipitously galvanizing American fears and provoking a U.S. reaction in kind, they could well find themselves ultimately worse off in the strategic balance than they might have been otherwise.

On the other hand, the Soviets have given every indication—both at SALT and elsewhere—that they are determined to test the United States at every step to see what the traffic will bear and to acquire the most expansive and diversified inventory of weapons that U.S. tolerance and Soviet resources will permit. Although this behavior is not exclusively a product of Soviet military doctrine, it certainly accords with the basic injunctions of that doctrine, which hold that nuclear war—however gruesome to contemplate—is not impossible, that its occurrence would place great demands on Soviet capabilities, and that the best way to prevent it is to exert every practicable effort to prepare for it.

VICTORY IS POSSIBLE

Naturally associated with this doctrinal stress on the need for a credible war-waging posture is the conviction that some meaningful form of victory, even in high-intensity nuclear war, is theoretically attainable if the proper military actions are executed in a timely fashion. To be sure, two important qualifications must be attached to this statement. First, the fact that Soviet doctrine stipulates a requirement for the capability to wage nuclear war and insists that it would be irresponsible not to assume that victory is theoretically achievable does not mean that the Soviet military leadership ipso facto prefers war to peace or places any less emphasis than its American counterpart on the overriding importance of deterrence. It does attest, however, to a recognition that deterrence can fail despite the best efforts of both sides to prevent it, and that in such a circumstance, the Soviet armed forces have an obligation to do more than simply absorb the initial attacks of the enemy and then retaliate indiscriminately with their surviving forces for no political ends other than to inflict a punitive reprisal for the enemy's transgression. Instead, they have a perceived duty to make the best they can of an inherently bad situation by recognizing the situation for what it is, seizing the initiative, and doing everything possible to prevent an already dismal state of affairs from devolving into something worse. Second, the Soviet doctrinal belief in the possibility of victory is in no way an expression of sublime confidence that victory would be an automatic and natural consequence of compliance with the dictates of Soviet nuclear strategy in an emergency. It merely indicates that the Soviet high command—and presumably the Party leadership—regards victory as an objective to be consciously striven for with every reasonable effort, ranging from determined peacetime investment in adequate strategic forces and other war survival measures to bold and assertive strategic initiatives should deterrence come under imminent and unambiguous risk.

One frequently finds declarations in Soviet military commentary such as the following statement by the late minister of defense, Marshal Grechko, that in the event of a new world war, "we are firmly convinced that victory in this war would go to us." Such remarks are far more reflective of exhortation than serious strategic analysis. It is a considerable overstatement to assert categorically that "the Soviet Union thinks it could fight and win a nuclear war." In all probability, Soviet military men are not fundamentally different from most other professional soldiers the world over: knowing more intimately than anyone else what the real rigors and agonies of combat are like, they are among the last to seek a fight, the least convinced things will go easily, and the most acutely sensitive to the fact that one can never be sufficiently prepared.

On the other hand, one also occasionally encounters remarks in the Soviet literature to the effect that "any a priori rejection of the possibility of victory is harmful because it leads to moral disarmament, to a disbelief in victory, and to fatalism and passivity. It is necessary to wage a struggle against such views." Statements of this genre are another matter altogether and deserve the most serious attention of Western military planners. While they bespeak no confident expectation that Soviet victory in war is foreordained, they strongly suggest that the Soviets are fully committed to confronting the specter of nuclear war with their eyes open.

IT PAYS TO STRIKE FIRST

Surprise, initiative, mass, shock, and momentum have been among the most recurrent themes in Soviet military writings during the past decade and a half. Occasionally one can even find direct assertions that "preemption in launching a nuclear strike is the decisive condition for the attainment of superiority over [the enemy] and the seizure and retention of the initiative." The sources of this Soviet fixation on the need for being able to "frustrate" and "break up" an enemy attack are not easy to pin down, although doubtless the experience of the Nazi invasion in 1941 and the traditional Bolshevik emphasis on the importance of quashing undesirable sequences of events before they get out of hand are prominent among them. In all events, Soviet doctrine is heavily laced with endorsement of preemption as a preferred strategy at the edge of war, on the premise that whatever uncertainties there might be at the moment of decision, inaction would probably carry greater risks than proceeding with an attack if the survival of the Soviet state were in jeopardy.

This image of preemption is in no way comparable to the Western notion of a "splendid first strike" aimed at so thoroughly degrading the enemy's capacity to wage war that he would be physically deprived of any options to inflict significant retaliatory harm. It is highly unlikely that the Soviet military leadership harbors any delusions that it either currently possesses such a capability or stands within grasp of it in the foreseeable future. The standard distinctions in Western strategic discourse between "first strikes" and "second strikes" (as well as between "tactical" and "strategic" nuclear operations) are entirely alien to the idiom of Soviet military philosophy. The Soviet belief in the merits of going first rests less on any assumption that doing so will substantially disarm the opponent than on a conviction that tremendous psychological and military advantages can be gained by getting the initial jump on the adversary and forcing him constantly to operate in a reactive mode.

This intellectual orientation of Soviet doctrine may partially explain the evident Soviet determination to acquire a credible hard-target kill capability against U.S. silo-based ICBMs, even though the U.S. alert bomber force and deployed SSBN fleet would remain survivable. One can readily imagine a favored Soviet crisis scenario in which a portion of the Soviet ICBM force is launched in a preemptive counterforce attack against the U.S. ICBM inventory, home-ported SSBN fleet, and command and control infrastructure. Following such an attack, the United States would find itself in a state of utter societal chaos, left with a sharply diminished retaliatory arsenal and a highly degraded battle management capability, and facing a Soviet adversary who not only remained militarily untouched but also stood poised with a large residual nuclear force and a fully alerted air defense capability. In such a situation, Soviet planners might believe, the rational response for the U.S. leadership would be to retain its surviving forces as instruments for negotiating a settlement from a position of weakness rather than to execute a punitive retaliation against Soviet cities, which would only trigger a devastating Soviet counterresponse in kind. Even if the United States were to opt for some sort of limited nuclear reprisal rather than merely capitulating forthwith, the Soviet Union would, by the logic of this thinking, still retain the upper hand in the engagement. Whatever losses it might sustain, it would nonetheless remain in the favored position of pursuing objectives it had established in advance in a conflict whose rules were overwhelmingly of Soviet making.

There is no evidence in Soviet doctrinal writings that Soviet military leaders believe they could preempt against the United States with impunity. The rationale behind their emphasis on preemption is certainly not to pursue the key to an easy victory (or the illusion that such a victory might be possible). Rather, it seems to reflect a conviction that the least miserable option at the brink of a hopelessly unavoidable nuclear catastrophe would be to strike first and decisively so as to secure a measure of initiative and control, without which even a Pyrrhic victory would remain beyond reach.

RESTRAINT IS FOOLHARDY

Part and parcel of the Soviet doctrinal emphasis on timely preemption is a thoroughgoing rejection of Western crisis-management concepts such as demonstration strikes, escalation control, limited nuclear options, and other signaling ploys for intrawar bargaining and communication of resolve. Soviet writings typically dismiss such concepts with open scorn as naïve American notions that fail to appreciate the harsh realities of modern warfare. Partly this attitude reflects deep-seated Soviet military skepticism about the likelihood that nuclear force application can be subjected to finely tuned control under the stresses and confusion of battle. Primarily, however, it reflects an abiding doctrinal axiom that any half-measures once the threshold of war has been crossed would risk sacrificing the initiative and compromising the prospects for a prompt and decisive victory. As one Soviet writer has put it, "any delay in the destruction of [the enemy's] means of nuclear attack will permit the enemy to launch nuclear strikes first and may lead to heavy losses and even to the defeat of the offensive." Implicit in this doctrinal orientation is the notion that deterrence is solely a passive peacetime function of deployed forces in being. Once deterrence fails, the task of strategy is not to continue the process of diplomatic dialogue through the measured use of violence, but to employ nuclear force with whatever intensity necessary to defeat the enemy militarily in the shortest possible time.

NUMBERS MATTER

As noted earlier, Soviet doctrine does not categorically insist that absolute superiority over the enemy is a precondition of acceptable strategic preparedness. Nor does it maintain that there is some magic level of deployed forces whose achievement will assure strategic sufficiency. Hardware is only one ingredient in the composition of Soviet strategic power. An equally important ingredient in Soviet eyes is strategy, and an effective strategy adroitly pursued can significantly compensate for qualitative deficiencies in the Soviet arsenal. At the same time, Soviet doctrine seems to indicate—and the pattern of recent Soviet arms acquisition seems to confirm—a Soviet belief that strategic adequacy requires the deployment of as much weaponry as Soviet fiscal and technological assets and such external constraints as arms control agreements and the tolerance of the United States will allow. Although some Soviet statements since the beginnings of SALT have professed a willingness to settle for some roughly defined strategic "equivalence" to the United States (seemingly ruling out any determination to seek manifest superiority), these statements have been occasioned primarily by the political requirement for Soviet compliance with the spirit of détente and do not reflect any underlying belief that once having achieved such "equivalence," the Soviets can complacently rest on their laurels. The concept of "parity" is purely a Western legal construct artificially transposed to the realm of strategic affairs and has no discernible counterpart in known Soviet military thought. In practice, the Soviet insistence on "equivalence" has tended to mean that the Soviets will not countenance accepting anything less and will seek to acquire as much beyond it—through self-serving negotiatory tactics at SALT and careful probing of U.S. resolve—as they can reasonably get away with.

This belief in the value of abundant forces is apparent across the entire spectrum of Soviet military activity. For theater war contingencies, the Soviets have produced 50,000 tanks, a truly dramatic achievement that exceeds that of the United States four times over. Their army is twice the size of ours. Their navy is also substantially larger. They are currently producing fighter aircraft at more than double the rate of the United States. At the strategic level, there is similar evidence of this doctrinal penchant for quantity in the large inventory of heavy Soviet silo-based ICBMs (numerically constrained only by SALT), the Soviet refusal to incorporate land-mobile ICBM limits into the SALT I Interim Agreement, the incipient proliferation of SS-20 MRBMs with their attendant ambiguity regarding rapid convertibility to long-range SS-16s, and the Soviet indisposition to accept the reduced ICBM numerical ceiling embodied in the original Carter SALT proposal of March 1977. These activities may or may not represent visible signs of an underlying effort to achieve significant strategic advantage "on the cheap" within the framework of SALT and détente, but they certainly attest to a closely held Soviet conviction that when it comes to strategic preparedness, there is safety in numbers and one can never have more than enough.

The sources of this belief in the value of amply endowed forces go far back into Soviet history and doubtless include traditional Soviet self-perceptions of inferiority, as well as the bitter memories of the costs of inferiority left by the near-disastrous Nazi onslaught of 1941. More recently, they have been reinforced by the embarrassing debacle the Soviets suffered in the Cuban missile episode of 1962. There has been much debate among Western analysts over whether it was the incontrovertible U.S. strategic superiority that principally enabled the United States to emerge from that crisis so successfully. Whether or not the United States in fact exploited its superior nuclear posture with as much clever finesse as some observers claimed it did shortly after the event, there is every reason to believe that the Soviets, for their part, learned a lasting lesson about what it means to be on the *inferior* side in a nuclear showdown. In considerable part because of the Cuban venture, Khrushchev lost his job and was supplanted by a new regime with more traditional strategic values. Promptly thereafter, a massive program of force expansion and modernization was set into motion that has continued unabated to this day. The new leadership, by every indication, bound itself to an all but enshrined commitment never again to allow the Soviet Union to lapse into a state of such perceived military weakness as to permit such easy humiliation at the hands of its principal adversary.

To say that Soviet doctrine places an important premium on numerical plenty (indeed, on as large a margin of military advantage as may be feasible) is not to argue that Soviet military planners harbor any belief that strategic superiority can either supply "instant courage" in crises or that it necessarily constitutes a tool that can be employed in specific and preplanned ways to exact enemy concessions in coercive diplomacy and war. There is nothing in the Soviet military literature even remotely comparable to the kinds of sophisticated—if frequently unpersuasive—arguments one characteristically finds employed by proponents of strategic superiority in the West. The Soviet case for strategic advantage is more diffuse and tends to regard numerical force preponderance principally as a comfort-inducing hedge against future contingencies whose precise character cannot be anticipated. In peacetime, such preponderance affords Soviet political leaders the freedom to act in crises with a favorable edge in self-assurance by shifting the burden of anxiety onto the opponent. In wartime, it would presumably provide Soviet commanders a cushion of reserve forces against the uncertainties of combat and thus help underwrite a more audacious strategy than might otherwise be possible.

SOVIET DOCTRINE IN PERSPECTIVE

So much for the essentials of Soviet military doctrine as they appear on the books. It remains now to consider what they mean in practical terms as determinants of Soviet force structuring and as guides to Soviet behavior in crises that could erupt into war.

To begin with, it bears repeating that doctrine serves many purposes besides simply prescribing criteria for weapons development and use. It provides a systematic body of official "truths" for reinforcing Soviet military morale and reaffirming the conviction of Soviet soldiers that they retain an important purpose even in an age of deterrence, in which the principal rationale of strategic weapons is to prevent wars rather than fight them. The repeated stress in Soviet writings that nuclear weaponry has not invalidated the possibility of achieving victory is perhaps the most eminent example of a doctrinal tenet that exists in considerable (though by no means exclusive) measure for this purpose.

Doctrine also provides a convenient set of bureaucratic rationales for the armed forces to employ in advancing their institutional interests in the competitive arena of Soviet budgetary politics. The ambiguity in Soviet doctrine regarding whether a future world war would be short or protracted offers a ready justification for large strategic reserve forces. The doctrinal insistence that no such war could be won without combined-arms operations serves, among other things, to help assure that all of the armed services receive a respectable piece of the action in the allocation of military roles and resources.

Finally, doctrine plays an important part in the Soviet strategic dialogue with the United States and aims to manipulate the perceptions and expectations of the U.S. leadership by casting Soviet military power in the best possible light. The emphatic Soviet disavowal of such U.S. strategic concepts as limited nuclear targeting and the equally adamant Soviet insistence that any war would be intense and uncompromising from the outset have the partial aim of forewarning the United States that the Soviet Union will not abide by U.S. rules in the event of war and neatly typify how doctrinal principles collaterally serve Soviet propaganda ends.

With these allowances accounted for, however, there remains much in Soviet doctrine of serious operational consequence for Soviet defense planners. The imprint of doctrine has been most vividly apparent in the physical complexion of Soviet force developments during the past decade. It goes without saying, of course, that Soviet doctrine is primarily the product of military men, whereas the ultimate responsibility for Soviet resource allocation and force structuring inheres in the civilian Party apparatus. It is also clear that the civilian leadership is under no compulsion to rubber-stamp the institutional preferences of the armed forces. Nonetheless, the entire range of Soviet military activity since the mid-1960s has accorded surprisingly—and disturbingly—with the central doctrinal themes highlighted above.

This is not meant to imply that the Soviet force posture since Khrushchev's ouster has been a product of unrestrained doctrinal determinism or that doctrine has, in any sense, blindly "driven" Soviet military procurement choices. There are observable inconsistencies between certain edicts of Soviet military doctrine and the realities of contemporary Soviet military preparedness, perhaps most notably apparent in the relatively low readiness of Soviet strategic forces for prompt combat employment. Soviet writings constantly harp on the critical importance of maintaining the Soviet military machine peaked for launch on a moment's notice. Yet in contrast to the United States, which continuously maintains approximately half of its SSBN boats on operational patrol, the Soviet navy deploys only a handful of its ballistic missile submarines on station at any given time and leaves the rest concentrated in their highly vulnerable home ports. Similarly, unlike the U.S. Strategic Air Command, which constantly maintains a third of its bomber force on five-minute strip alert, Soviet Long-Range Aviation is not known to observe any comparable practice. One could fairly argue that these are not significant anomalies, since Soviet doctrine posits preempting at some point during a gradually intensifying crisis, in which the Soviet military would presumably have more than ample opportunity to generate its forces to full alert status. The fact remains, however, that such anomalies explicitly belie a recurrent refrain in Soviet declaratory commentary.

Furthermore, Soviet military doctrine, with few exceptions (most notably on the question of whether a conventional war in Europe would "inevitably" escalate to the nuclear level), has remained more or less internally consistent and conceptually stable since around 1960, well before the post-Khrushchev weapons build-up began to lend real teeth to Soviet military pronouncements. The sharp discontinuity between the extravagant war-fighting rhetoric of Soviet military writings and the minuscule capability of actual Soviet strategic forces during the early 1960s clearly accentuates the fact that it has always been hard-nosed internal politics, leadership preferences, and institutional interest adjudication rather than automatic obeisance to the doctrinal catechism of the Soviet military that determine the character of Soviet strategic programs and policies.

On the other hand, it goes without saying that if there is a convergence of leadership predispositions with doctrine, then the latter becomes critically important as an explanatory factor. Although the evidence is largely presumptive, there is good reason to surmise that something much like this occurred shortly after the Brezhnev-Kosygin regime assumed power. The latter part of the Khrushchev era, one may recall, was a period of considerably turbulent Party-military relations, fed by Khrushchev's refusal to satisfy the demands of his marshals and exacerbated by the abortive Cuban missile venture, whose outcome most of the military and many in the Party felt was largely due to Khrushchev's inadequate defense preparations. With the advent of the new leadership in 1964, a fundamental change seems to have occurred. This is not the place for a detailed reconstruction of that period, but it is a reasonable inference from known events that following an intense Party-military controversy in 1966 and 1967 over the nature of the Soviet security problem, a mutual accommodation was struck between the Party and the military, in which the armed forces were granted most of their program requests that Khrushchev had left unrequited in return for a renewed spirit of institutional cooperativenss in the defense policy process. Moreover, Khrushchev's political successors appear to have become increasingly persuaded by much of the logic of Soviet military doctrine and assimilated it into their own belief system (if they were not indeed already substantially persuaded even while Khrushchev remained in power).

Tacit proof of this hypothesis may be inferred from a number of subsequent developments. For one thing, there has been a remarkable degree of quiescence, if not outright amity, in Soviet Party-military relations since 1967 that seems to entail far more than mere surface calm. Senior Soviet military figures have been heard to intimate openly to Westerners that "things have been a lot easier" since Khrushchev's departure and the patching up of Party-military conflicts over resource allocations that ensued. Second, there has increasingly appeared to be a blurring of the former institutional separation of Party and military in Soviet defense decision making since the late 1960s. The current minister of defense, Dmitri Ustinov, is a civilian with longstanding ties to the Soviet defense industrial community. His appointment to that position broke a long tradition of assigning it to professional military men. The chairman of the important Military-Industrial Commission, L. V. Smirnov, is also a civilian. Ustinov is additionally a voting member of the Politburo, as was his immediate predecessor, Marshal Grechko, prior to his death in 1973. Brezhnev, for his part, has become a self-appointed marshal of the Soviet Union. And all of these figures interact closely and regularly on defense policy matters in a number of high-level joint political-military planning committees with an apparent degree of harmonious collegiality that would have been unthinkable during Khrushchev's incumbency.

Finally, there is the inescapable fact that recent developments in Soviet weapons acquisition and military construction bear unmistakable earmarks of being significantly informed by the criteria of Soviet military doctrine. To list only the most obvious of these, there is the vigorous Soviet pursuit of a credible hard-target kill capability through the proliferation of increasingly accurate MIRVed ICBMs. There is evidence of growing Soviet interest in preserving a capability for wartime force reconstitution at both the theater and strategic levels. There have been repeated demonstrations of Soviet interest in acquiring the requisite antisatellite capabilities to deny the United States the wartime use of its space-based command, control, communications, and surveillance capabilities, upon which its own strategic force effectiveness heavily depends. Notwithstanding the ABM Treaty, there continues to be a highly robust Soviet research and development effort in advanced antiballistic missile technology and no evidence whatever that the Soviet military has relinquished its traditional emphasis on the importance of strategic defense in modern warfare. The Soviet air defense network, for which we have no comparable counterpart, is widely known to be the most extensive in the world and continues to grow in effectiveness and sophistication. Finally, there is the whole spectrum of war-survival measures that the Soviets have been implementing in recent years, ranging from their hardened grain-storage facilities and controversial population-defense program to their less noted but far more significant steps to acquire a redundant command and control capability for assuring central leadership management of any military emergency. None of these activities would be necessitated by a deterrent policy based on "assured destruction" assumptions, yet each constitutes an indispensable component of any strategy seriously aimed at preparing for the eventuality of major nuclear conflict.

Certainly this complex of programs requires more in the way of explanation than simply the reductionist assertion that it was hatched from Soviet military doctrine. It exists partly because of normal program momentum, partly because it is economically and technologically feasible, partly because Russians simply do things that way, and partly for a whole gamut of additional institutional, political, and cultural reasons. At the same time, there is little about it that is palpably incompatible with Soviet doctrine, and enough that accords with the war-survival injunctions of that doctrine to strike any reasonable observer as being far too consistent to be coincidental. Soviet doctrine is manifestly a combat-oriented operational philosophy that treats the possibility of nuclear war as a threat that cannot be wished away, and that orientation is the dominant hallmark of the comprehensive Soviet military build-up that has been under way, SALT and détente notwithstanding, throughout the past decade. If for no other reason than this extraordinarily close correlation between theory and reality, it seems appropriate to conclude that at least as far as peacetime force development is concerned, Soviet military doctrine is very much a vital factor bearing on the shaping of Soviet strategic policy.

As for the extent to which Soviet doctrine provides reliable insights into the way the Soviets would comport themselves at the actual brink of war, there is obviously less that can be said with confidence. For one thing, however explicit Soviet doctrinal writing may be in its depiction of the Soviet security problem, it is hopelessly elusive regarding what specific measures might be taken to cope with it were deterrence to fail. From everything available in the published Soviet military literature, we still lack any clear sense of what actual Soviet nuclear war plans involve, and we could be gravely misled if we tried to infer them solely from the known doctrinal indicators. To use a crude analogy, enunciated Soviet military doctrine is somewhat comparable to the U.S. Joint Strategic Objectives Plan (JSOP), a highly formal and widely coordinated national document that posits broad definitions of the strategic situation, general peacetime and wartime goals of U.S. military forces, and rough criteria for achieving those goals that most members of the U.S. political-military community can comfortably live with. Soviet doctrine is not in any sense, however, a source of specific "how to" guidance for the Soviet political leadership, and it tells us nothing whatever about the sorts of detailed target lists, laydown strategies, and preplanned rates of fire that doubtless figure in the Soviet counterpart to our SIOP.

Second, Soviet doctrine may provide a valuable intellectual ordering device for Soviet military planners, but it certainly is not binding on the Soviet civilian leadership. Blessed as they are with both natural conservatism and a total lack of prior experience at nuclear war, the Soviet leaders would doubtless feel powerful compulsions toward circumspection and restraint in any crisis that appeared in serious danger of nuclear escalation. At such a moment of truth, they might well conclude that what appeared reasonable enough when briefed in calmer times by the general staff had suddenly become the consummate height of strategic insanity. Moreover, the Soviet force posture is now in the process of acquiring a rich breadth of potential that will soon permit far more sophisticated options than anything currently addressed in the Soviet doctrinal literature. Whatever that literature may say about the importance of massive preemption at the outset, the riskiness of incremental force application, and so on, the Soviet leadership still retains the intellectual and organizational capacity for improvisation under stress. It is altogether plausible that Soviet leaders would feel no compunctions about throwing the whole book of doctrinal edicts out the window in a crisis if they felt they had a better way to address the problem.

What such a better way might look like is, of course, impossible to say in advance. The Soviet leaders themselves are probably as unsure as anyone else. The best that can be said is that Soviet military doctrine tells us something, though far from all, about the way the Soviet leadership thinks about strategic problems and provides some general hints about the sort of mind-set they would probably take with them into a major nuclear confrontation. Like all doctrines, however, it is merely a conceptual road map, not a rigidly binding route plan, and offers little of predictive value about future Soviet behavior other than to indicate that, up to now, Soviet leaders have tended to concentrate more than their American counterparts on what to do should deterrence fail. Because of that, they would probably arrive at the threshold of any actual nuclear crisis at least having given somewhat more systematic thought to the choices and dilemmas they faced.

Decision making in Soviet weapons procurement

Arthur J. Alexander

INTRODUCTION

Why does the Soviet Union acquire the number and sort of weapons it does? Why, for example, does it have more than 40,000 tanks, when 20,000 would be twice as many as any other country possesses? Why does it continue to produce new tanks at a rate of 4,000 per year—four times the American production rate? Several explanations must be considered: (1) historically based culture and values; (2) military-political doctrine; (3) the "objective" situation (the "threat" and the capabilities available to meet the threat) and the "rational" response; (4) organizational relationships, decision-making practices, and bureaucratic routines; (5) internal political power and accommodations; and (6) personalities.

The principal emphasis in this article is whether, and to what degree, the existing organizational structures, bureaucratic routines, and decision-making practices influence the size and shape of the Soviet force posture. *Would outcomes be different if processes were different?* After accounting for the effects of history, doctrine, situation, politics, and personality do organizational forces have an additional, detectable, and independent effect? The search for explanations of Soviet weapons procurement behavior in organizations and decision making is justified in part by the increasingly bureaucratized nature of Soviet institutions. This is characterized by centralized authority, rigidly hierarchical organization, inflexible outlook, and conservative reactions to change.

Soviet weapons procurement since World War II has proceeded in phases, the present phase dating back to around 1959.[1] In the first phase, expenditures declined sharply between 1945 and 1950 as Stalin cut back the size of the military and virtually suspended production of conventional arms, except for deployment of the first generation of jet fighters and a copy of the American B-29 strategic bomber.

The second phase began when the Soviet Union, partly in response to the American decision to fight in Korea, built up its own forces and gave support to

North Korea. From 1950 to 1954, expenditures, concentrated on procurement, jumped sharply. Stalin's death and the end of the Korean War allowed the new leadership to cut back the production of armaments, especially aircraft.[2] Khrushchev also cut back or canceled large naval programs initiated by Stalin. Manpower, too, was reduced throughout the latter half of the 1950s to pre-Korean War levels. One of the few sectors to experience growth was the ballistic missile program, which Stalin initiated and Khrushchev carried into production with the first generation of medium-range ballistic missiles. The missile design bureaus also tested the first intercontinental-range ballistic missiles in 1956, and by the end of the decade Khrushchev could announce their initial deployment.

The Soviet military build-up that continues into the late 1970s is estimated to have begun in the 1959-60 period.[3] This turnaround in military production coincided with Khrushchev's Seven-Year Plan for 1959-65. Since 1959, all sectors of Soviet military production have exhibited periods of rapid growth. The Central Intelligence Agency (CIA) has estimated total expenditure growth for this period at approximately 5 percent per year; William Lee's estimates, however, are closer to 9 percent.[4] Disaggregated procurement data indicate that, while all sectors have participated in the build-up, growth has been neither continuous nor simultaneous for all types of weapons. Reequipment and research and development (R&D) cycles, shifting doctrinal requirements, and the gradual filling in of perceived gaps produce "the complex periodization" observed by John Erickson. Whereas production of armored personnel carriers grew from very low levels in the 1950s to more than 4,000 per year in the 1970s, helicopter production only began to grow in the late 1960s.[5] Logistics support, long a weak link in Soviet military capabilities, benefited in the 1970s from the overall availability of funds. The pace of missile development and production proceeded with several ups and downs that, because of the large scale of the missile programs, have influenced the shape of the estimated aggregate expenditures curves. For example, the mid-1960s aggregate decrease in expenditures occurred when the initial intermediate-range ballistic missile (IRBM) program tapered off in the early 1960s and the rise of intercontinental ballistic missiles (ICBMs) had not yet fully compensated for this decline. The total expenditures curve then followed the rapid rise in ICBMs and submarine-launched missiles, which peaked in 1968-69, fell during 1972, and then rose again as the next generation of ICBM entered production.[6]

Within the Soviet services the chief budgetary advantage has fallen to the Strategic Rocket Forces, which did not even exist twenty years ago. Their procurement expenditures have also been the most volatile, reflecting system procurement cycles. The budget of the Air Defense Forces, with the smallest absolute share of total spending, fell by 20 percent from 1970 to 1975.[7] The ground forces have the largest share of the budget, but in recent years it grew relatively slowly, while air force growth was second to the Strategic Rocket Forces, and the navy grew at the same rate as total military spending. Over the longer period since 1960, it is more difficult to identify major trends, except for the Strategic Rocket Forces and the post-Khrushchev spurt in the land forces. Deployment of land, sea, and air weapons has been substantial over this period: Indeed, some commentators note the recent absence of visible interservice rivalries, suggesting that the general availability of funds has muted the potential competition for budgetary shares.

Whether military expenditures are seen as a drain on a nation's resources depends on, among other things, the size of these expenditures relative to national resources and their relative growth rates. According to CIA estimates, "when measured according to a definition of defence activities roughly comparable to that used in the US, the Soviet defense effort absorbs some 11-12 per cent of Soviet gross national product."[8] Lee's independent estimates show a higher defense burden on the national economy: 14-15 percent.[9] However, a more accurate picture of the drain on the economy of military hardware procurement is provided by the proportion of Soviet durable output allocated to national security uses, which Lee places at approximately 19 percent in 1975—compared with 11 percent in 1960.

On the basis of either Lee's military growth rate of 9 percent or the CIA's more modest 5 percent, defense expenditures in the Soviet Union have not been a declining proportion of gross national product (GNP) and may indeed have been increasing. This results not only from the growth of the military but also from the declining growth rate of the national economy, which has fallen steadily since the end of the post-World War II reconstruction. In 1975, GNP rose by only 2.5 percent, falling from an average annual rate of 4 percent in 1971-74, and more than 6 percent in the 1950s.

In summary, the long-run growth of Soviet military expenditures in general, and weapons procurement in particular, is impressive because of its persistence and scope, especially when compared with the more volatile behavior of the United States. Although the Soviet build-up is not new, cumulatively it has assumed striking proportions. Behind the continuity of the aggregate figures lies some redistribution across services and a shifting emphasis on new roles and doctrines: the revolution in military-technical affairs signaled by nuclear weapons; the new ocean-going role of the navy; and the reemergence of the ground forces under the politically accepted doctrine of the possibility of wars to be fought and won—with or without the use of nuclear weapons. Each service has had a period of equipment expansion, with the Air Defense Forces falling behind in recent years.

THE ORGANIZATION OF DEFENSE PROCUREMENT

As reflected in figure 1, the structure of governance in the Soviet Union is bifurcated, with the Communist party leadership and bureaucracy maintaining their historical primacy in policy formulation and supervision and with government agencies responsible for implementing policy. The Party is led by the Politburo, which is formally elected by the 240-member Central Committee. In fact, the position is reversed, since the Central Committee is largely chosen by the Politburo, its func-

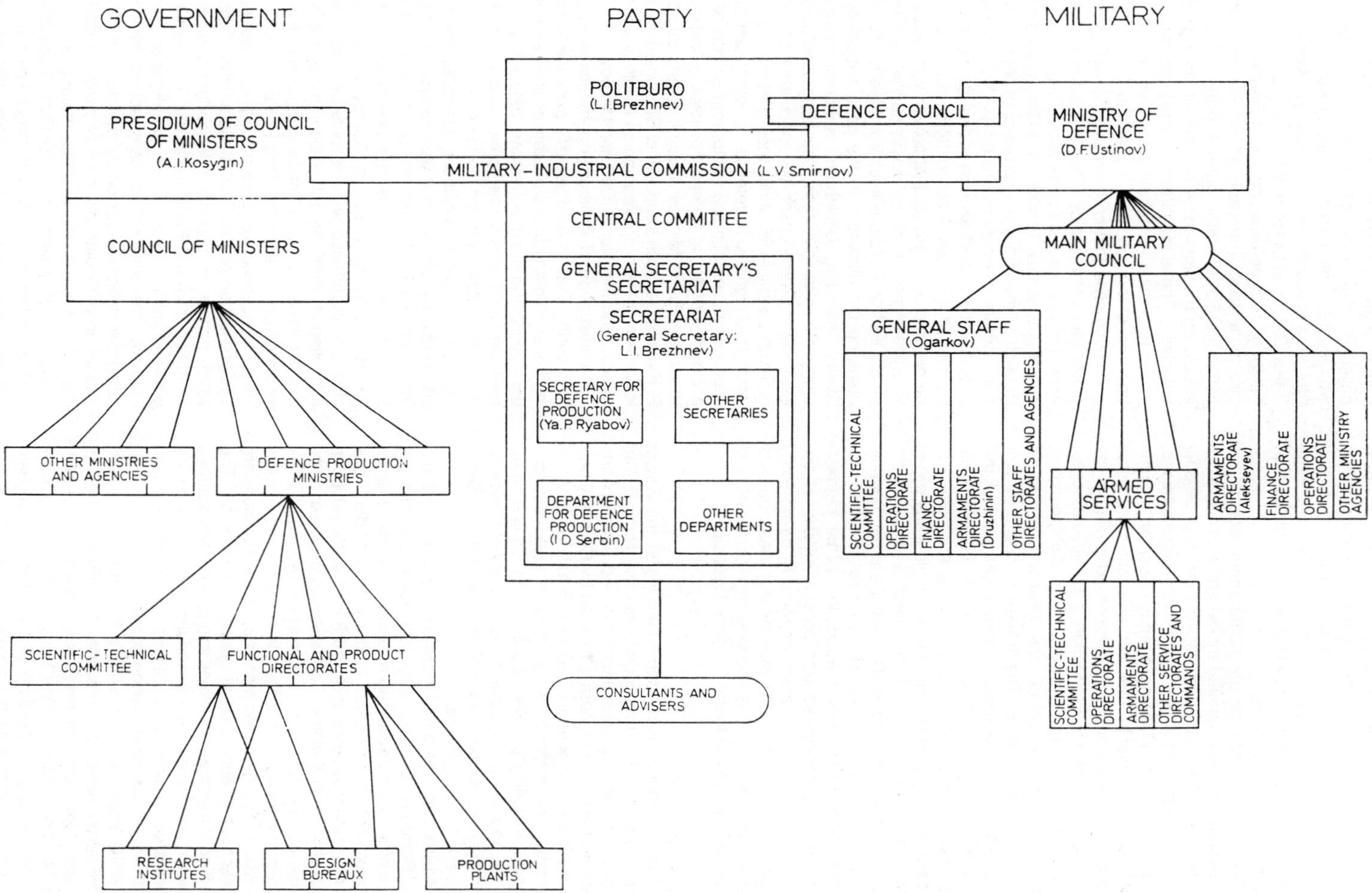

Figure 1. Principal organizations in Soviet weapons procurement

tion almost completely eclipsed by the senior body. Serving the Politburo is the Central Committee Secretariat, headed by ten secretaries supervising twenty-four specialized departments that oversee Party activities and the implementation of Party policy by government agencies.

The highest body on the government side is the Council of Ministers, chaired by the prime minister. Included in the Council of Ministers are chiefs of production ministries and other major state organizations, such as the State Planning Agency (*Gosplan*). It is in the ministries' plants that actual production takes place. Weapons production is the responsibility of the Ministry of Defense Production and several other ministries, such as those for aviation and shipbuilding. Most R&D and design of new weapons also takes place in these ministries. The military production sector is supervised by a secretary and Department of the Central Committee Secretariat. The military—that is, the Ministry of Defense—is somewhat anomalous in regard to Party control. There is no single Party organ that supervises all military affairs; and even this patchwork coverage is incomplete. The Defense Council, composed of a subgroup of Politburo members together with the military leadership, is the highest-ranking body concerned with political-military affairs and policies. However, there appears to be no Party organization charged with supervising these policies nor with providing the customary secretariat services of analysis and advice to the Defense Council.

POLITBURO

The Communist party dominates life in the Soviet Union, and the Politburo dominates the Party.[10] The present group of around fifteen full and seven candidate (nonvoting) members is headed by Central Committee General Secretary Leonid I. Brezhnev.[11] Members hold major posts in key Party and government bodies, including the Secretariat of the Central Committee, regional Party committees, Council of Ministers, and major ministries, such as Defense, Internal Security, and Foreign Affairs.

As the supreme policy-making body of the country, the Politburo deals not only with defense affairs but also with the whole panoply of issues arising in a large, modern nation. It has final authority over all decisions of national importance and also finds itself involved in relatively minor matters. Centralization of power combined with bureaucratic conservatism requires the direct intervention of the political leaders in a wide variety of issues. The demands placed upon the Politburo are consequently enormous in scope and in detail. The staffing through which issues are framed, the sources of information and analysis, and the possibilities for the generation of alternative policies are therefore crucial to the entire decision-making process.[12]

While each of the members has his or her own specialized tasks, responsibility for major issues is shared. Members have the right to raise any issue over the head of the responsible Politburo member or government agency.[13] Meetings of the full group are held weekly, although special consultations may be called more frequently if especially important or unexpected problems arise.[14] During the Nixon-Brezhnev Moscow summit meeting in March 1974, for example, a hastily called Politburo meeting (for which Marshal Grechko was recalled from Iran) was held to discuss a "conceptual breakthrough" in the Strategic Arms Limitation Talks (SALT). In October of the same year, two days of meetings between Kissinger and Brezhnev were capped by a special session of the Politburo, following which the Soviet Union agreed to the critical issue of equalizing the aggregate number of strategic delivery vehicles.[15] These meetings were presumably called to inform the Politburo, debate the issues, and receive the approval of the collective leadership.

A ruling style that combines individuality with collegiality can be unwieldy when revisions to previously accepted positions are considered, especially new and divisive proposals. This seems to be avoided generally through a time-consuming process of prior consultation and careful consensus building, through subgroup specialization, and also by sidestepping particularly troublesome issues. Most matters, in fact, are said to be decided by unanimous approval, with actual voting rarely taking place. If consensus cannot be reached, a small, ad hoc Politburo subcommittee is charged with resolving the dispute.[16] In the past, especially under Stalin, standing Politburo subcommittees were charged with specific tasks, including defense and foreign affairs. Some observers speculate that such subcommittees still exist. While their present, formal existence is uncertain, a defense "cluster" can be identified, composed of those Politburo members who take a closer interest in defense policies. It may include Brezhnev, Prime Minister Kosygin, Party Secretary A. P. Kirilenko (a close supporter of Brezhnev), M. A. Suslov (a senior Party spokesman on ideology and foreign affairs), and Minister of Defense Ustinov.

An illustration of Politburo operations in foreign affairs during Stalin's leadership is particularly illuminating because many of the processes still seem to be in use. A Politburo subcommittee chaired by Molotov exercised tight control over foreign affairs. The Ministry of Foreign Affairs "moved along on its own momentum as long as existing Politburo directives covered the contingencies with which it was confronted. If a policy issue arose which could not be disposed of on the basis of past instructions, the Commissar of Foreign Affairs referred the matter to Molotov. Usually, matters of lesser importance were resolved at this level or in consultation with the full subcommittee. If Molotov thought the issue was of major importance, the matter would go on the agenda of the Politburo."[17] The Politburo was supplied with background memoranda by the foreign section of the Central Committee Secretariat, which had at its disposal independent sources of information from the Party hierarchy. The secret police provided yet another channel of intelligence. The Politburo was therefore not at the mercy of the data and recommendations supplied by the ministry. The secretariat, in particular, played a key role as staff to the Politburo in nonroutine decision making and in supervising the policy decision of the Party leadership.

That the Politburo has been directly involved in specific weapons development and procurement decisions is attested to by the memoir literature of the Stalin and Khrushchev periods. This involvement typically took the form of interventions in continuous activities intended to stimulate developments in new directions, to solve problems, or to resolve controversies.[18] On a more regular basis, all large, nonrecurring expenditures are considered by the Politburo. Not only are budgets and aggregate resource levels approved by the Politburo, but so are numbers of weapons. It is claimed that the political leaders have canceled many programs,[19] and programs with cost overruns are sent to them for reconsideration.[20] Moreover, expensive, complex, high-technology weapons are said to demand greater technical as well as greater political control. Therefore, individuals such as Defense Minister and Politburo member Ustinov, or Chief of the General Staff Ogarkov, with their strong backgrounds in engineering-technical management, may be expected to loom larger in the decision-making process than their predecessors. It has even been suggested that it is because of their technical competence that they have been placed in their present positions.[21]

Despite the importance the leadership places on national security, the Politburo's central role in all aspects of Soviet life forces one to question its ability to deal other than superficially with most defense issues.[22] One could visualize a process of routine approval of most matters, closer scrutiny of the most expensive or politically sensitive projects, and reconsideration of those projects with cost overruns that would disrupt previously approved plans and budgets. Three conclusions may be inferred from these points: (1) most attention is probably paid to political issues of budget and shares; (2) international politics focuses attention on an important subset of strategic and other weapons; and (3) the content of most programs is determined by bureaucrats and technicians. However, the contents and costs of very expensive, prominent programs cannot be ignored, since they intrude directly into the internal politics of the budgeting process. For example, Khrushchev clearly saw that the strategic build-up he supervised required a sacrifice in other social goals: "I decided that we had to economize drastically in the building of homes, the construction of communal services, and even in the development of agriculture in order to build up our defences."[23] He also described Stalin's crash program for the construction of cruisers and destroyers as "terribly expensive. It involved diverting huge sums of money from the development of . . . other forms of warfare, not to mention the funds it diverted from our overwhelming nonmilitary needs."[24] Due to the all-encompassing scope of Soviet government and budgets, the demands of one sector cannot help but be compared with the requirements of another. Changes in budgetary shares are most noticeable and likely to stimulate political debate. A desire to avoid political controversy would therefore have considerable impact on the ability to reallocate among sectors and on policy-making more generally.

Devolution of authority to the working level is described by Hough as one of the major characteristics of the Brezhnev Politburo.[25] Hough argues that by allowing the specialized government complexes autonomy in policy and by giving nearly all these groups incremental budget increases each year, Brezhnev avoids the anger that Khrushchev's "voluntarist" and "subjective" intervention provoked in Party and government circles. Although the Party formally retains control of the defining of goals, and has even strengthened its hold on the various control mechanisms, the trend toward "scientific" decision making based on specialized knowledge has informally shifted policy formation to the specialized complexes.[26]

Even if Hough is basically correct about the main tendencies of devolution of authority and incremental budgeting, choices must still occasionally be made: the environment may be stable but it is not completely static. Of major influence in policy choices are the sources of alternatives that are considered. In particular, it is necessary to examine the possibility of individual Politburo members obtaining analytical and factual support on military issues that may not be consistent with the corporate military view, the dominant political policies, or the status quo. Given the individual authority of Politburo members, it is possible that they form alliances with parts of the bureaucracies—for example, with a military service or a research institute—that might provide independent policy analysis. Petrov stresses that formal structures within the upper Party leadership mean little, and that personal and family ties, shifting political alliances, and past and present informal associations among the governing elite are crucial.[27] A few examples have come to light of individuals bypassing intermediate levels of authority and going directly to the top with problems and ideas. Marshal Varentsov, for example, wrote a top secret letter to Khrushchev about poor management in missile production, lack of funds, and other deficiencies. Unfortunately for Varentsov, Khrushchev was not in Moscow at the time, and the letter was handled by Suslov, who informed Minister of Defense Malinovsky and Ground Forces Commander Chuykov of the complaints. Varentsov's superiors were naturally upset by this attempt to bypass them, and he suffered "very serious troubles" as a consequence.[28]

The aircraft designer Alexander Yakovlev also described how he bypassed "the usual steps of going through the ministry and air force, and instead went directly to Stalin" with an innovative design. Yakovlev felt stymied by the standard routines, yet recognized the seriousness of ignoring them: "I had no other recourse; I was afraid that my proposal might get bogged down in going through normal channels."[29] In this case, Stalin's enthusiastic support of Yakovlev was communicated to the minister of aviation production, who quickly fell in behind the leader's intervention. Interestingly, Beria opposed the selection of the Yakovlev design and offered a proposal of Lavochkin as an alternative. However, Stalin's original choice prevailed.[30]

This last example demonstrates the importance of politicians (Beria, in this case) having access to technical advice if they even hope to counter decisions made by the leaders. Another illustration of a quest for independent analysis involves the visits of Politburo member M. Solomentsev to the Central Institute for Mathematical Economics (TSEMI) in the early 1970s to discuss the possibility of TSEMI constructing an alternative five-year economic plan to the official plan prepared by the State Planning Agency.[31]

These cases illustrate links between technical experts and those in high Party positions, including the top leadership. It has been difficult, though, to uncover cases of military officers, allied to members of the Politburo, supplying advice and expertise in opposition to previously accepted policies or the view of the high command. The recent appointment of G. V. Romanov to full membership of the Politburo may provide an avenue for such advice in the future. Romanov, a shipbuilding engineer, was first secretary of the Leningrad Party organization and had close ties with the Leningrad navy base and navy schools; he is considered to be a navy supporter.[32] It must be emphasized, however, that the use of these ties as an entrée into Politburo deliberations is purely conjectural. Moreover, close personal ties, for example, between Khrushchev and Defense Minister Zhukhov, or between Brezhnev and Defense Minister Grechko, are as likely as not to be avenues for political influence on military affairs.

There are instances of military officers differing with the view of the General Staff, but they are not clear-cut examples of the availability of well-argued alternatives to prevailing opinions. In the early 1960s, a retired senior officer from the General Staff, Maj. Gen. N. A. Talensky, wrote on nuclear deterrence and arms control in a manner that supported Khrushchev's view and departed significantly from conventional military analysis. However, Talensky, ensconced at the Institute of Marxist-Leninist History, lacked the institutional role that could serve as a formal basis for participation in the development of defense policy.[33] Talensky's deviation from the dominant military viewpoint, even though he was a retired officer in an academy of science institute, earned him harsh condemnation from the military after Khrushchev's fall from power.

What becomes apparent from these cases are the serious risks, recognized by all participants, attendant in not going through established channels. However, these risks and the range of alternatives available to political participants must depend on the state of the political landscape. The greater the degree of collegiality, the more one would expect a greater diversity of opinion to reach the top. This is the central argument of "interest group" theorists, but the evidence for changes in the pattern of influences on political choices has yet to be demonstrated.

CENTRAL COMMITTEE SECRETARIAT

The Secretariat of the Central Committee[34] of the Communist party has been called the most influential organ of the Party, largely because of its position at the summit of the Party apparatus, its nationwide control over appointments, and because it in part staffs the Politburo.[35] The secretariat is also responsible for overseeing the implementation of policies emanating from the political leaders. It is consequently at a central node of policy and decision making, sitting astride information flows, analyses, and policy formulation and implementation.

These jobs are managed by ten secretaries, headed by a general secretary (first secretary from 1952 until 1966). About half of the secretaries are also Politburo members, which establishes part of the interlocking system of governance of Soviet society that links the Party to policy formulation and implementation. Each secretary has specific responsibilities, which are administered by a number of departments and a permanent professional staff estimated to number about a thousand.[36]

In the early days of Brezhnev's rise to full authority, the new leadership debated the role of the general secretary and, indeed, of the full Secretariat.[37] That debate was resolved in favor of the general secretary's overall direction of the Central Committee apparatus, and the secretariat's responsibility for the "creative supervision" of the execution of Politburo decisions on matters of government. Under Khrushchev, all ten secretaries had a seat in the Politburo, but immediately after his fall their representation was limited. This development and others have had the effect of diminishing somewhat the central role of the secretariat.[38] Its political importance as a whole was reduced against that of the Politburo; sources of expertise and information were diversified by bringing more groups into the staff;[39] the defense minister, with a seat on the Politburo since 1973, may now be able to bypass the normal routines of the secretariat and refer military issues directly to the General Staff for staffing and review.

A countervailing tendency must also be noted. The regularization of decision making under Brezhnev has enhanced the power of the secretariat by allowing it to function with clearer lines of authority and less interference than hitherto.[40] Brezhnev's careful selection and cultivation of the secretaries and their staffs has given him a control over the organization Khrushchev did not possess. The most important result of these links, according to Soviet participants, is the flow of information to the general secretary. Western political scientists emphasize the solid political base Brezhnev built in the secretariat, extending to the Central Committee and the rest of the Party apparatus.[41]

Brezhnev himself was the secretary responsible for heavy industry and defense production from 1957 to 1960.[42] He was succeeded in the mid-1960s, after a few years of confused authority, by Dmitri F. Ustinov, who became minister of defense in 1976. The post has probably now been given to Yakov Ryabov. Ustinov's lengthy involvement in the high-level supervision of defense industry dating back to the early 1940s, and his close association with the heads of the defense production ministries, probably gave him a great deal of personal power over Soviet armaments programs. It is therefore not clear as to whether his successor carries the same authority. Directly under this secretary is the Department of Defense Industry, headed since the late 1950s by I. D. Serbin. It is responsible for overseeing Party affairs in the military-production ministries, and also for the implementation of weapons R&D and production policies.[43] There are also Defense Industry departments within regional (*Obkom*) Party organizations to provide independent checks on the progress and problems of projects at a local level, and to deal with these issues both horizontally (with local government bodies) at the source, and vertically through the Party hierarchy.[44]

The staff of the central Party apparatus performs functions somewhat similar to the staffs of U.S. Congressional committees. They are involved in a combination of politics, analysis, and investigation. The staff of the Defense Production Department totals perhaps 90-100 professionals,[45] closely comparable to the staffs of Congressional committees dealing with defense matters.[46]

The secretariat staff, on the whole, are said to be highly capable, experienced individuals, somewhat younger and better educated than the government administrators they supervise.[47] The secretariat staff also have the undeniable benefit of the authority of the Party leadership to back them in their dealings with their nonapparatus counterparts. Even the most junior responsible workers ("instructors") can telephone instructions, for example, to the first secretary of the Central Committee of a Union Republic, to a deputy minister of a production ministry, or to the director of a research institute.[48] Instructors also have access to information gathered by the Soviet Secret Police (KGB).[49] These junior staff are said to be "treated like little kings when they travel in the provinces, as local officials are anxious to have them write good reports."[50]

Important decisions are often made informally, in fact, by the responsible staff who then, with the enlisted support of the Central Committee hierarchy, move the proposal toward formal passage. The Central Committee Secretariat thus acts as more than an adviser to the political leadership. It performs extensive executive functions, both indirectly through submission of policies to the Politburo for formal approval and directly through intervention in government activities.[51] Its members are called upon to mediate knotty issues that have been assigned to ad hoc bodies before they reach the Politburo.[52] Jurisdictional conflicts do not usually arise because the primacy of the Party is recognized by everyone. However, Politburo members can raise objections to secretariat activities at Politburo level.

As mentioned above, the Department of Defense Production oversees the political and substantive activities of the defense production sector; however, there is no organ in the secretariat formally responsible for purely military affairs or for defense policy. The Main Political Administration of the Soviet Army and Navy (MPA), which operates simultaneously as a Central Committee Secretariat department and as a directorate in the Ministry of Defense, oversees Party political work within the military services. Most of this work involves the detailed supervision of Party activities in military units, although occasionally MPA officers publish authoritative articles on doctrine, especially on the relationship between political authority and military affairs, that are consistent with the tasks of maintaining a correct Party line and building morale.

The Administrative Organs Department deals with personnel selection and promotion, particularly of Party members, throughout the military and KGB. Its present head is N. I. Savinkin, who succeeded N. R. Mironov in 1968. The links of the Party apparatus with the military have been well established.[53] Since 90 percent of all officers belong to the Party, the influence of this department on the military leadership can be substantial. However, its direct impact on weapons procurement is probably quite small.

In an assessment of the contribution of the secretariat to policy formulation, two points are important. First, it is likely that the secretariat departments become allied with, and to a large extent dependent on, the ministries they supervise. Second, however, the departments have an overview that is larger than that of any single ministry and a perception of their own role that goes beyond the goals of ministries and enterprises. Therefore, one would expect, in general, a congruence of interests between the secretariat and the military-production sector; but on interministerial or intraministerial questions there is less reason to assume a community of interests.[54] Frequent and intimate contact between Party and government officials, personnel transfers between Party and government, cooperation in the drafting and working out of major decisions, and many other transactions that bring Party staff and those they supervise into prolonged contact, result in a general similarity of views. In this sense it is correct to speak of a military industry-Party complex in which the Department of Defense Production has more in common with the military products ministries than it does with the other departments in the secretariat. Indeed, Hough argues that because of the specialization within the Central Committee Secretariat, department heads and staffs have a narrower perspective than many local Party officials.[55]

The secretariat staff is therefore unlikely to be a source of independent analysis of military-production questions that differ appreciably from the points of view of the ministries they supervise, even though differences over details are probable. Moreover, the secretariat has no institutional capacity to criticize military policies. However, individual secretaries, especially those with the authority and background of a man like Ustinov, might be expected to engage in debate on a personal and political basis rather than on institutional grounds. But pressures could just as well work in the other direction—*from* the Politburo and other Central Committee secretaries *to* the secretary for defense production.

SECRETARIAT OF THE GENERAL SECRETARY

Each of the secretaries of the Central Committee has a small personal staff.[56] Since the early 1970s, the size and importance of Secretary General Brezhnev's staff has grown in proportion with his own authority. This staff, headed by G. E. Tsukanov, is believed to rank as a Central Committee department, although it is not listed as one.[57]

These twenty to twenty-five experts specialize in foreign affairs (with different individuals responsible for the United States, Eastern Europe, and other regions), industrial matters, and the armed forces, although the division of labor is not always clear and there is some sharing and switching of responsibilities.[58] The rank of Brezhnev's secretariat has been indicated by the relative position of staff members in official dispatches, which places them above deputy foreign ministers and ambassadors.[59] This importance is apparently consonant with their responsibilities.

One of the more important tasks has been controlling the flow of information from the Central Committee Secretariat, through the general secretary, to the Politburo. Immediately after Khrushchev's fall, Central Committee secretaries and departments submitted information and recommendations directly to the Politburo. As Brezhnev gained control over the secretariat, clearance was required from him before information was given wider distribution to Politburo members. Since about 1970, submissions have been first sent as a matter of routine to Brezhnev's secretariat.[60] The secretariat also appears to review substantive proposals before they are finally submitted to the Politburo. The reviews, covering both form and substance, may request additional information or the views of various officials. The staff may also draw attention to additional options, including the consequences of the possible decisions.[61]

Appointment of government ministers (KGB, foreign affairs, defense) to the Politburo in the past decade has been suggested as one factor contributing to the rise in eminence of Brezhnev's secretariat. Typically, the Central Committee Secretariat oversees government operations, but if government officials also sit on the Politburo, this supervision is short circuited. Brezhnev's personal staff therefore may take on the additional responsibility of overseeing these particularly sensitive and poltically significant areas.

OUTSIDE ADVISERS AND CONSULTANTS

The growing complexity and increased technical content of defense and other national policies require a diversity of specialized expertise not ordinarily available to the Soviet leadership through its established staff organizations. Compartmentalized government agencies often do not have the breadth of knowledge needed to cope with rapidly changing events and unpredictable technologies. The use of experts from outside the Party apparatus and government is therefore a necessary concomitant to national policy making, and its growth is a notable feature of recent Soviet decision-making practices. This advice is obtained from institutions expressly established to provide it, from consultative groups, and from consultation with individuals on specific matters.

Institutions analyzing international affairs blossomed in the late 1960s, apparently under the guidance of the International Department of the Central Committee. For example, a consultants group was attached to the International Department, chaired in the past by a deputy to department head Ponomarev, and before that by academician Georgii A. Arbatov, director of the Institute for the Study of the USA and Canada.[62] The leading organizations advising the Politburo and secretariat on international affairs are two academy of sciencies institutes: Arbatov's USA Institute and the Institute for the World Economy and International Affairs (IMEMO). The growth of these organizations was motivated less by a desire to circumvent military expertise (which was deemed to be satisfactory) than to acquire broader data and analyses, and to correlate military issues with political, economic, and sociological considerations.[63] The institutes are staffed in part by former military and security officers; one of their tasks is to study the military affairs and strategy of the United States and other countries. A good deal of this research is published openly in academic journals and books; some research, however, is directly requested by and privately provided to the Central Committee Secretariat, Brezhnev's secretariat, or Brezhnev himself.[64] Much of this private advice, often provided on a "crash basis," is transmitted via the institutes' directors, who are personally close to their clients in the leadership. Occasionally, institutes may initiate studies and circulate them through published documents and personal contacts among leading officials. The status accorded to the institute directors and their close relationships with the leaders enable them to make an independent contribution to the cumbersome decision-making process.[65]

Military advice per se is still largely the monopoly of the Ministry of Defense, although the few retired or loaned high-level officers now found in some research institutes and their civilian associates carry out research on non-Soviet military affairs. The new sources of analysis may provide the seed bed for more extensive research in the future, but for the present it seems to be constrained by the jealously guarded monopoly of the General Staff and the pervasive secrecy surrounding military matters. For example, a staff member of IMEMO has disclosed that the General Staff objected to the institute's compiling defense statistics of a non-Soviet country, protesting that this was not an appropriate function for a civilian research institute. On the other hand, a staff member of the USA Institute has claimed that the Politburo has entrusted it and IMEMO with the task of forming alternative disarmament strategies to those provided by the General Staff.[66] However, the academic writers are unfamiliar with the details of Soviet arms control policies and receive their information through non-Soviet publications. They affect the process, therefore, by addressing general issues rather than the technical items of specific policies.[67]

There are contacts between the political leaders and individual scientists and experts on a less formal level. Khrushchev's links with scientists and weapons designers are a case in point. The aircraft designer A. N. Tupolev, for example, often came to him with ideas for new projects. Tupolev's country house in the Crimea adjoined Khrushchev's, and the designer would wander over with folders of new ideas that he would describe to the first secretary.[68]

Other Politburo members have attempted to supplement information coming through official channels by informal consultations with academic experts. Soviet émigré scientists have described a symbiotic relationship between politicians and research institutes: the institutes provide analyses and advice, and the Politburo member acts as a patron of the institute, protecting its budget and its position.[69] Such informal advice is often viewed with suspicion by the Central Committee Secretariat experts and by the ministries, but Politburo members are powerful enough to ignore these feelings.[70]

Ad hoc Politburo committees nominated by Brezhnev are being increasingly used to resolve complex issues on which there is not an immediate consensus.[71] Other committees can be convoked by Brezhnev's secretariat to develop specific policy recommendations. Since these committees are without any staff, they must draw on experts from the government and from research institutes of the Academy of Sciences.[72] Brezhnev's secretariat plays a key role in supervising the staffing of these high-level consultations, thereby controlling—or at least monitoring—the flow of information. However, bureaucratic barriers impede advice to the top policy makers as ministers and administrators interpose themselves between expert and potential client. This problem has been considered serious enough for Brezhnev's secretariat to ask the State Committee on Science and Technology for recommendations on freeing the flow of scientific advice. This may simply be another way for Brezhnev to control scientific information and advice, or it could be a genuine attempt to solve a vexing problem.[73]

In recent years, many "hard" scientists and social scientists have joined the staffs of both the Central Committee and Brezhnev's secretariat. Although no longer members of the working scientific community, they have the background and training to absorb technical advice. When called on by the Central Committee for consultation, experts consider it a special honor. In some instances, the process has been compared to testifying before an American Congressional committee; at other times, it is a consulting arrangement where the scientist does his work either at his own institute or at the Central Committee offices.[74]

Neither the Foreign Ministry nor the Central Committee departments conducts regular research on foreign affairs. Whenever a new problem arises or an old one takes on a new twist, there is a frantic search for outside expertise. A Central Committee secretary's request for an emergency study requires that work on other projects at a research institute be temporarily placed on one side.[75] Also, a part-time pool of experts is available to the Central Committee as a "consultative group."[76]

"Hard science" advice to the secretariat is given on a less regular basis than that of the social sciences and appears to deal with a more limited range of problems. At a more technical level, ministries involved in defense production often contract with research institutes in the Academy of Sciences for help in solving specific problems. But here the work is defined within narrow limits and restricted by great secrecy.

DEFENSE COUNCIL AND MAIN MILITARY COUNCIL

The Defense Council (*Sovvet Oborony*) of the Soviet Union, placed under the Presidium of the Supreme Soviet by the 1977 Constitution, links politicians and the military at the highest level.[77] Essentially a subcommittee of the Politburo and chaired by Brezhnev, perhaps with military participation, it is responsible for the task—as Soviet writers describe it—of "leadership of the country's defense." This task is broader than and separate from "leadership of the armed forces." The latter concerns specifically military questions, and is the job principally of the military leadership itself.[78] The former includes, in addition to military issues, "questions of internal and external policy, of the economy, ideology, and diplomacy of the state."[79] The leadership of the armed forces is today the task of the Main Military Council, which is subordinate to the Defense Council.

These two bodies have had checkered careers, having been expanded, contracted, altered, merged, eliminated, and restored. Their precise composition, roles, and methods of operation are shrouded in secrecy, but the available information can be filled out somewhat through analogy to past practices and present routines. A Council of Workers' and Peasants' Defense formed to lead the defenses of the fledgling government during the Civil War (1918-20) gave way to the Council of Labor and Defense (1920-37), which was superseded but not completely replaced by Stalin's Defense Commission (1932-37). Following the purges of the late 1930s, the Spanish Civil War, and the rise of the threat from Hitler, military power was centralized in the Committee of Defense (1937-41); during the wartime years of 1941-45, this was transformed into the State Committee of Defense (GKO: *Gosudarstvenyy Komitet Oborony*). The GKO, chaired by Stalin, wielded absolute authority in the state and was concerned especially with the mobilization of economic resources for the war effort until it was abolished in 1945.

Leadership of the armed forces was the task of variously named military councils of the army and navy until 1941, when a combined General Headquarters, or *Stavka,* was created to direct the overall wartime strategic command. At the end of the fighting, the *Stavka* was dissolved and replaced by a Higher Military Council. Our knowledge of this body is confused, perhaps because it combined in one organization the two functions carried out separately during the war by the GKO and *Stavka.* In October 1958, at the time of Khrushchev's dismissal of Zhukhov, the Higher Military Council (which Zhukhov was accused of trying to liquidate) was described as "the collective organ composed of members and candidate members of the Politburo, military and political leaders of the army and fleet."[80] Penkovsky also noted the existence of a council, chaired by Khrushchev, with three additional Politburo members and the Minister of Defense, his deputies, branch commanders, and other senior military officers.[81] This rather large body was directly subordinate to the Politburo, met regularly, and was often involved in quite detailed matters.

Some time between the early 1960s and 1967, this body was apparently split into two groups: the present Defense Council charged with leadership of the nation's defense, and the Main Military Council, which assumed authority for detailed military policy together with command and control of the armed forces.[82]

The exact composition of the Defense Council is not known, and there is consequently some disagreement among analysts' speculations. Brezhnev is known to be the chairman, and all sources agree that Prime Minister Kosygin and former President Podgorny were members. Marshal Grechko and Party Secretary Ustinov were both said to be members, and one writer, citing an interview with a former member of the Soviet General Staff, claimed that the chiefs of the General Staff and Warsaw Pact forces were also on the Defense Council.[83] Podgorny's removal from the Politburo, Marshal Grechko's death, and the assumption of the Ministry of Defense post by Ustinov may mean that only three Politburo members are now on the Defense Council: Brezhnev, Kosygin, and Ustinov. Some analysts suggest that other political and military leaders might attend meetings dealing with topics germane to their interests or expertise: the foreign minister, the KGB head, the Internal Affairs minister, or the chairman of the Military-Industrial Commission.[84]

The Main Military Council is a collegial group advising the minister of defense. It includes the minister of defense, his first deputy chairman, deputy chairmen (which include the service commanders), the chief of the Main Political Administration, and the chairman of the Defense Council. In wartime, the Main Military Council would become the headquarters of the Supreme High Command, operating much like the *Stavka* in World War II.[85]

The Defense Council has the job of planning the country's economic mobilization in wartime and supplying the military in the light of the council's perceptions of doctrine and threat. It is said to be primarily concerned with major weapons developments and procurement programs, manpower levels, and budget allocations.[86] In line with its budgetary responsibilities, the Defense Council provides the guidelines at the beginning of the planning process and would make recommendations to the Politburo regarding the final plans of the minister of defense and military-production ministries.[87] In wartime, the Defense Council would presumably assume the same functions as Stalin's GKO.

During the SALT negotiations, the Defense Council was the chief instrument through which the political authorities became involved in the process of military decision making.[88] Wolfe argued that it was in this group that the final policy decisions on SALT were resolved on behalf of the Politburo as a whole.[89]

The Defense Council, then, is potentially the key political policy-making body for military affairs in the Soviet Union, supplying the full Politburo with recommendations while receiving from it the broadest guidelines on priorities and budgetary allocations. The Defense Council approves doctrinal and strategic formulations, gives overall budgets to the military, reviews final plans, and approves weapons programs.

Formally, the Defense Council is said to have an advisory role,[90] but it is difficult to imagine that advice on military affairs offered to the Politburo by a group that included the general secretary of the Party, the prime minister, and the defense minister would be ignored or overruled. On the other hand, there is the distinct possibility that the Defense Council serves only at the pleasure of the general secretary and the Politburo, that it reports at their bidding, and that it exists more for crisis management than for regular consideration of political-military affairs. Indeed, some writers say that it meets only infrequently in order to consider major disagreements or deal with problems of critical national importance.[91]

Given the heavy responsibilities and workloads of the Defense Council members, it does not seem unreasonable to argue that its involvement in defense matters is limited. If this were indeed the case, then day-to-day leadership would necessarily be devolved to the Main Military Council and the Ministry of Defense, with only the most important political decisions, resources allocations, and major military movements reserved for the Defense Council. This devolution of detailed leadership to the military would be even more complete if the Defense Council had no independent staff but depended on the General Staff of the Ministry of Defense. Although evidence on this point is fragmentary, it appears that neither the Central Committee Secretariat nor Brezhnev's secretariat possesses the necessary resources to provide military advice. Indeed, former Defense Minister Malinovskiy wrote in 1964 that Soviet defense policy was made "only after conferences with the representatives of the General Staff."[92] Khrushchev too made several references regarding political consultation with the General Staff before making important military policy decisions. Although such consultation would be a natural and expected prelude to policy formation, there is no suggestion in these writings that technical advice was either sought or available elsewhere. If it is the case that the Defense Council must rely on the military for advice and expertise, political contributions to military-political decision making are deprived of an independent analytical foundation and would therefore follow military desires in most detailed matters, or fall back on broader political judgments for the rarer disagreements with military advice.

MINISTRY OF DEFENSE

Almost all military activities in the Soviet Union are under the aegis of the Ministry of Defense (MOD). These activities will be discussed in three sections: centralized ministry activities, the General Staff, and the five branch services of the armed forces.[93] Agencies with weapons acquisition responsibilities exist in each of these areas, although their specific tasks have not been clearly delineated by outside analysts. Indeed, the very existence and names of some of these organizations remain in doubt.

The ministry tends to have a more political complexion than the professionally oriented General Staff, even though all posts within it are occupied by military personnel. The exception is the present minister, Dmitrii F. Ustinov, a civilian with extensive experience in military production, economic planning, and the Party secretariat. Ustinov is one of the few civilians to occupy this position since Leon Trotsky was removed from the post in 1925.[94] Ustinov is a Politburo member, as was his predecessor, Marshal Grechko, who was appointed to the Politburo in 1973. Politburo membership for the defense minister marked a change from past practices when only political marshals were so honored.[95] Serving under the minister are three first deputies: the chiefs of the Warsaw Pact and General Staff and a deputy who aids in administration. The chief of the Main Political Administration also has the protocol rank of a first deputy minister.

In the past, the Warsaw Pact commander was considered to be second in command to the minister of defense, with the chief of the General Staff in third position. However, recent observations reverse these rankings. This is thought to be the result of a growing overall role for the General Staff, especially as the top-level commanders attempt to gain a firmer hand on command and control of the armed forces while the Ministry of Defense focuses on administration and resource allocation.[96] Personalities were also important in this reversal of rankings: until his death, the former head of the Warsaw Pact, Marshal Yakubovsky, was too senior and powerful to be relegated to third place; but death and the rising eminence of Chief of the General Staff Ogarkov apparently were sufficient to allow an underlying trend of growing General Staff influence to emerge.

There is some evidence of internal conflicts between central ministry agencies and the General Staff.[97] Penkovsky, for example, described tensions between Defense Minister Malinovsky and the General Staff and noted a lack of respect by the General Staff for their minister.[98] At the SALT talks, the Ministry of Defense and General Staff contingents often acted independently and reported via separate channels to the Politburo, the defense industry, and academic institutions, although it was difficult for American negotiators to identify their functional differences.[99] These organizational divisions illustrate the more general phenomenon of varied and competing interests among military leaders in the ministry, General Staff, and services with their differing stakes in particular weapons program and postures.[100] Such disagreements provide the Party with opportunities for control over a less-than-monolithic military establishment; disagreements may even be promoted by Party leaders precisely in order to gain control.[101]

Roughly parallel structures exist in the central MOD organization, the General Staff, and the main staffs of the individual services. Thus, there is a ministry-level directorate for armaments, as well as a General Staff element for armaments. Similarly, in the air force, for example, an Armaments Directorate reports directly to the air force commander, and an agency in the air force's main staff also deals with armaments. The lines of authority appear to be ordered somewhat according to a matrix style of management, with the service armaments element falling under the immediate chain of command of the commander but also receiving guidance from its ministry-level counterpart. To complicate matters, the General Staff at the ministry level and the main staffs at the service level are charged with the responsibility of coordinating and directing the activities of ministry and service agencies. One interpretation of the evidence is that the staffs formulate policies, and the central agencies implement them under staff guidance. As will be shown below, we have a fairly good understanding of the service armament directorates, but the detailed operations of the other MOD agencies dealing with weapons procurement remain unclear.

The rank of deputy minister is held by the five service commanders and the chiefs of several directorates.[102] The armaments directorate of the Ministry of Defense, created in 1970, is headed by General Alekseyev, who had been chairman of the General Staff's scientific-technical committee for the previous ten years and was one of the chief Soviet delegates to SALT. This was not the first time an armaments agency was established in the ministry: several times in the past, organizations had been set up to handle major reequipment programs. This post was created in 1929 to carry out the technical reconstruction of the army under the first Five-Year Plan.[103] It was abolished in 1936 but reappeared from the late 1940s to the early 1950s, apparently to manage the strategic missile program. From 1953 to 1957 there was also a deputy minister for Radar and Radio-engineering. From this evidence, it appears that during periods of major development and construction programs of new equipment, an agency in the Ministry of Defense was created to manage the job—tanks and aircraft in the early 1930s, strategic missiles in the 1950s, and electronics in the late 1950s.

These programs absorbed large amounts of resources, and their impact on the economy would have been particularly severe because of the *new* requirements for skills, materials, and production capabilities. Such programs would have been kept under the watchful eyes of the political leadership, which is perhaps easier to accomplish in the ministry than in the jealously guarded preserves of the General Staff. However, the present specific function of the ministry's armaments directorate can only be surmised on the basis of past patterns and present trends. These suggest that it is responsible for major new programs characterized by high levels of priority, uncertainty, and costs, perhaps providing a link between force planning and weapons procurement.

As with the civilian sector, plans are one of the important tools for achieving coordination of weapons development and production. Although detailed planning is the responsibility of the General Staff, this is done under the initial guidance and continued control of the financial and other sections of central ministry organs.[104] This separation of functions would provide the minister with an independent check on General Staff planning activities. The planning cycle establishes the calendar for the resource allocation process and thereby inserts rigidities into the intraplan period.[105] However, the military is more capable than civilian industry of escaping from the worst of these rigidities, because of the priority given to military production and the authority vested in such agencies as the Military-Industrial Commission so as to ease bottlenecks.

GENERAL STAFF

The Soviet General Staff sits at the center of the weapons requirements process. Typically, it neither originates nor gives final approval to weapons programs, but all requests and proposals flow through the organization, conflicting demands are adjudicated there, and service claims are tailored to meet procurement budgets and planning goals.

An important task of the General Staff is the resolution of interservice conflicts over resource allocations. Conflicts that cannot be settled at this level may involve direct discussions between the service commanders and the defense minister, perhaps within the context of Higher Military Council deliberations.[106] General Staff involvement in resource allocation problems arose, for example, when Khrushchev called for a build-up of tank forces in preparation for a Berlin showdown in 1961. A controversy broke out in the General Staff over finances when it thought that too much money had been allocated to tank troops, depriving other services and weapons of planned funds.[107]

The General Staff's present authoritative position with respect to armaments dates from around the period of Khrushchev's removal. Its assumption of a greater role in weapons procurement coincided with the dissatisfaction of the Soviet political leadership with general economic efficiency and technological innovation that began to show itself in a major way in the mid-1950s. This uneasiness spread to concern with military efficiency and innovation by the mid-1960s, at the same time that doctrinal debates in the post-Khrushchev era were wrestling with the possibilities of actually fighting a nuclear war—a major change from the Khrushchev doctrine of avoiding and deterring general nuclear war.[108] A former General Staff officer highlighted this change by remarking that professionalism, which had always been the hallmark of the military leaders controlling weapons acquisition, moved from competence based on the *use* of weapons to an emphasis on technical experts who know how to *build* them.[109]

The Stalinist system of economic planning and the R&D that dominated economic affairs until the mid-1960s was designed to enforce political priorities centered on the growth of gross output in heavy industry (including military production). The important shift in economic growth strategy in the 1960s emphasized high productivity and technological innovation. The institutions and incentives developed to accomplish the Stalinist goals required modification to meet the new demands. In particular, three problems demanded attention by military planners: (1) the increasing cost of modern weapons; (2) efficient choice of which weapons to produce; and (3) the need for increased flexibility in weapons R&D as science (with its unpredictability) drew closer to technology.[110] There was growing concern that although the system was effective in supporting established priorities and in improving weapons types that were already in production, the selection of new priorities and the development of weapons that were "new in principle" was unsatisfactory.[111]

Erickson argues that the military was given the go-ahead for a military procurement program in the mid-1960s to achieve strategic parity with the United States and to buttress its conventional war-fighting capability—provided that it made the most effective use of the resources allocated.[112] The General Staff was selected as one of the loci for accomplishing the desired changes. (The other organization that seems to have increased its role in military-economic relations was the Military-Industrial Commission.) Within the General Staff, several agencies are responsible for weapons R&D and procurement, including a main operations directorate, a central financial directorate, a scientific-technical committee, and an armaments directorate.[113]

The main operations directorate enters into weapons procurement because of its central role in the formulation of general military policy and the main lines of future weapons development. The central financial directorate would be concerned with the budgetary side of weapons planning, trimming the military requirements to fit the planned availability of funds.

The General Staff's scientific-technical committee may have been established around 1960, when General Alekseyev was appointed to his post. There is some evidence that this committee plans the directions of military-related research throughout the economy and also in the Warsaw Pact countries.[114] It is said to have close connections with both *Gosplan* and the State Committee for Science and Technology.[115] The committee would also be called upon to provide technical advice on new weapons proposals. As part of this task, it may have the overall responsibility of managing scientific-technical committees formed to review and follow each proposal and project throughout the R&D process.[116] The committee is also said to be the center of operations research activity devoted to the selection of new weapons.

The armaments directorate of the General Staff is headed by Colonel General Druzhinin, a principal author of a book describing the potential uses of cybernetics and computers in military decision making and control. Most of the General Staff work in requirements, planning, and coordinating weapons procurement probably takes place in this directorate; the new analytical planning techniques also come from this organization. Erickson, however, makes the case that it was not by making institutional changes that the role of the General Staff was altered, but rather by shifts in personnel—the appointment of key officers with technical management experience who redefined the role and function of their position. It was the appointment in 1968 of General Ogarkov as first deputy chief of staff (with unspecified responsibilities) that signaled the enlarged role of the General Staff in military-scientific work. His duties were thought to include supervision and management of the scientific-technical committees in the General Staff and services, and overseeing weapons programs and R&D.[117] His appointment also suggests a liaison between the General Staff and the Military Industrial Commission. (The armaments directorate in the Ministry of Defense is now said to perform a similar task.) While in this post, Ogarkov also acted as the chief Soviet military representative to the SALT talks.

The difference in role between the scientific-technical committee and the armaments directorate of the General Staff seems to be that the committee acts as a technical review organization charged with establishing the technical feasibility and monitoring the progress of those projects put forward by the armaments directorate. These functions are duplicated at a lower level in the services, and parallel similar activities in the industrial ministries and the Military-Industrial Commission.

MILITARY SERVICES

Most requests for new or improved weapons, as well as the initial estimate of the number required, emanate from the individual military services. These requirements can come from several service sources that reflect the organizational structure of the General Staff and Defense Ministry: the armaments directorate, the scientific-technical committee of the main staff, the operations directorate of the main staff, or the field commands.[118]

The services' armaments directorate maintains regular contacts with the research institutes, design bureaus, and industrial plants of the industrial ministries.[119] The commander of this organization in the Soviet air forces has described his close relationship with research institutes of the Ministry of Aviation Production. In particular, he noted his personal ties with the Central

Aerohydrodynamics Institute (TSAGI) and its director. On the other hand, his dealings with design bureaus appeared to be more distant: "We go to a design bureau with a project and they say, 'We can do part of it now and the rest in five years!' So then we go to another bureau and ask them. They too might say they can do some part, but not another. And so we go from one bureau to another and find out what they think can be done."[120]

The central role of the armaments directorates in requirements generation goes back to before World War II. The artillery designer Grabin stated, "As a rule, our plant received its tactical-technical requirements for the development of new guns from the Main Artillery Directorate." He added, however, an important amendment: "But several guns were developed on our own initiative."[121] The relative importance of the armaments directorate continues, but other organizations also contribute to the initiation of requests for weapons.

The main staffs of the services are the most likely additional source of new requests, both from the services' scientific-technical committee and from the operations directorate. As suggested in the previous section, scientific-technical committees are probably responsible for planning research and for managing project review bodies. In this position, they would be alert both to technical opportunities, on the one hand, and to development problems on the other. They would thus be in an ideal position to make recommendations from a technical point of view. In contrast, the operations staff would have the outlook of the equipment user and would be expected to make suggestions based on particular mission responsibilities or on field-demonstrated problems and needs. Field commanders would promote even more applications-orientated tactical-technical requirements than the operations staff.[122] In the navy, fleet commanders are said to have a significant impact on naval policy, including force procurement. Differences in fleet composition are one piece of evidence to suggest divergent opinions on program priorities.[123] The orientation or bias of requirements would thus seem to be partly determined by their origins: as one moves from the scientific-technical committee to armaments directorate to operations staff to field commanders, one would expect a shift from technical to mission influence.[124]

As part of its job of monitoring weapons projects through development and production, the armaments directorate sends teams of military representatives to facilities that have substantial military R&D or production contracts.[125] The military representatives formally accept equipment on behalf of the military customer and insure that quality and performance meet the specifications laid out in contracts.[126] They can also work out independent cost estimates to compare with the enterprise's figures. The authority vested in the military representatives gives the military customer a unique advantage in the Soviet Union, where customers typically operate in a market dominated by the seller.

Some sources claim that the military representatives, often retired officers, are unqualified for their jobs. But the generality of these observations is disputed by those who say that the representatives take their jobs seriously. A good reason for the military representatives to perform well is that they can be tried in the courts for criminal negligence if they accept inferior products. Examples have been described of special commissions formed to investigate the failure of military equipment in the case of tank turrets and welded submarine structures. In these cases, the military representatives were jailed for their contributions to the failures.[127] This is not to say that military representatives do not occasionally collude with plant managers, but these activities are often intended to further the military's own goals.[128] Despite their potential power within the plants, the military representatives perform primarily a control rather than management function. They are able to achieve high quality because of the dominance of the buyer and because of the priorities in materials, equipment, and manpower given to military production.

Although the military representatives help insure the quality of military products, the military customer must also pay (though perhaps not the full costs) for this advantage. The costs of meeting military quality standards can be substantial, since the plant must use higher quality materials, more skilled workers, and more stringent quality control. The higher cost of labor and materials is compounded by higher rejection rates of unacceptable products. Nevertheless, it is in this way that the military is assured of higher quality products than are commonly found elsewhere in the Soviet economy.

COUNCIL OF MINISTERS

The Council of Ministers, at the apex of administrative, executive, and planning functions in the Soviet government, is responsible for the implementation of policies originating in the Party. The Council of Ministers includes the chiefs of almost sixty ministries, seventeen state committees, a handful of agencies such as the State Bank, and the chairmen of the Councils of Ministers of the fifteen Union Republics. With more than 100 members, this body is too unwieldy to manage the Soviet economy. Like the organization of the Communist party of the Soviet Union, a smaller Presidium of the Council of Ministers is the locus of real policy making. Led by the prime minister (chairman of the Council of Ministers), the Presidium contains the deputy chairmen, including a deputy responsible for the defense industry sector.[129] Meeting weekly, the Presidium is a kind of inner cabinet whose members exercise a high degree of authority in coordinating broad areas of national administration. Since 1964, the prime minister has been Aleksei Kosygin.

In accordance with its job of working out the details of broad Politburo policies, the Presidium of the Council of Ministers must allocate specific resources for designated products among the Soviet Union's numerous ministries and enterprises. Defense production is just one of the many claimants on available resources, and although the Presidium can be expected to give defense the priority demanded by the political leadership, other economic goals are also important. Since defense priorities can have the effect of disrupting plans elsewhere and thereby reducing overall efficiency, special bodies have been created over the years to deal directly with the peculiar requirements and special priorities of military production. The Military-Industrial Commission, chaired by the deputy chairman for the defense industries, is the working group responsible for supervising, coordinating, and planning defense R&D and production and for assuring the smooth meshing of military requirements with the rest of the economy. (The Military-Industrial Commission is described in the following section.)

The transformation of the leadership's priorities into the detailed commands needed to direct the activities of many thousands of enterprises producing tens of thousands of products throughout the economy is the responsibility of the State Planning Commission (*Gosplan*), operating under the Council of Ministers. *Gosplan* has a separate division that develops the military production plan and integrates it with the rest of the economy. This military plan is transmitted separately to enterprises, which must satisfy its goals as a first priority. However, *Gosplan* influences weapons procurement more through its planning procedures than through its active involvement in policy making or implementation.

The chief method of Soviet planning lies in the simple practice of adding to the relevant *ex post* figures a certain percentage of growth. That is the foundation of all the technique, all the methodology of Soviet planning. The rest is secondary. The topmost level of the governing bureaucracy is responsible for establishing or reordering priorities in the light of past achievements. These rankings supplement the basic planning technique by directing resources in short supply to the highest priority sectors. This basic technique of planned and formal incrementalism has been described as perfectly suited to the bureaucratic organization of Soviet economic management. Although there are many inherent advantages in this approach, there are several important disadvantages. The chief defect is that "it congeals tempos and proportions. The method is by its nature conservative."[130] Not only does it lead to inflexibility between planning periods, but the immense complexities involved in revising and regenerating plans and allocations produce great rigidity within the periods. Since national economic management is planned at the center, the director of *Gosplan* sits on the Presidium of the Council of Ministers, where he has personal contact with the managers of the Soviet economy, including the deputy chairman for defense industry.

L. V. Smirnov has been deputy chairman of the Council of Ministers for defense industry since 1963, when he succeeded the ubiquitous Ustinov, who had held the position for more than five years. He is also chairman of the Military-Industrial Commission. Smirnov emerged as an active participant in the SALT talks in May 1972, when he was said to have been particularly effective as a "tough and skilful negotiator" with "a technician's grasp of the issue" superior to anyone else on either side of the table.[131] Smirnov's background as foreman and factory director in a defense plant, as a research institute director, and as chairman of the State Committee on Defense Technology (the successor organization to the Defense Production Ministry during the *Sovnarkhoz* experiments) gave him ample preparation for his present job.

But Smirnov is by no means the only man with a defense-industry background in high administration circles. In the early 1960s, military industrialists were in virtual control of the economy, holding three out of eight seats in the Council of Ministers Presidium, the deputy positions in the long- and short-term planning bodies, and the leadership of the economic organs in the Russian republic.[132] Since then, death, reassignment, and reorganization have reduced this concentration, although five members of the present Presidium have strong backgrounds in the defense industry. A possible reason for the prominence of military industrialists in the early 1960s is that the military and their allies in heavy industry were trying to isolate military production from Khrushchev's experiments of managerial decentralization. With experienced military-industrial people in key economic positions, the effects of regionalization could be mitigated. This attempt seems most evident with the creation of the Supreme Council of the National Economy (Supreme *Sovnarkhoz*) in 1963, with Ustinov made both its chief and also a first deputy chairman of the Council of Ministers.[133] The Supreme *Sovnarkhoz,* closely connected with the defense industries, was reluctantly accepted by Khrushchev.

This episode was just one example of the frequent industrial reorganizations throughout the post-World War II period in a series of attempts to increase efficiency and stir innovation. Peacetime conversion, the establishment and disbanding of "superministries" following Stalin's death, Khrushchev's experiments with regional rather than industrial principles of organization, and the consequent reversion to industrial forms after Khrushchev's fall marked the industrial scene for twenty years. The ability of the defense industry to sail through the several storms and emerge relatively unscathed depended in part on the positions of prominent defense industry alumni in the Presidium and elsewhere.

MILITARY-INDUSTRIAL COMMISSION

The Military-Industrial Commission (VPK: *Voennopromyshlennaia kommissiia*) is a working commission of the Council of Ministers with representation from the military-industrial ministries, the Ministry of Defense, the State Planning Agency, and probably the Central Committee Secretariat. Chaired by Deputy Chairman of the Council of Ministers Leonid V. Smirnov and presumably with a large staff, the VPK is the principal coordinating body for military research, development, and production. It also plays a key role in technical evaluations of new weapons proposals.[134] Although the VPK is nominally an organ of the Council of Ministers, there is some speculation that, in practice, it may be closely associated with, and may perhaps be responsible to the secretary for defense production of the Central Committee.[135]

In 1918, an executive committee responsible for Soviet military industry replaced a prerevolutionary group with a similar name and function. It seems to have operated until the beginning of World War II, when it was absorbed by the State Defense Committee. The State Defense Committee was itself abolished after the war, and it is not known when the VPK resumed operation in its modern form. It may have regained its role at the time of political dissatisfaction with military production efficiency in the 1960s. The military may also have been seeking better coordination of industry in the period of Khrushchev's dispersion of industry.[136] References to such a body began to circulate among Western analysts in the late 1960s. But, as with so many of the institutions associated with the Soviet military, there is little detailed description of the history, responsibilities and operation of the VPK.

As planner and coordinator of military R&D and production throughout the economy, the VPK is called upon to review proposals for new weapons with respect to their technical feasibility and production requirements. These proposals would come up through the various production ministries for final approval by the VPK. Project-related scientific-technical committees may also have VPK members, and in any event their activities would be expected to be scrutinized by the VPK.[137] The VPK draws up a concrete work program in the form of a "draft VPK decision" for the project, including the tasks assigned to specific organizations, timetables, funding arrangements, and detailed design specifications. When approved by the VPK leadership and Council of Ministers (most probably a *pro forma* approval), the draft document becomes a VPK decision, which is legally binding on all parties concerned. As part of its functions, the VPK would also be required to assess the impact of weapons programs on other sectors of the economy.

Weapons-related work throughout the economy carries the highest priority. The VPK is very likely to be the agency that polices these priorities. In doing this, it would have to allocate scarce resources among competing priorities, act to alleviate bottlenecks, expedite shipments, and generally keep things running smoothly.[138] However, keeping things running smoothly in the military-industrial sector necessarily creates disruptions elsewhere, imposing a cost on the economy that may not be fully recognized and is certainly not included in state budgets.[139]

The VPK also manages military-related R&D and coordinates research with the Academy of Sciences, although Western analysts do not know the relationship between these tasks and the research planning and administration carried on by the various scientific-technical committees of the Ministry of Defense and the State Committee on Science and Technology.[140] Soviet scientists describe some research institutes in the Academy of Sciences as being under VPK control. The VPK is also said to have a role in coordinating military-related R&D in the Warsaw Pact countries.

Despite the overall involvement of the VPK in most aspects of weapons acquisition, most sources emphasize that it is an implementing organization, rather than one that originates policy. Policy, they say, comes from the Politburo, the Defense Council, and the General Staff. It is the job of the VPK to see that the policies are fulfilled. Nevertheless, because the VPK provides information, performs technical analyses, and screens recommendations it has earlier approved, it must have a more than marginal influence on the type and number of weapons produced.

DEFENSE INDUSTRY

Soviet weapons are produced in eight ministries reporting to a deputy chairman of the Council of Ministers. They are controlled by the VPK and are also supervised by the Defense Production Department of the Central Committee Secretariat. Research and development on new and improved weapons takes place, for the most part, in research institutes and design bureaus in these ministries, with support provided by Academy of Sciences institutes and laboratories in institutions of higher education. Although the defense production ministries operate to some extent under the same system of incentives and constraints as the civilian sector, several mechanisms have been adopted to shield military-related efforts from the more deleterious effects of the economic system.

The present eight ministries evolved through reorganizations of older bodies and creation of new ones. On the eve of World War II, a single Commissariat of Defense Production was responsible for most weapons.[141] In 1939, the monolithic structure was split into several commissariats concerned with production, such that by 1945, seven separate production ministries existed for aircraft, mortars, tanks, ships, etc. These were recombined after the war into three ministries: for ships, aircraft, and armaments, with the last two brought together in a superministry for military production after Stalin's death. This concentration lasted for less than a year when, in addition to aviation resuming its former identity, new ministries were established for electronics and nuclear weapons. Ballistic missile production was assigned to a new ministry in 1965, and the manufacture of electronic components was separated from final electronic products in 1961. The defense production ministries were the last to fall under Khrushchev's regional reorganization (the *Sovnarkhoz* period) in 1958 and were the first to resume their ministerial status in 1965. During that seven-year period, defense production was administered by state committees, which retained central control of R&D and perhaps some production as well. In 1968, a new ministry became responsible for conventional ammunition, and in 1974 the Ministry of the Means of Communication was hived off from the Ministry of Communication. The following nine core ministries are today responsible for defense production:[142]

Ministry of Defense Industry	—conventional weapons
Ministry of Aviation Industry	—aircraft, engines, parts, air-breathing missiles
Ministry of Shipbuilding Industry	—ships and submarines
Ministry of Electronics Industry	—electronic components
Ministry of Radio Industry	—electronic products
Ministry of Medium Machine Building	—nuclear weapons
Ministry of General Machine Building	—ballistic missiles
Ministry of Machine Building	—ammunition
Ministry of the Means of Communication	—telecommunications equipment

A number of other ministries, though predominantly civilian, also contribute to the military effort. These include the ministries for automobiles, tractors, chemicals, and instruments.

The ministries are organized in a fairly standard way,

with Chief Administrations reponsible for functional tasks, including one for R&D, and others responsible for various product groups.[143] In the Ministry of General Machine Building, for example, there are four administrations for the production of ground equipment, rocket motors, control instruments, and missile production and assembly. In the Aviation Ministry, as in most ministries, an advisory Scientific-Technical Council is charged with reviewing new proposals and overseeing R&D.[144]

The heads of the chief administrations and other deputies form a ministerial council to advise the minister on the running of his organization, but the minister himself is usually endowed with sufficient authority and competence to dominate his subordinates.

The defense industrial sector operates within the general Soviet system of planned allocations and outputs, created to meet Stalin's goals of industrial growth under central Party leadership and control. Quantitative norms were the key indexes for assessing performance under this regime. Though relatively successful in developing the gross capabilities of the Soviet economy, this system has no automatic mechanism for fostering technological progress, largely because of its centralized control and emphasis on quantitative goals.

The leadership's new emphasis on quality rather than quantity brought the issue of innovation to the center of attention, with technological change promoted as the source of increased productivity and growth.[145] This is nowhere more true than in the military sector. The problem of innovation and technological change is one that Soviet military industry has faced since the first Five-Year Plan in the early 1930s. The Soviet leadership addressed this problem by giving the sector a priority and attention not enjoyed by others.[146] Priority resulted in the allocation of relatively large and scarce resources (including manpower) to the military sector. Particularly important for technologically advanced industries, priorities allowed a planning flexibility not enjoyed elsewhere in the Soviet economy.

High-quality manpower (including scientists and other technical workers) has been drawn to military R&D and production by larger salaries and bonuses than can be earned elsewhere and by nonpecuniary benefits such as housing.[147] However, there is growing doubt as to whether these inducements weigh as strongly now as in the past.[148]

In scientific work, it appears to be the universal experience of those familiar with both sectors that military-related research is granted a much greater quantity and quality of laboratory equipment than nonmilitary projects.[149] According to Soviet émigrés, whereas budgets from the Academy of Sciences were quite stable, military research budgets typically grew at an annual rate of about 5 percent. These budgetary practices meant, for example, that unpromising work that would lead to cancellation of the project in ordinary research would be granted funds for a different approach in military work; or that several research teams could attempt to reach the same goal by alternative processes, thus lending both competition and the benefit of parallel developments to the chosen projects.[150] The enforceability of contracts from defense production ministries seems to increase as one moves from research to production.[151] Production contracts are said to have the force of decrees issued by the Council of Ministers (probably through the VPK). Military representatives insure that the products delivered meet the specifications stated in the contracts. Some scientists in academy institutes felt, though, that contracts were not as stringent for scientific work as for production articles, since specification of scientific results is notoriously difficult.[152]

The military industry has other advantages. Its leadership has been remarkably stable. Most of the ministers and responsible persons in the Council of Ministers and Central Committee Secretariat have experience of military production dating back to the late 1930s.[153] The average tenure of the ministers in their present job amounts to more than twelve years.

With their years of experience and long familiarity with each other, with the Party, and with government industrial leadership, one would expect a community of shared values and interests—the basic necessities of "interest group" politics. Indeed, this group, along with its military customers, did appear to wield political influence during the period of Khrushchev's industrial decentralization, but this may have been designed as much to preserve their ability to perform their basic industrial tasks as to guard organizational empires. It is, in fact, the level of professional managerial competence of the military industrial leaders that appears to be most highly valued. Their value to the nation is indicated by cross-postings to manage new industrial sectors; by promotions to high positions in government, Party, and planning organizations; and by their technical contributions to matters such as SALT.[154]

The long tenure and wartime experience of the military industrial managers is likely to have induced a strong sense of the value of continuity in design and production. The intense emphasis on production during the war, and Stalin's insistence that change be held to a minimum to avoid disrupting production lines influenced the organization and procedures by which weapons are developed and produced.[155] Despite the privileged position of the defense industry, the managers have learned that continuity is the best guarantee of meeting planned output goals. While particularly true for the more traditional and conventional weapons such as tanks and aircraft, these values are embedded in a managerial ethos that continues to shape much in Soviet weapons procurement.

Over the years, several other organizational practices have evolved to implement the priority given to the military production sector. Concentration of production within a single plant, ministry, or the defense production sector insures greater control over resources than does dependence on the vagaries of uncontrollable suppliers. The Aviation Ministry, for example, produces sheet aluminum, magnesium alloys, shaped metal products, plastics, and rubber products. Commonly used components such as instruments, machine tools, rivets, nuts, and bolts, instead of being produced efficiently by a single supplier, are manufactured by all branches of defense industry; missile electronics, for example, are produced by the Ministry of General Machine Building.[156] The provision of excess capacity is another method for meeting the stringent demands of the military. Whereas most Soviet industry strains to meet its planning goals, a good deal of slack is found in the military product sector.[157] Normally, this excess capacity is used to produce a wide range of civilian goods, but the plant and manpower are available if necessary to meet a surge in demand or other unexpected requirement. In a widely quoted statement, Secretary Brezhnev declared in 1971 that "42 per cent of the entire volume of the defense industry's production is for civilian purposes."[158]

Each of the military industrial ministries, in addition to production, controls its own research institutes and design organizations. A key role in Soviet military R&D has been given to design bureaus and their chief designers. Their organizational position, however, varies across ministries. In the aviation industry, experimental design bureaus (OKB: *Opytno konstruktorskie byuro*) are established independently of research institutes and factories, although the OKB have their own shops where prototypes can be built.[159] In tank, artillery, and small arms, design organizations are attached to the production plants.[160] Shipyards have their own design bureaus, although some analysts speculate (on the basis of similarities in designs) that a central design bureau exists as well.[161] Ballistic missiles are designed in research institutes of the Ministry of General Machine Building. This pattern, probably more the result of historical development than planned, seems to consist of design and development moving from research institute to independent design bureau to factory as a technology matures. This movement was quite explicit in aviation when the Tupolev design group separated from TSAGI in the early 1930s. Helicopter design, being less well advanced, was retained in the research institute, with design bureaus being established only after the war.

The importance of designers stems partly from their technical competence (based to some degree on continuity of design experience), and also from their position at the central node between research and product, user and planner. They supply to the always chaotic R&D process a leadership and coordination made even more necessary in the Soviet Union by the absence of a responsive economy. It is the chief designer who is identified with the success or failure of a project. With these responsibilities, designers possess a degree of autonomy in running their organizations uncommon in the Soviet Union.[162]

Budgets and manpower levels of defense industry research institutes and design bureaus are relatively independent of production trends, exhibiting much less of the cyclical ups and downs of American weapons development teams as they follow the award or cancellation of contracts. This institutional stability results in a regular progression of designs and prototypes, as well as a level and quality of experience that only comes from the actual creation and test of new ideas in working hardware. The availability of improved weapons in prototype form may also make the follow-on production decision more likely than does the American military-political process of selling a plan instead of a product.

The success of a design bureau, despite its medium-term stability, depends in the long-run on the success of its products. The importance to the ultimate health of the organization of getting its designs accepted for production creates incentives for entrepreneurial behavior. The aircraft designer Yakovlev described these pressures as they existed in his group in the early 1950s, when Stalin ordered a concentration of resources on the Mig-15 designed by the rival Mikoyan bureau: "I was very worried about the situation developing in our design bureau. You see, behind me stood 100 people who might lose faith in me as the leader of the design collective." Yakovlev personally approached Stalin for permission to proceed with his own design. Stalin assented, and Yakovlev produced the Yak-25, which was later deployed in Soviet tactical aviation.[163]

A key feature of Soviet industrial organization is the great difficulty for newcomers to break into established industries. The creation of a new design bureau or the allocation of production capacity to a new product requires ministerial and planning approval; in some cases, it requires intervention from the top of the political leadership. Since little institutional provision is made for new technologies or products that are not a natural extension of current work, promotion of a new product requires either breaking into the system with the support of higher authorities or else creating new organizations outside the regular channels.

An illuminating example of the barriers to entry is provided by the 1960s debate over dirigibles.[164] The aviation ministry strongly opposed dirigibles, and their enthusiastic supporters attempted to promote them in the two ways mentioned above. The dirigible enthusiasts sought the aid of *Gosplan,* which saw sufficient merit in their plan to direct the Ministry of Aviation Industry to hear the arguments of the dirigible proponents before the Ministry's Scientific and Technical Commission. At first, the commission simply refused to consider the arguments, but in the end it relented. However, the hearings were described as "a dialogue of the deaf," the sessions being compared to "a first-class funeral prepared in advance."[165] Attempts to establish design bureaus outside the Aviation Ministry brought forth the blunt statement of aircraft designer Mikoyan: "If dirigibles are to be built, they will be built in the Aviation Ministry, and we are not going to do it."[166] Recognizing the need for higher-level intervention than they had so far obtained, the dirigible proponents called for national Party support, but they apparently never received enough to break down the barriers erected by the established organizations.

SOVIET ORGANIZATIONAL PROCESSES

A number of forces combine to give organizational life and decision making in the Soviet Union a peculiarly Soviet style that influences how as well as what decisions are made. This style has been described by journalists and other close observers of Soviet life and analyzed by psychologists, sociologists, historians, economists, and political scientists. The cultural influences on behavior, for example, have been variously ascribed to climate, geography, serfdom, the Orthodox Church, Tsarist autocracy, communal village life, swaddling practices, and child-rearing patterns. But in addition to strong cultural forces, structural and political influences affect decision making. Significantly, most of these forces act in the same direction, even though their relative strength is uncertain and their effect difficult to disentangle. However, there is fairly strong agreement concerning the salient features of organizational behavior—conservatism, petty bureaucratic obstructionism, secrecy, and departmentalism. Since the concept of conservatism is raised so frequently in this chapter, it may be useful to elaborate here on its usage. First, it must be considered in relative terms; the implicit standard of comparison is the United States or other industrialized Western societies. However, within the Soviet Union, the military is considerably more innovative than the civilian sector, partly because the former faces international competition of a particularly forceful nature. Second, I focus on the process rather than on outcomes; although, in general, conservative processes will have conservative results, this need not always be the case, as the Mig aircraft history in the next section demonstrates. Incrementalism, maintained continuously and for a long time, can produce substantial change. Third, while most bureaucracies are conservative in the sense that they will continue along the trajectories on which they are launched, the trajectories themselves can vary, and, I would argue, the laws of motion for Soviet bureaucracies are different from examples closer to home. Finally, Soviet conservatism is balanced by interventions from the leadership; consequently, it is not possible to offer a priori judgments as to which set of forces will prevail. Some periods have been marked by vigorous experiments and innovative thrusts, while others have been dominated by conservative principles. Leadership movements and politics therefore cannot be ignored.

ORGANIZATIONAL CONSERVATISM

Conservatism (continuity, insufficient change, flaccidity of initiative) is a prominent feature observed in most sectors of Soviet society, from the lowest levels to the top of the country's leadership. Many examples of the results of conservatism have already been cited, and more will be described in the next section. These include continuity in the design and production of weapons, certain doctrinal concepts unchanged for fifty years or more, and the difficulty experienced even by the top leadership in persuading design and operating organizations to try new ideas. The striking weakness of innovation in production enterprise has been well described by Berliner, and although his explanations for this behavior in terms of the structure of rewards, prices, autonomy and organizational arrangements is convincing, the study is not broad enough.[167]

Bureaucratization. Several analysts have cited personal relationships within Soviet bureaucracies as keys to understanding Soviet administration. Understanding and anticipating the desires of one's superiors is an example. A man with his own ideas or a reputation of being too knowledgeable can find himself in difficulty.[168] Consequently, one finds little enthusiasm for change that does not carry the imprimatur of superiors. In many instances, it is necessary to go to the very top of the hierarchy to find the stimulus to initiative.[169] Such tendencies were intensified by the fears developed during the Stalinist era, when failure or other unacceptable activities often resulted in removal from office—or worse. Particularly under Stalin, passivity was cultivated among the masses and within the ranks of the Party. "All initiative from below was disregarded or suppressed. Powerful individuals or small groups of senior officials took decisions and gave orders."[170] Official ideology congealed into procrustean conformity that brooked no challenge or criticism. The paralysis of initiative, learned and relearned by Stalin's bureaucrats, did not suddenly disappear at Stalin's death. Only now is the first post-Stalin generation of managers and advisers assuming authority.[171]

The bureaucratization of most aspects of Soviet life both describes and explains much about Soviet organizational processes.[172] Bureaucracy in the Soviet Union is long-standing and all-embracing.[173] Fainsod argues that this is an outgrowth of the totalitarian imperative that tends to transform the nation into a hierarchy of public servants operating within a framework of disciplined subordination to state purposes.[174] Like bureaucratic functionaries everywhere, the Soviet bureaucrat is noted for his "narrow and finicky adherence to the technicalities and a bullheaded stubbornness not to venture an inch beyond the rules."[175] When combined with centralization of authority, it leads to excessive concentration in Moscow, suppression of local initiative, red tape and delay in communications, difficulty of coordination, and a tendency toward ministerial and organizational self-sufficiency.[176]

Bureaucratic inertia has been intensified by the evolution of the Soviet Union into a complex and differentiated society that has spawned a demand for the advice and knowledge of experts and specialists. This is reflected by a shift in Party membership, for example, from revolutionary generalists to specialists.[177] While some see this transition as leading to increased efficiency,[178] others argue persuasively that specialization is more apt to generate increased departmentalism and rigid barriers to alternative opinions. Indeed, the latter are some of the more important preservers of conservatism. Although competition is promoted in certain critical areas such as weapons design, and although multiple channels of administrative information are maintained through government agencies, Party networks, and the KGB, in the majority of areas the single most important origin of critical technical information and policy alternatives is the operating agency charged with implementing a policy.[179]

Plans can be instruments of change if imposed by independent authorities from above. However, plans are often not exogenous to the operating agencies but are the subject of intense lobbying. Katz reports from émigré sources that, because the most important factor in receiving rewards is the kind of plan written for an organization, much of its effort during the preceding year goes into seeking an acceptable plan.[180] Representatives and lobbyists are sent to the central authorities in Moscow to promote the plans desired by their employers. They struggle with every means at their disposal to obtain quotas that will be easy to meet. As one top manager put it, "We do not need an objective plan or an economically perfect plan. What we need is a plan we can comfortably fulfill and overfulfill."[181] Efforts do not stop here. The more powerful or influential attempt to shift burdens to other sectors of the bureaucracy or economy, thus diffusing lines of authority and confounding the responsibility for possible failure.[182]

Secrecy and departmentalism. Secrecy is endemic in Soviet society: as a historically accepted value, as a written regulation, and as enforced by the bureaucracy and the KGB. Russian secrecy has been commented upon by foreigners for at least 150 years. The Marquis de Custine,[183] a French nobleman traveling in 1839, wrote, "In Russia, secrecy presides over everything; secrecy—administrative, political, social."[184] While true of public affairs generally, secrecy is most vigorously applied to all aspects of military activities. Departmentalism follows from secrecy but also has independent sources. Secrecy and departmentalism together force decisions to be made at higher levels throughout the bureaucracy. Secrecy is consistent with certain dominant character traits of Soviet citizens, but the habit of secrecy also has more mundane uses: the covering up of bungling; the suppression of awkward facts; and the preservation of a monopoly of information and expertise.

The effects of secrecy are rampant at all operational and planning levels. In military R&D, engineers typically work on a small piece of a mechanism, often without knowing the identity or use of the final product. Only a chief designer has the overall project in clear enough view to be able to make many of the design decisions that in other countries are normally delegated to lower levels. Secrecy retards the flow of scientific information and the efficient management of R&D, since details have to be continually referred upward for consideration. In R&D, it is one of the reasons why the chief designer has assumed his leading role in development.

Higher-level military planners are not immune from the problem. Khrushchev, for example, described a naval staff exercise he witnessed: "One of our commanders gave a report on how our fleet met and routed the enemy in the map exercise." Interrupting the briefer, Khrushchev asked, "Have you really assessed the situation correctly? If this were a real war and not just a map exercise, your ships would all be lying on the bottom of the sea by now." The commander looked up in surprise. Khrushchev went on: "You haven't taken into account the missiles which the enemy would certainly be using against you from his shore defences and his missile-launching planes. We have such a system ourselves, so surely the other side has it too." The perplexed commander replied: "I've never heard of missile-launching planes before. You're telling me something entirely new." Khrushchev noted that the information must have been classified and ordered that the naval commanders be briefed on the weapons available to both sides.[185]

This kind of secrecy even existed and was jealously protected by the military at the highest negotiating levels at SALT I. In one often-quoted exchange, General Ogarkov, the General Staff representative, took an American delegate aside and requested that the characteristics of Soviet weapons should not be discussed in front of the Soviet civilian delegates, who included a deputy minister of foreign affairs.[186]

Other forces also narrow the range of subjects that an individual or agency handles. Education is generally quite narrow, and career patterns confine individuals to rigid areas of expertise. There is very little interchange of personnel among government, military, industry, and academic circles, or movement between ministries and branches of the economy.[187] The planning and control systems create little incentive for attention to be paid to related matters beyond the periphery of defined organizational responsibilities.

An organization like the Military-Industrial Commission, which cuts across organizational boundaries, is therefore required to break through the barriers erected by secrecy and departmentalism. For the most part, however, even the Military-Industrial Commission would be expected to deal only with technical problems within its sphere of competence. It would be unlikely to consider trade-offs among weapons. Similarly, the Department of Defense Production in the Central Committee Secretariat is unlikely to wander beyond its assigned titular responsibilites.

Central Committee Secretaries, perhaps deputy chairmen of the Council of Ministers, and certainly the Defense Council and Politburo, rise above the confines of secrecy and departmentalism. This is a group of perhaps twenty to twenty-five people with ultimate authority to make decisions based on narrowly channeled information from monopolized origins, with limited possibility of lower-level conflict, feedback, or competition. The political structure tries to correct the narrowness of the communications channels by creating many of them. The Party, government, and secret police send information to the top in a system of multiple supervision, checks, and counterchecks. But the multiplicity of channels is unlikely to make up for the lack of alternative sources of expertise and analysis. Soviet participants in the system claim that the leadership is cut off from the day-to-day flow of events. The multiple channels are most useful for reporting technical matters of how the system is performing—such as problems, failures, malfeasance—facts that one group or another might either deliberately withhold or simply fail to transmit because of biased viewpoints. But these channels are insufficient to prompt questions as to whether, for example, the General Staff position on tank/antitank warfare is well thought out and solidly based; even if such questions were raised, it would be difficult for outsiders to provide a factual, analytical alternative. A consequence of secrecy and departmentalism, therefore, is that the military monopolizes information, expertise, and analysis of military issues.

HIGH-LEVEL INTERVENTIONS AND POLICY FLEXIBILITY

The strong tendencies toward conservatism and inflexibility impel the high-level leadership to assume the leading role in initiating change.[188] This is usually accomplished by way of intervention in the decision-making process.[189] A commitment to activism is in keeping with the precepts of the Party that decry passivity and inflexibility as traits to be vigorously overcome, particularly since they are seen to be undesirable tendencies embedded in the Russian character.[190] Although the leadership recognizes its role, and Party precepts attempt to instill a set of operating rules in the leadership that differs from those of the masses, the leaders are heir to the same Russian history and culture as those they lead, and their subordinates throughout Party and government are less fully motivated to Bolshevik activism. Initiative from the top is therefore episodic, and implementation is a continual struggle.

Sudden alterations between two courses of behavior are described as "one of the distinctive characteristics of the Soviet system."[191] Shock treatment from the center is considered necessary to overcome the overcaution and apathy of the rank and file and to respond to changes in the environment. However, once a new line is set, there is a marked tendency to operate mechanically.

Decrees and directives ordering change, however, unless accompanied by shake-ups in personnel and organizations (including, in the past, wholesale disciplinary actions), have rarely had the desired effects, even when organizations have been restructured. One example is the series of attempts over the years to rationalize and invigorate the computer industry. Decrees, restructuring, appointment of supervisory bodies, and the assignment of a "czar" have done little to bring the Soviet Union close to the levels of computer usage seen in the other industrialized countries.[192] Lower-level obstructionism, group interests, conservatism, and the operation of powerful and continuing incentives to act contrary to government decree have confounded the proclaimed policy.[193]

Occasionally, however, the assignment of a difficult job to an individual with recognized managerial talent, when backed up by "real" authority and perhaps with a new operating organization, has been successful.[194] There seems to be a greater ability to grant the requisite authority to accomplish a well-specified task—build an H-bomb, an intercontinental ballistic missile, a truck factory—than to achieve a more diffuse goal—to improve agriculture or develop an efficient computer industry. This is perhaps because a single project with a simple definition of success can be insulated from the general conservative tendencies by vigorous management and high-level priority and pressure. It is, however, more difficult to insulate and motivate an entire industry or sector of the economy. Military industry has been particularly singled out for intervention and priority. It is there, for example, that vigorous managers have been nurtured—Ustinov, Vannikov, Rudnev, Korolev, Tupolev are names associated with the management, development, and production of armaments, electronics, missiles, and aircraft. Ustinov and Rudnev, as technical managers, have been moved from job to job throughout the military-industrial sector to manage the new, high-priority tasks.

However, despite these and other means designed to launch the preferred sectors into more innovative trajectories, organizational activities continue to be governed, in the main, by deeply rooted, conservative tendencies and a structure of incentives that favors continuity. In periods when high-level interventions are more rare because of an explicit nonintervention policy or oligarchical power sharing, the military-industrial sector is more apt to go the way of other Soviet institutions, deviating but little from the tracks in which it has been moving.

SOURCES OF SOVIET ORGANIZATIONAL BEHAVIOR

As was said at the beginning of this section, Soviet political culture and organizational behavior have been ascribed to many sources. Convincing arguments have been made on behalf of all of these as influences on Russian character, and no doubt all—especially in combination—are part of the story. Long-standing traditions would make more recent development of marginal importance. Secrecy, lack of personal initiative, communal decision-making processes, deference to higher authority, a "narrow and finicky adherence to technique or rule"[195] have been observed by travelers and other observers of Russian society for generations. However, it is difficult to determine the relative influence of any one force; one cannot easily "hold other things constant" while altering a variable to determine its net effect. This problem, spelled out two decades ago by Daniel Bell,[196] has been addressed by Joseph Berliner.

Cultural effects. Berliner's working hypothesis in his study of technical innovation is that "there is little reason to believe that cultural characteristics are so different from those of other advanced industrial nations as to offer a major part of the explanation in differences in performance. . . . Given the appropriate social structure—organization, prices, incentives, decision rules—the economic behaviour of Soviet men and women is not likely to be very different from that of other peoples."[197] Berliner, however, does not discuss whether structure in the Soviet Union is itself based on culture. The present study does not address this question either but seeks the sources of behavior eclectically in culture, structure, and the nature of collective leadership in oligarchic politics.[198]

The manifestations of the Russian cultural heritage have been described by journalists and analyzed by researchers. The results of these different approaches are remarkably consistent. The Harvard Project on the Soviet Social System in the early 1950s studied intensively more than 3,000 World War II émigrés from the Soviet Union, all of whom completed a long questionnaire. In addition, detailed interviews about their life history and a battery of psychological tests were given to selected subsamples. Similar tests were given to American subjects for comparison. Many of their results are pertinent to organizational processes. The Russians, for example, expected their leader "to be the main source of initiative in the inauguration of general plans and programs and in the provision of guidance and organization for their attainment. The Russians do not seem to expect initiative, directedness, and organizedness from an average individual. They therefore expect that the authority will of necessity give detailed orders, demand obedience, . . . to insure performance."[199] This impression is supported by other results. The Russians thus seemed much more "passively accommodative to the apparent hard facts of situations."[200] In one test, a situation was given where the tools and materials for a job failed to arrive. The Russian subjects focused on whether the outcomes would be good or bad for the actor, "while the Americans at once sprang into a plan of action for resolving the situation."[201]

Another source of accommodation to authority, which also runs throughout Russian literature, is supported by the psychological studies. This is a view that impulses and desires are forces that need watching, and that the control of impulses is properly effected by outside authorities rather than by self-control. "They appear to feel a need for aid from without in the form of guidance and pressure exerted by higher authority."[202] Without firm leadership, there would be anarchy.

The conclusions of the Harvard study were tested thirty years later to determine whether the intervening years had changed the basic outlooks of Soviet citizens. American and Soviet émigrés to Israel were compared. By and large, the new study confirmed the findings of the earlier one.[203] The Soviet respondents were more inclined to favor strong leaders, with the government providing a guiding, educational role. They "set a narrower boundary to freedom, beyond which the realm of anarchy beings."[204] They suggested that "some Soviet type discipline would help to prevent Israeli democracy from turning into anarchy."[205]

In a cross-cultural comparison of bureaucratic processes, Crozier links Soviet cultural influences to autocracy and the pressures for production. Subordinates have had to internalize autocratic rule to the point where they accept arbitrariness as given. But they cannot help protecting themselves. One way is to remain passive, slow, and apathetic. A second is to use the traditionally strong informal groups as protective networks.[206] Central power then exerts pressures that are more and more disproportionate to objectives. Illegal activities undertaken to meet the state goals generate guilt and then dependency, since the leaders can crack down at any moment on the guilty parties.[207] Since the rulers cannot trust anyone, they construct checks and counterchecks. The source of this endless pattern is a discrepancy between goals and the subordinates' real abilities. The results of this are difficulty in identifying error, loss of informational feedback, and bureaucratic rigidity.

Crozier sees the bureaucratic system as founded on the dilemma of trust and suspicion. Apathy and small-group protection invite yet more pressure to make the system work in spite of the impossibility of trusting people.[208] Soviet administrators seem more wary of taking risks than do American bureaucrats, tending to rely on established precedent, existing structures, and accepted procedures rather than on individual initiative. A prominent cause of this is a characteristic of Soviet personal relations called *Kto-Kovo* (who-whom). The principal questions for Soviet officials are who is stronger than whom; who is the dominator, who the dominated; and who are the users, who the used? With this logic, there can be no neutrals.[209] Opposition to initiative, which would normally be dealt with by compromise in the West, produces tests of power in Soviet bureaucracy. Compromise assumes a rough equality between the parties, a notion that does not arise instinctively in Soviet officials. Such tests of power, which can be dangerous for losers, are therefore usually avoided, and so is change.

In many ways, the Soviet system now provides the average Russian with the social conditions that permit him to act out his national characteristics, and one could argue that the regime retains its power, in part, not because everyone is cowed but rather because it has support from the populace.

Structural effects. Three structural characteristics of the system are particularly relevant to decision-making processes throughout the military-industrial sector: the monopoly of expertise, the decision-approval process, and the economic sector's unresponsiveness to innovation and change. Many of these points have been discussed in passing, but they deserve more explicit treatment at this point.

Party networks are significant channels of information from operating levels to the leadership. As noted in the first section, however, Party coverage of the military is incomplete. The military maintains, as far as possible, a monopoly over military analysis and expertise. They are abetted in this practice by the pervasive secrecy over military matters. Issues of force posture and doctrine are gathered into the General Staff for debate, and the results are presented to the political leadership as the agreed military position. In the strong communal environment of the military leadership, individual commanders are unlikely to present views contrary to the established "corporate line" on those occasions when the commanders are called before the Politburo. Before the line is established, however, there is often ample evidence of considerable debate, especially when it is initiated by the high military command.[210] However, the debate takes place *within* the military, with virtually no participation by outsiders. Once the issue is resolved, the evidence suggests that further debate is cut short, and in many instances there may be no previous debate at all.

The military have actively discouraged discussions of military matters by outsiders, although there are glimmerings of growth in this area in the several research institutes supplying policy advice to the political leadership.[211] As a consequence of the military's near-monopoly, politically initated changes in military policy, or reallocation of resources within the military sector or between the military and other sectors must be made on the basis of nonanalytical considerations. Some support for this conjecture comes from the Soviet approach to technical matters related to arms talks. "They seem to adopt very simple, basic, uncomplicated positions and attitudes on SALT. . . . They give the impression that they are mystified or bored by all of the analytical think tank discussion and debate and argument that goes on in the United States."[212]

A possible reason for different models of reaching decisions between capitalist countries and the Soviet Union is that in the capitalist societies, especially in the United States, a normative approach to government administration is derived from the profit-making sector, where incentives lead to maximizing and optimizing behavior, and where bargaining and compromise are based on fair solutions (fair in the sense that both parties voluntarily agree to bargain). In the Soviet Union, solving problems typically involves finding a solution that is only marginally better than not finding one. For profit-oriented firms in capitalist economies, prices and technical relationships between inputs and outputs are in some degree knowable and known. Government administration, following the lead of the socially dominant sector, apologizes for not being able to duplicate business practices and constantly seeks to approximate that experience. The Soviet Union has little of this profit-orientated tradition. Decision making is bound up with a different set of criteria: political, organizational, intuitive, and technical—to the extent of asking, "Will it work?" To Westerners, Soviet decision making often seems crude, simple, and nonanalytical.[213] For the Soviet decision maker, the key questions are: Will we come out ahead or behind? Will we be better off or worse? Much in the Soviet approach that appears to be nonanalytical may, therefore, be explained by a different set of goals and understanding of what constitutes an acceptable agreement.

The structure of decision-making processes within the military-industrial sector places additional constraints on change. Attempts to do something differently—develop and produce a new type of weapon, for example—are vetted by technical committees, operational staffs, and military councils of the individual services, General Staff, and Ministry of Defense. On the government side, a similar process takes place as a proposal makes its way to the Military-Industrial Commission and thence to the Presidium of the Council of Ministers, the Defense Council, and the Politburo. At each stage, the inherent conservatism of the organizations is likely to challenge a proposed change. Since proposals for change implicitly call into question the correctness of the earlier decisions, challenges would be particularly severe for new policies or for alterations to previously decided policies. While change is difficult for any bureaucracy, this source of systemic conservatism is especially potent in Soviet organizations. Approval of a change at a lower level raises the possibility that a superior level of review would reverse the decision—a position that few Soviet decision makers or organizations would find satisfactory. Approval to continue a past policy is easier because it is known that all levels agreed on it. Therefore, unless a change were initiated from the top, forces within the system against change are pervasive and strong.

The character of the economic system, on which military development and production depend, has similar effects. In the centrally planned Soviet economy, supplies are allocated far in advance of actual need. Optimistic planning targets create a general shortage of materials, where a buyer may be required to accept an inferior product or go without. Given the central role of quantitative allocations, resources are not fungible; a simple money budget is not adequate to guarantee the availability of resources that have not been planned and allocated in detail. Since the Soviet economy has no automatic mechanisms for fostering technological progress, new products and production techniques must be deliberately planned and introduced by bureaucratized administrative bodies. While many of these economic problems were more severe in the past than they are today, such shifts as have taken place are only partial. The basic system of the past forty-five years continues.

The pattern of weapons design, development, and production is in part a response to the economic system. Unreliability of supply makes designers reluctant to ask for new components, or to go to suppliers with whom they have not dealt in the past. Supply problems create incentives to use previously developed components that may not be optimal from an overall standpoint, but that can be counted on to perform to known specifications. The rigidities of the planning process allow little flexibility in substituting one material or device for another, or in making reallocations within a given budget level. All of these conditions encourage an evolutionary approach that minimizes the necessity for flexibility and reallocation. The employment stability of R&D organizations, the detailed plans and regulations, the great difficulty for new organizations to break into established fields, the penalties of failure, and the practices and procedures by which R&D is managed all lead to military procurement conservatism.

Military industry has been insulated from the worst vicissitudes of the civilian economy by a variety of techniques, which include its being given priorities over materials, equipment, and personnel, and coordination by the Military-Industrial Commission. While more favored than the civilian sector, the Soviet military cannot entirely escape from the perversities and inefficiencies of the rest of the economy. The military sector can be isolated, buffered, and given priorities over civilian demands, but such strategies are neither costless nor completely successful. Furthermore, with the increasing complexity of modern weapon systems that incorporate a broader range of technologies and resources than in the past, the military is likely to become increasingly dependent on the rest of the economy and will find it more difficult in the future to avoid the effects of the civilian sector's patterns of behavior.

Political effects. The several sources of conservatism mentioned above—culture, bureaucratism, secrecy, structural forces, etc.—could be countered by a vigorous and innovative political leadership. However, since the days of Khrushchev's one-man rule, the oligarchy that replaced him has not emerged as a group seeking many major changes. The reason usually given for the group's rather stolid performance is that the balancing of power within a collective leadership requires caution and compromise, marked by stalemates and immobility. Since attempting to balance contending factions is unstable and inherently produces a contest for supreme power, and because policy making is increasingly complex, the collective arrangement has become static in its search for stability.[214]

This state of distributed power was deliberately sought by the leaders who removed Khrushchev. The means of achieving this included keeping the posts of Party and government leadership in separate hands; reducing opportunities for patronage;[215] distributing leadership seats in the Politburo, the Secretariat, and the Council of Ministers to avoid concentration of power; and maintaining countervailing sources of power among the topmost leaders.[216]

Despite Brezhnev's ability to fill many posts in the

first and second leadership levels with people of his choice, his colleagues' attempts to control patronage have colored life at the top. A normal rate of turnover in senior posts would place strains on the leadership group in their handling of politically significant appointments. One reaction has been to reduce turnover. This policy was given the title of "stability of cadres." One analyst claims that there is a fairly explicit understanding within the oligarchy and between it and the secondary leadership "whereby the latter are asked to curb any ambitions they might have for rapid advancement —in exchange for security of tenure and protection against encroachments."[217]

Relations within the Soviet leadership produce a natural concern to avoid "rocking the boat," meaning (in policy terms) hesitant and perhaps contradictory decision making, or simply avoiding decisions.[218] Despite a recent transformation from a more truly "collective" leadership in the late 1960s to a group "headed by Brezhnev," collectivity continues to prevail at the top. This is not to say, however, that politics is abandoned. Indeed, several scholars speak of the "reemergence of politics," but the essence of the new Soviet politics requires "a balancing, incremental perspective on many issues," with incrementalism as the "hallmark of the system."[219]

Until the structure of leadership changes, perhaps with new alignments and accommodations, new leaders, new power factions, or new problems and perspectives, incrementalism is likely to continue to dominate Soviet politics, and hence will continue to be a hallmark of Soviet decision making.

*WEAPONS ACQUISITION DECISION MAKING**

DECISION MAKING FOR CONVENTIONAL WEAPONS

Requirements generation and development decisions. The requirement for a new weapon can originate in many places. The most usual is in the using service, probably in the operations directorate of the service staff. The armaments directorate also plays a large part, since it is the service organization sitting between the designers and research institutes in the production ministries and the ultimate users represented on the service's staff. The armaments directorate would have the job of translating the military need into a set of "tactical-technical requirements"—the formal document that defines the specifications of the future weapon. Occasionally, the requirement may arise at a higher level—the General Staff, the Ministry of Defense, or even the political leadership. The higher the origin, the more likely that the weapon is intended to meet broader strategic or political requirements. Vertical and short take-off and landing (V/STOL) aircraft are an example. Aircraft designers Yakovlev, Mikoyan, and Sukhoi were directed to develop V/STOL aircraft in 1965, despite the absence of a specific military requirement.[220] The political intervention in this case could have been intended to assess the alternative technologies for possible future use aboard the small aircraft carriers the Soviet Union would deploy in the late 1960s.

Despite the fact that most requirements have their formal origins in the military services, the weapons design bureaus play crucial roles. We rarely hear the complaint, so often voiced in the United States, that the military sets the requirement (often to impossible levels of performance), with the designer expected to respond as best as he can.[221] Indeed, in the Soviet Union, the situation is often reversed. The military customers complain that they are forced to accept the conservative ideas of the designers—typically, revised versions of earlier products. In any event, the armaments directorates would have had close dealings with the design bureaus and research institutes and would be thoroughly familiar with the technologies becoming available to the designers and with their ideas for future developments. So although the requirement passes from the military to the production ministries, it is often conceived informally in the design offices that are selected at a later date to fulfill the project. Thus, it is "no accident" (as it is often phrased in the Soviet Union) that the Mikoyan design bureau, whose motto since its establishment in the late 1930s has been "Speed and Altitude," has turned out a succession of record-breaking aircraft in just those performance dimensions emphasized in the motto.[222] Nor is it an accident that requirements have continued for large ICBM boosters to be turned out by the large-booster design bureau, or solid-fuel rockets by the solid-fuel design bureau.

In some instances, designers have taken primary responsibility on themselves for promoting a new weapon. The reasons for this kind of entrepreneurial behavior are several. The design bureau may be running out of projects with little near-term prospect for additional work. Although budget continuity could be expected to tide an organization over ups and downs in workload, a continuous series of downs could have undesirable consequences for the organization's future. However, the usual pattern seems to be that designers see certain technical capabilities with potentially great military value that are held back by the standard operating procedures.[223]

Aircraft designer Tupolev's seaside chats with Khrushchev illustrate another avenue of technical entrepreneurship. According to Khrushchev's reminiscences, Tupolev "often came over to see me. We'd sit near the beach and talk. More often than not, he'd bring a folder and go over his latest ideas with me."[224] One of these ideas was for a nuclear-powered bomber, which Khrushchev and the leadership turned down because of its restricted payload and speed. However, because of the potential of the technology, Tupolev was authorized to continue research on nuclear aircraft. The entrepreneurial nature of these proposals was explicitly noted by Khrushchev. "To put it crudely, you could say he [Tupolev] was like a businessman dealing with a good customer. 'Here's my product,' he was saying. 'If you want it and can afford it, I can build it for you.'"[225] Khrushchev went on to imply that Tupolev's activities

*This section, while based on the description and analysis of previous sections, fills in many of the gaps in a consistent though speculative manner. In many instances, therefore, the text is more assertive than is warranted by the quality of the information. Citations noted earlier will not be repeated here.

on behalf of his own designs were not unusual for designers.[226] What was unusual was the good grace with which he accepted the rejection of his proposals.[227]

Constraints within the system on the development process further influence the requirements for new weapons.[228] Uncertainty of supply created by the tautly run, centrally administered economy and the inflexibility of planning make designers reluctant to ask for new components, or go to suppliers with whom they have not dealt in the past. Supply problems create incentives to use previously developed components that may not be optimal for the overall system but that can be counted on to perform to known specifications. With quantitative planning allocations, a simple money budget does not guarantee the availability of resources that have not been planned and allocated in detail. When one adds to these economic pressures the demands of a doctrine based on the mass use of armies and weapons, one can understand the incentives for designers to adopt an R&D strategy that emphasizes simplicity of equipment, common use of components, and a preference for gradual change as the means to increase performance. Though there is occasional grumbling over the performance and mission limitations of individual weapons, the military leaders seem to have accepted this state of affairs in part exchange for large numbers of weapons and a sizable and expanding budget.

R&D approval mechanisms. It is one thing to create a requirement for a new or improved weapon system; it is quite another to be granted the budget and materials for its development. Some initiatives can be financed out of design bureau or research institute budgets, but projects cannot get very far, especially if prototype construction and test requires substantial resources, unless the project is "sold" to a potential customer and one's own production ministry. However, preliminary design work requiring only a few of the more talented people in the design bureau is sufficient to generate a proposal for use in negotiations with potential users. From that point, the steps toward approval proceed in two parallel routes: through the ministerial/government hierarchy, and up through the military.

In the ministry, a proposal would first be vetted by a scientific-technical committee of experts to assess the technical feasibility of the design. It would then go up to the directorate overseeing the particular organization making the proposal, and then to the minister's office. A ministerial collegium composed of the deputy ministers and other leading administrators would probably also review it. From there, the proposal would be reviewed by the Military-Industrial Commission to determine resource requirements, special needs, the impact on other military programs, and the demands placed on the civilian economy. The process culminates in the publication of a VPK decision, the inflexibility of which means that weapons designs are frozen at a comparatively early stage.

Military approval begins at the service's armaments directorate, perhaps with a review by a service military-technical committee. The service general staff would also determine whether the design met the military requirements of the using command and fitted into the overall plan of that service. Having been approved by the service's Military Council (composed of the commander in chief and his deputies), the proposal would be forwarded to the General Staff, whose operations directorate would review it in the light of the overall force structure projected in the Ministry of Defense's long-term plans and budgets. The General Staff's scientific-technical committee would judge the technical characteristics. The armaments directorate of the Ministry of Defense could perform a systems analysis of the new weapon to calculate costs, benefits, and alternative approaches to the same mission. The proposal's economic impact would probably be determined so that the military would already know many of the industrial consequences before the proposal reached the Military-Industrial Commission. If it was approved on all counts, the Main Military Council of the Ministry of Defense would recommend the proposal to the Defense Council for final approval by the political leadership. With the recommendation of the Military-Industrial Commission, the Defense Council would approve the proposal and, if the resource requirements were large or if it raised other politically sensitive issues, it would be placed on the agenda of the full Politburo for approval and perhaps even discussion.

In order to eliminate unwelcome surprises along the tortuous path toward approval, most proposals—especially for new ideas—would most likely have been previewed and briefed before the formal procedures. If disapproval seemed probable, the idea would probably be withdrawn to avoid risking the ignominy of rejection. The stability of leadership in the government would allow the managers at all levels to have developed "old-boy" networks to solve problems behind the scenes, with the intention of overcoming the inherent rigidity of the bureaucratic system. All concerned have an interest in assuming that a project goes smoothly—or does not go at all.

The dual-approval path encourages conservatism.[229] Assent is most probable for a design resembling one previously approved. Deep-rooted feelings bias the decisions in favor of those weapons that have been established in manufacturing, accepted by the commands, and operated by the troops. If such a weapon can be improved, the process favors keeping it going.

Prototype construction and testing. In the Soviet Union, the decision to develop a weapon is often conceptually and organizationally distinct from the decision to produce and deploy it. This is in contradistinction to the United States, where production is often implied in the original authorization to develop the weapon (although this practice is now slowly changing). For many Soviet weapons types, prototypes are generally built and tested—often competitively—before decisions on production are made. Prototype construction and operational testing provide information on the costs and performance of the new weapon that is critical for the production decision. The use of prototypes and the progressive incorporation of new technologies and subsystems permit production decision making to proceed with many of the inherent uncertainties of a new program reduced or eliminated. In some cases, limited production is also undertaken with small quantities deployed for troop test. This seems to have been the course of events leading to the new T-72 tank, where interim models were produced by the hundred and demonstrated in large field exercises and in troop training.[230] The information gained from the interim models formed the basis for the next stage of development. The Bounder strategic bomber was an example of a prototype developed but never produced due to marked performance deficiencies discovered when the aircraft was flight tested.[231]

With naval vessels, however, the size, cost, and construction time often make it unfeasible to build a prototype first and then use the test information to decide on production, largely because the resulting program delays would be unacceptable. However, the Soviet Union seems to have canceled many series of ships in the middle of a production run when information was acquired during production or operations, or when technology or the threat changed. In these cases, the parts in the pipeline have been used to equip the next model.[232] Khrushchev commented that unexpectedly high costs in two ships, discovered after production had already begun, led to a reconsideration of the wisdom of building them. In one case, the leadership decided to cancel the series and melt down the cruisers that were being produced but were not yet completed. In the second, the decision was made to go ahead with construction as a concession to the military, who strongly favored the ships.[233]

Many of the advantages of building prototypes are gained, even for ships, by introducing a weapon system into service progressively. Thus, a surface-to-surface missile was fitted in its most primitive form to the last four (of more than thirty) Kotlin-class destroyers. Several years later, a new ship (but with an old steam propulsion unit), specifically designed to carry the missile in its developed form, was produced (Kynda-class), followed in four years by a fully developed ship with new propulsion and a refined missile (Kresta).[234]

A desire to maintain parallel and perhaps competitive design capabilities may unintentionally furnish an incentive to produce *both* alternatives developed to fulfill a single mission. ICBMs are an illustration of this: in the 1970s four new ICBMs (SS-16, SS-17, SS-18, SS-19) replaced three missiles deployed in the 1960s (SS-9, SS-11, SS-13). Each of these missiles had somewhat different characteristics, but it is not evident that they were all needed for strategic purposes. Rather, it could be argued that a large-booster design bureau's product is represented by the SS-9 and SS-18, and a solid-propellant design group is represented by the SS-13, mobile SS-16, and SS-20 IRBM (which composes the first two stages of the SS-16). A third design group turned out the SS-11 and perhaps SS-17 and SS-19. Another possible reason for multiple deployment is that each of the missiles incorporated a different mix of technologies and weapons characteristics: launch techniques, guidance, booster, warhead, multiple independently targetable reentry vehicle (MIRV), accuracy and hard-target capability. If the reliability of the technology or the environment in which the weapons were to be used were uncertain, diversity would be a way of hedging decisions.[235]

There may be a more subtle effect of design bureau activities on production decisions. The relatively stable budgets of the R&D organizations finance a continuous stream of new weapons embodying current technology and increased performance. While not every prototype incorporates an acceptable combination of mission capability and costs, the availability of a new weapon in working hardware may make the follow-on production decision more likely than in the American case, where it is often necessary to make decisions based on a plan instead of a prototype. On the other hand, the relatively small amount of resources required for experimental prototypes avoids a premature bureaucratic commitment to projects. I would conjecture that where large development projects are unavoidable (perhaps, for example, in a new generation of ICBM), the production decision is virtually assured from the start because of the mobilization of organizations and resources behind the program. For this reason, such programs may be examined by the Politburo in the R&D planning stage to insure political review before the bureaucratic machinery takes over.

A multiplicity of prototypes, either from the same design bureau over time or from competing design groups, increases the likelihood that an acceptable version becomes available for deployment. Consider, for example, the output of the Mikoyan design bureau, developer of the Mig series of aircraft. Three points are evident. First is the sheer number of different designs produced by this one organization. Second, cumulative improvement has been the chief means of advancing performance within the several families of aircraft. Third, experimental prototypes have been the means for bridging the gap between series.[236] The uncertainties of technology, performance, and costs are thus allayed both by the construction of experimental prototypes to investigate major changes and by the more usual reliance on gradual improvements. Controlling uncertainty in this manner significantly eases the decision to produce a new weapon; performance, costs, and resource requirements can be fairly well established; fewer surprises are likely to upset plans made well in advance of production decisions; and the continuity that comes from incrementalism, standardization, and the established style of a single design organization minimizes the disruption that sharp changes would effect in the Soviet economic system.

The list of Mig aircraft also demonstrates that large jumps in capability in deployed aircraft were actually arrived at in a rather conservative manner. Consider, for example, the Mig-21. This delta-wing interceptor was preceded by a swept-wing prototype with an earlier engine (Ye-50), a swept-wing prototype with the production engine (Ye-2A), a delta-wing prototype (Ye-5) with the same fuselage and engine as the Ye-2A, a preproduction series (Ye-6 or Fishbed B) based on the Ye-5, and finally the definitive production version (Mig-21F or Fishbed C) with refined aerodynamics and an up-rated engine. However, this version was limited to a clear-weather interception mission. Only later did the Mikoyan design bureau add search-track radar, increased fuel reserves, external ordnance load points, and ground-attack avionics. The latest models of the Mig-21 have roughly double the range and payload of the first deployed version, and the mission capabilities have expanded apace.

This listing of aircraft also provides some insight into the pervasive influence of designers and their predilections on weapons procurement decisions. Consider the high-altitude Mach 3 Mig-25 (Foxbat). The commonly accepted explanation of its origins is that it was built to a requirement to intercept the B-70 bomber being developed by the United States in the 1960s. However, the story takes on a different complexion when we note that the design bureau motto since the 1930s has been "Speed and Altitude," and that the performance of a continuous series of aircraft put the motto into effect. A case in point was a Mikoyan-built rocket-powered interceptor in 1946 (I-270) that reached 59,000 feet and 612 miles per hour. In the late 1950s, several prototypes of the Mig-19 were configured with rocket-boosters to reach altitudes of over 75,000 feet and Mach 1.7 speeds (SM-21 and SM-50). From 1957 to 1961, the Ye-75 family of prototypes was designed around different combinations of wings and engines based on a scaled-up Mig-21 concept. The final version of this series, the Ye-166, established several world records for speed and altitude and was powered by the engine that was to appear in the Foxbat prototype two years later. Finally, the Foxbat prototype Ye-266 first flew in 1964, and itself set new world records. Although the wings and engine inlets on the Ye-266 were departures from the preceding design bureau efforts, the engine had been used earlier, and the design, in general, sought to avoid rather than to confront technological limits.[237] The B-70 bomber was canceled in the late 1960s, shortly before the Soviet procurement system began producing the first of several hundred Mig-25s—a production run that continued into the late 1970s.

Production decisions. Formulation of plans and budgets for military procurement precedes requirements generation and weapons development. The budget, as the more general of the allocative devices, sets the overall defense and service constraints, while the plan assigns materials, manpower, plant, and equipment to specific uses. However, because the outcome of R&D is unpredictable, plans may not mesh with evolving needs as weapons proceed through the development process.[238] Consequently, when the weapon is to be produced, resources must often be reallocated within the plan. The inevitable squeezes on budgets and plans are resolved, for the most part, in two places: the General Staff and the Military-Industrial Commission. The task of the General Staff at this stage is to adjudicate between competing military demands; the Military-Industrial Commission has the job of juggling projects among ministries and plants and stretching scarce materials to meet the needs of certified users. The Military-Industrial Commission would also coordinate its activities with the Council of Ministers, which has a broader purview of the entire industrial sector.

The commitment of large programs to production would also require the approval of the Defense Council and Politburo. It is in those bodies that broader political, international, and economic considerations would be brought to bear on the decision. For most decisions on weapons production, Politburo review is likely to be *pro forma,* but in the event of a cost overrun large enough to jeopardize the plan or adversely affect other military and civil production plans, the Politburo would reconsider a project. For this reason, military-industrial planners would strive to hold costs to planned figures. This is done in two ways. First, the design process itself tends to control costs through the emphasis on simplicity, common use of components and subsystems, gradual change, and limited performance and mission capabilities.[239] Second, according to informants who have participated in the system, cost estimates are padded. The best ex ante estimates are adjusted upward by a factor that attempts to account for uncertainties, such as difficult technical problems or extra costs required for obtaining materials and parts in short supply; then that estimate may be doubled. During production, the military carefully monitors costs through detailed cost accounting checked by military representatives stationed at the plants.

Owing to the impact on the economy of military production, weapons procurement decisions would tend to be more conservative than either the formulation of requirements or R&D decisions. Economic and social goals, competing claims for investment and consumer goods, and broad political accommodations and priorities can be thrown away by major new military programs. Weapons that would minimize disruption and change, and maintain the continuity of existing production patterns, would therefore be chosen. Production proposals meeting these criteria would presumably be favored over those that called for new techniques or resources. Soviet weapons procurement is an obstacle course the hurdles of which are regularly spaced and of a standard height. To negotiate it successfully, strategies that insure steady progress are employed. Radical solutions that might ultimately pay off would do little good if the contestant were tripped by the first hurdle. Nevertheless, even radical projects are sometimes undertaken.

DECISION MAKING FOR "NEW IN PRINCIPLE" WEAPONS

Since the industrialization of the first Five-Year Plan, which created the foundation for a modern military-industrial sector, the Soviet Union's leaders have been instrumental in initiating major weapons projects that have departed significantly from previous experience. Decision-making patterns for these projects have been quite different from the routines for conventional equipment. Having no organizational precedents, the new projects are affected by fewer constraints than established programs.

Though exceptional and infrequent, such novel, high-priority projects have had important consequences for force posture and military capabilities. Occurrences of this class of weapon may be increasing. In the past ten to fifteen years, high-level attention has been directed to bringing science and application closer together; one area of concern has been the development of science-based military capabilities that are "new in principle." Despite the fact that analysis of such weapons is complicated by their very uniqueness, some tentative generalizations appear to be warranted. Discussion will be focused here on the development of nuclear weapons, ICBM, and a hypothetical scenario for charged-particle beam devices.

Nuclear weapons development. Soviet nuclear physics research in the 1930s was integrated with the international scientific community. However, when in 1940 the United States failed to respond to the publication of the Soviet discovery of spontaneous fission, the Soviet Union was convinced that a large secret project must have been under way in the United States.[240] The Nazi invasion disrupted research, but by late 1941 one of the authors of the paper on spontaneous fission, G. N. Flerov, who had been following the foreign literature on the subject, wrote to Stalin and the State Defense Committee, urging that "no time be lost in making a uranium bomb." The government at this time was beginning to receive information that top-secret work in nuclear physics was in progress in the United States and Germany. Stalin then turned to a group of leading physicists for advice. A program was subsequently initiated under I. V. Kurchatov, but the effort was very modest in comparison to the Manhattan Project, with perhaps fifty people involved. This work was directed by the Internal Affairs Ministry, which was also responsible for the country's uranium mines. Beria had been given general supervision of armaments and munitions industries during the war.

By 1945, several ministries were involved in the production of uranium and graphite, and in the creation of a mechanism to generate a supercritical mass of uranium. The explosion of the first American nuclear device in July 1945 led to an immediate order from Stalin to hurry things up. In September 1945, a Scientific-Technical Council associated with the Council of Ministers was established to oversee the program. Chaired by Munitions Minister B. L. Vannikov, who had previously been a consultant on the project, the committee included industrial managers and scientists and a representative from the Ministry of Internal Affairs, which continued to administer the program. The Council of Ministers assumed direction of the program in 1946 under a supraministerial agency (the First Main Directorate) headed by Vannikov, although Beria's Internal Affairs Ministry retained some residual authority. This work led to the successful detonation of a nuclear device in August 1949. The Ministry of Medium Machine Building, established in 1954, took over most nuclear responsibilities. The establishment of a ministry signaled the maturity of the new industry and relegated it to a more routine status than it had earlier enjoyed.

Holloway notes that evidence of the American program in 1941 and the weapons explosions in 1945 were the chief motivating circumstances behind the Soviet decisions.[241] However, the Soviet Union proceeded with a major, high-priority development of the hydrogen bomb immediately after the explosion of its first atomic bomb in 1949, without waiting for American test results to support the decision.[242] Soviet scientists first recognized the possibilities of making a fusion bomb during their research on the fission bomb; this work then benefited from the expansion of the nuclear program in 1945 and test results in 1949, from which important data and confirmation of theory were obtained.

The points to note in this brief description of Soviet nuclear weapons development include the following: physicists performed the initial research without paying explicit attention to weapons applications; they were the first to notice military potential; scientists brought this information directly to party leaders and the primary military planning organization (State Defense Committee); the Party sought advice from a group of scientists; the Party and government formed an ad hoc scientific-technical committee to oversee developments; following American activities in 1941 and the first nuclear detonations in 1945, Stalin was instrumental in accelerating the research; the scientific-technical committee was then transformed into a supraministerial agency; and, with the growing maturity of nuclear technology, this agency was given ministerial status.

Intercontinental missiles and sputniks. Several Soviet organizations, staffed largely by enthusiasts, carried out rocket research in the 1930s, receiving much of their support from the army. During the war, this effort was directed to projects promising quick returns; the highly effective Katyusha rocket artillery was one of their most outstanding achievements, but investigations were also conducted into liquid-propellant rocket boosters for aircraft and several other projects. There was no work on ballistic missiles comparable to German development of the V-2 but, by the end of World War II, a number of Soviet scientists had considerable experience in rocketry and a solid theoretical base for future work.[243]

In 1944, Soviet scientists had received information on the German V-2 and on other developments, including the Sanger project—an intercontinental bomber boosted by rocket power and intended to "skip" along the top of the atmosphere to achieve long range. The Soviet scientists drew the attention of the political leaders to these developments, and when Soviet forces overran the Peenemunde rocket bases in Germany, Soviet scientists went along to assess the German efforts and to help round up equipment and experts. By the end of 1945, several defense industry plants in the Soviet Union were converted to rocket production under the direction and coordination of a special committee subordinate to the Council of Ministers. This committee was headed by Chief Marshal of Artillery Nedelin and by the ubiquitous military-industrial managers Ustinov and Vannikov. German experts were put to work for the Soviet Union in design bureaus in Germany, but in October 1946 about 40,000 of them were transported to the Soviet Union.[244]

At first with German help, and then quickly on their own, Soviet scientists worked to improve the V-2. In 1946, an Academy of Artillery Sciences was established to oversee the development of military rockets. The emphasis of design at this time was on extreme technical simplicity, partly in reaction to the complexities of the V-2.[245] The goal at this period was first to match the German achievement and then to surpass it.

A major policy problem in 1946–47 seemed to be that of whether the Soviet Union should remain dependent on German designs and aid or whether it was capable of producing a booster and perhaps a satellite without external help. Several Soviet scientists argued on behalf of native capabilities; Stalin's son, Maj. Gen. Vasily Stalin, and Beria's deputy in the Ministry of Internal Affairs, Gen. Ivan A. Serov, have been identifed as opposing this view. Both Vasily Stalin and Serov had played crucial roles in the search for and organization of German scientists, and these efforts may have predisposed them to favor the continued use of the Germans. As experience was gained with the construction, launch, and improvement of the V-2 toward the end of 1946, moves were made to increase the domestic efforts. One of the original Soviet rocket research institutes, the Gas Dynamics Laboratory, turned to the development of powerful liquid-propellant rocket engines for long-range missiles. The rocket scientist Sergei P. Korolev was named to head another group in late 1946, and he took up these duties in February 1947. In April 1947, a series of Kremlin meetings discussed the rocket projects. The first meeting, apparently chaired by deputy prime minister Georgy Malenkov, included the chiefs of *Gosplan,* Air Force Armaments Minister Ustinov, and aircraft designers Yakovlev and Mikoyan. Malenkov noted that the V-2's range was too short for it to qualify as a strategic weapon. "Who do you think we can frighten with it? Poland? Turkey? . . . Our potential enemy is thousands of kilometres away. We must work on the development of long-range rockets."[246] The discussion turned to the Sanger project as a solution to the problem of long range. Others suggested a research program to develop a large booster. The result of that meeting was the formation of a government commission to study the Sanger project and other possible alternatives.

On the next day, a joint session of the Politburo and the Council of Ministers Presidium further considered the problem of long-range rockets. Many of the participants of the previous meeting attended, plus Stalin, Beria, Molotov, and others. Stalin was very interested in the transoceanic rocket bomber.[247] After considerable discussion on how to proceed, a decision was made to form a second high-powered rocket development committee, chaired by General Serov, which was to present a feasibility study by August 1947.

Few organizational details of Soviet rocket activities over the next few years are available, but rocket R&D continued, and two IRBMs, the SS-3 and SS-4, were developed. In 1954, the powerful RD-107 and RD-108 engines entered final development. (Except for minor differences, these were similar engines.) By 1957 they were used to power the SS-6, the first Soviet ICBM. It was at this time that the United States announced her intention to launch an earth satellite. Korolev reported to the Central Committee that the Soviet Union's own missile was more powerful than the American one, and the Soviet Union could launch a satellite before the United States.[248] The Central Committee responded, "This is a tempting business, but we'll have to think about it." Following a few months of thought and a series of rocket tests in the summer of 1957, Korolev was summoned to the Central Committee headquarters and told to go ahead with launching a satellite.[249] This was accomplished in October 1957.

The Ministry of General Machine Building had been established in 1965 to consolidate ballistic missile development and production activities, but Soviet space activities have never come under central authority. From about the time of the first sputnik, responsibility for space projects seems to have been under an organization referred to as the State Commission. Korolev was the deputy chairman of this commission, whose first head was K. N. Rudnev, another of the ubiquitous military-industrial managers.[250] This coordinating body lies outside the Academy of Sciences and includes high-level representatives from the major participating groups: Party, military, scientists, and industry. Since the participants are people in positions of authority, they can intercede quickly when bottlenecks and other stumbling blocks threaten programs, despite the fact that the space program as a whole remains a loose, ad hoc arrangement of institutions.

The following points emerge from the circumstances discussed here: scientists were the first to initiate work in rockets; they also recognized the potential of the German work and alerted the government; the crucial stimulus came from Stalin after the war through his insistence on the importance of Soviet work on long-range missiles; ad hoc groups of experts were formed to advise the leaders and supervise the development work; the Central Committee played a key role in approving the first space launches; and space activities continue to be supervised by a coordinating committee rather than by a unified authority.

Energy beams. The Soviet Union is spending large resources on high-energy beams. The investment in this field over the past ten years has been estimated by American intelligence analysts at $3 billion for just one test installation.[251] A hypothetical project history of this potentially revolutionary weapon may be illuminating in its own right, but it also supplies a context in which to bring together the evidence of the two preceding examples, the organizational and process analyses presented earlier, and other relevant information about Soviet science management as it affects nonroutine decision making.

Particle beam work seems to have reached a sizable scale around 1967, when three sets of influences merged to create a research-based project devoted to the possibility of a major weapons breakthrough:

1. Research on high-powered lasers and on controlled thermonuclear reactions led certain scientists to see potential military applications for their research.
2. The military and political leadership gradually saw that the antiballistic missile (ABM) weapons of the Air Defense Force's (PVO) antimissile branch were ineffective, thus challenging the very *raison d'être* of the ABM forces. The ABM Treaty, which limited further deployment of ABM systems, made this organization's future even more insecure.
3. At about this same time, Soviet analysts of science and technology, together with the Soviet leaders, became concerned about their ability to initiate and develop capabilities that were "new in principle." Believing that such capabilities flowed directly from science, it therefore seemed necessary to bring science and application closer together through various organizational and management techniques.

A growing concern of Soviet analysts and military-science policy in the 1960s was that the "research-production cycle" was not flexible enough to cope with rapidly changing scientific opportunities.[252] One particular anxiety was that "scientific opportunities and military requirements will not coalesce quickly enough to ensure the development of the most advanced weapons."[253] Departmentalism and secrecy were seen to aggravate this problem. The existing process appeared to be effective in supporting established priorities, but selecting new programs for the highest state priorities was complex and hazardous. Some analysts contended that whereas in the past military requirements placed demands on scientific possibilities, since World War II, scientific research has been presenting more and more possibilities for weapons development.[254] It came to be believed that Engels's notions about the relationship between demand and science were no longer valid; Engels claimed that "if industry makes a technical demand it moves science forward more than ten universities."[255] One writer suggested that the reverse is now true; with the development of science and the complexity of military R&D, the direction of influence is now "from science to military affairs, since contemporary science is able to find ways of raising the combat capabilities of the army and navy which are *new in principle.*"[256]

Attempts were subsequently made to bring science and requirements closer together. The General Staff increased its capacity for technical analysis and weapons selection, with much of its effort centered on formal systems-analytical techniques. Of greater importance has been the promotion to leading positions of men with experience in developing weapons that were "new in principle." These appointments include generals Ogarkov and Alekseyev to head the General Staff and its scientific-technical committee and Ustinov to the Ministry of Defense. But perhaps of greater significance has been the sensitivity of the military, industrial, and political leadership to the general problem of bringing science and application closer together.

In few areas does science dominate requirements as much as it does in controlled thermonuclear reactions and other high-energy power-generating technologies. For several decades, the Soviet Union has devoted considerable attention and resources to key aspects of magnetohydrodynamics, high-powered lasers, fusion research, and high-intensity microwave beams and is among the world's leaders in several areas of science. Many of the potential outcomes of this research are eminently useful to the civilian economy. But intelligence analysts have also perceived a growing possibility that much of this research could also be put to military use and that, in fact, a significant proportion of the Soviet work has been redirected to the military mission. One of the missions is conjectured to be the use of high-powered lasers or focused, high-energy, charged-particle beams as an antiballistic missile or antiaircraft weapon.[257]

Since the early 1960s, several major research groups active in the investigation and application of high-current, high-energy, pulsed electron beams have grown steadily.[258] The major part of the research has been conducted by half a dozen Academy of Sciences institutes.[259] A large number of institutes of secondary importance, connected with the Academy of Sciences, universities, and industrial ministries, have also been affiliated with this work.[260] Despite the large number of institutes, their geographical and administrative dispersion, and the wide range of activities in which they are engaged, there appears to be close coordination among them.[261] Coordination is demonstrated, for example, in the complementary nature of research topics concerned with high-performance energy conversion in which large energy concentrations impact on a small volume in a short time. Another indication is the participation of leading scientists in the guidance, review, and consultation rendered to the scattered researchers.[262]

Although much of the research is applicable to fusion, some analysts have concluded that the work, taken as a whole, is more relevant to weapons development than to peaceful tasks. The absence of organizational affiliation information for many authors of scientific papers suggests this. One of the major participants, L. I. Rudakov, does not indicate an institutional connection in his publications although through his coauthors he has been associated with several organizations over the years.[263] The relationship of this research to the military is strengthened by the claim that some of the work is under the direct control of the PVO.[264]

The PVO's rocket-defense (ABM) branch went through a series of ups and downs in the 1960s, ending the decade mainly on a "down." Deployment of the Griffon ABM around Leningrad in the early 1960s was a technical failure and was never completed. Initially, however, it stimulated high hopes in Khrushchev, who remarked in July 1962 that the Soviet Union "had missiles which could hit a fly in outer space."[265] This view echoed that of Defense Minister Malinovsky voiced a few months earlier: "The problem of destroying missiles in outer space had been successfully solved."[266] Within a year or so, however, other voices raised doubts about the ABM capabilities of Soviet weapons. Strategic Rocket Troops Commander General Krylov, for example, said in late 1963 that "existing systems of anti-missile defence cannot repulse nuclear missile strikes."[267]

The SA-5 high-altitude interceptor was deployed in the mid-1960s on the so-called Tallinn Line in what was probably an attempt to defend against the limited-range Polaris A-1 missile, but American deployment of the longer-range A-2 and A-3 models rendered the SA-5 ineffective in the ABM role. An improved ABM missile, the Galosh, was shown for the first time in the Moscow parade of November 1964. The decision to deploy the Galosh was apparently considered in the next few months. Brezhnev claimed in July 1965 that the Politburo was open to suggestions from the military on ABM if the program could be proved to be effective and could be properly managed.[268] The system was, in fact, deployed shortly after that, but by 1967 its effectiveness was also challenged. Whereas Galosh may have been useful against single-warhead missiles, American plans to field MIRV demonstrated the possibility of saturating any reasonable ABM deployment. Several prominent marshals and generals, including Grechko, who was soon to become minister of defense, denied that the Soviet ABM system was capable of destroying all incoming missiles. The PVO chief tried to rebut this challenge, but, only a month or so later, a highly placed source from within the PVO declared that the current state of technology made it necessary to continue research on missile defense and that the time was not ripe for continuing deployment: "One is required to carry on a lot more research, developmental work, and experiments."[269]

The PVO had in fact been associated during the 1960s with research on technologies other than missiles for ballistic missile defense. Ghebhardt suggests (admittedly on weak evidence) that Khrushchev's interest and support of cosmic ray research, and potential breakthroughs in laser technology, helped to promote the demise of the Griffon system.[270] He speculates that progress in laser research around 1963 attracted attention and support from both military and political leaders. According to other sources, the Soviet Union had by 1967 succeeded in producing laser effects that could neutralize ICBM guidance and fissionable material.[271]

The repeated difficulties with ABM missile developments, loss of support for existing systems from both political and military leaders, and, finally, the 1972 ABM Treaty with the United States (which prohibited further deployment) created a severe crisis for the ABM forces within the PVO. The incentives to investigate completely different technologies were clearly present throughout the 1960s and were reinforced in the latter part of the decade. Moreover, bureaucratic lags would probably have left a good portion of the PVO antimissile budget intact, despite the technical failure of the weapons on which the organization depended.

Scientists, for their part, could have been seeking an alternative source of support for their high-energy physics research. They may also have seen the potential for great breakthroughs in air defense from some combination of lasers and other energy-projection techniques. A senior scientist, following the precedents noted earlier for the development of nuclear weapons and sputniks, probably presented this case to the Central Committee Secretariat, either to the Science Department or the Defense Production Department. (Ustinov would certainly have been involved.) Prior personal contacts between the scientists and military men would have encouraged PVO representation in support of the proposed research. If the Secretariat accepted these ideas, a draft decree would have been prepared for Politburo approval; following approval, a leading institute would be made responsible for overall conduct of the effort; a scientific management committee would also have been formed to provide coordination, to resolve conflicts, and to oversee priorities.

The Secretariat and Politburo were probably made aware of the need for close cooperation between the military and scientists by the papers and analyses being written at the time on the problem of developing capabilities that were "new in principle." The new regime of Brezhnev and Kosygin was also emphasizing both the commitment to scientific decision making and the reliance on the views of experts. Energy beams for ballistic missile defense or other military uses epitomized the kind of application the analysts contemplated and the leadership promoted. Representative of the best of Soviet science, and at the frontier on a world-wide comparison, the potential rewards of coalescing science and defense were so revolutionary that it could have been difficult not to have gone ahead with the project.

Once the project won approval and began to grow, bureaucratic momentum and conservatism, as described throughout this chapter, would generate the forces necessary to keep it going, despite the considerable doubts that Western scientists raise about basic technical feasibility. Explaining why such a project continues after ten or fifteen years is quite different from speculating on how it began.[272]

CONCLUSIONS AND IMPLICATIONS

The question raised at the beginning of this chapter was whether Soviet organizational arrangements, decision-making practices, and bureaucratic routines have an independent effect on Soviet force posture. The evidence suggests that bureaucratic arrangements and political structure have a synergistic effect, which is summarized in the following points. The military actively maintains a thorough (but not complete) monopoly of information and expertise on military affairs and armaments, on strategic and tactical thought, and on the relationship among doctrine, tactical-technical concepts, and weapon requirements. This monopoly is coupled with conservatism and incrementalism in the creation of military-industrial alternatives that limit innovation and change. The political leadership must intervene to initiate greater change, but the nature of the collective leadership of the past fifteen years favors continuity. Therefore, we can expect the present trends to continue until the leadership widely supports major forces for reallocation and change as a result of one or more of the following: altered composition of the collective leadership, a new generation of leaders, significant change in the threat, or crisis elsewhere in the system (e.g., economy, agriculture, technology).

It must be recognized that these rather bald assertions are based on fragmentary evidence, historical analogies, systemic regularities, imagination, and a good deal of intuition. These conclusions and others put forward in this chapter are best thought of as hypotheses to be tested by the unfolding evidence of the operation of the Soviet system, both in its internal details and in its outward manifestations. Nevertheless, I believe the evidence reviewed here supports the main thrust of my conclusions.

MONOPOLY

Suppose, for purely hypothetical purposes, that Prime Minister Kosygin thought that tank production was more than adequate for the needs of the Soviet Union and wanted to transfer a tank plant to tractor production. Where could he find support to buttress his argument? Independent groups like the International Institute for Strategic Studies (IISS), the Rand Corporation, the Brookings Institution, Congressional committees, university researchers, or free-ranging journalists are not found in the Soviet Union. Potential sources of information, expertise, and analysis to provide alternatives to the military's views are limited to established, official bodies in the Central Committee apparatus, Council of Ministers, Production Ministries, and

Military-Industrial Commission. These organizations could supply analyses on overall costs, specific resource requirements, technological feasibility, production efficiency, and, perhaps, alternative weapons designs to perform the specified missions, but none could challenge the size or nature of potential enemy threats or of the preferred means and quantities of armaments for meeting the threat. These issues are reserved for the military. If a challenge to military practices were raised in the Politburo, the question would probably be referred to the Defense Council or Central Committee Secretariat, both of which would find it necessary to go to the Ministry of Defense for detailed staff analysis. Only an individual like the Central Committee secretary for defense production would be likely to have the breadth of vision to review such matters. Below that level, whether in Party or government, secrecy and compartmentalism would restrict the analysts' access to the information required, even if the organizations could be given the job in the first place.

Nevertheless, the Politburo can call on experts to present testimony on policy problems, and a Politburo member could presumably ask military professionals to give their views on disputed questions. This is more likely for a new issue than for a policy on which the General Staff had already established a position. It could be a career-wrecking act for an officer to support policies in conflict with those promulgated by his superiors. Similarly, it would be a rare military leader who would form an alliance with a Politburo member and support him in disputes with the other elements of the military and political establishment. However, before a position is established, there may be more openness and debate, with the possibility of diverse views from the military reaching the political leadership. This seems to have been the case during the controversy over strategic doctrine in the early 1960s, when a number of military and political authorities examined the consequences of nuclear-strategic weaponry. This debate, however, bore little of the technical data of Western arguments over the same issues, with their detailed calculations based on missile numbers, warhead size, accuracies, and hard and soft target capabilities, all in relation to sharply delineated models of deterrence, counterforce, countervalue, and other strategic variants. Indeed, the Soviet view that these issues are primarily political rather than technical suggests that Kosygin's hypothetical policy issue raised earlier is not phrased in the way Soviet politicians would frame it, and that the search for sources of policy alternatives in organizations may miss some important actors.

Rather than searching the organization charts for key actors, we should perhaps focus on specific individuals. Indeed, people like Arbatov at the USA Institute, Smirnov at the VPK, Serbin at the Defense Industry Department of the Central Committee Secretariat, or Ustinov, wherever he may be, are called on as individuals with broad experience and a lifetime career in defense affairs. The evidence to assess the implications of using individual expertise, however, is conflicting and fragmentary. For example, the former director of the disarmament section of the Institute of World Economy and International Relations (IMEMO) has stated that the institute was not given access to secret data on Soviet arms and weapons programs and had to rely on Western sources such as the *Military Balance* for information.[273] Whether the institute's director had personal access to the Soviet data and could provide adequate advice must remain an open question. However, I would note that the rigid compartmentalism at the lower levels of the Soviet bureaucracy is counteracted by a high degree of informality at the very top. As a staff member of the USA Institute explained it, "The lines between the top leadership and the problems to be solved are short and direct."[274] Nevertheless, the possibility of there being interactions at a high level would not invalidate the organizationally based conclusions of this article.

CONSERVATISM AND INCREMENTALISM

The forces of conservatism in Soviet life are many and strong. They are based on cultural, organizational, structural, and other influences. Their major effect is to preserve past trends and patterns and to make the new look much like the old. The best guide to what will happen tomorrow is what happened yesterday. Having said that, and having emphasized this point throughout the article, I believe some modification is necessary to avoid an excessively distorted view.

The management of affairs in the Soviet Union requires great stamina, imagination, and subtlety—characteristics that generate many proposals for changes to make things run more efficiently. Such changes are easier to accommodate if reallocations between sectors are not required, but they do occur. Nevertheless, what we know about Soviet citizens and institutions suggests that, in comparison with many Western nations, Soviet organizations are less likely to promote innovation and change. *Relatively* speaking, policy making in the Soviet Union tends to be more gradual than observed elsewhere. To draw an analogy, one could liken general administrative affairs in the Soviet Union to the way in which traditional postal services are run in many Western countries. A nation with a post office mentality is not aggressively innovative.

Even when a sector has a high priority, the leadership depends on bureaucracies to implement its policies. The bureaucracies' activities are governed by criteria of success, explicit and implicit, which may frustrate the goals of the policy makers or lead to less-than-efficient outcomes. An example of this involves the high-priority area of agricultural modernization, where the Ministry of Reclamation may compel the leadership to adopt programs favored by the bureaucrats, despite the fact that both the minister and his political superiors recognize that alternatives may be more desirable and that the experts' recommendations are based upon a peculiar set of incentives. The bureaucratic recommendations from within the Reclamation Ministry are to do more of what has been done for the past fifteen years: i.e., to build large new water delivery networks.[275] The land reclamation program has been described as a major test of the leadership's ability to control the state bureaucracy where the leadership presumably possesses the authority but not the tools to exert its control over many detailed decisions.

Similarly, I would expect that recommendations coming from the Defense Ministry would call for large military forces and growing procurement of all types of weapons, regardless of changes in the Soviet Union's external environment. These recommendations would undoubtedly be justified by carefully worked out and sincerely held arguments. There could very well be active debate within the military over the detailed structure of the doctrine, especially the specific weapons needs, but it would be a most un-Soviet General Staff that could disseminate a doctrine supporting a policy such as Khrushchev's deterrence policy, which promoted the goal of smaller forces.

Budgetary continuity and predictable political support could, somewhat paradoxically, permit greater flexibility at lower planning levels than would variability in budgets and support. Within the general framework established by the present political leadership, military planners can probably expect long-term growth within understood limits and thus promulgate doctrinal needs in anticipation of the actual availability of weapons. Doctrine and armament norms provide a blueprint for growth. In this context, the General Staff could approve the Strategic Rocket Forces missile program this year, knowing that the navy will get its new carrier next year, and that the army's tank production reached desired levels last year. The services are confident that delay will not necessarily kill their favored programs nor affect their relative positions. Under this umbrella, the Ministry of Defense or General Staff possesses enough leeway to raise tactical and technical questions that may affect future weapons plans. These debates need not be as threatening as they might be elsewhere because the High Command controls the ground rules, and because they are confined within the professional military arena. An example of this is the recent debate on the role of armored personnel carriers, tanks, and mechanized infantry tactics.[276] However, an unexpected change either in technology or in the threat facing the Soviet Union may disrupt these well-laid plans and internal accommodations. An expensive new radar system or interceptor designed to counter an American cruise missile is liked by no one except the Air Defense Forces—and then only if it means a budget increase rather than a reallocation from previously planned projects.

POLITICAL INTERVENTION AND POLITICS

The tendency for Soviet organizations to persist in deep-rooted patterns of behavior means that any redirection requires intervention from the top. In the past, radical shifts in policy were a notable characteristic of Soviet behavior. Such shifts were seen to be necessary to overcome caution, apathy, and bureaucratic conservatism of the rank and file. It was also necessary to respond to accumulated minor changes in the environment, which, because they had not elicited timely marginal adjustments, necessitated periodic major changes of course.

The history of the Soviet Union from the assumption of power by the Communists until World War II is full of examples of significant policy redirection. In the immediate postwar years, policy making solidified, but the post-Stalin period was one of major change in reaction to the consolidation, tight controls, and petrification of the political system under the last years of Stalin's leadership.[277] Khrushchev's cycle of reforms and revisions, however, left the Party and government in near chaos. Partly in reaction to the excessive fluidity of the Khrushchev era, the post-Khrushchev leadership sought to stabilize and consolidate the system. Another reason for the reduction in major changes and intervention was Brezhnev's and his colleagues' seemingly genuine desire for scientific decision making—meaning, in practice, a devolution of authority to experts at the working level. But perhaps the chief cause of policy incrementalism is the nature of the collective leadership, where a balancing of power requires caution and compromise. This is not to say that change does not take place, but that it requires great effort and persistence to build support over a sometimes considerable period of time. This was apparently the case with the new constitution, which took more than ten years to win approval, and with the reallocation of investment to agriculture, which also required gradual change over nearly fifteen years. The Politburo today is therefore less likely to initiate change than before, and the bureaucracy is more likely to be in control of its day-to-day affairs, with the "day to day" extending to the "year to year."

Even though incrementalism has become the hallmark of the system, over a period it can yield substantial change. The Soviet Union in the late 1970s is not the same as it was in 1965, and its military strength has not been stationary. But just as political decisions made by Khrushchev in the late 1950s and by the Brezhnev leadership in the mid-1960s established a twenty-year trajectory in military affairs, modification of that trajectory would also require political decisions. However, analysts of Soviet politics raise considerable doubt as to whether the present group of leaders could make such adjustments short of major crisis or change. There is even considerable doubt as to whether the successors to the political elite of the 1970s would find it possible—or desirable—to alter the status quo unless forced by outside events. Recruitment into the leadership "presents a picture of remarkable traditional gradualism."[278] The elite is more homogeneous than ever before, with both the first and second team of leaders products of the prewar Stalinist generation, beneficiaries of the Great Purge, achieving their great success during World War II. In the late 1930s, they were the youngest group of leaders in the industrialized world. Today they are among the oldest.

According to an argument put forward by Thomas W. Wolfe, the present political and military leadership shares a common outlook on issues affecting Soviet security.[279] This outlook embodies an attitude toward the positive value of military power and holds that overwhelming military strength pays dividends beyond deterrence alone. Stemming from Soviet tradition and experience, this view implies a tendency not to regard military expenditure as a social cost, as is generally the case in the West.[280] Other aspects of the shared outlook described by Wolfe are that the Soviet Union must look out for its own security and not trust others to take care of that for it, that it cannot feel secure until those that threaten it pose little danger, that the capitalist adversary is increasingly antagonistic, and that deterrence is best served by the ability to fight and win wars—nuclear or otherwise. Since most of the participants in Soviet political-military decision-making are said to share this outlook, day-to-day variation in leadership coalitions may have only a marginal effect on military expenditures.

Some of these values are deeply rooted in Russian history, but others result more from the particular experience of a generation that was raised in the revolution and was reaching preeminence in World War II. While it is perhaps impossible to establish the relative weights of different experiences, some analysts have speculated that the generation reaching positions of authority in the postwar period (but that have not yet reached the top leadership ranks) are more indifferent to ideological issues, stress freedom of action in daily decision making, are more responsive to popular demands for improved material conditions, and see a greater need to avoid terror in the maintenance of discipline.[281] This generation is only now reaching the top political levels, having been held back by the stability—due to longevity and explicit policy—of the present officeholders.

Not until this postwar generation of leaders appears on the scene (with substantially different personal histories and values molded by other events, in an environment with its own, probably economic, pressures for change) can we expect the Soviet Union to face the world and its own security in a way differing much from that of the past twenty years. However, given the ages of both the incumbent team and their likely successors, a new generation could dominate the high-level leadership as well as lower level Party and governmental positions within less than a decade.

POLICY IMPLICATIONS

What are the relative weights of organizational relationships and decision-making practices on the size and shape of Soviet force posture? It has been demonstrated in this article that they do have an effect, but their relative importance has not yet been assessed. It must be emphasized that any such assessment must be subjective, given the state of the evidence and analytical techniques. Also, these forces are not independent of one another, especially in the long run. For example, the organization of the Soviet economy is related to the drive to build up the military industry. The following is my estimate of the proportional influence of the specified classes of forces on aggregate defense expenditures, *holding each of the others constant:*

History, culture and values	40-50 percent
Internal politics and personalities	20-30 percent
International environment, threat and internal capabilities	10-30 percent
Doctrine	5-15 percent
Organizations and decision making	10-20 percent

Since culture and values develop from the past, and their effect on the present changes only slowly, I consider that approximately half of the Soviet commitment to security can be considered to be fairly constant. Therefore, in an era of relative stability in internal politics, the *relative* weight of organizational relationships and bureaucratic routines loom large, although from a longer-term perspective they shrink in comparison to politics and the perceived threat. Changes that could take place in the longer term might result from people coming to power with different views of history, doctrine, and international relations.

But what of the shorter run? Most issues that reach the political leadership for a decision are likely to have marginal impact on overall procurement patterns, and the views of the bureaucracies concerned would be weighted very heavily on these decisions. Politics are drawn into play when resource commitments are large and new, when controversies emerge among competing claimants, or when international politics intrude into the decision-making process. If this description is correct, it implies that Western efforts to influence Soviet weapons procurement will not be effective if couched in rational, cost-benefit analytical terms. Instead, it is necessary to force the Soviet leadership to consider the matter in political terms. Organizationally, it means forcing the matter to be placed on the Politburo agenda for more than routine consideration. It requires presenting the issue of the Soviet military build-up so that other things desired or feared by the Soviet leadership are pitted against each other. Despite the centralization of power, the incrementalist nature of Soviet decision making conceivably renders the Soviet Union less rather than more able than the United States to command a significant shift in procurement in response to changing conditions, particularly in periods when political disputes are carefully avoided. The essence of politics is national choice among competing alternatives, and where the alternatives involve actions by other nations, making a choice cannot be avoided. Debates over strategic concepts, Western calculations on efficient Soviet force postures, or information given to the Soviet leaders on the true costs of their defense establishment will probably not have the same effect as the deliberate invocation of political pressures. But such a policy has its risks, mainly because the results cannot be predicted with any accuracy.

Another approach is to promote Western actions that would call for large and unplanned Soviet countermeasures, thus making the Soviet leaders aware of the political nature of their activities. Since strategic cruise missiles, for example, could require massive investments in radars and interceptors, the Soviet Union may be drawn into negotiations over their deployment. However, this type of "bargaining chip" strategy is also risky. The Western nations must be prepared to go ahead with the proposed actions on their own merits, even if a quid pro quo is not forthcoming and the response of the Soviet Union is again unpredictable. As was the case with the American B-70 strategic bomber and Soviet Foxbat countermeasure, either the Soviet reaction could turn out to be much cheaper than assumed by Western analysts or the Soviet Union could make political moves in other areas.

A third approach is the education of potential secondary sources of expertise in the Soviet bureaucracy. Since the leadership does call on individuals and organizations outside the military for expert advice, these advisers can be given the detailed information not available from their own secrecy-ridden, compartmentalized, monopolized sources. The reliance placed on Western information and analysis, however, is likely to be less than that placed on their native resources—biased as they may be.

A senior American service officer has written that Soviet conservatism and caution, together with the need to mobilize internal political support for a new policy, make it difficult for Soviet policy makers to back away from a chosen course of action. To be effective in their efforts to influence Soviet policy, Western inputs must be felt relatively early in the Soviet formulation of policy. This requires constant dialogue at all levels to transmit both straightforward information as well as political messages.[282]

In summary, decision-making practices and organizational movements are important, especially in the short run, when political activities are quiescent and changes in the threat are minor. But contemplation of policy changes by parties either internal or external to the Soviet Union demands the recognition that politics cannot be ignored, and that they are a game that two can play. For a nation whose leaders have been nurtured in the belief that issues of economics, war, and international relations are, above all, political, the Soviet military build-up of the past two decades can be actively addressed only in political terms.

NOTES

1. Discussion of these phases is adopted from William T. Lee, "Soviet Defense Expenditures in the Tenth Five-Year Plan," *Osteuropa Wirtschaft*, no. 4 (1977).

2. The Mig-15 and Mig-17, for example, were produced in the thousands annually in half a dozen plants in the early 1950s. Within a few years of the end of the Korean War, total fighter aircraft production fell to considerably less than a thousand per year. Alexander Boyd, *The Soviet Air Force since 1918* (London: MacDonald & Janes, 1977), pp. 213, 218.

3. Lee, "Soviet Defense Expenditures," p. 8. Most analysts agree that the build-up extends back at least to the rise of Brezhnev in 1965 or the Cuban Missile Crisis period in 1962–63; those with longer memories or better data trace it back a few years earlier. Henry Brandon, for example, writing in the *Sunday Times* (London) described evidence shown to him by intelligence analysts: "But graphs I have been shown indicate a remarkably gradual increase in Russian expenditures over the past fifteen years" (16 January 1977). John Erickson states that "*the* Soviet military buildup as we have come to know it began in the late 1950s (accompanied by an upturn in military expenditures) and has been followed by 'a military buildup' with specific and important modernization phases imposed on it rather like in the fashion of Dean Swift's fleas—a factor which accounts for the complex periodization and differing time scales" ("Soviet Military Capabilities," *Current History*, October 1976, p. 98).

4. U.S., Central Intelligence Agency (CIA), *A Dollar Cost Comparison of Soviet and U.S. Defense Activities, 1967-1977*, SR78-10002, January 1978; CIA, *Estimated Soviet Defense Spending in Rubles, 1970-1975*, SR76-10121U, May 1976; William T. Lee, *The Estimation of Soviet Defense Expenditures, 1955-1975* (New York: Praeger, 1977), pp. 114-16.

5. U.S. defense posture statements show production rates for several classes of Soviet equipment from the mid-1960s.

6. CIA, *A Dollar Cost Comparison;* and *Estimated Soviet Defense Spending.*

7. Five-year growth figures from 1970 to 1975 are given in CIA, *Estimated Soviet Defense Spending*, p. 11.

8. U.S., Congress, Joint Economic Committee, Subcommittee on Priorities and Economy in Government, *Allocation of Resources in the Soviet Union and China, 1976*, 94th Cong., 2nd sess., 1976, p. 24.

9. Lee, "Soviet Defense Expenditures," p. 98.

10. The Politburo (Political Bureau) was renamed the Presidium of the Central Committee in 1952, toward the end of the Stalin era. In addition to some changes in the group's structure, the title of the Party chief was also changed from general secretary to first secretary. The traditional structure was restored following Stalin's death in 1953, and the traditional names were brought back into use in April 1966. It is these names that are used throughout this article.

11. Politburo members began using the formulation "the Politburo headed by Brezhnev" in early 1974. Before then, they were careful not to single out an individual as superior to the other members of the collective leadership.

12. This point is made by Thomas W. Wolfe, *The SALT Experience: Its Impact on U.S. and Soviet Strategic Policy and Decisionmaking*, R-1686-PR (Santa Monica, Calif.: Rand Corporation, 1975), p. 28.

13. Politburo procedures are discussed by Vladimir Petrov, "Formation of Soviet Foreign Policy," *Orbis* 17, no. 3 (Fall 1973): 827-31; Kenneth A. Myers and Dmitri K. Simes, *Soviet Decisionmaking, Strategic Policy, and SALT*, ACDA/PAB-243 (Washington, D.C.: Center for Strategic and International Studies, Georgetown University, 1974), pp. 11, 26; Theodore Shabad, "Brezhnev, Who Ought to Know, Explains Politburo," *New York Times*, 15 June 1975; Merle Fainsod, *How Russia Is Ruled*, 2d ed. (Cambridge, Mass.: Harvard University Press, 1963), ch. 10.

14. During the five-year interval between the twenty-fourth and twenty-fifth Party congresses (30 March 1971 to 24 February 1976), the Politburo met 215 times, or an average of 43 times per year (F. Petrenko, *Pravda*, 11 April 1976).

15. Wolfe, *The SALT Experience*, pp. 58, 160.

16. Similarity between certain features of Politburo procedures and those of the *Mir* are striking. Until well into the twentieth century, the *Mir* was the peasants' village communal assembly that governed and regulated life in the community. An elder was elected but did not stand out until it was necessary for him to take the opinion of a meeting. "Disputes would generally subside into a common recognition that one decision rather than another was equitable or inevitable. Sometimes the Elder was obliged to count heads, and in such cases the minority always accepted the majority verdict. . . . To betray the *Mir* was for the Great Russian, the greatest possible, the only unpardonable sin. . . . The peasants said, 'The *Mir* cannot be judged. Throw all upon the *Mir*, it will bear all.'" Wright Miller, *Russians As People* (New York: E. P. Dutton, 1961), pp. 80-81.

17. This example is taken from the first edition of Fainsod, *How Russia Is Ruled*, pp. 282-83.

18. Stalin's pervasive involvement in the weapons acquisition process included actions concerning tanks, aircraft, artillery, nuclear weapons, and missiles. Khrushchev's directing role in the Soviet space program is described in Leonid Vladimirov, *The Russian Space Bluff* (New York: Dial Press, 1971). Khrushchev himself portrays his interventions on ICBM, naval construction, and nuclear aviation in Nikita S. Khrushchev, *Khrushchev Remembers*, vol. 2: *The Last Testament* (Harmondsworth, England: Penguin Books, 1977), pp. 49-90.

19. Khrushchev described canceling a series of cruisers after only two or three had been built, but not yet outfitted, when it was determined that they would cost much more than planned (ibid., pp. 62-63).

20. Interviews by me and my colleagues with former Lieutenant General Mikhail Milstein, previously of the General Staff and now with the Institute for the Study of the USA and Canada, and with Georgii Arbatov, director of the same institute.

21. John Erickson, *Soviet Military Power* (London: Royal United Services Institute, 1971), p. 16.

22. Khrushchev, for example, described a proposal by Naval Commander in Chief Kuznetsov to rebuild the navy at "absolutely staggering costs." A memorandum outlining the proposal was first circulated among Politburo members, apparently only a few days before it was to be considered at a Politburo meeting. At the meeting, Khrushchev proposed delaying the decision for a week to give the members a better chance to study the proposals. There were thus only a few days for the Politburo as a whole to analyze a complex issue of naval policy. Khrushchev, *Khrushchev Remembers,* pp. 55-56.

23. Khrushchev, *Khrushchev Remembers,* vol. 1, p. 544-45. Looking back on those sacrifices, however, Khrushchev was proud of the role he played in modernizing Soviet forces.

24. Khrushchev, *Khrushchev Remembers,* vol. 2, p. 50. In this single chapter on the navy, Khrushchev mentions the costs of naval systems and programs twelve times.

25. Jerry Hough, "The Brezhnev Era: The Man and the System," *Problems of Communism* (March-April 1976).

26. Hough supports his argument by reference to the ever-increasing number of hospital beds turned out by the doctor-dominated health system, and by the railroad-dominated transport system's emphasis on railroads and the downgrading of roads and trucks (ibid., p. 15).

27. Petrov, "Formation of Soviet Foreign Policy," p. 824.

28. Oleg Penkovsky, *The Penkovsky Papers* (New York: Doubleday, 1965), pp. 300-301.

29. A. S. Yakovlev, *Target of Life,* AD674316 (U.S. National Technical Information Service, Dept. of Commerce), translated from *Tsel'-Zhizni* (Moscow: Izdatel'stvo Politicheskoi Literatury, 1966), pp. 394-95.

30. Ibid., pp. 396-97. Beria's opposition was apparently based on some internal political scheming.

31. Aron Katsenelinboigen, "Soviet Science and the Economist/Planners," in *Soviet Science and Technology,* ed. John R. Thomas and Ursula Kruse-Vaucienne (Washington, D.C.: National Science Foundation, 1976), p. 241.

32. Dmitri K. Simes, *Foreign Policy, Arms Control, and Strategic Issues in the Soviet Media,* (Georgetown University, Center for Strategic and International Studies, Monthly Reports, 19 April 1976), pp. 6-7.

33. This example is taken from Edward L. Warner III, "The Military in Contemporary Soviet Politics: An Institutional Analysis" (Ph.D. diss., Department of Politics, Princeton University, April 1975), pp. 161-65.

34. Included under this heading are the ten Party secretaries, the department heads, and the departmental staffs. The organization is also referred to as the central Party apparatus or the Central Committee apparatus. Staff members are often referred to as the *apparatchiki.*

35. Leonard Schapiro, *The Government and Politics of the Soviet Union,* 5th ed. (London: Hutchinson, 1973), p. 65.

36. Ibid. A former member of the Secretariat estimated the number of "responsible staff workers" at just over 900 and the number of other personnel at 2,400, including "responsible nonstaff workers." "Responsible" workers are professional or expert personnel, as opposed to "technical" workers such as secretaries and guards. "Staff" posts are permanent, whereas nonstaff jobs are temporary, or are filled by consultants. Mervyn Matthews, interview with the pseudonymic A. Pravdin, *Survey* (Autumn 1974), p. 95. Another estimate put the number of responsible workers at 1,300-1,500 on the basis of an assumed twenty-five departments. However, since the actual number of departments was twenty-three, the personnel estimate should be reduced to approximately 1,200-1,400. This estimate includes nonstaff as well as staff workers and is not inconsistent with the other estimates. A Avtorkhanov, *The Communist Party Apparatus* (Chicago: Henry Regnery, 1966), pp. 209-10.

37. The period in 1966-67 when Brezhnev consolidated his power in the Central Committee is described by Michel Tatu, *Power in the Kremlin* (London/New York: Collins/Viking Press, 1979), pp. 516-22.

38. A former consultant to the Secretariat notes a general suspicion and jealousy between that organization and other advisers close to Brezhnev. Brezhnev's personal secretariat, for example, was disparagingly known as "that kikish bunch," though there were no Jews on the staff. Boris Rabbot, "A Letter to Brezhnev," *New York Times Magazine,* 6 November 1977.

39. Sources of expertise and analysis are also now found in a secretariat attached to Brezhnev's personal office, research institutes, consultants, and ad hoc advisory committees.

40. Marshall D. Shulman, "SALT and the Soviet Union," in *SALT: The Moscow Agreements and Beyond,* ed. Mason Willrich and John B. Rhinelander (New York: Free Press, 1974), p. 113.

41. Teresa Rakowska-Harmstone, "Toward a Theory of Soviet Leadership Maintenance," in *The Dynamics of Soviet Politics,* ed. Paul Cocks et al. (Cambridge, Mass.: Harvard University Press, 1976), p. 67. Also, Sidney Ploss, "Politics in the Kremlin," *Problems of Communism,* May-June 1970, pp. 12-13.

42. Christian Duevel, "Link of Central Committee Secretary Ryabov with Defense Industry Corroborated," *Radio Liberty Research,* RL-31/77, 9 February 1977. The recent edition of the *Soviet Military Encyclopedia,* as quoted by Duevel (p. 2), mentions that Brezhnev, on the instructions of the Central Committee, "took charge of the questions of the development of heavy industry and construction, the development and production of modern military technology and weapons, the equipment of the armed forces with them, and the development of cosmonautics."

43. The secretary of defense production, and perhaps also his subordinate department, are said to be a link between the political and military leadership. The department's staff, for example, was claimed to have been active in the SALT I negotiations. See Myers and Simes, *Soviet Decisionmaking, Strategic Policy, and SALT,* p. 26.

44. For evidence on Obkom Defense Industry departments, see Jerry Hough, *The Soviet Prefects* (Cambridge, Mass.: Harvard University Press, 1969), p. 17.

45. This number is derived from the assumption that the Department for Defense Production is one of the larger departments. Estimates of responsible staff and nonstaff personnel for some other departments are: Science, 41-43 staff, 35 nonstaff; Propaganda, 48-51 staff, 35 nonstaff; Organization, 60 staff, 30 nonstaff. Matthews, interview with A. Pravdin, p. 95.

46. The staffs of the Senate and House Committees on defense and the defense subcommittees of the Appropriations Committees number approximately sixty-five people.

47. Shulman, "SALT and the Soviet Union," p. 114; Petrov, "Formation of Soviet Foreign Policy," p. 248. Although disputed by some observers (for example, Matthews, interview with A. Pravdin, p. 101), the point is made even more sharply by Hedrick Smith, who was told of a split in the Secretariat between the leaders at the top and the staff who had gained a "reputation for being too sophisticated, too educated, and too worldly to be fully trusted with the top jobs." Hedrick Smith, *The Russians* (New York: Quadrangle/New York Times Book Co., 1976), p. 293.

48. Matthews, interview with A. Pravdin, p. 78. He also describes how an instructor can be promoted out of the Secretariat to the position of deputy minister in a ministry he supervised.

49. After the death of Stalin, some departments established sectors of from three to five people to gather their own information, conduct surveys, and do analyses of this information for the Secretariat leadership. In 1971, however, these activities were restricted by a special internal Party decree, and the departments reverted to greater use of information from traditional channels. It was speculated on at the time that the leadership did not like this kind of departmental independence. Ibid., p. 98.

50. Ibid., p. 98.

51. Petrov, "Formation of Soviet Foreign Policy," p. 827; Matthews, interview with A. Pravdin, p. 98. Similar activities

with respect to scientific affairs were also described in interviews with several Soviet émigré scientists.

52. Thomas Wolfe, *Soviet Interests in SALT: Political, Economic, Bureaucratic, and Strategic Contributions and Impediments to Arms Control,* P-4702 (Santa Monica, Calif.: Rand Corporation, 1971), p. 18.

53. Savinkin was a career MPA officer before moving to the Party apparatus, and then served as Mironov's deputy. Mironov's career included a wartime stint as a high-level political officer, followed by several years in the KGB before moving on to the Secretariat. Both men attended an important military-Party conference in 1962 to discuss improvements in political training of officers and the role and authority of Party organizations in the military. Savinkin frequently attends military conferences and ceremonies and regularly signs obituaries of leading military and (most interestingly) people involved in defense production. Roman Kolkowicz, *The Soviet Military and the Communist Party* (Princeton, N.J.: Princeton University Press, 1967), p. 169; Warner, "The Military in Contemporary Soviet Politics," p. 81. A 1976 meeting of military Party workers called to "improve the standard of Party work . . . and increase the effectiveness of Party influence" was attended by MPA Chief General Yepishev, Administrative Organs Department Head Savinkin and his deputy, and the commanders of all the services (*Krasnaya Zvezda,* 8 July 1976, p. 2).

54. These points are made by Jerry Hough, "The Party *Apparatchiki,*" in *Interest Groups in Soviet Politics,* ed. H. Gordon Skilling and Franklyn Griffiths (Princeton, N.J.: Princeton University Press, 1971), pp. 80-83.

55. Ibid., p. 84.

56. Matthews, interview with A. Pravdin, p. 96. The chairman of the Council of Ministers also has a Secretariat, but very little is known about this organization except the name of its chief, Boris T. Batsanov (Herwig Kraus, "Members of the CPSU Auditing Commission as of 1 May 1978," *Radio Liberty Research Bulletin,* RL107/78, 15 May 1978, p. 1).

57. Leonard Schapiro, "The General Department of the CC of the CPSU," *Survey* (Summer 1975), p. 60.

58. The armed forces assistant may be V. A. Golikov, a former colonel and war veteran (Matthews, interview with A. Pravdin, p. 96). Another source claims, however, that the organization contains neither top military men nor specialists in military/strategic technology (Myers and Simes, *Soviet Decision-making,* p. 30). Golikov is the author of a survey article on agriculture and is said to be Brezhnev's assistant for agricultural policy (Ploss, "New Politics in Russia?," *Survey,* Autumn 1973, p. 29).

59. Myers and Simes, *Soviet Decision-making,* p. 16.

60. Ibid. There may be some confusion here between the secretariat of the general secretary and the General Department of the Central Committee. The General Department, called the Special Sector under Stalin, is charged with the formal control of documents in the Central Committee and the Politburo. The Special Sector also functioned as Stalin's personal secretariat, and although its functions (and name) were altered by his successors to eliminate the personal services it provided, the organization remains closely associated with Brezhnev's private secretariat. Schapiro, "The General Department of the CC of the CPSU," pp. 58-59.

61. Petrov, "Formation of Soviet Foreign Policy," pp. 823-24.

62. Simes, *Foreign Policy,* p. 5.

63. These points are made by Carl G. Jacobsen in "Soviet Thinks Tanks" (Paper presented at Harvard University, Center for International Affairs).

64. IMEMO Director Inozemtsev has said that at least 15 percent of his institute's work is for the Central Committee.

65. Petrov, "Formation of Soviet Foreign Policy," p. 843.

66. Alexander O. Ghebhardt, "Implications of Organizations and Bureaucratic Policy Models for Soviet ABM Decisionmaking" (Ph.D. diss., Columbia University, 1975), p. 199.

67. Douglas F. Garthoff, "The Soviet Military and Arms Control," *Survival,* November-December 1977, p. 246.

68. Khrushchev, *Khrushchev Remembers,* vol. 2, p. 72.

69. An example is Politburo member M. Solomentsev's use of the Central Institute for Mathematical Economics. Some analysts claim that IMEMO has close ties with Politburo members Suslov and Ponomarey and that the former member Shelepin used the Institute of the International Workers Movement as his personal "brain trust."

70. Petrov, "Formation of Soviet Foreign Policy," p. 844; and interviews with Soviet scientists.

71. Shabad, "Brezhnev, Who Ought to Know"; Myers and Simes, *Soviet Decision-making,* pp. 11-12.

72. Petrov, "Formation of Soviet Foreign Policy," pp. 826-30.

73. Myers and Simes, *Soviet Decision-making,* p. 22.

74. This is drawn from interviews with Soviet émigré scientists. In addition to the signal honor involved in these consultations, the scientists also describe themselves as being apprehensive and a bit scared about the order.

75. Petrov, "Formation of Soviet Foreign Policy," pp. 841, 843. But as one scientist told me, "It is not always necessary to solve the problem. One just has to look busy until it goes away."

76. Ibid., p. 830. Such a position seemed to be held, for example, by A. M. Rumyantsev, a member of the Central Committee and director of the Institute of Sociology in Moscow. However, when Rumyantsev set up a semiofficial Association of Social Prognosis attached to the Academy of Sciences but outside the direct control of the Central Committee Secretariat, the Secretariat opposed this move and was instrumental in its demise. Matthews, interview with A. Pravdin, p. 99.

77. The implications of the Defense Council's relationship with the Supreme Soviet are not clear. It may have been a mechanism to assure Brezhnev's leadership of the military when he became president of the Supreme Soviet or to raise the Defense Council to a status higher than that of a Politburo subcommittee.

78. Much of the following paragraphs is taken from the organizational history traced by John McDonnell, "The Organization of Soviet Defence and Military Policy-making," *Domestic and Foreign Dimensions* (New York: Praeger, 1977).

79. Marshal Grechko, quoted in ibid., p. 66.

80. Vladimir Petrov, *Partiinoe Stroitel'stvo v Sovetskoi Armii i flotte, 1918-1961* [Party construction in the Soviet army and navy, 1918-61] (Moscow: Voenizdat, 1964), p. 462.

81. Penkovsky, *Penkovsky Papers,* pp. 133, 151-53.

82. McDonnell, "The Organization of Soviet Defence," pp. 79-82. The possibility of a reorganization of these functions is supported by the fact that Soviet military writings in 1967 listed the Main Military Council as the primary organ of collective leadership of the armed forces, rather than of the country's defense. In 1969, the first mention in the West of the Defense Council was made in a U.S. Congressional testimony by a member of the Department of State's Bureau of Intelligence and Research (David Mark, statement before U.S. Congress, Subcommittee on Economy in Government of the Joint Economic Committee, *The Military Budget and National Priorities,* Part 3, 91st Cong., 1st sess., June 1969, p. 956).

83. Edward L. Warner III, "The Bureaucratic Politics of Weapons Procurement," in *Soviet Naval Policy,* ed. Michael MccGwire, K. Booth, and J. McDonnell (New York: Praeger, 1975), p. 73.

84. Harriet Fast Scott, "The Soviet High Command," *Air Force Magazine,* March 1977, p. 53; Douglas F. Garthoff, "The Soviet Military and Arms Control," pp. 245-46; and Raymond L. Garthoff, "SALT and the Soviet Military," *Problems of Communism,* January-February 1975, p. 29. It should be noted that many of these analysts, particularly the Garthoffs, either have had intensive dealings with Soviet military and political leaders or in their various positions have been privy to U.S. intelligence and analyses. Therefore, they may be more

authoritative than might be presumed from the absence of bibliographic references in their writings.

85. Scott, "The Soviet High Command," p. 54.

86. McDonnell, "The Organization of Soviet Defence," p. 72.

87. Warner, "The Bureaucratic Politics of Weapons Procurement," p. 73.

88. Shulman, "SALT and the Soviet Union," p. 112.

89. Wolfe, *Soviet Interests in SALT,* p. 28.

90. Myers and Simes, *Soviet Decision-making,* p. 20.

91. Ibid., pp. 20, 26.

92. Quoted in Warner, "The Military in Contemporary Soviet Politics," p. 76.

93. The five services, listed by Soviet protocol ranking, are Strategic Rocket Forces, ground forces, National Air Defense Forces, air forces, and navy.

94. Ustinov was made a marshal—the highest Soviet military rank—shortly after his assumption of defense leadership.

95. Marshal Zhukov had been a Politburo member for a few months in 1957, following his support of Khrushchev against the "antiparty faction." However, he was then demoted for, among other things, attempting to insulate the military from Party control.

96. These points are made by Gen. James Wold (U.S. air attaché, Moscow), *Air Force Magazine,* August 1977, p. 6; Peter Kruzhnin, "The Soviet Armed Forces in 1977," *Radio Liberty Research,* RL286/77, 16 December 1977, p. 3; Simes, *Foreign Policy,* p. 8.

97. Mobility and job turnover are much less than in the American military, and, consequently, the opportunity for parochialism to develop is considerably greater.

98. Penkovsky, *Penkovsky Papers,* p. 217.

99. Myers and Simes, *Soviet Decision-making,* pp. 27, 28, 31.

100. Raymond L. Garthoff, "SALT and the Soviet Military," p. 26.

101. Myers and Simes, *Soviet Decision-making,* p. 20.

102. The organization of the Ministry of Defense, General Staff, and services is described by Scott, "The Soviet High Command"; and "Organization of Soviet Aerospace Services," *Air Force Magazine,* March 1977.

103. This background is covered in Warner, "The Military in Contemporary Soviet Politics," p. 84n; and in David Holloway, "Science, Technology, and the Soviet Armed Forces" (Paper prepared for the Workshop on Soviet Science and Technology, George Washington University/National Science Foundation, November 1976), pp. 17-18.

104. Warner, "The Military in Contemporary Soviet Politics," and Holloway, "Science, Technology, and the Soviet Armed Forces," p. 16.

105. In 1965, for example, Politburo member Shelepin (among others) noted the renewed high priority of military production but suggested that this priority would not be reflected until the next Five-Year Plan (quoted in Vernon V. Aspaturian, "The Soviet Military-Industrial Complex: Does It Exist?," *Journal of International Affairs* 26, no. 1 [1972]: 26n).

106. Erickson, *Soviet Military Power,* pp. 16, 21.

107. Warner, "The Military in Contemporary Soviet Politics," p. 70. This information was obtained from a General Staff officer.

108. The case for political dissatisfaction over military efficiency and technological innovation is put forth by Holloway in "Technology and Political Decision in Soviet Armaments in Policy," *Journal of Peace Research,* no. 4 (1976); and in Erickson, *Soviet Military Power.*

109. Interview with Gen. M. Milstein, 10 May 1977.

110. Holloway, "Science, Technology, and the Soviet Armed Forces," p. 27.

111. Ibid., p. 28; and Holloway, "Technology and Political Decision," p. 262; Arthur J. Alexander, *Armor Development in the Soviet Union and the United States,* R-1860-NA (Santa Monica, Calif.: Rand Corporation, 1976), pp. 51-53.

112. Erickson, *Soviet Military Power,* p. 11. Erickson notes that the existence of an economic constraint is supported by Soviet military complaints "that costs ought *not* to be the final arbitrator, but rather the efficacy and the requirement for the weapon."

113. Many analysts point to the Soviet military's new attachment to *technique* to help meet the new policy goals; for example, network and cost-effectiveness analysis, programing methods, planning-programing-budgeting systems (PPBS), and technological forecasting. It is my own opinion, however (based on a review of the attempted introduction of these techniques into the economic sphere), that while they may prove marginally useful for improving low-level processes, they are almost useless for the problems considered here and may, in fact, divert attention and resources from the main task.

114. Holloway, "Technology and Political Decision," p. 25n.

115. John Erickson, "Soviet Military Operational Research: Objectives and Methods," *Strategic Review,* Spring 1977, p. 68.

116. For a description of how such project committees operate in aviation, see Alexander, *R&D in Soviet Aviation,* R-589-PR (Santa Monica, Calif.: Rand Corporation, 1970), p. 19.

117. Penkovsky, *Penkovsky Papers,* p. 142.

118. The precise title of what is here called the Armaments Directorate is not known, and in fact, the organization of the function seems to vary across the services. The navy, for example, has a chief for shipbuilding and armaments who supervises several technical departments: shipbuilding, ship repair, and weapons development. See James A. Barry, Jr., "Soviet Naval Policy: The Institutional Setting," in McCGwire and McDonnell, "The Organization of Soviet Defence," p. 113. The existence of scientific-technical committees in the military services is asserted by Matthew P. Gallaher and Karl F. Spielmann, Jr., *Soviet Decision-making for Defense* (New York: Praeger, 1972), p. 20; such committees are also mentioned by Holloway, "Technology and Political Decision," p. 25.

119. Warner, "The Military in Contemporary Soviet Politics," pp. 71, 75; and interview by author with Colonel General Mishuk, commander of the Armaments Directorate of the Soviet air force.

120. Mishuk interview. The independence of design bureaus and the search for competitive alternatives by the customers is also described by Khrushchev. Aircraft designer Tupolev, for example, refused Stalin's order to build an intercontinental bomber, "explaining that the limits of contemporary technology made such a task impossible to fulfill." Stalin then turned to the designer Myasishchev, who built the Mya-4 (Bison) to meet Stalin's requirement. When Khrushchev asked the rocket designer Korolyov whether ballistic missiles could be developed with shorter reaction times, and the designer said, "No," Khrushchev turned to another design bureau headed by Yangel for a solution to his problem. Khruschchev, *Khrushchev Remembers,* pp. 70, 83.

121. V. Grabin, "Contribution to Victory," *Technika i Vooruzhenie,* no. 5 (1970), pp. 7-8.

122. "Tactical-technical requirements" is the phrase used to specify missions, performance characteristics, and their priorities. These have been mentioned for a wide range of systems, from tanks to ICBMs. The documents themselves can be quite short, especially when compared to similar American documents, perhaps only a few pages long in many instances. See Alexander, *R&D in Soviet Aviation,* p. 18.

123. Barry, "Soviet Naval Policy," p. 118.

124. A source of difference in organizational bias arises in the air force from the educational background of aviation engineering personnel who attended special academies (for example, the Zhukovsky Air Engineering Academy) rather than the regular staff schools.

125. Military representatives (*Voennye Predstavitali,* or, more commonly, *Voenpred*) are discussed by Mikhail Agursky, *The Research Institute of Machine-Building Technology*

Soviet Institution Series, paper no. 8, (Hebrew University of Jerusalem, September 1976), pp. 9-12; by Warner, "The Military in Contemporary Soviet Politics," p. 79; and in interviews with the planning director of a large plant producing military and civilian products.

126. An anecdote illustrating the differences attributable to military production standards was related by a laboratory director in an association (*Obeedineniia*) of plants producing both civilian and military products. Pumps of similar design and construction were produced in two plants of the same size: a secret plant for military products and an open, civilian plant. Output from the secret plant was 5,000 units per year, whereas the civilian plant turned out 20,000 units. The laboratory was called in to investigate the productivity differentials when the local Party organization recognized the discrepancy after the two plants had been brought together.

127. These examples are based on the hearsay evidence of several Soviet interviewees. Another example concerned the rowlocks of ships' small boats, which were to be made of a specially treated alloy. On one occasion, when the specified alloy was not available, another was substituted. During naval maneuvers the small boats were launched, and almost simultaneously, rowlocks began to fracture throughout the fleet as the sailors put their arms to the oars. This case also led to an investigation and jail terms.

128. For example, a decline in military production below planned output goals, followed by a surge the following month, may be juggled in the account books by the military representative to show that the plan was met in both months. In this way, the plant retains its bonuses for achieving the plan in both months, and the customer gets its output while maintaining good relations with local management.

129. Schapiro, *The Government and Politics of the Soviet Union,* p. 117. The size and composition of the Presidium has varied greatly—from six to fourteen, for example, in a two-year period in the early 1950s. Since the mid-1960s, the number was stabilized in the ten-to-twelve range. McDonnell, "The Soviet Defense Industry as a Pressure Group," in *Soviet Naval Policy,* ed. MccGwire, Booth, and McDonnell, p. 92n.

130. Igor Birman, "From the Achieved Level," *Soviet Studies* 30, no. 2 (April 1978): 161, 164, 167.

131. John Newhouse, *Cold Dawn: The Story of SALT* (New York: Holt, Rinehart & Winston, 1973), p. 252.

132. These points are outlined in detail by McDonnell, "The Soviet Defense Industry," pp. 95-101.

133. Ustinov was said to have been "foisted upon Khrushchev" by a joint coalition of the Politburo, Council of Ministers, and military (Aspaturian, "The Soviet Military-Industrial Complex," p. 16).

134. Information on the VPK has become available in the past few years from several sources, including interviews conducted by the author with ex-members of the general staffs of several Warsaw Pact countries and Soviet scientists from both the Academy of Sciences and industrial branch research institutes. See Warner, "The Military in Contemporary Soviet Politics," pp. 71, 74, 78; McDonnell, "The Soviet Defense Industry," p. 93; Agursky, *The Research Institute,* p. 5; Garthoff, "SALT and the Soviet Military," p. 29; Wolfe, *Soviet Interests in SALT,* pp. 35-37; Andrew Sheren, "Structure and Organization of Defense-Related Industries," in *Economic Performance and the Military Burden in the Soviet Union* (Washington, D.C.: Joint Economic Committee, 1970), p. 124.

135. Wolfe, *Soviet Interests in SALT,* p. 35. The close association between these two bodies is supported by two interviewed scientists who referred to the organizations interchangeably when describing their own participation in high-priority research.

136. In a speech of April 1963, Khrushchev announced that Smirnov was replacing Ustinov in a job where Ustinov had been "responsible and answerable for the defence industry." This position may have been the VPK or a predecessor organization. Tatu, *Power in the Kremlin,* p. 344.

137. Warner, "The Military in Contemporary Soviet Politics," p. 78.

138. The planning director of a plant producing both military and civilian products noted in an interview that to meet military production plans, he never had to resort to the various semilegal bartering methods and favors (*blat*) that were commonly used on the civilian side. Interestingly, this planning director had never heard of the VPK. To manage priorities, he depended on the ministry, which presumably interacted with the VPK.

139. This point is discussed by Gur Ofer, *The Opportunity Cost of the Nonmonetary Advantages of the Soviet Military R&D Effort,* R-1741-DDRE (Santa Monica, Calif.: Rand Corporation, 1975), pp. 15-20. An anecdote related by a former British Foreign Office commercial counselor in Moscow illustrates this kind of disruption. The minister of the Chemical Industry angrily concluded a telephone conversation to greet his British guests. Still fuming, he explained that he was being required to divert a particular plastic from the ministry's regular plan to meet the demands of the Aviation Ministry. The minister complained that the Tu-144 supersonic transport project had already disrupted his plan and that this new incident was a second interference. After calming down, the minister shrugged and remarked that somehow they would find a way to work things out.

140. One scientist described two types of secret research that he knew about: work done directly under military supervision and that done under the VPK.

141. Commissariats were renamed ministries in 1946.

142. Information on the history and organization of defense industry is taken from McDonnell, "The Soviet Defense Industry," pp. 87-90; and Holloway, "Science, Technology, and the Soviet Armed Forces," pp. 6-12.

143. Agursky, *The Research Institute,* pp. 6, 30.

144. Examples of the operation of this council are given in Heather Campbell, *Controversy in Soviet R&D: The Airship Case Study,* R-1001-PR (Santa Monica, Calif.: Rand Corporation, 1972), pp. 22, 30.

145. Brezhnev dubbed the Five-Year Plan beginning in 1976 "The Plan of Quality."

146. Two kinds of priority are described by participants in Soviet industry and science: military priority, which is currently managed by the VPK, and state-Party priority, which is administered by the Central Committee. The latter can range from the Tu-144 supersonic transport to the Baikal-Amur railroad, and from eliminating pollution in Lake Baikal to the creation of artificial diamonds.

147. The planning director (referred to earlier) noted that a machine operator earning 170 rubles per month on civilian production could make 200-220 rubles on military orders. However, the salary differential typically enabled the plant to place higher-quality machinists in the military job.

148. Agursky, *Research Institute,* pp. 21-29. Agursky and others argue that many of the advantages formerly available only to workers on military projects are now more widespread and that the disadvantages—most prominently, secrecy—have increased. Some observers suggest that a less imaginative and adventurous type is, in fact, now attracted to military work precisely because of the protection afforded by secrecy and the ease in obtaining resources for scientific work. These opinions, however, are not universally held among the Soviet émigrés interviewed.

149. Many scientists and laboratories apply for military projects in order to build up their equipment or to generate work for colleagues and graduate students. It is generally expected that most scientists in the elite institutions will devote some part of their effort to secret projects for the good of the laboratory.

150. In interviewing Soviet scientists, one heard repeatedly that if a project carried a VPK priority, "money is no object." This view was echoed by the chief of the Armaments Directorate of the Soviet air force. When asked how he would have responded to a problem such as was found in the defective landing gear of the U.S. air force C-5A cargo aircraft, he re-

plied, "That's no problem. You find the problem and correct it, just like the U.S. air force did. Money is no problem."

151. Aircraft designer Alexander Yakovlev described the contracting process (to a colleague of the author) in the following terms: "After considerable negotiations with the customer as to *what* will be produced, the designer signs the contract and symbolically hands over his testicles with the contract. When the aircraft is delivered as specified, he gets his testicles back." Considering the risks, designers are naturally conservative in what they will agree to.

152. One ploy described by a research director was deliberately to subcontract the most difficult part of a job to another institute. Failure to produce could then be blamed on the subcontractor. Sometimes there were four or five levels of subcontracting, thus diffusing responsibilities through several layers of performers.

153. This point is made by McDonnell, "The Soviet Defense Industry," pp. 91-101. Death is now beginning to thin their ranks, forty years after they first rose to industrial leadership.

154. VPK Chairman Smirnov and Minister of Radio Industry Pleshakov were both members of the Soviet SALT delegation (Garthoff, "SALT and the Soviet Military," p. 29).

155. Alexander, "Weapons Acquisition in the Soviet Union, United States, and France," in *Comparative Defense Policy*, ed. Frank B. Horton III, A. C. Rogerson, and E. L. Warner III (Baltimore: Johns Hopkins University Press, 1974), pp. 427, 430.

156. Holloway, "Science, Technology, and the Soviet Armed Forces," p. 10.

157. Civilian industry attempts to do the same thing in a "semilegal" way. Hidden reserves—that is, excess capacity, large inventories, and overmanning—are carefully accumulated by industrial managers, but without the official sanction given to the same practices in defense industry.

158. Quoted by Holloway, "Science, Technology, and the Soviet Armed Forces," p. 9.

159. See Alexander, "Weapons Acquisition," pp. 429-30.

160. Warner, "The Military in Contemporary Soviet Politics," p. 75; and Holloway, "Science, Technology, and the Soviet Armed Forces," p. 13.

161. J. W. Kehoe, Jr., "Warship Design: Ours and Theirs," *U.S. Naval Institute Proceedings*, August 1975, p. 65; and MccGwire, "Soviet Naval Procurement," in *The Soviet Union in Europe and Near East* (London: Royal United Services Institute, 1970), p. 74.

162. This does not mean that design bureaus operate without constraints. A considerable number of technical rules and planning regulations act on the periphery of the organization, influencing the course of events. It is internal managerial autonomy that the designer possesses. This is in contrast to the high degree of participation by outsiders in detailed project management often found in American weapons developments. See Alexander, "Weapons Acquisition," p. 433.

163. Yakovlev, *Target of Life*, p. 394.

164. Campbell, *Controversy in Soviet R&D.*

165. Ibid., pp. 3, 36.

166. A. Mikoyan, "A chem plokhi samolety i vertolety?" [But what is wrong with airplanes and helicopters?], *Literaturnaia Gazeta*, 14 February 1968, p. 10.

167. Joseph Berliner, *The Innovation Decision in Soviet Industry* (Cambridge, Mass.: M.I.T. Press, 1976).

168. Smith, *The Russians*, p. 294.

169. The Soviet historian Roy Medvedev comments, "It cannot be denied that our leaders work very hard. How could it be otherwise.... There are far too many things that could be handled perfectly well at middle levels of administration, yet are still decided at the top.... Khrushchev spent 14 to 16 hours a day working on the details of his numerous reforms" (*On Socialist Democracy* [New York: Alfred A. Knopf, 1975], p. 296).

170. Ibid., p. 295.

171. This point is made by, among others, T. R. Rigby, "The Soviet Leadership: Toward a Self-stabilizing Oligarchy," *Soviet Studies*, October 1970, p. 172.

172. A large number of activities conducted by private individuals or organizations in most Western countries are state functions in the Soviet Union.

173. Lenin saw bureaucratic vices as a major force to be combated in the new regime. In 1922 he wrote to a deputy, "We have all sunk into a rotten swamp of bureaucratic departments" (quoted by Medvedev, *On Socialist Democracy*, p. 294).

174. Fainsod, *How Russia Is Ruled*, p. 387.

175. Smith, *The Russians*, p. 265.

176. Fainsod, *How Russia Is Ruled*, p. 395.

177. Michael P. Gehlen, "Group Theory and the Study of Politics," in *The Soviet Political Process*, ed. Sidney I. Ploss (Waltham, Mass.: Ginn & Co., 1971), p. 43.

178. Medvedev, *On Socialist Democracy*, 299.

179. Berliner notes, for example, that "the decisions made by the central planners are heavily influenced by the proposals made by the enterprises in the draft plans.... The enterprise is commanded to do what it had originally decided to do" (Berliner, *The Innovation Decision*, pp. 15-16).

180. Zev Katz, "Insights from Emigrés and Sociological Studies on the Soviet Economy," *Soviet Economic Prospects for the Seventies*, U.S. Congress, Joint Economic Committee, Washington, D.C. (1973), p. 93.

181. Ibid.

182. Fainsod, *How Russia Is Ruled*, p. 418. An émigré laboratory director described to me how his institute would accept a particularly difficult research problem and then subcontract the "impossible" parts to another institute. Subcontracting could go on like this for several more levels, with no single organization ultimately responsible for fulfillment of the original task.

183. Quoted in Smith, *The Russians*, p. 348.

184. A retired Soviet general told me of attempts to publish some relatively innocuous information on Soviet civil defense in an attempt to defuse Western speculations on Soviet intentions. He claimed that ingrained habits of not revealing anything of a military nature were extremely difficult to overcome and that the problem had been wrestled with for some time before it was finally decided to publish the information.

185. Khrushchev, *Khrushchev Remembers*, pp. 59-60.

186. Newhouse, *Cold Dawn*, p. 192.

187. Aspaturian, "The Soviet Military-Industrial Complex," pp. 18-19.

188. "High-level leadership" includes the Politburo, Party Secretariat, and Presidium of the Council of Ministers. In some cases, the term can also encompass ministers and agency heads. Interventions involving major redirections of previous policy would require the near-unanimous active support of Party and government leaders, whereas less important decisions could be made by the individuals assigned the specific functional responsibility with assent of the leading Party and government organs.

189. Although some major policy changes have been identified as beginning at the grass-roots level and working their way upward—the dissolution of the machine tractor stations is an example—most policy advice from operating organizations seems to be to continue past practices. On the machine tractor stations, see Theodore Friedgut, "Interests and Groups in Soviet Policymaking: The MTS Reforms," *Soviet Studies* 28, no. 4 (October 1976). Friedgut makes the point that sectoral initiatives have a greater chance of being heard by the leadership if a new policy is presented as a beneficial reallocation of resources within a sector rather than as a transfer from one sector to another (p. 525). He also points out that other conditions must be met to initiate change from below: "Any initiative from below was totally dependent on the central authorities abstention from veto" (p. 534). Initiative was not regarded as improper as long as it proceeded through recognized channels, but when aspirations toward autonomy were expressed,

official objections were raised (p. 538). The persons promoting change possessed demonstrated loyalty, professional expertise and success, and freedom from political entanglements (p. 540). It should be apparent that the number of cases meeting these criteria is small.

190. Nathan Leites, *The Operational Code of the Politburo* (New York: McGraw-Hill, 1951). "Any tendency toward passivity must be opposed" (pp. 25-30); "There must be no doctrinaire attitude against changes in strategy and tactics" (pp. 31-36).

191. Raymond Bauer, Alex Inkels, and Clyde Kluckholn, *How the Soviet System Works* (Cambridge, Mass.: Harvard University Press, 1957), p. 84. In economic affairs, such shifts were seen in the adoption and subsequent abandonment of the New Economic Policy in the 1920s, and in Khrushchev's more recent regional decentralization and the reversal of his policies by Brezhnev and Kosygin in the 1950s and 1960s.

192. Heather Campbell, *Organization of Research, Development, and Production in the Soviet Computer Industry,* R-1617-Pr (Santa Monica, Calif.: Rand Corporation, 1976), esp. sect. 3, "Party-Government Intervention in the Soviet Computer Industry," pp. 24-60.

193. "Although the instructions seemed clear enough, later evidence indicated that they were not carried out in full. Apparently, such a directive from the Soviet party and government did not carry enough weight to abolish, totally, the negative effects of ministerial parochial interests and jealousies" (ibid., p. 44).

194. "Real" authority must often be identified by results rather than by independent prior judgments of priority or power. That is, it is difficult to know from the documentary evidence whether a task has been granted the required priority, importance, resources, authority, "clout," and whatever else is required to get the job done.

195. Miller, *Russians as People,* p. 96. Associated with such bureaucratic tendencies are pervasive efforts to work around the bureaucratic obstructions. Successful operators have learned how to manage these legal and illegal activities, but it can take enormous energy and time; so although subtle maneuvering around the rules takes place, they still act as an impediment to initiative and change.

196. Daniel Bell, "Ten Theories in Search of Reality," reprinted in *The End of Ideology* (Glencoe, Ill.: Free Press, 1960).

197. Berliner, *Innovation Decision in Soviet Industry,* p. 519.

198. A direct test of Berliner's hypothesis is a recent study comparing economic performance in East Germany (GDR) and West Germany (FRG), two countries sharing a common (but not identical) cultural heritage. This study shows that since 1960, economic growth rates and producitivity increases in the two economies are almost identical. The GDR performance is much better than that of the Soviet Union, whose economic structure is the model for East Germany's. According to other indices, the FRG has performed somewhat better than the GDR. These results suggest that while structure does have the suggested effects, culture plays at least as strong a role. Paul Gregory and Gert Leptin, "Similar Societies under Differing Economic Systems: The Case of the Two Germanies," *Soviet Studies* 29, no. 4 (October 1977): 519-42.

199. Alex Inkeles, Eugenia Hanfmann, and Helen Beier, "Modal Personality and Adjustment to the Soviet Sociopolitical System," reprinted in Inkeles, *Social Change in Soviet Russia* (Cambridge, Mass.: Harvard University Press, 1968).

200. Ibid., p. 120.

201. Ibid., p. 116.

202. Ibid., p. 115. The American subjects asserted that their ability for self-control legitimates their desire for autonomy.

203. "There is a striking continuity in some areas with the findings of the Harvard refugee project" (Zvi Gitelman, "Soviet Political Culture: Insights from Jewish Emigrés," *Soviet Studies* 29, no. 4 (October 1977): 562).

204. Ibid., pp. 560, 563.

205. Ibid., p. 554.

206. Michel Crozier, *The Bureaucratic Phenomenon* (Chicago: University of Chicago Press, 1964), p. 229. The closeness and intensity of personal relationships is noted by most observers and analysts.

207. In addition to illegal activities conducted to meet state goals, semilegal and illegal market activities to advance personal welfare appear to be an increasingly important part of life in the Soviet Union. See, for example, the chapter "Corruption" in Smith, *Russians,* pp. 81-101.

208. Ibid., p. 231.

209. Ibid., p. 264. This is also a conclusion of Leites's studies on Bolshevik behavior. See, for example, the comments on Leites by Bell, "Ten Theories," p. 340.

210. The recent antitank debate is an example of this. See Philip Karber, "The Soviet Anti-Tank Debate," *Survival,* May-June 1976.

211. The involvement of civilians in the several negotiations on disarmament (SALT, MBFR, Indian Ocean disarmament, etc.) has helped to educate the nonmilitary participants in the technical details and arcane mysteries of military policy.

212. Don Cook, "Russian Approach to Talks Frustrating to Americans," *Los Angeles Times,* 8 January 1978, p. 22.

213. Decision procedures are treated in detail in the next section.

214. Rakowska-Harmstone, *Soviet Leadership Maintenance,* p. 75.

215. Since 1965, however, Brezhnev has been partially successful in thwarting the intent of the leadership in limiting patronage opportunities. As of 1976, ten out of sixteen full members of the Politburo, three out of six candidate members, and all five Central Committee secretaries not in the Politburo had links with Brezhnev. Similarly, many important regional party posts and government positions are now filled by Brezhnev men. Ibid., p. 69.

216. These points are established by Rigby, "The Soviet Leadership," p. 175.

217. Ibid., p. 179.

218. An example of the clumsiness involved in collective decision making is seen in the account of a Soviet-Egyptian meeting that was subjected to long interruption when agreement and signatures of Brezhnev, Kosygin, and Podgorny were required for approval to warn the Somalis that a coup d'état was being prepared against them. The Egyptians thought that approval of the entire Politburo may even have been required. The Egyptian participants were said to have been struck by the awkwardness of the procedure and felt that they had gained insight into their own difficulties in dealing with the Soviet leadership. Robert Conquest, "Continuing the Stalemate Tradition," *Soviet Analyst* 5, no. 7 (25 March 1976): p. 1.

219. Hough, "The Party *Apparatchiki,*" p. 68.

220. D. C. Winston, "Russia Seeks Supersonic VTOL by 1970," *Aviation Week and Space Technology,* 24 June 1968, p. 211.

221. In the United States, the dominance of doctrine and requirements over technology is long-standing. In the 1920s and 1930s, for example, the requirements process in tank development tended to be unidirectional. "Doctrine was enunciated as a theoretical exercise; specifications were drawn from doctrine; technology was asked to respond." Tank designers complained of "too great a faith on the part of the nontechnical people that any difficulty can be overcome by research and development." Alexander, *Armor Development,* pp. 55, 79.

222. The output of this bureau will be discussed in more detail later in this section. The record-breaking aircraft include I-224 (4A) (highest altitude of any Soviet piston-engine aircraft); I-225 (5A) (fastest Soviet piston-engine aircraft); and Ye-66, Ye-166, Ye-266 (world records for speed and altitude).

223. Examples include Yakovlev's letters to Stalin and the Central Committee, Grabin's and Petrov's artillery designs, and Koshkin's and Morozov's autonomous activities leading to the T-34 tank.

224. Khrushchev, *Khrushchev Remembers,* p. 72.

225. Ibid., p. 73.

226. Yakovlev mentions that when he proposed building a new fighter to use a new engine that was becoming available, Stalin replied that he had received a similar offer from Mikoyan as well (Yakovlev, *Target of Life,* p. 396).

227. "He wasn't like *most* designers and specialists. If you don't accept their proposals, they get mad and stay mad for some time" (Khrushchev, *Khrushchev Remembers,* p. 73).

228. Alexander, *Armor Development,* ch. 8, and "Patterns in Soviet Military R&D," pp. 44-53.

229. Intimidated by this dual-approval process, the frustrated Yakovlev felt forced to bypass it when he wanted to create "something new in quality": "I decided to skip the usual steps of going *through the Ministry and through the Air Force*" (*Target of Life,* pp. 394-395, emphasis added).

230. "New Russian Tanks on Winter Exercise," *International Defense Review,* July-August 1975, p. 487; J. Gratzl, "T-64: Some Thoughts on the New Soviet Battle Tank," *International Defense Review,* January-February 1976, pp. 24-26.

231. Roy Braybrook, "A Mighty Failure: The Bounder," *Flying Review International* 20, no. 3 (December 1964).

232. MccGwire, "Soviet Naval Procurement."

233. Khrushchev, *Khrushchev Remembers,* pp. 62-64.

234. MccGwire, "Soviet Naval Procurement," p. 83.

235. However, to complicate the analysis, whereas the earlier SS-8 and the SS-13 were produced in limited numbers (from sixty to seventy), perhaps to maintain design bureau and production capability, other Soviet missiles were developed but never deployed (SS-10, SS-12, SS-14, SS-15, SS-16). Some of these were mobile or IRBM, but they demonstrate that not every Soviet missile developed is produced.

236. Many of these experimental prototypes turned out to be dead ends (the VTOL Fishbed G, for example), whereas others were stepping stones from one generation to another. The Flipper, Ye-166, and Ye-266 series of prototypes successively explored the high-altitude, high-speed regime that led progressively from the Mig-21 to the quite different Mig-25 Foxbat.

237. For a description of the Foxbat technology, see *Strategic Survey, 1976* (London: IISS, 1977), p. 15. The engine inlet configuration of the Ye-266 had appeared a few years earlier on the American A-5 Vigilante.

238. Despite the Soviet development style that considerably reduces R&D uncertainties, the very nature of the activity carries with it considerable residual uncertainty that cannot be eliminated and must be dealt with.

239. Cost comparisons between American and Soviet weapons have indicated lower Soviet costs of about 50 percent for tanks, and more than 60 percent for jet engines. While differentials of these magnitudes may not be universal, lower costs generated by the Soviet design process are likely to prevail across a wide variety of equipment, especially when based on mature technologies. Alexander, *Armor Development,* pp. 120-22.

240. Herbert York, *The Advisors: Oppenheimer, Teller, and the Superbomb* (San Francisco: W. H. Freeman, 1976), p. 30. Much of this description is taken from York and from David Holloway, "Military Technology," in *The Technological Level of Soviet Industry,* ed. R. Amann, J. Cooper, and R. W. Davies (New Haven and London: Yale University Press, 1977), pp. 451-55.

241. Holloway, "Military Technology," p. 452.

242. Public disclosure of American H-bomb research came three months after the first Soviet fission explosion. Although the Soviet Union probably knew of earlier American work on fusion weapons, the Soviet initiative in fusion developments appears to have been largely of the Soviet Union's own doing. York, *The Advisors,* p. 452.

243. A number of German scientists who were forcibly sent to the Soviet Union after the war described their contribution to Soviet rocket developments as mainly that of transferring the technical and mechanical experience gained in actually building the long-range V-2 rockets. Soviet theory was thought to be as advanced as the German. Nicholas Daniloff, *The Kremlin and the Cosmos* (New York: Alfred A. Knopf, 1972), p. 47.

244. In addition to rocket experts, the German contingent included aircraft, electronics, and nuclear engineers and scientists.

245. Daniloff, *The Kremlin and the Cosmos,* p. 43. According to German recollections quoted by Daniloff, "They [the Soviet Union] relied on ordinary metals; they did not spend much time in the laboratory experimenting with exotic fuels but preferred to depend instead on liquid oxygen and kerosene." This approach was echoed ten years later during specific development when the designer Korolev proposed "that nothing should be done to complicate the construction of the first sputnik; it should be made as simple as possible." It came to be known as the "PS" (simplest sputnik). Vladimirov, *Russian Space Bluff,* p. 58.

246. These meetings have been reported by G. A. Tokaty-Tokaev, a participant who left the Soviet Union in 1948, quoted in Daniloff, *The Kremlin and the Cosmos,* p. 48.

247. Stalin must have been actively seeking technical advice on the subject because at about this time he had a long discussion with Korolev on long-range rocket possibilities (ibid., p. 97).

248. Ibid., p. 102.

249. Ibid.

250. Ibid., p. 80.

251. Clarence A. Robinson, Jr., "Soviets Push for Beam Weapon," *Aviation Week and Space Technology,* 2 May 1977, p. 17.

252. Much of this paragraph is taken from Holloway, "Science, Technology, and the Soviet Armed Forces."

253. Ibid.

254. David Holloway, "Technology and Political Decision in Soviet Armaments Policy," *Journal of Peace Research,* no. 4 (1976), p. 262.

255. Karl Marx and F. Engels, *Selected Correspondence* (Moscow: Foreign Languages Publishing House, n.d.), p. 548. Interestingly, most of the research in the West shows that Engels continues to be correct, even in the proportions he mentioned. Many studies indicate that 70-80 percent of innovations are stimulated by demand. Nevertheless, the problem for the Soviet Union is how to deal with the remaining 20-30 percent. For evidence on the relationships between demand and technology on innovation, see James M. Utterback, "Innovation in Industry and the Diffusion of Technology," *Science,* 15 February 1974.

256. V. Bondarenko (1971), quoted by Holloway, "Technology and Political Decision," p. 263.

257. It is not my purpose here to argue either for the feasibility of beam weapons or whether, indeed, Soviet research is actually directed in a major way toward military goals (although there is evidence for the latter point). Rather, I shall assume that the main thrust of the research is weapons related and proceed from that assumption. The first major public exposition of the particle beam threat was Robinson, "Soviets Push for Beam Weapon," pp. 16-23.

258. The Rand Corporation has published several reports dealing with technological developments relevant to Soviet charged-particle beam research: Simon Kassel and Charles D. Hendricks, *Soviet Development of Needle-Tip Field Emission Cathodes for High-Current Electron Beams,* R-1311-ARPA (1973); Kassel, *Soviet Development of Flash X-Ray Machines,* R-1053-ARPA (1973); Kassel and Hendricks, *Soviet Research and Development of High-Power Gap Switches,* R-1333-ARPA (1974); and Kassel and Hendricks, *High-Current Particle Beams, Part 1: The Western USSR Research Groups* R-1552-ARPA (1975).

259. The principal research institutes include the Khurchatov Institute of Atomic Energy and the Lebedev Physics Institute, in Moscow; the Physical-Technical Institute, in Kharkov; the Physical-Technical Institute, in Sukhumi; the Institute of Atmospheric Optics, in Tomsk; and the Nuclear Physics Institute, in Novosibirsk.

260. A U.S. government review of this research identified "hundreds of laboratories and thousands of top scientists" working on the technology necessary for production of high-energy beams (Robinson, "Soviets Push for Beam Weapon," p. 21).

261. Kassel and Hendricks, *High-Current Particle Beams,* p. 1.

262. Ibid., p. 9.

263. Ibid., p. 11. Rudakov's coauthors have been with the Khurchatov Institute, in Moscow, and the Institute of Nuclear Physics, in Novosibirsk.

264. Robinson, "Soviets Push for Beam Weapon," p. 16.

265. Shabad, "Khrushchev Says Missile Can Hit Fly in Outer Space," *New York Times,* 17 July 1962, p. 1.

266. Quoted in Ghebhardt, "Implications of Organizations," p. 17.

267. Ibid., p. 32.

268. Ibid., p. 60.

269. Ibid., p. 95.

270. Ibid., pp. 46-47.

271. *U.S. News and World Report,* 6 February 1967, p. 36.

272. Many American scientists doubt whether the Soviet effort in charged particle beams will be successful, citing several severe physical problems that must be overcome. Commenting on why the Soviet Union continues the research at a multibillion dollar rate, given the enormous obstacles, one intelligence analyst said, "Never underestimate the possibility of bureaucratic continuity in a country like the Soviet Union and the inability to kill a project, even if it fails to produce results" (Henry Bradsher, "The Death Ray Debate: Do the Soviets Have It?," *Washington Star,* 23 March 1977, p. 1).

273. Igor S. Glagolev, "The Soviet Decision-making Process in Arms-Control Negotiations," *Orbis,* Winter 1978, p. 770.

274. Quoted in Gallaher and Spielmann, *Soviet Decision-Making for Defense,* p. 26.

275. Thane Gustafson, "Transforming Soviet Agriculture," *Public Policy,* Summer 1977, pp. 296-303.

276. Karber, "The Soviet Antitank Debate."

277. Seweryn Bialer, *The Soviet Political Elite: Stability, Legitimacy, and Change* (Report prepared for the U.S. Department of State, Columbia University, 1977), p. 37.

278. Ibid., p. 40.

279. Thomas W. Wolfe, *The Military Dimension in the Making of Soviet Foreign and Defense Policy,* P-6024 (Santa Monica: Rand Corporation, 1977), pp. 35-40. Also given as testimony before the Subcommittee on Europe and the Middle East, Committee on International Relations, U.S. House of Representatives, 11 October 1977.

280. Ibid., p. 39.

281. These analytical conclusions are summarized by Bialer, *Soviet Political Elite,* p. 43.

282. Marshall Brement, *Organizing Ourselves to Deal with the Soviets,* P-6123 (Santa Monica, Calif.: Rand Corporation, 1978), p. 5.

Part three

EUROPE

Greenland
(Denmark)
0
400 Kilometers
0
400 Miles
Jan Mayen
(Nor.)
Murmansk
Arkangel'sk
Norwegian
Sea
Reykjavík
Iceland
Sweden
Finland
Faroe Is.
(Den.)
Norway
Helsinki
Leningrad
North
Bergen
Oslo
Stockholm
Tallin
Moscow
Göteborg
Baltic
Sea
Riga
Atlantic
Edinburgh
Glasgow
North
Sea
Denmark
Copenhagen
Belfast
Vil'nyus
Minsk
U.S.S.R.
Dublin
Ireland
United
Kingdom
Hamburg
Amsterdam
Neth.
London
German
Berlin
Dem. Rep.
Warsaw
Poland
Wrocław
Kiyev
Ocean
Brussels
Bel.
Federal
Bonn
Republic
of Germany
Lux.
L'vov
Prague
Czech.
Paris
Bratislava
Kishinev
Munich
Vienna
Austria
Budapest
Hungary
France
Bern
Switz.
Liech.
Romania
Lyon
Italy
Belgrade
Bucharest
Black Sea
Bordeaux
Yugoslavia
Bulgaria
Monaco
San Marino
Sofia
Marseille
Andorra
Istanbul
Ankara
Portugal
Madrid
Corsica
Rome
Tirana
Albania
Barcelona
Lisbon
Spain
Naples
Greece
Turkey
Sardinia
Balearic Is.
Athens
Gibraltar
(U.K.)
Algiers
Tunis
Sicily
Rabat
Malta
Valletta
Mediterranean
Sea
Crete
Tunisia
Morocco
Algeria
Tripoli
Libya
Egypt
Boundary representation is
not necessarily authoritative

THE DEFENSE POLICY OF THE UNITED KINGDOM

David Greenwood

The United Kingdom is a Great Power in reduced circumstances. But over the years, like the heads of those aristocratic households of the nation with whom fate has dealt similarly, British governments have displayed a remarkable talent for keeping up appearances.

On any realistic assessment the country is a middle-rank European power, standing below both the Federal Republic of Germany and France according to most indices of military capacity. Yet the British voice is heard on global security issues, even where the influence that the United Kingdom can exercise is negligible; for the national self-perception is emphatically not that of a "mere" regional actor. In practice the defense effort is concentrated on the North Atlantic and Western Europe, with posture and provision settled more or less exclusively within the Atlantic Alliance framework. Policy makers look beyond these horizons, however, at least when voicing aspirations in declaratory pronouncements. The United Kingdom's defense organization too is on the grand scale, despite the fact that at the start of the 1980s the nation cuts a less formidable military figure than ever before. Until very recently three service bureaucracies, each imbued with its own traditions and attentive to its own priorities, competed for resources under central supervision but not effective central authority. It is only the insistent pressure of financial and manpower constraints, together with the emergence in the higher direction of the Defense Ministry of strong personalities willing to wrestle with unwelcome choices, that has brought about change of late. Nevertheless the main characteristic of the present-day national order of battle is "balance" in both the interservice and intraservice senses. A small strategic nuclear force is complemented by comprehensive conventional capabilities in all three branches of the armed forces, which continue to receive near-equal shares of annual appropriations. The Royal Navy no longer has attack carriers or a fully fledged amphibious warfare capability, but in all other respects the United Kingdom retains a balanced fleet. The army has recently

The author wishes to thank Rae Angus for help in collecting material for this essay, and Margaret McRobb for secretarial assistance.

undergone "restructuring" but remains a true all-arms force. Short of combat planes and fast jet pilots though it may be, the Royal Air Force has, and plans to continue to have, the wherewithal to perform the full spectrum of tactical air missions.

How much longer it will in fact be possible to maintain across-the-board competence—and sustain the armaments base that permits considerable self-reliance if not complete self-sufficiency—is open to question. Suffice it to say that there is resistance to speculation about, and no disposition to effect, further radical change in the defense effort. In reduced circumstances or not, in the 1980s the United Kingdom will *try* to conduct its international security affairs in the style to which policy makers and planners are accustomed.

International environment

RELATIVE POWER POSITION

British politicians and the British people acknowledge, but acknowledge reluctantly and not unreservedly, that the United Kingdom nowadays rates as a medium power in an essentially regional setting. The reluctance is understandable in the light of historical experience, as is the fact that it is tinged with regret. After all, prior to and during the Second World War the British claim to independent Great Power status was incontestable. Moreover, it seemed for a time in the later 1940s that, while clearly unable to aspire to superpower stature, the nation might establish for itself a special position no more than one place below the United States and the Soviet Union in a national global pecking order. The international community actually accorded such recognition, for example, when the United Kingdom became one of the permanent members of the United Nations Security Council. British policy makers were certainly not in doubt at this time about where they wished the country to stand. A decolonization program was launched, but at the same time there was a determination to perform an active post-Imperial global role. Responsibilities were resumed in the Near, Middle, and Far East. A leading part was taken in fashioning postwar European security arrangements. And the atomic weapons development begun during World War II was continued. All these testify to a distinctive self-image.

On reflection, however, it is apparent that there was really little hope that the United Kingdom could carve out a permanent niche of this sort. In retrospect it is clear that the decisive acts of postwar British diplomacy were the construction of a European alliance with demanding mutual obligations, expressed in the Brussels Treaty of 1948, and the achievement of an American commitment to the defense of Western Europe with the signing of the North Atlantic Treaty in April 1949 and the subsequent establishment of the North Atlantic Treaty Organization (NATO). These were initiatives in which the imperatives of interdependence prevailed over the impulse to independence. To be sure, tension between the demands of the European and Atlantic affiliations and those of world-wide obligations dominated British policy making through the 1950s and 1960s. One or two vestiges of it are still discernible. There was never much doubt how the tension would be resolved, however, with Western European and North Atlantic concerns assuming greater significance as wider global aspirations steadily receded.

Since the early postwar years such have been the changes in strategic circumstances and the United Kingdom's relative economic position that not only has the nation relinquished its Great Power standing for "club membership" in NATO (and, since 1972, in the European Economic Community, or EEC), but it also cannot properly count itself more than an "ordinary member" of these fraternities. That much is evident from the summary statistics in table 1,

Table 1
Selected defenses expenditure statistics, 1978

Country	Total U.S. dollars (billions)	Per capita U.S. dollars	Percentage of GDP
United Kingdom	$14.1	$252	4.7%
Federal Republic of Germany*	25.4	429	4.1
France	17.8	333	4.0
Netherlands	4.2	303	3.4
Belgium	3.1	312	3.3
Portugal	0.6	63	3.3
Norway	1.3	313	3.2
Italy	6.1	107	2.6
Denmark	1.3	247	2.5
Canada	4.1	173	2.0
United States	105.1	481	5.0

Source: Statement on the Defense Estimates, 1979 (London: HMSO, 1979), figure 5, p. 16.
*Figures based on expenditure *including* Berlin aid.

which show selected indicators of the British defense effort in relation to those of allies and partners. On one measure—defense spending as a percentage of Gross Domestic Product (GDP)—the United Kingdom does rank above other West European countries. But more than anything else this reflects the expense of all-volunteer forces and a large equipment budget in an economy with an indifferent growth record. As far as the actual value of defense outlays is concerned, the British figures lie below those of France and West Germany (and, of course, far below those of the United States), while defense expenditure per head in the United Kingdom is less than that in half a dozen other European states. These statistics are the telling expressions of the United Kingdom's relative standing at the end of the 1970s.[1]

Having established the position that the United Kingdom now occupies, I shall now discuss two related questions that invite consideration. First, how does the nation perceive the threats and challenges to its security (and values) in the Atlantic Alliance setting? Second, in what ways are decisions about posture and provision still affected by "rank consciousness"—that is to say, by reluctance to settle for "ordinary membership" in NATO (and the EEC)?

THREAT PERCEPTIONS IN THE ALLIANCE SETTING

Of these questions the first is the easier to answer, at least in principle. As a member of NATO, the United Kingdom simply subscribes to the general Alliance assessment of "the threat." What is that assessment? What is the contemporary western view of the aspirations, intentions, and military capabilities of the Soviet Union that provides the essential frame of reference for British policy choices?

No truly authoritative analysis exists, strange though that may seem. The final communiqués of NATO's regular ministerial meetings are couched in a stereotyped language that is singularly uninstructive. The frequent pronouncements of the supreme commanders have to be recognized for what they are: the evaluations of senior naval and military officers whose dual obligation is to keep the potential adversary's capabilities under review and to keep politicians, parliaments, and public opinion in Alliance states aware of the need to match those capabilities. As for the international staffs in Brussels, "hawks" and "doves" contend there, as they do in national capitals.

Some view of "the threat" clearly does animate Atlantic Alliance members, however; otherwise they would dismantle the organization. Yet it evidently is not a hard-line perception of a permanent protagonist, unambiguously hostile, with alarmingly superior forces. It is, rather, a more complex appreciation, encompassing numerous judgments about aspirations, intentions, and capabilities. Impressionistic evidence suggests that if there *were* an "agreed assessment" it would run along the following lines.[2]

Quite what the Soviet Union's basic aspirations are is hard to discern. In the content and terminology of Moscow's rhetoric, however, ideological currents run strongly. Since long-run policy goals derive from these fundamental impulses, the presumption must be that they remain in uncompromising opposition to western liberal, democratic values.

Under the heading of *intentions*—meaning short- or medium-term policy objectives—a distinction has to be made between political (diplomatic) conduct and possible military activity. On the political plane, much Soviet behavior suggests that East-West détente is an instrument of diplomacy, to be wielded as opportunity offers in the promotion of state interest. On the other hand, the Soviet Union clearly acknowledges shared interests with the United States and its allies, not least in avoiding nuclear war; moreover, the West has sought to allay Soviet fears arising from perceptions of insecurity and to establish durable structures of cooperation, e.g., in economic relations. The ambiguity or ambivalence here is problematical. But one thing is obvious: as yet the basis for presuming generally beneficent intent is fragile. Thus, NATO countries judge it prudent to combine flexibility in exploring arms control opportunities and developing commercial ties with firmness of commitment to the maintenance of countervailing military power. In the military sphere itself, since a rough balance of forces does exist at present there is no solid foundation for suggestions that "the Russians are coming" on NATO's central front (or elsewhere). At the same time the absence of a direct, immediate threat of aggression does not justify complacency; for, as the preponderant military power in Europe even now, there is a sense in which the Russians have already arrived. Furthermore, it is evident from recent events in parts of Africa and Asia that, should the commitment of Western powers ever appear to be in doubt, the Soviet Union would probably extract strategic benefit from military advantage.

If this reasoning is correct, much hinges on assessment of the balance of military capabilities between East and West: at the intercontinental level; at the continental strategic level (which is where the Soviet intermediate- and medium-range ballistic missiles enter the reckoning), and at the European theater level (where shorter-range nuclear systems and conventional forces are relevant). Is the "Soviet threat" in these areas thought to be increasing, diminishing, or staying more or less the same?

Rigorous measurement is impossible. There are structural asymmetries at each level, for example, not to mention qualitative differences. It is, however, practicable to gauge the direction of change by comparatively coarse calculation. On this the consensus is that Soviet and Warsaw Pact capabilities have been enhanced of late relative to those of the Western powers. At the intercontinental strategic level there is "essential equivalence," because the superpowers' inventories are regulated by the agreements reached in the Strategic Arms Limitations Talks (SALT). At the continental strategic level it is the view of the United Kingdom and other European members of NATO that the Soviet Union enjoys a crucial advantage, principally because of the SS-20 missile deployments; the envisaged introduction of an extended-range Pershing (and cruise missiles) may or may not be an effective counter. As for the balance in European theater forces, the extent and pace of modernization and restructuring in Warsaw Pact formations recently is generally thought to have exceeded that achieved in NATO, and the momentum continues.[3]

Right-wing politicians in Britain (and elsewhere) are inclined to argue from this sort of analysis that NATO's force levels are barely adequate and the Alliance may be courting disaster. In fact, a much more decisive superiority would probably be necessary before even a reckless Soviet leadership would contemplate use of arms to upset the European status quo. It should be added, however, that the perception of how the balance is shifting itself confers benefits on the Soviet Union, both in Europe and (perhaps more significantly) elsewhere.

Existing dispositions for deterrence and defense need to be kept in good repair on this assessment. It is also incumbent upon NATO to exercise due vigilance against the possibility of the Soviet Union's acquiring options that would disturb strategic stability. Efforts to buttress the "partnership" elements in the inter-bloc relationship and to develop the existing structure of "confidence-building measures" in Europe are worth making, but only against the background of continuing prudent military provision.

Long and even tortuous though this "threat assessment" may be, it is in terms such as these that decision makers in the United Kingdom construe the *external* threats to national security. It is a nicely judged evaluation and one that accounts for both the care British governments have taken to sustain the contribution to NATO during periods of adjustment in defense dispositions and the cautious British approach to various East-West negotiations.

What of *internal* threats? Have defense policy makers and planners in the United Kingdom had to pay attention of late to domestic challenges to the nation's sense of security (and cherished values), in addition to those posed by the political and military power of the Soviet Union and Warsaw Pact?

In two quite different ways, they have. In the first place, as in many other West European countries, there has been concern about the problems that Martin Hillenbrand has diagnosed most cogently in arguing that "the health of the Western Alliance can be no better than the economic and resulting social and political strength of its various component countries."[4] Accordingly, politicians have approached the allocation of resources to defense with a clear understanding that committing funds to military purposes beyond economic capacity, or to the detriment of key social programs, could be as damaging as inadequate provision. That is to say, they have recognized that how judiciously the budgetary balance is struck between defense and other activities may be as important to security (broadly defined) as the actual sums allotted. The United Kingdom has not, however, been beset by the kind of economic distress and political turbulence experienced in Turkey or Italy, which has caused serious anxiety about the social stability of the state and potential vulnerability.

The nation's only "internal security" problem, properly so called, is the situation in Northern Ireland. This has had—and continues to have—a direct and significant impact on defense decision making, as regards force levels and deployments. But it is really a law-and-order problem writ large, and the armed forces are engaged in a policing task under the rubric of military aid to a civil power. The situation is designated "the Northern Ireland emergency," and the idea that troops might have to assume permanent responsibility for keeping the peace and rooting out terrorists there is anathema to the authorities, as it is to public opinion.

Has the United Kingdom genuinely come to terms with the fact that—as the statistics cited indicate—it now ranks as a medium power in a regional setting? Are British policy makers content not only to accept the kind of threat assessment that has been outlined as representing the overall NATO view but also to make an "ordinary member's" contribution to the Alliance's order of battle? Or is the nation's "distinctive self-image" still influential in program decisions and, if so, why and how? Brief remarks on these matters are now in order.

SELF-IMAGE AND STATURE

As has been suggested already, over the last thirty years or so British governments and the British people have become reconciled to the United Kingdom's inability to maintain the status of a major world power. At the same time, the imprint of what Kenneth Waltz called "hard residuums of national habits and deep-set attitudes towards international affairs" remains discernible in the approach to defense choices.[5] The station in international political life for which decision makers regard the country as suited, and which they hope it can occupy, is that of a leading regional power. The prevailing national self-image sets the United Kingdom at least on a par with the most substantial medium powers in Western Europe—France and the Federal Republic of Germany—despite the fact that both of these states operate from stronger and more buoyant economic bases and commit greater resources to defense. Evidence of the influence of this "rank consciousness" is apparent in the structure and deployment of the armed forces and the substance and tenor of debate about options for the future.

Looking back over the British defense experience since 1945, the adjustment in the national self-perception can be seen to have taken place in four phases. In the immediate aftermath of the Second World War it appeared (as has been noted) that a special position one rung below the superpowers might fall naturally to a nuclear weapons state and one determined (*a*) to play if not a "mid-Atlantic" at least an "offshore European" role within NATO, and (*b*) to discharge a variety of post-Imperial global responsibilities. In the first half of the 1950s, although it was apparent that there would be difficulties sustaining this stance, in fact it was formalized: in 1954-55 the United Kingdom joined the South East Asia Treaty Organization (SEATO) and signed the Baghdad Pact, leading to the formation of the Central Treaty Organization (CENTO); an unprecedented commitment was made to the peacetime stationing of forces in Europe, under the aegis of the Western European Union (WEU); and the government embarked on development and production of the new thermonuclear weapons and a ballistic missile delivery system. There followed a decade, 1956-64, in which policy makers lacked a firm sense of direction (it was at this time that Dean Acheson made his celebrated comment that Britain had "lost an Empire but not yet found a role"), and appraisal of critical decisions in this period has been likened to "logging a succession of tacks and jibes and course corrections, some of them very coarse corrections."[6] Not until a fourth phase—covering 1965-74—was a decisive reshaping of the defense effort and reordering of priorities effected, via a succession of defense reviews in which all but the last traces of world-wide involvement were progressively eliminated, permitting consolidation of the commitment to the defense of Western Europe.[7]

Looking at present provision and plans for the 1980s, however, the evidence that the national self-image remains distinctive is readily apparent. Retention of influence and prestige within NATO is seen to depend on possession of a particular kind of military establishment and on the payment of a "club subscription" that, in its comprehensiveness if not its scale, stands comparison with that of any of the European members of the Alliance. Thus, even after the "extensive and thorough" defense review of 1974-75 the United Kingdom makes—and plans to continue to make—significant and high-quality contributions to NATO's order of battle at sea, on land, and in the air; in all three elements of the triad (conventional forces, theater nuclear weapons, and strategic nuclear capabilities); and to the ready forces in each of the Alliance's major command areas (Atlantic, Channel, and Europe).

Moreover, there are *some* traces of the former position as a state with substantial world-wide interests: for example, the practice of occasional naval deployments to the Indian Ocean and the presence of ground and air force contingents in Belize and Hong Kong. More important, perhaps, discussion about future program possibilities is characterized by continuing emphasis on retention of the distinctive elements in the British defense effort: the strategic nuclear force, the comprehensive and balanced conventional capabilities (with ships of high quality, the most advanced land and air systems), the "spread" of the investment in Europe and the North Atlantic. If, therefore, speculation about the future could rest wholly on inclination and intention, one would have no hesitation in predicting that through the 1980s British defense planning will reflect the same self-perception as has characterized decision making in the later 1970s, and that the part that the United Kingdom will seek to play in international security affairs will continue to be that of the "major power of the second order."[8]

Yet further redefinition of the "appropriate" role for the nation is not out of the question. Reference has already been made to the continuing pressure of financial and manpower constraints on defense. It is becoming increasingly difficult year by year to sustain all-around competence and commitment in a credible way—i.e., with units up to strength and equipment up to date. If budgetary stringency continues, "keeping up appearances" may therefore become impracticable. This is not the place for detailed consideration of what changes might be wrought if further defense reviews should become necessary. Suffice it to say that prevailing notions of what is an acceptable *scale of provision* could be set aside, and the *pattern of provision* might undergo modification—for example, through reassessment of the priority accorded to the ground/air forces contribution to NATO's central front vis-à-vis the national investment in maritime forces.[9]

Limited adjustment to present plans would not, of course, make necessary wholesale reconsideration of national perceptions (or aspirations) concerning role and stature. But even modest change might entail abandoning any pretense to a leading position among the European members of the Alliance. And substantial diminution in the defense effort, or radical reshaping, would make it legitimate to ask whether the United Kingdom's standing had not become that of a "major power of the third order"—ranking alongside Italy rather than France and West Germany.

On balance what seems most likely is that there will be further marginal change in the scale of British defense dispositions during the 1980s with limited structural modifications. In these circumstances planners may have to wrestle with the choice between preserving a distinctive across-the-board contribution to NATO and defining a feasible specialized contribution. That is to say, they may have to ask what should be the United Kingdom's role within NATO, much as their predecessors had to ask questions about Britain's role in the world.

Valuable and necessary though it is to take a view of the United Kingdom's place in the international environment, and to establish what perceptions of threats to the nation's security and concepts of the nation's stature animate decision makers, the foregoing discussion really does no more than lay a general foundation for more specific analysis. Attention must now be directed to the determinants of policy, posture, and provision; to procedural matters; and to some of the principal features of the current and planned future defense effort and issues arising in debate about it.

Elucidation of the United Kingdom's security objectives, of the defense strategy derived therefrom, and of the main parameters of military doctrine for the implementation of that strategy would seem to be the obvious point of departure for this further detailed examination, at least in principle.

National objectives, national strategy, and military doctrine

There is undoubtedly an appealing logic and clarity about the idea that states decide on their aims, devise an approach to the attainment of desired ends, and develop appropriate concepts of operations for their armed forces in a systematic progression. Following such a deductive process would certainly seem the rational way to do things. But reality is not like that. Objectives may not be clearly delineated, and, of those that are, some do not find expression in firm goals but remain as loosely defined aspirations. In making *policy* proper—"a flow of purposive action over a period of time" in John Garnett's neat formulation—there is abundant evidence of the difficulties nations have in achieving complete consistency.[10] Choice of a becoming security *posture* is a troublesome business too, given the contradictory impulses that impinge on decision making about force structures, levels, equipment, and deployment. Even if a country is successful in investing its defense arrangements with a certain coherence, there may be problems over provision of the resources of manpower, materiel, industrial capacity, technical ingenuity, and organizing ability necessary to sustain them.

On this reasoning, understanding of the basic determinants of the United Kingdom's defense program and budget—which is another way of defining the subject matter of this section—is in fact unlikely to be advanced by speculation about some imaginary "rational deductive" construct that links objectives, strategy, and doctrine in British official thinking. For in practice there is probably no such thing. It is more instructive to conduct a survey of the judgments and assumptions underlying the current national defense effort as they relate to aspirations, policy, posture, and provision.[11]

ASPIRATIONS

Much of what can be said about fundamental aspirations has been anticipated in earlier remarks on the international environment and the view policy makers have of the United Kingdom's place within it. Restating the essential points briefly: British defense decision making is rooted in concern with *security* and *status*. Security connotes freedom to order the nation's affairs according to its own interests and values, implying freedom from fear of invasion, intimidation, or coercion. The only challenges that appear seriously to threaten are those posed by the Soviet Union. The values that infuse the Soviet system—and that Moscow is committed to propagate—are regarded as antithetical to those of western democracies. More immediately, the Soviet Union and its allies present a potential military threat to Western Europe. The only practicable response to these challenges is countervailing power, expressed in political cohesion and matching military might, provided within the framework of the Atlantic Alliance (and, in certain respects, the European communities). Considerations of stature, or prestige, enter the reckoning because the United Kingdom aspires to cut a certain kind of figure in international affairs: that of a leading regional power with a global vision.

POLICY

Of the nation's actual policy objectives, the central one is: to help deter aggression against either the United Kingdom itself or its European allies. National and regional security are regarded as inseparable. At the same time it is recognized that credible deterrence is dependent upon continuing association with the United States, given the link this implies to American strategic power. Total reliance on the United States in this connection entails certain risks, however. Because of this, successive governments have judged it prudent to maintain a semiindependent strategic retaliatory force. It is acknowledged, nevertheless, that dissuasion by the threat of punitive retaliation lacks credibility for many (if not most) contingencies. If attack by conventional forces is to be deterred, NATO needs the capacity to mount a conventional defense at least sufficient to deny Warsaw Pact forces a quick and easy victory. Indeed, a conventional war-fighting strategy is considered essential to the maintenance of deterrence, not to mention its desirability should deterrence fail—hence the substantial British contribution to the Alliance's conventional strength.

Retention of extraregional influence is also an important policy goal, despite the fact that the United Kingdom's Imperial disengagement is all but complete. To some extent this stems from a desire to be more than an "ordinary" European power. To some extent it is a simple consequence of past involvements, disengagement having left a legacy of minor responsibilities that policy makers feel cannot—or should not—be wholly set aside.

Recurring tension between the competing pulls of independence and interdependence is discernible in these judgments and assumptions. There is also a separate tension field in the policy arena, generated by the imperatives to preserve security through maintenance of adequate forces and the incentives to do what can be done to enhance security through arms control. Under the latter heading, the United Kingdom participates in several disarmament forums under United Nations auspices and has been responsible for important initiatives in some of them. The national commitment "to pursue negotiations in good faith on effective measures relating to cessation of the nuclear arms race" and to actual nuclear disarmament is, however, a nominal one for all practical purposes. Nor does the United Kingdom pay more than lip service to the desirability of general and complete disarmament.[12]

On the other hand, there is a genuine interest in progress toward regional arms control agreements. As a signatory to the Final Act of the Conference on Security and Cooperation in Europe (CSCE), the United Kingdom subscribes to both the provisions about agreed confidence-building measures (e.g., notification of maneuvers) and the obligation to widen the scope of those provisions. In the discussions on Mutual and Balanced Force Reductions (MBFRs) a negotiated rundown of NATO and Warsaw Pact force levels is sought, within the so-called guidelines area. The rationale for engagement in these exchanges is self-evident. It would serve British interests to moderate the intensity of the military confrontation in Europe and establish a military balance there at a lower level of forces, always provided this can be done on the basis of "undiminished security."

What has been achieved in the CSCE is strictly limited, however, and hopes of a substantial agreement in the MBFR talks seem to have receded rather than grown as the negotiations have continued. In the circumstances, therefore, the emphasis in British (and NATO) policy is firmly on the side of maintaining the Allied apparatus for deterrence and defense vis-à-vis the Soviet Union and Warsaw Pact countries. Accordingly, it is pertinent to ask how NATO views the task of countering the perceived political and military threat from the East. To what concepts of operations and to what strategic and tactical doctrines do member nations subscribe? What sort of stance has been taken up in Europe and the North Atlantic? And what, therefore, are the foundations of the defense posture assumed by the United Kingdom as a member of the Alliance?

POSTURE

Deterrence and defense rest on the ability to counter any form of aggression in an appropriate and credible manner. The wherewithal must exist to meet a conventional attack with a conventional riposte, at least in the first instance (and preferably for as long as possible). At the same time NATO's strategy of flexible response embodies the notion of graduated escalation. That is to say, the expectation is that governments would threaten the use of theater nuclear weapons if the ability to sustain a conventional defense were in question; such a crossing of the nuclear threshold would pose the risk of escalation to the use of strategic weapons. The concept of the NATO triad is thus central to the Alliance posture.

On the weight to be assigned to the different elements in the triad, the formal NATO position is that substantial conventional capabilities are the *sine qua non* of flexible response. That the United Kingdom endorses this view is clear from official policy statements, viz.:

> A strong conventional defence . . . would keep the nuclear threshold high. At least, it would delay the moment when NATO might need to use nuclear weapons and so make time for diplomatic attempts to end the conflict. At best it would demonstrate to the enemy that he had underestimated NATO's resolve and cause him to withdraw.[13]

Clearly, the effectiveness of an initial conventional defense is crucially dependent on warning. Alliance doctrine supposes that any aggression in Western Europe or the North Atlantic would be preceded by "political warning time" during which redeployment and reinforcement of front-line forces could be undertaken. Put another way, it is thought unlikely that any Warsaw Pact attack would be sudden or that it would take NATO by surprise. This too accords with British thinking.

Though committed to the idea of graduated escalation, neither the United Kingdom nor any other NATO country discounts the possibility that both protagonists in a European land/air conflict might wish not to resort to nuclear weapons. This produces a double burden. In the first place there is a requirement for conventional forces-in-being and forces-in-place adequate to withstand the shock power of a Warsaw Pact attack, i.e., to prosecute a "short war" of great intensity. If the period of conventional warfare should be protracted, however, there is the need to provide for the "long war;" that is to say, to think about sustenance, including the movement of troops and materiel from the United States—and hence for reserves *and* forces to protect air and sea lines of communication (within the theater and between Europe and North America).

How does the United Kingdom's contribution to NATO's order of battle fit into this postural framework? The roles of maritime forces are related to safeguarding the "forward areas at sea." Ground and air forces—principally 1 (British) Corps and Royal Air Force Germany—are earmarked for assignment to the Supreme Allied Commander Europe (SACEUR) to implement, alongside allies, the concept of operations for "forward defense" in northwest Europe itself. Principal assigned missions for maritime forces are surveillance and presence in peacetime, antisubmarine warfare, and mine countermeasures in the event of hostilities. The allotted task of 1 (BR) Corps is to defend its slice of NATO forces' layer-cake dispositions as far to the east as possible, by fighting a succession of tactical blocking engagements against a superior weight of Soviet and Warsaw forces (relieved perhaps by occasional limited counteroffensives). The priority missions for the United Kingdom's tactical air power are medium- and long-range attack against such targets as Pact airfields and supply lines, with some aircraft tasked for closer support and others withheld to provide a capability for nuclear strike.

Year-by-year decision making on defense is greatly facilitated by the existence of the frame of reference that the Alliance's posture and doctrine provide. At the same time, it is no secret that there are differences of view among the NATO nations about (1) how the flexible response strategy should be implemented, (2) whether the linkages between the different elements in the triad are sound, (3) how the balance between "short war" and "long war" capabilities should be struck, and (4) whether there *is* a danger of sudden or surprise attack, assumptions about warning time notwithstanding. Where the United Kingdom stands on some of these issues can be considered in due course. For the moment other matters take precedence. *Why* the United Kingdom provides what it does to the NATO order of battle is implicit in the foregoing discussion of the Alliance's posture. To illuminate the rationale of *what* is provided, and *how much,* examination of decision makers' judgments and assumptions about what constitutes "appropriate" provision is in order.

PROVISION

Whereas fundamental aspirations and decisions about policy and posture are framed in the light of the international environment and a nation's sense of its place in it (with special reference to perceived threats), ideas about "appropriate" provision for security tend to reflect what sort of defense effort the state's domestic resources and competencies permit it to mount. Put another way, it is in settling military provision that governments' choices are most affected by internal influences. Hazel and Williams have suggested that in the United Kingdom three kinds of judgment are influential in this context: (1) "those which determine the political choice about the scale on which resources should be committed to security purposes, as opposed to other claims on the national budget"; (2) "those which impinge on the allocation of resources within the defence establishment, i.e., among the Services"; and (3) "those made within the individual Services about (for example) what warships are most suitable for what missions, how field force formations should be structured and equipped, the performance characteristics required of combat aircraft."[14]

On the allocation of resources to defense, a key guideline reflected in the current and planned future program is that the share of GDP so allotted should not be significantly greater than that assigned by European allies. Whether approximate parity in defense/GDP proportions is a rational criterion for deciding the size of the defense effort is debatable. But British governments in the 1980s, as in the 1970s, face severe economic problems and are committed to major social programs. In such circumstances, perhaps nominal equality of sacrifice with other European states is as much, if not more, than politicians are prepared to ask of the electorate. (Provision on this scale is, of course, broadly acceptable to allies too.)[15]

Regarding the division of funds *among the services,* it has already been stated that importance is attached to the maintenance of balanced forces with a more or less full range of capabilities. Possession of *all-around* military competence is, among other things, one of the main bases of Britain's claim to a special status among the European members of the Atlantic Alliance. Little or no consideration is given, therefore—if indeed it ever was—to the idea of collectively balanced forces propounded when NATO was first established (requiring and permitting imbalances at the national level).

Several specific judgments and assumptions about *individual service* force levels, structures, equipment, and deployment underlie the current program and budget. It is appropriate to spell them out in some detail, as far as the three principal elements in the national order of battle are concerned.[16]

The first is that the United Kingdom should continue to provide substantial European theater ground forces. The British Army of the Rhine (BAOR) has rarely mustered its nominal strength of 55,000 troops and is costly in foreign exchange. But no major reduction has been seriously contemplated. Political and military judgments combine to make the force *level* virtually sacrosanct. A crucial consideration is the commitment under the Paris Agreements of 1954. This is not just a matter of adherence to a formal treaty. The rationale of the original undertaking remains valid. BAOR helps reassure those who would be apprehensive if the Bundeswehr were the only substantial power on the central front. A large contribution also entitles the United Kingdom to a prominent voice in Alliance councils and confers a claim to leading command positions. Furthermore, it indicates how highly the continental commitment is rated, demonstrating to partners that this goes beyond an interest in fighting to the last European soldier. (In addition, since 1968 it has been assumed that to reduce the Rhine Army's strength would be particularly ill advised while negotiations are under way with the Warsaw Pact countries on the subject of mutual force reductions.) As for the force *structure,* planning for the 1980s presumes that armament norms, existing ratios of armored units to mechanized infantry, and suchlike require little change. In choices about equipment, although the current program embodies provision for more light antitank weapons (for instance), armor retains its prominent position within the divisional structure, both to match Warsaw Pact tank capabilities and to provide the means for counterpenetration and, if appropriate, counterattack.

For navy general purpose combat forces the key judgment underlying current and planned provision is that it is essential to have a balanced fleet, including some ships of high quality, many less capable general purpose surface units, and a variety of smaller vessels. The operational justification for such a force structure lies in the flexibility it affords, making it feasible to cope with whatever Soviet challenges may be presented in the eastern Atlantic. This is true whether one considers wartime missions (acquiring sufficient "sea control" to safeguard the transatlantic line of communication) or the provision of peacetime presence (to forestall any Soviet efforts at intimidation). Also, a balanced fleet is one thing that other European members of NATO lack; it therefore differentiates the United Kingdom from its European partners (and, incidentally, validates retention of residual post-Imperial global aspirations).

Of the critical assumptions on the basis of which the air force general purpose forces program is configured, most are similarly rooted in regard for flexibility and versatility, against the background of the inexorably rising cost of advanced systems. The presumption is that only sophisticated aircraft are capable of operating in the hostile environment of modern air warfare. Given budgetary constraints, however, only relatively few of the requisite quality can be acquired. Therefore, the argument runs, it is necessary to procure versatile, multirole aircraft. Yet these, by their very nature, are the most expensive. This is a vicious circle, from which there is no obvious escape when mission priorities necessitate emphasis on the most demanding tasks and hence the most complex (and costly) systems. It is this position in which the United Kingdom finds itself, however. Current tactical air doctrine ascribes prime importance to (1) the offensive counterair mission (attacks on enemy air bases undertaken to suppress the threat to NATO's own air capabilities and ground formations) and (2) deep interdiction (attacks on theater reserves and supply lines). Lower priority is attached to battlefield interdiction and the attainment of local air superiority over the battlefield.

Running through these remarks is the clear message that, in each of the services' major mission programs, existing assumptions about structure are regarded as virtually immutable. Procurement of new equipment is thus based primarily on a "replacement" philosophy. The predisposition is to replace existing weapons with superior but essentially similar systems, like succeeding like. This is one of the most significant assumptions made about provision. Among other things it means that new technologies tend to be evaluated, and therefore adopted, only to the extent that they are compatible with the existing structure and organization of the armed forces. Opportunities to carry out some missions differently, to dispense with others, and generally to alter mission priorities may be overlooked as a result of the inclination so fostered to focus more or less exclusively on improvements at the margin.

It is no part of the business of this section, however, to pursue the implications of the "replacement" philosophy, or indeed of any of the other determinants of the size and shape of the defense effort reviewed thus far. The United Kingdom's security objectives, strategy, and doctrine have been illuminated, albeit from an oblique perspective; that is as far as the exposition in this part of the chapter needs to go.

Having said that, there are, however, certain glosses to be added—principally to facilitate comparison with other countries' circumstances—before taking up the third major theme: the decision-making process. For convenience these are grouped together in the following paragraphs.

OTHER OBSERVATIONS

An obvious first question is: what part, if any, do ideology and culture play in the determination of objectives (or the means chosen to pursue them)? Decision makers in the United Kingdom would resist any assertion that they play a significant role, arguing that over the years British defense and overseas policy has been animated by practical concern for "the national interest" rather than enthusiasm for propagation of a particular set of values. In one respect they would be right. Pragmatism earned Britain the tag "perfidious

Albion,'' and more than one statesman has acknowledged an inclination to fashion policy according to whatever suits the nation's purpose for the time being. As far as the recent past is concerned, however, there are two respects in which they would be wrong. As the British stance on the CSCE's Basket Three provisions illustrates, there is a definite commitment to certain ideas (or values)—like the virtues of democracy on the Western model, respect for individual freedoms and ''the open society''—that the nation seeks not only to protect but also to promote and extend. In addition, the United Kingdom's participation in disarmament and arms control negotiations, and the general tenor of debate about chemical, biological, and even nuclear weapons, testify to some respect for humane, Christian values.

Various questions concerning the extent of consensus and controversy on security matters also suggest themselves. Does one find broad agreement on policy goals? Are there major disputes about posture? Is the scale of provision for defense an issue in party politics? It is necessary to distinguish among the different contexts in which debate may take place in order to answer these questions satisfactorily. For instance, while no one would claim that defense in general is a salient topic in the political community, let alone among the population at large in the United Kingdom, within the defense establishment—and a military-industrial-academic community—exchanges on a range of subjects are commonplace (with wide differences of opinion entering many). Also, there are factions within the major political parties that hold positions on the size and composition of the defense effort far removed from those at the center of gravity of British security politics.

Except in rare instances, public opinion has not been directly influential on defense policy choices in recent years. According to one analyst this is because popular attitudes are generally favorable to, or indifferent about, the issues. Apathy has something to do with this. More important is the fact that defense and overseas policy is regarded as an area in which the government of the day carries authority and exercises leadership.[17] It does not follow that popular attitudes have had *no* influence on planning. In fact, ''they have impinged subtly, obliquely, indirectly, within the central process of 'setting national priorities.' ''[18] That is to say, defense has been subject to the effect of insistent pressure for the allocation of larger shares of total public spending to health, education, welfare, and other social security programs. Nor does acknowledgment of governments' authority in international political affairs generally mean that they have absolute freedom of maneuver. Quite the contrary: they must act within limits set by their sense of what the public will stand.

Looking at electoral politics, that defense has a low salience is both a consequence and an explanation of the state of public opinion. It also reflects the fact that in elections parties concentrate on issues of public concern on which they believe their own position to be distinctive. Defense is not such an issue in the United Kingdom. No formal accord exists among the principal parties. But the importance of NATO and the need to pay an appropriate ''club subscription'' constitute common ground. There is agreement too on most postural questions. Although some debate takes place within the political community, there is no continuing treatment of topics like the role of nuclear weapons in Alliance doctrine, or ''short war''/''long war'' theses, or mission priorities. Recent contributions to discussion from Conservative politicians have been few and far between. Material from Labor party circles has tended to focus either on the scale of provision for defense as opposed to social services' spending, or on specific issues like nuclear weapons programs or military-industrial conspiracy theories.[19]

In the defense establishment, however, there *is* argument about strategy and doctrine. Behind the facade of consensus that political convenience and constitutional propriety require, there is no lack of controversy on matters concerning policy, posture, and provision. No substantial studies have been written exposing the bureaucratic politics of British defense comparable with (for example) the work of Hammond, Schilling, and Snyder on overall program issues, or that of Ingemar Dorfer on particular procurement decisions.[20] But there is sufficient indirect, fragmentary evidence to confirm that major choices do generate disagreements (sometimes profound ones) and that strong constituencies exist for certain courses. Furthermore, each single service bureaucracy is naturally inclined to ''fight its own corner'' as and when necessary. Yet none of this amounts to more than the legitimate contention of opposing viewpoints and priorities. If the air force, with the aerospace industry lobby, presses the case for greater emphasis on maritime patrol aircraft vis-à-vis surface ships or submarines for antisubmarine warfare tasks, this is likely to ensure full exposure of the merits of the alternatives rather than degenerate into a bout of ''no-holds-barred'' institutional infighting between the services.[21]

Valid though an analytical approach based on specifying judgments and assumptions may be for elucidating national objectives, strategy, and doctrine, it has one serious disadvantage. No easy differentation is possible between (*a*) external influences on policy, like the state's place in the international environment and its relationships with adversaries and allies, and (*b*) internal influences, such as military, economic, technological, or psychosocial capacities. From one standpoint, of course, this shortcoming can be counted a merit. External and internal inputs to the decision-making process are, in fact, inextricably interwoven: differentiation for expository convenience can be misleading. On the other hand, to facilitate comparison of the British situation with that in other countries, there is value in a brief examination from this perspective of the essential domestic determinants of policy, posture, and provision.[22]

Economic factors have to be given pride of place—if that is what it is—in such a scrutiny. For the United Kingdom they have been influential in at least four different senses (and still are). First and most fundamentally, in some degree a nation's economic philosophy determines who its friends are. In this sense, the United Kingdom's Atlantic and European affiliations are the natural ones for a state that favors the "mixed economy" form of organization. Second, when developing these connections in the later 1940s, British statesmen were (among other things) ensuring reasonable provision for security despite relative economic weakness. The acknowledgment of interdependence originated in a practical recognition of the country's lack of capacity to sustain a fully independent role in world affairs, and the wisdom of this assessment has been borne out by events. It is in the actual evolution of the defense effort since 1945 that the impact of economics in a third sense is evident. General and specific resource constraints have been directly instrumental in prompting the significant transformation that has taken place.[23]

Despite the diminution in the *scale* of the British defense effort (according to the familiar indicators of military stature) and the contraction in its geographical *scope,* the nation retains more or less balanced forces whose equipment is kept reasonably up to date; in addition, a high proportion of the armed forces' systems and materiel continues to be procured from domestic industry. This last characteristic is the clue to the fourth sense in which economic factors enter the United Kingdom's defense calculations. Having a comprehensive armaments base that there are economic, social, and technological policy interests in supporting has been—and seems likely to continue to be—influential so far as the *pattern* of the defense effort is concerned. The point here goes beyond registering the familiar fact that from time to time procurement choices are determined by employment considerations or a desire to preserve a stake in some area of high-defense technology. The contention is that having all-around research, development, and production competence means the existence of a structure of interests and incentives for the maintenance of all-around military capabilities.[24]

The technological theme in this argument is worth an additional gloss. It is arguable that the case for the adoption of concepts of operations in which greater emphasis might be placed on simpler, more rugged warships or combat aircraft gets less than a fair hearing in the United Kingdom because the country is wedded to high-technology solutions to defense equipment problems for reasons that have little to do with military effectiveness. The point cannot be pursued here. But the idea that nations "live up" to their technological competence may be worth some attention from students of comparative defense policy.

Of the other "domestic determinants" of security arrangements that invite mention with facilitation of comparative studies in mind, *geography* deserves a brief word. Although this issue has not been highlighted thus far, it would be wrong to overlook how the United Kingdom's dispositions and priorities reflect the strategic location of the British Isles. The nation stands at the western end of NATO's northern flank and forms the southern part of that Greenland-Iceland-Faeroes-Scotland gap, which is the key "choke point" on the Soviet Northern Fleet's access route to the North Atlantic and to NATO's potentially critical sea line of communication (SLOC). The European end of that SLOC—and the interface with the intratheater SLOC—is the United Kingdom, which is therefore the key "rear area" for Allied Command Europe. Nor does it fulfill this role only with respect to reinforcement and resupply. It is from the comparative safety of bases in England that much of NATO's tactical air power might be expected to operate in the event of actual hostilities on the European continent.

Drawing the relevant "strategic maps"—either in this fashion or literally—can enhance understanding of any state's defense policy. It is not too far-fetched to say that the United Kingdom's present-day objectives, strategy, and doctrine could be inferred directly from reflection on (*a*) the familiar cartographer's representation, showing the British Isles as continental Europe's "offshore islands," and (*b*) the sort of view of the country's geostrategic setting that Geoffrey Kemp has recently produced.[25] What is equally true is that until the later 1940s it was necessary only to examine a political map of the world—showing the dominions, colonies, and other dependencies of the British Commonwealth (depicted, usually, in an arresting shade of red)—to acquire a sound overall appreciation of why, then, the United Kingdom defined its security priorities on a global scale and made its naval and military dispositions accordingly.

Aspirations, policy judgments, assumptions about what constitutes a becoming posture and "appropriate" provision—all framed against the state's perception of its place in the international environment and the threats it faces—these are the essential *inputs* to the United Kingdom's defense decision making. In a simple world it might be permissible to proceed from this point to consideration of *outputs,* to what British governments do and plan to do in defense, given these circumstances. Yet no student of national security affairs would make the mistake of supposing that the institutions, personalities, and procedures of the planning, programming, and budgeting apparatus can be regarded as "black boxes" or mere ciphers or formalized routines. Quite the contrary: in the United Kingdom, as elsewhere, some insight into how decisions are made is a prerequisite for full understanding of the decisions themselves.

The defense decision-making process

British institutional arrangements for defense policy making and planning are best illuminated, in the first instance, by examination of the organizational structure and bureaucratic procedures. To complement an account along these lines, a review of those constraints that have impinged on decision makers recently and those likely to operate in the 1980s is also included in this section.

STRUCTURE

Enumeration of *all* the institutions and agencies that could be said to be engaged in the defense decision-making process is out of the question. It is necessary to simplify matters, for manageability's sake. This is most conveniently done by consideration of (1) the central organization of the Ministry of Defense itself, which must obviously be the focus of attention; and (2) some of the main "other participants," ranging from the body to which the secretary of state for defense is formally accountable (Parliament, especially the House of Commons) to those that simply seek to influence program and budget choices (e.g., interest groups).[26]

Florence Nightingale once wrote of the nineteenth-century War Office that it was:

> a very slow office, an enormously expensive office, a not very efficient office and one in which the minister's intentions can be entirely negatived by all his sub-departments and those of each of the sub-departments by every other.[27]

No doubt it would be possible to find people with experience of the post-1964 Ministry of Defense prepared to voice similar sentiments. The set-up created then brought together a small coordinating Defense Ministry and three virtually autonomous service departments (Admiralty, War Office, Air Ministry) to form a centralized Ministry of Defense with a nominally strong Central Staffs element and three nominally subordinate single-service management organizations (navy, army, and air force departments). Later, a separate apparatus—the procurement executive—was added to deal with equipment acquisition. The redrafting of the organization charts did not, however, immediately expedite decision making; nor did it produce substantial manpower economies. Moreover, the service departments retained considerable de facto autonomy, and in "the continuing defense review" of 1964-68, senior officers and officials frequently behaved as though animated more by a determination to protect their own projects and priorities than by a commitment to fashion the "right" program. To be sure, the minister's intentions were not "entirely negatived," but they were occasionally frustrated.

All in all, however, this cynical assessment does less than justice to the 1964 reorganization itself and the subsequent evolution of the machinery of defense decision making. Authoritative central direction of the overall defense effort *is* possible from the office of the secretary of state for defense, if the incumbent uses the levers of power at his disposal. The junior ministerial posts in the ministry ceased to provide potential bases for serious challenge to such direction in 1967. The chiefs of staff organization still does—within limits set by constitutional propriety—provided the chief of the defense staff does not regard himself as simply a moderator, holding the ring among contesting single-service viewpoints. Recent holders of the post have emphatically not seen themselves in this light, however. In any event, from the top civil appointments in the hierarchy—the permanent undersecretary of state and the second permanent undersecretary, together with the procurement executive's chief and the chief scientific adviser—there is considerable scope for the exercise of guidance and control in the interests of coherent policies and programs. What is more, in the last few years "the center"—i.e., those parts of the ministry directly answerable to either the chief of the defense staff and his deputies or the permanent undersecretaries—has come to exert a stronger influence than hitherto. (Whether the same can be said of the procurement executive is less clear.)

It would be wrong, however, to convey the impression that the individual service chiefs and their departments do no more than follow the dictates of the higher command, whether it be in debate about equipment choices, on questions of tactical doctrine and concepts of operations, or even over major policy options. After all, these organizations are the principal repositories of technical expertise within their respective domains and the locus of responsibility for day-to-day administration and accounting, and it is to the service rather than the ministry that the personnel of the armed forces regard themselves as owing allegiance. Accordingly, it is with the departments that the initiative lies in procurement matters; the central staffs keep lines of communication with them in good repair at all times, and even a tough chief of the defense staff (or secretary of state) hesitates to act in the teeth of opposition from one or more service chiefs. In fact, taking an overarching view on the centralization/decentralization theme, the British system may well have reached the stage where—in structural terms—a useful balance between "the center" and the services now obtains, providing scope for constructive adversary politics within an overall framework delineated by higher authority.[28]

Regular consultation with other government departments is, obviously, a key feature of decision making in defense; thus, the first category of "other participants" in the process to be considered must be the cabinet colleagues of the secretary of state for defense. External defense being an aspect of foreign policy, the defense minister clearly liaises particularly closely with the foreign secretary. The former's concern with the well-being of the nation's armaments industries—and hence their international competitiveness and export performance—in fact gives him or her a distinctive interest in overseas policy. This is paralleled by an interest in domestic industrial policy, entailing close consultation with the Department of Trade and Industry. (Conversely, industrial capacity, employment, and regional policy considerations regularly cut across security policy preoccupations.) Within the "national security" field, strictly defined links with the Home Office are obviously important, not least where questions of military aid to the civil power are involved. Finally, all responsibilities of the secretary of state for defense are discharged, as Hastie-Smith has put it, "to the accompaniment of a running dialogue with the Chancellor of the Exchequer about the cost of the defence budget and the ability of the economy to sustain it."[29]

Of the institutions outside government with power or influence vis-à-vis the defense program and budget, a clear distinction should be drawn between those that do have formal *power* and those that do no more than exercise *influence* (or try to do so). The elected Chamber of Parliament, the House of Commons, is of paramount importance under the first heading. In the United Kingdom the executive governs subject to its ability to command a majority in the House of Commons. In this sense all its decisions are subject, directly or indirectly, to Parliament's consent. But there is a particular discipline associated with the House of Commons' control of the purse. And as far as defense is concerned, there is a need to "carry" the House of Commons in the vote not only on each year's budget (the estimates) but also on annual legislation regarding each service. Yet these are *formal* powers, for to reject outright what the government proposes is to take an extreme course in British politics, possibly precipitating a general election. In practice, therefore, the House of Commons "can, in normal circumstances, only influence the Government . . . by the strength of the argument which it brings to bear . . . in debate and otherwise."[30] A corollary is that special significance attaches to the role of certain parliamentary committees, notably that which acts as interlocutor with government on defense program and budget issues (the Defense and External Affairs Subcommittee of the House of Commons' Select Committee on Expenditure), and that which acts as Parliament's watchdog on the actual use of resources (the Public Accounts Committee).

Reviewing these core components of the "structure"—the Defense Ministry, other government departments, and Parliament—the questions arise: which are the key positions, and how far can the idiosyncrasies of a particular occupant affect the decision-making process? It is worth digressing briefly to consider the matter.

First and foremost, it is obvious that the top political appointment, that of defense secretary, is a crucial one, and that a strong-minded and strong-willed holder of the post can make a mark on the defense program. The Conservative Duncan Sandys certainly did that in the late 1950s. Following his *Outline of Future Policy,* planning took off in several new directions, driven by little more than the minister's conviction that these were the right directions (although, in retrospect, they appear to have been totally the wrong ones). Sheer force of personality seems to be the only explanation for the episode, the minister taking free rein to indulge his penchant for asking fundamental questions and answering them himself, in defiance of professional advice.[31] In the second half of the 1960s, Labor's Denis Healey managed a no less decisive reshaping of the defense effort, establishing the main contours of policy for the next decade and more. However, his was an entirely different method of working. The Healey style involved extensive consultation—but of an informal nature, with an emphasis on ad hoc groups, telephone calls, and personal advice rather than regular meetings of formal committees (according to John Baylis).[32] At the same time the minister's personal imprint is discernible in all that was done during his tenure of office, and in the way in which things were explained in the Defense White Papers of the period. In fact, at this time, "there is no point in seeking a focus of policy decision-making anywhere in the Ministry . . . outside the office of the Secretary of State."[33]

On the military side, the office of the chief of the defense staff can count for as much or as little as the incumbent wishes. It is generally supposed that in the mid-1960s Lord Mountbatten used his immense personal prestige to considerable effect in minimizing interservice squabbling during the childhood and adolescence of the newly centralized ministry. Circumstantial evidence indicates that in the mid-1970s Field Marshal (now Lord) Carver played an important part in preventing the 1974 Defense Review from degenerating into either indiscriminate application of the law of equal misery among the three services or uncritical slaughtering of the least sacred cows in the equipment program. It appears that in 1977–79 Marshal of the Royal Air Force Sir Neil Cameron fluttered the dovecotes of the ministry by insistence on a more imaginative assessment of new technological opportunities, and more systematic appraisal of medium- and longer-term program possibilities in general, than the machinery was accustomed to making. But these are the only recent holders of the highest uniformed appointment in the United Kingdom to have projected any kind of image other than that of the secretary of state's unobtrusive military counselor. Nor has any individual service chief emerged from the shadows into the popular, or the political, limelight in recent years. The last to do so was Admiral Sir David Luce, who resigned from the post of chief of the naval staff in 1966 in protest against cancellation of the first of a new class of attack carriers.[34]

Under no circumstances would the top civil servants of the Ministry of Defense enter the limelight. Yet the permanent undersecretary occupies a powerful position and may, indeed, have the decisive voice on many issues, especially if the minister is relatively unassertive and the chief of the defense staff is inclined to be self-effacing. Likewise on weapons acquisition decisions, short-term political and military appointees are reluctant to fly in the face of the advice of the head of the procurement executive and the chief scientific adviser. Yet perhaps no single mandarin within the ministry is as influential year in year out as the official who writes the script for the "running dialogue" that the secretary of state for defense holds with the chancellor of the exchequer: the permanent secretary at the treasury charged with oversight of the public sector and hence of public expenditure as a whole. This is because, anticipating a thesis to be elaborated later, expenditure *is* policy, and in reality the budgeting process is the central mode of defense decision making.[35]

Lying outside "official circles" are those "other participants" in defense decision making able to exercise limited influence on selected issues. The most important are interest groups, whose activities may include (1) direct consultation with the authorities on certain matters, (2) the lobbying of Parliament, and (3) efforts to shape public attitudes. The number of such groups involved in defense affairs in the United Kingdom is fairly small, and most that show a direct concern play generally supportive roles. These groups have influenced policy less in recent years, however, than those with little direct interest in defense. In David Capitanchik's words:

> ... debates about defence have revolved around questions of resource allocation. Trade unions, child action and anti-poverty groups (plus many others) have been pressing for greater expenditure on health, education and social welfare. And ... resources have indeed been switched from defence to these other public purposes.[36]

This is not to say that specifically defense-oriented groups wield no influence. Those representing economic interests—certain manufacturers' associations and organized labor in defense-related industry and defense-dependent localities, for instance—clearly do bring pressure to bear to some effect from time to time, while on welfare questions like pensions the veterans organizations invariably get a hearing. But it is really *only* in relation to the economic and social aspects of policy choices that interest groups command attention. Such organizations as have sought to effect substantive change in security policies have had indifferent fortunes. The Campaign for Nuclear Disarmament (CND) enjoyed considerable visibility in the 1950s and 1960s and was instrumental in the 1960 Labor party conference's rejection of an official policy statement and adoption of a unilateralist resolution. But that 1960 conference decision was reversed a year later, and at no time since has the CND come so close to realizing its objectives. Organizations currently seeking an end to the army's presence in Northern Ireland as an internal security force—of which the main ones are Troops Out and the British Withdrawal from Northern Ireland Campaign—are unlikely to fare better. If any "extramural" bodies can be said to impinge on key defense decisions in the United Kingdom it is the attentive publics, in specialist research institutes and some academic centers, who make it their business to analyze policy options. These can generate "solid and articulate support for, or opposition to, given lines of policy."[37] They do not, however, tend to initiate debate on radical departures in policy, although occasionally a commentator's sequence of argument that is dismissed as misguided or ill informed at first appearance turns up in official pronouncements at some later stage.

PROCEDURES

Organization charts, it is said, show how things would work if it were not for the personalities involved. This is only one of their shortcomings, however. Knowledge of the formal institutional structure involved in an activity like defense policy making and management may be *necessary,* but it is assuredly not *sufficient* for understanding of the decision-making process. It must be matched by an appreciation of the bureaucracy's procedures. In particular, elucidation is required of planning, programming, and budgeting practices. This is certainly true in the United Kingdom, where for all practical purposes settling the program and budget is the central defense decision-making process.

Reflection on the nature of budgeting confirms that, in fact, this is generally and necessarily the case, for budgeting is not bookkeeping. It is the act of "systematically relating the expenditure of funds to the accomplishment of planned objectives"[38] or "the translation of financial resources into human purposes."[39] Government budgeting is, therefore, the setting of national priorities, including the balancing of claims on resources for national security goals against those for personal consumption, industrial investment, social infrastructure, and social services. Defense budgeting entails the refinement and elaboration of security priorities, i.e., deciding what is to be done and what resources are to be allotted to what purposes over time. That this must be the heart of the business is self-evident, for every policy choice has expenditure implications and every budgetary allocation registers some decision about policy, posture, or provision. In a phrase: expenditure *is* policy.[40]

Redefining the task here in this light, the question is: how are resources allocated *to* defense and *within* defense in the United Kingdom? Essentially there are four stages:

1. Assessment of the resources likely to be available for all purposes, public and private, military and civil;
2. Decisions regarding the proportion of available resources over which government should take command, by taxation or borrowing, to finance collective provision;
3. Decisions about the allocation of those resources committed to public purposes among competing claimants, viz., the defense effort and civil expenditure programs;
4. Decisions on the content of the defense program, viz., the size and shape, equipment, and deployment of the armed forces, both front-line and support elements.

For present purposes the main emphasis can be given to the third and fourth stages, particularly the fourth. But it is important to be aware of the content in which defense decision making actually takes place. It is also important to recognize that resource allocation procedures in practice are concerned with ongoing expenditure programs and, therefore, with whether more or less should be assigned to public rather than private ends (stage 2); with whether the balance among public sector outlays should be altered (stage 3); and with whether this or that element in the national order of battle should be strengthened or run down, this or that weapon system developed and produced (stage 4). In short, most decisions are made in incremental or marginal terms. Only exceptionally is an entire line of expenditure open to outright severance or massive extension.

A further, but no less important, point is that, in the United Kingdom as elsewhere, examining or imagining new possibilities, making plans, monitoring progress on present policies, and mulling over past experiences are activities that go on continuously and simultaneously. Formal resource allocation, geared to the annual budget cycle, does not require the compression of choices into one cosmic operation. Rather, the yearly routine constitutes a bringing together, for overall appreciation and adjustment (if necessary), of numerous decentralized choices and decisions. A British defense official's description of the position is as follows:

> Decisions about the programme are taken . . . as need arises and as necessary information or the results of studies become available. They are taken in the knowledge of their impact on the planned resources at the previous review and in the knowledge that their effects will be taken into account in the next review. The purpose of the reviews is, indeed, to *bring together* the expected cost of existing policies including decisions taken in the interval since the last survey was made. (Emphasis added)[41]

The survey referred to in this observation is the annual Public Expenditure Survey, a governmentwide exercise that encompasses the first three of the "four stages of budgeting" and hence the allocation of resources *to* defense.

It would be tiresome to describe the origins and practice of this survey in detail. Suffice it to say that each year the Treasury orchestrates a complex operation in which, first, a medium-term (five-year) assessment of economic prospects is made. To adopt a well-worn metaphor, this stage seeks to establish how large the "national cake" is expected to be and leads naturally to consideration of how it should be sliced. The second stage is concerned—to prolong the metaphor—with where the initial cut of the knife should be made, determining how much the state gets and how much private citizens or private enterprise keep to use as they will. What is settled at this juncture is the burden of taxation and the extent of borrowing (or redemption of debt) on the one hand and the overall public expenditure total on the other. The size of the latter figure emerges after discussion of (*a*) general economic factors plus the government's overall political and social strategy, and (*b*) the amount needed to accommodate at least the minimal bids of spending departments. These deliberations take place under the auspices of a Public Expenditure Survey Committee (PESC), hence the shorthand term for the process: the PESC procedure. They merge imperceptibly into exchanges concerned with the third stage: apportionment of the total public expenditure figure among competing claimants, including the decision on how much to allot to defense as opposed to other things. This is the core of the public expenditure review exercise. It yields a set of projections for all government spending, analyzed according to programs (reflecting functions or objectives) and stretching to a four-year distant planning horizon, which is published in a Public Expenditure White Paper. The projections in the 1979 document, based on the 1978 survey and covering the period to 1982-83, are shown in table 2. Among other things, these data indicate the place of defense in British public expenditure priorities; in line with an earlier argument, the defense program whose aggregate cost

Table 2
Public expenditure in the United Kingdom, by major program, 1979/80 to 1982/83

	£ millions at 1978 survey prices			
Program	1979/80	1980/81	1981/82	1982/83
Defense	7,178	7,394	7,420	7,420
Overseas aid, etc.	1,892	2,004	2,005	2,141
Agriculture, trade, industry, etc.	4,108	4,019	3,988	3,990
Loans to nationalized industries	1,450	800	700	1,000
Roads and transport	2,867	2,862	2,842	2,833
Housing	5,237	5,495	5,617	5,728
Other environmental services	3,122	3,152	3,157	3,151
Law and order, etc.	2,137	2,180	2,231	2,274
Education and science	8,817	8,876	8,928	8,926
Health and personal social services	8,406	8,523	8,692	8,873
Social security	15,835	16,112	16,349	16,549
Other services	1,985	2,027	2,102	2,106
Northern Ireland	2,023	2,002	2,025	2,040
Total programs	65,056	65,446	66,057	67,032
Contingency reserve	800	1,400	2,000	2,500
Subtotal	65,856	66,846	68,057	69,532
Debt interest	2,300	2,400	2,400	2,300
Total public expenditure	68,156	69,246	70,457	71,832

Source: The Government's Expenditure Plans, 1979–80 to 1982–83, Cmnd 7439 (London: HMSO).

is shown in the tabulation becomes the point of reference for all subsequent defense decision making. In other words, the defense program is a *rolling* program: each annual review cycle is based on the inherited program.[42]

Neglecting the fact that, being concerned with managing as well as planning, the Ministry of Defense has to prepare budget estimates on other than a functional basis for administrative purposes, the crucial question can now be addressed: how is resource allocation *within* defense conducted? How are defense priorities set? How is the breakdown of the program total decided upon? More specifically, how are decisions made about endorsement or amendment of the program-in-being, as a matter of routine or in special circumstances (and including the incorporation of weapons research, development, and production choices)?

Obviously in an organization as large as the Defense Ministry there are several loci of decision making. There has to be "suboptimization" or a factoring out of the problems that arise in settling the precise composition of the defense effort. Simplifying brutally, the broad pattern of priorities is sketched by the central policy staffs in the light of the nation's security objectives and the part military power can play in pursuing them, thus defining the desired defense effort. These ideas lie behind any special studies that may be conducted, and equipment proposals are evaluated against this background. They enter the routine budgeting exercise via assumptions formulated by the central Program and Budget (P&B) division—to guide preparation of the ministry's input to the PESC procedure. Below this level, however, there is much choice among alternatives on a subproblem basis.

Outside the domain of "special studies" and major equipment proposals, the service departments enjoy substantial autonomy. Provided their decisions are consistent with the higher-level criteria embodied in the P&B guidelines, which are reiterated or revised annually, they enjoy freedom of maneuver to make numerous decentralized choices. For the most part this means incremental decisions with reference to manageable subproblems, on which systematic, quantitative problem-solving techniques can be brought to bear. Indeed, this is where cost-effectiveness analyses, operational research, and value engineering feature in the resource allocation process.[43]

Equipment acquisition is formally centralized, under the aegis of the procurement executive, but there is some de facto delegation. Good accounts of procurement procedures exist elsewhere. For present purposes it is sufficient to note that their main characteristic is a sequence of phases and thresholds—from concept formulation to the introduction of a system into service—that provides ample opportunity for both analysis and adversary politics and that probably goes as far as institutional arrangements can to ensure that only equipment that is both necessary and cost effective attracts funding.[44]

Resource allocation within defense, however, deals with more than how much more or less to allot for purposes which are exclusively the concern of a single service, or whether to include a new weapon system in the program. Priority setting involves questions of deployment and force structures, and it is occasionally necessary to ask whether it is worth maintaining some capability at all. Because issues like these arise regularly—and require careful investigation when they do—"special studies" must be considered part of the machinery of routine decision making. But it is in "special circumstances" that such exercises come into their own—most notably when a change of government takes place, so the entire inherited program comes under scrutiny. Major defense reviews of this sort are the occasion for fundamental reconsideration of the place of defense in the pattern of national priorities (see table 2) and for associated reconsideration of the pattern of security priorities.

Such an exercise was initiated by the incoming Labor government in 1974. It is useful to note the main features of this undertaking, partly as a case study in across-the-board appraisal of the defense program and budget and partly because—being the most recent example of the *genre*—the 1974 review established the structure of priorities present in the current program and budget.

The expenditure projections that Labor inherited foreshadowed outlays rising more or less in line with the (then) expected growth in GDP, as shown below:

	1975/76	1976/77	1977/78	1978/79	Average 1979–84
Inherited program (£m at 1974 survey prices)	4,000	4,070	4,150	4,300	4,450

However, the party was committed to reducing defense's share of national resources to a level close to those of other European members of NATO, to make possible "savings" amounting to several hundred million pounds over a period of years, these being sought in order to permit additional spending on the main civil programs. On taking office, therefore, studies were set in hand to develop *options* for the 1975–84 budget, based on different interpretations of "essential defense needs" and of the feasible scale and pace of expenditure reductions.

No one knows what possibilities were considered. But it is clear that an implicit ranking of national commitments was present in official thinking. Maintenance of the strategic nuclear force, the maritime capabilities for Atlantic defense, and the contribution to the Alliance's land/air forces in the Allied Forces Central Europe (AFCENT) area were assigned a coequal top priority, together with provision for the security of the "home base" (i.e., the United Kingdom itself). The specialist reinforcement forces for contingencies on NATO's flanks (including naval, ground, and air force components) rated a somewhat lower priority. The already much attenuated national capacity for operations outside Europe and the remaining extra-European garrisons were regarded as the most dispensable elements in the program.

From a set of "costed options" drawn up along these lines, ministers chose and in due course announced the revised program. This embodied continuing provision for the strategic nuclear force (but not for a replacement) and envisaged no far-reaching change in force structures or force levels for the "top priority" tasks (apart from some "stretching" of weapons procurement schedules and a reorganization of 1 [BR] Corps and other field force formations). But significant reductions in the specialist reinforcement forces were foreshadowed, e.g., deletion from the program of funds for new commando carriers and intimations that the United Kingdom would take a more stringent view of its obligations to southern flank security. And the government announced withdrawal of remaining ground and air forces from Singapore/Malaysia, Indian Ocean bases and Malta; "early reductions" in Cyprus and a major reduction in the Hong Kong garrison; and the discontinuance of routine peacetime naval deployments east of Gibraltar—in short, virtual abandonment of extra-European activities. All this made it possible to envisage expenditure projections as follows:

	1975/76	1976/77	1977/78	1978/79	Average 1979–84
Revised program (£m at 1974 survey prices)	3,700	3,800	3,800	3,800	3,790

(The considerable difference between the actual money values in this budget profile and those in table 2 is attributable to the differing price bases: the United Kingdom suffered double-digit inflation between 1974 and 1978.)

As for the transformation effected in the actual composition of the program, as expressed in the functional analysis of expenditure, the data in table 3 are illuminating. This tabulation shows the actual allocation of resources within defense, in percentage terms, for selected years (including the most recent figures available at the time of writing). The contrast between the pre- and post-1974 review defense effort is evident. So too is the fact that the current program and budget continue to reflect the pattern of priorities laid down in the late 1970s.[45]

CONSTRAINTS

Having examined the institutional structure and bureaucratic procedures involved in British defense decision making at some length, what now of the principal constraints that policy makers and planners have confronted in the past and may be expected to face in the future? Most students of the United Kingdom's security affairs would nominate budgetary limitations as the most persistent and pervasive influence. Following the sequence of analysis used in discussing resource allocation to and within defense:

1. Because of the British economy's poor growth record (and indifferent growth prospects), the re-

Table 3
Functional analysis of British defense expenditure, by major program, selected years, 1969/70 to 1979/80

<table>
<tr><th></th><th colspan="4">£ millions at 1978 survey prices</th></tr>
<tr><th>Program</th><th>1969/70</th><th>1973/74</th><th>1977/78</th><th>1979/80</th></tr>
<tr><td>Nuclear strategic force</td><td>2.6</td><td>1.2</td><td>1.5</td><td>1.5</td></tr>
<tr><td>Navy GP* combat forces</td><td>12.3</td><td>12.4</td><td>13.3</td><td>13.2</td></tr>
<tr><td>European theater ground forces</td><td>8.9</td><td>14.8</td><td>17.2</td><td>17.5</td></tr>
<tr><td>Other army combat forces</td><td>6.7</td><td>1.9</td><td>1.1</td><td>0.9</td></tr>
<tr><td>Air Force GP forces</td><td>16.2</td><td>14.7</td><td rowspan="2">16.3</td><td rowspan="2">17.0</td></tr>
<tr><td>Air mobility forces</td><td>4.3</td><td>3.4</td></tr>
<tr><td>Mission programs</td><td>51.3</td><td>48.4</td><td>49.5</td><td>50.1</td></tr>
<tr><td>Support programs</td><td>48.7</td><td>51.6</td><td>50.5</td><td>49.7</td></tr>
<tr><td>Total</td><td>100.0</td><td>100.0</td><td>100.0</td><td>100.0</td></tr>
</table>

Source: Statements on the Defense Estimates, 1969, 1973, 1977, 1979 (London: HMSO). (Functional analysis tabulations.)
Note: Figures have been reallocated to take account of some attribution changes over the years.
*General purpose.

sources available for all purposes have not been sufficient of late (and do not seem likely to be sufficient in the 1980s) to allow the nation to enjoy high consumption, undertake substantial industrial investment, maintain a "welfare state" able to satisfy rising social security expectations, *and* sustain the kind of defense effort that yields not only a reasonable sense of security within the international system but also the status to which the once Great Power aspires;

2. Their predecessors having countenanced a steady increase in the share of GDP absorbed by the state for collective provision, all governments taking office since the early 1970s have sought to contain the growth of public expenditure as a whole;
3. Faced with rising entitlements under various social security schemes and pressures on other civil programs, successive administrations have been disposed to regard the defense effort as offering most scope for economies in these circumstances (although the Conservative government elected in 1979 declared that it did *not* subscribe to this view).

In consequence, defense's share of GDP has edged downward steadily over time and it may well continue to do so.

If growth prospects were to improve and the Thatcher government's assault on civil public spending programs were to be sustained, budgetary constraints as such would, of course, be less pressing. That there will inevitably be "less money for defense" in the 1980s is not, therefore, a completely foregone conclusion. But there is another side to the economic facts of defense life. In the foreseeable future, as in the past, it *does* seem inevitable that cost factors will operate in such a way that the British will get "less defense for their money" (as will most other countries). On the *manpower* side, an improvement in pay relative to civilian alternatives could be required to preserve manning levels in the all-volunteer forces. In addition, more money is likely to be needed for social expenditures to mitigate the effects of "turbulence" on service families. On the *equipment* side, a set of interlocking vicious circles operates. Technological innovation is sought so that existing missions can continue to be performed effectively in the face of the protagonist's new challenges. Thus, each succeeding generation of weapons systems must be more sophisticated than the last. As a result, both initial acquisition and overall lifetime costs go higher. To accommodate higher unit costs, quantitites are reduced. This limits the scope for learning and scale economies, adding a further twist to costs. And the prospect of fewer units serves as an inducement to make each one do more—that is, to require multirole or general purpose capabilities—which entails building systems of yet greater complexity, and hence even greater expense. Budgets are, therefore, increasingly taken up with fewer and fewer, costly but complicated, items.[46]

Nor is it wholly a matter of costs. Keeping both regular and reserve formations up to strength could become more problematical for the United Kingdom as time goes by because, although demographic trends are not unfavorable through the 1980s, there are people who would not be attracted to the profession of arms at any price. In striving to keep the forces' equipment up to date, account has to be taken of the erosion of the United Kingdom's technical competence and competitiveness in certain areas. Inability to contemplate independent development of some of the most advanced systems already acts as a constraint on program choices.

Economic constraints on decision making may be the most evident and tangible. But are they the only ones? Clearly not. For one thing, practically speaking, each of the "judgments and assumptions" about policy, posture, and provision reviewed in the previous section is a constraint for year-to-year programing and budgeting. Options for neutralism on the Swedish model or an independent stance under the North Atlantic Treaty *à la française* simply do not enter the policy reckoning. Neither unilateral efforts at doctrinal innovation nor radical postural alternatives are seriously contemplated. Nor do British decision makers spend time speculating about reintroducing conscription or emulating the Canadian experiment in service integration, while concern for the defense industrial base sets limits to the enthusiasm with which collaborative procurement opportunities are pursued. In sum, although ministers, officials, and senior serving officers are most conscious of how budgetary stringency and their personal and procurement problems constrain choice, in fact they operate within a much more complex framework of explicit and implicit limitations on their freedom of action.

Recurring issues: defense policy outputs

The outcome of the defense decision-making process is the current program and budget. It has been shown that in the financial year 1979/80 the United Kingdom planned to devote over £7,000 millions (at 1978 survey prices) to military purposes, and that medium-term projections for public expenditure as a whole incorporate provisions for steadily rising outlays through the first half of the 1980s (see table 2). But what exactly is the money to be spent on? By answering this question it is possible to see exactly how the British have resolved—at least for the time being—the complex choice problem involved in settling the size, shape, equipment, and deployment of the armed forces in the light of existing doctrine and strategy, security objectives, and international political aspirations.

Having exposed in this way the contemporary conception of the United Kingdom's security priorities, as expressed in the allocation of resources to functions, it is sensible to ask next what changes (if any) are either already implicit in the program or likely to occur because current intentions are the subject of controversy. It is instructive also to note certain institutional features of the planned defense effort: specifically, how decision makers envisage acquiring the arms and mustering the armed forces for it.

Expectations about the outcome of arms control negotiations invite attention too, for achievement of a significant breakthrough in any one of several forums could have far-reaching implications (as, of course, could encountering a major impasse). Nor would an essay of this sort be complete without some remarks on the circumstances in which, rather than contemplating force reductions, the United Kingdom might feel impelled to augment its defense effort—either to bolster deterrence in Europe or with actual operations in mind. In short, there is an extensive agenda of topics for consideration in this final section.

THE CURRENT PROGRAM AND BUDGET

Just as defense's place in the pecking order of national priorities is most clearly demonstrated in the functional analysis of total public expenditure, so the content of the defense program itself is most usefully illuminated by the functional analysis of defense expenditure and personnel. Each year data on the outlays and manpower associated with particular defense purposes are set out in the United Kingdom's *Statement on the Defence Estimates*. Detailed figures are revealed only for the immediately forthcoming year, but fragments of evidence and informed inference allow valid observations to be made reaching further ahead. The functional divisions used in the *Statement on the Defence Estimates, 1979* and the main values for the 1979–80 "first-year slice" of the current program are shown in table 4. The following paragraphs consist of summary comment on each of the individual programs for which data are presented.

Of the major mission programs the strategic nuclear force is the least manpower intensive and not particularly costly. But it represents the single most powerful element in the national order of battle: the four nuclear-powered ballistic missile submarines (SSBNs), each carrying sixteen Polaris missiles, backed by the resources of the Clyde Submarine Base. Compared with the strategic weaponry of the superpowers, the Polaris force's capability is modest. However, it is in the program—and its replacement is under active consideration—because it contributes to the overall deterrence posture of the Atlantic Alliance and, being a European force, that contribution is held to be more significant than a simple measurement of its destructive power might suggest (though that itself is not negligible). Moreover, symbolizing as it does the United Kingdom's status as a nuclear weapons power, the presumption is that it yields political as well as military utility, conferring prestige and some influence.[47]

Yearly outlays for navy general purpose combat forces account for about 26 percent of the total amount directly attributable to mission programs in current budgetary projections (about 13 percent of aggregate defense spending). At present the fleet consists of over 150 warships, designed to provide the capacity to conduct a varied range of operations at or from the sea: for example, amphibious and airborne landings, protection of shipping (and self-defense), offensive and defensive antisubmarine warfare, mine hunting, and provision of naval "presence" (including offshore policing). Its "balanced" look is, of course, a reflection of past procurement

Table 4
Functional analysis of British defense expenditure and manpower, 1979/80

Program	Expenditure* (£m)	Percentage of total	Manpower (000s)	
			Service	Civilian
Nuclear strategic force	126	1.5%	2.5	4.4
Navy GP combat forces	1,131	13.2	32.2	8.2
European theater ground forces	1,496	17.5	98.4	27.7
Other army combat forces	81	0.9	14.4	6.8
Air force GP forces	1,462	17.0	53.8	11.4
Mission programs	4,296	50.1	201.3	58.5
Reserves and auxiliary formations	148	1.7	2.5	3.5
Research and development	1,151	13.4	1.3	33.2
Training	777	9.1	76.2	21.0
Production, repair, and associated facilities (UK)	590	6.9	9.7	87.2
Other support functions	1,481	17.3	39.0	59.9
War stocks and miscellaneous expenses	115	1.3		
Support programs	4,262	49.7	128.7	204.8
Grand total	8,558	100.0	330	263.3

Source: Statement on the Defense Estimates, 1979, Cmnd 7474 (London: HMSO), annex B, pp. 68–69.
*Defense estimates (at forecast outturn prices). The grand total here, £8,558 millions, corresponds to £7,178 millions at 1978 survey prices (see table 2). Forecast outturn prices represent, as the phrase suggests, the prices that will actually have to be paid during the 1979/80 fiscal year. Survey prices relate to price levels at the end of the preceding calendar year.

choices. But the current program embodies plans for new construction, which means that the future fleet too will have this character. In the 1980s there will be no attack carrier, and plans for a new generation of purpose-built Commando ships were struck from the program some years ago. Thus, the Royal Navy's former ability to project power ashore will be lacking. It will, however, have *some* competence in all other aspects of naval warfare. Overwhelmingly, roles and missions derive from NATO's maritime strategy, while the flexibility that a balanced fleet confers is regarded as a worthwhile asset in its own right "as an insurance against the unforeseen."[48]

Something like one-third of the total bill for the 1979–80 front line is accounted for by European theater ground forces, making this the most costly of the major mission programmes. As far as uniformed manpower is concerned, it is even more dominant. Almost 100,000 of the 330,000 members of the British armed forces serve with the program's three main components: the Berlin garrison is about 3000 strong; the British Army of the Rhine and Home Forces muster about 58,000 and 37,000 respectively. (In addition, the formations employ about 28,000 civilians in the United Kingdom and Germany.)

The troops stationed in Berlin, constituted as the *Berlin Field Force,* consist of infantry and some support units. They play a political role, providing part of the symbolic Western presence in the precarious enclave which is Greater Berlin itself; their military mission—to contribute to the Western powers' plans for safeguarding the security of their sectors of the city—is relatively unimportant compared with their political purpose, although the Force does pose problems for a would-be aggressor and the military presence does yield day-to-day benefits (e.g., in intelligence).

Although not without political significance, the business of the principal British ground forces on the European mainland—BAOR, comprising *1 (BR) Corps* (the combat element) and support units organised under *Rhine Area*—is to carry conviction in performing assigned military missions. The fighting formations are four armoured divisions (1, 2, 3, and 4 divisions), the 5th Field Force and an artillery division. They have places in the "layer-cake" dispositions to which NATO's contingents in AFCENT would deploy in the event of actual or threatened hostilities; and there, once brought up to full strength by reinforcements and reserves, they would be responsible for mounting a conventional "forward defence" in the first instance, employing theatre nuclear weapons if the process of controlled escalation which is the essence of the Alliance's flexible response strategy were to be implemented. The emphasis in their equipment (and training) reflects the expectation that to discharge this task would call for mechanised operations with extensive use of armour.

The combat elements of *Home Forces,* under the aegis of the Headquarters United Kingdom Land Forces (UKLF), consist of both regular troops and Territorial Army (TA) units. They are organised in three Echelons corresponding to their three essential roles: to reinforce BAOR (First Echelon), to provide reinforcement for Allied Command Europe (ACE) generally (Second Echelon), and to defend the United Kingdom itself (Third Echelon).

No changes in either the essential force structure or the force levels of this major component of the national defense effort are envisaged in the current program and budget. What is in prospect for the 1980s is considerable refurbishing and replacement of equipment. As for deployment, the only factor for change might be a transformation of the security situation in Northern Ireland. Present policy is to develop the Royal Ulster Constabulary as "the instrument for the maintenance of law and order," with the volunteer Ulster Defense Regiment and units of the regular army as "the essential buttress of this policy for as long as is necessary"—implying that a rundown of the latter is hoped for but not anticipated.[49]

In striking contrast to earlier times, other army combat forces—i.e., those stationed outside Europe—account for less than 10 percent of the army's strength in the current program (and about 1 percent of the total defense budget). These forces now consist of the Hong Kong garrison (mainly Gurkha troops); the Cyprus garrison plus contingents serving with and supporting the United Nations force in Cyprus (UNFICYP); a battalion in Gibraltar; and a battalion group in Belize. Their budgetary burden is trifling compared with their political and strategic value.

High and rising expenditures are a feature of the air force general purpose combat forces program, however. This fifth and last of the budget's major mission categories encompasses all the Royal Air Force's front-line squadrons and immediate support. For 1979-80 its bill was almost as great as that for European theater ground forces; because expensive reequipment is under way it seems likely to rise, absolutely and relatively, through the early 1980s. Under an austere command structure—Strike Command in the United Kingdom and Royal Air Force Germany, fielding about 800 and 150 aircraft, respectively—the United Kingdom disposes of a comprehensive tactical air arm. Its roles, derived from NATO's concepts of operations for defense of the North Atlantic and Western Europe, include maritime and overland strike (i.e., the delivery of nuclear munitions) and attack (nonnuclear weapons); offensive support of ground forces, including intimate close support and shallow (or battlefield) interdiction; air defense of the United Kingdom and surrounding sea areas, and of assets and forces in Germany or elsewhere; maritime patrol, surveillance in peacetime, antisubmarine operations in war; and reconnaissance, complementary to the strike/attack, offensive support, and maritime roles. In addition to combat planes for these tasks, the RAF's fixed-wing inventory includes transport and training aircraft. There are also rotary-wing squadrons to provide mobility for the army in the field, for search and rescue, and for communications duties. In fact, the United Kingdom has—and, on present plans, will continue to have—capabilities for the full spectrum of tactical air missions, including the most demanding of these, namely, deep interdiction and long-range offensive counterair operations.[50]

All the funds budgeted for defense *could* be apportioned among the five mission programs, for the whole of defense expenditure is ultimately directed to provision of the capabilities that have been surveyed. But this does not happen in fact. To be serviceable for force planning purposes, a functional analysis of expenditure should attribute to a particular purpose those costs (and only those costs) that are "assuredly and inescapably bound up with having that function . . . in the overall programme and budget" or, putting it another way, "the sums which one could certainly expect to save if the function . . . were dropped from the programme."[51] This rules out exhaustive attribution. Consequently, in British budgetary practice the costs assigned to mission programs include only those of the training, logistic, and administrative support that is inextricably associated with—indeed, inseparable from—the performance of operational tasks (i.e., an *integral* part of having the capability "on the books"). Other support activities, which cannot sensibly be apportioned among principal missions, are costed independently in six further programs (see table 4). Brief remarks on each are in order.

Volunteer reserves and auxiliary formations represent a modest claim on the United Kingdom's defense spending, and in 1979-80 a mere 2,500 Service personnel were ascribed to this program. The latter figure is misleading, however, for it refers only to those engaged full time in running the formations in question, which themselves muster over 170,000 in the Regular Reserve and about 75,000 in the Territorial Army. This manpower is an important component of the British defense effort, given that it is only by assimilating individual reservists and volunteer units that the services—and particularly the army—can be brought up to wartime strength. Indeed, this program should be regarded strictly as provision for part of the "teeth" of that effort rather than the "tail."[52]

Each of the other programs, however, is much more clearly "support." Two are concerned with what may be termed personnel-related support, and three are concerned with procurement-related activities. Under the former heading, the 1979-80 estimates record funding of £777 millions for training and almost twice as much on other support functions, which includes not only the higher direction of defense and the armed forces but also service pensions. Training in the United Kingdom is predominantly organized along single-service lines; this is a pattern that there is neither a declared intention nor strong impulse to change, although "rationalization" proposals are canvassed from time to time. Parts of the heterogeneous other support functions too may lend themselves to rationalization by integration. Of the subprograms here, "local administration, communications, etc. . . ." and "family and personnel services" remain largely single-service responsibilities, but it is likely to become increasingly difficult to justify (for example) retention of a more or less autonomous health, education, and welfare apparatus for each of the services. Likewise, regarding the Ministry of Defense itself, some currents continue to run in the direction of further integration; as has been noted, however, the present mixture of part centralized bureaucracy and part arena for the interplay of service departmental frictions and factions is not self-evidently dysfunctional. Under the procurement-related support heading fall, first, outlays for research and development—that is, fundamental research plus actual development work on systems, conducted partly in industry and partly in the government's own establishments. A continuing high and broadly based commitment to R&D can be expected to remain a feature of British defense provision for as far ahead as one can see. There is a trend toward greater involvement in collaborative acquisition arrangements. But, in order to be in the reckoning for cooperative ventures and to be in a position to appraise what Alliance partners offer, a sound and comprehensive national competence in military technology is judged imperative. A second program embraces the overheads of production, repair, and associated facilities in the United Kingdom. These comprise (1) Her Majesty's Dockyards and other establishments that make up the Royal Navy's support organization, (2) the counterpart army organization, most of which comes within the ambit of a logistic executive (army), and (3) the Royal Air Force's maintenance units, depots, and other facilities. Having undergone considerable reshaping in the 1970s (including a general paring down in post-1974 defense review exercises aimed at "trimming the tail without blunting the teeth" of the British armed forces), these organizations appear set for a period of comparative stability in the 1980s.[53] Finally, the presence in the functional analysis of the program war and contingency stocks serves as a reminder that arms and armed forces are powerless without ammunition (on which, incidentally, the United Kingdom is tending to spend rather more than has been usual hitherto as assumptions about appropriate stock levels have been reexamined).

CHANGE AND CONTROVERSY

Planning in defense means looking toward a ten-year distant horizon and beyond. Accordingly, within the current program certain changes are already foreshadowed; for the later years there are aspects of provision on which what will be done is not finally settled, because the critical choices have yet to be made and are indeed the subject of controversy within the defense decision-making and analytical communities.

Of the areas of uncertainty and controversy in British defense at the start of the 1980s, none is more critical than the future of the strategic nuclear retaliatory force. It also happens to be an area that has been greatly illuminated by studies available in the open literature, notably, the evidence assembled (and published) in 1979 by the House of Commons' Defense Committee.[54] It would be impracticable to try to summarize the arguments in the debate. Suffice it to note that the options open to the United Kingdom effectively narrow down to:

1. Leaving the strategic nuclear arena completely;
2. Continuing with a ballistic system like Polaris either independently or in partnership with the French or with continuing American help;
3. Turning to a cruise missile force either independently or with European collaborators or by buying into a European nuclear force based on equipment acquired from the United States.

The first course does not lack advocates, and there is a good statement of the case for it in the evidence submitted to the House of Commons' committee by Robin Cook (with Dan Smith).[55] However, the arguments against renunciation have hardened of late because of (*a*) the emphasis in Soviet military programs on weapon systems that cover targets in Western Europe, and (*b*) enhanced dangers of nuclear proliferation, which a unilateral British abandonment of a strategic force would do nothing to diminish. In any event, the Conservative government that took office in 1979, with a majority that gives it a life expectancy of four or five years, has indicated its firm intention to proceed to acquisition of a replacement for the Polaris force. So from a purely practical point of view, options 2 and 3 are the serious candidates. A follow-on ballistic system would require American help (or acquiescence) and/or French assistance if it were not to be inordinately expensive, although the costs of the missile might be offset by fitting it to a cheaper delivery vehicle than an ocean-going SSBN.[56] Adoption of the cruise missile alternative, in one of several theoretically feasible basing modes, is less attractive if some continuing "independence" for the British deterrent is a consideration (for a variety of reasons that cannot be elaborated here). On the other hand, there are strong arguments for not forgoing cruise missile options, on both substantive and "bargaining chip" grounds.[57] Such is the complexity of the issue that it would be foolhardy to speculate about how it will eventually be resolved. Among the significant influences will be the attitude of the United States to "assistance" and the extent to which the SALT process impinges on this; the progress of thought on the "Eurodeterrence" question (not least among Europeans themselves); and the matter of expense, including the impact of a replacement program on other components of the defense budget (not to mention American and European views on *that*).

Should it become a question of "making room" in the budget for a new sea-based system, one direction in which compensatory "savings" might be sought is the funding for the Royal Navy's general purpose combat forces. The projected evolution of the fleet as envisaged in the present program is summarized in table 5. Current front-line units constitute a balanced navy, and the intention is to preserve a broad "mix"

Table 5
Projected evolution of the United Kingdom's fleet in the 1980s

Type/Class	Numbers in service		
	1980	Mid-1980s	1989
Assault ships	2	1	0
ASW carriers/cruisers	2	2	3
Cruisers	2	1	0
Destroyers			
Sheffield class	7	12	14
Bristol class	1	1	1
County class	6	3	0
Frigates			
Broadsword class	3	8	12
Amazon class	8	8	8
Leander class	26	24	13
Others	7	0	0
MCMVs (coastal)	19	11	13
Offshore patrol vessels	5	7	7
Surface fleet	88	78	71
Fleet submarines (SSN)			
Trafalgar class	0	3	6
Swiftsure class	6	6	6
Dreadnought/Valiant class	6	5	3
Patrol submarines (SS)	14	1	0
Submarines	26	15	15
Grand total	114	93	86

Source: Greenwood, note 47.

of capabilities embodied in complementary, specialized ship types. Modernization within this structural framework is the keynote for the 1980s, based on a comprehensive series of "replacements." There will be fewer ships, however, because some substitution of quality for quantity is planned. Improvements in every aspect of naval technology are envisaged: ship construction, propulsion, sensors, data processing, communications, and weapon systems.

Several question marks hang over the plans, however. As has been noted, there is some dispute within NATO about whether existing doctrine and force structures place sufficient stress on the importance of withstanding an initial, sudden land/air attack. Obviously, if this debate were to lead to pressure for increased investment in forces-in-being, the wisdom of costly provision for protecting the Atlantic SLOC might be questioned. A more likely contingency, perhaps, is that the bill for the 1980s fleet may simply turn out to be higher than governments are prepared to pay, especially if they are having to find money for a new strategic nuclear force. Embracing the "short war" thesis might then be a way of rationalizing a major revision of construction plans.

European theater ground forces too are to undergo modernization within the existing structural framework, if the current program runs its course without disruption or amendment. But there are controversies about this as about the naval program. One concerns new conventional weapons technologies. The core issue is: should thought be concentrated on how best to exploit novel designs and developments to enable forces configured as at present to perform familiar tasks in accustomed ways; or should there be a more fundamental consideration of how they might be utilized? Related to this is the discussion on whether the Alliance should plan on fuller use of techniques of precision and discrimination.[58] In addition, in the 1980s it may be thought prudent to place added stress on the readiness and fighting efficiency of regular formations rather than their number, and on the mobility and effectiveness of reserves rather than nominal strengths. This could be one consequence of efforts to minimize NATO's vulnerability to sudden attack and to enhance capabilities for prosecuting a "short war" of great intensity.[59]

Some of these themes in doctrinal debate also have potentially profound implications for the British investment in tactical air power. Does the planned evolution of the force structure, based on a particular view of mission priorities, appear "right" for the 1980s? Is the emphasis on complex aircraft with multirole capabilities "appropriate," given the cost/quantity trade-off problem?

The forces of "conservatism" and "sophistication" appear to be dominant in current plans, but they are under challenge. The arguments that could most affect the United Kingdom's future choices are those related to the wisdom of persisting with manned aircraft for deep interdiction and close support. A strong *prima facie* case can be made for adopting unmanned systems for the former role and for giving up the latter altogether, placing greater emphasis on battlefield interdiction and local air superiority/air combat among tactical air mission priorities. The evolution of the Royal Air Force's program may well be influenced by the logic upon which this case rests.[60]

It would be foolish to pretend that all the pressures for change and all the matters for controversy concerning the individual major mission programs of the United Kingdom's defense budget have been covered in the foregoing paragraphs. But the issues touched upon *are* the salient ones. Running through these arguments about separate programs, however, is a more basic question related to the "balance" of the defense effort as a whole. If policy makers and planners do have to "make room" for a Polaris successor system in the 1980s, or just simply put up with financial stringency, are they likely to try to make the defense pound stretch to cover a program as at present envisaged, or will they find it necessary to choose where the United Kingdom's defense priorities really lie? Put specifically, will it be possible to maintain "balanced forces," both in the intraservice sense (a balanced fleet, an air force able to handle all missions) and in the interservice sense (a balanced contribution to NATO)?

No one can say that it *will* come to this, of course.

There may be a preference for "keeping up appearances" for a while longer, maintaining the semblance of all-around competence but with the forces generally undernourished, short of up-to-date equipment, and with fewer and fewer units properly up to strength. However, if that option should be rejected, the conclusion is likely to be that:

> The United Kingdom can continue to maintain a first-rate balanced Fleet *or* the kind of contribution it now makes to the Alliance's ground forces' order of battle in Northern Army Group *or* a "full spectrum" tactical air force but *not* all of these.

Thus, in the 1980s it may be necessary for the British to decide whether the most telling contribution they can make to Alliance, and specifically West European, defense is (1) maintenance of their maritime effort with some diminution of the subscription to forces for land/air warfare on the central front, *or* keeping the armored divisions of 1 (BR) Corps and the combat squadrons of RAF Germany (plus associated home-based forces) properly up to scratch, even if this means a reduction in maritime forces.[61]

ARMS AND ARMED FORCES

So far the "outputs" of the defense decision-making process in the United Kingdom have been considered exclusively in terms of the functional analysis of expenditure. This is because what illuminates security policy priorities most sharply is examination of how much money is devoted to what purposes (and why). Resources are allotted to defense not to raise armed forces and purchase arms as ends in themselves but with the performance of roles and the pursuit of objectives in mind. At the same time it *is* sailors and ships, gunners and guns, pilots and aircraft that the money is actually used to buy. It is pertinent, therefore, to ask certain supplementary questions about the British defense effort, based on this alternative perspective. In particular, to complement the dissection of the current program, it is useful to look briefly at arrangements and prospects for obtaining the manpower and acquiring the equipment required for that program.

Present plans envisage that, after twenty-five years of virtually uninterrupted decline, the strength of the British armed forces will level off in the 1980s at around 320,000 overall (navy: 74,500; army: 160,000; air force: 87,500). All will be voluntarily recruited; and even if the services are beset by manning problems there is no likelihood of a return to conscription. Whether intake targets will in fact be met is uncertain. Of the factors to which recruitment is sensitive some should be generally favorable (from the services' standpoint). The labor market outlook for the United Kingdom in the medium term is one of continuing high unemployment, and forces' pay should not be allowed to get out of line with remuneration in comparable civilian occupations. On the other hand, the general attractiveness of the service career is not what it used to be. Contraction in the geographical scope of the defense effort means that the opportunity for travel to exotic places is no longer an inducement. Because of developments in civil industrial training, the opportunity to "learn a trade" is not the attraction it once was. There is some evidence also that, over time, fewer and fewer people are willing to accept that (partial) regulation of social and recreational activities that is—and will remain—a feature of the service life.

It is sometimes suggested, however, that the most influential factors on potential recruits (and those contemplating reengagement after a short initial enlistment) are the esteem in which the armed forces are held in society at large and the congeniality of the working and domestic environment. On this argument the United Kingdom ought to have fewer manpower problems. The military profession necessarily "stands apart" from the rest of society, because units may be physically isolated and because a sense of distinctiveness is important for *esprit de corps*. Yet there is no great sense of alienation among the armed forces, nor are they themselves regarded as a separate "state within the state." Management styles in the services have become less rigid and hierarchical, the blurring of old "officers and men" distinctions being particularly noticeable in activities with a high technological content. On the domestic side, considerable attention has always been paid to personal welfare matters in the British armed forces (helped by the individual's association with ship, regiment, or squadron wherever possible); finally, the general standard of housing and other facilities that service personnel enjoy compares favorably with that in European armed forces.[62]

Weapons acquisition. The acquisition of arms for the services is undertaken, as has been noted, by the Ministry of Defense's procurement executive. The procedures involved are complex but coherent, as has been explained.[63] In 1979–80 over £2,500 million was budgeted for production of new equipment and spares; almost half that sum (£1,150 million) was for research and development. In both activities the United Kingdom is highly self-reliant, but not wholly self-sufficient. Imports represented 8 to 10 percent of the equipment budget in the late 1970s (but may account for a fractionally higher share through the early 1980s). The country's main current suppliers are the United States, from whom missiles (e.g., Lance) and military electronic equipment are being bought; France and the Federal Republic, most transactions coming under the rubric of collaborative deals (e.g., the helicopter "package" with France, the Tornado program with West Germany); and Belgium, with whom the United Kingdom is developing a new family of tracked armored vehicles, and from whom small arms and ammunition are purchased.

Erosion of the domestic armaments base has been taking place for some time, albeit at a modest rate. The effect has been to make the United Kingdom anxious to arrest the process. Hence, there is a greater disposition to participate in cooperative ventures, which permit preservation of the national stake in (or access to) relevant technologies at acceptable cost. But there is also a contradictory impulse: to cling to what is left, and therefore to be prepared to contemplate independent national development and production if the "right" collaborative opportunity does not present itself. It is impossible to predict in which future procurement choices the one or the other force is likely to prove dominant. A momentum for more cooperative solutions is building up, partly in response to general Alliance-wide pressures for more effective use of the considerable resources that NATO assigns to weapons acquisition, partly because of particular pressures on the eastern side of the Atlantic for "rationalization" of the European armaments base. At the same time, the United Kingdom has shown little inclination to compromise on its national preferences in naval equipment programs. The new main battle tank under development for the army is an independent venture (although open to others' participation). And if allies do not favor a VTOL/STOL type for one of the next generation combat aircraft, the possibility of the United Kingdom "going it alone" in this direction cannot be ruled out completely.

Obviously, much depends on the extent to which domestic political, economic, and social arguments enter the decision makers' reckoning. In the next decade neither general economic conditions in the United Kingdom nor employment prospects in some of the regions and localities where defense-related industries are sited will make it easy for governments to opt for off-the-shelf purchases from abroad or collaborative projects in which the British share of the work may be quite modest. Added to this is the fact that the nation's key defense contractors are state owned (at present), so that their future viability is a matter of political calculation rather than commercial performance. (And even if complete or partial denationalization were to take place, the government's interest in the well-being of these enterprises could hardly be diminished. For one thing, there would be a commitment to demonstrate that private ownership "works"; for another, the businesses would remain the nation's principal stake in high technology and, on that account, candidates for special treatment.)

Faced with a stark choice between, on the one hand, giving lower priority to preservation of jobs and competence and, on the other, standing aside completely from major initiatives to promote cooperation in the development and production of armaments, the United Kingdom would probably opt for the former, however. Certainly this would be the preference of Conservative administrations, by all indications. And it is the Conservatives who will be making defense procurement policy decisions in the first half of the 1980s at least.[64]

ARMS CONTROL OR ARMED CONFLICT?

Few commentators would dispute the emphasis in this chapter on the United Kingdom's defense effort, seen as a subscription to an Atlantic Alliance whose reason for being is to deter aggression. It is through the contribution of capabilities to NATO forces in Europe and in the north Atlantic that the nation seeks to safeguard its security. To say that, however, is to prompt two questions. Does the preoccupation with armed forces and armaments mean that no hope is entertained of security through arms control? Does the commitment to deterrence mean that no British decision maker envisages the employment of the country's forces in armed conflict (other than in defense, should deterrence fail)?

At the level of aspirations—and declaratory policy—the United Kingdom has high hopes, if not great expectations, about arms control. In the *Statement on the Defence Estimates, 1979,* support was registered for the SALT negotiations and the view expressed that "the Agreement as it seems to be emerging will enhance stability by setting firm and wide-ranging constraints, both quantitative and qualitative, on the strategic nuclear armouries of the two super-powers." In the same document the nation's involvement in the MBFR talks was recorded, together with the sentiment that an agreement here could contribute to "a more stable relationship and to the strengthening of peace and security in Europe." On the CSCE, the White Paper noted the failure to agree on further military confidence-building measures (at the Belgrade meeting) but entered a reminder that all participants will "continue to implement all the provisions of the Final Act." It also voiced a hope for early agreements on "a properly verifiable multilateral treaty banning nuclear explosions in all environments"—i.e., a comprehensive test ban (CTB).[65]

These remarks should not, however, be taken to imply that the United Kingdom has no reservations about the SALT process and would welcome an early MBFR agreement. Nor do they mean that the next practicable confidence-building measures under the CSCE rubric or a CTB would pose no problems. In fact, British (and other European) policy makers have been decidedly ambivalent about some SALT II provisions, not so much for what they say as for what they could imply. What the protocol might mean for cruise missile deployment options and how account can be taken of European interests in the future negotiations to which the Statement of Principles refers are just two topics among several relevant in this connection. Bringing the Soviet Union's "continental strategic forces"—notably, the SS-20 missiles and Backfire bombers—within the ambit of some negotiating forum is obviously a particular interest; until a satisfactory formula is found, the incentive to bring the exchanges on MBFRs to a definite conclusion is clearly diminished. Nor is that the only inhibition in these discussions. It now appears that some of NATO's own proposals may have been ill advised. As for the CSCE, notification of movements of forces (as opposed to notice of maneuvers) is the next logical step in the development of a regime of confidence-building measures; that is an obligation that a state trying to "keep up appearances" could find especially irksome. Finally, it is readily apparent what commitment to a CTB might mean for a nation facing a decision on replacement of its strategic nuclear forces (with the expectation that either American help or independent development effort is likely to be required).

Evidently the short answer to the first question posed in this section is that, at the practical policy level, some hopes are entertained. But the whole British approach to arms control is tempered by realism. That, it can be argued, is no more than prudence requires. A more cynical judgment would be that what really animates the United Kingdom in arms control endeavors is not so much a desire for enhanced security through acceptance of mutual restraints but rather the opportunity to set some bounds to the growth of Soviet military power without too much loss of freedom of action for itself and its allies.

Answering the second question is more problematical. Formally, the only circumstances in which the active use of military force would be contemplated by the United Kingdom are in the event of a failure of deterrence in the NATO area. All the elements in the national force structure have assigned roles and missions derived from the Alliance's strategy, and they are equipped and deployed accordingly. Little is heard today of the assertion made in 1968 that they possess a "general capability" for operations outside Europe; certainly no explicit attention is paid to the possibility of their employment in intervention actions.

Reflection on recent history counsels caution, however, when it comes to the obvious inference that active employment of forces is unlikely, if not inconceivable, in the foreseeable future. In the first place, when explicit reliance on deterrence for all contingencies was espoused by British planners in the early 1950s it coincided with a period of intense activity for general purpose forces in fulfillment of extra-European commitments, prompting Richard Rosecrance's remark that the British "had a marvellous doctrine for other people but they applied it to themselves."[66] Post-Imperial global obligations loom less large now, of course. But the use of forces outside the NATO area but under Alliance auspices, or at least in concert with those of allies, is not unimaginable: for example, in the event of certain developments in southern Africa or the gulf. In the second place, it is noteworthy that, even since the concentration of the defense effort on Europe and the North Atlantic, there have been occasional instances of the active use of force for strictly limited national ends. Warships mounted the Beira patrol as part of sanctions enforcement against Rhodesia and were "in action" during the fisheries disputes with Iceland in the mid-1970s. Ground and air forces have operated (and still do) in Belize; one assumes that they would do so in the event of crisis or hostilities in other places where the United Kingdom has residual colonial responsibilities. Lastly, the Northern Ireland "emergency" *is* an internal security operation, notwithstanding the fact that it is conducted under the rubric of military aid to the civil power.

Enumerating these instances tends to reaffirm the original assertion rather than contradict it, however. For in relation to the scale of the defense effort they amount to minor policing tasks. Nor does one really expect the British armed forces to be called upon to fire shots in anger during the next decade other than in contexts such as these (with the possible exception of peace-keeping operations under United Nations auspices).

Summary and conclusion

Molding an account of British defense policy to the common format devised for the "country chapters" of this volume is not a straightforward undertaking. Nevertheless, the logical progression is serviceable. It has been shown that the United Kingdom inhabits an international environment in which there are challenges to its security and within which the nation is conscious of its status. The perceived threats to security are almost exclusively those posed by the Soviet Union and its Warsaw Pact allies; the response to them has been framed within an Atlantic Alliance setting, for national security is judged to be inseparable from that of the NATO area as a whole and capable of being safeguarded only by acknowledging interdependence. At the same time there is a residual independent streak in the British psyche of which one manifestation is the kind of forces furnished to the Alliance.

It is against this background that national objectives, national strategy, and military doctrine must be appraised. The basic judgments and assumptions that lie behind the state's aspirations, its actual policy, the posture it has chosen to assume, and its provision for defense quite clearly derive from NATO's goals, strategy, and concepts of operations. The United Kingdom would, however, like to cut a certain figure in Alliance—and particularly European—circles; this is evident too, notably in the commitment of forces to each of the three components of the NATO triad (strategic nuclear, theater nuclear, and conventional arms); in all three elements (sea, land, and air); and within each of the three Alliance Command Areas (Atlantic, Channel, and Europe).

National aims and assumptions are inputs to the defense decision-making process. In the United Kingdom this involves an institutional structure, whose core components are the central staffs and service departments of the unified Defense Ministry, and a set of bureaucratic procedures centered on management of the "rolling" defense program and budget. It follows that the obvious frame of reference for consideration of defense policy outputs is the ministry's current program and budget: its actual content, the changes foreshadowed in it, and any unsettled matters. As it happens, analysis along these lines brings the argument full circle, for the composition of the present and planned defense effort displays the emphasis on NATO, yet bears the imprint of the desire to make a distinctive contribution to the Alliance. Tension between interdependence and independence is likewise discernible in debate on unresolved issues. In short, defense dispositions are now made—and will continue to be made—in accordance with the United Kingdom's prevailing self-image, that of the Great Power in reduced circumstances. Be that as it may, it is unlikely that "keeping up appearances" will prove a feasible policy beyond the short run. Sooner or later it will be necessary to abandon the facade of all-around competence; that will amount to a last acknowledgment that, for the once substantial global and imperial power, things are not what they used to be.

"Earth's proud empires pass away" is the hymnist's reminder that this is neither more nor less than should be expected. Not that the appropriate sentiment in such a situation is brooding nostalgia; better to take consolation from a poet and inspiration from a pop song. For the first purpose the British might reflect on Dryden's perceptive lines:

Not heav'n itself upon the past has pow'r
But what has been has been and I have had my hour.

As for the second, they may have noted that in the spring of 1979, while the nation's planners were reviewing the defense program for the next decade, the best-selling record in the United Kingdom was the defiant "I Will Survive."

Notes

1. International comparison of defense efforts is, of course, a hazardous undertaking. For a useful discussion of some of the problems, see Stockholm International Peace Research Institute, *The Meaning and Measurement of Military Expenditure,* SIPRI Research Report no. 10 (Stockholm: SIPRI, 1973). For data permitting broader comparisons than those in table 1, see R. L. Sivard, *World Military and Social Expenditures, 1978* (Leesburg, Va.: WMSE Publications, 1978), and International Institute for Strategic Studies, *The Military Balance, 1979–80* (London: IISS, 1979).

2. The following paragraphs contain some material originally used for my "Adequacy and Appropriateness of Western Military Expenditures," *Ditchley Journal* 5, no. 1 (Spring 1978): 74–86 (especially pp. 76–79). For a deeper analysis, see *Prospects of Soviet Power in the 1980s,* Adelphi Papers, nos. 151 and 152 (London: IISS, 1979), especially the papers by William Hyland, Jean Laloy, and Andrew Marshall.

3. One of the most useful assessments of the conventional theater balance available is Congressional Budget Office, *Assessing the NATO/Warsaw Pact Military Balance* (Washington, D.C.: Government Printing Office, 1977). On continental strategic forces' issues (and data) see R. Metzger and P. Doty, "Arms Control Enters the Gray Area," *International Security* 3, no. 3 (Winter 1978–79): 17–52.

4. M. J. Hillenbrand, "NATO and Western Security in an Era of Transition," *International Security* 2, no. 2 (Fall 1977): 21–22.

5. K. N. Waltz, *Foreign Policy and Democratic Politics* (Boston: Little, Brown, 1967), pp. 7, 161–62.

6. D. Greenwood, "Defence and National Priorities since 1945," in *British Defence Policy in a Changing World,* ed. J. Baylis (London: Croom Helm, 1977), p. 196. (The argument in the present paragraph is largely based on the material in this essay.)

7. For a detailed analysis of the British defense experience in the third and fourth phases, see D. Greenwood and D. Hazel, *The Evolution of Britain's Defence Priorities, 1957–76,* Aberdeen Studies in Defence Economics [ASIDES], no. 9 (Aberdeen: Centre for Defence Studies, 1977–78).

8. The phrase occurs, significantly, in the *Report of the Review Committee on Overseas Representation,* Cmnd. 4107 (London: Her Majesty's Stationery Office [HMSO], 1969), p. 22. (I am indebted to my colleague Jim Wyllie for this reference.)

9. There is full discussion of the point below.

10. J. C. Garnett, "Some Constraints on Defence Policy-Makers," in *The Management of Defence,* ed. L. W. Martin (London: Macmillan, 1970), p. 30.

11. See D. Hazel and P. Williams, *The British Defence Effort: Foundations and Alternatives,* ASIDES, no. 11 (Aberdeen: Centre for Defence Studies, 1977/78), on which I have drawn heavily in the remainder of this section.

12. The quoted phrase is from article 6 of the Non-Proliferation Treaty (NPT), which entered into force in 1970.

13. *Statement on the Defence Estimates, 1976,* Cmnd. 6432 (London: HMSO), chap. 1, para. 29, p. 10.

14. Hazel and Williams, *British Defence Effort*, pp. 13 and 14.

15. For data and some interesting arguments on the burden-sharing issue, with particular reference to the British case, see G. Kennedy, *Burden-sharing in NATO* (London: Duckworth, 1979).

16. There are further details on the major programs covered in the next three paragraphs below.

17. See D. B. Capitanchik, "Public Opinion and Popular Attitudes towards Defence," in *British Defence Policy*, ed. Baylis.

18. Ibid.

19. G. Pattie, *Towards a New Defence Policy* (London: Conservative Political Centre, 1977), and *Sense about Defence*, Report of a Labour party defence study group, (London: Quartet Books, 1977), are recent examples of "party" material.

20. W. Schilling, P. Hammond, and G. Snyder. *Strategy, Politics, and Defence Budgets* (New York: Columbia University Press, 1962); I. Dorfer, *System 37 Viggen* (Oslo: Scandinavian University Books, 1973).

21. But see C. Mayhew, *Britain's Role Tomorrow* (London: Hutchinson, 1967) and B. Reed and G. Williams, *Denis Healey and the Policies of Power* (London: Sidgwick and Jackson, 1971) for suggestions of "in-fighting" in the 1960s.

22. For an essay specifically directed to "determinants," see J. Baylis, "Defence Decision-making in Britain and the Determinants of Defence Policy," *Journal of the Royal United Services Institute for Defence Studies* 120, no. 1 (March 1975): 42-48.

23. See D. Greenwood, "Constraints and Choices in the Transformation of Britain's Defence Effort since 1945," *British Journal of International Studies* 2, no. 1 (April 1976): 5-26, for details on this point.

24. For an invaluable survey of the defense industrial base see the second part of R. Angus, *The Organisation of Procurement and Production in the United Kingdom*, ASIDES, no. 13 (Aberdeen: Centre for Defence Studies, 1979).

25. G. Kemp, "The New Strategic Map," *Survival*, March-April 1977, map 6.

26. For fuller accounts of the central organization, see F. A. Johnson, *Defence by Ministry* (London: Duckworth, 1979); M. Howard, *The Central Organisation of Defence* (London: Royal United Services Institute [RUSI], 1970); and R. M. Hastie-Smith, "The Tin Wedding: A Study of the Evolution of the Ministry of Defence, 1964-74," in *Seaford House Papers* (London: Royal College of Defence Studies, 1974). On "other participants," see Baylis, "Defence Decision-making," and Capitanchik, "Public Opinion."

27. Letter to Sidney Herbert, 1859, cited in Hastie-Smith, "Tin Wedding," p. 27.

28. But see note 21.

29. Hastie-Smith, "Tin Wedding," p. 38.

30. First Report from the Select Committee on Procedure, Session 1968-69, *Scrutiny of Public Expenditure and Administration*, House of Commons Paper 410 (1968-69), Evidence, appendix 1, para. 3, p. 237.

31. Baylis, "Defence Decision-making," pp. 42-43.

32. Ibid.

33. Howard, *Central Organisation of Defence*, p. 39.

34. See Mayhew, *Britain's Role Tomorrow*, for an account of the episode.

35. See H. Heclo and A. Wildavsky, *The Private Government of Public Money* (London: Macmillan, 1974) for a superb analysis of the Treasury's role in managing public expenditure (and hence public policy making).

36. Capitanchik, "Public Opinion," p. 271.

37. Ibid. p. 175.

38. A. Schick, "The Road to PPB," *Public Administration Review* 26, no. 4 (December 1966): 27.

39. A. Wildavsky, *The Politics of the Budgetary Process* (Boston: Little, Brown, 1964), p. 1.

40. This argument is set out more fully in D. Greenwood, *Budgeting for Defence* (London: RUSI, 1972), which also contains a fuller exposition of the procedures described in the next few paragraphs of this section.

41. Second Report from the Expenditure Committee, Session 1971/72, House of Commons Paper 141 (1971-72), appendix 33, para. 8.

42. For an official description of the PESC procedure, see *Public Expenditure White Papers: Handbook on Methodology* (London: HMSO, 1972). (But cf. Heclo and Wildavsky, "Public Money.")

43. Greenwood, "Budgeting," pp. 38-43.

44. The best concise and up-to-date account of the procurement process is in the first part of Angus, *Procurement and Production*.

45. For a full exposition of the 1974 Defence Review, see Second Report from the Expenditure Committee, Session 1974-75, *The Defence Review Proposals*, House of Commons Paper 259 (1974-75), and two articles in *Survival* 17, no. 5 (September-October 1975) under the heading "Setting British Defence Priorities" (the first of which is by the minister who conducted the exercise, the second by me).

46. L. Freedman, *Arms production in the United Kingdom: Problems and Prospects* (London: Royal Institute of International Affairs [RIIA], 1978), p. 13.

47. There is a fuller elucidation of the content and rationale of this mission program and of those discussed in later paragraphs in D. Greenwood, *The United Kingdom's Current Defence Programme and Budget*, ASIDES, no. 10 (Aberdeen: Centre for Defence Studies, 1977/78), pp. 4-55.

48. *Statement on the Defence Estimates, 1975*, Cmnd. 5976 (London: HMSO), chap. 1, para. 17.

49. *Statement on the Defence Estimates, 1978*, Cmnd. 7099 (London: HMSO), p. 22.

50. For a tabulation of Royal Air Force types and squadrons classified by missions, for the present and the mid-1980s, see Greenwood, *United Kingdom's Current Programme*.

51. Greenwood, *Budgeting*, p. 50.

52. There is a wealth of information on Reserve forces and their roles in the Sixth Report from the Expenditure Committee, Session 1976-77, *Reserves and Reinforcements*, House of Commons Paper 393 (1976-77).

53. For additional material on the support organizations, see the *Statement on the Defence Estimates, 1979*, Cmnd. 7474 (London: HMSO), chap. 5.

54. Sixth Report from the Expenditure Committee, Session 1978-79, *The Future of the United Kingdom's Nuclear Weapons Policy*, House of Commons Paper 348 (1978-79), hereafter cited as HC 348 [1978-79]. See also I. Smart,

The Future of the British Nuclear Deterrent: Technical, Economic, and Strategic Issues (London: RIIA) and the summary of this analysis in *International Affairs* 43, no. 4 (October 1977): 557–71.

55. HC 348 (1978–79), pp. 138–51.

56. HC 348 (1978–79), pp. 85, 96.

57. HC 348 (1978–79), pp. 84–87.

58. See the arguments in J. J. Holst and U. Nerlich, *Beyond Nuclear Deterrence: New Aims, New Arms* (New York: Crane, Russak & Co., 1977).

59. See Hazel and Williams, *British Defence Effort*, pp. 26–39.

60. For detailed arguments, see, for example, S. Canby, *The Alliance and Europe: IV—Military Doctrine and Technology*, Adelphi Papers, no. 109 (London: IISS, 1975), and my essay in E. Feuchtwanger and R. A. Mason, eds., *Air Power in the Next Generation* (London: Macmillan, 1979).

61. The quoted passage in this paragraph is from my lecture to the Royal United Services Institute for Defence Studies, 23 May 1979, on *The Scope of Britain's Defence Effort in the 1980s*. On the general theme, see also L. Freedman, "Britain's Contribution to NATO," *International Affairs*, January 1978, pp. 30–47, which in turn draws on the analysis in my *Defence Programme Options to 1980–81*, ASIDES, no. 6 (Aberdeen: Centre for Defence Studies, 1976).

62. A useful statistical study on recruitment is G. A. Withers, "Armed Forces Recruitment in Great Britain," *Applied Economics* 9 (1977): 289–306.

63. See above and the reference to Angus, *Procurement and Production*.

64. A relevant factor here may be the Conservatives' greater enthusiasm for the United Kingdom's European affiliations at a time when greater European cooperation in arms development and production is being actively canvassed. See, for example, the arguments in "A European Armaments Policy" (Report to the Twenty-Fourth Ordinary Session of the Assembly of Western European Union, 31 October 1978 Doc. no. 786).

65. *Statement on the Defence Estimates, 1979*, Cmnd. 7474 (London: HMSO), chap. 1.

66. R. Rosecrance, *Defense of the Realm* (New York: Columbia University Press, 1968), pp. 178–80.

BRITISH DEFENSE POLICY: A BIBLIOGRAPHICAL ESSAY

Chris L. Jefferies

Premier among several organizations that do research in the British defense policy field is the Royal United Services Institute for Defence Studies (RUSI) (Whitehall, London SWIA 2ET). Established by royal charter, its purpose is "the study of British Defence and Overseas Policy and for the promotion and advancement of the science and literature of the three services." The institute publishes a quarterly journal and the reports of occasional seminars it sponsors on various subjects relating to British defense. In addition, since 1974, the institute has edited the annual *RUSI and Brassey's Defence Yearbook* (formerly *Brassey's Annual: The Armed Forces Yearbook*), a volume that explores significant events of the past year in the fields of defense and international relations, as well as weapons development and technology. The reader will find the quarterly *RUSI Journal,* the seminar reports, and *RUSI and Brassey's Defence Yearbook* most useful.

The Centre for Defence Studies at the University of Aberdeen, Scotland, has been active in both research and publishing in the field of British defense policy with the issue of its *Aberdeen Studies in Defence Economics* (ASIDES) series. The ASIDES papers are published and circulated to make available the results of the center's current research in the economic aspects of defense. Though the emphasis of the studies is economic, such a focus provides a most useful basis for studying all other aspects of defense policy. Copies of the studies can be obtained for a nominal fee by writing the secretary, Centre for Defence Studies, University of Aberdeen, Edward Wright Building, Dunbar Street, Aberdeen AB9 274, Scotland.

The International Institute for Strategic Studies (IISS) (18 Adam Street, London WC2N 6AL) has long been active in the area of defense policy. Its Adelphi Papers, monographs that explore "the social and economic sources and political and moral implications of the use and existence of armed forces," occasionally also examine issues of British defense policy as well as the broader strategic issues that have an impact on them.

Sources of information often underestimated but which must not be overlooked are the official publications of the British government. Although they may not be as widely available in the United States as are other sources, they are available at major university libraries through interlibrary loan programs—or from the British Embassy in Washington. These publications provide an authoritative source of information on changes in defense policy and related expenditures in annual and supplemental statements on defense commonly known as White Papers. (They are entitled *Statement on the Defence Estimates,* 19--.) Additional sources are the reports of the Defence and External Affairs Subcommittee on the House of Commons Select Committee on Expenditure, although these are not too widely available.

American sources

In the United States there are several institutions that occasionally address British defense policy. The Inter-University Seminar on Armed Forces and Society (Social Science Building, University of Chicago, 1126 East 59th Street, Chicago, Ill. 60637) publishes the quarterly *Armed Forces and Society,* a journal that addresses civil-military relations, military institutions, arms control, and conflict management. The periodic and continuing Sage Research Progress Series on War, Revolution, and Peacekeeping is another relevant source. The Carnegie Endowment for International Peace (11 Dupont Circle N.W., Washington, D.C. 20036) publishes *Foreign Policy* on a quarterly basis; the Foreign Policy Research Institute (3508 Market Street, Philadelphia, Pa. 19104) publishes *Orbis: A Journal of World Affairs,* also a quarterly; and the Council on Foreign Relations (58 East 68th Street, New York, N.Y. 10021) publishes its *Foreign Affairs* five times annually. Of these institutions, the Inter-University Seminar publishes the most on British defense policy issues.

Defense policy histories

An understanding of contemporary British defense policy requires, at a minimum, the study of its most recent history. Since the end of World War II, British policy has undergone many important changes as the country has retreated from being a world empire and begun to develop a "European" perspective on defense issues. Even today this transition is reflected in policy debates and deliberations.

Several sources (among the many) are particularly useful in providing an understanding of the historical forces shaping today's British defense policy. C. H. Bartlett, in *The Long Retreat* (London: Macmillan, 1972), addresses the turbulent period from 1945 to 1970 in a general analysis of the period's defense policy. Phillip Darby, in *British Defense Policy East of Suez, 1947-1968* (London: Oxford University Press, 1973), focuses on the "retreat from empire." A most comprehensive and useful series of analytical essays on the period of 1945 to 1976 is found in *British Defense Policy in a Changing World,* edited by John Baylis (London: Croom Helm, 1977).

In addition to the books listed above are several monographs and articles that give a briefer and more condensed account of the period from 1945. John Baylis's article, "British Defense Policy," in *Contemporary Strategy* (edited by John Baylis et al.) (New York: Holmes and Meier, 1975), is largely a historical account focusing on the adjustments caused by the devolution of empire. He focuses on the efforts to balance commitments and capabilities, conventional and nuclear forces, total and limited war, and service autonomy and centralization. David Greenwood and David Hazel have written a study—*The Evolution of Britain's Defence Priorities, 1957-76,* ASIDES no. 9 (Aberdeen: Centre for Defence Studies, University of Aberdeen, 1977)—that traces the major changes in Britain's defense effort since 1957 (with emphasis on the changing strategic perspectives) and analyzes the trends of military manpower and defense budgets. In *British Defense: Policy and Process,* ACIS Working Paper no. 13, (Los Angeles: Center for Arms Control and International Security, UCLA, 1978), Arthur Cyr analyzes the period from an American perspective, identifying the economic problems (of which the withdrawal from empire is a reflection) and the resulting adjustments in strategic doctrine and world role. Finally, in brief form, a most informative article by P. M. Kennedy in the *RUSI Journal* (December 1977), entitled "British Defense Policy Part II: An Historian's View," summarizes the political, social, and economic constraints and influences on British defense policy.

Doctrine, thought, and policy

David Greenwood's *Some Economic Constraints on Force Structure and Doctrine* (Aberdeen: Centre for Defence Studies, 1977) illustrates how fiscal constraints in the form of reduced budget allocations have indeed forced Britain to reevaluate its defense role and policy. Another monograph, also coming from the Centre for Defence Studies at Aberdeen, is entitled *The British Defence Effort: Foundations and Alternatives,* ASIDES, no. 11 (1978), by David Hazel and Phil Williams. It deals with the sequential relationship between defense doctrine and policy actions in an analytical framework of four parts: national security *aspiration* based upon societal values; the operational *goals* (or policies) required to fulfill these aspirations, elaborated into a body of strategic and tactical doctrines; the national defense *posture* that prescribes the roles and missions of the armed forces to implement policy; and, finally, the *provisions* in terms of money, materiel, and manpower to allow the fulfillment of roles and missions. Using this analytical framework, the study examines alternative defense provisions, postures, policies, and aspirations in a most informative manner. It ultimately challenges the traditional doctrinal assumptions requiring a "balance" between strategic and conventional forces, between maritime and continental ground forces, between the interservice missions and capabilities, and among the elements of the maritime forces. The study follows the pattern established by Washington, D.C.'s Brookings Institution (see its annual *Setting National Priorities*) by focusing upon alternative uses of military budget allocations.

In a more traditional analysis of British military and defense doctrine are several articles of use to the student of British defense policy. Ian Smart, in a lecture given at the Royal United Services Institute in May 1977 (see *RUSI Journal,* December 1977) identifies six "axes of uncertainty" affecting British defense policy and doctrine: whether to abandon an imperial role; whether to abandon a global role; the proper relation between defense and economic policy; the proper long-term role of defense as an instrument of policy; the nature of the threat to national security; and the balance between the larger Atlantic community and the narrower European community. Until Britain resolves these uncertainties, Smart argues, British policy will be unclear and imprecise.

Michael Carver, former chief of the United Kingdom Defence Staff, addresses three issues in an article on "Britain's Defense Effort," in *RUSI and Brassey's Defence Yearbook, 1977-78* (London: Westview Press, 1977): the pull between demands of warfare on the Continent and war at sea or abroad, the importance and role of NATO commitments, and the declining budget resources available to provide for defense needs. A useful article outlining the evolution of British strategic thought is by Neville Brown in *Comparative Defense Policy,* vol. 1 (Baltimore: Johns Hopkins University Press, 1974).

On strategic nuclear doctrine and policy are two studies, both by Ian Smart. The first, entitled "Beyond Polaris" and found in *International Affairs* (October 1977, pp. 557-71), examines two issues: should Britain continue as a nuclear power, and with what will Britain replace its aging Polaris strategic force? The second is an earlier study, *Future Conditional: The Prospects for Anglo-French Nuclear Cooperation,* Adelphi Papers, no. 78 (London: IISS, 1971), in which Smart explores the possibility of an Anglo-French force and concludes that political issues seem to preclude extensive cooperation. The strategic-nuclear issue is also addressed in already-cited works by Arthur Cyr and by Greenwood and Hazel.

Addressing the question of Britain's commitment to a strictly European force is Sherwood S. Cordier, *Britain and the Defense of Western Europe in the 1970s* (New York: Exposition Press, 1973). In a category by itself is David Greenwood's *The United Kingdom's Current Defence Programme and Budget,* ASIDES no. 10 (Aberdeen: Centre for Defence Studies, University of Aberdeen, 1978). Based upon the fiscal year 1978/79 defense portion of the national budget, Greenwood presents a systematic analysis of the budget to determine: (1) how government resources will actually be spent, (2) how military forces are assigned specific roles and missions, (3) what force structures and force levels will be maintained, and (4) what changes (if any) in policy, posture, or provision are implicit in the national budget. This study is a most useful analysis of policy through the "back door"—the bottom line of defense policy as it is funded; that is, what government actually plans to do rather than just what government officials say will be done.

Defense processes and institutions

Equally important to our understanding of British defense policies is knowledge about the defense decision-making processes and institutions. Indeed, both the "who" and the "how" have significant impact upon policy. Before identifying specific readings, however, the point must be made that all of the works assume a basic understanding of the British governmental processes in contrast to the American: the difference between the British parliamentary system, in which the power of the legislature and executive are "fused," and the American presidential system, in which the power of the legislature and executive are "separated."

While there are many works analyzing the British governmental decision-making process in general, there are few that focus on the defense decision-making process. This may be due to the fact that in a parliamentary system, the process by which defense decisions are made appears to be little different from that by which all policy decisions are made. Certainly there are few, if any, full-length studies on the subject (such as is found in Allison's *Essence of Decision* about U.S. decision making). Nevertheless, there are several articles and monographs available from which a reasonable understanding of the British defense decision-making process and institutions can be gleaned.

One of the best is Richard Neustadt's "London and Washington: Misperceptions between Allies," in *Alliance Politics* (New York: Columbia University Press, 1970). Although somewhat dated, it is nonetheless useful because it focuses on several key differences in the decision-making processes of the United States and Great Britain that are still typical of the two systems. The contrast between the processes provides a good understanding of the British system.

A more recent source is an article by John Baylis entitled "Defense Decision-making in Britain and the Determinants of Defense Policy," *RUSI Journal,* March 1975. In this piece he identifies several forces that affect the defense decision process and the policies themselves: personal characteristics of the decision makers, the machinery of decising making, the role of interest groups and public opinion, and economic and international determinants. As a quick reference to and an overview of defense decision making, it is an excellent source. Arthur Cyr, in the previously cited *British Defense: Policy and Process,* identifies some of the same factors as Baylis, but he does so in comparison with the U.S. process and perspective.

Of some use, but in a narrower area, is an article by G. H. Green ("British Policy for Defence Procurement," *RUSI Journal,* September 1976) that summarizes the procurement process and the factors influencing it. Of particular note is his focus on the role of the defense industry in British defense policy (a counterpart British "military-industrial complex"?); economic factors and the overseas markets; and the issue of transatlantic versus European cooperation in joint research, development, and production of weapons systems.

Not to be underrated are sources that address the defense budget and the budget process. Two works are most useful from this perspective. The first is a comparative study by Richard Burt entitled *Defense Budgeting: The British and American Cases,* Adelphi Papers, no. 112 (London: IISS, 1974–75), in which he reviews the American process and the characteristics unique to it, and then, using that as a basis of comparison, does the same for the British process. He addresses the institutional frameworks, the mechanics of the budgeting process, and, finally, the perspective of the bureaucracy and budgeting. For those students with a basic understanding of parliamentary and presidential systems, this piece will be of great benefit.

The second work is concerned with just the British budget process. *Budgeting for Defence* (London: RUSI, 1972), by David Greenwood is an analysis of the financial year 1972/73 budget concerned with the variety of budget decisions, with the processes by which the programs and budgets are decided, and with their outcomes. Far more than just an analysis, however, the study also discusses budget principles and planning, budget procedures, and budgetary changes over the past decade.

Civil-military relations

Although not a major concern of British defense policy itself, civil-military relations is an issue that can enhance understanding of the societal constraints on policy, particularly in a democracy. In "British Forces and Internal Security" (*Brassey's Annual,* 1973), C. N. Barclay reviews the role that British troops have played since the nineteenth century in maintaining internal order and security, noting that there is still a role for internal security today and in the future—particularly in Northern Ireland.

John C. M. Baynes, in "British Military Ideology" (*Comparative Defense Policy,* previously cited), studies the military officer in British society by examining the social strata from which officers are drawn, their political indoctrination, the military's role in British society, allies and enemies, and domestic politics. A third source is by Adam Roberts, London School of Economics, who addresses directly the issue of civil-military relations in "British Armed Forces and Politics," *Armed Forces and Society* (August 1977). He does so from the viewpoint of British military involvement in politics and in domestic disturbances.

Summary

This essay does not claim to be exhaustive, but it does present at least a cross-section of representative readings dealing with major, relevant aspects of British defense policy: an historical perspective from 1945; the important issues of ideology, doctrine, and policy; the defense decision-making process and institutions; and civil-military relations. If one were inclined to go even further in a study of British defense policy, most of the sources identified above also have bibliographic references that could be pursued. In this regard, David Greenwood's chapter in this volume also contains a list of additional sources that can be found by consulting the notes at the end of his chapter.

THE DEFENSE POLICY OF FRANCE

Alan Ned Sabrosky

Prologue: the linking of power to purpose

One basic proposition lies at the foundation of my appraisal of the defense policy of the French Fifth Republic. This is that the defense policy of any nation, great or small, must ultimately be judged in terms of its ability to link military power to political purpose. This means that a country's strategic doctrine and force posture must not only be logically consistent with one another in a purely military sense, but they must also be directed toward, and consonant with, the attainment of clearly identifiable and operationally defensible political goals. The fact that armed forces have both political and military utility, with the former being of greater importance over time than the latter, ought never to be forgotten by those charged with the formulation and implementation of defense policy.

France, for one, has not forgotten. The essential linkage between a nation's foreign and defense policies, while often less closely made than should properly be the case, is remarkably evident in the case of France under the aegis of the Fifth Republic. The conclusion that France's "defense policy has been seen [by Paris] as one of, if not the, most important instrument to achieve the objectives of French foreign policy"[1] is very much on the mark. That is, unlike some countries, France has never been so sanguine about the state of world politics that it has been willing to entrust the preservation of its interests to international good will or the skill of its diplomacy and to ignore what has been called "the ancient lesson of power in world politics."[2] The central role of military power in world politics, however, has not meant the subordination of broader national interests to the dictates of defense. Military power is properly seen in France as a means to an end, not an end in itself. As a consequence, changes in French ambitions and national goals have wrought changes in French strategy and have contributed to the subsequent restructuring of the forces needed to sustain and apply it. Precisely what has been wrought, and why, will be discussed in this chapter.

International environment

Nothing defines the parameters within which a nation can (or must!) act more than its relative power and attributed status in the international order. To a certain degree, the entire decade of the 1970s was seen in France to be an era of change, with the end of that decade being an historic "hinge" around which new balances of power and new relations of forces were being established.[3] One of the key elements therein, at least from the French perspective, was the passing of bipolarity and the movement toward some postbipolar distribution of power in the world. Few anywhere, least of all in France, believed that a true form of "multipolarity" or "polycentrism" had yet emerged. But it did suggest that nations other than the superpowers were acquiring a greater ability to exercise a greater degree of influence in world politics than had been the case before. That diffusion of power and influence, the French usually assumed, would eventually work to France's advantage.[4]

To say that the world was changing, and that power was becoming more diffuse, certainly did not mean that any single third nation could confront either of the superpowers on anything approaching equal terms, and the French defense community clearly harbored no such illusions. On the contrary, the essential bipolarity of world politics at the level of strategic nuclear weapons was highlighted more starkly than before by the apparent fluidity of international relations below that level. What was different, at least from the French point of view, were the changes taking place in the network of relationships that existed between the superpowers. Put bluntly, the power of the Soviet Union was seen to be in the ascendancy (difficulties within the so-called socialist camp notwithstanding), whereas that of the United States was seen to be declining relative to that of its principal rival. And while the possibility of collaboration between the superpowers on some issues could not be entirely discounted as an outgrowth of détente, their rivalry seemed sufficiently enduring to preclude a long-term superpower entente.[5]

After the two superpowers, power was seen in France to have diffused in a variety of ways. China might well become a Great Power in the next century, but—for the moment—it obviously remained a large, developing country beset by a number of internal and external challenges. Japan was an industrial giant with relatively little political-military influence and less ability to underwrite its own security, even though the possibility that it might feel compelled to acquire a more substantial military capability to secure its industrial lifeline could not be ignored. Europe was considered to be little more than an economic consortium, lacking a unified defense and foreign policy apparatus and dependent on the United States for its own security. The rest of the world, although possessing in some respects great influence (as in the case of the OPEC cartel), was generally handicapped by its own measure of political instability, military vulnerability, and economic need.[6]

The position of France in this international hierarchy is that of a global middle power with substantial regional influence. It is the world's third-ranking nuclear power *and* the third-ranking naval power, with a substantial conventional ground and air capability as well. France's economic capabilities are on a par with its military power, even though its standing in the balance of economic power behind both Japan and the Federal Republic of Germany (FRG) suggests that its relative military prominence may be due as much to Japanese and West German self-restraint as to French efforts. Still, France's aggregate standing as a nation that is at least tied for fourth place in the international order seems well assured.[7] Indeed, the fact that France is strong in both military and economic terms gives it, as Roger Morgan has noted, "a certain degree of freedom of action . . . that Britain does not possess and that West Germany cannot exploit to the same degree because of . . . its historical legacy."[8]

Despite these assets, it is undeniable that France alone is no longer a Great Power by any objective measure one might want to use, nor is it truly possible for France to become one again.[9] What is rather remarkable about France, however, is the extent to which it has tended to act as if it were still a major nation whose "voice is often heeded and strong because of its independence vis-à-vis the two superpowers."[10] And what is even more remarkable is the degree of success France has enjoyed as a result of its efforts. It is, in D. Bruce Marshall's words, an "interesting case" as the only middle power that plays an independent role outside of its own region.[11]

Precisely what this greater freedom of action and extraregional independence mean for France is more difficult to determine accurately. Power and preferences must be coordinated well if policy is to be effective and security is to be enhanced. That France is a global middle power (albeit with limitations) that desires to be first among equals *after* the two superpowers defines the limits of France's capabilities and ambitions. How they are put to use, and their implications for French defense policy, are shaped by the role France has assumed within the Western community and the threats to it that it perceives in the world at large.

Broadly speaking, there are three possible roles open to France within the Western community, each of which has different implications for French strategy, doctrine, and force posture. First, France could pursue an *independent* role in all essential respects, in either a global or a European context. Second, it could assume an *Atlanticist* posture, cooperating with other Western Europe nations and the United States as part of a general Western security community. Third, and finally, France could adopt a *European* stance, associating itself with one or more Western European nations, but in all cases without the participation (formal or informal) of the United States.[12]

While each of the above roles, if wholeheartedly embraced, would clarify France's defense options, Paris has found itself unable to make any definitive decisions that would provide it with both status and security at an acceptable cost. The notion of Western Europe as a center of power independent of the superpowers has largely fallen by the wayside in recent years. Without underestimating more general difficulties, France has simply been unwilling to accept either the unavoidable compromises to its own national sovereignty or the enhanced position of West Germany that such an association would inevitably entail. The idea of some more narrowly defined pact among the Western European middle powers, or at least between France and either Great Britain or West Germany, likewise has little chance of success. Neither Britain nor Germany is inclined to replace American protection with French assistance, and France will not countenance an American presence that would unavoidably subordinate the role of France herself in any such arrangement.[13]

It is this latter characteristic that makes the idea of formally rejoining the Atlantic Alliance's integrated military organization so unattractive to France. From the beginning of the Cold War onward, as Marianna P. Sullivan has observed, "the subordination of French defense policy to that of the United States when the latter's responsibilities expanded globally as those of France contracted was not easily tolerated by a nation that regarded itself as a historically great power."[14] Indeed, it was France's unwillingness to countenance that subordination, coupled with the presumed unreliability of the United States in the aftermath of Dien Bien Phu (1954) and Suez (1956), that fueled both an aversion to overt dependence on the United States and the adoption of an independent course of action in world politics in general.

That France has preferred an independent role rather than a more limited European or Atlanticist one does not necessarily mean that reality corresponds to that preference. On the contrary, the increasing precariousness of that "independence" is all too apparent to some French analysts, one of whom concluded acerbicly that "independence no longer exists in a world where interdependence and dependence are the rule."[15] This interpretation becomes even more pointed in the military sphere than in the realm of politics. It has been properly pointed out that "an autonomous defense would obviously be worthless if it could not be exercised under all circumstances, in all forms of conflict."[16] Yet few French people, even among the most ardent advocates of French independence in world politics, seriously believe that "France alone" can safeguard itself and its vital interests in all circumstances.

The result of these factors is a French approach to world politics that grudgingly acknowledges both France's ultimate dependence on the United States for its own security and the importance of cooperating with other Western European countries to enhance the security of Europe as a whole. Yet at the same time, France clings to an assertive independence whenever actual or perceived threats to French interests or slights to French ambitions are concerned. This French desire to have the game both ways—that is, to act independently where possible and to rely on others where necessary—actually inhibits France's efforts to define a realistic security policy. Instead, it promotes the "equivocation" noted by David S. Yost[17] that reflects an implicit attempt to rationalize an otherwise contradictory and seemingly inconsistent set of French foreign and defense policies and actions.

Nevertheless, it would be wrong, I believe, to dismiss French policies and ambitions as mere manifestations of an irrational and unreasonable quest for a lost grandeur. On the contrary, the French position is far from being quixotic. Both French policies and French ambitions have their roots in (*a*) a complementary set of foreign policy assumptions that define the parameters within which French defense policy is formulated and (*b*) France's own historical experience from World War II through the present.

There are actually two separate subsets of foreign policy assumptions of varying significance. First, there are the externally oriented policy assumptions that bipolarity is inherently unstable, that the growing power and predictability of Soviet behavior stand in stark contrast to the declining power and unpredictable behavior of the United States, and that Germany (or even the Federal Republic of Germany alone) is at best an unknown quantity as far as the long-term interests and ambitions of France are concerned. These assumptions, as I will discuss later in this section, both reflect and shape French perceptions of possible threats to France. Second, the internally oriented assumptions emphasize the significance of France's *mission civilisatrice* (or, more modestly, its unique role in the world), the overriding importance of preserving national sovereignty even when collaborating with other nations, and the fundamental role of military power—and especially an independent nuclear capability—as the principal guarantor of status and security in the modern world.[18]

Further, France's approach to defense and foreign affairs is strongly influenced by its own recent historical experience with allies and adversaries alike. It also reflects a conscious (and far from wholly successful) effort to overcome the legacy of defeat in World War II (1940), reinforced by the successive defeats in Indochina and Algeria, and lent additional weight by the Suez debacle in 1956. From the French perspective, in fact, history has taught the twofold lesson that allies can be as unreliable as adversaries are implacable, and that France must have an independent ability to safeguard its interests and security if it wants to avoid being little more than a pawn on the diplomatic chessboard.[19]

The first step toward applying that lesson to France's

foreign and defense policy was taken by General Charles de Gaulle. As president of France, de Gaulle exercised a significant influence on the course of French policy. His so-called grand design of independence, prestige, and Continental leadership eventually gained widespread acceptance in France. In many respects, it served to give the French people both a degree of unity and a renewed measure of self-esteem, which had been badly shaken in the preceding years. Nor was his policy without substance. De Gaulle's proposal for a "triumvirate" of Western powers and his later withdrawal from the integrated military structure of NATO, for example, had a common point of departure: that of "elevating France to the publicly recognized position of a great world power."[20] When a prominent Gaullist wrote in 1978 that "a great foreign policy cannot be constructed without the help of a conceptual key that permits one to decipher the nuances and the subtleties of international realities,"[21] he was both defining the purpose of Gaullism and alluding to its success.

What is even more noteworthy is not that a Gaullist foreign and defense policy could have been proposed in the aftermath of successive military defeats abroad and amidst political discontent within France itself; it is that the basic principles of Gaullist foreign and defense policy retain considerable appeal today, and—albeit in somewhat modified form—remain at the heart of the policies of the current non-Gaullist president. Today, as under de Gaulle and his successor, Georges Pompidou, France essentially asserts its claim to the same degree of diplomatic freedom of maneuver accepted by the United States and the USSR for themselves. The notion that France is both an autonomous power and a military power has been underscored in various forums and reiterated by numerous members of the government.[22] A Great Power must, by definition, have activist and interventionist foreign and defense policies. There is much truth to David Watt's observation that

> President Giscard [after the 1978 elections] branched out all over the place with independent initiatives that revived a positive form of Gaullism instead of the merely negative one practiced by himself and his predecessor in the immediate past. The French military expedition to rescue Europeans stranded in Zaire . . . and the hosting of the four-power Western summit in January 1979, all pointed to a reversion to an activist French diplomacy designed to re-establish France as a member of the Alliance directorate, as General de Gaulle himself frequently proposed.[23]

There is no indication today that France, even under the Socialists, is likely to alter either its assumed role as an independent power or its perception of itself as a nation that, as Jacques Chirac once put it, "has always defended something greater than her own comfort."[24] It would probably take an internal or external disaster of considerable magnitude to compel a reconsideration of France's fundamental policy assumptions and a subsequent reappraisal of its defense policy. Barring such an eventuality, France is likely to remain committed to the self-defined fourfold task of upholding peace, organizing Europe, cooperating with other nations on economic matters of common concern, and enhancing "the influence of France as an independent and generous country."[25] It goes without saying that France is equally likely to attempt to maintain the defense capability dictated by those objectives.

The pursuit of those objectives will be undertaken by France as an independent country, as that is interpreted from the French perspective. Still, France has certainly not isolated itself from other countries, and retains a surprising network of contacts in addition to those associated with the European community and the European Parliament proper. The most obvious of these associations is France's membership in the United Nations, and specifically France's participation in the United Nations peace-keeping force still in place in Lebanon. In part, the assignment of French contingents to that force is a function of the French belief that "an active peace-keeping role" is important if France is to remain a viable permanent member of the United Nations Security Council.[26] But it also reflects France's ability to act in certain ways, in certain parts of the world, that the other permanent members of the Security Council—and particularly the superpowers—could not do without attracting a potentially unacceptable degree of opposition.

The French relationship with NATO is more complex. In 1966, of course, France announced that it would withdraw the following year from the Alliance's integrated military organization, but not from the Atlantic Alliance as a whole—a distinction that would have seemed somewhat forced to NATO's founders, I suspect. Nevertheless, that decision ostensibly reflected France's agreement with the broad political objectives of NATO, but not with what Paris saw to be the infringement of national sovereignty implicit in the Alliance's common defense organization. This intriguing reading of what the very concept of collective defense entailed, however, had a less abstract foundation as well. That was France's general unwillingness to subordinate French policy to that of the United States (which Paris saw to be dominating the Alliance), coupled with growing concern about the reliability of the American commitment to its European allies. Neither French concern, it should be noted, has abated greatly to this day, although the intensity of the French apprehension seems to have declined to a certain extent.[27]

The net effect of this has been to place France in an ambivalent position with regard to NATO. The French, and particularly the Gaullists, find their dependence on U.S. protection to be particularly galling. Yet there remained an equally strong suspicion in most political circles that "NATO had not outlived its utility"—a suspicion that even found a surprising number of adherents on the French Left.[28] Thus, France is not represented on NATO's Defense Planning Committee, the Nuclear Defense Affairs Committee or its Nuclear Planning Group, or the Eurogroup, although French "observers" are sometimes present. France also declares that French forces will act only on orders from Paris in the event of another war on the Continent. At the same time, however, France collaborates with selected NATO countries (other than the United States) on an ad hoc basis for the development and production of various weapons systems and is a member of the Independent European Program Group (which, incidentally, includes ten members of the Eurogroup) for similar cooperative efforts on a larger scale. France also maintains observer and liaison staffs at NATO headquarters in Brussels, and units of the French armed forces have begun to take part in NATO maneuvers with increasing frequency.[29] Most important of all, at least from NATO's point of view, is the fact that "the 2nd French Corps [which is not integrated with NATO forces] is stationed in Germany under a status agreement reached between the French and German governments. *Cooperation with NATO forces and commands has been agreed between the commanders concerned*" (italics added).[30]

Finally, there is France's complex set of relationships with various African countries, principally those in the so-called French community. France's relationship to NATO probably attracts more attention outside of France, and is certainly more important in terms of French security. But in the Gaullist lexicon (and that of its non-Gaullist supporters), security and status are inextricably linked, and France's role in Africa is often seen to be a more significant indicator of French status than what France does in NATO-Europe.

In Africa, France is what may be termed a postcolonial power that has assumed a neocolonial role, albeit in a rather restrained sense. The French commitment to a number of African countries is based on a complicated blend of historical involvement, contemporary security, and economic interests, and the French need to act like a truly independent power. At present, France has defense agreements with seven African countries, including Senegal, the Ivory Coast, Gabon, and the Republic of Djibouti, and has military aid and technical assistance agreements with as many as eighteen African nations. Over 14,000 French military personnel are stationed in twenty African countries in both advisory and security roles. Moreover, as the French intervention in Zaïre illustrates, France has designated part of its own rapid deployment force for service in Africa should such contingencies arise there.[31] In sum, the French, as Chief of Staff General Guy Mery once stated, "have many friends in Africa who trust us and who expect a great deal from us,"[32] and France fully intends to meet their expectations as a matter of mutual self-interest. The fact that France can do so without producing great opposition from other African nations is a measure of its success in this regard.

The interesting notion that France remains out of formal military alliances that it cannot dominate (e.g., NATO) but engages in those that it can lead (e.g., with the still-developing African nations) does not necessarily mean that France is unable to define actual or potential threats to its own security.[33] At one level, for example, there is the obvious problem of the superpowers. France believes that some form of détente is extremely important, but only if it is global and reflects an acceptance of the status quo in Europe and elsewhere.[34] Independent of détente (or perhaps in conjunction with it), there is a recognition in Paris that Europe in general, and France in particular, "remains today extraordinarily dependent on American power and extraordinarily vulnerable to Soviet power."[35] Neither condition, it should be noted, is pleasing to France. The threat from the Soviet Union is not discounted, although it is generally understood to be more political than military in character. But the fact that all of Western Europe in its present political configuration simply cannot assure its own security against the Soviet Union without American assistance implies, at least in the view of some influential French analysts, the existence of an implicit form of American hegemony that is itself a political threat to the ambitions, if not the actual security, of a nation such as France.[36]

A second level of possible threat is more sensitive and less widely understood. This is reflected in the need, as former President Giscard remarked in 1974 and others in his administration have repeated afterward, to guard against "other [nonnuclear] powers that might threaten French soil."[37] What country could that mean? The answer, of course, is Germany—united or not. This concern both mirrors and contributes to the curious admixture of political confidence and military apprehension in the French attitude toward the Federal Republic of Germany noted several years ago by Marc Ullmann.[38] Indeed, the unusually close linkage that conventionally exists between France's foreign and defense policies makes the contradiction between them on the matter of French-German relations both more astonishing and more detrimental to the formulation and implementation of a realistic French defense policy.

It cannot be denied, to be sure, that the relationship between Giscard and FRG Chancellor Helmut Schmidt has been of great importance. It has certainly facilitated a greater degree of cooperation between France and the Federal Republic of Germany than some would once have considered to be possible.[39] This appears to have become particularly noteworthy as the state of Soviet-American relations has become more uncertain.[40] It is also interesting to note that the overt public attitude within France is somewhat more favorable than that which appears to exist in a more subdued form in official or "elite" circles in that country. A 1978 survey, for instance, found that 33 percent of those polled considered the FRG to be France's "best friend" (reflecting, however, a slight decline from earlier surveys).[41] But public opinion in any country is a notoriously poor guide to policy, and the relationship between the two countries forged by Giscard and Schmidt is more personal than it is national. There is simply no guarantee that either leader's successor will be able, or even inclined, to work out a similar accord, or that public opinion in France will continue to countenance such an endeavor. It seems that, in general, the French simply do not trust the Germans not to act like Germans (as the French interpret such behavior) over the long term, and thus pose a political—if not a military—danger to the interests and the ambitions of France. The strength of the *Bundeswehr* and the relative robustness of the West German economy do nothing to allay French concerns.[42]

Other than the superpowers and the Germans, French decision makers of most political persuasions perceive relatively little in the world that might pose a direct threat (as that is conventionally defined) to the security of France. Certainly, France's military position and continental status make it difficult for most nations to pose a military threat to that country. There are indirect threats, to be sure, posed by the internal vulnerability of France to domestic unrest (as in 1968) and by its external vulnerability to interruptions in the supply of key strategic raw materials, most notably oil (as evidenced by France's reaction to the 1973-74 Arab oil embargo). France's internal security apparatus is intended to deal with the former, while its relationships with the OPEC countries and—in case of extreme need—its intervention forces provide some measure of security against the latter. And while these potential threats cannot be ignored, the French defense establishment does not consider them to be central concerns today.

National objectives, national strategy, and military doctrine

The relationship that normally exists among goals, strategy, and doctrine is complex and subject to misinterpretation. In the case of France, however, that relationship has been remarkably consistent over time, once one understands the assumptions on which French foreign policy is based and their implication for French defense policy. To a considerable extent, in fact, France's foreign policy has defined the objectives and specified the principles governing the selection of an appropriate strategy. The latter, in its turn, has dictated both the appropriate means (or force structure) and the preferred employment doctrine for them.[43] Indeed, France has done better than many other countries in this respect, perhaps because, as Edward Kolodziej has suggested, "France's military doctrine went beyond narrow considerations of battlefield use of military force. . . . [It was intended] to strengthen France's internal and external position in competing with other states [and] . . . responded to changes in France's foreign and domestic environment."[44]

In accordance with the assumptions underlying French foreign policy and France's adoption of an independent role in world affairs, the French defense establishment has been tasked with four general operational missions. These are to (*a*) secure France at home and French interests abroad, (*b*) participate in the defense of Europe in the event of another continental war (e.g., in case of a Soviet attack) in conjunction with the other members of the Atlantic Alliance, (*c*) permit France to act as an independent power outside of Europe as a means of underwriting French prestige, and (*d*) join in international peacekeeping missions under the auspices of the United Nations as part of France's obligations as a permanent member of the U.N. Security Council.[45] These missions, it should be noted, reflect the concatenated input of considerations of security and status, of pragmatism and prestige.

FRENCH STRATEGY: A TALE IN TWO PARTS

France's national strategy and military doctrine are both guided by, and modified in accordance with, changes in the priority given to these missions. In the broadest sense, French defense policy as a whole during the Fifth Republic has tended to conform to the general principles laid down by General de Gaulle, occasional deviations therefrom notwithstanding. Those precepts entailed "freedom of decision with respect to the employment of its [France's] forces, cooperation with allies and recourse to nuclear weapons to defend its vital interests."[46] The fact that France's freedom of action, as suggested earlier, was sharply restricted by the realities of France's position in the world, that cooperation with allies occurred erratically because Paris insisted that it take place only on France's own terms, and that recourse to nuclear weapons would mean the certain destruction of France's tangible interests in defense of its intangible pretentions—all have found little acceptance in French strategic circles.

To say this does not mean that French defense planners, policy makers, and analysts have adhered rigidly to a single strategic doctrine. On the contrary, the French literature on this subject is remarkably open, candid, and sophisticated—more so, in certain respects, than that which obtains in some other countries.[47] More to the point, however, is the fact that in the years since de Gaulle first came to power, France has followed two broad national strategies. Each strategy was linked explicitly to the French nuclear force, yet had major implications for French defense policy and the French armed forces in a more general sense. The first was based on the idea of the *sanctuarisation totale* ("total sanctuary"); the second, and more recent, approach is that of the so-called *sanctuarisation élargie* ("enlarged sanctuary").

The initial operationalization of the *sanctuarisation totale* as a basis for strategic planning saw the appearance of a de facto "fortress France" mentality. That which was seen to be worth preserving was France itself, and secondarily French interests overseas, regardless of the fate that might befall those countries with which France was associated. Thus, only direct threats to the territorial integrity and sovereignty of France would have to be deterred, or fought if deterrence failed. In its initial incarnation, it included the notion of *la défense tous-azimuts* ("all-horizon defense"). This was a declaratory policy that denied the existence of any specific threat to France and insisted instead that France must be prepared to ward off an attack from any direction. This fascinating notion, however, rapidly gave way to a more explicit recognition of the threat posed by the Soviet Union, a recognition that crystallized in the aftermath of the Soviet invasion of Czechoslovakia in 1968.[48]

This change in threat perception, on the other hand, did alter either the priorities assigned to the French armed forces or the basic doctrine for their employment. In both cases, pride of place was given to the *Force Nucléaire Stratégique* [FNS] ("strategic nuclear force"), first called the *force de frappe* ("strike force") and later renamed the *force de dissuasion* to emphasize its deterrent function. The primary objective of the FNS was obviously to deter attacks against France itself. If that deterrence failed, the French—in accordance with the accepted precepts of their own somewhat limited version of the doctrine of massive retaliation—would attack the aggressor's population and industrial centers with all the military resources at their disposal. Second to the FNS were the *Forces d'Intervention* ("intervention forces"), renamed the *Force de Manoeuvre* ("field force") in 1964. These included both a five-division regular army, with supporting air and naval general purpose forces, and a light airborne/air-transportable force. The former was deployed in France and in the southwestern part of the Federal Republic of Germany, whereas the latter—although largely based in France—was organized for use in Africa and other parts of the Third World where France had interests and allies (or clients) to be safeguarded. Third and last were the forces of the *Défense Operationnelle du Territoire* [DOT] ("territorial defense"). This would include approximately 100 regiments, plus supporting units, intended for internal security as well as a source of replacements for the regular forces during wartime.[49]

The origins of this rather ambitious and explicitly self-centered strategy are as obvious as its flaws. To a considerable extent, the concept of a *sanctuarisation totale*—and especially the extraordinary notion of *la défense tous-azimuts*—reflected de Gaulle's personal irritation with the United States and Great Britain for their refusal to countenance France's proposal for a Western "triumvirate" more than it did a rational strategic appraisal of France's capabilities and options.[50] In a certain sense, de Gaulle essentially decided to take France out of a political-military game in which the other players would not acknowledge it as an equal whose basic opinions were worth considering, and defined French strategy accordingly. Militarily, the likelihood that France could be a "sanctuary alone" in the event of an East-West war is actually as improbable an idea as that of "France alone" in a world of competing superpowers—a notion that even the Gaullists dismissed in all but the most limited sense of the term.[51] The fact that a France that truly saw any other power as a potential threat was also a France no other nation could truly trust could have but one meaning. This was that the strategic consequences of the attempt to implement a strategy of *sanctuarisation totale* were a prescription not for independence and security but for isolation and an unprecedented degree of insecurity and vulnerability should war occur—or even threaten—between the opposing superpowers and their allies.[52]

On the other hand, the concepts of *sanctuarisation totale* and *la défense tous-azimuts* (to focus on the more extreme doctrine) did have certain advantages. To be sure, these do not seem compelling in an absolute sense, but they nonetheless had attractions for a power such as France. Politically, they did emphasize French independence in world politics and a degree of nonalignment in the essential East-West power game.[53] That neither that independence nor that nonalignment may have been wholly attainable or realistic does not necessarily diminish their symbolic value to Gaullist France. Militarily, it would have been extremely difficult for France to have upgraded all of its armed forces at the same time in the 1960s, especially when one considers the political and economic liabilities of the Algerian war still being borne by France. Thus, given the prevailing French belief that another nonnuclear war on the Continent was extremely unlikely to occur, it made good strategic sense for France to concentrate on an independent nuclear force with its attendant political appeal. Finally, the associated doctrine of massive retaliation was not without its adherents in the United States and elsewhere, especially when one is dealing with a relatively limited strategic nuclear capability. This is particularly applicable in the Western European context, moreover, where it has been remarked that "the firebreak between TNWs [theater nuclear forces] and national strategic forces is not so clear-cut as it is for Americans."[54] That is, when it is all too likely that the battlefield will be one's own national territory either at the beginning of a war or shortly thereafter, a European alternative to massive retaliation is much more difficult to formulate persuasively than is the case with the United States.[55]

Nevertheless, the advent of the 1970s saw a number of developments that forced a reconsideration of French strategic thinking.[56] Soviet-American relations seemed to be improving in the early days of détente, and the French generally recognized that a continuation of that process would quickly erode whatever political and military leverage an independent, "fortress France" strategy might give Paris in the game of nations. That this détente coincided with a continuing Soviet military build-up in Europe was no less disturbing to French defense planners, who tended as a matter of principle to take a more cautious view of the emerging era of superpower amicability than was the case with many Americans. Further, the economic and technological costs of France's independent approach to matters of defense had been high, and—while unlikely to become absolutely prohibitive in the near term—were certain to increase in the future. There was also a growing sense of the limitations associated with an independent nuclear force maintained and enlarged at the expense of other arms. There was an inevitable complementarity between nuclear and conventional forces, as Defense Minister Yvon Bourges later acknowledged, and to link the defense of France solely to the strategic nuclear force was unsound in both a political and a military sense. Even the doctrine of massive retailiation was attacked (albeit indirectly) as a reflection of "a policy of all or nothing" that "in reality . . . would be scarcely credible" in the evolving strategic balance of power.[57]

Having found itself in a dilemma similar to that of the United States in the mid- to late 1950s, although for somewhat different reasons, France undertook a comparable redefinition of its defense policy and military establishment. At the strategic and doctrinal level, two principal changes occurred. First, the idea of France as a total sanctuary was discarded and replaced by the concept of the *sanctuarisation élargie* ("enlarged sanctuary" or "enlarged security area"). This meant that French forces would now be expected to engage an opponent in areas approaching France—the classic *bataille de l'avant* ("forward battle")—in place of the earlier "fortress France" notion implicit in the concept of the *sanctuarisation totale*. Second, the nuclear-heavy doctrine of massive retaliation joined the strategy of the *sanctuarisation totale* in the dustbin of French defense policy. In its place was a doctrine of flexible response, remarkably similar to that of NATO, which envisioned a graduated mix of strategic nuclear forces, tactical nuclear forces, and conventional forces capable of matching different types of threats in different conflict situations.[58]

The political and military implications of this dual shift in French defense thinking have been considerable. The strategy of *sanctuarisation élargie,* in the words of one astute observer, "means no more and no less than closer cooperation with [France's NATO] allies."[59] It certainly implied France's willingness (or acceptance of the unavoidable need) to participate in a NATO battle against the Warsaw Pact, whether or not France was formally a part of that alliance's integrated military organization, even if France itself was not under attack or in imminent danger of being attacked by the forces of the Warsaw Pact. This point was not lost on the Gaullists and their sympathizers, for whom "the new strategic concepts tended to place battlefield confrontation above deterrence and were thought to sacrifice the autonomy of French military policy in the name of European solidarity within the [NATO] alliance."[60]

The impact of this change in strategy on the French military establishment was equally profound and was first reflected in the *loi de programmation, 1977–82*. This program outlined four French defense objectives in accordance with the new strategy and doctrine: (*a*) to maintain France's nuclear capability at the level required for it to remain credible, (*b*) to provide France with a balanced mix of nuclear and classical (conventional) forces, (*c*) to increase the level of operations, and (*d*) to devote more resources to the well-being of those military personnel required for the more extensive strategy to be operationalized.[61]

The new program obviously meant that the strategic nuclear force would not only be retained but also would be revitalized in keeping with the French notion of dissuasion through nuclear sufficiency.[62] The overseas intervention capability would be retained in fact, if not in name, with its principal components (the Eleventh Parachute and Ninth Marine divisions) keeping their original missions.[63] But the major change necessitated by the doctrine of "flexible response" supporting the strategy of the *sanctuarisation élargie* was a significant augmentation in the conventional forces assigned to a Continental role, with the army and the navy being the principal beneficiaries. Indeed, two of the principal goals of the new program seem to have been to upgrade the entire army to the qualitative level of the intervention forces and to enhance the ability of the navy to do more than protect France's ballistic missile submarine (SNLE) Force.[64] The resulting force, it was believed, would give France the more balanced military capability it required in the evolving world order.

Balanced or not, one thread of continuity runs through French strategic and doctrinal thinking since the first French atomic test in 1960—the presumably enduring importance of nuclear weapons in French security planning.[65] Indeed, to speak of French defense policy at any point over the past two decades is to speak of the *force de dissuasion,* a situation that is most unlikely to change appreciably in coming years. This is largely because of the intense French belief that only nuclear weapons can underwrite French security and insure that other countries will "give it [France] its rank in the concert of nations."[66] Some, of course, may consider that French self-assessment to be overdrawn. But it cannot be denied that France's strategic nuclear force at least gives it the option (to return to David Yost's formulation) of equivocating forcefully!

The operational rationale underlying the French strategic nuclear force throughout its existence has been the principle of proportional deterrence.[67] This is in many respects a "poor man's principle" of deterrence, which is commonly associated with the nuclear forces—present or projected—of middle powers. It reflects a belief in the presumed rationality of a potential aggressor, such that the latter would be deterred by the threat of nuclear retaliation capable of inflicting damage certain to exceed whatever gains conquest might produce. There is neither a claim to possessing strategic parity with respect to the probable threat force nor even an attempt to approach such a capability with respect to the superpowers. There is simply an acceptance of the attainability of a degree of strategic sufficiency that, as Pierre Gallois put it in the specific case of France, entails only "being capable of instilling in a would-be aggressor the fear of reprisal great enough to make the stake represented by France, a relatively modest stake, a prize that cannot be coveted with impunity."[68]

More important than the theory of deterrence on which the French strategic nuclear force is based, however, is the question of its actual employment. That is, when, and under what circumstances, would it be unleashed against the putative aggressor? One such case would obviously be a direct attack against France alone. In this case, the French strategic nuclear force would punish the aggressor for its presumptuousness. A more likely contingency, however, would be in the event of an attack (almost certainly from the Warsaw Pact) that subjected France and NATO Europe to a similar threat. Although the French have always asserted that the primary function of their strategic nuclear force is to safeguard France, they have also tended to argue that the existence of the French nuclear force also serves the interests of NATO Europe by increasing the risk of escalation that an aggressor would have to consider in addition to the U.S. response.[69] When only France is threatened, Paris would clearly be the sole judge of the necessity for using the strategic nuclear force. Even in the case of a threat to both France and NATO Europe, however, the French strategic nuclear force would be launched when the *French* leadership believed the attacker had crossed the so-called critical threshold of aggressiveness. This is the point at which France would believe it had no other choices left except battlefield defeat or unconditional surrender. Moreover, the French decision would be made independent of the United States and its allies, *regardless of whether or not NATO itself concurred in the French decision.*[70] France, in short, claims the right to act for other countries that it denies to them with respect to France itself.

There is admittedly some sound basis for the French position as outlined above. The Russians obviously cannot be certain that France would not act in accordance with its declaratory policy and use its *force de dissuasion* as a *force de frappe* if deterrence failed, even if the United States and the other NATO countries argued for restraint or even for surrender. This in itself may add to Soviet uncertainty and, thus, truly enhance the general deterrent posture of NATO as a whole. The fact that France, unlike the United States and Great Britain, shares to a certain extent the Soviet predisposition to emphasize both the deterrent and the war-fighting roles of nuclear weapons[71] cannot have escaped the attention of the Soviet leadership or be reassuring to it.

Here, as elsewhere, however, there is another side to the coin. It is distinctly possible that Soviet uncertainty with respect to France's probable reaction may induce Moscow to strike the relatively vulnerable French nuclear forces at the beginning of a general offensive, or even in the midst of a particularly intense crisis in East-West relations. This would have the effect of pulling most, if not all, of France's nuclear "teeth," possibly inflicting substantial losses on France's population and industrial base (depending on the scope of the Soviet attack), and making a mockery of French "independence" and the *force de dissuasion.* In such an eventuality, the French strategic nuclear force would have been a magnet precipitating an attack that might otherwise not have occurred—the precise opposite of what it was intended to accomplish.

Further, the French concept of flexible response is, in practice, not all that flexible, even as the French rationalize it.[72] In fact, as Edward Kolodziej has bluntly pointed out, it rests "on a sharply constricted model of a graduated response strategy . . . [with] few escalatory rungs."[73] Yet even that limited degree of flexibility may be excessive, at least as far as the

French strategic nuclear force is concerned. For the credibility of the very concept of proportional deterrence (especially for one with France's capabilities) is linked inextricably to what Graeme Auton has described as "its automaticity, that is, its affinity to the American massive retaliation doctrine of the Eisenhower years."[74] Ironically, it seems that the French attempt to bring their nuclear doctrine more into accord with the realities of contemporary world politics may actually have weakened its deterrent power instead of enhancing it. That is, France appears to have rejected a doctrine whose implementation "would involve suicide"[75] and to have replaced it with a doctrine whose existence invites murder.

THE STRATEGIC NUCLEAR FORCE RECONSIDERED

The flaws and inconsistencies (obvious and otherwise) in French nuclear doctrine in particular necessarily invite questions concerning the validity of the rationale underlying the French fixation with a national nuclear force. And on reflection, it appears that Wolf Mendl was correct when he wrote that "one suspects that there is a far more pragmatic basis to French [strategic] policy than its theoreticians would have us believe."[76]

That basis, I am convinced, lies in the dual character of France's strategic nuclear force. Every military instrument of national policy has both political and military functions, as I indicated in the prologue, and the French strategic nuclear force is no exception.[77] Unfortunately, there has been a tendency in most discussions to place undue emphasis on the military role of the *force de dissuasion*. One should not forget that there is also a political dimension that I suspect, is a far more useful guide to understanding France's affinity for its less than overwhelming and awe-inspiring nuclear arsenal.[78]

There is, in the first place, the fact that the possession of an independently controlled national nuclear force is widely seen in France (and in many other countries as well) to be synonymous with that country's prestige, status, and autonomy in the world. Unless the French come to believe that such considerations are irrelevant or anachronistic, it is virtually certain that France would retain the *force de dissuasion* even if no actual or potential military threat to France existed or could be envisioned by the most pessimistic French defense planners. The retention of that independent French nuclear capability would be dictated by France's domestic and international political concerns, the overriding importance of which must not be underestimated.

Second in importance to status in French eyes is the diplomatic leverage seen to be implicit in the very existence of a national nuclear force. It is generally conceded that even de Gaulle recognized that the diplomatic value of a French strategic nuclear force probably exceeded its military utility, and his successors do not seem to have forgotten that lesson.[79] As Pierre Dabezies has remarked, France's "nuclear force gives her some freedom of action and . . . ensures that she cannot be ignored."[80] It must be conceded that there is at least some truth to the wry comment of one French writer to the effect that the fact that France is the only European country to have "land-based missiles capable of reaching Soviet territory" has not resulted in France's being "handicapped in her relations with the Soviet Union."[81] In fact, a fair assessment of French-Soviet relations would probably conclude that the opposite situation actually obtained.

The third political aspect of the *force de dissuasion* is related closely to the questions of European security and France's self-proclaimed belief in its rightful place at the head of Europe, that is, as the only Continental power to possess an independent nuclear force (excluding the extra-Continental British force, which is linked to that of the United States). The evolution of any European political union could easily mean that "France would constitute the nucleus of an . . . independent system of common security."[82] That such a development would enhance French status and increase the likelihood that France would dominate such a polity is usually left unspoken, but it is difficult to believe that the French (or any other Europeans!) are ignorant of the implications of their own doctrine in this matter.

To give precedence to the political rationale for the French strategic nuclear force, of course, does not mean that the *force de dissuasion* lacks a military rationale for its existence. On the contrary, many French analysts now assert that France's strategic nuclear force has a twofold military role to play. One is to give France the option of *acting* like a power in the world, exerting influence and employing conventional forces in ways and places that might otherwise not be possible. The second reason, which usually receives greater attention, is to deter the Soviet Union from attacking or threatening the national territory and sovereignty of France itself.

There is some objective basis for the first military rationale, at least if France is dealing with (*a*) nations that do not possess nuclear weapons of their own, and (*b*) issues that do not call into play the interests and the strategic nuclear forces of the superpowers themselves. Had the French possessed their own atomic weapons in 1954, for example, they could conceivably have used them in a final effort to save their besieged garrison at Dien Bien Phu, precisely as they hoped the United States would do for them in the stillborn "Operation Vulture."[83] It is equally likely that, in 1956, a nuclear-armed France would have resisted outside pressure from both the Soviet Union and its then-recalcitrant American "allies" to withdraw from Suez. This resistance could have taken the form of giving Moscow the option of exchanging

Russian cities for French ones, and precipitating a Third World War, in defense of Cairo and the Egyptian army. Put simply, both of these examples are illustrative of a cardinal French principle regarding nuclear weapons and foreign policy. This rule is that a state that lacks nuclear weapons can be told to cease and desist if it should act solely in defense of its own interests outside of its national territory. A state with its own nuclear arsenal, however, would rarely be asked to do so and cannot be compelled to refrain or withdraw in most instances at an acceptable cost to the third party. That France may misapprehend the situation does not alter the impact of this point of view on French defense policy in general, and on France's national nuclear force in particular.

Despite the perceived utility of the *force de dissuasion* as a facilitator of French military intervention abroad under certain circumstances, its more important declared military role involves the application of the aforementioned concept of proportional deterrence to France's military relationship with the Soviet Union. Many considerations affect this role's definition and prospects for success. In the final analysis, however, the key issue is whether the French nuclear contribution would matter if the Soviet Union had decided to throw its own military forces against Western Europe.

The answer to this question, in my opinion, is clearly *no*. Any Soviet decision to invade Western Europe would necessarily have taken account of the possibility that the conflict ultimately could result in a strategic nuclear exchange between the superpowers—the classic "central sanctuary" war. The Soviet leadership would also have to have concluded that the political-military objectives to be secured, and the potential gains to be realized, were worth both the risk of such an exchange and the losses they would incur if it took place. Otherwise, the Soviet attack would almost certainly not occur as a matter of deliberate policy. It should be readily apparent that a Soviet leadership that would not be deterred by the strategic nuclear retaliatory capability of the United States is highly unlikely to be deterred by the relatively marginal damage that might be inflicted by France's handful of manned bombers, IRBMs and SLBMs, even if they survived to strike a blow. The probability that they would not survive to do so, as I have suggested earlier, in the context of a general European war, is extremely high.

There is also little reason to suppose that an independent national nuclear force under French control would be able to accomplish the lesser (in European terms) objective of inducing the Soviets to refrain from attacking France itself, regardless of the fate of the remainder of Western Europe. It would require an extraordinary degree of self-restraint for the French leadership to observe Soviet columns cutting their way through NATO forces and rapidly approaching French territory and still to withhold their nuclear weapons in the hope that the USSR would not violate France's territorial integrity. It would require even greater self-restraint for the Soviet forces to make such an approach and continue to refrain from striking the French nuclear installations on the assumption that the French would resist the temptation to launch the *force de dissuasion* against Soviet targets. Such mutual self-restraint, it should be obvious, is all too unlikely, given the parameters of a European war. Yet even if that mutual self-restraint did obtain, the net effect would be to leave France "Finlandized"—devoid of its former partners, dependent on the USSR in all key respects, and utterly bereft of the status and prestige to which it now clings so adamantly. France, in short, might survive as a nominally independent state, but it would also be a political pauper.

The dubious military utility of the French strategic nuclear force with respect to the Soviet Union invites other questions concerning its possible military role in other threatening situations that do not involve the USSR, either in Europe or as an indirect threat to French interests abroad. And here, as was discussed in the first section of this chapter, the only other potential threat of any significance that France perceives is that posed by Germany. Indeed, it appears that while France still tends to discount the imminence of a Soviet military threat to France, it recognizes both the political and the military value of a nuclear counterweight to German conventional and military power.[84] The mere fact that the *Bundeswehr*'s conventional capabilities exceeded those of France was even used as a basis for arguing that France had to augment its own conventional forces to preclude a European defense based only on German conventional and French nuclear forces.[85] One rarely considers a strong ally to be of such concern. The reality that the primary political-military function of the French strategic nuclear force is to give France a measure of secure leverage over the Germans is something that analysts of French defense policy cannot ignore, no matter how sensitive the point might be. It is certainly unlikely that either the Germans or the Soviets are ignorant of it.

CONSTRAINTS ON FRENCH STRATEGIC CHOICE

The influence of perceived threats and preferred roles on French strategic choice is apparent from the preceding discussion. Yet it should be equally apparent that other factors within France itself have also been significant in the past and are likely to have a major impact on the retention or possible redefinition of French strategy and doctrine in the future. Five such factors seem particularly noteworthy: (*a*) France's geographical position, (*b*) the state of the French economic and technological base, (*c*) French public opinion, (*d*) the declared policies of the principal political parties in France, and (*e*) the political stability of France as a nation.

The most obvious constraint on French ambitions and strategies is that which is not readily amenable to change. This is the geographical location of France. In general, as Pierre Gallois has remarked, "France has [a] specific role to play [in the nuclear age] which is defined by her continental position and the limited resources at her disposal to defend the security of that position."[86] France's Continental position places demands on French defense planners aggravated by its relative vulnerability but moderated by the presence of the FRG (and NATO forces, including the U.S. Seventh Army, stationed on German territory) as a buffer between France and the most likely source of a military threat to France. Granted, the respite (in both spatial and temporal terms) such a buffer zone offers France is much more limited today than would have been the case even twenty years ago. But the fact that some respite is possible allows French planners to formulate a strategy, articulate a doctrine, and prioritize their forces in a way that would simply not be feasible if France were located in the same situation as, for example, the Federal Republic of Germany.

In today's security environment, of course, both the possession of and the direct access to key strategic raw materials are of at least as much importance as a nation's geographical position, and probably are more important. The fact that France lacks sufficient quantities of at least one key strategic resource—oil—and has no direct geographical access to contiguous sources of oil means that France is a Continental power that must act as both a "Continental" and a "maritime" power (as both terms are generally understood today) to secure both its position and its resources. The former dictates some general war capacity for deterrence and, if deterrence fails, defense. The latter necessitates the possession of substantial power projection capabilities to give France the potential to undertake offensive operations overseas with reasonable prospects of success. Both are difficult for a middle power such as France to achieve.

This consideration is underscored by France's economic and technological situation. The French economy is by no means insubstantial, nor is its economic system notably inefficient, except, perhaps, in comparison with those of Western Europe's economic giant, the FRG. Nor is French technology grossly antiquarian. Of the Western European countries, only France has been able to field a competitive air superiority plane, and in other areas (such as nuclear power technology) France has also done remarkably well. But in some respects, such as nuclear weapons technology, France lags behind even the United Kingdom (to say nothing of the superpowers). Indeed, the far more demanding problem of overcoming existing technological shortcomings and forestalling an impending technology gap of considerable dimensions relative to the most advanced industrial states weighs heavily on French planners.[87] There is much validity in the conclusion reached by one French strategist to the effect that France has the financial and technological capacity for both nuclear deterrence and internal security (within the limitations outlined above) but lacks a similar capacity to conduct independent conventional operations anywhere without at least some external assistance.[88] The fact that France's self-proclaimed independence both requires it to have the capacity it lacks and contributes to the existence of that inadequacy is illustrative of the dilemma confronting the French defense community today.

To a certain extent, the existence of that dilemma is made more bearable (if not more amenable to resolution) by the degree of political support that obtains in France for its current role in world politics, and particularly for the maintenance of an independent national nuclear force. This is immediately apparent when one considers the state of French public opinion on these issues. As table 1 indicates, there is more popular support for French participation in some

Table 1
Public support for alternative security roles for France, 1979

Security alternatives	Preference, by Party				
	Communists	Socialists	Giscardists	Gaullists	All
Western Alliance	23%	51%	64%	62%	47%
Europe only	(15)	(34)	(35)	(28)	(28)
Europe and United States	(8)	(17)	(29)	(34)	(19)
Alliance with USSR	7	1	—	1	2
Independence/neutral	47	32	18	24	30
No opinion	23	16	18	13	21

Source: Jerome Jaffre, "France Looks to Europe," *Public Opinion* (March/May 1979), p. 17.
Note: Findings reflect responses, in a French national poll conducted 18–24 January 1979, by Louis Harris, to the question "which solution seems to you best for France?"

form of a Western security community than there is for an independent security position. When one disaggregates the data to ascertain support for the three alternative roles France considers pursuing, however, a somewhat different picture emerges. Then it appears that a slight plurality of 30 percent support an independent role, followed by 28 percent in favor of the European option and—a distant third—19 percent in favor of the Atlanticist course of action. The apparent support for the European alternative is modified by the fact that a two-to-one majority do not want a European security community to evolve as part of the European community.[89] That is, for many Frenchmen there is a difference between security in collaboration with other independent European countries on the one hand and security as part of an integrated Western European polity at the sacrifice of some measure of French autonomy on the other. The former is clearly preferred and would seem to suggest some additional support for an independent role.

What has been described as the French electorate's current (and apparently enduring) predisposition to "remain jealous of their national autonomy"[90] is paralleled by the impressive reservoir of popular support for the French national strategic nuclear force. This support, it is worth noting, was not always present. During the 1960s, in fact, there was much public opposition to the *force de dissuasion*. By the early 1970s, however, public opinion had shifted sharply in favor of the *force de dissuasion*, to the point where today support for it constitutes one of the two "stable poles" in French views on defense-related issues. Certainly, the three-to-one majority believing that the *force de dissuasion* is essential to the defense of France reflects a commanding position that is unlikely to erode rapidly in the 1980s.[91]

As in most political democracies, public opinion in France "sets general constraints"[92] on the formulation and implementation of its defense policy, although—as in the early years of the *force de dissuasion*—those constraints are obviously not necessarily binding. But unlike some countries, in France, the views of the principal political parties accord with those of the electorate, once one controls for party identification as in table 1. In terms of partisan public opinion, the differences between self-identified Gaullists and Giscardists are slight, with the Gaullists being somewhat more predisposed than the Giscardists to either an independent or (ironically) an Atlanticist role for France. Further, the Socialists appear to be somewhat closer to the Gaullists and the Giscardists on this issue than to their erstwhile Communist allies. This is especially true with respect to the desirability of a Western security community in general and a European role in particular. Interestingly enough, not even Communist voters seem overly enthusiastic (at least openly) about a military alliance with the Soviet Union, preferring instead an independent stance.[93]

To a surprising degree, the policy positions taken by the leadership of the principal parties coincides with those preferred by their respective electorates, a phenomenon that is admittedly more common in Europe than it is in the United States. The position of the formally dominant Center-Right coalition, based on Giscard's own *Union pour la Démocratie Française* and the Gaullists, was strengthened by its better-than-expected showing in the 1978 elections, where it won a majority of ninety seats in the National Assembly. Until May 1981, this governing majority remained reasonably solid. The policies of the Giscardist-Gaullist coalition's leadership need no elaboration here, since they were both official policies of the French government and parallel the views of their respective supporters, as indicated in table 1. It should nevertheless be noted that the Gaullists retained considerable influence on those areas where the positions of the two factions diverged somewhat. The Gaullist fixation with French independence, for example, led to a situation after the 1978 elections in which (in the words of one observer of the French political scene) the "Gaullists not only forced Giscard to concede that France would veto any extra powers of the [European] Parliament [that might infringe on French autonomy], but actually threw out, in December [1978], the bill financing European elections in France."[94]

The position of the Left in France is far more complex. For a time before the 1978 elections, it seemed that a united coalition of the Socialist (PS) and Communist (PCF) parties would gain a majority in the National Assembly and, thus, be in a position to put François Mitterand, the PS leader, into the presidency eventually. The two parties even went so far as to bury their differences (rather than one another!) and define a "common program" on a wide range of policy questions. But contradictions in the "common program" (many of which were in the realm of defense and foreign policy), plus the PCF's unwillingness to take second place to the Socialists in the final round of the 1978 elections, precipitated the Left's electoral defeat and presaged the break-up of the PS-PCF coalition.[95]

This political divorce essentially brought the Socialist and the Communist parties back to their original—and rather different—views on French defense policy. Both parties have endorsed France's withdrawal from the integrated military organization of the Atlantic Alliance (i.e., NATO), but beyond that point of agreement, there is little consensus.[96] Broadly speaking, the Socialist leadership wants France to remain within the Atlantic Alliance as a whole, albeit while seeking to exercise a European option as an alternative. The Socialists essentially consider "independence," at least as the Gaullists or even the Giscardists define it, to be a chimera in the modern world, although some of the younger members of the PS do advocate a strongly independent role for France "as a way out of the need to make a choice between Washington and Moscow."[97] The PS is also grudgingly willing to retain the *force de dissuasion,* although Socialist leaders at different times in the past have argued for a national referendum on the French nuclear force and the inclusion of part of that force in some general arms control agreements.

The basic position of the French Communist party is markedly different on each of these points, despite some changes in recent years—most notably with respect to the *force de dissuasion,* which is now endorsed by the PCF's leadership, at least in the absence of a general program of nuclear disarmament. The PCF also supports the now-defunct notion of *la défense de tous-azimuts,* something that the conventionally pro-Soviet position of the PCF within the international Communist movement makes it difficult for others to accept truly as an accurate reflection of the PCF's orientation. Moreover, the Communists—unlike the Socialists—want France to leave the Atlantic Alliance as well as its integrated military organization. Indeed, the PCF is nominally so supportive of an uncompromisingly independent role for France that its position has been described wryly by Pierre Hassner as "Gaullocommunism" rather than "Eurocommunism."[98] And, in general, there remains much accuracy in Neil McInnes's earlier argument that the "PCF... is anti-German, anti-American, hypernationalist and violently opposed to the least abridgement of French sovereignty.... [PCF] influence in Paris could not fail to be a serious embarrassment not only to Western defense and European unification but to the simplest forms of international cooperation. Marchais [the PCF leader] is the poor Frenchman's de Gaulle."[99]

The fragmentation of the PS-PCF coalition and the intensity of the animosity that exists between both leftist parties and the Giscardist-Gaullist coalition underscore a more fundamental political concern in France. Political stability and societal cohesion are essential for the effective formulation and implementation of any defense policy. Yet it is precisely those conditions whose existence is most problematical in the case of France. More than in many other Western societies, class and party divisions in France are particularly strong. Even where there is something approaching a national consensus (e.g., on the role of France vis-à-vis the United States), the consensus tends to break down on the more basic question of which party should guide France—that is, who should rule. It has been suggested that the events of 1968 dramatized "the vulnerability of France's political system to disorder."[100] Regrettably, little seems to have changed since that time to modify that judgment. This may be indicative of a potential long-term political fragility seemingly belied at this time by France's power and presidential assertiveness.

THE FUTURE OF FRENCH STRATEGY

The last-mentioned reservation notwithstanding, continuity rather than change seems likely with respect to France's current strategy and doctrine.[101] France's leadership, in short, is likely to continue reasserting French independence in world politics and the paramount importance of a national nuclear force as the ultimate guarantee not only of independence but also of sovereignty itself.[102] It is equally likely that France will continue to espouse some form of a doctrine of flexible response. This is largely because it is now possible (perhaps necessary) for France to think in terms other than those associated with "massive retaliation."[103] But it is also partly because doing so permits France to cooperate more extensively with its formal Atlantic Alliance partners than has been the case in recent years without overtly forgoing its nominal independence. Even the recent decision to augment French general-purpose forces as part of the shift to the strategy of the *sanctuarisation élargie* meshes well with the original concept of the *force de frappe* ("strike force") advanced in the mid-1950s by General Paul Ely. General Ely saw that as "a broad military concept which would include both nuclear and conventional forces,"[104] rather than nuclear forces alone. France clearly seems to be moving in that direction, as evidenced both by the promulgation of the strategy of the *sanctuarisation élargie* and by the terms of the *loi de programmation, 1977–82.*

On the other hand, there are some ongoing difficulties with the above that may have a significant impact on French strategy in the 1980s, even if France's domestic divisions do not become acute and its economic and technological situation does not worsen. In a sense, its reliance on the notion of proportional deterrence and a belief in the ultimate (if not absolute) value of the nuclear *force de dissuasion* do appear to represent "a new kind of Maginot Line mentality" (*une sorte de nouvelle mentalité ligne Maginot*)[105] whose consequences for France could be as disastrous as were those of the original Maginot Line, for reasons I have discussed above. Further, the doctrine of flexible response may well be more appropriate in today's strategic environment. But it does add an element of uncertainty regarding France's response to an ultimate provocation that may also undermine both French independence and the deterrent value of the *force de dissuasion.*[106] Precisely how France can extract itself from this particular dilemma is not entirely clear.

The May 1981 election of François Mitterrand as

president and the victory of the Socialists do not at this writing appear to indicate any major change in the direction of France's defense policy. However, it is still too early for a complete assessment.

The defense decision-making process[107]

Broadly speaking, the French defense policy process encompasses three principal stages: (*a*) *planification* (the determination of what is desirable for an adequate long-term defense), (*b*) *programmation* (the identification of what is possible in the middle term, usually considered to be a period of five to six years), and (*c*) *budget* (the specification of what can actually be done in the short term, usually a single year).[108] The underlying assumption is that the requirements defined in each stage of the process will shape the next stage, thus insuring not only continuity of planning but also a high degree of congruence among strategy, force posture, and available defense-related resources utilized to maximum effect.

In this particular case, reality comes remarkably close to design. For a variety of historical, constitutional, and institutional reasons, the defense decision-making process in the French Fifth Republic probably approximates the classical "rational actor model" to a greater extent than is the case with any other Western country.[109] And despite a somewhat uneven policy output,[110] there is little doubt that it is marked by much the same "high degree of coherence and consistency"—to say nothing of relative success—that is commonly attributed to France's more general performance in foreign affairs.[111]

The French defense policy process has been aptly described by David S. Yost as an admixture of "parliamentary impotence and executive dominance."[112] There is certainly no question about the extent to which effective power in this process resides in the executive branch, and specifically with the president of the republic. The president is constitutionally and practically the one who has "supreme responsibility" in defense matters, is "the lone judge on the eventual use of nuclear weapons," and "personally exercises the power of decision and control on the use of the armed forces in the event of war."[113] It is also clear that the National Assembly, unlike the Congress in the United States, lacks the ability to pose any serious threat to the paramount position of the president and his staff in the defense policy process. In Edward Kolodziej's words, "French parliamentarians, associated with the defense policy process, accept a secondary, and even passive, role. . . . Oversight hearings and fact finding missions . . . are not a normal part of the French parliamentary system."[114]

Two recent developments have added weight to the simple reality of presidential dominance of the defense policy process by enhancing the overall position of the executive branch therein. One is the codification of that process into the three-stage sequence of planification-programmation-budget; the second is the existence of certain deliberate ambiguities in the current *loi de programmation, 1977–82*. The increased concentration of power in the presidency, however, does not mean that it has become easier for outsiders to understand. On the contrary, the complexities and intricacies of the defense policy process within the executive branch are considerable, owing in no small measure to the fact that "the French [defense policy] process has much more in common with the centralized, secretive, executive-dominated British system . . . than with the pluralistic [American system]."[115]

Yet if the formulation of French defense policy is centralized at the highest level, the implementation of that policy assuredly is not. At the most general level, it is accurate to say that the prime minister is only "an agent of the President" on these matters, and that the defense and foreign ministers have only a "restricted freedom of action" in the execution of presidential decisions.[116] But at a more specific level, responsibility for the actual implementation of defense policy decisions devolves on (*a*) the General Secretariat of National Defense and (*b*) the Ministry of National Defense.

The position of the General Secretariat of National Defense in France corresponds to that of the National Security Council in the United States.[117] Established in 1962, the General Secretariat of National Defense has the principal responsibility for coordinating the implementation of specific defense policies, both within the defense establishment proper and between it and other ministries and agencies of the French government. Headed by a ranking general officer, the General Secretariat (*a*) staffs and oversees the activities of defense planning committees, (*b*) participates in various stages of defense-related negotiations with foreign governments, (*c*) provides liaison among governmental and nongovernmental organizations carrying out defense-related tasks, and (*d*) assists the prime minister and the minister of national defense as directed. The position and direct access to the president, prime minister, and minister of national defense that the secretary general of this organization possesses independent of the regular military chain of command give the holder of this office an unusual degree of potential influence on French defense policy—a potential that is often realized.

The position of the Ministry of National Defense within the French government obviously parallels that of the Defense Department within the United States (see figure 1).[118] The minister of national defense has two principal sets of assistants: (*a*) senior civil servants, who head and staff the Ministerial Delegation for Armaments, the General Secretariat for Administration, and the Office of the Comptroller General of the Armed Forces, and (*b*) ranking military officers on the Committee of Chiefs of Staff, the directorate of the Gendarmerie (a paramilitary national police force) and Military Justice, and the offices of the inspector general of each of the individual services and the Gendarmerie, all of whom report directly to the minister of national defense independent of their respective chiefs of staff.

Each of these organizations or agencies has its own particular function. Those in the first set are principally concerned with the administration of the armed forces, whereas those in the second set deal with the operation of the military. Of the former, the Ministerial Delegation for Armaments (DMA) has the most influence. It has what are called state missions and also industrial missions. The state missions include the type of weapons system planning, procurement, and research and development (R&D) functions one would conventionally associate with a governmental agency of this variety. The DMA is supported in the execution of these missions by a number of technical/operational divisions and administration boards. The industrial missions, on the other hand, are a singular French phenomenon that requires the DMA to function as part of the general armaments industry—a military-industrial complex in fact as well as in name![119] Indeed, cooperation and coordination between the public and private sectors of defense-related industries—sectors whose spheres of influence overlap to a considerable degree in practice—are both extensive and cordial. This reduces (but does not eliminate entirely) both administrative workloads and the incidence of industrial noncompliance with policy requirements and obligations. Both the character and the consequences of this special relationship have been well summarized by Arthur J. Alexander, who wrote that dealings "between the French government and [defense] industry are on an intimate basis, with a great deal of administrative discretion practiced by executive agencies. . . . [A] sense of partnership pervades the relationship, . . . [which] reduces the need for official regulation and surveillance."[120]

Primary responsibility for the operation of the armed forces falls under the purview of the chiefs of staff.[121] There are four chiefs of staff, three of whom head their individual services (army, navy, air force) and are generally responsible for the material and operational readiness of them. In addition, there is also an armed forces chief of staff whose general responsibility to the minister of national defense for the overall readiness of the French armed forces makes him *primus inter pares* on the Committee of Chiefs of Staff in peacetime. In wartime, he becomes chief of the General Staff, with the three service chiefs available as his deputies for specific operations. All of the service chiefs, however, enjoy the right of direct access to the minister of national defense on matters related to the normal operation of their respective services. Regular meetings of the Committee of Chiefs of Staff (usually on a monthly basis), with the minister of national defense presiding, deal with matters of import to the defense establishment as a whole. Finally, a Supreme Council composed of senior general officers deals with service-specific matters.

Despite the nominal coherence and general efficiency of the French defense policy-making process, there are a number of constraints that inhibit its functioning, reduce the quality of its output, and, in the words of one scholar, "constitute virtually permanent [and detrimental] aspects of the process of defense policy formation in France."[122] First, the anomalous position of France within the Atlantic Alliance necessarily reduces France's access to American financial and technical assistance, and thus to much of the most advanced U.S. defense technology, although France's participation in the Independent European Program Group and the activities of American private industry are mitigating factors. At least in the technical aspect of defense, however, "France alone" entails more burdens for French planners than would be the case if France had adopted wholeheartedly either an Atlanticist or a European role.

Second, the actual administration of French defense policy is less efficient in some respects than its architects would wish it to be. In addition to the perhaps not unexpected range of managerial and cost-related problems one often finds in nationalized or quasi-nationalized industries and so-called state corporations, there is the more fundamental administrative problem posed at all levels by the ubiquitous French civil service. The civil service in France is, in a certain sense, closer to the British than it is to the American model, being not only powerful but also well trained and professional. Yet while such a bureaucratic apparatus promotes administrative continuity and facilitates the implementation of policies and programs it endorses, it also—like all bureaucracies—may delay or kill initiatives that it opposes. And independent of bureaucratic preferences on specific defense-related programs, the fact that the French civil service includes a substantial number of middle- and upper-level personnel appointed under Gaullist administrations certainly inhibits any major departures from Gaullist policies and objectives.[123] Inflexibility at any of the three stages in the planification-programmation-budget sequence, as well as in the actual implementation of them, necessarily flaws the process as an integrated whole. The

Figure 1. French defense organization

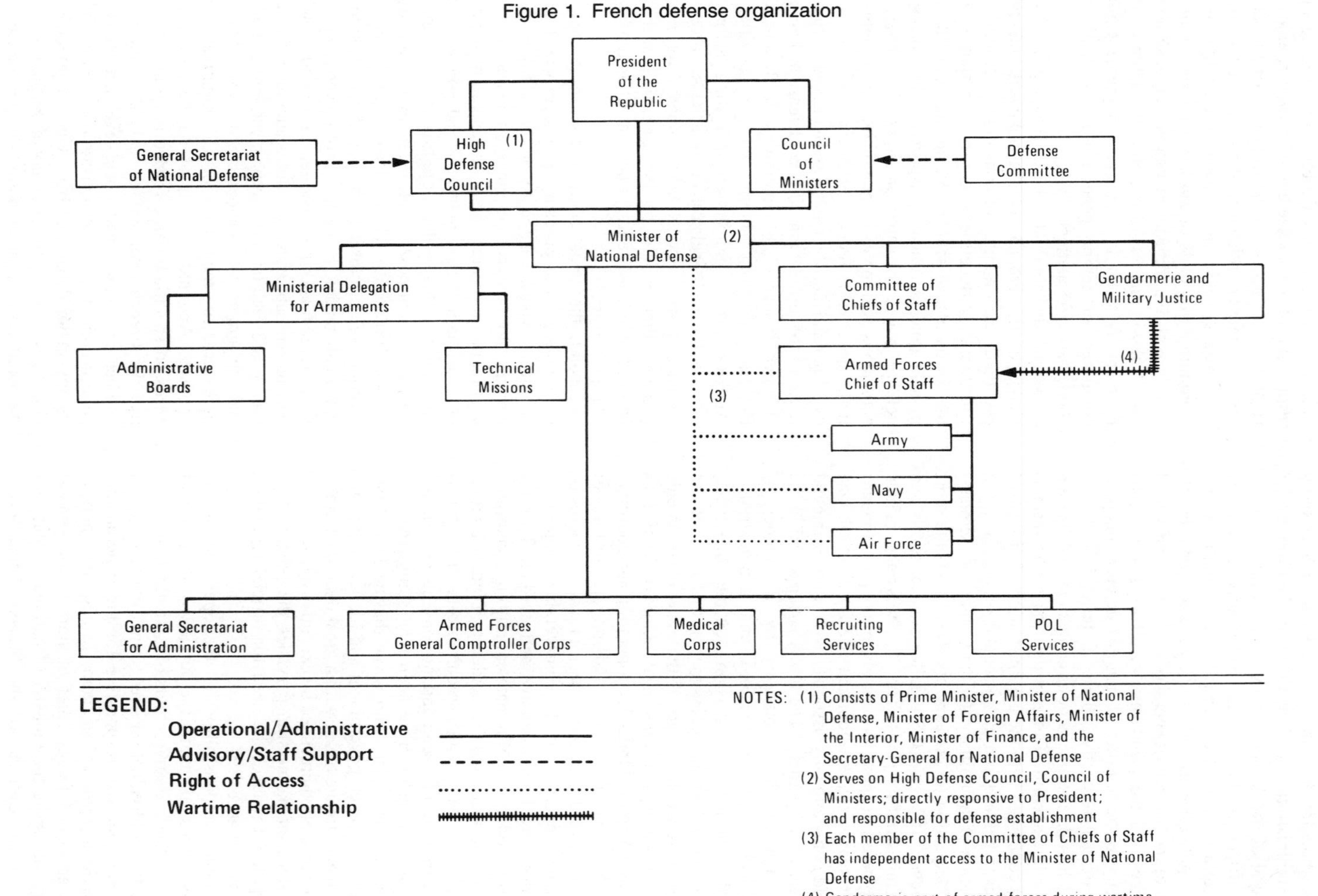

NOTES: (1) Consists of Prime Minister, Minister of National Defense, Minister of Foreign Affairs, Minister of the Interior, Minister of Finance, and the Secretary-General for National Defense
(2) Serves on High Defense Council, Council of Ministers; directly responsive to President; and responsible for defense establishment
(3) Each member of the Committee of Chiefs of Staff has independent access to the Minister of National Defense
(4) Gendarmerie part of armed forces during wartime

bureaucracy is in a position to do just that, if it so chooses.

Third, there is the question of finance—that is, of the share of the budget that can be devoted to defense in both a relative and an absolute sense. Manpower costs are increasing in France as in the other Western countries. As in other countries, higher manpower-related costs mean either higher defense budgets in an absolute sense or reduced outlays for research and development, procurement, operations, and maintenance, with outlays kept constant. The fact that French pay scales, while better now than in recent years, remain unusually low by Western standards has given rise to demands for further improvement that portend an intensification of this particular problem in the future.[124] This difficulty is compounded by the increasing cost of operations, which (when added to rising manpower-related costs) reduces the funds available for procurement. This problem is particularly acute for the general-purpose forces, given that the French nuclear forces absorb approximately one-third of the appropriations that are available for weapons and equipment.[125] At some point, it would seem, compromises will have to be made somewhere if France is to have what it considers to be an adequate defense at a politically acceptable and budgetarily feasible cost.

Against these liabilities must be balanced certain assets on which those charged with the planning and implementation of France's defense policy can draw. The French preoccupation with an independent role in world politics gives France's defense decision-making process an unusual degree of resiliency in the face of external opposition or criticism. Indeed, such criticism is invariably counterproductive, at least from the perspective of foreign governments. This is because it usually produces a measure of popularly supported official recalcitrance that virtually guarantees that France will adamantly pursue whatever policy provoked opposition from abroad, simply to demonstrate France's status as an independent power of consequence in the world. Nor is domestic opposition outside of the normal political process of considerable significance (except, perhaps, when it results in mass risings in the streets of Paris!). On the contrary, there is usually remarkably little public debate on the substance of defense policy that has much chance of significantly altering or shaping that policy.[126] A perusal of the French literature in this field also suggests that French defense officials, uniformed and civilian alike, present their cases and dismiss their critics with a degree of aplomb all but unknown in the United States and certain other Western countries.

There are, of course, more tangible assets available to France. Whatever its inadequacies, the relative strength and robustness of the French economy give French defense planners access to a reservoir on which to draw that their counterparts in some Western nations (e.g., Great Britain and Italy) simply do not enjoy. French technology, as indicated earlier, is certainly not backward in many respects. French industry, despite the political divisions and union activism that reflect France's class and party structure, nonetheless has a reasonably competent and stable labor force.[127] And finally, unlike the population in most of the past century and a half, the current French population is described as "young and growing,"[128] as well as being increasingly well educated relative to earlier years. This places France's defense manpower situation, at least, in a far more favorable situation than that with which the United States and Great Britain have to contend. It also permits France to make certain choices with respect to the use of the manpower that a declining prime recruiting pool might foreclose.

Most of the strengths and weaknesses of the French defense decision-making process are apparent in the current *loi de programmation, 1977–82*. That comprehensive program was intended to begin the implementation of the previously discussed long-term decision (*planification*) to move to a strategy based on the concept of the *sanctuarisation élargie* ("enlarged sanctuary"), a doctrine of flexible response, and a correspondingly greater degree of emphasis on reorganized and upgraded general purpose forces. The proposed outlays to be made in accordance with this program, reflecting the goal of allocating 20 percent of the entire budget to defense, are presented in tables 2 and 3.

A careful appraisal of the *loi de programmation, 1977–82* indicates a number of disparities between design and execution of this program.[129] First, the goal of allocating 20 percent of the state budget to defense has not been met. Actual expenditures have therefore varied from what was actually intended and projected, both in an absolute sense and among the five principal budget categories used in tables 2 and 3. This has resulted in an uneven development of forces and an equally uneven acquisition of weapons and material for the armed forces. Second, and partly because of the above, it seems that many of the principal program objectives of the *loi de programmation, 1977–82* have not been met in the budgets for 1977, 1978, and 1979 and seem unlikely to be met in 1980. Finally, despite the relatively greater emphasis to be given to the general purpose forces in light of France's new strategy and doctrine, only a minimal redistribution of funds among the services was projected in the program, and only marginal changes actually seem to have occurred to date. It would appear that bureaucratic and budgetary forces combined in this case to make the present and the future more like the past than might have been anticipated by someone

Table 2
Projected defense expenditures according to Loi de programmation, 1977–82

Budget category	1977	1978	1979	1980	1981	1982	Total 1977–82
Strategic forces and military R&D	11,670	13,145	14,795	16,470	18,495	20,570	95,145
Army	18,400	21,080	24,025	27,280	30,975	35,170	156,930
Navy	9,780	11,355	13,200	15,450	17,975	20,955	88,715
Air force	12,225	14,150	16,490	19,405	22,670	26,880	111,820
Gendarmerie	5,925	6,730	7,645	8,655	9,875	11,000	49,830
Total	58,000	66,460	76,155	87,260	99,990	114,575	502,440

Source: Richard Woyke, "The Process of Change in French Defense Policy," *Aussenpolitik* 28/1 (1977): 8.
Note: Sums given are in millions of francs.

contemplating the potential implications of the *sanctuarisation élargie* and "flexible response" for French defense policy.

Much the same, I believe, can be said about the French defense decision-making process in a more general sense. French ambitions will continue to guide French planning and have a major influence on those decisions affecting the structure, composition, and armament of the French armed forces. The process itself is virtually certain to remain centralized, and power will continue to remain concentrated in the presidency, regardless of foreseeable domestic political developments. And finally, it is all too likely that the outcome of that process will continue to be uneven, just as "the history of military program-laws under the Fifth Republic is one of great accomplishments—but also of delays, cutbacks, and outright cancellations in equipment programs."[130] That concatenation of overcommitment at the level of *planification,* rigorous planning at the level of *programmation,* and flawed execution at the level of the *budget* is, unfortunately, unlikely to be altered in the coming years—the almost inevitable consequence of a defense policy dictated more by French pretensions than by French power.

Recurring issues: defense policy outputs

The outcome of this complex interplay of role selection, threat perception, strategic choice, and defense decision-making process is a relatively large and sophisticated military establishment. Five specific resultants of this interplay will be examined here: France's (*a*) current state of civil-military relations, (*b*) force posture, (*c*) weapons acquisition system and arms trade, (*d*) arms control and disarmament policy, and (*e*) use of force abroad.

CIVIL-MILITARY RELATIONS

The multifaceted role of the armed forces in the French defense decision-making process is suggestive of the ambivalent place held by the military in French society as a whole. For a variety of historical and cultural reasons, the French military (and particularly the army) is seen by different groups to embody both the spirit of the nation and a potential threat to the constitutional order of the Fifth Republic. Historically, the armed forces have been the guardians and the instruments of French grandeur, and an integral part of society. This is reflected today in the broad-based popular support for the *force de dissuasion* and the assumed primacy of military power in world politics. But at other times in France's past, the armed forces have been used by the government or the so-called ruling classes to suppress the "common people" at home and to oppress indigenous colonial peoples abroad. The notion that the military is at heart the repository of reactionary political forces, at least among the officer corps, represents this perspective. The activities of the "Secret Army Organization" (OAS) and the abortive coup d'état during the Algerian War are but the most recent stimuli to this set of concerns.

Table 3
Percentage distribution of projected defense expenditures, 1977–82, from table 2

Budget category	1977	1978	1979	1980	1981	1982	Total 1977–82
Strategic forces and military R&D	20.1%	19.8%	19.4%	18.9%	18.5%	18.0%	18.9%
Army	31.7	31.7	31.5	31.3	31.0	30.7	31.2
Navy	16.9	17.1	17.3	17.7	18.0	18.3	17.7
Air force	21.1	21.3	21.7	22.2	22.7	23.5	22.3
Gendarmerie	10.2	10.1	10.1	9.9	9.9	9.6	9.9
Total	100.0	100.0	100.0	100.0	100.0	100.0	100.0

Source: Computed from budget data in table 2.

The affirmative view of the armed forces, of course, is most popular with present and former members of the officer corps, as well as with the aristocracy and the bourgeoisie. It finds the greatest degree of political support in the ranks of the Gaullists and the Giscardists. Conversely, the more critical view of the French military is particularly common in the enlisted ranks (especially among the conscripts), the working classes, and the intellectuals. Not surprisingly, the Socialists and the Communists tend to adhere to this position, although many do serve in all ranks—enlisted and commissioned alike—of the armed forces. But both perspectives exist—indeed, sometimes coexist—within French society.

It is the ambiguous character of civil-military relations in France that, more than any other single factor, dictates the model of military service that now obtains. That model is neither one of selective service (as practiced in many countries in Western Europe and elsewhere), nor of an all-volunteer or professional force (what the French would call the *armée de métier*). It is instead a form of "national service" or "national conscription" that was adopted in 1959 and today provides approximately one half of the personnel in the regular armed forces.[131]

This system, which is seen as a means of resolving the conflicting perspectives of the position of the military in French society, was adopted and persists for three basic reasons. First, budgetary considerations make national conscription popular with the government. Short-term conscripts cost less, in terms of pay and benefits, than either long- or short-term volunteers in an advanced industrial society. Second, the career military are favorably predisposed to this model of military service. This is partly because national conscription allows the armed forces to avoid manpower shortfalls or unwanted force reductions simply by culling the annual cohort of French youth. But it is also because the career military see military service as a means of forging a sense of national identity and allegiance to France among the conscripts, many of whom come from what the military would consider to be "politically suspect origins." And finally, national conscription is heartily endorsed by the Left for the opposite reason that it is supported by the career military. Put bluntly, the Left sees national conscription as a leavening influence on the military and fears that an all-volunteer force would eventually become the instrument by which the Right would suppress the Left.[132]

The existence of such a broad base of support for the concept of national conscription, however, does not mean that it escapes criticism. On the contrary, the fact that such a high proportion of the French armed forces is composed of conscripts serving a single year on active duty has engendered criticism from both of France's political wings. The Left essentially lobbies for a reduction in the length of mandated service, an improvement in pay and working conditions, and the right of military personnel (or at least the conscripts) to unionize and engage in collective bargaining with military "management." Gains have been made on some of these issues in the past, and there is no indication that the Left intends to relax its efforts to create what it considers to be a more humanistic form of military service. The one area where it has not enjoyed any success concerns the creation of military unions. Since the Left could well expect to dominate such unions, it sees them not only as a means of improving pay and working conditions but also as an additional safeguard against what it considers military "adventurism," especially against the Left itself. The French government is not unaware of the possible consequences of military unionization and is adamantly opposed to it. That position, too, is unlikely to alter, at least as long as a Center-Right coalition governs France.[133]

On the other side of the political spectrum, the Right (along with many professional soldiers) tends to believe that a single year of service is simply too short in an era of increasingly sophisticated military technology. There is also some concern about the reliability (in both a political and a military sense) of the conscripts, especially in the event of civil strife in France or an intervention in some part of the Third World. To hedge against that possible unreliability while retaining the national conscription model of military service for its acknowledged advantages, two regular French divisions (plus, of course, the Foreign Legion) are composed entirely of volunteers.[134] These are the Eleventh Parachute Division and the Ninth Marine Division, formerly part of France's *forces d'intervention extérieures* ("foreign intervention forces") and now the French government's implicit "ace in the hole" for dealing with militarily demanding and politically sensitive situations at home or abroad. There has also been a more conscious effort to make the armed forces in general and the army in particular more popular with the people by having them engage in a wide range of what would be called civic action programs, especially in the areas outside of the major urban centers. Doing so, it is apparently reasoned, may help soldiers and civilians alike to think better of one another, to their mutual benefit as well as to the benefit of France itself.

These countervailing tendencies are likely to persist as long as the system of national conscription remains in effect. Nor is there any indication that it will be replaced in the foreseeable future. There admittedly has been an increase in the number and intensity of the calls for France to follow the American and British examples and recruit its armed forces on an all-volunteer basis while concurrently reducing their size. This, it is argued, would provide France with a military establishment possessing the expertise and reliability necessary for modern warfare, but at an acceptable cost.[135] It is unlikely, however, that such calls will be heeded. This is essentially because it is politically impossible at the present time for the French government to replace the system of national conscription, regardless of its inefficient and uneconomical use of personnel.[136] That is, the flaws in national conscription are not yet considered great enough across the French political spectrum to overcome the liabilities associated with the alternatives to it.

FORCE POSTURE

A perennial question when appraising the defense policy of any nation, as Paul Viotti once pointed out, "is whether doctrine guides the evolution of force posture or . . . the converse is true."[137] In the case of France, as I have suggested earlier, the former generally holds true. The sequential linking of doctrinal changes to modifications in force posture does not always operate well, of course, as was pointed out in the preceding discussion of the *loi de programmation, 1977–82*. But to a remarkable extent, especially for a Western country, "France's doctrine responded to changes in France's domestic and foreign environment [and shaped the French armed forces accordingly]."[138] I have already discussed how changes in France's domestic and foreign environment have altered French strategy and doctrine. The question to be addressed here is the cumulative impact of those changes on France's military force posture.

To address this question, I will examine five principal aspects of the French force posture: (*a*) aggregate trend data on defense efforts, including the projected impact of the *loi de programmation, 1977–82;* (*b*) the nuclear forces, strategic and tactical alike; (*c*) the general purpose forces [GPF], with specific reference to the reorganization and augmentation of the army; (*d*) the reserves and organized territorial defense forces [DOT]; and (*e*) the future direction of trends bearing directly on French force posture.

In the first place, the aggregate trend data on French defense efforts presented in table 4 depict both a substantial allocation of human, financial, and material resources to defense and less of an effort than might be anticipated if one took France's proclaimed ambitions at face value. This is particularly apparent when one compares French defense efforts with those of its closest and less overtly ambitious Western European neighbors: Great Britain (the only other nuclear-armed Western European country) and the Federal Republic of Germany (France's political-military *bête noire*). It is clear, on the one hand, that France's absolute outlays for defense are considerable. As will be seen in the remainder of this section, they have given France one of the largest and most sophisticated military establishments in the world, with a reasonably well balanced mix of forces nominally unmatched in overall quality except by the two superpowers.[139] France's "military participation ratio" (MPR)[140]—that is, the percentage of 18-to-45-year-old males in the armed forces—is currently 4.7 percent, higher than that of its European "middle power" counterparts and above that of all NATO countries except Greece, Turkey, and Norway. The result is a French defense establishment of nearly 510,000 active-duty personnel, of whom approximately 54 percent are one-year conscripts.[141]

Nevertheless, these efforts, while sufficiently impressive in an absolute sense, simply do not seem commensurate with what would be required to lend substance to France's claim to be the leading power of Western Europe, capable of acting independently in world politics and professing to stand immediately behind the superpowers in the eyes of the world. France spends less (in current dollars) on defense than the FRG in every category in table 4, and only slightly more than Great Britain except in terms of the proportion of government spending allocated to defense. It also devotes approximately the same percentage of its gross national product to defense as the FRG (a surprising fact, given France's nuclear forces and concern about the Germans, coupled with the FRG's significantly larger gross national product), and barely two-thirds that of Great Britain, which has its own nuclear force and a gross national product one-third smaller than that of France.[142] One would have expected a country with France's ambitions and fears to do more for its own defense than is actually the

Table 4
Trends in French defense efforts

Category	1976	1977	1978	1979	% Change 1976–1979
Military personnel[1]	513	502	503	509	−0.7
Military outlays[2]	12.9	11.9	15.2	18.8	+46.0[3]
Per capita outlays[2]	241	224	285	349	+44.8
Defense outlays as percentage of budget	20.6	16.3	17.0	17.5	−15.1

Source: International Institute for Strategic Studies, *The Military Balance, 1979–1980* (London: IISS, 1980), pp. 24, 92–96.
[1]In thousands; regular/active-duty personnel only.
[2]Estimates based on current exchange rates in U.S. $ million.
[3]In current dollars; real growth, controlling for inflation, was 11.2 percent between 1976 and 1978 [1979 data not available].

case. Certainly a defense effort equivalent to that of Great Britain would have produced a military establishment whose size and capabilities would be more in keeping with France's declared role, strategy, and doctrine.

To a certain extent, of course, the current *loi de programmation, 1977–82* is intended to rectify some of the most glaring inconsistencies between proclaimed ends and available means. It does represent at least a nominal departure from some of the classical Gaullist views on preferred military priorities. The declared French determination to maintain the strategic nuclear force while up-grading the overall military establishment is certainly evidence of France's determination to rectify the situation. What is less evident, however, is France's ability to do so. To be sure, the greater emphasis being given to reorganizing the army and upgrading all of the general purpose forces has delayed somewhat the planned modernization of the *force de dissuasion*. But the latter (which has approximately 20,000–25,000 personnel) is still projected to receive essentially the same amount of funds for new equipment as the general purpose forces (which have over 480,000 personnel).[143] Thus, there is some reason to question the actual extent of the proposed changes on French force posture, even discounting the apparent problems of implementation discussed earlier in this chapter.

Whatever the precise scope of the changes projected in the current *loi de programmation*, France's nuclear forces seem likely to continue to enjoy a commanding position in the French military hierarchy. Those forces now compose the strategic nuclear forces (FNS) of the *force de dissuasion*, whose role has been considered earlier, and an increasingly wide range of tactical nuclear weapons (TNWs), both of which are being upgraded as part of the current program.[144] The more important nuclear capabilities, of course, are those associated with France's chosen instrument of status, autonomy, and security: the FNS. It is worth emphasizing that the size and utility of the FNS are "not determined in relation to the force level of potential adversaries."[145] Instead, the FNS is presumed to have both intrinsic and extrinsic value to France by virtue of its very existence.

That existence, it should be noted, is more than nominal. Occasional disparaging remarks (largely from outside France) to the contrary notwithstanding, the *force de dissuasion* has at its disposal a strategic triad of nuclear-powered ballistic missile submarines (SSBNs), land-based intermediate-range ballistic missiles (IRBMs), and manned bombers. This is a mix of strategic offensive forces that, as table 5 illustrates, gives the French FNS more diversity and operational flexibility than its British and Chinese counterparts possess.

The first leg of France's strategic triad to become operational was the manned bomber force. It now consists of thirty-three Mirage IVA strike aircraft (plus sixteen others in reserve), supported by eleven KC-135F tankers for in-flight refueling. Each bomber is configured to carry one seventy-kiloton AN-22 nuclear bomb. The Mirage IVA force is projected to remain in service until 1985, given the improved navigation and penetration capabilities with which it is now being equipped. After 1985, some of the Mirage IVA aircraft will be retained, either as reconnaissance aircraft or as air-to-ground missile carriers. Their current function within the FNS, however, will largely be assumed by light mobile ballistic missiles or by nuclear-armed cruise missiles, depending on the outcome of studies now under way.

Table 5
Strategic force mixes of selected middle powers

Country	ICBM or IRBM	SLBM	Manned Bomber
France	yes	yes	yes
Great Britain	no	yes	no[1]
China	yes	no	yes

Source: International Institute for Strategic Studies, *The Military Balance, 1979–1980* (London: International Institute for Strategic Studies, 1980).

[1]Great Britain does retain a force of *Vulcan* attack/strike bombers, which, although nuclear-capable, are no longer assigned to its strategic forces.

The second component of the FNS is the land-based intermediate-range ballistic missile (IRBM) force based in silos on the Plateau d'Albion in southern France. This force, organized under the aegis of the First Strategic Missile Group, has at its disposal eighteen SSBS S-2 missiles in individual silos, each of which is capable of delivering a 150-kiloton nuclear warhead against targets at ranges up to 1,800 miles. (Initial plans to deploy nine additional IRBMs were subsequently canceled.) These silos are currently being retrofitted with the new SSBS S-3 IRBM, an improved missile capable of delivering a 1-megaton thermonuclear warhead to a range of approximately 3,000 miles. The retrofitting of all eighteen IRBM silos with the new missile will be completed in 1982.

The third element of the FNS is generally considered to be the most important. This element is the ballistic missile submarine force. There are two principal reasons for this judgment. One is the relatively greater potential survivability of the SSBN force. The other is its substantially greater contribution to France's aggregate strategic striking power. The SSBN force presently consists of five nuclear-powered ballistic missile submarines of the Redoubtable class. The first four to become operational are each equipped with sixteen M-20 submarine-launched ballistic missiles (SLBMs) carrying a 1-megaton warhead up to 3,000 miles. The fifth, and last, SSBN of this class is the *Tonnant*. It carries sixteen of the new mirved M-4 SLBMs, each of which has three 100–150-kiloton warheads and a range in excess of 4,000 miles. The first four SSBNs of this class will have been retrofitted with the M-4 SLBM by 1985. After much debate, it has been decided to proceed with the construction of a sixth SSBN. This vessel, named *L'Inflexible*, is scheduled to become operational in 1985. It, too, will carry sixteen M-4 mirved SLBMs and is intended to be the prototype of a new generation of SSBNs that will be needed to replace the Redoubtable-class vessels when they begin going out of service (owing to age) in 1995.

Although less central to the functioning of France's nuclear deterrent than the *force de dissuasion*, Paris also has at its disposal a diverse and growing array of tactical nuclear weapons. The "dean" of the French TNW force is the Pluton, a relatively short-range (about seventy-five miles) missile carrying a single fifteen-to-twenty-five-kiloton warhead, which first became operational in 1974.

The five operational Pluton surface-to-surface missile (SSM) regiments with a total of thirty-two Pluton missiles are not intended to wage a tactical nuclear battle, as that is usually defined in Soviet and American military circles; however, they are supposed to be used as the final "shot across the bow," warning an attacker to stop or undergo an attack by France's strategic nuclear forces. It is largely for this reason that they are based in France.

The upgrading of the French TNW force is proceeding apace. A replacement for the Pluton is now being studied. In addition, approximately sixty of the French air force's Mirage III and Jaguar fighter-bombers have been configured to carry a single ten-to-fifteen-kiloton AN-52 tactical nuclear bomb apiece. Similar weapons are to be placed on the Super-Etendard carrier-based attack bombers. Finally, a new air-to-ground standoff nuclear missile is under development, probably intended for deployment on the Mirage 2000, with its advanced penetration capabilities, when this plane becomes operational by 1985.[146]

The combination of strategic and tactical nuclear weapons described above and summarized in table 6 clearly gives France an impressive nuclear strike capability at the present time. Projected and authorized programs can only enhance that capability in the future. Whether even that enhanced capability will suffice in what is virtually certain to be an increasingly demanding strategic environment in the 1980s is another matter entirely. A number of proposals to upgrade further the *force de dissuasion* have been presented to date, and others are under consideration. The more interesting include a suggestion to concentrate more heavily on the SSBN force, perhaps having as many as twelve such vessels operational at one time; a recommendation to consider developing an antiballistic missile (ABM) capability to provide some security to French cities and the IRBM force; and a plea to implement an extensive civil defense program.[147] Whether this or any other feasible mix of damage-inflicting and damage-limiting plans will be operationalized is as problematic as the long-term viability of the FNS in the changing world order.

While the FNS and the TNW capabilities are being upgraded, the general purpose forces are being both upgraded and reorganized in conjunction with France's new strategy and doctrine. The army is the principal beneficiary of this process, followed by the navy and the air force in that order. The reorganization of the army began in 1976–77. At that time, France began moving toward a ground force structure that would have a larger number of smaller maneuver divisions with an enhanced capability to conduct mechanized operations. The earlier structure had been based on two army corps and deployed a total of five mechanized and two light divisions, plus independent regiments and brigades and supporting units. The reorganized army structure will have three corps headquarters and a total of sixteen divisions or division force equivalents, eight of which will be ar-

Table 6
French nuclear delivery vehicles

Type	Number deployed (7/1979)	Date of first deployment	Range in statute miles	Warheads and yields
IRBM (SSBS S-2)	18	1971	1,875	1 × 150 kt
IRBM (S-3)	[18][1]	1980–82	3,000	1 × 1 MT
SLBM (MSBS M-20)	64	1977	3,000	1 × 1 MT
SLBM (M-4)	—	1985[2]	4,000	3 × 100–150 kt
Bomber (Mirage IVA)	33	1964	2,000[3]	1 × 70 kt
TNW (Pluton)	32	1974	75	1 × 15–25 kt

Source: International Institute for Strategic Studies, *The Military Balance, 1979–1980* (London: International Institute for Strategic Studies, 1980), p. 90; Gérard Vaillant, "Défense en France," *Défense nationale* (August-September 1978).
[1]These IRBMs will replace the older SSBS S-2 IRBMs.
[2]These will replace the older MSBS M-20 SLBMs and will also be installed on the fifth and sixth French SSBNs.
[3]Maximum speed: Mach 2.2.

Table 7
Divisional force structure

Unit type	Army list in 1978	Army list in 1982
Field army headquarters	First Army	First Army
Corps headquarters	I Corps II Corps	I Corps II Corps III Corps
Armored divisions	1st, 3rd, 4th, 5th, 6th, 7th, 10th	1st, 2nd, 3rd, 4th, 5th, 6th, 7th, 10th
Mechanized divisions	8th	—
Infantry divisions	14th, 15th	8th, 12th, 14th, 15th
Marine divisions	9th	9th
Alpine divisions	27th	27th
Parachute divisions	11th	11th

Source: Francis Carjean, "Armée de terre," *Défense nationale* (February 1979), pp. 146–49.

mored divisions, manned by 327,000 personnel (nearly two thirds of whom are conscripts).[148] The army's force structure in 1978 (midway through the reorganization) and that projected for 1982 (at the completion of that process) appear in table 7.

To these principal maneuver formations must, of course, be added the French Foreign Legion. This is a traditionally all-volunteer force whose 10,000 troops are organized into seven regiments available for use in an interventionary role.[149] There are also five surface-to-air missile (SAM) regiments equipped with the Hawk and Roland SAM weapons systems and a total of 12 helicopter groups or regiments with nearly 700 helicopters, plus supporting elements.[150]

As figure 2 illustrates, the fifteen maneuver divisions are based either in or adjacent to the territory of metropolitan France. Seven of the eight armored divisions will be located in the northeast, including three in the FRG. Other major army garrisons outside of France are located in Berlin (two mechanized/light armored regiments with 2,000 troops), Djibouti (4,000 troops), and Chad (1,800 troops), with smaller contingents in Gabon, the Ivory Coast, and Senegal. A parachute regiment with supporting en-

Figure 2. Divisional deployment/areas of responsibility

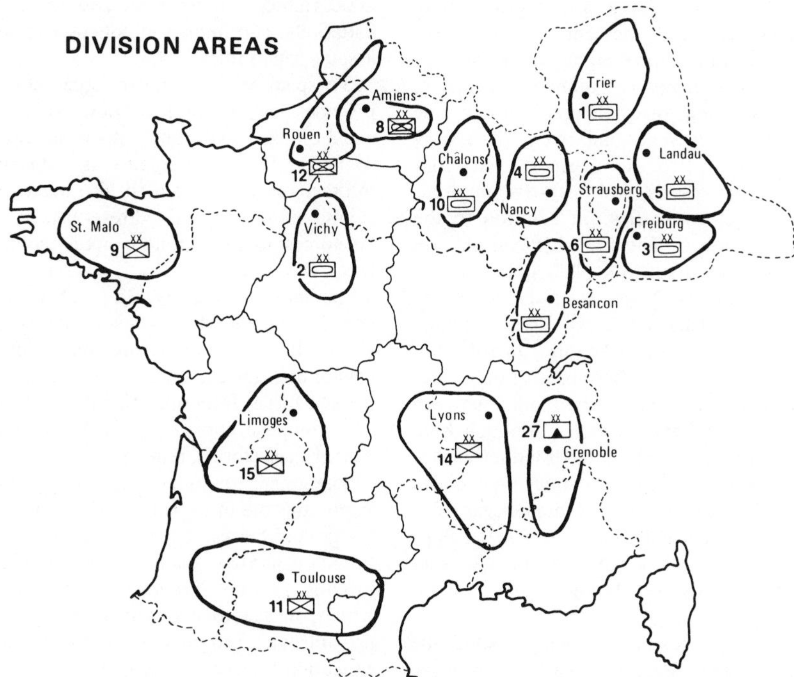

Source: Wilfred L. Ebel, "The French Republic," *Military Review* 59, no. 8 (1979): 53.

gineer and logistics units is in Lebanon under U.N. command.

Like that of the army, the navy's position in the French defense establishment is being augmented. For many years, the purpose of the French fleet was to deploy and to protect the SSBNs of the *force de dissuasion*. All of that is now changing. The French navy will retain its original mission and will continue to give precedence to it. But it has also been tasked with the full range of sea control and power projection missions one conventionally associates with a major naval power. Specifically, the French navy is now charged with (*a*) participating in the *force de dissuasion;* (*b*) securing the maritime approaches to France and its overseas territories; (*c*) securing France's access to resources and its essential lines of communication; (*d*) conducting operations in support of French interests, especially in the Mediterranean; and (*e*) carrying out what Minister of National Defense Yvon Bourges has described as "the essential mission of giving, by its presence in the world, an impression of France's status."[151]

The naval forces available to France seem to be simultaneously impressive in an absolute sense and inadequate in all but a purely nominal sense for the missions they have been assigned. That is, the French navy has been tasked with the requirement of carrying out missions suitable for the great power France would like to be, but it has at its disposal only the capabilities of the middle power that France actually is. In 1979, the French navy had approximately 70,000 personnel, some 28 percent of whom were conscripts. It operated forty-eight major surface combat vessels (including two medium attack carriers with forty aircraft each, one helicopter carrier, one cruiser, nineteen destroyers, and twenty-five frigates), twenty-three patrol submarines, sixty-four light surface combat vessels, and forty-five amphibious ships and fleet auxiliaries, in addition to the SSBNs described above. The French naval air arm has over 120 combat aircraft, plus helicopters, transport, and utility aircraft. Major naval bases are located at Cherbourg (Channel fleet), Brest (Atlantic fleet and SSBN), Lorient (Atlantic patrol submarines), and Toulon (Mediterranean fleet). The bulk of the French navy is currently divided between the Mediterranean and the Atlantic, although both attack carriers are stationed in the Mediterranean, while the SSBNs operate in the Atlantic. France also maintains a sizable presence in the Indian Ocean. The French squadron there usually has over a dozen ships and submarines on station at any one time. A small naval detachment is also on station in the West Indies.[152]

These forces and dispositions notwithstanding, the dual need to (*a*) bring aggregate capabilities more into congruence with assigned missions and (*b*) replace aging ships has necessitated a fairly ambitious naval construction program. Both of France's attack carriers will have to be replaced in the 1980s, and studies are now in progress to determine the optimal mix of launching platforms and aircraft types. It is also planned to have five nuclear-powered fleet attack submarines (SNA) under construction by 1982. Additional shipbuilding may include a nuclear-powered helicopter carrier equipped to handle V/STOL aircraft and as many as eight destroyers, five frigates, twenty-one light surface combat vessels, and fourteen amphibious ships and fleet auxiliaries, depending on the precise funding decisions that are subsequently made.[153]

Finally, the French air force now has nearly 104,000 personnel (40 percent of whom are conscripts) and nearly 500 combat aircraft. It is organized into four principal operational commands. The Air Defense Command has 8 squadrons with 120 interceptors, 9 SAM battalions equipped with the Crotale SAM system, and supporting elements. The Tactical Air Force Command has 21 operational squadrons with more than 340 aircraft and its own supporting units. The Air Transport Command operates 17 squadrons and a total of 190 aircraft and 90 helicopters. Finally, the Training Command has approximately 400 aircraft, some of which are obsolescent combat aircraft that, if necessary, could be pressed into active service in a secondary role. Projected acquisition programs for these operational commands include the Mirage F-1B/R and Mirage 2000 fighters, at least six additional Crotale SAM battalions, and improved helicopter transport and air assault capabilities.[154]

To speak of the regular forces alone, of course, provides an incomplete view of French military capabilities. Like most other advanced industrial societies, France maintains an extensive organized military reserve system. It also makes use of a substantial number of trained reservists to bring its regular forces to full strength upon mobilization.[155] In fact, when fully mobilized, reserves would compose 47 percent of the army, 38 percent of the air force, and 24 percent of the navy. Interestingly enough, given France's preoccupation with its nuclear capabilities and the obvious importance of keeping its nuclear forces fully operational at all times, reservists also compose approximately 10 percent of the personnel these forces require to be at full strength.[156]

The greatest number of reservists playing the most important role in French mobilization schemes are in the ground forces. There are actually three classes of French reservists. Each class has a different role and mission within France's mobilization program, which, in accordance with French doctrine, "make possible a progressive mobilization . . . [whose] execution is decentralized."[157]

The first class of reservists includes those required to bring the regular divisions and their supporting units to full strength. Approximately 90,000 reservists would be needed at present for the French maneuver forces to become fully manned and operational. When this phase of mobilization were completed, reservists would compose 15 percent of the personnel in the active divisions, 24 percent of corps troops, and between 62 and 72 percent of the personnel in the army's combat service and combat support units. The second class of reservists consists of those assigned to the territorial defense forces (DOT). These are composed largely of organized reserve units, including fourteen reserve divisions with regular cadres assigned to them in peacetime to facilitate mobilization. Approximately 80 percent of the personnel in the fully mobilized DOT divisions would be reservists. The third class of reservists, the Gendarmerie, is really a fully operational paramilitary force recruited largely from the armed forces but with a small proportion (about 10 percent) of conscripts. It has extensive internal security functions in peacetime and would be partly responsible for rear-area security during crises or war.[158] A summary of the mix of regular and reserve personnel in the French ground forces as of 1977-78 appears in table 8.

It should be readily apparent from the preceding discussion that France has not yet made a number of important decisions that will necessarily have a significant impact on its force posture.[159] It seems likely, for example, that both the concept of the *sanctuarisation élargie* and the doctrine of flexible response will be retained if at all possible. This suggests that an increasing emphasis ought to be given to the general purpose forces and the strategic mobility forces with an eye to augmenting France's power projection capabilities. It is also likely that France will continue to place its greatest reliance on the *force de dissuasion* as the preeminent guarantor of French security and status. What is more problematical is France's willingness to devote the resources (financial and otherwise) necessary to create and to maintain a balanced force capable of fulfilling the ambitious set of missions assigned to the French military. Indeed, one thing seems certain, regardless of what may appear in a given *loi de programmation*. This is that the *force de dissuasion* will be maintained at all costs, regardless of the reductions that maintenance might entail in other parts of the French defense establishment. A nation that sees status and security to be so inextricably linked, both to one another and to the *force de dissuasion,* cannot be expected to forsake the desirable merely to enhance its ability to attain what is merely possible. France, in this case, is most unlikely to do the unexpected.

WEAPONS ACQUISITION AND THE ARMS TRADE

For a military establishment to be effective, it is obviously necessary for its doctrine and force posture to be congruent with one another. But it is also necessary for it to be sufficiently well armed and equipped to be able to carry out its assigned missions. This requires a country either to produce or to have ready access to whatever military material its defense establishment needs.

In the case of France, the combined dictates of political autonomy and military necessity have made it essential for France to become largely self-sufficient in terms of weapons system research, development, and production. Independent powers, by France's definition, simply cannot afford to be dependent on others for the means of their own security. This is because such dependence implies a potential political vulnerability to the supplier that France considers to be unacceptable. American opposition to the French desire for a national nuclear force also has required France to develop the full panoply of nuclear weapons system technology essentially on its own. Finally, the French decision to withdraw from NATO in 1967, and France's unwillingness to participate in the Eurogroup collaborative weapons research and development consortium when it was first formed because of its ties to the United States, reinforced these tendencies toward self-sufficiency in the production of defense material.[160]

The net effect of these factors has been France's development of the second largest defense industry in Western Europe, surpassed in sheer size only by that of Great Britain. France not only produces some of the most advanced weapons systems and associated

Table 8
French army reserve mobilization

Force category	Peacetime strength	Reserve strength	Total mobilized strength
Maneuver forces	130,000	90,000[1]	220,000
Territorial defense forces (DOT)	60,000	160,000	220,000
Gendarmerie	66,000[2]	84,000	150,000
General totals	256,000	334,000	590,000

Source: Anthony S. Bennell, "The Effectiveness of Supplementary Military Forces," *Supplementary Military Forces: Reserves, Militias, Auxiliaries,* ed. Louis A. Zurcher and Gwyn Harries-Jenkins (Beverly Hills, Calif.: Sage, 1978), p. 51.
[1]Reserves for the entire army total approximately 300,000.
[2]Projected active-duty strength of the *Gendarmerie* is 78,500, including 6,000 conscripts.

technology in the world[161] but it also is the only Western European country to have an independently developed comprehensive nuclear weapons research and development program capable of producing a wide range of warheads, delivery vehicles, and guidance systems for both strategic and tactical purposes. In addition to the nuclear weapons systems described in table 5, France also independently produces the entire range of conventional weapons and other material needed by its armed forces.[162]

The fact that the French defense industry produces for France does not mean that France abjures cooperative armaments research, development, and production efforts with other countries, at least as long as the United States is not directly involved therein. On the contrary, French participation in such projects on either a bilateral or a multilateral basis is extensive and growing. French membership in the so-called Group of Six for defense industrial cooperation and in the aforementioned Independent European Program Group is the most noteworthy example of the latter. Less extensive cooperative ventures in which France has participated, however, have already met with considerable success. The most wide-ranging arrangements to date appear to have been with Great Britain. These have resulted in the development and production of the Jaguar fighter-bomber, the Martel AS-37 and AJ-168 air-to-surface missiles, the Puma and Gazelle tactical assault and armed liaison/transport helicopters, and the Lynx helicopters configured in either an antisubmarine warfare (ASW) or armed general-purpose mode with extensive antitank capabilities, among others. France has also engaged in cooperative efforts with other Western European countries. Prominent among these programs are the Franco-West German Euromissile (which brings together the Aerospatiale and Messerschmitt-Bölkow-Blohm firms) production of the HOT and Milan antitank and the Roland surface-to-air missiles; the development of a new minesweeper of L'Eridan class in conjunction with Belgium and the Netherlands; and the Otomat naval surface-to-surface missile developed jointly with Italy.[163] France's one concession to an American-sponsored system has been its recent subscription to the AWACS (airborne warning and control system) used by NATO.[164]

From the French perspective, France's increasing level of participation in the cooperative development of weapons systems does not invalidate its fundamental belief in the importance of an autonomous defense capability in all respects. Most of the major and secondary weapons systems employed by the French armed forces are of French origin and manufacture. This situation is unlikely to change appreciably in the near future. But it is also recognized in France that international cooperation in terms of the development and production of sophisticated weapons systems is essential in an increasingly interdependent and complex world, even for a nation such as France, which prizes its own independence. This is underscored by France's turn to the strategy of the *sanctuarisation élargie* and the increasing scope of informal French cooperation with NATO forces. Both lend weight to the guarded French assertion that "cooperation is not a goal in itself, but a means of [strengthening France] ... by [increasing the level of] standardization or interoperability."[165] That such cooperation should be limited to Western European countries is merely indicative of France's continuing interest in leading the Continent, if such should become possible at some point in the future, since French isolation would clearly be politically counterproductive in this respect.

Necessity, it seems, can be a demanding taskmaster. Unfortunately, neither necessity nor the presumed requirements of a new strategy can wholly eradicate the constraints on French cooperation with other countries in this area. All of the other Western European countries have different political and economic concerns that do not always coincide to enhance the prospects for international cooperation in the development and production of armaments with France. French nationalism, as suggested above, is also something of a problem, as is French opposition to the United States. The fact that France is not predisposed to engage in cooperative ventures (other than the previously mentioned AWACS) in which one of the superpowers is a participant means, in effect, that cooperative efforts with France foreclose direct access to U.S. technology.[166] This at the very least constrains both French efforts and the willingness of other NATO countries to cooperate with France.

Less openly discussed in many circles than French cooperation in the design and production of armaments in Western Europe is the importance of arms sales abroad to the well-being of the French defense industry. What has been described as "the deepening dependence of French industrial capacity on arms exports" is reflected in the fact that (according to French sources) French arms sales between 1965 and 1975 exceeded $8.2 billion, much of it to Third World countries.[167] Indeed, French arms sales in Africa in particular have often appeared to be a less overt form of intervention. This is because they provide France with both a presence and a degree of political leverage it would not otherwise possess. They also provide a basis for more direct French intervention in support of a good customer-client under certain circumstances. Examples of French arms sale agreements with selected foreign countries (either completed or contracted) in 1978–79 include the sale of (*a*) Mirage F-1 fighters to Spain and Jordan, (*b*) Mirage F-5 fighters to Argentina, (*c*) Puma helicopters to Spain, Lebanon, and Argentina, (*d*)

AMX-30 and AMX-13 tanks to Iraq, Lebanon, Singapore, and Saudi Arabia, (*e*) A69 frigates to Argentina, (*f*) Exocet surface-to-surface naval missiles to Ecuador, and (*g*) HOT and Milan antitank missiles to Syria. Even China has contracted to buy the HOT and Milan missiles and the Crotale SAMs from France.[168]

There are a number of actual or potential disadvantages to such extensive arms sales, however useful they may be to the health of the French defense industry. The most obvious liability is that French arms sales in the Third World, and particularly in Africa and the Middle East, mean that those countries in which France may have the greatest need (in the case of the OPEC countries) or the greatest inclination (in the case of Africa) to intervene will be better able to defend themselves against France and to resist French influence than would otherwise be the case. The fact that such arms sales reflect short-term domestic and balance-of-trade concerns rather than long-term security interests, and may therefore be counterproductive, has not gone unnoticed in France.[169] But it is equally clear that an avenue of escape from that dilemma (which, it must be conceded, is of some concern to all Western advanced industrial societies) is not readily apparent. What this means is that "in France's case the possibility of controlling military exports is hostage to the goal of economic growth. Unless the latter problem can be solved [by other means], progress in the former is likely to be slow whether the Right or the Left rules."[170]

ARMS CONTROL AND DISARMAMENT POLICY

The conflict between economic interests and security concerns inherent in France's arms sales throughout the Third World has its parallel in the dialectic between political preference and national security, which is implicit in France's approach to the problem of arms control. That approach is shaped by five factors. These are (*a*) the belief that France's own forces, nuclear and conventional alike, threaten no one; (*b*) the certainty that actual or potential threats to French security and interests do exist; (*c*) the conviction that arms control may be a means to enhanced security for France but that it is not an end in itself whose attainment has any particular intrinsic value; (*d*) the view that arms control, in the sense of arms reductions, must be undertaken first by the superpowers; and (*e*) the distinction made between vertical proliferation (the acquisition of additional weapons systems of a certain category by states that already possess systems of a similar class) and horizontal proliferation (the acquisition of weapons systems previously absent from a country's arsenal), especially with regard to nuclear weapons.[171]

The implications of these considerations are readily apparent in France's approach to problems of arms control and disarmament in the increasingly more heavily armed world. Instead of making the usual functional distinction between nuclear and nonnuclear weapons systems, France makes a geographical distinction between "*existing nuclear zones,* that is to say those that are already covered by the nuclear deterrent, and *those that are not* [i.e., nonnuclear zones]."[172] In the case of the nuclear-free zones, which largely encompass the Third World, France's official policy is to refrain from introducing nuclear weapons technology where such technology does not now exist. France also purports to encourage countries that do not now possess nuclear weapons to refrain from acquiring them elsewhere or developing them indigenously. In exchange for that mutual self-restraint, France "guarantees" that it (*a*) "will not use nuclear weapons against them or on their territory [against a third party]," and (*b*) "will give them access to the peaceful uses of atomic power"—that is, to the so-called civilian nuclear technology.[173]

There are a number of rather obvious problems with this approach to the question of nuclear nonproliferation. One is that no nation truly believes that another will exercise unilateral self-restraint when its own interests (especially its actual or perceived vital interests) appear to be threatened. Certainly, the fact that the French acquisition of nuclear weapons in the first place reflected in part a reaction to France's forced withdrawal from one intervention (Suez in 1956), coupled with its proclivity to intervene in Africa and its dependence on OPEC oil imports, cannot be entirely reassuring to some countries in at least those areas of the world.

Second, even if France did not intend to use its own nuclear weapons against or on the territory of a nonnuclear Third World country, French restraint does not imply security for the latter. Such forbearance on the part of Paris, after all, is no guarantee against coercion by another nuclear-armed state, or even by a more powerful conventionally armed country. Pakistan learned in 1971, for example, that the political encouragement and military self-restraint of the United States were inadequate assistance during its war with India. There is no reason for other Third World countries to assume that a militarily weaker country such as France would demonstrate greater fidelity, or that conventional assistance from France would suffice in such a situation. Thus, like France itself in the 1960s, a legitimate concern for status and security independent of other countries could lead many nations in the Third World to want to emulate France's own example and develop a national nuclear force.

Third, and perhaps most important, is the fact that there is a very real potential contradiction between the declared French opposition to introducing nuclear weapons into nonnuclear zones, and France's equally clear willingness to provide countries within such zones with nuclear technology for peaceful purposes. As the Indian detonation of its own nuclear device demonstrated, it is extremely difficult for a donor country to police *in toto* the way in which a recipient nation makes use of that technology without violating the latter's sovereignty in what would probably be considered an unaccepted degree. This alone supports the contention that there is no clear French determination today to impede nuclear proliferation. That is, despite protestations to the contrary by some officials, it does appear that "Giscard's France has not really committed itself to the fight against the spread of nuclear weapons."[174]

With respect to the existing nuclear zones in general, and Europe in particular, France believes that two conditions must be met before effective arms control can become a reality; these are that (*a*) the superpowers take the lead in reducing their own strategic nuclear arsenals and (*b*) the disparity in conventional forces favoring the Soviet Union and the other Warsaw Pact nations be eliminated. Only when these preconditions have been met, assert the French, can one seriously proceed with more general and comprehensive arms control and disarmament programs involving other concerned countries, such as France itself.

This position leads France to approve of the SALT process in general, and the SALT II accords recently negotiated (but not ratified as of 1982) between Moscow and Washington in particular, at least in principle. France has apparently decided against publicly criticizing the terms of SALT II, despite occasional indications that some members of the government have certain private reservations about some of them. This is simply because anything that restricts the Soviet and American strategic nuclear arsenals in any way necessarily enhances the utility of France's own *force de dissuasion,* or at least reduces the absolute level of outside threats to its survival.[175]

France takes quite a different view of both the MBFR (Mutual and Balanced Force Reduction) talks under way in Vienna and the proposed negotiations on SALT III. The MBFR talks are seen to be "detrimental to détente" and counterproductive in a more general sense. This is because France believes that any MBFR agreement that could be reached with the Soviets "would shift the already existing imbalance in Europe further in the East Bloc's favor."[176] Such a development would obviously run counter to one of the two fundamental French preconditions for arms control in Europe. A similar reluctance appears in the French attitude toward the proposed SALT III talks on the limitation of "gray area" (theater nuclear) weapons systems. This reluctance has its origins in the French conviction that France's participation in a SALT III accord would only weaken French security without correspondingly significant concessions from the superpowers themselves. Negotiating limitations to France's own strategic nuclear force (which has largely theater-specific capabilities) would therefore undermine "the independence of her [France's] own deterrent capability," since "France's nuclear force is [from its perspective] a 'central system' which secures France's vital interests against any attack."[177]

Given these assumptions (correct or not), it is not surprising that France has determined to abstain from any undertaking that it believes might adversely affect the theater military balance in general, or the position of the French nuclear *force de dissuasion* in particular. Indeed, French participation in any program or negotiations to control nuclear weapons in Europe is asserted to depend on the reduction of both international tension and conventional force levels in Europe. Achieving these objectives, in fact, is the principal aim of the "Conference on Disarmament in Europe" proposed by France to "increase confidence-building measures" and "improve the balance of military potential" in Europe "from the Atlantic to the Urals."[178] Pending the realization of that rather ambitious scheme, France will continue to enhance its own nuclear forces, proceed with underground nuclear testing, and forgo participating in any other arms control negotiations or nuclear test ban talks. The fact that France's seeming indifference to what it refuses to consider a legitimate problem may itself be self-defeating in the long run appears to receive little acceptance in official French circles. France may not threaten anyone else, of course, but there is no good reason for anyone else to trust it when it implicitly mistrusts others. Thus, French intransigence on this question may have the same deleterious impact on the proposed continent-wide disarmament conference as France's earlier intransigence had on the stillborn European Defense Community (EDC). The failure of the EDC was extremely unfortunate, but the failure of arms control in Europe may be fatal to France as well as to its ambitions.

USE OF FORCE

France's preoccupation with the military trappings of status and its ambivalent attitude toward arms control are reflected to a certain extent in its use of the French armed forces for political purposes. Those occasions when force has either been threatened or actually employed highlight both the strengths and the weaknesses of France's strategy and force posture. Both of the latter, as I have discussed, have undergone a change in recent years. But France still lives with the legacy of the *sanctuarisation totale* and the FNS-heavy strategy of massive retaliation, a legacy that will not be overcome quickly or easily.

Despite that legacy—or perhaps because of it—France assigns considerable importance to a reputation for the effective employment of its nonnuclear forces abroad in selected situations. Consciously or not, this concern reflects a certain logic on France's part. France's interpretation of independence in world politics necessitates both the capability and the willingness to employ military force when challenged. The only way that willingness can actually be demonstrated is to use that force occasionally. Otherwise, one lacks credibility. Moreover, the fact that France has not emphasized its nonnuclear forces until recently has made their occasional employment abroad all that more significant to France. That is, if those forces that had not been given primary attention did well when deployed outside of metropolitan France, the possibility that those forces that had received such attention—that is, the *force de dissuasion*—would do likewise if necessary could be enhanced in the eyes of other countries.

Be that as it may, France has used its armed forces overseas in four separate capacities.[179] First, France has used its navy to provide a military presence or a show of force in certain parts of the world. The fleet maintained in the Indian Ocean, for example, was until recently the largest Western force in that region. The naval squadron deployed to North Africa early in 1980 was widely seen as indicative of a demonstration of support for French interests in that region. Second, French forces perform relatively passive functions in countries with which France has military assistance agreements. In this capacity, they serve as advisers, instructors, technical specialists, and coordinators for a wide range of civic action programs from road building and related engineering tasks to public health and medical assistance. Third, France currently has units deployed with the United Nations peace-keeping force in Lebanon. Fourth and finally, France employs its armed forces abroad in explicit support of French interests, especially in Africa, supporting friendly governments or intervening to create a favorable political situation.

The third and fourth categories are obviously of greatest interest in the present context, simply because they provide the greatest test of the reliability and the efficiency of the French troops under the most adverse conditions they are likely to encounter short of a battle in defense of France itself. As indicated earlier, France maintains that participating in international peace-keeping operations is both the obligation and the mark of an independent power. The year before French forces were sent to Lebanon under the United Nations colors, Giscard had indicated a willingness to send French forces to that country on his own. For a variety of reasons (including sheer prudence), Giscard decided against taking that form of unilateral action. The subsequent United Nations appeal for contingents to police the cease-fire being negotiated in Lebanon thus provided France with an excellent opportunity to achieve its initially desired presence in the region in a less demanding multilateral political framework. That was an opportunity France did not let pass.

It is in Africa, however, that the French use of military force for political ends has been most notable. In recent years, there has been a marked increase in the incidence of French interventions (overt and covert) in Africa. This has reached the point where France has come to be variously characterized as a neocolonial power or a de facto Western gendarme in that region. Prominent among such interventions have been the introduction of French forces to support friendly governments in Gabon (1964) and Chad (1968); the operations in Zaïre (1978) to rescue trapped Europeans and to repel a Katangese invasion force; and the overthrow of Central African Emperor Bokassa I (1979), which reliable sources reported "was arranged and orchestrated by France" and carried out in the presence of French troops.[180] In the last instance, for once, French interests were seen to be better served by overthrowing a government instead of maintaining the status quo, as France has usually been wont to do.

In each case, French interventions appear to have been characterized by a judicious linking of military means to political ends. Neither domestic opposition nor foreign displeasure seems to have had a discernible effect on French actions. The single possible exception to this general rule may have been Giscard's abortive suggestion concerning a unilateral French intervention into Lebanon in advance of the United Nations force. Further, French interventions seem to have been motivated by a combination of three factors whose individual importance certainly varied in specific cases. One factor was a clear desire to secure France's traditional interests in the Third World, and specifically in Africa. A second consideration was that French interventions abroad allow France to demonstrate an ability to exercise influence independent of the superpowers, especially in areas where it would be extremely difficult (in a political sense) for other Western powers to act. The third factor is the least tangible but, in many respects, the most important. This is that French interventions provide an opportunity to enhance the grandeur of France.[181] The acclaim France received following its rescue operation in Zaïre, for example, was itself the best reward France could have been given for its efforts, and the hope of receiving it may well have contributed to the French decision to act in the first place. Certainly it was in keeping with past manifestations of French ambitions and interests.

There is also every indication that France intends to enhance its ability to undertake such operations in the future. Plans are now being implemented to give French intervention forces the additional training and air transport required for "the execution of combat missions in tropical or equatorial climates."[182] It is readily apparent that all of that, and more, is sorely needed. France's interventions may well have been politically impressive, but militarily they highlighted the operational shortcomings that were the almost inevitable consequence of the disproportionate attention France had given the *force de dissuasion* for so many years. The French force that intervened in Zaïre, for instance, was able to deploy only with the aid of American air transport and logistics support.[183] Such assistance cannot have been received as an unmixed blessing by a status-conscious country such as France. After all, how could one truly claim to be an independent power if it was necessary to seek outside aid for such a relatively minor operation? It seems that in many respects France's interventions and commitments in Africa, and the constraints on them, underscore what has been called "the basic traditional dilemma of France's defense policy—high objectives and limited means."[184] It is by no means certain that France will be able to resolve that dilemma in the 1980s. On the contrary, the situation may actually worsen. This is because "France is probably reaching the limits of its current power projection capabilities . . . but France is assuming new commitments anyway."[185] Once again, it is a matter of policy being dictated by ambitions rather than by objective considerations of the realities of world power.

Epilogue: the defense policy of France in retrospect

The preceding analysis necessarily produces a complicated view of French defense policy. On the one hand, it is difficult not to be impressed with the breadth of French strategic thinking, as well as the extent to which French strategy has shaped that country's force structure and employment doctrine. It is also apparent that France has achieved much more than an outside observer might have anticipated when de Gaulle first came to power. In fact, given what France has accomplished with its relatively limited resources, one might well wish that American defense policy had been directed and managed as well as that of France. "Gaullism," at least as it has been practiced by the presidents of the Fifth Republic, is not necessarily good for the Gaullist state's allies. On the whole, however, it seems to work remarkably well for the Gaullist state itself. Certainly there is much truth to the argument that "France [today] possesses a flexibility of military options unmatched by any other Western European nation. . . . Only a very bold or exceedingly stupid aggressor would challenge the French military by attempting to invade French soil."[186]

On the other hand, there is good reason to question France's ability to maintain its current political-military position in the future. Certainly the problems with France's current strategy, the competing budgetary demands that must be reconciled, and the host of other difficulties that have been identified in this chapter do not augur well for France. Indeed, they suggest that France may yet have to accept some additional erosion of its autonomy and some attenuation of its military capacity to act as an independent power in the world, no matter how unattractive such a course of action may be to the French.

Further, it is difficult to escape the conclusion that France's present and projected strategy and force posture reflect pretensions more than they do a realistic response to that country's security options and requirements, *given France's actual position in the hierarchy of nations*. This is not a matter of an overly ambitious strategy dictating an inappropriate force posture, or vice versa; it is that both French strategy and French force posture are at the service of a political ideal whose attainment exceeds French capabilities. Nor is it likely that France will take the corrective measures necessary to rationalize these disparities. Past performance and present practices both suggest that the French fixation with the appearance of status and security will increase as France's ability to achieve either of them independently declines. This portends a future deterioration in French military power and its already somewhat tenuous linkage to French political purpose. Such a development would exacerbate existing inconsistencies in French policy and call into question the fundamental assumptions on which that policy is based.

Perhaps the greatest single cause of this situation is the political equivocation discussed earlier that is still characteristic of France's foreign policy. France has simply not yet reconciled itself to its present position in the world, nor has it yet been willing to focus its efforts entirely on a specific role in world politics. It still pursues, at different times and on different issues, variants of independent, Atlanticist, and European policies intended to allow France to interact with other nations while postponing a final resolution of the basic contradictions in its declared interests. Unfortunately, France's inability—or unwillingness—to decide among these three broad political alternatives not only distorts the debate on French foreign policy but also inhibits the formulation and implementation of a comprehensive defense policy fully attuned to the global geopolitical reality within which France reluctantly must act.

A final question that arises concerning French defense policy is not restricted to France itself. It is simply whether any middle power, even one with France's capabilities and aspirations, can truly be said to have an independent ability to safeguard its own vital national interests, much less the coherent defense policy such a capability would presuppose and require. It could easily be argued, I believe, that any nation that concedes its ultimate dependence on another country for defense against outside aggression (as France does with respect to its dependence on the United States to deter the Soviet Union) really has a defense policy capable of dealing only with residual issues of marginal significance. In such a case, the domestic component in that nation's defense policy would be of far greater importance than the international security environment within which it must act.

It is this situation that seems to account for the inconsistencies in French defense policy. Under these circumstances, both the debate over and the actual direction of French defense policy serve principally for the internal rationalization and legitimization of France's military establishment and ambitions. Seen in these terms, and coupled with a recognition of France's continuing desire for prestige and its deep-seated concern about the Germans, French strategy and force posture become more readily understandable. That they may not become any more realistic is unfortunate, but still something with which we all may live, if only because France itself has more to lose from its intransigence than do the countries in Europe and elsewhere with which France must deal. That, perhaps, is but one of the many grim ironies with which France and other nations must come to terms in the emerging international security system of the 1980s.

Notes

1. John Baylis, "French Defense Policy," in *Contemporary Strategy: Theories and Policies,* ed. John Baylis, Ken Booth, John Garnett, and Phil Williams (New York: Holmes & Meier, 1975), p. 287. For other general critiques of French Defense policy, see Wichard Woyke, "The Process of Change in French Defense Policy," *Aussenpolitik* 28, no. 1 (1977); James Bellini, *French Defense Policy* (London: Royal United Services Institute, 1974); Wilfred L. Ebel, "The French Republic," *Military Review* 59, no. 8 (August 1979); and Lothar Rühl, *La Politique militaire de la Ve République* (Paris: PLON, 1976).

2. Alan Ned Sabrosky, "America's Choices in the Emerging World Order," *International Security Review* 4, no. 3 (Fall 1979): 247.

3. Guy Doly, "Sécurité de la France et Union européenne," *Politique Etrangère* 43, no. 3 (1978): 265.

4. Jean François-Poncet, "Speech of May 3, 1979, to the National Assembly on Foreign Policy," *Journal Officiel,* 4 May 1979, p. 2; and Wolf Mendl, *Deterrence and Persuasion: French Nuclear Armament in the Context of National Policy, 1945-1969* (London: Faber & Faber, 1970), pp. 15-16.

5. Yves Laulan, "Une Défense asservie," *Contrepoint,* no. 27 (1978), p. 44; Doly, "Sécurité de la France," pp. 274-75; François de Rose, "The Future of SALT and Western Security in Europe," *Foreign Affairs* 57, no. 5 (Summer 1979): 1067; and Marcel Merle, "Le Système mondial: réalité et crise," *Politique Etrangère* 43, no. 5 (1978): 499-500.

6. Jean-Baptiste Margeride, "Le Japon, nouvelle puissance militaire?" *Défense Nationale,* May 1978; Doly, "Sécurité de la France," p. 274; Pierre M. Gallois, "French Defense Planning: the Future in the Past," *International Security* 1, no. 2 (Fall 1976): 22; John C. Cairns, "France, Europe, and 'The Design of the World,'" *International Journal* 32, no. 2 (Spring 1977); and Valéry Giscard d'Estaing, "La Défense de la France," *Défense Nationale,* July 1976, pp. 8-9.

7. Ray Cline, *World Power Assessment, 1977* (Boulder, Colo.: Westview, 1978), pp. 132-33. See also Pierre Lellouche, "France in the International Nuclear Energy Controversy: A New Policy under Giscard d'Estaing," *Orbis* 22, no. 4 (Winter 1979), esp. pp. 951-52; and Jim Browning, "France Scuttles British Sea Power," *Washington Star,* 29 January 1978.

8. Roger Morgan, "The Foreign Policies of Great Britain, France, and West Germany," in *World Politics: An Introduction,* ed. James N. Rosenau, Kenneth W. Thompson, and Gavin Boyd (New York: Free Press, 1976), p. 163.

9. For concurring views spanning two decades, see Amaury de Riencourt, "The French Dilemma," *Orbis* 2, no. 1 (Spring 1958): 115; and Doly, "Sécurité de la France," pp. 271-73.

10. Gen. Guy Mery, "Address to the Institute for Advanced Studies in National Defense of April 3, 1978, on France's Defense Policy," Washington, D.C.: French Embassy 78/68 (1978).

11. D. Bruce Marshall, "Recent Developments in French Strategic Doctrine" (Manuscript presented at the biennial meeting of the Section on Military Studies of the International Studies Association, Kiawah Island, S.C., 8-10 November 1978), pp. 1-2.

12. Sabrosky, "French Foreign Policy Alternatives," *Orbis* 19, no. 4 (Winter 1976); and Doly, "Sécurité de la France," pp. 279-80.

13. For discussions of the issues and problems involved in a European security association independent of the United States, see David Watt, "The European Initiative," *Foreign Affairs* 57, no. 3 (1979): 577; Jean Klein, "France, NATO, and European Security," *International Security* 1, no. 3 (Winter 1977), esp. p. 41; François-Poncet, "French Foreign Policy," p. 10; Jean-Louis Burban, "Le Parlement européen et les problèmes de défense," *Défense Nationale,* February 1978; Mery, "France's Defense Policy," p. 19; Graeme P. Auton, "Nuclear Deterrence and the Medium Power: A proposal for Doctrinal Change in the British and French Cases," *Orbis* 20, no. 2 (Summer 1976): 396-99; Flora Lewis, "Debate on French Military Policy Breaks into Open," *New York Times,* 19 August 1977; Joseph I. Coffey, *Arms Control and European Security* (New York: Praeger, 1977), p. 24; and Wynfred Joshua and Walter F. Hahn, *Nuclear Politics: America, France, and Britain,* The Washington Papers, vol. 1, no. 9 (Beverly Hills, Calif.: Sage, 1973).

14. Marianna P. Sullivan, *France's Vietnam Policy: A Study in French-American Relations* (Westport, Conn.: Greenwood Press, 1978), p. 7.

15. Doly, "Sécurité de la France," p. 265.

16. Edmond Combaux, "French Military Policy and European Federalism," *Orbis* 13, no. 1 (Spring 1969): 145.

17. David S. Yost, "French Defense Budgeting: Persistent Constraints and Future Prospects" (Manuscript presented at the biennial meeting of the Section on Military Studies of the International Studies Association, Kiawah Island, S.C., 8-10 November 1978), p. 35.

18. Sabrosky, "French Foreign Policy Alternatives," pp. 1432-35.

19. This is discussed briefly in Morgan, "Foreign Policies," p. 164.

20. Elliott R. Goodman, "De Gaulle's NATO Policy in Perspective," *Orbis* 10, no. 3 (Fall 1976); Sabrosky, "French Foreign Policy Alternatives," pp. 1430-32; Sullivan, *France's Vietnam Policy,* ch. 1; and Charles A. Micaud, "Gaullism after De Gaulle," *Orbis* 14, no. 3 (Fall 1970): 657.

21. Jacques Chirac, "France: Illusions, Temptations, Ambitions," *Foreign Affairs* 56, no. 3 (April 1978): 499.

22. See, for example, Giscard d'Estaing, "La Défense de la France," pp. 7-8; Louis de Guiringaud, "Trois Aspects de la politique étrangère de la France: défense, détente, désarmament," *Défense Nationale,* March 1978, pp. 11, 22; and François-Poncet, "French Foreign Policy," p. 11.

23. Watt, "European Initiative," p. 587.

24. Chirac, "France," p. 489.

25. François-Poncet, "French Foreign Policy," p. 1.

26. International Institute for Strategic Studies, *Strategic Survey, 1978* (London: International Institute for Strategic Studies, 1978), pp. 22-23.

27. Walter Schutze, "Défense de l'Europe ou défense européenne: les institutions," *Politique Etrangère* 43, no. 6 (1978): 662-64; Frederic M. Anderson, "Weapons Procurement Collaboration: A New Era for NATO?," *Orbis* 20, no. 4 (Winter 1977): 974-75; Laulan, "Une Défense asservie," p. 43; Denise Artaud, "De Wilson à Carter: mythes et réalités de la politique américaine en Europe," *Défense Nationale,* January 1979, p. 60; and Laulan, "Europe: l'appel aux armes," *Contrepoint,* no. 29 (1979), p. 29.

28. Sue Ellen M. Charlton, "European Unity and the Politics of the French Left," *Orbis* 19, no. 4 (Winter 1976): 1462.

29. International Institute for Strategic Studies, *The Military Balance, 1978-1979* (London: International Institute for Strategic Studies, 1978), p. 16; Anderson, "Weapons Procurement Collaboration," pp. 973-77; and Ebel, "The French Republic," p. 50.

30. *Military Balance, 1978-1979,* p. 17.

31. Mery, "France's Defense Policy," pp. 3-4, 6-7; Pierre Lellouche and Dominique Moisi, "French Policy in Africa: A Lonely Battle against Destabilization," *International Security* 3, no. 4 (Spring 1979): 109, 111-15; and *Défense Nationale,* January 1979, p. 171.

32. Mery, "France's Defense Policy," p. 4.

33. For a discussion of the evolution of "threat perception" in French defense policy, see Edward Kolodziej, "French Military Doctrine," in *Comparative Defense Policy,* ed. Frank B. Horton, Anthony C. Rogerson, and Edward Warner III (Baltimore: Johns Hopkins University Press, 1974), pp. 245-56.

34. Giscard d'Estaing, "Press Conference of June 14, 1978," *Défense Nationale,* August-September 1978, p. 192; Giscard d'Estaing, "Press Conference of February 15, 1979," *Défense Nationale,* April 1979, p. 194; François-Poncet, "French Foreign Policy," p. 4; and Jean Laloy, "Coexistence pacifique ou paix?," *Défense Nationale,* May 1978, p. 22.

35. Laulan, "Europe," p. 29.

36. Robert Touleman, "Les Chemins de l'indépendance," *Défense Nationale,* February 1978, esp. pp. 17-19; Laulan, "Une Défense asservie," p. 43; Doly, "Sécurité de la France," p. 275; and Sabrosky, "French Foreign Policy Alternatives," p. 1434.

37. See Giscard d'Estaing's remark on 24 October 1974, as reported in *Le Monde,* 26 October 1974. See also Raymond Barre, "Discours prononcé au Camp de Mailly le 18 juin 1977," *Défense Nationale,* August-September 1977, p. 9.

38. Marc Ullmann observed that "all of the inconsistencies of French policy spring from one single, but basic contradiction: *France's foreign policy is based on an attitude of trust toward West Germany, whereas her defense policy reflects an attitude of distrust of that country*" [italics in original]; see his "Security Aspects in French Foreign Policy," *Survival,* November/December 1973, p. 267. For concurring views, see Baylis, "French Defense Policy," pp. 289-90; and Mendl, *Deterrence and Persuasion,* p. 33.

39. Lellouche, "France," pp. 955-56, 963.

40. "Paris and Bonn Take a Stand," *Newsweek,* 18 February 1980.

41. Jerome Jaffre, "France Looks to Europe," *Public Opinion,* March/May 1979.

42. *Strategic Survey, 1978,* p. 103. See also Claus Arndt, "Bilan de la politique de détente entre les deux états allemands," *Politique Etrangère* 42, no. 6 (1977): 593-99.

43. P. Lacoste, "Problèmes contemporains de politique et de stratégie navale," *Défense Nationale,* October 1978, p. 48.

44. Kolodziej, "French Military Doctrine," p. 257.

45. Yvon Bourges, "Speech of June 15, 1978," quoted in Gérard Vaillant, "Défense en France," *Defénse Nationale,* August-September 1978, p. 165; and Stephen S. Roberts, "French Naval Policy outside of Europe" (Manuscript presented at the biennial meeting of the Section on Military Studies of the International Studies Association, Kiawah Island, S.C., 8-10 November 1978), pp. 7-11.

46. Jean Klein, "La Gauche française de les problèmes de défense," *Politique Etrangère* 43, no. 5 (1978): 534.

47. See Marshall, "French Strategic Doctrine"; Kolodziej, "French Military Doctrine"; Pierre Gallois, *The Balance of Terror: Strategy for a Nuclear Age* (Boston: Houghton Mifflin, 1961); Raymond Aron, "La Force de dissuasion et l'Alliance atlantique," *Défense Nationale,* January 1977, pp. 37-38; the writings of André Beaufre, including *An Introduction to Strategy* (New York: Praeger, 1965), *Deterrence and Strategy* (New York: Praeger, 1966), *Strategy of Action* (New York: Praeger, 1967), and *Strategy for Tomorrow* (New York: Crane, Russak, 1974); and the writings regularly published in *Défense Nationale, Stratégie,* and *Nation Armée,* among others.

48. Sullivan, *France's Vietnam Policy,* pp. 14-15; Bayliss, "French Defense Policy," p. 301.

49. Baylis, "French Defense Policy," p. 297; and Lellouche and Moisi, "French Policy in Africa," pp. 116-17. The latter would be supplemented, especially in an internal security role, by the organized reserves (DOT) and the paramilitary Gendarmerie.

50. Bellini, *French Defense Policy,* p. 49.

51. The classic statement of this position appears in Michel Debré, "La France et sa défense," *Revue de Défense Nationale,* January 1972, p. 7.

52. For a discussion of the problems associated with *la défense tous-azimuts,* see Combaux, "French Military Policy," pp. 147 ff.

53. Sullivan, *France's Vietnam Policy,* pp. 14–15; Bayliss, "French Defense Policy," pp. 301 ff.

54. Auton, "Nuclear Deterrence and the Medium Power," p. 372.

55. We sometimes forget that the NATO strategy of flexible response has a collateral benefit (at least from the American perspective) of allowing the United States some additional time to resolve an East-West conflict short of a Soviet-American nuclear exchange.

56. For a good summary of this subject, see Marshall, "French Strategic Doctrine," pp. 5–6; and Flora Lewis, "Paris Military Parade Reflects New Strategy," *New York Times,* 15 July 1977.

57. Yvon Bourges, as quoted in *Défense Nationale,* January 1979, p. 182. See also Gérard Vaillant, "Défense en France," *Défense Nationale,* August–September 1978, p. 165.

58. Lellouche and Moisi, "French Policy in Africa," pp. 120–21; Marshall, "French Strategic Doctrine," p. 23; *Strategic Survey, 1976,* pp. 67–69; and Robert R. Ropelewski, "French Emphasizing Nuclear Weapons," *Aviation Week,* 2 August 1976.

59. Woyke, "Process of Change in French Defense Policy," p. 10.

60. Klein, "La Gauche française," p. 23; and Gallois, "French Defense Planning," pp. 27–31.

61. For a discussion of this plan, see Jacques Tine, "France's Military Effort in the Lead-up to the Eighties," *NATO Review,* June 1979, esp. p. 11; and *Défense Nationale,* February 1979, p. 146.

62. Barre, "Discours," p. 10; and Yvon Bourges as quoted in *Le Monde,* 10 November 1977.

63. Indeed, the 1977 "Bastille Day" parade saw France emphasizing its intervention forces.

64. Lellouche and Moisi, "French Policy in Africa," p. 128n. See also Ropelewski, "French Emphasizing Nuclear Weapons"; Vaillant, "Défense en France," p. 169; Gen. Guy Mery, "Une Armée pour quoi faire et comment?" *Défense Nationale,* June 1976, p. 16; Mery, "France's Defense Policy," pp. 15–20; and Roberts, "French Naval Policy outside of Europe," pp. 24–25.

65. For discussions of the development of French nuclear weapons and doctrine, see Mendl, *Deterrence and Persuasion;* and W. L. Kohl, *French Nuclear Diplomacy* (Princeton, N.J.: Princeton University Press, 1971).

66. Mery, "Une Armée pour quoi faire et comment?," pp. 13–14.

67. For discussions of this concept, see Marshall, "French Strategic Doctrine," pp. 2–3 ff.; Mendl, *Deterrence and Persuasion,* pp. 15–16; Gallois, "French Defense Planning," p. 25; and Auton, "Nuclear Deterrence and the Medium Power," pp. 373–76. For an interesting treatment of the doctrinal similarities underlying the French and Chinese nuclear forces, see B. W. Augenstein, "The Chinese and French Programs for the Development of National Nuclear Forces," *Orbis* 11, no. 3 (Fall 1967).

68. Pierre Gallois, "The Future of France's *Force de Dissuasion,*" *Strategic Review* 7, no. 3 (Summer 1979): 37.

69. Pierre Hassner, "A NATO Dissuasion Strategy: A French View," in *NATO and Dissuasion,* ed. Morton A. Kaplan (Chicago: University of Chicago Press, 1974), p. 97; and Gallois, "The Future of France's *Force de Dissuasion.*"

70. Roy C. Macridis, "French Foreign Policy," in *Foreign Policy in World Politics,* ed. Roy C. Macridis, 5th ed. (Englewood Cliffs, N.J.: Prentice-Hall, 1976), p. 109.

71. Walter F. Hahn and Wynfred Joshua, "The Impact of SALT on British and French Nuclear Forces," in *Contrasting Approaches to Strategic Arms Control,* ed. Robert L. Pfaltzgraff, Jr. (Lexington, Mass.: D. C. Heath/ Lexington Books, 1974), p. 154.

72. Roberts, "French Naval Policy outside of Europe," p. 19, discusses in a maritime context the French notion of "graduated/flexible response."

73. Kolodziej, "French Military Doctrine," p. 252. Kolodziej's remark actually predated the formal shift in doctrines but it applies with particular force to the current doctrine of flexible response.

74. Auton, "Nuclear Deterrence and the Medium Power," p. 374.

75. Ibid., p. 375.

76. Mendl, *Deterrence and Persuasion,* p. 16.

77. For summaries of these functions, see Hahn and Joshua, "The Impact of SALT on British and French Nuclear Forces," pp. 155–56; and Mendl, *Deterrence and Persuasion,* p. 18.

78. For a discussion of the French understanding of the political utility of military power, especially with respect to the *force de dissuasion,* see Bayliss, "French Defense Policy," pp. 287–91.

79. General Guy Mery, "Réflexions sur le concept d'emploi des forces," *Défense Nationale,* November 1975, p. 20; idem, "Une Armée pour quoi faire et comment?" p. 13; Baylis, "French Defense Policy," p. 288; Mendl, *Deterrence and Persuasion,* p. 207; Kolodziej, "French Military Doctrine," p. 254.

80. Pierre Dabezies, "The Defence of France and the Defence of Europe," in *Defence Yearbook, 1974* (London: R.U.S.I./Brassey's, 1974), p. 116.

81. De Rose, "Future of SALT," p. 1066.

82. Gallois, "French Defense Planning," p. 31.

83. For a summary of "Operation Vulture," see Bernard B. Fall, *Hell in a Very Small Place* (Philadelphia: J. B. Lippincott Co., 1966), pp. 293–314.

84. Hahn and Joshua, "The Impact of SALT on British and French Nuclear Forces," p. 153; James O. Goldsborough, "The Franco-German Entente," *Foreign Affairs* 54, no. 3 (April 1976): 507.

85. The French apprehension about a potential "balance of imbalances" between the French nuclear forces and the FRG's conventional forces is extremely interesting. Allies rarely apply such yardsticks to one another's own forces, which are assumed to complement each other. That France does not make such an assumption, at least on the basis of its declared policy, adds weight to the implicit French mistrust of the FRG.

86. Quoted in Marshall, "French Strategic Doctrine," p. 9.

87. *Strategic Survey, 1976,* pp. 69–70; and Auton, "Nuclear Deterrence and the Medium Power," p. 370.

88. Doly, "Sécurité de la France," p. 279.

89. Jaffre, "France Looks to Europe," p. 17.

90. Ibid.

91. Jean-Marc Lech, "L'évolution de l'opinion des Français sur la défense à travers les sondages de 1972 à 1976," *Défense Nationale* (August-September 1977): 51, 54, 56. The specific responses to the question, "Could a country such as France properly assure its defense without

the *force de dissuasion?*'' were as follows (a ''yes'' vote indicates a belief that the *force de dissuasion* is necessary):

	Yes	No	No Opinion
1973	25%	52%	23%
1975	20%	60%	20%

92. Morgan, ''The Foreign Policies of Great Britain, France, and West Germany,'' p. 167.

93. For an appraisal of the basis of the Socialist party's position on defense and foreign affairs, see Michael M. Harrison, ''A Socialist Foreign Policy for France?,'' *Orbis* 19, no. 4 (Winter 1976), esp. pp. 1489 and 1495.

94. Watt, ''The European Initiative,'' esp. pp. 574 and 578.

95. For discussions of these developments, see Klein, ''La Gauche française''; Chirac, ''France,'' esp. pp. 491–92; Watt, ''The European Initiative,'' p. 574; and Ronald Koven, ''Two Faces of Defeat,'' *Washington Post,* 22 March 1978.

96. For a general discussion of the divergent views of the PS and the PCF on French foreign and defense policy, see Howard Machin and Vincent Wright, ''The Search for Identity in Unity,'' *Comparative Politics* 10, no. 1 (October 1977), esp. p. 61; Flora Lewis, ''Left Wing in France Fails to End Discord,'' *New York Times,* 15 September 1977; Klein, ''La Gauche française,'' pp. 534–35; and International Institute for Strategic Studies, *Strategic Survey, 1977* (London: International Institute for Strategic Studies, 1978), p. 73.

97. Ronald Koven, ''Mitterand, Young Activists Transform Socialist Party,'' *Washington Post,* 7 March 1978.

98. Pierre Hassner, ''Eurocommunism and Western Europe,'' *NATO Review,* August 1978, p. 23.

99. Neil McInnes, *Eurocommunism,* The Washington Papers, vol. 4, no. 37 (Beverly Hills, Calif.: Sage, 1976), p. 70.

100. Combaux, ''French Military Policy,'' p. 145.

101. For a summary of Giscard's strategic approach, see Woyke, ''The Process of Change in French Defense Policy,'' pp. 11–12.

102. André Mattei, ''Le Facteur nucléaire,'' *Politique Etrangère* 43, no. 6 (1978): 677–78; Hahn and Joshua, ''The Impact of SALT on British and French Nuclear Forces,'' p. 155; Macridis, ''French Foreign Policy,'' p. 108.

103. Auton, ''Nuclear Deterrence and the Medium Power,'' p. 393.

104. Baylis, ''French Defense Policy,'' p. 296.

105. Guy Doly, *Stratégie, France, Europe: Sécurité de la France et Union européenne* (Paris: Les Editions Media, 1977), p. 205.

106. Marshall, ''French Strategic Doctrine,'' p. 26; Klein, ''La Gauche française,'' p. 41; Gallois, ''Future of France's *Force de Dissuasion,*'' pp. 40–41.

107. For an excellent study of the French decision-making process, see Yost, ''French Defense Budgeting.''

108. Henri Beauvais, ''Planification et programmation dans les armées,'' *Défense Nationale,* May 1978, esp. pp. 53–54.

109. For a discussion of this model and its implications for the decision-making process, see Graham Allison, *Essence of Decision* (Boston: Little, Brown, 1971), ch. 1. Note that *rationality* is used in the text as an approximation of a gain-maximizing process that takes account of interests, options, and consequences.

110. Yost, ''French Defense Budgeting,'' pp. 13–16.

111. Morgan, ''The Foreign Policies of Great Britain, France, and West Germany,'' pp. 168–69.

112. Yost, ''French Defense Budgeting,'' pp. 17–22.

113. France, *White Paper on National Defense* (1973), vol. 2, ch. 1, pp. 7–8.

114. Edward Kolodziej, ''Measuring French Arms Transfers: A Problem of Sources and Some Sources of Problems with ACDA Data,'' *Journal of Conflict Resolution* 23, no. 2 (June 1979): 197.

115. Yost, ''French Defense Budgeting,'' pp. 22, 34–35.

116. Morgan, ''The Foreign Policies of Great Britain, France, and West Germany,'' p. 165.

117. For an overview of the General Secretariat of National Defense, see the French *White Paper on National Defense,* vol. 2, ch. 1, pp. 8–9.

118. Ibid., chs. 1–2.

119. Bellini describes this as part of what he calls France's Scientific-Military Complex. See his *French Defense Policy,* ch. 4.

120. Arthur J. Alexander, ''Weapons Acquisition in the Soviet Union, the United States, and France,'' in *Comparative Defense Policy,* ed. Horton, Rogerson, and Warner, pp. 439, 442. For an unusually perceptive discussion of this phenomenon, see pp. 438–42 in Alexander's study.

121. *White Paper on National Defense,* vol. 2, ch. 1, pp. 9–12.

122. Yost, ''French Defense Budgeting,'' p. 1. Yost describes these constraints in considerable detail on pp. 23–34.

123. Jacques Isnard, ''Rethinking French Defense,'' *Manchester Guardian* (*Le Monde*), 24 August 1974; Stanley Hoffmann, ''Toward a Common European Foreign Policy?,'' in *The United States and Western Europe,* ed. Wolfram Hanrieder (Cambridge, Mass.: Winthrop Publishing Co., 1974), p. 83.

124. For an interesting treatment of this problem as part of France's general defense budget, see Philippe Lecarrière, ''Problèmes financiers de la défense,'' *Défense Nationale,* January 1977.

125. Doly, ''Sécurité de la France,'' pp. 277–78; *Le Monde,* 19 November 1977.

126. Yost, ''French Defense Budgeting,'' pp. 34–35.

127. Alexander, ''Weapons Acquisition,'' p. 442.

128. Morgan, ''The Foreign Policies of Great Britain, France, and West Germany,'' pp. 163–64.

129. Yost, ''French Defense Budgeting,'' pp. 6–13.

130. Ibid., p. 16.

131. Ebel, ''The French Republic,'' p. 55.

132. Michel L. Martin, ''Conscription and the Decline of the Mass Army in France, 1960–1975,'' *Armed Forces and Society* 3, no. 3 (May 1977): 392–93.

133. Much the same phenomenon appears throughout Western Europe, as well as in the United States. See Anthony S. Bennell, ''The Effectiveness of Supplementary Military Forces,'' in *Supplementary Reserve Forces: Reserves, Militias, Auxiliaries,* ed. Louis A. Zurcher and Gwyn Harries-Jenkins (Beverly Hills, Calif.: Sage, 1978), pp. 64–65.

134. It has been suggested that being composed of volunteers ''allows their use in combat overseas.'' See Lellouche and Moisi, ''French Policy in Africa,'' p. 128n. It should be

noted that the so-called Marine Division is the lineal descendant of the French colonial infantry and should not be confused with the amphibious assault forces with the navy.

135. A particularly forceful presentation of such arguments appears in Philippe Debas. *L'Armée de l'atome* (Paris: Copernic, 1976).

136. Bennell, "Supplementary Military Forces," p. 53.

137. Paul R. Viotti, "Introduction to Military Doctrine," in *Comparative Defense Policy,* ed. Horton, Rogerson, and Warner, p. 190.

138. Kolodziej, "French Military Doctrine," p. 257.

139. China's armed forces and defense outlays are considerably larger than those of France, of course, and some other countries (e.g., India) have more personnel in their active-duty military establishments. See International Institute for Strategic Studies, *The Military Balance, 1979-1980* (London: International Institute for Strategic Studies, 1980), pp. 94-97. Few, however, can approach the technological sophistication and operational effectiveness of the French armed forces.

140. Stanislav Andreski, *Military Organizations and Society,* 2nd ed. (Berkeley, Calif.: University of California Press, 1968).

141. *Military Balance, 1979-1980,* pp. 24, 96-97. As noted earlier, of course, France's continuing population growth rate suggests a reduction in this percentage if manpower levels are held constant.

142. Ibid., pp. 20, 24-25, 92, 94-96.

143. Tine, "France's Military Effort"; Woyke, "The Process of Change in French Defense Policy"; Yost, "French Defense Budgeting," pp. 5, 11-13; and *Strategic Survey, 1976,* pp. 70-71.

144. Ropelewski, "French Emphasizing Nuclear Weapons"; Yost, "French Defense Budgeting," pp. 4, 8-10; Gérard Vaillant, "Défense en France," *Défense Nationale,* January 1979, pp. 157-59 and *Défense Nationale,* August-September 1978, pp. 165-70.

145. Mery, "France's Defense Policy," p. 13.

146. Vaillant, "Défense en France," *Défense Nationale,* August-September 1978, p. 166; Baylis, "French Defense Policy," p. 304; *Military Balance, 1979-1980,* p. 90; Bellini, *French Defense Policy,* p. 76; Ebel, "The French Republic," p. 52; and *Défense Nationale,* June 1978, p. 171.

147. Mery, "France's Defense Policy," pp. 20-26; Auton, "Nuclear Deterrence and the Medium Power," pp. 396-98; Gallois, "Future of France's *Force de Dissuasion,* p. 38; Ivan Margine, "L'Avenir de la disuasion," *Défense Nationale,* April 1978.

148. For discussions of these changes, see *Défense Nationale,* January 1978, p. 143; *Défense Nationale,* January 1979, p. 160; *Défense Nationale* (February 1979), pp. 146-49; *Military Balance, 1978-1979,* pp. 22-23; and *Military Balance, 1979-1980,* pp. 24-25. Among other changes, the French army is proceeding with the integration of female officers and NCOs into the forces, but not in what the U.S. Army would call the combat arms. See *Défense Nationale,* October 1978, pp. 166-67.

149. Ebel, "The French Republic," pp. 53-54.

150. *Military Balance, 1979-1980,* p. 24.

151. *Défense Nationale,* August-September 1978, p. 169; and Roberts, "French Naval Policy outside of Europe."

152. *Military Balance, 1979-1980,* pp. 24-25; *Jane's Fighting Ships, 1979-1980* (New York: Franklin Watts, 1979); *Défense Nationale,* October 1978, p. 181.

153. *Défense Nationale,* January 1978, pp. 151-56; and *Défense Nationale,* January 1979, pp. 170 ff.

154. *Military Balance, 1979-1980,* p. 25; *Défense Nationale,* February 1978, pp. 148-54; and *Défense Nationale,* January 1979, pp. 163-67.

155. For a comprehensive discussion of the French reserves and mobilization system, see Bennell, "Supplementary Military Forces," pp. 50-54; Gérard Vaillant, "Vers une adaptation de notre système des réserves?," *Défense Nationale,* March 1979; and *Défense Nationale,* April 1978, pp. 149-50.

156. Vaillant, "Vers une adaptation de notre système des réserves?," p. 135.

157. Bennell, "Supplementary Military Forces," p. 51.

158. Vaillant, "Vers une adaptation de notre système des réserves?," p. 135; Bennell, "Supplementary Military Forces," p. 52; Pierre Michel, "La Nouvelle Orientation de la défense opérationnelle du territoire," *Défense Nationale,* January 1978.

159. French defense/force posture options in the 1980s are discussed in Bellini, *French Defense Policy,* ch. 6; and for an intriguing proposal, see Philippe Debas, "Pour une cavalerie légère nucléaire," *Defense Nationale,* January 1978.

160. The decision to withdraw, of course, was made by de Gaulle in 1966.

161. Anderson, "Weapons Procurement Collaboration," p. 974.

162. See, *inter alia, Military Balance, 1978-1979,* esp. pp. 92-100; and *Military Balance 1979-1980,* p. 98, for descriptions of the operational characteristics of some French weapons systems.

163. *Military Balance, 1978-1979,* pp. 92-97; *Military Balance, 1979-1980,* p. 98; *Défense Nationale,* March 1979, pp. 150-51; Bellini, *French Defense Policy,* esp. p. 57; and Frank T. J. Bray and Michael Moodie, *Defense Technology and the Atlantic Alliance: Competition or Cooperation?* (Cambridge, Mass.: Institute for Foreign Policy Analysis, 1977).

164. *Politique Etrangère* 43, no. 5 (1978): 613.

165. Marc Defourneaux, "Indépendance nationale et coopération internationale en matière d'armements," *Défense Nationale,* February 1979, esp. p. 48.

166. Bray and Moodie, *Defense Technology.*

167. Kolodziej, "Measuring French Arms Transfers," p. 212; Ebel, "The French Republic," pp. 55-56.

168. *Military Balance, 1979-1980,* pp. 103-07.

169. See, for example, Jacqueline Grapin, "Des armements pour quoi faire?," *Défense Nationale,* January 1978.

170. Kolodziej, "Measuring French Arms Transfers," p. 225.

171. For an overview of the French perspective on this issue, see Mery, "France's Defense Policy," pp. 9-15.

172. Ibid., p. 11 (italics in original text).

173. Ibid.

174. Lellouche, "France," p. 954.

175. François-Poncet, "French Foreign Policy," p. 4; Mery, "France's Defense Policy," p. 14; Jeffrey G. Barlow, "European Reactions to SALT II," *Backgrounder*

Number 75 (Washington, D.C.: Heritage Foundation), 23 February 1979, pp. 9-10, 11-12.

176. Woyke, "Process of Change in French Defense Policy," p. 9.

177. Council of Ministers, "Communiqué of January 10, 1979," *Défense Nationale,* March 1979, p. 161; François-Poncet, "French Foreign Policy," pp. 4-5; Watt, "The European Initiative," pp. 585-86.

178. Mery, "France's Defense Policy," p. 14; François-Poncet, "French Foreign Policy," p. 5.

179. *Défense Nationale,* February 1978, pp. 146-47, 158.

180. Ronald Koven, "French Troops, Negotiations Pushed Bokassa off Throne," *Washington Post,* 22 September 1979; and *Strategic Survey, 1978,* p. 15.

181. Dennis Chaplin, "France: Military Involvement in Africa," *Military Review,* January 1979, esp. p. 45; and Lellouche and Moisi, "French Policy in Africa," p. 33.

182. *Défense Nationale,* June 1978, pp. 161-62.

183. *Politique Etrangère* 43, no. 5 (1978): 619; and *Strategic Survey, 1978,* p. 16.

184. Lellouche and Moisi, "French Policy in Africa," p. 128.

185. Yost, "French Defense Budgeting," pp. 33-34.

186. Ebel, "The French Republic," p. 50.

FRENCH DEFENSE POLICY: A BIBLIOGRAPHICAL ESSAY

Lester G. Pittman

French defense studies generally concentrate on foreign affairs and nuclear strategy without paying much attention to the formulation or the economics of defense policy. The best general source of information for the student who reads French is the monthly publication *Revue de Défense Nationale* (known simply as *Défense Nationale* since 1973). This is a semiofficial journal that prints key articles and speeches on defense policy. Another source of current defense information is the daily newspaper *Le Monde*. Other useful publications are the journals of the three services: *L'Armée, Force Aeriennes Françaises,* and *La Revue Maritime*. The prestigious Institute of Higher Studies of National Defense in Paris also publishes its own journal, *Défense*.

For the student who does not read French, a good source with which to keep current is the bulletin of the French Embassy Press and Information Service (972 Fifth Avenue, New York, N.Y. 10021). English translations of some significant articles from *Défense Nationale* are printed in *Survival,* the publication of the International Institute for Strategic Studies (IISS) in London. Articles that analyze French defense policy can be found in British journals such as *Survival* and the *Royal United Services Institute* (*RUSI*) *Journal* and in the many American journals on international affairs and defense studies.

As suggested above, comprehensive books on French defense policy are rare. Two exceptions are Bernard Chantebout's *L'Organization générale de la défense nationale en France depuis la fin de la Seconde Guerre Mondiale* (1967) and the RUSI defense study, *French Defense Policy,* by James Bellini (London: Royal United Services Institute for Defence Studies, 1974). A good survey of the French perspective on European security and the evolution of French defense doctrine is "French Military Doctrine," by Edward A. Kolodziej, in the first edition of *Comparative Defense Policy,* ed. Frank B. Horton III, Anthony C. Rogerson, and Edward L. Warner III (Baltimore: Johns Hopkins University Press, 1974).

Much has been written on French nuclear strategy and defense policy in relation to European security. A good place to begin might be with general books on European security, for example, *NATO: The Entangling Alliance* (Chicago: University of Chicago Press, 1962), by Robert E. Osgood; *The Security of Western Europe* (London: C. Knight, 1972), by Bernard Burrows and Christopher Irwin; and the RUSI defense study, *European Security, 1972-1980* (Princeton, N.J.: Princeton University Press, 1971), by Neville Brown. Because General de Gaulle did much to shape foreign and defense policy in the Fifth Republic, his writings and biographies are another valuable source. For the issues surrounding France's withdrawal from the military organization of NATO, one should consult Henry Kissinger's *Troubled Partnership* (New York: McGraw-Hill, 1965), especially chapter 2, "The Protagonists: The United States and France"; and *NATO without France,* Adelphi Papers, no. 32 (London: IISS, 1966), by Kenneth Hunt. Two excellent books on French nuclear strategy that also include other defense issues are Wolf Mendl's *Deterrence and Persuasion* (New York: Praeger, 1970) and Wilfrid Kohl's *French Nuclear Diplomacy* (Princeton, N.J.: Princeton University Press, 1971). A good article on the same subject is Raymond Aron's "French Deterrent Capabilities and the Atlantic Alliance" (*Atlantic Community Quarterly,* Summer 1977).

There are a number of other works that deal specifically with the evolution of French strategy since 1958, including the traditional Gaullist view of security issues outlined in Kolodziej's "Revolt and Revisionism in the Gaullist Global Vision'' (*Journal of Politics,* May 1971) and in Mendl's ''Perspectives of Contemporary French Defense Policy'' (*World Today,* February 1968). A classic statement of the independent French nuclear strategy is General Ailleret's ''Directed Defense'' (*Survival,* February 1968). For the changes in policy following 1968, see Kolodziej's ''France Ensnared'' (*Orbis,* Winter 1972), Edmond Combaux's ''French Military Policy and European Federalism'' (*Orbis,* Spring 1969), and General Forquet's ''The Role of the Forces'' (*Survival,* July 1969). Two articles that illustrate the consistency of Gaullist security ideas before and after 1968 are Michel Debré's ''The Principles of our Defense Policy'' (*Survival,* November 1970) and his ''France's Global Strategy'' (*Foreign Affairs,* April 1971). Marc Ullmann's ''Security Aspects in French Foreign Policy'' (*Survival,* November–December 1973) offers a critique of defense policy under President Pompidou. Finally, defense policy is brought up to the presidency of Giscard d'Estaing in Pierre Gallois's ''French Defense Planning: The Future in the Past'' (*International Security,* Fall 1976); Jean Kelin's ''France, NATO, and European Security'' (*International Security,* Winter 1977); Alan Sabrosky's ''French Foreign Policy Alternatives'' (*Orbis,* Winter 1976); Pierre Lellouche's ''France in the International Nuclear Energy Controversy: A New Policy under Giscard d'Estaing'' (*Orbis,* Winter 1979) and ''La France, les SALT et la securité de l'Europe'' (*Politique Etrangère* 44, no. 2 [1979]); and D. Bruce Marshall's ''Recent Developments in French Strategic Doctrine'' (Paper presented to the conference of the International Studies Association, section on military sutides, November 1978). For an examination of French defense budgeting, one should consult David Yost's ''French Defense Budgeting'' (*Orbis,* Fall 1979).

Individual works on specialized or related topics provide additional information. John Ambler's *French Army in Politics, 1945–1962* (Columbus: Ohio State University Press, 1966) is an excellent book on civil-military relations. A brief but comprehensive introduction to the French experience in revolutionary warfare is found in Peter Paret's *French Revolutionary Warfare from Indochina to Algeria* (New York: Praeger, 1964). Surprisingly little has been written on the significant military involvement of France in the Third World. Several good articles on this subject, however, are General J. Mitterand's ''La Place de l'action militaire extérieure dans la stratégie française'' (*Review de Défense Nationale,* June 1970), Kolodziej's ''French Mediterranean Policy: The Politics of Weakness'' (*International Affairs,* July 1971), Jacques Isnard's ''French Arms Exports'' (*Survival,* April 1971), Dennis Chaplin's ''France: Military Involvement in Africa'' (*Military Review,* January 1979), and Pierre Lellouche and Dominique Moisi's ''French Policy in Africa'' (*International Security,* Spring 1979).

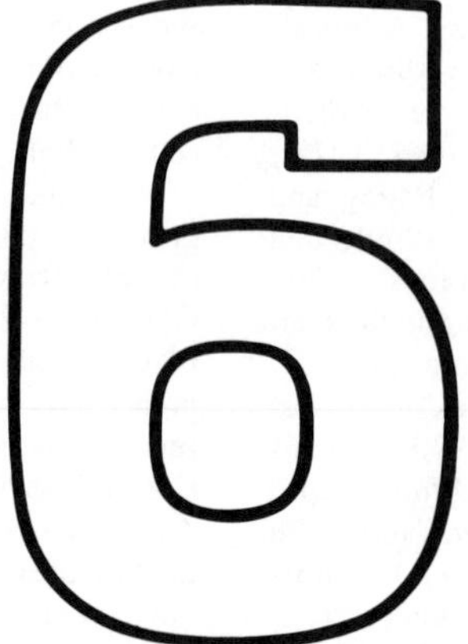

THE DEFENSE POLICY OF THE FEDERAL REPUBLIC OF GERMANY

Catherine McArdle Kelleher

To omit the Federal Republic of Germany from the list of major military powers in the 1980s would seem inconceivable. By almost every measure, the Federal Republic ranks as the second power in the Atlantic alliance. Thirty-five years after Germany's unconditional surrender in World War II, Bonn compares favorably with Britain and France in the size and capability of its military establishment. The German economic miracle continues, and West Germany has emerged from its state of "political dwarfdom" as a major international actor.

I would like to thank several scholars for their help and generosity during the preparation of this chapter: Dr. Richard Eichenberg, of Florida State University, who both commented extensively on the project and gave freely of materials developed for his dissertation, "Defense-Welfare Trade-offs in German Budgeting," submitted to the Department of Political Science, University of Michigan, 1981; Lt. Col. Michael Freney, U.S. Air Force, who gave of his time and his own research materials; Dr. Helga Haftendorn, of the Free University of Berlin, who gave a very useful commentary on the chapter; and Lt. Col. Step Tyner, U.S. Army, who provided critical comment and comfort on the final draft.

A focus on German defense policy alone, however, suggests as many paradoxes as unquestioned accomplishments in these three decades. All stem from Germany's unique military-political position, which, almost by definition, precludes the formulation of an exclusively German national defense policy. German strategy and doctrine are founded on the NATO framework; in the words of the 1979 White Paper, "The Bundeswehr is conceived as an armed force in an alliance."[1] German security rests in the last analysis on the deterrent threat of the American nuclear guarantee. German political rehabilitation was achieved largely through its status as an alliance partner—dependent but equal, reactive to the initiatives of others yet respected for its sacrifice and responsiveness. This remains true even as wider Atlantic interdependence has replaced direct dependence.

Much of this is not surprising, given the circumstances and conditions of German rearmament (table 1). The essential bargain was "No NATO without Germany; no Germany without NATO." Entry into the Western alliance structure—first the proposed integrated European Defense Community, then finally NATO itself—was the essential precondition for the restoration of German sovereignty. The German military effort was to be tightly controlled, both to right the military balance vis-à-vis the East and to assure an appropriate military balance within the West. German forces were essential, but only to the maximum levels (500,000) set forth in the separate Western European Union (WEU) treaty.[2] Germany was to be well armed but to renounce national production not only of atomic, biological, and chemical weapons but also of most major armament classes.

In the 1980s, the alliance orientation of German defense policy reflects another central concern: the harmonization and coordination of American and German defense resources.[3] For both states, the involvement of the thirteen other NATO members is essential—politically, militarily, and from the perspective of regional balance. But the core of NATO's ability to deter or to sustain conflict requires the linking of German and American capabilities. Without this, neither the present form nor the present substance of the alliance could be maintained.

Much of this simply reflects the relative capabilities of these two states.[4] But there are also some basic political axioms at issue. An independent German military capability outside the alliance or even a significantly lower proportionate German contribution of troops and money would be unacceptable to most, if not all, of the allies. So, too, would be a precipitous decoupling of American forces and any withdrawal of the American political and military guarantee of German security. The only conceivable alternate guarantor/protector for the Federal Republic would be a far stronger France or an integrated European defense system, but neither is presently feasible nor perhaps desirable.[5]

Without question, there are a number of domestic and international pressures that might produce a more independent German defense policy. In much of what follows I will examine these in their historical evolution and present state—a change in the nature of East-West confrontation in Europe, a major shift in the form and scope of American military and political involvement, a splintering of European political cooperation, or continuing perturbations in the domestic context of German national security policy. The probabilities of these changes differ widely but no one can be totally excluded as impossible over the next decade.

The basic argument of this essay, however, is that there are many good reasons why a more independent German defense policy will not emerge. For the present governing elite and its conceivable successors, the place of the Federal Republic as NATO's second power ensures most of their foreign policy goals. Political dialogue with the United States is now constant; German access is more automatic than that granted any other ally. Germany's role within NATO serves as both the base and an operational limit for relations with East and West Europe. This role provides the best, most credible structure for deterrence and the only hope of direct defense. And in the short term, it minimizes the political risks to Bonn of achieving continental dominance in an area of great historical sensitivity.

Finally, it forecloses few options of interest to the Federal Republic in a future as yet unforeseeable. A traditional postwar listing of possible German goals would include reunification, European military integration, nuclear independence, or a return to a looser alliance structure for coalition warfare. More recent additions might be an extra-European military role (say, to insure oil security) or a reduction to a smaller standing military establishment under terms of negotiated arms limitation or stabilization. But whatever the nature of future choice, the Federal Republic's present opportunity for maneuver is substantial. Its centrality in all NATO decisions is assured; costs, programs, and doctrines have long been negotiated, not just imposed. German leadership and initiative are now assumed—as perhaps also is German irritation at failures in the performance of others. The Federal Republic serves as a critical alliance channel to France and to Eastern Europe, as a direct and indirect supporter of the weaker NATO states, and as a major source of increasing analytic capability and policies for effective alliance management.

The critical variables, now as throughout Germany's last decades, seem to be the nature and strength of Germany's American connection. I will return to this again and again in the following examination of the nature and process of German defense decision making.

Table 1
Chronology of German Rearmament

Year	Event
1945	Unconditional surrender and demilitarization.
	Occupation by American, Soviet, British, and French forces.
1948	Breakdown of Four-Power governance.
	Initial informal discussion on German rearmament.
1949	Federal Republic of Germany established under provisional Basic Law.
1950	First formal discussion of German rearmament within NATO.
	France proposes European Defense Community (EDC).
1951-1952	EDC negotiations over size, structure, and armament of German forces.
1954	Defeat of EDC.
	Western European Union (WEU) established as framework for German rearmament within NATO.
1955	Germany enters NATO.
1956	First German forces inducted.
1965	Rearmament completed; twelve divisions assigned to NATO.

International environment

By most objective measures the Federal Republic of Germany ranks as a middle military power in the postwar international system.[6] Like Britain, France, and to a lesser extent China, it is a state with major political and military capabilities, a strong regional base, and a potential for a broader global reach. Germany's nonnuclear status is anomalous, the product of its past, the particular timing of its rehabilitation (1955), and increasing superpower control over nuclear proliferation. Somewhat discordant, too, is Bonn's constant rhetorical emphasis on the vulnerability of the Federal Republic, its limited room for maneuver, and its exclusively European domain of influence. Germany is unquestionably a second-tier state within the present and foreseeable international structure. At a minimum, its distinguishing characteristics are the size and capabilities of its military forces, the continuing level of the direct and indirect defense allocations, and its commitment to military excellence equal to that pursued by its major alliance partners, including the United States.

Almost from its inception in 1949, the Federal Republic has sought primary identification with the West.[7] The initial relationship showed Chancellor Konrad Adenauer's talent for making virtue of political necessity. The Federal Republic, after all, was a creature of the Cold War split among the victors of World War II. The Western powers, and especially the United States, were both occupation powers and founding fathers. Adenauer understood that in the short run, they alone would guarantee German security against internal and external threats and allow German reentry into the postwar international community. Reunification, if at all, would be a long-term process. It would require a series of dramatic changes not only in the international environment but also in German political structures and attitudes, bankrupted by Naziism and military defeat.

In the intervening decades, the Adenauer concept has led to a virtually inextricable involvement of the Federal Republic in the West. In the Atlantic framework, the Federal Republic is now the major European partner of the United States. Achieving this status in the mid-1960s represented the belated triumph of Adenauer's concept concerning the best means of ensuring and controlling American involvement in German security. For Adenauer's successors, the initial circumstances were hardly propitious (see table 2). On the one hand, there was Gaullist France, formally estranged from NATO's integrated defense and pressing Germany in several respects for a choice between Europe and American alliance. On the other was the declining Britain, unwilling to cede the "Anglo-Saxon connection" it had had with the United States throughout the postwar period, and ever chary of German capabilities and intentions.

American expectations about Germany's new role were no less risk laden. In the mid-1960s, the American preference was unquestionably for a junior partner, for a military organization and doctrine "made in America," and an ally willing to follow through on American conceptions. Doctrinal disagreements—such as those over the employment of forces or the control of escalation—were issues for consultation and German education, not joint decision making among equals. Germany was to be the European discussion partner in two respects: first, as the sounding board for American concerns, and second, as the medium for indirect Continental influence (with the Federal Republic as persuader, example, or threat) mostly, it was hoped, vis-à-vis the French.

Events and growing interdependence over the last decade have led to a far more equal and differentiated German partnership. A number of people, especially in the Nixon administration, foresaw still greater German sharing of alliance power and responsibility.[8] The Federal Republic would be the explicit European "pole," the synthesizer, coordinator, and, if necessary, "director" of European security efforts and organization. The United States would extend its European deployments, at least in the short run, and remain alliance leader and general strategic reserve. The Federal Republic, however, would come to have equal decision-making power over issues including nuclear use and arms control negotiations with the East, and would receive fundamental American support for its foreign policy and economic initiatives. Eventual German nuclear ownership or direct military involvement outside of NATO would not be precluded, although the United States preferred that such involvement be through the medium of a European force. The final organizational outcome would have to be left to time, and to the progress of German-Franco-British maneuvering. But it might well approach the initial "two pillars" concept put forth by John F. Kennedy or the vision of European-American bigemony supported by Franz Josef Strauss upon occasion.[9]

Others under Nixon, and the majority within the Carter administration, favored a more limited division of labor. Within the NATO military framework, Germany was an "almost equal"—except, in accordance with Bonn's own preference, in areas involving the direct control of nuclear weapons. Equality, though, involved the assumption of both positive and negative burdens in alliance decision making. Germany had the right to criticize American initiatives but also the responsibility to propose alternatives and to promote approval among Europeans as well as Americans (e.g., on NATO force modernization, reserve readiness, long-range theater nuclear forces, and

Table 2
Principals in West German defense policy making, 1955-81

Parliament	Coalition Parties	Chancellor	Foreign Minister	Defense Minister
1st (1949-53)	CDU/CSU, FDP, and others	Konrad Adenauer, CDU	Adenauer	
2nd (1953-57)	CDU/CSU, FDP	Adenauer, CDU	Adenauer (-1955)	Theodor Blank, CDU (1955-56)
			Heinrich von Brentano, CDU (1955-)	Franz Josef Strauss, CSU (1956-)
3rd (1957-61)	CDU/CSU	Adenauer, CDU	von Brentano, CDU	Strauss, CSU
4th (1961-65)	CDU/CSU, FDP	Adenauer, CDU (-1963)	Gerhard Schröder, CDU	Strauss, CSU (-1962)
		Ludwig Erhard, CDU (1963-)		Kai-Uwe von Hassel, CDU (1963-)
5th (1965-69)	CDU/CSU, FDP	Erhard, CDU (-1966)	Schröder, CDU (-1966)	von Hassel, CDU (-1966)
	CDU/CSU, SPD (Grand Coalition)	Kurt Georg Kiesinger, CDU (1966-)	Willy Brandt, SPD (1966-)	Schröder, CDU (1966-)
6th (1969-72)	SPD, FDP	Brandt, SPD	Walter Scheel, FDP	Helmut Schmidt, SPD (-1972)
				Georg Leber, SPD (1972-)
7th (1972-76)	SPD, FDP	Brandt, SPD (-1974)	Scheel, FDP (-1974)	Leber, SPD
		Schmidt, SPD (1974-)	Hans-Dietrich Genscher, FDP (1974-)	
8th (1976-80)	SPD, FDP	Schmidt, SPD	Genscher, FDP	Leber, SPD (-1978)
				Hans Apel, SPD (1978-)
9th (1980-)	SPD, FDP	Schmidt, SPD	Genscher, FDP	Apel, SPD

Note: CDU = Christian Democratic Union
CSU = Christian Social Union
FDP = Free Democratic party
SPD = Social Democratic party

airborne warning and control systems). After almost ten years of military stagnation, German initiatives for reform and renewal were imperative, and increased financial responsibilities were the key to allied acceptance.

Rather different expectations about Germany's "partner" role have been intermittently voiced by other Central Front states. Germany is seen as the most influential European "representative," the source of criticism and correction for a too-often preoccupied United States. The specific focus of concerns has varied, largely as a function of European perceptions of either too much American leadership and control in the early 1970s or the diffuse, capricious style of more recent years. But a general catalog of criticisms includes: (1) the American obsession with war-fighting requirements rather than components for the primary deterrence system, (2) recurring American tendencies toward implicit "decoupling" of strategic nuclear forces and a limited conception of the "Eurostrategic" balance,[10] and (3) unpredictable American behavior vis-à-vis the Soviet Union in the pursuit of essential détente and arms limitations.

Germany is clearly the once and present king of Europe, within the formalities of the European community and outside of it. Adenauer's initial conception was of Europe as the framework for German economic recovery and political rehabilitation. Integration with the rebuilding economies of France and the Low Countries was to ensure the submerging of German economic nationalism as well as the paying of Germany's just debts. Too, the interlocking of the French and German economic destinies would serve as the practical basis for enduring Franco-German reconciliation.

The German economic miracle of the 1950s and 1960s has left Germany as Europe's banker and economic spokesman. Together with France, it has acted in Europe to insure a favorable but equitable balance—as in its continuing financial support of both Britain and Italy.[11] Germany has also defended broader economic interests and political-economic preferences in a number of diverse arenas outside of Europe, primarily in the trans-Atlantic dialogue with the United States. But there has also been direct German economic intervention in its own interests and in those of its European partners in the turmoil of the Portuguese revolution, the chaos of Chile, and the confusion of Turkey and Pakistan.

Coexistent with these primary Western allegiances, however, are several special relationships with the East. All reflect Germany's unique historical and geopolitical position. All segments of the West German political spectrum support the fullest possible human links to the "other Germany," the German Democratic Republic (DDR). Reunification may no longer be a major national objective even in the long run; the precedent-breaking treaties of the 1970s formally recognized the existence of "two states in the German nation."[12] Both the Federal Republic and the DDR remain competitors—politically and ideologically, abroad and at home. The symbolizing of Berlin continues to be an always neuralgic point open to manipulation. But ties remain—in the family relationships revived under the détente of the 1970s, in the continuing economic ties, however exploitative they appear to other Western states. Less evident is the continuing cautious interweaving of leadership perceptions in both East and West Germany about the requirements of European security and stability. Primary alliances and bases for national legitimacy lie elsewhere, but the potential for greater "within-nation" identification and integration remains.

Less symbolic but of perhaps greater short-run significance are the other German ties to the East. Beginning with Chancellor Willy Brandt's drive for "normalization" in the early 1970s, Germany's *Ostpolitik** has resulted in an increasing German presence in Eastern Europe.[13] In part, it builds on traditional German commercial and economic dominance in the region. It also reflects German support for the "European" policies of these states, pursued cautiously within the Conference on Security and Cooperation (CSCE) or mutual and balanced force reduction (MBFR) framework and ever-mindful of the limits of Soviet toleration. German championing of these causes is relatively low key, given the political risks and the persistence of virulent anti-Germanism.

More troublesome for many in the West has been the evolving German-Soviet relationship. The Adenauer concept was framed in the emphatic anticommunist and anti-Soviet tones characteristic of most Western foreign policies of the mid-1950s. *Ostpolitik* and "normalization" in the late 1960s and early 1970s have led to a formal treaty of mutual assurance (1969), myriad new economic and cultural interchanges, and far more continuous political dialogue.[14] Détente in Europe has been Bonn's primary goal, a process valued both for improving the human landscape in the short term and for the prospect of longer-term European stability.

There are many in the opposition Christian Democratic Union (CDU), as outside of Germany, who see danger in this thickening of German-Soviet ties. Some cite the precedent of Rapallo, the separate Moscow-Berlin agreement concluded in the 1920s at the expense of the West. Others, most notably American National Security Advisers Kissinger and Brzezinski, have proclaimed the danger of "Finlandization" or of Bonn's seduction into "self-Finlandization." Defenders of the ties, particularly those within the ruling Social Democratic party (SPD), stress the fairly narrow dependencies that have been created on both sides—in long-term loans as in energy supplies, in technology transfers as in the promotion of greater human rights and in sanctioned emigration of ethnic Germans from the East. They also cite Adenauer's decision to open formal relations with the Soviet Union in 1955, far ahead of any other communist state and in direct contradiction of German policy toward any state with formal relations with East Germany. His justification was simply that the interests at stake—political, military, and economic—were too important to be ignored or postponed. This argument is seen as even more valid after thirty years of military confrontation and arms build-up in Central Europe.

The posture of primary identification with the West but with clear, continuing communication to the East is at some variance with the broad German consensus on the nature of the direct threats to German security. Without question, most see the sources of direct threat to be principally the Soviet Union and secondarily its East European allies.[15] In its simplest form, the threat is military or political-military. Many view a direct Soviet invasion or even use of direct military pressure as of very low probability (figure 1). Some cite the attractiveness of an intact Western Europe for the Soviet Union or even its political intractability for Soviet occupation. Others doubt Soviet incentives to invade or Soviet willingness to forego the easy gains of the détente period in the areas of economic support and technological transfers from Western Europe.

Most in West Germany, though, do perceive their status as the European state most exposed and vulnerable to Soviet military and political presence. However slight the probability of direct Soviet action, should conflict occur, West Germany will be the battlefield or the foremost trench. Berlin is the farthest outpost, the dramatic tripwire that will signal the onset of pressure and invasion.

**Ostpolitik* is a reference to the West German foreign policy of improved relations with the Soviet Union and Eastern Europe.—Ed.

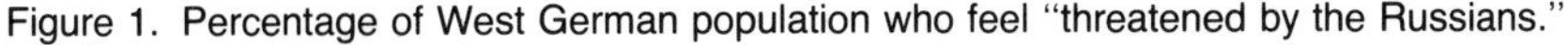

Figure 1. Percentage of West German population who feel "threatened by the Russians."

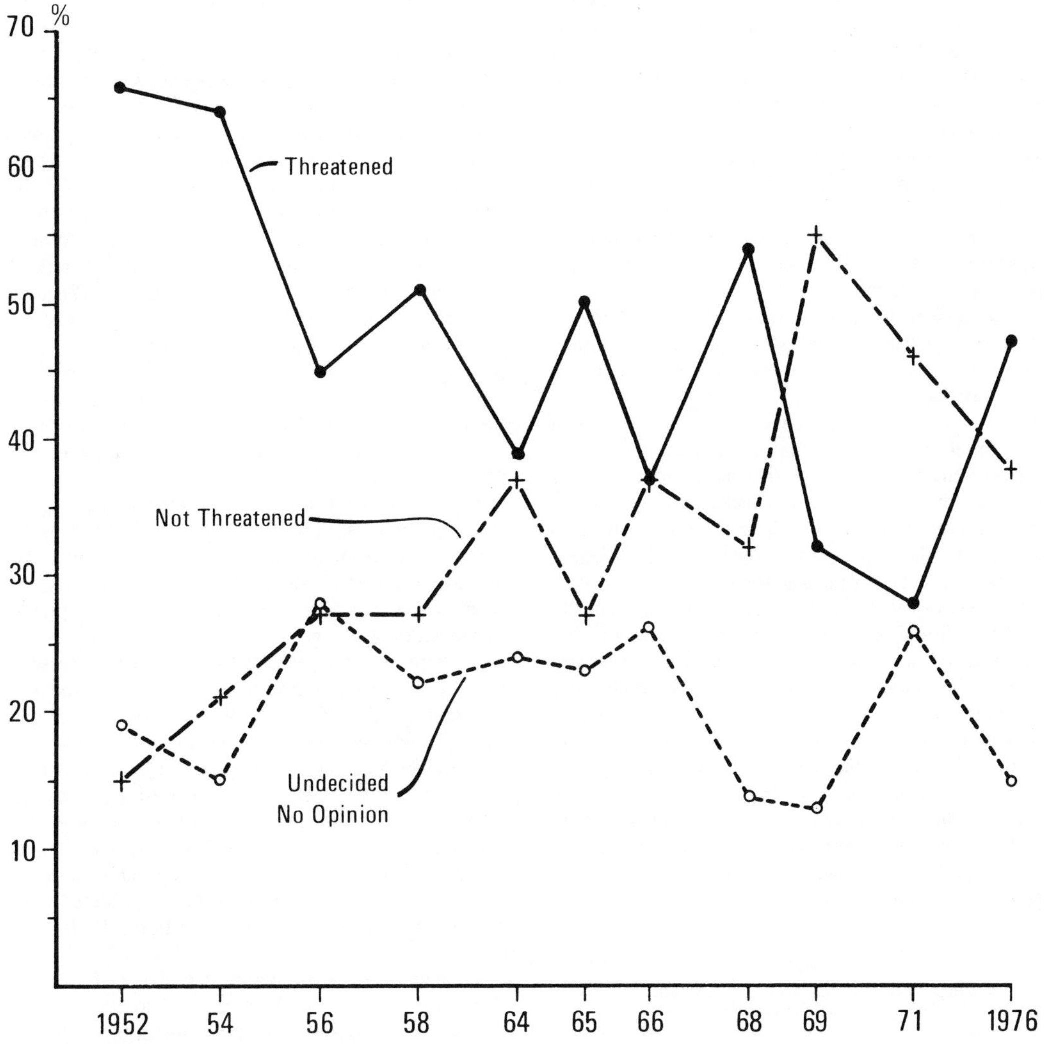

Text of survey question: "Do you have the feeling that we are threatened by the Russians or that we are not threatened?"
Source: Data provided by Richard Eichenberg.

It is from this perspective that there is particular German sensitivity to changes in Soviet military capability or increases in troop levels in the East.[16] From day to day, to be sure, there is no pervasive mood of gloom or anxiety; many would assert the outbreak of a European conflict now to be "unthinkable." Moreover, successive German leaderships of all political persuasions have found it prudent continually to downplay detailed threat analyses or even the range of damage to life and property which might be expected. Yet there is a surprisingly widespread appreciation of the Soviet conventional potential stationed in the German Democratic Republic or of the general destabilizing effects of recent SS-20 deployments by the Soviets. If not always "six feet tall," the Soviet military adversary is seen as powerful, ever ready, and totally responsive to the decisions of the Soviet political elite.

A countering capability is seen to come only through the involvement of the United States and NATO in the defense of the Federal Republic. In the 1950s and 1960s, when the probability of Soviet action seemed higher, this was a point of overwhelming national consensus. The withdrawal of even a small number of American conventional forces occasioned elite demands for reassurance and remedial action (as in 1956, 1962, and throughout the mid-1960s). In the period of "normalization" and increasing strategic parity of the 1970s and 1980s, there has been a cooler tone, and far less tendency to identify the threat as imminent or exclusively military.[17] There is more frequent criticism of American force posture decisions and weapons acquisitions (e.g., the B-1 or the MX). But there is still majority agreement on the inescapable need for an American guarantee of German security in détente and in confrontation, in peacetime and in conflict. And as figure 1 and table 3 partially record, the strength of this perception has increased over the low points of the early 1970s.

A more probable threat is seen as Soviet attempts to use political means for the same objective, to divide the Federal Republic from its Western allies. Those on the Right, in the German CDU-CSU as in the United States, cite continuing Soviet efforts to use both the carrot and the stick in relations with the Federal Republic. One Soviet tactic is to encourage, through popular agitation, German opposition to an important alliance program—such as the deployment of long-range theater nuclear force (LRTNF) systems (1980–81) or the earlier neutron bomb plans (1978–1979).[18] Simultaneously, Moscow holds out the prospect of a negotiated "equitable" settlement (e.g., an immediate moratorium on all LRTNF deployments East or West) or the threat of a worsening of relations (e.g., a break-off of CSCE contacts or an increase in the visitors fee for family DDR trips).

At least equally unpalatable are Soviet attempts to invoke "the German threat" as a divisionary tactic. In the 1950s and 1960s, the rhetorical specter of a revanchist West Germany, inheritor of the Nazi past, provided considerable incentive in Soviet attempts to tighten Soviet-Eastern European relations. *Ostpolitik* efforts of the 1970s as well as the general improvement of bilateral ties, especially with Poland, have removed most but not all of the impact of this Soviet instrument.[19] A nuclear-capable Federal Republic, and a competent, ready Bundeswehr as the strongest conventional European force—both are images that still touch remembered fears and current suspicions.

Less successful now, too, are Soviet efforts to discredit German initiatives within the West. Anti-Germanism is still a potent force among the Left in almost all European states; German economic success is also not the subject of universal admiration, especially by other European Socialists.[20] Yet the general thickening of Western European political relations and the continuity of Franco-German rapprochement, especially under Giscard and Schmidt, make Soviet charges less relevant or credible. Few of the Europeans dependent on German economic leadership are supportive of direct challenges to German preferences, in NATO as in the EC.

From Adenauer onward, German leaders have seen the greatest risk as being Soviet attempts to weaken the Bonn-Washington link. Adenauer repeatedly cited as his dreaded nightmare the prospect of a Soviet-American agreement on an acceptable European order, concluded over the head of, and at the expense of, the Federal Republic. Every lessening of superpower confrontation in the 1950s seemed threatening—the "Geneva spirit" of 1955, the London Conference on Disarmament in 1957, the Eisenhower-Khruschev discussions at Camp David in 1959. To counter this, Adenauer used a number of tactics—his personal contacts with Eisenhower and Secretary of State John Foster Dulles, repeated pleas for formal and informal reassurance, and even occasional forays into American domestic politics, as in his "unofficial" backing of Nixon in the 1960 election.

Adenauer's fears grew with the advent of the new Kennedy "superpower" approach to the Soviet Union and in relation to his declining political power within the CDU. His demands for reassurance became continuous, his criticism of the new president more strident and targeted for use by Kennedy's enemies. The high point came in the mid-1960s, with Lyndon Johnson's insistence on the Nuclear Nonproliferation Treaty (NPT) with the Soviet Union.[21] To Adenauer and Franz Josef Strauss, both then out of power, this was a superpower attempt to impose a "nuclear Versailles." It restricted options for a German national force that were of no tangible interest but gave the Soviets new rights of control and inspection vis-à-vis the Federal Republic.

In the 1970s, such criticisms became far less frequent and more muted, as Washington pursued a policy of "benign neglect" toward European affairs and Bonn was caught up in its own Eastern initiatives.

Table 3
Importance of Bundeswehr as perceived by survey respondents

	Survey response		
Year	Important/ Very Important	Unimportant/ Not So Important	Superfluous
1969	63	24	4
1970	68	20	5
1971	62	22	5
1972	66	25	4
1973	63	22	5
1974	58	32	7
1975	74	16	2
1976	79	10	1
1977/78	79	17	2
1979	80	15	2

Source: Ralf Zoll, "Militaer und Gesellschaft in der Bundesrepublik: Zum Problem der Legitimitaet von Streitkraeften," in *Wie Integriert ist die Bundeswehr?* Ralf Zoll, ed. (Munich: Piper Verlag, 1979), p. 48.

The one point of continuing neuralgia was the risk implicit in Soviet-American cooperation in arms limitation, SALT I and especially SALT II. Chancellor Helmut Schmidt, for example, charged that the 1977–78 SALT II discussions were highly questionable:[22] issues vital to European security were being discussed without real consultation with the European allies or even much consideration of their interests, particularly in the area of theater nuclear systems.

German tactics to counter this threat take several directions. The most usual is to underscore the primacy of the American connection and to press German demands through every channel, public and private. Successive German governments, moreover, have favored the development of new integrative structures within NATO to deal with thorny questions or to provide for "automatic" decision sharing with the United States. The most dramatic new forums, not surprisingly, were suggested in the area of nuclear control in the 1960s—a NATO nuclear force under a NATO commander, a Western Four (United States, United Kingdom, France, and the Federal Republic), and the much-discussed Multilateral Nuclear Force (MLF).[23] None ultimately was adopted, although a final alternative, the NATO Nuclear Planning Group (NPG), established in the late 1960s with assured German participation, has achieved a considerable measure of success.

An increasing number of the German elite in the 1970s came to question how much more congruent or predictable the German-American connection could become. Most saw the core problem to lie in the nature of the American decision-making process (e.g., extensive interagency bargaining and the confused, sometimes unstable institutional links in the American system) as well as in the competing American interests in other areas of the world (e.g., Asia). The trauma Watergate imposed on American alliance leadership (as in all areas of political behavior), the repeated communication crises of the Carter administration—all strengthened these arguments. In broad outline, the theme was the same as that pushed by the first postwar leader of the SPD, Kurt Schumacher.[24] Only Germany could define and further German national interests; the solutions could not be wrung from a policy of fixed alliances with West or East, or even perhaps from one primarily based on military strength.

There is, however, a substantial elite group, particularly in the left wing of the SPD, who see independent German-Soviet ties as an equally valuable counter, particularly in combination with a continuing *Westpolitik*. Some statements, for example, those by former Chancellor Willy Brandt or by SPD leader Egon Bahr, suggest *Ostpolitik* as an antidote to unwelcome superpower agreement, or an unwarranted sacrifice of German interests or stakes in an international game in which Germany has only veto rights. This is also true vis-à-vis France's efforts from time to time (e.g., de Gaulle in 1966 or even Giscard in 1980) to assert its preeminence as the Soviet discussion partner in Europe. Whatever the subject—trade, arms control, or a final political settlement of the World War II legacy—the attempt to bargain for but also about Germany is to be resisted.

A final threat, widely perceived among German elites if not by the mass public, is that stemming from the Germans themselves. Critics on the Right see the source most simply as a flawed national character. Perhaps the most dramatic expression is found in Adenauer's reaction to the 1954 failure of the European Defense Community, which would have totally submerged German military units in a European whole:

> I am one hundred percent convinced that the German national army, to which Mendes-France [then French premier] is forcing us, will be a great danger to both Germany and Europe. When I am no longer there, I do not know what will happen to Germany if we have not yet succeeded in creating a united Europe. . . . The French nationalists would rather [have] a Germany with a national army than a united Europe—so long as they can pursue their own policy with the Russians. And the German nationalists think exactly the same way; they are ready to go [i.e., pursue their own independent policy] with the Russians.[25]

On other occasions, Adenauer also cited the fatal German fascination with *Schaukelpolitik,* the playing off of East and West so successfully pursued by Bismarck in the 1870s.

The contemporary Right critique focuses in Germany, as elsewhere, on the threat posed by unprecedented economic prosperity and declining popular willingness for civic duty or national service.[26] In simplest terms, Germans, like all Western peoples, are "too fat to fight." This is asserted whether the particular targets are ill-kempt conscripts or unruly students, welfare cheaters or domestic speculators.

The internal threats judged most dangerous by most Germans, in the 1970s and at present, cluster around the preservation of civic order. The attribution of the particular source of risk is again often dependent on the ideological orientation of the commentator. Those on the Right see the continuing, sometimes violent, demonstrations of students, antinuclear protestors, squatters, environmentalists, the unemployed, and "marginal groups." First and foremost, however, is the threat of terrorism, domestic and international, as epitomized by the activities of the Baader-Meinhof gang or the Red Brigade.

Those on the Left are more likely to find the sources of threat in the repressive, constricting nature of existing German society and state. They point to the widespread popular panic about terrorism, to the resulting programs of the late 1970s to curtail civil liberties in order to capture or deter terrorist activity.

Their arguments focus on the future: at what point will the requirements of internal security and those of external security become so fixed that the nature of both individual life and German society in general will be irretrievably transformed?

Both perspectives are articulated most forcefully only at the extremes of the German political spectrum. But both suggest an implicit fear shared by many Germans, all too mindful of the chaos and the consequences of the Weimar period. The threat from outside Germany is at least definable and amenable to partial solution. The threat of an enemy boring from within raises questions and calculations about national identity and national values that few in the German elite are willing to define or able, politically, to confront.

National objectives, national strategy, and military doctrine

Given this range of perceived threats, what is the national security strategy of the Federal Republic? First and in the short run, it is primarily to seek security against external political threat and military attack through membership in the Atlantic alliance, and, in particular, in maintaining the closest possible ties to the United States.[27] For this purpose, NATO is only secondarily a fifteen-member organization. Its essence is the military-political core of the Central Front states—the United States, Britain, Canada, Denmark, the Benelux states, the Federal Republic, plus an informally tied France. This is the basis on which to mount an effective Western military capability for deterrence and defense, up to the involvement of strategic nuclear forces.

The centrality of the United States in this effort stems, in the majority German view, from a number of sources. The most obvious is its military and political preeminence. The United States may have lost its strategic advantage in an age of Soviet-American nuclear parity. American economic dominance has faded even in terms of potential wartime mobilization, as in World War II. The claim to overall technological superiority has also fallen before successive challenges from Western allies as from the Soviet Union. Chancellors and ministers have commented recently on the sorry readiness levels of some American units in Germany or on problems of equipment and morale.[28]

Yet for most of the German elite, the U.S. military capability remains the last best guarantee of German security. American forces (the conventional ones but especially the nuclear ones) are the make-weights that offset Soviet military power. The 200,000 or so American troops stationed on German soil are living proof of American commitment to the integrity of the Federal Republic; so, too, are the approximately 400,000 American military dependents. Further, the substantial members of tactical nuclear forces (TNF) in West Germany constitute at least one indicator of American willingness to threaten and if necessary initiate escalation to general nuclear war.[29]

Of significance, too, is the parallel involvement of the other Central Front states in maintaining a multilateral military presence on German soil (figure 2). The size and capabilities of the seven national contingents vary considerably; their deployments clearly reflect the early stratification of occupation force assignments. The 50,000 or so French troops are stationed under a separate Franco-German agreement, concluded in 1966. But together, these national commitments provide, first, an equalizing and legitimizing framework for German national capabilities and, second, multilateral reinsurance guarantees for the American security commitment.

Increasingly, though, the German elite sees détente policy as the second major "pillar" of a national security strategy.[30] The time frame is far more long term than that of defense policy; the goals are definable only in general terms: "to reduce and control possibilities of conflict between East and West under conditions specific to East-West relations."[31] But the clear principle was established over the decade of the 1970s by Brandt and Schmidt: defense without simultaneous efforts to reduce the probability of threat and, thus, the need for defense is self-defeating and politically unacceptable.

From this perspective, the long-term answer to German security dilemmas lies in steps, taken together with allies and adversaries, to limit the level of military capability on both sides of a divided Europe.[32] Images run the gamut from the full-scale force disengagement model first proposed by Germans and others in the 1950s to the more contemporary depiction of a series of small cuts or even mutual confidence-building measures (CBMs)* which will enhance perceptions of stability. A surprisingly broad popular consensus, too, supports arms limitation. The people are critical of SALT but support it as an essential process. They welcome all initiatives to discussion—the work in the Conference on Security and Cooperation (CSCE), the U.N. Special Session on Disarmament (SSOD), or the recent French proposal for a European Disarmament Conference (CDE).

In the 1970s, this consensus was reflected in a number of official debates and decisions.[33] Popular support for the process of arms control negotiations has been widespread, even when results—as in the talks on Mutual and Balanced Force Reductions in Europe (MBFR)—have been mostly atmospherics.

*Such measures include mutual notification between the NATO and Warsaw Pact countries of major exercises and the exchange of observers of such maneuvers.—Ed.

Figure 2. Force deployments on German territory

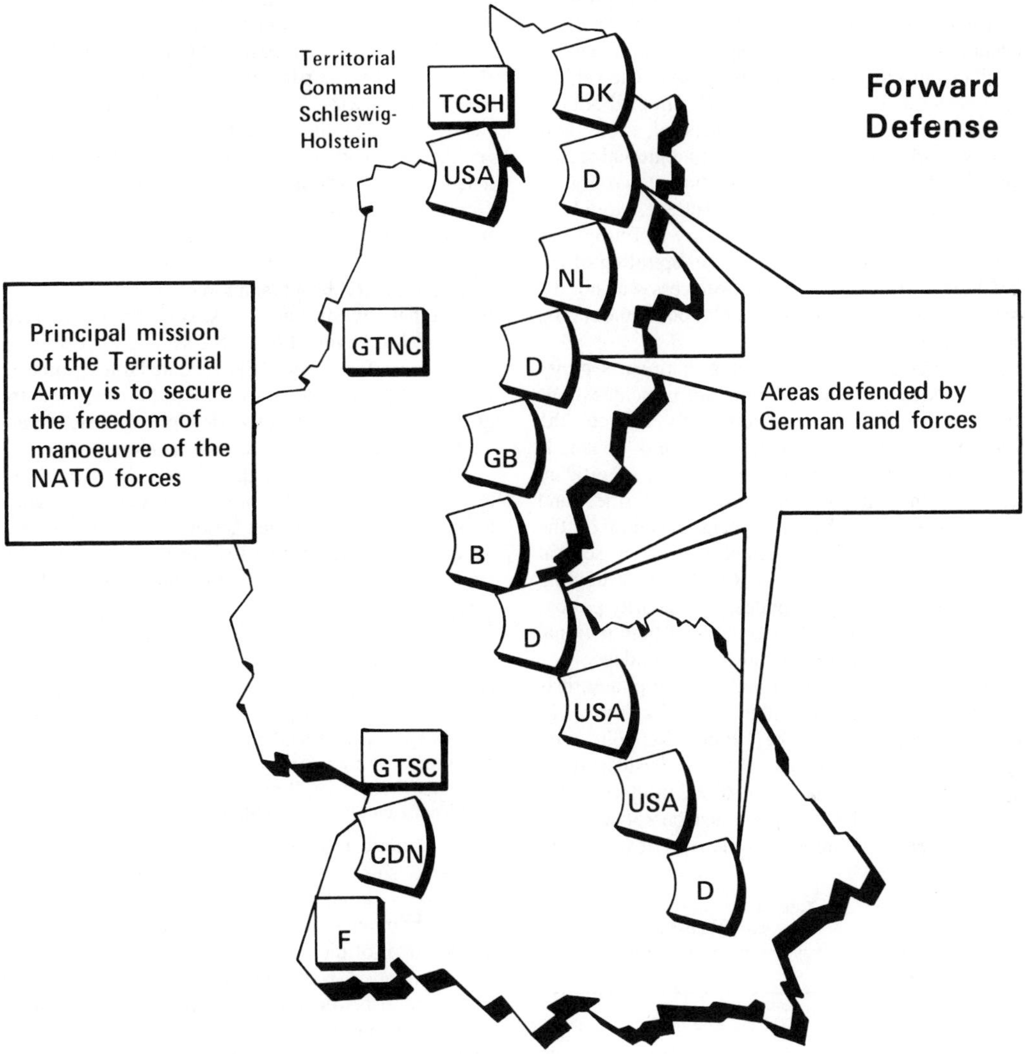

Source: White Paper, 1979, p. 21.

Note: German Forces

D = *Bundeswehr* (army)
GTNC, GTSC, TCSH = territorial defense commands

Allied Forces

B = Belgium
CDN = Canada
DK = Denmark
F = France
GB = Great Britain
NL = Netherlands
USA = United States

Promises for future talks are seen by many on the Left and the Center as long-term investments in avoiding misperceptions and increasing European dialogue, if not increasing integration between East and West.

Perhaps the most dramatic evidence of this basic argument came in the context of the LRTNF debates of 1979–80.[34] Chancellor Schmidt had initiated the call for these new force deployments, citing the gap in the spectrum of deterrence revealed by Soviet deployments of the mobile SS-20 missiles. The NATO allies had set up a special High-Level Working Group

(HLG) to consider various force options and deployment possibilities. Under direct, continuous pressure from within his own SPD-FDP governing coalition, Schmidt also had to make acceptance contingent on simultaneous efforts to limit these forces. The vehicle was a Special Group (now the SCG) directed both to consider the arms control impacts of these new weapons and to prepare for negotiating mutual reductions with the Soviet Union. Only thus, it was argued both within the Bundestag and outside it, would the West work toward long-term stability in Europe, or avoid setting off yet another upward spiraling of the East-West arms race in Europe. Success was not assured or perhaps not even attainable, but without this, there would be no deployments.

Both strands of present German national security strategy, however, leave a number of basic questions unanswered. In some measure, this reflects the judgment of German political leaderships that it is prudent to do so. But at least an equally significant reason is the unique dilemmas of priorities and modalities imposed by the special position of the Federal Republic. In the metaphor used by several German scholars, the Federal Republic is struggling to create a new type, or ''model,'' of security policy, one that acknowledges the demands of both national responsibility and international interdependence.[35]

First, in relation to traditional defense policy, it is clear that reliance on the United States for its primary security has always left the Federal Republic with significant costs and doubts. The most basic of these turns on the level and form of national military forces (table 4). At one level, these must be sufficient to meet the political conditions of the American guarantee: the demonstration of continuing German (and European) efforts to sacrifice for one's own defense. It was under this Congressional requirement that American forces were first sent to Europe, and this is the core of the recurring alliance debate about equitable burden sharing.[36] For the first decade of rearmament (1955-65), the Federal Republic was allowed to set the pace and scope of its military development. Thereafter, Washington pressed forcefully for a German effort up to the 500,000-troop maximum set in the Western European Union Treaty of 1955. At present, the Federal Republic provides over half of NATO's Central Front land forces, about one-third of the combat aircraft, and almost all of the Baltic naval forces.[37] Moreover, it holds the second largest effective reserve force pool, the second largest force of nuclear capable launchers and platforms, and the greatest European capacity for rapid defense expansion and general economic mobilization.

Table 4
German armed forces, 1980-81

Branch of service	Troops
Army	
Total strength	335,200
Conscripts	176,000
Organization	
Field army	272,000
3 corps	
12 division	
6 armored	
4 armored infantry	
1 mountain	
1 airborne	
Territorial army	38,000
Navy	
Total strength	36,500
Conscripts	11,000
Air Force	
Total strength	106,000
Conscripts	38,000
Reserves	
All services	750,000

Source: International Institute for Strategic Studies, *The Military Balance, 1980-1981* (London: IISS, 1980)

There are many within the alliance who would like to see the Germans take on more burdens. A characteristic tone opposing such action was set by Defense Minister Georg Leber in a 1975 response to reports of American interest in a 600,000-man Bundeswehr:

> There are many arguments against that. It is not as if the Federal Republic of Germany led a charmed life—not from an economic perspective either—and could afford everything. But more importantly if the Germans were to increase their army while others were to reduce theirs, inner-European problems would arise with certainty, because of the excessive weight that such a German army would then have in a circle of the Western European military powers. And I must preserve Europe from that.[38]

The American definition of sufficiency leaves unanswered some of Bonn's basic political worries. Adenauer's initial fear was that sufficiency would entail a permanent status of inequality for Germany, the purveyor of the footsoldiers or the cannon fodder for the alliance. Every German soldier might mean less allied effort or more specialization on advanced military functions (e.g., Admiral Radford's plan in 1956 for reduction to small American ''atomic units'' attached to allied forces.)[39] Sufficiency, therefore, had to be interpreted as a commitment to forces of equal armament, organization, and readiness. Moreover, it was American forces that set the standard that all alliance forces should eventually reach. The Federal Republic would suffer only one categorical disadvantage (no direct possession of nuclear munitions), but this would be true of most Continental states.

German fears about the implications of the sufficiency standard took on a somewhat different character in the 1960s and early 1970s. The most public of them concerned sufficiency as a justification for the withdrawal of American forces and the ''Europeanization'' of the Central Front defense. Adenauer and his CDU successor, Ludwig Erhard, consistently opposed American reductions of even relatively limited size as a weakening of the basic security guarantee. Efforts to legislate cuts through a series of "Mansfield Amendments" in the United States Senate met similar, if less dramatic, resistance. What was at dispute was an arbitrary or formal American drawdown, which disturbed deterrence or undermined public confidence. Simultaneously, for example, the Erhard (CDU) and Kiesinger (CDU-SPD) governments accepted the stripping of American units to the benefit of operations in Vietnam. In 1973, the Brandt government (SPD) allowed the reequipping of Israel from American stocks in Germany. Present German reactions to American force changes are far more restrained, but changes are also less frequent or severe.

Worries continue about another interpretation of sufficiency—that under NATO's doctrine of flexible response. American pressures for greater conventional build-up began under the Kennedy administration in the wake of the Berlin crisis of 1961–62.[40] The Federal Republic was the ally most responsive to the challenge, and accelerated its build-up by more than 25 percent. It was far less supportive of American demands for greater reserves and force sustainability, and consistently criticized American plans for a conventional effort in Central Europe of up to 90 days duration. Along with the other allies, the Federal Republic finally agreed to flexible response as official NATO doctrine, set down in NATO's MC 14/3* of 1967. But German unofficial policy opinion and the opinions of many defense leaders remained critical toward the "extended conventional exchange" concept.[41]

The German stance stemmed in part from a more pessimistic assessment of the East-West conventional balance than that current in Washington in the mid-1960s and 1970s.[42] An unspoken German fear—that the invoking of the American guarantee would come too late, if at all—was fundamental to this. The dread was of a defense first, say, at the Rhine, leaving a substantial part of Germany to suffer cycles of occupation, then liberation.[43] As a condition of alliance membership, the Federal Republic had insisted from the outset on the absolute principle of forward defense. This meant formal alliance adherence to the defense of German territory as close to the borders of East Germany and Czechoslovakia as possible and as soon as possible after the onset of conflict.

Added insurance came through Bonn's policy, begun in the 1950s, of encouraging settlement and plant location as close to the border areas as practicable. By 1979, estimates showed that at least 25 percent of the West German population and industrial plant base were within 100 kilometers of the demarcation line.[44] Should conflict occur, the military and human costs of these policies would be great, particularly when added to the expected confusion of massive westward movements of refugees from East Germany and elsewhere. But in peacetime this policy added, in German eyes, another component to deterrence. It was a credible indicator that neither Soviet "salami tactics" (e.g., a "grab" for Hamburg or a limited invasionary probe) nor a negotiated settlement on the basis of *de facto* occupation or control (e.g., that tried by the Soviets in the 1950s and early 1960s against several Berlin enclaves) would be unanswered.

Divergences in German preferences about the timing of nuclear use still remain, but the debate is largely conducted in vague verbal formulations. American political leaders tend to talk in terms of days, of "use as late as possible." Germans, within the SPD as well as the CDU, suggest that it may be a question of hours as well, with the preferred formulation being "as early as necessary." Flexible response itself is sufficiently vague—at least in peacetime—to accommodate both points of view.

There is also far more explicit reference to the fear of American "decoupling." Under strategic parity, the argument in Bonn goes, the United States will be far more willing to accept (1) war termination on the basis of a nuclear war limited to Europe which leaves the United States homeland unscathed, or (2) a short conventional war in which American forces are attacked but no escalation to nuclear weapons occurs. The German ruling elite, most dramatically Chancellor Schmidt himself, rejects both options as contrary to the core bargain of the alliance and ultimately to the long-term security of the United States itself. Any suggestion is to be rejected that admits the possibility of (1) a separable "Euro-strategic" balance, or (2) either a Soviet or American "sanctuary" in the event of European conflict.

The causes for this insistence are to be found in both elite and mass attitudes toward defense policy in general. Both groups are agreed that the principal bulwark of German security is a policy of credible, effective deterrence. At the simplest level, this rests on a fundamental belief akin to that underlying the American "massive retaliation" doctrine of the 1950s. The best deterrent is the specter of total nuclear war, which will result almost automatically from the first use of nuclear weapons. Any doctrine that allows the possibility of (1) limited nuclear use (e.g., selected nuclear options in any number), or (2) the limitation of nuclear effects (i.e., the neutron bomb or other "clean" nuclear devices) undercuts the operation of deterrence. The low risk of Soviet action against Western Europe will remain so only if the Soviets are convinced of both the certainty of American involvement and the probability of rapid escalation to strategic nuclear exchange.

*This is a reference to a NATO Military Committee document outlining the alliance commitment to the doctrines of flexible response and forward defense.—Ed.

A related attitude cluster concerns the impossibility of an adequate conventional effort by the NATO states. Many of the dimensions cited parallel those mentioned regarding nuclear war—the devastation to the German population and property alone, the dread of the occupation-liberation cycle, the continuing possibility of nuclear initiation by both sides. The more knowledgeable also point to the uncertainty introduced by an autonomous French nuclear force. (At least officially, the *force de frappe* is to be used as soon as French borders, if not French deployments in Germany, are threatened.)[45] Others, especially on the Left, point to the simple quantity of TNF held by American, German, and allied forces.

The central argument is not new: that the West and Germany itself will not (and perhaps cannot) accept the economic, political, and social burdens required for conventional mobilizations of the needed magnitude. Defense policy analysts point to the experience of the past—the continuing failure to meet any of the conventional improvement goals, let alone the ambitious 96-division level (M + 30 days) established at NATO's outset.[46] Even in times of direct crisis—Berlin in 1958–59 or 1961–62, or Czechoslovakia in 1968—the Central Front allies have made only marginal increases in the force levels or the allocation of national resources for defense. The final assertion is always that the Federal Republic cannot mount such an effort alone or bear an even more inequitable burden than at present. German sacrifice would make no essential difference and might risk major economic disadvantage, foreign political charges of revived German militarism, and widespread political disaffection in West Germany.[47]

The less specific public attitudes seem related to the low probability accorded the outbreak of European conflict and to an understanding of national security as having both economic and political requirements. Prevalent images are of the cutbacks higher defense expenditures would impose on domestic prosperity in general and social welfare rights in particular.[48] This would both lessen support for the government and strengthen internal dissidents—just as was true in the Weimar period (figure 3).

Somewhat paradoxically, there is another German fear of at least equal intensity: that the United States will use nuclear weapons too quickly in Germany's defense.[49] In the 1950s this fear surfaced in the emotional "*ohne mich*" (without me) campaigns against nuclear armament. The mass marches on Easter, the continuing stream of appeals from intellectuals and scientists, the attempt to organize antinuclear plebiscites—all characterized the most emotional of the rearmament debates.

After a period of relatively limited activity, the antinuclear movement revived in intensity in the 1970s, in Germany as throughout Europe.[50] The proximate sparks to debate came from various sources: (1) an unclassified systematic study by a respected scientist, Carl Frederick von Weizäcker, on the effects of nuclear conflict on the Federal Republic; (2) the strength of antimilitarism among the European youth movement; and, finally, (3) the neutron bomb controversy.* The LRTNF decision of December 1979 to base extended-range Pershing and ground-launched cruise missiles on European soil provided an opportunity both to assert and to win allegiance to an "alternative view." The left wing of the SPD was particularly active, acting at times in concert with organized groups in the Benelux states, in Scandinavia, and in England.

At its serious core, this perspective raises two questions. The first emphasizes the inability of the German government to control the decision to use nuclear weapons, even those stationed on its own soil or earmarked for its own dual-capable systems.[51] As presently configured, German forces closely resemble those of the United States in terms of equipment with dual-capable weapons across the tactical spectrum. Warhead release will come only in times of NATO-defined crisis, and it will be implemented only after authorization by the American president and by the NATO and national decision makers designated in still-secret NATO guidelines.† What direct influence the Federal Republic will have in actual conflict is uncertain.

A second question is whether, even in peacetime, the Federal Republic will bear the political costs of American decisions to acquire more TNF for European deployment. As was forcefully argued in February 1979 by Herbert Wehner, the SPD parliamentary chief, the levels of nuclear destructive power already held by East and West are awesome.[52] Further Western acquisitions will perpetuate, if not accelerate, the arms race and result in "defensive" Soviet counteracquisitions. The result will be even greater reliance on nuclear weapons and, in time of conflict, an almost automatic employment of TNF.

It is in this context that détente as the best hope for long-term German security receives the greatest elite support. Nuclear arms limitation on a realistic, mutual basis is the next step to stabilizing European détente and therefore is a primary domestic political requirement. However deemed necessary, the acquisition of a new weapon system must be evaluated within this framework. Moreover, there now seems good and sufficient reason to examine the nuclear-

*This is a reference to proposals to deploy enhanced radiation weapons (ERW) that maximize initial radiation while minimizing blast effects. In a counterforce mode such weapons are said to be useful against tanks or troop concentrations. Opponents note that if it is used in populated areas there would be large numbers of human casualties with minimum damage to buildings and other structures.—Ed.

†In short, the United States retains control over nuclear weapons assigned to West German units.—Ed.

Figure 3. Four opinions on defense spending among the West German population

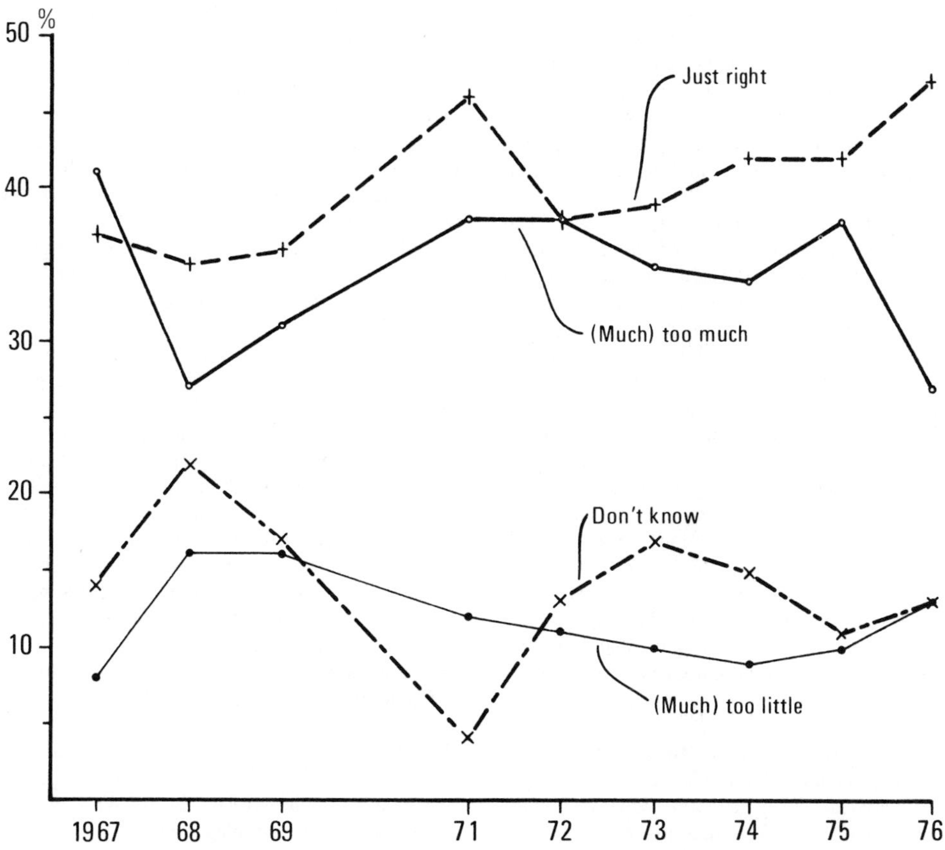

Source: Surveys conducted by the EMNID Institute for the German Ministry of Defense. *See* Federal Ministry of Defense, Information and Press Staff, *Hinweise fuer Oeffentlichkeitsarbeit* (Bonn, 14 September 1979).
Text of survey question: "Security costs money. In your opinion, does the Federal Republic spend much too much, too much, just the right amount, too little, or much too little on defense?"

based strategy of the alliance and ask "how much is enough?"

Many in the German elite contend that this view of détente and arms limitation is fundamentally different from that pursued by the United States. Their criticism is two edged. The original Kissinger-Nixon concept of détente in the early 1970s was overly optimistic, with a fatal fascination for (1) a series of progressively more comprehensive global arms control regimes, (2) "bargaining chip" deployments, and (3) attempted linkages of political incentives in Europe to constraints on Soviet behavior elsewhere. Equally flawed in the opposite direction were the formulations of the Carter administration, particularly after Afghanistan. Détente cannot be an arbitrarily defined, stop-and-go process, affected by national threats and punishments and hostage to events that do not critically affect fundamental Western interests. Moreover, the American electorate must be brought to value arms limitation in its own terms, not just as something "given" to the Soviet Union or subject to reconsideration every four years.

Left unanswered, however, are a number of troublesome issues of process and substance. After the prolonged debates of the early 1970s, there are still widely differing conceptions, even among proponents, about the requirements and priorities of détente. Opposition critiques obviously come from a number of sources. There are a number far on the German Right who argue that it results from wishful thinking or the start of the "self-Finlandization" process discussed above.[53] Commentators outside of

Germany trace the roots to the unusual stability and calm in the Europe of the 1970s and the Soviets' ability to exploit the atmospheric gains of détente. They postulate that any dramatic interruption of détente—the invasion of Poland or other East European countries as opposed to the deployment of weapons systems such as the SS-20s—will limit elite attribution of benefits and popular expectation of a continuing process of stability and increasing mutual confidence.

These arguments are often given greater weight in the face of the radical critique of defense efforts launched by the Left.[54] Individual spokesmen and group actions stress the nonproductivity of defense investment, the automatic conjuncture established between government and defense industries, and the economic exploitation involved in a system of military conscription. True national security, in this view, lies in the satisfaction of individual economic and social rights and the guarantee of a new quality of life. Both goals cannot be met by a highly militarized society or a state that is required by its principal ally to sacrifice more and more national resources for Western defense against a slight or nonexistent Soviet threat. In the exaggerated student activist formulation, it is the United States that thus constitutes a grave threat to German national security and that, by its emphasis on military preparedness, may undermine long-term prospects for détente and European stability.

Proponents of détente—Left, Right, and Center—reject the arguments of both sides as simplistic and overly ideological. They are somewhat less sure, however, in their own formulations about how détente is to be maintained or expanded. In arms limitation, however flawed its approach, it is the United States that is to be the principal Western negotiator with the Soviet Union. Coordination and consultation with the European allies is assumed, yet actual direct involvement is to be avoided. West Germany can warn, stimulate, and maneuver; more than this will raise questions of intra-European balance and about Germany's special political and military vulnerabilities.

Moreover, the task of achieving West-West consensus on the balance to be struck between defense and détente is clearly formidable. At what point will the efforts toward détente and arms limitation be judged to have served adequately the goals of stability, even if no East-West agreement results? Will not at every stage the potential for limitation, real or perceived, appear to domestic publics, if not to political elites, to outweigh the tactical advantages of deployment? Might this not extend to all new systems, even conventional systems that can be defined as upsetting the existing balance and thus undermining progress toward détente?

One further issue is the past alliance division of labor, in which Germany and the other European allies have tolerated American actions and decisions (e.g., Vietnam or MX) as long as these did not directly affect the American guarantee or involve European resources. Increasingly assertive German demands that the United States do nothing to damage European détente results in an expanded agenda for trans-Atlantic bargaining. The potential for continuing domestic German disagreement and Soviet political manipulation appears substantially increased. And the level at which the benefits of détente would be outweighed by the costs imposed on Western political and military capabilities are uncertain, if not undefinable.

At the level of detailed proposals, the question of realistic bargaining strategies becomes even more difficult. The immediate German agenda seems to emphasize three points: (1) the specifics of a SALT III and LRTNF limitation cannot be left to unilateral American decision, (2) limitations sought must transcend the American definition of security requirements (e.g., the artificial strategic-tactical division), and (3) there must be trans-Atlantic risk sharing in terms both of final limits and of negotiating tradeoffs. This means, for example, that European-based nuclear systems, American or German or other, should be considered not as separate capabilities but rather as parts of "integrated force packages" that would also include some central system elements. How an equitable balance across such aggregates would be calculated is left for future negotiations, presumably—as in MBFR—in the West-West arena as well as in the East-West context.

Bonn's assertion of more autonomous policy in these areas has also stimulated major American criticism and questioning. At a superficial level are the mistaken charges of European "pacifistic" leanings.[55] More serious is the analysis of the inherent contradictions between Bonn's stress on the indivisibility of arms control and the relative divisibility of détente. Often heard, too, is the charge that Germany is more interested in dialogue per se than in short-term results—as experience in MBFR over the past decade seems to indicate.

This leaves German policy makers with perhaps the most fundamental dilemma of all in balancing policies toward defense and détente. In détente, the principal interlocutor is the Soviet Union; in arms limitation efforts, the United States and the Soviet Union are of almost equal importance. German anxieties about the American position stem, in part, from the problems of recent years. But they also basically reflect German and European concerns that the United States pursues and will continue to pursue a different set of interests and values. Even with increased coordination, the probabilities of long-term convergence on significant arms limitations are at best uncertain—and perhaps very low.

Extremists in the Federal Republic argue that the point of divergence is already here and the implications for Germany's continued reliance on NATO must be drawn.[56] Most in the German elite at present will admit only to the existence of these dilemmas. Perhaps, as in the past, the passage of time alone will mute the issues and sanction, if not resolve, apparent contradictions.

The defense decision-making process

Not surprisingly, the German defense decision-making process is finely attuned to American policies and to decisions within the NATO framework.[57] Many of the critical decisions immediately after World War II were made by the Western founding fathers. The Adenauer government could achieve at most only delay or marginal change. The twenty-five years since rearmament have underscored the importance of German-American consultation—for agenda setting, bargaining, and even the revocation of previous alliance considerations. In many respects, the German defense decision-making process is as constrained as German defense policy. It is circumscribed by the same lack of a separable national profile; external actors and preferences penetrate German deliberations at every stage. The framework for maneuver and change is fairly narrow. The day-to-day expertise and analytic independence have developed slowly, with considerable encouragement, pressure, and training stemming from the United States. It was not until the early 1970s, for example, that autonomous German defense planning staffs began to take a major role in the internation studies within NATO (e.g., those set by the NPG), or to develop national options in the areas of manpower, training development, and equipment management.

The continuing significance of external influence over the policy process is made more salient by the often unfocused character of the domestic political debate in these areas. As in most European states, the level of elite interest in defense issues is low and quite sporadic. The parliamentary system adds three more constraints: strictly organized, infrequent public debates; tight party discipline; and the inherent advantages accruing to the proposals of the government. Public hearings are almost unknown; Cabinet debate is confused by the principles of both the "primacy" of the chancellor and the ministerial "responsibility" for functional areas. The form and substance of defense questions, therefore, are usually of major concern to only a handful. This small group includes party defense experts, a few defense correspondents and involved defense intellectuals, and the sizable defense bureaucracy, civilian and military.

Indeed, as Helga Haftendorn and her colleagues have argued, security policy suffers generally from overbureaucratization and fragmentation (figure 4).[58] Both the Foreign Office (AA) and the Defense Ministry (MOD) have major staffs to implement their somewhat overlapping responsibilities. The new organization of the chancellor's office allows for a third major competitor from time to time. Added to the usual problems of coordination engendered by bureaucratic competition and partial information are

Figure 4. Institutional structure for arms control and security policy decision making

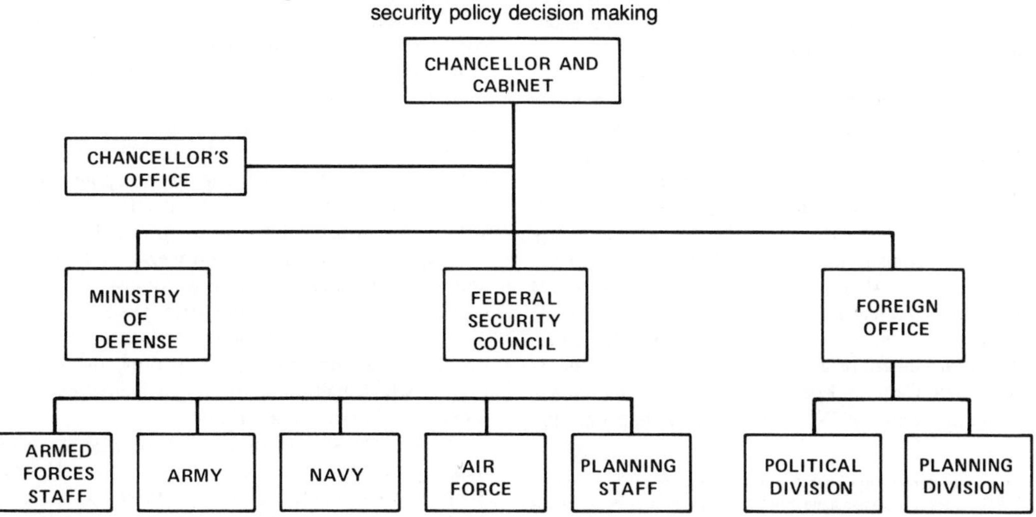

the difficulties injected by simultaneous negotiations and coordination with external organizations—NATO staffs and political authorities. A final overlay is frequent communications with various American authorities—those military and political leaders actually present on German territory, official representatives in Bonn and at Supreme Headquarters of Allied Powers Europe (SHAPE), and those in Washington. Not only are a series of frequent official "bilaterals" involved but also constant informal discussions and information sessions.[59]

The result, too often, is a decision-making system mired in details, overloaded with communications, and relatively unresponsive to immediate political shifts or unfamiliar events. Unlike the United States, Germany has no external source of domestic expertise which can be easily mobilized or which has credibility or legitimacy. Parliamentary skill is too often limited to a few "assigned" party experts; general expertise is somewhat limited even within the MOD, let alone within the more traditional diplomatic circles in the Foreign Office. There are only a handful of external research institutes concerned with security issues, and even fewer that do not have a systematic progovernment or antigovernment stance. Indeed, until the 1970s, national defense analysis at the level of either the media or civilian experts was relatively rare and was thought somewhat antiintellectual, if not irrelevant to Germany's national priorities and international constraints. Popular contributions were and still are virtually nonexistent.

Clearly, these are criticisms that can be leveled in some measure at the defense decision-making process in every advanced industrialized democracy.[60] What is striking about the German case is the contrast between the size and expense of the defense effort and the relatively limited scope of attention to (and participation in) defense decision making. The lack of a separate national policy is one factor but it is not the only explanatory factor.

The only circumstances under which the scope of defense decision making expands are those that also make informed, open debate difficult or politically risky. Over the past three decades, this type of debate has generally concerned four different types of issues: (1) nuclear armament and control (1956, 1958, 1962, and 1979–81); (2) maladministered, costly weapons acquisitions (e.g., the F-104 fighter in the 1960s or the MRCA *Tornado* in the 1980s); (3) ministerial malfeasance (e.g., Strauss in 1962); or (4) "excessive" NATO "requirements" in force structure or armament (e.g., the level of German concurrence with Carter's 3 percent real increase in defense spending* and LRTNF). More often than not, the Cabinet has already completed preliminary discussion and its first move is to restrict debate. The reaction is an intensified challenge, often spilling over into the extraparliamentary parties or to mass publics. In all but a few cases, the chancellor controls the outcome, but only after private compromise and usually some compensating action in another, perhaps unrelated, sector. The furor then trails off, to lie relatively dormant until the next spark.

However constricted the present system, it nonetheless represents a considerable evolution from that first established in the early 1950s.[61] In rearmament as in most matters, the personality and preferences of Konrad Adenauer were critical. In the views of many, the chancellor was "a compleat civilian," interested in rearmament only as an instrument to gain Germany's political rehabilitation and integration with the West. Military argument divorced from political calculation was of little importance to him, despite the best efforts of successive defense advisers, civilian and military. What he believed critical was to retain full control in his own hands of all German foreign and military affairs, and to restrict involvement and information to the smallest possible official circle.

The first steps toward a separate defense policy-making structure were taken by Franz Josef Strauss, defense minister under Adenauer from 1956 to 1962.[62] Ambitious, brash, hard driving, and well schooled in defense questions by American Occupation authorities, Strauss soon pulled the Defense Ministry through its initial organizational confusion and contradictions. His aim was always to establish the primacy of the minister—in external alliance negotiations as well as in domestic discussions, in questions of nuclear doctrine and psychological defense as in determination of recruitment practices and troop levels. His battles with the opposition SPD were legion; he was always useful for colorful press copy because of his sweeping pronouncements on all issues of Western defense and civilization.

In the last analysis, however, Strauss remained dependent on Adenauer. It was critical to have the chancellor's support for particular decisions (e.g., the acquisition of nuclear-capable weaponry or the stretch-out of Bundeswehr recruitment) as well as his willingness to use Strauss as a "trial ballooner" or "point man" for public controversy at home and abroad. The outcome was that Strauss never succeeded in developing a ministerial system for planning and analysis or for continuing interagency coordination with the primary competitor, the Foreign Office, which had, and still has, principal responsibility for "international affairs."

The present system of German defense decision making received much of its impetus from Helmut Schmidt, first as defense minister (1969–74) and now as chancellor.[63] Like Strauss, Schmidt brought to his

*This is a reference to Carter administration pressure on America's NATO allies to increase annual defense expenditures by 3 percent above the inflation rate.—Ed.

MOD tasks ambition, considerable expertise, and a proclaimed faith in professionalism. He also faced a far more tractable agenda—with far fewer battles with critical allies and domestic opponents over basic defense issues. He enjoyed far more latitude to foster discussion and analysis, both within the Ministry of Defense and in coordination with the Foreign Office and other involved agencies.

Schmidt also was accorded greater flexibility in organization within the ministry. For example, he created a new personal planning staff, set up a special "expert" commission on force structure questions for the 1980s, and attracted a number of promising military and civilian staffers to ministry service. These plus numerous smaller changes were then consolidated, albeit at a lower level, by Schmidt's successor, Georg Leber, of the SPD.

Schmidt faced some process constraints similar to those Strauss confronted. The perennial question reemerged regarding the preeminent authority of the Foreign Office in international affairs not directly concerned with military specifics—such as in positions on arms limitation, NATO policy guidelines, and bilateral relations. Despite successive challenges, Schmidt and his planning staff gained little exclusive control.[64] The minister also found himself in several continuing battles with the top military leadership. In one case, Schmidt was charged with "politicizing" the military, or with creating "SPD generals." He, in turn, suggested the need for greater "professional" responsiveness to the policy shifts set down by the new SPD-FDP coalition, and for continuing adherence to ministerial discipline regarding public critiques by serving officers.

As chancellor, Schmidt has sometimes pursued a similarly activist role in reforming the defense decision-making process. Security policy coordination has received new resources within the chancellor's office; the chancellor has taken a more forceful leadership role in the Cabinet, the smaller Federal Security Council (a Cabinet committee), and the still smaller meetings of the relevant ministers (Foreign Office, Defense, and Finance, most usually). But Schmidt has been constrained by both political and operational realities. He must preserve the careful political balance within his coalition. The FDP's Hans-Dietrich Genscher takes a harder, more pro-American posture, while, at least initially, Defense Minister Apel was the rising star of the SPD and enjoyed considerable support from its more détente-oriented left wing. Moreover, electioneering and times of economic crisis have meant that Schmidt's usual role (and that of the Cabinet in general) is basically one of approving postures already negotiated by the Foreign Office and the MOD.[65]

The role of the military leadership in this process has not really expanded with the greater legitimacy now accorded the Bundeswehr in general. The organizational structure of the ministry is, of course, designed to ensure civilian control and is somewhat parallel to that in the United States. The defense minister has the "power of command" over the armed forces in peacetime.[66] In a "state of defense," this power passes to the chancellor, and operational wartime command to the designated NATO commanders. The formal role of the Chief of Staff of the federal armed forces (Generalinspekteur der Bundeswehr) is to serve as "military adviser to the Minister . . . and the Federal Government." Together with service Chiefs of Staff (army, air force, navy, and health), he acts in the name of the Bundeswehr Defense Council. The respective chiefs function officially both as leaders and as administrative heads of their ministerial divisions.

Informally, the visible participation of the military leadership in decision making was highest in the first decade of rearmament. One clear reason was Adenauer's use of "good generals"—especially the honored Speidel and Heusinger—to gain acceptance of the new Bundeswehr.[67] His targets were both internal—former military officers and more conservative (or nationalistic) groups—and external—the victorious Allied military, particularly respectful of German tradition and experience. Another reason was simply the force of the personalities and personal experiences involved. Those accepting higher command in the fledgling Bundeswehr had been major figures in World War II, and had already emerged from both the postwar de-Nazification process and the relegitimization under the Federal Republic. They had little to lose and perhaps much to gain in publicly pointing out mistakes in, say, NATO's nuclear employment doctrines (e.g., General Trettner) when private persuasion had failed.[68]

The principal reasons, however, reflect the basic principles of postwar civil-military relations (to be discussed further below). There are still major factions of the German political spectrum that view an active engaged military role as inappropriate, if not dangerous. Moreover, if the Bundeswehr is basically analogous to other state agencies and institutions, it must and will follow their pattern.[69] The result is often as fragmented and bureaucratic an approach to defense decision making as that in the Foreign Office or elsewhere (see figure 4). Lack of coordination, incremental decision making, sensitivity above all to budget constraints, and loyalty to the "usual" and "that invented here"—all are to be expected, and perhaps preferred, by the civilian leadership, within the ministry and the broader political elite.

Particular insights into these process characteristics can be gleaned from even a brief survey of German defense spending patterns (figures 5 and 6). The allocation of resources to defense and within the defense establishment is unquestionably the most visible phase in the decision making process and one

Figure 5. German defense spending by party in power (in billions of 1970 Deutschmarks)

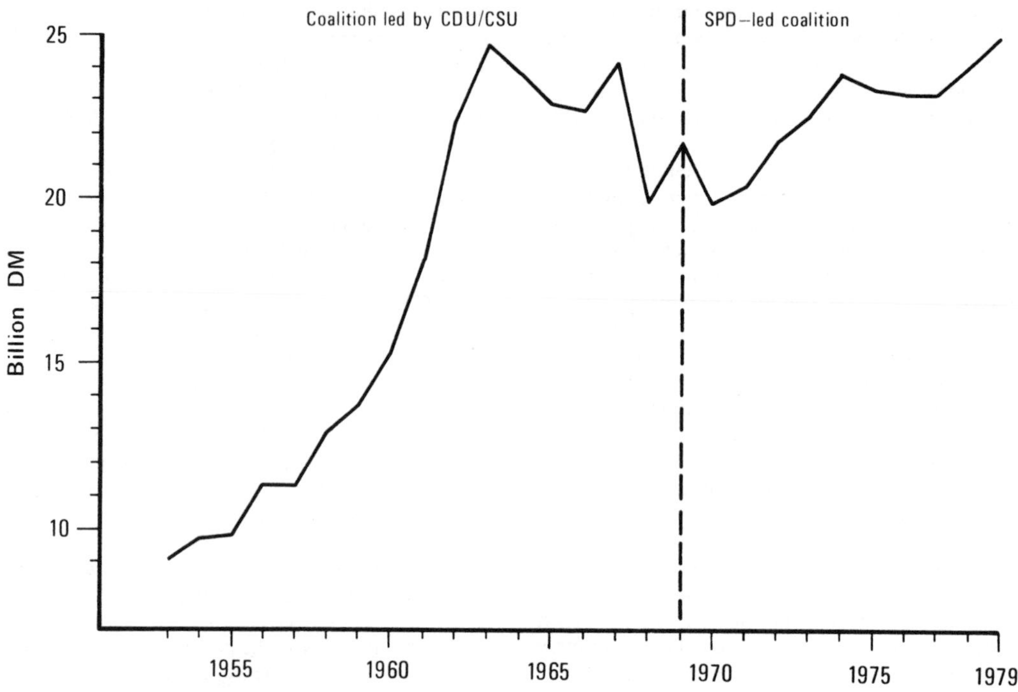

Source: Eichenberg, "Defense-Welfare Tradeoffs in German Budgeting."
Note: Includes defense budget, stationing costs of allied troops, and civil defense outlays, but not federal border guards or Berlin assistance.

of the most hotly contested, inside and outside the ministry. To be sure, only the indirect traces of major acquisition decisions or doctrinal shifts are discernible. But budgetary analysis does capture the essential trends and allows an estimate of the operating ground rules for decision making.

As analyzed in an innovative study by Richard C. Eichenberg, German postwar defense budgeting exhibits three major process characteristics.[70] The first is the significance of time, in terms of the relative strength of MOD claims on both total governmental resources and bargaining within the MOD. In constant dollars, defense spending builds to a high in the first decade of rearmament then undergoes a decade of perturbation, and returns to its former levels (see figure 5). Despite preferred party images and electoral rhetoric, the CDU- and SPD-led coalitions have participated almost equally in high levels of expenditure. Both appear equally constrained by the rearmament-replacement cycle (as the SPD has discovered since 1975) and American pressure for greater alliance burden sharing (evident in the Kennedy push of the early 1960s and the Carter initiatives of the late 1970s).

The differences in levels also appear to be a function of the total amount of resources available to the central government. Eichenberg found that, of all the changes in ministerial spending, those in the MOD pattern were most closely correlated with changes in overall federal spending. Moreover, the dip in spending in the mid-1960s corresponds closely to that imposed by the "Erhard recession" on all federal expenditures. The budgetary solution—the Middle-Term Finance Plan—imposed spending ceilings and established relatively fixed ratios between the money available to the MOD and that for other ministries over five-year planning cycles.

More critical differences and some contradictions are evident in the shifts between budget categories over time (see figure 6). In the initial rearmament phase, the major share went to procurement—to the "equalization" of German armament with the most modern held by other allies. As shown in table 5, the total shares claimed by the army and the air force were almost equal, despite the very different manpower levels (350,000 versus 100,000). The battles over budget shares consumed considerable attention in the period 1956 to 1960, when the final terms of build-up were fixed.

More surprising, perhaps, is the steady upward

Figure 6. Three categories of West German defense spending (budget authority)

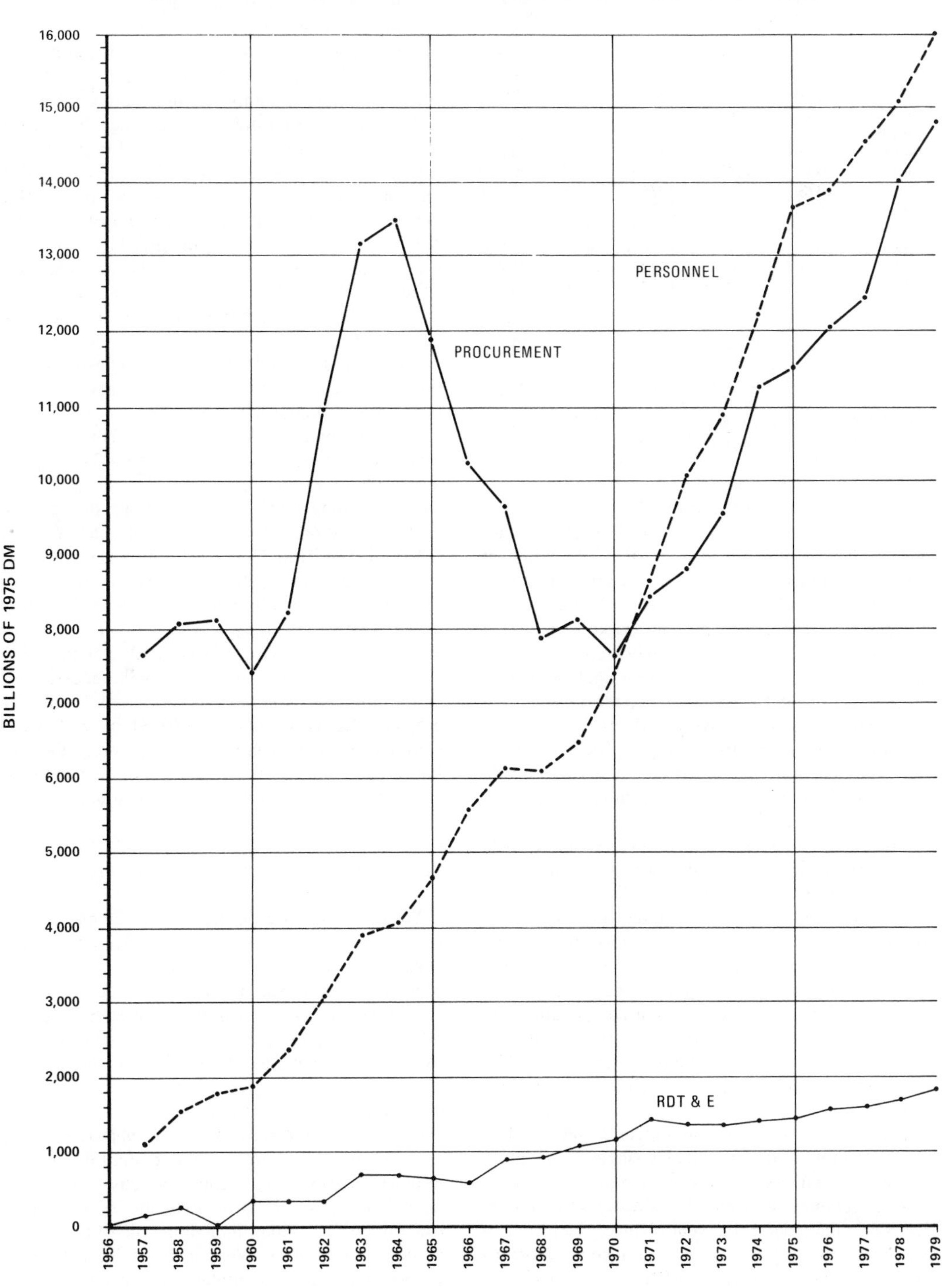

Source: Eichenberg, "Defense-Welfare Tradeoffs in German Budgeting."

Table 5
Total weapons procurement costs for the Bundeswehr by service category, 1957–69 (in millions of marks)

Year	Army	Navy	Air Force	Other	Total
1957/58	1539.8	262.3	553.1	39.9	2395.1
1958/59	601.8	599.8	1097.3	46.2	2345.1
1959/60	1042.3	462.9	702.8	46.0	2254.0
1960[a]	745.9	386.2	901.6	33.9	2067.6
1961	987.1	464.3	1414.8	73.7	2939.9
1962	1473.7	634.1	2075.5	85.8	4269.1
1963	1559.3	593.4	2630.5	83.6	4866.8
1964	1475.9	885.7	1572.6	78.4	4012.6
1965	1325.1	691.7	1158.5	64.7	3240.0
1966	1271.7	550.1	739.5	122.1	2683.4
1967	1652.1	742.7	1107.5	73.5	3575.8
1968	1177.1	589.0	1236.5	46.7	3049.3
1969[b]	1477.1	456.7	1575.1	72.9	3581.8
Total	16328.9	7318.9	16765.3	867.4	41280.5

Source: Bundes Presse- und Informationsamt, *Weissbuch 1970: Zur Sicherheit der Bundesrepublik Deutschland und zur lage der Bundeswehr* (Bonn, 1970), pp. 197–98.
[a]Reflects shortened fiscal year (April–December 31).
[b]Estimated costs.

curve of personnel costs. From 1956 to 1966, this supply reflects the accretion of manpower, military and civilian, within the new MOD. Thereafter, it typifies a situation faced by most European states. Soldiers, even conscripts, are now to be paid wages comparable to those of civilian workers, with the same benefits and cost-of-living pay increases. These costs have risen as steeply as personnel outlays in other governmental agencies, since the interrelation has been fixed legislatively. Moreover, without additional costly perquisites (e.g., officer universities), the Federal Republic would not have been able to overcome the severe shortages among junior officer ranks and NCOs.

This steady increase in manpower costs is made more difficult by a related development: heightened public assertion of a defense spending ceiling. The trends reflected in public attitudes (see figure 3) suggest a general acceptance of whatever the existing defense expenditures are or have recently been. True to its rhetoric, the membership of the CDU/CSU is somewhat more in favor of increased spending, but not by an overwhelming percentage. Incrementalism is clearly the dominant strategy in terms of public acceptance as well as the rules of intraministry harmony.

Eichenberg's study indeed suggests that much of the bargaining about marginal changes takes place within the MOD itself, and often at fairly low levels. The budget total for defense has already been more or less set in the federal five-year planning budget. Unless there are surprises—e.g., the recent disastrous multi-role combat aircraft (MRCA) *Tornado* cost overruns—it will remain relatively fixed. The amount of interagency bargaining or horse trading is limited by the lack of a clear executive coordinating body (e.g., the Office of Management and Budget) or a strong tradition of parliamentary oversight. Further, a good portion of social welfare expenditure occurs at the state level; both this practice of compartmentalization and the principle of ministerial autonomy are, and will almost certainly remain, sacrosanct.

This leaves the portion of the leverage that exists in the hands of those outside the Federal Republic. The forum may be the recurring bilateral negotiations with the United States about appropriate burden sharing, or it may be in the wider context of the annual NATO planning exercise, symbolized by national responses to the NATO Defense Planning Questionnaire (DPQ). But these represent arenas for the exercise of influence by other actors, military and political. NATO "requirements" can also be (and have often been) mobilized when either domestic negotiations need additional support or a service finds a major project under unfriendly fire.

Clearly, however, the German role is far more autonomous and assertive than in the past. This is partly the result of experience: the Federal Republic has taken a leading role in the Euro-group deliberations on budgetary projections, in the formulation of the NATO Long-Term Defense Improvement Program (LTDIP), and in production consortia (as for the MRCA-*Tornado*). Moreover, changes in the domestic economy as well as the growth of a domestic defense industry have placed real constraints on German abilities, not to mention willingness, to act as the alliance's foremost supporter of cooperative projects. As the events of 1980–81 have shown, a German chancellor can now argue publicly about the fair share borne by specific allies and demand equal consideration for German economic strains.

Recurring issues: defense policy outputs

What are the specific outputs of defense decision making? How are these different from those produced by processes more distinctly national in character? I will examine, in varying degrees of detail, outputs in four critical issue areas: civil-military relations, weapons acquisition, force structure decisions, and perceptions of the utility of force.

CIVIL-MILITARY RELATIONS

Central to any discussion of German defense policy, present or future, is the evolution of civil-military relations since the first days of rearmament.[71] The reasons are obvious: the legacy of Prussian military tradition, the unique role of the military in the downfall of the Weimar Republic, and the still controversial issue of military responsibility for the crimes of Naziism, within Germany and in external conquest. The defeat of German militarism had been a primary war aim of the West. For the Europeans in particular, the principal issue in rearmament was how to restore the best in the German military experience without also threatening the beginnings of West German democracy or the reestablishment of European order. In the words of Franz Josef Strauss, "The new German army was to be strong enough to threaten the Russians but not the Belgians."[72]

The basic answer was the concept of *Innere Führung* (the citizen in uniform) as the core organizing element of the German armed forces. As worked out in the early 1950s principally by Wolf Count von Baudissin, the basic principles explicitly rejected the two most troublesome civil-military models from the past.[73] The first was that of the incipient state-within-the-state, in which the autonomous, aristocratic military establishment set its own standards and loyalties without necessary regard for an overriding political authority or democratic ethic. This was an extreme or romantic interpretation of the "Prussian system," founded on the basis of self-sacrifice, self-imposed duty, loyalty to discipline, and Spartan simplicity. The individual and the institution were to be indistinguishable, with the highest achievement seen as service to the state but not necessarily the existing government (as in Weimar).

The second rejected model represented perhaps the obverse: the politicized, submissive military of the Nazi period. Hitler attempted to break "the Prussian system" by systematically changing the basis of professional authority to one dependent on the Nazi party, and ultimately on loyalty to himself alone. His creation of "people's generals" (such as Rommel), his establishment of the *Waffen-SS* as a rival organization, his constant probing of military loyalty—all were elements leading toward a redefinition of professional responsibility ("only obeying orders") and of organizational competency and discipline.

As it has evolved over the past twenty-five years, *Innere Führung* has emphasized civilian supremacy in several different respects. As noted above, the authority of the elected political leadership—the minister and the chancellor—is unquestioned, in crisis as in peacetime. More importantly, the soldier is viewed first and foremost as a citizen, with rights and responsibilities to be respected by the military establishment and with a future existence not defined by his present military career. His tasks involve a personal decision regarding the ethics of his profession and his own choices within broad guidelines on behavior vis-à-vis subordinate and superior, ally and adversary. It is a system designed to recognize rights to unionize and to pursue freedom of conscience, to achieve political legitimacy without submission or superiority.

Not surprisingly, the achievements of the *Innere Führung* program have not always matched these ideals. A major initial difficulty was finding people to implement and administer the program. The problem was not with the top leadership (that had been solved by the rigorous screening carried on by politicians and citizens), it was that the majority of the first lower and middle officer ranks had served in the Wehrmacht. Even a decade of civilianization seemingly had not prepared them to make such a radical adjustment or to move from theory to operational practice. Those who supported the program most strongly were, or were perceived to be, outsiders or loners, perhaps even those who had never understood the requirements of military tradition.[74]

A related source of difficulty was the expectations of the West German population as a whole. Again two rather different conceptions were involved; the requirements were neither congruent nor subject to compromise. The first conception was that of the traditionalists, who saw unionization or direct political education, civilian dress, and second career training as alien to the best of German tradition. They found comfort in the adverse reactions of older officers, such as General Albert Schnez, the army inspector from 1969 to 1971, who repeatedly challenged his minister and the SPD-FDP government on these issues.[75]

The second strand was a virulent antimilitary reaction, particularly among the first two postwar generations. In this perspective, military characteristics were largely antithetical to the ideal of a democratic society or a nonmilitaristic Germany. Those attracted to this profession were viewed as either dupes or antidemocrats, or perhaps those who could not make it "outside." Conscription, too, was seen as little better than forced labor or exploitation by the state; the concept of patriotic service had been irretrievably damaged by Nazi practices.

These views received strong support from external sources during the first decade or so of rearmament. Obvious channels were the Soviet Union and Eastern Europe; by dint of political will, all of the emotional baggage of Naziism was attributed to West, not East, Germany. Bonn was almost always described as "revanchist," ready to march again. More subtle but equally painful were a number of incidents in the West: Eisenhower refusing to shake General Speidel's hand despite his NATO command, the integrated NATO staff's reaction to German uniforms, the popular demonstrations in France and Holland against "rehabilitated" officers from World War II.

The passage of time has blunted many of these difficulties.[76] The prewar military generation has now largely passed from the scene. At least toleration, if not acceptance, is assured to the Bundeswehr by the vast majority, abroad as at home. Education in *Innere Führung* principles is now a regular and legitimate component of military training at all levels. A good portion of the initial "high dudgeon" has been replaced by a greater tolerance toward the military past, more practical examples of the ethical choices to be made, and group seminars based on mutual acceptance and questioning. The problems of other Western military establishments—especially the French and American—have brought new understanding for some of Germany's past dilemmas.

Still at question, however, is where the limits of individual responsibility for criticism within state service truly lie. Over the past two decades, ministerial discipline has been imposed on a number of critical voices within the Bundeswehr, from both the Left and the Right. In each case, the critic proclaimed his right of conscience to bring his case before the public, and has cited the parallels in past German history.

Even individual interpretations of military tradition have become matters of controversy, most dramatically within the Bundeswehr but also in the larger political context. As the *White Paper, 1979* statement of principles shows, the organizational response to the dilemmas reflects more caution and careful balancing than leadership or suasion, moral or political. Tradition in the Bundeswehr:

1. cannot be anything except what is justified under the Constitution
2. must not be allowed to contradict the social system of values and standards
3. must be in relation to peace
4. must not be restricted to the history of the Bundeswehr
5. must not be allowed to concentrate solely upon events and figures in military and belligerent history
6. must subscribe to understanding amongst nations and to overcoming chauvinism
7. must not be allowed to degenerate into traditionalism
8. when ordered and prescribed, is incompatible with the governing image of the enfranchised citizen
9. calls for sympathy from the civilian population
10. is also a question of patience.[77]

A cause of even greater uneasiness for some is the questionable congruence of civilianization, especially in the exercise of authority and in dress and personal style, with the requirements of professional efficiency and the hierarchy of command. Here Germany has done at least as well as other allied governments facing the same challenges (Holland, France, and, to a degree, the United States). But there are still major gaps and discrepancies, ever-present fuel for critical attacks from all sides.

These issues may well become more significant as the Bundeswehr confronts the demographic squeeze of the mid-1980s.[78] Until now, it has conscripted only 80–85 percent of each eligible class; conscripts in the 1970s have constituted only 45 percent (220,000) of the total active manpower. Successive legislation has also made it relatively easy to gain a Bundeswehr exemption on grounds of religious or ethical conviction. And with a relatively short term of service (fifteen months), the shortfall among conscripts has become relatively negligible.

From 1988 onward, however, present projections foresee a growing manpower deficit (figure 7). The immediate impact will be felt in the number of available conscripts, but parallel effects can be expected in the ranks of both the short-term volunteers (two- to fifteen-year enlistees) and regular forces (officers and senior NCOs). There are a number of remedial actions now under study—a longer conscript term, greater financial and career incentives for volunteers, a change in the conscript-enlistee ratio—but all turn on basically the same issues: what type of military organization is deemed necessary by German society, and which sacrifices, if any, must be made to preserve the painfully crafted character of the present Bundeswehr? At present, it is yet another issue that is foreseeable but not yet on what the political elite believes to be the unavoidable political agenda. And as long as the United States continues to suffer related manpower shortfalls, the external price to be paid is neither immediate nor perceived as particularly risky.

WEAPONS ACQUISITION

The basic outlines of German weapons acquisition have already emerged in the earlier portions of this essay. The Federal Republic began rearmament with virtually no national weapons production capability.[79] Moreover, under the terms of the Western European Union Treaty, it was specifically prohibited from the manufacture on German soil of any system judged to have "offensive capabilities." The initial equipment for the Bundeswehr came from allied, principally American, stocks already deployed in Europe.

The intervening decades have seen a gradual, then wholesale lifting of the WEU restrictions. Virtually the only one of significance to remain is the "voluntary" pledge of Chancellor Adenauer to renounce atomic, biological, and chemical production. The few others still in force—e.g., that on cruise missile production—will presumably be lifted as a matter of course.

These outcomes reflect not only Germany's clear alliance status but also the care and caution Bonn has continually exercised in this sensitive area.[80] The scope of autonomous production in major weapons classes is painstakingly defined; many German weapons emerge from coproduction or licensed production arrangements. Unquestionably, the economies of scale in high-technology manufacture are a major reason. But so, too, is Bonn's continuing determination to avoid unnecessary symbols of national independence, and to secure as much military integration as possible. The major national programs that do exist—e.g., the Leopard tank—often repre-

Figure 7. Available versus required conscript manpower

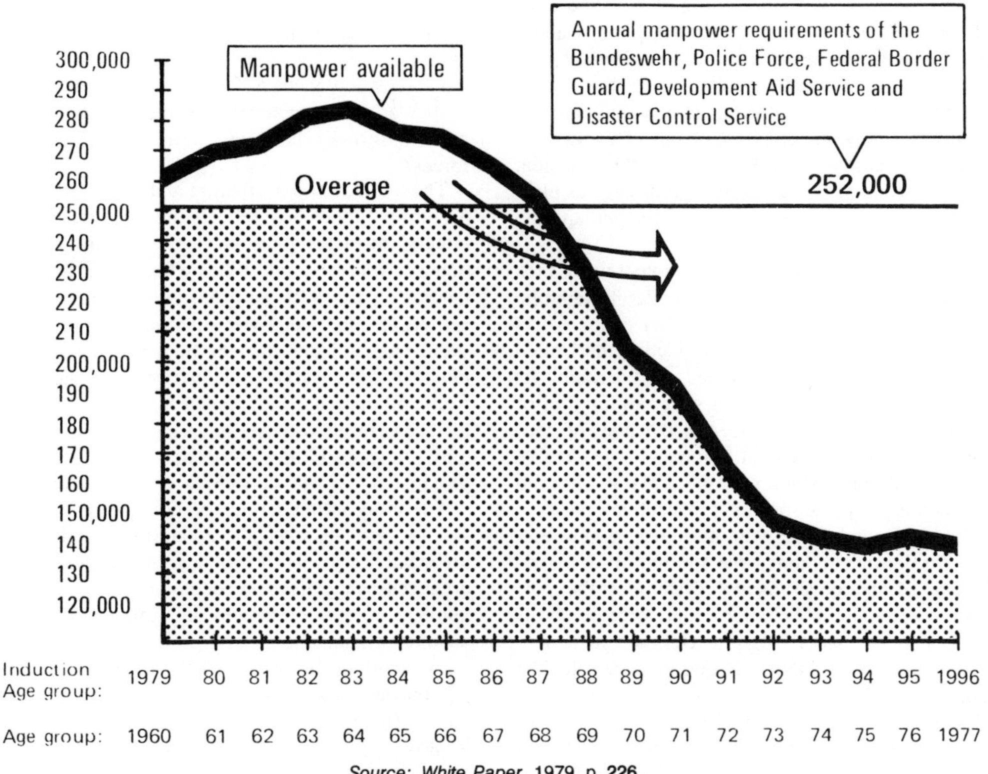

Source: White Paper, **1979, p. 226.**

sent an alternative to desired coproduction—as in the failed main battle tank (MBT) program with the United States.

Under these conditions, Bonn's continuing pressures for greater rationalization and standardization within NATO have been consistent. Germany is one of the most vocal advocates of the "two-way street" concept—of greater trans-Atlantic sharing of contracts and technological development—first supported by the Carter administration then left to fade. The demonstrable successes of German joint efforts have been few, even within the European framework.

As shown in figure 5 above, weapons procurement has proceeded in two cycles. According to *White Paper, 1979,* a total of 48 billion DM went to weapons purchases from 1970 to 1979, with an additional 13 billion DM for research and development.[81] The stated budgetary goal since the latter part of the 1970s has been to insure that at least 30 percent of each budget is devoted to capital expenditure. These include, however, all types of purchases, at home and abroad, as well as construction contracts for military facilities, infrastructure, and housing.

What will be the future direction of German acquisition policy? All available evidence suggests that there will be a more "national" approach, even in aircraft in the wake of the *Tornado* disaster.* There are suggestions that even planned purchases will be further stretched out, with present equipment being kept on line for perhaps another decade. Defense Minister Hans Apel suggested in early 1981 that the Federal Republic, even in its more affluent days, probably could not have continued major tank, aircraft, and ship purchases in the light of inflation and cost overruns.[82] Just as in the recession of the mid-1960s, the solution will be in a less ambitious acquisition schedule and perhaps more reliance on the maintenance and progressive improvement of deployed systems.

There would seem to be little chance to rely on external markets or direct sales. The United States is seen by a number of German analysts to have returned to a policy of "buy American." Most of the European states are under the same pressures as the Federal Republic—high unit costs, a commitment to

*The author is referring to cost overruns and performance problems experienced in the early 1980s.—Ed.

preserve domestic employment, and an interest in a strong national technological base. The 1976 aircraft "sale of the century"—the selling of both the F-16 and the *Tornado*—have also raised questions about how to manage the next transition to a new weapons generation (already partially planned for the 1990s) in a projected period of constrained economic growth and strong, competing domestic claims. This was one of the first items to vanish from the MOD agenda; there are strong pressures in the Bundestag, as elsewhere, to apply stretch-out policies for perhaps the next decade.

Foreign military sales are also constrained in a number of ways.[83] In 1981, the Federal Republic ranks as the fifth largest arms supplier in the world but lags by a considerable margin behind the United States, the Soviet Union, France, and Britain. Its policies have been quite circumspect and mindful of existing regional arms balances in the light of continuing left-wing criticism at home and considerable sensitivity abroad. Moreover, the 1981 public and parliamentary opposition to prospective sales to Saudi Arabia and Chile will introduce a new element to sales calculations—the strength of domestic criticism of the governmental system of the purchaser. The failure of Schmidt to deliver fully on his promises to the Saudis, despite German oil dependence, will also constitute a strong precedent for the future.

The expectation, therefore, must be of an arms policy somewhat more national in orientation, but following familiar lines. The German interest in alliance standardization will remain strong, if only because the connections between the persistence of twenty-nine different gas nozzles and German national security are relatively clear cut. There are also indirect benefits to be calculated, credit for the transfer of obsolete equipment to Greece and Turkey under a complicated NATO burden sharing arrangement being only one direct example. But there will be new economic constraints, and a far more cautious German approach to coordination and coproduction.

THE FORCE POSTURE OF THE FEDERAL REPUBLIC

The present force posture of the Federal Republic is remarkably like that negotiated in the first rearmament discussion. The personnel levels are perhaps the most stable component: 70 percent for the army (*Heer*), with 50 percent of all conscripts; 22 percent for the air force (*Luftwaffe*), with 30 percent of all conscripts; and 8 percent for the navy (*Marine*), with 20 percent of the total conscript manpower.[84]

Many of the questions treated in other chapters regarding the fit between doctrine and structure are relatively less important in the German case given the pervasive alliance orientation. All of Germany's tactical air capability, for example, is under NATO command (two and four Allied Tactical Air Force), even in peacetime. All German land forces are major *assigned* elements under NATO's northern and central commands. At a minimum, this implies a responsiveness to the planning and doctrine of the alliance. In operational terms, it means relatively constant communication and joint exercises with other Western forces deployed on German soil. There are also particularly strong bonds—some fostered, others more informal—between German and American forces.

The amount of perturbation and challenge in force posture policy clearly reflects the size and degree of integration of the three services. The army unquestionably was the hardest hit by the manpower uncertainties of the 1970s and shortfalls in junior officers and NCOs. Its manpower situation has now at least stabilized, and the changes in pay and recruitment practices have garnered higher performance marks from both national and alliance authorities. Nonetheless, it is faced with the huge training and administrative responsibilities associated with inducting approximately 50,000 conscripts every quarter.

The army is the service branch whose twelve divisions have absorbed the greatest external pressure for increased levels of efficiency and, therefore, for organizational change. A rough measure of this is the number of major changes in American army divisional organization (three). The German pattern (now three) has been somewhat more resistant to precipitous shifts but generally has followed suit eventually. The most recent plan has involved measures to improve (1) combat efficiency, (2) the army "tooth-to-tail" ratio, and (3) the number of trained personnel available for reserve duty and unit training for cadre divisions readily expandable in times of tension.

In many respects, it is the German air force that is the closest counterpart of an American service. In part, this reflects a planned similarity; much of the Luftwaffe initial pilot training is conducted in the United States in close connection with similar American units. Specific technological requirements beyond those of either army or navy units constitute another parallel element, with a third being constant interaction within the NATO tactical air commands.

The smallest of the three services, the navy has maintained perhaps the most autonomous profile. Its missions are largely confined to Baltic defense and North Sea security, with a small mixed force of naval air support, fast frigates, and shallow-draft submarines. Pressures to expand the scope of naval operations continue, both from within Germany and from its allies. But for the foreseeable future, it will probably continue to operate in the area of "German defense" set down in legislation, with principal attention given to the coastal defense function.

The fourth "regular" service is that of the separate Medical and Health services, organized under their own service *Inspekteur*. Their functions are quite simply "preventive medicine, medical care, and the treatment and evacuation of casualties." They will remain under national command even in wartime and will render support when possible to both civilians and the medical services of the other NATO forces.

The final element within the German defense establishment is the territorial army (TV), organized under the army to provide for home defense under national command in wartime. The TV has long been a stepchild of the Bundeswehr establishment, understaffed and underequipped. Continuing NATO pressure for greater reserve capabilities has led to new plans for establishing cadre divisions with more modern equipment. Moreover, there will be a strengthened ready reserve force and a more extensive program of reserve duty training. Some twelve home defense brigades will reach close to full strength in a period of heightened warning; all in all, perhaps a million troops can be mobilized in the first two weeks of conflict.

PERCEPTIONS OF THE UTILITY OF FORCE

In discussing German perceptions of the utility of force, an analyst begins with a largely hypothetical framework. No German regular forces have been used since the German entry into NATO. There have been no instances of direct force use on the Central Front; indeed, German forces are deployed at some distance from the East German or Czechoslovak border to prevent accident or incident. By Four Power agreement they have also been excluded from any functions directly related to the successive Berlin crises. The only use of German force came in the freeing of a captured German plane in Mogadishu, and this was undertaken by the special antiterrorist unit of the federal border police, a separate paramilitary organization.[85]

There are few in Germany, or within NATO in general, who are dissatisfied with the stability this implies regarding the Central Front. A number of German analysts suggest a second reason: the avoidance of even the probable confrontation of East German and West German troops. The Bonn government has never doubted the loyalty of West German troops, even under such conditions, or the necessary task of targeting East German forces and cities. The East German leadership has made similar pronouncements. The separation of the two states, in many senses, has increased with time. But for at least some West German observers, it is a question that cannot be answered confidently until conflict occurs.

West Germany has steadfastly refused to allow its troops to become involved outside the European "zone of German defense." Perhaps the most dramatic confrontation came in the mid-1960s, when President Lyndon Johnson pressured Bonn to send at least a token force to Vietnam. Chancellor Erhard responded that this was beyond the spirit of the German Constitution; moreover, it would have constituted an intolerable political and psychological burden for German forces and German society.

In recent years, there have been some renewed calls in the United States for greater German participation in the maintenance of a favorable international order. The security of the Persian Gulf and, thus, of European oil supplies, has been emphasized as an issue of particular significance for Germany. More or less serious schemes have been a German naval presence in the gulf, direct German support for an alliance rapid-deployment force, or even the inclusion of some German units in American-led RDF.

Most German political leaders have rejected all of these suggestions for the same reasons as were given in the mid-1960s. However more self-confident and assertive they may be on NATO affairs, most of the German political elite believe the cost of extra-NATO involvement will still be too high. They have offered a number of alternatives: (1) substantial economic assistance to two Western "anchors" in the region, Turkey and Pakistan; (2) the assumption of certain unspecified functions in Europe to allow greater American flexibility; (3) increased diversification of energy imports and utilization, and (4) increased diplomatic links with the gulf states. The Federal Republic has argued in bilateral and NATO discussions that, taken as a package, these constitute a fair share toward stabilization of the gulf region and alleviation of energy vulnerability.

For the foreseeable future, German reluctance to expand the scope of its force commitments will almost certainly continue. There are obvious technical and economic constraints; German forces, for example, cannot be projected easily beyond national borders without relying on other states. The most important limitations will still be political and psychological, in terms of domestic constituencies as well as external allies and adversaries. Even in the case of an energy embargo, the range of nonmilitary instruments available to any future German government would seem considerable.

The pivotal question would seem to be the degree of importance American leadership will attach to direct German participation. Under present conditions, the question has not really been raised. And there is good reason, now as in 1965, to expect German resistance, if not direct opposition. One solution often discussed is a formal expansion of NATO's area of responsibility. But this would be highly questionable, given present alliance politics, and West German ambivalence, Left and Right, on this subject is already quite marked.

Epilogue

Throughout this essay, the analysis has focused on what seem to be the underlying contradictions of postwar German defense policy. The Federal Republic is the second NATO power in all but direct nuclear capability, yet it has no separable national defense profile. Its forces are among the most numerous and most effective in the West, yet the structure and doctrine of the Bundeswehr reflect alliance compromise and American political necessity more than they do German conceptions and choices. Finally, the Federal Republic is now clearly a power with global impact. But its defense policy remains firmly anchored in the requirements of the Central Front, and it is likely to remain so.

There is no necessary reason for the speedy resolution of any of these contradictions. In many respects, they reflect the basic German-American bargains under which rearmament was sanctioned. The present international order is permissive; it is hard even to imagine a systemic challenge that would force greater congruence, much less a radical reorientation, of German national security efforts.

The critical variable would seem to remain the strength and durability of the German-American relationship. This relationship has already withstood a number of major shifts and substantive disputes. Yet the basic issues are (1) the convergence of national interests in a preferred European order, and (2) the benefits to both of linking national security resources. The arguments of the past now seem challenged on several sides—the new significance attached to Persian Gulf security by the United States or the primacy that the Federal Republic occasionally seems to accord the maintenance of European détente, whatever the global context. These challenges will be all the more intense if present projections of continuing economic constraints on both states do indeed come true.

Much will depend, as it always has, on the perception of long-term mutual benefit in the relationship. There is much to build on in terms of both direct cooperation and indirect networks of communication. The most probable and hopeful production will be a continuation of the basic German-American connection in the interests of European stability, well beyond the decade of the 1980s.

Notes

1. Federal Republic of Germany, Federal Minister of Defence, *White Paper, 1979: The Security of the Federal Republic of Germany and the Federal Armed Forces* (Bonn: Federal Minister of Defence, 1979), p. 25.

2. This and later historical discussions are drawn from my earlier book, *Germany and the Politics of Nuclear Weapons* (New York: Columbia University Press, 1975).

3. Several recent treatments include the essays collected by Wolfram Hanrieder in his *West German Foreign Policy, 1949-1979* (Boulder, Colo.: Westview Press, 1980), especially those by Hillenbrand, Wörner, and me.

4. By German calculations, in 1978, the total defense expenditures of the NATO states were divided into the following shares: United States, 59.0 percent; FRG, 11.5 percent; France, 10.0 percent; United Kingdom, 7.9 percent; Italy, 3.4 percent; Holland, 2.4 percent; Canada, 2.3 percent; with the remaining 3.5 percent divided among the rest. The figures reflect total U.S. spending and exclude Greece and Turkey. See *White Paper, 1979,* pp. 276-77.

5. For recent suggestions along these lines, see James Bellini and Geoffrey Pattie, *A New World Role for the Medium Power* (London: Royal United Service Institute for Defense Studies, 1977).

6. Kelleher (*Germany and Nuclear Weapons,* "Epilogue") suggests one measurement scheme; Bellini and Pattie, a related one.

7. The best treatment in English of this initial period is Robert McGeehan, *The German Rearmament Question: American Diplomacy and European Defense after World War II* (Urbana: University of Illinois Press, 1971).

8. See here the related treatment in my essay, "Germany and NATO: The Enduring Bargain," in *West German Foreign Policy,* ed. Hanrieder, pp. 43-60.

9. Compare, here, the essays of Kissinger, Nerlich, and Hassner in Kenneth Myers, *NATO: The Next Thirty Years* (Boulder, Colo.: Westview Press, 1980).

10. Perhaps the earliest full statement of the "decoupling theme" is Andrew J. Pierre's "Can European Security Be Decoupled from America?," *Foreign Affairs,* July 1973, pp. 761-77.

11. See the concise treatment of the evolution of these relationships in the late 1970s in Wolfram F. Hanrieder and Graeme P. Auton, *The Foreign Policies of West Germany, France, and Britain* (Englewood Cliffs, N.J.: Prentice-Hall, 1980), pp. 33-49.

12. The principal treaty was, of course, the Treaty on the Basis of Relations, or the so-called Basic Treaty between the Federal Republic and the German Democratic Republic, signed in December 1972. The original source was Chancellor Willy Brandt in 1969. See Gebhard Schweigler's *National Consciousness in Divided Germany* (Beverly Hills: Sage, 1975).

13. *Ostpolitik* is usually defined as FRG relations with the Soviet Union and East European states other than the DDR. The relevant treaties here are: (1) the German-Soviet treaty of August 1970, (2) the German-Polish treaty of December 1970, and (3) the German-Czech treaty of 1973. These together with the Four Power Agreement on Berlin of October 1970 and the Basic Treaty of 1972 constitute the legal foundation for Bonn's "normalization" program. See on this Michael Kreile, "Ostpolitik Reconsidered," in *The Foreign Policy of West Germany: Formation and Contents,* ed. Ekkehart Krippendorff and Volker Rittberger (Beverly Hills: Sage, 1980), pp. 123-46.

14. See Kreile, "Ostpolitik Reconsidered," pp. 134-39.

15. Compare the contrasting chapters in the official *White Paper, 1979:* "Accommodation," pp. 41-52, and "The Military Balance," pp. 99-121.

16. For a contrasting view, see Christian Potyka, "Die vernachlässigte Offentlichkeit," in *Sicherheitspolitik,* ed. Klaus-Dieter Schwarz, 2nd ed. (Bad Hunnef-Epel: Osang Verlag, 1976), pp. 365-78.

17. See *White Paper, 1979* formulation, "A policy of détente is part of a perceptive security policy," p. 42.

18. See my article on LRTNF, "The Present as Prologue," in *International Security,* Spring 1981; and Alton Frye, "Nuclear Weapons in Europe: No Exit from Ambivalence," *Survival,* May/June 1980, pp. 98-106.

19. See Kreile, "Ostpolitik Reconsidered," pp. 123-46; and Wolf-Dieter Karl, "Entspannungspolitik: Der Weg von der Konfrontation zur Kooperation in den Ost-West Beziehungen," in *Sicherheitspolitik*, ed. Klaus-Dieter Schwarz, pp. 127-50.

20. For a brief synthesis of these arguments, see Frieder Schlupp, "*Modell Deutschland* and the International Division of Labour: The Federal Republic of Germany in the World Political Economy," in *Foreign Policy of West Germany*, ed. Krippendorff and Rittberger, pp. 33-100.

21. See Kelleher, *Germany and Nuclear Weapons*, pp. 296-301.

22. See his famous Alistair Buchan Memorial Lecture of October 1977, reprinted in *Survival*, January/February 1978, pp. 2-10.

23. For further details on these various alternatives and the evolution of the German position, see Kelleher, *Germany and Nuclear Weapons*, chapters 7, 9, and 10.

24. For further details, see Lewis Edinger, *Kurt Schumacher: A Study in Personality and Political Behavior* (Stanford: Stanford University Press, 1965).

25. As reported in *Der Spiegel*, 6 October 1954, pp. 5-7.

26. For a more detailed development of this theme, see Catherine M. Kelleher, "Mass Armies in the 1970's: The Debate in Western Europe," *Armed Forces and Society*, Fall 1978, pp. 3-30.

27. For a further development of this theme, see Kelleher in *West German Foreign Policy*, ed. Hanrieder, pp. 43-60.

28. See the comments by Minister Matthöfer and Chancellor Schmidt reported in press accounts through the spring, summer, and fall of 1980 and translated in the Foreign Broadcast Information Service, *Daily Report: Western Europe*.

29. See *White Paper, 1979*, pp. 107-10, 125-27, for the most concise statement of the German interpretation of the role and potential of European-based TNF.

30. See Helga Haftendorn's discussion in her "West Germany and the Management of Security Relations: Security Policy under the Conditions of International Interdependence," in *Foreign Policy of West Germany*, ed. Krippendorff and Rittberger, pp. 7-31.

31. *White Paper, 1979*, pp. 42.

32. Ibid., pp. 42-43, 55-84.

33. See the various essays on both processes in the volume edited by Helga Haftendorn, Wolf-Dieter Karl, Joachim Krause, and Lothar Wilker, *Verwaltete Aussenpolitik: Sicherheits-und entspannungspolitische Entscheidungsprozesse in Bonn* (Cologne: Verlag Wissenschaft und Politik, 1978).

34. See Kelleher, "Present as Prologue," for further details.

35. See Krippendorff's introductory essay to *Foreign Policy of West Germany*, pp. 1-5.

36. See McGeehan, *German Rearmament Question*.

37. *White Paper, 1979*, pp. 24-26.

38. As quoted in Walter F. Hahn, *Between Westpolitik and Ostpolitik* (Beverly Hills: Sage, 1975), p. 70.

39. Kelleher, *Germany and Nuclear Weapons*, pp. 49-56.

40. Ibid., chapter 6.

41. Ibid., chapter 8.

42. See, for example, the discussion of the Soviet threat in the first two white papers under Schröder in 1969 and under Schmidt in 1970.

43. See the further discussion of this throughout Kelleher, *Germany and Nuclear Weapons*, and Hanrieder and Auton, *Foreign Policies of West Germany, France, and Britain*, chapter 1.

44. For this reason alone, the report of columnists Evans and Novak that in the summer of 1977 the Carter administration was considering defense along the Weser-Lech perimeter occasioned immediate Bonn protests and criticisms. See Hanrieder and Auton, *Foreign Policies of West Germany, France, and Britain*, p. 25.

45. See the essay by Sabrosky in this volume.

46. This was the original goal set at the Lisbon conference of 1952. See McGeehan, *German Rearmament Question*, for further details.

47. See the Leber comment quoted above.

48. See below for a report of empirical results on "guns v. butter" achieved by Richard C. Eichenberg in his doctoral dissertation on this topic, "Defense-Welfare Tradeoffs in German Budgeting," submitted to the Department of Political Science, University of Michigan, June 1981.

49. One example of the somewhat inflammatory popular commentary on this issue is a 1981 *Stern* article by Wolf Perdelwitz, "Die versteckte Atommacht," 19 February 1981.

50. See Kelleher, "Present as Prologue."

51. The decision rules are left unpublished, in part for reasons of what the Germans view as "credible deterrence." For discussion of earlier demands for a national veto right, see Kelleher, *Germany and Nuclear Weapons*, chapter 8.

52. The Bundestag debate on these issues took place in March 1979, but Wehner and others had been raising questions in the fall of 1978. On this, see the discussion in "The Modernization of NATO's Long-Range Theater Nuclear Forces" prepared by the Congressional Research Services for the House Committee on Foreign Affairs (96th Cong., 2nd sess.), 31 December 1980.

53. This is clearly not the position of the CDU centrists, as is clear from, for example, the essay by sometime shadow Defense Minister Manfred Wörner in *West German Foreign Policy*, ed. Hanrieder, pp. 37-42. But see the remarks attributed to Richard Allen in the *New York Times*, 29 March 1981.

54. See John Vinocour's report on Chancellor Schmidt's criticism of these groups, *New York Times*, 5 April 1981.

55. Compare the somewhat different evaluation developed by Martin Muller in Haftendorn et al., *Verwaltete Aussenpolitik*, pp. 167-89.

56. See the *Stern* interview given by the retired Luftwaffe Colonel Alfred Mechtersheimer, "Atomarer Selbstmord und Umwegen," 3 April 1981, pp. 74 ff.

57. This account relies in large measure on the work of Helga Haftendorn, alone in *Foreign Policy of West Germany*, ed. Krippendorf and Rittberger, and with her associates in *Verwaltete Aussenpolitik*.

58. *Verwaltete Aussenpolitik*.

59. See Hillenbrand's discussion in "Germany and the United States," in *West German Foreign Policy*, ed. Hanrieder, pp. 73-91.

60. Clearly this is reflected in the various national essays in this volume and in Hanrieder and Auton, *Foreign Policies of West Germany, France, and Britain*.

61. On Adenauer's system see Wolfram Hanrieder, *West German Foreign Policy, 1949-1963* (Stanford: Stanford University Press, 1967), and the one volume of Adenauer's own memoirs published in English: *Memoirs* (Chicago: H. Regenery Co., 1966).

62. Strauss is clearly one of the most colorful and controversial figures in postwar German political life. His works in English include *The Grand Design* (New York: Praeger, 1965).

63. Schmidt has also published two major books on defense policy, both available in English: *Defense or Retaliation* (New York: Praeger, 1962), and *The Balance of Power* (London: Kimber, 1971).

64. Haftendorn, "West Germany and Security Relations," p. 12.

65. Haftendorn et al., *Verwaltete,* p. 13, lists a few interesting exceptions from the early 1970s.

66. *White Paper, 1979,* p. 140.

67. Kelleher, *Germany and Nuclear Weapons,* chapters 1 and 2.

68. Ibid., pp. 215-18.

69. See the special collection of essays edited by Ralf Zoll on German civil-military relations published in *Armed Forces and Society* 5 (Summer 1979): 523-686.

70. See Eichenberg, "Defense-Welfare Tradeoffs in German Budgeting."

71. The literature on German civil-military relations, prewar and postwar, is substantial. In addition to the sources cited in *Armed Forces and Society* 5 (Summer 1979): 523-686, there are numerous political texts—e.g., from the Right, Dieter Portner, *Bundeswehr und Linksextremismus* (Munich: Olzog, 1976), and from the Left, Ulrich Albrecht, Henning Schierholz, and Joseph H. Helmut Thielen, eds., *Anti-Wehrkunde: Basistexts zur politischen Bildung* (Darmstadt: Luchterhand, 1975).

72. In interview accounts in the 1960s, my sources quoted the French as the Europeans to be soothed. Other sources attribute this remark to Adenauer and to Schumacher.

73. See Wolf Graf von Baudissin, *Soldat für den Frieden* (Munich: S. Piper, 1969).

74. Compare, on this point, Wilfrid von Bredow, *Die unbewältigte Bundeswehr* (Frankfort: Fischer Taschenbuch Verlag, 1973), and Wido Mosen, *Bundeswehr: Elite der Nation?* (Neuwied: Luchterhand, 1970).

75. More recent incidents, reflecting the generational change, have involved "Left" critiques of governmental decisions—e.g., the "Bastion" affair of 1979.

76. *White Paper, 1979,* pp. 188-205.

77. Ibid., pp. 197-99.

78. Ibid., p. 226.

79. The actual restrictions are contained in the various protocols modifying the "Brussels Treaty," the Western European Union treaty, reprinted in U.S., Senate, Committee on Foreign Relations, *Protocols on the Termination of the Occupation Regime in the Federal Republic of Germany,* 83rd Cong., 2nd sess. (1954), executives I and M.

80. See the range of critiques cited in the excellent bibliography attached to Krippendorff and Rittberger, eds., *Foreign Policy of West Germany.*

81. *White Paper, 1979,* p. 275.

82. Quoted in *Frankfurter Allgemeine Zeitung,* 15 March 1981.

83. See U.S., Senate, Committee on Foreign Relations, *Protocols.*

84. *White Paper, 1979,* pp. 137-86.

85. The Frontier Police are a separate "third force" under the control of the Ministry of Interior, although this special antiterrorist unit, GSG9, operates under direction from the chancellor as well.

WEST GERMAN DEFENSE POLICY: A BIBLIOGRAPHICAL ESSAY

Terry L. Heyns and Barbara U. Riley

For a general treatment of West German foreign policy which also touches on security matters, an excellent source is a volume written by Wolfram F. Hanrieder and Graeme P. Auton entitled *The Foreign Policies of West Germany, France, and Britain* (Englewood Cliffs, N.J.: Prentice-Hall, 1980). Another source is the chapter by Josef Joffe in Roy C. Macridis, ed., *Foreign Policy in World Politics,* 5th ed. (Englewood Cliffs, N.J.: Prentice-Hall, 1976). One of the best anthologies on the subject to be published in recent years is Wolfram Hanrieder's *West German Foreign Policy, 1949-1979* (Boulder, Colo.: Westview Press, 1980), which contains articles on various aspects of foreign and defense policy including Catherine M. Kelleher's "Germany and NATO" and Hans Morgenthau's "Prospects of German Foreign Policy."* Manfred Wörner, chairman of the Armed Services Committee in the Bundestag, also provides a very authoritative view in his "West Germany and the New Dimensions of Security," published in the same volume.

Of particular note is the Summer 1979 edition of *Armed Forces and Society,* a special issue on civil-military relations in West Germany edited by Ralf Zoll. Included are articles by American and German scholars on the Bundeswehr, legitimacy and civil-military relations, public opinion and security policy, political socialization and draftees, the German offi-

*See below, pp. 365-67.

cer corps, and other topics. With respect to officer training, Wolf Graf von Baudissin, a retired army general, addresses the question of *Innere Führung* (internal leadership instilled with a sense of purpose) in his "Internal Leadership in the Federal German Army," *NATO Review*, December 1978. Citizen integration in the German armed forces is also discussed. Jon L. Lellenberg proposes an enlargement of the citizen in uniform concept by substantial expansion of the Territorial Army in *The Citizen-Army Concept in Germany: Political-Military Implications* (Palo Alto: Stanford Research Institute, Strategic Studies Center, 1974). Justification for such a move includes several socioeconomic factors (and their effects on German public opinion), which are not discussed in any detail by official West German government publications. Lellenberg also argues that an expanded role for the Territorial Army would help to overcome some glaring NATO deficiencies, such as a lack of defense in depth. Another viewpoint, especially interesting to the student of military affairs, is presented by Trevor N. Dupuy in his article "The Current Implications of German Military Excellence" (*Strategic Review* 4 [Spring 1976]). Colonel Dupuy discusses several factors that he feels enabled the Germans to reach unparalleled standards of military excellence in world wars I and II. He also suggests that the Soviet military is currently pursuing the same course.

The threat posed by the Soviet military is an essential consideration in West German defense policy. The vulnerability of NATO nations, especially the Federal Republic of Germany (FRG), to a Soviet blitzkrieg is discussed by Steven L. Canby in "European Mobilization, U.S. and NATO Reserves," *Armed Forces and Society* 4, no. 2 (February 1978). Mr. Canby warns that the NATO partners rely too heavily on U.S. strategic power, and that the present strength, organization, and distribution of NATO forces is insufficient to overcome a Soviet strategy for a war of short duration.

A clear statement of the multidimensional West German perception of the threat is provided by Ulrich de Maiziere's article, "Strategic Balance—Deterrence—Defense Planning: A German View of the Strategic Situation in Central Europe," *RUSI and Brassey's Defence Yearbook, 1977/1978* (London: Royal United Services Institute, and Boulder, Colo.: Westview Press, 1977). General Maiziere, who was chief of staff of the FRG's armed forces from 1966 to 1972, emphasizes the importance of NATO, the adherence to a strategy of forward defense, and the necessity of nuclear weapons to a credible deterrent. These same topics are addressed by Georg Leber in "Principles Underlying German Defense Policy," *Atlantic Community Quarterly* (Summer 1976). An American scholar, Catherine M. Kelleher, focuses more closely on the sensitive question of nuclear weapons and West German defense policy in her book, *Germany and the Politics of Nuclear Weapons* (New York: Columbia University Press, 1975).

Nuclear defense issues must also be seen within the context of overall defense policy. Current statements of defense policy goals are contained in the addresses of Chancellor Helmut Schmidt ("Peace and Security within the Atlantic Alliance," *Bulletin* 5, no. 9 [11 October 1978]) and Defense Minister Hans Apel ("Sicherheitspolitik, 1979" [Bonn: Bundesministerium der Verteidigung/Information- und Pressestab, 16 February 1979]). It is interesting to note the use of familiar American defense jargon even in the original German text. Official German language government publications often refer to international agreements concerning defense policy to which the FRG is a signatory. A collection of these agreements and other pertinent documents (such as excerpts from the FRG's constitution and various policy statements) is available in English in *Documents on Disarmament and Arms Control* (Bonn: Press and Information Office of the Federal Government, Federal Republic of Germany, Bundesdrückerei, 1978). The German version, *Abrüstung und Rüstungskontrolle* (Bonn: Auswärtiges Amt, Referat Offentlichkeitsarbeit; Köllen Druck & Verlag GmbH, 1978), includes additional statements and speeches of interest.

Government White Papers, also published in English by the FRG Press and Information Office, vary widely in content and format. The *1971/72 White Paper*, for example, is devoted primarily to a discussion of force structure reorganization, whereas the *1975/76 White Paper* is particularly useful in policy definition. Each edition contains a progress report on new programs.

"West German Foreign and Defense Policy," by Elmer Plischke (*Orbis* 12 [Winter 1969]), traces the historical development of German postwar foreign policy and defense posture. Evolution in defense and foreign policy since the Adenauer era is characterized as methodological rather than as a reflection of basic changes in fundamental national goals. The nonaggressive intent of defense policy and the "citizen in uniform" concept of the military are emphasized as manifestations of a democratic society. In specific reference to the United States, Alex A. Vardamis treats "German-American Military Fissures" in the Spring 1979 issue of *Foreign Policy*. Vardamis also places German defense policy within the overall context of the Atlantic Alliance, the West Germans no longer being completely dependent on the United States as far as their foreign and defense policy is concerned. The Winter 1979/80 edition of *Foreign Policy* also includes three articles by Melvin Croan, Josef Joffre, and David Schoenbaum under the heading "The Germanies at Thirty."

As previously mentioned, the above works provide

only a beginning. The serious student will, of course, wish to do extensive reading about German policy from the German viewpoint and in the original language. The members of the Deutsche Gesellschaft für Auswärtige Politik have collaborated on a multitude of comprehensive works dealing with numerous aspects of foreign and defense policy. An extensive bibliography (including the prestigious Europa-Archiv) is available from the institute. These works are extremely well researched and of considerable interest, but *Sicherheitspolitik vor neuen Aufgaben,* ed. Karl Kaiser and Karl Markus Kreis, is especially useful for its definition of current defense policy issues.

Finally, the publications of the nongovernmental International Institute for Strategic Studies in London are a continuing source of reliable information concerning defense matters. Adelphi Papers (twelve to fourteen per year) and articles in the bimonthly *Survival* often treat topics related to West German defense policy. The annual *Strategic Survey* and *Military Balance* address doctrine and force posture.

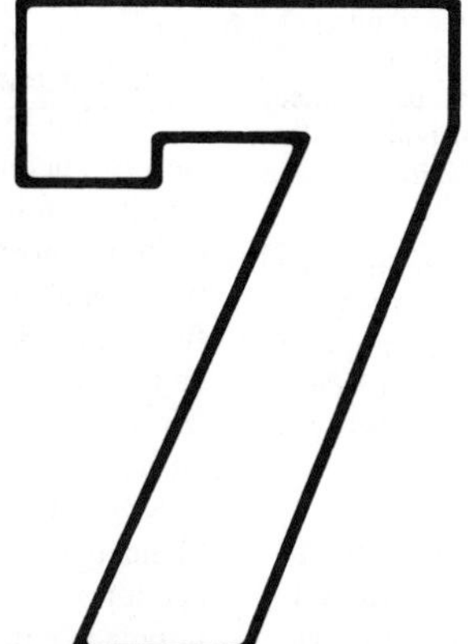

THE DEFENSE POLICY OF SWEDEN

William J. Taylor, Jr.

International environment

Aptly characterized as a "lesser power," Sweden is, nevertheless, the fourth largest country in Europe in geographic area. Given its reputation as one of the most advanced industrial nations of the world, whose defense industry has produced the sophisticated Viggen fighter aircraft and the S tank, it is sometimes difficult to remember that Sweden's total active duty forces number only 66,100 and that its total defense budget for 1981/82 was only $3.6 billion.

Sweden's 1978 GNP of $84.9 billion is large compared to its Scandinavian neighbors (Norway, $39.4 billion; Denmark, $55.3 billion; and Finland, $30.8 billion), but far smaller than its great power, European neighbors to the south (e.g., Federal Republic of Germany, $634.2 billion; France, $463 billion; and Britain, $302 billion).[1] Sweden is highly dependent on its international commercial relations. Its share of world trade is about 3 percent. Approximately 20 percent of its total production and half of its manufactured goods are exported, principally to the industrialized countries; the United States is Sweden's principal trading partner.

Sweden ranks high in the total of development assistance provided to the less developed countries and relatively low (twelfth) among the world's arms suppliers to the Third World.[2] In terms of general international measures of both military and economic capabilities, Sweden must be placed in the category of lesser powers. However, as will be explained later, Sweden's position in the Nordic balance is of central importance. Indeed, its position in the international political system can be understood best in the context of this Nordic balance. Forged in the aftermath of World War II, this balance describes both a perceived condition and a long-term objective of Swedish national security policy. The balance emerged in the Nordic area as a pattern of regional security policy based fundamentally on the Cold War confrontations between East and West that emerged after the war. One noted scholar has described the basic facts of the balance as follows:

—Denmark and Norway are members of NATO but have in peacetime neither nuclear weapons nor allied troops on their territories. But both countries reserve the right to reverse this situation by a unilateral decision. Norway has very limited forces in the area adjacent to the Soviet naval base system on the Kola Peninsula.

—The Swedish security policy of nonalignment in peace, aiming at retaining neutrality in war, is supported by a defense establishment with low peacetime preparedness but with great mobilizable strength.

—The security policy of Finland is conducted within the framework provided by the Treaty of Friendship, Cooperation and Mutual Assistance (TFCMA) with the Soviet Union. Like Sweden, Finland has a large wartime establishment, but, unlike Sweden, Finland rotates the training of the conscripts in order to maintain constantly a number of army units in sufficient preparedness in peacetime. Technologically, Finnish defense is restricted both by the peace treaty after World War II and by limitations in her economic and industrial resources.

—Iceland is far more an Atlantic than a Northern European country in a purely strategic sense. She is the only NATO-aligned Nordic country with allied forces—however limited in numbers—based on her territory on a permanent peacetime basis (in accordance with agreements between Iceland and the United States since 1951).[3]

Sweden is one of the few nations that was able to remain outside two devastating world wars. In fact, Sweden has not been involved as a belligerent in war since the Napoleonic era, and Swedes want to keep things that way. There is a broad public consensus that Swedish policy should be geared toward "total defense," which explicitly includes military, civil, economic, and psychological defense. The Swedish budget appropriates funds for precisely those categories to serve the principal function of protecting the nation.

THREATS TO SWEDISH SECURITY

In the 1970s there was a widespread opinion that the probability for a conventional, major conflict in Europe between the power blocs is about the same as the probability for a nuclear war.[4] Swedes came to believe that the détente of the 1970s had lowered the probability of war between the Soviet Union and NATO. In the event of war between the superpowers, there was a widespread perception in Sweden that there is little of strategic value to either the Soviets or NATO that would make a direct attack on Sweden worthwhile. At present, there are few Swedish natural or manufactured resources for which the potential East-West belligerents do not have alternative sources. Control of Swedish territory in either the North or along Sweden's Baltic coastline cannot be considered of vital strategic significance in war, although overflight, use of Swedish airfields, and reduction of a potentially hostile nation in one's rear might be marginal strategic concerns. To the extent that Swedes do perceive a military threat in time of war, it is from the Soviet Union, not the NATO allies—although Swedish public officials will never say so in public.

Thus, there was a low and diminishing perception of threat from direct military aggression. However, as will be discussed later, Swedish defense policy has been designed to hedge the bet.

In an age of rapidly increasing interdependence, it has become clear to both the public and decision makers in Sweden that the availability of material resources is important to their security. As in most of the industrialized states, the critical resources for Sweden are energy resources—enough and at reasonable prices. Sweden is heavily reliant on crude oil and petroleum imports. The most obvious alternative is nuclear energy; the most explosive political issue in Sweden in the late 1970s was the use and expansion of nuclear power plants. Swedish coalition governments fell over the issue, but by 1979 it became clear to most that there were few realistic alternatives, and a modest expansion of nuclear power facilities was mandated by the government. Sweden's policies for economic defense (described later) involve stockpiling resources critical to national security.

Sweden is a parliamentary democracy that has long blended socialist traditions with a largely capitalist economy. An advanced, industrialized state whose populace enjoyed for many years the world's highest standard of living, Sweden's welfare spending has increased markedly in recent years. Some suggest that government support for inefficient industries and the wage demands of Swedish labor unions may price Swedish products out of the international market. Unit labor costs in Sweden rose by as much as 40 percent in 1975–76. The rate of income taxation is among the highest in the world and is rising. In brief, although Sweden is not alone among the advanced industrialized countries, its economy is in difficulty.

A longer-term threat perceived in Sweden, perhaps to a greater extent than in some other industrialized countries, is the growing disparities between the rich industrial world of the North and the poor, underdeveloped countries of the South. In fact, the potential for North-South conflict has assumed a more prominent place in public debate than has the potential for East-West confrontation. Although this may stem partly from a desire by Swedish decision makers to downplay the East-West confrontation for Swedish and general Nordic security reasons, there is a genuine concern among the more informed Swedish public that international security cannot be attained over the long term while there remain gross inequalities between rich and poor nations (just as the welfare-state psychology suggests that inequalities between rich and poor within states breed conflict). Sweden manifests its concern for North-South problems by substantial economic development assistance to less developed countries.

NO ENTANGLING ALLIANCES

Through a combination of decisions over the years, Sweden has adopted a foreign policy of "nonalignment (or 'freedom from alliances') between power blocs in peace, aiming at neutrality in war."[5] The foreign policy objective is de facto neutrality unsupported by international guarantees or by conventional international law, as in the cases of Swiss or Austrian neutrality.

Sweden is not a member of NATO, although its western and southern neighbors are. There simply is no question that Sweden's general orientation is toward the West in security, trade, sociopolitical, and psychopolitical terms. Yet, strategic considerations mandate that Swedish policy pronouncements downplay those orientations. Sweden consciously adopted a position in 1948-49 to remain a neutral buffer state with its own relatively strong defense. This has been a keystone of the Nordic strategic balance. On the one hand, Sweden's position made it easier for Norway and Denmark to join NATO on "minimum conditions" (no foreign troops or nuclear weapons on their territories). On the other hand, Sweden's choice not to join the western alliance structure and to remain a "buffer" may have assisted Finland's attempts to retain some independence from the Soviet Union. Having fought and lost two wars with the Soviets, the Finns sought the optimal range of trustful ties with their eastern neighbor, free of military occupation. This may have been possible in part because the Soviets perceived no hostility from Sweden or possibility of NATO military formations along Finnish borders that would require the presence of Soviet ground units.

The Swedish refusal to join the European Economic Community (EEC), despite potential economic benefits, was driven in large part by Swedish perceptions that the EEC and NATO were related in important ways and, thus, EEC membership could lead to an erosion of Swedish nonalignment in peacetime. Sweden chose instead to restrict its role in the economic framework of the West to the conclusion of a trade agreement with the EEC.

The Swedish policy of arms acquisition also has been geared partly to the policy of nonalignment in peacetime. That is, Sweden chose to produce its own major weapons systems in Sweden, rather than purchase them elsewhere. Admittedly, support for Swedish industry played a major role in this approach. Indeed, the classic case of the decision in 1958 to produce the Swedish AJ37 Viggen aircraft was consistent with both nonalignment and support for Swedish industry. For several years, that aircraft has been one of the most sophisticated in Europe and has provided a major element of Swedish defense capability. As will be shown later in this chapter, a tentative 1979 decision not to produce in Sweden the next generation follow-on to the Viggen raised implications for the Swedish policy of nonalignment in peace, aimed at neutrality in war.

National objectives, national strategy, and military doctrine

The goals of Swedish security policy were reiterated by the undersecretary of state for defense in introducing the five-year defense program budget for the period 1977/78 to 1981/82:

> . . . to assure the nation's freedom of action in all situations by means we ourselves choose, so that within our borders we can preserve and develop our society in accordance with our own values in political, economic, social, cultural and all other respects, and at the same time work in the world for international détente and peaceful development.[6]

To achieve these goals, successive governments and all four major political parties have concluded that Sweden requires a strong, all-around (but non-nuclear) "total defense" to preserve its credibility. They have found no contradiction between defense preparations and deep involvement in international work for disarmament.[7] Swedish defense is deemed to play an important role in maintaining the Nordic balance by preventing instabilities that might result in direct confrontation in the Nordic area between the superpowers.

There has been a long-term consensus behind these goals of Swedish security policy and, many are prepared to argue, a straight-line projection of Swedish attitudes. As we shall see later in examining the role of Swedish mass media and public opinion, the validity of straight-line projections may be dubious.

SWEDISH POLITICAL VIEWS

There is in the Swedish mass psyche a thread of skepticism about the intricacies of world politics and the merits of defense expenditure. Being citizens of a relatively small country that has experienced the whims of history in the past, many Swedes now feel that they have something to contribute to the construction of a new, more stable international system. Some people outside Scandinavia find these aspirations of Swedes and other Scandinavians perplexing or even irritating. However, such aspirations should be understood in the context of nations that, in sociological terms, have moved in many ways from war societies to postwar societies. This contention means simply that these nations have achieved a degree of "security community" among themselves. Such a community entails a natural inclination to settle differences by means other than war. But it does not mean that Sweden or the Nordic countries have in any way given up the notion of national security as a military concept. They will defend themselves if attacked, but they also measure their national security in economic and social terms.

Most Swedes feel that they can express their opinions quite freely, without necessarily being suspected of advancing only the narrow interests of their own country. Since Sweden has been for many years in a relatively fortunate position economically and in many other respects, it might even be a natural thing for Swedes to voice concerns of a more general nature, expressing certain moral or idealistic tenets of international politics. However, Swedes can be hard-nosed when it comes to their own security. Although the idealist tradition in Swedish foreign policy has had its impact on defense discussions, realist and idealist traditions always coexist. It is the mixture of idealist and realist elements in foreign and defense policies that varies with the times, according to domestic political situations and levels of tension in relations among the world's major powers.

No doubt there is a connection between these philosophical tendencies and the fact that parties on the moderate left have dominated Swedish politics ever since World War I. Although they have not been in power for that entire period, the Social Democrats (SDs) have been clearly dominant. This party has in general tended to be more idealistic than the more conservative groups. Since the advent of universal franchise, the latter have not been as successful in obtaining governmental power in Sweden as in many other European nations. Whether SDs and Liberals have become politically ascendant as a result of widely held beliefs in foreign policy or national security areas is clearly debatable. But, through their policies, they may have reinforced existing public sentiment in these fields. There is, evidently, a very close connection between public images in relation to domestic and foreign policy. In Sweden, a moderate leftist is likely to hold world views that might be labeled "dovish" in American parlance.

Although the SDs lost in the Swedish general elections of 1976 and 1979, they remain clearly the largest and strongest *single* party in Sweden (154 seats in a 349-seat Parliament). The SDs traditionally emphasize domestic welfare over defense, and they have forged the opposition to the new-generation Swedish fighter aircraft. The SDs were in power in 1958 when the decision to produce the Viggen aircraft was made, but the Swedish economy was in far better condition in those days and defense priorities were easier to sustain. In 1981, the choices are much tougher.

The SDs are fully supportive of the policy of nonalignment in peace, aimed at neutrality in war. The point, however, is that major defense programs, reduced through insufficient funding, impact on what defense policies a nation has the capability to pursue. The old political saw, "Show me your programs and I'll tell you your policy," has real meaning. The Swedish policy of nonalignment in peace and neutrality in war is based fundamentally on a strong *national* defense. A shift to domestic welfare spending at the expense of defense spending can erode Swedish basic defense policy. The case study of defense decision making later in this chapter indicates that a change of Swedish national priorities could be in the offing.

DEFENSE DOCTRINE

Swedish defense doctrine is based fundamentally on the realities of a divided Europe and deterrence of "marginal attack." Swedish strategic planners assume that:

> ... a power which might threaten or even attack Sweden will always have a substantial part of its resources tied up for other purposes, for example to counter any expected or unexpected confrontation with the other superpower. Thus only a marginal part of the military strength of a superpower could be used in an attack on Sweden.
>
> ... provided that the goal in Sweden is limited and the country can defend itself, the value of controlling Sweden or part of Sweden will not be worth the cost of conquest.[8]

As stated before, Swedish doctrine calls for "total defense." Military, civil, and psychological defense, as well as the responsibility for coordinating total defense, reside with the Ministry of Defense. The Ministry of Trade coordinates economic defense. The program subsumed by each of these categories of total defense will be discussed below in the context of decision-making constraints.

Military strategy planned for meeting the marginal attack has in reality been a combination of territorial defense based on rapid mobilization of a large conscript army armed with relatively inexpensive weapons *and* a peripheral defense based principally on high-technology aircraft and naval forces defending well beyond Sweden's land and sea boundaries. In the late 1960s and early 1970s emphasis was on the latter. However, at a time of 14 percent inflation, the essence of a current defense debate is the cost and wisdom of attempting to carry out both strategies simultaneously.[9]

STRATEGIC CONSIDERATIONS

Sweden's policy of neutrality presupposes a "*tous-azimuts*" strategy under which total defense preparations should provide the capability to meet an attack from any quarter. A glance at a map underscores Sweden's strategic position between the superpowers and their allies. In fact, in the 1940s and 1950s Swedish forces were tasked with defense against attacks both from the Baltic and through Finland. These missions were redefined in 1963 to provide for either one or the other, not both simultaneously. In any case, three considerations would erode the "*tous-azimuts*" strategy. First, Sweden defense planners have long considered the military threat to be from the Soviet Union, and their sympathies clearly lie with the West.[10] An example was the 1962 defense report of the supreme commander that was based on a Baltic attack from the east and showed the Soviet Union as the aggressor. (Of course, the Soviet ambassador protested strongly about this report to the Swedish minister of foreign affairs.) As we shall see, there has been every reason for Swedish defense planners to retain that view, although they have gone to great pains in public pronouncements to deny it. Second, Swedish planners cannot have missed the qualitative build-up of Soviet forces on the Kola

Peninsula in recent years, including a standing force of two category 1 motorized divisions, airborne units, and some 300 Soviet aircraft.[11]

Although operating with extreme uncertainties, Swedish defense planners traditionally have assigned the country a low strategic value, but this has been over a period prior to the realities of the slow but sure Soviet build-up on the Kola Peninsula. The principal strategic significance of a nation depends, at least in part, upon its location and its resources. In terms of location, it is the strategic significance of Norway that makes the major difference. Whether one believes that Norwegian (and Danish and Swedish) strategic utility resides in their position "behind the lines" of Soviet strategy, or that the deployment of new technology on the Kola Peninsula (mainly naval) points to the nonutility of occupying territory,[12] it remains necessary to come to grips with five major considerations. First, it is possible that the Soviets would not want to commit major naval forces to large amphibious landings, preferring to hold them in reserve initially.

Second, the Soviets might consider that:

> The rapid transit of ground troops to the north could be facilitated by the use of Finnish territory and rail links, "doubling up" on Soviet capacity. Swedish airspace could be utilized simply by over-flying for high priority missions or some form of "pre-emptive occupation" on the pretext of NATO's making use of Swedish facilities—a number of scenarios suggest themselves, all with the background that the Soviet Union could not leave Sweden out of its military calculations.[13]

Third, the Swedish transportation system might offer the Soviets means of rapidly placing conventional forces in strategically important locations simultaneously in Norway and Denmark. Swedish air bases and airports might be viewed as being of additional value.[14]

Fourth, a Soviet thrust through the Baltic into the Atlantic would necessarily mean elimination of Norway's coastal defenses and neutralization of Swedish coastal defenses.[15]

Fifth, if Soviet military operations against Norway were completed successfully, it is difficult to imagine the Soviets ignoring a "neutral," capitalist country with a mobilized, technologically sophisticated armed force of 750,000 intact in its newly acquired "front yard." The ideological and political costs of doing so might be viewed by Soviet leaders as simply too high.

Finally, there is concern that the rapid increase in deployments of Soviet SS-20 missiles in the East and the NATO decision to install Pershing II and cruise missiles in the West portend violation of Swedish neutral air space in time of war. Some have suggested recently that the very threat of NATO sea-launched or air-launched cruise missiles in the Norwegian sea area could cause the Soviets to seek movement forward of early warning sites and airbases, thus increasing the threat of invasion through Sweden. This combined with the joint U.S. and Norwegian decision of January 1981 to stock equipment in central Norway for a U.S. marine brigade could change the strategic situation for Sweden. The threat of cruise missiles has led to calls for fewer fighter aircraft and more and better capabilities for air defense with surface-to-air missiles. This could become a serious, divisive issue in interservice relations in Sweden.[16]

Despite (or perhaps because of) these strategic considerations, Swedish defense planners have few alternatives. They cannot formally align themselves against what must be perceived as the principal military threat for several reasons. There is a clear public consensus in Sweden for a policy of neutrality; this is part of the Swedish psyche. Such alignment would almost certainly guarantee in time of war between the superpowers the Soviet attack that Sweden seeks to avoid. However, even though they do not plan on direct NATO support, defense planners probably must consider the extent to which NATO force commitments to the northern flank would reduce at the margin Soviet capabilities against Sweden. It should be noted that some have denied explicitly that the United States would come to Sweden's aid in the event of Soviet attack.[17]

FACTORS AFFECTING THE STRATEGIC DEBATE

Consideration of the first, five-year total defense program (FY 1977/78 to 1981/82), simultaneous with long-range perspective planning for defense fifteen years into the future, raised serious debates in the Swedish defense community that have continued to the present. These debates have been over the most fundamentally important defense matters, i.e., threat assessment, budget constraints, strategy, weapons systems, and the future of the aircraft industry.

Threat assessment. Some have suggested that Swedish defense planners envision a change in the primary threat from naval invasions through the Baltic or on the Norwegian coast to a swift Soviet land invasion across Finland and northern Sweden "to secure the northern Norwegian coastline in order to control the ice-free approaches to the vast military complex at Murmansk."[18] The invasion would be based in part on large tank and mechanized infantry forces. Modernization of Soviet amphibious and land forces on the Kola Peninsula is taken as evidence to support this view.

Budget constraints. With a high rate of inflation over the last several years, and under the pressure of increasing military manpower costs and insistence on a larger share of the budget for welfare programs, the size of the entire defense budget has been called into serious question. The opportunity costs for defense spending, in both resource and international political terms, are seen as extraordinarily high in some quarters.

Strategy. The threat assessment and budget constraints noted above have given rise to harsh debates over defense strategy between the advocates of perimeter defense on the one hand and territorial defense on the other. The equipment and manpower requirements for these two strategies are different.

Weapons systems. Debates over defense costs and strategy have focused on the technology, costs, and capabilities of the most expensive element of Swedish defense materiel—aircraft. Given the lead time required for research, development, production, and delivery of new fighter aircraft, the decision should have been made in 1976 concerning the follow-on to the AJ37 Viggen in order to have the new aircraft in the air force inventory in the early 1990s, before the Viggens are phased out (about 1995). The new aircraft would remain in service until 2015. Thus, the recent debates are about a critical weapon system for defense over the next thirty to forty years. These debates on the future are couched in memories of the past, especially the enormous cost overruns after the 1958 decision to produce the Viggen, an aircraft with a price tag double the original estimates on which the parliamentary decision was based. The Social Democrats who backed that decision have not forgotten.

Survival of the aircraft industry. The three principals in military aircraft production are SAAB-Scania (airframes), Volvo Flygmotor (engines), and L. M. Ericson (target acquisition and display systems). Although industrially diversified, all three depend in part upon government defense contracts. The size and nature of the contracts make a great deal of difference to these firms. A decision to continue with a modified Viggen impacts adversely on their R&D programs. A decision for a limited number of a new aircraft involving new technology impacts adversely on production programs. Either decision is related to the willingness and international political capability of the government to sell Swedish military aircraft abroad. An alternative to these bleak industry scenarios argued in some quarters is a partial shift by the three aircraft industries into nonmilitary manufactures.

The B3LA was one of the two major fighter aircraft under consideration in these debates from 1976 to 1978. In December 1978, after a bitter political struggle, the B3LA was found to be too costly. A similar but less costly version called SK38/A38 was proposed. The SK38 was a trainer version of the A38. The other major contender was the AJ37/A20, a modified Viggen. For reasons that will be developed throughout the remainder of this chapter, these alternative aircraft became the center of disputes involving almost every aspect of the defense decision-making process.

The defense decision-making process

There are a few basic considerations central to understanding the institutions involved in decision making for Sweden's defense. The first is that, despite a very large public administration sector, the number of people involved in the decision-making process is small. Second, with the exception of the various government ministers, a very small number of others in a ministry, and members of the Parliamentary Defense Committee (some of whom change when governing coalitions change), the vast majority of key people in defense decision making remains stable. Third, some of the civilians in key positions of the decision-making bureaucracy normally hold reserve military commissions, meaning that there is some commonality of background. Finally, because of these three factors, people in the defense policy decision-making process have known each other, many very well, over many years. This makes a difference in the way business is conducted.

The major institutions involved in decision making for total defense are portrayed in figure 1. At the highest level, the critical interaction is between the government (governing coalition) and the parliament (Riksdag) because the latter must appropriate defense funds requested in the government's annual budget bill submitted by the minister of the budget each January. Each fourth year the parliament considers a five-year defense program budget. The Parliamentary Defense Committee is critical in forging the consensus and influencing the votes required for passage of a given defense bill.

THE PARLIAMENTARY DEFENSE COMMITTEE

In a unicameral parliament of 349 voting members elected every three years on the basis of proportional representation, the Defense Committee is one of sixteen standing committees involved in studying legislative propositions. The committee has fifteen members, whose political affiliations are representative of relative party strength. Thus, reflective of the 1976 national elections—in which a Center party coalition displaced the Social Democrats for the first time in over forty years—the Defense Committee included eight members of the coalition (Center party, 4; Conservative party, 2; Liberal party, 2) and seven members from the Social Democrats.

Committee membership does not change frequently, and since the mid-1950s Defense Committee expertise on defense issues has grown. However, given the minuscule staff available to the committee, a parliamentary premium on compromise, and the central role of the cabinet, the impact of the committee is not great. Given the fact that the Swedish voter votes for parties, not individuals, the committee member does not have to "play to the public" in voting on defense matters. The selection of members is carried out by party caucus and members generally vote their party positions. Selections for special parliamentary committees on defense matters are conducted in the same manner, and the voting behavior of members is predictable along party lines. The pressures for party conformity are great, as is the case in most parliamentary systems; this is decidedly unlike the American system, where party discipline over most issues is tenuous at best.

The constitutional charge to the Defense Committee is to "prepare matters concerning military defense, civil defense, psychological defense, economic defense, noncombatant service, and financial benefits to conscripts." When the parliament is in session, the committee carries out its duties in meetings twice a week (on Tuesdays and Thursdays). Like meetings of all other parliamentary committees, Defense Committee meetings are in closed session. The members of the committee conduct periodic visits to military installations and are in frequent contact with military officers assigned to positions in Stockholm. Individual members and the committee as a whole maintain contact with the defense industry. For example, in 1978 the committee made several trips to SAAB-Scania, the largest corporation in the Swedish military aircraft industry, whose future will be affected significantly by alternatives in government procurement of the follow-on to the Viggen 37 aircraft. Given this connection, the American observer tends to think in terms of a "military industrial complex" and the activities of business lobbyists. Although the former exists in a special sense (to be discussed below), the latter does not exist in any formal sense comparable to registration of lobby groups in the United States.

There also exists a special cooperative relationship between the Defense Committee and the Foreign Relations Committee; the two deal with some similar matters, especially in the context of considering the five-year defense program.

THE CABINET

Although the fundamental laws of the land are the province of the elected parliament, effective political power resides in the cabinet and the parties of the governing coalition it represents. Parliament designates the prime minister, who appoints all other ministers. As Sweden entered the 1980s, there were twenty ministers (including five women) represented in the cabinet. Most of the ministers normally are also members of Parliament who vacate their seats and give up their right to vote during their tenure in the cabinet (a substitute from the same party fills the vacated parliamentary seat).

Figure 1. Swedish organization for total defense

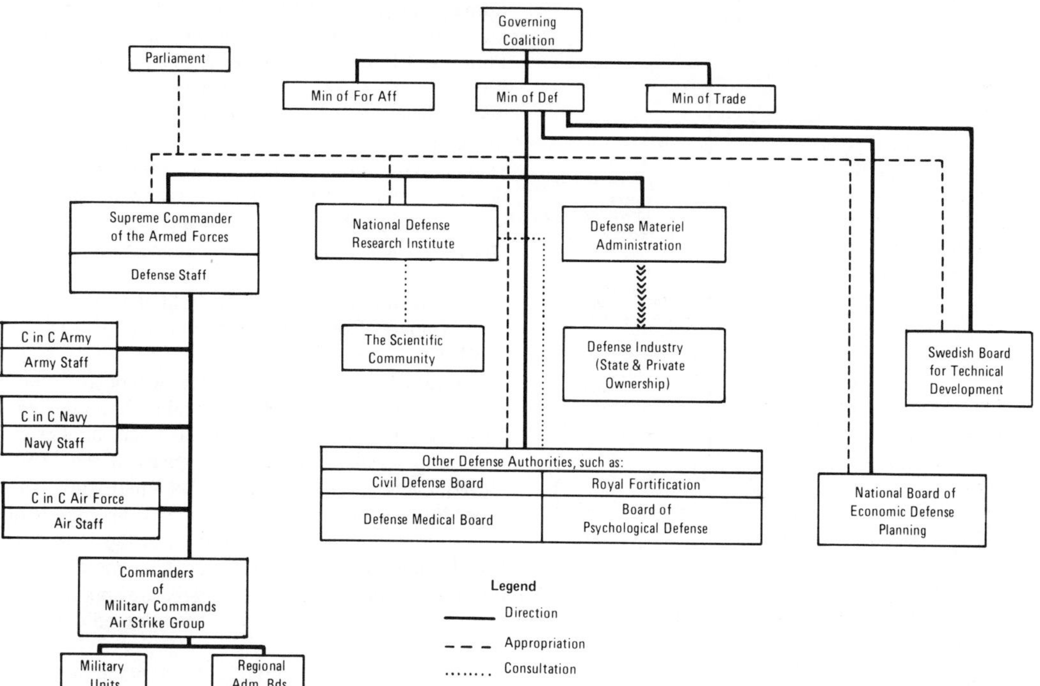

THE MINISTRY OF DEFENSE

The minister of defense is charged with coordination among ministries in matters affecting national defense. Responsible to the minister, the principal manager for work performed in the ministry is the under secretary of state for defense (see figure 2). Unlike most countries, the Swedish Defense Ministry is responsible for policy framework and guidance, but the various central authorities, agencies, and boards concerned with defense matters are responsible for execution. Although shown in figure 1 as "directing" these other agencies and boards, the defense minister, like each of the other thirteen heads of ministry, does not have the formal authority to issue formal instructions in his own name; all directives, including those to the military staffs, are issued in the form of decisions made by the government as a whole. In practice, however, many defense decisions are made by the defense minister himself.

Government decisions on defense and other matters are routinely made at Thursday meetings, presided over by the prime minister and held in the cabinet office in Stockholm's Government Building. These meetings normally last less than a half hour and are generally a formality for ratifying decisions already made. For exceptional issues that the defense minister feels require prior discussion within the government, there is the rather unique Swedish forum of frequent lunches in the chancery that are normally attended by members of the government. In this informal setting, the minister has the opportunity to "test the waters" on issue positions, iron out differences, coordinate approaches, and exchange information. Major questions are generally addressed at formal government meetings held several times per week, for which agendas are distributed in advance. Agenda items are normally presented by a ministry civil servant who is a principal action officer for the item and who is best qualified to answer more specific questions. However, the civil servants do not remain for subsequent discussions among members of the government, and there are no minutes for such meetings.

Excluding armed forces personnel assigned to military units and personnel assigned to military district staffs, the number of people who work on defense matters might approximate 10,000 military and civil servants, depending on which organizations are counted under defense. Civil servants enjoy almost complete tenure. They are appointed for life and can be removed before retirement only for cause and through legal process. The vast majority of defense employees are office and building staff members assigned to the many agencies and boards shown in figure 1. As with all the ministries, only a very small number of individuals (about 150) are assigned to the office of the minister of defense, and only a very few are involved in policy decision making (see figure 2). Some of the more important and influential of these are assigned to the Secretariat for National Security Policy and Long-Range Defense Planning (SSLP), a body created in 1972. This secretariat, totaling eleven people and headed by Lennart Grape, is a prime mover in "perspective planning" (fifteen to twenty years into the future); it is also intimately involved in defense system planning and program planning. The secretariat's principal analytical approach is systems analysis. There has been a close connection between members of the SSLP and the National Defense Research Institute (FOA). In fact, in the late 1960s Dr. Grape moved from a position in FOA to head the SSLP.[19]

The SSLP is divided into three ad hoc reference groups: international, domestic, and scenario design, each with a separate director. The large number of studies undertaken under the auspices of the SSLP clearly cannot be performed by its small staff. The procedure for performing the studies is analogous to the interdepartmental group system of the U.S. National Security Council staff. That is, members of different staffs, agencies, and boards are appointed to membership on study groups for the limited duration of a study project.

Important in every step of defense planning is the Planning and Budget Secretariat (PBS). The few individuals in PBS are responsible for drafting the

Figure 2. Swedish Ministry of Defense

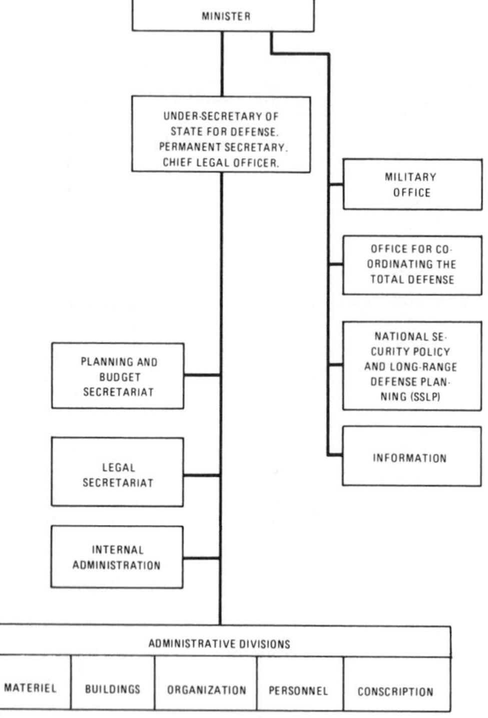

five-year defense plans and for coordinating the annual defense budget throughout all major organizations involved in the total defense.

MILITARY STAFFS

The armed forces of Sweden, like the agencies and boards, are not directly responsible to the minister of defense. Rather, in both peace and war they are under the overall command of the supreme commander (SCO) of the armed forces, who is directly responsible to the government. The commanders in chief of the three services are not in the operational chain of command. The command line goes directly from the SCO to six military regional commanders and the Air Strike Group, then to the operational unit commanders.

The defense staff working directly for the SCO numbers approximately 425 people. The overall responsibilities of the staff are those of the SCO: operational war planning; readiness; those aspects of mobilization, training, tactics, organization, equipment, and personnel as relate to operations; coordination of the long-term planning for development and direction of the armed forces; balance among the differing requirements of the armed forces; management of budgeting within the armed forces; and execution of all operations in wartime. The division of particular staff responsibilities is shown in figure 3. The service staffs number 420 army, 325 navy, and 350 air force. Each has a chief of staff responsible to the service commander in chief for direction of peacetime administration, training, and organization of military units in the various services, as well as for force development and military research and development. Each of the service staffs has an augmentation of operations analysts from the National Defense Research Institute.[20]

THE NATIONAL DEFENSE RESEARCH INSTITUTE (FOA)

FOA (from the Swedish *Försvarets Forskningsanstalt*) was established in 1958 to rationalize the fragmented operational research efforts of the three services that developed after World War II. With more than 1,500 employees (about a third with academic degrees), it is Sweden's largest research organization and it plays a major role in defense planning. FOA is divided into a planning and administration unit and five departments, as shown in figure 4.[21]

The Central Planning and Administration Unit has three bureaus that assist the Managing Board and director general and coordinate budgeting, research planning, personnel planning, and administration. It is important to note that this organization plays a major role in recruiting, training, and placing operations research specialists throughout the defense organization.

Department 1 performs studies and planning rang-

Figure 3. Swedish defense staff

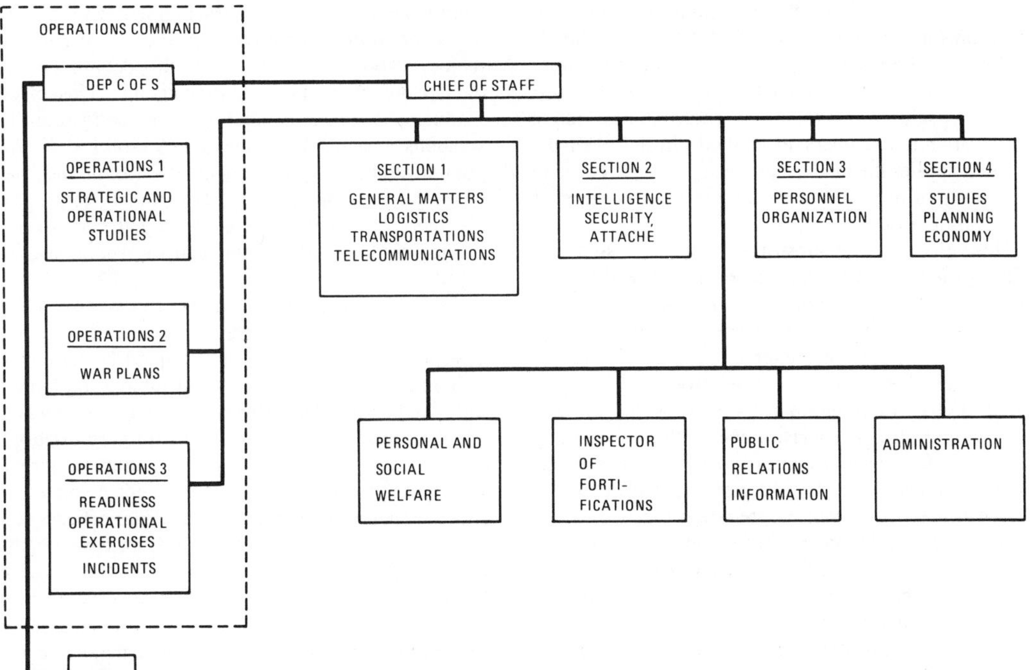

Figure 4. National Defense Research Institute

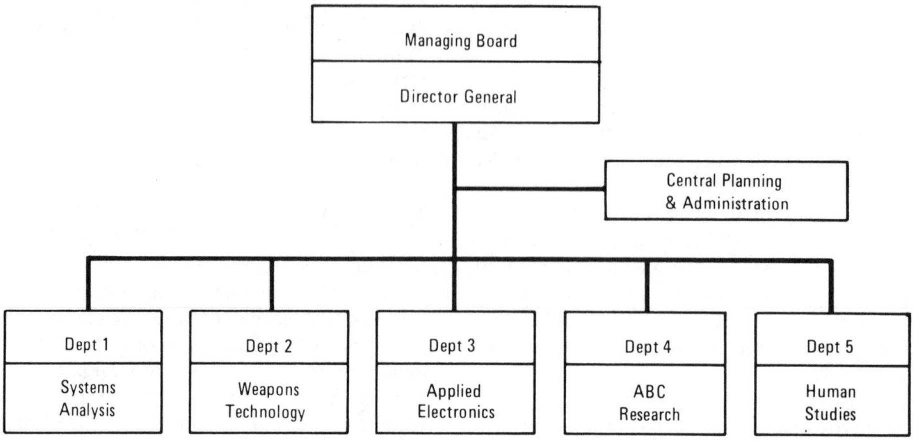

ing from weapon systems to defense policy and is responsible for operations research organization and training across the defense organization. Department 2 deals in applied physics, chemistry, and mathematics centered on weapons and weapon systems research. This department is also responsible for analysis and reporting on worldwide nuclear weapons technology and for operation of a seismological array station. Department 3 works on military and civilian applications of electromagnetic and acoustic waves in such fields as communication, guidance, and navigation. FOA 3 also studies the electromagnetic and radiation effects of nuclear explosions and protective measures against them. Department 4 studies the effects of (and protection against) chemical and biological warfare agents and nuclear explosions. The scientific disciplines involved in these studies range from organic chemistry to applied physics. Department 5 applies the medical and behavioral sciences to the study of mankind in war and to the environment of total defense.

Like the heads of most agencies and boards, the director general of FOA is responsible directly to the government, but he reports to the minister of defense. The priorities for various research activities are assigned to FOA by the supreme commander, and requests for allocations must pass through his defense staff. FOA has program responsibility for defense research in other agencies, meaning that this agency has a major role every four or five years in coordinating and developing a five-year program plan for defense research, as well as preparing the budget for annual appropriations.[22] The operations research people placed through the defense organization have close relationships with FOA. In fact, FOA appears to have a defense "omnipresence."

For fiscal year 1977/78, for example, the appropriated FOA budget was approximately $45 million. Additionally, FOA received both public and private grants for specific research contracts. Unlike the defense research organizations of some other countries, FOA is concerned primarily with applied and some basic research, *not* with development of defense materials.[23] The latter is the responsibility of the Defense Materiel Administration.

THE DEFENSE MATERIEL ADMINISTRATION (FMV)

A central agency in defense decision making is the Defense Materiel Administration. It is one of the largest organizations (a staff of over 3,800) and is the central authority for the procurement and maintenance of military equipment.[24] Project officers for major weapons systems work in this department and the liaison with civilian industry in close. Cost calculations and recommendations on budgeting for weapons systems from the director of FMV carry great weight in government decisions and parliamentary appropriations, although FMV requests to contract for weapons must go through the appropriate service commander in chief and the supreme commander.

The general officer who heads FMV has the potential for exercising considerable power and influence. The position traditionally is occupied by an exceptional senior officer with a bright future, and there is every indication that officers consider assignment in FMV to be career enhancing. In a military establishment where overseas "operational action" is largely confined to participation in UN peace-keeping activities, it appears that many of the brighter officers seek involvement in those organizations in Sweden that enjoy high priority and prestige. In the Swedish technocratic society FMV is such an organization, and within FMV high priority appears to be given to the position of project officer for a major weapon system.

DEFENSE COMMISSIONS

The use of special commissions for program planning or to study current problems is a characteristic feature of the Swedish administrative system.[25] Although the number varies, there are generally in the neighborhood of 300 commissions at work.[26]

The use of such commissions in defense planning is typical. Defense commissions are formed every four years to take a five-year look at defense programs. There was such a group in 1974, and another formed in March 1978 began its work toward the five-year defense program to begin after 1982. This commission was chaired by Gunnar Petri, the under secretary of state for defense, and had thirteen members—including representatives from government agencies and several members of the parliament, some of whom were also members of the Parliamentary Defense Committee.

The second major type of commission to study problems is typified by the B3LA Commission, which began its work in the spring of 1977 to consider the impact of a decision to adopt either a modified Viggen (A20) or a new aircraft (B3LA) to replace the Viggen 37. This commission was headed by Gunnar Nordbeck. Another example is the Air Industry Commission formed in 1978 to restudy the issue of the successor to Viggen 37. However, this fifteen-member body, directed by retired army General Sten Wåhlin, studied the impact upon the entire aircraft industry of a decision *not* to produce either A20 or B3LA—or both. This group included members of government from the different parties, representatives from industry and the trade unions, and technical experts.

The reports of these commissions can carry great weight, and the course of commission deliberations is of much interest to all concerned in defense decision making.

THE DEFENSE INDUSTRY

With a GNP estimated at $84.9 billion in FY 1979/80, Sweden spent $3.33 billion, or 3.5 percent, on defense.[27] A very high percentage (over 70 percent) was devoted to military personnel costs, due in large part to wage inflation and real cost increases brought about through union pressures in a highly unionized, advanced industrial society.[28]

Unlike the other Scandinavian countries, Sweden's defense industry has been relatively large and thriving. The four major corporations involved in defense R&D and production are SAAB-Scania in Linkôping, Volvo-Flygmotor in Trollhättan, L. M. Ericsson in Mölndal, and Bofors in Karlskoga. The first three are involved principally with military aircraft, and Bofors is engaged in producing a wide variety of gun and missile systems. Each of these major corporations has a large number of subcontractors for weapon systems components.

Sweden's industrial productivity has been high indeed. By 1977 Sweden held second place in the world's GNP per capita, the main impetus for which has been increased output per capita. There have been three principal trends in Swedish industry since the mid-1950s. First, there has been increasing concentration of industrial production into increasingly larger firms through business mergers. Second, the traditional leading sectors of Swedish manufacturing based directly on iron and wood have gradually lost their importance, and production emphasis has been shifted toward engineered and chemically processed goods involving high technology. Engineering has become the leading industrial sector. Third, Swedish manufacturing firms have expanded much more rapidly abroad than in Sweden, with engineering manufacturers leading the way.[29]

Research and development expenditures involve approximately 1.4 percent of the GNP, and most R&D (about 65 percent) is done by the largest manufacturers in partnership with central government agencies. In recent years, firms employing more than 1,000 persons carry more than 80 percent of industry's R&D bill and account for about half of the production and slightly less than half of employment within the industrial sector.[30]

Although figures are not available, it is certain that R&D for weapons systems and other defense-related systems constitute a very high proportion of the total R&D effort. Of course, many of the defense R&D efforts also have civilian applications.

Swedish industry is highly unionized at every level. The dominant organization for manual workers is LO (Swedish Confederation of Trade Unions), which has a membership of 1.9 million, about 90 percent of the organizable blue collar workers. The principal organization for white collar workers is the TCO, which has twenty-four affiliated unions and a membership of about 880,000 (or 75 percent of organizable white collar workers). In an arrangement unusual in many countries, the dominant employer organization is SAF, which has more than 28,000 member firms employing some 1.3 million people.[31] These unions figure largely in major business and government decisions on defense production.

The leading defense manufacturers in Sweden do not formally "lobby" the government; it is not necessary for two major reasons. First, given Sweden's policy of nonalignment in peacetime, the traditional view has been that buying weapons systems in Sweden helps keep the nation independent of other advanced industrialized nations that are members of alliances. Second, given the movement toward concentrating industry through business mergers, there has been little room for competition in contract bidding. Rather, the relationship with the government appears to be a matter of technology salesmanship among the relevant service staffs (the defense staff, the National Defense Research Institute, and the Defense Materiel Administration) and contract negotiations principally with the Defense Materiel Administration.

Traditionally, lobbying in the cabinet and the parliament has been unnecessary. Describing the situation of the late 1950s, one observer noted: "By the time the politicians are brought into the process they usually have little option left but to justify the production order."[32] And one high official in government stated in an interview that "even if they had to lobby, they wouldn't be very good at it."[33] However, given downward pressures on the defense budget, the increasing political importance of decisions on major weapon systems, and a consequent necessity for earlier cabinet-level scrutiny of proposed defense expenditures, it is possible that business lobbying will increase. None of this is to imply that the defense industry and various government officials do not lobby with foreign industrial producers of weapons systems components over licensing arrangements; both do and in concert.

THE NEWS MEDIA

Many in the Swedish defense organization and in the defense industry would appear to be somewhat paranoid about the news media. Some assert that the media are "controlled" largely by the socialists and that it is very difficult for defense decision makers to get even-handed treatment on policies and programs for total defense. Others deny that this is true, pointing out that the papers with the largest circulations are owned by the nonsocialist parties.

It is true that the media tend to give short shrift to Swedish defense matters. To the extent that the media focus on foreign policy, they prefer to inform the public on détente, international peace keeping, and international development assistance. True, too, understanding that outspoken support for defense spending is unpopular or genuinely convinced that conditions for peace are not necessarily founded in strength or, perhaps, guilty of wishful thinking, many politicians have tended to focus on international peace. As Ingemar Dörfer has expressed it: "Swedes tend to believe what their government has been telling them; that détente is here to stay."[34]

Television in Sweden is unique by American standards. Similar to many European nations, there are rarely any daytime programs and only two channels in the evenings. TV production is controlled by an independent board that is highly subsidized by the government. Programs appear to be selected or designed much more for their cultural value than for public leisure or public information. The TV Board appears to believe that the Swedish public is not (or should not be) interested in defense policy. However, there are programs on such issues as arms control and disarmament. Some Swedish defense officials have tried, unsuccessfully, to persuade the TV Board that defense and defense information are important.

In general, the Stockholm newspapers are reluctant to print articles on defense: *Svenska Dagbladet,* which is conservative and defense oriented, is the exception; others, such as *Dagens Nyheter* (Liberal) and *Aftonbladet* (Socialist), are generally skeptical or antidefense; the Communist paper *Ny Dag* is clearly antidefense. Like the TV Board, the press argues that the Swedish public is not interested in defense.

An example of the general media position is the case of the press reporter Maj Wechselmann, who gained notoriety several years ago for having "blown the cover" on the military-industrial complex involved in the high cost overruns (almost double original estimates) of developing and producing the Viggen 37 aircraft. An ardent opponent of defense spending in general, and especially in the case of the B3LA/A38 controversies, she was awarded the peace prize for 1978 from the Swedish Peace and Arbitration Society, a pacifist organization.[35]

As in any constitutional democracy, defense decision makers in Sweden bear the burden of systemic political constraints from which authoritarian regimes are relatively free. Then too, their alternative choices in defense policy are shaped or conditioned by geopolitical factors, by technological developments and trends only partially under their "control," and by the increasing realities of resource scarcity.

POLITICAL CONSTRAINTS

Governments in parliamentary systems usually wish to avoid taking stands on crucial political issues unless they can be relatively confident they can win. The reason is obvious; unlike the American system, a vote on a major issue can result in the "no confidence" vote that spells the demise of a governing coalition.

The Swedish government was faced with just such a crucial issue in October 1978—the necessity to make a fundamental decision on the expansion of nuclear energy. Prime Minister Fälldin's Center party repudiated a compromise he had struck with his coalition partners (who had pushed for expansion of nuclear energy) to delay putting two additional nuclear power plants on line until the nation's energy agency pronounced that safe means of waste disposal had been found. The Center party sought additional concessions that the prime minister could not get and Fälldin resigned.

Concerning a parliamentary decision on the next generation of fighter aircraft, although the decision had major implications for the future of Swedish defense and defense industry, no party wished to take responsibility before the 1979 elections. A common delaying tactic in such instances is to have commissions undertake studies of the issue. A companion tactic is to fund research and development on alternative aircraft systems incrementally so that opponents are confronted with sunk costs so great that a decision not to adopt a new Swedish-manufactured fighter aircraft would be clearly irrational on economic grounds.

As will be discussed below, one alternative for future Swedish aircraft production and a means of reducing per unit costs would be foreign sales; however, at least two political constraints would tend to counter any such move. First, even if members of the defense establishment advocated this alternative, they would be constrained by the Foreign Ministry's intent to keep arms sales abroad below 1 percent of total Swedish production. Second, such a position could run afoul of the country's foreign policy of neutrality—even if it could survive the onslaught of Swedish public opinion.

RESOURCE CONSTRAINTS

Aside from such human resource constraints implied by the potential loss of trained R&D personnel in the aircraft industry, there are other major resource constraints to be sure. The most obvious is funding for military defense in the light of real or politically perceived opportunity costs for domestic programs at a time when the Swedish economy is in dire straits. *The Swedish Budget for 1978/79* painted a bleak picture: the nation's balance of payments situation had deteriorated, inflation was unacceptably high, foreign markets had deteriorated, production had fallen three years in succession, unemployment had been kept at manageable levels only by substantial efforts in labor market policy, and the nation's budget deficit had grown.[36]

In this milieu and against a background of rising military manpower costs and rising costs of defense production, the constraints are obvious. Defense decision makers have been confronted over the past several years with what amounts to a budget "ceiling" that keeps falling in constant currency. Although the budget for military defense rose from $1.5 billion in FY 1973 to $3.33 billion in FY 1980, the military defense share of the GNP dropped from 4.6 to 3.5 percent during the same period. The net result has been to force defense decision makers to reduce drastically in military equipment, numbers of military units, and both conscript and refresher training, and to plan for strength reductions by about 2,000 people in the central authorities and military staffs by 1985. The picture can be made to appear even worse if one contrasts recent forecasts of the future with the situation of the mid-1950s:

> The mobilizable front line forces will decline into between half and one third of the force structure in the mid-1950s, one generation earlier. The Air Force will go from a 17 wing Air Force in 1955 (compared to a 26 wing US tactical Air Force now) to a 7 wing essentially Viggen Air Force in 1988. The air defense fighter force, the strongest in Western Europe in 1955 with 33 squadrons, will eventually have 8 Viggen squadrons.[37]

Of course, one can argue that the more sophisticated weapon systems of the present and projected future have far greater capability than earlier generations and, thus, one needs far fewer. But this is a current and unresolved argument among military force development planners everywhere.

Military defense, albeit the largest part by far of "total defense," is still only one area of defense where resource constraints are important.[38]

Swedish Total Defense Costs, 1978/79
(millions of Swedish Kroner)

Military defense	13,543.7	
Civil defense	291.8	
Economic defense	480.0	
Miscellaneous	117.0	
Total defense	14,432.5	($3.14 billion)

Civil defense is based on training for both men and women between the ages sixteen and sixty-five who would comprise a wartime organization of approximately 210,000 people. The civil defense mission is to protect the population against the effects of conventional warfare, with a secondary mission of providing protection against ABC weapons within reasonable cost limits. Throughout the more highly populated areas, there is an impressive array of rock and concrete shelters. Though such defense is directed by the Civil Defense Administration, primary responsibility resides with local authorities, with all financing eventually to be provided by the national budget.[39] Resources for this activity are constrained not only by opportunity costs but also by public mood. For example, perceptions on détente and nuclear mutual assured destruction between the superpowers make it difficult for decision makers to convince the public and the parliament that protection against ABC weapons requires much funding.

Economic defense planning, directed by the National Board of Economic Defense, is centered on Sweden's ability to withstand independently blockade and wartime situations involving essential resources such as energy supplies, raw materials, food, fertilizer, and clothing, and to convert quickly from peacetime to wartime industrial production. Caught in the typical economy-ecology dilemma of the energy crisis, which has been an issue toppling two successive governments, major emphasis in economic defense is on stockpiling crude oil.[40]

As with all industrialized nations, international trade and international division of labor affect Sweden's prosperity in peacetime and economic security in war. Yet, as the prime minister put it in 1978:

"Our economic links and commitments must not become so strict as to make it impossible for us to keep out of a European conflict between East and West."[41] Peacetime resource constraints are thus linked to the political constraints of a foreign policy of neutrality in war.

The miscellaneous costs of total defense include psychological defense, equipment for emergency hospitals in wartime, and the development of certain communications capabilities. Properly so, Swedish planners are concerned about the capabilities of an aggressor to penetrate their communications systems, with all that implies for emergency command and control and psychological defense.

Resource constraints are real in Swedish peacetime defense planning. It is clear that Sweden is more or less constrained in defense capability based upon various crisis scenarios envisioning short or long wars.

CHANNELS OF DECISION MAKING

The current long-range planning system for Swedish defense is based on a study begun in 1965 when the Ministry of Defense was reorganized. The system was applied on an experimental basis in 1968 and was accepted in principle by the parliament in 1970. In 1972 the Swedish Planning, Programming, and Budgeting System was implemented fully (see figure 5). The system contains four major elements: (1) Studies of international developments and construction of cases of aggression in the form of "crisis scenarios"; (2) Prospective plans dealing with a time perspective of fifteen to twenty years; (3) System plans for major weapon systems; and (4) Five-year program plans, rolled every year.[42]

Figure 5. Main links in Swedish PPBS

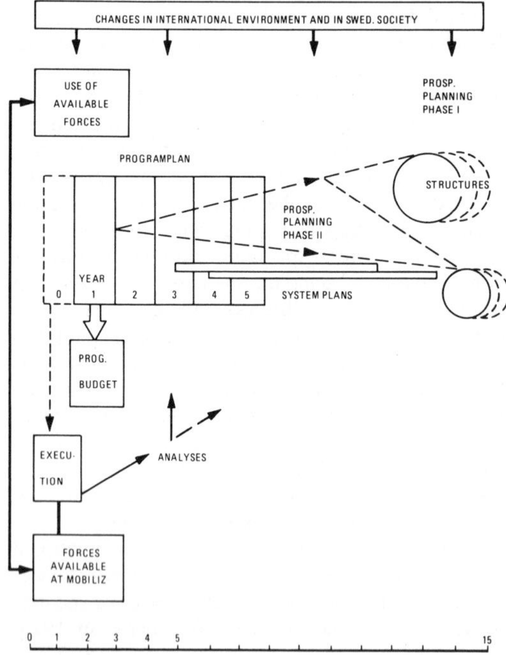

Part of the responsibility of the Ministry of Defense for coordinating all defense matters in peacetime is to decide which types of threat to plan for. Should Sweden plan for deterrence, and at what levels? for reducing the consequences of war, and in what respects? for contributions to stability in the Nordic region, and how? for territorial denial? To serve this function, crisis scenarios are developed on the basis of possible international developments that are of particular relevance to Swedish defense policy. Studies focus on international, regional, and national politicomilitary, technological, economic, and social developments that may lead to cases of aggression or crises affecting Swedish interests. Study results are formally written as documents called "cases of aggression" or "crisis scenarios." This is primarily the work of the SSLP that manages these studies designed to suggest basic guidelines for planning.

Perspective plans fifteen to twenty years into the future are basically the frameworks for alternative defense structures under different budgetary constraints. This work is done principally by the defense staff under the direction of the supreme commander. Considered are alternative compositions of the armed forces derived from given goals (cases of aggression or crisis scenarios), including prescribed internal restrictions describing: (1) basic operational principles, (2) objectives of main allocation programs, and (3) characteristics of essential systems.[43] The studies of defense structures provide background for R&D policies, a basis for parliamentary decisions concerning defense five-year program plans, a long-term planning framework used by other branches of total defense, and background for military staff exercises and maneuvers. They serve also as mechanisms for coordinating the long-term planning activities of the many boards and agencies involved in total defense.[44] The perspective plan describes the most important relationships among system plans.

System planning provides the link between perspective plans and program plans (see figure 6). The perspective plan outlines the ways in which future alternatives can be realized. A system plan is a detailed plan for the development of *one* such alternative system, which can be as large as the armed forces as a whole, or main allocation programs, or as small as a specific weapon system (with subprograms, program elements, or equivalents), such as air defense units. Testing the feasibility of system plans against program plans provides the feedback loop for revision of the perspective plan, which is provided to the Ministry of Defense and subsequently to the parliament as a basis for program plan decisions.[45]

Five-year program plans are developed every

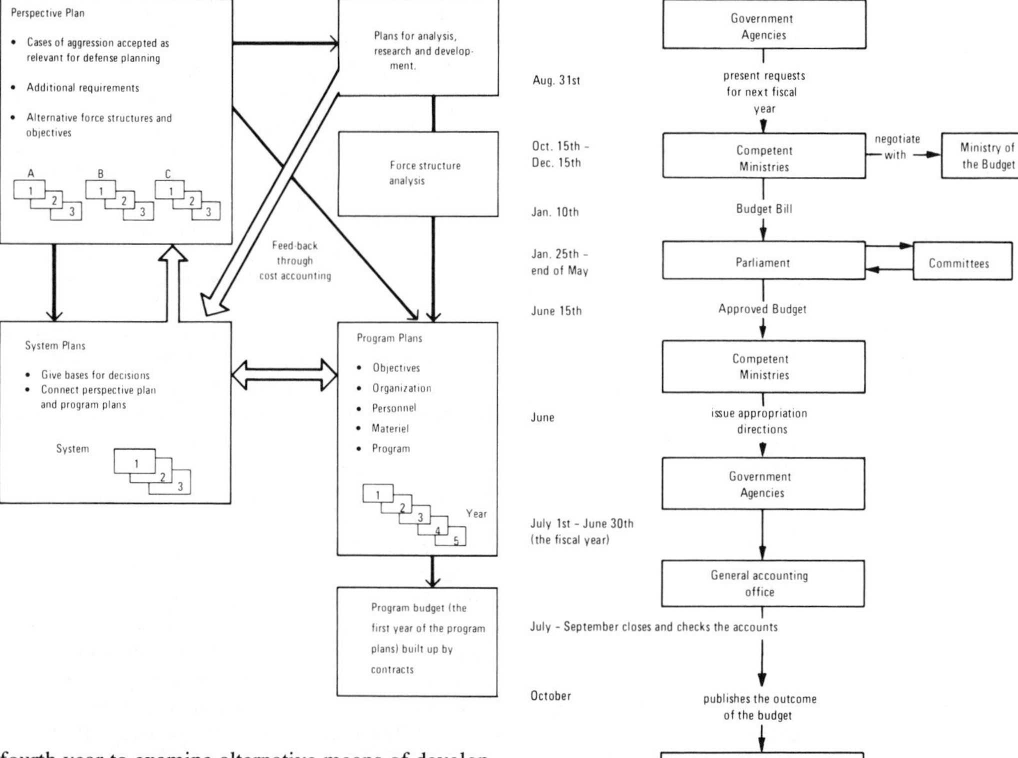

Figure 6. The connection between plans

Figure 7. Swedish budget procedure

fourth year to examine alternative means of developing different categories of defense capital over the planning period, in order to satisfy specific operational goals. Included are considerations of commitments for the future based on ordered (but not supplied) material and assumed priority programs, such as conscript training.[46] When defense capital equals demand, a program plan is feasible and rationally could be adopted. Whether or not a particular program budget will be adopted is, of course, a political decision.

Annual defense budgeting is based on the Swedish fiscal year, which runs from July 1 to June 30 (see figure 7). The work of the Ministry of Defense for this budget begins during the winter of the preceding calendar year, based on directives from the Ministry of the Budget. All defense agencies must have their budget requests to the Defense Ministry no later than August 31. These requests are formally registered in the ministry and, given the right to public information under the Freedom of the Press Act, often receive broad press coverage. From August 31 to December 15 the defense budget is prepared and negotiated with the Budget Ministry.

The government's budget bill (about 4,000 pages), including an economic policy statement, the draft budget, and a survey of the national economy, is submitted to the parliament by January 10. The formal trace of the budget through the parliament is shown in figure 8.[47]

The channels of the Swedish defense decision-making process are followed formally. Whether or not the process "works" or works "as intended" is another matter. For example, it would be important to know what the correlation is between program budgets and actual defense expenditures from year one through year five. Unless the correlation were relatively high, given the opportunity costs of the resources devoted to program planning (and thus through the feedback loop through systems planning to perspective planning), alternative planning procedures might be in order. A thorough time series analysis would be required for such analysis of the efficacy of the system.

Recurring issues: defense policy outputs

CIVIL-MILITARY RELATIONS

Ministers of Defense have been outspoken concerning the lack of defense information received by the Swedish public. In 1978 Eric Krönmark criticized

Figure 8. Swedish parliamentary budget procedure

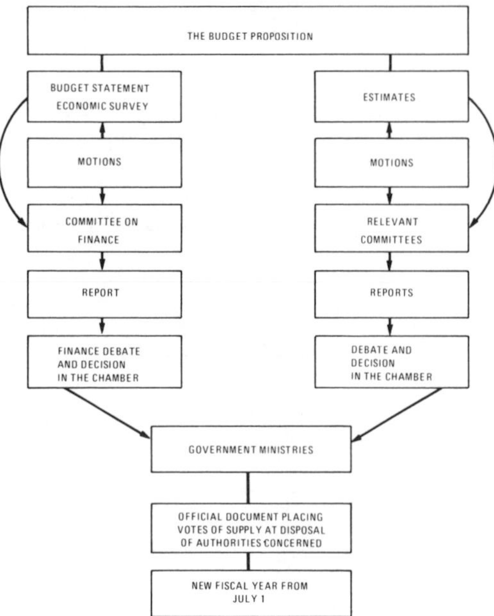

the inadequacy of defense information in the school system—to which the director general of the Swedish Board of Education replied to the effect that defense gets its prescribed share in the curriculum, but the pupils find the subject uninteresting.

Surveys indicate that the defense minister is correct. In 1977 the National Psychological Defense Planning Committee surveyed 1,011 people in 115 districts concerning their views on total defense. The results are instructive (but note the comparison of maximum and minimum values):[48]

a. the significance of military defense diminished from 64 percent in 1975 to 54 percent;
b. credence in the importance of civil resistance and guerrilla defense increased from 23 to 28 percent;
c. credence in the war-deterrent effect of Sweden's armed forces diminished sharply, from 55 percent in 1974 to 31 percent;
d. credence in Sweden's ability to keep out of a major European war decreased from 38 percent in 1965 to 23 percent;
e. in 1977, only 20 percent of Swedes believed that the country could defend itself, compared to 30 percent in 1975; and
f. moderate Party supporters were the most positive on defense (about 57 percent), as compared to 26 percent for Social Democrats and 4 percent for Communists.

On March 1, 1978, the newspaper *Dagens Nyheter* concluded "Diminished Interest in Total Defense" in reporting another survey by the National Psychological Defense Planning Committee. The survey found that:

a. nearly 60 percent knew nothing about the tasks of economic defense in wartime;
b. only 8 percent knew what defense cost annually;
c. half of those interviewed did not know what "psychological defense" implied;
d. only 16 percent were aware that important information on evacuation in time of war could be found in the telephone directory; and
e. defense knowledge was greater on the Moderate (Conservative) side and diminished the further to the left one looked.

Support for the military conscription system in Sweden appears to be waning somewhat. Whereas in 1973, 90 percent of the population supported it, by 1977 the figure had dropped to 80 percent. Declining support is most noticeable among the young. In 1977, 65 percent of those between eighteen and twenty-nine were in favor, with 28 percent against and 7 percent undecided.[49]

The trend in Swedish public opinion as the country entered the 1980s appeared to be a belief that peace had broken out in Europe, a belief based on perceptions in 1972 that détente was on its way and on views in 1977 about the usual Swedish timelag in perception of what is going on in European security. However, the Soviet invasion of Afghanistan in December 1979 changed this perspective rather dramatically.[50]

Although the Swedish public is not well informed about defense matters, one can conclude that in general the Swedes are not antidefense or antimilitary and that they are generally willing to support defense but, at a time of high inflation, they are concerned about rising defense costs. There appears to be a growing public tendency to doubt the threat of war,[51] to view the military as a necessary evil to be funded at lower levels, and to want the military to perform its routine functions without interfering excessively with the important business of the welfare state.

FORCE POSTURE

Obviously, current force posture weighs heavily in decisions on defense plans and programs for the future. Sweden's current force posture is larger than most would think and, depending upon one's assumptions about war scenarios in northern Europe, could weigh significantly in the strategic balance. The active duty strength of the armed forces as Sweden entered the 1980s was 66,100, with a total strength of approximately 750,000 which is to be mobilized within seventy-two hours to fight on their own territory.[52] Added to this are about 100,000 troops in the home guard.

The air force has 430 operational combat aircraft (plus 20 in storage), including nine squadrons of the sophisticated Viggen attack and reconnaissance aircraft, with more due to be phased into the inventory to replace the older Draken aircraft. In numbers, this air capability is twice as great as that of Norway and Denmark combined and in numbers of combat aircraft only 90 less than the capability of the U.S. Air Force/Europe. Viewed another way, the Swedes theoretically can mount a higher fighter sortie rate than the United States Air Force.[53] It should be noted that the total number of combat aircraft in the Swedish inventory will be reduced as the four new versions (attack AJ37, reconnaissance S37, fighter-interceptor JA37, and trainer SK37) replace older aircraft.

The army has an active duty strength of 44,500 that includes 36,000 conscripts at any given time serving their required 7½ to 15 months of training. Fully mobilized, the army has more than 500,000 troops organized in 28 brigades (24 infantry and 4 armor) under six military district commanders reporting in wartime to a military supreme commander.[54]

The navy has 14 submarines and about 175 other ships and boats, half of which are landing craft. Torpedo boats with surface-to-surface missiles are to replace destroyers. The navy also commands fixed and mobile coastal artillery battalions that are partially armed with surface-to-surface missiles.[55]

Swedish defense shares the current manpower cost problems typical of western Europe and the United States. Attempts at cost reductions impact on the number of active duty units available, how well manpower can be trained and retrained, and unit morale—all of which raise questions about military capability and readiness.[56] And the Swedish armed forces are one of the world's six fully or partially unionized military institutions. In fact, the Swedish and Norwegian armed forces have the longest unbroken traditions of military unionism, and neither appear to have significant problems with military unions. Almost all Swedes belong to unions and find nothing particularly unique about membership while in military uniform.[57]

Like the military establishments of the other Western democracies, the Swedish armed forces are not without their problems, but their military personnel appear highly professional, motivated, well trained, and capable of carrying out the missions assigned them by the government.

WEAPONS ACQUISITION

As Ingemar Dörfer has pointed out so well, Swedish defense policy has little to do with science and a great deal to do with technology.[58] Sweden suboptimizes in the technology of weapons acquisition, relying on a balance of technological change between the superpowers. In practice this means that, as long as the East does not outstrip the West in weapons technology, Sweden can rely on Western technology to sustain Swedish defense requirements. This frees the Swedish government from the first two steps of a full-blown R&D program for weapons acquisition, steps Sweden cannot afford. They are:

1. the formation and empirical verification of theories about parameters of the physical world;
2. the creation and testing of radically new physical concepts, components, devices, and techniques;
3. the identification, modification, and combination of feasible or existing concepts, components, and devices to provide a distinctly new application practical in terms of performance, reliability, and cost; and
4. relatively minor modifications of existing components, devices, and systems to improve performance, increase reliability, reduce cost, and simplify application.[59]

This means that Swedish weapons programs are for the most part within "the state of the art," eliminating many R&D uncertainties. However, this creates major external uncertainties and definite constraints. Sweden must purchase either major weapon systems or their technology from either the Soviets or the advanced industrialized states of the West—meaning principally the NATO allies. Declining to purchase weapon systems on the principle of nonalignment in peace or neutrality in war, Sweden has purchased Western technology in the form of contract licenses for major components of major weapon systems. The clearest example is the acquisition process for the Viggen AJ37. Swedish planners opted and contracted for the U.S. Pratt and Whitney JT8D engine, which is manufactured under license by Volvo-Flygmotor for the Viggen airframe built by SAAB-Scania.

Viggen cost overrun problems notwithstanding, another major defense problem of suboptimization has recently arisen. A major alternative for solving current and projected problems of the Swedish aircraft industry was to sell the Viggen in large numbers abroad. In 1977 and 1978 India seriously considered purchasing the Viggen. However, the U.S. license contract (and the current U.S. arms export laws) for the Pratt and Whitney engine specify no sale to third parties without U.S. approval. In August 1978, Secretary of State Cyrus Vance informed Minister of Commerce Burenstam-Linder that the United States opposed the sale.[60] This is clearly an important technological constraint, which Swedish defense decision makers must suffer on aircraft systems as long as they suboptimize by purchasing the systems based on contracts with the West. The possible alternatives are not happy ones: (1) optimizing by following steps 1 and 2 in the aircraft system acquisition process, which Sweden cannot afford; (2) purchasing the tactical aircraft in toto from the West, which denigrates nonalignment and would probably adversely affect the R&D component of Sweden's leading industrial sector—engineering; (3) contracting or purchasing from the Soviet Union, which would be politically untenable and would probably exacerbate Swedish arms sales problems; or (4) doing without fighter aircraft, which would make Swedish deterrence of the marginal attack much less credible (the Swedish army commander in chief has disagreed with this view) and would probably lead to the demise of the aircraft industry and consequent loss of thousands of jobs by civilian technicians.

Clearly, Swedish defense planners are not confronted with these technological constraints on most weapon systems, only on the ones *most* important to Swedish defense as presently conceptualized.

WEAPONS ACQUISITON AND THE FIGHTER AIRCRAFT CONTROVERSY: A CASE STUDY

Attempting analysis of the process underlying a major decision not yet finalized and on which definitive statements may not be forthcoming for many months or years is admittedly a risky business. Yet, some of the informal fundamentals of the Swedish defense decision-making process can be drawn from the undertaking even at this point.

Research, development, testing, evaluation, and production require long lead times even in the Swedish system, which suboptimizes in the weapons acquisition process. By 1995 the present Viggen system should be replaced by a follow-on system. By then the Viggen 37 system will become obsolete—structurally "worn out" and well behind the fighter aircraft technological power curve. The decision to begin the R&D process in order to have the follow-on aircraft *in the inventory* should have been recommended in 1974 or 1975 and made in 1976 or 1977. In February 1979, a decision was finally made by the Ullsten government. In essence, the decision was to cease work on new aircraft alternatives and to develop the existing pursuit version of the Viggen to give it attack capability, to form another aircraft committee to study trainer aircraft alternatives, and to examine the future possibilities of collaboration with other countries in developing fighter aircraft.[61] In December 1980, Parliament finally voted to provide funding for the study of yet another version of future fighter aircraft, the JAS.

Constraints affecting the decision-making process were several. First, there were the resource constraints described earlier in this paper based upon current and foreseeable conditions of the Swedish economy. There were important cost-benefit comparisons of the leading alternative systems, the A20 on the one hand and the B3LA or A38 on the other. The data involved in this comparison are not now available and may not be for some time. However, existing evidence suggests that, although the A20 may have been a less expensive alternative in the short run, the B3LA or A38 would have been less expensive over the long term (see figure 9). The B3LA/A38 included new technology involving the air frame, engine, instrumentation, and armament; over the first five years, R&D would have cost an estimated $8.3 to 11.0 million more each year than the alternative.[62] The A20 involved modification of current Viggen technology. Included in these calculations was a major consideration of the state of aircraft research and development, and alternatives to it, at the time decisions would have to be made about the follow-on to either the A20 or the B3LA. Projecting alternative costs over the next five years is clearly more concrete (and perhaps more persuasive to the layman) than projecting for the long term. Most politicians taking stands on resource questions in the late 1970s certainly did not expect to be in the politi-

Figure 9. Aircraft cost comparison concept

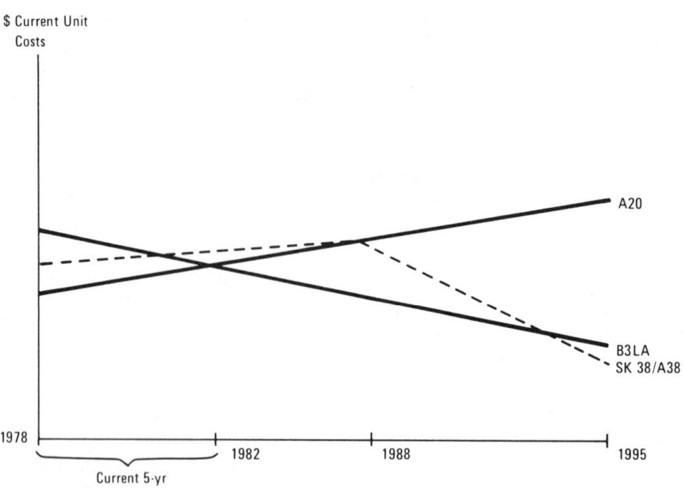

cal arena in the 1990s to see the culmination of the long research, development, testing, evaluation, and production processes.

In 1973, with the deep involvement of the defense staff, air staff, FMV, and FOA, the system plan for air attack systems laid out alternatives that were incorporated in Systems Plan Number 2. In preparation for the 1977 five-year defense decision that would involve enormous commitments of Swedish resources and, in the light of the then-current controversy over the large cost overruns involved in the Viggen system, the Social Democrats created the Thunberg Commission in 1974 to examine the total defense picture. Given the timing for decisions on future aircraft production, that commission should have, but did not, recommend the follow-on to Viggen. The Viggen controversy was still too hot politically.

Another commission was formed specifically to examine the aircraft issue. In the fall of 1976 the choice was between the A20 at relatively the same cost or the B3LA at added cost. But politics intervened in the form of the September 1976 national elections. The Social Democrats were ousted and the B3LA issue went into limbo. The parliament decided not to fund the program for 1977/78 and to "wait and see." In the spring of 1977 yet another group, the B3LA Commission (or Nordbeck Commission), was tasked to look deeper into the issue of aircraft alternatives. This commission, headed by Undersecretary of State for Defense Gunnar Nordbeck, included representatives from the Ministries of Defense and Budget, the armed services, and the defense industry. This group was to examine the alternatives and consequences of funding (i.e., an affirmative decision) and to recommend an aircraft to be funded in the 1978/79 budget. Again, in the context of a Swedish economy in decline, the parliament postponed a decision.

Yet another commission, referred to earlier, was formed in 1978 to restudy the issue, examining this time the consequences for the Swedish air force and the aircraft industry of a decision *not* to fund a Swedish-manufactured follow-on to Viggen. This group, the Air Industry Committee, submitted its report to the Ministry of Defense in October 1978. This study of the B3LA was to be available in mid-October 1978 to be used in finalizing the defense request for the budget bill to be submitted to the parliament in January 1979; in fact, the study was not available. The fundamental conclusions of the Air Industry Committee report were that the costs of alternative systems over the long run were not significantly different and that, although the major aircraft corporations could absorb some of the impact of not producing a new fighter aircraft in Sweden, there would be significant adverse consequences for the Swedish aircraft industry.

A month before the Air Industry Committee report was released, one of Prime Minister Fälldin's last moves before stepping down was to instruct Defense Minister Krönmark to find a less expensive B3LA alternative. Krönmark directed FMV to study such an alternative. Thus, even before the Air Industry Committee's report had been submitted, the basis for a new aircraft with essentially the same capabilities as the B3LA at a lower cost had begun; the new aircraft was the SK38/A38.[63]

The politics of choice. The second "wait-and-see" decision by the parliament was a bit more than that. On April 25, 1978, the parliament approved a $7.1 million appropriation for the B3LA project, or at least for pursuing R&D on alternative aircraft. However, on May 30, 1978, the Socialist, antidefense Stockholm daily, *Aftonbladet,* printed the story "B3LA: Secret Contract between Government and SAAB." Allegedly, Minister of Defense Krönmark had, without consulting the Parliamentary Defense Committee, come to a secret understanding with SAAB-Scania's chairman, Marcus Wallenberg, for contracts to be placed from 1978 to 1980 for a total of 119 pursuit Viggens (AJ37). And, the price of these Viggens allegedly hinged on whether SAAB were contracted to build the B3LA; if not, the price would be $10.7 million higher.

The reaction was immediate. The Social Democrats (SDs) picked up on the story: "We have been deceived. The Government should put its cards on the table concerning Wallenberg's and the Defense Minister's secret contract," demanded Social Democrat Maj-Britt Theorin in Parliament. On June 2, the prime minister confirmed in parliamentary hearings that such an agreement had been signed.[64] The minister of defense replied angrily that the "leaked" information was a security violation and that the offender should be punished. Beneath the surface of this now-critical popular issue lay longer-term interests and stands developed by competing factions.

The Social Democratic minorities in the various committees formed to consider the B3LA had consistently opposed the project and the increased defense budget expenditures involved. Their party leader, former Prime Minister Olaf Palme, was especially irritated by the fact that SDs had not been selected to participate on the Nordbeck B3LA Commission, despite the argument used by Prime Minister Fälldin that this group had not been "politically composed."[65] The Social Democrats took the position that if the Fälldin government decided to go with the B3LA, the SDs would cancel the project when (and if) they returned to power in the fall 1979 elections. They knew that they were not without important support because the supreme commander, Stig Synnergren (an SD), had protested in writing against the nature of the government's negotations with SAAB-Scania, linking Viggen 37 prices to future B3LA contracts.[66] The *Aftonbladet* expressed surprise on May 30, 1978, that the B3LA affair seemed to have a rapid momentum of its own and that flexibility for a decision appeared to be diminishing rapidly.

The armed services. There are fundamental, now almost traditional, differences between the ways in which the Swedish armed forces view defense requirements. More than 85 percent of all Swedish commissioned officers of all services prefer the Conservative party and only 3.9 percent the Social Democratic party.[67] However, army officers appear to be more inclined toward the philosophy of the Social Democrats, to be more traditional, and to be more egalitarian. In fact, they appear to be more typically Swedish. Navy and, especially, air force officers appear to be much more oriented toward the West and its technology and thus to be less traditional in outlook. The army is much more concerned with inner-directed territorial defense of Sweden. The air force and the navy focus on "perimeter defense" of Sweden well beyond its shores. These general predispositions have enormous influence on the stands the various services take on the alternatives to the follow-on to Viggen 37.

The army territorial defense advocates have argued that:

> Total defense must take the form of a defense with staying power.... Capacity for stubborn and enduring defense is more important than great initial strength....
>
> Military defense... should in the future continue to be built up so that in all essential respects it will be balanced and will make defense in depth possible with a concentration of forces on frontiers and coasts....
>
> Priorities should be allocated... in accordance with the principle that it is better to obtain a larger number of technically less advanced weapon systems than a few technically advanced ones.[68]

Territorial defense, thus defined, does not require long-range, technologically sophisticated aircraft capable of striking an attacker at sea well beyond the Swedish coastline. Rather, weapon systems should be oriented toward close support of ground units. The army, and especially the army commander in chief, General Nils Sköld, was aware that ever higher costs of aircraft technology at a time of declining defense budgets and increasing manpower costs probably would result in diminished funding for army programs.

In 1979 interservice rivalry was intense.[69] The army fought to preserve the conscription system and reservist refresher training; to acquire funding for attack helicopters, surface-to-surface conventional antitank missiles, armored personnel carriers, and troop concentrations; to modernize ground force weapons; and to arm aircraft now in the inventory (SAAB 105 aircraft) for the close air support role.

This emphasis places the army at odds with the air force and navy, both of whom have argued for the importance of a strategy based on attacking "the enemy's invasion units during the most vulnerable phase: the sea crossing."[70] The argument was for a "high-low" mix of attack aircraft in which the A20 stood for the high (expensive, technologically sophisticated, high altitude, supersonic) and B3LA or A38 for the low (relatively inexpensive, low altitude, subsonic). Both the air force and the navy, but especially the former, were concerned that postponement of the aircraft decision would lead in the 1990s to an obsolete Viggen 37 and SK60 (modified SAAB 105) air force with consequent high maintenance costs and flying hazards. The air force and navy found sympathy with the technologically oriented Defense Materiel Administration and Defense Research Institute. A major problem for all the services is that the budget appears to be dictating strategy. That is, strategy cannot be developed in the abstract but must consider current and projected force structure. Strategy without the weapon systems to carry it out is irrelevant at best.

The defense industry. The defense industrialists are Swedes interested in Swedish security; they are also entrepreneurs interested in making a profit and preserving the future health and vitality of their corporations. SAAB-Scania was representative in pushing for a quick decision on Swedish production of the new fighter or the A20. SAAB's management argued that the costs could be kept reasonable because the B3LA or A38 would involve lighter materials and reduced size and complexity of electronic gear. The industry arguments relied on the defense staff formula of "effect plus survival equals efficiency in war" and cited added benefits of the new fighter for all the services, including its use as a support weapon for the army.[71] The position used as "the bottom line" in pressing for a favorable decision on the new aircraft was that "If the... project does not go through, the aircraft industry in Sweden will collapse and as many as 12,000 people could lose their jobs."[72] Despite the degree of validity of the SAAB-Scania argument, the ardent defense critics have countered that:

> The management at SAAB has always known how to conduct extortion against the State. The most effective threat for ensuring continued orders has been to propose the closing down of the largest metal industry in Linköping.
>
> The SAAB directors themselves have also gone to the ministries, though as long as there was a Social Democratic government it was just as effective to work on the unions and utilize their access to government offices. Then the directors would also refer arrogantly to the workers' initiative.[73]

The trade unions. The potential impact of aircraft decisions upon the aircraft industry certainly is not lost on the major trade unions. The future of defense production for SAAB-Scania, Volvo-Flygmotor, and L. M. Ericsson involves a large number of employees. It made a difference to the two major unions representing white collar workers primarily in R&D jobs (TCO and SACO) and to the major union representing blue collar workers concentrated in production jobs (LO) what kind of decision was made. Unions rely on their parties to represent their views in the government. If only the A20 were adopted, then much less R&D employment would be required. If the decision were made to purchase new aircraft abroad, both R&D and production jobs would be lost. In the event of the latter, some have suggested retraining for employment in industries producing civilian manufactures. But this was not a viable solution for the unions, which preferred the status quo and asked for examples of growing industry in the civilian sector that could train and absorb, for example, the 5,000 people employed by SAAB in Linköping. The unions had representatives on the Aircraft Industry Committee, one each from LO, TCO, and SACO. The representative from LO was a Social Democrat, the TCO representative (from SAAB) was a Conservative, and the SACO representative leaned toward the Social Democrats. Any decision by the government must come to grips with union pressures through the political parties; the unions have made their concerns very clear and their representatives have argued predictably. In September 1978 the TCO representative, Ben Ottoson (union chairman at SAAB-Scania and a Moderate), insisted that adoption of the A20 would be disastrous for white collar employment at SAAB-Scania and Volvo-Flygmotor, arguing that employment analysis by the Defense Ministry was one sided.[74] At least from the unions' perspectives, the best decision would have been the "high-low mix" that the air force and navy advocated—the best of all worlds for both white and blue collar workers. In fact, more technicians could soon be hired because the average age of the force was relatively old, over fifty in the case of SAAB's technicians.[75]

Public opinion. The general lack of knowledge concerning defense matters on the part of the Swedish public could only be made worse by what they may have read or heard on television about the B3LA/A38 controversy. Newspaper articles were confusing at best in portraying the issues involved. The costs involved were variously estimated; the B3LA was reported variously as a "go" and a "no go"; the final decision was reported just over the horizon time and time again, and the impacts of alternative decisions were reported in contradictory ways. It is safe to say that there was no public consensus in Sweden for or against a B3LA/A38 (or A20, or both) program. One might hypothesize that this was an acceptable state of affairs for the government, permitting relative freedom of choice, and certainly better than a public consensus against a program the government might prefer.

The government. Either government spokespersons were inconsistent in their statements on the new aircraft or they were variously misinterpreted in press reports. Prime Minister Fälldin was reported as both for and against the program.[76] Minister of Defense Krönmark lent support to various alternative proposals—from Swedish manufacture of the B3LA to collaborative programs with Italy or Switzerland.[77]

Prior to the fall of Prime Minister Fälldin's Center party coalition on 5 October 1978, Krönmark was quite specific in stating the following about the aircraft decision:

1. no one in the government had opposed the B3LA;
2. the only real skeptics were a number of younger Center party people and even fewer Liberal party people;
3. the program (presumably a high-low mix of A20 and B3LA) was costing 400 million Swedish kroner ($9.7 million), of which industry paid 100 million Sw. kr. ($2.4 million) for fiscal year 1978;
4. the decision could not be postponed for another year for reasons of expense and long-term national security;
5. the problem of finding jobs for a couple of thousand displaced, qualified technicians would be manageable.[78]

Despite the vocal opposition of the Social Democrats and Prime Minister Fälldin's insistence that the aircraft decision would have to be founded upon a broad political unity, Krönmark took the position in the summer of 1978 that the government had "confidence in the Defense Materiel Administration and Aircraft Industry people,"[79] and that Prime Minister Fälldin would decide in favor of the B3LA without the cooperation of the Social Democrats if the basis for the project were sound.

However, the new minority government of Liberal party Leader Ola Ullsten, with the weakest parliamentary support since 1936, did not have such confidence. Caught between strong SD advocacy of the A20 and Moderate party advocacy of the B3LA, by November 1978 the new defense minister, Lars de Geer and his undersecretary, Gunnar Petri, saw the SK38/A38 alternative as a possibly attractive compromise. De Geer announced in the parliament on November 20, 1978, that the B3LA was no longer being considered.[80] By mid-December, Prime Minister Ullsten had established two new aircraft committees. One was a parliamentary committee, with an SD as chairman, to study the employment situation and production alternatives in the Linköping region. The other was a committee under Supreme Commander Lennart Ljung to compare the operational and cost aspects of the A38 and A20 projects. Appointment of the latter study caused serious political conflict both within and outside the Ministry of Defense.

In late November, the director of the Ministry's

Materiel Section, Ingemar Engman, a known supporter of the Social Democrats' proposals for a guerrilla-type defense organization (and, hence, less spending on sophisticated and expensive weapons systems), went outside his line of authority to write and publish a letter to the supreme commander. In the letter Engman indicted both the A38 alternative and the means by which the proposal for it was made. He cited the impropriety of FMV in forwarding the proposal directly to the government rather than to the supreme commander; he pointed to alleged inadequacies in the FMV analysis of the A38; he asserted that the A38 was a B3LA in disguise; he claimed that, because the A38 engine would be manufactured in the United States, the Volvo-Flygmotor plant at Arboga would be closed down; and he joined in the Social Democrats' argument that a plane-for-plane comparison clearly favored the A20 over the B3LA or A38.[81] An FMV spokesman, Air Force Lieutenant Colonel Sven Hökborg, who was also the project officer for the B3LA and A38, quickly denied that either engine alternative (British or American GE404) would be built abroad.[82]

The unions were quick to make their views known. Indicative of the issue's divisiveness, one element of the unions broke ranks with its own party. Ingvar Fahlsten, union chairman at the SAAB Aircraft Division (largely a Social Democratic trade union) insisted that an A20 decision would be disastrous for white collar employment in development work at SAAB.[83] On the other hand, Olaf Palme reiterated the Social Democrats' unanimous and irrevocable rejection of the B3LA and all its variants.[84]

By late December 1978, the supreme commander was committed to providing an early February 1979 comparison of the A38 and A20 alternatives. Early on, he went on record, stating that his report would take the form of a perspective plan to the year 2000, that negotiations with industry would be of decisive importance to his study, and that neither the A20 nor the A38 would be built in previously planned numbers within the present budget.[85]

Although there was mounting pressure from all quarters in early 1979 for an "immediate" decision on the next-generation fighter aircraft, and although the A38 option appeared to be a happy compromise, there appeared to be also increasingly sound reasons why the Ullsten government might find it politically prudent to stall the decision even further.

Given the weak parliamentary support of the Liberal party coalition, a major decision either way—to adopt the A38 alternative or to reject all alternatives—could have constituted in early 1979 a major election issue that, in combination with other issues, would guarantee a Social Democratic victory in the fall 1979 elections.

How could a major decision be avoided? In theory at least, if a decision maker knows that the best case (a consensus in favor of a preferred policy position) is not possible, and if the decision maker wishes to avoid the worst case (a consensus against the preferred policy), there is a short-term option. That option is to fragment public opinion so that there is no consensus either way. How could this be accomplished in the case of the fighter aircraft controversy? Clearly, outright denial of a follow-on to Viggen would have had high political costs with FMV, FOA, the defense industry, some of the unions, the air force, and the navy. On the other hand, adoption of a high-low aircraft mix would have carried high political costs with opposition parties, the army, and with Sweden's pacifist groups. But, there was a middle way that had at least the appearance of being a compromise. On February 24, 1979, *Svenska Dagbladet* reported the government's proposals:

—Discontinue the development work on the SK38/A38, formerly known as the B3LA.
—Develop further the pursuit version of the Viggen and give it attack capacity.
—Purchase a light, armed trainer, simpler and cheaper than the A38.
—Appoint the Supreme Commander to study these alternatives (aircraft committee Number 12).
—Increase work in the space industry field.
—Set up an industrial fund of 300 million kroner to facilitate a changeover to civilian production.
—Start work on heavy missiles.
—Examine the scope for collaboration with other countries in the future.[86]

By the time of these proposals, the defense community itself was fragmenting rapidly over the fighter aircraft issue. The head of the FMV, General Ove Ljung, criticized the supreme commander, General Lennart Ljung, for his economic analysis, which permitted the government to equivocate on the fighter decision. The air force commander in chief, General Dick Stenberg, was also critical of the supreme commander's position.[87] Olaf Palme had abruptly summoned a press conference and indicated that the trainer aircraft alternative might be acceptable to the Social Democrats.[88] In the wake of the government's decisions, the chairmen of the four trade unions at SAAB-Scania and Volvo-Flygmotor demanded employment guarantees for all employees in the aircraft industry.[89] Former Supreme Commander Stig Synnergren, was reported to support a variant of the trainer alternative.[90] Former Foreign Minister Karin Soder was reported in March 1979 to have summed up the developing situation aptly: "Karin Soder considers that since there is no longer any proper agreement on the aircraft question, the Defense Committee should be able to study the question of what attack aircraft Sweden should have in the future."[91]

"Final" decisions on the follow-on to the Viggen must await parliamentary debate and final vote. At this writing, there is no reason to believe that the positions of the contenders will be altered significantly. There is much at stake:

1. the future of an independent Swedish aircraft industry, "the very source of pride of the technostructure";[92]
2. the future directions of Swedish "nonalignment" —to the extent that strategy is affected by the source of acquisition for major weapons systems;
3. the viability of Swedish perimeter defense; and
4. the future of the army's conscript system.

Given the politics of compromise in Sweden's parliamentary system, it would be surprising if there were clear "winners" or "losers" in this competition for scarce public resources. Nevertheless, all the contestants perceive that there is much at stake and one might expect continued, intense debate.[93]

Notes

1. International Institute for Strategic Studies, *The Military Balance, 1979-1980* (London: IISS, 1979), pp. 79-80.

2. Stockholm International Peace Research Institute, *World Armaments and Disarmament: SIPRI Yearbook, 1978* (Stockholm: SIPRI, 1978), p. 226.

3. Nils Andrén, "The Nordic Balance: An Overview," *Washington Quarterly* 2, no. 3 (Summer 1979): 1-2.

4. See Idem, "The Security and Defense of Sweden," *FOA Reprints, 1976/77: 14* (Stockholm: National Defense Research Institute, 1977), p. 29.

5. Nils Andrén et al., *The Future of the Nordic Balance* (Stockholm: Ministry of Defense Sweden, Secretariat for National Security Policy and Long-Range Defense Planning [hereafter SSLP], 1977), p. 85. For further background, see Johan Jorgen Holst, ed., *Five Roads to Nordic Security* (Oslo: University Press, 1973), pp. 208-12.

6. SSLP, *Swedish Security Policy and Total Defense* (Stockholm: SSLP, 1977-1), p. 2.

7. Ibid., p. 3; and *The Swedish Budget, 1978/79* (Stockholm: Goteborgs Printers AB, 1978), p. 86.

8. Andrén et al., *Nordic Balance*, p. 94.

9. Ingemar Dörfer, "The Nordic Balance in Perspective: Sweden" (Paper prepared for the Seminar on International Security Problems in the Nordic Area, Georgetown Center for Strategic and International Studies, 15-16 June 1978), pp. 7-23.

10. Katrina Brodin, *Surprise Attack Problems and Issues* (Stockholm: SSLP, no. 1975-3), pp. 15-16. See also North Atlantic Assembly, "Defense of the Northern Flank," November 1972, p. 39, and Thorbjorn Fälldin, *Swedish Security Policy* (Stockholm: Ministry of Foreign Affairs, Press and Information Department, 1978), p. 2.

11. John Erickson, "The Northern Theater: Soviet Capabilities and Concepts," *Strategic Review* 4, no. 3 (Summer 1976): 70-71.

12. Arthur E. Dewey, "The Nordic Balance," *Strategic Review* 4, no. 4 (Fall 1976): 7-8.

13. Erickson, "The Northern Theater," p. 8. See also pp. 76, 79 on the place of Sweden in probable Soviet calculations.

14. Nils Andrén, *The Security and Defense of Sweden* (Stockholm: National Defense Research Institute, 1976), p. 79, and Nils Ørvik, "Scandinavian Military Doctrines," in *Comparative Defense Policy*, ed. Frank B. Horton III, Anthony C. Rogerson, and Edward L. Warner III (Baltimore: Johns Hopkins University Press, 1974), pp. 265-66.

15. Erickson, "The Northern Theater," p. 70.

16. Ørvik, "Scandinavian Military Doctrines," p. 266; see also Martin Peterson, "Stockholm: Nonaligned and Nervous," *Washington Quarterly* 3, no. 3 (Summer 1980): 189; Colonel Carl Bjoreman, "Upset in the Power Balance Can Heighten Demand for Swedish Base Areas," *Dagens Nyheter*, 15 April 1980; Carl Bildt, "The Cruise Missile: Can Sweden Remain Neutral?" *Svenska Dagbladet*, 31 January 1980; Ingemar Ingman, "Replace Aircraft with Missile Systems," *Dagens Nyheter*, 20 October 1980; and "Alva Myrdal to Military Authorities: How Shall We Manage to Assert Our Neutrality?," *Dagens Nyheter*, 25 April 1980.

17. For example, see the denial at a meeting of the Swedish Institute of Foreign Affairs reported in *Svenska Dagbladet*, 4 May 1977.

18. *Aviation Week and Space Technology*, 15 May 1978, p. 16. See also John Erickson, "The Northern Theater," pp. 70-72; and Nils Ørvik, "Scandinavian Military Doctrines," pp. 265-67.

19. Sven Hellman, "Use of International-Security Studies," in *Trends in Planning*, ed. C. G. Jennergren, Stephen Schwartz, and Olov Alvfeldt (Stockholm: National Defense Research Institute, 1977), pp. 95-96. See also Ingemar Dörfer, *System 37 Viggen* (Oslo: Scandinavian University Books, 1973), p. 21. This book is a classic study of Swedish defense decision making.

20. *Operations and Systems Analysis: A Special Issue in English in a Series of Surveys* (Stockholm: National Defense Research Institute, 1969), pp. 9-10; "FOA in a Nutshell" (Stockholm: National Defense Research Institute, 1978), pp. 1-2.

21. From "FOA in a Nutshell," pp. 2-3.

22. Carl Gustav Jennergren, "The Planning Division of FOA, Its Development and Role," in *Trends in Planning*, ed. Jennergren, Schwartz, and Alvfeldt, pp. 19-23.

23. "FOA in a Nutshell," p. 2.

24. There are an additional 1,100 people in the ordnance and supply administrations in the military districts. See Pierre Vinde and Gunnar Petri, *Swedish Government Administration*, 2nd rev. ed. (Stockholm: Swedish Institute, 1978), p. 36.

25. The terms *committees* and *commissions* are used interchangeably in Sweden. Where this chapter refers to Defense Committee, the reference is to the Standing Parliamentary Defense Committee.

26. Vinde and Petri, *Swedish Government Administration*, pp. 24-25.

27. IISS, *The Military Balance, 1979-1980*, p. 34.

28. *Labor Relations in Sweden* (Stockholm: Swedish Institute, 1977), passim.

29. *Swedish Industry* (Stockholm: Swedish Institute, 1977), p. 3.

30. Ibid.

31. *Labor Relations in Sweden*, p. 2.

32. Dörfer, *System 37 Viggen*, pp. 95-96.

33. Interview in the Swedish Ministry of Foreign Affairs, 27 June 1978.

34. Dörfer, "The Nordic Balance in Perspective: Sweden," p. 19.

35. *Swedish Digest,* no. 31 (15 August 1978), p. 2.

36. *The Swedish Budget, 1978/79,* p. 47.

37. Dörfer, "The Nordic Balance in Perspective: Sweden," p. 6.

38. *The Swedish Budget, 1978/79,* p. 87.

39. SSLP, *Swedish Security Policy and Total Defense,* p. 6.

40. *The Swedish Budget, 1978/79,* p. 87.

41. Fälldin, *Swedish Security Policy,* p. 7.

42. Brita Schwartz, "Programme Budgeting and/or Long-Range Planning," in *Trends in Planning,* ed. Jennergren, Schwartz, and Alvfeldt, p. 41.

43. SSLP, *The Defense Planning System: Planning and Planning Documents* (Stockholm: SSLP, 1970), pp. 13-14. For a précis of the perspective plans developed in 1969, see *Svenska Dagbladet,* 7 May 1979.

44. Hellman, "Use of International Security Studies," pp. 101-3; Schwartz, "Programme Budgeting and/or Long-Range Planning," p. 46.

45. SSLP, *The Defense Planning System,* pp. 17-19.

46. Ibid., p. 19. Some suggest that the assumptions of the present conscript system should be reexamined. See Dörfer, "Nordic Balance in Perspective: Sweden," pp. 16-18.

47. Figure from the Swedish parliament (Stockholm: Administrative Office of the Riksdag, 1978), p. 11.

48. See *Svenska Dagbladet,* 14 December 1977.

49. Dörfer, "Nordic Balance in Perspective: Sweden," p. 19.

50. See Kurt Tornquist, "Attitudes about International Affairs and Defense," *Psychological Defense* (Stockholm: Board of Psychological Defense, 1980), pp. 6-9. The percentage of the Swedish public who perceived a threat to world peace by the Soviets increased from 15 percent in 1973 to 36 percent in 1980. During the same period those who perceived a threat to world peace by the United States declined from 20 percent to 10 percent. Seventy-one percent of those surveyed in 1980 were uneasy over tension in the world, as compared with 51 percent in the fall of 1979. Fifty-three percent in 1980 were of the opinion that there is a large risk of major conflict into which Europe can be drawn, as opposed to 39 percent in the fall of 1979.

51. Brodin, *Surprise Attack Problems and Issues,* pp. 14-15.

52. IISS, *The Military Balance, 1979-1980,* p. 33.

53. Dörfer, "Nordic Balance in Perspective: Sweden," p. 19.

54. Ibid., p. 19; *The Swedish Army* (Nacka: Essett Herzogs, 1977), pp. 3, 8.

55. Dörfer, "Nordic Balance in Perspective: Sweden," p. 19; IISS, *Military Balance, 1978-1979,* p. 31.

56. International Institute for Strategic Studies, *Strategic Survey, 1977* (London: IISS, 1978), pp. 119-24.

57. William J. Taylor, Jr., "Issues in Military Unionization," in *Blue Collar Soldiers?,* ed. Alan Ned Sabrosky (Philadelphia: Foreign Policy Research Institute, 1977), p. 24. See also William J. Taylor, Jr., "Military Unions for the U.S.: The Irrelevance of the European Experience," *Naval War College Review,* Winter 1978, pp. 85-86.

58. Dörfer, *System 37 Viggen,* pp. 17-18.

59. Merton J. Peck and Frederick M. Scherer, *The Weapons Acquisition Process: An Economic Analysis* (Boston: Harvard Graduate School of Business Administration, 1962), p. 24; quoted in Dörfer, *System 37 Viggen,* pp. 17-18.

60. *Swedish Digest,* no. 30 (8 August 1978), p. 1.

61. Warren K. Christolon, "Swedish Air Force: The End of an Era?," *Armed Forces Journal,* September 1979, p. 44.

62. For different estimates, see *Afonbladet,* 30 May 1978 (the high figure) and *Dagens Nyheter,* 1 June 1978 (low figure).

63. See Nordbeck's statement in *Svenska Dagbladet,* 16 November 1978; see also the statement of the FMV project officer for the B3LA and A38 (Sven Hakborg) in *Svenska Dagbladet,* 7 November 1978, and the Statement of Air Force Commander in Chief Dick Stenberg in *Dagens Nyheter,* 5 December 1978. All make the point that both the SK38/A38 and B3LA are based on the fundamental principles for the light attack aircraft operational requirements approved by the supreme commander in the 1977 systems plans.

64. Ibid.

65. See Olaf Palme's statement in *Svenska Dagbladet,* 19 October 1977.

66. *Aftonbladet,* 30 May and 3 June 1978.

67. Annika Brickman, "Military Trade Unionism in Sweden," *Armed Forces and Society* 2, no. 4 (Summer 1976): 537.

68. Quoted in Adam Roberts, *Nations in Arms: The Theory and Practice of Territorial Defense* (London: Praeger, 1976), p. 95.

69. *Defense and Foreign Affairs Digest* 6, no. 10, p. 47.

70. Gen. Hans Neij, chief of the Air Force staff, quoted in *Svenska Dagbladet,* 17 February 1977.

71. Tore Gullstrand, head of SAAB-Scania's Aeronautical Division, quoted in *Svenska Dagbladet,* 24 April 1977.

72. Ibid.

73. Maj Wechselman, quoted in *Dagens Nyheter,* 3 May 1978.

74. *Svenska Dagbladet,* 19 September 1978.

75. *Expressen,* 9 September 1977.

76. *Dagens Nyheter,* 2 July 1978.

77. Ibid.

78. Summarized from *Dagens Nyheter,* 2 July 1978.

79. Ibid.

80. See *Svenska Dagbladet,* 21 November 1978.

81. *Dagens Nyheter,* 28 November 1978; *Svenska Dagbladet,* 29 November 1978.

82. Ibid.

83. *Svenska Dagbladet,* 18 December 1978.

84. *Dagens Nyheter,* 2 December 1978.

85. *Svenska Dagbladet,* 23 December 1978.

86. *Svenska Dagbladet,* 24 February 1979.

87. *Svenska Dagbladet,* 14 and 21 February and 8 May 1979.

88. Ibid.

89. *Svenska Dagbladet,* 20 March 1979.

90. *Dagens Nyheter,* 3 April 1979.

91. *Svenska Dagbladet,* 9 March 1979.

92. Dörfer, *System 37 Viggen,* p. 80. Some suggest that manpower and other "operational" costs have eroded the Swedish technostructure and that the "technical services" (air force and navy) are rapidly losing ground to a "professional army" that is anathema to most Swedes. See, for example, Johan Tunberger in *Svenska Dagbladet,* 11 May 1979.

93. *Dagens Nyheter,* 12 May 1979.

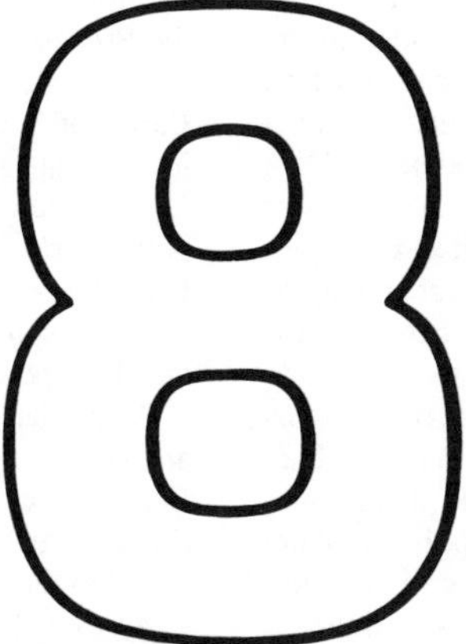

THE DEFENSE POLICY OF ROMANIA

David P. Burke

In November 1978 Nicolae Ceauşescu, president of Romania and secretary general of its Communist party, returned from a Moscow meeting of the Political Consultative Committee of the Warsaw Treaty Organization proclaiming and defending his refusal to raise his nation's defense budget in accordance with the wishes of his Soviet hosts. In the West this news drew brief attention to Romanian deviance within the Eastern European Communist alliance. For a while rumors circulated of menacing troop movements in the border regions of Romania's allies, but by the end of the year the affair was no longer news. Its main effect, in the United States at least, was to remind the attentive public that Romania was still (as the cliché puts it) "the maverick of the Soviet bloc."

By now Romania's deviance in foreign policy is familiar to students of international affairs. Among Western commentators, Romania is most frequently described as a country whose nearly Stalinist internal order has permitted it to practice unconventional policies in international politics and foreign trade without unduly tempting the Soviet Union to intervene, perhaps (as in Czechoslovakia) with the support and participation of other members of the Warsaw Pact.

This chapter contends that Romanian policy and the situation of Romania within the Eastern European political system are more complex and more deviant than generally supposed. Not only has the Romanian government managed to maximize its freedom of action by prudent maneuvering along the fine edge of Soviet tolerance, but it has also elaborated a defense policy unique in the Warsaw Pact, a policy whose content clearly indicates its authors' intent: to mobilize the entire Romanian people to ensure that any invasion would be met by prolonged resistance and guerrilla warfare. The purpose of this policy is clear: to add to the country's margin of safety by deterring attack by its most likely invaders, Romania's own allies.

This is not the prevailing view of Romanian defense policy among Western policy makers, and that alone makes a wider knowledge of Romanian defense desirable. However, broader policy considerations also argue for more attention to the Romanian case. For too long military planning in Washington and the Atlantic Alliance has begun by assessing something called the Warsaw Pact threat. It is typically arrived at simply by adding up the capabilities of the armed forces of the USSR and its European allies. When the results of this process are presented, they are often prefaced by a pro forma statement that one cannot really be sure what the governments of the non-

Soviet Warsaw Pact states would do in an East-West crisis, but that it is only prudent to assume that they would all fight at the side of the Soviet Union in any conflict between the USSR and NATO. This having been said, every tank, aircraft, and man added to the Polish, Hungarian, Romanian, and other Eastern European forces is taken as an additional unit of a threat which should be balanced or countered by a corresponding increase in the military capabilities of the Western Allies. This might have led to overreaction in the West, but in practice it has not. For various reasons Western governments have been unwilling to act fully on the basis of these threat assessments. Consequently, in the context of the arms race, the assumption of a monolithic Warsaw Pact threat has been simplistic, but not really dangerous.

Instead, the chief pitfall for Western policy makers stemming from the assumption of Warsaw Pact unity is the political blindness it encourages—a blindness to the diversity of interests and policies that exists among the countries of the pact. And that, especially in the midst of a European crisis, could be very dangerous indeed. To the extent that the leaders of the West see the Warsaw Pact as a monolith, and behave toward it as if it were one, they may actually drive its members together. Western statesmen may fail even to perceive opportunities based on differences within the pact that would permit them to reinforce deterrence or to cope with a crisis. This being so, the study of Romanian defense policy is particularly worthwhile as a consciousness-raising exercise. It is hard to look closely at Romania without increasing one's appreciation of Warsaw Pact diversity, for Romania's defense forces, like NATO's, are primarily a response to the Warsaw Pact threat, not a component of it.

International environment

Romania is a medium-sized country in the midst of a rapid and uneven emergence from poverty and underdevelopment. In 1977 its population was 21.7 million, approximately that of Canada or California. Among the non-Soviet members of the Warsaw Pact, only Poland—with some 31 million people—was larger. Romania's per capita gross national product of $2,372 was slightly higher than that of Hungary and a bit less than Poland's, but it was still quite low by Western European standards. In the same year the per capita GNPs of Greece and Ireland were some $500 more than Romania's, and Portugal's $572 less, but West Germany's was 3.4 times as great.[1]

Romania is a thorough-going Communist dictatorship. In the personalist regime of Nicolae Ceauşescu there is not a semblance of collective political leadership. Authoritarianism and the cult of the personality flourish as nowhere else in Eastern Europe. At the same time, the country is increasingly decentralizing economic decision making and continuing to practice the most unconventional foreign policy of any ally of the Soviets. Romania maintains correct relationships with Israel, Albania, and Chile; was the first Eastern European country to recognize West Germany; enjoys most-favored-nation status in trade with the United States; has cordial relations with China and particularly warm ones with North Korea. Ceauşescu tends these relations carefully, with particular attention to nonaligned and Third World countries and the non-European Communist states.

At the party level, Romania has particularly close and cooperative relations with the Spanish and Italian Eurocommunists, emphasizing the right of each national party to chart its own road to socialism. Since the Soviet and Cuban interventions in Africa, Ceauşescu has taken to denouncing the intensification of the "imperialist policy of force and diktat" and the "redivision of the spheres of influence and domination," while never directly mentioning the USSR.[2] Similarly, in the wake of the Soviet invasion of Afghanistan, the Romanians refrained from openly criticizing the USSR, but when the other allies of the Soviets were lining up to support the USSR against a U.N. General Assembly resolution calling for withdrawal from Afghanistan, Romania's delegation members eloquently absented themselves from the vote. However, despite all this, Romania remains a full member of the Warsaw Treaty Organization and of its economic counterpart, the Council of Mutual Economic Assistance (CMEA). In these organizations, as elsewhere, the keystone of Romanian foreign policy has been insistence on the independence, sovereignty, and equality of all states and on noninterference in their internal affairs. In practice this has meant the promotion of any relationship that promised to contribute to the economic development of Romania, to the security in power of its national Communist party under Ceauşescu's leadership, and to the increase of its government's ability to decide the country's fate for itself.

Three classes of threats exist which could affect the continuation of this independent policy and the security of the regime. Internal threats occasionally arise from Romanian dissidents and members of the country's ethnic minorities. Recently these have been met by a distinctively Romanian combination of open oppression and quietly facilitated emigration, though the major ethnic minorities (especially the Hungarians and Germans) do enjoy reduced but still extensive facilities for education and cultural expression in their own languages. These various internal threats have so far been fairly small scale—matters for the politicians and the secret police, not for the armed forces.

The external threats to Romania are two: involvement of the country in a NATO–Warsaw Pact war, and invasion by the Soviet Union and its other allies to end the country's deviant policies. The first threat is not ignored by the Romanians. They admit that an East-West war could happen, and that Romania and the rest of the world could be devastated by it. The vigorous efforts of the Romanian government in support of the Conference on Security and Cooperation in Europe, its position in support of mutual and balanced force reduction, and other efforts toward European arms control are in part directed at reducing this threat. So are at least part of its military efforts, particularly in air defense and civil defense against nuclear attack. However, Ceauşescu has repeatedly stated that the Romanian government does not believe that an East-West war is at all likely in today's circumstances.[3] It is not the focus of Romanian defense policy, though the worsening of international relations has drawn considerable Romanian comment since the Soviet invasion of Afghanistan. One danger remains: invasion of Romania by its Warsaw Pact allies. The main thesis of this chapter is that Romania's deviant defense policy can be understood only as a response to that threat.

National objectives, national strategy, and military doctrine

An understanding of today's Romanian defense policy requires a knowledge of its evolution and of the place of national security among the country's other objectives. Romania is an original signatory of the Warsaw Treaty. However, even at the birth of the alliance its attitude was slightly different from those of its allies. While other Eastern European delegates to the Warsaw Conference referred only to the Soviet liberation of their countries, Romania's Gheorghe Gheorghiu-Dej took a slightly less subservient and more independent line, speaking of the overthrow of the Fascist dictatorship by the Romanian people and their struggle "side by side with the Soviet army to crush the Nazi hordes."[4] Three years after the Warsaw Conference the Romanians persuaded the Soviets to withdraw their troops from the country, a diplomatic accomplishment unique among the states in which Soviet garrisons persisted after the postwar consolidation of Communist rule. This step set the scene for increasingly deviant policies in several fields.

Economic policy was the first area in which Romania parted company with the Soviets. From the date of its independence in 1877, Romania had been one of Europe's poorest countries, and for generations it stayed poor. On the eve of the Second World War its per capita income was between sixty and seventy dollars a year, a bit more than those of Yugoslavia and Bulgaria, and about on a par with that of Greece.[5] Nonetheless, the country had potential advantages. Though poverty stricken and overpopulated, Romania's agricultural areas were among the most fertile in Eastern Europe, and the country possessed the only major European oil fields outside the Soviet Union. To the Communist leadership of postwar Romania these assets were seen as a springboard for comprehensive (or as the Romanians prefer it, "many-sided") economic development. To the Soviets they represented Romanian natural advantages that ought to be emphasized in a nationally specialized and centrally planned economy embracing the Soviet Union and all of Eastern Europe. The vehicle for this policy would be the Council of Mutual Economic Assistance (CMEA).

However, the Romanian Communist leaders had no desire for their country to remain underdeveloped and dependent on agriculture and diminishing deposits of petroleum, or to have its economic future dictated by a Soviet-dominated CMEA. Instead, their economic policy has been one of forced development and diversification at the expense of both personal consumption and trade with their Communist neighbors. The result has been one of the highest long-term rates of economic growth in Europe, though it admittedly began from a very low base. The maintenance of this high growth rate is of key political importance in Romania, as the reward held out to the people for their sacrifices and their tolerance of a highly totalitarian regime has been the conversion of the country from underdevelopment to "medium-developed" status by the mid-1980s. To this and to the maximization of national independence, everything, except the security of the Communist regime, has been subordinated.

In its dealings with its CMEA partners, Romania has insisted from the beginning that economic relations be based on four principles: full equality of rights, respect for national independence and sovereignty, noninterference in internal affairs, and mutually advantageous cooperation. On April 27, 1964, the Romanian party's Central Committee gave these principles concrete effect and highlighted the country's growing assertiveness by flatly rejecting the CMEA's plans for supranational economic integration as "incompatible with national sovereignty."[6] After this veto, Romania's CMEA partners gradually accepted the four principles in the economic sphere. Meanwhile, Bucharest was elevating them to the status of guiding principles for all legitimate relations between fraternal Socialist states, including military relations. Thus, along with resistance to supranational economic planning and insistance on equality and independence in Party and state relations, the Romanians consistently resisted plans for greater military centralization and integration within the Warsaw Pact. This policy of military sovereignty became more active in late 1964, when Romania unilaterally reduced its period of compulsory military service from twenty-four to sixteen months. At about the same time, Western reporters were granted interviews with Romanian officials, who made pointed references to previous Romanian statements favoring the abolition of all military blocs and spoke of the need to find "new ways" of reaching decisions within the Warsaw alliance.[7]

In March 1965, at the height of this campaign, Gheorghiu-Dej died. He was succeeded as Party first secretary by his protégé, Nicolae Ceauşescu. Three months later Ceauşescu made a speech to a group of Romanian officers in which he pointedly ignored the Warsaw Pact and instead stressed Romanian national requirements for defense of the fatherland.[8] Almost simultaneously, a new Romanian constitution appeared; it contained language on declaration of war which stressed that such a decision would be a sovereign act of the Romanian government. At the same time the Romanians were reported to be dragging their heels regarding participation in the 1965 Warsaw Pact exercises and reducing their army from 240,000 to 200,000 troops.[9] (The linked policies of military frugality and avoidance of pact exercises have persisted to this day.)

The Soviet Union responded with its own proposals for reform of the Warsaw Pact. These proposals are believed to have stressed a tightening of Warsaw Pact structure and procedures, especially regarding coordination of foreign policy positions, and the maintenance or increase of Soviet domination of the pact's military command structure. The Romanians countered with a campaign of their own. On May 7, 1966, in an address on the anniversary of the founding of the Romanian Communist party (PCR), Ceauşescu denounced "military blocs . . . and the sending of troops to other countries" as an "anachronism incompatible with independence and national sovereignty."[10] He assailed the Soviets for meddling in Romanian affairs then and in the past, citing such delicate matters as the manipulation of national Communist parties by the Comintern, and the Nazi-Soviet pact under whose Secret Additional Protocol the USSR had detached and absorbed the Romanian provinces of Bessarabia and Northern Bukovina in 1940. The Romanians also leaked a proposal for Warsaw Pact reform (which they denied on May 18, thus drawing even more attention to it). The French Communist daily, *L'Humanité,* printed excerpts from the Romanian proposal. It called for prior consultation before the use of nuclear weapons and the rotation of the post of supreme commander of Warsaw Pact forces among officers of all member states. It also denounced the pro rata sharing of pact expenses among members, and declared that the presence of Soviet forces, except in East Germany, was no longer needed. If any country wanted such troops, the Romanians called for the host country to pay for them itself.[11]

Romanian-Soviet differences over defense and alliance policy continued unabated through the October 1966 Bucharest Conference of the Warsaw Pact and the CMEA and for the two years following it, though with varying intensity and often out of public view. The Warsaw Pact was not reformed to suit either Soviet or Romanian preferences. The essential difference between the two governments remained the degree of national or alliance (read Soviet) control over defense policy and national military forces. Only on these two issues was Romanian defense policy significantly deviant. On questions of doctrine, military organization, and the threat the forces were intended to meet, the Romanian military was essentially indistinguishable from the other Eastern European forces that had been recreated in the image of the Soviet army early in the Cold War. All that changed with the invasion of Czechoslovakia.

ROMANIA AND CZECHOSLOVAKIA, 1968

Intense political maneuvering within the Soviet Union and the pact preceded the decision of the USSR and five of its allies to invade Czechoslovakia.[12] However, Ceauşescu and his government had long opposed pact meetings devoted to the internal affairs of any Socialist country. As a result, they were excluded from the preinvasion pact conference in Dresden, and they were neither consulted on nor invited to the Czechoslovak-Soviet meetings at Čierna and Bratislava, at which concessions were extorted from the Dubček government. The Bratislava meeting also produced a statement pledging the signatories to "strengthen political and military cooperation in the Warsaw Treaty Organization."[13] In response to this, the Romanians protested that the problems of the pact should not be discussed at a meeting to which not all members had been invited.[14] Finally, both Tito and Ceauşescu traveled to Prague in a clear attempt to show solidarity with the Dubček government, Ceauşescu arriving to a warm welcome on 15 August. Five days later the invasion began.

Ceauşescu's response was immediate and courageous. He promptly denounced the invasion as a "flagrant violation of the sovereignty of a fraternal socialist country," and he warned that Romania would not permit a similar violation of its territory.[15] Unlike the Czechoslovaks, the Romanians prepared to fight. Significantly for later policy, Ceauşescu reactivated the Patriotic Guards. (This people's militia had been formed by the Communist party in World War II when the Soviets invaded and the country changed sides, but it had languished since the Party gained power.) For over a week there were rumors of the movement of Soviet troops to the Romanian border and of Soviet demands, as in the case of Czechoslovakia, for Warsaw Pact maneuvers on Romanian territory. The rumors were reportedly confirmed by American intelligence. In contrast to its behavior in the Czechoslovak case, the American government stated that it would view any Soviet intervention in Romania or Yugoslavia with utmost seriousness. As the crisis progressed Ceauşescu moderated his criticism, but he stood his ground.[16] The immediate threat of invasion passed, but Ceauşescu's response to it prefigured a radical reorientation of Romanian defense policy.

DEFENSE OF ROMANIA AS THE "CAUSE AND WORK OF THE ENTIRE PEOPLE"

In 1969, the tenth congress of the Romanian Communist party formalized and expanded the defense measures that had been taken in the wake of the invasion of Czechoslovakia. The congress declared that "the defense of the fatherland is the duty of every citizen; in today's conditions, in case of a war, not only the Army, but all citizens must be ready to fight in defense of the freedom, sovereignty and integrity of their homeland."[17] This concept was put forward at the congress as the basis of a doctrine of the "struggle of the entire people for the defense of the socialist fatherland," which was held to be a concept particularly suited to (and derived from) the stage of development through which Romania was passing, that of the construction of the "comprehensively developed socialist society."[18]

Since 1947 the armed forces had been directly subordinated to the Party. In 1969 the Council of Defense was established as the supreme organ for the direction not only of the armed forces, but also of the entire military power of the country. Ceauşescu, as secretary general of the Party, was made the president of the Council of Defense and supreme commander of the armed forces.[19] This step appears to have been taken not only to tighten and regularize Ceauşescu's direct control of the military, but also as a means for the coordination of basic defense organization and planning which, under the new concept, directly involved a growing circle of organizations and ministries outside the ministries of the armed forces[20] and interior.

The new defense concept was developed and given concrete form over the following three years, culminating in December 1972 with the approval by Romania's parliament, the Grand National Assembly, of the Law Regarding Organization of National Defense of the Socialist Republic of Romania.[21] Its preamble states:

> The Romanian people, dignified and courageous, have always defended with weapons in hand, their freedom and their right to independent life and development. Continuing these glorious traditions in today's conditions, when victory in an anti-imperialistic war of defense can be obtained only through general struggle of the whole people, all the country's citizens must be ready to fight, even at the cost of their lives, to safeguard the peaceful labor of the people and the sovereignty and integrity of the homeland. . . .
>
> The cause and work of the entire people, the defense of the homeland is the sacred duty of every citizen of the Socialist Republic of Romania, the supreme proof of love for their ancestral land, and of their devotion to socialism. Romanian citizens, men and women, without distinction of nationality, religion or occupation, have the right and the obligation to participate in one of the forms of military training established by law, to learn to handle the means of combat and to continuously improve their training to be ready at any time to fight with arms in hand for the defense of the socialist homeland.[22]

The first article of the law declares that the territory of Romania is "inalienable and indivisible," and it forbids the acceptance of any act of a foreign state, any occupation of national territory, or any general surrender that would affect the "sovereignty, independence or territorial integrity" of the country or weaken its defense capacity. It concludes by declaring any such act of acceptance to be null and void. The law goes on to state that the purpose of the organization of national defense is "to secure the conditions required for carrying out *defensive combat on the whole territory of the homeland*."[23] Any possibility of military operations outside Romania is pointedly ignored. Furthermore, not only must the Grand National Assembly (or the State Council between CNA sessions) act to mobilize or to declare war, but also a "state of war can be declared *only in case of an armed aggression against the Socialist Republic of Romania or against another state to which the Socialist Republic of Romania has obligations of mutual defense* assumed through international treaties, *if the situation were produced for which the obligation of a state of war is established*."[24] On this issue the Warsaw Treaty itself is rather vague. It covers only cases of "attack" on one or more of the pact members in Europe. In such cases it obligates each signatory to "come to the assistance" of the state or states attacked "with such means *as it deems necessary*," including armed force.[25] These words, borrowed directly from the North Atlantic Treaty, had been included in that document at the behest of the U.S. Congress specifically to limit the obligation to go to war.[26] Similarly, they do not strictly obligate Romania to declare war or to respond militarily in case of attack on a Warsaw Pact ally. Furthermore, the language of the Law regarding Organization of National Defense would seem to require the Romanian authorities to find that "armed *aggression*," not just an attack, had occurred, thus opening an enormous potential loophole for escaping the obligation to declare war.

The law provides for compulsory military service

for all citizens, women included, a provision unique in the pact and nearly unprecedented elsewhere.[27] While doing their compulsory service, men and women receive a small allowance (essentially just pocket money) from the military, and half their usual salary from their employer (one of several provisions of Romanian law that make it difficult to separate the country's military and civil budgets in terms that make sense in the West). Upon completion of their service, men and women pass to the reserve. However, this provision is complicated by the existence of several paramilitary organizations that, with the armed forces, are equally a part of the Romanian defense structure. Chief among these are the Patriotic Guards, the people's militia revitalized after the invasion of Czechoslovakia. The Law Regarding Organization of National Defense describes the Patriotic Guards as "armed combat units of working people from towns and villages, commissioned for the purpose of strengthening the defense capacity of the homeland."[28] The Patriotic Guards are Party rather than state organizations that function under their own staffs composed of active and reserve military officers and noncommissioned officers. Despite the subordination of the Patriotic Guards to the Party, membership is open to all Romanians, not just Party members. Their military equipment and weapons are provided by the ministries of national defense and interior and are normally stored at the workplaces where units of the Patriotic Guards have been formed.

The law provides for a Defense Council at each level of local government headed by the senior local official of the Party. The remaining membership of these councils consists of other officials of the Party and of the Union of Communist Youth, the local military commander, the chiefs of staff of the local Patriotic Guards and Antiaircraft Defense, and other key figures in organizations involved in the preparation and coordination of defense measures in each local government area. Coordinated by the defense councils, the Patriotic Guards operate directly under the leadership of local Party organs. However, in time of war, when military operations involving major units of the armed forces are being conducted in their areas, they are subordinated to the military units concerned.[29]

The role of the Patriotic Guards is very similar to that of the Territorial Defense Force in Yugoslavia. They are the main element responsible for the conduct of armed struggle against an invader by the masses of the population, supplementing the conventional, mobile units of the military services and enormously increasing the size of the forces opposing the enemy. They would be the main force in a prolonged resistance war, the chief practitioners of guerrilla warfare. Their numbers are large but almost universally ignored in Western estimates of the size of Romania's forces. In 1977, the first year it took notice of the Patriotic Guards, the International Institute for Strategic Studies (IISS) estimated the size of the Romanian conventional forces as 181,000, with 345,500 reserves. The institute credited the Patriotic Guards with a strength of 700,000 men and women, a figure confirmed to me as approximately correct by a senior Romanian officer.[30]

Reservists are encouraged to participate as members of the Patriotic Guards; those who do so receive priority for promotion without having to serve otherwise required additional time on active duty.[31] When mobilization is decreed, reservists in the guards remain with their Patriotic Guards units rather than joining the active forces,[32] a further indication of the centrality of the Patriotic Guards to the defense system. As a result, the IISS figures probably overstate the real size of available reserves and understate the proportion of the Patriotic Guards in the total defense forces.

Provision is made in the Law Regarding Organization of National Defense for universal military training of youth. For this purpose, the Union of Communist Youth, Romania's equivalent of the Soviet Komsomol, has been converted virtually into a paramilitary organization. Under the most recent revision of the law, training begins for all students, boys and girls, in the fifth grade and continues through the rest of school and at the workplace up to the age of twenty. The training is led by reserve military personnel using equipment and weapons provided by the Ministry of National Defense.[33]

In summary, the Law Regarding Organization of National Defense provides for a comprehensive structure to create and control the mobilization of a major portion of the Romanian population to respond in arms to any foreign incursion into the national territory. All citizens receive military training in school. Men and women continue this training during compulsory military service. When they return to civilian life, very large numbers of them continue to train in local units of the Patriotic Guards in the territory they are expected to defend in time of war.

Even before 1972, Romanian law provided that entry of any foreign military forces into the country without a public vote of the Grand National Assembly would be considered an invasion. Only in case of attack can a state of war be declared, and such a declaration can take place only by act of Romanian national authorities. If war begins, any act of surrender, even by the country's own authorities, is null and void. The 1972 law makes it very likely that an invasion would automatically result in the outbreak of a guerrilla war that not even the Romanian government could entirely call off. Furthermore, it repeats and strengthens the constitutional provisions that make declaration of war a Romanian national decision, while introducing new opportunities for the

Romanian government to count itself out of a Warsaw Pact military action that is not, in its view, a defensive war resulting from "aggression" against a pact member.

ELABORATION OF THE NEW DOCTRINE

Since the adoption of this new doctrine, the Romanian government and the party have sponsored an extensive body of writings in which the doctrine is explained, rationalized, elaborated, and legitimized by appeals to reason and to history. The basic argument presented in these works is that in today's world the nation is not withering away but is far from obsolete, and that the defense of the Romanian nation stands at the center of the country's military doctrine. Furthermore, national defense is an inseparable part of the construction of the new, socialist system: building and defending socialism are seen as two aspects of the same process. In one of his contributions to this literature, Col. Traian Grozea describes national defense as simply "a set of measures and actions designed to establish a climate of calm and security required by the development of society, against external aggressive factors which might try to violate our socialist nation's liberty and independence and, in case of aggression, whatever its form, to give our socialist state the capacity of repelling such aggression."[34] The emphasis on the participation of the broad masses of society in this task is explained as arising from the Romanian Communist party's concept of the role of the masses in history. The military is engaged both in the building and in the defense of the comprehensively developed socialist society. At the same time, the Romanian people as a whole participate in its defense.[35]

According to the doctrine, national defense is a process that begins in peacetime and continues in case of armed aggression. In peacetime all the nation's economic, political, ideological, administrative, and other elements are gathered together to prepare the nation's defense under the leadership of the Party and the government, and sole leadership by Romania's constitutional bodies continues in war. It is admitted that aggression against the Socialist countries obliges every Socialist state that has assumed international commitments of mutual defense to be ready to honor its pledges. However, the mobilization of defense efforts for situations "for which mutual assistance clauses have been established . . . can only be effected by the Party and by the Government bodies of the respective country."[36] In other words, for the Romanians alliance decisions on peace or war or alliance control of national military forces is impermissible. With that observation, alliance factors in Romanian defense policy are generally dismissed.

Furthermore, great emphasis is placed on the purely defensive character of Romanian doctrine: "to secure the free and independent development of socialist Romania . . . [and] the safeguarding of our own patrimony—*the national defense of this country has an exclusively defensive character.*"[37] In addition, "the laws of this country declare that defense cannot be limited or discontinued as a result of the actions of a foreign state or of any other circumstance."[38]

These defensive purposes require the existence of a material and technical base tailored to the requirements of the country. Thus, national defense is largely conditioned by the development of the country's industry. The goal is to maximize Romania's provision of its own means of defense, for "state sovereignty in matters of defense can be fully exercised only if one can also secure the necessary means of struggle by one's own effort."[39] Consequently, reliance on foreign sources of weapons is minimized in favor of domestic production, both of foreign weapons built under license and of original Romanian designs.

In case of war, national defense will be carried out "in the military, political, economic, diplomatic, and other fields in a multitude of forms and procedures." But, "in the case of an aggression carried out by an enemy who has a great superiority of military forces and weaponry, national defense will assume the form of a *general people's war.*" This form of war is "*an armed riposte given not only by the armed forces, but by the entire people rising up to fight the army of the invader.*"[40] One of the main purposes of this struggle would be to frustrate any attempt by the invader to gain a lightning victory. As Grozea put it:

> As regards *the duration of the confrontation,* it is to be expected that the aggressor will aim to obtain a decision and will try to achieve it in the shortest possible time.
>
> When the duration of the war is longer than the aggressor expected, a situation is created, whose consequences are unfavorable to him. The gradual reduction in the intensity of his blows, the lower rhythm of his actions and delays caused by the large-scale participation of the mass of the people in the defense struggle thwart the intentions of the aggressor of presenting the world a "*fait accompli.*"[41]

The identity of the invader in the war toward which all these efforts are directed is always left prudently unstated. However, the occasional, nearly pro forma, references to NATO and the West in Romanian expositions of defense policy usually have the flavor of a non sequitur. It is difficult to conceive of a scenario for a war, except an invasion by one or more of Romania's Warsaw Pact allies, that would fit the circumstances described by Traian Grozea in his discussion of nuclear weapons:

> It can be expected that a war launched by the aggressor against this country *would be waged, in the main, with classical armament.* This hypothesis has in view that the enemy, having a great superiority as to the number of troops

and technical means, would be certain of a balance of forces on the basis of which he could believe that he is capable of obtaining military victory without having to resort to nuclear weapons (if he has such weapons). Moreover, the fundamental political nature of the type of conflict to which the riposte is the war of the entire people is not very favourable to the deployment of the rocketry and nuclear weapon arsenal from the viewpoint of the propaganda aims pursued by a possible aggressor. . . . At the same time, it should be noted that the use of nuclear weapons would produce the danger of generalizing the war, of increasing its area, whereby the publicly declared aims of the aggressor at the start of hostilities, which as a rule refer to a local war, would lose all meaning.[42]

Col. Iulian Cernet divides wars of the entire people into three possible stages, not all of which must be experienced in any particular struggle. If the enemy is defeated in the first stage, for example, the remaining two would not occur. Cernet's first stage is the "generalized national effort made to repel enemy aggression or to thwart the enemy's principal aims."[43] The strategic aim in this stage is to repel the invader, but if that cannot be done, to inflict the largest possible losses on him, to stop his offensive, and to maintain control of one or more parts of the nation's territory. In this stage Cernet foresees defensive air operations as well as naval operations and amphibious landings. While this stage of the war is predominantly defensive, it would be marked by offensive strikes against the invader, linked to the armed struggle of the entire population in the areas penetrated by the enemy.[44]

The second phase Cernet describes as "the attrition (destruction) of the forces of the occupation and the creation of conditions leading to the liberation of the country's territory."[45] This is the stage of war of resistance to the occupier. In discussing it, encouragement is taken from the experience of occupied countries in the Second World War. Cernet specifically cites the case of Yugoslavia (this is fairly unusual in Romanian defense writings, though Yugoslav experience and contemporary defense policy provide an obvious parallel to Romanian doctrine). In Yugoslavia the Germans achieved a density of three servicemen per square kilometer of occupied territory and five soldiers per 100 inhabitants. In Romania that would require between 700,000 to 1,000,000 troops, which the Romanians believe would be difficult for an enemy to sustain over the long run, especially since a long-lasting armed resistance would be likely to create "external complications" that would force the enemy to shift some of its initially deployed forces out of Romania.[46] In words the Romanians are too prudent to use, the war might spread. Soviet relations with the rest of Eastern Europe, Yugoslavia, NATO, and China provide a wealth of opportunities for this to happen.

The third stage of a war of the entire people is the liberation of the "temporarily occupied territory" (a favorite Romanian phrase). It is difficult to say exactly what military operations would occur during this phase, although offensive actions would dominate whatever fighting occurred. As Cernet notes, "internal and external conditions" could shape a great diversity of situations.[47]

As for the duration of each phase, Cernet holds out the prospect of a long war. Again drawing on the experience of the Second World War, he notes that the first phase in countries attacked and occupied by the Germans lasted from one day (Denmark) to fifty (France). The second stage, the resistance in occupied Europe, lasted from four to five years. For examples of the third stage he points to, among others, the final offensive of the Yugoslav People's Army, the national insurrection in northern Italy in 1945, and the August 1944 insurrection in Romania.[48]

SUPPORTING LITERATURE AND PROPAGANDA

Since Romania's adoption of the doctrine of the war of the entire people, there has been an outpouring of literature and propaganda in support of it. A series of books has been published by the military publishing house, Editura Militară, in Bucharest. Some of these have been translated into foreign languages. Of those in English, *National Defense: The Romanian View* is particularly valuable and to a large extent typical of the entire body of literature.[49] Like many other works of its kind, it was produced by a collective of military writers (in this case ranging in rank from captain to major general) working under the auspices of the Studies and Research Center for Military History and Theory.

A striking characteristic of this literature is its appeal to Romanian history to support the new doctrine, and its failure to admit that Romania has learned anything useful from the Russians. A striking example is *Istoria gîndirii militare Romaneşti* [History of Romanian military thought], a collection edited by Corneliu Soare in 1974. It is an exhaustive, occasionally fascinating, survey of its subject from the Middle Ages to the adoption and implementation of the post-1968 doctrine (discreetly ignoring the period from 1941 to 1944 when Romania was a German ally). Throughout the 404-page book, forty foreigners are cited, from Napoleon to Morris Janowitz. Only four are Russians: a scholar who praised a Romanian lord in the sixteenth century; Ivan the Terrible, because the praise was addressed to him; and two others (Maj. Gen. V. Zemskov and a certain Dragomirov), one in a footnote and the other as a writer cited by the Romanian interwar theoretician Mircea Tomescu.[50] The book simply ignores the period of intense Soviet influence (to put it mildly) from the end of World War II to the late 1950s.

In this literature every aspect of Romanian history that involved arming broad masses of the people or popular support (direct or indirect) of military operations or of partisan or guerrilla warfare is summoned up as a precursor of the country's present defense policy. Even the depredations of Balkan outlaws from the sixteenth to the nineteenth centuries are interpreted in that light.[51] Specially favored subjects are the use of the masses of peasants and townspeople in the resistance to the Ottomans by the lords of the Romanian lands in the fourteenth through the sixteenth centuries,[52] the questions of arming the masses and of partisan warfare in the early years of Romanian independence in the nineteenth century,[53] and the participation of the people in the fighting against the Germans within Romania that followed the country's change of sides in World War II.[54] The last case is interpreted as a national anti-Fascist insurrection at the call of a government primarily influenced by the working people's parties led by the Communists. A special point is made of the discipline and national will shown by the "turning of weapons by the whole Romanian Army" against the German ally in 1944,[55] an intriguing emphasis in view of the fundamentally counter-ally character of today's Romanian defense policy.

The propaganda effort conducted by the Party within the armed forces has also been importantly affected by the demands of the new doctrine. For example, the illustrated monthly, *Viaţa Militară,* published by the High Political Council of the Ministry of National Defense, devotes regular attention to cooperation between the armed forces and the Patriotic Guards and to the participation of the army in the military training of youth.[56] Women in the armed forces are also regularly featured in the magazine.[57] A particularly striking contrast to Soviet practice is the Romanian effort to link the armed forces to the pre-Communist era. The armed forces are depicted as the same units, the same army, that has fought for the Romanian homeland since the foundation of the modern state in the nineteenth century, an army preserved, democratized, and perfected by the Romanian Communist party. Unit museums are full of pictures, artifacts, and battle flags from the First World War and before. Similarly, the Mărăşeşti Division, named for the great battle of 1917, was recently presented the Order of Defense of the Fatherland and commended by Ceauşescu on the hundredth anniversary of its formation.[58]

The defense decision-making process

Little is known about the details of defense decision making in Romania. Except to laud the genius of Ceauşescu and the leading role of the Romanian Communist party, little is published on the subject in Romania, and it has not been an important focus of foreign studies, either academic or governmental.

There is little doubt, however, that final decision-making power is firmly concentrated in the hands of Nicolae Ceauşescu, who combines in his person the roles of head of state, head of the Party, supreme commander of the armed forces, and chairman of the Defense Council. The last institution is the key organ for the formulation and coordination of defense policy at the national level. In addition to Ceauşescu, the membership of the Defense Council includes the prime minister and the ministers and heads of the central organs of the Party and the state directly involved in political, military, and economic preparation for war and the execution of defense measures.[59] In this its composition parallels that of its counterpart councils at the local level.

The scope of responsibility of the Defense Council is comprehensive. It is charged with establishing the basic conception of the defense system, approving the measures for organization of the armed forces and Patriotic Guards, and approving their mobilization and action plans. It also approves measures for troop deployment and organization of the national territory for defense and plans for economic mobilization, logistic support of local air defense, evacuation and dispersal of the population, as well as plans for "providing the material means necessary for the country's defense and security."[60] In an emergency it is the Defense Council that would determine whether to call upon the State Council or the Grand National Assembly (GNA) to declare a state of emergency, of full or partial mobilization, or of war. In case of surprise attack, the Defense Council would take "the necessary measures for repulsing [*sic*] the invader" and directly control national mobilization and combat actions.[61] The council is, in theory, responsible jointly to the Central Committee of the Party and the Grand National Assembly, or between GNA sessions, to the State Council. However, this subordination means little in practice. The GNA meets only briefly, and Ceauşescu heads the Defense Council, the State Council, and the Party's Central Committee. What he approves in one is almost sure to be approved in the others.

The actual process of defense decision making appears to involve the development of general defense policy under Ceauşescu's direction within the Defense Council, and the preparation of legislation and plans within the various ministries and Party organs whose heads sit on the council. These proposals are submitted to the Defense Council for revision and approval, with further approval (if needed) by the Central Committee, State Council, and Grand National Assembly. Approved proposals are referred back for execution to the national organs of the state and Party. All of this occurs with President Ceauşescu in the chair of each of the key decision-making bodies except the largely ornamental Grand National Assembly.

No doubt, bureaucratic politics play a role in this process as in all complex governmental organizations, but the extent will remain difficult to determine without access to players or former players in the system. Some of the necessary data should be available from high-level defectors such as Maj. Gen. Pacepa, who left in 1978, but for the time being access to such persons is difficult and the results of their interrogation are locked in the files of Western intelligence agencies.

One factor, however, is clear: the important influence of Ceauşescu's personality on the process. It seems to account for some of the more peculiar aspects of Romanian defense policy. Ceauşescu is a Romanian nationalist whose public pronouncements hint strongly that he sees himself as a modern Communist version of Romania's warrior princes—Michael the Brave, Stephen the Great, and Vlad the Impaler are examples—who figure so importantly in the flood of nationalist historical writings published since Ceauşescu came to power. He admires the military for their discipline in a country whose people are not particularly famed for that quality. In the early to middle 1970s, when Ceauşescu was conducting an emotional campaign against indiscipline and managerial sloppiness in the civilian economy, these aspects of his personality were reflected in his repeated references to the army as a model of national dedication and discipline to be emulated by civilian enterprises. The high point of this era was the startling decision to hand over such enterprises as the national airline, TAROM, to the military as part of the Ministry of National Defense. This resulted in the world's only airline to be headed by a commander to boast a deputy commander for sales. In 1977, when Ceauşescu's outrage had cooled and TAROM's discipline was presumably adequate, the enterprise was returned to civilian control, taking many of its formerly military staff with it.[62]

Whatever the influences of bureaucratic politics and personality on Romanian defense policy, it is clearly formulated within very close restraints. The first of these is the limit of Soviet tolerance of Romanian policy deviance. Romanian sensitivity to this constraint is clear, not only in the broad outlines but also in the details of policy. Romanian production of non-Soviet weapons is an example. Long after the Romanian navy adopted the Chinese Hu Chwan hydrofoils and Shanghai motor gunboats as the first line of their coastal fleet, and the air force had adopted the French Alouette 3 as its standard light armed helicopter, photographs of them were pointedly excluded from Romanian military publications. Whenever helicopters or naval vessels were shown, they were the older Soviet models adopted or ordered before 1968. Then, gradually, the French and Chinese systems appeared, often in the background and always in photographs that featured equipment of Soviet design. Finally, after the passage of time, the non-Soviet systems moved to the foreground of photographs without accompanying Soviet weapons. At no time in this process was the country of design of the non-Soviet systems even suggested.

In the case of the IAR-93/Orao jet fighter-bomber, a Romanian-Yugoslav joint project, this sensitivity has again been apparent. Though this supersonic aircraft represents a technological breakthrough for Romania of the sort that would normally be highly publicized, for four years all information released on it came from Yugoslavia, where the aircraft was first publicly displayed in April 1975.[63] No photographs of Romanian IAR-93s appeared until 1979, when three of them took part in a formation fly-past at the August 23 national day parade in Bucharest. The same parade was used for the public unveiling of a domestically produced tank, based on the Soviet T-54/T-55 series, which had also been under development for years.[64]

The chief constraint on Romanian defense policy of domestic origin is budgetary. There is no doubt that, after maintenance of national independence and the Communist regime, comprehensive economic development is the overriding priority of the Romanian government. This limits Romanian defense expenditures, consistently the lowest in the Warsaw Pact as a percentage of GNP.[65] The 1978 crisis of the defense budget both underlines this fact and illustrates the interrelationship of defense budget constraints and Soviet tolerance of Romanian policy.

On November 22 and 23, 1978, the Political Consultative Committee (PCC) of the Warsaw Treaty Organization met in Moscow to discuss and coordinate defense and foreign policy between the member states. A major purpose of the meeting was to secure agreement on a general increase in defense expenditures, which was being urged by the Soviet Union. The meeting ended with Nicolae Ceauşescu and the Romanian delegation returning home after a public break with their allies on the issue, which the Romanians undoubtedly had known for some time would be on the PCC agenda.

That knowledge provides a key to Romanian activities both before and after the conference that indicate careful orchestration to maximize the chance that Romania could defy the Soviets on the budget issue and escape unscathed. The first event to note in that connection was Romania's conduct of extensive, and extensively publicized, military exercises in the first week of September in the Braila-Galati area in the northeast part of the country, near the Soviet border. The exercises were attended by Ceauşescu and a high-level group of government, Party, and security officials. A postexercise broadcast on Romanian radio described the maneuvers as "a verification of the training of our armed forces, . . . a verification of their capability to organize and lead complex combat actions in cooperation with patriotic guards and other formations from the national system of civil defense, in the spirit of the requirements of our party's military doctrine." The broadcast further described the determination of the armed forces "to fulfill the honorable mission to defend, together with all the people, freedom, national independence and sovereignty and our socialist fatherland's integrity."[66]

Two months later the Grand National Assembly met. The session began on November 3 with a presentation of the national Socioeconomic Plan for 1979 by Ilie Verdeţ, the first deputy prime minister and chairman of the State Planning Committee. Press accounts of the presentation stressed economic development and rising personal income and living standards; defense expenditure was not mentioned. Significantly, Verdeţ ended his report by stressing that real incomes of the population would increase 6.4 percent in the following year, pensions and children's allowances would be increased, the average "consumption fund" per family would rise from 9,200 to 9,700 lei, and the number of apartments built would total 236,000–76,000 over the number anticipated in the current five-year plan. The GNA approved the plan and budget on the same day.[67]

In the short time intervening before the PCC session, Ceauşescu paid a formal visit, apparently hastily arranged, to Yugoslavia, where he conferred at length with President Tito. Shortly after, he left for Moscow. His return and the policy break with the country's allies received extensive coverage in the Romanian media. This reached its peak with the coverage of three meetings, at which Ceauşescu spoke to representatives of the working class; of the peasantry, intelligentsia, and youth; and of the armed forces and Ministry of Interior. At all of these he stressed the untruth of any rumors that secret agreements had been reached in Moscow or that anyone except the legally constituted Romanian authorities would or could commit the Romanian armed forces to action. His speeches stressed the importance of disarmament and the responsibility of the Socialist states, as well as NATO, to take unilateral initiatives to reduce the levels of arms in Europe. Ceauşescu emphasized that his government was convinced that there was no imminent danger of war, and that under those circumstances "it would be a big mistake to increase military expenditures." To the representatives of the workers he emphasized that increased military expenditures would make impossible achievement of the recently approved program "for raising the people's material and cultural standard of living."[68]

At the meeting with the military and Ministry of Interior representatives two days later, Ceauşescu gave this point a different twist, flatly stating that "we must give a primacy of place to the fulfillment of the programme of socio-economic development."[69] But he went on to say that this was actually a military advantage:

> . . . any defensive war will be the war of the whole people and to resist any imperialist aggression the people will have to fight arms in hand, if necessary, and to destroy any aggressor by all means.
>
> That is why, the bigger our successes are in developing the productive forces, in the flourishing of science, culture and education, in raising the material welfare of the whole people . . . the more firmly will the people fight to defend these gains, and the more easily will it defeat anyone encroaching upon our socialist gains, the homeland's independence.[70]

When it came to the question of Warsaw Pact control of the Romanian armed forces, Ceauşescu's presentation to the military was more explicit and more emotional than it had been in the two preceeding meetings with civilians. Referring to an earlier conference with the military leadership, he recalled that he had said:

> . . . never would the Romanian army participate in a war of aggression against anybody. It will only wage a war of defense against an imperialist aggression and it will do its duties to the allies provided that the latter are subject to an imperialist aggression. Consequently, by preparing ourselves for a war of defense, against aggression, it is only normal that our army be directly tied—by its whole activity, by everything undertaken, by its military and political training—to our people, to our people only, that it be placed under the command of the Party and State bodies of Socialist Romania and only under their command! Never will we admit that any Romanian unit or soldier take order [*sic*] from outside! It is only from within, from within the country that they shall be given the order to fight! This also holds true in case some of our neighbours will be attacked and we shall have to come to their help. Those units to be designated for helping them will solely act upon orders from our Party and State bodies; it is only our people that will be in a position to commit them to fighting and solely upon orders from the Romanian Supreme Commander![71]

Whatever the Soviets had proposed at the PCC meeting regarding the wartime control of the forces of the Warsaw Pact alliance (or whatever rumors in Romania claimed the Soviets had demanded), Ceauşescu was clearly rejecting it. That this outburst took place on television before a uniformed military audience can only have added to its force.

Ceauşescu's last public shot in this engagement with the USSR was included in a major prime-time address on national radio and television on December 1, 1978, the sixtieth anniversary of the unification of Transylvania with the rest of Romania at the end of the First World War. This time, however, his passion was muted and the references to the budget dispute were embodied in a lengthy discussion of defense policy near the end of a very long speech.[72] From that point on the dispute was allowed to cool. In any event, the Soviets did not act against Romania, and the budget was not raised.

Ceauşescu had taken a genuine risk to keep defense spending within its traditional budgetary limits. But he had also been careful to link his defiance of the Soviets to the issue of national control of the Romanian armed forces and to his repeated assertions that the Romanian forces would resist *any* aggressor. It is hard to see this as anything but an attempt to deter a precipitate Soviet action against Romania. In a sense, the Soviets were also made to pay a political price for carrying the issue of defense spending to the point that the Romanians had to resist openly. In his speech to the military representatives on his return from Moscow, Ceauşescu went further on two issues than he had ever gone in public before, first by asserting that Romanian forces would remain under exclusively national, not Soviet, command even in a Warsaw Pact war with the West, and then by announcing that Romania would aid other Socialist states against aggression "no matter who the aggressor is" (since 1968 a Romanian code-phrase referring to a Soviet or Warsaw Pact invasion).[73]

One further constraint is also apparent in this incident: the force of public and elite opinion. The care exercised by Ceauşescu and the country's controlled media to explain to the people and to the military elite exactly what had and had not been agreed to in Moscow is impressive, as were he appeals made to the interests of the workers (improvement of living standards) and to the military (improved defense capability). Ceauşescu's explanation to the military of how low defense expenditures actually increase the country's defense capacity through the doctrine of war of the entire people is especially inventive.

Recurring issues: defense policy outputs

Romanian doctrine stresses the unity of the people and the armed forces. This signifies more than just the concept of the armed forces as the nation in arms which is common in countries, from France to China, whose forces are constructed, like Romania's, on the basis of universal military service. In Romania's case the distinction between the military and civilian sectors of society is further clouded by the doctrine of people's war, the widespread involvement of the armed forces in civilian production, and the rotation of cadres which is a distinctive feature of the Ceauşescu regime.

In Romania the term *military profession* would be taken as a reference to the permanent cadres of the forces of the Ministry of National Defense, and possibly of the Ministry of the Interior. In peacetime these cadres comprise two-thirds of air force and navy strength, and 60 percent of the ground forces.

In the absence of studies of public attitudes toward the military in Romania, such as those of Jerzy Wiatr in Poland,[74] one must fall back on indirect evidence. The internal propaganda media of the armed forces seek to inculcate the idea that to serve the fatherland militarily is to carry out an honorable duty and to share in a glorious tradition. However, there is no official support for the idea that the professional military is a special caste in any way superior to the citizenry as a whole. All those in the defense forces—professionals, conscripts, reservists, and members of the Patriotic Guards—are depicted as participating in the common task of national defense. If any group is singled out for special respect, it is those on active duty. The annual admission of the new class of conscripts and their swearing of the military oath is given widespread and respectful coverage in the military press. But this patriotic ceremony is a rite of passage experienced by the vast majority of Romanian men (and now women) in every generation since the country's independence. It honors all those who have formally accepted the duty of defense of the homeland, not just those who comprise the professional military cadre. From the beginning of their active-duty training, all Romanians are seen as defenders of their country, whether in the active forces, in the "people's defense formations," or as reservists subject to call to active service. The professionals are not singled out, and they are not the object of any special deference by the general public.

The legal obligation of military service is performed in various ways. Conscripts serve either full- or part-time service of sixteen months (two years in the navy) or short-term service of nine months. The short term can be served by students who have passed examinations for admission to institutions of higher education. Their service is completed before they begin their first year of studies. Other students in university-level institutions who have performed military training during their studies serve only two months on active duty.[75] After their compulsory military service, all Romanians are considered members of the reserve. Reserve military units in the American sense apparently do not exist in Romania. Instead, individual male reservists between the ages of twenty and forty-five are subject to recall for periods of training of up to three-months duration whenever necessary. From forty-five to fifty, they may be called up for only one period of at most three months. Reserve noncommissioned and commissioned officers may be called up for as much as two to three months every year or at longer intervals, or they may participate in a nonactive-duty training program of fifty-six hours distributed over a four-and-a-half-month period. Women reservists are legally subject to service from ages eighteen to forty-five, though it is unclear under what conditions and for what periods they would actually be called up. Finally, persons in the Patriotic Guards and other people's defense formations can meet their military obligations through regular participation in their unit training programs.[76]

The blurring of the distinction between military

and civil society that is inherent in the doctrine of defense as the "cause and work of the entire people" is increased by the extensive participation of the armed forces in civil production. Military units assist in the harvest and work widely in construction and in other industries. For these activities the troops draw extra pay from the civilian enterprises that contract with the Ministry of National Defense for the use of military labor. These activities necessarily reduce the amount of military training that can be conducted during the period of compulsory military service. This distresses some senior officers, but civil labor is by now a well-established feature of Romanian military life.[77] The absorption of entire industries by the armed forces, as typified by the experience of TAROM, now seems to be a thing of the past. However, military personnel as individuals can still be found in civilian functions where specialized skills are in short supply. An example is the Romanian merchant marine, where rapid expansion has resulted in the assignment of professional naval officers to duty aboard merchant vessels.

Frequent and widespread transfer of senior personnel in politically sensitive positions is a feature of Ceauşescu's governing style. This rotation of cadres has the salutary effect of reminding incumbents that their careers are in the hands of their leader. It also inhibits the development of potential Ceauşescu rivals backed by well-established bureaucratic and regional constituencies. Senior military officers are not immune to this rotation, especially when they reach ministerial or subministerial rank or the top political officers' positions. Rotation of top military cadres often involves a change from military to civilian status, as in the recent appointment of the chief political officer of the armed forces to be head of the Bucharest municipal government.

WEAPONS ACQUISITION

Whenever practical, Romania produces its own weapons. Increasingly these are of non-Soviet design. Romanian industry now produces the majority of weapons types in the hands of its forces, though for the most part national production is concentrated in comparatively low-technology fields. This, however, is changing. The ground forces are equipped with both the Soviet BTR-50 and BTR-60 armored personnel carriers and the newer Romanian TAB-70 and TAB-72 (both of which are based on the BTR-60 design). The TAB-70 and 72 are sophisticated vehicles and apparently not just copies of their Soviet precursors. Their hull contours are slightly different, and the Romanians claim they are faster. Modern, amphibious fighting vehicles, their eight-wheel design permits high-speed movement on roads and excellent off-road performance. In the water they rely on an advanced hydrojet propulsion system. The next obvious step beyond these armored fighting vehicles is an indigenous Romanian tank. As mentioned above, it appeared publicly in 1979. Like the TAB-70 and TAB-72, it turned out to be a variation on a Soviet design, the T-54/T-55 series, already in Romanian service. The Romanian tank, however, is easily distinguished from its Soviet forebear by the armored skirting protecting its treads and differences in details of its external equipment.[78]

The Romanian navy has not procured a Soviet vessel since 1968. The two main equipment programs for the navy since that time have both involved domestic production of vessels of Chinese design, the Shanghai-class motor gunboat and the Hu Chwan-class hydrofoil motor torpedo boat. The hydrofoil is capable of a maximum speed of fifty knots, and both types are equipped with different sets of weapons from the same vessels in Chinese service. As the navy is essentially a coastal force, these small, high-speed vessels comprise the first line of the country's maritime defense.

The air force more than the other Romanian services relies on high-technology, and hence foreign-built, weapons. While it has the largest proportion of Soviet weapons systems in its inventory, much of the effort to switch to domestic production of military equipment is centered on the air force. Except for President Ceauşescu's personal Boeing 707 and the Czechoslovak L-29 trainer, all jet aircraft currently in Romanian squadrons are Soviet designed and built. Most are obsolete or obsolescent and will have to be replaced with new aircraft soon if the air force is to remain at all credible as a fighting force. The only likely source of a modern all-weather interceptor is the Soviet Union, but, as noted above, the Romanians are cooperating with the Yugoslavs to develop a new fighter-ground attack aircraft called the Orao in Yugoslavia and the IAR-93 in Romania. This project is particularly interesting, as it involves a remarkable transfer of Western defense technology to a Warsaw Pact country. The aircraft is powered by two Romanian-built Rolls Royce Viper jet engines, and production versions of the fighter will be equipped with an afterburner specifically designed for it by Rolls Royce. Maximum speed of the afterburner-equipped aircraft at altitude is estimated at Mach 1.65 (946 knots, or 1,089 miles per hour). The IAR-93 is primarily intended for ground and naval support, but with the afterburning Viper engine its high-speed, rapid rate of climb (1 minute, 36 seconds to reach 36,000 feet), and service ceiling (over 52,000 feet) should permit it to assume a secondary clear-weather intercept mission. The aircraft is equipped with landing gear of French design and with electronics, auxiliary equipment, and instruments from several countries of Western Europe.[79]

The most numerous military helicopter in Romanian service is the French Alouette 3, built in Romania by ICA-Brasov as the IAR-316. It is used in the utility, observation, and light armed-attack roles. Of the 130 built in Romania by 1979, 45 were in military service. In addition to the Alouette 3, Romania has recently built large numbers of domestically designed trainers and light agricultural aircraft, as well as over 300 British-designed Britten Norman Islander twin-engine light transports. In 1978 and 1979 the Romanians acquired licenses to build two versions of the British Aerospace BAe 111 jet transport aircraft and its Rolls Royce Spey turbofan engines for the domestic and export markets.[80]

Since World War I Romania has had a tradition of aircraft design and production whose strength is out of all proportion to the country's wealth and general level of technology. This tradition was interrupted by the Soviets in the postwar years. The redevelopment of the industry has had a high priority in the Ceauşescu period. The military payoff is now in sight. When the IAR-93 and BAe 111 projects and their engines are added to Romania's current production of the Alouette 3 and domestic light and training aircraft, the country will have the most advanced and diversified aircraft industry in Eastern Europe. It will surpass Poland and Czechoslovakia, whose industries were favored by licensed production of first-line Soviet aircraft in the 1950s when Romania's was suppressed. Within a few years time, the Romanian aircraft industry should be able to supply all the country's needs for first-line military aircraft, except for all-weather interceptors and medium and heavy helicopters. A license to produce the latter should be relatively easy to acquire in Western Europe.

FORCE POSTURE

The various components of the Romanian defense system are tailored specifically to apply the doctrine adopted after the invasion of Czechoslovakia. The army (in Romanian usage, *army* means all the armed forces of the Ministry of Defense) today remains a conventional force equipped with "classical" weapons. With a peacetime strength of 180,500, it is the third largest non-Soviet force in the Warsaw Pact, ranking after those of Poland and Czechoslovakia.[81] Besides its defense functions, it continues to promote the foreign policy of the Party and state by "its relations of friendship and collaboration with other armies." These relations are explicitly *not* limited to the Warsaw Pact. Indeed, the Romanian army is described as developing "relations of friendship and cooperation with the armies of all the socialist states, with those of the countries engaged on the path of a progressive, independent policy, and with the armies of other states."[82] In the struggle to defend the country against aggression, the army provides the main mobile striking force, "since it is not directly linked to certain territorial areas," as the Patriotic Guards would be.[83] Though the army comprises the land forces, the Territorial Air Defense Forces, the air force, and the navy, the geographical and military conditions of Romania are described, with other factors, as giving the greatest weight and principal role to the land forces.

The total strength of the land forces is 140,000, of whom some 95,000 are conscripts. Its main units are two armored divisions, eight motorized rifle divisions, and two mountain brigades with supporting artillery, surface-to-surface missile, antitank, and antiaircraft organizations.[84]

Within the land forces the infantry has seen the greatest recent development. Its reequipment has stressed antitank weapons and transport and combat vehicles, all built in Romania. Its training (and that of the rest of the army) for operations in a people's war has been modified to stress operations against armor and low-flying aircraft (especially helicopters), demolition operations, and the use of improvised weapons. Today's training also stresses independent operations by small groups of troops, operations against enemy forces superior in numbers, and infantry combat operations by other arms (artillery, engineers, etc.).[85]

The Romanian air force, with 437 combat aircraft, also ranks third in size in Eastern Europe, though only 50 more aircraft would cause it to exceed the combat strength of the air force of France or West Germany.[86] In 1978 the air force was separated from the Territorial Air Defense and established as a separate service with its own distinctive uniform, essentially on the same organizational level as the navy. This approximates the organization of military aviation that existed before the Romanian forces were restructured on the Soviet model in the late 1940s. For technical reasons, the air defense forces of the Warsaw Pact countries are the most closely linked part of the alliance's military forces in peacetime. They are in constant operational communication with the Soviets. The change in the status of the air force left only the Romanian radar warning net and antiaircraft missiles and artillery under the command of the Territorial Air Defense and thus in close daily contact with the Soviets and the other pact forces. In Romania, air defense interceptor aircraft still operate under control of Territorial Air Defense during operations, but their chain of command, like that of all other military aviation, now runs to an air force headquarters, which answers only to national authorities.

The bulk of Romania's aging air force is devoted to air defense and close air support, though it is tasked and equipped to conduct all air operations except strategic bombing. Under the new defense doctrine its fighter-bomber squadrons, in addition to their usual broad range of ground and naval support missions, are trained and tasked to support the Patriotic Guards and resistance formations.[87] In the next several years these squadrons should be reequipped with the previously described IAR-93 supersonic fighter-bomber.

The navy's main task is to defend Romania's 153 miles of seacoast from "possible aggression by sea."[88] As the Black Sea is virtually a Soviet lake, the implications of this mission seem clear. The navy's main sea-going forces are its mine warfare craft and its high-speed gunboats and hydrofoils. The navy is also responsible for riverine operations on the Danube. With 10,500 personnel, it is smaller than the navies of Poland and East Germany, and slightly larger than the navy of Bulgaria.[89]

In Romania the Frontier Guards are part of the Ministry of Defense rather than Interior, as is the case in the other Eastern European countries and the USSR. Concern with the threat posed by the country's neighbors is shown in the Frontier Guards mission of "localizing and resolutely coping with possible frontier provocations, incidents or violations, and with the first surprise strikes of an aggressor." The Frontier Guards work in close cooperation with the people's defense formations in the border areas. This cooperation is described as "organized and conducted permanently, both in peace and in war."[90]

The Ministry of the Interior is responsible for Romania's internal security. In addition to the open and secret police elements typical of a Communist dictatorship, it also has security troops that can take direct part in combat operations. The ministry is also the country's chief intelligence and counterintelligence organ, charged with "uncovering in due time the existence of political, economic, ideological, military and other actions which can be indicative of preparations for an aggression on our state and its objectives," as well as "thwarting the actions started by foreign intelligence organizations."[91]

The 700,000 Patriotic Guards are organized as territorial defense forces and are equipped with light weapons. Their basic organization parallels that of conventional ground forces: from platoon to battalion with individual rifle, mortar, obstacle and demolition, antitank grenade, scouting, and other units. In theory, at least, the Patriotic Guards are volunteers. They wear a distinctive khaki fatigue uniform and beret without visible insignia of rank. In addition to training in the use of explosives and their own weapons, they are also trained to capture and use enemy weapons. There is permanent and close cooperation between the staffs of the Patriotic Guards and those of the army and the Ministry of the Interior.[92] Ceauşescu himself has stressed the importance of continuing cooperation between the conventional forces and the Patriotic Guards, admonishing the army that it is

> necessary that throughout organizing the military training account should be taken of the existence of these people's formations, that broad collaboration should be established with them, as well as joint actions even during training and exercising, that there should be close cooperation between the army and these fighting units.[93]

The Patriotic Guards are expected to conduct local operations, both offensive and defensive, but defense is given priority. Their main task is to defend their home localities and workplaces and the approaches to them. Not even in wartime would they be full-time forces. When they are not on operations they are expected to continue their normal work, and even to increase output as required by defense needs. Occasionally they might be sent to other areas, but, as mentioned above, the army remains the main mobile force available for defense and strike operations. When operating within the action perimeter of a major army unit, and thus under its command, Patriotic Guards would usually work jointly with reconnaissance and security units (where their local knowledge would be very useful) in defense of local objectives, and on the flanks or in secondary sectors of the major unit's area of responsibility.[94] Patriotic Guards units outside the area of operations of major conventional units remain subordinate to their own county or municipal staffs and carry out operations under their direction or that of the local Defense Council. In the "temporarily occupied" territory, they would form the backbone of the resistance forces.

Local Air Defense is also organized on a "volunteer" basis in Romania, and its functions are, by and large, similar to those of comparable organizations in the Soviet Union and the rest of Eastern Europe. However, under the doctrine of the war of the entire people, Local Air Defense units are also responsible for cooperation with the army and Patriotic Guards and for participation in combat actions. In such cases their main roles would be combat security, logistics, and medical support. They would also perform various wartime tasks for the protection of material goods by sheltering and other means. In territory occupied by the enemy, this task would continue. Operating underground, they are expected to use all means to protect valuable property.[95]

ARMS CONTROL

Especially since the invasion of Czechoslovakia, Romania has been a vigorous and consistent advocate of arms control, and especially of arms reduction in Europe. For a country whose main security threats are invasion by its neighbors and almost incidental involvement in an East-West nuclear war, this policy seems entirely logical. Romania has coupled its advocacy of arms reduction with pronouncements in favor of abolition of both NATO and the Warsaw Pact, and, failing that, of their military command structures. In their dealings with their Warsaw Pact allies, Romanian officials regularly and publicly note that even if the pact were abolished, they could still rely on Romanian support under their bilateral defense treaties, the implication clearly being that the pact and its military command are superfluous.

As long as the pact exists, however, Romania seems determined to play its full part in the alliance's command structure, though it prohibits pact exercises on its soil if they involve more than command staffs and communications personnel. Foreign troop units are forbidden to enter Romania, and Romania will not send its troops abroad for exercises. Participation in Warsaw Pact command and policy-making organs, however, does play an important role for Romania. It prevents its allies from charging that it has abandoned the pact (one of the main Soviet justifications for the 1956 invasion of Hungary); it provides a useful source of intelligence on pact forces, plans, and capabilities; and it permits Romania to participate in foreign and defense policy coordination within the alliance and thus possibly to influence decisions that may affect its interests profoundly. Despite these advantages, the Romanian government would apparently consider the abolition of the Warsaw Treaty Organization to be a net gain for its security, a step toward the demilitarization of Europe, and thus a complement to its arms control goals.

Romanian arms control policy and its several themes were summarized by Ceauşescu in his New Year's Eve message at the end of 1979:

> The most ardent imperative of our time, the vital desideratum of all peoples, is the achievement of disarmament, nuclear disarmament in the first place. While ensuring a balance which should not endanger the security of any side, one must do everything for the systematic reduction of military expenditure, of military effectiveness and armaments, the withdrawal of foreign troops within their national borders, the dismantling of military bases and dissolution of military blocs, and the building of a world without weapons and without wars. The huge funds that are spent today on arming should be directed only towards ensuring the people's economic and social progress, toward the continual improvement of life on our planet.[96]

None of these words conflicts directly with Soviet policy, so Moscow can hardly object to them. But if they were converted even partially into fact, the threats to Romania from involvement in an East-West war and from an invasion by its allies would both be reduced.

Concluding comments

It remains to draw some conclusions from Romanian defense policy. Clearly, one should not take everything the Romanians say about it at face value. Like most part-time volunteer military organizations, the Patriotic Guards are probably of very uneven quality. It is also possible that the Romanian people would participate in an all-people's war with less widespread dedication now than in 1968, when the new defense policy was conceived. Since then, the regime has clamped stifling restrictions on artistic and literary expression, and the disaffection of many intellectuals has been widely reported. Unrest among the workers was underlined by the 1977 strike by miners in the Jiu Valley. The consumer still suffers from inflation and massive diversion of funds to industrial investment. Freedom of political action is virtually nil. Recent visitors have been struck by the drabness of life and widespread apathy and sullenness of the people. It is possible that large numbers of Romanians would now sit out a war of the entire people—possible, but the Soviets cannot count on it. As long as that is so, Romania's deterrent defense policy seems well founded—at least as well founded as and much more clearly directed than any apparent alternative toward the main threat to Romania's security, an attack on the country by its own allies.

Romanian defense policy also invites certain conclusions regarding the country and its Warsaw Pact associates. It appears that in its defense policy the Romanian leadership has preserved just enough attention to the Warsaw Pact and to bilateral defense commitments to minimize the risk of invasion on the pretext of abandonment of the pact (as in Hungary in 1956). At the same time, Romania's strict internal order reduces the Soviet temptation to invade to extinguish a possibly contagious Communist heresy (as in Czechoslovakia in 1968). The country's defense policy of war of the entire people is clearly intended to complement these policies through deterrence by creating a credible threat of delay, bloodshed, and possible widening of the war should the country be invaded.

Romania has kept open the option of participation in a Warsaw Pact war if one should be forced upon it, but the whole doctrine of war of the entire people indicates that the Romanians do not believe that the threat of a war at the side of their allies is nearly as great as that of invasion by them.

For the United States and its NATO allies, the importance of Romania's deviant defense policy lies mainly in that fact. Romania pays relatively little attention to nuclear or coalition warfare. Instead, its doctrine assumes a massive invasion by ground forces that enter a Romania whose transportation net and economy are still largely functioning. There is only one plausible source for such an invasion, and it is not the NATO alliance.

Looking beyond Romania, what does this suggest for the Western allies? First, to the extent that the Romanian case is relevant, the conception of a unitary Warsaw Pact threat that has dominated Western thinking about the defense of NATO Europe is faulty, and potentially dangerous. In the military sphere, as in many others, the countries of the pact are no longer necessarily puppets or clones of the Soviet Union. Moreover, to treat them as such, especially in a crisis, could force them into a war on the side of the USSR. Second, the Warsaw Pact itself is not a "black box" that responds monolithically to external stimuli or to the orders of the Soviet high command. It is an international alliance with its own internal politics.

If NATO's deterrent succeeds in some future crisis, the politics of the pact are likely to be a key factor in its success. This is so for two reasons: first, because prudence might cause the USSR to back away from a crisis that threatened to force internal differences in the Warsaw Pact to the surface and thus call into question Soviet dominance of Eastern Europe. Second, during a crisis political maneuvering within the pact by its non-Soviet members might powerfully reinforce deterrence. The leaders of the non-Soviet Warsaw Pact states have nothing to gain and much to lose if there is even a serious threat of East-West war. It could seriously destabilize their regimes. Consequently, they might well be the most effective voices urging caution on the Soviet leadership and attempting to strengthen the influence of whatever members of the Soviet Party and government elite might be arguing against the recourse to war. An antiwar position by the bulk of the non-Soviet Warsaw Pact governments would thus seem to be the most likely outcome of a serious European crisis, but only as long as war and the destruction of their societies did not appear inevitable to them and to their people.

On the other hand, grave dangers lie in conceptions of the Warsaw Pact within the minds of Western politicians and military planners which are based on the false assumption of a monolithic response by the pact countries to the will of the Soviet government. Such an assumption invites Western statements, actions, and dispositions of forces that, in a crisis, could turn pact unity into a self-fulfilling prophecy and convert the governments of some of its non-Soviet members into advocates of a disarming Soviet strike against NATO. Romanian defense policy reminds us how unrealistic the dangerous assumption of Warsaw Pact unity is.

Romania is unquestionably the most deviant (or simply the most independent and diplomatically gifted) of the countries of Communist Eastern Europe. One might argue that sweeping conclusions should not be drawn from such an extreme case. This may be true. But if I may end this chapter with a guess, it would be that a close reading of the laws, policies, and military literature of the other non-Soviet members of the Warsaw Pact would reveal smaller, though growing, differences with the Soviets that point to quietly spreading fissures within the pact and to increasingly outdated views of that organization in the minds of many Western military and political leaders.

Notes

Portions of this chapter are adapted from "Defense and Mass Mobilization in Romania," published in *Armed Forces and Society*, November 1980. I am grateful to the editors of the journal for their generous permission to include that material here. I would also like to acknowledge the generosity of Col. Nicolae E. Călin, military, air, and naval attaché of Romania in Washington, who provided many of the Romanian materials drawn upon for this study. I am also grateful to Dr. Richard Staar, of the Hoover Institution, Stanford University, and to my colleagues Jiri Valenta, Edward Laurance, and Boyd Huff of the Naval Postgraduate School for their very helpful comments on earlier versions of this study.

1. International Institute for Strategic Studies, *The Military Balance, 1978–1979* (London: IISS, 1978), pp. 13–15, 19–28 (hereafter cited as *Military Balance, 78–79*).

2. For example, see "Ceauşescu: 19 November Report to the 12th RCP Congress," U.S. Foreign Broadcast Information Service, *Daily Report: Eastern Europe*, supplement, 10 December 1979 (series cited henceforth as FBIS *Eastern Europe*).

3. This point was made particularly in connection with Romania's 1978 refusal to increase its defense expenditures at the behest of the Soviet Union and its other allies. See "Speeches of President Nicolae Ceauşescu at Meeting of the Working Class, Peasantry, Intelligentsia, Youth, Army, and the Ministry of the Interior," *Lumea Supplement* (Bucharest, November 1978?), pp. 3, 9, and 14 (cited hereafter as Ceauşescu November 78 Speeches).

4. Robin Allison Remington, *The Warsaw Pact: Case Studies in Communist Conflict Resolution* (Cambridge, Mass.: MIT Press, 1971), p. 57. The emphasis is Remington's.

5. David Floyd, *Rumania; Russia's Dissident Ally* (New York: Praeger, 1965), p. 30; Maurice Baumant, *The Origins of the Second World War* (New Haven: Yale University Press, 1978), p. 300.

6. Thomas W. Wolfe, *Soviet Power and Europe, 1945–1970* (Baltimore: Johns Hopkins Press, 1970), p. 303.

7. Ibid., p. 304.

8. Ibid.

9. Ibid.

10. Cited by ibid., p. 307.

11. Ibid., p. 307.

12. For a superb treatment of the internal Warsaw Pact and domestic Soviet political maneuvering that led to the invasion, see Jiri Valenta, *The Soviet Intervention in Czechoslovakia: Anatomy of a Decision* (Baltimore: Johns Hopkins University Press, 1979).

13. Quoted by Remington, *Warsaw Pact*, p. 104.

14. *Scînteia* (Bucharest), 8 August 1968. Also cited in Remington, *Warsaw Pact*, p. 104.

15. *Scînteia*, 22 August 1968.

16. Remington, *Warsaw Pact*, pp. 106–8.

17. Cited in Ilie Ceauşescu, "Considerente referitorare la politica militară promovată de PCR pentru transformarea armatei române intri-o armată de tip nou şi dezvoltarea acesteia conform doctrinei militare a luptei intregrului popor (August 1944–1975)" [Considerations regarding the mili-

tary policy promoted by the Romanian Communist party for the transformation of the Romanian Army into an army of a new type and its development in accordance with the military doctrine of the struggle of the entire people], in *File din istoria militară a poporului român* [Pages from the military history of the Romanian people], ed. Ilie Ceauşescu (Bucharest: Editura Militară, 1975), vol. 3, p. 242.

18. Ibid., p. 243.

19. Ibid., p. 235.

20. In 1972, in keeping with the new defense policy, the Ministry of the Armed Forces was renamed the Ministry of National Defense.

21. Romania, Council of State, *Legislaţie privind organizarea de Stat, Legea nr. 14/1972, privind organizarea apărării naţionale a Republicii Socialiste România* [Legislation regarding state organization, Law no. 14/1972, regarding the organization of national defense of the Socialist Republic of Romania], hereafter cited as Law no. 14/1972.

22. Ibid., preamble.

23. Ibid., articles 1 and 3 (emphasis added).

24. Ibid., article 6 (emphasis added).

25. Warsaw Treaty, article 4, as cited in Remington, *Warsaw Pact,* p. 203. Provisions of Romania's bilateral treaties with its allies are similar, though in some cases more strictly binding.

26. Lester B. Pearson, *Mike: The Memoirs of the Right Honourable Lester B. Pearson,* ed. John M. Munro and Alex I. Inglis (Scarborough, Ont.: New American Library of Canada), vol. 2, p. 62.

27. Law no. 14/1972, article 28.

28. Ibid., article 104.

29. Ibid., articles 14–21 and 104–17.

30. *The Military Balance, 1977–1978* (London: International Institute for Strategic Studies, 1977), p. 15, and confidential interview, October 1977. The figure of 700,000 for Patriotic Guards strength was carried over to *Military Balance, 78–79,* p. 15.

31. Law no. 14/1972, article 104c.

32. Confidential interview, October 1977.

33. Law no. 14/1972, articles 118 and 119, and Romania, Council of State, *Decret al Consiliului de Stat pentru modificarea Legii nr. 33/1968 privind pregătirea tineretului pentru apărărea patriei* [Decree of the Council of State for amendment of Law no. 33/1968 regarding training of youth for the defense of the homeland], article 4.

34. Traian Grozea, "General Characteristics of National Defence," in *National Defence: The Romanian View,* ed. Iulian Cernet and Emanoil Stanislav (Bucharest: Military Publishing House, 1976), p. 75.

35. Ibid., p. 76 f.

36. Grozea, "General Characteristics," p. 80.

37. Ibid., p. 82 (the emphasis is Grozea's).

38. Ibid.

39. Ibid., p. 85.

40. Ibid., pp. 87, 88, and 89 (the emphasis is Grozea's).

41. Ibid., p. 96 (the emphasis is Grozea's).

42. Ibid., p. 99 (the emphasis is Grozea's).

43. Iulian Cernet, "The Political and Strategic Aims of the War of the Entire People," in *National Defence,* ed. Cernet and Stanislav, p. 106.

44. Ibid., p. 108 f.

45. Ibid., p. 106.

46. Ibid., pp. 110–12.

47. Ibid., p. 113 f.

48. Ibid., p. 116 f.

49. For full citation, see note 34. The book was originally published in Romanian in 1974 by Editura Militară (Bucharest) under the title: *Apărărea natională a României socialiste: Cauză şi operă a întregului nostru popor* [The national defense of socialist Romania: cause and work of our entire people].

50. C(orneliu) Soare, ed., *Istoria gîndiri militare Românesti* [History of Romanian military thought] (Bucharest: Editura Militară, 1974), pp. 13, 53, 337.

51. Constantin Căzănişteanu, "The Armed Struggle of the Entire People: Romanian Traditions," in *National Defence,* ed. Cernet and Stanislav, pp. 35–37.

52. For examples, see Ştefan Pascu, " 'Oastea de ţara,' oaste populară în tarile române în secolele XIV–XVI" ["The country's army," a people's army in the Romanian lands in the 14th through the 16th centuries], in *Armata Republicii Socialiste România: Tradiţii si contemporaneitate* [The army of the Romanian Socialist Republic: its traditions and its present], ed. A. G. Savu (Bucharest: Editura Militară, 1975), p. 21 ff; Ion Cupsa, "Contribuţia lui Ştefan cel Mare la dezvoltarea artei militare româneşti" [The contributions of Stephen the Great to the development of Romanian military art], in *File din istoria,* ed. Ceauşescu, vol. 3, p. 71 ff.; and Constantin Căzănişteanu, "Armed Struggle of the Entire People," pp. 29–34.

53. For examples, see Teodor Popescu, "Gîndirea social-politic despre înarmarea maselor oglindita in presa civilă, dezbatarile parlamentare şi legislaţia militară din timpul domniei lui Alexandru Ioan Cuza" [Sociopolitical thought on the arming of the masses reflected in the civilian press, parliamentary debates, and military legislation during the rule of Alexander Ioan Cuza], in Ilie Ceauşescu, ed., *File din istoria* 1 (1973): 69; and Constantin Căzănişteanu, "Războiul de partizani in gîndirea militară romanească din veacul al XIX-lea" [Partisan warfare in 19th-century Romanian military thought], in Ilie Ceauşescu, ed., *File din istoria* 2 (1974): 21.

54. For examples, see Stefan Păslaru, "Date privind sprijinirea ormatei de către masele populare în lupta pentru desăvirşirea eliberarii teritoriului naţional (septembrie-octombrie 1944)" [Data concerning the support lent to the army by the people's masses in the struggle for the completion of the liberation of the national territory, September-October 1944], in Ceauşescu, ed., *File din istoria,* vol. 1, p. 245; and Ion Dumitru, "Marturii documentare din archivele statului despre insurecţia naţională armată antifasciste şi antiimperialistă" [Documentary testimony in the state archives on the antifascist and antiimperialist armed insurrection); and A. G. Savu, "Consideraţii privind întoarcerea armelor de către întreaga armata română in august 1944" [Considerations regarding the turning of weapons by the entire Romanian army in August 1944], in *Armata Republicii Socialiste România,* ed. Savu, pp. 73, 89, respectively.

55. See, for example, Savu, "Consideraţii privind întoarcerea armelor."

56. Recent examples are *Viaţa militară* (Bucharest) 2 (1979): 27, and 3 (1979): 24 f.

57. For example, *Viaţa militară* 3 (1979): 32.

58. "La jubileul Diviziei 'Mărăşesti' " [On the jubilee of the Marasesti Division), *Viaţa militară* 3 (1979): 8 f.

59. Mihai Vasiliu, "The Conduct of National Defence," in *National Defence,* ed. Cernet and Stanislav, p. 255.

60. Ibid.
61. Ibid.
62. Interview with D. Mihailescu, New York office of TAROM, 17 July 1979.
63. *Aviation Week*, 21 April 1975, p. 19.
64. *Viaţa militară* 9 (1979): 9 f.
65. The estimated figure for Romanian defense expenditure in 1977 was 1.8 percent of GNP. The comparable figure for the USSR has been variously estimated at from 11 to 15 percent. The 1977 defense expenditure for the non-Soviet Warsaw Pact countries other than Romania ranged from a high of 5.77 percent of GNP for East Germany to a low of 2.32 percent for Bulgaria. See *Military Balance, 78-79*, pp. 11-15.
66. *FBIS Eastern Europe*, 11 September 1978, p. H1.
67. Bucharest AGERPRESS quoted in *FBIS Eastern Europe*, 6 November 1978, pp. H2-H7.
68. "Ceauşescu November 78 Speeches," pp. 3, 4.
69. Ibid., p. 13.
70. Ibid., pp. 13-14.
71. Ibid., p. 15.
72. *FBIS Eastern Europe*, 4 December 1978, pp. H18-H24.
73. *Military Balance, 78-79*, p. 15.
74. An example is Jerzy J. Wiatr, "Military Professionalism and Transformations of Class Structure in Poland," in *Armed Forces and Society: Sociological Essays*, ed. Jacques van Doorn (The Hague: Mouton, 1968), pp. 229-39.
75. Law 14/1972, article 31.
76. Ibid., articles 29, 31, and 65-67; Emanoil Stanislav, "The Structure of the National Defence System," in *National Defence*, ed. Cernet and Stanislav, p. 167.
77. Confidential interview, October 1977.
78. *Viaţa militară* 9 (1979): 9.
79. John W. R. Taylor and Kenneth Munson, eds., *Jane's All the World's Aircraft, 1979-80* (New York: Franklin Watts, 1979), p. 99; Nicolae Chericov, "Orao: Detail Changes for Production Model," *International Defence Review* 3 (1976): 343 f.
80. Taylor and Munson, *Jane's All the World's Aircraft*, pp. 159-61; *Military Balance, 78-79*, p. 15.
81. *Military Balance, 78-79*, p. 15.
82. Iulian Cernet et al., "The Components of the National Defence System," in *National Defence*, ed. Cernet and Stanislav, p. 172 f.
83. Ibid., p. 174.
84. *Military Balance, 78-79*, p. 15.
85. Cernet et al., "Components of the National Defence System," p. 173.
86. *Military Balance, 78-79*, pp. 15, 23, and 24.
87. Cernet et al., "Components of the National Defence System," p. 178.
88. Ibid.
89. *Military Balance, 78-79*, pp. 13-15. My students who have served aboard U.S. naval vessels on recent Black Sea deployments report that their ships were almost constantly shadowed by those of the Bulgarian and Soviet navies, but never by the Romanians. This may indicate that the relative lack of cooperation between the Romanian and other Warsaw Pact land and air forces also extends to the sea.
90. Cernet et al., "Components of the National Defence System," p. 176.
91. Ibid., p. 181.
92. For a recent illustrated article on such cooperation, see *Viaţa militară* 2 (1979): 24 f.
93. Quoted in Cernet et al., "Components of the National Defence System," p. 186.
94. Ibid., pp. 186-88.
95. Ibid., pp. 189-95.
96. *FBIS Eastern Europe*, 10 January 1980, p. H4.

Nuclear deterrence and the medium power: A proposal for doctrinal change in the British and French cases

Graeme P. Auton

Early in 1974, Secretary of Defense James Schlesinger announced changes in the targeting doctrine for U.S. strategic forces that reopened the debate over strategic adaptability, closed more than a decade before. Instead of relying upon massive countervalue second-strike retaliation, or "assured destruction," America's strategic deterrent would depend on a more flexible force and targeting posture, one providing the American president with a broader range of options for a more selective use of nuclear weapons against a wider array of civilian and military targets. This change of emphasis embodied four essential requirements:[1] (1) the U.S. deterrent should be capable of "riding out" a surprise nuclear attack and of subsequently penetrating enemy defenses with flexible counterstrikes, while still withholding "an assured destruction reserve for an extended period of time"; (2) command and control facilities should be able to "direct the employment of the strategic forces in a controlled, selective, and restrained fashion"; (3) forces should be capable of executing "a wide range of options" in response to a similarly wide range of potential enemy provocations, and should possess the "capability for precise attacks on both soft and hard targets, while at the same time minimizing collateral damage"; and (4) the total U.S. force posture should have "essential equivalence" with that of the Soviet Union; that is, it should maintain an "overall balance" in which Soviet advantages in some areas are canceled out by U.S. advantages in others.

The new outlook was a response to the increasing incredibility, in some circumstances, of a Catonic strategy of city annihilation which sought greater destructiveness in stragetic forces at the expense of flexibility or "usability." If assured destruction assumed as its overriding objective avoidance of resort to nuclear weapons through the guarantee of immediate population targeting once the nuclear threshold was crossed, Schlesinger's commitment to strategic adaptability recognized that implementation of such a doctrine would be needlessly suicidal in the event of more limited (perhaps accidental or irrational) provocations—such as a limited attack on U.S. military installations, or an attack on America's European allies. This realization was reinforced by the steady growth of Soviet strategic forces, which promised to give Moscow a wider range of strategic options, and which threatened to put Washington in the position of launching countercity attacks first. In short, critics of the assured destruction concept—including Secretary Schlesinger and President Nixon—believed it intolerable that the United States should "have no option as a deterrent to a broad range of possible threats other than a massive attack that would destroy Soviet population and industry."[2]

The strategic reassessment in the United States is important to medium nuclear powers—and to Britain and France in particular—because a similar debate ought to be taking place within their governments; indeed, a basic reconsideration of the doctrinal underpinnings of smaller nuclear forces is long overdue. As Marc Geneste recently observed, "Official strategic thought in Western Europe has slept comfortably during a quarter-century under the U.S. nuclear umbrella."[3] If it did nothing else, Schlesinger's announcement, coming at a time of superpower strategic parity, reinforced the argument that America's "extended deterrence," on which European security has for so long depended, is no longer credible. Europeans will have to fend for themselves.

While it would be unrealistic to expect medium powers to assume a strategic posture that even the United States has long rejected—that of a first-strike disarming counterforce capability against a superpower—it is not unreasonable to pursue the possibility of greater medium-power strategic adaptability in terms of targeting options. As Van Cleave and Barnett have noted, and as Secretary Schlesinger argued, there is a wide difference between major counterforce capabilities, on the one hand, and greater selectivity and flexibility in targeting, on the other.[4] In presenting the argument for

Reprinted from *Orbis, a Journal of World Affairs* 20, no. 20 (Summer 1976): 367-99, published by the Foreign Policy Research Institute, Philadelphia, Pa., by special permission.

flexibility on the part of medium nuclear powers, this essay will take note of the strategic dilemma in which they have traditionally found themselves, will propose one possible way out of the dilemma, and will consider the implications of this proposal for force structures and notions of "sufficiency." Two limitations to the analysis should be stated at the outset: First, I will be principally concerned with the strategic relationship between a medium power (Britain or France, or the two together) and a superpower (the Soviet Union); I will not consider the relationships among lesser nuclear powers, or between such powers and nonnuclear states. Second, many of the political and organizational problems pertaining to medium nuclear forces (and specifically to the British and French efforts) will not be treated. No effort will be made, for example, to deal with the political and diplomatic uses of (and incentives behind) medium nuclear forces; nor will the reliability of America's military commitment to Europe be considered; nor shall I delve into the political and legal problems surrounding Anglo-French nuclear cooperation. These issues have been discussed extensively elsewhere. What follows will be mainly an analysis of strategic doctrines, options, and capabilities.[5]

Four crucial factors have shaped and constrained the development of West European nuclear deterrents and strategies. First, although some future "united Europe" could probably bear the economic burden of a "superpower" strategic force, the absence of economies and technologies of scale, reinforced by persistent nationalism, has limited the size of the two existing independent deterrents.[6] Despite much speculation about alternative schemes for a "European" nuclear force, and about the benefits of Anglo-French nuclear cooperation, the obstacles to such developments—ranging from the legalities of Anglo-American nuclear-sharing provisions to the enduring historical and political insecurities of nation-states—have remained formidable. It is unlikely that a viable "European" deterrent will emerge soon, or that cooperation in nuclear decision making will advance much beyond the prevailing arrangements in NATO's Nuclear Planning Group (NPG); therefore, it is unlikely that significantly larger or more rationalized (with regard to a division of labor) European deterrents will come into being. Political and economic factors will remain limiting. In this study "European deterrents" will be taken to mean the British and French independent forces without any implication of their formal merger or integration; for one thing, as I shall discuss, there are important technological and doctrinal differences between the British and French nuclear efforts.

Second, the "state of the art" in West European nuclear technologies has lagged behind that of the superpowers. This is especially important in the French case, where a lag of several years in developing multiple warheads and longer-ranged SLBMs (submarine-launched ballistic missiles) has deprived the *force de frappe* of the strategic advantages such developments yield in terms of target coverage and overall system invulnerability.[7] In the British case, too, technological inadequacies have had serious consequences, compelling a reliance on the United States for crucial system components and support elements such as strategic intelligence.[8] Economic factors account for much of the problem. Major improvements in independent nuclear weapon and delivery system technology are unlikely to take place without massive increases in national defense expenditures or, alternatively, some pooling of West European resources. At present, political conditions are not conducive to either of these courses.

Third, geography has placed critical constraints on the effectiveness of West European deterrents. The relative proximity of Britain and France to the NATO "front line" and to the Soviet Union drastically reduces the warning time their deterrent forces would have in the event of a Soviet nuclear strike, and—more troublesome—compresses the time frame in which London and Paris would have to devise responses to a Warsaw Pact conventional assault. The limited warning time in the event of a nuclear strike, reduced to three to five minutes from the ten to thirty minutes available in the American case, means that ground-based European deterrent systems such as aircraft or the French SSBS (*sol-sol balistique strategique*) force are especially vulnerable to preemptive attack. Thus, both Britain and France have been compelled to turn to submarine-launched systems, though even ballistic missile submarines (SSBN) are influenced by the geographic factor, since very low frequency (VLF) communication systems for relaying information to them could be "taken out" in a matter of minutes.[9]

The second part of the geography-time problem—relating to a Warsaw Pact conventional assault—raises a controversial question: if tactical nuclear weapons (TNWs) were ultimately used by the West to compensate for its conventional inferiority and to buy time, to what extent would such weapons provide a "firebreak" separating conventional conflict from strategic nuclear exchange? Again, geographic factors—proximity to the front line and the "compactness" of European territory—are crucial. Recent French thought, including that of André Beaufre, has argued that TNWs *could* provide a firebreak, and that their *selective* early use might allow national strategic deterrents to be held in reserve in the case of less-than-total provocations.[10] Yet it must be remembered that the important variable is how the Warsaw Pact would use its TNWs, and that from a West European perspective a TNW is not automatically a "flexible response" weapon: it may be used selectively against military targets, but it may also be used against cities, and the level of collateral population destruction it can cause is very high. As Geneste remarked, most of "the nuclear arsenal specifically designed for European defense still consists of the blind 'blunderbusses' of the 1950s, likely to devastate friend and foe alike if used."[11]

Thus, for West Europeans the firebreak between TNWs and national strategic forces is not as clear-cut as it is for Americans: if East-bloc TNWs were used British and French "strategic" assets, the distinction between tactical and strategic nuclear weapons would become—in London and Paris—purely academic. Early commitment of TNWs might therefore only speed the rate of escalation to strategic nuclear conflict.

Fourth, domestic political factors have influenced the

evolution of the British and French deterrents. Domestic *support* for nuclear deterrents has stemmed from an unwillingness to bear the political and economic costs of large, conscripted conventional forces of the sort that would obviate resort to nuclear weapons. Europeans have been less interested in defense than in deterrence; they have had no desire to see a "limited" war waged on European soil, and they have been acutely aware that extensive conventional deployments would dilute the credibility of nuclear deterrence. Governments have thus found it politically expedient to opt for rigid nuclear strategies of massive retaliation and to stand under the umbrella of Washington's nuclear guarantee (although both actions have become progressively less credible in recent years).

At the same time, domestic British and French *opposition* to the independent deterrents—based on considerations as various as doctrinal skepticism, pacifism, and the allocation of scarce resources—has been powerful, and has on occasion produced concrete changes in force structures and weapons procurement. In Britain this was most evident in the extended debate over the nuclear deterrent preceding the 1964 general election, a debate that resulted—largely out of economy considerations, but with an increment of unilateralist socialist sentiment thrown in[12]—in the Labor government's reduction of the Polaris force from five to four submarines and cancellation of the TSR-2 low-level strike aircraft. (In retrospect it seems likely that a Conservative government would have stayed with five SSBNs.) Likewise, the French government has experienced spates of parliamentary opposition to the *force de frappe,* critics taking the view either that the deterrent should be abandoned altogether or that its development should take place in an Atlantic or European, rather than national, context.[13] Ultimately, the domestic political factors influencing British and French nuclear developments have worked to dilute overall European force postures. Parliaments and publics have seen little need to support major defense expenditures, nuclear or conventional, in part because of the continued extension of American guarantees.

These major constraining factors have tended to produce deterrents that, compared to those of the superpowers, are small, technically less advanced, more vulnerable (both in delivery systems and support elements), and politically more controversial. Since these characteristics have been common to the British and French nuclear forces, a similarity of strategic doctrines has emerged—a similarity derived most of all from the belief that the limited size of the two forces circumscribes the targeting options open to them. The underlying rationale has been "proportional deterrence" or the "unacceptable damage" doctrine. According to this concept, a smaller nuclear power may deter a much larger one if it can threaten the latter with a level of destruction that outweighs the benefits of aggression. Edward Kolodziej has summed up this argument for the French force:

> Sufficient striking power to destroy only so much of the enemy's vital centers that he would be deterred from attacking a smaller nuclear power was necessary, not annihilation of the enemy homeland. France might be destroyed in the nuclear exchange, but the aggressor would presumably absorb more damage than could be reasonably offset by the anticipated benefits of his attack on France.[14]

In short, "the prospective enemy would be foolish to attack France and expose himself to damages greater than the worth of France to his political designs."[15] Estimates of what constitutes an unacceptable level of damage depend ultimately, of course, on the psychology of the adversary power's leadership; it is possible, as General Ailleret once argued, that "only a few nuclear weapons, astutely applied . . . could . . . by themselves . . . break the adversary's will, without it even being necessary to generalize such bombardments."[16]

In practice, proportional deterrence has two important subsidiary characteristics. First, it is principally a countercity doctrine, and does not attempt damage limitation through destruction of the opponent's offensive forces. Cities provide the most "efficient" targets for inflicting unacceptable damage: they are large and "soft," and their position is constant. Thus, Andrew Pierre, writing about justifications for the British deterrent, notes that "the threat of just one nuclear weapon reaching Moscow or Leningrad might be sufficient to deter the Soviet Union from . . . launching an attack upon Britain."[17] Second, a key characteristic is its automaticity, that is, its affinity to the American massive retaliation doctrine of the Eisenhower years. In the early 1960s the rigid doctrine of employment that grew up around the British and French nuclear forces dictated that total retaliation would instantly follow "the slightest sign of aggression";[18] escalation to thermonuclear exchange and widespread population destruction would be unavoidable and would be justified by clear prior communication of the "rules of the game" to the putative foe. Any retaliatory threat less severe than this—less "total" and "automatic"—would, it was thought, undermine deterrence, make conflict in Europe more "thinkable," and increase the chances of Soviet aggression.[19]

Only since the late 1960s has some modification of the automaticity of European deterrence postures taken place, mainly on the part of the French. Early in 1969 General Fourquet outlined a shift in French strategy from massive retaliation to graduated response (*la réplique graduée*), a doctrine more in line with official NATO thinking, which envisaged "testing the enemy's intentions," first with conventional forces, then with tactical nuclear weapons, "thus affording governmental authorities time to weigh the necessity of resort to a strategic nuclear strike."[20] A further hedge on "automatic" retaliation was provided by fostering what Beaufre refers to as strategic "uncertainty"—that is, uncertainty in the Kremlin about whether or not, and under what conditions, the *force de frappe* would be launched against Soviet cities.

Despite these modifications in French strategic thinking, the targeting doctrine for the *force de frappe*—as for Britain's independent deterrent[21]—has continued to be principally a countercity one, with the implicit threat of rapid escalation to nuclear "city busting." Indisputably, implementation of this threat to Soviet cities would involve suicide. The alternative most commonly perceived in London and Paris would be to do nothing strategic-nuclear unless the East bloc resorted to nuclear attacks against the British and French homelands first, in which case either (1) Western Europe would be overrun by Warsaw Pact conventional forces and the national deterrents would prove useless, or (2) the Soviet Union would initiate strategic nuclear strikes, leaving Britain and France the option of delivering a retaliatory "blow from the grave." Obviously, this would be no real alternative at all.

Proportional deterrence, in the traditional mode described here, presents serious problems of credibility, especially when the conjunction of instant massive retaliation—perhaps involving first use of nuclear weapons—and countercity targeting is considered. If the East bloc launched a successful conventional assault on Western Europe, or if the Soviets delivered a counterforce nuclear strike against components of the British and French deterrents and other military targets, British and French leaders—given their professed strategic doctrine—would have no choice but to escalate the conflict to the level of population targeting and "city busting." It simply has not been believable that they would do so. As Richard Rosecrance has observed, such notions presume "an almost inhuman *elan*"; they demand "too much resolve."[22] The asymmetry between the Soviet and West European deterrents would yield the Soviets a much larger increment of political and diplomatic maneuverability, and permit them the option of waiting while forcing London and Paris to cross the countervalue threshold first (or do nothing). In a theoretical sense, British and French strategic doctrines have embodied all the weaknesses of Thomas Schelling's "brinkmanship," turning the "threat that leaves something to chance" into an "irrevocable commitment," and possibly confronting European decision makers with a difficult choice between automating an incredible threat and conceding defeat altogether.[23]

It is not hard to draw parallels between this dilemma and the situation confronting Secretary Schlesinger prior to the change in American targeting doctrine. In America's case, assured destruction became inadequate in the late 1960s because the growth of Soviet strategic capabilities narrowed "the range of circumstances in which an all-out strike against an opponent's cities [could] be contemplated."[24] Given a variety of less-than-total threat scenarios, a change of emphasis in U.S. targeting doctrine was unavoidable. In the case of Europe, where Soviet strategic superiority has been a fact of life from the beginning, this same logic presumably should have compelled a similar change in British and French thinking. Indeed, it is possible that proportional deterrence—the automatic or near-automatic infliction of unacceptable damage through city destruction—never was the correct strategic concept for medium powers like Britain and France, uniquely vulnerable to superpower countervalue attack because of their compact size and high urbanization.

What alternatives are available for two medium powers sitting close to the periphery of the Soviet bloc? How might any medium power enhance its deterrence capability against a superpower? These questions must be approached with two facts in mind: (1) it is impossible to divorce the deterrent value of a nuclear force from its war-fighting capability, should deterrence fail; and (2) it is likely that limited, "nonapocalyptic" provocations would dominate the early stages of any European conflict. If deterrence ultimately relies on the "usability" of strategic forces, and if limited conflict would prevail in the early part of a European war, effective West European deterrence would seem to require a capability for employing nuclear weapons in a flexible and selective way, without large-scale risk to civilian populations. Van Cleave and Barnett have distilled the basic assumptions underpinning this argument:

> Since deterrence is some product of capability and credibility, the capability to use nuclear forces in a rational and nonapocalyptic fashion, when compared with the credibility of massive strikes in response to nonmassive attacks, and when the adversary has his own massive capabilities in reserve, may become a better—and infinitely safer—deterrent. Contrary to what many seem to believe, increasing the credibility of use does not promote a breakdown of deterrence and the ultimate use of nuclear weapons. The objective is deterrence, and if both capability and credibility of the use of strategic weapons are sufficient, deterrence will be strengthened.[25]

If the only conceivable use of a deterrent consitutes national self-immolation, it is difficult to see how it might be used at all, especially by a medium power against a larger opponent with an intrinsic capability for much greater strategic flexibility. The prescription is clear: medium powers must escape the kind of logic asserting that the only effective targets for smaller deterrents are cities and civilian populations; i.e., they must reject the contradictory notion that medium nuclear forces have a deterrent value but no war-fighting utility. *A range of options is required which allows for the measured and selective employment of nuclear weapons against a wide array of targets, in order to avoid immediate escalation to a level of destruction that could not credibly be pursued.* In what follows I shall consider this argument in terms of providing the West European strategic deterrents with a more flexible targeting policy.[26]

But to return to a point already raised: in talking about strategic force "flexibility" or "adaptability," or about "measured deterrence," I am *not* talking about a comprehensive counterforce capability against the Soviet Union. Such a capability—if one calculates for delivery system reliability, system accuracy, and future Soviet ABM (antiballistic missile) and ASW (antisubmarine warfare) developments—would seriously test the resources of the United States, and is certainly beyond the capacity of either of the European deterrents now operational or any conceivable integrated "European" deterrent. What I am talking about is much more limited: targeting flexibility sufficient to enable "controlled, selective, restrained, and precise attacks" against both military and civilian targets, without assuming either (*a*) a comprehensive counterforce capability or (*b*) the necessity for instant escalation to Catonic city destruction.[27] The range of options for employing nuclear forces is not one of stark "either/or" choices; rather, it lies along a continuum and allows for a mix of targets holding out the prospect of containing strategic conflict—even, it will be argued here, for medium powers with capabilities markedly inferior to those possessed by the Soviet Union and the United States.

What sort of strategic nuclear response would a flexible or adaptable medium power targeting doctrine call for? At minimum it would require (1) an ability to inflict a high level of damage on a variety of "soft" counterforce and other nonpopulation targets, damage that in itself might prove "unacceptable," and (2) a residual ability to inflict an unacceptable level of countercity destruction. In the event of a Warsaw Pact conventional assault on Western Europe, or some other limited provocation, the British and French governments would have an initial option (in addition to conventional defense and the possible employment of TNWs) of striking at vulnerable counterforce targets in the Soviet Union, the loss of which, while not registering a devastating impact on Soviet society or even on the prosecution of limited nuclear war, would seriously impair Moscow's short-term position in the broader context of the Soviet-American strategic relationship.

Barry Carter has noted the following categories of "selective" targets in the Soviet Union vulnerable to hits by a small number of incoming warheads:

> 1. There are many nonmilitary, industrial targets, outside urban centres that would require only one or two nuclear warheads each: such targets include manufacturing plants, power plants, and the two construction yards [for] missile submarines [one at Severodvinsk on the White Sea, the other near Vladivostok on the Pacific].
> 2. Except for "hardened" targets, most military targets could be destroyed by only one or two warheads each; such targets include air defence sites [including phased-array early warning and ABM radars], military airfields, major army bases and submarine bases [in which perhaps half of all Soviet SSBNs would be docked or undergoing refit, barring considerable warning time].
> 3. Even for hard targets such as missile silos, nuclear weapons storage facilities and command posts, the use of small numbers of warheads will create a high probability of destruction.[28]

Insurance against a Soviet countercity reprisal for such limited and selective strikes would be provided by that increment of European nuclear forces left in reserve, presumably enough to threaten several large Soviet cities beyond the reach of the Moscow ABM network. Of course, the USSR might launch limited counterforce or otherwise "selective" retaliatory strikes of its own in an effort either to destroy what remained of Europe's deterrent forces or to demoralize European populations without inviting condign destruction of Soviet cities. The assumption is, however, that at this point there would be powerful incentives on both sides for controlling conflict and preventing its escalation to mutual city targeting.

The advantages of this more adaptable targeting doctrine are twofold, and reflect the benefits Schlesinger claimed for the American shift to strategic adaptability. First, since the initial use of nuclear weapons would not have apocalyptic consequences, the threat to resort to it in the event of dire provocation would be more credible—much more credible, certainly, than the threat of massive countercity strikes. Deterrence would therefore more likely succeed in preventing conflict in the first place. Moreover, the selective destruction of Soviet counterforce targets would constitute "unacceptable damage" to the extent that it threatened the strategic balance between the Soviet Union and the United States. As Geneste has argued, the "sanctuarizing" of West European nation-states—their possession of means of strategic nuclear retaliation—is one way of threatening Moscow with what are, for it, strategic losses in exchange for tactical gains.[29] Thus, in a multinuclear world, "Soviet perceptions of what constitutes 'unacceptable damage' might be lower than when a more bipolar power balance existed."[30]

Second, if deterrence failed, the incentives for containing further escalation of a conflict would be high after selective counterforce targeting. The seriousness of West European intent to carry out the deterrent threat would have been clearly established, yet the level of collateral civilian damage would still be quite low. Large urban areas would remain unscathed, hostages of the nuclear capacity both sides held in reserve. The desire to prevent destruction from mounting once the counterforce threshold had been crossed would more likely impel the two sides toward accommodation than would the aftermath of immediate city targeting.

Six major criticisms of medium-power strategic adaptability ought to be considered at this point. After I have assessed these criticisms, I will go on to discuss the technical requirements of the flexible strategy.

First, a now familiar critique is that doctrinal flexibility would make the use of nuclear weapons less costly and more "thinkable," thereby increasing the chances that a nuclear war would occur. Further, it is argued that once the nuclear threshold has been crossed, even in a limited or "selective" way, escalation to all-out city targeting is inevitable. Though both these notions seem plausible, there is no hard evidence to support either. To quote George Rathjens:

> Certainly the underlying premise of the flexible options policy is to make a nuclear response credible, but this need *not* imply an increased likelihood of nuclear war, for *if* the credibility is sufficient, the likelihood of a whole range of provocations may be reduced, and the compound probability of a provocation followed by a nuclear response may be less than in the case of continued reliance on "the threat that leaves something to chance." Similarly, the effect of greater emphasis on flexible options on the probability of an all-out nuclear exchange must be indeterminate: the probability could be greater or less than if no change in emphasis were made.[31]

The theory that even the most limited use of nuclear weapons in Europe would violate the nuclear taboo, thereby making it easier for all nuclear powers to unleash their deterrent forces, assumes that nuclear weapons have a dynamic of their own, irrespective of the political purposes for which a conflict is waged. Obviously, if a war is fought for limited objectives (as, from a Soviet perspective, it would have to be in Europe), nuclear weapons would best be used—if used at all—in a limited and restrained fashion. It can hardly be contended that a flexible strategy would make nuclear usage so much more "attractive" or "thinkable" to Britons and Frenchmen that the decision to resort to nuclear weapons would be taken lightly.

Second, it may be argued that adoption of a flexible options doctrine would give the Soviets added incentive to launch a disarming first strike against European deterrents. This is for two reasons: (1) despite the considerations raised with respect to the first criticism, Moscow might perceive an enhanced European willingness to use nuclear weapons in accordance with the new doctrine; and (2) a Soviet "selective" first strike could be prosecuted secure in the knowledge that the European response, should elements of the British or French deterrents survive, would most likely be a counterforce one. This is a difficult problem to grapple with. It would seem, though, that profound uncertainties would remain from the Soviet perspective: uncertainty about whether a European response, if one was possible, would remain rationally "limited"; and uncertainty about the reaction of the United States, regardless of the dictates of American national self-interest. Besides, as I mentioned in dealing with the first criticism, it is untrue that a flexible options strategy is essentially more provocative or unstable; Soviet incentives for launching a counterforce first strike against European deterrents would probably be no higher in a strategic adaptability targeting universe than in a massive countercity one.

Third, it can be argued that uncertainty works the other way, with no assurance that the Soviet response to a selective European nuclear strike would also be selective; Moscow might respond to a counterforce first strike with countervalue retaliation, even though some European nuclear weapons remained unlaunched. As Wolfgang Panofsky has pointed out, no matter what doctrine one adopts for the use of his own nuclear forces, there is no guarantee that an adversary will adopt the same doctrine; civilian populations will remain at risk.[32] Soviet military analysts have directed much criticism at what they call Western doctrines of "flexible reaction" and "realistic deterrence," yet such criticism seems aimed mainly at notions of conventional pause, not at discriminate nuclear targeting policies.[33] The overwhelming logic of reciprocity would work against responding to selective, precise counterforce strikes with massive countervalue retaliation where the party that undertook a counterforce first strike retained a residual capacity to inflict unacceptable urban damage.

Fourth, it can be argued that after a "first-stage" counterforce exchange between Europe and the Soviet Union, European governments would be back in the unenviable position of having only a countercity strategy open to them if pressed to further action—but this time with the bulk of their deterrent forces expended. This problem would arise in the event that a key calculation proved erroneous: namely, that Moscow would be willing to try for accommodation after an initial counterforce exchange. There are two responses: (1) it is doubtful that Britain and France would be in a position that much worse than if they had stayed with countercity massive retaliation in the first place (at least the option of a lower level of civil destruction would have been tried); and (2) it would be possible, even at this stage, to keep targeting options open, though outwardly manipulating the possibility of launching a countercity third strike.

Fifth, a series of technical objections has been raised regarding the suitability of SSBNs as launching platforms for "selective" or "measured" nuclear strikes. Kosta Tsipis has argued (*a*) that submarine navigation systems are so unreliable that the uncertainty of an SSBN's position at missile launching time makes SLBMs useless against anything but large, soft countervalue targets like cities, and (*b*) that a coordinated attack by SSBNs is impossible because of the lack of reliable, sustained two-way communication between submarines and their political authorities.[34] Both these statements are highly misleading. As Herbert Scoville has noted, "the present technology has advanced to the point where the location and attitude of the submarine could in principle no longer be the critical factor in obtaining missile accuracies down to less than an eighth of a mile."[35] Moreover, one-way communication from land to submarine would in most cases be sufficient (in fact preferable, since two-way communication would reveal each submarine's position).[36] This does not mean that submarine and missile navigation systems will not need to be improved (for the French force large improvements are needed in these areas) or that greater redundancy will not have to be built into VLF communication networks (the European Achilles' heel). But it does mean that technological factors are ultimately permissive and represent no long-term obstacle to flexible deterrence strategies.

One further criticism—less sweeping than Tsipis's assertions—falls into this same category. It can be argued that if British and French SSBNs launched, say, two-thirds of their missiles in a preliminary counterforce (or "selective targeting") attack, leaving the remaining third in reserve, they would likely reveal their positions and make it possible for the Soviets to "track back" and destroy them.[37] This danger, however, would hardly represent a much greater problem than now exists with respect to Soviet ASW capabilities: smaller SSBN forces such as the British and French are already more vulnerable than larger forces to a "peacetime" war of attrition (in which submarines would "disappear" under suspicious circumstances) and to active tracking from port. These latter liabilities are in no way sensitive to targeting doctrine. The eventual solutions are technological: longer-ranged SLBMs to provide a more extensive ocean area in which to patrol and hide, improved ASW countermeasures, deployment of more SSBNs. The important point in the present context is that an Anglo-French shift to a flexible targeting doctrine would not appreciably increase the vulnerability of West European SSBNs to Soviet ASWs.

Sixth, it can be argued that the level of offensive nuclear forces required for even a limited counterforce and selective targeting capability would exceed the size of current European deterrents by a wide margin. Moreover, future political and economic constraints may prevent any significant increase in these forces' size. However, the kind of measured deterrence previously outlined does not require major expansion of European deterrents beyond that already planned; barring radical improvement of Soviet ABM or ASW capabilities, relatively modest additions to the size and quality of West European nuclear forces will suffice for most foreseeable contingencies. Table 1 provides a rough breakdown of the current status of the British and French deterrents. If—given adequate political warning time—half of all their SSBNs could be on sta-

Table 1
British and French strategic nuclear forces, 1976

Britain
4 SSBNs, each with 16 Polaris A-3 (UGM-27C) with 3 × 200 KT MRV warhead, range 2,880 st. mi.
50 nuclear-capable Vulcan B2 bombers, range 4,000 st. mi. (aging—not currently deployed in nuclear role), 3 squadrons Buccaneer S2 strike aircraft, range 2,000 st. mi. (number deployed in nuclear role unknown)

France
4 SSBNs, each with 16 MSBS M-1/2 with 1 × 500 KT single-shot warhead, range 1,550 st. mi. (M-1) to 1,900 st. mi. (M-2); a fifth SSBN is under construction; a sixth is being studied.
18 SSBS S-2 IRBM. (in hard silos) with 1 × 150 KT single-shot warhead, range 1,857 st. mi.
36 Mirage IVA bombers with 1 × 60 KT bomb, range 2,000 st. mi.; 16 more in reserve (also 11 KC-135F tankers)

Source: The Military Balance, 1975–1976 (London: IISS, 1975).

tion, these would presently be able to launch 128 warheads against targets. This is hardly a negligible capability when we consider the range of other delivery systems that Europeans might also use in a nuclear confrontation. As Geoffrey Kemp has observed, a flexible targeting strategy is "less sensitive to delivered MTE [megaton equivalents] and more sensitive to missile accuracies";[38] given a modicum of offensive force sophistication, a large number of military and isolated industrial targets in the Soviet Union could be jeopardized by a concerted Anglo-French effort.

I shall now consider the technical requirements of medium-power strategic sufficiency and attempt to appraise what sort of capability exists—or economically could exist—for fulfilling the prerequisites of a flexible nuclear strategy. Notions of strategic sufficiency cannot be divorced from targeting doctrines, of course, and targeting doctrines in turn depend upon the simultaneous consideration of (*a*) the characteristics of targets, and (*b*) the capabilities of nuclear delivery systems. In what follows I will discuss, first, counterforce, or "selective," targets (the object of initial West European nuclear strikes) and, second, countervalue targets (those Soviet cities against which European deterrents would retain a residual third-strike capacity). I will then proceed to analyze the capabilities of West European nuclear delivery systems.

COUNTERFORCE, OR "SELECTIVE," TARGETS

In Barry Carter's crude typology of "selective targeting" introduced earlier, he delineated three categories of such targets: (1) industrial, outside urban areas; (2) "soft" military; and (3) "hard" military. The blast survivability of these targets—measured in psi (pounds per square inch) blast overpressure—would range from 3 to 5 psi for radar antennas, unprotected aircraft, and air bases to 30 psi for industrial machinery and 300 to 1,000 psi for hardened missile silos and command posts.[39] Required missile accuracies would vary accordingly, depending on warhead yield. Such select targets have varying degrees of economic and strategic importance. The destruction of command and control centers, radar installations, nuclear warhead stockpiles, and conventional-force staging areas would have a serious short-term impact on the Soviet strategic position but a negligible long-term one (given time for reconstruction). The targeting of certain nonpopulation segments of the economic infrastructure, on the other hand, might have more lasting effects. Relevant here would be energy sources, transportation networks, and heavy industrial plants.[40]

For the medium power interested in forcing Moscow into a negotiated settlement before the destructiveness of war became overwhelming, the former category of targets—those that are strictly military and short-term sensitive—would be most important. They would be crucial to the Soviet-American and Sino-Soviet strategic contexts, and therefore would be most "cost effective" in terms of inflicting the highest degree of nonpopulation "hurt" in relation to the number of warheads launched.

COUNTERVALUE TARGETS

A flexible options strategy would entail a residual ability to hold some Soviet cities "hostage." Kemp has distinguished eleven major Soviet urban-industrial concentrations, and at least six of these would constitute prime targets for European nuclear forces: Moscow, Leningrad, the Ukraine (Khar'kov-Donetsk-Rostov), Kuybyshev-Volgograd, Sverdlovsk, and Baku.[41] Moscow presents a special problem for medium powers because of its ABM network, sanctioned under SALT I; while it would certainly be possible for at least the British deterrent to penetrate Moscow's defenses, few missiles might be left for other targets, and it would be difficult to pursue a flexible options strategy. A credible threat to the five major urban targets outside the Moscow region, however, would require no more than the sixteen MRVed (3 × 200 KT) Polaris aboard one British SSBN, and if the missiles were upgraded to a MIRV capability (Kemp suggests 6 × 40 KT) the boost vehicle requirement would drop even further.[42]

Table 2 gives two sets of figures for the number of warheads to two different yields that might be targeted against these five urban concentrations. The first set—based on Kemp's calculations—assumes a requirement for a uniform blast overpressure "footprint"

Table 2
Warheads required for urban targets outside Moscow

City	Area (sq. mi.)	5 psi uniform footprint		"unacceptable damage"	
		1 MI	40 KT	1 MI	40 KT
Leningrad	250	4	35	2	17
Khar'kov	105	2	15	1	7
Donetsk	96	2	13	1	7
Rostov	87	2	12	1	6
Kuybyshev	134	2	19	1–2	9
Volgograd	86	2	12	1	6
Sverdlovsk	150	3	21	1–2	10
Baku	77	2	11	1	5
Total		19	138	10–12	67

of 5 psi over the entire area of a city. The second set, taking into account the fact that destruction would rarely require an entire city to be subjected to the same blast overpressures (in part because of thermal and radiation effects), postulates the number of warheads that would more realistically be required to inflict "unacceptable damage." Calculation of this second set of figures is based on a 5-psi blast overpressure covering roughly half the area of a city, with the understanding that lesser (though still destructive) overpressures would spread out to peripheral areas and that "large numbers of survivors, including many injured people, would probably cause greater overall problems for a regime than a city's total destruction."[43]

Both sets of figures presuppose a low air burst (scaled height 900 to 1,000 feet), yielding a 5-psi footprint of 60 sq. mi. for a 1-MT warhead, 7.2 sq. mi. for a 40-KT warhead.[44] A 1-×-1-MT single-shot warhead would have a blast effect slightly less than that of the 3-×-200-KT MRV cluster currently mounted on British Polaris (note: an MRV does *not* possess the target separation characteristics of a MIRV); 40 KT is the likely yield of each warhead if the British Polaris were MIRVed to a 6-×-40-KT configuration. (Poseidon and Trident 1, by the way, might carry a 10-×-50-KT warhead with countermeasures.)

If the estimates in table 2 are correct, inflicting "unacceptable damage" on the five urban-industrial concentrations outside Moscow would involve delivering the warheads of between ten and twelve missiles to their targets. Accounting for delivery system and warhead reliability (factors I will turn to in a moment), fourteen or fifteen SLBMs would have to be held in reserve for the third-strike countervalue stage of a European flexible options strategy. This calculation is important: subtracted from the total size of a deployed nuclear force, it yields what Michael Intrilligator has called the "counterforce proportion" of the deterrent—the number of missiles (and other delivery systems) initially available for a selective counterforce first strike.[45] In the event that residual countervalue targeting was based on the cities listed in table 2, the counterforce proportion of the British force would be—at a minimum—seventeen to eighteen SLBMs (assuming 50 percent of British SSBNs "on patrol"), plus other nuclear delivery systems (e.g., aircraft). Effective Anglo-French cooperation would permit an even bigger initial counterforce strike.

DELIVERY SYSTEMS

Calculations of delivery system capabilities must take into account a variety of variables while remaining sensitive to targeting doctrine. Variables to be considered in the case of SLBM forces include: the on-patrol coefficient of SSBNs; the ASW survival probability of SSBNs; the reliability of missile launching systems; the reliability of each reentry vehicle (RV); the single-shot kill probability (SSKP) of ABM interceptors (where relevant); the accuracy, or "circular error probability," (CEP) of warheads; the peak overpressure resistance of targets (in psi); and the long-term effects of warhead detonation (radiation, fallout, and the like). Some quantification of these factors for existing strategic systems is possible.

On the basis of American and British experience, an SSBN on-patrol coefficient of about 0.5 is attainable (though it drops as low as 0.25 for the British for considerable periods of time, and has recently hovered around 0.4 for the United States).[46] That is, no more than half of all European SSBNs can be expected to be on station at any particular time. For my purpose I will optimistically assume a 0.5 on-patrol coefficient.

Kemp has given an ASW survival probability of about 0.8 for SLBM forces of fewer than ten boats with missile ranges of less than 2,500 n.m. (2,877 st. mi.).[47] Such speculation is of limited utility, however. A submarine might launch half or two-thirds of its SLBMs before succumbing to ASW, or it could be sunk before firing any missiles at all. This range of uncertainty makes it difficult to calculate ASW's impact on the chances that a warhead will successfully reach its target. One further point: the ASW survivability of an SLBM force does not correlate simply with the number of SSBNs on station; MIRVing missiles may also enhance the overall ASW resistance of a deterrent, to the extent that an SSBN launching half of its MIRVed Poseidons before being sunk would cause more damage than another submarine that got off all sixteen of its single-shot missiles.

The reliability of both missile launching systems and RVs has been put at 0.9 by Kemp; multiplying the two together (0.9 × 0.9), one comes up with a total system reliability factor of 0.81. That is, barring ASW and ABM, 81 percent of all warheads launched should reach their targets.[48] I will use this figure in the present analysis as a general "rule of thumb."

Under the terms of SALT I and the 1974 superpower Protocol, the Soviets may deploy up to 100 ABM interceptors around Moscow. Actual deployment has fallen well below the permissible maximum, however: in 1975 only 64 Galosh long-range ABM launchers were in place around the Soviet capital.[49] The SSKP of these interceptors has been estimated at 0.4 for the established system against RVs with sophisticated penetration aids; it could rise to 0.8 for a more advanced ABM system against RVs lacking significantly improved penetration aids.[50] Of course, ABM effectiveness drops markedly against MIRV systems, but the British Polaris so far carries a simpler MRV—possessing ABM vulnerability analogous to that of a single warhead[51]—and the French SLBM carries only a single-shot warhead.

A CEP of between 0.2 and 0.25 n.m. (0.23–0.29 st. mi.) recently claimed for American missiles could well be better than that. It would probably be safer to attribute a somewhat larger figure to the British Polaris and an even larger one to the French SLBM. Nonetheless, the accuracy of both West European systems is most likely sufficient for the "soft" and semihardened targets envisaged in the selective options strategy advocated here. In connection with CEP, it is important to keep in mind that against hardened or semihardened targets, RV accuracy is more important than yield in megatonage; "an improvement in accuracy by a factor of two has the same effect against a hardened target as increasing yield by a factor of eight."[52]

A calculation of the relationship among all these factors will begin to give some indication of the British and French capabilities. In the British case we might use the following formula to determine the number of warheads likely to reach their target: Britain has 4 SSBNs, each with 16 missiles, and each missile contains 3 MRV warheads (3 × 200 KT). This gives a total of 192 warheads in 64 missiles. Next, if we discount ASW and ABMs, we may work out the answer thus:

192×0.5 (on-patrol factor)=96×0.81 (system reliability)
=77.76 warheads on target

Owing to the characteristics of MRVs, these 77 or 78 warheads would be dispersed in no more than 32 clusters (having been launched by 32 boosters, half of the British SLBM force "on station"). A similar calculation for the French SLBM force—taking into account four SSBNs, a total of 64 warheads (1 × 500 KT) and a 0.5 on-patrol factor—will yield 25.92 warheads on target. Obviously, as table 3 indicates, the "on-target" figures for both the British and French forces would be substantially higher were their systems upgraded to MIRV capability. This suggests that the British government ought seriously to consider MIRVing its present Polaris or somehow acquiring Poseidon or Trident 1. In the following section I will consider more fully the range of options for future British and French strategic force structures. It should be remembered, meanwhile, that both Britain and France retain nuclear delivery systems other than submarine-launched missiles, though SLBMs will comprise the backbone of the two deterrents in the foreseeable future.

Naturally, European offensive capabilities would be degraded by any substantial improvement in Soviet ASW technology or a "thick" deployment of ABMs by the USSR (were SALT I completely abrogated). Under such circumstances, European MIRVing or construction of more SSBNs would be necessary. The impact of extensive Soviet ABM deployments can be seen if we look at the requirements for penetrating the Moscow ABM network allowed under SALT I; such an analysis will also tell us about the advisability of targeting Moscow as part of a West European flexible options strategy. Kemp has devised the following equation for determining minimum penetration requirements for Moscow (assuming 100 ABM launchers and interceptors, an SSKP of 0.8, and a target coverage requirement of 8 warheads). In the equation, x = the number of warheads against which one interceptor is fired; y = the number of warheads against which two interceptors are fired; 0.2 is the probability of one warhead surviving an attack by one interceptor (derived from the 0.8 SSKP); 0.04 (that is, 0.2 × 0.2) is the probability of one warhead surviving an attack by two interceptors; 8 is the number of warheads required to penetrate; and 100 is the total number of interceptors that can be fired:[53]

$$8=0.2x+0.04y \textit{ and } 100=x+2y$$

Working out the equation, x and y both equal 33.33 (Kemp's results are slightly different); $x + y$ (the total number of warheads intercepted, of which 8 would survive and penetrate to target) = 66.66, or 67 warheads that would have to be launched against Moscow.[54] Accounting for offensive system reliability (67 divided by 0.81), 82.716 (83) warheads would have to be launched in the first place.

Clearly, this kind of offensive requirement is formidable for a medium power; in the British and French cases, Moscow might not be worth targeting until the strategic delivery systems of both nations are upgraded. Still, Moscow—by virtue of its role as *the* locus of Soviet administrative and political authority—would be a valuable target for a medium power to threaten, and, it might be argued, there are mitigating circumstances. The more important are that (*a*) fewer than 100 ABMs have in fact been deployed around the Soviet capital; (*b*) the current Galosh system may have not an SSKP of 0.8 but a much lower one (0.4 perhaps); and (*c*) in accordance with the formula for "unacceptable" urban damage used in table 2, it would probably be sufficient to hit Moscow with 4 warheads of moderate yield. Even if we still grant an SSKP of 0.8, the penetration requirement for 4 warheads against 64 interceptors (the number of Galosh emplaced in 1975) is considerably lower than the requirement for 8 warheads against 100 interceptors. Thus, where $4 = 0.2x + 0.04y$ *and* $64 = x + 2y$, we obtain the following: $x = 15.11$, $y = 24.45$, and $x + y$ (the number of warheads that would have to be arrayed against Moscow's defensive system) = 39.56 (40). Accounting for offensive system reliability (40 divided by 0.81), 49.383 (conservatively, 50) warheads would have to be launched initially, a figure substantially lower than the 83 given for the first calculation.

Carrying this same argument further, a wide range of penetration requirements and RV-ABM relationships might be hypothesized. Table 4 summarizes some of these requirements for the Moscow ABM system, using four different "warhead on target" and "number of ABM" mixes (an SSKP of 0.8 is assumed constant). The warhead requirement listed in the fourth column (warheads launched) is in one sense quite conservative, since incoming RVs would carry decoys and other countermeasures that might degrade the effectiveness of an ABM system; thus, fewer warheads might be needed.

Even the last and least demanding requirement listed—that for 4 warheads "on target" against 64 interceptors—might be difficult for either Britain or France to meet independently. True, the British Polaris fleet "on station" could launch 96 warheads, but these

Table 3
Warheads on target for various SLBM configurations

Missile and warhead	On station: Missiles	On station: Warheads	Warheads on target
Polaris, 3 × 200 KT MRV	32	96	77.76 (78)
French MSBS, 1 × 500 KT	32	32	25.92 (26)
Polaris, 6 × 40 KT MIRV	32	192	155.52 (156)
Poseidon, 10 × 50 KT MIRV	32	320	259.20 (259)

Table 4
Warheads required to penetrate Moscow's ABM system

Required number of warheads on target	Number of ABM interceptors (SSKP of 0.8)	Required number of warheads for penetration	Required number of warheads launched (reliability 0.81)
8	100	67 (66.66)	83 (82.716)
4	100	56 (55.56)	69 (69.135)
8	64	51 (50.68)	63 (62.962)
4	64	40 (39.56)	50 (49.383)

would be concentrated in 32 MRV clusters, each with a vulnerability to ABM similar to that of a single-shot warhead. Moreover, the penetration aids built into the British Polaris are not as well developed as those in the American Poseidon. Even if the British SLBM force managed to penetrate Moscow's defenses and deliver 2, 3, or even 4 warheads on target (causing damage of an "unacceptable" magnitude), no SLBM would be left for other targets, and a commitment to the flexible options strategy would be very difficult. Were the British and French SLBM forces combined (128 warheads, but a maximum of only 64 ABM targets), the targeting of Moscow might still preclude flexible options.

The lesson is clear: until at least the British force is MIRVed, Moscow should not be targeted as part of a flexible West European deterrent strategy. It makes more sense to reserve for a countervalue third strike only sufficient SLBMs to destroy the cities listed in table 2; this would permit a fairly large initial "counterforce proportion," especially if British and French targeting could be coordinated.

My analysis of the requirements for penetrating Moscow's ABM network can give only a rough idea of the consequences if the Soviets decided—in part because of the growth of "third-power" nuclear capabilities—to construct a more extensive ABM system, one covering most major Soviet cities. There are already indications that such a decision has been made, in defiance of the porous strictures of SALT I.[55] Perhaps most disturbing are reports that the Soviets have tested SA-5 Griffon and SA-2 Guideline surface-to-air (antiaircraft) missiles in an ABM mode; when one considers that Soviet SAM defenses are the most extensive in the world, the implications of making these missiles (or follow-on variants) dual capable—that is, antiaircraft *and* ABM—are highly unsettling.[56] It would be impossible for the West to tell whether SAMs deployed around Soviet cities were genuinely for antiaircraft defense, or whether their real use would be as point defense ABM interceptors. Moreover, the Soviets have continued to test and deploy radars that would be useful for ABM defense.[57] The only reliable antidote to these measures from the Anglo-French standpoint is a large and expensive upgrading of European deterrent forces.

This study has discussed that the British and French nuclear forces, as they are presently structured, are adequate for a rudimentary kind of flexible targeting strategy. It would be foolish, though, to conclude that their present size and structure will always be sufficient, and that no new efforts and expenditures will be needed to maintain nuclear sufficiency; I have shown that one development—more extensive Soviet deployment of ABMs—would necessitate a major overhaul of European nuclear capabilities. SALT I managed, temporarily, to forestall the necessity for this overhaul. Yet, even if our suspicions about Soviet cheating on SALT prove false and thicker Soviet ABM defenses are not developed, there will inevitably arise a need for upgrading the British and French deterrents.

At present both forces face four fundamental problems: (1) the possibility of heavier Soviet deployment of ABMs, which will require the MIRVing and eventual enlarging of European offensive forces; (2) the improvement of Soviet ASW capabilities, counteraction of which will necessitate longer-ranged SLBMs and—ultimately—new, quieter, and more numerous SSBNs; (3) the vulnerability of European VLF communication systems, which will require building more redundancy into present systems or procuring airborne VLF transmitters; and (4) the inadequacy of independent European strategic intelligence capabilities (crucial where a flexible options strategy requiring selection of vulnerable counterforce targets is to be implemented), which will involve as its remedy more intensive development of European satellite technology. Most of these problems are in the short run susceptible to a qualitative "quick fix"; over a longer period of time, however, quantitative enlargement of the British and French forces and their support elements will be inevitable, especially in response to ABMs and ASW.

BRITISH OPTIONS

For the British, five basic options stand out. First, more SSBNs could be constructed to carry the present Polaris A-3 (with either an MRV or a single-shot warhead). The construction of just one additional SSBN (at an immediate cost of $225 to $250 million) would ensure a minimum of two submarines on station at all times, something the present force of four boats cannot guarantee.[58] Doubling the number of SSBNs, to a total of eight boats, not only would double the number of warheads on target, but would dramatically improve the deterrent's "on-patrol" coefficient while increasing invulnerability to ASW. The cost of raising the British force to this level would run between $900 million and $1 billion, long-term maintenance costs being twice those for the present deterrent. A major problem with this approach is that it would not make optimal or efficient use of each SSBN unless it were combined with an upgrading of missiles, which would compound the expense.

Second, the four existing SSBNs could be fitted with a MIRVed Polaris. This option, while doubling the number of warheads on target (assuming a refit to 6 × 40 KT) and improving the capacity to penetrate ABM defenses, would not carry the collateral benefit of an enhanced "on-patrol" coefficient associated with option one. Nonetheless, its cost is attractive—$100 to $200 million per boat, or $400 to $800 million total—and British warhead technology is permissive; there are some indications that this might be the approach finally adopted. Of course, a warhead even more sophisticated than the 6-×-40-KT MIRV suggested here might be developed; also, an optimal solution might involve combining this approach with the construction of, say, one additional SSBN.

Third, Britain could buy Poseidons from the United States, assuming that Washington would sell. Were the British able to buy or duplicate the American "front end" for the missile (that is, the postboost vehicle, including the MIRV propulsion and guidance system), installing Poseidons in existing SSBNs would more than triple the number of warheads on target (the Poseidon C-3 carries ten to fourteen MIRVs) and—owing to more advanced electronic countermeasures—would further increase ABM penetrability. The cost, including submarine conversion, might run to $250 million per boat, or $1 billion for the entire force; this could be competitive, however, since Poseidon's longer useful life would allow costs to be amortized over a longer time frame. As with option two, this approach, given sufficient funding, could be combined with acquisition of additional SSBNs.

Fourth, London could delay conversion of its SSBN until Trident 1 became available, assuming—once again—that Washington would sell. Besides drastically increasing the number of warheads on target,[59] Trident 1, because of its 4,600-st.-mi. range, would improve ASW survivability by enabling SSBNs to patrol in a wider ocean area.[60] Procuring the even longer ranged Trident 2 system, including the new generation Trident submarine (which will carry twenty-four SLBMs) is another possibility, but the cost of this system, available in the middle or late 1980s, has been *conservatively* estimated at more than $1 billion per boat, which might well rule out independent British acquisition.

Fifth, Britain and France could strike out on their own and jointly develop an indigenous European strategic deterrent. Even if a "joint" Anglo-French force proved politically impossible, the two nations might develop hardware in common for their separate independent deterrents. Certainly technological factors would be permissive; as Ian Smart has noted, the strengths, and weaknesses of British and French nuclear technologies are uniquely complementary.[61] The costs of this approach would be high, but probably not prohibitive, given effective and complete Anglo-French cooperation. Some appreciation of costs may be derived from the fact that during the twelve years of 1960-1971, France, in developing its own deterrent, spent 2.6 times what Britain spent on nuclear forces.[62] Considering recent moderate levels of British and French military spending, an increase in defense expenditures sufficient to finance an independent effort would not be out of the question.[63] Nonetheless, if Britain can continue to secure U.S. nuclear cooperation it is unlikely—from London's perspective—that a totally independent Anglo-French course will prove attractive.

FRENCH OPTIONS

Because the French effort has been largely an independent one, future options for improvement of the *force de frappe* may not be so variegated. It has sometimes been asserted that the French deterrent is not only more independent than the British, but also more "well rounded"—comprising, besides SLBMs, IRBMs in hard silos in Haut-Provence and a force of Mirage IVA supersonic bombers. To confuse a succession of stop-gap measures for a "well-rounded" deterrent, however, would be a mistake. The aging Mirage IVAs are vulnerable to preemptive attack—despite their dispersion to a number of airfields—and have a doubtful capacity for penetrating Soviet defenses. The IRBM (SSBS) force is "open to the same doubts about survivability as now surround all the land-based missile forces of the Superpowers in a period of increasing missile accuracies,"[64] except that in the French case these doubts are compounded by the small size of the force and its close proximity to the Soviet Union.

Thus, while the French are apparently concerned about a followon aircraft to replace the Mirage IVA (if a 1974 interview with General Grigaut is any indication),[65] the brunt of France's deterrence capability will fall increasingly on the MSBS submarine-launched missiles. French SLBMs currently present three special problems: (1) it is not certain that submarine navigation and warhead guidance systems have been perfected to the point where a fairly low CEP can be guaranteed; (2) the range of even the second-generation MSBS (M-2) is insufficient at 1,900 st. mi.; and (3) the single-shot (1 × 500 KT) warhead mounted on the missile does not afford the target coverage and ABM penetration advantages of a MIRV or even an MRV. Future French efforts will likely be aimed at correcting these deficiencies.

The range of French alternatives is in many respects similar to that for the British. There are four main options. First, Paris could compensate for its SLBM warhead and range problems by constructing more SSBNs. Five submarines are presently planned (four will be operational in 1976), and a sixth is being studied; it might not be unreasonable to plan an eventual force of eight. Six SSBNs would permit forty-eight missiles on station (assuming a 0.5 on-patrol coefficient), and eight SSBNs would permit sixty-four; the larger number would, in addition, compound Soviet ASW problems. The French have been secretive about costs, but we may assume that, for this option, costs would be at least as high as those for raising the British forces to the same size, and probably higher.

Second, Paris could stay with the five or six SSBNs currently planned and concentrate on MIRVing and extending the range of its SLBM. If we assume a minimal degree of success—a 3-×-50-KT MIRV on a missile with a 2,800-st.-mi. range (the range of a Polaris A-3)—a force of five submarines could launch at least 96 targetable warheads (given two SSBNs constantly on station) and would be able to patrol in wide areas of the North Atlantic presently outside the launching range of French SLBMs. This option would require large additional R&D expenditures; if it were combined with option one, the costs involved would be very high.

Third, France could try to obtain more extensive

technical cooperation from the United States, or perhaps even purchase SLBMs from Washington outright. This alternative, if history is any guide, seems politically unlikely; nonetheless, a change in American attitudes is not impossible. As Pierre has observed, a more equal American treatment of Britain and France in nuclear matters, now that France is indisputably a nuclear power, might be beneficial to Washington.[66] The one or two technical problems raised would by no means be insurmountable: namely, how easily could French SSBNs be converted to take American Polaris or Poseidon missiles, and how quickly would France be able to develop sophisticated warheads in the event that Washington provided boosters only?

Fourth, as I noted in discussing British options, there would be a certain logic to Anglo-French nuclear cooperation. If it took the form of joint development of hardware, France would gain access to more advanced British warhead technology, offering in return its experience with boosters and satellites. On the other hand, if London continues to receive American assistance, making this kind of cooperation less likely, the Anglo-French connection might at the least concern itself with coordinating British and French targeting strategies in order to eliminate targeting redundancies and reduce doctrinal conflicts. Less demanding though collaboration in targeting plans might be (compared with joint development of hardware), it would become very important if—as Kemp has suggested—future improvement of Soviet ASW or ABM capabilities put a premium on larger, well-coordinated SLBM forces.[67]

Ultimately, the direction the evolution of the British and French deterrents will take involves not only technical variables but also broad political and socioeconomic priorities. Though I have not dealt with the political and strategic rationales of European nuclear forces, or with the allocative dilemma confronting European societies, this does not mean that the British and French deterrents can be viewed in isolation from politics or from wider strategic issues. It is just that these subjects must properly be the focus of another study.

Given the parameters of the present analysis, what major conclusions can be drawn? I have shown that special constraints operate on the development of the British and French deterrents, that the old doctrine for their use is no longer credible (if it ever was) and that a doctrinal reorientation toward a flexible options strategy is necessary if European nuclear forces are to retain their usefulness. For London and Paris this last point constitutes the main lesson of Schlesinger's 1974 revision of the American targeting emphasis, and it has not been completely lost on Europeans; there have been persistent calls recently for a "renaissance" of European military thinking.[68] In looking more closely at European deterrent forces, I have shown that a flexible options strategy *is* a feasible alternative. True, maintaining its feasibility in the future will necessitate some economic sacrifices on the part of Britons and Frenchmen. But if we accept the proposition that one of the nation-state's prime functions is to provide as much as is reasonably possible for its own defense and for independent means of dealing with unforeseen contingencies, the relatively modest sacrifices involved are worthwhile.

In the broader West European context, it seems possible that the independent deterrents—provided they pursue a more selective targeting strategy—may constitute part of the answer to the dilemma of European defense in a time of increasing pressure for American withdrawal. Six years ago David Calleo argued that the phenomena of American disengagement and European nuclear arming were two sides of the same coin; the second, involving a regional nuclear balance of sorts, was a natural compensation for the first.[69] The same point may be argued today, perhaps with even more meaning in the light of the vacuous diplomacy of CSCE and the inertia of MFR.[70] Whether the British and French deterrents remain "independent," whether they are "held in trust" for all Western Europe, or whether a West European nuclear force finally emerges, the fact is that European nuclear weapons are here to stay. What the present study has advocated, more than anything else, is intelligent planning for the day when the use of such weapons may be contemplated.

NOTES

1. *Report of Secretary of Defense James R. Schlesinger to the Congress on FY 1975 Defense Budget and FY 1975-1979 Defense Program,* 4 March 1974 (Washington, D.C.: Government Printing Office, 1974), pp. 44-45.

2. G. W. Rathjens, "Flexible Response Options," *Orbis,* Fall 1974, p. 677.

3. Marc E. Geneste, "The City Walls: A Credible Defense Doctrine for the West," ibid., Summer 1975, p. 478.

4. Cf. William R. Van Cleave and Roger W. Barnett, "Strategic Adaptability," ibid., Fall 1974, p. 667.

5. Discussions of nuclear strategy pitched at this level often seem to have an air of unreality about them. "Realistically" it can be asserted that the chances of a nuclear confrontation occurring in Europe are slim, that the chances that Europeans will by themselves undertake a nuclear showdown with the Soviets are even more remote, and that neither East nor West has any interest in seeing Europe devastated in another war, nuclear or conventional. Such arguments stress the need to look at adversary *intentions* as well as capabilities, posit the likelihood of precrisis political warning time, and (often rightfully) criticize the kind of thinking that subsists on hypothetical war scenarios instead of seeking real solutions to real political problems.

This sort of critique also has its weaknesses. Thus, it is argued that the Soviet bloc has no immediate interest in invading Western Europe and assuming the anxieties, burdens and dislocations such an effort would involve; that, therefore, independent European deterrents should be dismantled, or American troops in Europe brought home. The same logic could be applied to Soviet designs vis-à-vis North America (presumably Moscow has no immediate interest in the costs and burdens of a frontal attack in this area), yet few would argue for dismantling the U.S. strategic deterrent. American analysts' prescriptions for scuttling European nuclear forces usually reflect a profound inability to stand in European shoes. The fact is that independent European deterrents will continue to exist and grow, and any argument predicated on dismantling them is unrealistic. If it is true that President Giscard d'Estaing has in his public statements downplayed the importance of the nuclear threat to France, it is also true that he has not offered to stop development of the *force de frappe.*

6. On West European defense and problems of technological/economic scale, see Klaus Knorr, "Economic Factors in Future Arrangements for European Security," in *European Security and the Atlantic System,* ed. William T. R. Fox and Warner R. Schilling (New York: Columbia University Press,

1973), pp. 1-33; John C. Garnett, "European Security and the Enlarged Community," in *The Defence of Western Europe,* ed. John C. Garnett (New York: St. Martin's, 1974), pp. 57-86; and René Foch, *Europe and Technology* (Paris: Atlantic Institute, 1970).

7. France has trailed Britain in multiple warhead design, nuclear explosives, guidance systems, computers, nuclear submarine design, and submarine propulsion systems. It has maintained a lead over Britain in missile boosters, logistics, and satellite technology. See Ian Smart, *Future Conditional: The Prospects for Anglo-French Nuclear Cooperation,* Adelphi Papers, no. 78 (London: International Institute for Strategic Studies [IISS], 1971), pp. 10-14.

8. "Apart from supplying *Polaris* missiles and passing on many organizational and managerial lessons, the United States has provided the complete launching and fire control system for British SSBNs (including the gas system for the underwater ejection of missiles) and the vital Ships' Inertial Navigation System (SINS) equipment. Having acquired these, it is reasonable to suppose that Britain... could duplicate them, but it is also clear that, without them, the British programme would have had a much more troubled history" (ibid., pp. 12-13).

9. Britain and France have not built a great deal of redundancy into their VLF networks. The British have use of facilities at Rugby, England; Halifax, Nova Scotia; and Simonstown, South Africa. The two French VLF stations are at Rosnay in the department of Indré and at Pencrau in Finistere.

10. See André Beaufre, *Strategie pour demain: les problèmes militaires de la guerre moderne* (Paris: Plon, 1972).

11. Geneste, "City Walls," p. 480.

12. Michael R. Gordon, *Conflict and Consensus in Labour's Foreign Policy, 1914-1965* (Stanford, Calif.: Stanford University Press, 1969), pp. 269-82.

13. Wilfrid L. Kohl, *French Nuclear Diplomacy* (Princeton, N.J.: Princeton University Press, 1971), pp. 169-70; on French popular, scholarly, and military criticism of the *force de frappe,* see pp. 170-77. See also P. T. Friedrich, "Defense and the French Political Left," *Survival,* July/August 1974, pp. 165-71.

14. Edward A. Kolodziej, *French International Policy under de Gaulle and Pompidou: The Politics of Grandeur* (Ithaca, N.Y.: Cornell University Press, 1974), p. 102.

15. W. W. Kulski, *DeGaulle and the World: The Foreign Policy of the Fifth French Republic* (Syracruse, N.Y.: Syracuse University Press, 1966), p. 111.

16. Quoted in B. W. Augenstein, "The Chinese and French Programs for the Development of National Nuclear Forces," *Orbis,* Fall 1967, p. 858.

17. Andrew J. Pierre, *Nuclear Politics: The British Experience with an Independent Strategic Force, 1939-1970* (London: Oxford University Press, 1972), p. 306.

18. Aerienne M. Fourquet, "The Role of the Forces," *Survival,* July 1969, p. 207.

19. Meantime, the efficacy of the U.S. nuclear umbrella would be maintained by the "triggering" effect of European national deterrents, and (in French thought) by the uncertainty engendered by multiple centers of nuclear decision making.

20. Kohl, *French Nuclear Diplomacy,* pp. 162-63.

21. The British defense establishment has done little to refine strategic doctrine beyond stressing the role of its deterrent as an adjunct of American nuclear power. The British have made less of the distinction between tactical and strategic nuclear weapons, and official Whitehall estimates that a European conflict would escalate quickly to the nuclear level have remained basically unchanged.

22. R. N. Rosecrance, *Defense of the Realm: British Strategy in the Nuclear Epoch* (New York: Columbia University Press, 1968), p. 23.

23. I am here assuming some familiarity with Schelling on the part of the reader. On the "threat that leaves something to chance" and the notion of an "irrevocable commitment"—the two components of Schelling's "brinkmanship"—see his *Strategy of Conflict* (New York: Oxford University Press, 1960), pp. 119-31, 187-203. For a critique of Schelling, see Philip Green, *Deadly Logic: The Theory of Nuclear Deterrence* (Columbus: Ohio State University Press, 1966), pp. 129-55.

24. Schlesinger, quoted in Van Cleave and Barnett, "Strategic Adaptability," p. 667.

25. Van Cleave and Barnett, "Strategic Adaptability," p. 661.

26. The "selective targeting" and "flexible response" concepts also apply to tactical nuclear weapons (TNWs), but in a way that—owing to geographic factors—is subtler for West Europeans than for Americans. From a European perspective that "flexible response" characteristics of TNWs must ultimately be measured in the same way as the flexible response characteristics of strategic weapons—i.e., the extent to which their accuracy and yield, and the doctrine for their employment, enable their use in a selective and discriminate manner against isolated counterforce (or other nonpopulation) targets.

27. Cf. Van Cleave and Barnett, "Strategic Adaptability," p. 666.

28. Barry Carter, "Flexible Strategic Options: No Need for New Strategy," *Survival,* January/February 1975, pp. 26-27.

29. Geneste, "City Walls," p. 490.

30. Geoffrey Kemp, *Nuclear Forces for Medium Powers, Part 1: Targets and Weapons Systems,* Adelphi Papers, no. 106 (London: IISS, 1974), p. 28.

31. Rathjens, "Flexible Response Options," p. 686.

32. Wolfgang Panofsky, "The Mutual-Hostage Relationship between America and Russia," *Foreign Affairs,* October 1973.

33. Cf. Lt. Gen. I. Zavyalov, *Krasnaya zvezda,* 19 April 1973, trans. Foreign Broadcast Information Service (FBIS), 24 April 1973, p. M-4. Also, G. A. Trofimenko, *Strategiia global'noi voiny* [The strategy of global war] (Moscow: Voenizdat, 1968), pp. 128-45. For an overview of the Soviet critique of limited war concepts, see Thomas W. Wolfe, *Soviet Power and Europe, 1945-1970* (Baltimore: Johns Hopkins Press, 1970), pp. 211-13, 451-52. On Soviet views of the political context of limited war, see Christopher D. Jones, "Just Wars and Limited Wars: Restraints on the Use of the Soviet Armed Forces," *World Politics,* October 1975, pp. 45-53.

34. Kosta Tsipis, "Anti-Submarine Warfare and Missile Submarines," in *The Dynamics of Arms Races,* ed. David Carlton and Carlo Schaerf (New York: Wiley, 1975), pp. 38-39.

35. Herbert Scoville, Jr., "Missile Submarines and National Security," in *Arms Control: Readings from Scientific American,* ed. Herbert F. York (San Francisco: Freeman, 1973), p. 240.

36. Ibid., pp. 241-42.

37. Given a modicum of Anglo-French cooperation, ways of minimizing this danger might be devised. With a larger SLBM force, the entire missile complement of one or two submarines might be held in reserve for a countervalue third strike.

38. Kemp, *Nuclear Forces for Medium Powers,* Part 1, pp. 7-13.

39. Ibid., pp. 16-17. For a detailed analysis of target survivability characteristics, see U.S. Atomic Energy Commission, Samuel Glasstone, ed., *The Effects of Nuclear Weapons,* rev. ed. (Washington, D.C.: Government Printing Office, 1962).

40. Strictly speaking, these are "selective" targets only so long as their destruction does not entail high collateral population damage.

41. Kemp, *Nuclear Forces for Medium Powers,* Part 1, pp. 7-13.

42. MRV: multiple reentry vehicle; MIRV: multiple independently targetable reentry vehicle.

43. Geoffrey Kemp, *Nuclear Forces for Medium Powers, Parts 2 and 3: Strategic Requirements and Options,* Adelphi Papers, no. 107 (London: IISS, 1974), p. 27.

44. Ibid., pp. 5-6. For Kemp's calculation of warhead requirements for a 5 psi uniform footprint, see pp. 23-26.

45. Michael D. Intrilligator, *Strategy in a Missile War:*

Targets and Rates of Fire, UCLA Security Studies Project no. 10 (Los Angeles: University of California, 1967), p. 1.

46. Cf. Smart, *Future Conditional,* pp. 14-15, and Carter, "Flexible Strategic Options," p. 30.

47. Kemp, *Strategic Requirements and Options,* p. 9.

48. Ibid., p. 6.

49. *Report of Secretray of Defense James R. Schlesinger to the Congress on the FY 1976 and Transition Budgets, FY 1977 Authorization Request and FY 1976-1980 Defense Programs, 5 February 1975* (Washington, D.C.: Government Printing Office, 1975), pp. 11-16.

50. Kemp, *Strategic Requirements and Options,* p. 7. One element relevant to SSKP: in general, long-range area defense ABMs and their radars are less able than point defense systems to discriminate between real warheads and decoys. Cf. Richard L. Garwin and Hans A. Bethe, "Anti-Ballistic Missile Systems," in *Arms Control,* ed. York, pp. 170-72.

51. Ted Greenwood, *Qualitative Improvements in Offensive Strategic Arms: The Case of MIRV* (Cambridge, Mass.: MIT Center for International Studies, 1973), pp. 269-70.

52. Van Cleave and Barnett, "Strategic Adaptability," p. 658n.

53. Kemp, *Strategic Requirements and Options,* p. 10.

54. Multiply $8=0.2x+0.04y$ by 50. Result: $400=10x+2y$. Now subtract $100=x+2y$. *Result:* $300=9x$. Calculating it out, x then equals 33.33 and y equals 33.33. (Kemp is at variance; he gets $x=34.4$.)

55. Charges that the Soviets have violated either the spirit or the letter of SALT I have focused on (1) construction of new ICBM silos in excess of the number allowed under the 1972 Interim Agreement; (2) violation of silo dimension restrictions; (3) replacement of light SS-11-type ICBMs with heavy SS-19-type ICBMs; (4) testing of SAMs in an ABM mode; (5) upgrading and testing of air defense radars in an ABM mode; and (6) interference with U.S. means of compliance verification. The Soviets have also been accused of developing (though not deploying) mobile (rail- or truck-mounted) ICBM launchers, something not specifically prohibited by SALT I.

56. Cf. Clarence A. Robinson, Jr., "Further Violations of SALT Seen," *Aviation Week & Space Technology,* 3 February 1975, p. 12; also Colin S. Gray, "SALT I Aftermath: Have the Soviets Been Cheating?," *Air Force Magazine,* November 1975.

57. Clarence A. Robinson, Jr., "Soviets Push ABM Development," *Aviation Week & Space Technology,* 7 April 1975, pp. 12-13.

58. This cost estimate and subsequent ones obviously involve some degree of "guesswork," based on appendix C of Kemp's study (*Strategic Requirements and Options,* pp. 31-34) and on Schlesinger's annual report for FY 1976 and FY 1977, pp. 11, 30-33. Kemp's summary is particularly good.

59. Depending on the range and type of countermeasures desired, Trident 1 might eventually carry anywhere between ten and fourteen MIRVs. See Norman Polmar, *Strategic Weapons: An Introduction* (New York: Crane, Russak, 1975), p. 154.

60. A partial measure is conceivable here: British MRV or single-shot warheads could be coupled with the American Trident booster, though the advantage of obtaining only the Trident's added range might not justify the refit cost involved.

61. Smart, *Future Conditional,* pp. 8-17.

62. Ibid., p. 18. Using Smart's figures (British expenditures, \$4.9 billion; French expenditures, \$12.77 billion), British spending equaled only 38.37 percent of French outlays.

63. For 1972-75 military spending was as follows:

	Britain		*France*	
	Expenditures ($ million)	% GNP	Expenditures ($ million)	% GNP
1972	7,889	5.0	7,360	3.9
1973	9,033	5.2	9,818	3.7
1974	9,900	4.9	9,102	3.5
1975	10,380	5.2	12,250	3.4

Source: The Military Balance, 1975-1976 (London: IISS, 1975), p. 76.

64. W. Martin, *Arms and Strategy: The World Power Structure Today* (New York: David McKay, 1973), p. 42.

65. "Entretien avec le Général Grigaut, Chef d'Etat-Major de l'Armée de l'Air," *Défense Nationale,* October 1974, pp. 75-92.

66. Andrew J. Pierre, "Britain and European Security: Issues and Choices for the 1970s," in Fox and Schilling, *European Security,* p. 99.

67. Kemp hypothesizes an eventual West European requirement for perhaps ten or fifteen Poseidon-type SSBNs. Accepting this figure for the sake of argument, and conservatively estimating costs at \$250 million for the refit of each existing SSBN and \$400 million for the construction of each new one (including missiles and warheads), the initial outlay would be between \$2.8 and \$4.8 billion if Britain and France pooled their resources and forces. Long-term maintenance costs would be added to this.

68. In France, former Gaullist Minister Albin Chaladon has called for a fundamental rethinking of European military strategy, and in Germany the same demand can be found in Miksche's *Vom Kriegsbild* (Stuttgart: Seewald Verlag, 1975) and in the writings of Gen. Johannes Steinhoff. Still, most European concern for Schlesinger's reorientation seems to have focused on its implications for the American military commitment to Europe. Cf. "La Doctrine d'emploi des arms stratégiques américaines et la défense de l'Europe," *Défense Nationale,* October 1974, pp. 93-100.

69. David Calleo, *The Atlantic Fantasy: The U.S., NATO, and Europe* (Baltimore: Johns Hopkins Press, 1970), pp. 142-43.

70. CSCE: the Conference on Security and Cooperation in Europe; its Final Act was concluded in Helsinki in August 1975. MFR: mutual force reductions (formerly MBFR: mutual and balanced force reductions).

Defense budgets and policy

Chris L. Jefferies

Budgets and *policy* are two terms guaranteed to tax the interest and attention of even the most ardent student of government: *budgets,* because it evokes the dry image of incomprehensible columns of figures, statistics, and bookkeeping; *policy,* because it is an overly generic, often ill-defined, reference to what someone in government thinks should be done. This essay is an attempt to illustrate in a comparative context not only that the study of budgets need not be a dull and taxing effort at research, but more importantly that the study of defense budgets can be a very useful means to define defense policy in precise and unmistakable terms; that is, a nation's defense budget can give a clear indication of its defense policy.

INTRODUCTION

Beyond a mere statistical listing of governmental expenditures, a governmental budget is many things serving diverse purposes: "a political act, a plan of work, a prediction, a source of enlightenment, a means of obfuscation, a mechanism of control, an escape from restrictions, a means of action, a brake on progress, even a prayer."[1] At the "bottom line," though, a government's budget is its plan of how the scarce resources available to it will be allocated and distributed to benefit society. Because there are always competing claims for these limited resources, however, the budget also determines who wins and who loses. Thus, it also represents practical politics associated with the distribution of influence within government and society. It reveals "the norms by which men live in a particular political culture—for it is through the choices inherent in limited resources that consensus is established and conflict is generated."[2]

Most important for our consideration, however, is the budget itself, and the fact that it is a government's statement of what it feels ought to be done. In other words, regardless of political maneuvering, attempts at obfuscation, or governmental rhetoric, we can turn to the budget for clarity because it is the final and ultimate statement of policy. It is a commitment "memorialized by money."[3]

For example, since funds have continued to be programmed and appropriated for testing and development of a penetrating manned bomber for use after the middle to late 1980s, U.S. defense policy must still be interpreted as including some manned-bomber capability after the B-52 becomes obsolescent, even though President Carter canceled actual production of the B-1 follow-on manned bomber.[4]

Another example is French withdrawal in the 1960s from the command structure and joint-force deployments of NATO. While maintaining the French commitment to European defense, this move reflected a policy preference for independence from domination by the superpowers or other European states. Indeed, it signaled France's intention to follow its own defense policies and strategies. Close examination of France's budgets reveals a consistency or congruency between budget trends and policy statements in favor of European defense. Thus, when economic problems in 1967 and 1968 required cuts in France's defense budget, the tactical forces for European operations were least affected. Even France's nuclear forces, the symbol of its policy independence and self-determination, suffered a greater share of the reduction than did its forces programed for European defense.[5]

In both of the examples presented above, defense budgets give a clearer indication of defense policy than the policy statements themselves. This is not to argue, however, that policy statements do not give an indication of a nation's defense policy or that there are no links between budgets and policy statements. To the contrary, it is more meaningful to analyze defense policy statements and budgets together to gain an accurate indication of a nation's defense policy. The study of a defense budget is therefore useful in this regard because it can be used to confirm, contradict, or clarify the articulated defense policy statements; it can give a clearer indication of the true direction of the policy.

In an ideal world, the link between policy statements and budgets is rational and straightforward: a nation's values are reflected in policies, which, in turn, are reflected in governmental programs that are funded in a governmental budget (see figure 1). Of course, the world seldom conforms to this "ideal" presentation; the sequence may not follow this rational pattern at all.

Security is only one of several demands placed on government by society and must compete with other claims for the same limited resources available to government. Unless it "wins" in competition, the formally stated defense policy may not accurately be reflected in a defense budget. It may even be the reverse: economic and budgetary constraints may limit otherwise logically calculated defense policies and requirements. Thus, President Carter, partly in an effort to reduce the size of the FY 1978 Defense Budget, canceled production of the B-1 manned bomber and opted instead for cruise missiles to be launched from modified B-52s. This decision, made in large part for budgetary reasons, reversed the logical order suggested by figure 1, directly affecting American defense policy in general

Figure 1. Defense policy and budgets: a rational sequence

National Values/Goals
↓
Governmental Policies
↓
Government Programs
↓
Government Budgets

and U.S. nuclear strategy and force employment doctrines in particular.

Are the defense policies articulated by a national government consistent with the budgetary provisions required to implement these policies? If so, then it is likely that we will be able to understand the defense policy of a particular country merely from its formal policy statements. If not, then examination of the country's budgetary provisions will provide a clearer picture. Moreover, a lack of consistency or congruency between statements and budget provisions may even provide us with an indication of an impending policy shift, made necessary by a major and significant imbalance between a nation's articulated policy and the means to carry it out. The examples that follow demonstrate use of the budget to clarify an implied policy, to indicate an impending policy change, and to confirm the stated policy.

CASE ONE: POLICY CLARIFICATION

The U.S. defense budget is usually accompanied by published statements seeking to justify various budgetary line items, thus providing a somewhat more explicit statement of the foreign policy implications of these expenditures.[6] Even if these statements were not published, however, many of the same inferences could be drawn merely from examining the budget figures directly. In the 1970s, foreign policy statements on the question of using force to assure availability of oil and other resources were often deliberately vague, even though hints of that possibility were made from time to time. Budget documents, by contrast, were somewhat more revealing. For example, a 1979 statement identified budget proposals to "increase the firepower and mobility of the Army and Marine infantry divisions to respond to threats outside the NATO area," and the 1980 budget stated that a Marine Corps objective is "maintenance of the Fleet Marine Forces at a high level of combat-readiness for service . . . as national security may require." In his FY 1980 military posture statement (part of the budget process), the chairman of the Joint Chiefs of Staff observed that "in the Middle East and Persian Gulf, . . . U.S. and allied dependence on oil from that region make peace there a matter of U.S. national interest." Again, "U.S. forces which can protect and advance U.S. interests in the Middle East/Persian Gulf region include naval forces in the Mediterranean and a small Middle East naval force. . . . U.S. forces from the Pacific and European theaters participate regularly in the Persian Gulf region."

With respect to specific capabilities, the 1974 budget responded to the 1973-74 oil supply crisis by including funds to reorganize the armed forces for greater flexibility and "hitting power" and to speed overseas reinforcements "including the formation of lightly armed ranger battalions, four new heavy reserve brigades, and a tri-cap (triple capability) division mixing armor, helicopters, and infantry." More recently, the 1980 budget provided for a "quick-reaction" force of about 110,000 troops which could quickly be deployed to "world trouble spots." The army was to designate a "unilateral corps" of two or more divisions to be backed up by air force, marine, and navy forces. This force was further identified as a key element in a White House review of how the United States should respond if the U.S. sources of Middle East oil were threatened.

In this case, although official foreign policy statements were often vague, identifying military activity in the Persian Gulf region as only a possibility, budgetary provisions suggested a more definite policy. In short, examination of the defense budgets served to *clarify* the defense policy.

CASE TWO: POLICY CHANGE

In the period following the end of World War II, Great Britain continued to aspire to the status of a major world power. Occupying one of the permanent seats on the U.N. Security Council, the United Kingdom also became a member of NATO, CENTO, and SEATO. In addition to participating in a regional pact with Australia and New Zealand, the United Kingdom also retained its ties and defense obligations with former and newly independent colonies. The third power to achieve nuclear power status, Britain's force posture and deployments generally reflected those of a world power, with the defense budget up to 1958 averaging about 9 percent of GNP.[7]

In their global role, the British depended on the use of a highly mobile strategic reserve ground force, stationed mainly in the United Kingdom, to respond to emergencies in their global commitments. In 1956, however, an event occurred that most policy historians have considered a watershed in British defense policy: the nationalization of the Suez Canal by Egypt precipitated a major effort by Britain, together with France and Israel, to seize the Canal by force. The failure of Britain to achieve its military objectives fully, though not its fault alone, nonetheless demonstrated that Britain was considerably weaker than both the nation's leaders and the world had believed. Beyond the political questions involved, the failure was, in part, a reflection of Britain's inability to respond to the crisis given the limited numbers of forces available. The Suez crisis began to make clear that, because of the continued assumption of great power status, these military forces were continually being called upon to perform a wide variety of tasks all over the world.[8]

Jointly with Australia and New Zealand, Britain continued to provide for defense in Europe, the Mediterranean (Gibraltar, Malta, Cyprus), the Persian Gulf (Kuwait, Bahrain, Oman, Aden, the Trucial States), Africa, the Caribbean, the Indian Ocean region, and Southeast Asia (Singapore, Malaysia, Hong Kong). With the granting of independence to former colonies, the transition to local rule necessitated policing, antiterrorist, and antiinsurgent operations "as the tide of nationalist sentiment demanding independence grew. . . . The fact remains that the armed forces were often left to 'hold the ring' against indigenous rioting and terrorist activity as politicians reluctantly worked out their timetables of withdrawal."[9]

Indeed, manpower was being reduced, as well as expenditures for the weapons systems needed to perform the tasks. Personnel strength was reduced from 719,000 in 1957 to 446,000 in 1962—a reduction of 38 percent. By 1967 manpower levels reached 417,000—a reduction of 42 percent.[10] While attempts were made in the early 1960s to reduce defense expenditures, they were done without a corresponding reduction in global commitments. British defense forces were clearly overstretched in terms of capability to carry out assigned tasks. Certainly the incongruency between national goals—articulated in a stated policy that deemphasized conventional force capabilities and emphasized nuclear deterrence instead—suggested the need for a shift in policy to reduce commitments, or a shift in force posture, structures, and budgets to increase conventional capabilities.

The shift began in the mid-1960s, largely brought about by financial constraints. In October 1964 a Labor government took office. It quickly became apparent that in order to redress the nation's deteriorating balance of payments position, as well as to fulfill campaign promises to increase spending on social programs, a reduction in the allocation of budget resources to defense was necessary.

Several attempts were made subsequently to reduce defense expenditures, which resulted in the cancellation of several weapons systems, including a Polaris submarine and a new carrier, and the development of a new tactical strike and reconnaissance aircraft. It was not until 1966, however, that the incongruency between policies and capabilities focused upon the armed forces stationed abroad in support of longstanding global commitments; clearly, these forces were a major factor contributing to the unfavorable balance of payments. Although attempts were made to withdraw certain forces from "East of Suez" (while emphasizing that Britain would maintain a "special capability" for extra-European operations), by 1968 it became clear that the heretofore Great Power global role aspired to by Britain would have to end. Thus, on January 16, 1968, the government formally acknowledged the end of Britain's major world role and stressed that the British defense effort would concentrate in Europe and the North Atlantic in conjunction with allies: "Britain will not undertake major operations of war except in cooperation with allies. . . . We will not accept an obligation to provide another country with military assistance. . . . Finally, there will be no attempt to maintain defense facilities in an independent country against its wishes."[11]

Budget patterns reflected the policy change. The percentage of the budget allocated to the European Theater Ground Forces (NATO) showed a significant increase (from 7.4 percent in 1965/66 to 17.2 percent in 1977/78) which was consistent with stated policy. Also significant was the fact that, from 1965/66 to 1977/78, the percentage of the budget allocated to naval and air force general purpose forces remained about constant—12-13 percent and 17-18 percent, respectively. With fewer naval and air forces required outside the European area, the forces freed from deployment abroad would now be committed to NATO.[12] Moreover, policy statements were consistent with this budgetary shift: "Britain's basic security depends on the strength of the North Atlantic Alliance, and it is to the North Atlantic Treaty Organization (NATO) that by far the greater part of Britain's military forces is committed. Britain makes a major contribution to the full range of deterrent capabilities, both conventional and nuclear, required to maintain NATO's defense posture."[13]

In summary, this case has illustrated that inconsistencies between stated policies and existing capabilities may be inferred from examination of the defense budget (see table 1). Such inconsistencies tend, in time, to be resolved either through increase in expenditure consistent with needed capabilities or, as in this case, a shift in national objectives reflecting given levels of expenditure.

CASE THREE: POLICY CONFIRMATION

Perhaps more than with any other country, France's defense policy and budgets have demonstrated longstanding coherence. Foremost among the inputs to French defense policy has been a strong sense of national pride that has manifested itself in a demand for national independence and has been the unifying force in policy formulation. Even more than a means to achieve the basic national goals of security and prosperity, the French have considered independence an end in itself. Given France's history of foreign invasions

Table 1
The United Kingdom: policy change

Item	1955–65	1965–75
National values/goals	Security	Security
Defense policies	Nuclear deterrence; world/commonwealth commitments	Defense of Western Europe/North Atlantic
Programs (force postures/structures)	Strategic nuclear forces/strategic reserve forces in U.K. for world-wide deployment	Interdependent nuclear forces; conventional capabilities tailored to European defense
Defense budget	*Decreased* conventional forces (manpower cuts)	No independent nuclear force follow-on; conventional force (army, navy, air force) funded for Europe
Congruence?	No. Indicated need for either policy change or increase in conventional capability.	Yes. Policy statements confirmed by budget.

and occupations, it is thus not surprising that France has been obsessed with national independence, including a distrust of formal alliances. Indeed, it has been France's alliances that have caused some of the greatest suffering and ignominy; alliances have not only failed to preserve France's territorial integrity, but in the case of World War I, they have obligated it to fight. This desire for total independence of action has been the unifying thread in French defense policy during the last twenty years.

Following de Gaulle's return to power in 1958, French policy began to reflect the overriding desire of self-determination as a means to assure security. France withdrew from the integrated force and command structure of NATO, since these ties reduced flexibility and national autonomy. NATO was requested to move its headquarters out of France, and other nations with troops in France under status-of-forces agreements were required to leave. Not only did de Gaulle want to avoid being restricted by active alliance ties, but he also wanted no foreign troops in France, especially American ones, that might provoke the only major potential adversary at the time, the Soviet Union, into invading France.

The Soviet Union, its extraordinary political and military power coupled with a basically antagonistic ideology, has indeed been perceived as the major threat to France. After withdrawing from the command structure of NATO (although not from the alliance itself) and expelling U.S. troops, de Gaulle moved to establish an independent foreign and defense policy to reduce the threat from the Soviet Union; he pursued his own policy of "détente" and developed an independent nuclear deterrent.[14] Since de Gaulle, France's defense policy has been to maintain independent (free from alliance restrictions) armed forces, both conventional and nuclear.

In the early 1960s, France began the development of a strategic nuclear force structure with weapons deliverable first by manned bomber, then by land-based missiles, and finally by submarine-launched ballistic missiles.[15] But nuclear forces were not to provide France's only deterrent; conventional ground and air forces were also to play a major role. One of France's greatest concerns has been that a prolonged conventional war—particularly the type likely to be fought within the NATO alliance—would be fought on French soil. Thus, the deployment of French armed forces is based on the "trip-wire" concept: ground forces assigned to the field will trigger the threat of a nuclear response—either strategically on Soviet cities, or tactically in the field—if conventional forces cannot contain a Soviet or Warsaw Pact invasion before the fighting spills into France.[16] France's force posture reflects this strategy—three armored divisions are stationed in West Germany, two regiments are stationed in Berlin, and the remainder (beyond a few small units assigned overseas) are deployed in France.

Examination of the budget confirms formal policy statements. A full 16 percent (but only about 4 percent of the total military forces) of the 1979 budget was earmarked for strategic nuclear forces. This high figure, in contrast to just 1.5 percent in Britain's budget for nuclear forces, reflects the high cost of an independent capability. France must bear the cost of all research, development, deployment, and operation. (Britain's smaller joint force has been able to avoid high developmental and deployment costs by cooperation with the United States, which supplies the missiles while Britain supplies the warheads.) In addition, France is concerned about subsequent follow-on systems, and is continually upgrading its strategic forces with new missiles (submarine-launched missiles are being replaced with follow-on systems; the ground-launched S-2 missiles are being replaced with the S-4).[17] Moreover, an additional 2 percent of France's 1979 budget was allocated to tactical nuclear forces, making the total portion of the budget allocated to nuclear defense over 18 percent.

By far the greatest portion of the budget allocated to conventional forces goes to the army, which received 19 percent of the 1979 budget. Farther down is 13 percent for tactical air forces, most of which is allocated to close-air support of ground troops. Only 12 percent of the budget is apportioned to conventional naval forces. The imbalance in favor of ground forces clearly indicates France's concern with the conventional ground threat from Warsaw Pact forces. Forces assigned abroad (Djibouti, Senegal, Ivory Coast, Gabon, Chad, and Lebanon as part of the U.N. peace-keeping mission) receive 3 percent of the total budget, compared to about 1 percent of the United Kingdom's budget. (France appears to have only a slightly greater overseas, or "global," role than Britain, measured by this criterion.)[18]

In summary, France's link between national goals and values, through defense policy, force posture, and structure to the defense budget, illustrates unusual congruency. It reflects France's articulated concern for an independent defense policy and capability. Policy statements are confirmed by the budget (see table 2).

In conclusion, I have tried to illustrate, with these brief examples, that the study of a nation's defense budget is a meaningful and useful way to determine its defense policy. If congruence does not exist between policy statements and the budget, then we must look more closely at the budget to get a clearer understanding of what the policy actually is. Indeed, the mere discovery of incongruence, particularly if it is substantial, may indicate a forthcoming shift in formal policy statements.

Table 2
France: policy confirmation

Item	1958–80
National values/goals	Security
Defense policies	Independent nuclear force; conventional force "trip-wire" concept
Programs (force postures/structures)	Strategic nuclear triad force (ground, air, sea); large ground force deployment
Defense budget	Large percentage for nuclear forces; follow-on strategic system replacements; conventional force budget focused on ground forces
Congruence?	Yes. Policy statements confirmed by budget.

NOTES

1. Aaron Wildavsky, *The Politics of the Budgetary Process*, 2d ed. (Boston: Little, Brown & Co., 1974), p. xxiii.
2. Aaron Wildavsky, *Budgeting: A Comparative Theory of Budgeting Process* (Boston: Little, Brown & Co., 1975), p. xii.
3. Ibid., p. xiii.
4. Joseph A. Pechman et al., *Setting National Priorities: The 1979 Budget* (Washington, D.C.: Brookings Institution, 1978), pp. 266-67.
5. David Greenwood, "France, West Germany, and the United Kingdom," in *Comparative Defense Policy*, ed. Frank B. Horton III, Anthony C. Rogerson, and Edward L. Warner III (Baltimore: Johns Hopkins University Press, 1974), pp. 361-62.
6. The sources of subsequent citations are various annual U.S. budget-related documents, including *The Budget of the United States Government, Report of the Secretary of Defense, and United States Military Posture* (Joint Chiefs of Staff). All are published by the U.S. Government Printing Office. For critiques of the annual budget, see the annual publications of such groups as The Brookings Institution and the American Enterprise Institute.
7. William P. Snyder, *The Politics of British Defense Policy, 1945-62* (Columbus: Ohio State University Press, 1964), p. 183.
8. John Baylis, "British Defense Policy," *Contemporary Strategy* (New York: Homes & Meier, 1975), p. 273.
9. Ibid., p. 271.
10. David Greenwood and D. Hazel, *The Evaluation of Britain's Defense Priorities, 1957-76,* Aberdeen Studies in Defense Economics (University of Aberdeen, Scotland, 1978), p. 21.
11. The 1966 Defense Review as quoted by Ian Smart, "British Defense Policy, Part 1," *RUSI Journal,* December 1977, pp. 9-10.
12. These and the preceding figures are taken from Greenwood and Hazel, *Defense Priorities,* pp. 21, 23, 32.
13. "Defense," *Britain, 1975: An Official Handbook* (London: H. M. Stationery Office, 1975), p. 111.
14. Pierre M. Gallois, "French Defense Planning," *International Security* 1, no. 2 (Fall 1976): 17, 26.
15. Greenwood, "France, West Germany, and the United Kingdom," p. 345.
16. Wynfred Joshua and Walter F. Hahn, *Nuclear Politics: America, France and Britain* (Center for Strategic and International Studies, Georgetown University, 1973), p. 18.
17. *The Military Balance, 1978-1979* (London: International Institute for Strategic Studies, 1978), pp. 22-23.
18. Figures from the budget of France are taken from Ministère de la Defense, *Project de Loi de Finances pour 1979* (Paris: Imprimerie Nationale, 1978), pp. 25-28.

The future of France's *force de dissuasion*

Pierre M. Gallois

The recent advances registered by American and Soviet technologists in the accuracy of ballistic missiles have validated France's national nuclear arsenal in a spectacular way. At the time the mobile element of the French atomic force—its missile-launching submarines—was launched, it could not be foreseen that this component would become absolutely essential to France's security. In an era of relentless progress in weapons technology and corresponding vulnerability of military forces, one of the weapons that is still viable because of its ability to survive a surprise attack is the nuclear-tipped missile launched from a mobile platform—particularly from a submarine platform.

France is today the only country on the continent of Europe, within range of accurate Soviet weapons, that by dint of its mobile means of nuclear reprisal is in a position to neutralize the advantages conferred upon a possible Soviet military initiative by the increasing accuracy of Soviet ballistic weapons. This French capability assumes sharper significance at a time when all of NATO Europe lies under the shadow of new and accurate Soviet "Eurostrategic" weapons. The growing vulnerabilities of the NATO nations—in a political as well as military sense—are weighing ever more heavily on the conduct of those countries, and consequently on the cohesion of the alliance.

THE LARGE CONSEQUENCES OF A SMALL CEP

The British general Fuller divided the history of the means and methods of combat, from ancient times to the present day, into three phases. First was hand-to-hand fighting, followed by fighting from a distance with bows and arrows and the first firearms. The third historical phase entails combat over very long ranges, in which the distinctions between contending fighting forces and civilian populations, between armaments and material goods, have all but disappeared. Hiroshima represented the culminating point of this third phase.

Today mankind is entering into a fourth phase of combat, in which it becomes possible to attack over tremendous distances using highly accurate weapons, with a destructive yield that is adapted to the nature and size of the target attacked. Hence, it appears that any fixed military target of known geographical coordinates which is located on the earth's surface and inadequately protected is prey for destruction. Only mobile arms with sufficient concealment can escape these new offensive capabilities. Should a reinforcing rationale be needed for the development of French nuclear weapons, particularly their mobile components, then certainly the spectacular improvements in the accuracy of ballistic missiles offer a decisive argument.

Beginning with the first tests of ballistic missiles by the Soviet Union, the calculations by military experts had to take into account the inaccuracies of fire. In the initial phase of missile development, the state of the ballistic art was generally expressed in terms of a CEP (circular error probable) of three to four kilometers. Somewhat later, after the famous Soviet tests of February 1959, the CEPs of Soviet guided missiles at their maximum range began to be estimated, in Europe at least, at about two kilometers. In order to compensate for these probable inaccuracies, the missiles needed a commensurately large destructive yield to take out their target. This meant that the nuclear warheads mounted in the first generations of Soviet ballistics missiles carried an explosive yield measured in megatons, or even tens of megatons.

Little by little, however, ballistic missile accuracies have improved substantially—to the point where not only large targets like population and industrial complexes, but also airfields, tank and munitions depots, command posts, and pipelines have become hostage to long-range strikes. Even such minute targets as the silos that protect ballistic missiles have become vulnerable to attack.

It is still likely today that explosive charges on the order of 20 to 25 megatons would be necessary to destroy an American ICBM silo resistant to high pressures equal to or lower than 300 psi—assuming that the CEP of the attacking Soviet missile is between 900 and 1,000 meters. A rough calculation shows that if the CEP of the same missile were to drop from 1,000 to 100 meters, a 50-kiloton warhead would suffice to knock out the target. Soon increases in accuracy by a factor of ten will make the corresponding destructive yield divisible by 500.

These spectacular improvements in long-range missile accuracies lie at the root of the rampant anxieties expressed in the United States about the modernized Soviet ballistic arsenal. The anxieties focus on the growing vulnerability of the land-based American Minuteman ICBMs in their silos and thus upon the possible negation—in practical strategic terms—of the land-based leg of the U.S. strategic triad. The search for redressive solutions to this problem in the United States has turned to several options for a mobile deployment of a modernized ICBM force.

But the implications of the accuracy improvements in missiles are impacting not only in the United States and the Soviet Union. These implications essentially are as follows. First, in line with greater accuracy, the yield carried by their strategic and tactical weapons will be progressively reduced in order that their destructive radius may correspond to the size of the target. Some fifteen years ago, a ground-to-surface target of one hectare (two and a half acres) protected by concrete of 21 psi could have been destroyed only by a warhead of several megatons. Today, 100 kilotons would suffice. Tomorrow, 1 or 2 kilotons will do the job.

Second, as a consequence of these reduced yields of warheads, "collateral damage" will become progressively constrained. This factor is enormously important for Western Europe. For many years the assumption has been widespread that resort to nuclear weapons in Europe would have the effect of destroying the very assets that war is meant to protect or to conquer. During NATO's "Carte Blanche" exercise in 1955, the estimated nuclear devastation of Western Europe was numbing in its magnitude. Consequently, the European members of NATO were urged to defend themselves with conventional weapons and to trust that the Soviets would impose similar restrictions on themselves.

The improvements in the accuracy of ballistic weapons throw everything back into the melting pot. The portents are clear that already today, and progressively in the future, the ravages of conventional warfare in Europe would be more sweeping than those of an attack with ballistic missiles waged with the advantage of surprise and directed selectively against the weapons and forces of the European NATO countries. Not too long ago an American general officer explained that, in the event of a conflict, the armored brigade he commands would take up positions in a portion of German territory comprising some 185 urban clusters. The latter would be transformed into centers of resistance, and each building into a blockhouse. After a few hours of fighting, no building would stand. And one can imagine the destruction flowing from an attritional engagement involving 10,000 or 15,000 tanks, followed by artillery barrages, on highly and densely urbanized German territory.

On the other hand, airfields, munitions depots, artillery stores, tank concentrations, and other military targets in the NATO countries are usually located some distance from populated areas. The selective destruction of such high-value targets could be carried out by means of highly accurate strikes by missiles with warheads in the kiloton range. Such disarming "surgical" operations would entail only slight collateral damage and promise to the victor the conquest of industries and economies that survived the conflict almost intact.

Such a scenario of conflict may seem surprising. Its viability, to be sure, depends on two conditions: initiative and surprise exercised by the aggressor.

Now, the initiative of conflict in Europe rests strictly with the Warsaw Pact. The very ethos of the Western democracies renders it inconceivable that they would ever contemplate a turn to aggression. Whatever differences may divide them from the totalitarian countries, and irrespective of the behavior of those countries, the Western nations will alway prefer the road of negotiations. Therefore, if war were to erupt in Europe, it could be conceived and carried out only at the initiative of the Soviet Union.

Moreover, in contrast with the military activities that the Soviet Union has supported in recent years in such remote regions as Southeast Asia and Africa—where Moscow has been able to leave the actual combat to friendly local forces—in any major European conflict Soviet forces would be directly embroiled. This means, first of all, that no real parallel can be drawn between a war in Europe and conflicts in the Middle East, Africa, or Asia, where the Red Army itself has never been engaged.[1] It means, secondly, that if the Soviet Union were to make the momentous decision to initiate a conflict in Europe, it would do so only on the assumption of assured success. Consequently, it would, if necessary, use all appropriate weapons at its disposal. For this reason alone, it is naïve to believe that the Soviets will accept such restraints on their conduct of conflict as the Allies, for their part, seem willing to impose upon themselves.

Reference was made to the conditions of initiative and surprise. Surprise is a function both of the initiative and of the type of forces that would be used. Surprise could not be achieved by the Soviet Union through the massing of a large number of armored and motorized divisions and their westward advance. It could easily be attained, however, if several hundred multiple-warhead ballistic missiles could inflict a disarming blow upon the NATO European countries.

The fact that the westward rush of Soviet armored divisions still captivates the thinking of the NATO staff no doubt is attributable to historical flashbacks, particularly Hitler's invasions of Poland and France forty years ago. In the meantime, however, an ever-expanding arsenal of new weapons consigns the Blitzkrieg of the Third Reich to the relics of the past. A massive invasion of Western Europe would work above all to the disadvantage of the Warsaw Pact forces, who would thus forfeit the element of surprise and become mired in operations that would be likely to deny the quick, preemptive success that Soviet planners would be looking for. The new, accurate long-range weapons hold out a much more attractive option for combining the advantages of initiative and surprise.

THE SURVIVABLE WEAPONS OF NATIONAL SURVIVAL

If the implications of the new technical advances in the accuracy of ballistic weapons have been dealt with here at some length, it is to underscore that all military planners, particularly those in Western Europe, will henceforth have to take this new factor heavily into account. The Soviets now possess four striking advantages in this field: they have at their disposal an imposing and diversified military apparatus; they can grasp the initiative in all operations in which they would engage their forces: they can organize their armed interventions in such a manner as to retain the advantage of surprise; finally, they are adding to their panoply ballistic weapons that are becoming increasingly accurate while progressively adapting their destructive power to the targets to be struck.

There is no ambiguity in Soviet doctrine, which follows closely on the heels of technical advances in Soviet armaments. General M. Shtemenko has written: "The breakthrough of a prepared defense will be accomplished not by gnawing through as happened in the last war, but by the launching of nuclear strikes and overcoming it by fast movements of tanks and motorized rifle troops."[2] Field Marshal Grechko was even more explicit: "The operational and tactical missile units comprise the basis for the firepower of the ground troops. . . . The missile troops are capable of hitting any targets located at ranges of from several score to many hundreds of kilometers with great accuracy . . . using nuclear ammunition. . . . The missile troops of the ground forces are continuing to develop. Here, chief attention is being given to a further rise in the range and aiming precision of the missiles."[3]

The same concept is developed in *The Basic Principles of Operational Art and Tactics:* "The principle of simultaneous action against the enemy to the entire depth of his deployment and upon objectives of the deep rear has acquired an increasingly realistic basis with the adoption of nuclear weapons."[4] With a range of some 3,500 kilometers and a CEP of about 250 meters, SS-20 missiles, even if they were deployed east of Moscow, could effectively hit targets throughout the entire depth of NATO deployments.

For a democratic country like France, which has neither territorial ambitions nor aggressive intentions, the only reasonable security policy is that of ensuring the continued survival of the retaliatory weapons with which it intends to deter any other power from attacking its territory or threatening the free exercise of its sovereignty. Since France also has to take into account the new Eurostrategic weapons, the only recourse is to the kind of passive defense that consists of the constant concealment of its retaliatory weapons from external attack. But France's territory is both too small and too densely populated to host reprisal weapons that are continuously on the move. That leaves the spaces of the ocean and the air.

Since 1972, the *Redoutable,* France's first nuclear-powered missile-launching submarine of the present series of six, has been plying the ocean on operational patrols. At the outset, this submarine was equipped with sixteen missiles with a range of 2,500 kilometers, each carrying an atomic warhead. Four additional units similar to the *Redoutable* have been built, but the missiles have been progressively modernized, from the M-1 model (range of 3,000 kilometers) to the M-2, which has a range of more than 3,000 kilometers, and then on to the M-20, equipped with a thermonuclear warhead and penetration aids, and finally to the M-4, with a range of more than 4,000 kilometers and provided with multiple reentry vehicles (MRVs). The sixth French nuclear submarine, the *Inflexible,* will be armed with these M-4 missiles, and the other submarine units will be successively refitted with them. By 1985 France will operate six nuclear-powered missile-launching submarines, two or three of them on permanent patrol.

The number of these submarines may appear small, especially when compared with the American and Soviet fleets. But French strategy lays claim only to the concept of minimum deterrence: being capable of instilling in a would-be aggressor the fear of reprisal great enough to make the stake represented by France, a relatively modest take, a prize that cannot be coveted with impunity.

But the French force of submarine-launched missiles also holds out a promise for the possible, if perhaps remote, future. If one day the mosaic of states that comprise Western Europe were to transform itself into some kind of political union or even a confederation, one of the most decisive contributions to this unity would be a nuclear force of relatively numerous missile-launching ships capable of inflicting damage that would be proportionate to the considerable stake, much larger than that of France alone, represented by Western Europe as a whole. In this respect, France occupies a privileged position on the old continent. It is the only European power that could someday supply its neighbors with the instruments of their ultimate defense in the nuclear age. This form of security could be provided under conditions similar to those that the United States grants to its European allies, but with a credibility all the stronger because France shares a direct geographical destiny with her European partners.

But no matter what destiny awaits France and its European neighbors, the number of missile-launching submarines put into service by the French navy will probably be increased. Voices have already been raised in the National Assembly in favor of the construction of new submarine units and the maintenance of a fleet of eight or even twelve ballistic missile-launching nuclear submarines. Such an effort would naturally entail a reallocation of French military resources, with the navy's share being appreciably increased. If we take into account the advent of new weapons, particularly of the precision weapons that condemn static systems—and if we also consider the extension of the maritime zones to be patrolled within the 200-nautical-mile limit—it seems absurd to try to cling to the traditional balance among France's three armed services. Consequently, without increasing the total French national defense budget, an internal redistribution of funds should provide the submarine force with the share that it rightly merits, if only because the evolution in weapons technology dictates such a reallocation of defense expenditures.

THE IRBMS IN THE ALBION PLATEAU

France's strategic deterrent force is based on a "triad" of components: naval, land, and air. The land component is composed of eighteen IRBMs in silos scattered over the rocky expanse of the Albion plateau in Haute-Provence (in the southeast of France, close to the Mediterranean Sea). Those missiles carry a 150-kiloton warhead each and have a 2,500-kilometer range.[5] The force of eighteen IRBMs is divided into two units of nine IRBMs. The command post of each is represented by a kind of capsule that is suspended in a cavity hollowed out in the rock at a depth of roughly 400 meters or 1,200 feet.

Some fifteen years ago, consideration was given to the ultimate deployment of six units of nine IRBMs each, or fifty-four IRBMs. Twenty-seven of these were to become operational in an initial phase, and this figure was to have been doubled to fifty-four IRBMs in a second phase. Due to the lack of funds—and also because of a somewhat limited interest in the IRBM force by the French air force, which was in charge of the project—the second phase of the project was never carried out. Moreover, the first phase was scaled down from three units to two units of nine IRBMs each when it became obvious that the improved accuracy of their IRBMs would enable the Soviets to destroy the silos containing the French missiles with a relatively small number of nuclear warheads.[6]

Ten years ago, taking into consideration the lower accuracy of the Soviet missiles, the calculation showed that hundreds of megatons would have had to be used to knock out the fixed land-based component of France's triad. The heavy radioactive fallout from such massive explosions would have been driven by the earth's rotation and the prevailing wind eastward toward the Soviet Union. This fallout would still have carried very serious effects beyond a 2,000-kilometer range. Thus, the potential aggressor would have paid dearly for the preemptive destruction of the IRBMs on the Albion plateau. Today, the higher accuracy of missiles permits the use of fewer offensive missiles with smaller-yield warheads. As a consequence, the radioactive fallout generated by a corresponding attack would be greatly reduced.

But the missiles on the Albion plateau, even in their modest number of eighteen, still play a role by putting every potential aggressor within the range of the IRBMs before a dilemma: either the aggressor threatens France's territory without having first destroyed those missiles and therefore risks the destruction of some of his population and economic centers, or he destroys those missiles at the same time he launches his overall offensive, but in so doing he reveals his determination to attain his objectives at any price, thus justifying reprisals by SLBMs launched from French nuclear submarines.

Instead of increasing the number of IRBMs located on the Albion plateau, the French government has preferred to improve their performance. The S-2 missiles will be replaced next year by the S-3 model with a 3,000-kilometer range and a one-megaton warhead.

Thus, the fixed component of the French strategic triad will see its survivability threatened as a result of the greater accuracy of the Soviet missiles. Nevertheless, in the light of increases in the yield and range of the IRBMs, the initiator of a conflict involving France would continue to face the risk of the devastating effects of the improved IRBMs on his own territory.

THE AIRBORNE COMPONENT OF FRANCE'S TRIAD

In December 1956 just after the Suez crisis, France inaugurated a preliminary project for a supersonic bomber capable of carrying atomic projectiles some 2,000 kilometers.[7] Starting in 1963, air units equipped with Mirage IV-A bombers were deployed upon a dozen military airfields: a total of sixty-six bombers were built. As long as the principal strategic threat to France loomed in enemy bombers, and sufficient warning of attack enabled crews on alert to take to the air, these Mirage bombers represented a deterrent potential that could not be ignored. Attacking at low altitudes, and at a speed close to Mach 1, they would have been able to cope with a small number of important targets without suffering excessive losses. However, the advent of accurate ballistic weapons and the concomitant potential of surprise attack will result in the transformation of existing bombers into long-range reconnaissance aircraft, preferably to be used in limited conflicts beyond French borders rather than in the contingency of a major surprise attack against France itself.

France could weigh at least three alternatives to the present airborne element of its strategic nuclear forces: a new long-range bomber; a mobile land-based ballistic missile; and a transport plane able to launch ballistic missiles or cruise missiles from a stand-off position.

In contrast with those of the United States and the Soviet Union, France's geographical position does not allow it to maximize an airborne alert for its bombers because of the limited airspace available for long-range training flights. In financial terms as well, it would be difficult for France to create a large fleet of heavy bombers.

A second alternative relates to the mobile land-based ballistic missile. The Soviet Union, commanding vast and sparsely populated territories and a closed society, can make use of such missiles, as is demonstrated by the SS-16 ICBM and the SS-20 IRBM. On the other hand, for France, an "open" society with a limited territory and dense population, the mobile land-based ballistic missile is not a viable solution. The ground-launched cruise missile confronts the same problems. Beyond the fact that its penetration capability is low, its survival could be ensured only by constant movement over erratic routes through rather densely populated territory.

There remains the alternative of the relatively slow, long-range airplane equipped with air-launched ballistic or cruise missiles. The French General Staff once considered a ballistic missile-launching bomber at roughly the same time that the U.S. Air Force was testing the Skybolt missile. Costly and complex, the concept of a ballistic missile-launching bomber was abandoned on both sides of the Atlantic.

Today, however, the combination of the slow plane and air-launched cruise missiles (ALCMs) is arousing new interest. To be sure, this looms as a costly alternative—in the United States as in France. Yet, in the context of existing defense budgets and the national security stakes attached to the survival of second-strike capabilities, the expenditures for such a solution would not seem excessive.

Let us consider the example of a commercial airline that owns about a hundred twin- and four-engine planes. Anxious to make a profit, this company has its equipment fly between ten and fourteen hours per day over the routes that it serves. This means that nearly one-half of this fleet of 100 planes is in flight at the same time, and for at least three hundred days a year. Assuming that this company at least covers its expenses, its annual turnover figure would be about 7 billion francs. By economizing on the frills of a commercial enterprise, a military agency could construct a similar fleet of aircraft at a total cost of below 5 billion francs (approximately $1 billion). For this price, it could simultaneously maintain aloft some fifty aircraft (especially because planes with a lower specific consumption could replace long- and medium-range commercial aircraft for which speed is a commercial asset). If we note that France's defense budget is about 80 billion francs, this means that a capability of some fifty aircraft constantly on station and carrying some 500 cruise missiles would entail only about one-sixteenth of France's total defense outlays.

These and other alternatives are being researched in France by the general staffs of the military services and armaments departments. Everyone knows that strategic retaliatory forces must evolve at the same pace as technological innovation—that at the same time existing arms must be improved and deterrence sustained with new weapons. Subsonic and supersonic cruise missiles, air-to-ground supersonic missiles carried by rapid planes attacking at low altitudes, mobile land-based ballistic missiles with a greater range than that of the existing Pluton missile (a tactical weapon)—all these are the subjects of research contracts and, in some cases, orders for production.

THE MODEST BUT ABSOLUTE AMBITIONS OF A MEDIUM-SIZED POWER

Six missile-launching submarines and ninety-six MRV missiles, eighteen missiles in silos, and a maximum of fifty nuclear-armed aircraft—this arsenal may seem diminutive in comparison with those of the United States and the Soviet Union. But in the late twentieth century, nuclear weapons have profoundly revamped traditional military force relationships to the point where concepts of quantitative and even qualitative superiority or inferiority, while still of political interest, have lost in military significance.

Shortly after his arrival in the White House, President Carter appeared to adopt not only the notion of "sufficiency" that had already been advanced by President Nixon but also that of minimum deterrence based on 200 to 250 strategic delivery vehicles. In relative terms, such an American force would not differ substantially from what France considers necessary to assure its own security against a major threat. Later, after becoming more familiar with the international scene, Mr. Carter no longer spoke of minimum deterrence. A principal reason clearly relates to the circumstance that, in contrast with France, which does not guarantee its military aegis to any country, the United States intends to keep watch over the security of its allies in Europe and the Far East. This vast mission implies, at least in political terms, the possession of military resources that balance those of the Soviet Union—even though the word *balance* has lost its earlier meaning.

If SALT appears to many experts as a useless and even dangerous exercise, this is so because there is no relationship between the precise accounting set up by the negotiators and the responses of public opinion. Accustomed to traditional measurements of military power, and believing that the most heavily armed nation is also politically the strongest, the general public cannot comprehend the fine distinctions made by experts when they trade off multiple warheads against numbers of launchers, or warhead yield against accuracy. Thus, two forms of logic coexist: the complex logic of experts, who are content with certain inferiorities, and the simpler logic of the public, which assigns military superiority—and thus political supremacy—to the side that boasts the largest and most complete inventory of military capabilities.

It goes without saying that for France the nature and size of its strategic nuclear forces have to cater to other criteria. France is located close to a military giant who, bent upon achieving supremacy over American power, has completely unsettled the balance in Eurasia—in the East vis-à-vis China and in the West in the face of the West European nations. And this military giant holds the advantage of all initiatives—for war, for peace, and for intermediary contingencies. If there were to be an armed conflict in Europe, it could not be a minor affair because the Soviet Union would perforce be involved.

As far as France is concerned, the purpose of such a conflict would not be to "gnaw away" a small piece of national territory or to occupy an island along its coasts. Indeed, in defense matters, France confronts an "all or nothing" prospect. In its case, the expedients of "crisis management" or the fine distinctions of "flexible response" appear as the theoretical constructs of scholars which, while they may excite intellectual debate, have little relevance to the realities of national survival. France's strategic capabilities are at the same time limited as well as absolute. Therefore, France's nuclear forces can be relatively rudimentary—on condition that their survival is assured—and no comparison can be made with the strategic arsenal of one or the other superpower.

To be sure, the deterrent value of the French strategic force may weaken as the years pass. The potential enemy might become able to amputate this strategic force through preemptive attack. He could blunt the French force through measures of active and passive defense. The nature of the likely reprisal following the use of French forces might loom so terribly as to throw the credibility of their use increasingly into question. All those things could come to pass. But two facts remain. One is the uncertainty about the destructive effects of France's arsenal and about the behavior of the men responsible for its use. The other is the certainty of toppling from a known, rationally conducted conflict into the unknown of an irrational nuclear war, and one waged for a prize that would hardly be worth the risk. To be able to deter at a lesser cost than is imposed on the Great Powers for this purpose is an advantage that falls to medium-sized powers. France has striven to seize this opportunity.

NOTES

1. During the Sino-Vietnamese conflict, the USSR could have created a diversion by opening a "second front" along the thousands of kilometers of frontier it has in common with China. Moscow took great care not to do that.
2. As cited in P. M. Derevianko, *The Problem of the Revolution in Military Affairs* (Moscow: Voenizdat, 1965).
3. Field Marshal A. A. Grechko, *On Guard for Peace and the Building of Communism* (Moscow: Voenizdat, 1971).
4. V. Y. Savkin, *The Basic Principles of Operational Art and Tactics* (Moscow: Voenizdat, 1972).
5. For France, a ballistic weapon with a range of 2,500 kilometers can be considered strategic, while in the United States it might be characterized as a theater weapon.
6. It is obvious that the number of ballistic weapons needed for neutralizing the silos decreases as accuracy improves. Better still, this improvement of accuracy will reach a point where "fratricidal" effects will be eliminated. Someday, two low-yield warheads exploding within a small time interval, one on the ground, the other aboveground, will be sufficient for the destruction of a 300-psi silo.
7. The program was launched after the French parliament, with a large majority, approved the establishment of a strategic-nuclear force. The Hungarian crisis and the Suez crisis had brought to light both the Soviet threat and the precariousness of military alliances.

The prospects of German foreign policy

Hans J. Morgenthau

The broad outlines of the foreign policy of the Federal Republic of Germany are determined by three factors: the geopolitical position of the country, its aspirations with regard to other countries, and the aspirations of other countries with regard to it.

Since Germany's unification in 1870, its position among the nations has been determined by two considerations: the German people are by nature the most populous and disciplined people of Europe, and they have at their disposal the greatest industrial potential on the continent. In consequence, if nature were allowed to take its course, Germany would of necessity have become the master of Europe. It is this mastery that other European nations refuse to accept and that to prevent they have waged two world wars in one generation. This contradiction between the natural endowments of the German people and the political viability of the continent constitutes for the non-German world the German problem. How to reconcile these two elements of the contradiction has been the besetting issue for Germans and non-Germans alike.

Bismarck suffered from the *cauchemar des coalitions,* the fear that the great powers of Europe, especially France and Russia, would conclude a grand alliance in order to destroy the natural preeminence of Germany in Europe. On the other end of the political spectrum, Clemenceau confirmed Bismarck's fear when he declared that there were 20 million Germans too many. The division of Germany in consequence of the distribution of military power at the end of World War II and of the Yalta and Potsdam agreements similarly sought to reconcile German power and European freedom by cutting Germany down to size.

It is a testimony to the inherent strength of the German people that even the truncated Germany of today has again become the foremost industrial and military power on the continent. It is a testimony to the drastic changes that German power and foreign policy have undergone that the preeminence of Germany is no longer perceived by the other European nations as a threat to Europe. Three factors are responsible for that change.

The political balance of power that emerged from the distribution of military power at the end of World War II reduced all nations of Europe to the status of second- or third-rank powers, which to a greater or lesser extent had to lean, or were compelled to lean, for protection upon one or the other of the superpowers. The extent of that dependence determined the ability of those nations to pursue an independent foreign policy. Thus, the Federal Republic of Germany had to follow the American lead, as East Germany had to follow the Soviet lead.

This inability to pursue an independent foreign policy has been greatly enhanced by the stationing, in virtual permanence, of foreign troops in West and East Germany. This presence of foreign troops made it impossible for both Germanies to pursue, without the consent of the respective foreign powers, adventurous policies that might involve the nations concerned in international complications or even war.

Finally, a succession of West German governments and the electorate supporting them have drawn a lesson from Germany's defeats in two world wars and the human and material devastation accompanying those defeats. It is the same lesson Bismarck drew from the contemplation of Germany's geopolitical position, which became the basis of his foreign policy: the position of Germany in the center of Europe, surrounded by potentially hostile nations, makes it imperative for Germany to avoid a two-front confrontation. It requires either a Western or an Eastern orientation.

This imperative of caution and self-restraint has been greatly enhanced by the geographical position of Germany between the two nuclear superpowers. A war between the United States and the Soviet Union would most likely be a nuclear war, and the two Germanies would hold the forward positions, inviting total destruction.

The Federal Republic of Germany has opted for the West for two basic reasons. Its eastern frontier follows the line of military demarcation established between the Red Army and the Western armies at the end of World War II. The military governments established in the Western zones of occupation considered it their main purpose to preserve the status quo of that de facto partition. That purpose was powerfully and in all probability decisively supported by the refusal of the German people—freely and clearly expressed in the West and mutedly in the East—to exchange the tyranny of the Nazis for that of the Communists.

That refusal, as applied to the German Democratic Republic, was expressed by the early West German governments through the Hallstein Doctrine, which denied the legitimacy of the East German government and assumed the representation of both Germanies by the government of the Federal Republic of Germany. By the same token, the Hallstein Doctrine proclaimed the illegitimacy of the partition of Germany and presented reunification of the two Germanies as the foremost aim of West German foreign policy.

This aim was essentially limited to rhetorical proclamations, since the Soviet Union was no more willing to relinquish its military hold upon East Germany than the Western powers were to relinquish theirs on West Germany. Unable to pursue its claim of exclusive representation with anything even approaching efficiency, and conscious of the permanent importance of West European and American support, the Federal Republic of Germany pursued in reality a policy of Western integration, as exemplified by the West German membership in the European Community and in NATO. Thus, while West German rhetoric was turned to the East, the political and military realities pointed toward the West.

The treaties of 1970 with the Soviet Union and Poland, augmented by subsequent treaties with other Eastern bloc nations and the Final Act of Helsinki of 1975, mark a turning point in the foreign policy of the Federal Republic. They imply the recognition by the Federal Republic of the territorial status quo in Central and Eastern Europe and of the sovereignty of the East German government. They abolish for all practical purposes the Hallstein Doctrine. However, that does not mean that reunification as a goal of the Federal Republic's foreign policy has also been abandoned. The Federal Republic still refuses to accept the partition of Germany as legitimate and, hence, definitive, but regards reunification as impossible for the foreseeable future for reasons of ideology and the distribution of military and political power. When one considers the prospects of the Federal Republic's foreign policy, one must not lose sight of the possibility that reunification, now hardly anything more than a mirage on the distant horizon, might become a real goal of the Federal Republic's foreign policy.

The decline of American power and influence tilts the balance of power in favor of the Soviet Union and, in consequence, increases the insecurity of the nations of Western Europe. These nations—ambivalent toward the United States, whose support they need but resent—may then perceive themselves as having been abandoned by the United States and having to face, on their own, a Soviet Union unchallengeable in its military power. This state of mind would give the Soviet Union its long-sought-after opportunity to stabilize what it calls European security, which is in truth a euphemism for its own. Seen from the vantage point of the Kremlin, European security requires the reduction, if not the elimination, of American power on the Continent, the consequent emasculation of NATO, and the isolation of the Federal Republic of Germany. The nations of Western Europe, isolated from each other and from the United States, would then no longer be able to maintain a viable balance of power vis-à-vis the Soviet Union and would have to accommodate themselves to the Soviet hegemony over the Eurasian land mass.

This accommodation—were the Federal Republic of Germany to join in it—would signify a drastic change in the distribution of world power. The Western orientation of the Federal Republic has been derived from calculations of comparative political, military, and economic advantage. That orientation has not remained unchallenged from within the Federal Republic, even while rational calculation argued powerfully in its favor. If the development I have indicated above were to come to pass, rational arguments could indeed support an Eastern orientation. Traditionally fearful of the "Russian bear," a West Germany deprived of assured American protection would have to move into a neutral, if not friendly, political and military position vis-à-vis its towering neighbor to the east. That position would be greatly strengthened by the complementary relationship of the West German and Soviet economies. The Soviet Union has obviously decided to supplement its own efforts at industrial modernization with a massive influx of Western technology. The Federal Republic is one of the most highly developed industrial nations, dependent on large-scale exports for its prosperity. Once the political, military, and economic ties among the Western European nations and between them and the United States are loosened, the Soviet Union could offer a profitable alternative.

What argues against this possibility is not only the ideological cleavage between East and West and the distribution of military and political power, but also—and most emphatically—the interests of the Soviet Union, the Eastern bloc nations, and the Western powers. Even a truncated West Germany has become the most important economic and military power west of the Elbe River. Even this truncated West Germany affects France, if not the other Western European nations, as a competitor, if not a threat. The Western military and economic integration of the Federal Republic has served to mitigate that competition and to stave off that threat. However, even in the organizations effecting that integration, the natural preeminence of Germany has made itself felt. NATO has become for all practical purposes an American-German alliance, and the German mark is, together with the Swiss franc, the strongest currency in Western Europe.

When, with all these factors in mind, one raises the question of the prospects for the foreign policy of the Federal Republic, one realizes how narrow the space is within which the foreign policy of the Federal Republic moves today and will be able to move in in the foreseeable future. The solution of the issue of reunification depends only remotely upon the Federal Republic and primarily upon the Soviet Union. The Soviet Union will not give up its hold upon the German Democratic Republic, a refusal that precludes reunification, unless it receives an equivalent. One could imagine an Eastern orientation of the Federal Republic in the sense of severing its intimate military and political ties with the West. Instead, a united Germany, the kingpin of the Finlandization of Western Europe, would maintain its formal independence but lean politically and militarily upon the Soviet Union. There is very little likelihood that such a reorientation of the foreign policy of the Federal Republic will soon take place. But the history, first of Prussia and then of Germany, shows that the Eastern alternative has not been alien to Prussian and German statecraft and that it could materialize again as a viable option, given circumstances (especially in the nuclear field) favorable to it.

The Federal Republic, restrained in the East to relative immobility for the foreseeable future, must seek in continuing Western integration its main outlet for an active foreign policy. It must temper that activism with a considerable measure of self-restraint, always conscious of its preeminent power and the unacceptability of that preeminence to the other nations of Western Europe.

Thus, the prospects for an active foreign policy of the Federal Republic are dim. That dimness results from the Eastern political situation in which the Federal Republic finds itself, from the restraints that its neighbors in the East and West impose upon it, and from the self-restraint that the Federal Republic has imposed upon itself and is likely to continue to practice in the future.

Part four

THE MIDDLE EAST

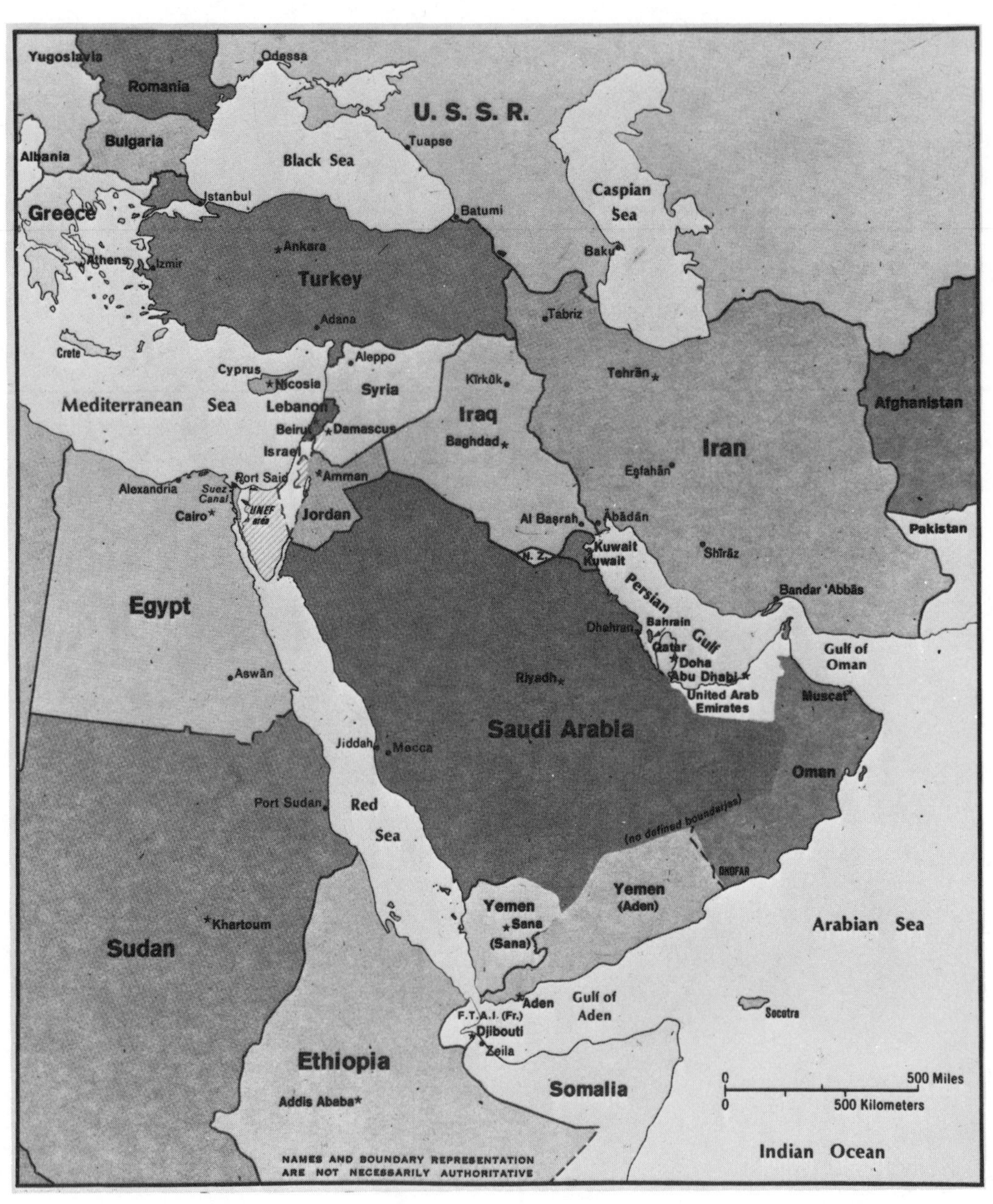
Yugoslavia
Odessa
Romania
U. S. S. R.
Bulgaria
Tuapse
Albania
Black Sea
Caspian
Sea
Istanbul
Batumi
Greece
Ankara
Baku
Athens
Izmir
Turkey
Adana
Tabriz
Crete
Aleppo
Cyprus
Nicosia
Syria
Kirkūk
Tehrān
Mediterranean Sea
Lebanon
Iraq
Afghanistan
Beirut
Damascus
Baghdad
Israel
Iran
Alexandria
Port Said
Amman
Eşfahān
Suez Canal
UNEF area
Cairo
Jordan
Al Başrah
Ābādān
Pakistan
N. Z.
Kuwait
Kuwait
Shīrāz
Persian Gulf
Bandar 'Abbās
Egypt
Dhahran
Bahrain
Qatar
Gulf of Oman
Doha
Aswān
Riyadh
Abu Dhabi
United Arab Emirates
Muscat
Saudi Arabia
Jiddah
Mecca
Oman
Port Sudan
Red Sea
(no defined boundaries)
DHOFAR
Yemen (Aden)
Yemen
Sana
(Sana)
Khartoum
Arabian Sea
Sudan
Aden
Gulf of Aden
F.T.A.I. (Fr.)
Socotra
Djibouti
Zeila
Ethiopia
Somalia
0
500 Miles
0
500 Kilometers
Addis Ababa
Indian Ocean
NAMES AND BOUNDARY REPRESENTATION
ARE NOT NECESSARILY AUTHORITATIVE

THE DEFENSE POLICY OF ISRAEL

Bard E. O'Neill

International environment

During its thirty-two years as a state, Israel has had a defense policy that has been determined primarily by the threats that its leaders have perceived from the international environment. The content of these threat perceptions, in turn, has been a product of a complex interplay of historic, geographic, and demographic factors.

THE CREATION OF A JEWISH STATE

The declaration of Israel's statehood in May 1948 was the culmination of a long, arduous, and frequently violent struggle on the part of Jews to create an independent state in the area of their ancient Biblical kingdoms known as Palestine (see figure 1). The main impetus behind this enterprise came not from the small Jewish community that had resided in Palestine since the time of the Roman conquest in 63 B.C., but rather from European Jews who were part of the Diaspora (i.e., the Jews who had dispersed throughout the world during the time of the Roman Empire and thereafter). Although the Jews had never abandoned hope of one day returning to Palestine, their interest in the area remained largely religious until the emergence of a nationalist movement among Eastern European Jews in the latter half of the nineteenth century. A conjunction of two political trends accounted for the new political activism of the Jews: the rise of nationalism in Europe and increased discrimination and violence against them in Eastern Europe, particularly Russia.

Both nationalism and anti-Semitism led a number of Jews to conclude that the security of the Jewish people could never be assured unless they attained a national home. The most prominent proponent of such thinking, an Austrian by the name of Theodor Herzl, wrote a major pamphlet entitled *Der Judenstaat* [The Jewish state], in which he made the case for a Jewish national state. Inspired by Herzl, Jewish nationalists met in Basel, Switzerland, in August 1897 and endorsed the aim of creating a Jewish home. Whereas Herzl had not indicated the location of such a home, the Basel conferees proposed that it should be in Palestine. Moreover, they established the World Zionist Organization (WZO) as the major instrument for its actualization. In the years between the Basel conference and World War I, the Zionists expanded their organization internationally, encouraged settlements in Palestine, set up a national fund to buy land, and made intensive, albeit unsuccessful,

Figure 1. The evolution of the state of Israel

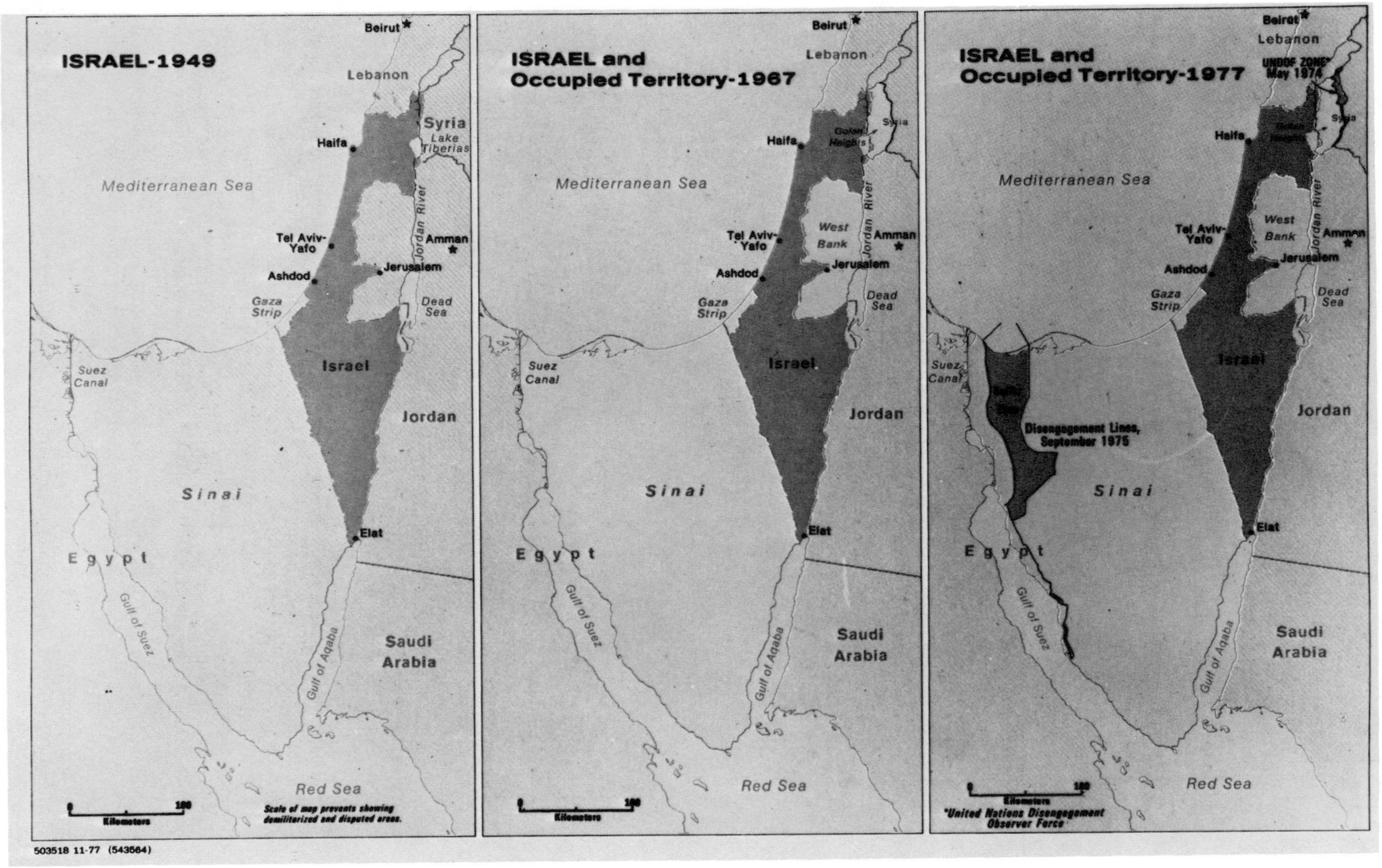

ISRAEL-1949

Scale of map prevents showing demilitarized and disputed areas.

ISRAEL and Occupied Territory-1967

ISRAEL and Occupied Territory-1977

*United Nations Disengagement Observer Force

503518 11-77 (543564)

efforts to persuade the major powers, especially Turkey, to adopt policies favorable to the achievement of their ultimate aim.

When the British consolidated power in the area during the war, they too were subjected to Zionist pressure. Motivated by a desire to secure Jewish support for the war, the British government engaged in talks with two important British Zionists, Dr. Chaim Weizmann and Lord Lionel Walter Rothschild. Although the British had previously agreed to an Arab demand for postwar independence in the Arabian peninsula (except Aden) and the area of Palestine, Lebanon, Syria, and Iraq, they had made such support subject to reservations and exclusions of territory because of their concern for French interests. Shortly thereafter, the British added to the confusion generated by their imprecise pledges to the Arabs by dispatching a letter to Lord Rothschild on 2 November 1917 (known since then as the Balfour Declaration) in which they indicated that Britain viewed with favor the establishment of a national home for the Jews in Palestine as long as it did not prejudice the civil and religious rights of the non-Jewish communities located therein. During the succeeding years, the wording of this declaration was interpreted in different ways by different people. In the meantime, the WZO stepped up its support for immigration to Palestine, thereby incurring Arab resistance; over the course of the next two decades, there was intermittent violence between the Jews and both the British and local Arabs, whose own sense of nationalism was stirring.

The accomplishments of the Zionists during this period were limited not just by Arab and British opposition but also by a failure to gain the support of a large segment of European Jewry that rejected Zionism on various religious, ideological, and practical grounds. However, most of this Jewish opposition to Zionism was soon shattered by Adolf Hitler's ascent to power in Germany and his adoption of virulent and violent anti-Semitic policies. As the German chancellor implemented his so-called final solution, a monumental act of genocide that took the lives of over six million Jews (known as the Holocaust), many previous skeptics in the Jewish community concluded that the campaign for an independent Jewish state deserved active and immediate support. As a consequence, political and material backing from international Jewry rose substantially.[1]

As Jews continued to arrive in Palestine, Arab resentment increased. Although several commissions of inquiry reviewed the problem, a viable solution remained elusive. When World War II began, the British government quickly found itself preoccupied with survival and therefore postponed any major decision, confining itself instead to the immediate issue of regulating Jewish immigration. In the aftermath of the war, a weakened Britain, beset with severe economic difficulties, decided to transfer to the United Nations what seemed to be an unsolvable problem. After several months of intensive and skillful lobbying by the Zionists, the U.N. approved a partition plan on November 29, 1947, which made provision for both Jewish and Arab states.

When both the Palestinian and other Arabs rejected this decision, fighting ensued between the two sides. Taking advantage of the absence of a U.N. plan to implement the partition resolution, the Zionists seized the initiative by acquiring weapons and training the forces necessary to defend their community and to sustain the state that would be established when the British withdrew in May 1948. As things turned out, the Palestinian Arabs proved unable to mobilize and organize the capability necessary to undercut the partition plan. A poorly coordinated (but nonetheless threatening) intervention of regular Arab military forces failed, and provided the Jews the opportunity to take control of the Negev desert in the south and the western Galilee sector in the north during the breakdowns in cease-fire arrangements that punctuated the fighting in 1948. As a consequence, Israel expanded to a size far more defensible than it had been under the partition plan.

THE LEGACY OF THE HOLOCAUST

Two aspects of the Holocaust left a lasting impression on those who would be charged with the responsibility for formulating national security policy for Israel in the years ahead. First, the Holocaust focused attention on the basic question of physical survival. Unlike their counterparts in other states, Israeli leaders believed that it was inadequate to define security as the safeguarding of political values and structures and a way of life; for them, security had come to mean the very existence of a people.[2] Second, the experience of the Holocaust led to the further conclusion that physical security was too important to be left to others, since, even in moments of extreme peril, sympathetic friends might be indecisive. From the Jewish point of view, this was a painful and costly lesson that had been learned from the unwillingness of the Allies to undertake any measures for relief and rescue at the height of the Holocaust, even when such measures would not have conflicted with the military objectives or required the use of military power.[3]

In one sense, then, the birth of Israel came at a time of both individual and collective trauma and insecurity. Moreover, the insecurity was reinforced immediately when the nascent state was invaded by neighbors who made it clear that they viewed Israel as an illegitimate entity created by the West to atone for German sins. Aside from accentuating Israeli feelings of insecurity, the 1948 war also underlined the emphasis on self-reliance, since Israeli appeals to the U.N. early in the fighting went unheeded.

DEMOGRAPHIC AND GEOGRAPHIC VULNERABILITY

Although the Arabs were greatly demoralized by the outcome of the 1948 war, they pledged themselves to the eventual eradication of the Jewish state. Inasmuch as the Arabs enjoyed a 50 to 1 manpower advantage (32.3 to 0.65 million), such hostility was of no small concern to Israel. The fears that it engendered were further magnified by the geographic facts of life. In the words of one scholar, "Israel's geostrategic position until June 1967 was a strategist's nightmare."[4] Surrounded by four belligerent Arab states and vulnerable to a blockade from the sea, it was "a state under siege."[5] The total area of Israel was close to 8,000 square miles, and the length of its borders was 615 miles on land and 159 miles on sea. There were no natural obstacles along the land borders.

In the south, Israel is contiguous to Egypt's Sinai peninsula, a barren and sparsely populated region (see figure 2). Because of its large size and terrain, and Egyptian control of the few obstacles that could impede an invading force, the Sinai was conducive to the massing and movement (in the northern and central sectors) of large forces not far from Israeli population centers. Although the mountainous southern part of the peninsula was not suitable for the movement of modern military forces, it was still important, since the location of Sharm el-Sheikh near the Strait of Tiran allowed it to control shipping in the Gulf of Eilat.

Another area adjacent to Israel is the Gaza Strip, located in the northernmost part of the Sinai and running some twenty-six miles along the Mediterranean coast. Originally intended as part of the Palestinian Arab state, it was occupied by Egypt in 1948 and placed under a military government. Its pre-1948 population of 70,000 swelled to 261,000 as the result of an influx of refugees from the fighting. In 1948, it served as the main base of the invading Arab armies and for attacks on the western Negev. By 1952, it had become a staging area for unorganized guerrilla attacks on Israeli settlements. Three years later, these attacks were placed under the control of Egyptian military intelligence and increased considerably.

From a security point of view, the border with the West Bank poses the most serious problem. Like the Gaza Strip, the West Bank was to have been part of the Palestinian Arab state but during the fighting in 1948 fell under the control of Jordan. It was formally annexed to Jordan in 1950 despite objections from the Arab League. Since the West Bank is next to the narrow waist of Israel, which at one point is only nine miles wide from the Mediterranean coast to the border, it was possible that a surprise attack by Jordanian armored forces might cut the country in two, thereby severing the north-south lines of communications. Short of that, almost all of the heavily populated and industrialized central section of Israel was within Jordanian artillery range. Furthermore, the West Bank could be (and eventually was) a base for periodic guerrilla attacks against Israel, occasionally supported by the Jordanian army. The city of Jerusalem, meanwhile, was surrounded on three sides by Arab forces and thus vulnerable to being quickly isolated from the rest of Israel (see figure 3).

Finally, in the north, Israel is bordered by Syria's Golan Heights, which overlook the Hula Valley and Northern Galilee (see figure 4). After 1948, the Syrians heavily fortified the area and from time to time shelled Israeli settlements below.[6]

National objectives, national strategy, and military doctrine

NATIONAL SECURITY OBJECTIVES

While there was no precise, overall codification of national strategy, much less a detailed longer-term plan for the orchestrated use of resources to attain political aims, on a more general level, several interrelated elements became discernible as the leaders of the new state moved to grapple with a host of formidable problems, including the consolidation of political control, economic development, social integration of immigrants from diverse backgrounds, and the provision of national security.[7] The most salient of these elements was the overriding emphasis placed on security and its corollaries, namely, the pursuit of peaceful acceptance of Israel by its Arab neighbors, the commitment to become as self-reliant as possible with respect to defense matters, and the construction of a strong military establishment.

In establishing priorities, Israel's first Prime Minister, David Ben-Gurion, saw "no alternative for Israel but to grant a central status to considerations of national security."[8] The centrality of security, as Dan Horovitz has pointed out, was an outgrowth of an essentially pessimistic view of the international environment held by Israeli personalities of various ideological and political persuasions. Such pessimism was rooted in the conception that survival involved not just the safeguarding of the state but the physical existence of all Jews in Israel as well. This conception, in turn, derived from the unhappy historical experiences of the Jews described in the previous section. Added impetus to the importance ascribed to security was provided by the "strategic data" of the Arab-Israeli conflict. In Horovitz's words:

> As a result of these data Israeli security conceptions have emphasized Israel's narrow security margin, resulting from a quantitative inferiority in population and resources and a lack of strategic depth. It is against this background that we must see the Israeli tendency to worst-case analysis as a guiding line in the formulation of foreign policy, which in these circumstances tends to be subordinated to the needs of security policy.[9]

Figure 2. The Egyptian border: Sinai and Gaza

EGYPTIAN BORDER: SINAI AND GAZA
Mediterranean Sea
Gaza
Gaza Strip
(Israeli-occupied)
Port Said
Jerusalem
West Bank (Israeli-occupied)
Hebron
Dead Sea
Be'er Sheva
Al Arish
104 km. 62 miles
Al Qanṭarah
Abū 'Uwayjilah
ISRAEL
Quseima
Suez Canal
Great Bitter Lake
Bi'r Jifjāfah
54 Km. 30 miles
Suez
U.N. Buffer Zone
JORDAN
11 km. 7 miles
SINAI PENINSULA
(Israeli-occupied)
Elat
Al 'Aqabah
Gulf of Suez
Gulf of Aqaba
SAUDI ARABIA
Aṭ Ṭūr
Sharm-esh-Sheikh
Strait of Tiran
Tiran
EGYPT
Red Sea

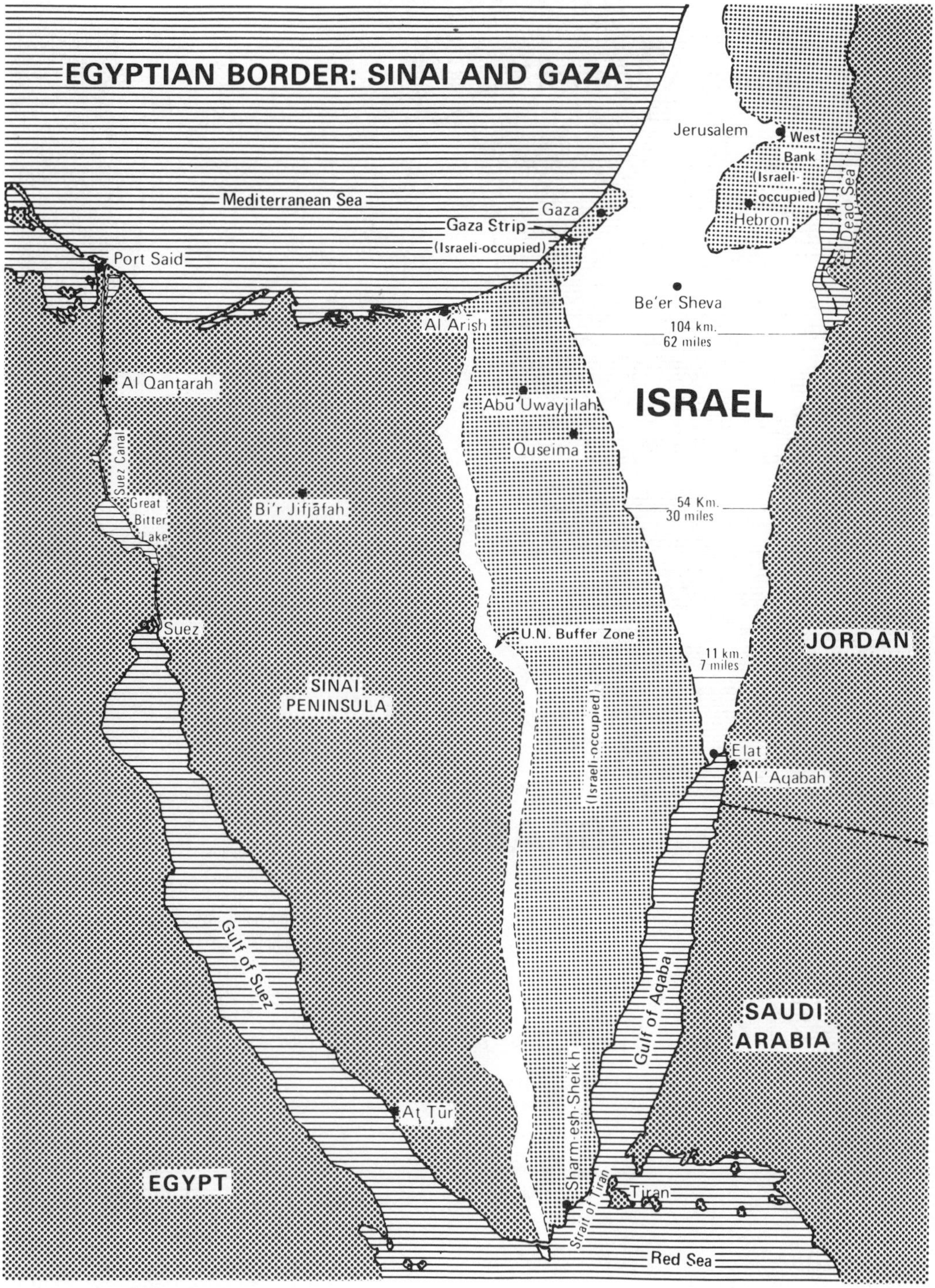

Figure 3. The Jordanian border

Figure 4. The Syrian border

The primacy accorded to security policy could be seen in all aspects of national strategy, beginning with its long-term goal.

Succinctly stated, the ultimate national strategic goal of Israel was defined as (and remains) peace with the Arab states. By peace, Israel did not have in mind agreements to avoid the use of force; instead, peace was conceived to be the full normalization of relations (i.e., diplomatic representation and international links in the areas of communications, trade, culture, travel, and so forth) with its neighbors. Only the actualization of peace along these lines, Israelis believed, could yield meaningful security. However, since Arab bellicosity relegated the goal of peace to a long-term pursuit, Israel was compelled to concentrate its efforts on the more proximate objective of insuring the physical security of Israel's land and people. Although Israeli leaders understood that military victory alone could not bring peace, they did hope that as time passed, the Arabs would become convinced that Israeli military strength rendered the destruction of the state improbable and futile and thus would come to terms.[10] But from the vantage point of the late 1940s, that day was reckoned to be far into the future. In the meantime, Israel would have to focus its national assets on the immediate aim of guaranteeing survival of the state. In pursuit of this aim, a pragmatic foreign policy and military strength were emphasized.[11] As far as military strength was concerned, Israel stressed a capability that would deter Arab attacks by posing potentially high costs and few gains and that, if it failed, would enable Israel to defeat enemy forces.

SELF-RELIANCE

An intermediate strategic objective, greatly influenced by the Holocaust and the 1948 war, was to become as self-reliant as possible where security was concerned. Despite the commitment to self-reliance, however, the realities of international politics and Israel's limited capabilities necessitated a degree of flexibility. Although preferring a policy of nonalignment vis-à-vis the Great Powers, Israel soon found that Soviet policies, such as restrictions on emigration and growing support for the Arabs, were inimical to its interests. Consequently, by the early 1950s, Israel had, in effect, aligned with the West. The shift toward the West marked a return to a policy of seeking the support of one Great Power that had been pursued in relation to Great Britain during the mandate but that had been dropped in the period following independence. By reverting to a policy of obtaining the support of one Great Power, Israel stood to benefit in three ways: first, the legitimacy of Zionism would be increased; second, the military and economic sectors could acquire badly needed material assistance; and third, the Arabs might come to realize that violent opposition to Israel was no longer a sensible policy.[12]

As things turned out, the concrete payoffs of aligning with the West were slow in coming. Therefore, the assurance of physical survival continued to rest on armed strength and self-reliance and the associated need to enhance the country's economic and military capabilities. In the economic sphere, this meant that educational, technical, and human resources had to be marshaled for development. As the years went by, the impressive achievements of the Israeli economy became a mainstay in the drive for self-reliance, albeit at substantial cost to a civilian sector that was simultaneously called upon to pay the costs of absorbing new immigrants.

The economic efforts directed toward self-reliance worked out reasonably well until a Soviet decision to provide Egypt with arms in 1955 stimulated an already fledgling arms race. From that point onward, Israel's dearth of national resources and heavy industry compelled it to look abroad for sophisticated (and expensive) equipment. Although German reparations, American loans, and contributions from Jews outside Israel helped to defray the costs, Israel gradually incurred heavy international debts.[13] Yet, the realization that absolute self-reliance was impossible did nothing to attenuate the commitment to minimizing foreign dependence as much as possible through the production of military hardware in Israel. Indicative of the diversion of economic resources to the security sector were both the high taxes and percentage of GNP allocated for defense and the substantial time that most Israelis spent in the military as either regular soldiers or reservists (see below).[14]

MILITARY POWER AND SECURITY

The high expenditures for the armed forces provided further evidence that Israeli political leaders considered a strong military capability as the centerpiece of national strategy. Recognizing that military strength required a good deal more than money and weapons, the leaders of the defense establishment turned their attention to the vital question of organization between 1948 and 1953.

On May 31, 1948, a government order was issued establishing the *Zvah Haganah Le Israel* (given the Hebrew acronym *Zahal*), or, as it is known in English, the Israeli Defense Forces (IDF).[15] The largest of several Jewish underground military organizations, the Haganah, became the foundation of the only legal military force in Israel. Despite opposition from left- and right-wing parties seeking to maintain their own armies, Ben-Gurion prevailed in a determined effort to create a single military force subject to civilian control. As far as basic structure was concerned, the leadership opted for a unified command for *Zahal* in which there would be one general headquarters and a chief of staff (*Ramatkal*) commanding all the military branches. At this point, also, the tradition of appointing very young chiefs of staff was established (the first two were in their early thirties).

The overriding organizational task during the incipient years of the IDF was to transform the segmented units of the 1948 war into a cohesive and modern military force capable of engaging regular armies equipped with air elements, armor, and artillery. Accordingly, the previous situation, wherein brigades tended to operate in one region from which their troops were recruited, was changed into one characterized by centralized control under the general staff headquarters. New units were no longer recruited on a local basis or confined to single areas of operations. Moreover, the country was divided into three major areas of command—the north, central, and south.

To cope with the demographic disparity vis-à-vis the Arabs, Israeli strategy stressed continued immigration. Cognizant that success in this endeavor would still leave *Zahal* far short of the number of recruits required for a large standing army, Yigal Yadin, the first chief of staff, devised a universal system of reservists in which every citizen was transferred to a reserve unit after completion of his mandatory tour of regular duty. Upon entering the reserves, individuals were to continue training, sometimes up to forty-five days a year, and to advance in rank until age fifty-five. Large military exercises were held to test the reserve system. In light of its small regular army and sizable reserve components, *Zahal* became a veritable citizens' army.[16] Because of the time required to mobilize and deploy the reserves, a premium was placed on advance warning from a high-quality intelligence apparatus. Furthermore, management of such a complex system required the IDF to devote a considerable effort to the education and training of a new generation of officers.

Although the strategic imperative of upgrading military capability was well served by these organizational and educational policies, it ran into trouble when it came to weapons acquisition, because the Western powers were reluctant to provide arms (the United States, in fact, refused to supply arms). Hence, the Foreign Ministry—then in charge of foreign weapons procurement—scrambled to obtain whatever weapons it could, rather than wait until preferred weapons might become available. This had three notable effects on national strategy: first of all, it led Israel to hoard and accumulate arms; second, it stimulated greater efforts to acquire equipment abroad; and third, it reaffirmed the wisdom of having a domestic arms industry.[17]

The effort to obtain advanced weapons abroad finally paid dividends in the mid-1950s. After strenuous efforts by the defense ministry and the IDF, close ties were established with France. As a consequence, the IDF was able to acquire up-to-date weapons for the first time, weapons that shortly thereafter were employed against Egypt.

THE 1956 WAR

The troubles with Egypt were precipitated by incidents along the Gaza Strip border. In response to alleged Egyptian aggressive activities, Israel carried out large-scale reprisal attacks. One of these, which took place in February 1955, was a reaction to decisions by Egypt's President Gamal Abdel Nasser to seek advanced weapons and to sanction attacks inside Israel by Egyptian-trained guerrillas.

By the summer of 1956, the interjection of major power interests made a bad situation worse. Disconcerted by Egypt's purchase of Soviet arms via Czechoslovakia and its recognition of Communist China, the United States withdrew an offer to help finance Cairo's main development project, the Aswan Dam. In reaction, Nasser nationalized the Suez Canal, a move that resulted in British and French collaboration with Israel. As fall approached, Israel became increasingly concerned about guerrilla raids and the arms being shipped to Egypt. When Egypt moved to form an alliance with Jordan and Syria, there were trepidations that, in time, the balance of power in the area might shift in favor of the Arabs. To preclude any serious threat to *Zahal's* ability to defend the state, Israeli leaders decided to act before Egypt consolidated its military strength and the new alliance.

After finalizing military plans with Britain and France, Israeli forces invaded the Sinai in late October. Besides the objectives of eliminating guerrilla bases and decimating Egyptian military power, Israel hoped to compel Egypt to conclude a peace settlement on Israeli terms and to acquire strategically important territory. By early November, an Israeli military victory was all but confirmed by the withdrawal of Egyptian forces westward over the canal. However, in the course of the next few months, American pressure, Soviet threats, and the possibility of sanctions by the U.N. forced Israel to relinquish its gains and France and Britain to accept Egypt's nationalization of the Suez Canal. Though obviously unhappy with this turn of events, Israel nonetheless had achieved some of its other aims. Large amounts of Egyptian military hardware were destroyed, and the Strait of Tiran was opened to Israeli shipping. In addition, the United States declared, *inter alia,* that it was prepared to exercise the right of freedom of navigation through the Strait of Tiran and to join with other nations to secure this right.[18]

The relative ease with which *Zahal* moved across

the Sinai in the 1956 war testified to the improving military capability of Israel. Although the war gave Israel over ten years of peace, it did little to alter basic national strategy, especially the elements of self-reliance and commitment to a powerful IDF.

As noted above, despite Egypt's defeat in the field, international pressure forced Israel, Britain, and France to yield their territorial gains and to accept Nasser's nationalization of the Suez Canal. Nasser's successful defiance of "imperalism" made him a hero in the eyes of Arabs throughout the Middle East. Motivated by (and taking advantage of) his new stature, the Egyptian leader sought to assert his leadership in the Arab world through diplomacy, propaganda, subversion, and, in the case of Yemen, military force. This preoccupation with Pan-Arab matters did not allow Israel to rest easy, however. Since aspirations for Pan-Arab leadership were hardly compatible with accommodating the perceived common enemy of the Arabs, namely Israel, there was no modification of the professed long-term Arab aim of destroying the Jewish state. In spite of Nasser's orientation toward Arab affairs, Israel could never be sure that Egypt and its allies would not one day turn their attention to the "Zionist problem." And, since the Egyptians and the Syrians were being equipped, trained, and advised by the Russians, the longer-term possibility of a military move could not be ruled out. In short, the Sinai war did not eliminate Israeli fears about the future, particularly since the geostrategic vulnerabilities along the borders had not been rectified.

In view of this situation, Israel devoted considerable time, effort, and resources to both analyzing and adjusting military doctrine (see below) and modernizing *Zahal*. Since the defense establishment was unable to acquire all the weapons it desired, the IDF depended increasingly on improvisation and its own technical know-how. In addition to enhancing its conventional capability, Israel also channeled resources into nuclear research and development.

THE 1967 WAR

In the spring of 1967, Israel's military capability was again tested when Nasser arbitrarily closed the Strait of Tiran, requested U.N. peace-keeping units to leave the Sinai, and augmented his military forces in the Sinai. While Israel mobilized its reserves and the daily costs of this undertaking mounted, the Western powers procrastinated over whether or not to send ships to open the strait. Frustrated by the inaction of the West, concerned about the Arab military threat, and enticed once again by an opportunity to strengthen (if not solidify) their military superiority by redressing the unfavorable geostrategic situation that had existed for nineteen years, Israeli generals argued for a swift preemptive attack. Once approval was given by Prime Minister Levi Eshkol, a dawn air attack all but eliminated the Egyptian air force. Following this decisive blow, the IDF moved with alacrity in a period of six days to seize the Sinai and the Gaza Strip from Egypt and, thereafter, the West Bank from Jordan and the Golan Heights from Syria. The geostrategic conditions in the conflict area were thereby dramatically changed in a very short span of time.

The seizure and occupation of the three Arab territories posed a dilemma for Israeli strategists. On the one hand, the indefinite retention of the areas brought over one million Arabs under Israeli control. Aside from the potential problems of ruling an antipathetic population, Israel had to contemplate the long-term effect on its democratic political ethos that indefinite rule without equal rights might have. On the other hand, an expeditious return of the territories to Arab control would mean going back to the disadvantageous geographic circumstances that prevailed before the war, something that security planners were loath to do, particularly after the Arab leaders met at the summit in Khartoum during August 1967 and resolved that there would be no recognition of, nor settlement and negotiations with, Israel. The policies adopted by the Israeli government were consistent with existing national strategy.

The magnitude of the Israeli victory in 1967 left few doubts about the military superiority of the IDF. Yet, in spite of the Israelis' demonstrable advantages, the Arabs did not seek the peace that national strategists had long hoped they would. Instead, the major Arab states demanded the return of all occupied areas and a restoration of Palestinian rights. While confining their main efforts to the diplomatic arena, the Arab states began the slow process of refurbishing their armed forces.

It did not take long for Israel to realize that the war had increased, rather than mitigated, Arab hostility. Nowhere was this more evident than in Arab support for commando and terrorist attacks against Israelis by Palestinian guerrilla organizations that had proliferated after the war. Although many of these groups were controlled by Arab states, others, such as *Al-Fatah* ("the largest"), were independent. The stated purpose of the Palestinian groups, many of which coordinated their activity through an umbrella organization called the Palestine Liberation Organization (PLO), was to expunge Zionism. From the Israeli point of view, the support of the guerrillas (known collectively as the *fedayeen* ("men of sacrifice") by the Arab states appeared to be yet another indicator of their determination to annihilate the Jewish state. This, in turn, had the effect of reconfirming major elements of national strategy.

As in the past, security remained the most important consideration. Unlike the past, the conditions for providing security, particularly the geographic ones, were vastly improved. Aside from removing various threats that could have been posed by nearby Arab forces, the occupation gave the Israelis defense in depth for the first time and provided natural defense barriers (e.g., the Jordan River and the Suez Canal). Moreover, it enabled the IDF to build and disperse new bases and facilities. The dispersal of air bases was especially important given their vulnerable prewar concentration in a few areas due to Israel's small size. Retention of the Sinai allowed Israel to construct four new air bases and a number of smaller airfields.

The security value of the territories to Israel increased as a result of *fedayeen* attacks along the borders, particularly the border with Jordan. Through the establishment of fortified settlements (*Nahals*) and military outposts, Israel was able to engage Palestinian guerrilla units (though not urban terrorists) in relatively open terrain a good distance from Israel's heartland.

There was, however, no gainsaying that retention of the territories strengthened Israel's military capability and thereby enhanced overall national security. Thus, while Israel indicated a willingness to return large portions of the territory and population, it insisted on controlling other areas for security reasons.[19] The degree of *Zahal's* military superiority that resulted from this new situation accentuated the importance of deterrence in Israeli strategic thinking. Although still committed to a strong war-fighting capability, the security establishment came to believe that the Arabs would be deterred from starting a major war because they would suffer unacceptable costs while having little chance of achieving their aim of destroying Israel. What Israel did not count on was the Arab states' conducting a major war for limited aims.

THE 1973 WAR

Israel's refusal to meet Arab demands that it return to the 1967 borders eventually led Nasser's successor, Anwar al-Sadat, to begin preparations for war. Although Nasser's initial attempts to dislodge the Israelis from the territories had been primarily diplomatic, by 1968 his despair with the continued impasse led him to start intermittent hostilities against IDF units along the canal. As Israeli casualties from artillery and commando raids began to rise in 1969, the Cabinet approved the use of air strikes deep inside Egypt. Unable to contain the Israeli Air Force (IAF), Nasser finally agreed to a cease-fire in the summer of 1970. In September, the Egyptian president died of a heart attack.

Shortly after assuming power, Sadat was confronted with an internal threat from the left (the so-called centers of power). In the spring of 1971, he eliminated this opposition and then turned his attention to the dispute with Israel, promising to wage a "battle of destiny." Much to his displeasure, he found that the military was in no condition to engage *Zahal*. Consequently, he appointed a new defense minister, who was charged with preparing the armed forces for a war with Israel. Meanwhile, Sadat relied on diplomatic efforts to bring pressure to bear on Israel, albeit with little effect. By the spring of 1973, Sadat became convinced that a limited war was the only way to create a new diplomatic situation that would eventually lead to a return of the occupied territories. Hence, he moved to obtain Syrian agreement to join the conflict. While the plans and preparations for war were being finalized over the summer, Egyptian diplomats went about lining up Arab and Third World support.

On October 6, 1973, the Arab armies attacked the IDF on both the southern and northern fronts, inflicting heavy casualties and achieving significant territorial gains.[20] Despite some very tense moments early in the conflict, especially in the north, where Syrian forces drove to the doorstep of northern Israel, the IDF eventually routed the Syrians and threatened to do likewise to the Egyptians.

In spite of their eventual military success, the Israelis were shocked by the war, particularly by the Arab ability to gain strategic surprise and to achieve initial military objectives. In retrospect, the close call in the Golan Heights was of special concern.

The October War had the effect of underscoring once more the basic elements of national strategy. The improved military capability of the Arabs, coupled with their continued disinclination to recognize Israel, accented the stress on national security. In fact, Israel became preoccupied with security matters as it sought to ascertain why things went so badly at the beginning of the conflict. One outcome of the postwar assessment was a decision to upgrade military strength substantially, through doctrinal changes, reorganization, improved training and maintenance, greater discipline, and a massive arms acquisitions program. A factor that played a key role in the renewed attention to arms acquisition was the belief that the dramatic rise in postwar oil revenues would enable the Arabs to rebuild their forces with huge quantities of costly, sophisticated equipment. Another factor was the realization that the West's dependence on oil had made it more responsive to the Arabs. During the conflict, the Europeans refused to sanction the transit of supplies to Israel for fear of provoking the Arabs, and immediately after the war, both the Europeans and the Japanese endorsed the Arab demand that the occupied territories be returned.

The shift by Europe and Japan provided further impetus for an already greater emphasis on self-reliance that derived from perceived American hesitation in resupplying Israel. Whatever the truth in the debate over whether or not the United States deliberately held up supplies, Israel experienced some anxious moments when the first few days of fighting drastically reduced its inventories. In light of this, *Zahal* committed itself to acquiring enough arms to wage a prolonged war without depending on any outside source.

From the Israeli standpoint, the war also reinforced the strategic importance of the territories. Although the Arabs argued that the war proved that territory could not provide security, the Israelis drew the opposite conclusion when they asked themselves what would have happened without the defense in depth provided by the Golan Heights and Sinai.

THE SADAT INITIATIVE

As time went by, the Israeli assumption that the Arabs would accept Israel only when they could not defeat it was partially vindicated. The reason for this, of course, was Sadat's gradual move toward an accommodation with Israel, which began with public acknowledgments that Israel's destruction was not a realistic aim and culminated with his Jerusalem visit in December 1977. By 1979, the Egyptian decision to normalize relations with Israel brought the long-sought-after acceptance and legitimacy; however, since the other Arab states (except Oman and the Sudan) bitterly castigated Sadat as a traitor, and since many issues were still unresolved, the essential ingredients of national strategy were unchanged.

PRESENT AND FUTURE STRATEGIC CONSIDERATIONS

One of the striking features to emerge from this review of national strategy is the remarkable consistency of its major components from 1948 to the present. While there is little reason to doubt the continuation of this state of affairs, the policies of the Likud, the right-wing-led coalition that came to power in 1977, raised some important longer-term questions regarding strategy. These questions revolve around two issues: first, negotiating separate peace accords with the Arab states, as opposed to a comprehensive settlement, and second, the expansion of the domain that is to be secured. Regarding the former, Israeli leaders have differed over the years. Some believed that separate agreements would diminish the overall capability of the Arabs to threaten Israel and therefore would lead to its eventual acceptance by most Arab governments. The key to this approach was the aim of disengaging the strongest Arab military force, Egypt, from the conflict. Others felt that separate agreements were unlikely, given the reluctance of major Arab regimes to go it alone, since such a policy would mean reliance on their own, rather than collective Arab capability, in bargaining with Israel—an obviously inferior position. Moreover, it was argued that since any Arab state that broke ranks would be faced with subversion sponsored by other Arab nations, it would be an unstable partner over the longer term. For those Israelis who held this latter view, the only answer was a comprehensive solution that involved all parties to, and major issues in, the dispute.

In practice, Israeli governments had vacillated between the two approaches, depending on what seemed feasible or advisable given the diplomatic conditions and international pressures at various points in time. For example, although two limited disengagement agreements were negotiated with Egypt and one with Syria between 1973 and 1975, Egypt's reluctance to proceed further without its Arab allies created yet another impasse and led the major outside power involved in the negotiations, the United States, to press for an overall solution. Although not in total agreement, the Israeli leadership shifted course, only to see the renewed multilateral effort fail because of Israel's refusal to talk to the PLO and the Arabs' inability to agree among themselves on conditions for new talks (particularly on the role of the PLO) and on the nature and composition of an Arab delegation. The unanticipated decision of Sadat to visit Israel then brought a dramatic reversal that resulted in the Egyptian-Israeli peace treaty.

The major question that these events have posed is whether or not the treaty with Egypt has convinced Israeli leaders that separate negotiations with the Arab states are the only way to accomplish their ultimate goal of peace, even though the treaty is technically linked to the requirement for pursuing a comprehensive solution. If this proves to be the case, the preferences for separate negotiations could become a cardinal element of national strategy. Yet, since significant opponents of the separate approach exist outside the government, its durability will remain a matter of conjecture for some time.

The second matter that bears on present and future national strategy relates to the definition of what is to be secured. Is it pre-1967 Israel or an expanded Israel that has incorporated sizable portions of the territories, most especially the West Bank? Once again, there are different positions. As far as the Likud government is concerned, the West Bank is part of Eretz Israel ("the land of Israel") and thus it should remain under Israeli control. Conversely, others, most notably the Peace Now Movement, believe that most or all of the territories should be returned. Some even contend that an independent Palestinian state should be established in the West Bank and Gaza Strip, a proposal that is anathema not only to the government but also to the opposition Labor party. In order to forestall such an eventuality and in order to move toward its objective of securing Israeli control over the West Bank, the Likud has supported increased Jewish settlements while promising limited autonomy to the Arab inhabitants.

In view of vigorous Arab protests and international criticism, as well as domestic dissent, the final outcome remains in doubt.[21] Should the Likud persist and be successful, a question will arise as to whether

Israel's planners will identify new buffer zones in areas currently under Arab control that are deemed important for the security of "greater Israel." If they do, it could mean heightened sensitivity to Arab military deployments in these regions similar to that which existed in the areas surrounding Israel prior to the 1967 war.[22] Although admittedly speculative, such questions are nonetheless important to contemplate because of their potentially important effects on national strategy.

Military doctrine

In view of the high priority Israel persistently has accorded to security and military strength, the nexus between national strategy on the one hand and military doctrine (i.e., the guiding principles for the application of military force) and force structure on the other has been inherently close and self-evident over the years. In part, this is due to the fact that the same historic, geographic, demographic, and economic factors that have played such an important part in determining national strategy have also influenced military doctrine and force structure. Since events on the battlefields during Israel's wars obviously have had significant effects on the evolution of doctrine, the military aspects of Israeli history will receive more direct attention in this section.

THE FORMATIVE YEARS: 1948–55

When Israeli strategists began the task of consolidating doctrine and planning for future hostilities in the early 1950s, they were guided by two basic assumptions, according to Maj. Gen. Israel Tal: one was that the destruction of enemy forces bestowed only a temporary advantage on the IDF in view of Arab materiel and human resources; the other was that captured territory would be difficult to hold because of the international opposition it would generate. Thus, conquered territory was viewed as conferring a strategic advantage and a bargaining chip for peace negotiations.[23] The recognition of the enemy's capability to rebuild following a defeat, the advantages the Arabs had by virtue of their numbers and resources, and the importance of territory compelled Israeli strategists to fashion a doctrine and force structure that would fully exploit the advantages of the Jewish community, most notably its high motivation, organizational abilities, and educational achievements. Since the effects of these attributes had already made themselves felt during the War of Independence, when the Jews were forced to fight on separate fronts against an adversary superior in troops and firepower, the origins of many of the enduring features of doctrine can be traced to that conflict.

To offset the Arab advantages during the War of Independence, Israeli military leaders found it necessary to mobilize the entire war potential of the Jewish community. In the absence of strategic depth, border settlements came to play an important role, namely, containing enemy advances until regular units could be transferred to their areas. To assure quick movement and concentration of power, a unified command structure was adopted. Once forces were concentrated against the Arabs, however, the problem of how to cope with the enemy's greater firepower had to be solved. The Israeli answer was to maximize surprise by following the strategy of the indirect approach, i.e., doing the unexpected in space, time, and direction. Because of the success in this undertaking, both the indirect approach and flexibility in planning and operations became essential ingredients in IDF military doctrine.[24] On the tactical level, this meant placing a high premium on competent middle- and lower-echelon commanders who were willing and able to adjust to changes on the battlefield (as opposed to adhering slavishly to textbook plans and standard operating procedures).

During the early years of statehood, the principle of transferring the war to the enemy's territory as quickly as possible through highly mobile, deep-penetration operations became part of military doctrine. To do otherwise and engage the enemy inside Israel was considered too costly in view of the state's small size, concentrated population, and economic assets.

The force structure that emerged from the War of Independence was primarily infantry oriented; air and naval components were small. Between 1949 and 1953, it underwent a number of organizational changes, the most important of which was the previously discussed institution of the reserve system. Border settlements retained their role as a first line of defense until the reserves could be mobilized.

The main instrument of attack remained the infantry. It was to receive fire support from tanks that functioned as mobile artillery. Accordingly, the pace of advance was necessarily dependent on the speed of infantry movements; little thought was given to the use of armor as a spearhead.

When Moshe Dayan became chief of staff in 1953, he did not alter the infantry's central role. However, he did place great emphasis on the further development of an offensive spirit. Although he subscribed to the indirect approach, Dayan recognized that it could not be used in all cases. Thus, he saw to it that the IDF was trained for direct assaults on fortified positions. Whether following the direct or indirect approach, Dayan believed in attacking forcefully and aggressively, even if it resulted in somewhat higher casualties.[25]

The emphasis on offensive spirit could be seen in the policy that the IDF adopted to deal with guerrilla attacks. Instead of responding with similar types of actions, as had been done from time to time, the IDF carried out reprisals against military targets. The purpose was to deter future attacks by increasing the costs to the Arab states and demonstrating to the Arab governments that their armies could not prevent retaliatory measures.

Whether dealing with guerrillas or planning for the possibility of conventional warfare, the IDF continued to accord primacy to the infantry despite entreaties from commanders of the armored corps who wished to operate in large concentrations rather than as small ad hoc groups supporting the infantry. It was only in the last few days prior to the 1956 war that Dayan suddenly reversed course and approved the use of tanks in large formations, a change of thinking that proved more successful than had been anticipated.[26]

During Dayan's tenure, the IAF was treated much the same way as the armored corps, in that its principal mission was to protect and support the infantry. Given the importance of the reserve components in the IDF, the air force was charged to ensure that mobilization met little interference and that aid was given to contain enemy advances until mobilization was completed.[27] From the IAF point of view, the successful fulfillment of such objectives was contingent on the ability to perform two important missions: the achievement of air superiority (by striking enemy air units on the ground if possible) and the interception of enemy aircraft threatening Israel. To accomplish these missions at a reasonable cost, the IAF opted for compact fighter-bombers in lieu of more expensive and less flexible bombers.[28]

In addition to the missions noted above, the IAF also acquired primary responsibility for the defense of Israel's coastline. While the Israel Defense Forces Navy (IDFN) provided support in this undertaking, major importance was not assigned to its activity. In fact, the primary strategic maritime objective, maintaining Israel's lines of communication with the outside world, was given to the merchant marine.[29] The role of the IDFN continued to be circumscribed until after the Sinai war.

MOBILITY, FIREPOWER, AND QUICK VICTORY: 1956–66

The Sinai war and the analyses that came in its wake influenced military doctrine and force structure in a number of ways. The swift Israeli drive across the Sinai indicated that the aim of a rapid military victory was attainable; Dayan believed that such a victory was imperative in order to avoid external political or military interference. The strategy of indirect approach, deception, and surprise once again emerged as a key element of success. Although the advantages of preemptive attack also became apparent, it was not until the postwar Arab military build-up that "it became a principle to deliver the first blow whenever a threatening situation developed as a result of the concentration of regular Arab forces in the proximity of [the] borders."[30]

The roles of the various components of the IDF were also affected by the war. In view of the new stress on combining mobility and firepower, the armored corps replaced the infantry as the principal instrument for decisive action; consequently, it was enlarged, personnel of higher quality were recruited, and extraordinary gunnery standards were established (and achieved).[31] Since the other land forces were tasked with supporting the armored corps, they were mechanized.

Like armor, the IAF's star rose as a result of the Sinai campaign. The key part that air superiority played in the Israeli victory motivated Israel to augment its aircraft inventory through the acquisition of French Mystères and Mirages and to devise new programs to enhance the quality of its pilots. Successful efforts were also made to modify aircraft to suit local conditions and to shorten their turn-around time by improving maintenance procedures.[32] Within the IAF, meanwhile, there was an increasing belief that the force should be committed first and foremost to the offensive. As the IAF commander, Ezer Weizman, continually importuned: "Israel's best defense is in the skies of Cairo." Such thinking led to detailed planning of operations to catch the Arab air forces on the ground before takeoff.[33]

Unlike the armored and air force components of the IDF, the importance of the navy was not significantly upgraded. Yet, even though there were few improvements in the IDFN's force structure, the navy was called upon to support the doctrinal principle of quickly transferring the battle to the adversary's territory by blockading enemy ports in time of war.

THE VINDICATION OF DOCTRINE AND FORCE STRUCTURE: 1967

As the fateful spring of 1967 approached, the IDF's doctrine and force structure were oriented toward swift, intense offensive operations inside enemy territory, led by armored and air force units. Though constantly alert to the opportunity to conduct indirect attacks, the IDF was prepared for direct assaults on the Soviet-inspired deep linear defense posture of Egyptian forces in the Sinai. Where it was impossible to outflank the enemy, Israeli doctrine called for heavy armored attacks along a narrow front near the center of the adversary's defense system. The air force was to attack antitank defenses, provide close support, and disrupt the enemy's rear areas. Heliborne operations would also be used for the last named. Should armored units arrive earlier than the mechanized forces, they would be encouraged to attack immediately in order to prevent the opposition from reorganizing.[34]

Israeli military doctrine was implemented in 1967. In the midst of mounting tensions that had their origins in border hostilities during the fall of 1966, the Soviets misled Nasser with exaggerated reports about an Israeli build-up against Syria. This brought a series of Egyptian moves described earlier (closing the Strait of Tiran, requesting evacuation of U.N. forces, and increasing forces in the Sinai). After some hesitation following the mobilization of their forces, Israeli leaders finally initiated hostilities. Consistent with the strategy of the indirect approach and the principles of attacking first and transferring the war to enemy territory, the IDF began operations with massive, devastating, and simultaneous predawn attacks against Egyptian airfields by aircraft sweeping in from several directions. Taken by surprise, the Egyptian air force was obliterated. As the air attacks were taking place, Israeli armored units launched a general offensive against Egyptian land forces. Shortly thereafter, Jordanian artillery opened up against Jerusalem, and ground units seized part of the city. The Israelis responded with a counterattack that hurled the Jordanians back and engaged them at several points along the front. Although the Syrians entered the war with air and artillery attacks, the Israelis adhered to the principle of dealing with the strongest opponent first by adopting a defensive posture against the Syrians until offensive operations were completed on the Egyptian and Jordanian fronts.

Within four days, a combination of direct and indirect attacks in the Sinai had routed Egyptian forces and enabled the IDF to achieve all of its objectives. Though the IAF received much of the credit for the success of the Sinai battles, the speed and thoroughness of victory was also due to other factors, including the quality and leadership of Israeli commanders, swift maneuvers in the field, excellent intelligence, good communications, and impressive logistical support. In contrast, the Egyptian forces fared poorly in all these areas, thus undercutting otherwise courageous efforts in a number of specific situations.

Though the sea battles were of secondary importance, it should be noted that the outnumbered IDFN took to the offensive early in the war; as a result of these naval operations, Egyptian missile boats and submarines were prevented from inflicting any appreciable damage.

Though intense, the battle for the West Bank and Jerusalem was over within fifty hours. Once again, the expeditious accomplishments of military objectives was due largely to the air-armor tandem.[35] Much the same was true on the Golan Heights, where the Israeli commander, Gen. David Elazar, relying on the strategy of the indirect approach, mobility, and envelopment, put Syrian forces to flight within two days.[36] The magnitude of the Israeli military victory was aptly summarized in *Paris Match,* June 24, 1967, by Gen. Andre Beaufre, one of France's leading strategic thinkers:

> In these three campaigns the Israeli armed forces demonstrated their high quality from the uppermost to the most modest levels. Such a series of successes rules out the idea of an accidental stroke of good luck. Sinai three days, Jordan two days, Syria two days—this decidedly is systematic lightning war.
>
> The recipes used are all well known: Surprise, resolve and speed, air superiority, a large degree of decentralization of command, ardent troops unencumbered by the complex of rigid and inhibited actions which still prevails all too often in the European, and even the American armies, a simplified logistics system. The utmost of maneuver is thus made possible. . . .
>
> All this was known. But perhaps never before has an execution been seen which was so close to perfection; nor has a victory which was more rapid and more complete.[37]

THE INTERPLAY OF OFFENSE AND DEFENSE: 1968–72

It was somewhat ironic that the same war that vindicated major elements of military doctrine also had the longer-term effect of undermining some of them. Although the offensive orientation that had stressed speed, mobility, and the like had proved its worth, the strategic depth provided by the newly occupied territories engendered some important defensive warfare inclinations. Nowhere was this more true than in the Sinai, where Israel decided to establish a quasi-static defense line along the Suez Canal (the Bar Lev Line) that was manned by small numbers of troops who were charged with holding the line during a conflict while the rest of the IDF gathered forces for a counterattack.[38] With the passage of time, the newly acquired defensive depth also raised questions about the need for the kind of preemptive attack that was so decisive in June 1967. As things turned out, Israeli military commanders remained committed to the notion of striking first but found their arguments overruled by the political leaders in the hours just before the 1973 war. Though international political considerations (i.e., fear of a negative U.S. reaction) were correctly cited as the overriding reason for not attacking first, it must be recognized that there was no anxiety that Israel faced an immediate nearby threat, as in 1967. The difference, of course, was the existence of the Sinai buffer zone.

The vulnerability of the Bar Lev Line had become apparent one year after the 1967 war, when Egypt began the so-called War of Attrition, a combination of artillery attacks and commando raids along the canal designed to inflict substantial casualties on Israeli forces. The IDF's first reaction was to relieve pressure along the canal by carrying out deep commando raids against lightly defended targets inside Egypt. The military purpose of this offensive riposte was to demonstrate that Israel could dictate its own terms of fighting and to compel Egypt to withdraw forces to the rear. When this brought a lull in the fighting, the IDF undertook a crash program to shore up the canal fortifications.

In June 1969, Nasser recommenced the War of Attrition. Since intensified commando attacks failed to bring an end to the fighting, the Israelis resorted to air attacks, first along the canal and then deep inside Egypt. At this point, the Soviet Union came to Egypt's assistance by building a formidable air defense system in the areas of important targets and cities, directing defensive operations, and flying missions. As the Egyptian air defense network was gradually moved toward the canal, the IAF began heavy round-the-clock bombing of air defense installations. However, though it finally gained the upper hand, Israel reluctantly yielded to American pressure for a cease-fire in the summer of 1970.

Both the 1967 war and the War of Attrition left their marks on military doctrine and force structure.[39] The IAF emerged from the June conflict as the most important part of the IDF, a development that was underscored by its performance in the War of Attrition. As a result, the IAF inventory was improved both quantitatively and qualitatively through the acquisition of American aircraft (most notably F-4 Phantoms, which had greater range, payloads, and versatility). Moreover, the IAF devoted more attention to electronic and counterelectronic warfare following its confrontation with the air defense system installed by the Russians during the War of Attrition. Efforts were also made to improve radar control systems through computerization and to upgrade the reconnaissance capability. In addition, the fighting gave a major boost to domestic production. The Israeli Aircraft Industry (IAI) produced several aircraft of its own, developed its own electronic equipment, and acquired the ability to repair and service all planes in the IAF arsenal.[40]

While the 1967 war reinforced the centrality of the armored corps within the land forces, there was more (but insufficient, as it turned out) attention paid to integrating armor with mechanized infantry and mobile artillery. Furthermore, the armored forces had to adjust to the new geostrategic situation by adopting a defensive posture along the Suez Canal. This did not mean that offensive operations were neglected. Indeed, considerable efforts were devoted to planning and training for armored operations across waterways.

As part of its preparation for the future, the armored corps was doubled in size. New tanks were acquired from abroad, and both old tanks and captured Russian tanks were converted and improved by adding new guns, engines, and range finders. All the guns and most of the ammunition were produced in Israel.

As far as the infantry was concerned, the 1967 war convinced the IDF of the need for a unified training system that would remove the distinction between elite and regular units. Accordingly, all combat personnel were trained for airborne, mechanized, and counterguerrilla operations.[41]

Although the June war did not alter the lower priority accorded to the IDFN, the naval force structure underwent a fundamental transformation. The post-June war sinking of the destroyer *Eilat* by Egyptian sea-to-sea missiles and the disappearance of a submarine en route to Israel intensified existing doubts about the utility of large warships in the region while underscoring the wisdom of a previous decision to produce missile boats. As those boats became operational, they were fitted with Gabriel sea-to-sea missiles produced by the IAI. Though small submarines were also given attention, the missile boat eventually became the backbone of the IDFN.[42]

One of the more notable developments after the 1967 war was the substantially greater part the domestic arms industry had come to play in improving the air, land, and sea forces. Despite the national strategic objective of self-reliance noted previously, Israel had made only modest progress prior to the war because of the limitations imposed by its small size. Although Israel still continued to recognize the impossibility of producing all of its weapons and equipment, it nonetheless concluded that greater sacrifices could and should be made in order to decrease its dependence on outsiders, especially during emergencies. The immediate cause of this conclusion was the decision of its main supplier, France, to embargo Israel during and after the war. The outcome was an Israeli commitment to produce as many weapons as feasible, given cost calculations, and with respect to essential weapons, to proceed even if the price were high. To offset the increased expenditures involved, sales to other countries were emphasized.[43]

The newly flourishing domestic arms industry, together with the qualitative and quantitative improvement of the force structure, the new geostrategic situation, and morale, leadership, and training problems in the Arab armies gave the IDF a clear margin of military superiority through the early 1970s. In fact, Israel's confidence that its military superiority would deter the Arabs from starting a major war was so high that intelligence indicators of impending hostilities in early October 1973 were dismissed. The prevailing assumption was that the Arabs would not go to war because they had no hope of winning. Since the Israelis further assumed that winning to the Arabs would mean the destruction of Israel, little or no attention was paid to the possibility that their adversaries might initiate major hostilities in order to achieve limited objectives.

THE OCTOBER WAR: REAPPRAISAL AND REBUILDING

It was evident that the Israelis had seriously miscalculated Arab intentions when the Egyptians and Syrians attacked on October 6, 1973. Though this is not the place for a detailed account of the October War, a summary of events is important because of the far-reaching effects the conflict had on *Zahal*.

In their initial planning for the war, the Egyptians and Syrians had come to realize that destruction of the IDF was impossible in view of its superior position. In the light of this situation, they set tough but limited objectives for themselves. The preeminent political goal was to generate a new diplomatic process that would eventually lead to a return of the occupied territories. In order to bring the desired results, the Arabs believed that the passivity of the superpowers would have to be transformed into active pressure against Israel. In Sadat's view, the United States was the key because of the leverage it derived from Israeli dependency on American economic and military assistance.[44] If the United States was to use this leverage on behalf of the Arabs, its interests in the area had to be threatened. In more specific terms, the Arabs hoped to take advantage of both the increasing Western need for petroleum and fears of a superpower confrontation that could result from a gradual escalation of hostilities. Besides creating international pressure on Israel, the Arabs also intended to add internal pressures through the infliction of heavy losses on the IDF.

Success on the battlefield was critical for the achievement of these political aims. It was also necessary for creating a psychological climate conducive to negotiations involving Israel. Before the war, such negotiations were inconceivable to the Arabs because of the belief that they would be tantamount to supplication. The only way Arab leaders thought this state of mind could be changed was to redeem their honor and dignity (a very important consideration in Arab culture) through a military success that would leave them in a position of perceived strength.[45] If everything went as planned, there would be another important benefit, namely, an enhancement of the legitimacy of the governments in Cairo and Damascus.

Thanks to an elaborate and brilliant deception plan, as well as a monumental Israeli intelligence failure, the Arabs achieved strategic surprise. During the early fighting, the Arabs were able to inflict costly defeats on the IDF and to achieve significant territorial gains. In the south, the Egyptians crossed the canal, destroyed the Bar Lev Line, and consolidated control of a narrow beachhead running the length of the canal, while in the north the Syrians drove through the Golan Heights. The reluctance of the Egyptians to send their forces beyond their air defense umbrella and into the Sinai allowed Israel time to mobilize its reserves and concentrate on the perilous situation in the Golan, where the Syrian offensive had advanced within a few miles of Northern Israel.[46] The Egyptian Minister of Defense rationalized his conservative approach with this explanation:

> In order to advance we had to wait for armor to enter the field, then for the mobile antiaircraft missiles to enter the field, regardless of opportunities that others saw or I saw.
>
> If I had thrown in my forces after the [opportunities] experts are talking about without adequate defense against the enemy's air superiority, I would have been putting the whole burden on the air force, which would have exceeded its capacity.[47]

Following heavy fighting in the Golan Heights, *Zahal* went on the offensive and drove halfway to Damascus, a turn of events that brought frantic Syrian appeals to Egypt to relieve pressure by moving forces forward in the Sinai. By the time Egypt responded, Israel had already begun to redeploy units to the Sinai; shortly thereafter, both sides engaged in a massive armored confrontation. When this confrontation checked the Egyptians, the High Command in Cairo decided to move additional forces across the canal, thus setting the stage for Israel's use of the strategy of the indirect approach.

Implementing a plan that had been conceived and successfully tested in maneuvers after the 1967 war, the Israelis sent armored columns across the canal. Although the success of this bold stroke was very much in doubt during the early hours because of stiff Egyptian resistance, the IDF finally secured the crossing point, moved forces across the canal, surrounded the rear of the Egyptian Third Army in the south, and posed a similar threat to the Second Army in the north. At this point, heavy pressure from the superpowers brought an end to the fighting, thus sparing the Egyptians a potentially disastrous defeat.

Despite the favorable military outcome, there was little rejoicing in Israel. The anxious moments and heavy casualties that the IDF experienced early in the war led to a wide-ranging reassessment of military matters that included a critical look at doctrine and force structure.

One of the first elements of doctrine scrutinized after the war was the principle of delivering the first blow. Though eminently successful in 1967, a first strike was eschewed in 1973 because of the aforementioned concerns about the American reaction and the defense in depth provided by the occupied territories. As one of Israel's leading generals put it:

> After the Six-Day War, our defense concept changed. Thanks to the strategic depth we had acquired, we no longer clung to the principle of the "first blow," and we also believed that we had reached safe harbors and could allow

ourselves to conduct a defensive war. All this was correct insofar as the question of our national existence was at stake, but it was wrong with regard to the possibility of Arab success in gaining limited military objectives. We certainly did not intend to allow the Egyptians and Syrians to conquer the Suez Canal or the Golan Heights from us by force of arms.[48]

Such views notwithstanding, there were reasons to doubt whether a preemptive attack would have been as decisive in 1973 as it was in 1967. To begin with, the Arabs had not only developed and implemented aircraft revetment and dispersal plans but they had also constructed a massive air defense system against both high- and low-altitude attacks.[49] Furthermore, they were psychologically prepared for a possible air assault by the IAF.

As things turned out, Israel leaders were not convinced that war was imminent until early on the morning of October 6. Although a decisive preemptive attack was questionable for the military reasons just noted, there was still the possibility of a damage-limiting or spoiling blow.[50] However, because Prime Minister Golda Meir took the United States at its word it would be hard pressed to support Israel if the IDF struck first, she turned aside a first-strike proposal by the chief of staff.[51] Since many Israeli leaders came to the conclusion that not striking first had been a mistake, a preemptive move in the face of a future large-scale Arab military build-up has now become more probable. Yet, it cannot be viewed as a certainty in the light of possible American political opposition, the preparedness of the Arab states, and the mitigating effects that the early warning systems installed in 1975–76 would have.[52]

The doctrinal emphasis on offensive operations, transferring the battle to enemy territory as soon as possible, dealing with the most threatening enemy first, and following the indirect approach was reinforced by the 1973 war. Early reverses during the hostilities were attributed by many to the defensive posture along the canal that enabled the Egyptians to dictate the terms of battle and seize the initiative. The fact that armored forces were dealt major setbacks when they moved against the Egyptians shortly after the fall of the Bar Lev Line did not diminish the preference for offensive operations; indeed, as postwar analyses concluded, the failures were due to inadequate preparation, faulty coordination, and poor control and leadership by the Southern Command. After the containing of enemy advances in the Golan Heights and the Sinai, it was offensive—first into Syria (the most threatening front) and then across the canal into Egypt—that ultimately proved decisive in that they transferred the initiative to the IDF and allowed it to dictate the terms of battle. As a consequence, the Israeli defense establishment renewed its commitment to offensive warfare. Illustrative of this situation was the serious consideration devoted to a range of offensive options for a future conflict that included the possibility of outflanking Syrian forces by means of invasion through either Jordan or Lebanon, even if these states were to avoid involvement in future hostilities. Other options raised by the IDF were air strikes against the supporting Arab states and amphibious operations against Egypt's long coastline.[53]

The reaffirmation of offensive warfare was also designed to support another element of strategic doctrine that deserves brief mention here—the stress on quick victory. As suggested above, the Israelis were denied a complete military victory on the Suez front because of Soviet and American political intervention (the very sort of thing Dayan had warned against when he was chief of staff). The length of the conflict had given both superpowers enough time to contemplate their responses and enabled them to avoid (though narrowly) a rapid Israeli *fait accompli*. Besides failing to attain a total victory over the Arab armies, the IDF also incurred heavier losses due to the prolonged fighting, a point that brings me to an evaluation of the effects of the war on the tactical aspects of Israeli military doctrine.

On the tactical level, Israeli military doctrine stressed a number of themes prior to the war: initiative and flexibility by local commanders (as long as they achieved assigned objectives), high-quality middle- and lower-echelon commanders, highly motivated personnel trained to use modern equipment, good maintenance, and minimization of casualties.[54] The war had important effects on all of these.

After an exhaustive inquiry, the blue ribbon panel that was established to analyze all aspects of the war, the Agranat Commission, concluded that initiative and improvisation played a key role in extricating *Zahal* from a very difficult situation.[55] Yet, at the same time, it reaffirmed the fact that commanders exhibiting flexibility and initiative cannot afford to do so at the expense of the objectives assigned to them, by pointedly noting that a major reason for failure in the Sinai early in the war had been an "erosive deviation" from the objective set by the chief of staff.[56] On the Golan Heights, by contrast, the adroitness and flexibility of Israeli commanders during both the defensive and offensive phases of the fighting was a key factor in battlefield success.[57]

The Golan fighting also demonstrated the importance of middle- and lower-echelon officers of high quality. As the Agranat Commission pointed out, the initiative and resourcefulness of junior- and field-grade commanders, who were forced by circumstances into independent and isolated actions, influenced the outcome of the entire campaign.[58] For example, despite being outnumbered twelve to one in the early going, the armored corps achieved an impressive twelve-to-one kill ratio.[59] Active front-line leadership was not without costs, however, since 24 percent of those killed in action were officers, a 4 percent rise above 1967.[60]

While the performance of lower-ranking officers was no doubt reassuring to the IDF, the same could not be said of all the major commanders. One of the most significant opinions of the Agranat Commission was that the southern front commander, Maj. Gen. Shmuel Gonen, did not possess the qualities necessary for moving, deploying, reinforcing, and supporting forces in accordance with the strategic aims of a major command. Specifically, Gonen was charged with not preparing thoroughly for the early containment battle (there was no detailed operational plan); failing to ascertain whether his forces had arrived in full and were properly deployed; overlooking the need to review and approve the plans of his commanders; conducting the battle without effective command of his forces, with the consequence that he was not properly informed of developments; hastily moving forces without due regard for whether the objectives of higher command levels were achieved; changing the objectives of his *Ugdot* ("battle groups") without giving them information about Egyptian and Israeli forces; causing a general erosion of both the objectives and method imposed by the chief of staff; and being impatient to cross the canal before the essential conditions for such a move had been created.[61]

In explaining why it believed Gonen had failed, the commission argued that although he possessed courage and comprehensive professional knowledge and expertise in the operation of the means used by *Zahal,* Gonen was lacking the "special administrative command expertise and know-how . . . required to coordinate the forces of a regional and theater command at the right time and place."[62] What all this suggested, of course, was that the skill and achievements of forces on the tactical level could be undercut by poor high-command-level leadership. While the IDF has always been aware of this, the Agranat critique had the effect of increasing the sensitivity to the need for assuring quality and proper preparation for high-echelon command as well as for middle and lower levels. To assure that the process for appointing top commanders was as thorough as possible, a permanent committee of commanders was tasked with reviewing the credentials of candidates and advising the chief of staff.

The importance of well-trained and motivated personnel in relation to modern weapon systems, and high standards of equipment maintenance, was borne out in the October War. For example, the high operational readiness rate (over 90 percent) and the impressive turn-around time for aircraft, which were made possible by both superb maintenance and the renowned skills of the pilots, enabled the IAF to average 2,000 sorties per day and to achieve an air-to-air kill ratio of sixty to one.[63] That the armored corps experienced similar success was no doubt due to a demanding training program, which was described as follows in an article completed just prior to the war:

> Conscripts get several months of recruit training before arriving at the armor school where they study individual tank subjects (gunner, driver, communications) and then have tank unit training. Thus, Israeli soldiers wait some months before becoming full-fledged tank crew members. The training is intense, twelve hours a day for five days a week and six hours on the sixth day (one entire day of the training week is reserved just for maintenance). Those selected for officer training will have served almost two years before becoming a platoon leader, four to five years before getting command of a tank company.[64]

Despite the success of training programs such as this, the IDF could not rest on its laurels because the Agranat Commission expressed apprehension about a perceived diminution in regimen and discipline which it felt had created some "grave difficulties."[65] To arrest this adverse trend, greater emphasis was placed on expanding and strengthening training programs.[66]

The final tactical principle of doctrine, the minimization of casualties, was the subject of national attention after the war. In twenty days, an estimated 2,500 Israelis were killed, 2,000 wounded, and 508 missing in action.[67] As bad as these figures appeared, they could have been worse were it not for several decisions made during the conflict. The objective of sparing lives, for instance, was one of the reasons for the adoption of a cautious campaign on the Golan Heights that was marked by the use of close air support and heavy artillery barrages before infantry and armored formations carefully moved through Syrian lines; it was also said to have been one of the factors dissuading the IDF from moving on to Damascus.[68]

The human cost in 1973, together with an estimate that another three-week war using improved technology might result in a staggering 8,000 casualties, heightened the IDF's concerns about battlefield losses. For the most part, resolution of this problem was viewed as a function of strategic doctrine and force structure. With regard to the former, the emphasis on swift, offensive warfare by concentrated and integrated forces was considered the best way to minimize loses; with respect to the latter, primary reliance on air and armor, supported by artillery and infantry forces, as well as on the use of advanced weapons (especially precision-guided munitions), was believed conducive to fewer casualties. As one observer put it:

> The obsession of Israel's military leaders since 1973, therefore, has been to restore the ability of their aircraft and tanks to operate freely on the battlefield, where those reservist infantrymen must venture on to it, to give them the maximum possible chance to survive. More than before, this has meant a concentration on new kinds of weapons.[69]

Once the postwar analyses were completed and the IDF began to implement many of its recommendations, it became clear that the strategic and tactical elements of military doctrine that had evolved over the years were to be reconfirmed rather than altered. Both short-term and, especially, long-term war plans reemphasized familiar principles of strategic doctrine (offensive orientation, surprise, striking first, fighting in enemy territory, quick victory, the indirect approach, and so forth) in addition to the tactical elements discussed above. At the same time, however, it is important to note that, as in 1973, IDF plans and deployment patterns did not rule out defensive operations, at least for a time. On the West Bank, for example, many of the settlements established since 1967 became part of a defensive network designed to impede an enemy thrust until the IDF was mobilized and moved into positions where it could conduct offensive operations if they were deemed necessary.[70]

In the final analysis, the major changes that occurred after the 1973 war were in the area of force structure rather than doctrine. A major effort was undertaken to improve all facets of the IDF: support functions (intelligence, logistics, and maintenance), the combat arms (both regular and reserve components), and weaponry.

The initial scheme for strengthening the IDF was set forth in a 1974 plan called Matmon B, which defined military requirements in such a way that Israel would have the capacity to conduct rapid, intensive offensives against its neighbors before external powers could intervene.[71] It involved substantially higher manpower levels and "an enormous increase in weapons inventories, accompanied by qualitative improvements of a similar magnitude."[72] To accomplish its aims, the IDF not only stepped up the acquisition of sophisticated hardware abroad but also encouraged domestic arms producers to expand and increase their output.[73]

In the land forces, the number of tanks rose by 1,000, artillery pieces by 700, and armored personnel carriers by several thousand. In addition, antitank weapons were purchased in large quantities from the United States.[74]

The IAF capability was also upgraded considerably by adding over 200 combat aircraft, including American F-4Es, A-4Ns, F-15s, and F-16s. The F-15 was particularly noteworthy in that it generally was considered to be the best fighter aircraft in the world. To cope with the surface-to-air missiles that had caused serious problems in the war, a large number of precision-guided munitions, air-to-surface missiles, and electronic countermeasures were introduced. To extend the combat range of fighter-bombers, old Boeing KC-97 tankers were retired in favor of jet tankers modified from Boeing 707s by IAI.[75] Air defense was also improved considerably through the acquisition of the E-2C airborne early warning aircraft, improved Hawk surface-to-air missiles, Chaparral antiaircraft missiles, and antiaircraft guns.[76] Finally, as the well-publicized Entebbe raid in 1976 showed, the IAF had also developed the ability to control, move, and supply forces far from Israel.

Although most of the effort to strengthen the IDF structure focused on the land and air forces, the IDFN was not neglected. For example, missile boats were increased from fourteen to twenty-one, Harpoon antiship missiles were ordered from the United States, and Israeli-built reconnaissance aircraft entered service.[77]

Force structure improvements were not limited to the addition of greater and more sophisticated equipment to the arsenals of the land, air, and sea components, since postwar assessments had identified several related issues that needed serious attention. These included requirements for sound intelligence, greater coordination of the combat arms, more efficient mobilization procedures, better maintenance, and improved discipline. After careful analysis, a series of corrective steps was taken with respect to each.

The intelligence issue was considered most critical because of breakdowns on the national and field levels. How an intelligence apparatus renowned for its dexterity could have blundered so badly was a question addressed by the Agranat Commission. Not surprisingly, the answer was that interpretation, not collection, was to blame. Both structural and psychological shortcomings accounted for this.[78]

Intelligence had been structured in such a way that only one agency, Military Intelligence, with a staff that ironically was described as "refreshingly small" just prior to the war, was responsible for interpretation and analysis.[79] Within a unitary structure such as this, the estimates of Military Intelligence were dominant. As things turned out, the absence of contending views was nearly fatal because Military Intelligence misinterpreted various Arab moves in the days preceding the outbreak of hostilities. The prewar view of the head of Military Intelligence, Maj. Gen. Eliahu Zeira, was that a conventional attack was improbable because the Arabs had little chance of victory.[80] Similar opinions were also expressed by other military leaders, such as the 1967 hero Gen. Ariel Sharon.[81] Judgments like these led both military and academic analysts to dismiss Arab warnings as nothing more than a penchant for rhetorical flourishes that masked a lack of capability.[82]

In view of the strategic surprise the Arabs gained by virtue of this situation, Israeli leaders concluded after the war that the intelligence system had to be restructured in such a way that contending interpretations could be voiced (multiple advocacy). Hence, the capability of both the civilian intelligence organization, *Ha Mossad L' Tafkidim Meyuhadim* ("the Institute for Special Tasks"), and the Foreign Ministry to provide independent interpretation and analysis of Arab capabilities and intentions was strengthened.

While both the Mossad and the Foreign Ministry reportedly have channels to the political leadership, Military Intelligence has retained its preeminent status, in part because it has more resources at its disposal and can request inputs from the civilian agencies.[83] As far as field-level intelligence is concerned, numerous improvements were made in response to deficiencies identified by both the Agranat Commission and independent observers.[84]

A second major problem, coordination of the combat arms, was manifest early in the war, when Egyptian infantry using antitank rockets played a major role in several Israeli defeats. In retrospect, the Israelis traced their difficulties to a failure to integrate infantry, armor, artillery, and air elements sufficiently on the battlefield. As a consequence, the IDF paid much greater attention than before to preparing its components for combined operations in a future war.[85]

During the war, the IDF also experienced difficulties in three related areas: mobilization, which Chaim Herzog characterized as "hastily improvised"; maintenance of equipment, which reservists complained was often shoddy; and lax discipline, which the Agranat Commission believed was partially responsible for equipment readiness problems, as well as other shortcomings.[86] In response to the first two criticisms, the IDF instituted a number of reforms (e.g., dry storage and better protected and decentralized vehicle and equipment depots located closer to the anticipated battlefronts) and carried out exercises that reportedly enabled it consistently to achieve full mobilization in thirty-six hours. While improvements in the area of discipline were more problematical in view of the informality and egalitarian values of Israeli society, there was a discernible tightening up, particularly under Ra'fael Eytan, who became chief of staff in 1978. Nevertheless, the IDF had still not resolved all its difficulties, as was clear from a 1979 comptroller's report that identified continued deficiencies in the areas of maintenance, safety, discipline, and field intelligence.[87]

As the new decade of the 1980s began, there was a general consensus among analysts that the force structure improvements and reforms had left the IDF stronger than ever. Though budgeting constraints, which stemmed from national economic problems and the costs of redeploying from the Sinai to the Negev (as required by the Egyptian treaty), were forcing cutbacks in a number of areas, there was little doubt that the IDF was capable and ready to conduct operations in accordance with existing military doctrine.[88] That doctrine, fashioned in four wars, provided the IDF with a series of consistent and reliable guidelines for the conduct of large-scale warfare on the conventional level.[89] How the IDF dealt with other levels of conflict (i.e., insurgent and nuclear), however, remains to be discussed.

COUNTERINSURGENCY

From its very beginning, Israel had to cope with terrorist and guerrilla attacks from adjacent Arab states. Since the *fedayeen* organizations were controlled and supported by the Arab governments, the Israelis established a policy of holding the Arab governments responsible and therefore carried out small-scale reprisals against targets in the Arab states.[90] By the mid-1950s, the reprisal actions had taken the form of large-scale operations against military objectives in Arab States. The purpose was to demonstrate the weakness of the Arab armies and to increase the costs of supporting the insurgents to the point where the Arab regimes would discontinue their support.[91] Although this policy did bring periodic lulls, it did not end *fedayeen* raids. While the longest period of calm came after the 1956 war, raids began again in 1966 and played a role in triggering a series of events that culminated in the 1967 war.

After the Arab defeat in 1967, the insurgent threat took on a new, more serious, dimension. Although still receiving assistance from various Arab states, several Palestinian organizations acquired an independent political status. Consequently, the Palestinian resistance became an amalgam of groups, some of which were autonomous (e.g., Al-Fatah, the Popular Front for the Liberation of Palestine, and the Democratic Popular Front for the Liberation of Palestine) and others of which were controlled by Arab governments (e.g., Sa'iqa by Syria and the Arab Liberation Front by Iraq). Although these organizations differed in terms of ideology, strategy, and tactics and were constantly engaged in internecine power struggles, they shared the common goal of destroying the Israeli state. They also agreed that the only way this aim could be accomplished was by means of a protracted people's war that stressed familiar insurgent techniques (i.e., political organization, terrorism, and guerrilla warfare). Thus, between 1967 and 1970, Israel was faced with guerrilla raids from across the border (especially Jordan), and terrorism and political organization efforts inside the occupied areas (and sometimes within Israel itself). From 1971 until the late summer of 1973, the guerrilla threat receded, but internal terrorism continued. Moreover, a new dimension, terrorist attacks outside the Middle East (transnational terrorism), was added. The period after the 1973 war until 1980 was largely one of internal terrorism conducted by groups either inside the territories or infiltrating from Lebanon.

The Israeli doctrine for coping with this expanded revolutionary insurgence was a multifaceted one that went beyond reliance on *Zahal*. To preclude the insurgents from establishing a wide base of popular support among the Arabs, a series of political and economic steps were taken to restore and improve normal life patterns. The administrative policy of the military government stressed noninterference, a minimal Israeli presence, and freedom of movement in the occupied areas. Economic policy, meanwhile, was designed to increase the standard of living in the occupied areas to the point where it would give Arabs a stake in stability.

To deal with guerrilla raids and terrorism, a series of coercive measures were taken. The guerrilla threat was handled mainly by the IDF. Besides retaliatory attacks inside Arab states that harbored guerrillas, the IDF adopted a range of counterguerrilla actions that had been effective elsewhere. These included the building of security barriers along the borders, counterguerrilla raids, and, most importantly, extensive patrolling by small units along the borders.

The internal terrorist threat was reduced significantly by a skillful blend of carrot-and-stick techniques. Active popular support for the *fedayeen* was largely neutralized by the aforementioned administrative and economic policies, while terrorists were apprehended by the police and intelligence apparatus. To put teeth in the antiterrorist program, a number of sanctions were used: curfews, cordon and search operations, detention without trial, deportation, and the destruction of the homes of terrorists and suspected supporters. With few exceptions, the military courts imposed long prison sentences on those found guilty of terrorist acts, membership in illegal organizations, possessing unauthorized weapons, and the like.

The response to the problem of transnational terrorism involved both the IDF and intelligence agencies. Since the attacks abroad were frequently planned in Lebanon, the IDF conducted various kinds of punitive attacks against Lebanon, and in 1976 it demonstrated a willingness to respond outside the Middle East with the surprise raid inside Uganda. By and large, however, operations against the terrorists outside the region were carried out by Mossad. Such operations included assassination of Palestinian terrorists and the mailing of letter bombs.

By the mid-1970s, the main elements in Israeli counterinsurgency doctrine had become clear. In keeping with principles developed in other nations over the years, it combined political, economic, and military measures. Moreover, different threats were handled with different responses by appropriate arms of the government. Within this context, the actions of *Zahal* were generally in line with the offensive orientation that marked its conventional warfare doctrine and operations. The IDF consistently, albeit not always successfully, sought to deliver hard blows to the *fedayeen* with search-and-destroy operations and air attacks and to achieve surprise with unanticipated raids (e.g., a heliborne attack against the Beirut airport in 1968 and the Entebbe operation). Nowhere was the proclivity for the offensive more in evidence than in the 1979–80 campaign of continuous air, ground, and naval attacks against Palestinian guerrillas and bases in Lebanon. Although beset with problems and counterproductive policies from time to time, the counterinsurgency campaign was, on balance, successful in reducing violence to manageable levels. It also led some elements in the resistance to consider the possibility of settling for a small Palestinian state rather than pursuing the seemingly futile quest to eliminate Israel.[92] What the counterinsurgency campaign could not do was resolve the problem once and for all, since that required political decisions at the highest level to cope somehow with the intensification of Palestinian nationalism and increased identification with the PLO which had become apparent in the West Bank and Gaza Strip by 1979.

NUCLEAR POLICY

While the understanding of Israel's military doctrine and force structure on the conventional and insurgent levels of conflict is enhanced by substantial data and public commentaries by present and former leaders of the security establishment, the general public knows relatively little about nuclear weapons, and much less nuclear war-fighting doctrines, given the dearth of verified empirical evidence on the subject. Beyond Israel's stated policy that it will not be the first party to introduce nuclear weapons into the Middle East, a veil of secrecy and sensitivity has descended. As a result, analyses of the Israeli nuclear weapons question have been highly conjectural and sometimes contradictory.[93] Considerable disagreement obtains on whether Israel has, or is close to achieving, a nuclear capability, as well as on the political, psychological, and military aims that nuclear weapons might feasibly serve. Although one expert, Alan Dowty, has cast doubts on the existence of nuclear weapons in Israel by pointing out that officially there are no indications that Israel has acquired the ability to separate plutonium from other byproducts necessary for the manufacture of nuclear weapons, others (reportedly including the CIA) estimate that the IDF could assemble and deliver between ten and twenty bombs.[94] The seriousness of this possibility has engendered considerable debate and discussion of the possible objectives that such a capability might achieve. In general, the most prevalent thinking is that if Israel does possess nuclear bombs, they are probably weapons of last resort.[95] They would be used to prevent the physical destruction of Israel if that seemed to be an imminent possibility. Thus, nuclear weapons have been viewed as a final deterrent to genocide and, if deterrence fails, as a means to inflict massive losses on any aggressor poised to overrun Israel. This policy has been linked to the commitment "never again" to permit the killing of defenseless Jews that occurred in the Holocaust.[96]

The assumptions that Israel has nuclear weapons and that they are to be used only in response to the most extreme peril leads to the conclusion that the military utility of nuclear weapons is severely restricted.[97] The possibility of employing such weapons in a tactical, limited manner on the battlefield (similar to NATO's plans) seems to be negligible in view of the major build-up of Israeli conventional forces between 1974 and 1980. Yet, how long this situation will continue is a speculative matter, especially since no less a personage than Dayan has questioned whether over the longer term Israel could continue to match an Arab military build-up fueled by petrodollars. If it cannot, Dayan has suggested that an open reliance on a nuclear deterrence might be necessary.[98] Needless to say, should this ever occur, Israel's military doctrine and force structure would be profoundly affected.

The defense decision-making process

Up to this point, the discussion of Israeli defense policy has focused on the substantive dimensions of defense policy, i.e., national strategy, military doctrine, and force structure. How major decisions have been made with respect to these is a question of institutional setting and process.

INSTITUTIONAL SETTING: THE MAIN ACTORS

The locus of defense decision-making power in Israel has always been the prime minister and Cabinet. Within the Cabinet, the Ministries of Foreign Affairs and Defense traditionally have exercised the greatest influence; of the two, the Ministry of Defense clearly has been the most important. In fact, for eighteen of Israel's first twenty years, the prime minister served as his own defense minister. Although lacking a legal basis for the making of security policy, Ben-Gurion established a tradition that the minister of defense would deal with grand strategy and security, while the IDF would concentrate on operational matters and execute policy. However, the lines between the two were never clearly delineated, a point criticized by the Agranat Commission in 1975.[99]

In an effort to resolve this problem, a basic law was passed in 1976 that formally vested command in the government and made the minister of defense the highest authority over the IDF and its link to the Cabinet. The chief of staff was made responsible to the minister of defense for all *Zahal* matters. Although in general the Defense Ministry was to be in charge of technical and administrative matters (military research and development, production or procurement of material, and financial planning and budgeting) and the IDF General Staff was to retain responsibility for organization, training, and the planning and execution of military operations, the minister of defense could intervene in all IDF matters by virtue of his role as supreme commander of the IDF.[100]

As far as the organizational structure of *Zahal* is concerned, it has been composed of a General Staff whose permanent members are the heads of five branches (operations, manpower, quartermaster, planning, and intelligence); the commanders of the armored corps, navy, and air force; and the three area commanders of the ground forces. The General Staff has control over all IDF branches. Although not separate services, the navy and the air force have enjoyed a fair degree of autonomy. Until 1980, the ground forces lacked a single commander; instead, the north, south, and central commanders had equal responsibilities. The General Staff also exercises authority over more than twenty functional commands such as artillery, armor, and training.

The three ground force area commanders have been assisted by a deputy and staff officers for supply, training, manpower, and operations. Area commanders have responsibility for area defense and all ground force installations and combat units in their sectors.[101]

While the prime minister, Cabinet, Ministry of Defense, and IDF have been the most important institutions in the defense decision-making process, other actors have exercised intermittent influence from time to time. Among these have been the Knesset Committee on Foreign Affairs and Security, party leadership echelons, and the media.

INSTITUTIONAL INTERPLAY

While major defense policy decisions in Israel have been the result of a complex interaction of the actors noted in the preceding section, the influence of particular institutions in the process has varied over the years. Although precise calculations of relative power and influence have proved to be elusive, because of the intermeshing of actors (e.g., party leaders, Cabinet officials, and prime minister) and the secrecy that has surrounded defense policy making, several scholars have provided valuable insights and propositions about the decision-making process.

Aaron Klieman, for example, has contended that Israeli policy has been made in a setting where interpersonal relations at the highest level have been more important than bureaucratic considerations.[102] Although the prime minister has always been the pivotal figure in important defense decisions, in view of the authority vested in the office he holds, some prime ministers have been particularly dominant. The most striking example, of course, was the charismatic Ben-Gurion, whose constant preoccupation with security matters motivated him to act as his own minister of defense. While his forceful personality frequently has been cited as the principal factor in his accomplishments, especially the difficult task of unifying the various Jewish military forces after the War of Independence, Ben-Gurion's control of the Ministry of Defense put powerful institutional resources at his disposal, not the least of which were the Ministry's wide-ranging contacts with all the key elements of the government bureaucracy.[103] Although the Foreign Ministry's impact on foreign policy issues vacillated over the years, in the specific area of defense policy it had minimal influence, since Ben-Gurion viewed it primarily as an implementing agency. Moreover, Ben-Gurion sought little advice.[104] In cases where he did, it usually was provided by a small inner circle referred to as a "kitchen cabinet," made up of a few Cabinet members, Labor party defense experts, a few senior officials from the Ministry of Defense, the chief of staff, the director of military intelligence, a few other officers, and the head of the Security Service.[105]

When Ben-Gurion first retired and Moshe Sharett became prime minister in 1954, the Cabinet emerged as a key decision-making organ in defense matters. Even though Ben-Gurion returned as prime minister a year later, it was not until Sharett departed the government in 1956 that Ben-Gurion's influence and *modus operandi* again became dominant. In 1959, Ben-Gurion's reassertion of power was increasingly criticized as "authoritarianism" in the security sphere. On 31 January 1961, Ben-Gurion resigned, thus precipitating a Cabinet crisis that lasted several months.[106]

During the crisis, the smaller parties that the Labor party needed to form a coalition government pressed hard for institutional controls over security policy and for Labor's relinquishment of its monopoly over the major finance, foreign affairs, and defense portfolios. In November 1961, this crisis was resolved through the creation of the Ministerial Committee on Defense; however, since Ben-Gurion resisted interference in the security area, the new committee had exiguous impact.[107]

The succession of Ben-Gurion by Eshkol in 1963 eventually changed this situation. Membership in the Ministerial Committee on Defense was increased, and the committee became a powerful organ in defense decision making (Eshkol viewed it as being similar to a "war cabinet"). It retained this status until the early spring of 1967, when the entire Cabinet again became the main decision-making forum. While other institutions, such as the Knesset Committee on Foreign Affairs and Security and *Zahal*, exerted pressures on the top leadership through 1967, the Cabinet was, in Michael Brecher's words, "the ultimate arena for strategic-level decision making in policy issues involving party, personal, and institutional conflicts."[108]

Despite the lack of a systematic treatment of defense decision making in Israel for the last twelve years, similar in scope to Brecher's impressive work on the earlier period, a careful monitoring of policy making in Israel, as well as academic commentaries on the subject, suggests that the dominant role of the prime minister and Cabinet has diminished little.[109] At the same time, however, the 1973 war and the subsequent resignation of Golda Meir's government had the effect of increasing outside pressures on the decision makers, inasmuch as defense policy and, most especially, the IDF were subjected to more scrutiny and criticism than previously had been the case. That the advent of a right-wing government in 1977 did little to offset this trend could easily be seen in the constant debate over both the policies and the actions of the military government in the occupied territories and IDF reprisal actions against the Palestinian guerrillas in Lebanon.

Increased outside pressures notwithstanding, it is safe to say that the prime minister, as in the past, has remained the final arbiter on major defense policy matters. As far as the interest groups that have influenced security policy deliberations and outcomes are concerned, available evidence suggests that the Defense Ministry and the IDF have been the most important over the years. However, the reader should be cautioned that the paucity of detailed data and the lack of any systematic analyses of interest articulation by the IDF have made propositions regarding the relative influence of the Defense Ministry and the IDF necessarily tentative. Furthermore, much of the evidence that does exist must be gleaned from studies of other facets of defense policy, especially those dealing with civil-military relations.[110]

In the area of civil-military relations, two books by Amos Perlmutter, *Military and Politics in Israel* (1969) and *Politics and the Military in Israel* (1978), provide a number of useful insights. In general, Perlmutter contends that while the IDF has wielded considerable influence owing to the high priority attributed to defense matters and the access to the political leadership enjoyed by the chiefs of staff, the military has been subject and loyal to civilian authority since 1948.[111]

During the Ben-Gurion years, the IDF seemed to have had more prestige and influence than the civilian component of the Defense Ministry, largely because the prime minister forged a special and close relationship with the chief of staff and the High Command.[112] Although Ben-Gurion did not rely on the chief of staff for his principal military advice and the chiefs of staff rarely participated in Cabinet meetings, the High Command did influence strategy from 1948 to 1955. Such influence no doubt stemmed from the fact that the prime minister selected chiefs of staff who shared his basic views, including the belief that the Arabs were intent on encircling and destroying Israel. Ben-Gurion's confidence in the IDF permitted him to avoid involvement in day-to-day operational matters, a situation that had very important consequences for strategy. As Perlmutter has noted:

> *Zahal* was assigned operational responsibility for many crucial defence policies and, therefore, in its successful pursuit of these operational goals, *Zahal*'s strategy could determine to a large extent the course of Israel's foreign relations. *Zahal* became identified with national security; and national security became identified with Arab encirclement.[113]

Not all IDF and Ministry of Defense perceptions and policies went unchallenged, however. Between 1953 and 1955, the IDF's hard line toward the Arabs was opposed by Prime Minister Sharett and part of the Cabinet. Coincidental with this discord over basic policy orientations there was a struggle between the defense minister, Pinhas Lavon, and the IDF, caused by Lavon's attempt to assert control over operational matters. In the end, Lavon's efforts to reform the IDF-Defense Ministry relationship came to nothing, in part because he managed to alienate not only the foreign policy moderates but his erstwhile IDF allies as well. In fact, Lavon's IDF opponents went so far as to present false testimony against him before an ad hoc committee investigating a series of espionage failures that had led to the demise of a major Israeli spy ring in Egypt.[114] It is interesting to note that one of the reasons for the IDF's opposition to civilian involvement in operational matters was said to have been its fear that such intrusion would have undercut the doctrinal emphasis on quick and decisive offensive operations.[115]

The return of Ben-Gurion to power in 1955 strengthened the hand of the hard-liners, who immediately began preparations to deal with what was perceived to be an increasing threat from Soviet-armed Egyptian military forces. The prestige of *Zahal* and Ben-Gurion's allies was enhanced even further by the military success of the Sinai campaign. Parenthetically, it should be noted that one important trend during this time was a tremendous growth in the Defense Ministry's power, due to its deep involvement in the country's scientific, technological, and industrial affairs.

In 1960-61, the politics of defense in Israel were subjected to heavy criticism when Lavon attempted to exonerate himself of any wrongdoing during his previous tenure as defense minister. Although Ben-Gurion weathered a rather heavy political storm, and no major reforms were undertaken in the defense establishment, the so-called Lavon affair nonetheless set in motion a public examination of the centralizing tendency evident in the political and economic systems of Israel. This examination continued into the Eshkol administration.

The Eshkol years were marked by acrimonious relations between the prime minister on the one hand and Ben-Gurion and his allies on the other (even though Ben-Gurion had nominated Eshkol as his successor). While the politicians were immersed in various disputes, the IDF's power and influence gradually increased. Efforts by the deputy defense minister, Zevi Dienstein, to transfer several tasks (e.g., armaments, recruitment, and supply) to the IDF were successfully mitigated by the High Command, which feared that accepting responsibility for support functions would adversely affect operational capabilities. More importantly, the chief of staff, Yitzhak Rabin, emerged as the de facto minister of defense, according to Perlmutter. Since Eshkol, who held the defense portfolio, had little experience in military matters, he deferred to Rabin in the formulation of military strategy and, unlike his predecessors, acceded to IDF requests for larger military budgets.

The influence of the IDF during the Eshkol years was obvious during the 1967 crisis. Once Nasser announced the closure of the Strait of Tiran and increased his forces in the Sinai, the IDF moved ahead with military planning, mobilized reserve components, and argued for a preemptive war against Egypt. Following Eshkol's unsuccessful two-week pursuit of a diplomatic solution, heavy public pressure led him, reluctantly, to appoint Dayan as minister of defense. Since Dayan's views coincided with those of *Zahal*, the pressure on Eshkol mounted, and he finally reached a decision to go to war. While the principle of civilian supremacy had been upheld, there was no denying that IDF actions and advice had played an influential part in the decision-making process.[116]

Not surprisingly, the overwhelming victory of 1967 added once more to the prestige and influence of the defense establishment, especially the IDF. Yet, while experts agreed that *Zahal* wielded significant influence, they offered contradictory explanations for such influence. Perlmutter argued that Dayan's continuation as defense minister after the war ushered in a period of notably close relations between the civilians in the ministry and the IDF, mainly because Dayan was an assertive administrator, an acknowledged expert in military affairs, and an inspirational leader. The input of Chiefs of Staff Bar Lev and David Elazar (1971-74) and other high-ranking officers, many of whom were former colleagues or disciples of Dayan, was said to be considerable. In contrast to Perlmutter, Jon Kimche contended that the IDF's influence was due to Dayan's exclusion from matters relating to both national (grand) and military strategy.[117] Yet, although they disagreed on the matter of the defense minister's actual influence, both Perlmutter and Kimche concluded that the General Staff became the focal point for military advice to the political leadership following the 1967 war.[118] This state of affairs and its policy consequences was a major theme in a careful examination of the defense policy arena during the 1969–70 War of Attrition by Avi Shlaim and Raymond Tanter. Because the Shlaim-Tanter piece has provided one of the few detailed and revealing analyses of recent defense decision making, its findings merit brief attention.

After noting that the balance between civilian politicians and the General Staff shifted noticeably toward the latter following the 1967 war, Shlaim and Tanter investigated the decision to bomb Egypt (in reaction to Nasser's War of Attrition in 1969) with respect to the participants in the process and the objectives they wished to achieve. One of the conclusions reached by the authors was that the military had preponderant influence in the making of policy. The General Staff acted as the Cabinet's principal source of information and advice and, according to Shlaim and Tanter, this predisposed the Cabinet to agree to the military's proposal—the only option presented, as it turned out—to carry out deep-penetration bombing of Egypt as a means to end Egyptian violence. Although the military aspects of the bombing option had been carefully analyzed by the IDF, such was not the case with regard to the political ramifications. The political and psychological aims were never articulated in an exact manner and did not command a consensus. Likewise, the anticipated reactions of the Egyptians, and most especially the Russians, were badly miscalculated.[119] Since the Foreign Ministry was almost completely excluded from the decision-making process, both orderly and careful staff work on the costs, risks, and benefits of various options, as well as a regular flow of verified information, were denied the Cabinet. Under such conditions, the Cabinet members putatively relied on their general knowledge, informal conversations, and data gleaned from newspapers in forming their opinions. This led to a situation where short-term military realities shaped Israeli responses and no attention was paid to long-term implications. As Shlaim and Tanter put it: "There was a tendency to act on a day-to-day basis, guided solely by the dictates of military requirements."[120] That the IDF had exercised dominant influence was beyond doubt. That such dominant influence was conducive to formulating security policies that effectively integrated political and military considerations was not.

Although the extent to which these conditions continued after the War of Attrition is difficult to determine, the preeminent role of Military Intelligence in the days prior to the October War would seem to suggest that little change had occurred. At the same time, however, Prime Minister Golda Meir's refusal to accede to the chief of staff's preemptive strike option on the eve of the war demonstrated that IDF influence was not always translated into policy.

While it might have been expected that the problems experienced by the IDF in 1973 would have diminished its influence, apparently such was not the case. Indeed, the demise of Dayan and the weaknesses of, and rivalries among, the new leaders—Prime Minister Rabin, Defense Minister Shimon Peres, and Foreign Minister Yigal Allon—enabled the new chief of staff, Mordecai Gur, to exercise greater influence. Indicative of this was his inclusion in the government's delegation for negotiations with the Arabs. This led Perlmutter to submit that Gur's assumption of political responsibilities and contribution to national security policies rivaled that of Dayan between 1954 and 1957. Moreover, in his role as military adviser, Gur apparently enjoyed a status similar to that of Rabin under the Eshkol government.[121]

Whether Gur's successor (Eytan) has managed to continue this trend is hard to say, because his brief period in office has provided little more than speculative impressions. The situation has been further complicated by the presence of three strong personalities in key cabinet positions related to defense policy (Begin as prime minister; a dynamic former air force hero, Ezer Weizman, as Defense Minister; and Eytan as chief of staff). At this writing, the public record would seem to suggest that Begin has been a strong prime minister who acts decisively on basic high-level security matters. Weizmann, meanwhile, has played an active part in negotiations with Egypt, owing to his strong personal rapport with Sadat. Within the military establishment, he has been attentive to general strategic issues and managerial concerns. He has also shown particular interest in the future of the IAF.[122] While Eytan has tended to focus on operational matters, he has also been involved with broader policy questions, especially the issue of settlements in the context of security. Regarding the relationship between the Defense Ministry and the IDF, there is some ambiguity about the future, inasmuch as a new ministry planning staff has been created that may rival the IDF planning section when it comes to inputs to the defense minister. Whatever the case, the IDF continues to play an important part in day-to-day policy. Although its degree of influence may have waxed and waned over time, the IDF has always been a major actor in the policy process. Given the centrality of security in the context of national strategy, the continuous hostility of most Arab states, the constant emphasis on military strength, and the ever-present fear that a major miscalculation could lead to a national catastrophe, it would have been naïve to expect otherwise.

Recurring issues: defense policy outputs

As the state of Israel enters the 1980s, there is no reason to believe that security considerations will be any less important than in the past. Although the normalization of relations with Egypt has raised hopes that the Arab-Israeli dispute will be resolved, such an accomplishment clearly is a long way off, inasmuch as many Arab states have yet to reconcile themselves to the notion of a Jewish state in the region. Indeed, states such as Iraq and Libya continue to call for the displacement of what they refer to as "the Zionist regime." While others, such as Syria, Lebanon, Jordan, and Saudi Arabia, may be inclined to accept Israel at some future time, such acceptance is, minimally, contingent on a satisfactory resolution of the Palestinian and Jerusalem problems. Unfortunately, only an inveterate optimist could envisage a speedy and comprehensive resolution of these matters, in view of the profoundly divergent positions of the Arabs and Israelis with respect to each.

Leaving ideological commitments to the concept of Eretz Israel aside, security considerations strongly militate against major concessions by Israeli leaders, especially on the West Bank and Golan Heights questions. From the perspective of Israel's defense establishment, a comprehensive withdrawal in the context of belligerent relations with many of its neighbors would be highly imprudent. Such a belief creates a dilemma, for as long as the IDF remains in the occupied territories, those Arab governments that seem disposed to reach an accommodation with Israel are unlikely to adopt conciliatory policies. A major reason for this reluctance is, and no doubt will continue to be, the domestic uncertainty that prevails in the Arab world. The combination of unfulfilled aspirations, corruption, inefficient administration, and psychocultural disruption that has marked the modernization process in the Middle East has either undermined or threatens to undermine the legitimacy of most Arab governments. The resurgence of Islam at the turn of the decade has been the most dramatic symptom of this state of affairs. Faced with a recrudescence of Moslem fundamentalism plus anti-Westernism and sporadic political violence and an intensification of social cleavages, there is a high probability that Arab leaders will continue to perceive substantive concessions to Israel as an invitation to even more internal and external turbulence that may well lead to their own demise.

The implication of this predicament for the Israeli leadership is painfully obvious. Simply stated, as long as the hostile impasse with the Arabs remains, there can be no diminution of the priority ascribed to security and, as long as violence and bellicosity continue, a strong military will retain its status as an instrument of statecraft that is used variously to deter, punish, and, if need be, debilitate adversaries. This continued preoccupation with security and the concomitant diversion of national resources to the IDF will confront Israeli leaders with new and vexing questions related to doctrine, force structure, weapons acquisition, and arms control in the decade ahead. Over the short term, the trends in each of these areas, which were described earlier, will, in all likelihood, continue. Accordingly, Israel can be expected to pursue its quest for adequate supplies of advanced weapons that are conducive to both self-reliance and offensive warfare. With the possible exception of nuclear weapons, arms control measures are likely to be dismissed as unrealistic.

When one looks at the longer-term prospects for Israeli defense policy (beyond the mid-1980s), there is far less clarity. Although any number of specific issues related to doctrine, force structure, weapons acquisition, and arms control can be conjured up and assessed, there is one general consideration that has possible repercussions in all areas of defense policy. Essentially, that consideration involves Israel's ability to sustain the level of expenditures deemed necessary by its military leaders to maintain a favorable balance of forces against potential enemies that not only are acquiring large quantities of advanced weaponry but also are gradually demonstrating greater proficiency in utilizing that weaponry. Whether an increasingly troubled Israeli economy can manage this problem while simultaneously responding to rising demands from deprived social groups is an open question. If it cannot, Israel may be faced with some difficult choices. A disinclination to risk concessions to the Arabs, coupled with a perceived need to address domestic restiveness, may compel the government gradually to scale down weapons acquisitions and revise the force structure.[123] The consequent loss of flexibility and increased apprehesion inherent in such a development would probably result in renewed interest in arms control and explicit nuclear deterrence. Of the two, reliance on an explicit nuclear deterrence seems more likely to gain support, given the scant prospects of the Arab states' addressing the arms control issue without achieving their main objectives in the dispute with Israel. Under circumstances such as this, Moshe Dayan's previously cited question as to whether Israel could indefinitely compete with an Arab arms build-up fueled by oil revenues may be answered precisely the way he suggested, that is, by an open commitment to nuclear deterrence. Should that transpire, the Middle East surely will enter its most perilous period to date.

Notes

Since the large majority of readers are presumed to be English speaking, the notes concentrate on materials in English in order to be of practical value to those who may wish to pursue the subject matter further. Those interested in Hebrew sources will find a plethora of articles, monographs, newspaper commentaries, and books on Israeli defense matters; of particular importance is the Israeli Defense Forces journal, *Ma'arachot*.

1. At least some knowledge of the Holocaust is indispensable for understanding the conceptions underlying Israeli national strategy and defense policy. Those interested in the Holocaust will find a sizable corpus of literature. One especially useful account is Nora Levin, *The Holocaust* (New York: Schocken Books, 1973).

2. A former speechwriter for President Jimmy Carter captured the essence of this when he wrote: "For some the word 'security' may be an intellectual construct. For the Jew, security means life.

"For 2,000 years, Jews qua Jews have been the objects of calculated attempts at annihilation. And for 30 years the tiny nation of Israel, populated by the survivors of Hitler's unfulfilled Final Solution, has lived in constant danger of extermination, fighting four major wars, surrounded by 22 hostile Arab countries intent on the goal of a truly final destruction.

"Only an Israeli Jew can fully understand the psychic scars and strengths that are consequences of this unrelenting pressure; only Israeli parents can know a literal fear for the lives of their children; only a kibbutznik can appreciate the necessity of the 24-hour watch. The state of Israel and, in a broader sense, the Jewish people, have not only walked through the valley of the shadow of death, they have lived in that valley of death."

See Mark Siegel, "Security Means Life," *New York Times,* 26 March 1978.

3. *The Holocaust* (Yad Vashem, Jerusalem: Martyrs and Heroes Remembrance Authority, 1975), pp. 64-65.

4. Michael Brecher, *The Foreign Policy System of Israel* (New Haven: Yale University Press, 1972), p. 65.

5. Michael I. Handel, *Israel's Political-Military Doctrine,* Occasional Papers in International Affairs, no. 30 (Cambridge, Mass.: Harvard University, 1973), p. 1.

6. The geographic vulnerabilities of Israel between 1948 and 1967 are well known to analysts of the Arab-Israeli conflict, and they receive ample attention in the large body of literature on the conflict. Those interested in a succinct accounting of Israeli perceptions of the geostrategic situation may consult the following background papers published by Carta, Jerusalem, in 1974: *Golan Heights; The Gaza Strip; Judea and Samaria;* and *Secure and Recognized Boundaries.*

7. National strategy is considered here to be the systematic and orchestrated use of economic, military, diplomatic, and psychological capabilities to accomplish major goals and objectives articulated by leadership elites.

8. Dan Horovitz, "Is Israel a Garrison State?," *Jerusalem Quarterly* (Summer 1977), p. 69.

9. Ibid., pp. 68-69; quote p. 68.

10. The recognition that military victory could not by itself resolve the dispute with the Arabs is noted by Maj. Gen. Israel Tal, "Israel's Defense Doctrine: Background and Dynamics," *Military Review* (March 1978), p. 23.

11. For a discussion of the pragmatic nature of Israeli foreign policy, see Aaron S. Klieman, "Zionist Diplomacy and Israeli Foreign Policy," *Jerusalem Quarterly* (Spring 1979), pp. 99-109.

12. Ibid., pp. 100-103.

13. Handel, *Israel's Political-Military Doctrine,* p. 8.

14. Horovitz, "Is Israel a Garrison State?," pp. 71-72. Those interested in the economic costs of Israel's defense effort should consult the following analyses: Fred M. Gottheil, "An Economic Assessment of the Military Burden in the Middle East," *Journal of Conflict Resolution* (September 1974), pp. 502-13; and Paul Rivlin, "The Burden of Israel's Defense," *Survival* (July-August 1978), pp. 146-54.

15. *Zahal* and IDF are used interchangeably in this chapter.

16. For a good summary of the main features of the Israeli reserve system, see Irving Heymont, *Analysis of the Army Reserve System of Israel, Canada, United Kingdom, Federal Republic of Germany,* report prepared for Office of the Director for Planning and Evaluation, Department of Defense (McLean, Va.: General Research Corporation, 1977), pp. 6-15.

17. Handel, *Israel's Political-Military Doctrine,* p. 19.

18. For a succinct account of these developments, see Fred J. Khouri, *The Arab-Israeli Dilemma,* 2d ed. (Syracuse, N.Y.: Syracuse University Press, 1976), chap. 7.

19. The debate over the disposition of the territories produced a variety of proposals both outside and inside the government. By 1969, a scheme devised by Yigal Allon, known as the Allon Plan, became the unofficial basis of policy. The plan called for a 10-15-mile-wide security belt along the sparsely populated edge of the Jordan River, which would be considered Israel's new security frontier. Guarded by a string of paramilitary settlements, the strip would contain fewer than 20,000 Arabs. New towns were to be constructed to overlook the Arab population centers of Jericho and Hebron, and a 4.3-mile-wide corridor linking Jordan with the West Bank was to be created. With the exception of Jerusalem and areas near Latrun and Hebron, the area outside the paramilitary strip, which contained most of the Arab population, would either be permanently demilitarized and given an autonomous status or be linked to Jordan, depending on negotiations with the Jordanians. Moreover, Hussein's government would be asked to accept 200,000 refugees from Gaza. Besides providing for defense against conventional attacks—the Jordan River was a natural tank ditch—the Allon Plan, with its paramilitary settlements, was also directed at the problem of guerrilla infiltration. Clearly, the training of the *Nahal* personnel would allow them to carry out the patrolling and other tasks associated with territorial defense. Finally, to the south, Allon's scheme called for a demilitarized Sinai and a new Israeli town near Sharm el-Sheikh, to protect a north-south line to El-Arish which represented the Israeli withdrawal area. For information on the plan, see Abraham S. Becker, *Israel and the Occupied Palestinian Territories: Military-Political Issues in the Debate* (Santa Monica, Calif.: Rand Corporation, 1971), pp. 27-32; *Le Monde* (Paris), 11 June 1978; and *New York Times,* 18 and 24 June 1969.

20. Not surprisingly, the October War spawned a vast outpouring of literature. Those who wish to examine it in more detail should find the following to be useful: D. K. Palit, *Return to Sinai* (London: Compton Russell, 1974); Chaim Herzog, *The War of Atonement* (Boston: Little, Brown & Co., 1975); Edgar O'Ballance, *No Victor, No Vanquished* (San Rafael, Calif.: Presidio Press, 1978); Trevor N. Dupuy, *Elusive Victory* (New York: Harper & Row, 1978), pp. 387-605; Nadav Safran, *Israel, the Embattled Ally* (Cambridge, Mass.: Harvard University Press, 1978), pp. 476-534; and Mohammed Heikal, *The Road to Ramadan* (New York: Quadrangle, 1975).

21. A good example of domestic criticism may be found in "*Ha'aretz* Editor Discusses Israel's Isolation,"

Ha'aretz (Tel Aviv), 15 June 1979, in *Foreign Broadcast Information Service, Middle East and North Africa* (hereafter *FBIS/MENA*), 19 June 1979, pp. N7-N8.

22. This was precisely the topic of a recent analysis of possible Iraqi troop deployments along the Eastern front (Syria and Jordan). See "Analysis of Potential Threat on the Eastern Front," *Ha'aretz* (Tel Aviv), 13 April 1979, in Joint Publications Research Service, *Translations on Near East and North Africa,* 073523, 25 May 1975, pp. 76-78.

23. Tal, "Israel's Defense Doctrine," p. 23.

24. The profound influence of the strategy of the indirect approach on Israeli military leaders before, during, and after 1948 is attributed to the eminent British analyst Sir Basil Liddell Hart. On this point, see Brian Bond, "Liddell Hart's Influence on Israeli Military Theory and Practice," *Journal of the Royal United Services Institute* (June 1976), pp. 83-89; and Jac Weller, "Sir Basil Liddell Hart's Disciples in Israel," *Military Review* (January 1974), pp. 13-23.

25. Handel, *Israel's Political-Military Doctrine,* p. 25.

26. Ibid., p. 23. Bond, "Liddell Hart's Influence," p. 85, contends that, despite Dayan's reversal, tanks were to be used only in a support role. As things turned out, Israeli armored commanders flouted the High Command's orders and achieved major victories.

27. Zeev Schiff, "The Israeli Air Force," *Air Force Magazine* (August 1978), pp. 33-34.

28. Two additional considerations were believed important in the decision not to acquire bombers: one was the relatively short ranges within the potential target area; the other was the burden on Israel's scarce human resources that the larger air and ground crews required by bombers would have created. See Handel, *Israel's Political-Military Doctrine,* pp. 27-28; and Schiff, "Israeli Air Force," p. 34.

29. For a brief summary of the IDFN's evolution, see Lt. Comm. Reuben Porath, "The Israeli Navy," *U.S. Naval Institute Proceedings,* September 1971, pp. 33-39.

30. Tal, "Israel's Defense Doctrine," p. 27.

31. Yigal Allon, *The Making of Israel's Army* (New York: Universe Books, 1970), p. 65.

32. Handel, *Israel's Political-Military Doctrine,* pp. 43-45.

33. Schiff, "Israeli Air Force," p. 34.

34. Handel, *Israel's Political-Military Doctrine,* p. 41.

35. Nadav Safran, *From War to War* (New York: Pegasus, 1969), chap. 7.

36. On the successful use of the strategy of the indirect approach in 1967, see Bond, "Liddell Hart's Influence," pp. 86-88; and Weller, "Sir Basil Liddell Hart's Disciples," pp. 19-23.

37. Quoted in Safran, *From War to War,* p. 382.

38. The Bar Lev Line consisted of a series of fortified bunkers connected by a patrol road. It was to receive immediate support from air and artillery and tanks positioned a short distance to the rear.

39. On the war of attrition, see Lawrence L. Whetten, *The Canal War* (Cambridge, Mass.: MIT Press, 1974).

40. Schiff, "Israeli Air Force," pp. 35-36.

41. Handel, *Israel's Political-Military Doctrine,* p. 62.

42. Porath, "Israeli Navy," pp. 36-38.

43. Handel, *Israel's Political-Military Doctrine,* pp. 62-63.

44. Both before and after the war, Sadat repeatedly made this point by saying that the United States held 99 percent of the cards in the bargaining process.

45. The need to redeem honor and dignity was a constant theme before, during, and after the war. For a good illustration, see "Speech of President Hafez al-Assad over Damascus Radio and Television," Damascus Domestic Service, 6 October 1973, in *FBIS/MENA,* 9 October 1973, pp. F2-F4.

46. See *Aviation Week and Space Technology* (7 December 1973), p. 17. Some critics and observers have faulted this strategy as being overly cautious. Edgar O'Ballance, for instance, is of the opinion that Egyptian forces could probably have seized the Sinai passes by 7 October. See Edgar O'Ballance, "The Fifth Arab-Israeli War, October 1973," *Army Quarterly and Defence Journal* (U.K.) (April 1974), p. 317; and Robert R. Rodwell, "The Mideast War: A Damned Close-Run Thing," *Air Force Magazine* (February 1974), p. 40. Other analysts, by contrast, have pointed out that armor and mechanized losses were heavy when Arab forces ventured beyond their air defense cover. See Lawrence Whetten and Michael Johnson, "Military Lessons of the Yom Kippur War," *World Today* (March 1974), p. 104; and J. F. Koek, "The Middle East Conflict, October 1973," *Army Journal* (Australia) (December 1974), p. 5.

47. Cited in *Aviation Week and Space Technology* (7 December 1973), p. 7.

48. Tal, "Israel's Defense Doctrine," pp. 30-31; also see Samuel W. Sax and Avigdor Levy, "Arab-Israeli Conflict Four: A Preliminary Assessment," *Naval War College Review* (January-February 1974), p. 8.

49. Whetten and Johnson, "Military Lessons," pp. 103, 105.

50. For a contrary analysis that argues that a preemptive attack would probably have produced an overwhelming victory similar to 1967, see Kenneth S. Brower, "The Yom Kippur War," *Military Review* (March 1974), p. 33.

51. O'Ballance, "Fifth Arab-Israeli War," p. 320.

52. Bonner Day, "New Role for Israeli Air Force," *Air Force Magazine* (August 1978), p. 38. For a cogent discussion of the military advantages of preemption in a future war, see Steven J. Rosen and Martin Indyk, "The Temptation to Pre-Empt in a Fifth Arab-Israeli War," *Orbis* (Summer 1976), pp. 276-82. In discussions that I had with civilian and military planners in Israel, it became apparent that preemption was viewed as a dubious option in the face of incremental deployment changes by Arab forces surrounding Israel. Although the cumulative effect of such changes might constitute a serious threat, each change by itself might not be sufficient to justify a preemptive attack and the associated risk of adverse international, and particularly American, reactions. Accordingly, preemption would appear to be a viable option only when Arab redeployments had reached a point where their threat to the IDF was obvious.

53. Herbert J. Coleman, "Israel Shifts toward Long-Range Fleet," *Aviation Week and Space Technology* (10 March 1975), p. 19; Robert Holtz, "Israeli Air Force Faces New Arab Arms," *Aviation Week and Space Technology* (10 March 1975), pp. 15-18.

54. This convenient summary is borrowed from Handel, *Israel's Political-Military Doctrine,* pp. 67-68.

55. *Press Release Issued by the Commission of Inquiry, Yom Kippur War, upon Submission of Its Third and Final Report to the Government and the Defense and Foreign Affairs Committee of the Knesset* (Jerusalem: Ministry of Information, 30 January 1975), pp. 14, 33. Hereafter referred to as *Agranat Press Release.*

56. Ibid., p. 15.

57. See Herzog, *War of Atonement*, pp. 98–105.

58. *Agranat Press Release*, pp. 17–18.

59. Brower, "Yom Kippur War," p. 26.

60. *Armed Forces Journal International* (March 1974), p. 18.

61. *Agranat Press Release*, pp. 22–23.

62. Ibid., p. 22.

63. Brower, "Yom Kippur War," p. 26; Holtz, "Israeli Air Force," p. 16.

64. *Armed Forces Journal International* (October 1973), p. 68.

65. *Agranat Press Release*, pp. 28–30, 33.

66. Gen. Herzl Shafir, head of the General Staff branch, described the training programs in 1974 as "unprecedented in scope." He asserted that the IDF had succeeded in filling all the gaps left by the October War and in preparing all new conscripts. See *Jerusalem Post* in English, 13 April 1975, in *FBIS/MENA*, 17 April 1975, p. N6.

67. A. J. Barker, "Israel after the Yom Kippur War: Zahal Reflects on the Lessons," *Journal of the Royal United Services Institute* (June 1974), p. 28; and *Armed Forces Journal International* (March 1974), p. 18.

68. Brower, "Yom Kippur War," p. 27; Sax and Levy, "Arab-Israeli Conflict Four," p. 13.

69. Charles Holley, "IDF Strategy in 1977; Quick, Offensive Fighting," *Middle East* (September 1977), pp. 28–30, quote p. 29. As Holley notes, a primary reliance on the infantry would undoubtedly result in higher losses. See also "Chief of Staff Gur Discusses IDF Plans," Jerusalem Domestic Service in Hebrew, 24 September 1974, in *FBIS/MENA*, 24 September 1974, p. N5.

70. Former Chief of Staff Mordecai Gur put it this way during an interview in October 1974: "The distances between us and the important centers of the hostile countries are not great. Their armies are concentrated to a major and decisive extent along the borders. This means that if you succeed in finding the right political strategic and tactical path, you can definitely expect to terminate an engagement by what we term a blitzkreig. There is no reason to assume that a future war must be a long one. I certainly do not accept this." See Gide'on Levari, "Interview of the Month," Jerusalem Domestic Service in Hebrew, 26 October 1974, in *FBIS/MENA*, 30 October 1974, p. N7. Three years later, Jac Weller, "Armor and Infantry in Israel," *Military Review* (April 1977), p. 7, observed that "in Israel today, everything is offense oriented." A somewhat contrary view may be found in Charles Wakebridge, "Israel's Changing Military Posture," *Military Review* (June 1976), pp. 6–7. Wakebridge argues that although offensive doctrine may remain and be taught to *Zahal*, in practice many troops are in a static defensive disposition. That at least some Israelis see defensive actions as a distinct possibility was evident in discussions I had with one top civilian planner, who ruminated about the option of conducting a "surprise defense" in the West Bank. What he had in mind was reliance on the defensive network involving the settlements and an emphasis on creating unforeseen obstacles for an attacking force. Not surprisingly, a ranking military officer evinced some discomfort with this notion when it was broached with him during a later interview. At the same time, however, he conceded that cutbacks in defense spending and draft requirements had increased the importance of territorial defense.

71. Anthony H. Cordesman, "How Much Is Too Much?," *Armed Forces Journal International* (October 1977), p. 6.

72. W. Seth Carus, "The Military Balance of Power in the Middle East," *Current History* (January 1978), p. 29.

73. In 1978, the IDF's logistical center reported that it was ordering 34 percent of needed items from local producers, as compared to 20 percent in 1976, according to *Bamahane* (Tel Aviv), 23 May 1979. For a concise account of the achievements, aspirations, limitations, and motives for the domestic arms industry, see Holley, "Switch from Arms Purchase to Manufacture," *Middle East* (September 1977), pp. 31–33. Also see Louis Kraar, "Israel's Own Military-Industrial Complex," *Fortune* (13 March 1978), pp. 72–76; Philip J. Klass, "Electronic Warfare Capability Developed," *Aviation Week and Space Technology* (1 May 1978), pp. 55–61.

74. Carus, "Military Balance of Power," p. 30.

75. Holtz, "Israeli Air Force," pp. 15–18. The Israelis lost 37 percent of their fighter and attack aircraft in 1973.

76. In the last half of 1978, a doctrinal debate was reportedly taking place between air force leaders, who continued to stress the traditional missions and leading offensive role of the IAF, and ground commanders, who wished to see the air force concentrate on ground support operations. See Day, "New Role for Israeli Air Force," p. 38.

77. Carus, "Military Balance of Power," p. 30.

78. The analysis of the intelligence failure became a fertile topic for social scientists. The following are among the more insightful treatments: Michael Brecher and Mordechai Raz, "Images and Behavior: Israel's Yom Kippur Crisis, 1973," *International Journal* (Canada) (Summer 1977), pp. 475–500; Michael I. Handel, "The Yom Kippur War and the Inevitability of Surprise," *International Studies Quarterly* (September 1977), pp. 461–502; and Avi Shlaim, "Failures in National Intelligence Estimates: The Case of the Yom Kippur War," *World Politics* (April 1976), pp. 348–80. These authors and others address the psychological (e.g., images, attitudes, values, and beliefs of the decision makers) and structural dimensions.

79. *Armed Forces Journal International* (October 1973), p. 47.

80. Arab success was believed to be dependent on Egypt's ability to stage deep air strikes inside Israel. Since this was considered to be beyond Egyptian capability, war was thought to be unlikely. See Shlaim, "Failures in National Intelligence Estimates," pp. 352–53.

81. Sharon provided an insight into Israeli thinking prior to the war when he argued that the IDF presence along the canal left the Egyptians with no line of defense between Cairo and the canal, and that, because of this, Sadat would not attack because he would not want to fight near Cairo. In more specific terms, he called attention to two factors that would dissuade Egypt from attacking. In his words: "Operations that are the result of a simple drill, they do very well. But where you have to improvise, react to a changing situation, where the commander has to be forward, the kind of fluid situation a river crossing is—that is not one of their strong points. Thus, the Canal becomes a real obstacle for the Arabs.

"The second reason is the desert. [Sharon crossed Sinai twice, in 1956 as commander of the paratroopers and in 1967 as the head of an armored division.] A desert crossing is hard. It takes will power. You must conduct a mobile operation, take risks, make fast decisions, use initiative, do things even if contrary to what you were told before. That's not the strong point of the Arab. And you have to be good at close combat fighting, hand-to-hand, night combat. This is one of our strongest points. The Arab soldier doesn't have the psychological structure."

Quoted in *Armed Forces Journal International* (October 1973), p. 70.

82. Ibid., p. 47.

83. Interviews with Brig. Gen. Yoel Ben-Porat, 10 September 1979; Abraham Lif (Ministry of Defense), 22 October 1979; and Maj. Gen. Menachem Meron, 23 October 1979.

84. See *Agranat Press Release,* pp. 18–19; Sax and Levy, "Arab-Israeli Conflict Four," p. 11; O'Ballance, "Fifth Arab-Israeli War," p. 314; Koek, "Middle East Conflict," p. 13; Cordesman, "How Much Is Too Much?," p. 35; and Schiff, "Israeli Air Force," p. 38. Several officials with whom I discussed this matter pointed out that Israel's limited resources made it very difficult to have three strong intelligence structures. They made the point that factors other than a major reorganization (i.e., access, coordination, and interpersonal relations) were key considerations in fostering pluralism.

85. One reason for this state of affairs in 1973 may well have been the encouragement given to each arm to develop its own "philosophy of battle" and the concomitant belief that it could win a war without the help of other arms. See *Armed Forces Journal International* (October 1973), p. 64. On the efforts to improve coordination, see Weller, "Armor and Infantry," pp. 5–11; and Schiff, "Israeli Air Force," p. 38.

86. "The Middle East War 1973," lecture by Gen. Chaim Herzog, *Royal United Services Institute* (March 1975), p. 5; and *Agranat Press Release,* pp. 11, 19, 28.

87. Hirsh Goodman, "Tank in a Bag," *Jerusalem Post,* 23 March 1979; "Agranat Report: Highlights," *Middle East* (September 1977), pp. 26–27. Goodman describes "dry storage" as follows: "By this method, which is now in extensive use in the IDF, a tank is oiled, greased, fueled up, loaded with ammunition, packed with the crew's equipment and food, dusted off and placed in a gigantic zipper bag. It is then plugged into an air conditioning unit, which keeps the tank and its contents at a constant temperature and as fresh as a daisy for months on end without any running down of batteries, evaporation of fuel or deterioration of ammunition. In times of emergency, all a crew had to do is unzip the bag and drive off to battle." On the Comptroller's report, see *Jerusalem Post,* 10 May 1979.

88. *Jerusalem Post,* 9 July 1979.

89. The consistency in Israeli military doctrine is noted by Tal, "Israel's Defense Doctrine," p. 22, who argues that all military thinking since the 1950s amounted to little more than a series of footnotes to the military thoughts that were crystallized then.

90. *Fedayeen* means "men of sacrifice." Although it has generally been used to refer to Arab guerrillas, it has come to be associated with Palestinian insurgents.

91. Moshe Dayan, *Diary of the Sinai Campaign* (New York: Harper & Row, 1965), pp. 8–9.

92. For an expanded analysis of the Israeli counterinsurgency effort, see Bard E. O'Neill, *Armed Struggle in Palestine* (Boulder, Colo.: Westview Press, 1978), chap. 4.

93. At times, Israeli leaders have denied the existence of nuclear warheads. See *Newsweek,* 20 October 1975, for ex-Foreign Minister Yigal Allon's comments to this effect. Although, strictly speaking, such denials may be accurate, they do not necessarily mean that Israel lacks a nuclear capability. The reason for this is that the components for weapons may be ready for rapid final assembly.

94. Alan Dowty, "Nuclear Proliferation: The Israeli Case," *International Studies Quarterly* (March 1978), pp. 82–83. In contrast to Dowty, another observer states flatly that a separation plan was completed in 1969. See Special Correspondent, "Israel's Nuclear Weapons: Are They in Safe Hands?," *Middle East* (June 1976), p. 27. The CIA estimate was reported by the *Washington Post,* 15 March 1976. Those who are interested in pursuing the matter of nuclear weapons in Israel may wish to compare the following to Dowty's article: Yair Evron, "Israel and the Atom: The Uses and Misuses of Ambiguity, 1957-1967," *Orbis* (Winter 1974), pp. 1326–43; Fuad Jabber, "Israel's Nuclear Options," *Journal of Palestine Studies* 1, no. 1 (n.d.): 21–38; S. Jaishankar, "Israeli Nuclear Option," *India Quarterly* (January–March 1978) pp. 39–53; Robert J. Pranger and Dale R. Tahtinen, *Nuclear Threat in the Middle East* (Washington, D.C.: American Enterprise Institute, 1975); and Steven J. Rosen, "A Stable System of Mutual Nuclear Deterrence in the Arab-Israeli Conflict," *American Political Science Review* (December 1977), pp. 1367–83.

95. Moshe Dayan has reportedly indicated that a nuclear option should be used only if the country's existence were in danger. See Avraham Schweitzer, "The Importance of the Nuclear Option," *Ha'aretz* (Tel Aviv), 15 March 1976, in *FBIS/MENA* 16 March 1976, p. N3.

96. Many observers attribute this to the so-called Massada complex, by which they mean a determination to go down fighting rather than submit to destruction. However, since this refers to an act of mass suicide on the part of Jewish defenders about to be overtaken by the Romans at Massada in 73 A.D., the analogy is not compelling. This is because the nuclear policy of Israel putatively is designed to destroy the enemy if the state is being overrun. A better analogy might be Samson's act of bringing the temple down on his enemies as he was about to be killed. Hence, it may be more appropriate to refer to a Samson complex rather than a Massada complex. Short of using nuclear weapons if the existence of the state were threatened, Israel might threaten to employ them in order to obtain a rapid and major commitment by American forces to the defense of the country.

97. Dowty, "Nuclear Proliferation," pp. 87–97, presents an excellent summary and critique of the political, psychological, and military objectives that various scholars have suggested Israeli nuclear capability might be directed toward.

98. As Dayan put it: "We have come to a highly critical point in regard to exploiting manpower. The Arabs have inexhaustible conventional power. In facing the facts we cannot escape emphasizing a specific consolidation of our strength. Not another 1,000 tanks or 200 aircraft; we must confront growing Arab power with deterrent atomic weapons. The Arabs want to destroy us and what will cool their verve is the news that they can expect total destruction. We must bear in mind that we are a state with a population of 3 million. If we keep up the tempo of armament aimed at a conventional balance of power, we shall ultimately find every one of us busy tightening tank treads and maintaining aircraft."

See *Yedi'ot Aharonot* (Tel Aviv), 14 March 1976, as cited in *FBIS/MENA* 18 March 1976, p. N7. One analyst has pointed out that the acquisition of sophisticated equipment by itself might not enhance Arab capabilities because of limited maintenance capabilities. However, he also notes that the willingness of sellers to perform maintenance and to install logistics and command and control systems can offset this liability to an important degree. When combined with the IDF's increasing problems in training recruits from families that emigrated from backward countries, such a development threatens to reduce the technological gap that has always been a major Israeli asset. See Kenneth Preiss, "Some Aspects of Modern Technology and Regional Planning in the Defense of Israel," *Middle East Review* (Fall 1978), p. 38.

99. Amos Perlmutter, *Politics and the Military in Israel, 1967-1977* (London: Frank Cass & Co., 1978), p. 63; *Agranat Press Release*, pp. 25-27; Horovitz, "Is Israel a Garrison State?," p. 70.

100. Richard F. Nyrop, *Israel: A Country Study* (Washington D.C.: Government Printing Office, 1979), p. 255. Not all experts agree that the Basic Law provided sufficient clarity on the relations among the political leaders, the minister of defense, and the IDF. See, for instance, Peter Elman, "Basic Law: The Army, 1976," *Israel Law Review* (April 1977), pp. 232-42.

101. On the basic organization of the IDF, see Nyrop, "Israel: A Country Study," pp. 255-57; Edward Luttwak and Dan Horovitz, *The Israeli Army* (New York: Harper & Row, 1975), pp. 94-98. Weller, "Armor and Infantry," p. 5, has pointed out that the area commander's exclusive control over all ground forces has been resisted.

102. Klieman, "Zionist Diplomacy," p. 94.

103. Brecher, *Foreign Policy System*, p. 178. Jon Kimche, "Politics and the Israel Defense Forces," *Midstream* (June/July 1974), pp. 31-33.

104. Klieman suggests that the political stock of the Ministry of Foreign Affairs did not improve. After noting its "permanent downgrading," he went on to describe it as an auxiliary agency with "... little voice and even less influence in the actual formulation of policy." See Klieman, "Zionist Diplomacy," p. 96, and Horovitz, "Is Israel a Garrison State?," p. 70.

105. Brecher, *Foreign Policy System*, p. 175.

106. Ibid., p. 182.

107. Ibid., pp. 182-83.

108. Ibid., p. 185, and Kimche, "Politics and the Israel Defense Forces," p. 34.

109. Between 1967 and 1973, defense policies were conceived and designed by Prime Minister Meir's "kitchen cabinet" according to Perlmutter, *Politics and the Military*, pp. 63ff.

110. One reason for this is the IDF's discouragement of any research into its relations with the cabinet or other political groups. Ibid., p. 4.

111. Amos Perlmutter, *Military and Politics in Israel: National Building and Role Expansion* (London: Frank Cass, 1969), pp. 123-245, suggests the following five reasons why the IDF did not emerge as the ruling group in Israel: a tradition of civilian supremacy dating back to the preindependence era; a high level of political institutionalization; cohesive and stratified classes, groups, and parties; value and ideological congruence between civil and military sectors; and a rise of professionalism in and depoliticization of the IDF.

112. Perlmutter, *Politics and the Military*, pp. 197-98; Kimche, "Politics and the Israel Defense Forces," pp. 33-34.

113. Perlmutter, *Military and Politics*, p. 81; *Politics and the Military*, pp. 197-98.

114. Perlmutter, *Military and Politics*, pp. 87-89.

115. The specific issue involved was a Lavon proposal that a national security authority be established to oversee the Ministry of Defense. Ibid., p. 91.

116. Ibid., *Military and Politics*, pp. 105-8, 113-14; *Politics and the Military*, pp. 29, 40-42; and Horovitz, "Is Israel a Garrison State?," pp. 69-70.

117. Kimche, "Politics and the Israel Defense Forces," p. 34-35. One high-level officer with whom I talked was of the opinion that Dayan's exclusion was the result of his preoccupation with relations with the Arabs in the occupied territories rather than the actions of others.

118. Perlmutter, *Politics and the Military*, p. 66, indicated that the High Command became the exclusive source of advice to the political leaders, while Kimche, "Politics and the Israel Defense Forces," p. 35, stated that matters concerning military strategy "become the preserve of the High Command."

119. Anticipated reactions in Egypt included demoralization of the Egyptian people and the downfall of Nasser. As for the Soviet Union, there was little thought given to the possibility that Moscow might take command of, and massively rebuild, Egyptian air defenses.

120. Avi Shlaim and Raymond Tanter, "Decision Process, Choice, and Consequences: Israel's Deep-Penetration Bombing in Egypt, 1970," *World Politics* (July 1978), pp. 483-516, quote, p. 516.

121. Perlmutter, *Politics and the Military*, pp. 195-98.

122. As Sadat and Begin's relationship became closer in 1978-79, Weizmann's involvement in the diplomatic process seemed to diminish noticeably.

123. In specific terms, Israel's internal social and economic problems involve demands by disadvantaged Eastern Jews and Arabs for socioeconomic benefits, skyrocketing inflation, disappointing immigration trends, and emigration to the United States. Leaving these aside, there is another factor that may complicate matters for Israel, and that is the willingness of the United States to make adequate quantities of weapons, aid, and loans available in view of its own economic difficulties and the perceived need to strengthen its military forces in the decade ahead. On the last point, see Drew Middleton, "U.S. Military Can Match Soviet, Officials Say, but Not before 1990," *New York Times*, 7 January 1980.

MIDDLE EASTERN DEFENSE POLICY: A BIBLIOGRAPHICAL ESSAY

Mark G. Ewig

Attempting to write a bibliographic essay on the defense policy of nations of the Middle East is both a challenging and an ominous task. The diversity of the region, coupled with a substantial lack of unbiased information, contributes to this problem. Any essay that can serve as a rudimentary tool for examining the body of English language literature on this subject must be tempered with caveats. First, the reader must understand that this is not a comprehensive bibliography of the defense policies of the region or of any individual country. It rather seeks to acquaint the student with some of the major writings that exist. Second, in order to maximize student utility, all nonEnglish language sources are excluded. This creates several limitations because of the small amount of available literature. Israel, to some extent, is an exception. Last, most of the literature even peripherally associated with the topic tends to examine the role of the military within society rather than to explain defense policy or segments thereof. While this adds an important dimension to the puzzle at hand, it seldom presents a picture of the environment, strategy, doctrine and force structure, and decision-making processes that occur within the defense policy establishments in the region.

Without dispute, the military dimension plays a significant (and, some argue, predominant) role in Middle East politics. One of the first comprehensive surveys was *The Sociology of the Military: A Selected and Annotated Bibliography* (Chicago: n.p., 1969). This compendium consists of over 200 English-language listings in the field of civil-military relations. Those that pertain to the Middle East focus on examining the results of various military coups, and offer (or refute) the argument that military intervention politics facilitates modernization and political development. Often-quoted articles such as Majid Khadduri's "Army Officer: His Role in Middle Eastern Politics," in *Social Forces in the Middle East,* ed. S. N. Fisher (Ithaca, N.Y.: Cornell University Press, 1955), pp. 162–84; Manfred Halpern's "Middle Eastern Armies and the New Middle Class," in *The Role of the Military in Underdeveloped Countries,* ed. John Johnson (Princeton, N.J.: Princeton University Press, 1962), pp. 277-316; Dankwart A. Rutow's "Military in Middle Eastern Society and Politics," in *Political Development and Social Change,* ed. Jason L. Finkle and Richard W. Gable (New York: Wiley & Sons, 1966), pp. 386–96; James A. Bill's "Military and Modernization in the Middle East," *Comparative Politics* 2 (October 1969): 41-62; and a series of articles in *The Military in the Middle East: Problems in Society and Government,* ed. S. N. Fisher (Columbus: Ohio State University Press, 1963) have paved the way for further studies.

Amos Perlmutter, in an excellent review article entitled "The Arab Military Elite," *World Politics* 22 (January 1970): 269-300, notes that in the late 1960s scholars turned away from earlier descriptive works to in-depth studies of the causes of military intervention within societies. J. C. Hurewitz's *Middle East Politics: The Military Dimension* (New York: Praeger, 1969) attempted to look into the causes and consequences of military intervention. Eliezer Beeri's book, *Army Officers in Arab Politics and Society* (New York: Praeger, 1970), is a good companion piece to Hurewitz's volume, but goes much further. Not only does Beeri examine the struggles that brought the officers to power, but he also provides an excellent analysis of the officers' social origins and motivations. Fuad I. Khuri and Gerald Obermeyer look further at military intervention as a social process in "The Social Bases for Military Intervention in the Middle East," in *Political-Military Systems: Comparative Perspectives,* ed. Catherine McArdle Kelleher (Beverly Hills, Calif.: Sage Publications, 1974). Uriel Dann, in *Iraq under Qassem* (New York: Praeger, 1969), shows that the causes and consequences of military intervention can be examined as an independent analytical unit—a single military actor in a single nation-state (Qassem in Iraq).

Several other contributors in this area of civil-military relations are worth mentioning. William Thompson surveys a number of approaches to explain intervention in his "Toward Explaining Arab Military Coups," *Journal of Political and Military Sociology* 2 (Fall 1974): 237-50. Gabriel Ben-Dor, in his article entitled "The Politics of Threat: Military Intervention in the Middle East," in *World Perspectives in the Sociology of the Military,* ed. George A. Kourvetaris and Betty A. Bebratz (New Brunswick, N.J.: Transaction Books, 1977), succinctly summarizes much of this literature and adds his own behaviorally oriented approach to the study of military intervention. Ben-Dor goes a step further in "Civilianization of Military Regimes in the Arab

World," *Armed Forces and Society* 1 (May 1975): 317–27, by focusing on the disengagement of the military from direct rule and the factors that have increased regime stability (defined as the absence of coups) in the Arab Middle East during the past decade.

None of these works, however, can be portrayed as providing a detailed examination of the defense policies of Middle Eastern countries. Their main focus is on the role of the military in the political life of a particular society. Little material exists that examines the role of the military within the decision-making apparatus of the state. Consequently, the information that follows on the individual Middle Eastern states is in most cases fragmentary.

Syria

Perhaps the two best books to be consulted are Nikolas Van Dam's *Struggle for Power in Syria* (New York: St. Martin's, 1979), and R. D. McLaurin et al., *Foreign Policy Making in the Middle East: Domestic Influences on Policy in Egypt, Iraq, Israel, and Syria* (New York: Praeger, 1977). The former is an excellent account of the rise to power of President Assad and the Alawites, while the chapter on Syria in the latter looks at the military as an interest group within the national security policy-making arena and details Syrian political and military objectives. Other useful articles on Syria include Amos Perlmutter, "From Obscurity to Rule: The Syrian Army and the Ba'ath Party," *Western Political Quarterly* 22 (December 1969): 827–45; A. I. Dawisha, "Syria under Assad, 1970–1978: The Centres of Power," *Government and Opposition,* 13 (Summer 1978): 341–54; and Moshe Ma'oz, "Alawi Military Officers in Syrian Politics, 1966–1974," *Military and State in Modern Asia,* ed. Harold Schiffrin (Jerusalem: Jerusalem Academic Press, 1976).

Iraq

Very little information is available on Iraqi defense policy. McLaurin's *Foreign Policy Making* has a small section on the nature of Iraqi military policy. In addition to his previously cited book, Uriel Dann's article entitled "The Iraqi Officer Corps As a Factor for Stability: An Orthodox Approach," in *Military and the State in Modern Asia,* argues that the Iraqi military has prevented the domestic political situation from becoming potentially more chaotic.

Egypt

The best discussion of Egyptian national security policy can be found in McLaurin, *Foreign Policy Making.* Military policies and objectives are outlined, as well as the relationhip between the military and the Arab Socialist Union. Charles Holley has written an interesting essay on the changing role of the Egyptian armed forces since the Soviet arms embargo and Cairo's turn to the West as a source of military hardware, "Egypt's 'Other' Armed Forces," *Middle East Journal* 46 (August 1978): 28–30. Eliezer Beeri's "Changing Role of the Military in Egyptian Politics," in *Military and the State in Modern Asia,* provides a very general discussion on the demilitarization of the government of Egypt since the death of Nasser. P. J. Vatikiotis's *Egyptian Army in Politics: Pattern for New Nations?* (Bloomington: Indiana University Press, 1961) traces the rise of the military elite within Egyptian society. Amos Perlmutter, *Egypt: The Praetorian State* (New Brunswick, N.J.: Transaction Books, 1974), admits to the fragmentary nature of available information on policy formulation in Egypt as he traces Nasser's rise to power and the effective use he made of the military. Finally, William G. Sykes has written an interesting work entitled "Egyptian Arms Procurement in the Post-1973 War Era" (M.A. thesis, Naval Postgraduate School, Monterey, Calif., 1977), in which he explores the arms diversification process that began in Egypt following the 1973 war and the effect that switching to Western equipment has had on Egyptian capabilities.

Other sources that could be of some merit in examining any of the nations of the Middle East are the area handbook series prepared by the Foreign Area Studies of American University. Each of these books contains a section, "National Defense," which compiles basic facts on the armed forces of the country under consideration. A recent Rand report by A. H. Pascal et al. entitled *Men and Arms in the Middle East: The Human Factor in Military Modernization* (Santa Monica, Calif.: Rand Corporation, 1979) fills a major gap in the literature by assessing the contributions of improvements in the quality of manpower and organization to the military effectiveness of the major Middle Eastern states, excluding Israel.

From the above, it should be obvious that there is a dearth of defense-policy-related materials on most of the Arab Middle Eastern countries. On the other hand, abundant materials, though occasionally lacking in quality, are available which deal specifically with Israeli defense policy.

Israel

Amos Perlmutter writes copiously about civil-military relations in Israel. His book, *Military and Politics in Israel: Nation Building and Role Expansion* (New York: Praeger, 1969), adroitly traces the development and the role of the army in the determination of foreign and defense policy in Israel. A sequel, *Politics and the Military in Israel, 1967–*

1977 (London: Cass, 1978), continues this valuable study. A succinct synopis of these books is included in chapter 9 of Perlmutter's *Military and Politics in Modern Times* (New Haven: Yale University Press, 1977). Another excellent study of the Israeli Army is Edward Luttwak and Dan Horowitz's *Israeli Army* (New York: Harper & Row, 1975). The book focuses on the people and the ideas that have shaped Israeli defense policy since independence.

Several useful articles detail the relationship between the geostrategic environment of Israel and its defense policy. Moshe Dayan's "Israel's Border and Security Problems," *Foreign Affairs* 33 (January 1955): 250-67, forms the basis for several later articles on the unique geographic restraints faced by the Jewish nation. Merrill A. McPeak, "Israel: Borders and Security," *Foreign Affairs* 54 (April 1976): 426-43; and Yigal Allon, "Israel: The Case for Defensible Borders," *Foreign Affairs* 55 (October 1976): 38-53, should be read as companion pieces in order to understand the controversial nature of certain aspects of the territorial and security concerns of Israel. Dan Horovitz looks at the centrality of the security issue and its relationship to the allocation of resources within Israel in "Is Israel a Garrison State?," *Jerusalem Quarterly,* Summer 1977, pp. 58-75.

The argument that the territory acquired by Israel during the 1967 war paradoxically weakened Israel's security position is made by Walter Laqueur in chapter 3 of *Confrontation* (New York: Bantam, 1974). Likewise, Israel Tal, in "Israel's Defense Doctrine: Background and Dynamics," *Military Review* 58 (March 1978): 23-37, argues that the increased territory brought confusion to Israel's defense planning.

An excellent introduction to the doctrinal aspects of Israeli defense policy is the survey by Michael Handel, *Israel's Political-Military Doctrine* (Cambridge, Mass.: Harvard University Press, 1973) McLaurin's *Foreign Policy Making* also contains useful information that serves as an excellent primer on Israeli defense policy. These two sources should be read prior to examining the monumental works of Michael Brecher which, in my opinion, are the two best volumes available on Israeli defense policy, and which, I hope, will serve as models for studies of other Middle Eastern nations. Brecher's *Foreign Policy Systems of Israel* (New Haven: Yale University Press, 1975) gives a macroanalysis of the foreign-policy-making system using a structural-functional approach. The book provides an excellent discussion of the relationship between the Israeli defense and foreign ministries. A companion piece entitled *Decisions in Israel's Foreign Policy* (New Haven: Yale University Press, 1975) gives a microanalysis of the decision-making process utilizing a number of incidents and issues that have had a profound effect on Israeli foreign and defense policy.

There are a number of excellent works that contain case studies of Israeli defense doctrine. Abraham R. Wagner's *Crisis Decision-Making: Israel's Experiences in 1967 and 1973* (New York: Praeger, 1974) examines the environment, the strategies, and the process within the policy-making arena during the two latest Arab-Israeli wars. By his own admission, Wagner's coverage of the 1973 war includes only general observations. Other useful studies include Avi Shlaim and Raymond Tanter, "Decision Process, Choice, and Consequences: Israel's Deep Penetration Bombing in Egypt, 1970," *World Politics* 30 (July 1978): 483-516; Michael Handel, "The Yom Kippur War and the Inevitability of Surprise," *International Studies Quarterly* 21 (September 1977): 461-502, and Avi Shlaim, "Failures in National Intelligence Estimates: The Case of the Yom Kippur War," *World Politics* 28 (April 1976): 348-80.

The Arab-Israeli conflict in general and the October 1973 war in particular have led to a plethora of articles and books that provide helpful insights into the defense-policy-making process. Some helpful studies include Fred O. Khouri, *The Arab-Israeli Dilemma,* 2d ed. (Syracuse: Syracuse University Press, 1976); Chaim Herzog, *The War of Atonement* (Boston: Little, Brown & Co., 1975); Trevor N. Dupuey, *Elusive Victory* (New York: Harper & Row, 1978); Insight Team of the *London Sunday Times, Yom Kippur War* (New York: Doubleday, 1974); Nadav Safran, *From War to War* (New York: Pegasus, 1969); Abraham R. Wagner, *The Impact of the 1973 October War on Israeli Policy* (Washington, D.C.: American Institute for Research, 1975); and Nadav Safran, *Israel: The Embattled Ally* (Cambridge, Mass.: Harvard University Press, 1978). Other books that concentrate on the Arab perceptions of the situation include Mohammed Heikal, *The Road to Ramadan* (New York: Quadrangle, 1975); and John W. Amos II, *Arab-Israeli Military and Political Relations: Arab Perceptions and the Politics of Escalation* (New York: Pergamon, 1979).

Several studies have also examined the nature of a future Arab-Israeli conflict. Martin Indyk and Steven J. Rosen comment on the advantages of a preemptive Israeli strike in "Fifth Israeli War," *Orbis* 20 (Summer 1976): 265-85, while Rosen alone looks at the overall strategic aspects of another conflict in "What the Next Arab-Israeli War Might Look Like," *International Security* 2 (Spring 1978): 149-73.

Nuclear weapons and their impact on defense policies in the Middle East are well represented in the literature. Among some of the best sources are Robert Harkavy, *Spectre of a Middle Eastern Holocaust: The Strategic and Diplomatic Implications of the Israeli Nuclear Weapons Program* (Denver: University of Denver Press, 1977); Steven J. Rosen, "A Stable System of Nuclear Deterrence in the Arab-Israeli Conflict," *American Political Science Review* 71 (December 1977): 1367-83; and Robert Pranger and Dale Tahtinen, *Nuclear Threat in the Middle East* (Washington, D.C.: American Enterprise Institute, 1975). Other excellent sources include Alan Dowth, "Nuclear Proliferation: The Israeli Case," *International Studies Quarterly* 22 (March 1978): 22–33; Lawrence Freedman, "Israeli's Nuclear Policy," *Survival* 17 (May 1975): 114–20; and Yair Evron, "Israel and the Atom: The Uses and Misuses of Ambiguity, 1957–1967," *Orbis* 17 (Winter 1974): 1326–43.

This short essay has attempted to survey the available English-language literature on defense policy in the Middle East, presenting books and articles that will be beneficial to those studying the region. It should be apparent that the material presently available is highly skewed toward Israel, both quantitatively and qualitatively. The remainder of the panorama of Middle Eastern defense policy awaits in-depth study. There is clearly a need for more scholarly research on the defense policy processes of the Arab states.

Men and arms in the Middle East: The human factor in military modernization

Anthony Pascal, Michael Kennedy, Steven Rosen et al.

A host of factors come together with the human variables to influence the effectiveness with which a given society will exploit its military forces. The nature of the threat, strategic objectives, weapons available, terrain, and climate, of course, form the background against which the human factor is played out. And, for purposes of analysis, the human factor requires subdivision into the mental and physical characteristics of troops, qualities of leadership in officers, and organizational structures appropriate to the accomplishment of military missions. Some of the human factors are amenable to change through policy decisions; others are largely autonomous in their gradual evolution. We aim to provide an abbreviated summary of findings as to the directions of change in a list of what we have come to see as the critical variables. (Iran is one of the countries examined below, but data and commentary refer primarily to prerevolutionary Iran before the fall of the shah.—Ed.)

AUTONOMOUS VARIABLES

Population size confers obvious advantages. The determinants of the size of the required military force are largely exogenous and stem from the strategic situation facing the country. Other things equal, populous countries can more easily find the trainable manpower required in their military forces, assuming a fairly equal distribution of native abilities in each country. Civilian human capital programs—nutrition, health, education, training—will naturally enhance the effective supply.

In this connection, we explore here some national indicators of military effort in relation to each economy and labor force. The states of the region vary appreciably in commitment of national resources toward security ends. As shown in table 1, it is generally the oil-rich states—Saudi Arabia and Iran—and the confrontation states—Egypt, Jordan, and Syria—that devote large fractions of their national products; none, however, comes close to Israel's commitment. Iraq, so far, lags considerably in the fraction of GNP absorbed by the military, as does Turkey, which has neither the excess budgetary resources nor the immediate security problem.

A somewhat different picture emerges from the per capita statistics. Wealthy Saudi Arabia, to a lesser extent Iran, and beleagured Israel stand out. Populous states such as Egypt and particularly Turkey score low. The requirements of confrontation for Syria and Jordan and a favorable ratio between foreign exchange and population for Iraq tend to push them to the intermediate rank.

Table 1 indicates relationships between national populations and the size of the various military forces. By and large, the bigger the fraction absorbed by the military, the more intense will be the competition between the sectors. Clearly, however, low levels of demand for raw unskilled labor in the domestic economy (as in Turkey) will reduce the social cost of mass conscription. Moreover, the average level of skill in the population affects the results of the competition. In a sense then, Israel, where skills are highest, may be more capable of bearing the enormous burden of its military than Saudi Arabia, whose burden is small but

Reprinted here by permission of the Rand Corporation is an extract from a lengthier study under the same title prepared for the director of net assessment, Office of Secretary of Defense. See R-2460-NA, pp. 37–54.

Table 1
Military expenditures in relation to GNP and population in selected Middle Eastern countries, 1978

Country	Military expenditures (millions/dollars)	Military expenditures as a percentage of GNP	Military expenditures per capita (dollars)[a]
Egypt	2.8	21	70
Iran	9.9	14	280
Iraq	1.7	11	136
Jordan	0.3	23	100
Saudi Arabia	9.6	17	1215
Syria	1.1	17	151
Turkey	1.7	4	39
Israel	3.3	30	892

Source: The International Institute for Strategic Studies, *The Military Balance,* 1978–1979. These figures appeared more reliable to us than those presented by the U.S. Arms Control and Disarmament Agency in *World Military Expenditures and Arms Transfers, 1967–1976.* They are, for example, much closer to figures reported in classified intelligence sources.
[a]Based on CIA population estimates, *National Basic Intelligence Factbook,* 1978.

whose skill level is also low. Egypt, Iran, and Turkey employ considerably smaller fractions of their labor forces to meet military needs.

The advantages of a large population base in relation to the size of the armed forces are illustrated by table 2. For all of the populous states—Egypt, Iran, and Turkey—the military absorbs about 6 percent of the relevant population and about 10 percent of the population "fit" for service. These are also the states, aside from Israel, where the armed forces encounter the least relative difficulty in meeting skill needs. Saudi Arabia attempts no more than the "Big Three" in percentage terms, but the backwardness of its population makes it substantially more difficult to secure an effective military. Jordan and Iraq appear not too dissimilar in aspiration and Syria seems to try the hardest of all, exclusive of Israel. By deduction, what we have discovered about skill shortages in Jordan—that, for example, supplies of readily trainable men are soon exhausted—may apply as well to Iraq and even more pronouncedly to Syria. Israel plays in an entirely different league in terms of population skill levels, so even if it devotes the highest fraction of manpower to its military forces, it is able to attain the most in average military competence. Nonetheless, the cost of the standing army in economic product foregone is bound to be heavy there, as suggested in table 1.

Industrialization and attendant urbanization move society along paths that widen the option for building military power. Not only do physical resources for mili-

Table 2
Comparison of population and military forces for selected Middle Eastern countries, 1978

Country	1978 population (estimated, in millions)	Relevant population (males 15–49)	Number considered "Fit" to serve[a]	"Fit" population relevant population	Number of males reaching military age annually (eligible military age)	Number in military service[b]	Percentage of relevant population in military service	Percentage of "Fit" population in military service
Egypt	39.9	8.59M	5.60M	.65	384,000 (20)	511,800	6	9
Iran	35.3	8.08M	4.79M	.59	350,000 (20)	524,500	7	11
Iraq	12.5	2.64M	1.48M	.56	118,000 (18)	221,800	8	15
Jordan	3.0	624K	444K	.71	32,000 (18)	69,300	11	16
Saudi Arabia	7.9[c]	1.81M	1.02M	.56	66,000 (18)	87,400	5	9
Syria	8.1	1.82M	1.02M	.56	96,000 (19)	262,500	14	26
Turkey	43.1	10.67M	6.28M	.59	461,000 (20)	642,000	6	10
Israel	3.7	760K[d]	655K[d]	.86	60,000[d] (18)	199,600	26	31

Source: Central Intelligence Agency, *National Basic Intelligence Factbook,* 1978.
[a]"Fit" is defined as admissible for service in peacetime on physical and mental criteria.
[b]Includes National Guard equivalent units.
[c]Figure is in dispute even among intelligence sources; an estimate around 6-6.5M total is the consensus.
[d]Figures for Israel include *females* as well as males.

tary aggrandizement become more available but the entry into technological culture usually prepares the citizenry for participation in collective undertakings in which a modern outlook confers great advantages. Although it is undoubtedly true that the sense of collective purpose (notably the Israeli concern with national survival) enhances effectiveness, it is also the case that warfare has changed so dramatically that the general concomitants of urban industrial existence—the ability to work in organized teams with advanced equipment—outweigh the martially useful qualities generated in nomadic or rural societies—fierce loyalties, personal bravery.

In our review of comparative rates of national military modernization, the relative positions of Egypt and Iran, on the one hand, and Saudi Arabia and Syria, on the other, seem quite informative. Noting that each pair contains both rich and poor states, the former have demonstrated a superior capacity to translate elements of modernity from the economic sphere into the military. The choice made by Saudi Arabia and Syria, modernization of societies through the military vehicle, may have costs in strictly military terms. Turkey represents an interesting case in point. The Turkish attempt to modernize its social structure through military service appears to have degraded military effectiveness. To build a modern military in a traditional society may be a good development strategy; it is unlikely to win wars against a thoroughly modern opponent.

Given contemporary sources for technology and advanced economic organization, modernization will probably be accompanied by increased exposure to the West. When the Western influence extends into the military, to the supply of arms and the training of men, it seems to confer an additional advantage. The case of Jordan is illustrative. Jordan's small size and vulnerable strategic situation have affected its ability to swing substantial weight in past Arab-Israeli engagements. But Israelis, almost unanimously, rank Jordanians as man-for-man their most dangerous opponents in the air and on the ground. Most attribute the Jordanian edge to their long association with the British as military advisers and trainers. The contrast between the results of the British influence in Jordan and the Soviet influence in Egypt (pre-1973) provides further confirmation of the thesis.

Urban industrial societies generally have higher levels of per capita income for the mass of the population. For armies, general affluence confers its advantages through the physical stamina and mental competence of the troops. Among the countries we have examined, differentials in standards of living are not at present very great. Impressive statistics on per capita income in the oil-rich states mask an extreme maldistribution often characteristic of the early stages of economic development when affluence has not yet trickled down to the masses.

But rates of economic growth do differ appreciably across the selected countries. Those with expanding economies find it increasingly difficult to attract and retain needed talents in the military sector against the enticement of high wages and opportunities for advancement in civilian life. Iran and Saudi Arabia are examples. But even in the slow-growth and no-growth economies, competition for personnel enters through the lure of emigration. Hundreds of thousands of young Egyptians, Jordanians, and Syrians work in the gulf states and Libya, where oil export proceeds fuel a continuing economic boom.

Stable regimes can wield military power more effectively, not because they necessarily have superior supplies of human capital but because they can afford to organize people more efficiently. They are secure enough to attempt to delegate authority to its most appropriate level, having less fear that independent nuclei of power will threaten the existing structure. Delegation appears to be a prerequisite to the establishment of flexible and adaptive command structures.

Over and over we were struck by the critical contribution of decentralized decision making to the successful prosecution of war in the region. The 1973 war, on both the Sinai and Golan fronts, illustrated how hypercentralized military commands on the Arab side found it difficult to respond to unanticipated opportunities and threats: the Syrians ignored a possible opportunity to advance beyond the Golan Heights and into the Galilee Valley in the first few days of the campaign; the Egyptian canal crossing achieved such surprise as to make possible the occupation of the Mitla Pass and Abu Rudeis but the opportunity was not pursued; it took inordinate time for the Egyptian high command to react to the Israeli counterattack on the west bank of the Suez. Anecdotal evidence as to the superiority of Egyptian field commanders relative to the Syrians leads us to surmise that a portion of the edge in organizational adaptability displayed by the Egyptian military (compared with the Syrian) may be attributable to the regime stability factor.

Some have argued that the fear of insurrection directly affects training practices as well. Without live ammunition and combined force operations, the realism of exercises is much reduced and the preparation of the forces thereby diminished. But fearful leaderships seem reluctant to disperse the resources and to permit the lateral cooperation necessary to organize these sorts of exercises. The superior internal security situation in Egypt, compared with, say, that in Syria and Iraq, should in days to come begin to translate into better training and then greater potential battlefield responsiveness.

Regime insecurity has additional implications. Where loyalty to the existing government is an issue, the leadership will naturally stress faithfulness rather than competence in making assignment and promotion decisions. The Jordanians regularly favor Bedouins over Palestinians, the most educated and progressive component of the population, in sensitive military appointments. Evidence of the loyalty criterion is also seen in the dominance of Alawites in key Syrian command positions and a favoring of leaders originating in the town of Tikrit in the Iraqi forces. As an example of the consequences, many observers allege a sharply negative relation between rank and capability in the Syrian officer corps, although they perceive no such pattern among the Egyptians. Whether the high-quality junior officers observed in the Syrian forces in 1973 will be permitted to advance up the ranks and, if so, whether they will then be co-opted (and defanged) by the reigning establishment remains to be seen.

Most commentators agree that, aside from the "loyalty test," barriers to advancement based on ethnicity or social status have receded in all of the Arab societies as democratic and pluralistic ideas gain acceptance. Perhaps the clearest and most costly—in efficiency terms—of the remaining barriers affect women, particularly in the most traditional societies such as Saudi Arabia. Even with the severe labor shortages in the kingdom, women hardly participate in the civilian economy, let alone in the military forces. Jordan, Iran, and Egypt have much more readily accepted women in clerical and technical positions, even in the military, although a strong reaction by traditional elements is already apparent.

The military, of course, must compete with the civilian economy for the society's available talent. Given the level of effectiveness in conscription policy, the higher the prestige and the more attractive the conditions of the military calling, the easier the attainment of manpower goals. Turkey, where the warrior tradition reigns and the military career confers high prestige, meets its manpower objectives most successfully among the countries surveyed. Conscript quotas are easily met too because the living standards and the education and training opportunities compare favorably with civilian life. Military careers have lower relative prestige in Saudi Arabia and score lower still in Iran, with obvious negative implications for recruitment in those countries.

In the course of our study, we found that commentators consistently reflected on the cultural characteristics that affect the trainability and performance of Middle Easterners. These cultural characteristics appear to suffuse the entire weapons absorption and military modernization process, and we summarize comments on some of these traits here.

These characteristics plus an accompanying disregard for tools mainly affect maintenance operations, as in Iran, where maintenance is regarded as a dirty word. Iranians tend to perform quite well at "clean" electronics work.

In Saudi Arabia a reinforcing belief holds that contractors have been hired to do the dirty work, but Jordan and Egypt, owing to their different cultural backgrounds and more vocationally oriented educational systems, do not hold that belief to nearly the same extent. In the Middle East (as in much of the rest of the world) piloting airplanes is regarded as respectable, but driving tanks is dirty. Therefore, higher status people are attracted to the air forces.

Progress toward a more functional work ethic comes in fits and starts when the proper incentives are instituted. After exposure to U.S. military training, Iranian and Saudi students generally show that they can develop mechancial aptitudes and perform adequately, but they sometimes relapse upon return to operational assignments. The Turkish experience suggests that migrant workers who return from Western Europe may often absorb and subsequently use more efficient business practices. They may also create new demands for better public education and vocational training in the home country. Turkish involvement in NATO may have had similar effects in the specifically military sphere, as a result of some standardization in training practices, the participation in joint exercises, exposure to high standards of performance, etc.

Knowledge acquisition comes through drill, not analysis. Rote learning leads to mastery of routine tasks but does not develop the ability to see cause-effect and to ends-means relationships. This outlook suffices for systems in which operation and maintenance is based on repetitive steps, as in the TOW anti-tank system. But memorizing set procedures does not instill flexibility and ingenuity or the ability to adjust to unforeseen contingencies. One wonders whether the Arabs, for example, have absorbed the implications of mistakes made in the October War to the extent that Israelis have learned from their own weaknesses.

In Middle Eastern cultures, responsiblity tends to be treated as a shared social phenomenon rather than as something pertaining strictly to the individual. Concepts of right and wrong depend less on individual determination and more on what is deemed right or wrong by the world surrounding the individual—producing people who are sensitive and subject to public shame but feel a lesser sense of personal guilt.

Answering to society for all deeds creates pressures for officers and men to appear blameless, by keeping and saving "face," to escape censure. Face thus becomes an extremely important element of personal motivation and social interactions because it reflects the individual's worth and dignity. Keeping face often results in formal showmanship, and saving face requires excuses for failures and shortcomings and leads to shifting blame. The concern for face affects the predisposition to both offer and accept criticism.

The ability to put on a good show—the affixing of decals to the fuselage—may appear more important as a measure of success than a high operational readiness rate, the practical importance of which may even be downplayed. The imperatives of serving the group and keeping face also have pronounced effects on the classroom performance of military trainees. Students avoid showing ignorance by not asking questions. Instructors avoid provoking shame by not posing questions. Cheating carries little stigma and may, in fact, be seen as a way for students to help each other and to serve group goals. Refusing to help a colleague is thought dishonorable. U.S. instructors have had to take considerable care to design programs that will accommodate cultural differences. Otherwise, there would be little give and take in the classroom and poorer students would not receive remedial training.

The pervasiveness of what are often called "punishment" cultures in the Middle East also has military implications. For example, in Iran, if a civilian or military technician made an error, he could lose pay and risk incarceration or corporal punishment. This incentive system motivates some typical behavior patterns ranging from general inertia to the falsification of reports. In tactical flying, for example, concern for the safety of the aircraft often leads to very conservative training. In maintenance, fear of losing or damaging equipment means conservative testing and practicing. In Iran, at least, the harshness of the punishment culture has recently diminished. Some Western management techniques—discussion meetings that help identify problems without trying to cover up failures, devices to retrain mechanics who err—are being adopted in the military. Lesser adaptation is seen in Saudi Arabia.

Rigid hierarchy, centralization of command, and prescribed responsibilities mark Middle Eastern authority patterns. These translate into a penchant for staying in conventional channels in military operations. At working levels, skills and duties become highly compartmentalized and isolated. One's power base often depends upon, and is reflected by, hoarding of materials, parts, and personnel. Disgorging a hoard may require multiple signatures and forms so as to disperse responsibility.

The ideals of centralization cause middle-level personnel to reject decision-making responsibility and to pass even small matters up to higher commanders, who then become burdened with decisions on issues about which they lack necessary information. High-level authorities are expected to behave in a fairly rigid manner. Apparent obedience to orders is automatic even when the command is not fulfillable. The result of these conditions is to diminish the incentives and opportunities for showing innovation and flexibility. In pilot training, Middle Eastern students tend to place inordinate reliance on the instructor pilot, so they frequently fail to learn the systems and procedures thoroughly. This inhibits the development of flexibility in dealing with unexpected events.

Cultural constraints relating to local ideas of authority and responsibility are reflected throughout the processes of technology absorption. For example the Iranians had planned to purchase the most sophisticated C^3 (that is, command, control, and communications) technology in the world, but were installing only the vertical linkages upward to the Shah, and not the horizontal field linkages. The Arabs—except for the Jordanians—have had even more noticeable difficulties in adopting modern C^3 technology, again partly for cultural reasons: the reluctance to share resources, the concern to protect oneself from responsibility for failures, the lack of faith of superiors in the competence of subordinates. The resulting inflexibility degrades training exercises and, ultimately, adaptability on the battlefield.

CIVILIAN POLICY VARIABLES

Human-capital-building programs—basic and university education, technical and vocational training, public health, medical care, and nutritional improvements—obviously enhance the quality of the population base from which the military recruits its force. Some Israeli commentators perceived significant improvement in health and literacy among Egyptian prisoners captured in 1973 over 1967. However, spending on such programs comes out of the same national budget that finances direct military expenditures, and the civilian program inevitably benefits people who do not enter the military. A dedicated warrior state could conceivably concentrate its human capital improvement efforts exclusively on its soldiers, at least in the short run. All of the states we studied have adopted a more generous approach and have generally had comprehensive social programs. Those with the heaviest defense burden, such as Syria, have obviously had to make the most sacrifices on the social front.

Table 2 shows the 1978 total population estimates for the states surveyed together with the size of the relevant population, the "fit" population, and the military forces. An indication of the general extent and success of human capital programs can be surmised from the column indicating the fraction of the population aged fifteen to forty-nine deemed fit for military service. Although Israel leads the others at 86 percent, Jordan stands out among the predominantly Muslim states at 71 percent, and Egypt follows at 65 percent. All of the others cluster between 55 and 60 percent.

MILITARY POLICY VARIABLES

As we have discussed earlier, and as tables 1 and 2 bear out, countries that field large armed forces out of small or poorly prepared population bases encounter the most difficulties in meeting military manpower requirements, which explains the comparative difficulties noted in Syria, Jordan, and Saudi Arabia.

Recruitment methods vary widely among the states. Some, such as Egypt and Syria, conscript; others, such as Saudi Arabia, rely on volunteers. The choice depends on tradition, politics, and military needs. In some states—Egypt, for example—conscription can tap scarce skill supplies. In others, selectivity through "hiring" may be advisable, at least given the somewhat negative experience with conscription in Turkey. Retention policies also vary. The hitch lasts from twenty months to three years for enlisted men in each country. The period adopted represents a choice on the trade-off function between current capability, which is best attained through a standing professional force with years of experience, and mobilization potential, which is heightened by the processing of larger numbers of young men serving necessarily shorter hitches. The latter option will also appeal to Turkey, which sees its army as a modernizing and socializing vehicle for the larger society.

Generally, expertise in assignment—the matching of aptitudes and skills with positions—is quite underdeveloped in Middle Eastern militaries. Diagnosis and remediation receive short shrift. Political loyalties continue to weigh heavily in promotion decisions. Assignment problems emerge not only out of inexperience with the principles of personnel management but as a result as well of the often-observed inclination to strip the best human resources from the generality of units so as to staff the elite forces or the most recently acquired weapon system. Favoring SAM and antitank units in 1973 seems to have led to certain advantages for the Arabs, however. Iran seemed to have made the most progress in planning for force balance, but even there the priority unit syndrome produces adverse spillovers on personnel capabilities in the general run of units.

We have pointed out the inefficiences inherent in the maintenance of ethnic, sex, and class barriers to participation. The military forces of the states studied vary substantially in their openness to pluralism because the political price necessary to gain the advantages of wider access differs among them. The Iraqis distrust the Kurds, Jordanians restrict the Palestinians, Syrians discriminate against Shiites, each operating out of motives of regime security and political patronage. Integration of women violates deep-seated values in Muslim society of which the Saudi rulers seem most observant. Even in neighboring Iran, the shah's attempt to break with traditional sexual segregation evoked strong reactions.

Although our evidence is sketchy, class barriers have apparently been the earliest to fall, particularly in the ostensibly socialist states of Iraq, Syria, and Egypt. But in Egypt, particularly, we have noted a tendency—reflecting broader social values—to permit paper credentials to signify as weightily as demonstrated competence. The importance of merit rather than background or loyalty may differ by service within a given country. In Jordan, for example, the air force appears superior to the ground forces in its readiness to assign and promote officers on the basis of competence alone.

The Middle Eastern concern for face, also discussed earlier, adds complications in the development of rationalized personnel systems. Criticism evokes shame and becomes muted out of a reluctance to embarrass fellow soldiers. Add this to notions of shared rather than individual responsibility, and the result often is a failure to demote or discharge the inept. These problems show up most prominently at middle management levels. The Iranians appear to have diagnosed their difficulties and were making some progress in dealing with them by means of training reforms and debriefing sessions.

All of the states have experimented with the use of outsiders for the performance of certain specialized tasks. The Saudi military employed vast numbers of foreigners from South Asia, East Asia, and the West. The Iranians tapped foreign sources to meet skilled labor shortages and also developed the *homofar* system in which fairly high wages were paid to indigenous civilians with scarce skills on long-term contract to the military. The homofar concept offers attractive advantages to those other forces in the region in which acute civilian skill shortages do not preclude its use (e.g., Egypt, perhaps Syria and Iraq). The idea, however, seems not to have spread.

The employment of outside personnel certainly adds to immediate capability and most likely expedites the enhancement of indigenous military skills through on the job training (OJT). But such dependence also carries costs aside from the obvious ones inherent in higher compensation and, in the case of expatriates, the depletion of foreign exchange reserves. Civilian workers are generally less subject to military control and discipline than are their national military counterparts. When the outsiders are also expatriates who owe primary allegiance to some third power, the ability to make war on any sustained basis will be affected by the acquiescence if not approval of that third power.

Substitution of capital appears as one solution for labor shortages. Black box replacement in place of periodic maintenance is a concrete manifestation. However, the substitution may simply escalate skill requirements to a higher level. The instruments that diagnose the black boxes require maintenance. There is increased dependence on a sophisticated system to supply the black boxes where and when needed. Because skill shortages are even more severe at these levels, the alleged "capital substitution" solution may prove ephemeral.

Although necessary to prepare the forces for action, training is, as we have discussed in earlier sections, expensive in a number of senses: it uses resources and it degrades immediate response capabilities. The poverty of many of the countries in the region constrains training by limiting supplies of parts and expendables. Egypt and Jordan come prominently to mind.

The goal of catching up with the Israelis in proficiency drives the Arab forces to train more intensively. The improved Arab performance, particularly in antiaircraft and antitank units, demonstrated in 1973, testifies to the payoff from training. A side cost often intrudes, however. The better the training in technical subjects, the harder it is to retain the resulting electronics specialist or engine mechanic in the military force, given his alternative pay in the civilian economy. This problem has been most severe in Iran, Saudi Arabia, and Jordan, where the lure is emigration, but it is felt even in Turkey. The United States and Israel are not immune to this problem either.

Training often works best when the trainee is removed from the inhibitions of his accustomed sociocultural milieu. Acceptance of individual responsibility and criticism, innovative behavior, esteem for manual endeavors, and willingness to work long hours may be more easily inculcated in settings where these traits are approved and rewarded. Middle Eastern students often return from training stints in the United States fired with new attitudes and work styles. The use of bicultural liaison officers, assigned responsibility for discipline and behavior, who accompany their training contingents, had come to be seen by Iran as an effective device for reinforcing the positive effects. The Saudis have recently installed similar procedures. Always present, however, is the danger of reversion to traditional behavior following the return to the home country.

In none of the countries studied did we encounter any *absolute* barriers to training operators and logistics support personnel for sophisticated weapons. Even in Saudi Arabia, where manpower shortages and cultural inhibitions seem most severe, training takes. But we also found that it may require twice as long to produce a Saudi pilot, mechanic, or supply clerk with U.S. proficiency standards. In the other countries where the U.S. trains military personnel—Iran, Jordan, Turkey—the training period exceeds U.S. specifications but by lesser amounts.

Deriving the most benefits from practice requires that exercises be carried out with a large element of realism. The Egyptian predisposition for thorough planning and intensive training appears to have yielded impressive returns during the canal crossing that opened the 1973 war. Use of live ammunition, arrangements for joint operations—for example, air-armor-infantry—and the incorporation of uncertainty and fluidity to the mock battle situation best prepares troops and commanders for the test of war. But certain background factors in the Middle East militate against such devices. Ammunition is expensive. Interunit horizontal links are undeveloped as a consequence of both tradition and regime insecurity. The preparation of a flexible response capability goes against the Arab preference for well-specified and well-rehearsed plans. The yield derived from force exercises is thus diminished even when they occur. Without practice, skills acquired in training may atrophy to the point where the system simply loses its effectiveness.

Supply systems provide ample illustration of organizations where traditional patterns of authority and responsibility have constrained efficient performance. The reluctance to release accumulated hoards, the insistence on face-to-face transactions, the fascination with forms and stamps, and the disposition to seek higher-level approval for trivial decisions means, for example, that a parts inventory may remain in excess in one location while equipment is grounded for want of the same item at a nearby base. These difficulties appear even in Iran, where progress in logistics rationalization had moved faster. Malperformance is even more widespread in Saudi Arabia (but individual parts inventories there are larger).

Basic reforms in managerial style must precede significant progress in what we have labeled macro-level competence. For the Arab states that have fought Israel, failures in responsiveness and adaptability have been noted repeatedly. Even in 1973 the Egyptian and Syrian forces displayed rigid adherence to prespecified plans and overcentralized command structures. Armored attacks, for example, were organized in textbook fashion with little attention to terrain or enemy responses. Lateral coordination was weak, and central HQ quickly became overloaded with information and slow to respond. Although some attempts at reform are under way, progress in this area is difficult and time consuming. Other heretofore second-line states such as Saudi Arabia and Iraq have neither Syria's experience of past conflict to drive the lessons home nor the state of social development characteristic of Egypt and Jordan.

Iran had given some indication of rapid development in military management capability according to U.S. observers. Problems in evaluating Iranian progress stem from the paucity of tests for that system. Having fought no serious engagements against worthy adversaries, Iran's true abilities in this regard remained mostly a mystery. The Turks, with a long history of military relations with the West, gave a good account of themselves against the Greeks in Cyprus; but even they experienced difficulties in organizing the campaign.

In the medium term, the continuation of economic and social development and programs that increase the quality of a country's human capital will, in turn, enhance its military potential. Few states, perhaps, will opt deliberately to slow down the rate of economic growth expressly to ease recruiting problems. But given the supply of available manpower and an exogenously determined force size goal, policy choices represent alternative routes on the way to improved military effectiveness. There *is* a production function for military effectiveness, and its arguments include human resources, time, and perseverence. The primitive state of existing theory and the scantiness of data have prevented our research from estimating the size of the payoffs to be expected from personnel policies versus training versus exercises versus organizational reforms at functional and command levels. We have, we believe, identified the critical policy choices for the modernizing military. We reiterate the importance of the obdurate attitudinal variables that will impede the course of improvement associated with any change in strategy.

THE RELATIONSHIP BETWEEN MODERNIZATION AND THE MILITARY BALANCE

The unequal level of military modernization in different states affects their relative abilities to organize, maintain, operate, and obtain the greatest combat usefulness from given sets of equipment. Differences in organizational and managerial effectiveness, social and cultural milieu, manpower competence, combat experience, and military leadership greatly influence how effectively various systems are adapted to the particular requirements of different states. Indeed, it can be argued that although differences in the "human factor" are inherently more difficult to measure and quantify than differences in equipment, competence factors have historically had a greater effect on combat outcomes than have differences in weapons hardware.

Nowhere has this been more evident than in the Arab-Israeli wars. In 1967, the Israelis were outnumbered by more than 2:1 in combat aircraft and almost 3:1 in tanks, yet according to public reports they achieved an air combat kill ratio of 20:1 and a tank kill ratio of better than 7:1. In 1973, outnumbered again by 2.5:1 in both combat aircraft and tanks, the Israelis achieved favorable kill ratios of 40:1 in dogfights and 2:1 in tank kills. Some of these disparities are explained by differences in the performance characteristics of the equipment and some may be explainable by differences in casualty rates traditionally experienced between attacking and defending forces (particularly the tank kill ratio), but these factors alone cannot explain the greater part of the outcomes. Indeed, on some characteristics, such as unilateral advantages in night fighting equipment in 1973, the qualitative edge in hardware favored the Arabs. Observers agree that only by bringing in the human competence differential can the Israeli margin of superiority be explained and that individual and collective excellence has been the keystone of the favorable military balance enabling Israel to tolerate greatly unequal force ratios.

It follows that improvements in the ability of the Arabs to use different equipment effectively could, in principle, more greatly affect the military balance than mere improvements in the quantities or qualities of equipment inventories themselves. In theory, if the Arabs could close the manpower and organizational competence gap or introduce new systems whose simplicity of operations reduced the importance of the gap, they might decisively improve the military balance. The modernization issue is therefore at the very center of efforts to assess the future Arab-Israeli military balance.

Differences in the levels of modernization among the states we have examined in the Middle East are probably not as wide as in the cases of the other military balances of the region, but there are some disparities. Egypt has a significant advantage over Libya, and Iraq has considerably greater combat experience than Kuwait and Saudi Arabia. Although Iran lacks the combat experience of Iraq, it appears to be at a higher level of modernization, and the gap appears to be widening. Iran seems much further down the road of modernization than Kuwait or Saudi Arabia.* Finally, the Syrian-Iraqi balance is probably one of fairly equal levels of military effectiveness, although the advantages conferred on Syria as a result of more intensive war experience could tip the balance. Detailed comparisons in these cases are more difficult, as most of the recent combat experience of the region has involved opposed forces of Israel and the Arabs, and therefore most of the data points apply to this particular balance. Indeed, differences among the Arabs must be inferred from their unequal performance against Israel.

TIME TRENDS IN MODERNIZATION

When trends in modernization are related to the *future* military balance, it is important to recognize that not every increment of modernization by one side necessarily leads to a narrowing of the manpower and organizational competence differential and an improvement of the military balance in its favor. Conceivably, we could see the Arab-Israeli gap widening rather than narrowing, in spite of Arab successes in modernization, when we examine the elements of the modernity gap more closely.

First, the level of modernization, as it relates to military competence, is a relative measure, and improvements on one side must be related to improvements on the other. It is sometimes asserted that the Israelis are already close to 100 percent of the theoretically attainable "perfect" operation of military systems, whereas the Arabs have been operating at only 25 or 50 percent effectiveness, and that therefore improvements on the Arab side are bound to narrow the gap. But individual and organizational competence are not "perfectible." As in competitive sport, there is always the possibility of improvement, and Israeli improvements also must be taken into account.

Yet this objection is not as basic as some others. Although both the beginning and the advanced athlete can improve their performance, the rates of improvement that are possible for the beginner clearly exceed those possible for the front runner, and in this sense the gap will tend to narrow even if it never closes. Moreover, in the process of military modernization, there may be a point where a decisive qualitative transformation takes place, after which self-sustaining growth in military effectiveness becomes the norm. At the early stages of modernization there is primary reliance on foreign advisers, the social and cultural milieu resists improvements, and modern military systems remain foreign imports that cannot fully be absorbed by local personnel. But a later stage of modernization can build on the local accumulation of military capital, expertise, and experience; constant improvement is built into the system, and foreign technologies can be absorbed more rapidly. If the Arabs can achieve such a qualitative transformation, unilateral improvements may have an absolute effect on the military balance even if the Israelis also improve.

A second and more important objection is raised when levels of modernization are related to the operator and support personnel competence and organizational requirements imposed by the weapons being introduced. In practice, weapons differ in the level of skills they require of their operators, and the portion of combat outcomes explained by individual and organizational competence (as opposed to the inherent capabilities of the weapons themselves) is much greater for some systems than for others. For example, the effectiveness of long-range terminally guided, surface-to-surface missiles carrying large nuclear warheads against area targets is largely a function of the devices themselves and is quite insensitive to the skill of the operators. (But difficulties in programing the guidance systems may indeed vary with the skill of operators.)

In contrast, the effectiveness of an F-4 against a Mig-21 has been shown to be related more to pilot skill than to the inherent characteristics of the platforms and their weapon fits. (This was illustrated by the experience of U.S. Navy pilots in Indochina, who improved their dogfight kill ratios from 2.3:1 in the period 1965-68 to 12.5:1 in the period 1970-73 by going through the Dissimilar Air Combat pilot retraining program—a 400 percent improvement with the same equipment.) Also, the effectiveness of forces in the field is a function of the support systems backing them up, including all the elements in the maintenance, supply, and logistic train. Although for some systems the performance of the weapons themselves is the key, for many others what is done with the hardware is more important than its mechanical attributes.

To relate changes in the competence gap to changes in the military balance, we introduce an intervening variable: changes in the share of combat outcomes explained by human competence, itself a function of technology. Suppose, for example, that the Arabs marginally improved their competence "rating" compared with that of the Israelis. At the same time, new systems (e.g., advanced tactical fighters) were introduced whose operation and support *required* much greater competence. The net military balance might improve in favor of Israel even though the weapons were introduced on both sides and the rates of improvement in the human factor were greater on the Arab side. The key to this intervening variable between modernization rates and the military balance is the changing portion of the combat outcomes explained by differences in individual and collective competence.

This study has been concerned primarily with modernization itself; we have seen that, with varying degrees of success, fairly rapid improvements are being undertaken in a number of countries. Although no effort has been made here to examine the Israeli case, it is probably fair to conclude that, for the reasons given above, on at least some characteristics the competence gap is gradually closing, if only because the Arabs started a considerable distance behind. The

*We remind the reader that this report was written before the upheaval in Iran.

Arabs are also closing the qualitative gap in equipment by obtaining advanced European, Soviet, and American systems. These factors, combined with their quantitative superiority in weapons inventories and manpower, may lead observers to conclude that the net military balance is improving in the Arabs' favor and even that they are bound eventually to achieve strategic superiority.

But such an assessment may be altered when we consider the mission requirements of the various parties in greater detail, especially when offensive and defensive mission requirements are related to changes in prevailing military technology, as addressed below. The net assessment must also take account of the intervening variable between modernization and the military balance—the share of combat outcomes explained by human competence. To determine that share requires detailed study of future weapons inventories. It may be that the role of individual and collective competence is gaining importance more rapidly than the competence gap is narrowing.

It is important to distinguish two classes of competence questions: those pertaining to individual skills in the operation, repair, and provisioning of equipment sets (microcompetence); and those pertaining to collective capabilities to organize and operate forces effectively to fulfill military objectives (macrocompetence).

At the micro level, there are countervailing trends. For some systems, the introduction of highly sophisticated but simple-to-operate weapons will reduce the influence of human skill in military operations. The closer we come to the mythical automated battlefield, with push-button "fire and forget" weapons, the less individual competence and initiative will count. New systems vary greatly in the expertise demanded of their operators, but some simplify the skills required of the actual user on the front line. For example, the second-generation antitank missiles (TOW, Dragon, Milan) come closer to truly automatic guidance, once properly programed, than the first-generation missiles they replace; and the eventual introduction of third-genration systems will continue this evolution. Such developments reduce the advantage of technical sophistication and "brainpower" in the operation of weapons on the battlefield and act as an equalizer between armies of unequal skill (though even in these cases the supply and maintenance demands may be increasing).

For other systems, the importance of operator competence is growing. The F-15 is said to approach the limit of human mental endurance and capacity, because of the wide variety of platform and weapon control options that must be considered simultaneously. Even when one subsystem is improved for fairly automatic operation, as in the case of reliable all-aspect, fire-and-forget infrared-homing dogfight missiles, the optimal deployment of the platform and missile combination to obtain the greatest net utility from this advantage imposes greater than ever demands on the tactical ingenuity and inventiveness of the pilot, who must simultaneously consider all the other elements of the combat environment. Such developments increase the advantage of technical sophistication and widen the margin of inequality between forces of unequal skill.

Although it is difficult to derive summary conclusions at the micro level, at the macro level of competence the trends appear strongly to enhance the value of human effectiveness as a force multiplier. The effect of the technological revolution is to increase the demands on highly trained personnel and to heighten the advantage of an officer corps that can adapt, improvise, and manage efficiently. One factor is the molecularization of the battlefield. Because effective firepower is becoming increasingly light and compact, in the future mobile and fairly independent small units will often be used to threaten and destroy larger units in the Middle East and other places where the problems of target acquisition are reduced and there is a premium on mobility, concealment, and dispersal. More authority will have to be delegated to lower command levels, and the quality of junior officers and the intermediate ranks from captain to colonel will more heavily influence the effectiveness of the fighting forces. Improvisational tactics and operational flexibility will find their widest scope, and the net effect of the new technologies will enhance rather than reduce the importance of the qualitative human factor.

At the same time, maximum stress will be placed on the ability of the high command, control, and communication system where there is a proliferation of small units and a molecular pattern of deployment. This will multiply the advantage of the forces operating on interior rather than exterior lines, who are more readily able to concentrate against one vulnerable or high value point and then another. This advantage will be further enhanced when combined with "mechanical" force multipliers such as the Hawkeye E-2C downward-looking airborne radars and the integrated tactical ground environment computers.

Another factor at the higher levels of strategy and war planning is the very speed of technological change and innovation. An unprecedented number of systems incorporating new concepts are being introduced into this region simultaneously, and if there are future wars the participants will have to rely heavily on weapons never before operated under combat conditions. The performance of individual systems is bound to differ from simulations and results obtained on the testing ground. It will be necessary to modify organization, deployment, and tactics under the pressure of battle, and there will be substantial rewards to the side that is able to adapt more rapidly and absorb and integrate new equipment and ideas on shorter lead times.

In the coming years, a technological breakthrough or surprise is less likely to take the form of an unforeseen new weapon system per se than an innovative application of the known technology resulting from a superior understanding of its ultimate significance on the battlefield. Rapid adaptation of systems to meet new threats during the war, such as the devising of ECM responses to new radar threats, may be as important as the possession of the systems themselves. In these and other ways, the relationship between human capability and the rapidly changing equipment technologies may enhance the advantage of states favored by greater skills at the higher levels.

But these counterarguments and objections on the relationship between modernization and the military balance are complex and do not yield easily to quantification. If there is a narrowing of the competence gap combined with a narrowing of the qualitative gap in equipment, most observers will be attracted to the view that the military balance itself is improving for the Arabs correspondingly. Therefore, although the "objective" effect of modernization may not necessarily favor the Arabs, the subjective effect is quite likely to be a perception that the Arab military position has improved. It follows that whether or not modernization improves the military balance in favor of the Arabs, it will be perceived to do so, and to that degree military modernization will make the war option more attractive.

OTHER FACTORS IN THE MILITARY BALANCE

It is not possible to derive a net assessment of the regional military balance solely from the modernization factors examined in this report. A full study would have to examine in detail other elements such as: offensive and defensive mission requirements; the military geography of assumed conflict theaters; forces prepositioned in combat areas; forces that could be mobilized or redeployed within relevant time frames; external supplies or support units that might be lifted to the conflict theaters; comparisons of orders of battle, both quantitative and qualitative; and intelligence capabilities. In addition, scenario-specific assumptions must be made as to a number of contingencies, such as: the main military moves; whether tactical and strategic surprises are achieved; levels of mobilization over time; whether preemptive options are exercised; the contributions of expeditionary forces by third and *n*th states; the participation or nonparticipation of superpowers; and the specific locations of military actions. Finally, assessments must be made of the relative effectiveness of opposed systems (some never tested in battle) in given scenarios, such as: the state of the tank-antitank competitions; the fluidity of battle lines; the effectiveness of SAMs and SAM suppression weapons; the freedom of ground attack aircraft to operate effectively in various zones of the combat theater; electronic systems versus ECM versus ECCM; target acquisition and terminal guidance systems vs. stealth technologies, decoys, and other antisystems; and mobility-enhancement and mobility-denial systems.

Most of these issues clearly fall outside the narrow question of modernization of human capital. Yet, modernization levels do affect net assessments, and it would be desirable to conduct follow-on research. The following examples illustrate but do not exhaust the researchable questions.

First, modernization questions specific to particular technologies affect microcompetence in the absorption and effective operation of individual systems. For example, what is the potential of a given state to absorb and utilize numbers of a given aircraft, naval platform, land combat vehicle, weapon, or intelligence aid? How will the skill of operational personnel in this state compare with that of the adversary, and what will be the net effect on the military balance?

Second, does a given state have the organizational capability to structure given levels of combat manpower and equipment effectively into fighting units able to perform specified military tasks? This includes maintenance, repair, and logistic support; the ability to deliver combat units to critical points within restricted time frames; the coordination of command, control, communication, and intelligence under organizational stress; centralization and delegation of authority; and other elements of wartime management of fighting units.

Third, at the strategic level, is the national command authority able to proportion ends to means; to set mission requirements that are attainable by available forces and make optimal use of resources; to adapt war plans to take account of changing circumstances; to devise effective courses of action; and to integrate military and political objectives?

These issues of individual, organizational, and strategic competence have been addressed at a general level in this study, but a weapon-specific and mission-specific analysis is a task for the future.

CONCLUSIONS

With regard to states active in the Arab-Israeli balance, we have identified some significant trends of improvement in microcompetence, the factors affecting the performance of individuals. But the findings also suggest that no significant breakthrough is likely in macrocompetence, the organizational and managerial factors affecting the performance of fighting units. Therefore, it is unlikely that there will be a revolution in the net effectiveness of the Arabs over the next ten years, particularly if, as we have argued, competence itself has a growing influence on military outcomes.

With regard to the other military balances of the region, differences in comparative rates of modernization may be more significant. Iran before the upheaval seemed capable of a decisive improvement by achieving a qualitative transformation to ultimate modernity. If so, the military balance between Iran and the other states of the gulf might have been fundamentally altered.

These conclusions suggest that the Arab states will not be able to close the gap with Israel over the next decade, and that they would have lost ground in relation to Iran had trends there continued, in spite of the great effort being undertaken and the progress being made. The widespread belief that time is on the side of the Arabs, and that the wind of history is behind the Arab sail, is not fully supported by a detailed examination of trends in modernization and projections over the next decade within the confines of this analysis. However, the improvements that are being achieved are likely to affect perceptions of Arab military effectiveness, and to that degree they may affect the strategic choices that are made.

Part five

EAST ASIA

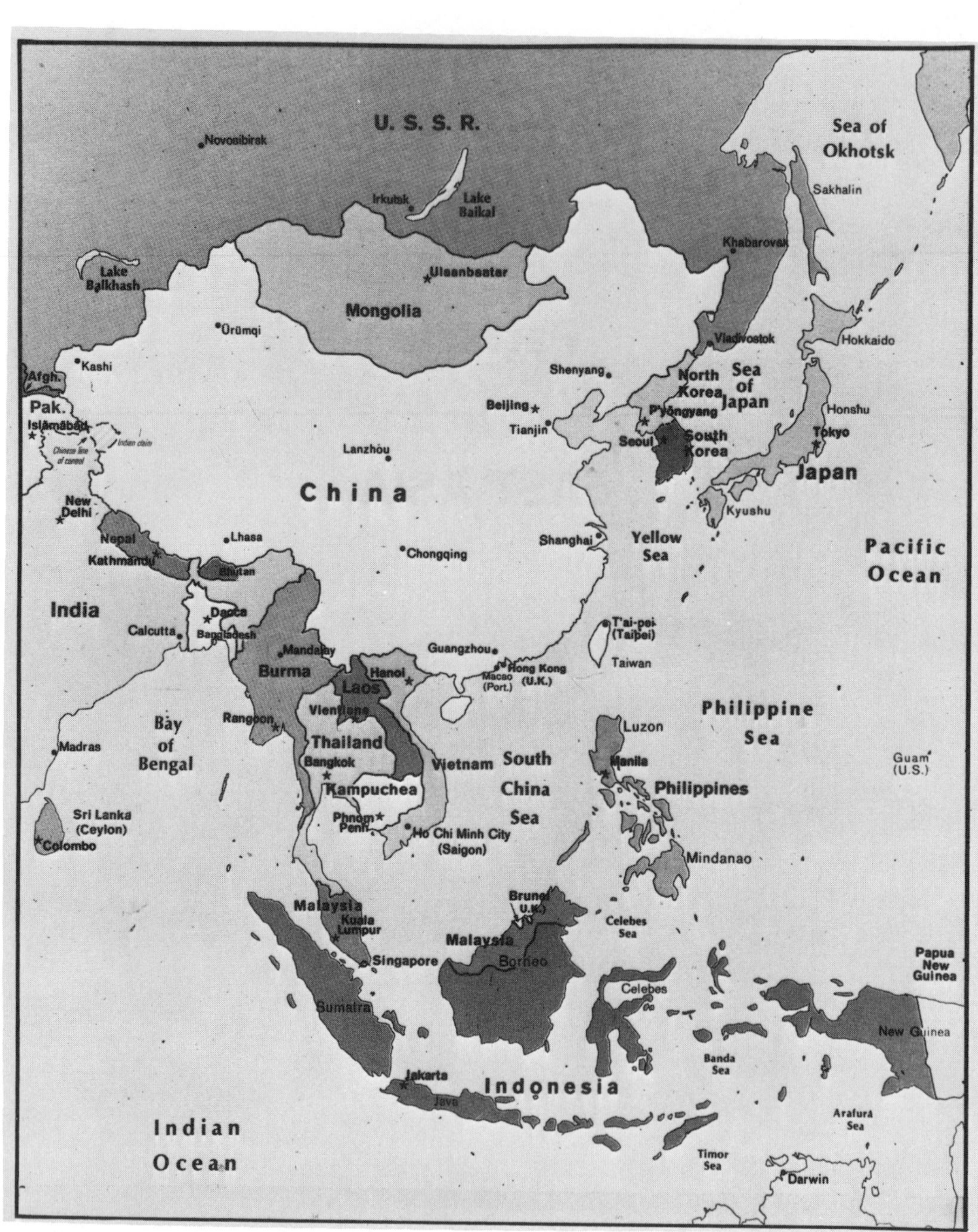
U. S. S. R.
Novosibirsk
Irkutsk
Lake Baikal
Sea of Okhotsk
Sakhalin
Khabarovsk
Lake Balkhash
Ulaanbaatar
Mongolia
Ürümqi
Vladivostok
Hokkaido
Kashi
Afgh.
Shenyang
North Korea
Sea of Japan
Pak.
Islāmābād
Beijing
P'yŏngyang
Honshu
Indian claim
Chinese line of control
Tianjin
Seoul
South Korea
Tokyo
Lanzhou
Japan
China
New Delhi
Kyushu
Nepal
Lhasa
Shanghai
Yellow Sea
Pacific Ocean
Kathmandu
Chongqing
Bhutan
India
Dacca
T'ai-pei (Taipei)
Calcutta
Bangladesh
Mandalay
Guangzhou
Burma
Hanoi
Hong Kong (U.K.)
Taiwan
Macao (Port.)
Laos
Vientiane
Philippine Sea
Bay of Bengal
Rangoon
Luzon
Madras
Thailand
Bangkok
Vietnam
South China Sea
Manila
Guam (U.S.)
Kampuchea
Philippines
Sri Lanka (Ceylon)
Phnom Penh
Colombo
Ho Chi Minh City (Saigon)
Mindanao
Brunei U.K.)
Malaysia
Kuala Lumpur
Celebes Sea
Malaysia
Singapore
Borneo
Papua New Guinea
Celebes
Sumatra
New Guinea
Banda Sea
Jakarta
Java
Indonesia
Arafura Sea
Indian Ocean
Timor Sea
Darwin

THE DEFENSE POLICY OF THE PEOPLE'S REPUBLIC OF CHINA

William R. Heaton, Jr.

International environment

Several factors bear upon Chinese perceptions of the international situation. One of obvious significance is the traditional Chinese sense of cultural superiority. Historically, the Chinese saw China as the "middle kingdom," surrounded by cultures of lesser civilization. Generally speaking, China was quite content to allow the foreign "barbarians" to come to China to partake of Chinese civilization; indeed, the most expansionist dynasties were usually non-Chinese, such as the Mongols or the Manchu. Many elements of this attitude are relevant today.

Much of the analysis in this document is based on the author's experience as a member of the National Defense University Delegation to China in April–May 1979. This delegation, the first U.S. military group to visit China since 1947, held extensive unofficial discussions with Defense Minister Xu Xiangqien and other senior Chinese military leaders, and visited a number of Chinese military facilities. The author is grateful to Paul Godwin, Harvey Nelson, and Jonathan Pollack, who read earlier drafts and made valuable comments and criticisms. The views expressed herein are those of the author and do not necessarily reflect those of the United States government or any governmental agency.

The Chinese are sensitive about their territorial boundaries. China's strategic border areas are, to a great extent, inhabited by minority peoples such as Tibetans, Mongols, Uighurs, Kazakhs, or the tribal peoples of southwest China.[1] Though numbering only about 6 percent of China's total population, the minorities have offered a continuing challenge to the Chinese Communist leadership. Official policy has ranged from almost forcible assimilation to special cultivation, but whatever the ebbs and flows of policy (and there have been several), the Chinese tend to view these peoples as their inferiors.

More complicated is how the Chinese view the West. During President Nixon's first visit to China in 1972 it was popular to conjure up images of the foreign barbarian approaching the throne of the emperor in the forbidden city. While such images make good newspaper copy, they fail to recognize the complexity of the Chinese view. Since the coming of the West to China in force in the 1800s, the Chinese have had a simultaneous admiration-rejection attitude. Perhaps no question has so perplexed various Chinese governments since the 1840s as how to respond to the West. At times the Chinese have tried to adopt Western technology while rejecting Western ideas, as did the self-strengtheners from about 1840 to 1894 or the Qing reformers from 1901 to 1911. At other times the Chinese have considered both, as they did during the alliance with the USSR from 1950 to 1957, or they have rejected both, as they did during the Boxer Rebellion of 1900–1901 or the Cultural Revolution of 1966 to about 1969. Indeed, one prominent scholar of China insists that the current "four modernizations" campaign in China is concerned with the essential question of precisely how China should interact with the West.[2] In this respect, Sun Shangqing, deputy director of the Institute of Economics, Chinese Academy of Sciences, has argued that China could acquire advanced science, technology, and management methods from the developed capitalist countries without the attendant evils and abuses of the capitalist system.[3]

Thus, the question of the type and degree of Chinese interaction with the West has been a contentious political issue. Contributing to this question is the Chinese perception of humiliation during the phase of "semicolonialism" experienced by China after the Opium War, which ended in 1842. For a hundred years the Western powers carved out spheres of influence in China, relegating the Chinese to inferior status in their own country. While the Eastern impact was not without benefit to China, this "century of humiliation" is generally regarded with some bitterness by the Chinese.

Nationalist feelings in China resulted directly from this sense of humiliation and led to political movements of Sun Yat-sen and the Kuomintang, and even the Chinese Communist movement. All of these groups agreed on the need to end China's humiliation, to eliminate the unequal treaties, and to restore China to a position of respect in the international community. It may well be said that the Chinese Communist movement was ultimately successful because it was more effective than other political movements in organizing around (and identifying with) these objectives. When Mao proclaimed the establishment of the People's Republic on October 1, 1949, he exclaimed: "The Chinese people have stood up!"

The desire for equality with the West continues to be an important element of Chinese perceptions. An editorial celebrating the opening of the 5th National People's Congress observed:

> In the present day world, being backward economically and technologically means being easily kicked around. For a whole century following the Opium War, China was kicked around and beaten. Unequal treaties humiliating the nation and forfeiting its sovereignty shackled our beloved country. Why was our country subjected to such humiliation? Why was she trampled underfoot? The corrupt social system was one factor and economic and technological backwardness was another. From Hung Hsiu-shuan to Sun Yat-sen, Chinese progressives waged indomitable struggles to build a prosperous and powerful China. But it was not until our great Chairman Mao Tsetung [Mao Zedong] integrated the universal truth of Marxism-Leninism with the concrete practice of the Chinese revolution, led us in overthrowing the three big mountains—imperialism, feudalism and bureaucratic-capitalism—which lay like a dead weight on the Chinese people, and founded the People's Republic of China that the Chinese people stood up.[4]

This quote demonstrates another key element of Chinese perceptions—that of backwardness. Since the purge of the "Gang of Four," the Chinese have been increasingly forthcoming about their economic poverty and scientific and technical retardation. The editorial cited above, while claiming that there has been some progress in science and technology in China since 1949, acknowledged that the gap between China and the developed countries has grown wider.

The Chinese perceive that China will acquire international respect only as it acquires power. The acquisition of power involves comprehensive modernization, the goal of the current four-modernizations campaign that seeks fulfillment by the year 2000. Yet, modernization is an extremely complicated and precarious goal. In the opinion of many scholars, China has a precarious position between agriculture and population, so a major test will be its ability to feed its population.[5] Beyond this, the Chinese must cope with a variety of economic and political questions.

Another variable that relates to Chinese perceptions has to do with the nature of the political system. While the nature of Chinese decision making is covered in greater detail in a later section, it is important to note here that ideology and authoritarianism are important aspects of Chinese perceptions. Officially, ideology is characterized as "Marxism, Leninism, and the thought of Mao Zedong." According to one prominent scholar of China, Maoist ideology is an attempt to make Marxist and Leninist concepts relevant to the experience of the Chinese revolution.[6] Maoist ideology is like any other extensive body of official dogma—it is often given a change in emphasis by various members of the elite to justify or explain certain courses of action. During Mao's lifetime, particularly when he personally directed political affairs, emphasis was placed on social change. Perhaps the high point of Mao's application of Maoist ideology was the Cultural Revolution, in which Mao and his supporters sought extensive change in political organization and social structure. Since Mao's death and the purge of the Gang of Four, his successors have accelerated the deemphasis of Maoist policies, paradoxically, all in the name of "Maoism."

The two most prominent slogans in China are "Let Practice Be the Sole Criterion of Truth" and "Seek

Truth from Facts." Mao's successors have turned to Mao's essay on practice as the primary source for the new policy of enhanced Party authority and economic and social stratification. With respect to politics, "de-Maoification" has resulted in two contradictory trends. On the one hand, the Chinese Communists believe that increased personal freedom is necessary as part of the drive for modernization. On the other hand, they also believe that the authority of the Party must be strengthened (the attacks on the Party during the Cultural Revolution brought China to the brink of anarchy).

A recent visitor to China who held discussions with an official responsible for Party ideology noted that the official threw up his hands and proclaimed that there was no more ideology in China. Though Maoist orthodoxy has come under fire, the underlying role of ideology should not be so lightly dismissed. All major policy pronouncements are couched in ideological terms, and, though basic tenets of Marxism-Leninism may have been altered to fit the Chinese experience, there can be no question but that current Chinese leadership is committed to a certain style of politics. The closing of "democracy wall" because it resulted in "damage to socialist democracy and the socialist legal system" bears ample witness to this point.[7]

In summary, Chinese perceptions are affected by historical experience, the sense of economic and technological backwardness, ideology, and the authoritarian nature of the political system. The following generalizations may be drawn.

(*a*) Among the Chinese there is a sense of traditional cultural superiority that contibutes to a feeling of humiliation with respect to China's dealings with the West from 1842 to 1949. How China should respond to the West is a fundamental question.

(*b*) The Chinese feel that China can avoid humiliation only if it is able to become a powerful and united country. China must acquire the attributes of national power through modernization.

(*c*) The current Chinese leadership is changing Maoist orthodoxy; nevertheless, ideology and an authoritarian political style will continue to influence Chinese perceptions.

These elements can be understood clearly as we focus upon the Chinese state perception of the international environment—the "three-worlds" hypothesis.

Official Chinese foreign policy pronouncements going back to 1948 have divided the world into three categories. During the period of the Sino-Soviet alliance the world was divided into the socialist camp, the imperialist camp, and the intermediate nonaligned zone. This view of the world was changed with the Sino-Soviet rupture, so by the time of the Cultural Revolution the Chinese were speaking of the United States and the USSR as one world, the intermediate zone consisting of industrialized countries as the second world, and the developing countries, including China, as the third world. Concerning this hypothesis, Mao stated in 1974 that in his view: "The United States and the Soviet Union form the first world. Japan, Europe and Canada, the middle section, belong to the second world. We are the third world. The third world has a huge population. With the exception of Japan, Asia belongs to the third world. The whole of Africa belongs to the third world, and Latin America too."[8]

Since that time, the three-worlds concept has continued to dominate China's security policy pronouncements. In November 1977, a year after Mao's death, the Editorial Department of *Renmin Ribao* [People's daily] published a comprehensive exposition of this thesis entitled "Chairman Mao's Theory of the Differentiation of the Three Worlds in a Major Contribution to Marxism-Leninism." This editorial explained that the three-worlds concept was a scientific Marxist-Leninist assessment of contemporary reality. The First World consists of the two hegemonic superpowers, the United States and the Soviet Union. These two countries, because of their imperialistic nature, are the greatest exploiters of the peoples of the world and will inevitably go to war with each other. The Soviet Union, however, is seen as the most dangerous source of war, since it is bent on an expansionist policy, while the United States is merely trying to retain its world position.[9]

The Second World includes the industrialized countries of Eastern and Western Europe, Canada, Japan, and Australia. In the Chinese view these countries have been dominated by the superpowers in the past, but are beginning to assert their independence and thus constitute a force that can be utilized in resisting the superpowers. Western Europe is especially crucial in this regard since it is there that Soviet hegemonism is directly aimed.[10]

China is seen as part of the Third World, and it is most important for China to work together with Third World countries that constitute the main force for defending against imperialism, colonialism, and hegemonism. Since these countries and peoples are the most exploited, they will be the most resolute in their resistance to imperialism. China must join with, and assist, the Third World in overcoming the splits and divisions engineered by the imperialists, but it can never become a superpower or a hegemonist.

The three-worlds thesis has been consistently restated by the Chinese leadership since that time, albeit with some modification. The main modification, however, is that world war may be averted by the formation of a united front, a point that will be examined in greater detail in the next section.

In his visit to the United States in early 1979, after the normalization of relations with China, Vice-Premier Deng Xiaoping restated the three-worlds view and discussed the formation of a united front, including the United States.[11] Again, in his report to the second session of the Fifth National People's Congress, Hua Guofeng stated: "Adhering to Comrade Mao Zedong's theory of the three worlds, we will strengthen our unity with the proletariat and the progressive forces of the world, with the socialist countries and various Third World countries, and unite with all the forces in the world that can be united in a joint effort to oppose the hegemonist policies of aggression and war."[12]

The three-worlds hypothesis succinctly summarizes Chinese perceptions of China's relative position within the international system. Through this concept China has undergone a subtle, yet fundamental transformation in statecraft. Instead of merely taking the side of the oppressed and opposing the oppressors, Chinese definitions increasingly resemble realpolitik, albeit with a distinctly Chinese quality.[13] The concept also gives rise to the Chinese strategy of forming a united front against hegemonism.

National objectives, national strategy, and military doctrine

According to the three-worlds hypothesis, the greatest threat to China comes from the hegemonism of the superpowers. More particularly, the threat is the Soviet Union, since it is seen as actively pursuing hegemonism. In support of this assertion, official Chinese sources note Soviet activities in Indochina, the Indian Ocean, Africa, the Middle East, and Europe.[14] The Soviet Union is particularly dangerous because it came late to imperialism and is therefore more vicious, rapacious, and predatory than other capitalist states. The USSR is more deceptive than other imperialists because it "flaunts the banner of Leninism" in order to undermine the oppressed peoples of various countries. The Soviet Union is more likely to rely on military force to achieve its objectives because its economic strength lags far behind that of the West.

In order to contain Soviet power and influence, the Chinese openly call for the creation of a "united front against hegemonism."[15] In concluding a peace treaty with Japan, the Chinese insisted upon the inclusion of an antihegemony clause. Similarly, when the United States agreed to an antihegemony clause in the announcement of normalization of relations it was considered by the Chinese to be a major foreign policy victory.[16] Deng Xiaoping also suggested that the United States was part of the united front.[17] It is somewhat ironic that one of the "hegemonic" superpowers could be considered to be part of the united front against hegemonism.

This is not to say that Chinese strategy need always be based on a fundamental antagonism toward the USSR. Many China scholars believe that the desire for modernization in China and the ideological shift will bring about a kind of détente between China and the USSR. It is doubtful that the close alliance of the early 1950s could be reestablished, however, or that tension and hostility could be greatly reduced. The problem of Soviet involvement in Vietnam and Afghanistan, and other Soviet-sponsored attempts to isolate and encircle China, augur against any Sino-Soviet rapprochement. Also, because of long-standing ideological differences, the Soviet Union is likely to pose some degree of continuing threat to China.

There can be no doubt that current Chinese policy demonstrates concern with the Soviet threat. While expressing support for the Third World, China promotes an anti-Soviet line in its dealings with Third World countries, particularly in the United Nations. The Chinese cite the Soviet invasion of Afghanistan, along with activities in Indochina, Africa, and the Middle East as evidence of Soviet plans for worldwide aggression. Meanwhile, China has assiduously cultivated ties with North Korea, Pakistan, Thailand, Japan, and other countries in an effort to ward off Soviet encirclement. A major factor contributing to the development of normalized relations between China and the United States was China's concern with the USSR. Under the concept of the united front against hegemonism, China's vital interests involve preventing the expansion of Soviet power in Asia and across the globe.

Besides containment of the Soviet Union, Chinese strategy also seeks to buy time to achieve modernization. By avoiding all-out war, China can devote more resources to trade and development. Consequently, Chinese policy seeks a balance between containing Soviet influence and avoiding the outbreak of war so as to give China time and resources to devote to the four modernizations. In the past few years some significant gains have been made.[18] Yet, the "defensive counterattack" against Vietnam* may well have increased the demand for devoting more resources to the military sector. China's developmental program has already undergone significant retrenchments; while growth may continue, increased military expenditures could undermine the current policies.

Between the third plenum of the Eleventh Central Committee in December 1979 and the fifth plenum in February 1980, the policy of forming a united front was given added emphasis. Also, the idea that war was inevitable was reversed. In January, Deng Xiaoping, in a major address before 10,000 cadres in the Great Hall of the People, said that one of China's main tasks in the 1980s was to "oppose hegemonism and safeguard world peace in international affairs."

*That is, the military invasion by Chinese forces in 1979, a response to Vietnamese involvement in Cambodia.-Ed.

Similarly, Ji Pengfei, director of the International Liaison Department of the Central Committee and a member of the Politburo, commented on past errors in Chinese foreign policy and called for a course that would promote stability and modernization.[19]

Related to the drive for economic modernization is the drive for social change, another element of national strategy. Maoist ideology emphasized a high degree of egalitarianism. Mao wanted to eliminate distinctions between social classes, mental and manual labor, urban and rural area, and so on. By contrast, Mao's successors are willing to tolerate a much greater degree of social inequality in order to achieve modernization. Thus, China now encourages more pay for better work, more incentives for skilled urban industrial workers, and production on larger private plots of land in rural areas. Nevertheless, while some of the more radical egalitarian policies have been discarded, the regime clearly remains committed to the achievement of socialism. The education system, the media, art, culture, and other communications continue to reflect advocacy of the virtues of hard work, selflessness, and diligence in building a new society. In the past, major political cleavages in China have been over the issue of social mobilization. It is an issue that will continue to be a matter of debate. It should not be forgotten, of course, that it was such issues that resulted in the Cultural Revolution and corresponding increase in military involvement in politics—a legacy still very much relevant to the contemporary scene.

The essence of Chinese strategy lies in the goals of the Chinese revolution: national sovereignty and independence, territorial unification, power, and economic and social change. The concept of the "united front against hegemonism" permits the Chinese leaders some flexibility in shifting among the various priorities. Indeed, much of the political conflict in China may be ascribed to conflict among the priorities, a subject that I will return to later. Under the banner of the "united front against hegemonism" China plans to achieve a position of regional prominence, and eventually global prominence. While China officially proclaims that it will never act like a superpower or seek hegemony, there can be no question that the united front concept is designed to bring China greater influence in the international community.

Within the context of the "united front against hegemonism," Chinese policy planners have articulated two basic concepts of military strategy and doctrine. The first is the concept of people's war, and the second is what Allen Whiting termed the "calculus of deterrence." Generally, the concept of people's war lies behind Chinese efforts to deter an attack; however, the concept has undergone considerable revision over the past few years.[20]

In 1965, when Lin Biao issued his call for "people's war" on the part of the "world countryside" against the "world cities," he reached back into the experience of the Chinese Communists in the War of Resistance against Japan for his model of Chinese military power. Although this concept has continued to play a significant role in defense policy planning, since the purge of Lin and the Gang of Four, Chinese spokesmen have referred to "people's war under modern conditions," which in fact is a revision of some classic Maoist assertions about people's war. For example, on the fifty-first anniversary of the founding of the People's Liberation Army in August 1978, Defense Minister Xu Xiangqian outlined the military strategy of the armed forces. Xu restated China's position that war among the superpowers is inevitable, but he argued that it can be postponed if a united front against hegemonism is successful. Xu went on to state the main principles of Chinese military doctrine:

> China must continue to make the most of its vast territory and large population, the superiority of its social system, the glorious tradition of people's war, and other favorable conditions to win victories through arduous and protracted people's war. . . .
>
> Future conflict will likely find China pitted against an enemy with superior military technology and better arms. However, because enemy military theory is decadent and reactionary and his war will be unjust, he will be no match for the Chinese armed with Chairman Mao's military thinking. . . .
>
> If any enemy dares to invade China the main forces of the country and local corps will annihilate large numbers of enemy troops. The militia will be mobilized to look for any opening to hit the enemy. Everyone will be a soldier, every village a fortress and every place a battlefield. No enemy can stand the attrition. . . .
>
> Chinese forces will defend key points, will prevent enemy forces from moving into Chinese territory unchecked, and will systematically lead them to battlefields of Chinese choice to wipe them out piecemeal: "Protracted war will change the balance of forces between ourselves and the enemy." . . .
>
> China will continue to modernize its armed forces and to improve training and equipment. It will pay attention to the experience of other countries and utilize all resources for improving the capabilities of the armed forces.[21]

According to Xu, people's war is essentially defensive:

> Active defense and luring the enemy troops in deep are the basic principles of our strategy for winning a future war against aggression. "Engaging the enemy outside the gates" has never been a good method of fighting. Ours is a socialist country and our social system determines that our strategic principle must be one of active defence. In coping with invaders, we must strike at the enemy after letting him in, and strategically we strike only after the enemy has struck.[22]

The problem is, of course, that since 1949 there has been no invasion of China. Chinese employment of military power has been in areas on China's periphery, sometimes in disputed territory, but also sometimes on foreign soil. While the Chinese claim that these actions are punishing or defensive, the actual employment of force calls into question a strict interpretation of the "defensive nature" of people's war.

Xu himself recognized the problem in a subsequent article in *Red Flag* entitled "Strive to Achieve Modernization in National Defense: In Celebration of the 30th Anniversary of the Founding of the People's Republic of China."[23] A striking feature of this article is the lack of reference to "people's war" even under "modern conditions." Rather, Xu asserts that: "Our military thinking must ally with the changing conditions. If we treat and command a modern war in the way we commanded a war during the 1930's and 1940's, we are bound to meet with a big rebuff and suffer a serious defeat."[24] Xu goes on to call for the modernization of weaponry, more research for the development of new weapons, more specialization of weapons for use under different conditions, more learning from foreign experience, and more and better training of personnel, particularly officers. On the latter point Xu argues that Mao's military thinking must be "developed" to fit the "new conditions of modern warfare and to solve new problems which may arise in modern warfare."[25]

One specialist on Chinese defense policy has pointed out that the essential elements of Maoist military doctrine are reliance on mass mobilization and principles such as the multifunctionality of the armed forces, political control of the military, the primacy of people over weapons, and the primacy of internal over external roles. Classical people's war strategy is a product of "traditions of the landscape" (terrain and continental location) and "traditions of the mind" (deception). Thus, modernization of China's armed forces will necessarily lead to the demise of the classic people's-war concept.[26]

Another astute observer of Chinese military policy, Jonathan Pollack, cautions that official Chinese statements must be qualified by several factors. First, it is highly unlikely that the USSR will attempt a massive ground invasion of China. Second, the Chinese leadership does not really anticipate a major war with the USSR.[27] This view was borne out by statements of high-ranking military leaders during discussions on our April–May 1979 trip to China. We were told that during the Chinese invasion of Vietnam the Soviet Union staged maneuvers along the Chinese border to try to bluff China, but did not take direct military action. One leader asserted (repeating a statement made to reporters by Deng Xiaoping): "We dared to touch the rear end of the tiger and he didn't turn to fight us. We think the rear end of the tiger can be touched."[28]

If the concept of people's war is increasingly being questioned in China, just what kind of military strategy and doctrine is evolving? As many students of China have pointed out, the country's principal preoccupation has been deterrence. The Chinese obviously believe that articulating a "people's-war" concept helps to deter a would-be aggressor. At the PLA Military Academy I asked the commandant, Xiao Ke, if enemy forces might simply avoid a massive invasion and use air power to halt the four modernizations or inflict a limited but humiliating defeat on China so as to gain political concessions. The response was that, in the Soviet view, the problem of China was too great to solve by a limited attack. Meanwhile, the best deterrent against a massive invasion was to prepare for one.

Indeed, the same attitude is evident in the continuing commitment to "dig tunnels deep and store grain everywhere." Work is continuing on the extensive system of underground tunnels in Beijing and other cities, and the Chinese continue to pay attention to civil defense, militia training, and other forms of preparation against attack. Our examination of the tunnels made us question their efficacy during an actual attack: nevertheless, there can be no doubt that they are psychologically important, both for their deterrent value in confronting a potential enemy and to the Chinese people. The idea that victory can be won in spite of technological inferiority is strongly held by most Chinese and lends credibility to China's defense posture.

Allen Whiting, one of the most prominent students of Chinese military doctrine, has examined the use of force by the Chinese in a variety of cases to demonstrate the Chinese approach. Whiting summarizes his findings on the Chinese calculus as follows:

1. The worse our [Chinese] domestic situation, the more likely our external situation will worsen.
   a. A superior power in proximity will seek to take advantage of our domestic vulnerability.
   b. Two or more powers will combine against us if they can temporarily overcome their own conflicts of interest.
   c. We must prepare for the worst and try for the best.
2. The best deterrence is belligerence.
   a. To be credible, move military force; words do not suffice.
   b. To be diplomatic, leave the enemy "face" and a way out.
   c. To be prudent, leave yourself an "option."
   d. If at first you don't succeed, try again, but more so.
3. Correct timing is essential.
   a. Warning must be given early when a threat is perceived but not yet imminent.
   b. The rhythm of signals must permit the enemy to respond and us to confirm the situation.
   c. We must control our moves and not respond according to the enemy's choice.[29]

Similarly, another analyst, applying the concept of "coercive diplomacy" developed by Alexander George and his colleagues, has examined the use of military force by the Chinese. Five distinct phases of Chinese actions were found: (1) probing, (2) warning, (3) demonstration, (4) attack, and (5) détente.[30] Furthermore, the analyst concluded that the Chinese emphasize centralization of the decision-making process in national security decisions. Local commanders are prohibited from carrying out actions without central approval and the political commissar system is designed to secure faithful execution of central decisions. Also, warning signals are designed to demonstrate intentions while preserving the possibility of tactical surprise. But, as Whiting has also demonstrated, there were "flaws" in the warning systems in the Korean and Indian conflicts because the warnings lacked credibility or did not provide sufficient lead time for opponents to reconsider their policy courses.[31] Concerning demonstrations, the analysis makes four points: (1) Beijing carries out extensive probes to determine the capability and intention of an opponent before escalating conflict; (2) Chinese demonstrative actions are designed to exploit weak links in the enemy defense posture resulting in Chinese superiority at the site of clashes; (3) the targets of Chinese actions are often the proxies or client states of its main adversary; and (4) Chinese demonstrative actions are usually initiated and terminated very quickly.[32] Also, the Chinese may engage in graduated or intermittent escalation so as to catch the opponent off guard. A subsequent study of China's "defensive counterattack" against Vietnam in 1979 revealed that while there were certain variations in phases and techniques, Chinese behavior in the Vietnam case was similar to that in other conflicts.[33]

Another aspect of military doctrine has to do with nuclear weapons. Chinese statements have repeatedly played down the role of nuclear weapons in war, but their political significance has been recognized. During the Cultural Revolution it was said that the "atom bomb of Mao's thought" was more powerful than the nuclear weapons of the reactionaries and the revisionists. Some Chinese leaders also made statements about China's ability to survive a nuclear attack more successfully than other countries. Nevertheless, as Pollack points out, "No Chinese military program was accorded a higher priority during the 1960's than the acquisition of an independent nuclear deterrent."[34]

The Chinese nuclear program thus appears to be one of "minimum" (or "finite") deterrence. According to Pollack:

> After an initial flurry of deployments—beginning with limited numbers of TU-16 bombers and MRBMs in 1970 and progressing to IRBMs in early 1972—the aggregate levels of Chinese delivery vehicles have increased very little since 1973. According to the most recently available data, China's strategic systems consist of approximately 30-40 IRBMs, 30-40 MRBMs, and 80 intermediate-range bombers. Other aircraft—an even older IL-28 medium-range bomber and the F-9 fighter-bomber—may to a limited extent supplement these forces. Still undeployed are either a sea-launched ballistic missile, or a limited-range, multistage ICBM, purportedly test-fired as early as 1970. (Very small numbers of the latter system, however, may now be operational.) The modesty of this effort and the virtual absence of any quantitative changes in deployment patterns in recent years are inescapable facts.[35]

The Chinese thus have devoted considerable resources to the nuclear deterrent, including the development of an SLBM, even though they publicly demean the role of these weapons in combat. According to one official, China developed nuclear weapons to offset the superpowers' monopoly. In his view, China did not need many nuclear weapons and did not plan to build many; rather, China's limited resources would be concentrated on the development of air defense and antitank defense. Consequently, it appears that the role of nuclear weapons is conceived of in political terms as much as in military terms.[36] The strong, yet limited, commitment to nuclear weapons development suggests that the minimum deterrence posture will continue to be an important element of Chinese national security policy.

A striking feature of the Chinese deterrent concept is that it has remained quite constant, while other aspects of strategy have radically changed. In the global context, China has shifted from an alliance with the Soviet Union and confrontation with the United States to a policy of cooperation with the United States and Japan and confrontation with the USSR.[37] The concept of people's war is also undergoing considerable redefinition, if not outright rejection. Yet the Chinese approach to deterrence has remained fairly consistent. Much of the reason for this has to do with Chinese capabilities—the Chinese have made a virtue of necessity—but it also has to do with the nature of the debate over strategy.

Paul Godwin has observed that deterrence has been China's overarching security policy. How deterrence can best be achieved has been the subject of vigorous debate. The evolution of the people's-war concept is evidence of the ongoing analysis of threats and capabilities in China. Godwin has referred to the "crisis of modernization" in China related to weapons systems, strategy, and doctrine. Many other observers agree that the modernization of the armed forces will contribute to the demise of the people's-war concept.[38] More will be said about the modernization debate later on. The point to be made here is that while the Chinese follow a policy of deterrence, they are altering their approach to how deterrence should be achieved. This is reflected in Chinese security policy debates, which are now leading to a decline in the "people's-war" concept and a more vigorous effort toward modernization.

The defense decision-making process

The role of bureaucratic politics in Chinese decisions has been described in many ways. The Chinese themselves speak of an ongoing dialectic between a correct, revolutionary line and an incorrect, bourgeois line. Lin Biao and the Gang of Four are said to have advocated and partially implemented a counterrevolutionary program during the Cultural Revolution. This program has now been thoroughly repudiated and discredited and the country now "follows the wise and correct policy of Chairman Hua and the Central Committee." Whoever is in power gets to define the correct line and to label opponents as counterrevolutionaries. When power changes, the line also changes. The history of the CCP is a constant struggle between right and wrong.

Some Western analysts have borrowed from the "two-line" dichotomy of the Chinese in proposing a two-group analysis. The "radicals" are highly motivated by ideological purity, value social equality over development, and prefer revolutionary fervor to political stability. The "moderates" or "pragmatics," on the other hand, feel that "it doesn't matter whether or not the cat is black or white—as long as it catches mice it is a good cat," development must precede equality, and stability is essential to power and development.[39] Still other analysts see a four-way split based on disagreement over how China should respond to the West, or a three-way split based on geography and career background.[40] All of these approaches have something to offer, but none is entirely satisfactory. Rather, the concept of shifting coalitions or informal groups seems more appropriate.

INFORMAL COALITIONS

An examination of interest group politics in China indicates that informal groups are based on four factors: ideological view, personality, career background, and the nature of the particular issue involved.

A great deal has been written about differing ideological perspectives. Within the broad rubric of Maoism, many different positions are evident. People such as Zhang Qunqiao and Yao Wenyuan, members of the Gang of Four, believed that material incentives for work were dangerous inasmuch as they encouraged a capitalist consciousness. Zhou Enlai and Deng Xiaoping, on the other hand, believed that wage incentives were in accordance with the socialist principle of "from each according to his work," particularly since the worker was producing in a socialist economy. Many other examples, far too numerous to repeat here, also testify to ideological diversity among the Chinese leaders. All consider themselves to be disciples of Mao, yet each understands the problem somewhat differently.

A factor usually overplayed by Chinese analysts on Taiwan and underplayed by Western analysts is that of personality. Informal groups in China are in part a reflection of who likes whom, who is settling scores, taking revenge, or venting one's spleen, or, conversely, who is helping a protégé or friend. For example, much of Jiang Qing's (Mao's widow and one of the Gang of Four) venom during the Cultural Revolution has been attributed to her resentment of Zhou Yang, the purged Minister of Culture. When Jiang herself was purged, the cartoons and public attacks betrayed a good deal of personal animosity on the part of her detractors. Perhaps a major reason for the rise of Hua Guofeng to the Party chairmanship was his ability not to offend anyone in particular.

A third factor concerns career patterns. This factor has been especially important and much analysis has been done on geographic background, career progression, the protégé system, and other related factors. William Whitson's analysis of the field army affiliation and generational ties of the high command are a clear example.[41] A more recent analysis of the Chinese Communist Politburo looks at whether career experience has been in the central military, regional military, state bureaucracy, or regional bureaucracy.[42] Also, there are ongoing efforts to identify members of the central committee, regional Party secretaries, high-ranking members of the state bureaucracy, and protégés, or supporters, of some leading figure. It is not uncommon to see analysis along the lines of Deng's power base being strengthened and Hua's being reduced (or vice versa), based on the appointment to (or dismissal from) a key position of a suspected supporter.

Issue orientation is the final factor. Various domestic and political issues arise and different positions are taken—often positions resulting from the factors previously mentioned. There have been sharp divisions over military policy, resource allocation, the pace of modernization, and other issues that have a significant bearing on defense policy. Yet, not everyone has a stake in all issues: a leader could conceivably be deeply involved in one issue but relatively unconcerned with another. At the same time, a decision maker not ordinarily concerned with an aspect of policy could have decisive impact on its outcome. For example, the agriculture minister may not be directly concerned with national defense policy, but his competition with the military for resource allocation will certainly affect the defense budget.

Since the purge of the Gang of Four there have been a number of shifts in the composition of the Chinese leadership. One of the most important was the second rehabilitation of Deng Xiaoping following the Eleventh Party Congress in August 1977. Some analysts believe that Deng's position was solidified by official appointments during the Fifth National People's Congress in early 1978, though Hua

Guofeng did not relinquish the premiership to Deng as many anticipated. During the third plenum of the Eleventh Central Committee, which met in December 1978, several persons who had been promoted during the Cultural Revolution were criticized and demoted, though they retained Politburo membership. Hong Kong newspapers discussed the existence of a "whatever" group and a "practice" group. The "whatever" group centered its position on the assertion that "whatever Chairman Mao said, we should try to do, and what he did not say, we should not do." The "practice" group argued from the slogans "Let Practice Be the Sole Criterion of Truth" and "Seek Truth from Facts." Those who were demoted were said to be of the former group; the winners were said to be of the latter group. Reportedly, those promoted to Politburo membership and other key positions during this period were Deng's protégés.[43] Indeed, the slogans pertaining to "practice" were prominently featured during 1979 and into 1980.

An excellent analysis of Chinese media since the third plenum posits the existence of three groupings. One, headed by Deng, is actively trying to rid the Party of another, the leftists, who remain in the Party apparatus. The third group, headed by Hua and Ye Jianying, has balanced between the other two in an effort to create a climate of stability in which China can pursue modernization. This analysis observes that since Deng has not been successful in ridding the Party of the residual leftist presence, political conflict is likely to persist in the future.[44]

During the fifth plenum, four members of the Politburo were purged, including Chen Xilian, former commander of the Beijing Military Region, and Wang Dongxing, Mao's former bodyguard. There were also significant changes in the composition of the high command and China's military regions. Then, during the September 1980 session of the National People's Congress, Hua and Deng resigned their State Council posts while retaining their Party positions. Zhao Ziyang, a Deng protégé and an economic reformer, replaced Hua as premier. These moves further entrenched Deng and his supporters and enhanced Deng's program of modernization and collective leadership.

The important point here, however, is that security policy is entwined with the fluid political situation in which leaders have persistently maneuvered to enhance their power and further their policy goals. While stability and unity are the main goals of present policy, the political struggle that continues could be disruptive of the achievement of consensus. Security policy decisions are likely to continue to reflect the nuances of debate and coalition building among the Chinese leadership. With this perspective in mind, it is now useful to consider the organization of decision making and policy implementation pertaining to defense policy decisions. Then we may go on to examine some of the key debates, including the contemporary debate over modernization.

ORGANIZATION OF DECISION MAKING

Like other countries organized along lines suggested by Marxist-Leninist ideology, China distinguishes between the Party and the state. The Party has the responsibility for defining the future and, acting as the vanguard of the proletariat, guiding society toward the realization of socialism. The organs of the state are to exercise the dictatorship of the proletariat, to implement the programs of the Party. The Party controls the state organs through a system of "parallel hierarchies" that assures proper implementation of Party decisions. This rule also applies to defense matters. Mao stated that "political power grows out of a barrel of a gun. The Party must control the gun; the gun can never be allowed to control the Party."

Mao's dictum notwithstanding, the history of Chinese communism has shown some tension between the gun and the Party. During the Cultural Revolution, for example, Party authority was frequently challenged, even within the military, and there was considerable disruption. The military provided administration in many areas of China; for example, at the end of the Cultural Revolution, fully twenty-one of twenty-nine provincial Party first secretaries were professional military officers. Also, during the purge of the Gang of Four their opponents used elite units of the PLA to carry out the purge.

There has not been a strict dichotomy between military and civilian roles among China's leadership because of the revolutionary heritage. China's protracted revolutionary war required that leaders develop skills in military affairs and civilian administration—a melding of the warrior and the bureaucrat. Long March veterans are gradually passing from the scene, but are still very influential in the highest levels of decision making. China today enjoys a much higher military representation in the Politburo and the Central Committee than the USSR and most other Communist states.

The highest authority for decision making is the Politburo and its standing committee. About a third of the members of this group are career military officers, and more have professional military experience, for example, as political commissars. Below the Politburo is the Central Committee, which has several commissions that relate to defense policy decisions, the most significant of which is the Central Military Commission. Party Organs are responsible for guiding the actions of state organs such as the Defense Ministry, the Foreign Ministry, and other ministries and agencies that have a bearing on national security. It is the nature of Communist societies that much of what the government does is deemed to have a bearing on national security. Accordingly, there tends to be a good deal of secrecy surrounding the decision-making process. In any event, the Party plays the leading role.

There are several ways in which Party organs control other policy bodies. One method the Party has used is that of insuring that key individuals hold multiple positions. Until the September 1980 National People's Congress session, Hua Guofeng, the Party chairman and the commander in chief of the armed forces, was also premier of the State Council. Deng Xiaoping, CCP vice-chairman, was also a vice-premier of the State Council and chief of staff of the PLA. While some leaders still hold multiple positions, such as Huang Hua, foreign minister and a vice-premier, and Xu Xiangqian, defense minister and a Politburo member, China is moving toward a sharper differentiation between Party and government, as evidenced by the 1980 changes in State Council membership.

Along with the Party apparatus concerned with military affairs is the state bureaucracy. The Ministry of National Defense is responsible for managing the budget after figures have been decided upon by top Party leaders. The Defense Ministry also handles conscription and demobilization and coordinates defense production with the National Defense Industries Office of the State Council.[45] The NDIO coordinates military production. There is also the National Defense Science and Technology Commission (NDSTC), which is in charge of military research and development and reports directly to the Central Military Commission.[46]

Often the composition of various Party and state organs demonstrates the existence of bureaucratic politics. For example, Nelsen observes that the composition of the very powerful Central Military Commission (CMC) has been highly political and fluid, with several reorganizations over the past several years.[47] Within the CMC there is a highly secret Control Group that acts as a check on CMC decisions. By observing which people receive which positions during Party or government shuffles, analysts can attempt to discern which of the informal groups is enjoying an advantage, even if only temporarily.

In early 1980 some major changes in the composition of the high command were announced in conjunction with the fifth plenum of the Eleventh Central Committee. Eight of China's eleven military region commanders were changed or reshuffled. Yang Dezhi replaced Deng as chief of staff of the PLA, and four new members were added to the Standing Committee of the Military Commission. A Hong Kong newspaper reported that Yang Dezhi, Yang Yong, Han Xianchu, and Wang Ping had joined Hua Guofeng (chairman), Ye Jianying, Deng Xiaoping, Liu Bocheng, Xu Xiangqian, Nei Rongzen (vice-chairman) Su Yu, and Geng Biao (secretary general) as members of the Standing Committee. These changes added younger people to the upper echelons of the high command and, according to the report, helped to pave the way for a stable leadership transition.[48]

Beyond the intricate system of formal organization is the informal network common to all bureaucratic organizations. The various Red Guard documents forthcoming during the Cultural Revolution shed considerable light on the complex pattern of personal relationships and bureaucratic infighting actually going on in China. The informal network is the spice of political life in China; however, a thorough examination of it here would be beyond the scope of this chapter.

SECURITY POLICY DECISIONS

Policy debates in China may be considered on two levels. The first, or general, level has to do with the debate concerning broad strategic questions. On the second level are debates over resource allocation, force posture, and other issues related to the broad questions. Space limitations preclude a full discussion of these issues in this chapter; however, those who want further information may consult the sources cited for much greater detail. Another cautionary note concerns the range of domestic issues that affects defense policy questions. Many of the hard-fought issues in Chinese political life concern domestic, social, and economic questions, as well as security questions. For example, much of the reason for the purge of Defense Minister Peng Dehuai, in 1959, had to do with his opposition to the Great Leap Forward and the organization of people's communes. Yet his purge also resulted in the appointment of Lin Biao and a reversal of the trend toward professionalization of the armed forces. A defense policy decision may, therefore, have its roots in issues only peripherally related to defense policy.[49]

Since the founding of the People's Republic, the central strategic issue has been that of China's relations with the superpowers. Initially, China decided to "lean to one side" and formed an alliance with the Soviet Union. By the late 1950s the alliance ran into trouble for various reasons and by the beginning of the Cultural Revolution of the Soviet Union was deemed a principal adversary. China's relations with the United States were a matter of considerable debate among the leadership throughout the period. Illustrative of the seriousness of the debate was the issue of how China should respond to the U.S. presence in Vietnam. According to a study by Harding and Gurtov, the debate centered on whether China should reorder military priorities and prepare for a U.S. attack or continue on a course stressing the ideological role of the armed forces. Lo Ruiqing, the PLA chief of staff and a principal in the dispute between powerful contending factions, was purged.[50]

The strategic debate extending from the late 1960s into the mid-1970s centered on whether the two superpowers were colluding or contending. Thomas Gottlieb shows that three groups—which he identifies as moderates, the military, and radicals—took differing positions on the international situation. According to Gottlieb, the moderates felt that the USSR was the principal threat and wanted to improve relations with the United States and to drive a wedge between the United States and the Soviet Union. The military wanted to avoid a confrontation with the USSR while gradually building up China's military capabilities. The radicals sought militant confrontation with both superpowers. Chinese policy during the Cultural Revolution indicated several shifts, depending upon which group was in the ascendancy. According to Gottlieb, the hand of the moderates was strengthened after the March 1969 border clash with the USSR along the Ussuri River.[51]

Kenneth Lieberthal carried Gottlieb's analysis into the 1970s and stated that the three groups (now identified as radicals, "hard" moderates, and "soft" moderates) continued the debate over the superpower relationship and how China should respond to it. In his analysis the radicals wanted to use political struggle to oppose the revisionism and subversion of the Soviet Union. The "soft" moderates advocated delaying tactics against the USSR by sending occasional peace feelers while building China's military. The "hard" moderates, by contrast, felt that the USSR would respect strength, not weakness, so China should put up a bold front. The radical position was undercut by the purge of the Gang of Four, but the "soft" and "hard" positions have alternated since 1976.[52]

In a somewhat different approach, Peter Sargent and Jack Harris undertook a number of studies focusing on China's assessment of the superpower relationship and the Chinese position on SALT. Their research examined the essence of the "collusionist" and "contentionist" positions and attempted to identify which Chinese leaders were taking which sides in the debate. Contrary to the findings of Lieberthal, they concluded that U.S. policies could have a decisive impact on how China responded to the USSR. Sargent and Harris paid particular attention to U.S. targeting doctrines and positions in the SALT and MBFR negotiations; whether or not the United States has a flagging will has been repeatedly debated by the Chinese.[53]

Within the context of the broad national security questions outlined above, there have been debates over the professionalization and modernization of the armed forces. From 1952 to 1958 there was a major effort to modernize and professionalize the PLA, based on the Soviet model.[54] After the purge of Peng Dehuai and the rise of Lin Biao, the trend shifted. There was a concerted effort to base the legitimacy of the PLA on its political role and particularly on its adherence to Maoist ideology. PLA ranks were abolished in 1965 and the PLA was made a model for Chinese society during the Socialist Education Campaign just prior to the Cultural Revolution.

Beginning in 1964 and continuing during the Cultural Revolution, a great deal of emphasis was placed on refitting air and naval weaponry, and the PLA air force and navy probably received an increased share of the budget. Also, more resources went into the development of China's nuclear deterrent. Resources were concentrated on strategic nuclear forces and air power, while political emphasis was placed on the PLA's role in society; great attention was given to the development of the militia. Apparently, this resulted in the neglect of conventional military forces, a charge now often leveled at Lin Biao and the Gang of Four. During the later phases of the Cultural Revolution and culminating in the purge of Lin was the debate over "steel versus electronics" between those who favored strategic nuclear weapons and those who wanted more money spent for tanks and other equipment for the modernization of the ground forces.

After the purge of Lin there was a slowdown on the development of nuclear weapons deployment, and perhaps also a decrease in the defense budget. There may have been some mistrust of the military after Lin's alleged coup attempt, but there was also some question about the strategy China had pursued. The attempts to refit or "backengineer" Soviet aircraft had met with dubious success; China continued to lag further and further behind in the development of modern weaponry. The political role of the armed forces was also debated.

After the purge of the Gang of Four, a number of significant changes were evident. The withdrawal of the military from civil administration, a process that had been occurring since the purge of Lin, was accelerated. More emphasis was placed on the fighting skills of the PLA as opposed to ideological reliability. The Gang of Four was said to have tried to mobilize segments of the militia to support a coup attempt, and it appeared that the role of the militia was being downgraded. In 1978 a conference dealing with the role of the political work in the armed forces reorganized the General Political Department and strengthened the hand of military commanders. In 1979 it was announced that there would be an increase in the defense budget and China showed increased attention to the development and deployment of strategic weapons.

Chinese leaders have repeatedly asserted that the modernization of national defense, one of the "four modernizations" would be based on the modernization of the other sectors, namely, agriculture, industry, and science and technology. Nevertheless, in recent years there have been distinct efforts to improve

China's defense capabilities, as the increase in budget attests. Within this context, there will continue to be debates over strategy, budget, the political role of the armed forces, and a variety of other questions that have arisen in the past.

What is essential to point out here is that the national security decision process in China reflects that importance of bureaucratic politics. The leadership of China has been a series of coalitions that contend for power while trying to build consensus over issues. National security decisions help to shape the coalitions and in turn are shaped by them. Within the organizations established to make and implement these decisions there have been frequent personnel changes. These personnel changes have been associated with changes in policy. Given the present political situation in China, we may expect that there will continue to be changes in China's approach to national security questions. These changes will probably arise from the issue areas sketched out in the following section.

Recurring issues: defense policy outputs

The previous sections have explained some of the trends in China's national security policy. Many of the problems, issues, and debates have been long standing and have continued into the present; only the most crucial may be examined here. These include the issue of territorial unification, civil-military relations and weapons acquisition as part of the modernization debate, force posture, China's position on arms control, and questions over the use of force.

TERRITORIAL SECURITY

It was observed at the beginning that territorial integrity is an important symbol of the Chinese revolution. As important to the Chinese as territory is the question of the unequal treaties by which territories were taken from China. The Chinese government has repudiated the unequal treaties and refuses to be dictated to on the basis of them. Notably, Vietnam, India, and the Soviet Union all possess territories taken from China by unequal treaties (in the case of Vietnam by France, India by Britain, and the Soviet Union by the czars). China claims that it does not want the territories back, only the completion of new agreements based on negotiations of equal sovereignty. All three countries have been suspicious of Chinese intentions and there have been border wars with all three.

China has given up territory in negotiations with other bordering states, or has held territorial questions in abeyance for other political reasons. For example, China deferred the dispute over the Senkaku Islands with Japan because of the need for better relations with Japan, but, should the situation change, the issue could resurface. China previously signed a border agreement with Mongolia, but there have been some troubles along the border because of Mongolia's support for the Soviet Union and because of the presence of Soviet troops in Mongolia.

Perhaps the outstanding issue is Taiwan.[55] Taiwan remains a symbol of China's unresolved civil war. As part of the normalization agreement between the United States and China, the United States gave Taiwan one year's notice of cancellation of the Mutual Defense Treaty and also expressed the hope that the Taiwan question would be resolved peacefully by the two parties. The United States also indicated that it would maintain economic and commerical relations with the people on Taiwan and would supply them with defensive arms.

The Chinese position on "liberating" Taiwan also softened. While maintaining that Taiwan was an integral part of China and that resolution of the Taiwan question could brook no outside interference, China appeared to be willing to allow the status quo to continue indefinitely. Vice-Premier Deng assured U.S. congressional representatives that Taiwan could continue with its own economy, its own government, and its own military and police forces.[56]

The Shanghai Communique and the documents of normalization in recognizing that Taiwan is a part of China may have eliminated Taiwan as a symbol of past humiliation, thereby reducing the prospect for a military solution. This could conceivably change if more radical leaders were to come to power in Beijing, if Taiwan were to try to declare independence, or if the U.S. government were to change its policy of proceeding with quiet (but significant) ties to Taiwan. The demand by some circles in the United States that the United States take a highly vocal and visible position in defense of Taiwan could conceivably remind the Chinese of past humiliation and create pressure to take military action.

For the time being it appears that the present leadership wants to try to avoid military action against Taiwan, action that would likely be costly at best and unsuccessful or disastrous at worst. Chinese leaders have repeatedly made overtures to Taiwan, all of which have been formally rejected. Nevertheless, there have been increased trade links between the two countries through Hong Kong and there are some hopes of greater contact in the future.

Taiwan does not pose a great military threat to China, but it is a vital issue for Chinese national security. It could become an even greater issue should the government on Taiwan opt to acquire nuclear weapons, an option that has been publicly rejected by Taiwan's leaders but that is not outside the realm of possibility. Another complication could arise should Taiwan decide to try to form a closer relationship with the Soviet Union. In any event, the most pressing issue is whether or not Taiwan will continue to be "part of China" or will become something else. An independent Taiwan has been rejected by both sides, but there are strong internal pressures on Taiwan to move in that direction. Accordingly, the issue will remain a security problem for Beijing.

Indeed, the question of territorial security has been a major factor in China's national security policy since the founding of the People's Republic. China still has many outstanding unresolved territorial problems. Some, such as those with the USSR and Vietnam, are of immediate significance. Others, such as those with Japan, the Philippines, and other countries, are now dormant but could flare up under various conditions. Finally, as discussed above, Taiwan will also continue to be a problem.

THE POLITICS OF MODERNIZATION AND THE MODERNIZATION OF POLITICS: WEAPONS ACQUISITION AND CIVIL-MILITARY RELATIONS

As has been noted previously, the principal slogan for China's developmental program is the "four modernizations," of which national defense is one. Concerning defense modernization, the defense minister stated:

> On the basis of accelerating our economic construction, we must strive to modernize our national defense at high speed and pay attention to learning from the advanced experience of other countries; at the same time we must make efforts to improve the arms and equipment of our army, navy, air force and militia so that there will be new-type conventional equipment and sufficient ammunition as well as better atom bombs, guided missiles, and other sophisticated weapons.[57]

Xu's statement indicates that the modernization of defense will be based on the development of the other sectors and will probably receive a lower priority in resource allocations. Nevertheless, China already devotes a considerable portion of industrial production to military purposes. Also, the defense budget announced in 1979 was a 20 percent increase over 1978.[58] Consequently, there is no doubt that considerable effort will be made to modernize the armed forces.

Modernization involves both weaponry and such political matters as strategy and doctrine, civil-military relations, and political indoctrination of armed forces personnel. Concerning weaponry, China has gone through several phases. During the period of the Sino-Soviet alliance, the PLA acquired considerable weaponry from the Soviet Union. After the Sino-Soviet dispute and the withdrawal of Soviet advisers, the Chinese began their own engineering and research and development efforts. The Chinese not only were successful in producing small weapons, but they also manufactured heavy weapons such as tanks and aircraft.[59] It should also be noted that China first tested a nuclear device in 1964 and has been developing and deploying nuclear weapons and strategic delivery vehicles sporadically since the late 1960s and early 1970s.

During this "self-reliant" phase, Chinese technology has increasingly lagged behind that of the USSR and the West. Consequently, in recent years they have expressed a desire to obtain arms and technology from other countries. In 1975 China concluded an agreement with Rolls Royce to produce the Spey 202 jet engine in a factory in Sian. The engine will be in full production sometime in the early 1980s. The Chinese have also shown interest in purchasing the British V/STOL "Harrier," and negotiations have proceeded intermittently for several years. Another item of interest is the Franco-German HOT antitank missile. Chinese military delegations have visited many countries on "shopping expeditions," but there have been few purchases. We were told that foreign technology was very expensive and that China wanted to continue to maintain self-reliance in arms acquisitions. Most authorities agree with the finding of Paul Godwin that the Chinese will resist "quick fix" military acquisitions, but will selectively adapt Western technology.[60]

Related to the question of weapons acquisition is that of military strategy and doctrine. As was noted earlier, the concept of "people's war under modern conditions" involves a transition from doctrinal emphasis on protracted war and minimum deterrence to a greater emphasis on conventional defense. Several analysts argue that the acquisition of technology will force changes in military doctrine. This could be the most traumatic aspect of modernization and will produce considerable tension within China's leadership.[61] Others question whether China's leaders can achieve consensus over the doctrinal issues brought on by new technologies.[62]

With respect to civil-military relations, one of the fundamental problems has been the question of the PLA role in society. Mao and his supporters believed that there should be a close relationship between the army and the masses, that correct political indoctrination was the most important part of military training, and that the military should participate actively in politics and administration. During the Cultural Revolution, the legitimacy of the armed forces was based to a large extent on ideological orthodoxy. The PLA abolished ranks including insignia and titles, urged soldiers to criticize officers, and ordered troop units to spend more time working on farms and engaging in propaganda and political study and less time in combat training. The PLA was called upon to replace the organs of the Party and the state in many areas of China during this period.

There has been significant change in this concept.

Without abandoning the principle that motivation of personnel is a vital factor, a principle with which every military organization in the world would agree, the Chinese have shifted to the position that correct ideological standpoints are demonstrated by improved military professionalism. The political reliability of the PLA is shown not by its ability to mouth Maoist slogans, but by its ability to provide national defense.

The General Political Department has revamped political education so that it now takes less time and emphasizes combat readiness. For example, a political directive from the air force Party Committee in early 1979 said that the thrust of political indoctrination in military work should be to try to get rid of the attitude of "waiting for new guidelines and new equipment," but should seek to achieve modernization. The directive stated:

> We must use the equipment we have now, be prepared for any future war, and defeat an enemy having superior equipment with our poor equipment. We must also insure that the modernization of the armed forces is not only a question of equipment, but a matter of preparing well to master the use of more modernized weapons and equipment.
>
> Promotion of work in all fields this year must be centered around education and training and bold changes must be made for all training manuals, methods and systems that are unscientific and incompatible with modern warfare. We must reform political education and oppose formalist methods of education that deviate from reality so as to let political work play a truly effective role in modernization.[63]

Similarly, speaking before the graduating class of the PLA Political Academy, the director of the General Political Department, Wei Guoqing, stated that modernization could be achieved only through a correct political view.[64] And Xiao Hua stated that a primary role of political indoctrination was to help officers and soldiers train for combat.[65] The shifting of political indoctrination to support modernization and professionalism in the armed forces will create more incentives for the mastery of technology by soldiers and a more favorable climate for weapons modernization. Undoubtedly, it will also bring some problems. Officers recruited and promoted on the political ethic of the Cultural Revolution have been challenged by the new ethic; however, several reports have mentioned resistance to the new ethic and a corresponding adverse influence on military performance.[66] Indeed, political struggles within the higher Party leadership could well continue to filter down to lower echelons.

A related question has to do with the role of the military in politics. One study shows that since the Cultural Revolution military representation at the highest levels declined somewhat during the period of Party reconstruction and then leveled off; however, it still continues to be an important segment. Military involvement at the regional level appears to have declined steadily, particularly at the first-secretary level.[67] This could be significant to overall policy, since the military is generally regarded as a conservative force in Chinese politics. For example, the military adopted a generally centrist position during the Cultural Revolution and tends to avoid excessive zeal in promoting social change.[68]

This conservativism is readily apparent in the socialization of China's senior military leaders. During our trip to China we visited the PLA military academy and held discussions with other officers responsible for professional military education. After reviewing the curriculum and holding talks with these officers we were persuaded that there is little to suggest that the military is committed to massive and rapid social change in China. Rather, most attention is focused on the immediate problems of national defense.[69]

An ongoing question has been the relationship between the PLA and militia. The Gang of Four is charged with having tried to separate the militia from the PLA and then use it as an independent base from which to launch a seizure of political power. The PLA has responsibility for training the militia and for providing some leadership; however, there is evidence that many PLA cadres resist being involved in militia work for various reasons. The present leadership of China apparently wants to avoid a situation whereby the militia becomes too independent while at the same time insuring that the PLA does not spend too much time in militia activities.

To foster good civil-military relations, the PLA is expected to undertake a variety of tasks. PLA units regularly participate in civil labor projects such as construction and road building. They are also expected to produce some of their own food and supplies so as not to constitute too great a burden on the people. The PLA also acts in disaster relief emergency missions and is often involved in responding to earthquakes, floods, and other natural disasters. PLA heroes are popularized in the media. For example, after the defensive counterattack against Vietnam, several heroes of the battle were sent on a tour throughout China to tell of their experiences. All of these activities help to elevate the already high prestige of the armed forces. At a time when modernization and professionalism require greater time and energy for soldiers, these tasks can serve to remind of the basic values of not being above the people and of working and integrating with the masses.

The image of close harmony between the PLA and the people was upset somewhat by a series of events at Beijing University in late 1979. Students protested the occupation of dormitories and other campus buildings by the Second Artillery Unit, which had moved onto the campus during the Cultural Revolution. When the PLA units refused to move, the students called a strike. A few days later, on October 13, 1979, PLA representatives agreed to vacate the facilities over a period of time and the matter was considered closed;[70] nevertheless, criticism of the PLA occurred subsequently in wall posters.

Another sensitive issue for the authorities has been the protests of PLA veterans who claim discrimination in work assignments and other areas. Similarly, some Chinese citizens have complained that PLA veterans get unfair advantage in employment. The publicity associated with these complaints cannot help but further exacerbate existing tensions.

Nevertheless, the armed forces will continue to be an important element in China's control of border areas such as Tibet, Xinjiang, and Inner Mongolia. These areas are particularly sensitive because of the minority populations. The Chinese government has encouraged *Han* colonization in many areas. Some of this colonization has been based on the PLA Production and Construction Corps, which operates farms, mines, factories, and other facilities in border regions. Visitors to China in the late 1970s reported that tensions between the Chinese and minority nationalities continue to be an important political factor in the border regions. The PLA pays considerable attention to the recruitment and training of minorities. Thus, it plays a dual role: by being stationed in the border regions and sponsoring colonization, it enhances political control and security; by recruiting and training minorities, it assists in socialization.[71]

As can be seen from the foregoing analysis, modernization will have an important impact on the armed forces. The PLA will retain such traditional roles as defending China, securing the border regions, acting as an agent of political socialization, and working in various civic projects. However, as it becomes more specialized in weaponry and organization, and as doctrine and strategy are redefined, the manner in which the PLA functions in its traditional tasks will be subject to reexamination. We have already seen that modernization is a contentious issue within the leadership; as the results of modernization appear, it seems likely that there will be even more questions and problems needing solution.

FORCE POSTURE AND COMMAND STRUCTURE

The People's Liberation Army consists of ground, air, and naval units and numbers about 4.5 million people. The PLA is one of the two largest military forces in the world, yet it is small as a proportion of the total population. Consequently, recruitment for the armed forces is highly selective and involves high physical, mental, and political standards. Membership in the armed forces is greatly esteemed, and is often an avenue for social mobility; there are far more applicants than successful candidates even though by law all able-bodied citizens have an obligation to serve. Women comprise about 1 to 2 percent of the armed forces.[72]

Most of the PLA ground forces are infantry, which is divided into two major components. One component is the thirty-seven or thirty-eight main force corps, which are sometimes referred to as armies. Each corps numbers about 93,000 troops at full strength and is subdivided into three divisions and smaller support units having most of the artillery, armor, and heavy equipment. The remainder of the main forces are armor, artillery, and railway divisions and signal and engineer regiments that could be used in conjunction with the corps during wartime. The second component is the regional forces, which have fewer troops or units and lighter weapons. Most of the regional forces are independent regiments and battalions.[73]

In addition to regular PLA units, China has three types of militia. According to early 1980 estimates, the *armed* militia numbers about 17 million. It receives regular training and is expected to be ready for combat, particularly in defending local areas. The backbone or *basic* militia numbers nearly 11 percent of the population and is chiefly responsible for village security and law and order in rural areas. It receives some training from the armed militia. The *ordinary* militia includes another 13 percent of the population; however, it exists primarily in name, since its organizational role remains undefined and it receives little if any training.[74] According to Defense Minister Xu, the militia would supplement regular units and would be brought into play in the event of an invasion of China. It would fight a war of attrition until the enemy was defeated.[75] There are some indications that militia units supported regular PLA forces during the "defensive counterattack" against Vietnam. If so, this would have tested the ability of regular PLA units and the militia to work together in a combat situation.

China is divided into eleven military regions, each constituting two or three provinces with the headquarters in a prominent city. (The exception is Xinjiang Military Region, which includes only Xinjiang.) The military regions are further subdivided into military districts equivalent to a province. Each military region has both main force and regional force units. As might be expected, most forces are positioned in the Shenyang and Beijing military regions. Because of the problems with Vietnam, forces in the Kunming Military Region have been strengthened in recent years.

The chairman of the Chinese Communist party, Hua Guofeng, serves concurrently as commander in chief of the armed forces and chairman of the Central Military Commission (CMC). The CMC includes central and regional military commanders and the leaders of all branches and service arms. It is headed by a powerful Standing Committee, chaired by Hua, with five vice-chairmen, five regular members, and Geng Biao as secretary general. Immediately below the CMC are three departments. The General Staff Department, headed by Yang Dezhi, issues military orders and is responsible for military operations. The General Political Department is presently headed by Wei Guoqing and is responsible for the system of political commissars that exists throughout the armed forces. The General Logistics Department, headed by Hong Xuezhi, is responsible for logistics, pay, medical care, and other support functions.

Some analysts have argued that because of the division of China into military regions with powerful military commanders in each military region, China could disintegrate under a situation of stress into a warlord-type situation such as existed in the early 1920s. Harvey Nelsen, however, has shown that, during peacetime, regional military commanders do not have control over the main force units stationed in their regions. Rather, their orders come directly from the General Staff. During wartime, the military regions would become operational war zones with regional commanders taking over tactical command of all forces, but during peacetime, they do not control main force units.[76]

The question has sometimes arisen concerning who actually commands military units—unit commanders, who come under the General Staff Department, or the political commisars, who come under the General Political Department. In August 1978 the General Political Department was reorganized; subsequently, many unit military commanders were made first secretaries of the Party organs within the armed forces, thereby strengthening their authority. Nevertheless, most analysts believe that working relations among unit commanders and political commissars are by and large harmonious. In his study, Nelsen challenges the idea that political commissars were more likely to stress correct ideological indoctrination as opposed to military professionalism.[77]

In addition to ground forces, China has a navy of about 300,000 personnel and 23 major combat ships. The Chinese navy is primarily a coastal force, though there are reports that it has one submarine with SLBM tubes and may begin SLBM tests. During our visit to a naval base near Shanghai, we toured several ships and noted their immaculate condition. However, they lacked such essentials as radar-guided fire control. Also, much of the upper echelon command structure of the navy is made up of army personnel who have had little experience at sea.

The PLA air force includes about 400,000 personnel and about 5,000 combat aircraft, including 80 TU-17 Badgers, 300 Il-28 and 100 Tu-2 light bombers, 500 Mig-15 and F-9 fighter bombers, 4,000 Mig-17/19, and about 80 Mig-21 fighters. Like that of the navy, most air force equipment is obsolescent.[78]

Chinese nuclear forces are continuing to expand. In addition to improving warheads, China is also developing new missiles, including a second-generation IRBM and an ICBM. The CSS-3, a multistaged rocket with a range of about 3,000 nautical miles, has been tested continuously since 1976.[79] A full-range ICBM, the CSS-X-4, has been under development for several years and is now reportedly operational, though at this writing it has not been fully tested.

The deployment of Chinese forces has reflected the concept of "people's war under modern conditions." In 1979, prior to the attack on Vietnam, China reinforced its troops along the borders of Vietnam and the USSR in anticipation of conflict.[80] We were repeatedly told by the Chinese that the Soviet Union had staged maneuvers along the Chinese border during the conflict, but that the Chinese had taken special measures to prepare for a possible Soviet attack. Modernization in equipment and doctrine may bring about change in China's defensive posture over the long run, but for the immediate future it seems likely that deployments will continue much as they have in the past.

ARMS CONTROL

The Chinese position on arms control has historically been closely related to the "collusion-contention" debate. Those who advocated that the United States and the Soviet Union were in collusion saw SALT and other arms negotiations as dangerous to the security of China. Those who felt that the two countries were in competition believed that little would come from the negotiations. The latter view gradually won out, but the Chinese view of arms control continues to be skeptical.[81]

The Chinese position has been outlined on various occasions. In one of the most detailed statements, Chinese Foreign Minister Huang Hua gave China's view before the Tenth Special Session of the U.N. General Assembly on Disarmament in May 1978. Among Hua's main points were the following.

> Genuine disarmament must begin with the superpowers. Only when they actually begin to disarm, rather than merely camouflage arms expansion with talk about disarmament, will progress be made. . . .
>
> China advocates the complete prohibition and thorough destruction of nuclear weapons. At no time and under no circumstances will China be the first to use nuclear weapons. . . .
>
> China supports the demands of small and medium-sized countries for the establishment of nuclear-free zones and peace zones, and has undertaken a due commitment toward the Latin American nuclear-free zone. . . .
>
> China stands for the dismantling of all military bases on foreign soil and the withdrawal of all armed forces stationed abroad. China has no bases or troops stationed abroad and will never ask any country to place bases or troops on Chinese territory. . . .
>
> China stands for the complete prohibition and thorough

destruction of biological and chemical weapons, and firmly upholds the 1925 Geneva Protocol for the Prohibition of the Use in War of Asphyxiating, Poisonous or Other Gases, and of Bacteriological Methods of Warfare. . . .

China holds that all countries have the right to develop nuclear weapons for peaceful purposes and is opposed to the attempt of the superpowers (on the pretext of nuclear non-proliferation) to hamper the development by other countries of their own nuclear industry.

Huang further demanded that the superpowers declare that they will not use nuclear weapons, and will withdraw their armed forces stationed abroad, destroy their nuclear arsenals by stages, reduce conventional arms, refrain from military exercises near the borders of other countries, and stop exporting weapons for the purpose of fomenting war and securing foreign domination.[82]

At the U.N. session, the Chinese delegation proposed a working paper on disarmament that contained the same points.[83] The final document adopted by the session was partially acceptable, but did not meet many of China's objectives. China felt that the superpowers had "smuggled a lot of sinister stuff" into it.[84] In May of 1979, China put forward another proposal to the U.N. Disarmament Commission, which was essentially a restatement of the earlier position. China stated that SALT II, like earlier arms agreements between the United States and the Soviet Union, cannot "cover up, still less limit, their intensification of the nuclear arms race." China also accused the United States and the Soviet Union of continuing to expand their conventional arms and of vying with each other to develop new weapons of mass destruction, as well as chemical weapons.[85]

China has shown increasing interest in conventional disarmament. The Chinese delegate to the U.N. conference on prohibiting or restricting certain kinds of conventional weapons in Geneva, An Zhiyuan, stated that, "to remove the dangers of war, it is necessary to place conventional disarmament on a par with nuclear disarmament." He reiterated China's position that genuine disarmament must begin with the superpowers.[86]

Some analysts have suggested that there has been a slight softening of the Chinese position on SALT. Originally China was said to have been adamantly opposed to SALT because it would only whet the appetite of Soviet hegemonism, confirm the declining role of the United States, and upset the balance of world power. However, after the normalization of relations with China, the visit of various Chinese leaders to the United States and U.S. leaders to China, Chinese opposition to SALT has been reduced to statements that SALT would not achieve anything. Public statements by Chinese officials have warned the United States and Europe not to let down their vigilance against the USSR because of SALT.

China has not ratified the Nuclear Test Ban Treaty or the Non-Proliferation Treaty and has continued to test nuclear weapons in the atmosphere, to the chagrin of Japan and other neighboring countries. China asserts that it will not submit to nuclear blackmail by other countries and must, therefore, continue testing. So far there is no evidence that China is willing to achieve restrictions on testing or arms, short of China's own proposals. Some advocates of SALT believe that China must somehow be included, possibly through an effort to limit the Soviet SS-20, which poses a threat to China as well as to Europe.[87]

It seems likely that China's approach to arms control will reflect its perceptions of the international situation. As long as the USSR is seen as being on an expansionist course and a threat to China's vital interests, China will oppose a situation that formally allows the USSR a predominant position. China also decries the position of the United States, but tends to see it as a response to the Soviet position. Consequently, the Chinese position will continue to reflect the politics of the united front against hegemonism.

STRATEGY AND THE USE OF FORCE

As China seeks to modernize its armed forces, the issues of strategy, doctrine, and force posture will become increasingly complex. It was noted previously that the manner in which China employs its armed forces has changed very little over the past thirty years, even though there have been radical changes in foreign policy, perceptions, strategy, and now doctrine. That changes may be contemplated is suggested by the Chinese experience in Vietnam.

After a build-up of several months and repeated warnings, Chinese forces invaded Vietnam along a 450-mile front on February 17, 1979. The invasion force met with increasing resistance, but succeeded in capturing the key objective—Long San. After that success, China announced that Vietnam had been duly punished and that the "defensive counterattack" would end. China called for negotiations and withdrew its forces by March 15. The Chinese claimed victory but the results were, at best, mixed. The military accomplishments were negligible. Both sides sustained about 3,000 killed and upward of 20,000 wounded and captured.[88] Vietnam continued its policy of driving out Chinese residents and of maintaining forces in Cambodia. Territorial disputes along the border were not resolved; however, the relationship between Vietnam and the Soviet Union was apparently enhanced. Vietnam got increased aid from the USSR and the Soviet Union stepped up its use of the naval facilities at Cam Ranh Bay and Vietnamese air bases.

On the other hand, China put Vietnam on notice that Vietnam could not act with impunity against a Chinese ally, Cambodia. This also let Thailand and other Southeast Asian countries know that China would not be pushed around by Vietnam, even if it meant risking war with the Soviet Union. Nearly all of the Southeast Asian countries refused to recognize the Vietnamese-backed puppet regime in Cambodia. Most countries, including the United States, supported the Chinese proposition that all foreign armed forces in Vietnam or Cambodia be withdrawn. It is also worth noting that the invasion required Vietnam to devote more resources and energy to defense and delayed Vietnam's modernization program.

The ultimate outcome was probably a political victory for China, but at great cost. The cementing of the Soviet-Vietnamese alliance in Asia may act as a constraint on China's achievement of regional prominence. Also, some analysts believe that military problems encountered in the "counterattack" have resulted in a stronger demand by the PLA for improvement in weaponry and a greater share of the budget. Indeed, the campaign was exclusively ground combat. Chinese aircraft did not become involved, nor did the Chinese navy. Both were held in abeyance rather than risk destruction by superior forces.[89]

The issue, then, is whether or not China can continue to utilize its armed forces as it has over the past thirty years. The ability to achieve a quick and decisive victory—as was the case with India in 1962 and South Vietnam in 1974 (over the Paracel Islands)—seems to be less feasible. Furthermore, such actions may generate greater pressure for devoting more resources for armed forces modernization, something that most leaders would now clearly like to avoid. The Chinese press gives hints that the leadership has debated the issue. Certainly, the military is trying to learn from the Vietnam experience, as we were repeatedly told during our visit in mid-1979.

Conclusion: the future of Chinese national security policy

The prospects of a closer security link between the United States and China have apparently improved with the Soviet invasion of Afghanistan, the visit of Secretary of Defense Brown to China in January 1980, and the decision to permit limited sales of defensive arms to China. On concluding his visit, Secretary Brown declared that while there would be no alliance between the United States and China, the two sides had parallel interests and would take parallel action.[90]

For its part, Beijing commented favorably on the U.S. decisions to increase defense spending and to organize opposition to Soviet activities in Afghanistan. China announced support for a boycott of the 1980 summer Olympics and indicated that it would provide material as well as moral and political support to Pakistan. The Chinese media expressed approval that the United States had finally awakened to the intentions of the Soviet Union.[91] There was even tacit approval for the creation of a 100,000-person quick-reaction force on the part of the United States to deal with contingency situations; such approval would have been unthinkable even a few years ago.

A *New York Times* report cited studies by the Defense Department pertaining to the issue of defense modernization in China, particularly the costs of weaponry. These studies also reportedly considered the strategic issues involved in the event of war with the Warsaw Pact and how China might participate.[92]

All of this suggests that both China and the United States are rethinking the problems of their security relationship and that both sides are taking steps toward greater cooperation. It has become a maxim that the period of enmity between China and the United States that endured for over two decades and contributed to two major wars in Asia was a result of mutual misunderstandings between the two countries. Were such misunderstandings to constitute the basis of new security links, the result could be even more devastating. As such steps are contemplated, it would be well to review some of the propositions explained in this chapter.

The first section of this chapter observed that Chinese perceptions are shaped by historical and ideological forces. China perceives itself as weak and thus in a subservient position to the superpowers. Nevertheless, it is possible for China to modernize and become a powerful national actor in Asia and eventually across the globe. China must avoid war in order to modernize, but must also resist the power of the Soviet Union, which China perceives as the greatest threat.

China's overarching national seucurity policy is to form a "united front" against Soviet power. The "united front" is a shifting coalition that involves all forces that can be involved at a given time. As the nature of the threat changes, so must the nature of the "united front." The "united front" is not an alliance, but an expedient policy based on self-interest. Within the context of overall strategy, China's military strategy and doctrine are shifting to accommodate gradual modernization. The concept of "people's war" is giving way to the concept of "people's war under modern conditions." China is continuing to improve its minimal nuclear deterrent, but will place most emphasis on conventional forces. China's force deployment and military strategy will continue to stress deterrence.

Chinese security policy is highly contingent upon the leadership that has been engaged in a series of ongoing debates over a variety of policy questions. The resolution of past debates has often been characterized by leadership change, frequently through purge. While some elements of security policy have remained reasonably constant (such as the deterrent principle), many elements have undergone change. Consequently, there is no guarantee that China's present policy on a variety of security policy questions will endure. Nevertheless, the Chinese military is an important part of the decision-making process and appears to have adopted a cautious approach to security questions.

Such issues as territorial security, modernization, force posture, arms control, and how to employ armed forces are among the subjects of contentious debate. While consensus may be achieved on some of these issues, evidence from the past indicates that these questions will not be easily resolved. Any of them could conceivably result in a leadership purge. During our visit to China we were assured by the defense minister that there was a unanimity of views within the Central Committee pertaining to questions of security policy. This could well have been the case at the time the assurance was given, but if the past is a reliable indicator, the unanimity could be fleeting.

Given the various components of Chinese security policy examined here, it should come as no surprise that Chinese reactions to a particular situation are complex. The Chinese attitude of "wait and see" when broached with the idea of a "hot line" or of reticence when questioned about the exact nature of a commitment to Pakistan seems quite appropriate to the situation. The Chinese will be very cautious in making concrete pledges and commitments; their decisions will reflect internal political considerations as much as external "objective" factors of the international environment.[93]

In remarks shortly after he departed China, Secretary Brown rightly noted that there are still marked differences between China and the United States. Among these are the attitudes toward the question of Korean security, the problem of territory (e.g., Taiwan and the dispute with Japan over the Senkakus), the Vietnam issue, and the question of how to deal with the Soviet Union, to name a few of the major ones. These issues need not constitute an irreconcilable enmity between China and the United States, but they must be considered realistically as any steps toward greater cooperation are undertaken.

The call here is not that greater security links should be avoided or rejected; rather, the pressing need is to consider the changing nature of Chinese security policy and the causes behind these changes. When this has been successfully accomplished, then it is proper to assess what role, if any, the United States might play in modernization, in involving China in arms control negotiations, in cooperating to aid Pakistan or other countries, or in a variety of other security links. The old adage that those who ignore history are condemned to repeat it may well be relevant as the United States and China find themselves on the brink of a new relationship. By clearing away misunderstandings and misperceptions in the security policy area, both sides will be greatly benefited. Only in this manner can the goal of bringing peace and stability to Asia and the world—a goal frequently articulated by both parties—be achieved.

Notes

1. The best book on the subject of Chinese-minority relations is June Dreyer, *China's Forty Millions* (Cambridge, Mass.: Harvard University Press, 1976).

2. Chalmers Johnson, "The Failure of Socialism in China" (Paper presented before the Eighth Sino-American Conference on Mainland China, Columbia, S.C., 18 May 1979).

3. Sun Shangqing, "Modernization: The Chinese Way," *Beijing Review (BR)*, 9 November 1979, pp. 21-23.

4. "A Major Move in Continuing the Long March" (portions of a joint editorial from *Red Flag*, *People's Daily*, and *Liberation Army Daily*), *Peking Review* (*PR*), 3 March 1978, p. 11.

5. On China's economy, see Robert F. Dernberger, "Prospects for the Chinese Economy," *Problems of Communism*, September-December 1979, pp. 1-15. Also see his section on China's economy in Allen S. Whiting and Robert F. Dernberger, *China's Future* (New York: McGraw Hill, 1977). Also see Nick Eberstadt, "Has China Failed?" (two parts), *New York Review of Books* (part 1, 3 April 1979), pp. 33-40; (part 2, 19 April 1979), pp. 41-45.

6. Franz Schurmann, *Ideology and Organization in Communist China*, 2nd ed. (Berkeley: University of California Press, 1968), pp. 24-33. An excellent source on Maoist ideology is John B. Starr, *Continuing the Revolution: The Political Thought of Mao* (Princeton, N.J.: Princeton University Press, 1979).

7. "New Site for Big Character Posters," *BR*, 14 December 1979, pp. 6-7.

8. Editorial Department of *People's Daily*, "Chairman Mao's Theory of the Differentiation of the Three Worlds Is a Major Contribution to Marxism-Leninism," *PR*, 4 November 1977, p. 111.

9. Ibid., see entire article.

10. There are numerous examples of this. In November 1978 the Party journal *Red Flag* stated: "Competing with U.S. imperialism for world hegemony, Soviet social imperialism is intensifying its preparations to encircle and out-flank Western Europe." Commentator, "The Plotter of a Siege Is Being Besieged," *Red Flag*, 11 November 1978, p. 77. Foreign Broadcast Information Service (FBIS), *Daily Report* (People's Republic of China), 29 November 1978, p. A9. An article published by New China News Agency (NCNA) in late December 1978 entitled "Kremlin Pushes Southward in 1978" stated: "The Kremlin's southward push stands out most noticeably in its global expansionist offensive this year. It is aimed at a strategic breakthrough from Soviet central Asia to the Indian Ocean, thereby outflanking Western Europe and menacing East Asia" (FBIS, *Daily Report*, 3 January 1979, p. A10). *Radio Beijing*, in January 1979, stated: "Over the past year, in order to encircle Europe the Soviets have stepped up their aggression and expansion for military bases seized in Asia and Africa" (FBIS, *Daily Report*, 30 January 1979, p. A18). Some

observers have referred to China as the Asian member of NATO because of its strong support for the alliance.

11. Deng Xiaoping, as interviewed in *Time,* 5 February 1979, p. 34.

12. Hua Guofeng, "Report on the Work of Government" (Paper delivered at the second session of the Fifth National People's Congress, 18 June 1979), *FBIS Supplement,* 2 July 1979, p. 29.

13. Robert E. Bedeski, "State and Revolution in China after Mao: Leadership, Sovereignty and the 'Three Worlds,'" *Pacific Affairs,* no. 51 (Spring 1978), p. 78.

14. In his report before the second session of the National People's Congress, Hua stated:

> Social-imperialism has become more adventurist. In Europe it has been steadily increasing its offensive military forces, threatening and blackmailing the West European countries. In Africa, the Middle East, the gulf area and South Asia, it has made use of agents, enlisted mercenary troops and resorted to infiltration and subversion and even incited armed invasion and military coups in its attempt to seize strategic areas and resources and control sea lanes with the aim of dominating these areas and throttling Europe by encircling it from the perimeter. In the same period, it has quickened its expansion in the Asian-Pacific region, where it has beefed up its naval and air forces, established and sought more military bases and continually flaunted its military strength. It has encouraged and assisted the Vietnamese authorities and even got directly involved in their assertion of control over Laos, their aggression against Kampuchea and their rigging up an "Indochinese federation," in order to realize step by step its fond dream of an "Asian collective security system" with Indochina as the base area. The aggressive and expansionist pursuits of the greater and the lesser hegemonists in Indochina, far from being a regional matter, are part and parcel of social-imperialism's global strategy for world hegemony. A host of facts proves that social-imperialism is the main source of tension in the international situation today. [Hua, "Report on the Work of Government," p. 28]

15. An excellent work on the application of the united front concept in Chinese foreign policy is J. D. Armstrong, *Revolutionary Diplomacy: Chinese Foreign Policy and the United Front Doctrine* (Berkeley: University of California Press, 1977). Also see William R. Heaton, "A United Front against Hegemonism: Chinese Foreign Policy into the 1980's" (National Defense University monograph 80-2, March 1980).

16. Zeng Oing, "A New State in Sino-American Relations," *Shijie Zhishi* [World Knowledge], no. 1 (January 1979), pp. 16-18 (FBIS, 7 February 1979).

17. Deng interview with *Time,* p. 34.

18. "Plans Readjusted, Policy Unchanged," *BR,* 27 July 1979, pp. 9-11. Also see the report by Yu Qiuli, vice premier of the State Council and minister in charge of the State Planning Commission to the second session of the 5th NPC. See *BR,* 6 July 1979, pp. 37-41; 20 July 1979, pp. 7-16.

19. Deng Xiaoping, "Current Situation and Tasks," as reported in *Cheng Ming* (Hong Kong), no. 29 (1 March 1980), pp. 11-23 (translated in FBIS, *Daily Report,* 11 March 1980). "Ji Pengfei Talks on PRC Future Foreign Policy," *Chung Pao* (Hong Kong), 10-16 March 1980 (FBIS, *Daily Report,* 18, 20 March 1980).

20. The terms *strategy* and *doctrine* are often used and confused interchangeably. Rather than become enmeshed in semantics, I have chosen to look at two principles of Chinese security policy—deterrence and "people's war." These principles are relevant for strategy and doctrine, however defined.

21. Xu Xiangqien, "Heighten Our Vigilance and Get Prepared to Fight a War," *PR,* 11 August 1978, pp. 5-9.

22. Ibid., p. 10.

23. Xu Xiangqien, "Strive to Achieve Modernization in National Defense: In Celebration of the 30th Anniversary of the Founding of the People's Republic of China," *Red Flag,* no. 10 (2 October 1979), pp. 28-33; United States Joint Publications Research Service (USJPRS), *China Report,* no. 74680 (30 November 1979), pp. 43-52.

24. Ibid., p. 47.

25. Ibid., p. 48.

26. Jack H. Harris, "Enduring Chinese Dimensions in Peking's Military Policy and Doctrine," *Issues and Studies,* July 1979, pp. 77-88.

27. Jonathan D. Pollack, "The Logic of Chinese Military Strategy," *Bulletin of the Atomic Scientists,* no. 34 (January 1979), pp. 23-24.

28. This remark was made during discussions with officials of the PLA Military Academy on 3 May 1979.

29. Allen S. Whiting, *The Chinese Calculus of Deterrence* (Ann Arbor: The University of Michigan Press, 1975), pp. 202-3.

30. Steve Chan, "Chinese Conflict Calculus and Behavior: Assessment from a Perspective of Conflict Management," *World Politics,* no. 30 (April 1978), pp. 391-410.

31. Ibid., p. 406.

32. Ibid., pp. 407-8.

33. Edward Ross, "China Punishes Vietnam: Chinese Conflict Management in Perspective" (Paper, Department of National Security Affairs, Naval Postgraduate School, Monterey, Calif., March 1979).

34. Pollack, "Chinese Military Strategy," p. 26.

35. Ibid., p. 26. He is citing figures from International Institute for Strategic Studies, *The Military Balance, 1978-1979* (London: IISS, 1978).

36. Xu's article in *Red Flag* in October contains comments similar to those made to us earlier. He said: "We must lay stress on the development of conventional weapons while continuously developing some nuclear weapons and other sophisticated weapons. We are developing nuclear weapons to break down the nuclear monopoly. We use them in defense. We do not base our victory in war on nuclear weapons."

37. For an excellent examination of this shift, see Jonathan D. Pollack, *Security, Strategy, and the Logic of Chinese Foreign Policy,* Policy Studies Monograph no. 2 (Berkeley: University of California Institute of East Asian Studies, 1981).

38. Paul H. B. Godwin, "China's Defense Dilemma: The Modernization Crisis of 1976 and 1977," *Contemporary China,* no. 2 (Fall 1978), pp. 63-85. Cf. Angus M. Fraser, "Military Modernization in China," *Problems of Communism,* September-December 1979, pp. 40-43.

39. An example of this approach in the scholarly literature is A. Doak Barnett, *Uncertain Passage: China's Transition into the Post-Mao Era* (Washington, D.C.: Brookings Institution, 1974).

40. Michel Oksenberg and Steven Goldstein, "The

Chinese Political Spectrum," *Problems of Communism,* no. 24 (January-February 1975), pp. 72-73. Discussion of the Oksenberg and Goldstein factional model may also be found in Kenneth Lieberthal, "China in 1975: The Internal Political Scene," *Problems of Communism,* no. 24 (May-June 1975), pp. 1-19.

41. William Whitson, "The Field Army in Chinese Communist Military Politics," *China Quarterly,* no. 37 (January-March 1969), pp. 1-29; William Whitson and C. Huang, *The Chinese High Command: A History of Communist Military Politics, 1927-71* (New York: Praeger, 1973); William Whitson, *Chinese Military and Political Leaders and the Distribution of Power in China, 1956-1971* (Santa Monica, Calif.: Rand Corporation, 1973). Factionalism among the Chinese military elite has been a subject of considerable debate. William Pang-yu Ting, in "Coalitional Behavior among the Chinese Military Elite: A Nonrecursive, Simultaneous Equation, and Multiplicative Causal Model," *American Political Science Review,* no. 73 (June 1979), pp. 478-93, outlines the debate among William Whitson, Harvey Nelsen, and William Parrish. Using mathematical equations, Ting proposes a model of factionalism based on professional interests and affective ties.

42. For example, see Kenneth Lieberthal, "A 'Second Revolution' Begins in China," *Fortune,* 23 October 1978; also, "China: The Politics behind the New Economics," *Fortune,* 31 December 1979, pp. 44-50.

43. Luo Bing, "The Fall of the Whatever Faction," *Zheng Ming,* no. 16 (February 1979), pp. 5-8 (FBIS, *Daily Report,* 30 January 1979, pp. N3-7).

44. Lyman Miller, "Chinese Political Debate since the December Third Plenum," *FBIS Analysis Report no. FB 79-10017,* 1 August 1979.

45. One of the best studies on PLA is Harvey Nelsen, *The Chinese Military System* (Boulder, Colo.: Westview Press, 1977), p. 13.

46. Ibid., 59-72. A report in July 1979 stated that the General Staff Department of the PLA was conducting classes on modernization for the NDIO and the NDSTC and various other military and civilian agencies. Subjects included nuclear weapons, strategic and tactical guided missiles, infrared rays, glimmer, lasers, and other advances in science and technology (XINHUA, 28 July 1979; FBIS, *Daily Report,* 30 July 1979).

47. Nelsen, p. 47.

48. *Wen Wei Po* (Hong Kong), 27 February 1980; FBIS, *Daily Report,* 27 February 1980.

49. On the military questions debated by the leadership at the time of Peng's purge, see Gregory J. Terry, "The 'Debate' on Military Affairs in China, 1957-59," *Asian Survey,* no. 16 (August 1976), pp. 788-813.

50. Harry Harding and Melvin Gurtov, *The Purge of Lo Jui-ch'ing: The Politics of Chinese Strategic Planning,* Rand R-548-PR (Santa Monica, Calif.: Rand Corporation, 1971).

51. Thomas M. Gottlieb, *Chinese Foreign Policy Factionalism and the Origins of the Strategic Triangle,* Rand R-1902-NA (Santa Monica, Calif.: Rand Corporation, 1977). Also relevant to this study is Michael Pillsbury, *SALT on the Dragon: Chinese Views of the Soviet-American Strategic Balance,* Rand P-5457 (Santa Monica, Calif.: Rand Corporation, 1975).

52. Kenneth G. Lieberthal, *Sino-Soviet Conflict in the 1970's: Its Evolution and Implications for the Strategic Triangle,* Rand R-2342-NA (Santa Monica, Calif.: Rand Corporation, 1978).

53. See the following reports by Peter L. Sargent and Jack H. Harris: *Chinese Assessment of the Superpower Relationship, 1972-1974,* no. BDM/W-75-128-TR (Vienna, Va.: BDM Corporation, 1975); *China and SALT,* no. BDM/W-76-066-TR (McLean, Va.: BDM Corporation, 1976); and *China, MBFR, and the New American Targeting Doctrine,* no. BDM/W-75-211-TR (McLean, Va.: BDM Corporation, 1977).

54. Ellis Joffe, *Party and Army: Professionalism and Political Control in the Chinese Officer Corps, 1949-1964,* Harvard East Asian monograph no. 19 (Cambridge, Mass.: East Asia Research Center, Harvard University, 1967). See especially pp. 40-43.

55. William R. Heaton, Jr., "U.S.-China Relations: Normalization and the Future of Taiwan" (Paper, Research Directorate, National Defense University, Washington, D.C., January 1979). Excerpts of this paper, which discusses the Taiwan question, were published in the *Deseret News* (Salt Lake City), 10 February 1979, p. 6S.

56. "Sino-American Relations: A New Turn" (Trip report to Committee on Foreign Relations, U.S. Senate, 96th Congr., 1st sess., Washington, D.C., January 1979). Commonly referred to as the Glenn Subcommittee Report, this document contains much useful information about U.S.-China relations. It also contains a section on Chinese military and defense policy (pp. 42-46). The statement by Vice Premier Deng is found in the "Introduction and Summary," pp. 3-4.

57. Xu, "Heighten Our Vigilance," p. 11.

58. *Washington Post,* 30 June 1979, p. A16.

59. Michael Westlake, "How Do You Update Copies of a Copy of a Copy?," *Far Eastern Economic Review,* 7 March 1980. This article discusses the difficulties of reverse engineering and projects the development of military aircraft in China.

60. Paul Godwin, "China and the Second World: The Search for Defense Technology," *Contemporary China,* no. 2 (Fall 1978), pp. 3-9.

61. Francis J. Romance, "Modernization of China's Armed Forces" (Paper delivered at the annual meeting of the Association for Asian Studies, Los Angeles, Calif., 30 March-1 April 1979). This paper was published subsequently in *Asian Survey* 20, no. 3 (March 1980): 298-310.

62. For example, see Jonathan D. Pollack, "Defense Modernization in the People's Republic of China" (Paper presented at the Workshop of the Development of Industrial Science and Technology in the PRC: Implications for U.S. Policy, St. George, Bermuda, 3-7 January 1979). See especially pp. 14-16.

63. XINHUA, 30 July 1979; FBIS, *Daily Report,* 31 July 1979, pp. L18-20. A meeting of the PLA Air Force Party Committee on political work in early 1979 concluded, among other things: "As to equipment, it will gradually be improved as the country advances toward modernization. For this reason we must use the equipment we have now, be prepared for any future war and to defeat an enemy having superior equipment with out poor equipment. We must also insure that the modernization of the armed forces is not only a question of equipment, but a matter of preparing well to master the use of more modernized weapons and equipment.

"Promotion of work in all fields this year must be

centered around education and training and bold changes must be made for all training manuals, methods and systems that are unscientific and incompatible with modern warfare. We must reform political education and oppose formalist methods of education that deviate from reality so as to let political work play a truly effective role in modernization." [XINHUA, 11 February 1979; FBIS, *Daily Report,* 13 February 1979, pp. E1-2]

64. XINHUA, 30 July 1979; FBIS, *Daily Report,* 31 July 1979.

65. Xiao Hua, "Bring the Powerful Force of Political Work into Play in the Modernization of the Armed Forces," *Red Flag,* no. 6 (June 1979), pp. 32-38; FBIS, *Daily Report,* 27 June 1979, pp. L21-30. See especially p. L28.

66. For example, see the report in *Guangming Ribao,* 4 August 1979; FBIS, *Daily Report,* 9 August 1979, pp. L12-14.

67. Ellis Joffe and Gerald Segal, "The Chinese Army and Professionalism," *Problems of Communism,* no. 27 (November-December 1978), pp. 1-19. See especially pp. 8-9.

68. Harlan W. Jencks, "The PLA in Politics: In Quest of Stability," *China under Communism: Revolution and Diplomacy, 1949-1976,* ed. Gilbert Chan (forthcoming); original paper available at the Center for Chinese Studies, University of California, Berkeley, March 1979.

69. William R. Heaton, Jr., "Professional Military Education in China: A Visit to the Military Academy of the People's Liberation Army," *China Quarterly,* no. 81 (March 1980).

70. XINHUA, 13 October 1979; FBIS, *Daily Report,* 15 October 1979.

71. William Heaton, "The Minorities and the Military in China," *Armed Forces and Society* 3, no. 2 (February 1977): 325-42. Also see idem, "The Chinese People's Liberation Army and Minority Nationalities," *Journal of Asian Affairs* 3, no. 2 (Fall 1978): 93-102. A panel at the 1980 conference of the Association for Asian Studies in Washington, D.C., considered Chinese defense policy issues in the 1980s. I highly recommend the papers presented there for insights into the modernization question. Listed in order of presentation, they include: Jonathan Pollack, "Chinese Security Issues in the 1980's"; Francis J. Romance, "China's Military Modernization: Major Impediments"; William Heaton, "Professional Military Education in the People's Republic of China"; David L. Shambaugh, "China's Defense Industries: Indigeneous Development and Foreign Procurement"; Richard Latham, "The Rectification of 'Work Style' in the PLA"; June T. Dreyer, "The Chinese People's Militia: Transformation and Strategic Role"; and Harvey Nelsen, "Personnel Policy in the PLA: Confucian Anachronism or a Model for the 1980's."

72. One of the best studies on the PLA is Harvey Nelsen, *The Chinese Military System* (Boulder, Colo.: Westview Press, 1977), cf. p. 20.

73. This information is drawn from Nelsen, *Chinese Military System,* pp. 3-4.

74. I am grateful to June Dreyer for providing me with this information about the militia.

75. Xu, "Heighten Our Vigilance," p. 10.

76. Nelson, *Chinese Military System,* p. 10.

77. Ibid., pp. 216-17.

78. See William Heaton, "Modernizing the Chinese Air Force" (Paper, Research Directorate, National Defense University, Washington, D.C., November 1978). Also see Paul H. B. Godwin, "The Chinese Tactical Air Forces and Strategic Weapons Program: Development, Doctrine, and Strategy" (Air University Documentary Research Study, Maxwell AFB, Ala., April 1978).

79. *Reuters,* 3 March, 1980; FBIS, *Daily Report,* 4 March 1980.

80. Fraser, "Military Modernization in China," pp. 42-43.

81. On the development of the Chinese position, see Ralph N. Clough et al., *The United States, China and Arms Control* (Washington, D.C.: Brookings Institution, 1975).

82. Huang Hua, "Superpower Disarmament Fraud Exposed" (Speech by the chairman of the Chinese delegation at the U.N. General Assembly Special Session on Disarmament), *PR,* 2 June 1978, pp. 5-13.

83. "Chinese Delegation's Working Paper on Disarmament," *PR,* 16 June 1978, pp. 22-24; "Who Should Disarm First?," *PR,* 16 June 1978, pp. 25-26.

84. "The Struggle Goes On," *PR,* 14 July 1978, p. 29.

85. "China's Stand on the Question of Disarmament," *BR,* 1 June 1979, pp. 16-88.

86. XINHUA, 12 September 1979; FBIS, *Daily Report,* 13 September 1979, p. A1.

87. Clough et al., *United States, China and Arms Control,* pp. 69-88.

88. Deputy Chief of Staff Wu Xiuchuan told French officials that the Chinese had suffered 20,000 casualties and the Vietnamese 50,000 (*Washington Post,* 4 May 1979).

89. On the Vietnam experience, see Heaton, "United Front against Hegemonism," the section on Sino-Vietnamese relations. Important aspects of exchanges between the two sides from the time of the conflict up to the present can be found in translations in FBIS *Daily Report* on an almost daily basis. Official statements of the Chinese position may also be found in *Beijing Review*. There are far too many references to be repeated here.

90. XINHUA, 14 January 1980; FBIS, *Daily Report,* 14 January 1980.

91. *Radio Beijing,* 21 January 1980; FBIS, *Daily Report,* 22 January 1980.

92. Drew Middleton, "Pentagon Studies Prospects of Military Links with China," *New York Times,* 4 January 1980.

93. An interesting situation developed during meetings between Secretary Brown and Vice Premier Deng. XINHUA cited Deng as urging all countries to "enter into an alliance to counter the Soviet Union's policy of global expansionism." Two days later XINHUA stated that there had been a mistranslation and that Deng actually "urged all countries to unite and deal seriously with the Soviet Union's global expansionism." While the original Chinese is closer to the latter, XINHUA's original "mistranslation" was probably intentional. The later decision to change from "alliance" to "unity" could well have been motivated by disagreements among the leadership over how strong a stance China should make over the Soviet invasion of Afghanistan. See XINHUA, 8 January 1980; FBIS, *Daily Report,* 8 January 1980; XINHUA, 10 January 1980; FBIS, *Daily Report,* 11 January 1980. On China's reluctance to appear too close to the U.S. in dealing with Pakistan, see the report by Don Oberdorfer, *WP,* 18 March 1980, p. A12.

CHINESE DEFENSE POLICY: A BIBLIOGRAPHICAL ESSAY

Richard J. Latham

Although several books and many articles have been written about China's military affairs, they do not fit conveniently into some of the conventional categories of analysis (i.e., doctrine, policy, strategy, force structure, deterrence) found in Western defense policy literature. Those who research Chinese military writings will discover, moreover, that there are other differences between the defense policy literature of the People's Republic of China (PRC) and that of the West. This will be especially true for those who have already explored the literature of SALT, disarmament, NATO, or U.S. and Warsaw Pact defense policies. First, there are almost no official Chinese documents or publications comparable to what is distributed by the U.S. Department of Defense, the U.S. State Department, or the Soviet Union's Ministry of Defense. Second, there is little substantive Chinese analysis of China's own defense policies. The few Chinese commentaries about defense policy usually were written after a particular policy or leader was discredited. Third, there is no scholarly writing being done today in the PRC about defense policy that is available outside the highest levels of the Chinese government. China's closest equivalent to a "think tank," the state-run Chinese Academy of Sciences, has not published any research dealing with matters of defense, nor has the Academy of Military Sciences of the People's Liberation Army (PLA). And finally, the scope of existing scholarship dealing with Chinese defense policy has changed little in twenty years. In short, what is called the literature of Chinese military affairs is almost entirely the product of foreign analysts and observers.

It is commonly acknowledged that China is now one of the major international political actors. There has been a tendency, however, to view China as having an equally powerful military force. There is an expectation, too, that there should be an extensive literature dealing with China's defense policies. To the contrary, China is not as militarily powerful as some mistakenly assume, and there is not an extensive defense policy literature compared to other major political and military actors. Beijing has a large standing army and a comparatively large number of combat aircraft, but the PLA has gone largely untested for over two decades. Equipment and weapon systems are mainly pre-1960 vintage. Although the Chinese have fought border skirmishes with the Soviet Union, India, and Vietnam, these encounters have not required Beijing to project its forces much beyond its own borders. China's generals and civil leaders have not totally failed to alter the military doctrine formed in the 1930s and 1940s, but there have been few circumstances in China's recent experience that have prompted a need for serious doctrinal reconsiderations.

The paucity of defense-related information coming from China exists for several reasons. First, China has long felt militarily insecure and threatened by foreign powers along its borders. That insecurity has caused an exceptional insistence on nearly absolute secrecy concerning even the most remote matters related to national defense. Second, the PLA has long been influenced ideologically by Mao Zedong's guidance on guerrilla warfare or "people's wars." Of course, Mao's dictum has not permanently arrested China's movement toward a more conventional force structure but it has dampened any published or professional discussion of defense policy. The extent to which contemporary Chinese editorialists struggle to justify the coexistence of modern weapons and strategies with the doctrine of "people's war" illustrates the continuing sensitivity of this issue. Since Mao's writings can be used to discredit any new military thought that may fall upon bad political times, PLA leaders are understandably reluctant to print publicly anything that can be used later as evidence of revisionism, opportunism, or nonorthodoxy. Third, a basic commitment to Party control of the PLA has created an important side effect. Some observers feel that an overemphasis on political activism in the PLA has diminished military efficiency and professionalism. Although the current regime in Beijing seems committed to a more balanced mix of military and political training, it is far from being a resolved issue. Even now, Chinese Communist party (CCP) and PLA theoretical studies, commentaries, and editorials seldom address defense policy by itself. Defense policy, to the extent that it is addressed at all, is mentioned obliquely and vaguely in the context of broader political or economic issues. Finally, China's professional military education (PME) academies have not visibly demonstrated an active role in analyzing, assessing, or proposing new perspectives about military doctrine, policies, and strategies. Although this is not surprising given China's rigid adherence to CCP guidance, this apparent lack of intellectual creativity in the military seems to have promoted a certain degree of sterility in the area of defense policy. Presumably, classified studies are written by the PLA, but there is no public discussion in any open CCP propaganda organs.

The remainder of this essay contains a selected bibliography that is divided into six categories: (1) primary research sources; (2) basic reference works; (3) military history; (4) military organization and personalities; (5) doctrine, policy, and strategy; and (6) civil-military relations. In most cases, only the more recent or most enduring scholarship has been listed. Much of the earlier writing about military affairs in China is outdated following nearly two decades of tumultuous changes in China's domestic and international political circumstances. Generally, mostly English-language works are listed, although some important Chinese-language sources are included. Articles dealing only with China's military capabilities have not been listed. Since Peking's weapon systems are limited in number and variety, most "bean count" articles have only updated earlier and understandably imprecise estimates. *Strategic Balance,* published by the International Institute for Strategic Studies (18 Adam Street, London WC2N 6AL), is the best yearly source of such order-of-battle data. Finally, no single research organization or journal is singularly concerned with Chinese defense policy. This bibliography, therefore, lists only those institutes and publications likely to have a continuing or specific interest in all aspects of modern China, including defense policy. Well-known Western journals that focus broadly on defense policy, national security studies, or international relations have not been listed.

Primary research sources

There is a variety of primary research sources, but many are in the Chinese language. The most authoritative Chinese publications include the following: *People's Daily* (Renmin Ribao, Beijing), the CCP's official propaganda organ; *Liberation Army Daily* (jiě fàng Jūn Bào, Beijing), the official newpaper of the PLA; and *Red Flag* (Hóng Qi, Beijing), the CCP's theoretical journal. Editorials are among the best indicators of policy shifts, especially the 1 July (anniversary of the CCP), 1 August (anniversary of the PLA), 1 October (anniversary of the PRC), and 1 January (New Year) editorials, which are frequently used to announce important policies. English translations normally can be found in *Daily Reports: People's Republic of China* (Washington, D.C.: Foreign Broadcast Information Service), a document containing transcriptions of radio broadcasts or English-language dispatches from Peking's official New China News Agency. Less timely articles that are taken from a variety of Chinese publications can be found in *Translations of the People's Republic of China* (U.S. Department of Commerce, Joint Publications Research Service). Hong Kong's *Dakong Bao* and *Wen Wei Bao* are two left-wing newspapers that are known to use, on occasion, well-placed CCP sources to "scoop" the mainland papers several days or weeks before important policies are publicly announced in Peking. The *Dakong Bao* also publishes a weekly English-language supplement based upon New China News Agency dispatches. The *Beijing Review,* formerly *Peking Review* (Beijing: Foreign Languages Press), is an English-language tabloid that frequently publishes important CCP government decisions and documents. Finally, the Institute of International Relations (64 Wan Shou Road, Mucha, Taipei, Taiwan) publishes *Issues and Studies,* a monthly journal concerned with modern Chinese affairs. Although this journal itself is not a primary source, it does occasionally include secretly obtained reprints of CCP Central Directives (*Zhōng-fǎ*). Within the PRC, these are closely held documents and are similar, in some respects, to U.S. National Security Council memoranda. These are the most concise and explicit statements of CCP policy.

Basic reference works

An invaluable but frequently difficult to obtain book is the *Handbook on the Chinese Armed Forces* (Washington, D.C.: Defense Intelligence Agency, 1976). Although this book is already several years old, it provides an excellent composite view of the PLA, its organization, general doctrine, and strategy. Harvey W. Nelsen's *Chinese Military System* (Boulder, Colo.: Westview Press, 1977) contains an important and more up-to-date treatment of the PLA. William W. Whitson has written or edited two books that are standard works for those who wish to understand the evolution of China's present military system: *The Military and Political Power in China in the 1970s* (1972) and *The Chinese High Command: A History of Communist Military Politics, 1927–1971,* coauthored by Huáng Chén Xia (New York: Praeger, 1973). "The Politics of Chinese Military Modernization, 1949–1977," a doctoral dissertation written at the University of Washington by Harlan Jencks, is expected to be published as a book. *The Politics of the Chinese Red Army,* edited by J. Chester Cheng (Stanford, Calif.: Hoover Institute on War, Revolution, and Peace, 1966), was once the single most important collection of PLA documents outside China. This book is a collection of classified documents concerning the PLA that were acquired by the U.S. Department of State and released through the Library of Congress in 1963. It will be useful for those who intend to examine Chinese defense policy roots in the 1950s.

Several academic journals have a continuing interest in contemporary China and occasionally publish articles dealing with Chinese military affairs. The *China Quarterly,* published by the Contemporary China Institute (School of Oriental and African Studies, Malet Street, London, WC1E 7HP), deals with Chinese defense policy on a continuing basis. The Center for Chinese Studies (Barrows Hall, University of California, Berkeley, Calif.) publishes *Asian Survey,* which also addresses China's military affairs. The *Australian Journal of Chinese Affairs* (Contemporary China Centre, Australian National University, P.O. Box 4, Canberra, ACT 2600, Australia) can be useful, as well as *Contemporary China* (Boulder, Colo.: Westview Press 80301). The *Journal of Asian Studies* (Association of Asian Studies [AAS], 1 Lane Hall, University of Michigan, Ann Arbor, Mich. 48109), once the only academic publication concerned with China and Asia in the United States, has shifted its focus to more historical scholarship in recent years. The AAS remains, however, the main professional organization of China scholars in the United States. The annual AAS conference is an important forum in which scholars frequently present papers dealing with China's military affairs. Finally, *Current Scene,* a former publication of the American consulate general, Hong Kong, has been an excellent source of information on all aspects of modern Chinese politics, economics, and military affairs; however, it ceased publication in 1978.

Military history

As so often is the case, defense policy becomes a politically "safe" research subject only after it becomes history. This is no less true in China. No mention of Chinese defense policy would be complete without referring to Sun Tzu's *Art of War* (London: Oxford University Press, 1963). This treatise on war from Chinese antiquity is probably most useful as a historical curiosity and as a source for prefatory quotations in Western military books. (Sun Tzu is rarely if ever regarded as an authority on war by the CCP or PLA.) Largely as a result of a growing interest in the history of warfare in China during the 1960s, Frank A. Kierman, Jr., edited *Chinese Ways in Warfare* (Cambridge, Mass.: Harvard University Press, 1974). This book deals mainly with the distant Chinese past and would not be useful to someone whose interests are decidedly modern. During the 1960s and early 1970s, the U.S. Army's Office of Military History in Taipei, Taiwan, published several books and monographs in limited numbers. Although these publications may never reach more than a handful of individuals, much of that research can be found in Whitson's two books mentioned above.

Military organization and personalities

A fair amount of material has been written about the organization of the PLA and cliques within the army. Besides the *Handbook on the Chinese Armed Forces,* Nelsen's *Chinese Military System,* Jenck's "Politics of Chinese Military Modernization, 1949–1977," and Whitson's work, the following books are also useful: Gerard H. Corr, *The Chinese Red Army* (New York: Schocken Books, 1974); Angus M. Fraser, *The People's Liberation Army* (London: Oxford University Press, 1967); and Samuel B. Griffith, *The Chinese People's Liberation Army* (New York: McGraw-Hill, 1967). An indispensable work on PLA personalities is Huang Chen-Xia's *Mao's Generals* (Hong Kong: Research Institute of Contemporary History, 1968). Unfortunately, this book is published only in Chinese. Huang, who worked closely with Whitson and was an unusually well-informed source of information, died unexpectedly and was not able to complete additional work on Chinese military cliques and factions. Finally, Ellis Joffe's *Party and Army: Professional and Political Control in the Chinese Officer Corps* (Cambridge, Mass.: Harvard University Press, 1967), although now somewhat dated, is an important study dealing with the roles of commanders and commissars in the PLA.

Doctrine, policy, and strategy

As suggested above, only a small number of CCP and PLA leaders discuss and determine military doctrine, policy, or strategy. There are no annual reports from the Ministry of Defense that outline China's defense policies, nor are there any White Papers that specify the regime's objectives. Our understanding of Chinese military affairs, therefore, is interpretative. Only after certain former ministers of defense, such as Lo Rui Qing (see Harry Harding, Jr., and Melvin Gurtov, *The Purge of Lo Rui Qing: The Politics of Chinese Strategic Planning* [Santa Monica, Calif.: Rand Corporation, 1971]) and Lín Biāo (see Michael Y. M. Kau, *The Lín Biāo Affair: Power Politics and Military Coup* [White Plains, N.Y.: International Arts and Science Press, 1975]) were purged have the Chinese revealed bare, and perhaps not altogether accurate, policy outlines that were advocated while those individuals were in office.

Several essays by Mao Zedong have influenced modern Chinese military practices. The relevancy of Mao's essays since he died (1976), as well as when he was alive, is debatable. In the short term, however, and notwithstanding an acknowledged need to modernize militarily in China, Mao's military writings will serve, when necessary, as a convenient standard of socialist orthodoxy. Any unsuccessful departure from the spirit if not the letter of Mao's guidance could serve as grounds for being purged. The Chinese are pragmatic, however, and ostensibly a *successful* departure from the principles of "people's war" could be rationalized as an acceptable practical variation. The *Selected Works of Mao Zedong* are printed in five volumes (Peking: Foreign Languages Press, 1961-77). The last volume was printed in 1977, after Mao's death. Also of value is Mao's *Selected Military Writings,* 2d ed. (Peking: Foreign Languages Press, 1966), a volume composed of essays extracted from the longer *Selected Works,* cited above. Samuel B. Griffith's *Mao Zedong on Guerrilla Warfare* (Garden City, N.Y.: Anchor Press/Doubleday, 1978) is a reprint of an earlier translation (1940) and book (1961) by Griffith (*Yu Chi Chan Guerrilla Warfare*). This volume includes a translation of Mao's 1937 pamphlet, *Guerrilla Warfare*.

Lín Biāo, China's minister of defense from 1959 to 1971, and at one time the heir apparent to Mao, wrote a small pamphlet called *Long Live the Victory of the People's War* (Peking: Foreign Languages Press, 1965). Although this was not Lín's first publication, he took Mao's ideas on "people's war" and applied them to wars of national liberation outside China. Following an abortive coup d'état in 1971—according to Chinese sources—Lín Biāo died in an aircraft crash while trying to flee to the Soviet Union. Understandably, Lín's pamphlet is no longer available in China, and his doctrine of wars of national liberation is no longer actively promoted, although it has not been totally rejected in theory. A comprehensive look at the concept of "people's war" is found in Chalmers Johnson's *Autopsy on People's Wars* (Berkeley, Calif.: University of California Press, 1973).

During the last two decades, several themes frequently have been evident in the literature dealing with PLA policy and strategy: (1) the Chinese perception of "strategic encirclement", (2) military modernization, and (3) Chinese nuclear weapon strategies. There have been other themes, of course, but these three have persisted with some regularity. Since the United States and the PRC normalized diplomatic relations (1 January 1979), and the Taiwan issue has truly become an "internal" issue for the PRC and Taiwan, only the Soviet Union, in Chinese eyes, remains as the force behind "strategic encirclement." American-Soviet détente, moreover, has heightened Chinese fear because détente presumably may allow Moscow to divert more military assets to the Sino-Soviet border area. Michael Pillsbury's *Chinese Views of the Soviet-American Strategic Balance: Salt on the Dragon* (Santa Monica, Calif.: Rand Corporation, 1975) is an excellent study of Peking's views on rapprochement. In "Peking's Counter-Encirclement Strategy: The Maritime Element," *Orbis* (Summer 1976), Francis J. Romance contends that China is "casting glances farther and farther seaward . . . as an integral element of an evolving counterencirclement strategy." *The United States, China, and Arms Control* (Washington, D.C.: Brookings Institution, 1975), by Ralph N. Clough et al., underscores China's distrust of Soviet intentions and fear of a weakened United States and NATO vis-à-vis the Soviet Union. Another informative article in Jonathan D. Pollack's "Sino-Soviet Relations," in *The Soviet Threat: Myths and Realities,* ed. Grayson Kirk and Nils H. Wessell (New York: Academy of Political Science, 1978).

In the late 1950s and early 1960s, much attention was focused on the development of China as a nuclear power. Even though the Soviet Union refused to give China a prototype of a nuclear bomb in the late 1950s, the Chinese succeeded in developing a weapon on their own (1964). One of the earliest and most prolific writers on this subject was Alice Langley Hsieh. Her research at the Rand Corporation eventually was published as *Communist China's Strategy in the Nuclear Era* (Englewood Cliffs, N.J.: Prentice-Hall, 1962). A more recent article by Hsieh is "China's Nuclear Missile Programme: Regional or Intercontinental?," *China Quarterly* (January-March 1971). Between 1962 and 1979, China's inventory of strategic weapons did not change substantially. Additionally, there were few if any new indicators of Chinese defense strategies and policies. The literature of this period, therefore, generally added only new data concerning PRC missile tests, satellite launches, and nuclear tests. For a more recent treatment of China's nuclear strategy options, see William T. Tow's "China Nuclear Strategy and U.S. Reactions in the Post-Détente Era," *Military Review,* no. 6 (June 1977). Harry Harding's "Making of Chinese Military Policy," in Whitson's *The Military and Political Power in China in the 1970s,* provides an informative analysis of how policy in the PLA is formulated. Jonathan D. Pollack addresses possible shifts in Chinese military affairs in "The Logic of Chinese Military Strategy," *Bulletin of Atomic Scientists* (January 1979); and Steve Chen examines Chinese conflict management in "Chinese Conflict Calculus and Behavior," *World Politics* 30 (April 1978). Finally, Paul H. B. Godwin has published two well-documented and useful studies at the United States Air Force's Air University, Maxwell Air Force Base, Ala.: *Doctrine, Strategy, and Ethics: The Modernization of the Chinese People's Liberation Army* (1977), and *The Chinese Tactical Air Forces and Strategic Weapons Program: Development, Doctrine, and Strategy* (1978).

Civil-military relations

The formative years of the CCP were during the era of "warlord politics" (see Lucian W. Pye, *Warlord Politics* [New York: Praeger, 1971]). It is not difficult to understand, therefore, Mao's strong insistence that "the Party commands the gun, and the gun shall never be allowed to command the Party." The performance and development of the PLA as a legally restrained participant in Chinese society since 1949 is complex and has varied over time. For a good analysis of the PLA's varying roles, see Michael Y. M. Kau's *People's Liberation Army and China's Nation-building* (White Plains, N.Y.: International Arts and Sciences Press, 1973).

Near the end of China's Cultural Revolution (1966–69), the involvement or "intervention" of the PLA in China's domestic politics began to reach a peak. As radical Red Guards forced the collapse of the Party, the PLA was required to assume political and managerial responsibilities in the civilian sector. Examples of the sizable literature written on this subject are: Parris Chang, "The Changing Pattern of Military Participation in Chinese Politics," *Orbis* 16, no. 7 (Fall 1972); Jurgen Domes, "Generals and Red Guards," *Asia Quarterly* 44 (October–December 1970); John Gittings, "Army Party Relations in the Context of the Cultural Revolution," in *Party Leadership and Revolutionary Power in China,* ed. John Wilson Lewis (London: Cambridge University Press, 1970); and Ellis Joffe, "The Chinese Army in the Cultural Revolution: The Politics of Intervention," *Current Scene* 8, no. 18 (7 December 1970). In "China's Military: The PLA in Internal Politics," *Problems of Communism* 24 (November–December 1975), Ellis Joffe draws attention not only to the PLA's role during the Cultural Revolution but also to the post-1971 period when the PLA began to resume its more conventional roles in Chinese society. Besides providing for national defense, the PLA also has been an active participant in economic production and the construction of industrial and transportation facilities. For examples of this civil-military interaction, see Bai Cheng-ta, "The Production-Construction Corps: A Survey," *Issues and Studies* 10, no. 2 (November 1973), and Ralph Powell, "Soldiers in the Chinese Economy," *Asian Survey* 11, no. 8 (August 1971). Finally, one of the most recent authors to address PLA-civilian relationships is Alan P. L. Liu. In "The 'Gang of Four' and the Chinese People's Liberation Army," *Asian Survey* 19, no. 9 (September 1979), Liu argues that there were radical efforts between 1974 and 1976 leading to "the denigration of the special status and legitimacy of the PLA in China."

Conclusion

During the 1980s, the literature on China's defense policy should become more sophisticated, less historically oriented, more factually substantiated, and less estimative. Indeed, there may even be a growth in official Chinese commentaries about defense policy matters. Since the Shanghai Communiqué of 1972, China has increasingly expanded its international contacts. Beijing also has purchased significant amounts of Western technology and equipment. China's diplomats have never been as widely exposed to the international community as they are now. And finally, for the first time since 1949, Western military attachés are being assigned to Beijing in growing numbers. In fact, in 1979 the PRC assigned military attaches to Washington, D.C., a United States National Defense University group visited the PLA's Academy of Military Sciences and other military installations, and a National Aeronautics and Space Administration (NASA) group visited China's satellite launch facilities. The net result of these interchanges and dialogue should be a much clearer understanding of Chinese defense policies and strategies by policy analysts outside China than has existed during the last thirty years.

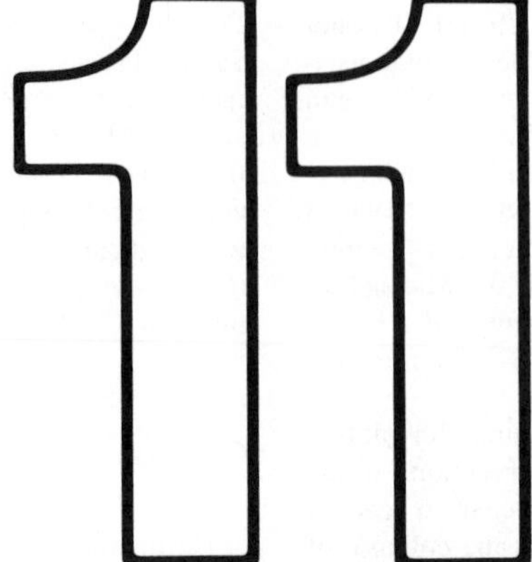

THE DEFENSE POLICY OF JAPAN

John E. Endicott

Before Japan's role in the international system is discussed and the areas of interest to comparative defense policy are treated, a setting is required that gives the reader an understanding of the very restricted environment in which defense policy exists in Japan.

In World War II, Japan experienced a defeat that was as traumatic an event as any experienced by any nation on earth. From rapid, dramatic victories early in the war, the invincible war machine of the empire of Japan soon came to a halt, tottered, and collapsed in ruin, accompanied by abject national poverty, near famine, and psychological shock. In rapid succession, Japan was told by U.S. occupation authorities that it would be stripped of its war-making potential and that elements of its militant past would be eradicated. Purges, land and Zaibatsu reform, general programs to democratize the state, and a constitution that renounced war as an instrument of national policy became part of this total postwar experience.

After remarkable progress was made along all these fronts to create the Asian version of Switzerland, it became all too apparent to American officials that more than a weak Japan was needed in long-term competition with Soviet power. This fact became abundantly clear when war on the Korean Peninsula broke out in June of 1950, requiring the redeployment of American troops and the creation of a Japanese defense capability to replace U.S. occupation forces.

Two years later, Japan regained its independence; the occupation ended, and on the same day that the peace treaty was signed, a U.S.-Japanese Mutual Security Treaty was initiated that tied Japan's defense—and future—to the West. This security arrangement and the establishment of the Self-Defense Forces became focal points for Leftist opposition. Also, soon after independence, in delayed reaction to the events of Hiroshima and Nagasaki and as a demonstration of regained sovereignty, an antinuclear aspect was added to the defense picture. Gradually, numerous ideas and concepts were created that surrounded the defense issue in Japan as restraints. Elements such as the three nonnuclear principles (no production, possession, or importation of nuclear weapons), no dispatch of Japanese forces overseas, no "offensive" weapons, and no export of weapons or the equipment necessary for their manufacture all became part of the Japanese defense policy experience. In addition to these matters of policy that were debated in the Diet, public opposition—even antipathy—to the Self-Defense Forces was an accompanying feature. This attitude was at a personal level and became so keen that defense personnel often commuted to work in civilian clothes to avoid the ice of public contempt. The defense environment of Japan that existed until the late 1960s, in essence, was not positive. The government, and especially the Defense Agency, measured all advances in defense capabilities first in political terms; overall military considerations were denigrated.

Gradually, changes in how Japan and the Japanese treat the defense issue are occurring; a new defense environment is coming into being. Largely due to events since 1969, the Japanese have become more tolerant of the Self-Defense Forces and the Mutual Security Treaty with the United States. In the international arena, the spectacle of socialist state fighting socialist state has destroyed the myth of socialist benevolence, and with it much of the theoretical base for leftist alternative defense policies, such as unarmed neutrality, that were once considered viable policy alternatives. The relative decline of U.S. military power in comparison to that of the Soviet Union has also introduced an updated sense of realism, and the rapprochement between China and the United States has removed a previously negative aspect of the Japanese defense pact with America. Domestically, almost thirty years of "good works" (disaster relief, civil assistance, etc.) by the Self-Defense Forces have also paid dividends. Attitudes have changed and are changing; in late 1979, as many as 86 percent of the general public supported the existence of the Self-Defense Forces. While such figures are a far cry from the militant opposition of earlier days, a deep-set antimilitary bias still exists among the Japanese public when it comes to consideration of the military instrument for national policy objectives. "Peace diplomacy" is still far preferred as the method to obtain national objectives, and only 15 to 20 percent of the population supports expanding the current limited size of the Self-Defense Forces.[1]

These are some of the factors that have generally constrained the military instrument in Japan and have led to the long-term, disproportionate influence of the United States in Japanese defense policy. The U.S. influence still exists, and may explain why considerations of Japan's strategy since World War II often begin with a statement of the viability of the U.S. defense establishment rather than a review of Japanese perspectives.[2] It is the relationship between the United States and Japan in the defense field that is changing at this very moment. An era of partnership among equals is being approached. The decade of the 1980s will reveal its degree of realization.

International environment

THE RELATIVE POSITION OF JAPAN IN THE INTERNATIONAL SYSTEM

Japan is a country with some unique characteristics. On the one hand, it is a respected member of the world economic system with a GNP, depending on the source, as large or larger than that of the USSR.[3] Its economic representatives have penetrated practically all markets of the world including the Council for Mutual Economic Assistance (COMECON), the Organization for Economic Cooperation and Development (OECD), and the Third and Fourth worlds. In an economic sense, by almost any standard, Japan stands as a superpower: its products, people, and performance have earned it the reputation of a heavyweight.

On the other hand, Japan is not a military superpower. While possessing considerable actual "defense" power, Japan has chosen to pursue policies that strictly limit the use of military power as an instrument of national policy.[4] In fact, although the Japanese fiscal year 1980 defense budget was the sixth largest in the Free World, and considerable military power exists in relative terms, Japan chooses to concentrate on defensive missions in and about its four Home Islands with the objective of deterring the arbitrary use of military power.[5]

WHAT THREATS EXIST?

Japan's refusal to use military power except in self-defense is to certain observers an admission of the inappropriateness of the military instrument for Japan in the era of modern weapons. While this may be the case not only for Japan but also for all nations, Japan's potential threats are indeed multifaceted. The belief in the nonutilitarian nature of military power comes largely from the nature of the complex network of dependencies that exists between Japan and many nations. (Refer to table 1 for a brief but graphic review of these dependencies.) Japan's interests are so wide and its dependencies so deep that it is faced with the dilemma that use of military power in one region might well create an unacceptable reaction in another. In the main, Japan views its interests as best served by an international stability that cannot be created by the use of force. Japan, in essence, is dependent on various states, but chiefly the United States, to maintain an international milieu that supports its continuing efforts for economic development.

An awareness of the economic threat is shared by the Japanese at large and is underscored by polling data in which nonmilitary threats to Japan were seen as most likely "in the next several years."[6] While

Table 1
Japanese dependence on imports, 1978
(raw materials imported as a percentage of total individual imports plus domestic production)

Crude oil	99.8%	Natural rubber	100.0	Wool	100.0
Coal	73.3	Iron ore	99.5	Cotton	100.0
Copper	97.5	Pulp	85.5	Soybeans	95.8
Bauxite	100.0			Wheat	93.8

Source: Japan, Ministry of Finance.

economic threats, primarily dependence on imported oil, are perceived as the most likely externally produced danger to Japan's stability, some popular recognition of a military threats does exist. In an April 1979 poll, 73 percent of respondents indicated that the Soviet Union posed a "current military threat" to Japan. Other countries that followed were China (PRC), with 8 percent; North Korea, with 6 percent, and South Korea, with 4 percent. This particular poll, while useful to some extent, failed to include the United States as one of the possible sources of military threat.[7] In a June 1979 poll conducted by the *Yomiuri Shimbun,* a prestigious Japanese newspaper, this omission was corrected. A total of 79 percent still identified the USSR as the main potential threat; China, North Korea, and South Korea placed one after another, but the United States placed second! A total of 21 percent of respondents who felt threatened (some 45 percent) chose America as the second most likely military threat to Japan.[8] To explain some aspects of these responses, a quick examination of the internal threats is necessary.

INTERNAL ASPECTS OF MILITARY THREATS

Since the end of the World War II U.S. occupation and the creation of the U.S.-Japan Mutual Security Treaty, there has been a degree of mistrust between the political Left and political Right in Japan—a mistrust that goes far back, it might be added. For years the Right has feared a Leftist-inspired revolt that would call in help from Japan's socialist neighbors; the Left, on the other hand, feared U.S. unilateral intervention in Japanese internal affairs (a kind of reimposed occupation), as well as a coordinated Rightist-sponsored coup that would feature joint military action by the Japanese Self-Defense Forces, U.S. forces in Japan, and selected Korean units from South Korea.[9]

These various threats of intervention were largely the fears or fantasies of the extremist fringes on the Japanese political scene, and an understanding of their mistrust of each other over the past three to four decades does much to explain the responses.

EXTERNAL THREATS

The uniformly high perception of a Soviet threat among the Japanese comes from historic animosity that has existed between the two Northeast Asian powers since the czar and Bakufu clashed over Hokkaido in the midnineteenth century. More recent events between the two countries have emphasized the irredentist claims of Japan for four islands (Etorofu, Kunashiri, Shikotan, and the Habomais) taken from Japan by the USSR in the closing days of World War II. Deployments of combat forces to these islands and a general enhancement of air, sea, and ground capabilities in the Far East in the late 1970s have contributed to a perception of a Soviet military threat at popular and governmental levels.[10] The Soviet invasion of Afghanistan in 1980 and the arrest of a former Japanese Ground Self-Defense Force major general on charges of spying for the USSR helped to focus the traditional anti-Soviet attitudes of the Japanese public.[11]

The notion of a Soviet "threat" as critically defined by the government of Japan stresses potential rather than actual threat. Clearly, increased Soviet activity throughout East Asia is noted by Japanese decision makers, but the likelihood of actual military attack upon Japan is held to be minimal; the primary threat to national security is still seen in terms of resource availability, especially oil.[12]

In this kind of moderate threat environment, military forces are considered as contributing only partially to the national security needs of Japan. Since the threat to security from internal sources is minimal and can be easily dealt with by the current defense establishment (including police), and since the threat from external sources is viewed as less than imminent, the national security needs of Japan are increasingly identified by elements of the government and the defense community as encompassing a broad range of items. These items include technological development, resource availability, assistance to Third World states, and, finally, a military capability to provide a minimum level of deterrence to external attack. Only by achieving progress in all these areas, it is argued, can Japan be secure and compete adequately in the world of the 1980s. Inattention to any one item could expose Japan to a threat possibly as serious as military attack, but this is not considered likely.[13]

WORLD VIEW

The interpretation of Japanese national security interests along the lines described above reveals the ascendancy of a particular world view in the Japan of the late 1970s. This world view is one that can be called internationalist; it has been in control of the main thrust of Japanese foreign and defense policy since the end of World War II and may remain predominant for some time to come. Its basic objective, as one of the historic world views in Japan, is to insure Japan's development and well-being through interdependency with the outside world, particularly the English-speaking world.[14]

Ever since the restoration of imperial power in the 1860s, this world view has competed with one that, in contrast, can be called self-reliant. The self-reliant view holds that the key to Japan's success is in introspective and autonomous development. Thus, from this perspective, an independence born of the absence of (or, at least, a minimum number of) dependencies can be created that will produce a Japan able to capitalize on its unique characteristics among states.

Control of foreign policy has alternated over wide

periods of time between advocates of these two perceptions. As one might expect, the 1930s and the World War II period witnessed the ascendancy of the self-reliant world view. Since World War II, the internationalist view, with close ties with the United States and the West, has been dominant.

While the above world views did contend with one another prior to World War II, they were primarily held by those with conservative political orientations. Since World War II, a third view—that of the political Left—rose to considerable power and served as a definite constraint on policy advocated by the two conservative world views. This Leftist world view held that since all socialist states were by definition benevolent toward other socialist states, no military power was needed in a Northeast Asia controlled by Leftist or socialist states. Calling for unarmed neutrality as the defense policy for Japan, the Japan Socialist party, in particular, led forces that acted as effective restraints on any moves to change the nature of Japan's military forces.

Developments between the socialist states in Asia since the 1960s, and especially during the late 1970s, have competely destroyed the myth of socialist benevolence. In addition to actual hostilities between socialist states, China (PRC) and Japan normalized relations. Chinese leaders chided Japanese socialists for their naïveté in defense policy and endorsed the U.S.-Japan Mutual Security Treaty. Fears among Japanese of being drawn into a war with the PRC because of U.S. "adventurism" evaporated, and with it the effectiveness of the Leftist world view.

The late 1970s and the year 1980 were witness to a dramatic transformation of the defense debate in Japan. The power, even willingness, of the Left to control and dampen this debate waned, and the debate over the basic defense orientation of Japan achieved new levels of sophistication. It is, in fact, this lack of traditional Leftist restraint (since World War II) that has led to defense issues being discussed more frankly and realistically by various Japanese without fear of censure or public condemnation. It has led some observers, especially the Soviets, to believe that Japan is about to rearm on a major scale. What is happening in Japan is that the defense issue is returning to the public arena—a healthy and nonprovocative state of affairs in a democratic society.

The vitality of the internationalist world view among Japan's elite still seems unquestioned, and the degree of Japan's interdependence on the world system is not likely to change appreciably over the next decade. Certainly the internationalist view that has directed Japanese policy since World War II is dependent on the continued involvement of the United States in Northeast Asia. Events of late 1979 and early 1980 indicate a renewed commitment by the United States to its world-wide defense obligations in the face of a deterioration of détente between the superpowers. This renewed U.S. commitment and the position achieved by Japan since the war may act to prevent the concept of self-reliance from becoming predominant again in Japan unless a cataclysmic change in the basic stability of the international system occurs. Changes, either economic or political, that threaten Japan's livelihood could force an appeal to other solutions. One such option would inevitably be the self-reliant one. However, even this world view would need to reflect the dependencies extant in modern Japan.

BASIC LINKAGES WITH THE INTERNATIONAL SYSTEM

Besides dependencies on resource suppliers, Japan bases its foreign and defense policies on a long-term military reliance on the United States and a general commitment to the United Nations system. Indeed, the U.S.-Japan Mutual Security Treaty is the key to understanding current Japanese defense policy. In a treaty first executed in 1952 and revised in 1960, the United States agreed to assist Japan (after required Constitutional procedures) in the defense of Japanese territory. Japan was not required, as in the case of NATO members, to assist the United States if America were placed under attack and Japan was not physically involved. While this is legalistically the case, an implied obligatory relationship has evolved over time. This can be seen in the case of the sanctions questions involving Iran and the Soviet Union where a high degree of political reciprocity was expected by the United States.[15] What might seem to be a lack of reciprocity in terms of treaty obligations has not, in fact, been upsetting to American officials. In return for the commitment to defend Japan, the United States retains a military presence in Japan—an invaluable logistics base in the event of involvement in the Korean Peninsula or other Asian areas.

More specifically, Japan depends on the United States for deterrence of nuclear threats or blackmail and actual use of nuclear weapons against Japan. In return, the United States has constantly encouraged the Japanese to develop and maintain a sound conventional capability that would deter insurgency and small- or medium-sized attacks from external sources. Such a capability would make it possible for Japan to defend itself, allowing more time for the United States to react.[16]

As the 1980s begin, support for the U.S.-Japan Mutual Security Treaty (MST) has reached new highs in Japan, largely due to increased Soviet belligerence and the collapse of the Leftist defense policy alternatives mentioned above. Acceptance of the MST has reached 61 percent of respondents in nationwide polls, and support for a national orientation toward the West has soared to 56 percent from 28 percent, where it stood in 1974.[17] Japan is firmly linked to the United States through the defense relationship, not to mention common economic and political objectives.

For their part, U.S. officials maintain that Japan—not China—is the principal pillar on which U.S.-Asian policy will be based for the indefinite future.[18]

All, of course, is not in complete accord between the United States and Japan, and some Japanese observers have become increasingly vocal in the degree to which they criticize the various economic and military pressures being applied by Americans on Japan. Pressures on the Japanese to increase their defense effort, to increase purchases of U.S. military hardware, and to develop common sanction policies toward Iran during the hostage crisis have worked in some quarters to weaken the confidence that is placed in the U.S.-Japanese relationship. A perceived lack of U.S. resoluteness during the late 1970s led to increased concern about U.S. credibility. Accordingly, specific doubts as to the commitment of the United States to defend Japan increased somewhat.[19] However, the greatest test of the alliance and Japan's principal link to the United States will come when access to finite amounts of oil results in competitive (and possibly confrontational) resource diplomacy.

National objectives, national strategy, and military doctrine

A consensus on Japan's national security objectives seems to be emerging from the Japanese policy process. In actuality, this new consensus will not differ as much in its substance from the past as in its breadth of support. What is happening is the development of a widened political support base for the U.S.-Japan security relationship and the existence of the Self-Defense Forces. Practically all political parties except the Japan Communist Party now support to some degree the fundamental security characteristics advocated by the Liberal Democratic Party since its creation in 1955.[20] While the broadening of the defense consensus is occurring, the articulation of a new framework that will perhaps better define the security objectives of Japan is also under way. This new framework has often been referred to in the Japanese media as overall or comprehensive security. While the exact nature has still to emerge from the consensus-building process, which is slow and demanding, part of the concept can be seen in what the Ministry of International Trade and Industry (MITI) published as a "think piece" in the summer of 1979.[21]

In this preliminary paper by a MITI study commission, a ten-year projection was drafted that outlined the objectives of Japan's broad national security policy. Security policy in itself was seen not only as encompassing military forces in being and deterring aggression by an enemy but also as including efforts to increase Japan's technological base, assure adequate resources, and realize diplomatic influence. Basic national objectives remained focused on insuring the economic well-being of the nation within the context of the U.S.-Japan Mutual Security Treaty, but the study did posit defense expenses in the late 1980s and 1990s as roughly 1.5 percent of the GNP.[22]

The pursuit of comprehensive security, with emphasis on economic well-being, has been dictated by external considerations as much as internal, and the genesis for such an economic focus can be seen in the traumatic defeat of Japan in World War II and the humiliation, despair, and abject national poverty brought about because of policies pursued in the 1930s and 1940s by the military elite of that period. As a result of the defeat and the experience of the U.S. occupation, the utilitarian value of military forces per se is still viewed as extremely low; however, Japan is not, after its history of militarism, given over to the pursuit of "pacifistic purity." A pragmatic society has seen that a very efficient military machine, unless supported by a technological and natural resource base of unquestioned excellence, cannot seek security solely by resort to the military instrument. This has not quite become the dogma of the land but, even in the late 1970s, only 38 percent of the Japanese thought that the future primary role of the Japanese Self-Defense Forces would be related to the forces' national security mission.[23] Items such as disaster relief, public welfare, and internal security were viewed collectively as more important tasks for the military to pursue. The Japanese generally continue to view their national security objectives as economic in nature—objectives that will contribute to the public well-being.

To place such emphasis on economic considerations, however, is not to say that Japan does not have certain key objectives that could be considered secondary goals—goals that would, it is hoped, be achieved through an active omnidirectional diplomacy, not through the commitment of military forces. Such goals in the security field would possibly encompass maintenance of the status quo or political stability on the Korean Peninsula; continuation of the Sino-Soviet competition in Northeast Asia; development of the PRC into a modern state as a foil to Soviet power; a return to normalcy in the Indochina area; maintenance of secure sea lines of communication throughout the world, but especially from the Persian Gulf; extension of the profitable economic relationship with Taiwan; and return of the four Northern Islands held by the Soviet Union.[24]

Most of these desiderata, while generally supportive of the status quo and international stability (except for the irredentist Northern Territories issue), have significant economic bonuses, and to most of these objectives Japan brings economic skill and determination. Perhaps the only objective that cannot be addressed in an economic sense is safe and secure sea lines of communication; this must be addressed in multilateral arenas such as the ongoing Law of the Sea Negotiations. It may be possible, after a period, to advance a package of economic incentives (development of Siberian resources) that could even cause the Soviets to reconsider their intransigence regarding the Northern Territories. Currently, Japan's leverage in connection with most of these objectives is weak. Attempts to use aid as an inducement to the Vietnamese government to alter its policy vis-à-vis Cambodia proved frustrating.

Unilateral Japanese strategies to further the realization of these policies could incorporate developmental aid in the case of developing states on the Indian Ocean littoral (especially Association of Southeast Asian Nations [ASEAN] states), transfer of advanced technology in the case of the PRC, and the proffer of necessary capital in the case of the USSR. In none of the current objectives does the military, as presently formulated, play any but the most minor of roles. Such is the legacy of the experience of World War II.

Before the specifics of Japan's national strategy and the deployment of the Self-Defense Forces are examined, it might be useful to review the domestic determinants of defense policy to better understand why the Japanese military is so severely limited in the role it can play in the accomplishment of national policy.

THE POLITICAL SYSTEM

Japan's parliamentary system of government has been dominated since 1955 by the Liberal Democratic Party (LDP). For many years this conservative party captured two thirds of the seats in the Diet; gradually it has lost this edge and now maintains the slimmest of majorities over the combined opposition parties. Luckily for the LDP, the "combined opposition" is only a term and not a reality; however, this too is changing. The LDP has consistently supported the U.S.-Japan Mutual Security Treaty and the existence of the Self-Defense Forces since the LDP's creation in 1955. These policies have become hallmarks of its defense policy. In opposition, the "progressive" (Leftist) parties initially advocated renunciation of the Mutual Security Treaty, abolition of the Self-Defense Forces, and adoption of the concept of unarmed neutrality. During the early periods of the Japanese defense debate, the LDP's two thirds majority permitted it to press forward with its foreign and defense policies in spite of vociferous attacks from the Leftist opposition. Repeatedly the Self-Defense Forces were termed by the political left as illegal and a contravention of Japan's antiwar constitution, especially article 9.

Over the years, however, the strength of the LDP and the primary opposition party, the Japan Socialist Party (JSP), has declined, with support gradually going to a collection of centrist parties that advocate various degrees of moderate-to-progressive socialist programs. At one time, such a drift of political power toward the center would have implied impending abrogation of the Mutual Security Treaty and radical restructuring of the Self-Defense Forces; however, as a result of the repudiation of the concept of socialist benevolence, these parties—the Democratic Socialist Party (DSP), Komeito (Clean Government Party), the Socialist Democratic Federation, and even the once-doctrinaire Japan Socialist Party (JSP)—have adopted a new pragmatism that brings them closer to the policy advocated by the LDP. In essence, a consensus that involves all parties of the right, center, and left-of-center—omitting only the Communists—and that supports the security treaty and the Self-Defense Forces, is beginning to emerge.[25]

While the political parties evince a new receptivity to the existence of the Mutual Security Treaty and the Self-Defense Forces, the underlying national will or inclination of the Japanese people remains basically against any policy that would result in a greater role for the military (as can be regularly demonstrated by polls taken by the government of Japan and other institutions).[26] The will reflects lessons learned by one generation that are perhaps even more emphatically held than those held by the American generation that determined never again to lose a peace or to allow incipient aggression to go unpunished. The Japanese public resists any move to use military force in other than defense of the islands, and any efforts that might weaken civilian control over the military. This is basic and is unlikely to change rapidly.

JAPAN'S NATIONAL STRATEGY

Because of its particular historic relationship with the United States and the lessons learned in World War II, Japan chooses to depend on the U.S. Mutual Security Treaty as its first line of defense. Deterrence of attack through the U.S. security commitment is fundamental to Japanese strategy. If deterrence fails, conflict could take on several forms. If the evolving struggle comes from within Japan and is characterized as indirect, fifth column, or small-scale direct, Japan will attempt to counter it through its own defense resources. If the attack is of major conventional proportions or involves nuclear threats or nuclear use, the United States would be expected to provide the necessary assistance.

Deterrence of a conventional attack through enemy knowledge of probable losses that would be suffered in such an effort will function during the 1980s as a most effective part of Japanese strategy. The Japanese have stressed Self-Defense Forces capabilities to destroy or badly degrade the ability of an enemy to project forces to the Home Islands. Emphasis, in fact, has been placed on efforts to secure lines of communication and "strengthen air-defense capabilities." But in the event of a successful invasion, the Ground Self-Defense Forces have been engaged in modernization programs to "improve mobility and fire power."[27]

While not officially admitting that the Soviet Union is the primary potential enemy, strongly indicative of national concerns are the location of key defensive units in Hokkaido and the creation of a new mechanized division with fire power strong enough to engage a Soviet main battle force successfully.

GENERAL ELEMENTS OF JAPAN'S DEFENSE POLICY

In addition to the political and overall strategic considerations in Japan's defense policy, there exists another body of extremely important features that control or establish the framework for consideration of defense issues in Japan. Within this general grouping is a subgrouping of elements that either became government policy or were reaffirmed as government policy in 1976 during the tenure of Prime Minister Miki Takeo and his defense adviser, Sakata Michita, Director General of the Defense Agency.

NATIONAL DEFENSE OUTLINE (TAIKO)

At the core of Japan's current defense policy is the National Defense Outline, or *Taiko* (refer to table 2). Subject to considerable pressure from the opposition parties but aiming to provide the necessary force levels for deterrence or defeat of possible small-to-medium-scale attacks, the government of Japan, after four successive build-up plans (refer to table 3), chose, in 1976, to place a limit on the size of the Self-Defense Forces. The size and general composition as projected by the *Taiko* would remain fixed as long as the following assumptions of the state of the world remained valid:

The United States and the Soviet Union will continue to avoid nuclear war as well as conventional war of total involvement.

The Soviet Union will continue to be occupied with European problems such as NATO confrontation and control of Eastern Europe.

There is little possibility of Sino-Soviet confrontation being resolved, although relations may be partially improved.

Table 2
Taiko: National defense program outline targets and actual defense force strength attained at the end of FY 1979 (March 1980)

Item	National defense program outline (standard defense force)	Defense force strength attained at the end of FY 1979
GSDF		
Self-defense official quota	180,000 troops	180,000 troops
Basic units		
Units deployed regionally in peacetime	12 divisions 2 composite brigades	12 divisions 1 composite brigade
Mobile operation units	1 armored division 1 artillery brigade 1 airborne brigade 1 training brigade 1 helicopter brigade	1 mechanized division 1 tank brigade 1 artillery brigade 1 airborne brigade 1 training brigade 1 helicopter brigade
Low-altitude ground-to-air missile units	8 antiaircraft artillery groups	8 antiaircraft artillery groups
MSDF		
Basic units		
antisubmarine surface ship units (for mobile operations)	4 escort flotillas	4 escort flotillas
antisubmarine surface ship units (regional district units)	10 divisions	9 divisions
Submarine units	6 divisions	5 divisions
Minesweeping units	2 flotillas	2 flotillas
Land-based antisubmarine aircraft units	16 squadrons	16 squadrons
Major equipment		
Antisubmarine surface ships	approx. 60 ships	59 ships
Submarines	16 submarines	14 submarines
Operational aircraft	approx. 220 aircraft	approx. 190 aircraft
ASDF		
Basic units		
Aircraft control and warning units	28 groups	28 groups
Interceptor units	10 squadrons	10 squadrons
Support fighter units	3 squadrons	3 squadrons
Air reconnaissance units	1 squadron	1 squadron
Air transport units	3 squadrons	3 squadrons
Early warning units	1 squadron	
High-altitude ground-to-air missile units	6 groups	6 groups
Major equipment		
Operational aircraft	approx. 430 aircraft	approx. 400 aircraft

Source: Japan Defense Agency, *Defense of Japan* (1979), p. 86.

Table 3
Development of defense capability build-up

Item	1st Build-up plan (1958–60)	2nd Build-up plan (1962–66)	3rd Build-up plan (1967–71)	4th Build-up plan (1972–76)
GSDF				
Self-defense official quota	170,000 troops	171,500 troops	179,000 troops	180,000 troops
Basic units				
Units deployed regionally in peacetime	6 divisions 3 composite brigades	12 divisions	12 divisions	12 divisions 1 composite brigade
Mobile operations units	1 mechanized combined brigade 1 tank regiment 1 artillery brigade 1 airborne brigade 1 training brigade	1 mechanized division 1 tank regiment 1 artillery brigade 1 airborne brigade 1 training brigade	1 mechanized division 1 tank regiment 1 artillery brigade 1 airborne brigade 1 training brigade 1 helicopter brigade	1 mechanized division 1 tank brigade 1 artillery brigade 1 airborne brigade 1 training brigade 1 helicopter brigade
Low-altitude ground-to-air missile units		2 antiaircraft artillery battalions	4 antiaircraft artillery groups (another group being prepared)	8 antiaircraft artillery groups
MSDF				
Basic units				
Antisubmarine surface ship units (for mobile operations)	3 escort flotillas	3 escort flotillas	4 escort flotillas	4 escort flotillas
Antisubmarine surface ship units (regional district units)	5 divisions	5 divisions	10 divisions	10 divisions
Submarine units		2 divisions	4 divisions	6 divisions
Minesweeping units	1 flotilla	2 flotillas	2 flotillas	2 flotillas
Land-based antisubmarine aircraft units	9 squadrons	15 squadrons	14 squadrons	16 squadrons
Major equipment				
Antisubmarine surface ships	57 ships	59 ships	59 ships	61 ships
Submarines	2 submarines	7 submarines	12 submarines	14 submarines
Operational aircraft	(approx. 220 aircraft)	(approx. 230 aircraft)	(approx. 240 aircraft)	approx. 210 aircraft (approx. 300 aircraft)
ASDF				
Basic units				
Aircraft control and warning units	24 groups	24 groups	24 groups	28 groups
Interceptor units	12 squadrons	15 squadrons	10 squadrons	10 squadrons
Support fighter units		4 squadrons	4 squadrons	3 squadrons
Air reconnaissance units		1 squadron	1 squadron	1 squadron
Air transport units	2 squadrons	3 squadrons	3 squadrons	3 squadrons
Early warning units				
High-altitude ground-to-air missile units		2 groups	4 groups	5 groups (another group being prepared)
Major equipment				
Operational aircraft	(approx. 1,130 aircraft)	(approx. 1,100 aircraft)	(approx. 940 aircraft)	approx. 510 aircraft (approx. 930 aircraft)

Source: Japan Defense Agency, *Defense of Japan* (1979), p. 70.
Note: Numbers of operational aircraft in parentheses denote total number of aircraft including trainers. The number of units is as of the end of each plan period.

The United States and China will continue mutual negotiations to adjust their relations.

The situation on the Korean Peninsula will generally remain as it is, with no major armed conflict.[28]

The original 1976 White Paper comments (pp. 38–39): "Given no major change in the above preconditions, there is little possibility of major armed aggression against Japan; however, the possibility of limited aggression, or of neighboring conflicts spreading to this nation cannot be denied."

Improvements in the nature of the Self-Defense Forces until the above assumptions were challenged would concentrate on qualitative upgrading of weapons systems, logistical infrastructure, and command and control systems. There has not been a serious reconsideration of these assumptions. However, in 1981 an internal LDP subcommittee was formed to review them.

THE 1 PERCENT BARRIER

Several other elements of Japan's continuing defense policy were established in 1976; these are perhaps more familiar to Western readers than the *Taiko*. Incorporated into cabinet-level decisions during the tenure of Prime Minister Miki Takeo was a measure to key defense expenditures to a fixed percentage point of the gross national product. While it may appear "unstrategic" to fix expenditure levels without reference to a threat by setting the defense level at a ceiling of 1 percent of the GNP, given the political environment of Japan, the measure was acceptable to all sides. For those who desired more money for defense, an expanding economy or GNP promised increasing real sums for defense. In bureaucratic terms, the amount, although fixed, was a guarantee that the Japan Defense Agency could at least have a planning figure that would approximate its actual annual budget. For those opposed to large increases in defense spending, the 1 percent figure was a ceiling that promised an end to concern over possible massive and rapid rearmament. The existence of a definite level also assured critics that they would be able to keep tight control over the specific contents of any defense agency budget. No fixed time span was considered for the 1 percent limit; it was to remain in effect "for the interim."[29]

Some critics of the Japanese defense effort contend that this method of determining defense expenditures errs in not considering the threat. As such, they maintain, Japanese programs tend to concentrate on front-line, high-cost equipment items with very little logistical back-up. This indeed seems to be the case, but it has been the natural consequence of several other policies also pursued by the government: failure to identify a specific threat because of a diplomatic policy that is omnidirectional; a belief by certain segments of the government that no imminent threat exists and, short of such a threat, that efforts should be focused on development of the nation's industrial base; a general reluctance on the part of the public to support any increase in the size of the Self-Defense Forces; and Liberal Democratic Party (LDP) concern with depoliticizing the defense issue.

1976 WEAPON EXPORT POLICY AND NPT RATIFICATION

Two other elements of Japan's current defense policy that were given official sanction in 1976 were the policies toward weapons export and nuclear weapons. The 1976 articulation of policy toward weapons exports came after defense contractors brought significant pressure on the Ministry of International Trade and Industry (MITI) to review the existing restrictive no-export policy that had been a feature of Japanese policy since 1967. In the wake of a business slump because of the world-wide oil crisis, some business spokesmen advocated a liberalization of export policy to help the economy. Rather than finding a panacea for underutilized production capability, the defense interest groups found that their efforts had backfired. Indeed, in 1976 the MITI issued updated guidance that not only banned the export of weapons but also disallowed the export of facilities with which to manufacture weapons. The other significant policy guideline to be realized in 1976 concerned nuclear weapons and was accomplished by the ratification of the Nuclear Nonproliferation Treaty (NPT). Japan's adherence to the treaty was certainly consistent with the basic strategy followed by Japan since World War II—dependence on the U.S.-Japanese security relationship and ultimately on the U.S. nuclear guarantee for the security of Japan.

OTHER ELEMENTS OF JAPANESE POLICY

In addition to the 1976 actions that reveal the policy constraints on Japanese defense policy, the constitution of Japan and the basic laws of the Japan Defense Agency and the Self-Defense Forces establish the legal environment within which Japan's defense establishment operates. The principles of civilian control, the all-volunteer nature of the Self-Defense Forces, the no "offensive" forces limitation, and the very nature of the rules of engagement should a crisis occur are found in these laws and their implementing legislation. So restrictive are some of these regulations that Gen. Kurisu Hiroomi, the chairman of the Joint Staff Council in 1978, publicly criticized existing procedures to deal with a surprise attack on Japan. He opined that it might be necessary for the Self-Defense Forces to take extralegal measures for Japanese forces to defend themselves if brought under attack.[30]

This critique of emergency procedures cost Kurisu his job, but it did start a review of existing legislation for possible corrective action. Efforts to create a unified command post were redoubled, and elemental means to insure effective combined operations will likely be completed in the early 1980s. In November 1978, *Guidelines for Japan-U.S. Defense Cooperation* was issued (the result of another initiative of 1976) and is expected to have an increasingly important impact on Japanese defense policy. These guidelines provide for enhanced cooperation in operations, intelligence, and logistics between the Self-Defense Forces and U.S. Forces Japan. Greater capability for coordinated operations is seen as a result of these guidelines that facilitate military-to-military contacts. The joint posture for deterring aggression, responding to any armed attack on Japan, and enhancing Japan-U.S. cooperation in situations concerning the Far East (outside of Japan) were addressed in the guidelines and made somewhat more precise. While only a beginning, these guidelines serve as a basis for achieving significant levels of U.S.-Japanese interoperability.[31]

Japan's grand military strategy, in summary, can be seen as dependence on the U.S.-Japanese Security Treaty and maintenance of a standing defense force that will provide the nucleus around which a larger force can be created if necessary. Accomplishment of this strategy is constrained by the following limitations: no nuclear weapons, no "offensive" weapons, no export of weapons, only 1 percent of the GNP for defense expenditures, strict civilian control, and no Japanese Self-Defense Forces in combat overseas.

There are many who insist that the mere existence of the Self-Defense Forces is a contravention of Article 9 of the Constitution. It is clear that the Japanese government has taken the view that the Self-Defense Forces do not challenge the Constitution but exist because of the basic right of all nations to self-defense, a right that was reaffirmed by the U.N. charter. To date, court tests of these views have sustained the government's position: as the capabilities of neighboring countries' forces improve, the nature of the Japanese defense will, of necessity, change. Within this context, even defensive nuclear weapons can be defined by the government as constitutionally allowable; however, the nuclear option has been forsworn by adherence to the NPT and numerous affirmations of the three nonnuclear principles.

OTHER DOMESTIC DETERMINANTS

The level of economic and technological development of Japan is, of course, not a factor that limits its defense potential. Japan manufactures, or has the capability to manufacture, most of its defense needs. As has been pointed out in several works, these needs could even include nuclear weapons and appropriate delivery vehicles. In the case of Japan, it is, as always, the political factor that has the greatest impact on defense policy. While Japan could produce practically all the weapons needed, this is frequently not done because of questions of economy of scale, technology transfer, or simple political realism. This issue will be treated at greater length later in the chapter.

POPULATION AND EDUCATION

Japan is experiencing a population inversion much like that of the United States. The proportion of the population 55 years of age and over will have increased from 16 percent of the labor force in 1975 to 23 percent by the year 2000.[32] As the population ages, the percentage of young people available for military service will decrease. Japan's particular situation, like that of the United States, is complicated by the "all volunteer" nature of service and the generally good state of the economy, which provides ample job opportunity in the private sector. Nevertheless, the problem of maintaining sufficient manpower will not be acute as long as the size of the Self-Defense Forces remains relatively small. Of course, given changes now being made in retirement age, there may also be some increase in the average age of personnel in the Self-Defense Forces. Current Ground SDF (GSDF) manning is at 86 percent of authorized levels, while the two other services stand at 96 percent. No attempt is being made to attain full strength at this time.[33]

Applications for various positions in the military run well above the need and, as long as the service maintains its current profile, manpower will not be a problem. Rates of competition for available openings for the National Defense Academy run seventeen to one for science and engineering and sixty to one for social sciences and humanities. Applications for noncommissioned officer candidate positions for the ground forces have a twenty-four to one ratio; for the maritime forces, nineteen to one; and for the air force, twenty-three to one.[34] Such levels of interest from high school graduates are impressive indeed. Since Japan boasts the highest literacy rate in the world and possesses an excellent educational system, there is no constraint on the military from this quarter. Only when military members attempt to attend Tokyo University for postgraduate degrees do problems arise, but the environment there is improving somewhat.

FORCE EMPLOYMENT

Controversy over emphasis on readiness of cadre forces has been a traditional element of the defense debate in Japan. While not exactly a debate on force employment per se, a steady stream of literature over the years has been available from two principal schools of thought that seem to have emerged concerning what Japan's posture should be on a day-by-day basis. The first stresses that Japan needs to stop buying high technology, expensive aircraft, naval vessels, and tanks if the missiles, ammunition, and basic logistical support infrastructure do not exist. One of the most outspoken proponents of this school is Kaihara Osamu. Kaihara frequently makes comparisons between Japan's Imperial Army and current forces. The rates of fire, according to Kaihara, even for battles in the late 1930s, consumed ammunition at rates unsupportable by the Self-Defense Forces as currently configured.[35] He insists that "the present Self-Defense Forces have become nothing more than window dressing," and the "Air Self-Defense Force is nothing more than a high-class flying club.[36]

The other school concentrates on creating capabilities for the Self-Defense Forces to perform a wide range of missions. Stressing development of experience with high-quality systems that can be provided with logistical back-up when a "real" threat emerges, this school places emphasis on training a cadre. With money tight and the threat low, this school advocates the acquisition of ships, planes, and tanks that will match any in the world. Also, it emphasizes the expandable nature of the Self-Defense Forces so that in an emergency they can be increased, while, at the same time, the industrial base can focus on necessary munitions to fill in the gaps in logistical support. From available data, and the fact that the Standard Defense Force concept was established during Sakata Michita's tenure as director general of the Defense Agency, it would appear that current policy places the primary emphasis on the cadre concept rather than on readiness. Until a major threat develops, the Self-Defense Forces will continue to be employed primarily to combat the all-too-numerous national disasters that frequent Japan—earthquakes, tidal waves, typhoons, and fire.

A debate is reportedly being conducted inside the Self-Defense Forces concerning force employment and the critical tactical question of where to defend Japan. In a debate reminiscent of the *san sen ron* ("three-line debate") of World War II, the three services contend with each other regarding the role of interdiction and island defense. Where is it best to stop an attacking force—at sea or in the air as it approaches, on the beaches, or through defense in depth? As one can see, solutions offered tend to stress the capability inherent in a particular armed service. Therefore, it can be assumed that the Air Self-Defense Force and the Maritime Self-Defense Force favor attacking forces as they approach Japan. The capabilities of the Ground Self-Defense Force, of course, can be brought to bear only after an enemy invading force has landed.

Japan is in the process of increasing exercises and training so as to improve integration of the complementary capabilities of its three services. Many U.S. observers place emphasis on increased air and naval capabilities for Japan and, during the 1980s, the Ground Self-Defense Force may even obtain a 100-mile-capable surface-to-surface conventional warhead missile. This would provide all three services with the means of stopping an invading force in Japan's territorial waters rather than on the Japanese islands themselves.[37]

The defense decision-making process

One of the most misunderstood aspects of the Japanese scene is the decision-making process. This process, whether relating to defense or any other policy issue, involves consensus building and not simple majority rule. Meticulous care is taken to bring as many of the decision makers as possible into general agreement on a subject before considering that consensus has been reached. Therefore, the process—where approximately 80 percent agreement is sought—can and usually does require time.

Since the Liberal Democratic Party (LDP) has run the government since 1955, decision making has generally focused on research and information gathering with the party structure itself. This process starts at the research council level among individual Diet members. Usually, as consensus is obtained, proposals flow upward to the LDP Policy Board for approval, on to the Executive Committee for endorsement, then to the Cabinet for concurrence and introduction into the Diet as a government-sponsored bill. Not until that time do opposition parties become actively involved.[38] Measures purely of defense interest must also be considered by the National Defense Council, and it was agreed early in 1980 that special Diet committees on defense would also be established. Initially, these special committees will provide for a multiparty discussion of defense issues; they may eventually be given the increased status of standing committees and become active players in the decision-making process. Thus, defense-related bills may soon be considered in a new atmosphere. This is increasingly likely as the LDP loses the power to introduce and pass legislation on its own strength. The impact of the opposition parties, especially those of the center, will be felt within the Diet, and what was once intraparty consensus will become interparty consensus.

When an issue is taken up in the LDP research councils, members of the government ministries concerned are invited to give testimony or provide information. At the same time, if it is an issue affecting the business community, an appropriate group of industrialists will take up the subject. For example, the Defense Committee of the Keidanren (an organization much like the National Association of Manufacturers) might send a representative or delegation to discuss an issue. Further, opinions can be made known through the many interfacing commissions and advisory bodies existing in Japan that consist of business, government, and LDP representatives. Thus, the entire conservative establishment, not just the LDP, will consider the same issue. Occasionally, opinions are so violently at odds that issues are set aside temporarily until consensus can be reached by cooler heads. Such was the divisiveness of the decision to ratify the Nuclear Nonproliferation Treaty (NPT). This particular treaty was signed in 1970, but it took six years to obtain a consensus sufficient to ratify the treaty in the Diet. A more in-depth review of the decision-making process with reference to the treaty reveals much of the nature of decision making in Japan.[39]

RATIFICATION OF THE NPT

The following observations are based on information that surfaced in the Japanese press concerning the decision to ratify the Nuclear Nonproliferation Treaty. Of the various LDP research councils and committees, the Foreign Affairs Research Council, the Diplomatic Affairs Committee, the Resources and Energy Research Council, the Science and Technical Committee, and the Security Affairs Research Council held deliberations to consider the ratification issue, and, occasionally, in order to expedite considerations, joint meetings among several of these groups were held.

Activity of the NPT issue in these councils only became intense when NPT ratification was selected as one of fourteen items that would be submitted to the 1975 Diet for consideration. This occurred in January 1975. The announcement of intent to ratify set off increased activity by the Ministry of Foreign Affairs. It was clear that, while the LDP consensus had yet to be realized within the party, the Foreign Ministry, as a bureaucratic actor, was fully committed to rapid ratification and was lobbying for rapid consensus development within the party. It was also apparent that the prime minister and his chief aide, the chief of cabinet secretary, were committed to ratification and were working toward that end.

After consideration of ratification by several research councils, the party response was sluggish. A series of conditions for ratification established in 1970 were reiterated as having to be met before the party councils would recommend ratification. In the midst of a growing stalemate, Prime Minister Miki contacted the chairman of the Foreign Affairs and Security Affairs Research Councils. He applied pressure on those two key deliberation bodies and got the "consensus process" moving again.

A single issue, "a free hand on nuclear devices" for the future, was seen to be the primary obstacle to consensus. The impasse was caused by "hawks" in the LDP, but once that issue was adequately dealt with, opponents of the NPT created other linkages and attempted to bog down the process. Gradually, however, other government agencies, elements of the business world, and top leaders of the LDP announced their support for ratification. Within the party, a Diet Members' League for Promotion of NPT Ratification was established, and press coverage became intense.

Prime Minister Miki kept applying pressure on the party deliberative councils while external international pressures (from the United States, the USSR, and Australia, to mention a few) were building and acted as further incentives for ratification. Opposition parties became more vocal on the issue as it neared time for introduction of the measure into the Diet.

A joint consultative conference among the various LDP councils was used to speed up the lengthy process. Since consensus could not be reached, the joint conference, to expedite matters further, decided to allow the chairmen and vice chairmen of the research councils and committees involved to resolve the initial party position. The chairmen approved ratification of the NPT but introduced six "matters of request" that represented the principal concerns of the representatives at the joint conference. These concerns were (1) promotion of the NPT structure world-wide, (2) strengthening of the Japan-U.S. Security Treaty structure, (3) strengthening of Japan's national security structure, (4) strengthening of the nonnuclear countries' security (some form of superpower guarantee), (5) promotion of nuclear disarmament, and (6) promotion of peaceful uses of atomic energy. Implicit in this restrained approval was that one of the three nonnuclear principles—that nuclear weapons will not be brought into Japan—would be applied with a certain degree of flexibility.

The Policy Board finally received the recommendations and proposed incorporating the requests as "abstract demands" in its recommendations to the Executive Board while emphasizing continued close cooperation in the future between Japan and the United States. This kind of issue-dodging was not appreciated by the research councils. The LDP Executive Board, in addressing the issue, promised to convey the extensive concerns voiced by the lower level and the party's secretary general to the prime minister. It then approved the bills relating to the ratification of the NPT, and they were forwarded from the party to the formal government structure to be presented to the Diet.

Party leaders met at the prime minister's offical residence for a liaison conference to map out Diet strategy. The group agreed to make "all-out efforts to realize ratification and approval of the Nuclear Non-proliferation Treaty at the current Diet session."[40] Diet deliberations were scheduled to begin in the Lower House Foreign Affairs Committee on 4 June. Other hearings in the Lower House Budget Committee were scheduled for later in the week.

Interpellation on the NPT bills by the opposition parties started in the Foreign Affairs Committee on 6 June. On the morning of 10 June, as management of legislation through the remaining days of the Diet became more critical, the LDP held a summit meeting to reexamine priorities. It was decided that "all efforts" would be directed toward an attempt to pass the Public Office Election Law and the Political Funds Control Law Revision bills. It was agreed that the NPT Ratification Bill would remain under observation, and a decision as to its subsequent steering would be made later.

The Japan Socialist Party (JSP), Komeito, and the Democratic Socialist Party (DSP) were also grappling with the NPT question. On 17 June, the JSP announced that it was postponing a final decision regarding its attitude toward NPT ratification; this delay was seen as increasing the difficulty of meeting the short time schedule left before the Diet session ended. A few days later, the LDP announced that it was "advisable not to try to ram the bill through the Diet . . . since the Japan Socialist Party has come out officially against the bill."[41] Thus, the NPT was not ratified in the 1975 session of the Diet. The LDP had failed to coordinate its intraparty views (the hawk faction never did concur in the matter), and the failure to consolidate membership views gave rise to charges that the party's executive leadership was running ahead alone.

To succeed with the 1975 effort, the LDP would have had to rely on substantial support from opposition parties, but this was not possible because the LDP had not coordinated interparty views to the extent required. Because of the lack of time, competition with other bills thought to be more important by government and LDP leaders, and failure to coordinate adequately with the opposition parties, the 1975 effort ground to a halt. The Miki cabinet had pledged at the outset of the session to obtain early Diet passage of five major bills: ratification of the NPT, the Antimonopoly Law Reform, the Electoral Law Revision, the Political Funds Control Revision, and ratification of the Continental Shelf Agreement with South Korea. Miki promised success on these five issues, as well as progress on the Sino-Japanese Peace and Friendship Treaty. This was more than the system could handle.

While the problem of consensus proved elusive in 1975, the backers of the NPT were more successful in 1976. I need not trace the debate in detail here, but a few points are appropriate. In 1976 the backers of the NPT concept were more organized. The prime minister and his allies, the Foreign Ministry, Defense Agency leadership, and the Diet Members Association for NPT Ratification, worked to give the measure top priority in the Diet. However, the Lockheed affair interfered and resulted in a boycott of Diet proceedings by most opposition parties.

Had it not been for the boycott, the NPT bills would have been passed by the Lower House, possibly in late March or early April of 1976. As it was, action was completed in the Lower House on 28 April, when the bills were forwarded to the Upper House, where they were passed on the last day of the session, 24 May 1976. Eventually, all parties supported the NPT except the Japan Communist Party, which adhered to a counterproposal that called for a complete ban on nuclear weapons. Thirteen members of the LDP violated party discipline and remained seated during the vote for ratification (they did not vote). Unanimity had not been reached, but a broad consensus certainly had been realized. These bitter-enders probably were the force that blocked or impeded the ratification process at all stages—even from the 1970 signing of the treaty. Their tenacity and the efforts of the rest of the party to include them in the consensus is representative of the decision-making process in Japan. Responsive in a timely manner, it is not; broad-based, it is.

The excursion into only the very obvious parts of the debate on one issue was done to make the point that the Japanese method for making important decisions that bind the nation for years to come is long and tedious. Consensus is a necessity and it represents a significant departure from Western traditions of simple majority rule. In the modern world of electronic technology, one might say that this represents a weakness in the Japanese political system. Whatever may be the case, unless the policy makers of the United States and other countries understand this particular intricacy of the Japanese system, demands will be made for quick policy responses that are just not possible.

THE INTRICACIES OF DECISION MAKING

Decision-making authority within the Japanese government bureaucracy is diffusive. In defense matters, the parliamentary system and the special Japanese adaptation of it provide for the National Defense Council (NDC) as a special clearing house for defense issues. Under article 62 of the Defense Agency Law, the NDC must approve long-range planning before the initiation of a plan, budgets, major equiment commitments, etc.[42] When the Japan Defense Agency presents its budget, or major new weapons procurement programs, it must do so in the NDC, where the prime minister, deputy prime minister, Ministry of Finance, Ministry of Foreign Affairs, Economic Planning Agency director general, and JDA director have membership. Others are invited as appropriate. These ministries and agencies that compose the National Defense Council, not in any way subordinate to the Japan Defense Agency, must consider the request. The power to deny Defense Agency requests represented by membership of the Ministries of Finance and Foreign Affairs on the NDC is considerable. The Japan Defense Agency, a junior member of the Japanese bureaucracy, can find itself as a supplicant before the council in presenting its major programs. The NDC forum does not have the power of the U.S. National Security Council (NSC), since it has only a small professional staff of seconded bureaucratic personnel who concentrate on defense-related studies; nor is it the location of substantive debate for the creation of policy alternatives. In essence, the National Defense Council is not a primary actor but more of a facilitator for interministerial consideration of defense policy that has been formulated elsewhere, generally in the LDP, the Ministry of Foreign Affairs, and the Japan Defense

Agency. To date, attempts to make it more like the American NSC have failed, primarily because of political and bureaucratic opposition to such a move.

While the decision-making process in the government centers on the NDC for formal presentation of defense budgets, the Japan Defense Agency must work out its draft budgets and major programs in close contact with the Ministry of Finance and the Ministry of International Trade and Industry and their representatives who are seconded to the Defense Agency. This, in essence, provides the major ministries a multifold opportunity to influence Defense Agency programs.

Within the Japan Defense Agency itself, decision making is largely handled by what is called the Naikyoku, or internal bureaus (see figure 1). Five bureaus—Defense, Personnel and Education, Health and Medical, Finance, and Equipment—function as the heart of decision making for overall defense policy. Staffed by professional civilians, these bureaus make all important decisions for approval by the director general or his administrative deputy.

The lack of military officer participation in the Naikyoku has been a long-term source of contention between the military and civilian members of the Japan Defense Agency. While some efforts have been made to introduce military officers into the Naikyoku, they have not resulted in changing existing authority patterns. Since some see this issue as a key to the concept of civilian control of the military, it might be a long time before a senior ranking military officer finds himself assigned to a position of authority in the Naikyoku. This is particularly true since the increased assertiveness of several Japanese generals (especially Gen. Kurisu Hiroomi) has rekindled concern over the adequacy of civilian control of the military. This concern for civilian control can be seen in the strict management of command authority that rests with the prime minister and runs down through the director general of the Japan Defense Agency to the military commander involved.

The Japanese system, as has been pointed out elsewhere, dampens the power of individual decision makers and stresses the group process. The role of consensus, in effect, acts to reduce the impact of charismatic leadership. In any event, one thing that remains a fact in Japan is the effectiveness of civilian control of the military.

Figure 1. Defense structure

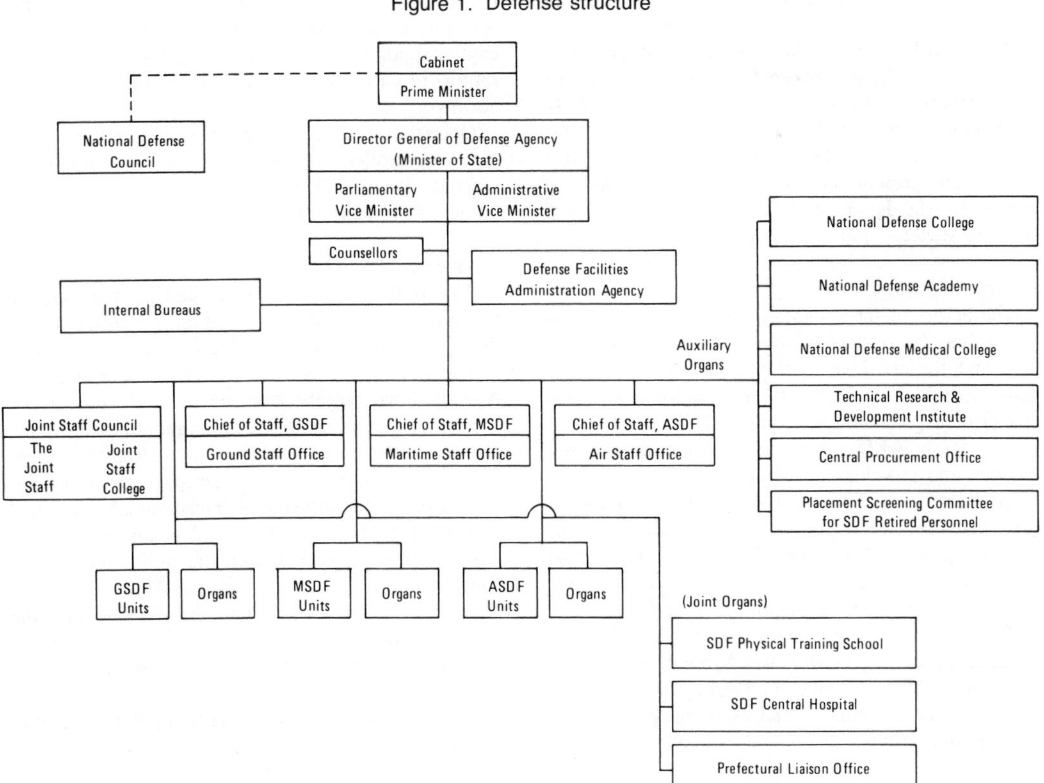

Source: Japan Defense Agency, *Defense of Japan* (1979).

Recurring issues: defense policy outputs

CIVIL-MILITARY RELATIONS

The Japan Self-Defense Forces must be given "full marks" for their efforts to improve relations with the civilian population. Polls reveal that most respondents feel positively toward the assistance provided by the military during and after natural disasters. In addition to disaster relief, the services also engaged in civic action projects and programs to reduce or moderate the impact of military bases on neighboring communities. Such items as noise abatement and TV interference payments to affected households are indicative of a defense establishment with a high degree of concern for the private or civilian sector.

Of course, it has all been a very uphill struggle. The postwar environment was extremely hostile at first and, as mentioned, most military personnel attempted to maintain as low a profile as possible in relations with civilians. Recent public attitudes demonstrate that the alienation of the military from the rest of the society is ending. Even in Okinawa, one of the most sensitive environments in all Japan, personnel recruiting can be conducted, and, for the first time in years, young *Jieitai* personnel have been invited to the coming-of-age ceremony (*seinenshiki*) in Naha.

As yet, officers of the Self-Defense Forces cannot attend the prestigious Tokyo University (*Todai*) for postgraduate work, but a few Tokyo University graduates are entering the military (three in 1978–79) to become officers. These items are indicative of a general and growing acceptance of the Self-Defense Forces by the Japanese. The military is gaining a place in society—not militarism.[43]

WEAPONS ACQUISITION

The actors of the Japanese weapons procurement system can be seen as falling into primary, secondary, and tertiary levels of involvement.[44] Primary actors would include the three individual services (the Ground, Air, and Maritime self-defense forces); the Research and Development Division, Equipment Bureau, and Development Division of the Japan Defense Agency; the Technical Research and Development Institute; and, of course, military industrial contractors such as Mitsubishi Heavy Industries and Nippon Denki. The primary actors, it will be seen, play an active role from beginning to end.

The secondary actors are the Defense and Finance Bureaus of the Japan Defense Agency, as well as politicians who represent certain policy or constituent interests. These secondary actors often resolve conflicts among primary actors and can have a very important role.

The tertiary actors consist of the Cabinet and the National Defense Council. While these two bodies may not be actively involved during most of the process, they have crucial roles to play if they choose to intervene. (The Lockheed case demonstrated that involvement and direction from above can happen in the Japanese system.)[45]

The first stage in weapons acquisition is played primarily between the service that has recognized an operational deficiency or requirement and the Technical Research and Development Institute (TRDI). A three-star general is assigned to the TRDI from each service. When the operational requirement is developed, the Defense Agency's Research and Development Division and TRDI consult to determine if the research will be accomplished domestically or not. At times, decisions to do research in Japan are made just to keep abreast of the latest developments in a particular field. This first decision is subject, of course, to some lobbying from domestic industrial representatives.

If a decision is made to do the research domestically, a research priority is established for the project. This is done by the Finance Bureau of the Japan Defense Agency with considerable input from the Equipment Bureau. Various industrial candidates are considered for the job on the basis of past performance and need. The word that a contractor is being sought is passed to potential contractors, and a source is selected to do the research. Some political input probably exists at this point if the project is significant in budget terms. However, if the matter is a routine research decision, politicians probably do not get involved.

Once the decision is made to do research, the matter is controlled by the TRDI. As a prototype is created, the TRDI follows the progress and approaches the next decision.

DEVELOPMENT DECISION

As a prototype comes down the line, the question is addressed as to its development potential. Up to this point, the issue has been primarily research oriented, and policy levels of the Japan Defense Agency have largely remained outside the effort. However, the question of development is very much a policy question and receives input from the agency's defense bureau that is charged with policy determination, the Ministry of International Trade and Industry (MITI), politicians, and business. Also involved are study teams from the individual service concerned, as well as the Defense Agency's Equipment Bureau, which often is closely tied with the MITI's wishes. If the equipment concerned is a major item, the influence of the MITI is particularly critical.

Basically, what is decided at this point is whether to buy the equipment in question, license-produce it, or produce it domestically, drawing on research already completed in the preceding phase. As can be imagined, contractor pressure for domestic production usually is heavy. Decision criteria usually include such technical questions as the benefit to Japanese industry if a technology transfer is involved and the quality of foreign equipment versus domestic alternatives. Another policy consideration is the question of impact on the U.S.-Japan Alliance. The questions of interoperability and standardization of American and Japanese weapons systems have to be addressed and can sometimes weigh quite heavily in the final decision. Besides technical and other defense policy considerations, a final decision includes, as in the United States, the impact of political influence. The MITI, various members of the Diet, and leaders in the government can make final recommendations that can have a disproportionate impact on the decision to buy or produce.

If a decision is made to produce the item domestically, agreement as to who will produce which components and accomplish the final assembly is done between business elements and the Japan Defense Agency. In most cases the industrial firms handling military orders have already agreed on the division of the contract. However, whether or not such a division takes place is dependent on government concurrence, not just acquiescence. In the event that a decision is made to license-produce, a letter of offer is issued to the foreign producer (probably to the U.S. government) and a reaction is awaited. Production involving Japanese firms is often accomplished with on-site representation of the Japan Defense Agency, thus assuring quality control and facilitating production.

While the capability of the Japanese industrial base to produce a wide range of military hardware is unquestioned, it suffers from a problem of underutilization.[46] This forces management to seek ways to diversify sufficiently into nonmilitary applications to enable maintenance of a skilled cadre. A former head of the Japanese Defense Committee of the Keidanren captured the frustrations of some producers when he stated that the Self-Defense Forces would change into "bamboo-spear units" unless capital expenditures were increased.[47] Keidanren reported the fiscal year 1977 percentage of defense production of various industries to be: aircraft manufacturing, 88.4 percent; shipbuilding, 2.5 percent; electric communication apparatus production, 56 percent; and vehicle production, 0.6 percent. Total defense production was only 0.38 percent of industrial production for fiscal year 1977 (April 1, 1977 through March 31, 1978).[48]

For the time being, the limited nature of the domestic market for military hardware will keep Japanese-produced equipment comparatively high priced. The quality will remain competitive, but the size of production runs dictates what amounts to continued subsidy through high costs paid by the government.

FORCE POSTURE

The force posture and deployment of the Japan Self-Defense Forces reflect their several roles. The most modern and well-manned ground units are stationed in the Northern Army opposite one of the possible Soviet invasion routes (see figure 2). Other forces are assigned throughout the main islands as garrison forces and reflect another role, that of preservation of peace and security in Japan itself. Levels of equipment held by the Self-Defense Forces are reflected in table 4.

The positioning of forces on separate islands is necessary in Japan because of the dictates of geography and good military tactics, but this does create mobility problems. As to the ability of Japanese forces to defeat an invasion, even Japanese observers cannot agree. It is likely, however, that the forces, as postured in the early 1980s, can accomplish those goals set out by Director General Nakasone in 1970: to create a force that can resist small-scale aggression successfully but one that must ultimately depend on the United States to repel any large-scale and determined invasion.

MILITARY DOCTRINE AND FORCE POSTURE

Military doctrine, as previously pointed out, does not control the force posture in Japan as such. The force posture has been largely a political creation and happens to be what can be supported with approximately 1 percent of the GNP. The coming decade will see a growing capability on the part of the Japanese to act as a cohesive force in resisting aggression, but for the near term, focus will remain on equipment and building up a cadre force as determined in the 1976 *Taiko*. The doctrine, as such, should be related to the characteristics of the Standard Defense Force as defined in the 1976 White Paper.

(3) Characteristics of Standard Defense Force

. . . Japan's defense forces are of the peacetime structure in nature. On the whole, they should be well-balanced and flawless, rather than capable of handling a specific, imminent threat of invasion. The necessary characteristic of such defense strength are listed below.

First, all defense functions must be arranged with no flaws, so that minimum action can be taken against any conceivable type of aggression with conventional weapons. If any functional defect existed, counteraction in that particular field of operations would be impossible, leaving an aggressor a free hand.

Our defense capability therefore requires all functions and data necessary for air, sea and land defense, including command and communications and the various auxiliary functions which supplement them, with no defects.

Second, these functions must be organized and systematized in accordance with Japan's topography, so that immediate defense action can be taken systematically against any invasion of our land, air or sea space. Proper balance and effective combination of combat units and logistics support are necessary for an integrated defense capability against aggression.

Third, during peacetime, quality volunteers must be enlisted and thoroughly trained to maintain personnel capacity. Emphasis must be placed on the SDF's positive cooper-

Figure 2. Force posture: deployment

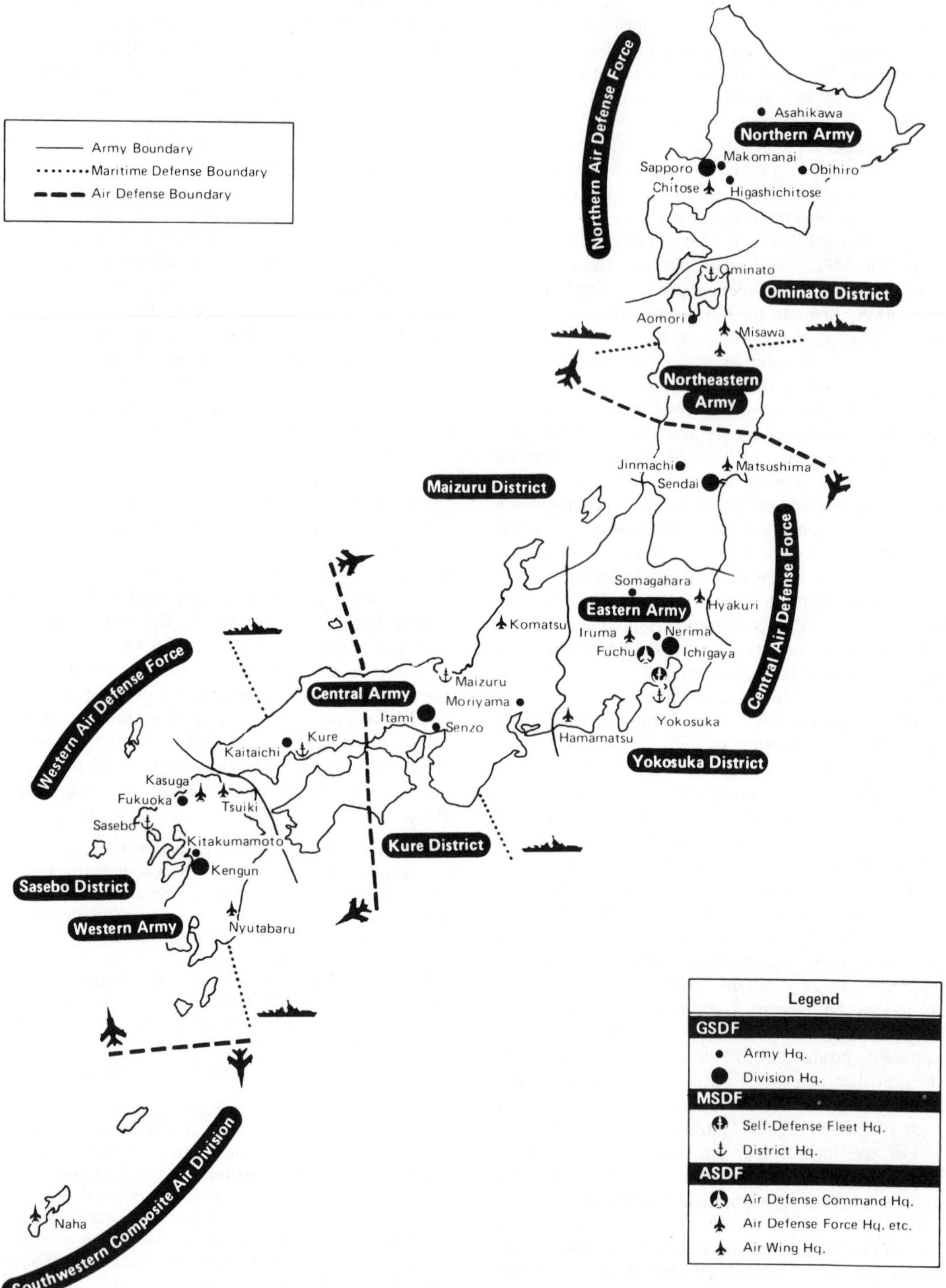

Source: Japan Defense Agency, *Defense of Japan* (1979), p. 12.

Table 4
Self-Defense Forces equipment: major equipment in service, as of 30 September 1978

Force	Equipment	Number
GSDF	Recoilless guns	1,290
	Mortars	1,860
	Field guns	960
	Rocket artillery	50
	Antiaircraft machineguns	360
	Tanks	810
	Armored personnel carriers	640
	Hawks	8 groups
MSDF	Destroyers	46 (95,000 tons)
	Submarines	14 (23,000 tons)
	Minelayers, minesweepers	39 (16,000 tons)
	Patrol ships	26 (6,000 tons)
	Tank landing ships	6 (10,000 tons)
ASDF	Fighters	410
	Reconnaissance planes	20
	Trainers	370
	Transport planes	40
	Rescue planes	55
	Nikes	5 groups

Source: Japan Defense Agency, *Defense of Japan* (1979), p. 13.

ation in public welfare, taking prompt relief and rescue actions in case of natural calamity or major disaster. This also requires an even geographic distribution of units, and necessary equipment and facilities must be kept in good condition.

. . . Standard Defense Force as such must include the following capabilities.

First, surveillance of the data-gathering activities in nearby air space and straits must be maintained at higher levels than in other fields.

Since Japanese military power is limited to self-defense and is based on a peacetime conception under the general international situation, it is extremely important to have efficient detection of military activity around Japan, and to be able to deal flexibily with any changes.

Second, the defense forces must be capable of responding quickly and effectively to indirect aggression (large-scale internal disturbances or uprisings caused by agitation or intervention of one or more foreign powers), invasion of air space or other unlawful military activity against Japan.

Third, the defense forces must be prepared to counter any potential small-scale armed attack, which would be likely to come by surprise. Therefore, logistics support such as personnel, equipment and ammunition supply and other functions must be ensured on an emergency response level.

Fourth, the development of operational functions and equipment must be effectively compatible with the Japan-U.S. security arrangement, for smooth cooperation with American forces.

Fifth, the defense forces must be capable of smooth expansion and strengthening should the Government find such necessary due to changes in the international situation. . . .

Should the international environment undergo some drastic change, this defense concept would, of course, require reexamination.[49]

ARMS CONTROL

Japan is committed to all aspects of arms control, both conventional and nuclear. In the conventional area, this commitment is clearly demonstrated by Japan's example of unilateral control. As pointed out previously, the government of Japan follows a program that prohibits the export of weapons as well as the facilities with which weapons are produced.

The three principles of no-weapons export that constitute government policy were reiterated as recently as 1976. This policy strictly delimits the export of weapons and is overseen by the Ministry of International Trade and Industry. Under this policy, exports are prohibited to Communist states (weapons and equipment on the Japan, U.S., and NATO Coordinating Committee List, except Iceland—the so-called COCOM List), to states undergoing U.N. sanctions, or to any state involved or about to be involved in conflict.[50] The government of Japan has, in essence, decided not to export anything that can be defined as an instrument of death. It is one of the most effective arms control measures in the international community.

NUCLEAR ARMS CONTROL

Japan ratified the NPT in 1976 and disavows any intent to produce nuclear weapons. Additionally, since the government of Prime Minister Sato, it has followed an explicit policy of not permitting the introduction of nuclear weapons, not manufacturing them, and not possessing them.

The antinuclear feeling of the Japanese people was first actively revealed in the early 1950s when the fishing vessel *Fukuryo Maru* was unlucky enough to receive fallout from U.S. nuclear tests at the Bikini Atoll.[51] This event acted as a catalyst to create an outpouring of antinuclear feeling, which has moderated somewhat over the years, but not much.

In addition to the NPT and the three nonnuclear principles, the antinuclear weapons bias of the Japanese people has been reflected by government actions with regard to SALT and talks for general disarmament. The government of Japan has endorsed the SALT process between the two nuclear superpowers but has been on the fringes of the negotiations. Prior to the U.S. determination to halt consideration of the ratification of SALT II as a result of Soviet involvement in Afghanistan, the Japanese government was concerned that in SALT III greater emphasis be placed on the question of regional nuclear balances.

In the meetings of the Committee of the Conference on Disarmament (CCD) in Geneva, under the auspices of the United Nations, Japan has consistently advocated general and complete disarmament and has made several proposals along this line regarding nuclear disarmament.[52]

USE OF FORCE

It is probably quite clear, at this point in the account, that Japan has not employed its defense forces in actual hostilities since their creation as a National Police Reserve. The government of Japan has even resisted efforts to involve the military in operations on behalf of the United Nations, taking the position that Japanese armed forces cannot be used overseas except for the defense of Japan. National opinion is still probably far from permitting such a use of the Self-Defense Forces.

The decade of the 1980s has started, however, on a very uncertain note. The erosion of respect for the norms of international diplomatic behavior, the increasing capriciousness of the holders of scarce natural resources, the continued adventurism of nonstate and some state actors, and the spectacle of Soviet forces being employed outside the traditional areas of Soviet military presence collectively have set a disturbing tenor for the new decade. Prime Minister Ohira was so shocked over the use of Soviet forces in Afghanistan that he termed the Soviet pressure in the northern islands of Japan "a potential threat."[53] This was followed by a statement by General Takeda, chairman of the Joint Staff Council, that called for a fundamental reassessment of the midterm operations estimated for planning.[54] Implicit in his statement was an increased emphasis on readiness, as well as a possible telescoping of the equipment objectives reflected in the midterm planning estimate, which lists objectives to 1984. By February 1980, the reaction to Soviet moves in Afghanistan had resulted in the two important defense policy formulation committees of the LDP, headed by Sakata Michita and Genda Minoru, endorsing a goal for Japanese fiscal year 1981 of 0.92 percent of the GNP for defense. They also went on record for an annual increase of 0.2 percent until the 1 percent figure is reached.[55]

While these events have prompted the above response, the tendency to base an evaluation of future Japanese defense policy on single-point analysis would fail to recognize the complex multidimensional nature of defense policy in Japan. While spokesmen for the Defense Agency often tend to capture the ear of eager U.S. reporters, they speak for only one agency in the Japanese system of government. It happens to be an agency with only a moderate amount of domestic bureaucratic power; it does not compare with the power of countervailing bureaucracies in the Japanese system such as Finance, International Trade and Industry, and Foreign Affairs. In an era of limited economic growth, the demands of other sectors of the Japanese government will have to be balanced with those of the Japan Defense Agency. Questions of alternative energy development, development of sophisticated technology for Japan's industrial base, and assistance to selected states of the Third World may take precedence, in certain instances, over calls for increased emphasis on the military element of national security. What does happen will only occur as a broad national consensus develops for greater defense in the face of a growing international threat.

The use of force by the Japanese state and its nationally based Self-Defense Forces can be projected in only one instance, that involving the direct invasion of Japan by hostile forces. In such a case, the Japan Self-Defense Forces would act to repel the invader, calling on the United States under terms of the Mutual Security Treaty.

Summary

Japan is a unique example of a successful economic state with military might not precisely in relation to its economic power. This position has given rise to criticism from elements in the United States that Japan does not pull its weight in defense matters. Such may be the case, but one must also ask what the United States has received in return from the Japanese relationship. It has received a forward base from which it may be possible to operate in the event of renewed hostilities in Korea, an advanced logistical and industrial system that may be called upon in times of emergency, and a base for stability in Northeast Asia that has been enhanced over the past three decades by the absence of a well-armed and possibly highly feared Japanese nation. While some portions of Japan's colonial empire may not mind a militarily strong Japan, there are some, especially Korea, who do not forget the severity of the colonial era.

Now that the seeds of democracy and civilian control of the military have had an opportunity to develop and take root, an increased military posture for Japan may not have the same immediate connotations of years gone by. Regardless of these sentiments, it is clear that Japan, as a nation, experienced the effects of a military unrestrained; it will be many years and will require a fundamental realignment of the basic assumptions of the Japanese polity before the military is once again given a substantial role in, first, the determination of, and second, the attainment of Japanese policy. When that time does come, the professional military officers in Japan will look more like their colleagues in the United States than their Japanese predecessors. It may be possible to forecast a significant Japanese naval presence in the North Pacific as the century nears its conclusion, but to imagine large military forces with missions on the Asian continent seems unjustified from the vantage point of 1980.

In any event, Japanese defense policy will continue to evolve as a product of a complex and multifaceted system of pressures—political, economic, and social, external and internal. The external pressures will be accommodated in the context of a cooperative policy with its principal ally, the United States. The internal pressures will continue to reflect the fundamental changes that have occurred in Japan's political system since World War II. The creation and maturation of new political constituencies insure that whatever Japan's response, it will be within the framework of a stable and democratic society.

Notes

1. See especially U.S. International Communications Agency (USICA), "Japanese Public Opinion Relevant to U.S.-Japanese Security Relations," *USICA Reasearch Memorandum,* 13 June 1979. Also, an *Asahi Shimbun* poll released 25 March 1980 revealed a figure of 25 percent willing to support a strengthened Self-Defense Force.

2. For example, p. 1 of *Summary of the Defense of Japan,* by the Japan Defense Agency and released by the Foreign Press Center, Tokyo, Japan, begins with a review of the U.S. factor.

3. *Japan Times,* 19 December 1979.

4. "In conformity with the spirit of Japan's Constitution, Japan's defense power is limited to purely exclusively defensive purposes" Japan Defense Agency, *Defense of Japan* (1979). Also see "Basic Policy for National Defense," as provided by Cabinet action of 1957, Japan Defense Agency, *Defense of Japan,* (1979), p. 64.

5. *Business Japan,* July 1979, p. 57. According to the *Nihon Keizai,* 29 August 1979, the Japan fiscal year budget request was 2,295.9 billion yen. Also see *Nihon no Boei* (1979), p. A-23, for a comparison of world-wide defense spending.

6. USICA, "U.S.-Japanese Security Relations," p. 5.

7. Ibid.

8. Ibid.

9. Interview with Dr. Nathaniel B. Thayer, professor, Johns Hopkins School of Advanced International Studies.

10. Japan Defense Agency, *Defense of Japan* (1979), p. 2.

11. *Asahi Shimbun,* 19 January 1980.

12. See especially Kubo Takuya on the Soviet threat, in *Asahi Shimbun,* 15 October 1979 (evening). He makes a distinction between "potential threat" and "manifest threat."

13. On comprehensive security, refer to *Tokyo Shimbun,* 21 March 1979; *Nihon Keizai,* 8 August 1970; and *Nikkeiren Times,* 26 July 1979.

14. For another interpretation of Japan's self-image, see Herbert Passin's "Socio-Cultural Factors in the Japanese Perception of International Order," in Japan Institute of International Affairs, Annual Review, especially pp. 69–71.

15. *Japan Times,* 19 December 1979.

16. Refer to *Washington Post,* 10 February 1980, p. A-20, for an assessment of U.S.-Japanese defense interaction.

17. USICA, "Japanese Public Opinion: The Self-Defense Forces and Security Links with the U.S.," *USICA Research Memorandum,* 27 April 1979, p. 3.

18. See the 6 March 1980 interview with Assistant Secretary of State Richard Holbroke in *Yomiuri.*

19. USICA, "Credibility of the U.S.," *USICA Research Memorandum,* 27 August 1979, p. 7.

20. Even the Japan Socialist Party, in the face of intense leftist opposition, is slowly moving away from its traditional revisionist policy. Moves to minimize policy differences with the Komeito to enable joint campaigning in the Upper House elections of June 1980 were striking. See *Asahi Shimbun,* 17 October 1979; *Mainichi,* 19 October 1979; and *Yomiuri,* 24 October 1979.

21. *Nihon Keizai,* 25 July 1979.

22. This represents an extrapolated figure derived from the 1990, 7 percent of GNP rate for national security, which would include defense, economic cooperation, and development of technology (*Nihon Keizai,* 25 July 1979).

23. Japan Defense Agency, *Defense of Japan* (1979), p. 203. The rates show 14 percent for domestic security, 33 percent for disaster relief, and 4 percent for community programs.

24. Japan Defense Agency, *Defense of Japan* (1978), p. 69.

25. *Asahi Shimbun,* 1 March 1980, and *Mainichi,* 3 March 1980.

26. USICA, "U.S.-Japanese Security Relations," p. 5.

27. Japan Defense Agency, *Defense of Japan* (1976), pp. 146–47.

28. Japan Defense Agency, *Defense of Japan* (1979), p. 70.

29. Japan Defense Agency, *Defense of Japan* (1976), p. 79.

30. Research Institute for Peace and Security, *Asian Security* (Tokyo: Research Institute for Peace and Security, 1979), p. 172.

31. Japan, Ministry of Foreign Affairs, *Guidelines for Japan-U.S. Defense Cooperation,* 28 November 1978; and Research Institute for Peace and Security, *Asian Security,* p. 173.

32. Nakagawa Katsunhiro, "Japan's Defense" (Manuscript, spring 1980), p. 5.

33. Research Institute for Peace and Security, *Asian Security,* p. 175.

34. Japan Defense Agency, *Defense of Japan* (1976), p. 155.

35. See especially "Japan's Military Capabilities: Realities and Limitations," *Pacific Community,* pp. 129–42, for Kaihara Osamu.

36. Ibid., p. 139.

37. *Daily Yomiuri,* 15 August 1979.

38. Nathaniel B. Thayer, *How the Conservatives Rule Japan* (Princeton, N.J.: Princeton University Press, 1969), pp. 207–36.

39. The account of the 1975 and 1976 debate over ratification of the NPT is largely taken from my article "The 1975–76 Debate over Ratification of the NPT in Japan," *Asian Survey,* March 1977, pp. 275–92. Please refer to the article itself for the details omitted in this review.

40. Ibid.

41. Ibid.

42. John Endicott, *Japan's Nuclear Option* (New York: Praeger, 1975), p. 65.

43. USICA, "Self-Defense Forces and Security Links With the U.S.," p. 3.

44. This short summary of the weapons acquisition process represents a synthesis of material found in Sungjoo Han's excellent account, "Japan's PXL Decision: The Poli-

tics of Weapons Procurement," *Asian Survey*, August 1978, pp. 769–84, and in the work by Kaihara Osamu, *Nihon Boei Taisei no Naimaku* (Tokyo: Jiji Press, 1977). Conversations with members of the Naikyuko and long-time observers of the Japanese scene are also reflected.

45. See especially Kaihara's *Nihon Boei Taisei no Naimaku*.

46. *Nihon Keizai*, 1 April 1980.

47. *Mainichi*, 25 May 1976.

48. Defense production data is from *Asahi Shimbun*, 13 February 1980.

49. Japan Defense Agency, *Defense of Japan* (1976), pp. 39–40.

50. John Endicott and William Heaton, *Politics of East Asia* (Boulder, Colo.: Westview Press, 1978), p. 226.

51. Jijimondai Kenkyujo, *Gensuikyo* (Tokyo: Jijimondai Kenkyujo, 1961), pp. 1-2.

52. Endicott, *Japan's Nuclear Option*, pp. 51-52.

53. *Asahi Shimbun*, 5 February 1980.

54. *Yomiuri Shimbun*, 31 January 1980.

55. *Nihon Keizai*, 18 February 1980.

JAPANESE DEFENSE POLICY: A BIBLIOGRAPHICAL ESSAY

James H. Buck

There is not a large body of scholarly books and articles that deal solely or specifically with Japan's defense policy. This is due, in part, to the relative unimportance and low visibility of the military component of Japan's foreign policy. In the twenty-five years since the establishment (1954) of the Japan Defense Agency and the Self-Defense Force (SDF), Japan has purposefully emphasized the political and economic aspects of foreign policy while keeping a very low military profile. At the same time, defense policy has been a lively, often divisive domestic political issue, especially with regard to the appropriate degree of Japan's reliance on, and military cooperation with the United States under the provisions of the U.S.-Japan Mutual Security Treaty. In general, most of the scholarly treatment of Japan's defense policy has been within the larger context of foreign policy.

In contrast to some other industrialized nations, Japan has not developed a body of concepts derived from or supporting its defense policy which deserves to be called military strategy in the usually accepted sense of the word. But this was also true of the pre–World War II period, for Japan has produced no strategists of world renown. Some conventional analytical categories (for example, deterrence, force structure and doctrine) have not been applied systematically to the SDF. This may be attributed to the unique constitutional status of the SDF, the explicit denial of an offensive mission to these forces, and perhaps the fact that there is little attraction to the study of relatively small armed forces, structured defensively in a nation seemingly remote from the great strategic military questions of the day.

At the same time, political leadership in Japan, beginning in 1970, has made concerted efforts to inform the Japanese public about the content of Japan's defense policy. A primary vehicle for this effort has been the publication by the Japan Defense Agency (in 1970, 1976, 1977, and 1978) of the authoritative volume entitled *Nippon-no-boei*, also available in English as *Defense of Japan*. The 1979 version is entitled *Boei Hakusho* [Defense White Paper] (299 pages). Each volume sets forth the major facts essential to the study of Japan's defense: the official view of the international military balance and the structure of conflict in the world; the Japan-U.S. security system; the domestic environment surrounding various defense issues. These volumes have readily available data concerning budget, personnel strengths, research and development activities, disaster relief activities, joint U.S.-Japan exercises, and SDF Organization. Two series of annual publication, not available in English, contain useful data on the SDF: *Boei Nenkan* [Defense yearbook] (Tokyo: Defense Yearbook Publishing Co.) and *Jieitai Sobi Nenkan* [SDF equipment yearbook] (Tokyo: *Asagumo* Newspaper Co.). The latter also publishes the newspaper entitled *Asagumo*, designed primarily for SDF members, which contains timely information on defense matters and publishes personnel reassignments. SDF personnel are informed regularly about a variety of defense topics, including policy statements and interviews of leading officials, by means of the monthly magazine *Boei Antena* [Defense antenna] published by the Office of the Director General of the Japan Defense Agency.

The government's more active role in seeking public support for defense policy objectives has long been assisted by the work of individual scholars affiliated with general research institutes, the most prominent of which has been the Nomura Research Institute. More recently, two defense policy research institutes have been formed. Masamichi Inoki heads the Research Institute for Peace and Security in Tokyo. In late 1979, this institute began publication of an annual report entitled *Asian Security,* which was to be serialized in the Tokyo English language daily, the *Japan Times*. The Japan Center for the Study of Security Issues, headed by Hideaki Kase, actually predates the Inoki Institute by a few months. It has formed collaborative bonds with a U.S.-based think tank, and has already embarked on several ventures. The Japan Center receives substantial support from private funds, and much of its analytical strength is centered in the Kyoto Sangyo Daigaku. In contrast, the Research Institute for Peace and Security (headed by Inoki) actually receives some support through budgeted funds from the government of Japan and represents one of the new departures in defense policy studies made possible since the mid-1970s.

Fairly comprehensive and representative Japanese works on defense policy include *Nihon Boei no Shinkoso* [New structure of Japan's Defense], by military affairs commentator Kaoru Murakami (Tokyo: Saimaru Publishers, 1973), a study of the SDF fourth Five-Year Plan and the military environment in terms of an equidistant foreign policy with China and the Soviet Union; *Jieitai wa Yaku ni Tatsu ka* [Is the SDF of any use?], by retired Air Self-Defense Force colonel and staff member of the National War College Takashi Tsuchida (Tokyo: Keizaioraisha Publishers, 1975); and *Kuni wo Mamoru* [To defend the nation], by Masamichi Inoki, former Kyoto University professor and former superintendent of the Defense Academy (Tokyo: Jitsugyo no Nihonsha Publishers, 1972).

The best single work on the sources and early development of Japan's postwar defense policy is Martin Weinstein's *Japan's Postwar Defense Policy, 1947–1968* (New York: Columbia University Press, 1971). It should be supplemented by John K. Emmerson's *Arms, Yen, and Power: The Japanese Dilemma* (New York: Dunellen, 1971), and by Franz Michael and Gaston Sigur, *The Asian Alliance: Japan and United Policy* (New York: National Strategy Information Center, 1972). Three collections of essays that include Japanese contributors and deal with defense policy in the general context of Japan-U.S. relations and the security of East Asia are: James W. Morely, ed., *Forecast for Japan: Security in the 1970s* (Princeton; Princeton University Press, 1972); Priscilla Clapp and Morton Halperin, eds., *United States-Japanese Relations: The 1970s* (Cambridge, Mass.: Harvard University Press, 1974); and Franklin B. Weinstein ed., *U.S.-Japan Relations and the Security of East Asia: The Next Decade* (Boulder, Colo.: Westview Press, 1978). All of these works are scholarly in tone, soundly descriptive, and analytical. Highly critical views of Japan's defense policy are found in Albert Axelbank, *Black Star over Japan: Rising Forces of Militarism* (New York: Hill and Wang, 1972), and in Harold Hakwon Sunoo, *Japanese Militarism: Past and Present* (New York: Nelson-Hall, 1975).

Some Adelphi Papers of the International Institute for Strategic Studies (IISS) contain informative articles on Japan's defense policy, for example, Richard Ellingworth's "Japanese Economic Policies and Security," no. 90 (October 1972); Kunio Muraoka, "Japanese Security and the United States", no. 95 (February 1973); and Masataka Kosaka, "Options for Japan's Foreign Policy," no. 97 (Summer 1973). Accurate order of battle (military equipment inventory) is available from *The Military Balance* published annually by the International Institute for Strategic Studies, London.

Public views of Japan's defense and foreign policy were traced through the 1960s by Douglas Mendel in several articles in *Public Opinion Quarterly* (Fall 1959, Spring 1966, and Winter 1972–73) and in *Asian Survey* (July 1967, August 1969, and December 1970). A more recent and comprehensive appreciation is John K. Emmerson and Leonard A. Humphreys, *Will Japan Rearm? A Study in Attitudes* (Washington, D.C.: American Enterprise Institute, 1973).

The Modern Japanese Military System, ed. James H. Buck (Beverly Hills, Calif.: Sage Publications, 1974), contains rather specific essays on the Japanese military tradition (Leonard A. Humphreys), recruitment and training in the SDF (Thomas M. Brendle), the constitutionality of the SDF (Theodore McNelly), defense policy and the business community (David R. Hopper), as well as more general essays on security policy by Martin Weinstein, Gastor Sigur, Evelyn Colbert, Douglas Mendel, and the editor. The authoritative study of Japan's naval forces is James E. Auer, *The Postwar Rearmament of Japanese Martime Forces* (New York: Praeger, 1973). An appraisal of naval requirements is found in David Shilling, "A Reassessment of Japan's Defense Needs," in *Asian Survey* 16 (March 1976). A look at the future is found in Linton Wells II, "The Sea and Japan's Strategic Interests, 1975–1985" (Ph.D. diss., The Johns Hopkins University, 1975).

Nuclear weapons and Japan's defense policy are treated in depth in John E. Endicott's *Japan's Nuclear Option: Political, Technical, and Strategic Factors* (New York: Praeger, 1974). Jay B. Sorenson has dealt with the subject in *Japanese Policy and Nuclear Arms,* Monograph Series no. 12 (New York: American-Asian Education Exchange, 1975). Japan's adherence to the Nuclear Non-Proliferation Treaty has been discussed in three articles in *Asian Survey:* Daniel I. Okimoto's "Japan's Non-Nuclear Policy: The Problem of the NPT," vol. 15 (April 1975); John E. Endicott's "The 1975–76 Debate over Ratification of the NPT in Japan," vol. 17 (March 1977); and Roger W. Gale's "Nuclear Power and Japan's Proliferation Option,'' vol. 18 (November 1978). A more recent treatment criticizing nonproliferation efforts is Ryukichi Imai, ''Non-Proliferation: A Japanese Point of View,'' in *Survival* (London: International Institute for Strategic Studies, March–April 1979). Japanese opinions on nuclear arms and a series of intriguing scenarios that might lead to a Japanese decision to develop nuclear weapons are outlined in Herbert Passin, ''Nuclear Arms and Japan,'' in *Asia's Nuclear Future,* ed. William H. Overholt (Boulder, Colo.: Westview Press, 1977).

Civil-military relations has virtually been ignored, with the exception of James H. Buck, ''Civilian Control of the Military in Japan,'' in *Civilian Control of the Military: Theory and Cases from Developing Countries,* ed. Claude E. Welch (Albany: State University of New York Press, 1976). This essay examines the origins and development of Japan's civil-military relations in the light of internal and external influences for the years 1870–90 and 1945–70.

Recent South Korean-Japanese relations are summarized in Hong N. Kim's ''Japanese-South Korean Relations in the Post-Vietnam Era,'' *Asian Survey* 16 (October 1976). Also in *Asian Survey,* Nathan White focuses on ''Japan's Security Interests in Korea,'' vol. 16 (April 1976). James H. Buck has written ''The Role of Korea in Japanese Defense Policy,'' *Asian Affairs: An American Review* (March–April 1977).

As the mission, force structure, and size of the SDF has changed little in the past twenty-five years, so also has there been little enlargement of the scope of writing and debate about the SDF. However, the latter seems to be changing. The mid-1978 resignation of General Hiroomi Kurisu, chairman of the Joint Staff Council, seems to have sparked a serious debate about the readiness of the SDF, about command and control, and about U.S.-Japan military cooperation (see Hiroomi Kurisu, ''Japan: The New Defense Debate,'' *Defense and Foreign Affairs Digest* 6, no. 10 [1978]: 32–33). This development is described in Henry Scott-Stokes's lengthy article in the *New York Times Magazine,* 11 February 1979, entitled ''It's All Right to Talk Defense Again in Japan.'' Important current considerations of Japan's defense policy are [cogently] portrayed by Michael Pillsbury in ''A Japanese Card?,'' *Foreign Policy,* 33 (Winter 1978/79).

The political framework of Japan's defense

Hisahiko Okazaki

Japanese public opinion on defense issues has undergone significant changes in the past twenty-five years. In a short-term analysis at any point in this period, the change has always been slow and subtle, and not without fluctuations. After this quarter century, however, the change has become clearly visible; the idealistic pacifism of the early postwar years has been gradually replaced by more realistic ways of thinking. In addition, Marxist-Leninist ideas, which once exercised an overwhelming influence on intellectuals in Japan, just as in many other countries in the early postwar period, have declined, and have been replaced by a middle-class status quo mind-set in the area of politics and by Keynesian theories in the field of economics.

However, it would definitely be premature to expect further radical change in Japanese attitudes toward defense issues in the foreseeable future, simply extrapolating this tendency into the coming years. It would also be erroneous to suppose that the political framework and setting of the defense debate in Japan are changing parallel to, or keeping pace with, changes in public opinion.

For example, in a public opinion poll of February 1979, 86 percent supported the existence of the Japanese Self-Defense Forces (JSDF) and only 5 percent were against it. When these figures are compared with the percentage of seats held by the different political parties in the Japanese Diet, this lack of parallelism is obvious. The governing Liberal Democratic party, the Democratic Socialist party, and the New Liberal Club definitely support the existence of the JSDF. Counting the Komeito (Clean Government party) as a supporter of the JSDF, 68.8 percent of the House of Representatives and 67 percent of the House of Councillors support the SDF. The Socialist party and the Communist party, which are opposed to the existence of the JSDF, hold 26.4 percent of the seats in the House of Representatives and 27.3 percent in the House of Councillors.

This discrepancy, in spite of the fact that the defense issue is one of the major dividing lines between these parties, is the product of complex psychological factors and equally complex social and political circumstances. Any tendency toward a narrowing of this discrepancy would probably be a long and complex process.

THE CONSTITUTION

The most important of all the political factors relevant to Japanese defense issues is undoubtedly the Japanese Constitution, enacted on 3 November 1946 during the occupation period. While realistic interpretations of the Constitution have gradually been established, it is necessary in any study of Japanese defense issues to bear in mind that the Constitution continues to be the central issue in the Japanese defense debate. The preamble to the Constitution says:

> We, the Japanese people, desire peace for all time and are deeply conscious of the high ideals controlling human relationship, and we have determined to preserve our security and existence, trusting in the justice and faith of the peace-loving peoples of the world.

As its most striking manifestation of this philosophy, the Constitution has article 9, which is unique in its approach to the questions of peace and war.

> Article 9. Aspiring sincerely to an international peace based on justice and order, the Japanese people forever renounce war as a sovereign right of the nation and the threat or use of force as means of settling international disputes.
>
> In order to accomplish the aim of the preceding paragraph, land, sea and air forces, as well as other war potential, will never be maintained. The right of belligerency of the state will not be recognized.

Unrealistic as they may appear to foreign students of international affairs today, these paragraphs reflect a way of thinking that was undoubtedly prevalent in that period.

Japan surrendered, accepting the Potsdam Proclamation of 26 June 1945, which defined the terms for the Japanese surrender as follows:

> . . . we insist that a new order of peace, security and justice will be impossible until irresponsible militarism is driven from the world. . . . Until such a new order is established and until there is convincing proof that Japan's war-making power is destroyed, . . . Japanese territory . . . shall be occupied to secure the achievement of the basic objectives we are here setting forth.

The occupation authorities adhered strictly to this policy in Japan in the very early stages of the occupation—to be more accurate, until it became clear that a cold war was inevitable.

Concurrently there existed high expectations, short lived though they were, concerning the role of the United Nations in maintaining the peace and security of the world. On 26 June 1945, exactly one month before the Potsdam Proclamation, the United Nations Charter was signed, constituting another proclamation of the postwar policy of the allied forces. The charter begins with the words:

> We, the peoples of the United Nations, determined to save succeeding generations from the scourge of war, which twice in our lifetime has brought untold sorrow to mankind . . . to ensure, by the acceptance of principles and institutions of methods, that armed forces shall not be used, save in the common interest.

It should be noted that the Japan-U.S. Security Treaty of 1951 states in article 4 that:

> This Treaty shall expire whenever in the opinion of the Governments of Japan and the U.S.A. there shall have come into force such United Nations arrangements . . . as will satisfactorily provide for the maintenance of international peace and security in the Japan area.

In these two documents, the Potsdam Proclamation and the United Nations Charter, we can see the two basic concepts of the Constitution. They are "no war potential" and "to preserve our security and existence, trusting in the justice and faith of the peace-loving peoples of the world." It is, moreover, not difficult to imagine the strong popular support for antiwar, absolute pacifist idealism in Japan, when one considers the miseries that followed the war and the defeat.

THE DEFENSE DEBATE

An immediate and obvious question arising out of article 9 of the Constitution is: "It is all right to hope to live in peace, but what shall we do if we are attacked in spite of all our peaceful efforts?" Practically all the defense controversies in postwar Japan originate from this question. A doctrinaire interpretation of the article produced the policy of unarmed neutrality, which is still the banner held by the Japan Socialist party, the second largest party in the Diet. Those advocating this course usually assume that war is unthinkable and can be avoided by peaceful means. When asked about the case where the "unthinkable" becomes a reality, their reply has to be "no military resistance." Another logical answer, though, is revision of the Constitution, which has always been part of the party program of the governing Liberal Democratic party.

The political circumstances surrounding Japan changed rapidly. The Korean War broke out on 25 June 1950, and in less than two weeks the occupation authorities ordered the establishment of a 75,000-man National Police Reserve, which later evolved into the present JSDF.

The Japan-U.S. Security Treaty was signed on 8 September 1951, on the same day as the peace treaty. The preamble to the Security Treaty is one of the most clear-cut and concise expressions of the Japanese defense policy line followed thereafter.

> . . . On the coming into force of that [Peace] Treaty, Japan will not have the effective means to exercise its inherent right of self-defense because it has been disarmed.
>
> There is danger to Japan in this situation because irresponsible militarism has not yet been driven from the world. Therefore Japan desires a Security Treaty with the U.S.A. . . .
>
> The Treaty of Peace recognizes that Japan as a sovereign nation has the right to enter into collective security arrangements, and further, the Charter of the United Nations recognizes that all nations possess an inherent right of individual and collective self-defense.
>
> In exercise of these rights, Japan desires, as a provisional arrangement for its defense, that the U.S.A. should maintain armed forces of its own in and about Japan so as to deter armed attack upon Japan.
>
> The United States of America, in the interest of peace and security, is presently willing to maintain certain of its armed forces in and about Japan, in the expectation, however, that Japan will itself increasingly assume responsibility for its own defense against direct and indirect aggression, always avoiding any armament which could be of an offensive threat.

The treaty was revised in 1960, when this explanatory preamble was deleted. However, the basic framework of Japanese defense thinking changed little; it continued to be that the United States would deter armed attack upon Japan and Japan would increasingly assume a defense responsibility, though always avoiding any armament that could constitute an offensive threat. Ever since then, the clearest line dividing government and opposition has been their positions on the Japan-U.S. Security Treaty and the JSDF.

While there has never existed any consensus between the government and opposition parties in the interpretation of the political situation, the judiciary has on occasion had to give decisions in cases involving the question of the legality of the JSDF. There have, in fact, been a number of important court decisions in the last few years concerning the legality of the JSDF, always after deliberation spanning many years (in the case of the Hyakuri Base Suit, more than twenty years). These decisions have certainly contributed to the change in public opinion favorable to the JSDF in the last few years.

In a Sapporo High Court appeal ruling of 5 August 1976 on the "Naganuma Incident," the High Court said that the organization, formation, and equipment of the SDF cannot be said, as was claimed by Naganuma residents, to be of an "apparently and clearly aggressive nature." "Whether the existence and other aspects of the SDF are compatible with Article 9 of the Constitution is a judgement related to sovereign act, and, as a political act of the Diet and Cabinet, it should be entrusted ultimately to the people as a whole for their political judgement. It is interpreted that the court cannot rule on this matter."

The Mito District Court ruling of 17 February 1977 on the "Hyakuri Air Base Suit" sets out a more elaborate and extensive argument.

(1) As an independent nation, Japan has an inherent right of self-defense, and if confronted by sudden and unjust external aggression, may resort to force in its own defense in order to thwart or eliminate such infringement. The first paragraph of Article 9 of the Constitution renounces war as sovereign right of the nation and the threat of use of force only when used as a means of settling international disputes. This paragraph is not to be interpreted as meaning that Japan has renounced war even as a means of achieving self-defense.

(2) It is appropriate to interpret the "aim of the preceding paragraph" in the first sentence of the second paragraph of Article 9, as referring to the prohibition of all war potential that can serve for an aggressive war or for the threat or use of force. . . .

(3) Accordingly, it would not be a violation of the Preamble and Article 9 of the Constitution for Japan to organize and maintain effective and appropriate measures to the extent necessary for national self-defense.

(4) The defense issues of a nation are issues that concern the foundation of the nation's existence. . . . Policy decisions as to the size of the organized force with Japan may maintain for exercising the right of self-defense are matters to be determined on the basis of comprehensive study of the changing international environment, the current international situation, scientific and technological development and other factors and the outlook for the future, and this necessarily requires expert political and technological judgement of a high order.

(5) Deliberation on matters of this type is, in principle, not a task for a court of law. . . . Nevertheless, it cannot be said that the existence of the SDF, including their purpose, organization, formation, equipment and characteristics, apparently and clearly constitutes the "war potential" referred to in the second paragraph of Article 9 of the Constitution. All the evidence examined by this court does not allow the court to conclude that the SDF constitutes apparent and clear war potential.

The legal arguments on the constitutionality of the SDF have by no means ended. In fact, the defendants are dissatisfied with the ruling on the Hyakuri Base Suit and have appealed to the Tokyo High Court, and we may expect a long, continuing legal argument that might possibly go up to the Supreme Court. Nevertheless, we can assume that, in the absence of a ruling to the contrary and considering the general atmosphere of public acceptance of the SDF, the legal arguments have also reached a point at which the right of self-defense and the existence of the SDF are accepted as constitutional.

LIMITS TO SDF CAPABILITIES

It can be seen in the above court rulings that although the courts declined to consider the existing SDFs to be unconstitutional, they maintained the position that their constitutionality is a matter of the scale, equipment, and capabilities of the SDF. This is not at all a new point. In fact, whether the particular weapons, etc., involved are within the limits of a capability of a defensive character, narrowly interpreted—in other words, not of an aggressive or offensive nature—has always been the central issue when debating any new addition to SDF capability. The government has always sought to show that the particular capability increase is necessary to maintain the minimum defensive SDF capability and is not of an aggressive or offensive character.

As a result of these Diet explanations given by the government, Japan's defense has come to be subject to many self-imposed restrictions. These restrictions range from matters that are considered to be directly related to interpretation of the Constitution to those that are no more than a reflection of general pacifist ideas and are only slightly related to the Constitution.

Some of these self-imposed restrictions have come to be regarded as quasi-constitutional prohibitions. Although they are, strictly speaking, no more than quasi-juridical restrictions, since the courts refuse to make any authoritative judgments, they have come to be regarded as de facto constitutional prohibitions through the following process. The government is obliged by opposition parties to express its opinion to the Diet that the particular weapon or activity involved would not be a violation of the Constitution. The criteria of employment, successfully advanced by the government in such debates, and repeated by the government in many sessions over a long period of time, tend to become, in effect, sacrosanct restrictive criteria that must be satisfied.

One such restriction is the prohibition of dispatch overseas of the SDF; there is a resolution adopted by the House of Councillors in 1954 which gives greater moral authority to the government's position previously reiterated on a number of occasions in the Diet.* Cooperation in U.N. peace-keeping activities by dispatching SDF members for noncombatant purposes is not considered by the government to be prohibited under the constitution. However, it would, in practice, be necessary to revise the relevant law if the SDF were going to be used for this purpose. The laws concerning the SDF are worded in such a restrictive manner that it was necessary to revise laws and broaden the scope of the activities of the SDF in order to enable SDF personnel to participate in Olympic Games overseas and for SDF personnel to transport Antarctic expedition teams in an SDF ice-breaker.

The concept of collective self-defense is also a highly constitutional issue. Under the United Nations Charter, Japan has the right of collective and individual self-defense. However, it is considered to be unconstitutional to go to the aid of an allied country with the armed forces of the SDF when Japan itself has not yet been attacked. This point is noteworthy, since there have been various unofficial suggestions by foreign politicians and scholars for revising U.S.-Japanese security arrangements, modeling them on those of NATO.

Some types of weapons have come to be regarded as unconstitutional in the course of Diet debate. Since such strategic weapons as ICBMs or B-52-type long-range bombers have the capability of devastating an adversary country, they are considered to exceed the purpose of self-defense. Of course, as even the opposition parties point out, it is difficult to draw a clear line between a defensive weapon and an offensive weapon. A good example is the arguments advanced in connection with the proposed purchase of interceptors, F-4 Phantoms, and F-15 Eagles. When Japan purchased F-4s, the government decided to strip them of their air refuel systems and air-to-ground attack capability in order to limit the capability of the aircraft to a strictly interceptor role. In the case of the proposed purchase of F-15s, the government has not felt obliged to do the same. Of course, there has been a change in the public's attitude and increasing political consciousness of the need for defense, but the explanation given by the government was that even with such equipment F-15s cannot be used for other than defensive purposes.

NUCLEAR INHIBITION

Another characteristic of postwar Japanese defense thinking is an aversion to anything nuclear. The origin of this widespread feeling is, of course, the unique experience of Hiroshima and Nagasaki, combined with the experience of the harm done to Japanese fishermen by the nuclear testing on Bikini Island. Also, there may still be, in some leftist thinking, a residual effect of the antinuclear "peace offensive" in the very early stages of the Cold War, when the Soviet Union had a very limited nuclear capability.

The government does not take the view that nuclear questions are necessarily constitutional issues, for the reason that some types of nuclear weapons can be used only for defensive purposes. Nevertheless, in view of this deep-rooted public aversion to anything nuclear, the government has imposed a number of restrictions on the use of nuclear energy.

One example of such self-imposed restrictions is the "three nonnuclear principles," which evolved in Diet debates and were subsequently formalized in a resolution adopted by the House of Representatives in 1971. The three principles consist of neither producing nor possessing nuclear weapons in Japan, nor introducing them into Japan.

Another restriction is the principle set out in the Fundamental Law on Nuclear Energy, which restricts the use of nuclear energy exclusively to peaceful purposes. Japan also ratified the Nuclear Nonproliferation Treaty in 1976. The first two of the three nonnuclear principles are thus enshrined in both the Fundamental Law on Nuclear Energy and the obligation under the Nonproliferation Treaty.

The third principle—not introducing nuclear weapons into Japan—is more controversial. It is not denied that the inability of the U.S. forces to bring nuclear weapons into Japan might, to some extent, constitute a constraint on its ability to extend the nuclear umbrella over Japan and defend the common interest of the two countries in the Far East. This question, however, should be considered within a larger political perspective, of which the following two factors are part: (1) the United States has other means of extending an effective nuclear umbrella over Japan and operating effectively for the common interest; and (2) the mutual trust between Japan and the United States is the main pillar supporting the U.S.-Japanese security relationship, and U.S. understanding of the Japanese people's feelings about nuclear matters, which are not at all unnatural in the wake of Japan's unique nuclear experience, will certainly increase that mutual trust.

ARMS TRANSFER

The question of the transfer of arms to foreign countries is not treated as a defense matter in Japan, and policy in this regard is decided by the Ministry of International Trade and Industry in consultation with the Ministry of Foreign Affairs. However, it may be worth touching upon this question, as it is one of the topics very often raised when foreign students of Japanese defense matters seek to explore what kind of regional defense role Japan could play, independent of other constraints such as the prohibition on overseas dispatch of the SDF.

Here again, the Japanese attitude is strict. Japan long maintained a policy of prohibiting the export of arms to (1) Communist countries, (2) countries under U.N. resolution arms embargo, and (3) countries involved or likely to be involved in the international conflicts. These restrictions were tightened in 1976 with a Diet statement of the formal view of the government so that (1) arms exports to the above three areas were banned, (2) the export of arms to other areas should also be refrained from, and (3) the same restrictions would apply to plants for the production of arms.

Almost the sole reason for these self-imposed restrictions, which certainly adversely affect the interests

*Overseas dispatch means here the dispatch of armed personnel for the purpose of the use of force.

of a part of Japan's heavy industry, is the manifestation of a "pacifist posture," which may seem strange to foreigners accustomed to think of Japan as an "economic animal." There are mixed foreign reactions to this policy. Some potential competitors for arms exports are not at all displeased with this policy and hope for the continuation of it. Some countries are disappointed by the unavailability of certain military equipment from Japan, which, for various reasons, they consider the most convenient place to obtain it. Some are irritated by Japan's reluctance to assume a larger role in regional security, while some consider it to be a wise policy, one enabling Japan to avoid involvement in international conflicts.

THE NATIONAL DEFENSE PROGRAM OUTLINE

The year 1976 was marked by two other important policy decisions concerning Japanese defense: the adoption of the National Defense Program Outline and the decision to keep the defense budget within 1 percent of the GNP for the time being.

The National Defense Program Outline was a kind of "new look" for Japanese defense planning. Since 1958 the JSDF had been built up in accordance with one three-year plan (FY 1958–60) and three successive five-year plans (FY 1962–66, 1967–71, 1972–76). These build-up plans produced a 180,000-man Ground SDF, a 4-escort flotilla Maritime SDF, and a 17-squadron Air SDF. The outline took the position that the SDF had reached approximately the size that was sufficient for the nation's defense in the prevailing international environment, and stressed, above all, the need for qualitative improvement, in both organization and equipment.

The thinking underlying this new policy was set forth at length in the Official Explanatory Note. According to this note, the principal reasons for arriving at the outline's conclusions are as follows: (1) public pressure demanding that the government set a clear target, or limit, for the defense build-up; (2) the existing imbalance between the fighting units and the rear support capabilities; and (3) the financial problem, including the shift in the Japanese economy away from high growth, sharp increases in the price of up-to-date equipment following the oil crisis, and difficulties in obtaining sufficient personnel and land for further expansion of size.

The outline, shaped principally by the above domestic motives, adopts the position that a large-scale invasion is not likely to take place in the prevailing international circumstances. From this follows the conclusion that the present size of the SDF is adequate.

The 1 percent limit was not, in fact, a part of the outline, but was decided a week later in the same circumstances. The adoption as late as 1976 of the outline and the 1 percent limit may seem curious to foreign observers, with the increasing support among the Japanese people for national defense and with other free world countries increasingly calling for a larger Japanese defense role. If one recalls, however, the mood prevailing in the first half of the 1970s, when détente seemed to be the wave of the future, and the financial state of affairs throughout the free world after the oil crisis, the motives and rationale of the outline may not appear so surprising.

Furthermore, there is still a long way to go to achieve the qualitative improvement of the SDF envisioned by the outline, and even to reach the 1 percent ceiling. For practical purposes, therefore, neither the outline nor the 1 percent limit will interfere with Japan's efforts to strengthen its defense in the near future.

THE DEFENSE GUIDELINES

Meanwhile, another new development that may have a far-reaching effect on Japanese defense has been taking place. As a result of the summit meeting between Prime Minister Miki and President Ford in 1975, a Japan-U.S. joint undertaking was initiated to produce draft guidelines for Japan-U.S. defense cooperation; these guidelines were adopted by the Japan-U.S. Security Consultative Committee and then approved by the Japanese Cabinet on 28 November 1978. Following the Cabinet's approval, the minister of state for defense ordered joint work to start under the guidelines.

Since the end of the occupation, Japan-U.S. cooperation under the Japan-U.S. Security Treaty has been one of the two pillars of Japanese defense, the other being the JSDF. Since Japan's military capability is strictly for defensive purposes, the Japan-U.S. security system is absolutely essential to deter aggression directed against Japan.

Although the purpose of the joint work is limited to studies, with neither government being under any obligation to implement the conclusions reached, the results of such study will certainly help each party to understand how the other sees the defense of Japan and to identify what will be necessary to achieve the common purpose in this region. This will constitute valuable progress, since in the past no consultations were conducted on the details of joint measures to be taken in the case of an armed attack on Japan.

SUMMARY AND FUTURE OUTLOOK

The political framework of the defense debate in Japan has a history originating in the defeat, the occupation, and the peace treaty; it has changed little in its basic concepts in the past quarter century. The pacifist ideal is still a guiding principle of Japanese politics. The Socialists, who still bear the banner of unarmed neutrality, do everything they can to curb any government move that appears to them to depart from the pacifist principles of the Constitution. The SDF has to be the "minimum size" necessary for self-defense. Although the word "minimum" is flexible enough to mean "of a strength matching any possible threat," it is, nevertheless, effective in checking the growth of the size and budget of the SDF.

In sum, Japanese defense is institutionally wedded to the Japan-U.S. Security Treaty. Looked at through the eyes of the average foreigner, Japanese defense is bound to appear limited, both in its size and in the scope of its activity; further, it is framed to be dependent on American support. There may be a more euphemistic way of describing it, but one has to admit that this view is essentially correct; I would prefer straightforward recognition of the facts to any unrealistic dream of "autonomous defense." After all, no country, except the United States and USSR, and perhaps China, has a truly autonomous defense today.

What will be the future of this built-in political framework of Japanese defense thinking? It is always risky to make predictions, but the odds are that there will be little change, or, at most, a change which has to be extremely slow. I assume this "immobilism" not because of the so-called Japanese pacifist psychology, the "peace-loving aspirations of the Japanese people," or any "sacred inviolability of the Constitution," which have been used so many times to explain this immobilism. Rather, I would give the following three reasons: (1) a middle-class status quo mind-set; (2) political, financial, and bureaucratic inertia; and (3) the geographical situation of Japan.

In every recent poll, more than 80 percent of the Japanese population describe themselves as middle class. This figure shows the remarkable stability of Japanese society. Furthermore, the Japanese middle class is different from that in Western societies in that they are heartily proud and satisfied to be middle class. The traditional simplicity of the Japanese life style means that people can feel satisfied as long as they have permanent jobs, even without material assets other than a television set and a refrigerator, and this gives them a sense of belonging to the middle class.

It is not at all difficult to imagine that such a society will be status quo minded. People accept the existence of the SDF at its present size and with its present function. They see no reason to demand changes, including expansion of the size of the SDF, and they would be reluctant to accept changes, unless they were forced to do so by outside circumstances. The public poll shows that 54 percent approve of the present size, 22 percent are for an increase, and 6 percent are for a reduction in size.

The existing political or financial inertia is partly a corollary of the above social situation. The treasury and the Diet are accustomed to spending only a small percent of the budget on defense. In the annual budget negotiations it is incredibly difficult for any ministry, not only the Defense Agency by any means, to increase its share of the budget by even 1 percent. As long as the people do not want a drastic change, politicians will not press for one either. Also, the nature of Japanese Diet debate tends to produce this immobilism. Government policy is always expressed in a very carefully phrased way. The opposition or the press never fails to question any new wording, creating an issue. Any expression, particularly one with a restrictive implication, once uttered in the Diet is likely to stay as an official government position and to eventually join the family of built-in restrictions.

Japan's geographic situation helps to maintain these attitudes in the Japanese nation and politics. Japan is an island country, and has exprerienced only two invasions in its history. The first was by a Mongolian invasion force, which was destroyed at sea by a typhoon and did not actually reach the Japanese islands. The second, the American invasion, would not have happened if Japan had not started the war first. In the postwar period, the U.S. deterrent force has always been effective; furthermore, the Republic of Korea has functioned as a buffer. These circumstances clearly do not give the Japanese people any great sense of urgency concerning an increase of its defense capability.

What would be possible motivations for further change? Specialists in the areas of Japanese politics and history have pointed out that all major changes in the Japanese political framework have come as a result of stimulus from abroad. The scenario that has been suggested most often is one where the southern part of the Korean Peninsula is overrun by Communist forces. That scenario is unlikely to materialize. A growing Soviet military build-up around Japan, a rumored American withdrawal from Asia, or an American demand that Japan increase its share of defense responsibilities is also given as possible outside stimuli that might push Japanese public opinion in the direction of a bigger defense capability. These stimuli would certainly have a substantial impact on Japanese public opinion, but the impact would not, by the nature of the stimuli, come in a drastic way and, therefore, would take time to produce any significant changes in the Japanese political framework concerning defense.

Undoubtedly there have been changes. Japanese public opinion increasingly supports the existence of the SDF and the Japan-U.S. Security Treaty. The annual budget of the SDF has grown to ten billion dollars, which makes Japan the ninth largest military power in the world in terms of expenditure. And this budget is steadily increasing, in parallel with the growth of the GNP, which is around 6 percent annually. This means that the Japanese defense budget growth is greater than the estimated 5 percent growth of the defense budget of the Soviet Union and the target of 3 percent growth the NATO countries have agreed to maintain. The joint study under the guidelines has begun and thus there will be closer ties for cooperation between the JSDF and the U.S. forces.

Nevertheless, it is always prudent for any strategist or scholar in the area of international affairs to assume that Japan will change very slowly and to build his strategy or theory on that premise. Barring some cataclysm, such as an economic crisis that threatens the stability of the entire middle class of Japan or the approach of a war, Japan and the JSDF will probably stay much as they are now, though with steady but slow amelioration.

Part six

CONCLUDING PERSPECTIVE

DEFENSE POLICY IN COMPARATIVE PERSPECTIVE: A CONCLUSION

Douglas J. Murray and Paul R. Viotti

Within the discipline of political science the comparative study of defense policy is an emerging subfield of study similar in many ways to another subfield, comparative foreign policy.[1] Comparative defense policy cuts across such traditional divisions as international politics and economics, public policy and administration, domestic politics and economics, and comparative political and economic systems. The purpose of this book is to contribute to the development of this subfield by constructing a framework within which to study the defense policy of a given state. Accordingly, the core of this work is the collection of individual country chapters. Our aim in this concluding chapter is neither to summarize those chapters nor to develop a comprehensive theory of comparative defense policy. Rather, by combining what has been written in this volume with comments made earlier in an informal conference of our authors, we hope to illuminate some of the conceptual issues related to this new field and thus create a better foundation for theory development.

The international environment

The comparative study of defense policy begins with the study of the international political system. Indeed, the study of the national security policy of any given state must originate with an examination of the international context within which the state, its bureaucratic agencies, and its decision makers are immersed. The absence of superordinate authority or world government that would maintain order among states gives rise to a security dilemma with which all states must cope. Although survival of the state is by no means the only objective states seek, this concern with national security is common to all. In a world of states that claim to be sovereign entities, there is no global authority that would provide security. Accordingly, given national security objectives, states formulate their own defense policies, attempting to develop the necessary strategies, doctrines, and force postures (which are discussed in part two of each country study chapter).

STRUCTURAL CONSIDERATIONS

One of the most important conceptual issues at the international level of analysis is the extent to which the external environment or international system determines (or constrains) the policy choices made by the decision makers of states. Certainly, international level considerations cannot be ignored. The relations between the superpowers, for example, affect the security calculations of the other states. Kenneth Waltz refers to this condition as the bipolar structure of the contemporary international system. If by *structure* we mean the distribution (or concentration) of capabilities or power within the global system, then a strong case can be made for bipolarity. In this regard, Waltz is quick to note that to say the world is *bipolar* is not to say that the superpowers *control* the policies of other states; it is only to say that, given their relative power positions, the United States and the Soviet Union pursue policies that have pervasive *influence*. These policies cannot be ignored.

Stanley Hoffmann, by contrast, argues that the world is asymmetrically multipolar. Central to his thesis is the view that power calculations vary from issue to issue. Thus, in such nonsecurity issues as international trade and monetary relations, he sees the world as decidedly multipolar. But even Hoffmann agrees with Waltz that in security or "strategic" relations the bipolar description applies. Although both would appear to agree on this point, Waltz rejects attempts by Hoffmann and others to disaggregate the concept of power. The classic view, expressed most clearly by E. H. Carr,[2] is that power is an integrity: it cannot be divided. Given linkages among issues, the attempt to separate the military, economic, and other components of power is artificial at best. Indeed, those who hold this view that power is an integrity observe that relations within the European Economic Community cannot be separated from the fact that these relations occur under a security umbrella tied to one of the superpowers. Similarly, seen from this perspective, the attempt to view the economic relations of East European countries as separate from the security relations these countries have with the other superpower is misleading.

In any event, few would disagree with the contention that policies pursued by the superpowers and relations between them affect the defense policy choices of other states; their impact is far greater than that of most lesser powers that have regional rather than global scope. Accordingly, given their relative importance, the defense policies of the United States and the Soviet Union are treated at length in Part Two of this volume.

As a reading of the Korb and Warner articles makes clear, the policies of the other superpower are a principal concern of both the United States and the Soviet Union. This is not an exclusive focus, of course. Both countries are also concerned with alliance management and threats posed by other countries. For example, the Soviet Union keeps a close eye on China, the European states (especially West Germany), and the countries of the Middle East and South Asia on the periphery of the USSR.

Some writers, however, object to bipolar and most multipolar conceptions of structure as oversimplifications that ignore the effect of such factors as the resource dependency of northern hemisphere countries upon those of the "South"—the less industrially developed states of the southern hemisphere or the "Third World." They point out, for example, that, when acting in concert, states belonging to the Organization of Petroleum Exporting Countries (OPEC) can assert considerable leverage over states dependent on them as a source of oil and natural gas. Resource availability is not just an economic issue. Indeed, national security depends upon maintenance of either domestic or external sources of petroleum and other mineral resources.

From this perspective, the Third World is more than just an arena or stage upon which superpower and other great power relations are played; structural images must certainly capture the systemic role played by Third World countries. Because bipolar and multipolar images as they are now represented tend to have an East-West focus, critics argue that structural images used by students of international relations should be made more sensitive to North-South considerations.

POWER: INTERDEPENDENCE AND PERCEPTIONS AS MODERATING FACTORS

Having noted the importance of power and its distribution as factors that affect defense policy choices, one must also acknowledge the limits of power as an explanatory variable. Neither superpower has the power to impose its designs on the other. But even in their relations with other states, the superpowers moderate their relative positions by their degree of dependency or interdependency.[3] For example, given the superpower status of the United States, one would expect American-Canadian relations to be dominated by the United States. In fact, Canada exercises considerable autonomy in its international relations concerning both security and nonsecurity questions. That Canada is not totally dependent on the United States in these issues contributes to the country's policy independence. Even in security matters, Canada is able to pursue a more independent path than one would otherwise suppose. In North American air defense, for example, Ottawa can be sure that the United States will provide for its own defense, even if Canada chooses not to participate in the arrangement.

Washington can be expected to make expenditures for North American air defense with or without Canadian contributions. Given this situation, it is the

United States that becomes somewhat dependent on Canada for its continuing contribution to the common effort—a contribution measured not only in dollar expenditures but also in terms of radar sites and associated communications nets that Canada's geographic location offers. In short, dependency by one party equates to some degree of leverage for the other party quite apart from "objective" power calculations.

Assuming that states are the principal actors, *sensitivity* interdependence addresses the external effects on other states of actions taken by a given state or group of states. Beyond mere sensitivity is the degree of *vulnerability* of various states to the actions of other states. One criticism of this state-centric approach to defining interdependence is that it does not take direct account of such *transnational* actors as multinational corporations, which operate across the boundaries of individual states. The same criticisms can, of course, be directed against this volume, given the country-study approach followed here.

In any event, there is no consensus among scholars as to whether global interdependence (however defined) is increasing, decreasing, or remaining substantially the same.[4] Even more contentious is the question of whether increasing interdependence is conducive to peace. That rising interdependence is associated with peace is certainly the common wisdom deeply set in the Western liberal tradition, but this causal relation has been challenged. Indeed, closer association of states may result in a higher probability of conflicts that could lead to war; from this perspective isolation from other states—an autarkic position—is the best posture for avoiding conflicts that lead to war.[5] On the other hand, those who believe that interdependence promotes peace argue that ties of mutual dependency make these relations too costly to break and thus make war less likely. Indeed, there are opportunity costs associated with breaking relations.

The power of states (usually defined as the capacity to influence) would also seem to be moderated by such factors as national will. Indeed, some scholars have considered power to be a multiplicative function such that power is the product of perceived will (or credibility) and capability. For example, as either credibility or capability decline, the overall power of the state is similarly reduced. From this perspective, the subjective dimension of perceptions is at least as important as "objective" calculations of capability.[6] Furthermore, it is argued that even the capabilities factor is moderated by perceptions.

SELF-PERCEPTIONS OF ROLE: OPPORTUNITIES AND THREATS

Although a common focus in security policy studies is on threats and threat perceptions, note should also be taken of the obverse side of the same security coin: perceived opportunities the state may wish to pursue.[7] Indeed, policy makers may see little or nothing within the international environment that would obstruct or otherwise impede the attainment of certain goals. To the contrary, other actors may be supportive of these purposes and be willing to collaborate in a common effort to achieve collective goals.

Decision makers hold certain images of the role their states should play internationally. A substantial change in power position relative to other states inevitably alters these perceptions; however, there is sometimes a considerable lag between changes in the "objective" situation and "subjective" realization (and acceptance) of a new role.

Britain is a classic case in point. As the Greenwood and Jefferies (budgetary) articles make clear, Britain attempted to retain its global position in the years immediately following World War II, and even developed its own strategic nuclear force. At most a middle power, however, Britain was finally forced to reduce its overseas commitments, withdrawing from east of Suez. No longer a global power, the United Kingdom has retained its close security linkage with the United States, but now has a Eurocentric security focus.

The French self-perception of its international role during and subsequent to the Gaullist period has been far greater than the country's capabilities as a middle power would immediately suggest. Alan Sabrosky notes the French attention to developing an independent nuclear force, maintaining its European-based forces under French national control, and retaining the conventional capability for selective intervention in Africa and the Middle East. Thus, France's relative position has been influenced by its self-image but constrained or moderated by its actual capabilities. In short, as illustrated by the British and French cases, the relative international power position of a given state is a function of both objective and subjective factors.

For its part, the middle rank position of the Federal Republic of Germany is further limited by the countries that occupied Germany following World War II. Nuclear weapons stationed on West German soil, for example, are under foreign control. Although the FRG contributes substantially to NATO defense in terms of both committed manpower and financial support, the country's offensive capability is severely constrained. Certainly division of the country between East and West and the continuing presence of allied troops are continuing reminders that very real external constraints on Germany's military role persist. Nevertheless, the FRG now has the strongest economy in Europe and, for that matter, also maintains the largest European ground force commitment to the NATO alliance. As both Catherine Kelleher and the late Hans Morgenthau point out, the FRG remains firmly committed to the West for security, but the thought-provoking possibility that Germany might one day turn again toward the East is explored in Morgenthau's article.

Japan is another middle power subject to constraints on its military capabilities. Like the FRG, Japan has accepted a lesser military posture while embracing a significant economic role. In the Japanese case, as John Endicott observes, defense expenditures have been limited by domestic preference to about 1 percent of the GNP. Indeed, it can be argued that reliance upon the American security umbrella has resulted in defense cost savings that would have made possible the large-scale aggregate investment of national resources in Japanese industry. It is also true, of course, that the United States benefits from the security relation with Japan. In addition to its contribution to regional stability, the United States derives considerable leverage from the Japanese security dependency that is linked not just to security issues but also to the entire range of socioeconomic and other nonsecurity issues that constitute the substance of Japanese-American relations. The converse, of course, is also true.

As becomes clear from reading William Heaton's article, the Chinese perceive themselves as part of the Third World. Although the military sector is one of the "four modernizations," the other three—agriculture, industry, and science and technology—have even higher priority in Chinese planning. Improvement in China's defense capabilities will undoubtedly occur, but there is little prospect that the country will be anything more than a regional power during the remainder of this century. Even in regional terms, the very real limits to China's capacity for using force were demonstrated in the "punitive" intervention in Vietnam and the attempt to influence events in Cambodia in the late 1970s. Although the possession of nuclear weapons and ICBMs will pose a continuing threat to other countries (notably the Soviet Union), mere possession of such a capability by no means confers great power or superpower status on China. Waltz makes this case very strongly in his essay. Even though the country has unquestioned potential, both militarily and economically, China will likely remain a middle power for the foreseeable future.

Among the ranks of lesser powers considered in this volume are Sweden, Romania, and Israel. The bases of Swedish neutrality are explored by William Taylor in the context of security in the northern "theater." Aside from traditional Swedish grounds to support such a policy, Finland serves as a useful buffer between Sweden and the USSR that allows Sweden to play a more independent role than might otherwise be possible. By contrast, Romania is situated on the western frontier of the Soviet Union. David Burke notes that in spite of this proximity, Romania maintains its military forces under national control even as it collaborates with the other members of the Warsaw Treaty Organization. Although there are certainly very real limits to Romanian policy independence in both economic and security matters, the country's self-image does resemble that of France in its attempt to carve out a somewhat more autonomous national role.

Although Israel, discussed by Bard O'Neill, is closely tied to the United States for its security, the country has attempted to reduce this dependency by developing its own defense industries. Security policy is subject to considerable controversy among Israelis, some favoring greater accommodation with neighboring Arab states and resolution of the Palestinian problem as the best long-term guarantee of security, while others continue to hold to a harder line. Even so, the perception of Israel as surrounded by hostile Arab states is pervasive. In its most extreme form, some have described the Israeli security dilemma as a "Masada" complex (a reference to the siege mentality exhibited in the first century A.D. when Jewish zealots committed suicide rather than submit to the Romans). Indeed, with the exception of Egypt under Sadat, Arab reactions to the legitimacy of Israel as a state have indeed been hostile (or at best skeptical). Without a doubt, this hostility has reinforced Israeli perceptions of insecurity that play such a large part in shaping the country's defense policy.

For their part, Arab leaders resent the great power intervention that resulted in the creation of Israel as a state, particularly since it was imposed on the region with what they regard as insufficient attention to the rights of Palestinian Arabs. Unfortunately, we have no country-study chapters on the Arab states in this volume. Given the extensive treatment that would be required by the common framework we devised, the scholars we contacted argued that the absence of sufficient data precluded such an effort at this time. Although considerable work has been done on civil-military relations and sociological aspects of various Arab military establishments, defense policy *per se* has not received much attention. The point is underscored in the bibliographic essay by Mark Ewig. We join him in calling for more work on Arab defense policy processes that can be the basis for future comparative efforts.

ALLIANCES AND INTERNATIONAL SECURITY REGIMES

Given the security dilemma that confronts states in an international environment that some have described as anarchic, there is at least some incentive for states to attempt reduction of uncertainties by creating a security *regime* or set of rules to make the behavior of states somewhat more predictable. International regime studies[8] can be understood as attempting to answer the question Where does order come from in a world that lacks a central superordinate authority? One answer, usually associated with scholars in the "realist" school, is countervailing power. Formation of alliances is an external means (as Waltz points out) by which states cope with the security dilemma. The literature on alliances is extensive and offers a variety of approaches to the subject.[9] Certainly politics within and between alliances is central to understanding the defense policies of most of the countries examined in this volume. Particular attention, of course, is directed toward both the Warsaw and North Atlantic treaty organizations as competing alliances.

Collective security—concerted action by "law-abiding" states against aggressors—was thought by some to be a substitute for alliance or "balance of power" politics,[10] but the experiences of both the United Nations and the earlier League of Nations have not built much confidence in collective security as a principal source of international order. On the other hand, members of international organizations have achieved some success in "peace-keeping" operations, whether serving as buffers between adversaries or engaging in the maintenance of areas torn by civil strife.[11]

Another source of international order is the voluntary construction by states of what has been referred to above as regimes, or sets of rules, that govern a state's behavior in various issue areas. The rules that are central to a given regime range from the least formal or implicit norms to the most explicit or formal rules that may even have the binding character of international law. Some regimes may have formal institutions associated with them, but such formal institutionalization is not prerequisite for a regime to exist.

The construction of regimes dealing with trade, the exchange of currencies, navigation, fishing, and other socioeconomic, technological, and scientific issues has been the subject of numerous studies, but there has been much less conceptual and empirical work done on the construction of international security regimes. Nevertheless, we feel the construct has considerable utility in the study of defense policy processes. Policy makers may actively seek to construct or maintain such regimes. In any event, established or agreed rules and norms will undoubtedly influence their defense policy choices.

Intraalliance politics would appear to be associated with one type of international security regime. Elsewhere we have referred to this type simply as an *allied regime*.[12] The other type or category is what we call an *adversary regime*. Examples of adversary regimes under construction during the last quarter-century are depicted in table 1. It should be noted, of course, that adversary regimes differ qualitatively from both allied regimes and nonsecurity regimes; indeed, conflict is the very essence of adversary regimes. The conflicting parties to an adversary regime,

Table 1
Adversary regimes: arms conflict and control

Conflict control	Arms control
Geographic	Strategic Arms Limitation (SALT)
Antarctica	Force Reductions (MBFR)
Space	Nuclear Nonproliferation
Nuclear Free Zones (Latin America)	Nuclear Test Bans
Seabed	Chemical Weapon Prohibitions
European Security (CSCE)	Biological Weapon Prohibitions
Tacit Spheres of Influence	Conventional Arms Transfers
Instrumental Means	
Communications	
Hot Line	
Nuclear Accidents	
Confidence-Building Measures (CSCE)	

Note: These regimes are in various stages of construction. Not all parties are adversaries, but most deal with adversary relations. Most are multilateral regimes, but some (notably SALT and Communications) are bilateral, superpower regimes.

however, do have a logical purpose in common with parties to allied and nonsecurity regimes. This common element—reduction of uncertainty—is a dominant motive for constructing all types of regimes. In fact, the uncertainty reduction purpose would appear to be as intense (and probably even more intense) in the process that results in the construction of an adversary regime as it is in the construction of other categories or types of international regimes. For example, the stakes are rather high in relations between the superpowers: the parties are driven to reduce uncertainty in what are inherently conflictual relations. The seeming contradiction in collaboration between or among adversaries can thus be accommodated by introducing the common purpose of uncertainty reduction.

Parties to arms and conflict control negotiations may express their purposes as being to reduce the likelihood of war, reduce damage or devastation should war occur, and reduce potential costs or defense expenditures that would result from continuing an arms race.[13] These purposes are clearly attempts to reduce uncertainty associated with adversary relations. That the parties may also be seeking to maintain the status quo (or seek advantage over other states) is a further example of an attempt to control environmental uncertainty.

In short, conflict remains central to adversary regimes, but the construction of such a regime can be understood as *routinization* of conflict relations. When policy makers agree upon rules (and even procedures) that make mutual behavior somewhat more predictable, they are obviously reducing uncertainty. More to the point, they are attempting to gain some control over an unpredictable external environment by agreeing to define the limits or constraints within which conflict will continue to take place.

National objectives, national strategy, and military doctrine

Given an understanding of the international environment within which the state is immersed, one can turn to an examination of national objectives, strategies for mobilizing national capabilities for these purposes, and military force employment doctrines. That strategy and doctrine in fact flow in such a logical pattern from national objectives is an assumption that conforms closely to a rational model of defense decision making. Although such a model is useful for organizing the discussion of strategy and doctrine in part two of each country study article, "nonrational" factors are treated explicitly in the exposition of decision-making processes that follows in part three.

A fundamental problem for defense policy makers is formulation of national objectives. At times these may be more implicit than explicit. Even when they are stated explicitly, different objectives may conflict in such a way that pursuit of one may preclude attainment of the others. In other instances there may be considerable uncertainty concerning objectives that should be sought, situations in which competing political factions often conflict. Decision makers would undoubtedly prefer to operate in response to clear-cut sets of objectives, but such simplicity is not typical of the complex world within which defense decision makers usually operate.

As we use the term, *national strategy* refers to the *grand strategy* of a given state. Successful implementation of national strategy typically calls for some consensus on methodology for the use of economic, diplomatic, military, and other "instruments of policy." In a particularly insightful article that relies heavily on the writings of Clausewitz ("The Forgotten Dimensions of Strategy," reprinted above), Michael Howard identifies four dimensions of strategy applicable to the use of the military instrument: the operational, the logistical, the social, and the technological.[14] Although the relative importance of each of these factors is arguable, ignoring any one of them in strategic calculations can have devastating consequences. In particular, Howard warns that the West appears "to be depending on the technological dimension of strategy to the detriment of its operational requirements, while [ignoring] its societal implications altogether."

Thus, Howard combines socioeconomic considerations (*viz.*, the social, logistical, and technological) with the purely military or operational elements of national strategy. In this volume we use the terms military *strategy* or force employment *doctrine* to capture the methodology associated with the military instrument. As such, we see military doctrine or strategy as subordinate to (or a component of) national or grand strategy. Doctrine, in turn, may give rise to particular tactics applied to specific situations or contingencies. The terms *strategy* and *tactics* in this narrower context refer merely to applications of doctrine. In any event, such applications can be differentiated from national or grand strategy and force employment doctrine, which are the focus of our country studies.

A common occurrence in most writing on defense policy is the blending of the meanings of terms such as *strategy* and *doctrine*. Although one can attempt to establish fairly precise analytical distinctions between the two, empirically they are very closely related. Indeed, national strategy and military strategy or doctrine as categories are not mutually exclusive. Nevertheless, we think it useful to treat national strategy and force employment doctrine as separate categories, even if they do overlap. *National strategy* is the more inclusive term that incorporates both military and nonmilitary factors; *military strategy* or *doctrine*, by contrast, is concerned exclusively with the ways and means of employing military forces for either deterrence or war-fighting purposes.

Military strategy or doctrine can be defined[15] as a methodology that *describes* the environment within which the armed forces must operate and *prescribes* the methods and circumstances of their employment. The primary function of such doctrine is to maximize the effectiveness of a state's military capabilities in support of national objectives. As such, military doctrine has at least two levels of definition. At the national or grand strategy level, military doctrine is concerned with coordinating the separate contributions of the armed services with the diplomatic, economic, and nonmilitary instruments of policy. At a lower level, each armed service also has its own military doctrine governing the employment of the forces under its command.

The traditional focus of military strategy or doctrine was on the use of force in an operational context—maximizing war-fighting capabilities. In the post–World War II era, however, the development of nuclear and other weapons of mass destruction resulted (at least in the West) in a considerable shift in doctrinal emphasis from war fighting to deterrence. (Only recently has there been any evidence of a shift in the opposite direction.) The perceived capability and willingness to use force are crucial to deterrence of war. Paradoxically, however, maintaining a deterrence posture is itself a use of force. Although one may argue that there has been a decline in the *operational* or *active* battlefield use of force among the industrial countries, one must also acknowledge the continuing presence of nuclear and nonnuclear arsenals for deterrence purposes as a *passive* use of force. In short, to the extent that deterrence based on the willingness to use the military instrument has substituted for war fighting, force remains centrally a part of international relations.[16]

A perennial question is whether doctrine guides the evolution of force posture or whether the converse is true. A review of the readings in this book suggests that doctrine and force posture are inextricably linked, although one may lag behind the other. Doctrine in the absence of requisite capabilities to implement it can hardly be very useful. On the other hand, acquisition of new military capabilities (as in a technological breakthrough or new access to foreign sources of weapons systems) can inspire new doctrines to govern the use of these new kinds of military forces.

Aside from the rational concern of providing the decision makers of a state with a logical framework or methodology for the acquisition and employment of its armed forces, military strategy or doctrine may also be made to serve several other functions.[17] For example, it may be designed to boost morale in the armed forces, balance domestic political factions, demonstrate adherence by the leadership to the tenets of a particular ideology, develop a popular consensus in support of the state's defense policies, contribute to alliance cohesion, and mislead or threaten adversaries. As a result of these often contending functional objectives, formally stated military strategy or doctrine may not be a true reflection of *de facto* or informal doctrine operative in a particular state. The analyst must, therefore, delve into the military practices of the country being examined. Indeed, many countries do not even have a formally and publicly articulated military strategy or doctrine, and one must, instead, turn to the body of information on doctrine established in large part by actual practice.

Warner argues that "the Soviets assign the highest priority to the deterrence of nuclear war," but pursue a "victory-oriented" or "war-winning approach to deterrence." With respect to targeting, Soviet declaratory doctrine assigns "highest priority to attacks on the enemy's military forces," but also emphasizes "extensive strikes against key industrial and political facilities."

Soviet defense efforts are focused in two geographical theaters of operation: Europe and the Far East, particularly along the Chinese frontier. According to Warner, war-fighting doctrine in these theaters holds that Soviet forces must rely on "massed, armored warfare" with "a commitment to seize the initiative at the outset of hostilities." Victory would be secured through "reinforcing efforts of all ground, sea and air forces"—the "combined arms concept." Moreover, Soviet forces would be "prepared to initiate extensive nuclear operations," including a strong predisposition to preempt "any enemy resort to the use of nuclear weapons." In any event, Warner notes that the Soviets would "mass their armor-heavy forces along selected main axes of attack," and seek to achieve a "series of simultaneous breakthroughs of the enemy's defenses."

Korb tells us that the United States is also committed to *deterring* nuclear war, "conventional attacks by the Warsaw Pact nations on Western Europe," and "smaller contingencies" elsewhere, particularly if such conflicts lead to "a crisis or conflagration in Western Europe." Certainly, the "keystone of U.S. strategic nuclear policy has been an assured second-strike capability" as necessary for maintaining a deterrence posture, but Korb also notes a collateral interest in being able "to engage in a controlled or limited nuclear exchange" should deterrence fail. Combining deterrence and war fighting, then, is at the core of the "countervailing strategy" that emerged in the late 1970s during the Carter administration. Although this military strategy was endorsed in a formal Presidential Decision in 1980, the idea that American strategy encompasses both deterrence and war-fighting concerns was not new. Indeed, the roots of the "countervailing strategy" lie in the Kennedy-Johnson and Nixon-Ford administrations of the 1960s and 1970s.

The United States retains defense commitments in Asia, particularly in South Korea and Japan. On the other hand, following the end of U.S. involvement in the Vietnam war, emphasis has shifted to the European theater and to the Middle East. Strengthening NATO through both conventional and nuclear force modernization and improving the capacity to deploy U.S. forces to the Middle East have been central American strategic concerns in the late 1970s and into the 1980s.

The military "balance" (or, to use Soviet terminology, the "correlation of forces") in the European theater favors Soviet and Warsaw Pact forces in numbers of personnel and armaments deployed there. The United States and its NATO allies rely on the alleged technological superiority of their forces to offset this quantitative advantage. Moreover, the presence of battlefield nuclear weapons in Europe and a commitment to NATO nuclear force modernization are central to the Western military position. Both sides also depend heavily on the integrity of their alliances and on effective command, control, and communications functions when engaged in combat operations. In addition to these social and operational dimensions, both face major logistical problems in any sustained war efforts, particularly if escalation to the use of nuclear weapons occurs. It is in this context that Howard's treatment of the elements of national strategy seems particularly relevant. Indeed, evaluating the military balance in Europe depends heavily upon the relative importance one places on each of the factors Howard identifies.

SOVIET-AMERICAN DOCTRINAL ASYMMETRY

As becomes clear from the Korb and Warner country studies and the readings by Ermarth, Pipes, and Lambeth, there is little, if any, doctrinal consensus between the United States and the Soviet Union. This is illustrated most clearly when one examines the record of the SALT negotiations during the late 1960s and throughout the 1970s.[18]

High-sounding phrases were adopted that implied a superpower consensus on strategic objectives—maintaining strategic stability, equality, and equal security (or the American corollary of essential equivalence). In fact, there is no certainty that both have had common objectives. Is the effort one of reducing the likelihood of war through pursuit of arms control? Are both sides seeking to maintain peace through deterrence? Even if both are so motivated—and there is no consensus on this point—do they share common doctrinal views on the ways and means leading to this outcome?

If deterrence is the aim, is it to be achieved through maintaining a credible assured destruction capability?[19] Deterrence based on so-called mutual assured destruction (MAD) has been the dominant American view, although not even American strategists are of like mind on the subject.[20] Simply stated, the MAD logic is that if each side retains the capacity and perceived willingness to wreak devastation on the other, then neither will be so foolish as to provoke such a war. Civilizations are held hostage in the hope that doing so will reduce the likelihood of war. The prospect of nuclear war is made so awful that neither side would rationally consider undertaking it. Populations are left with few, if any, active or passive defenses.[21] Following this MAD logic (or illogic), the more vulnerable people are, the less likely they will need protection, because, it is assumed, the mutual devastation of nuclear war and its likelihood are inversely related.[22] All of this, of course, rests on the assumption that states (or decision makers acting for them) will act rationally.

Is this the deterrence logic that is common to both sides? At least some American negotiators have assumed that it is.[23] The logic certainly seems compelling that if the United States can maintain a credible assured destruction capability vis-à-vis the Soviet Union, the latter will be deterred from starting a nuclear war, even if the Soviets do not agree with the doctrinal premises underlying the American position. But stating this misses a more fundamental point central to negotiating a strategic arms limitation agreement.

American doctrinal premises have led to advocacy of antiballistic missile (ABM) limitations and constraints on offensive systems that will preclude either side from achieving what is referred to as a credible first-strike posture. Consistent with this thinking, American strategic planners have not put much emphasis on civil defense preparations. By contrast, there is considerable evidence that the Soviets do not share the American assured destruction doctrinal perspective. To the extent that the Soviets wish to achieve a deterrent posture vis-à-vis the Americans (again, there is no consensus on this point), it is to be through maintaining a credible war-fighting posture. As Dennis Ross argues, for example, the Soviets may be seeking to achieve deterrence on the basis of "denial" rather than "punishment."[24] In short, if they have a credible nuclear war-fighting capability, what rational adversary would take them on in that mode? The adversary would be denied any rational purpose to be achieved from use of the military instrument and thus would be "deterred" from engaging in warfare.

If one accepts the view that Soviet and American strategies diverge along these lines, one can account for at least some of the difficulties experienced by negotiators in the SALT negotiations. Even if both sides aim to achieve deterrence (or peace through deterrence), then there is little agreement or consensus on the means to that end.[25] The Soviet preference for maintaining a war-fighting posture requires continuing commitment to both active and passive defenses,[26] as well as to offensive systems capable of destroying or reducing an adversary's war-fighting capabilities.

All of this assumes that both sides share the peace through deterrence objective. But not all students of the Soviet strategic literature are in agreement on even this point. For one thing, the concept of deterrence is far more prevalent in the American than in the Soviet strategic literature. Accordingly, some have argued that Soviet military thinking is more traditional than the American—that is, it remains much closer to the Clausewitzian text.[27] From this perspective, seeking (or maintaining) a credible war-fighting capability (regardless of whether it is employed in a nuclear or nonnuclear mode) is seen as justifiable in itself. Even if the Soviet Union does not want a war, if one were thrust upon the country it would wish to respond so as to maximize its chances of "winning" such an encounter, or at least minimizing the damage it need sustain. From this point of view, Soviet strategists have not conceded that such wars are inherently unwinnable. Nor have they accepted the Western premise that applying Clausewitz to nuclear wars is anachronistic.

An attempt to summarize this discussion of the uncertainties and doctrinal asymmetries in Soviet-American strategic relations is contained in table 2.

Table 2
Strategic doctrinal asymmetries

United States		Soviet Union	
Objectives	Means	Objectives	Means
Peace through deterrence	Credible assured destruction (second strike) capability	Defense? Peace through deterrence?	Credible war-fighting capability?
Damage limitation in event deterrence breaks down?	Some counterforce and active defense capability?	"Defense" in event of war?	War-fighting capability?

Not only do both sides harbor uncertainties about cause-effect relations, but this is also compounded by uncertainties over the calculations of the other.[28]

STRATEGY, DOCTRINE, AND THE MIDDLE POWERS

As General Gallois observes (in "The Future of France's *Force de Dissuasion,*" reprinted above), France enjoys "an advantage that falls to medium-sized powers": "to be able to deter at a lesser cost than is imposed on the Great Powers." Although one can criticize the French nuclear forces as too small (and highly vulnerable) to be entirely credible, Gallois argues that its contribution to deterrence rests on such uncertainties as "the destructive effects of France's arsenal" and "the behavior of the men responsible for its use."

Sabrosky is much less confident than Gallois concerning French capability for credible deterrence. Specifically, the French doctrinal commitment to "proportional deterrence" and "flexible response" would appear to have "few escalatory rungs." As Auton argues (in "Doctrinal Change in the British and French Cases," reprinted above), in the French context proportional deterrence really means minimum or finite deterrence. Although Auton examines "flexible options" that would include both counterforce and countervalue targets, he notes that, at least when used independently, both the British and French strategic nuclear forces now have "principally a countercity [targeting] doctrine" consistent with their minimum or finite deterrence postures.

The earlier French military doctrine of all-horizon defense that was closely tied to a "fortress France" mentality has been modified consistent with French objectives of securing national interests abroad and permitting the country to operate internationally as an independent power. French participation in the defense of Europe is certainly necessary if the country hopes to attain its other objectives. Nevertheless, notwithstanding efforts to avoid such a confrontation, if a war breaks out in Europe, the French would certainly prefer that it be fought on German soil. Thus, France has maintained forward deployments of forces in West Germany. One can assume that French military strategy or doctrine would call for the use of both conventional and tactical nuclear forces in Germany before absorbing an attack on French territory.

Unlike the French forces, British forces are fully integrated with NATO and explicitly contribute to the maintenance of the NATO "triad"—central strategic systems, theater nuclear systems, and conventional forces. Although British strategic nuclear forces can still be used independently to provide the country with a minimum or finite deterrence against an attacker, they have in fact been closely tied to American nuclear employment plans.

Aside from submarine-launched ballistic missile capabilities, the British royal navy would assist other allied navies in a joint attempt to keep the European and Atlantic sea lanes open in the event of war. Greenwood notes that among European navies the British, although certainly lacking the capacity for global deployment it once had, has the only "balanced fleet." British deployment of ground and air units in Germany is also a clear demonstration of the country's continuing commitment to NATO's theater nuclear and conventional defense capability. Although British forces have some capability for counterattack, force employment doctrine puts primary emphasis on "defensive" measures that would blunt any invasion by Warsaw Pact forces. The hope, of course, is that NATO defenses will be strong enough to deter any such attempt. Moreover, as Greenwood points out, the British have also supported various attempts to reduce tensions in Europe by endorsing such confidence-building measures between East and West as mutual notification of military maneuvers or training exercises.

The Germans are painfully aware that in any future European war Germany would be the primary battlefield. For obvious reasons, then, the country's planners favor a defense posture that would not provoke an attack, but would deter any attempt by adversaries to invade the country. The West Germans have also resisted talk of strategies in which forward-based troops would initially withdraw from the front lines, thus conceding a large proportion of German territory to an advancing enemy. Instead, West German doctrine has understandably maintained a commitment to forward defense that would blunt and, even more importantly, deter any invasion. Whether allied forces have the capability for a sustained forward defense or whether they would necessarily have to withdraw (in preparation for counterattack or as part of an attrition strategy) remains a subject of considerable controversy. Another matter of concern, of course, is when "tactical" or theater nuclear weapons would be employed. Given that the West Germans maintain the largest ground force contribution to NATO forces in Germany, observers ask whether the allies would necessarily have to escalate to nuclear weapons in the face of the advancing mass of Soviet and other Warsaw Pact forces. In some ways, it is this uncertainty, not only with respect to the threat from the East but also concerning the nature of the allied response, that explains West German commitment to reduction of tensions through confidence-building measures and arms control on the one hand and the much-heralded *Ostpolitik* of improved relations with the East on the other.

With respect to Japanese military strategy or doctrine, Okazaki notes that "Japan's military capability is strictly for defensive purposes" and in this regard "the Japan-U.S. security system is absolutely essential to [deterring] aggression directed against Japan." That Japanese security relies on close links with the United States is underscored by Endicott in his discussion of the U.S.-Japan Mutual Security Treaty. The Japanese Self-Defense Forces (SDF) are structured to cope with what has been defined as the central problem for Japanese military strategy or doctrine: stopping an invading force. By establishing and maintaining "capabilities to destroy or badly degrade the ability [of an adversary] to project forces to the Home Islands," the SDF would hope to deter any such attempt. Given this defensive character, Japanese military strategy is further constrained by explicit commitments not to acquire nuclear or other "offensive" weapons and weapons systems, not to sell or otherwise export weapons to other countries, and not to engage in overseas combat operations.

Finally, as Heaton notes, Chinese military strategy or doctrine has undergone some revision, but the concept of *people's war* remains central. In its earlier Maoist formulation, the concept also had global implications in that it referred not just to the defense of China but also to the efforts of the "world countryside," or Third World, directed against the imperialist, aggressive activities of the "world cities," or the industrial countries. Although this global aspect no longer receives the same emphasis, importance is still placed on total militarization of the Chinese population in the event of invasion with a protracted war of attrition waged against the invaders. So defined, people's war is very much a defensive military strategy, relying as it does on mass mobilization to resist invaders. The Chinese hope, of course, that potential adversaries will be deterred from invading if they perceive the futility of any such attempt.

Offensively, China does not possess the necessary air or sea lift capabilities for projection of its forces outside of the region. Cross-border deployments (such as the "punitive" invasion of Vietnam in 1979) also reveal the very real limitations on Chinese use of force even within the region.

Heaton observes that the Chinese do have an extensive (if not very sophisticated) civil defense program. Their offensive nuclear capability is very limited. Although it cannot be dismissed by the USSR and other states in the region, the Chinese deterrent is minimum or finite at best. The relatively small number of nuclear weapons in China's arsenal and the relative inaccuracy of the country's delivery systems severely limit their use in a war-fighting mode. Thus, even at the nuclear level, China's military doctrine would appear to be primarily defensive.

STRATEGY, DOCTRINE, AND LESSER POWERS

Burke tells us that Romania's planned response to invasion would be "defensive combat on the whole territory of the homeland." The resistance would include both regular and guerilla tactics involving military forces and allegedly the entire Romanian population. Although the country is a member of the Warsaw Treaty Organization, actual commitment of Romanian forces would decidedly not be automatic, but rather would be subject to decision by Party and government elements. War "would be waged" in Clausewitzian fashion of force employment doctrine for political purposes "with classical armament." Emphasis is placed on national resistance, attrition of enemy forces, and liberation of territory occupied by the enemy as the outcome of what is seen as a long-term struggle.

As Taylor points out, Sweden is committed to a "total defense" that includes military, civil, economic, psychological, and other dimensions. Emphasis is placed on both "territorial defense" with "rapid mobilization of a large conscript army" and a "peripheral defense" with deployment of "high technology aircraft and naval forces defending well beyond Sweden's land and sea boundaries." Maintaining a force posture commensurate with these "peripheral defense" objectives, given the costs that such high-technology weapons systems entail, has been a major issue of debate in Swedish politics.

Finally, Israel maintains a relatively small regular force, but relies heavily on rapid mobilization of reserves at times of national emergency. Particular emphasis is placed on mobility and, as demonstrated in the June 1967 war, on achieving surprise. As O'Neill notes, Israeli doctrine stresses "offensive operations, transferring the battle to enemy territory as soon as possible, dealing with the most threatening enemy first." The country is surrounded by Arab states, but Israel has been able to capitalize on divisions among them. Seizure in 1967 of the West Bank, Golan Heights, and Sinai Desert (including Gaza) and maintaining the capability for periodic intervention in southern Lebanon have provided buffers against Israel's adversaries. Similarly, making a separate peace with Egypt was a clear attempt to neutralize the threat of Israel's western front. Of course, the encirclement of Israel is also offset to some extent by the geomilitary advantage of internal lines of communication that allow for flexibility in the deploying of forces from one front to another and in maintaining logistical support for combat operations on more than one front.

The defense decision-making process

AUTHORITARIAN REGIMES

An understanding of a state's domestic politics is clearly central to the analysis of its defense policy. Indeed, the internal structure of states (to include organizational or bureaucratic elements) has direct impact on the defense decision process. Authoritarian regimes as in the Soviet Union, for example, make policy centrally, usually without open debate and without much need for compromise to resolve disputes among competing interests outside of government. To be sure, there is competition and political compromise within the ruling elite that takes alternative institutional and private views into account, but the domain within which the politics of policy choice takes place is a relatively narrow one.

Warner observes that in the Soviet Union it is the twenty-three-member Politburo that is at the center of defense policy formulation. Having said that, both Warner and Alexander (in, respectively, "The Defense Policy of the Soviet Union" and "Decision Making in Soviet Weapons Procurement," reprinted above) identify an array of other institutional actors that make inputs to (and participate in) the defense decision-making process. The nature of politics within this Party and government elite has indeed been the subject of controversy in the West. Roman Kolkowicz, for example, argues that the Soviet military is in an interest group that competes for political influence.[29]

An alternative interpretation is a more unitary image of military-Party relations provided by William Odom. Odom argues that the Soviet decision-making elite is not as factionally divided as the pluralist model of Kolkowicz would suggest.[30] Contrary to Kolkowicz, Odom does not see Party-military relations as essentially an adversary process. Rather, he sees both elements as sharing similar views—a "Party-military consensus" on "fundamental issues" and a basic compatibility of "institutional ethos."[31] The military is depicted as "an administrative arm of the party, not something separate from and competing with it."[32] Acknowledging that the military is a "political institution," Odom nevertheless states that

> the military's political life is bureaucratic in character, not parliamentarian and not lobbyist. . . .
>
> Personal cliques and coalitions of cliques take shape in bureaucracies, but they differ generically from interest groups. They cannot formalize themselves and thereby institutionalize the pursuit of an interest. In the Soviet bureaucracy, informal cliques and coalitions are established only at great risk; they probably do not extend beyond small face-to-face groups.[33]

Implicit in Odom's critique, of course, is the view that superimposing a Western pluralist model on Soviet politics is a bias that largely ignores "unique political and cultural contexts"[34] and thus distorts the reality of Soviet defense decision-making processes.

Heaton notes that in China, as in the Soviet Union, "the highest authority for decision making is the Politburo and its standing committee," but the military in China, unlike that in the USSR, has a much greater representation in the Politburo. According to Heaton, "about a third of the members" of the Politburo "are career military officers" and still other members have had "professional military experience." But this overlap of "military and civilian roles" that is part of the legacy of "China's protracted revolutionary war" does not lead Heaton to adopt Odom's unitary conception of Party-military relations. To the contrary, Heaton argues that "the concept of shifting coalitions or informal groups seems more appropriate."

Similarly, Warner argues that Soviet defense policy and, in particular, the Soviet defense budget are "purely the product of bureaucratic politics within the government and Party hierarchies." Alexander also sees the Soviet Defense Ministry as representing an institutional view favorable to "large military forces and growing procurement of all types of weapons" and opposed to competing interests. Thus, Kolkowicz's view receives more support from the contributors to this volume than that offered by Odom. With respect to Romania, Burke assumes bureaucratic politics to play a role in the defense policy process "as it does in all complex governmental organizations," but he concludes that there is insufficient data to confirm this supposition. Indeed, the absence of information about decision-making processes in Marxist-Leninist countries remains a major problem for Western scholars.

DEMOCRATIC REGIMES

Although there are marked differences among the countries explored in this volume, most of them can be labeled as democracies. Political authority and the exercise of power in some is highly centralized with fewer points of access to those in power, whereas in others, notably the United States, political authority is highly fragmented with many points of access to those exercising power and making policy choices. In addition to these structural differences, cultural variations are also significant. Thus, decision making in Japan is the oftentimes slow-moving politics of consensus building, whereas in Britain open conflict among opposing parties is central to the political process. The impact of culture on political process is striking, particularly when one considers that both Japan and Britain share the same formal political structure, a parliamentary regime in a unitary state.

Parliamentary regimes, as in the United Kingdom, West Germany, Sweden, Israel, and Japan, have a fusion of executive and legislative functions such that policy choice is made centrally within the Cabinet. (In most parliamentary regimes there is also little, if any, judicial check on the legislature.) There is still considerable debate and compromise both within and outside of the majority party or coalition that controls the government, but most of these politics occur within the Cabinet. Although the titles vary from country to country, the principal defense decision makers within the Cabinet are the prime minister and the ministers of defense, foreign affairs, and finance or treasury. Maintaining a consensus within the majority party is a major task undertaken by these and other Cabinet members that typically involves considerable political compromise. The necessity for compromise is underscored, of course, when no single party has a majority of seats in the legislature and the government is composed of a coalition of parties. In such cases, both the prime minister and the defense minister are usually members of the party in the governing coalition that has the most seats in the legislature.

Although the point has been made that defense policy making in parliamentary regimes takes place primarily within the Cabinet composed of ministers from the majority party or from the parties within the governing coalition, note is also taken of the crucial role played by bureaucracies formally subordinated to these government ministers. The career civil service members remain in place even as governments change. More than just a source of stability, these civil servants are repositories of information upon which the government ministers so heavily depend. Accordingly, as has been widely recognized, bureaucracies play a decisive role in shaping the alternatives among which policy makers are forced to choose. In other instances, of course, career bureaucrats can act as a conservative force by delaying or otherwise obstructing implementation of political decisions they oppose. Moreover, appreciation of this bureaucratic role is central to understanding defense policy processes in authoritarian and democratic regimes of all types.

France has a presidential regime with some separation of powers between legislative and executive; however, the executive has clearly been the more powerful branch since the Gaullist Constitution came into effect in 1958. A relatively strong executive, coupled with the fact that the country is a unitary state with ultimate political authority centralized in the national capital, results in a concentration of defense decision making comparable to that in parliamentary regimes. This is reinforced, moreover, by a political culture or tradition of strong bureaucracy centrally directed from Paris.

By contrast, the United States not only has a presidential regime of separation of powers within the central government, but also considerable division of powers between the central government and fifty state and thousands of municipal, county, and other local governments. Although local administrations exist in unitary states, they are strictly subordinated to the central government. There is no such subordination in American federalism. Indeed, when the federal dimension is combined with the existence of a strong legislative counterweight to any executive initiatives, the result is a highly fragmented political system with numerous points of access by interest groups to political authorities operating in a wide variety of places and on various levels. None of this is accidental, of course. Distrust of centralized political power is deeply set in the American political culture with roots early in the country's history. Indeed, the rationale for both separating and dividing power—a presidential regime in a federal state—is most clearly expressed in the *Federalist Papers*, especially numbers 10 and 51, written by James Madison.

Although West Germany also is a federal state with power and authority more dispersed than in other parliamentary regimes, defense decision making is viewed primarily as a national concern and thus is centralized within the Cabinet with inputs received from military elements, a relatively small defense bureaucracy, and political party factions such as the left wing of the Social Democrats (SPD). By contrast, in the United States such issues as defense procurement and military force deployments are issues that regularly draw the attention and participation of private interests, local officials, state governors, and representatives of both houses of the U.S. Congress. The attempt by the Defense Department to deploy the M-X ICBM system in Utah and Nevada is a classic case that clearly illustrates the political milieu within which American defense decision making takes place. Coalitions and countercoalitions of private and governmental actors, federal and state and local officials, and legislative and bureaucratic figures all participated in the process.

Interest group politics of this sort also exist in the parliamentary regimes already discussed, but usually not to the same degree. Fragmentation of political authority and a political culture that legitimizes the dispersion of power go a long way to explain the extreme pluralism of American political processes. Multiple points of access enable interest groups to flourish in a way not possible in democratic regimes with greater concentration of political authority and fewer points of access to those in political power. Interest group pluralism is by no means unique to American politics, but structural and cultural factors do strengthen the role that interest groups can play. Interest groups are relevant actors in other democratic regimes, but to a somewhat lesser extent.

It can also be argued that the nature of defense policy outputs themselves—decisions and actions—is directly affected by the type of internal political structure and the associated political culture. Thus, in the United States, where political power and authority are highly fragmented, decisions are reached (and almost always implemented) incrementally and as the result of considerable compromise. Although the politics of compromise and incremental choice is also present in parliamentary regimes, as a matter of degree the implementation of decisions and actions taken by these democracies do have a somewhat more comprehensive and coherent character. Certainly this is one inference that can be drawn from the country studies in this volume. (See table 3.)

ORGANIZATION PROCESSES AND BUREAUCRATIC POLITICS

The relevance of organizational processes and bureaucratic politics to understanding how defense policy is actually made has been underscored by the efforts of Graham Allison and others.[35] That defense decisions and actions do not necessarily proceed in a logical sequence from national objectives, strategies designed to coordinate the use of the state's capabilities, and employment doctrines governing the use of force is an argument that flows from their work.

On the other hand, some have cautioned against too heavy a reliance on organizational and bureaucratic variables.[36] To what extent, for example, does focus on organizational and bureaucratic factors obscure the importance of variables external to the decision makers? From this perspective, the specific decisions and actions taken may be shaped by decision maker and organizational perspectives in the "pulling and hauling" and coalition formation of bureaucratic politics, but the general course of policy is more a function of the international environment with which decision makers have to contend. How to account for the effects of individual perceptions in

Table 3
Comparing democratic regimes: formal internal structure

Type of political regime	Type of state	
	Unitary	Federal
Parliamentary	United Kingdom, Japan, Sweden, Israel	West Germany
Presidential	France	United States

general and for such personalities as a de Gaulle in France, a Brezhnev in the USSR, or a Mao in China in particular (not to mention other idiosyncratic factors) was a problem that confounded each of our country study authors. Personalities can and do change, but often there remains a degree of constancy in defense policy that survives alterations in domestic authorities.

Defense policy and the level of analysis problem

If relative constancy in the general course of defense policy is an accurate description applicable to most countries (and not everyone would agree that it is), is this to be explained by the dominance of such external factors as the relative distribution or balance of power within the international system that usually changes very slowly? Or is relative constancy to be explained by the nature of decision-making processes themselves—that they usually involve incremental or marginal changes from established policy? Is "any policy" really encumbered by all preceding policies and, in turn, does it encumber "all succeeding policies?"[37]

In a very real sense, the conceptual issue of how to study defense policy is the relative importance of the various "levels of analysis."[38] More than twenty years ago, the late Professor Fred Sondermann (to whom this book is codedicated) grappled with the linkage between foreign policy and international politics.[39] Sondermann noted the importance of the "international system which has profound impact upon the behavior of participants in that system's processes."[40] On the other hand, he also took note of the view that "international politics cannot be understood without a thorough examination of the policies of the states participating in that process" and the "complex web of factors and forces which affect governmental policies."[41]

In other words, how important are distribution of capabilities (or power), degree of interdependence, level of tensions, and other system-level variables as determinants of policy? To rely exclusively on such variables opens one to the criticism of system determinism—that states and other "actors" are mere automatons lacking any capacity for independent action. Ernst Haas describes the problem when he excoriates "determinists" who "see the components [of systems] as relatively unchangeable and arrange them in an eternal preprogrammed dance; the rules of the dance may be unknown to the actors and are specified by the theorist. The recurrent patterns discovered by him constitute a super-logic which predicts the future state of the system."[42]

On the other hand, instead of focusing on the "system" of states and other actors, some would argue that one will find the dominant variables to be the types of states (or their internal structure to include organizational and bureaucratic factors). Still others would argue that personality and the set of cognitive orientations and perceptions (or operational codes) of individual decision makers are central.[43] To adopt such positions, of course, is to open oneself to the charge of reductionism, ignoring external or environmental factors. Indeed, as Sondermann observed, "As one progresses down the path toward greater (and narrower) specificity, one does reach points which—however valid and interesting they are in themselves—are rather far removed from the subject of international politics which provided the starting point for one's inquiries."[44]

To say that systemic considerations, the type or structure of states and their associated political cultures, organizational and bureaucratic dimensions of this internal structure, and psychological variables are all important is not to say very much. Indeed, to say that everything is important begs the more relevant question of the relative importance of the different variables in explaining defense decisions and actions. Even more to the point, can we identify the conditions that affect the relative importance of systemic, state, organizational or bureaucratic, and individual-level variables? (See figure 1.)

A theory of comparative defense policy offering explanation and prediction would necessarily be built upon the answers to such questions. Because we do not pretend to have these answers, we do not claim to have provided a *theory;* our only claim is to have offered a *framework* for the comparative study of defense policy. We do contend, however, that the variables we have identified will be central to any theory of comparative defense policy, the development of which remains to be accomplished.

Figure 1. The Level of analysis problem

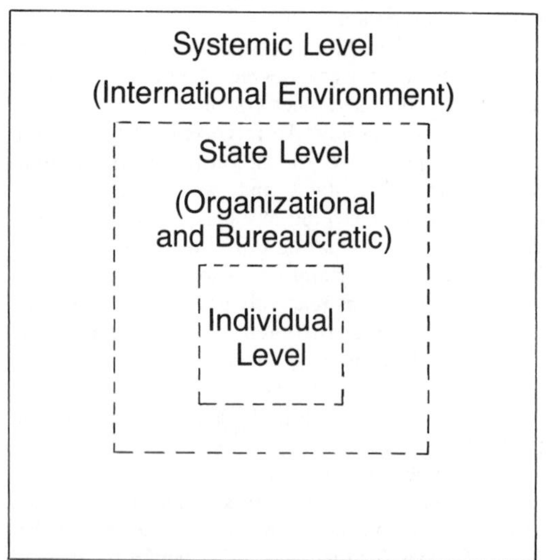

Notes

1. Path-breaking efforts in this field were James Rosenau's "Pretheories and Theories of Foreign Policy," in *Approaches to Comparative and International Politics,* ed. R. B. Farrel (Evanston, Ill.: Northwestern University Press, 1966), pp. 27–92; and idem, "Comparative Foreign Policy: Fad, Fantasy, or Field?," *International Studies Quarterly* 12 (September 1968): 296–329. Later efforts include Wolfram F. Hanrieder, ed., *Comparative Foreign Policy: Theoretical Essays* (New York: David McKay Co., 1971); James N. Rosenau, ed., *Comparing Foreign Policies: Theories, Findings, and Methods* (New York: John Wiley & Sons/Sage Publications, 1974); Patrick J. McGowan and Howard B. Shapiro, *The Comparative Study of Foreign Policy: A Survey of Scientific Findings* (Beverly Hills, Calif.: Sage Publications, 1973); and Maurice A. East, Stephen A. Salmore, and Charles F. Hermann, eds., *Why Nations Act: Theoretical Perspectives for Comparative Foreign Studies* (Beverly Hills, Calif.: Sage Publications, 1978).

2. See his *Twenty Years' Crisis, 1919–1939* (New York: Macmillan, 1939; and Harper Torchbooks, 1964), especially chapter 8. Carr states: "Power, which is an element of all political action, is one and indivisible" (Harper edition, p. 132).

3. For a well-developed discussion, see Robert Keohane and Joseph Nye, *Power and Interdependence* (Boston: Little, Brown, 1976).

4. For an empirical analysis that challenges the "conventional wisdom" of a continuing trend toward rising interdependence, see Richard Rosecrance, "Whither Interdependence?," *International Organization,* Summer 1977.

5. For a development of this argument, see Kenneth N. Waltz, "Conflict in World Politics," in *Conflict in World Politics,* ed. Steven L. Spiegel and Kenneth N. Waltz (Cambridge, Mass.: Winthrop Publishers, 1971), pp. 454–74.

6. For one of the better treatments of perceptual factors and their impact on international politics, see Robert Jervis, *Perception and Misperception in International Politics* (Princeton: Princeton University Press, 1976).

7. See, for example, the discussion in Kenneth N. Waltz, *Man, the State and War* (New York: Columbia University Press, 1959), p. 204.

8. See the Summer 1975 issue of *International Organization,* edited by Ernst B. Haas and John J. Ruggie. Cf. Ernst B. Haas, "Why Collaborate? Issue-Linkage and International Regimes," and Oran Young, "International Regimes: Problems of Concept Formation," in *World Politics* 32, no. 3 (April 1980).

9. A representative sample of this literature, but by no means an exhaustive list, would include Francis A. Beer ed., *Alliances: Latent War Communities in the Contemporary World* (New York: Holt, Rinehart & Winston, 1970); George F. Liska, *Nations in Alliance: The Limits of Interdependence* (Baltimore: Johns Hopkins University Press, 1962); William H. Riker, *The Theory of Political Coalitions* (New Haven: Yale University Press, 1962); and Julian Friedman, Christopher Bladen, and Steven Rosen, eds., *Alliances in International Politics* (Boston: Allyn & Bacon, 1970).

10. A classic study that examines balance of power, collective security, and world government as alternative

sources of order is Inis L. Claude, Jr., *Power and International Relations* (New York: Random House, 1962).

11. For a brief overview of U.N. peace-keeping operations, see M.L.J. Smith, "United Nations Forces: A Critical View," *Defence Force Journal*, no. 15 (March-April 1979), pp. 24-32.

12. See our "International Security Regimes: On the Applicability of a Concept" (Paper presented to the Annual Convention, American Political Science Association, August 1980).

13. For a good discussion of these objectives, see Jerome H. Kahan, *Security in the Nuclear Age* (Washington, D.C.: Brookings Institution, 1975), pp. 277-85. Of course, this is by no means an exhaustive list of goals, but it does seem to capture some of the most important. As a practical matter, other motives are often present, such as when negotiations are used to enhance the state's public image or as a platform for propaganda.

14. Cf. Howard's earlier article, "The Relevance of Traditional Strategy," *Foreign Affairs* 51, no. 2 (January 1973).

15. One of us addressed this subject in Frank B. Horton, Anthony C. Rogerson, and Edward L. Warner, eds., *Comparative Defense Policy* (Baltimore: The Johns Hopkins University Press, 1974), pp. 190-92.

16. The literature on the use of force and the question of whether it is declining is extensive. A representative sample would include Robert J. Art and Kenneth N. Waltz, eds., *The Use of Force* (Boston: Little, Brown, 1971); Klaus Knorr, "International Coercion: Waning or Rising?," *International Security*, Spring 1977; idem, "On the International Uses of Military Forces in the Contemporary World," *Orbis*, Spring 1977; and idem, "The Limits of Economic and Military Power," *Daedalus*, Fall 1975; Robert Tucker, "Oil: The Issue of American Intervention," *Commentary*, January 1975; idem, "Further Reflections on Oil and Force," *Commentary*, March 1975; Stanley Hoffmann, "The Acceptability of Military Force," Adelphi Papers, no. 102 (London: International Institute for Strategic Studies, Winter 1973); and Robert Johansen, *Toward a Dependable Peace* (New York: Institute for World Order, 1978).

17. See the discussion in Arnold L. Horelick, "Perspectives on the Study of Comparative Military Doctrine," and Benjamin S. Lambeth, "The Sources of Soviet Military Doctrine" in *Comparative Defense Policy*, ed. Horton, Rogerson, and Warner, pp. 192-216.

18. Good narrative accounts are John Newhouse, *Cold Dawn* (New York: Holt, Rinehart & Winston, 1973), for SALT I; and Strobe Talbott, *End Games* (New York: Harper & Row, 1979), for SALT II.

19. For a short overview of deterrence theory to include various critiques, see Robert Jervis, *Deterrence Theory Revisited*, Working Paper no. 14 (Los Angeles: University of California Center for Arms Control and International Security, 1978). Also see his *Perception and Misperception in International Politics*, chap. 3; and *The Logic of Images in International Relations* (Princeton: Princeton University Press, 1970), chap. 8. Cf. Alexander George and Richard Smoke, *Deterrence in American Foreign Policy* (New York: Columbia University Press, 1974); and "Failures of Deterrence," *World Politics* 30 (April 1978): 347-53.

20. For example, there is the seemingly endless debate on how much is enough (to include the finite or minimum deterrence positions). There is also the matter of how much "damage limitation" should be provided or whether such forces may be misperceived and thus be destabilizing.

21. Active defense is meant to include fighter-interceptor aircraft, surface-to-air (antibomber) missiles, and antiballistic missile defenses. Passive defense would include civil defense. Early warning defenses may also be considered passive defenses unless they are specifically tied to active defense systems.

22. Although earlier an advocate of MAD, Henry Kissinger has become one of its outspoken critics. See the reprint of a September 1979 speech to a NATO conference in *Washington Monthly* 2, no. 4 (Autumn 1979). As a hedge against total vulnerability, damage limitation has also been present in American strategic thinking (i.e., in the event of war, how can damage be limited or devastation of the U.S. be reduced?). Even here, emphasis has been more on offensive than on defensive measures, although development of an ABM was seen in the late 1960s as consistent with the damage limitation purpose.

23. Certainly this is the view expressed by former ACDA head Paul Warnke, confirmed in a discussion with one of us in April 1980 at Colorado College, Colorado Springs, Colo. It is also said to have been the view of Harold Brown, David Aaron, and Zbigniew Brzezinski, key figures in the Carter administration. See Talbott, *End games*, p. 52. Cf. Walter Pincus, "Past the SALT: An Interview with Paul Warnke," *New York Review of Books*, 14 June 1979.

24. See Dennis Ross, "Rethinking Soviet Strategic Policy: Inputs and Implications," *Journal of Strategic Studies* 1, no. 1 (May 1978). Cf. Fritz Ermarth, "Contrasts in American and Soviet Strategic Thought," reprinted above.

25. And, as Jervis observes, there is no consensus even among American strategic thinkers, much less (we would add) between the Americans and their Soviet counterparts. See his *Deterrence Theory Revisited*.

26. Those who view the Soviets as sharing the deterrence through assured destruction purpose note as evidence for this view that the Soviets did agree in 1972 to limit deployment of ABM systems. Opponents of this view, by contrast, argue that, given American technological advantages, the Soviets may have merely been attempting to keep the United States from achieving a lead in ABM systems. Thus, freezing an adversary's technology is offered as an alternative to the view that the ABM agreement was based on shared doctrinal premises. See the discussion in Stanley Sinkiewicz, "SALT and Soviet Nuclear Doctrine," *International Security* 2, no. 4 (Spring 1978): 99-100. Cf. Raymond L. Garthoff, "SALT and the Soviet Military," *Problems of Communism*, January-February 1975.

27. See Richard Pipes, "Why the Soviet Union Thinks It Could Fight and Win a Nuclear War," reprinted above.

28. The Americans wonder if the Soviets are really seeking to achieve deterrence and, if so, whether it is to be based on assured destruction or war fighting. On the other hand, U.S. talk of "city avoidance," "damage limitation," and even some advocacy of nuclear war-fighting capabilities when coupled with development of MIRVs, cruise missiles, and other high-accuracy systems may have given the Soviets pause to question articulated American doctrine. Actual American intentions notwithstanding, from the Soviet perspective, such systems can be construed as being as consistent with developing a war-fighting posture as with

merely maintaining an assured destruction, second-strike capability.

29. See Roman Kolkowicz, "Interest Groups in Soviet Politics: The Case of the Military," *Comparative Politics* 2, no. 3 (April 1970): 445-72.

30. See William E. Odom, "The Party Connection," *Problems of Communism* 22, no. 5 (September-October 1973): 12-26.

31. Ibid., esp. pp. 14-17.

32. Ibid., p. 23.

33. Ibid., pp. 24-25.

34. Ibid., p. 23.

35. For example, see Allison's "Conceptual Models and the Cuban Missile Crisis," *American Political Science Review* 62 (September 1969): 689-718; and idem, *Essence of Decision* (Boston: Little-Brown, 1971). Cf. Allison and Morton H. Halperin, "Bureaucratic Politics: A Paradigm and Some Policy Implications," *World Politics* 24 supplement (Spring 1972): 40-79.

36. See Stephen D. Krasner, "Are Bureaucracies Important? (Or Allison Wonderland)," *Foreign Policy*, no. 7 (1972), pp. 159-79, and Robert J. Art, "Bureaucratic Politics and American Foreign Policy: A Critique," *Policy Sciences* 4, no. 4 (1973): 467-90.

37. Fred A. Sondermann, "The Linkage between Foreign Policy and International Politics," in *International Politics and Foreign Policy*, ed. James N. Rosenau (New York: The Free Press, 1961), p. 14.

38. An early treatment of the level-of-analysis problem is Waltz, *Man, the State and War*. Cf. Harold Sprout and Margaret Sprout, *Man-Milieu Relationship Hypotheses in the Context of International Politics* (Princeton: Princeton University Center of International Studies, 1956). Another discussion of the problem is J. David Singer, "The Level-of-Analysis Problem in International Relations," in *The International System: Theoretical Essays*, ed. Klaus Knorr and Sidney Verba (Princeton: Princeton University Press, 1961), pp. 77-92. A more recent treatment is Waltz, "Theory of International Relations," in *Handbook of Political Science*, ed. Fred I. Greenstein and Nelson W. Polsby (Reading, Mass.: Addison-Wesley, 1975), esp. vol. 8, pp. 65-75. Finally, a useful discussion of the issues is Robert Jervis, *Perception and Misperception in International Politics*, esp. chap. 1.

39. Sondermann, "Foreign Policy and International Politics," pp. 8-17. The article was based on a paper presented to the annual meeting of the American Political Science Association, St. Louis, September 1958.

40. Ibid., p. 13.

41. Ibid.

42. See Ernst B. Haas, "On Systems and International Regimes," *World Politics* 17, no. 2 (January 1975): 151.

43. For one of the best treatments of perceptual factors, see Jervis, *Perception and Misperception in International Politics*. The concept of "operational code" has been developed by Alexander George. See his "'Operational Code': A Neglected Approach to the Study of Political Leaders and Decisionmaking," *International Studies Quarterly* 13 (1969): 190-222. Cf. Ole Holsti, "The Operational Code Approach to the Study of Political Leaders," *Canadian Journal of Political Science* 3 (1970): 123-57; and idem, "The Belief System and National Images," *Journal of Conflict Resolution* 6, no. 3 (1962): 244-52.

44. Sondermann, "Foreign Policy and International Politics," p. 14.

Glossary

ABC WEAPONS Atomic, biological, and chemical weapons. Procurement of any ABC weapons often stirs public controversy in democratic nations. The Geneva Protocol of 1925 prohibits the use of poison gas and bacteriological methods in warfare.

AIR DEFENSE FORCES OF THE USSR (PVO STRANY) One of five independent arms of the Soviet military services, the Air Defense Forces have historically received funding sufficient to deploy air defenses greater than those of any Western country. The forces include surface-to-air missiles (SAMs), antiballistic missiles (ABMs), and jet interceptors.

AIR-LAUNCHED CRUISE MISSILE (ALCM) A cruise missile launched from an airborne platform. *See also* Cruise missile.

ANTIBALLISTIC MISSILE (ABM) A defensive missile designed to intercept and destroy an offensive ballistic missile or its payload.

ANZUS TREATY A security treaty concluded in 1951 among Australia, New Zealand, and the United States. The treaty declared that an attack upon any of the members would constitute a common danger and that each would respond to it according to its constitutional processes.

ARMS CONTROL International agreements (implicit or explicit) that regulate the numbers, types, characteristics, deployment, and use of armed forces and armaments.

ARMS CONTROL AND DISARMAMENT AGENCY (ACDA) An independent American agency established in 1961 to conduct research and to develop arms control and disarmament policies. ACDA's director serves as a principal adviser to the president and the secretary of state on such matters.

ARMS RACE Competition between two or more countries or coalitions of countries that results in the cumulative proliferation or accretion of weapons; an increase in the destructive power of weapons possessed by those parties; and/or the build-up of their armed forces, incited by convictions that national security objectives demand quantitative superiority, qualitative superiority, or both.

ASSURED DESTRUCTION CAPABILITY A highly reliable ability to inflict unacceptable damage on any aggressor or combination of aggressors at any time during the course of a nuclear exchange, even after absorbing a surprise first strike. *See also* First strike; *Mutual assured destruction; Unacceptable damage*.

BALANCE OF POWER A system of power alignments in which peace and security may be maintained through an equilibrium of power between rival powers or blocs. In this condition, states enter into alliances with friendly states to protect or enhance their power positions. Critics argue that the balance of power may lead as easily to war as to peace, citing World Wars I and II as examples.

BALANCE OF TERROR A state of mutual deterrence between the superpowers based on the ability of each to deal a mortal blow to the other even while (or after) receiving such a blow itself.

BALLISTIC MISSILE A missile propelled into space by one or more rocket motors without reliance upon aerodynamic surfaces to provide lift. After thrust termination, the reentry vehicles follow ballistic trajectories determined mainly by gravity and aerodynamic drag, with only slight midcourse corrections and terminal guidance possible.

BALLISTIC MISSILE EARLY WARNING SYSTEM (BMEWS) An electronic system to provide warning of incoming enemy ICBMs so that U.S. strategic forces may be launched before enemy missiles hit.

BIOLOGICAL WARFARE The use of biological agents to debilitate or kill people and other forms of life.

BIPOLAR A world power distribution or structure characterized in the present period by the predominance of the United States and the USSR.

BOMBER A military aircraft designed to deliver nuclear or

conventional weapons against targets on the ground. Bombers are generally classified as heavy (e.g., U.S. B-52 and Soviet TU-95 Bear), medium (e.g., U.S. F-111 and Soviet TU-22M Backfire B), or light (Soviet Il-28 Beagle).

BREZHNEV DOCTRINE The Soviet policy of maintaining friendly Communist regimes in power in neighboring states, using force when necessary. The invasions of Czechoslovakia in 1968 and Afghanistan in 1979 demonstrated the doctrine in action.

BRIGADE A unit usually smaller than a division to which are attached groups and/or battalions and smaller units tailored to meet anticipated requirements. *See also* Division.

BRINKMANSHIP Demonstrated willingness on the part of an adversary to approach the brink of nuclear war with the intention of prevailing over an opponent during a crisis. The intent is not to go to war but to come closer to war than the opponent is willing to come.

BRUSHFIRE WAR A local war that can flare up suddenly and either subside prior to Great Power intervention or escalate to greater magnitude.

CAPABILITY The ability to execute a specified course of action. A capability may or may not be accompanied by an intention.

CAPITALIST ENCIRCLEMENT A Soviet term referring to the ring of capitalist nations surrounding the USSR that, in the Soviets' view, poses a security problem.

CBR (CHEMICAL, BIOLOGICAL, AND RADIOLOGICAL OPERATIONS) A collective term used only when referring to combined chemical, biological, and radiological operations. *See also* NBC.

CIRCULAR ERROR PROBABLE (CEP) A measure of weapons system accuracy used as a factor in determining probable damage to targets. CEP is defined as the radius of a circle within which a warhead has a 0.5 probability of falling.

CIVIL DEFENSE Passive measures designed to minimize the effects of enemy action on all aspects of civilian life, particularly to protect the population base. This includes emergency steps to repair or restore vital utilities and facilities.

CLOSE-AIR SUPPORT Air strikes against targets near enough to ground combat units that detailed coordination between participating air and ground elements is required.

COLD LAUNCH The technique of ejecting a missile from a silo before full ignition of the main engine. (Sometimes called "pop-up.")

COLD WAR A state of tension between adversaries in which measures short of sustained combat by regular forces are used to achieve national objectives. These measures may include political, economic, technological, sociological, paramilitary, and small-scale military efforts. The term *Cold War* is commonly used to characterize relations between the United States and the USSR from the late 1940s through the 1960s.

COLLATERAL DAMAGE Damage to areas not specifically targeted, caused by the effects of strikes extending beyond the immediate area of a target.

COMINFORM (COMMUNIST INFORMATION BUREAU) Stalin established Cominform in September 1947 as a successor to the Comintern (Communist International) to help integrate and consolidate the Communist countries under Soviet control. Nine Communist parties originally joined: those of the USSR, Poland, Czechoslovakia, Bulgaria, Hungary, Romania, France, Italy, and Yugoslavia. The organization soon encountered difficulties; Yugoslavia was expelled and in 1956 the bureau ceased to exist.

COMMAND, CONTROL, AND INTELLIGENCE A comprehensive concept that refers to an arrangement of facilities, equipment, personnel, and procedures used to obtain, process, and distribute information needed by decisionmakers to plan, direct, and control operations.

COMPELLENCE The process of influencing, through one instrument or a variety of instruments, another party either to initiate or to cease some specified action, which would not otherwise have been taken. Compellence is positive in nature, while deterrence is negative.

CONFERENCE ON SECURITY AND COOPERATION IN EUROPE (CSCE) The conference that led to the signing of the Helsinki Agreements of 1975. *See also* Helsinki Agreements.

CONFLICT SPECTRUM A continuum of hostilities that ranges from subcrisis maneuvering in Cold War situations to the most violent form of general war.

CONTAINMENT The United States post–World War II policy to prevent communism from spreading.

CONTINGENCY PLANS AND OPERATIONS Preparation for major events that can reasonably be anticipated and that probably would have a detrimental effect on national security; actions in case such events occur.

CONTROLLED RESPONSE Responding to a military attack with military action matched to the circumstances in a manner designed to avoid all-out nuclear war.

CONVENTIONAL WEAPONS Weapons that are neither nuclear, biological, nor chemical (except riot control, incendiary, and smoke agents).

Cordon sanitaire A territorial buffer between two opposing forces or states.

COST EFFECTIVE The description of a condition that matches ends with means in ways that create maximum capabilities at minimum expense—in colloquial terms, getting the most for your money.

COST SHARING An attempt by NATO members to distribute defense costs among themselves more fairly. The concept is in response to the perception that some states were paying more than their "fair" share of NATO's defense expenditures.

COUNCIL OF MUTUAL ECONOMIC ASSISTANCE (CMEA) CMEA (sometimes referred to as COMECON) was formed in January 1949 in response to the Marshall Plan and is the economic counterpart of the Warsaw Pact. Its stated objective is to promote the economic development of all members and it has, in practice, led to greater division of labor, coordination of five-year plans, and trade and economic ties that as a whole benefit the USSR. Members include the Soviet Union, Poland, Czechoslovakia, Romania, Hungary, Bulgaria, East Germany, and Albania.

COUNTERFORCE The use of strategic nuclear forces to destroy or render impotent the military capabilities of an enemy. ABM and air defense installations, command and control centers, army and naval facilities, nuclear stockpiles, bombers and their bases, ICBM silos, and ballistic missile submarines are typical counterforce targets.

COUNTERINSURGENCY ACTIONS Military, paramilitary, economic, political, psychological, and civic actions taken by a government to defeat insurgency forces.

COUNTERVAILING STRATEGY Secretary of Defense Harold Brown committed the United States to a countervailing strategy during the Carter administration. This strategy requires forces capable of responding to any attack such that the enemy could not hope to gain any rational objective; any enemy gain would entail offsetting losses. Specifically, forces must be able to: (1) survive a surprise attack, (2) be deployed in a controlled manner by national command authorities, (3) penetrate enemy defenses, and (4) destroy their assigned targets.

COUNTERVALUE A strategic concept that dictates the destruction or neutralization of such nonmilitary enemy assets as population centers, industries, resources, and institutions.

COUPLING Linking a lower-level conflict to the use of the U.S. strategic triad in order to deter aggression. The credibility of this coupling of central strategic and theater (or European-based) systems is an issue of continuing concern to European NATO members.

CREDIBILITY The perception by a nation that an opponent has both adequate forces and the national will to act in accordance with its publicized doctrine.

CROSS-TARGETING Attack planning that assigns a number of warheads carried by different delivery vehicles to a specific target with the goal of increasing the probability of target destruction.

CRUISE MISSILE A guided missile, the major portion of whose flight path to its target is conducted at approximately constant velocity. It depends on the dynamic reaction of air for lift and upon propulsion forces to balance drag.

CRUISER A large, long-endurance surface warship armed for independent offensive operations against surface ships and land targets. It also acts as an escort to protect aircraft carriers, merchantmen, and other ships against surface or air attack. It may have an antisubmarine capability. Its own aircraft-handling capability is restricted to one or two float planes, helicopters, or other short take-off and landing types.

CULTURAL REVOLUTION The People's Republic of China underwent a period of political violence and turmoil from 1966 to 1969 known as the Cultural Revolution. Mao Zedong initiated the revolution by forming the Red Guards to eliminate opposition to his policies. The guards' zeal became excessive and the People's Liberation Army assumed an enlarged role in the political system to help restore order.

DAMAGE LIMITATION Active or passive efforts (including counterforce and civil defense measures) designed to limit the level or geographic extent of devastation during war.

D-DAY The day on which an operation commences or is due to commence. This may be the commencement of hostilities or any other operation.

Défense (de) tous azimuts The use of defense forces geared to meet threats from any direction, usually used in reference to French refusal under de Gaulle to specify either superpower as the primary security threat. It was popularized as France's military policy under de Gaulle.

DEFENSE IN DEPTH The siting of mutually supporting defense positions designed to absorb and progressively weaken an attack, prevent initial observations of the whole position by the enemy, and allow the commander to maneuver his reserve.

DEFENSE PLANNING COMMITTEE The Defense Planning Committee of NATO was formed in 1966 after France left the integrated military organization. The fourteen-nation committee deals with issues related to alliance-integrated military planning and other matters in which France does not participate.

DEPRESSED TRAJECTORY The trajectory of a ballistic missile fired at an angle to the ground significantly lower than the angle of a minimum-energy trajectory.

DESTROYER A medium-sized warship configured to escort and protect other ships against air, submarine, and surface attacks. It may also be used for independent offensive operations against enemy ships or land targets. Some destroyers embark one or two helicopters.

DÉTENTE The relaxation of tensions in international relations that may be achieved formally or informally.

DETERRENCE Measures taken to prevent aggression by opponents and to inhibit escalation if combat occurs; the prevention from action by fear of the consequences. Threats of force predominate. It is a state of mind produced by one's perception of a threat of unacceptable counteraction by an opponent.

DETERRENCE BY DENIAL Deterring another power from a first strike by convincing the opponent that no military benefit could be gained by striking first. This basically counterforce posture requires deployment of damage-limiting and disarming forces and corresponds to the Soviet conceptualization of deterrence.

DIVISION When used in reference to ground forces, a division is a tactical unit that is self-sufficient in arms and services for the conduct of sustained combat. A division is larger than a regiment or brigade but smaller than a corps. The number of troops and the quantity of equipment in a division vary by country and by type (infantry, artillery, etc.). A typical infantry division may have 10,000–15,000 troops.

DOCTRINE The fundamental principles by which the military forces or elements thereof guide their actions in support of national objectives. It is authoritative but requires judgment in application.

ECONOMIC WARFARE The offensive or defensive use of trade, foreign aid programs, financial transactions, and other matters that influence the production, distribution, and consumption of goods and services. It seeks to achieve national security objectives by augmenting friendly capabilities and diminishing or neutralizing enemy capabilities and potential.

ELECTRONIC COUNTERCOUNTERMEASURES (ECCM) Electronic warfare involving actions taken to retain effective use of the electromagnetic spectrum despite the enemy's use of electronic countermeasures.

ELECTRONIC COUNTERMEASURES (ECM) Electronic warfare waged to prevent or reduce an enemy's effective use of weapons and tactics utilizing electromagnetic radiations.

EQUIVALENT MEGATONNAGE (EMT) A measure used to compare the destructive potential of differing combinations of nuclear warhead yields against relatively soft countervalue targets.

ERETZ ISRAEL The common Hebrew name of Palestine, which roughly corresponds geographically to Palestine under the British mandate boundaries.

ESCALATION Intensification or broadening of a conflict through the use of more powerful weapons, larger numbers of forces, or the geographic spread of the conflict.

ESCALATION LADDER Successive levels of intensity along the conflict ladder, with strategic nuclear warfare options as the uppermost rung.

ESSENTIAL EQUIVALENCE A policy that prescribes roughly equal force structure capabilities and effectiveness without demanding numerical equality of all weapon types.

EUROGROUP The Eurogroup was established in 1968 by ten Western European members of NATO. Its objective is to coordinate and improve the West European military contribution to the alliance through greater overall cooperation in defense matters.

EUROPEAN ECONOMIC COMMUNITY (EEC) An association established in 1958 with the purpose of promoting the economic welfare of members by abolishing trade barriers among signatories and adopting common import duties on items from other countries. Currently Great Britain, France, West Germany, Italy, Belgium, Luxembourg, Denmark, Ireland, and the Netherlands belong to the EEC. (Also known as the Common Market.)

EUROSTRATEGIC WEAPONS Nuclear weapons deployed by the USSR and designed for use against Western Europe (i.e., the SS-20 IRBM).

EXTENDED DETERRENCE Extension of the deterrent value of the United States strategic nuclear forces to protect other countries (most notably NATO and ANZUS members and Japan) from aggression.

FIELD ARMY An administrative and tactical organization composed of a headquarters, certain organic army troops, service support troops, a variable number of corps, and a variable number of divisions. *See also* Division.

FINITE DETERRENCE Deterrence predicated on minimum capabilities corresponding to precisely calculated needs. Cities are targeted.

FIREBREAK A psychological barrier that inhibits escalation from one level of conflict intensity to another, especially from conventional to nuclear warfare.

FIRST STRIKE The first offensive move of a war. As applied to general nuclear war, it implies the ability to eliminate effective retaliation by the opposition. *See also* Counterforce; Second strike.

FIRST-STRIKE CAPABILITY A military capability sufficient to eliminate effective retaliation by initiating an attack against the opponent's forces. It usually involves targeting nuclear weapons in a counterforce mode.

FISSION The splitting of an atomic nucleus (as by bombardment with neutrons) of certain heavy elements (such as uranium and plutonium), resulting in the release of substantial quantities of energy. *See also* Thermonuclear.

FLEXIBLE RESPONSE A strategy prescribing forces able to respond to a threat at any point along the conflict spectrum. Robert McNamara adopted flexible response as the U.S. strategy in the early 1960s as a replacement for massive retaliation, which was commonly perceived to be an almost immediate resort to nuclear weapons in response to Communist aggression.

FLIGHT In navy and marine corps usage, a specified group of aircraft usually engaged in a common mission; the basic tactical unit in the Air Force, consisting of four or more aircraft in two or more elements; a single aircraft airborne on a nonoperational mission.

Force de dissuasion The name commonly given to France's nuclear weapons, which are intended to provide the country with minimum deterrence.

Force de frappe A label applied to France's nuclear forces, as they would become a striking force should their deterrent power fail.

FORWARD-BASED SYSTEMS (FBS) U.S. nuclear forces based in Europe or on aircraft carriers capable of striking the USSR.

FORWARD DEFENSE The NATO strategy that dictates resistance to a Warsaw Pact invasion at the point of penetration, as opposed to an orderly retreat to more defensible lines. This strategy has been particularly espoused by West Germany, as it is German territory that would be lost by any falling back.

FORWARD EDGE OF THE BATTLE AREA (FEBA) The foremost limits of a series of areas in which ground combat units are deployed, excluding the areas in which the covering or screening forces are operating, designated to coordinate fire support, the positioning of forces, or the maneuver of units.

FRENCH COMMUNITY With the advent of France's Fifth Republic in 1958, a new constitutional arrangement established the French Community to preside over the country's overseas territories. These territories were given the choice of independence or autonomous status in the community. Initially only Guinea chose independence, but within three years several others made the same decision. In the last two decades, the formalistic community has largely given way to a series of bilateral agreements between France and its former possessions.

FRG Federal Republic of Germany

FRIGATE A medium to small surface warship armed as an escort against surface attack and either air or submarine attack. It may be capable of embarking and handling one or two helicopters.

FRONTAL AVIATION The primary mission of Frontal Aviation (USSR) has traditionally been to provide air support—air defense, ground assault, reconnaissance, and electronic warfare—to ground forces. This mission has been broadened of late to encompass air strikes against theater nuclear reserves and tactical air forces. Current inventory aircraft include the mainstay Mig-21/Fishbed as well as the Mig-25/Foxbat B, the Mig-23/Flogger, the SU-17/Fitter, the Fencer A, and various helicopters and medium transports.

FUSION The process, accompanied by the release of tremendous amounts of energy, whereby the nuclei of light elements combine to form the nuclei of heavier elements. *See also* Fission; Thermonuclear.

FY Fiscal year

GANG OF FOUR Four members of the Politburo of the People's Republic of China (Jiang Qing, Wang Hungwen, Chang Ch'un-Ch'ia, and Yao Wen-yuan) helped spearhead the radical thrust of the Cultural Revolution and were subsequently labeled the Gang of Four. Vying for political power following Mao's death, the Gang of Four was purged by the more moderate faction led by Hua Guofeng.

GAO Government Accounting Office (United States)

GDP Gross domestic product

GENERAL PURPOSE FORCES All combat forces not designed primarily to accomplish strategic offensive/defensive or strategic mobility missions. *See also* Strategic defense; Strategic mobility; Strategic offense.

GENERAL STAFF A group of officers in the headquarters of divisions (or larger units) that helps its commanders in planning, coordinating, and supervising operations.

GENERAL WAR Armed conflict between major powers in which the total resources of the belligerents are employed and the national survival of a major belligerent is in jeopardy. *See also* Limited war.

GOLAN HEIGHTS A 714-square-mile area in the southwestern corner of Syria with a long history of conflict in the Arab-Israeli dispute. Israel has been loath to relinquish the region since capturing it in the 1967 Middle East War, for it had long been used by guerrillas to shell nearby Israeli settlements.

GOSPLAN The Soviet State Planning Committee, which is responsible for the coordination and guidance of all economic planning in the USSR.

GRADUATED DETERRENCE A range of deterrent power that affords credible capabilities to inhibit aggression across much of the conflict spectrum.

GRADUATED RESPONSE The incremental application of national power to meet a security threat. This type of escalation allows the opponent to accommodate each level of power gradually.

GRAND STRATEGY The art and science of employing national power under all circumstances to exert desired types and degrees of control over the opposition by applying force, the threat of force, indirect pressures, diplomacy, subterfuge, and other imaginative means to attain national security objectives. *See also* National objectives.

GROUND FIRE Small arms ground-to-air fire directed against aircraft.

GROUND-LAUNCHED CRUISE MISSILE (GLCM) A cruise missile launched from a ground platform. *See also* Cruise missile.

GROUND ZERO (GZ) The point on the surface of the earth at or vertically below or above the center of a planned or actual nuclear detonation.

GUERRILLA WARFARE Irregular forces conducting military and paramilitary operations in hostile territory.

HARDENED SITE A site constructed to withstand the blasts and associated effects of a nuclear attack and likely to be protected against chemical, biological, or radiological attack. *See also* Hard target.

HARD TARGET A target fortified against nuclear blasts.

HELSINKI AGREEMENTS Signed on 1 August 1975, the Helsinki Agreements were the final act of the thirty-five-nation Conference on Security and Cooperation in Europe. The four sections of the agreement on East-West relations included measures on economic cooperation, humanitarian issues, and increased human contacts among nations, and plans for a follow-up conference. The West viewed the agreements on human rights as a major victory, but in exchange they, in effect, endorsed the post-World War II boundaries in Europe.

HI-LO MIX Mingling high-cost, high-performance items with relatively low-cost, low-performance items in any given weapons system to achieve the best balance between quantity and quality in ways that maximize capabilities and minimize expenses.

IAF Israeli Air Force

IDF *See* Israeli Defense Forces.

IDFN Israeli Defense Forces Navy

IMEMO Institute for the World Economy and International Affairs (USSR)

INDEPENDENT EUROPEAN PROGRAM GROUP (IEPG) An independent forum for European cooperation in defense equipment in which France can participate. Membership includes Belgium, Denmark, France, West Germany, Italy, Greece, Luxembourg, the Netherlands, Norway, Portugal, Turkey, and the United Kingdom.

INERTIAL GUIDANCE A guidance system designed to project a missile over a predetermined path, wherein the path of the missile is adjusted after launching by devices wholly within the missile and independent of outside information. The system measures and converts accelerations experienced to distance traveled in a certain direction.

INFRASTRUCTURE A term generally applicable for all fixed and permanent installations, fabrications, or facilities for the support and control of military forces.

INTELLIGENCE The product resulting from the collection, evaluation, analysis, integration, and interpretation of all information concerning one or more aspects of foreign countries or areas, which is immediately or potentially significant to the development and execution of plans, policies, and operations.

INTELLIGENCE ESTIMATE An appraisal of the elements of intelligence relating to a specific situation or condition with a view to determining the courses of action open to the enemy or potential enemy and the probable order of their adoption.

INTERCEPTOR AIRCRAFT A manned aircraft utilized for identification and/or engagement of aerodynamic threats (aircraft and cruise missiles).

INTERCONTINENTAL BALLISTIC MISSILE (ICBM) A ballistic missile with a range of 3,000 to 8,000 nautical miles.

INTERDICTION To prevent or hinder, by any means, enemy use of an area or route.

INTERMEDIATE-RANGE BALLISTIC MISSILE (IRBM) A ballistic missile with a range capability of 1,500 to 3,000 nautical miles.

INTEROPERABILITY The ability of the armed forces of different nations to operate each other's equipment and to interchange the components of such equipment. *See also* Standardization.

ISRAELI DEFENSE FORCES (IDF) The armed forces of Israel, consisting of the Israeli Air Force, the Israeli Ground Defense Forces, and the Israeli Defense Forces Navy.

JCS Joint Chiefs of Staff (United States)

JOINT FORCE A general term applied to a force that is composed of significant elements of the army, the navy or the marine corps, and the air force, or two or more of these services, operating under a single commander authorized to exercise unified command or operational control over such joint forces.

JOINT STRATEGIC CAPABILITIES PLAN (JSCP) A short-range, current capabilities plan that translates U.S. national objectives and policies for the next fiscal year into terms of military objectives and strategic concepts and defines military tasks for cold, limited, and general war which are in consonance with the actual U.S. military capabilities.

JOINT STRATEGIC OBJECTIVE PLAN (JSOP) A midrange objective plan that translates future (five to eight years forward) U.S. national objectives into military and strategic concepts and defines the basic military tasks for various types of war that may be accomplished with the objective force levels.

JSDF Japanese Self-Defense Forces

JSPD (JOINT STRATEGIC PLANNING DOCUMENT) A JCS planning document that provides advice on forces required, military objectives, and strategy for an eight-year period (United States).

KGB Committee for State Security (*Komitet Gosudarstvennoye Bezopasnosti*). The predominant state and internal security police organization of the USSR.

KILOTON The equivalent explosive power of 1,000 tons of trinitrotoluene (TNT), used as a measure of yield for nuclear weapons.

LAUNCHER A structural device designed to support and hold a missile in position for firing.

LAUNCH ON WARNING A doctrine calling for the launch of ballistic missiles when a missile attack against them is detected and before the attacking warheads reach their targets.

LEAD TIME The amount of time between the start of research and development on a weapons system and its operational deployment.

LIMITED WAR A conflict in which participants limit themselves in terms of objectives, forces, weapons, targets, and geographic areas.

MAIN POLITICAL ADMINISTRATION (MPA) The department of the Central Committee of the Communist party of the Soviet Union whose responsibility it is to maintain firm Party control of the military.

MANEUVERABLE REENTRY VEHICLE (MARV) A ballistic missile reentry vehicle that has the capability of changing its trajectory during reentry, thus making it more accurate and more survivable than reentry vehicles without this capability.

MANHATTAN PROJECT A term referring to the collective research and development efforts that led to the successful detonation of the atomic bombs over Japan in August 1945. The actual research and development took place at numerous sites in the United States and Canada with the help of scientists of several nationalities.

MASSIVE RETALIATION The strategic doctrine of the United States during the 1950s. As outlined by Secretary of State Dulles, it held out the possibility of a nuclear reaction to virtually any aggression that demanded a military response. Massive retaliation was adopted primarily to enable cuts in the Defense Department budget, for it allowed minimal expenditure on conventional forces.

MAXIMUM DETERRENCE Diversified, survivable deterrent power of such quality and magnitude that it affords optimum capabilities to inhibit aggression across the entire conflict spectrum. *See also* Deterrence; Minimum deterrence.

MEDIUM-RANGE BALLISTIC MISSILE (MRBM) A ballistic missile with a range of 600 to 1,500 nautical miles.

MEGATON The equivalent explosive power of one million tons of trinitrotoluene (TNT), used as a measure of yield for nuclear weapons.

MIG The name "Mig" stands for Mikoyan and Gurevich, noted Soviet aircraft designers, and refers to a type of Soviet tactical aircraft.

MILITARY ASSISTANCE ADVISORY GROUP (MAAG) A joint service group normally under the military commander of a unified command and representing the secretary of defense which primarily administers the U.S. military assistance planning and programming in the host country. *See also* Joint force; Unified command.

MILITARY ASSISTANCE PROGRAM (MAP) That portion of the U.S. security assistance authorized by the Foreign Assistance Act of 1961 (as amended) which provides defense articles and services to recipients on a nonreimbursable (grant) basis.

MILITARY BALANCE The comparative combat power of two competing countries or coalitions.

MILITARY DOCTRINE Fundamental principles by which the military forces guide their actions in support of national objectives. It is authoritative but requires judgment in application.

MILITARY NECESSITY The principle whereby a belligerent has the right to apply any measures that are required to bring about the successful conclusion of a military operation and that are not forbidden by the laws of war.

MILITARY STRATEGY The art and science of employing military power under all circumstances to attain national security objectives by applying force or the threat of force.

MINIMUM DETERRENCE Deterrent power predicated on the belief that countries possessing even few nuclear weapons are automatically guaranteed immunity from rational attack, since the penalty for aggression presumably would be intolerable. *See also* Deterrence.

MINUTEMAN A three-stage solid-propellant intercontinental ballistic missile that is the mainstay of the U.S. land-based strategic missile force. Designated as LGM-30.

MISSILE EXPERIMENTAL (MX) The MX is being developed as the next-generation U.S. ICBM. As it is a more accurate missile than the Minuteman, the increased survivability from enemy attack is to be achieved through mobile basing.

MOBILE MISSILE Any ballistic or cruise missile mounted on and/or fired from a movable platform, such as a truck, train, ground effects machine, ship, or aircraft. *See also* Minuteman.

MOBILIZATION The act of preparing for war or other emergencies through assembling and organizing national resources; the process by which the armed forces or part of them are brought to a state of readiness for war or other national emergency. This includes assembling and organizing personnel, supplies, and materiel for active military service.

MOBILIZATION BASE The total of all resources available, or that can be made available, to meet foreseeable wartime needs. Such resources include the manpower and materiel resources and services required for the support of essential military, civilian, and survival activities, as well as the elements affecting their state of readiness, such as (but not limited to) the following: manning levels, state of training, modernization of equipment, mobilization of materiel reserves and facilities, continuity of government, civil defense plans and preparedness measures, psychological preparedness of the people, international agreements, planning with industry, dispersion, and stand-by legislation and controls.

MOSSAD The oldest of Israel's five intelligence agencies. (While the Israeli intelligence community as a whole came under criticism following the 1973 Arab surprise attack, Mossad had been allowed only to gather—not assess—military intelligence prior to the 1973 war.)

MULTIPLE INDEPENDENTLY TARGETED REENTRY VEHICLE (MIRV) A missile reentry vehicle containing several nuclear warheads, each capable of striking a different target.

MULTIPOLAR Distribution of power among several blocs in the international community, as opposed to the two-way power division of a bipolar world.

MUTUAL AND BALANCED FORCE REDUCTION (MBFR) The acronym MBFR commonly refers to the talks that began in October 1973 between NATO and Warsaw Pact countries regarding force reductions in Europe. The USSR and East

European participants object to the inclusion of the term *balanced* and refer to the "MFR" talks.

MUTUAL ASSURED DESTRUCTION (MAD) A condition in which an assured destruction capability is possessed by opposing sides.

MUTUAL FORCE REDUCTIONS (MFR) The original name for the Mutual and Balanced Force Reduction (MBFR) talks between NATO and Warsaw Pact countries. The word *balanced* was included by the NATO countries seeking to reduce the asymmetry in force levels.

MUTUAL SECURITY TREATY (MST) Japan and the United States signed the Mutual Security Treaty in 1952 to ensure the defense of the Japanese island chain. In return for the right to maintain bases on Japanese territory, the United States assumed primary responsibility for the country's defense.

NATIONAL COMMAND AUTHORITIES (NCA) The president and the secretary of defense or their duly deputized alternates.

NATIONAL INTELLIGENCE ESTIMATE (NIE) A strategic estimate of capabilities, vulnerabilities, and probable courses of action of foreign nations that is produced at the national level as a composite of the views of the intelligence community. It can be formulated on a current topic or situation in a particular country at the direction of the director of central intelligence (DCI) and represents the pooled judgment of the U.S. intelligence community in policy making at the highest levels of government.

NATIONAL INTEREST A highly generalized concept of elements that constitute a state's compelling needs, including self-preservation, independence, national integrity, military security, and economic well-being.

NATIONAL OBJECTIVES The fundamental aims, goals, or purposes of a nation (as opposed to the methods of achieving those ends) toward which a policy is directed and the nation's energies are applied. These objectives may be short, medium, or long range in nature.

NATIONAL POLICY A broad course of action or guiding statements adopted by a government to help meet national objectives.

NATIONAL POWER The combined resources (political, economic, technological, social, scientific, military, and geographic) of a nation that comprise its capabilities or potential.

NATIONAL SECURITY COUNCIL (NSC) Created by the National Security Act of 1947, the primary functions of the NSC include policy coordination, advice, planning, and crisis management. While serving as the focal point for ideas and initiatives within the national security community, the council's nature and role vary greatly with the personality and desires of the president it serves.

NATIONAL STRATEGY The art and science of developing and applying the political, economic, psychological, and military powers of a nation during peace and war to meet national objectives.

NBC Nuclear, biological, and chemical weapons.

NEUTRALITY In international law, the attitude of impartiality, during periods of war, adopted by third states toward belligerents and recognized by the belligerents, which creates rights and duties between the impartial states and the belligerents. In a United Nations enforcement action, the rules of neutrality apply to impartial members of the United Nations except as far as they are excluded by the obligation of such members under the U.N. Charter.

NIXON DOCTRINE Pronounced by President Richard Nixon in 1970, the Nixon Doctrine pledged to U.S. allies that in deterring nuclear warfare primary reliance would remain with American forces, but at the local warfare level the primary defense burden would fall on the country threatened. The Nixon Doctrine (also known as the Guam Doctrine) reflected domestic pressures to reduce defense spending and overseas commitments.

NONALIGNMENT The political attitude of a state which does not associate or identify itself with the political ideology or objective espoused by other states, groups of states, or international causes, or with the foreign policies stemming therefrom. It does not preclude involvement, but expresses the attitude of no precommitment to a particular state (or bloc) or policy before a situation arises. *See also* Neutrality.

NONPROLIFERATION TREATY (NPT) The treaty to prohibit the spread of nuclear weapons or the technology to build them from states that do not possess this capability. *See* Arms control.

NORTH ATLANTIC TREATY ORGANIZATION (NATO) A regional military organization formed in 1949 by the North Atlantic Treaty. Its primary mission is to deter and defend the North Atlantic area against aggression by the Warsaw Pact nations. Current membership includes Belgium, the United Kingdom, Denmark, West Germany, Greece, Iceland, Italy, Luxembourg, the Netherlands, Norway, Portugal, Turkey, Canada, France, and the United States. France, while a member of the alliance, withdrew from NATO's integrated military command in 1966.

NTH COUNTRY A reference to additions to the group of powers possessing nuclear weapons—the next country of a series to acquire nuclear capabilities.

NUCLEAR CLUB A slang term referring to countries that have developed their own nuclear capability.

NUCLEAR FREE ZONES Areas in which the production and stationing of nuclear weapons are prohibited. The Treaty for the Prohibition of Nuclear Weapons in Latin America, which entered into force on 22 January 1968 (Treaty of Tateloco), established a nuclear free zone in Latin America.

NUCLEAR THRESHOLD The psychological line between conventional and nuclear warfare. The difficulty of crossing this threshold varies directly with a state's reluctance to use nuclear weapons.

NUCLEAR UMBRELLA The protection that the United States offers to friendly nations with its deterrent forces. This protection against aggression is provided by linking the security of another country to use of U.S. nuclear weapons.

NUCLEAR YIELD The energy released in the detonation of a nuclear weapon, measured in terms of the kilotons or megatons of trinitrotoluene (TNT) required to produce the same energy release. Yields are categorized as: very low, less than 1 kiloton; iow, 1-10 kilotons; medium, 10-50 kilotons; high, 50-500 kilotons; or very high, over 500 kilotons.

OAS Organization of American States

OECD Organization for Economic Cooperation and Development

OFFICE OF MANAGEMENT AND BUDGET (OMB) The agency in the Executive Office of the president having primary responsibility for efficient and economical conduct of government operations and for budget preparation and administration.

OPERATIONS RESEARCH The analytical study of military problems, undertaken to provide responsible commanders and staff agencies with a scientific basis for decision on action to improve military operations. *See also* Systems analysis.

ORDER OF BATTLE The identification, strength, command structure, and disposition of the personnel, units, and equipment of any military force.

OSD Office of the secretary of defense (United States)

OVERKILL Destructive capability beyond what is theoretically necessary to destroy specified targets and achieve designated security objectives.

OVERPRESSURE The pressure resulting from the blast wave of an explosion. It is referred to as "positive" when it exceeds atmospheric pressure and "negative" when resulting pressures are less than atmospheric pressure during the passage of the wave. *See also* Hardened site; Hard target.

PALESTINE LIBERATION ORGANIZATION (PLO) The PLO was established to represent the Palestinian Arabs. The organization has served as a base for much anti-Israeli guerrilla activity, and its role in the settlement of Middle East problems is an issue of contention, with Israel refusing to recognize it as the legitimate representative of Palestinian Arabs.

PARITY A force structure standard that dictates that overall military capabilities be roughly equal to those of a particular rival.

PASSIVE AIR DEFENSE All measures, other than active defense, taken to minimize the effects of hostile air action. These include the use of cover, concealment, camouflage, deception, dispersion, and protective construction (e.g., missile site hardening).

PAUSE In the defense of Western Europe, a moment of reflection imposed on any aggressor before the defense resorts to nuclear weapons, i.e., one function of NATO's conventional troop strength.

PAYLOAD The weapon and/or cargo capacity of any aircraft or missile system, expressed variously in pounds, numbers of bombs, air-to-air and air-to-surface missiles, chemical warfare canisters, guns, sensors, electronic countermeasures packets, etc., and in terms of missile warhead yields (kilotons, megatons). *See also* Throw-weight.

PCR Romanian Communist party

PD (PRESIDENTIAL DECISION) A document associated with the Carter administration.

PENETRATION AIDS ("PEN" AIDS) Techniques and/or devices employed by offensive aerospace weapon systems to increase the probability of penetration of enemy defenses.

PEOPLE'S WAR As defined by the People's Republic of China, People's War involves defending the country with simply armed infantry forces, guerrilla units, and a large popular militia. The requirements of minimum deterrence guide deployment of nuclear weapons. The sectors of Chinese society advocating People's War envision a significant political role for the armed forces, and constitute one pole in a continuing struggle over what military doctrine is to follow. *See also* People's War under modern conditions.

PEOPLE'S WAR UNDER MODERN CONDITIONS This concept implies a shift in doctrinal emphasis (versus People's War) for the armed forces of the People's Republic of China. Conventional defense is stressed more than reliance on militia forces, and the armed forces' political role is relatively reduced.

PLA (PEOPLE'S LIBERATION ARMY) The formal designation of the armed forces of the People's Republic of China.

PLUTON A French land-mobile, tactical nuclear weapon with a maximum range of 120 km and a warhead of 15 or 25 kilotons.

POLARIS The oldest U.S. SLBM.

POLITBURO The highest Soviet policy-making body, with ten to fifteen full members. Although the Politburo's operation is cloaked in secrecy, it is known that military influence in the body varies with the changing composition of its membership.

POLITICAL CONSULTATIVE COMMITTEE A Soviet-dominated, high-level Warsaw Pact committee composed of the Communist party first secretaries, heads of government, and defense and foreign ministers from each member. The committee ostensibly serves as the pact's policy-formulation organ.

POSEIDON The Poseidon gave MIRV capability to the U.S. SLBM arsenal.

PPBS (PLANNING, PROGRAMMING, AND BUDGETING SYSTEM) A resource management process used by the U.S. Department of Defense to provide military capabilities to meet defined national security objectives.

PRC People's Republic of China

PREEMPTIVE ATTACK An attack launched in anticipation of an enemy's intention to initiate hostilities.

PRESIDENTIAL REVIEW MEMORANDUM (PRM) Under the Carter administration, Presidential Review Memorandums functioned within the National Security System. They defined a particular security-related problem, set a deadline, and assigned the study to one of two NSC committees—the Policy Review Committee or the Special Coordinating Committee. The responsible committee investigated the issue and made a recommendation to the president on any action to be taken.

PRINCIPLES OF WAR A collection of abstract considerations which has been distilled from historical experience and which, applied to specific circumstances with acumen, assists strategists in selecting suitable courses of action.

PROLIFERATION The spread of nuclear weapons or nuclear weapon capability to an increasing number of countries.

PROPAGANDA Any form of communication in support of national objectives designed to influence the opinions, emotions, attitudes, or behavior of any group in order to benefit the sponsor, either directly or indirectly.

PROPORTIONAL DETERRENCE Medium powers can obtain proportional deterrence by deploying enough nuclear striking power to inflict unacceptable damage—damage that would outweigh any gain anticipated by the attacker—on any aggressor. Proportional deterrence is the foundation of France's *force de dissuasion,* as it theoretically protects France from superpower aggression even with a far smaller nuclear force.

PROTOCOL OF 1974 In conjunction with the ABM Treaty of SALT I, the 1974 Protocol limits the United States and the USSR to one ABM site each, with a maximum of 100 ABM launchers deployed.

PROXY WAR A form of limited war in which Great Powers avoid a direct confrontation by furthering their national security interests and objectives through conflict between representatives or associates. *See also* Limited war.

PSYCHOLOGICAL WARFARE The planned use of propaganda and other psychological actions having the primary purpose of influencing the opinions, emotions, attitudes, and behavior of hostile foreign groups in such a way as to support the achievement of national objectives. *See also* National objectives; Propaganda.

PVO-STRANY *See* Air Defense Forces of the USSR.

QUICK-REACTION FORCE A force of 100,000 troops proposed for the United States by President Jimmy Carter, with the capability of rapid deployment anywhere in the world.

R&D Research and development

REENTRY VEHICLE (RV) That portion of an ICBM or SLBM that reenters the earth's atmosphere carrying a warhead.

RESERVE COMPONENT Armed forces not in active service. U.S. reserve components include the Army National Guard and Army Reserve, the Naval Reserve, the Marine Corps Reserve, the Air National Guard, and the Air Force Reserve.

RESIDUAL FORCES Unexpended portions of the remaining U.S. forces which have an immediate combat potential for continued military operations, and which have been deliberately withheld from utilization.

REVOLUTIONARY WAR Efforts to seize political power by illegitimate and/or coercive means, destroying existing systems of government and social structures in the process.

SALT *See* Strategic Arms Limitation Talks

SANCTIONS An economic warfare tool, usually adopted by several states acting in concert, to compel a country or coalition of countries to cease undesirable practices or otherwise bow to the wielder's will. *See also* Compellence; Economic warfare.

SCC *See* Standing Consultative Commission.

SEA CONTROL The employment of naval forces, supplemented by land and aerospace forces as appropriate, to destroy enemy naval forces, suppress enemy ocean-going commerce, protect vital shipping lanes, and establish local superiority in areas of naval operations.

SECOND STRIKE The first counterblow of a war, generally associated with nuclear operations.

SECOND-STRIKE CAPABILITY The ability to survive a first strike with sufficient resources to deliver an effective counterblow. *See also* Assured destruction; First Strike; Mutual assured destruction; Unacceptable damage.

SENSORS Devices used to detect objects or environmental conditions. Examples are radars and optical systems used in missile and aircraft warning/tracking/engagement systems, seismographs used in detection of underground nuclear tests, and devices used to detect long-range emissions from nuclear tests that vent to the atmosphere.

SHORT-RANGE BALLISTIC MISSILE (SRBM) A ballistic missile with a range of up to 600 nautical miles. Currently deployed American SRBMs include the Pershing, Lance, and Sergeant. The USSR has deployed the Scud, Scaleboard, and Frog SRBMs, and France the Pluton.

SHOW OF FORCE The purposeful exhibition of armed might before an enemy or potential enemy, usually in a crisis situation, to reinforce deterrent demands.

SINO-SOVIET PACT OF 1950 The result of determined bargaining between Mao Zedong and Josef Stalin, the Sino-Soviet Pact of 1950 obligated each country to thirty years of mutual security and friendship. In it the Soviets also pledged to provide China with $300 million in economic aid and to return Manchurian rail and port facilities that they had acquired in 1945.

SLBM (SEA-LAUNCHED BALLISTIC MISSILE) A ballistic missile that is carried in and launched from a submarine.

SLCM (SEA-LAUNCHED CRUISE MISSILE) A cruise missile carried by and launched from a surface ship or submarine.

SOFT TARGET A target that is not significantly protected from the various effects of a nuclear blast.

SORTIE An operational flight made by one aircraft.

SQUADRON An organization consisting of two or more divisions of ships, or two or more divisions of aircraft (navy) or flights of aircraft (air force). It is normally, but not necessarily, composed of ships or aircraft of the same type. It is also the basic administration unit of the army, navy, marine corps, and air force. *See also* Flight.

SRBM *See* short-range ballistic missile.

SSBN (STRATEGIC SUBMARINE, BALLISTIC, NUCLEAR) A nuclear-powered submarine equipped to carry and launch ballistic missiles.

STANDARDIZATION The adoption of like or similar military equipment, ammunition, supplies, and operational, logistical, and administrative procedures among countries of a security alliance.

STANDING CONSULTATIVE COMMISSION (SCC) The SCC was established in December 1972 in accordance with the provisions of the SALT I ABM Treaty. It meets regularly and its aim, in the language of the treaty, is "to promote the objectives and implementation of the provisions" of the treaty and the Interim SALT Agreement.

STRAIT OF TIRAN A vital choke point between the Sinai Peninsula and Saudi Arabia which controls Israeli access to the Red Sea. Closure of the Strait of Tiran by President Gamal Nasser in the spring of 1967 helped bring on the 1967 Middle East War.

STRATEGIC A term relating to the power relationships that exist between nations and the ability of nations to control aspects of the international environment. It applies to the means of attack over intermediate or intercontinental ranges, usually in a nuclear mode.

STRATEGIC ARMS LIMITATION TALKS (SALT) The Strategic Arms Limitation Talks between the United States and the USSR were begun in 1969. SALT I, concluded in 1972, encompassed the Treaty on the Limitation of Antiballistic Missile Systems and the Interim Agreement on Certain Measures with Respect to the Limitations of Strategic Offensive Arms. The agreement essentially froze at existing levels the number of ballistic launchers, operational or under construction. The Protocol of 1974 to the Treaty on the Limitation of ABM Systems restricts each side to a single ABM site with a maximum of 100 launchers deployed. The SALT II negotiations began in November 1972 and a general framework was agreed on in May 1978. Three main elements comprise the SALT II framework:

1. A treaty imposing the following limitations:
   a. 2,250 strategic launchers.
   b. a sublimit of 1,320 MIRVed SLBM and ICBM launchers and aircraft-carrying long-range cruise missiles.
   c. a sublimit of 820 MIRVed ICBM launchers.
   d. a sublimit of 1,200 MIRVed ballistic missiles.
   e. no limit on the range of cruise missiles carried on heavy bombers.
2. A protocol including the following provisions:
   a. Only one new type of land-based ICBM system could be deployed by either side during the treaty's duration until 1985.
   b. Ground-launched and sea-launched cruise missiles with a range of over 600 km would be banned for three years, although research on these missiles would be permissible.
   c. The number of warheads on existing types of missiles

would be frozen at present levels. New MIRVed missiles would be limited to ten warheads per ICBM and fourteen warheads per SLBM.

3. A joint statement of principles for SALT III. These principles would serve as general guidelines for SALT III, and involve areas too controversial to have been agreed upon in SALT II.

STRATEGIC DEFENSE The strategy and forces designed primarily to protect a nation, its outposts, and/or its allies from the hazards of general war. It features defense against missiles, both land and sea launched, and long-range bombers. *See also* Strategic offense.

STRATEGIC DELIVERY VEHICLE A vehicle capable of delivering a strategic nuclear weapon. Manned bombers, sea-launched ballistic missiles, and land-based ballistic missiles are examples of strategic delivery vehicles currently deployed by the world's nuclear powers.

STRATEGIC MOBILITY The ability to shift personnel, equipment, and supplies effectively and expeditiously between theaters of operation.

STRATEGIC OFFENSE The strategy and forces designed primarily to destroy the enemy's war-making capacity during general war or to so degrade it that the opposition collapses. *See also* National interest; National objectives; Residual forces.

SUBMARINE A warship designed for under-the-surface operations with the primary mission of locating and destroying ships, including other submarines. It is capable of various other naval missions. SSNs are nuclear-powered submarines. *See also* SSBN.

SUBVERSION Action designed to undermine the military, economic, psychological, or political strength or morale of a regime. *See also* Propaganda; Unconventional warfare.

SUFFICIENCY A level of military strength that is adequate to achieve the objectives of a given country. Depending on various factors, superiority, equality, or inferiority of military strength vis-à-vis a rival power may be considered sufficient.

SURFACE-TO-AIR MISSILE (SAM) A surface-launched missile designed to operate against a target above the surface.

SURFACE-TO-SURFACE MISSILE (SSM) A surface-launched missile designed to operate against a target on the surface.

SURVEILLANCE The systematic observation of aerospace, surface, or subsurface areas, places, persons, or things by visual, aural, electronic, photographic, or other means.

SYSTEMS ANALYSIS As implemented by Secretary of Defense Robert McNamara during the Kennedy administration, systems analysis involves the application of cost analysis methods to maintain a credible global military presence.

TACTICAL A term referring to battlefield operations in general.

TACTICAL NUCLEAR WEAPONS Nuclear weapons with a range of less than 100 km. Examples include nuclear warheads delivered by artillery pieces and the French Pluton short-range missile.

TACTICAL NUCLEAR WEAPON (TNW) FORCES OR OPERATIONS Nuclear combat power expressly designed for deterrent, offensive, and defensive purposes that contribute to the accomplishment of localized military missions; the threatened or actual application of such power. It may be employed in general as well as limited wars.

TACTICS The detailed methods used to carry out strategic designs. Military tactics involve the employment of units in combat, including the arrangement and maneuvering of units in relation to each other and/or to the enemy.

TANK, MAIN BATTLE A tracked vehicle providing heavy armor protection and serving as the principal assault weapon of armored and infantry troops.

TARGET ACQUISITION SYSTEM A system that detects, identifies, and locates a target in enough detail to allow effective use of weapons.

TEAM B *See* National intelligence estimate.

TERMINAL GUIDANCE SYSTEMS A system that directs a missile between midcourse and its arrival in the vicinity of the target. The purpose of such systems is to achieve greater accuracy.

THEATER A geographical area outside the continental United States for which an American commander has been given responsibility. When used in reference to a level of conflict, it describes warfare below the strategic nuclear level yet above a localized conflict.

THEATER NUCLEAR WEAPONS Nuclear weapons below the strategic level yet with a range over 100 km (when targeted for use in a given theater, such as Western Europe). These weapons may be delivered by aircraft (medium and light bombers and tactical aircraft), MRBMs, IRBMs, or SSBNs.

THERMONUCLEAR An adjective referring to the process (or processes) in which very high temperatures are used to bring about the fusion of light nuclei, with the accompanying liberation of energy.

THERMONUCLEAR WEAPON A weapon in which very high temperatures are used to bring about the fusion of light nuclei, such as those of hydrogen isotopes (e.g., deuterium and tritium), with the accompanying release of energy. The high temperatures required are obtained by means of fission.

THINK TANKS Private companies specializing in defense-related research and analysis.

THREE-PERCENT GUIDELINE In response to the growing strength of Warsaw Pact forces, the NATO countries pledged themselves in 1977 to an annual growth rate in defense spending of 3 percent (real growth). This guideline has been met with varying degrees of success.

THRESHOLD An intangible and adjustable line between levels and types of conflicts, such as the separation between nuclear and nonnuclear warfare. The greater the reluctance to use nuclear weapons, the higher the threshold. *See also* Firebreak.

THROW-WEIGHT The throw-weight of a ballistic missile is the maximum useful weight that has been flight tested on the missile's boost stages and serves as an indicator of how large a warhead the missile can deliver. Conversion factors can yield an equivalent throw-weight for manned bombers.

TITAN A liquid-propellant, two-stage, rocket-powered intercontinental ballistic missile that is guided to its target by an all-inertial guidance and control system. The missile is equipped with a nuclear warhead and is designed for deployment in hardened and dispersed underground silos. Designated as LGM-25C.

TNT EQUIVALENT A measure of the energy released from the detonation of a nuclear weapon, or from the explosion of a given quantity of fissionable or fusionable material, in terms of the amount of trinitrotoluene (TNT) that would release the same amount of energy when exploded. *See also Kiloton; Megaton; Yield.*

TOOTH-TO-TAIL RATIO The ratio of forces in combat positions to those in support positions in a country's armed forces and in specific military organizations.

TRANSPORT AIRCRAFT Aircraft designed primarily for carrying personnel and/or cargo.

TREATY OF FRIENDSHIP, COOPERATION, AND MUTUAL ASSISTANCE (TFCMA) Bilateral treaties that the USSR has signed with East Germany, Finland, and a number of other states.

TRIAD U.S. nuclear forces include three components known collectively as the Triad. They are: ICBMs (550 Minuteman IIIs, 450 Minuteman IIs, and 54 Titan IIs), manned bombers (315 B-52s and 66 FB-111s), and SLBMs (Polaris and Poseidon missiles carried on 41 SSBNs).

TRIPWIRE CONCEPT Ground forces located near the border of a powerful potential invader can serve as a tripwire. Insufficient to repel the aggressor themselves, their engagement in a significant conflict would trigger large-scale escalation, usually entailing the use of nuclear weapons. U.S. troops in West Germany and French infantry divisions along the Franco-German border are both known by this term.

Trompe-l'oeil A visual deception.

TUBE ARTILLERY Howitzers and guns, as opposed to rockets and guided missiles. They may be towed or self-propelled.

TURNAROUND TIME The length of time necessary for servicing of an aircraft between operational missions.

UNACCEPTABLE DAMAGE The level of damage anticipated from a second strike which is high enough to deter an enemy from launching a first strike. National values and economic considerations help determine what level of damage is unacceptable.

UNCONVENTIONAL WARFARE A broad spectrum of military and paramilitary operations conducted in enemy-held, enemy-denied, or politically sensitive territory. Unconventional warfare includes but is not limited to the interrelated fields of guerrilla warfare, evasion and escape, subversion, sabotage, direct action missions, and other operations of a low-visibility, covert, or clandestine nature. These interrelated aspects of unconventional warfare may be prosecuted singly or collectively by predominantly indigenous personnel, usually supported and directed in varying degrees by (an) external source(s) during all conditions of war or peace.

UNIFIED COMMAND A command with a broad continuing mission under a single commander and composed of significant assigned components of two or more services. It is established and so designated by the president, through the secretary of defense with the advice and assistance of the Joint Chiefs of Staff, or, when so authorized by the Joint Chiefs of Staff, by a commander of an existing unified command established by the president.

VERIFICATION In arms control, any action, including inspection, detection, and identification, taken to ascertain compliance with agreed measures.

VLADIVOSTOCK ACCORDS President Gerald Ford and First Secretary Leonid Brezhnev met in Vladivostock in 1974 to discuss further limitations of strategic offensive arms. They agreed on four basic elements to be contained in a SALT II treaty: the new treaty would last through 1985; each side would be limited to 2,400 total nuclear delivery vehicles; each side would be limited to 1,320 MIRVed systems; and forward-based systems (such as U.S. nuclear-capable fighters in Europe) would not be discussed. *See also* Strategic Arms Limitation Talks.

VPK Military-Industrial Commission (USSR)

V/STOL Vertical/short take-off and landing

WAR-FIGHTING/WINNING DOCTRINE This doctrine prescribes forces equipped to conduct and win a conflict at any level, as opposed to forces under a deterrent doctrine, which are designed only to prevent the outbreak of war. War-fighting doctrine is usually associated with the USSR, whereas the United States has subscribed to war-avoidance doctrines.

WAR GAME A simulation, by whatever means, of a military operation involving two or more opposing forces, using rules, data, and procedures designed to depict an actual or assumed real-life situation.

WARHEAD That part of a missile, projectile, torpedo, rocket, or other munition which contains the nuclear or thermonuclear system, high explosive system, chemical or biological agents, or inert materials intended to inflict damage.

WAR POWERS ACT OF 1972 Initiated in response to dissatisfaction with presidential authority to conduct the Vietnam War, the War Powers Act reduces the president's authority to deploy armed forces abroad. Specifically, if the president commits American forces to battle on foreign soil, he must report his reasons to Congress within forty-eight hours and obtain Congressional approval of the commitment within sixty days; otherwise, the commitment must be halted.

WARSAW PACT An East European military alliance that is committed to the defense of the member states' territory. The signatories are the Soviet Union, Bulgaria, Czechoslovakia, East Germany, Hungary, Poland, and Romania. Signs of schisms in the Moscow-dominated alliance have thrown the wartime reliability of some members into question.

WEST BANK The United Nations Resolution of 1947 set aside 2,270 square miles west of the Jordan River for the establishment of an independent Arab state. Jordan subsequently gained control of the area by the Israel-Jordan Armistice Agreement of 1949. Israel captured the West Bank in 1967, an acquisition making Israel far more defensible. Currently, control of the West Bank is a matter of dispute between Israel and the various Arab countries.

WING, TACTICAL AIR A wing is a U.S. Air Force unit composed of one primary mission group and the requisite support personnel and facilities. A tactical air wing has fighter or attack aircraft as its primary mission group.

YIELD A measure of the destructive power of a nuclear weapon in terms of how much trinitroluene (TNT) would be required to produce an equivalent blast.

ZERO-BASED BUDGETING (ZBB) With the goal of matching expenditures to objectives, ZBB forces organizations to justify their total spending program for each new budget period. President Jimmy Carter implemented ZBB for the national government, and some state and local units also have used it. Different degrees of success have been reported.

ZERO-SUM GAME A situation in which a gain by one participant necessarily results in an equal and corresponding loss to the other.

Index